WHO'S WHO
OF BRITISH
MEMBERS OF PARLIAMENT

Volume
IV
1945-1979

Who's Who
of British
Members of Parliament

VOLUME
IV
1945-1979

A Biographical Dictionary
of the House of Commons

Based on annual volumes of
'Dod's Parliamentary Companion' and other sources

MICHAEL STENTON
Peterhouse, Cambridge

and
STEPHEN LEES
University of Cambridge Library

THE HARVESTER PRESS, SUSSEX

HUMANITIES PRESS, NEW JERSEY

First published in Great Britain in 1981 by
THE HARVESTER PRESS LIMITED
Publisher: John Spiers
16 Ship Street, Brighton, Sussex
and in the USA by
HUMANITIES PRESS INC.,
Atlantic Highlands, New Jersey 07716

Who's Who of British Members of Parliament Volume 4
© 1981 The Harvester Press Limited

British Library Cataloguing in Publication Data
Who's who of British Members of Parliament
  Vol. 4 : 1945-79
    1. Great Britain. Parliament. House of Commons—Biography
    I. Stenton, Michael   II. Lees, Stephen
  328.41 '07' 30922   JN672

   ISBN 0-85527-335-6

Humanities Press Inc.
ISBN 0-391-01087-5

Photosetting by Thomson Press (India) Ltd., New Delhi and
printed in Great Britain by
St. Edmundsbury Press, Bury St. Edmunds, Suffolk

Contents

Preface by Michael Stenton

Alterations to the original entries drawn from Dod's *Parliamentary Companion* have once more been made according to the principles set out in the Preface to Volume III. The main difference in the character of the post-1945 entries found in this volume is that the amount of 'post-parliamentary' detail is rather greater than that provided for the period 1918-1945. Such detail has been drawn—in a highly selective way—from what is readily available in handbooks and obituaries. These sources themselves reflect a slowly developing willingness in political circles to declare extra-Parliamentary interests. However, the reader must not be deceived by appearances: the weight of information supplied here is still far from complete as a biographical record. The commercial and interest-group connections which do not find expression in this volume, because unstated in the contemporary reference literature, may be at least as important as the more public ones.

With the publication of this fourth volume what began as a contribution to the history of Parliament can now be used as a tool of political 'science'. It is all the more timely then to renew the reminder that *Who's Who of British Members of Parliament* will not reveal its full usefulness unless it assists in the prompting as well as in the answering of good questions. Even a casual perusal of its contents raises interesting points. One is, for example, struck by the large number of railwaymen who became MPs. The miners, of course, have their mining areas, but the railwaymen seem to know how to recommend themselves. But the success of certain trade unions in obtaining Parliamentary representation has not been matched by equivalent success in the ministerial arena. If this seems a narrowly 'Westminster' sort of comment to make, it can be answered that an explanation of the discrepancy is more likely to be found in the internal history of trade unions than by the statistical analysis of Dod's entries or Hansard's columns.

Thus this Biographical Dictionary, whilst fulfilling its function as a chronicle of Parliamentary membership, points beyond Parliament as well as at it. In theory Parliament's powers are so overwhelming and limitless that a constitutional analyst is baffled before the miracle of its restraint and self-denial. Parliament has not sought to rule or to be particularly well-informed about the detail of ruling. The mother of parliaments would be better described as the nursery of ministers and the seminary of politicians. But is the whole explanation of this state of affairs internal to the party system as practised in the House of Commons and the unrelation of Whitehall to Westminster? Those who think not might start their investigations by looking at all the not-so-important people listed in this book—Parliament's parliamentarians rather than Whitehall's—not because the answers will be purely personal but because the search for prime causes and wider processes needs an empirical check.

PREFACE

It would be a pity if this Who's Who was used only for reference. Even in smaller and more parochial matters of the Parliamentary stage there is some profit to be had in browsing through its pages looking for quirks of public life. It is, for instance, remarkable how informative MPs are about their membership of Parliamentary delegations. Are these inter-parliamentary visitations of any importance, or are these sometime delegates honourably confessing to the enjoyment of an honest perk? Students of the prehistory of Britain's membership of the European Community will find it worth their while to notice how gently the British MP was accustomed to the idea of Continental debating assemblies by his experience of trips to the Council of Europe and the Western European Union. MPs continue to emerge from the diplomatic service—as they have done for many generations—but they now arrive from the domestic departments as well. Is this a trend to watch, or a trend that betokens something?

It is to be regretted that the twentieth century has seen the gradual extinction of the brief political tags and phrases which MPs formerly permitted in Dod's entries. The modern Dod is a much less lively list of office-holding and party-affiliation than was once the case. However, the editors have made an effort to include where possible items and detail which might have a bearing on an MP's inclinations or non-party attachments. Confessional affiliation is one such factor: the reader will frequently come, rather abruptly, across phrases such as 'a Methodist' or 'a Roman Catholic'. (Such an entry does not imply that the MP in question was prticularly active or ardent in support of his faith.) Anglicans, of course, excepting the important sub-group who show up clearly as leading Anglican laymen, are not so easily identifiable in the reference literature: the assumption that the English are a nation of honorary Anglicans will not go away. Amongst political issues it appears that the decision to join the EEC was preceded by the most complex pattern of cross-voting on a major matter in the entire post-war period. Even after seven years of membership party loyalties are still split along the same fractures. So far political fission—such as that provoked by free trade and Home Rule in the last century—has been avoided, but it remains a possibility. For this reason we have noted, in the relevant entries, when MPs did not conform to the majority position of their party at the important division of 28 October 1971. Perhaps some continuity of character with the Victorian generation of Dods has been maintained in this way.

M.S.

Acknowledgements

The Editors are indebted to Mr. D.L. Clarke, Librarian of the British Library of Political and Economic Science, for permission to consult the unpublished files relating to C. Cook, *Sources in British Political History 1900-51* and to Angela Raspin for providing access to them. They would again like to express their thanks to Dr. D. Menhennet, Librarian of the House of Commons Library, and to Michael Griffith-Jones, Head of the Reference Room. They are also grateful to Mavis Thomas for her painstaking work in the preparation of this volume and to Alastair Everitt for his guidance and his patience.

Advice to Readers

This is the fourth volume, which taken together with previous volumes, will supply biographies of every Member of Parliament to have sat in the House of Commons between 1832-1979. Volume I comprises more than 3050 lives for the years 1832-1885 inclusive. Volume II covers the years 1886-1918. Volume III covers 1919-1945 and Volume IV covers the period from 1945 to May 1979.

The foundation of the whole set of reference works is the long run of *Dod's Parliamentary Companion*, published annually (sometimes twice a year) since 1832 and still continuing. The fullest and best entry for each MP has been taken from this source, and supplemented where possible with important additional information. Yet the personal and idiosyncratic style of Charles Dod's Original entries has been maintained, with minor adjustment where events he mentions in the present tense have been rendered into the past. The biographies have then been organised into these new volumes, for ease of reference.

The following notes on the location of each biography in particular volumes, party labels, supplementary data which has been specially researched, changes of names and further guidance on supplementary sources will assist the user:

WHICH VOLUME IS AN MP IN?
In Volumes I, II and III the biography of an MP is printed in the volume whose dates cover the *end of his career in Parliament*. Volume IV covers all those who sat between 1945 and 1979 including those who were still Members at the 1979 dissolution. All those who sat both before and after 1945 have been included in Volume IV and there are a handful of entries which appear in both Volumes III and IV as an extra help to the reader.

WHICH VOLUME OF 'DOD' IS THE PRINCIPAL SOURCE FOR EACH LIFE?
In the majority of cases the very last entry has been used. After certain general elections Dod ran a second edition. Unless otherwise specified the first edition of Dod is the one which has been used. The year of Dod which has been used as the source has been clearly indicated in square brackets at the end of each entry.

PARTY LABELS
Those given by Charles Dod are used.

SUPPLEMENTARY DATA ADDED
Each entry essentially follows that of Dod but a number of consistent changes have been made to ensure that all the information appears in the same order. Some

variations used by Dod have been retained; Brecknockshire and Breconshire are used interchangeably, as also are Salop and Shropshire.

The consistent order that we have followed is: name, address, clubs, details of parentage, birth, marriage, education, career prior to entering Parliament, political principles or affiliations, views on controversial or important questions, full Parliamentary career including every occasion when a person unsuccessfully contested a seat, reason for finally leaving Parliament, subsequent career when known, and the date of death when this can be traced. It was found that Dod was less concerned in giving full information about the occasions when MPs were unsuccessful candidates and a considerable amount of checking and adding of details has been necessary. Neither could Dod include any information about contested seats after an MP had finally left Parliament. This information has been fully researched and added to the relevant entries. Usually this additional information appears after the details of the Parliamentary career, except for details about birth-date, parentage, education, and marriage—all of which have been inserted into the main body of the entry.

There were a number of successfuly candidates who entered and left Parliament between editions and no entries are to be found in Dod. In those cases we have provided all the information about the Parliamentary career, together with full details about any other seats contested either before or after they sat. We have added further information when this has been available.

If an MP is still alive at the time of writing this volume it has been indicated by a star at the end of the entry. When neither a star nor a date of death is given this shows that we have not been able to establish whether the subject of the entry is still alive.

CHANGES OF NAMES

A few individuals changed their family names during this period and there are sometimes discrepancies between the names recorded in standard reference books and those which appeared in *Dod's Parliamentary Companion*. As a general rule we have followed the *Parliamentary Companion* and where necessary cross references are given in the text and in the name index.

OTHER CONVENTIONS FOLLOWED

'Returned in 1945' etc., means elected at the general election in that year. 'Retired in 1959' etc., means that the sitting MP failed to contest his seat. There is no implication that the man took a sober decision to end his political career. Where the word is not used it is because there is something standing in the text constituting the formal cause of the MP's departure from the House of Commons: electoral defeat, a peerage, a government appointment, etc. To 'contest' a seat, or to be 'a candidate', is, by gentlemanly omission, not to be elected.

SUPPLEMENTARY SOURCES

Unlike their predecessors in the first three volumes of *Who's Who of British Members of Parliament* the majority of Members contained in this volume are still alive and those who are no longer with us have died in the last 35 years. The current and recent editions of *Who's Who* and the volumes of *Who Was Who* for the last three decades therefore contain entries for the great majority of Members included in this volume. *Kelly's Handbook*. . . similarly covers most of them but there remains a small band of MPs who are not included in these works or whose entries are very brief. What has happened to, for example, Lester Hutchinson, Charles Beattie or Sidney Schofield? There are also Members who disappear from the pages of *Who's Who* years before their death, perhaps because the Member deliberately wishes to be omitted, perhaps as a result of notoriety acquired in the law courts, or perhaps because the compilers of *Who's Who* are no longer able to locate them or to communicate with them. Tony Benn, Peter Baker and Henry Nicholls perhaps exemplify these categories. Conversely other Members remain in *Who's Who* for some years after their death: Arthur Moody is an example of this type. *The Dictionary of National Biography* contains entries only for the most prominent and even then, as yet, only for those who died before 1961. Most former MPs, but by no means all, received an obituary notice in *The Times* and all these obituaries have been used as a source of information for this volume. Obituary notices in other newspapers, national, regional and local, have also been used on occasions when it was necessary to check, clarify or supplement information already retrieved from other sources: for example Cyril Dumpleton's death was recorded in the *Dawlish Gazette*, James Ranger's in the *Croydon Advertiser*, Charles Howell's in the *Derby Evening Telegraph* and Edwin Taylor's in the *Bolton Journal*. Obituaries often prove to be valuable, not only because they include details not readily available elsewhere but also because they reveal mistakes in the other sources: the information provided on Sir Thomas Moore's date of birth by his *Daily Telegraph* obituary on 10 Apr. 1971 illustrates the point.

Burke's and Debrett's Peerages are often useful for those who were ennobled or knighted (and for MPs who were related to them) and they are supplemented by L.G. Pine, *New Extinct Peerage 1884-1971* (London, 1972). *Debrett's Illustrated House of Commons and the Judicial Bench* ceased publication in 1931 and is therefore valuable for only a small number of the Members included in this volume.

Official material of relevance includes the official return of election expenses published as a Parliamentary Paper after each General Election, *The Journal of the House of Commons* (which is useful for providing information on new writs and on the censure and expulsion of Members), *London Gazette* (for the dates of appointments to offices of profit under the Crown) and the lists of Members included in Hansard. *The House of Commons Weekly Information Bulletin*, and its companion for the House of Lords, only began publication in May 1979 but the wealth of useful information which is assembled conveniently in them induces a sense of regret that they were not published in an earlier period. Another interesting newcomer is the unofficial *House Magazine*, which was founded by Mike Thomas, the MP for Newcastle East, and since 1976 has been published weekly while Parliament is sitting.

Other works have been valuable in confirming or contradicting dubious statements in *Dod* and in supplementing some of the briefer entries. Notable among these are F.W.S. Craig, *British Parliamentary Election Results*, *Vacher's Parliamentary Companion* (which has been published at monthly or quarterly intervals since 1832), *Whitaker's Almanack* (annually since 1869), D. Butler and A. Sloman, *British Political Facts 1900-1979* (5th edition, London, 1980), *The Times Guide to the House of Commons*, published after each General Election (until 1966 with the title *The Times House of Commons*), C. Bunker, *Who's Who in Parliament* (London, 1947), *The Political Companion* (published at regular intervals since 1969) and *Who Does What in Parliament* (which appeared 5 times between 1970 and 1973). The annual *Municipal Yearbook* is useful for providing information on Members' service in local government. Details of their activities in Europe are provided by *Vacher's European Companion* (which has appeared quarterly since 1972) and by *The Times Guide to the European Parliament 1979*. Useful details of Members' Parliamentary and extra-mural interests are provided by M. Hulke, *Cassell's Parliamentary Directory* (London, 1975) and, on a rather more subjective level, in two works by Andrew Roth, *The MPs Chart* (6 editions between 1967 and 1979) and *The Business Background of MPs* (published 8 times between 1960 and 1975). Registers of universities, colleges and schools and membership lists of professional bodies and learned societies have also been useful.

Valuable information is sometimes contained in the *Annual Conference Reports of the National Union of Conservative Associations* and in the *Reports of the Annual Conference of the Labour Party*. Thomas Scollan's death seems to have been recorded only in the *78th Annual Report of the Scottish Trades Union Congress*. All Labour MPs will eventually be included in J.M. Bellamy and J. Saville, *Dictionary of Labour Biography* (London, 1972-), the first 5 volumes of which have been used for this work, and in J.O. Baylen and N.J. Gossman, *Biographical Dictionary of Modern British Radicals*, the first volume of which was published by the Harvester Press in 1979 but has not yet reached the twentieth century.

The Irishmen in this volume are far less numerous than in its predecessors since they are restricted to the 6 counties; for the most part they present no idiosyncratic problems of the kind posed by their Parnellite forbears at the end of the 19th century or the Sinn Feiners elected in 1918. However biographical information about the latter-day Sinn Feiners, Thomas Mitchell and Philip Clarke, who were deprived of their seats in 1955, and about the Unionist Charles Beattie, Mitchell's temporary successor in Mid Ulster, is not easy to find. Henry Boylan's *A Dictionary of Irish Biography* (Dublin, 1978) deserves mention here if only because, had it been published earlier, it would have been a useful source for the previous volumes of *Who's Who of British Members of Parliament*. Information on those Members who also sat at Stormont in the Government and Parliament of Northern Ireland can be found in *The Official Reports of Parliamentary Debates* for the Northern Ireland Senate and House of Commons (1921-72), *Journals of the Proceedings of the Assembly* (1973-74) and *Report of Debates of the Northern Ireland Constitutional Convention* (1975-76). Biographical information is also included in J.F. Harbinson, *The Ulster Unionist Party(1882-1973)* (Belfast, 1973).

Volumes 3 & 4 of C. Cook, *Sources of British Political History 1900-51* (London, 1977), list the papers of Members who sat between those dates and C. Hazlehurst and C. Woodland, *A Guide to the Papers of British Cabinet Ministers 1900-51* (London, 1974) is also extremely useful. For other Members it is necessary to have recourse to the National Register of Archives.

A special effort has been made to provide accurate information about all Government posts held by MPs. The only reliable lists—at least as far as junior ministerial posts are concerned—are those in D. Butler and A. Sloman, *British Political Facts 1900-1979* (5th edition, London, 1980). Efforts have also been made to discover the dates of death on the Members included in this volume since biographical information often derives from obituaries. The indexes at the Office of Population Censuses and Surveys have been used whenever the printed sources were contradictory, deficient or obviously inaccurate. For example the date of Charles Gibson's death was obtained from his death certificate. Local newspapers have also been consulted in appropriate circumstances, as mentioned above. Nevertheless a few gaps remain, and doubtless some inaccuracies also. The editors would be grateful for any further information and for corrections and significant additions to any of the entries in this volume and its three predecessors.

ABBREVIATIONS

The following abbreviations are used in this book: B means born; Bart. Baronet; bro. brother; Capt. Captain; Co. county; Col. Colonel; Coll. College; d. daughter; Dept. Deputy; educ. educated; eld. eldest; Gen. General; Gov. Governor; Hon. Honourable; jun. junior; Lieut. Lieutenant; Maj. Major; m. married Nr. near; PC. Privy Councillor; Pres. President; Rt. Right; Sec. Secretary; sen. senior; s. son; Visct. Viscount.

Who's Who of British
Members of Parliament, 1945-1979

ABSE, Leopold. 396 Cyncoed Road, Cardiff. 13 Cavendish Avenue, London. S. of Rudolph Abse, Esq., Solicitor. B. 22 Apr. 1917; m. 1955, Marjorie Davies. Educ. at Howard Gardens High School and London School of Economics. Chairman Cardiff Labour Party 1951-53. Member of Cardiff City Council from 1953-58. A Labour Member. Unsuccessfully contested Cardiff N. in 1955. Elected for the Pontypool division of Monmouthshire in Nov. 1958. Member of Home Office Advisory Committees on Penal System 1968 and Adoption 1972. Author of *Private Member* (1973). Chairman of Select Committee on Welsh Affairs from 1980.* [1979]

ACLAND, Sir Richard Thomas Dyke, Bart. of Columb John. 10 Gerald Road, London. Killerton, Exeter. S. of the Rt. Hon. Sir Francis Dyke Acland, 14th bart., MP. B. 26 Nov. 1906; m. 15 Apr. 1936, Anne Stella, d. of R.G. Alford. Educ. at Rugby, and Balliol Coll., Oxford. Barrister-at-Law, Inner Temple 1930, retired 1934. Unsuccessfully contested the Torquay division as a Liberal in 1929 and Barnstaple in 1931. Sat for Barnstaple from 1935-45 as a Liberal until Sept. 1942, thereafter as a Common Wealth Member. Unsuccessfully contested the Putney division as a Common Wealth Member in 1945. Elected for the Gravesend division of Kent as a Labour Member in Nov. 1947 and sat until he resigned in Mar. 1955 over his disagreement with the Labour Party's support for the manufacture of the hydrogen bomb. Expelled from the Labour Party in Mar. 1955 when he announced his intention of contesting the by-election in opposition to the official candidate; Parliament was dissolved before a by-election could be held and he unsuccessfully contested the general election in Gravesend in May 1955 in opposition to the official Labour candidate; the Conservative gained the seat. Succeeded to Baronetcy 1939; donated his family estate to the National Trust in 1943. Second Church Estates Commissioner 1950-51. Sen. Lecturer, St. Luke's Coll. of Education, Exeter 1959-74. Author of *Unser Kampf* 1940, and other works.* [1954]

ADAMS, Harold Richard. 86 Highlands Heath, Putney, London. S. of A. Adams, Esq.

B. 8 Oct. 1912; m. 1st, 1938, Joyce Love (divorced 1955); 2ndly, 1956, Peggy Fribbins. Educ. at Elementary School, Emanuel School, and London University. A Lecturer in Economics and Business Administration; late Assistant Commissioner for National Savings; joined E. Surrey Regiment 1940; served with 25th Army Tank Brigade in N. Africa and Italy; later Staff Officer Land Forces Adriatic. Fellow of Association Incorp. Statisticians. Assistant Whip Oct. 1947. A Lord Commissioner of the Treasury Feb. 1949 to Apr. 1950. A Labour Member. Unsuccessfully contested Canterbury in 1935. Sat for Wandsworth, Balham and Tooting division from 1945-50. Elected for Wandsworth Central in 1950 and 1951 and sat until he retired in 1955. Member of Wandsworth Borough Council 1938-40. Died 25 June 1978. [1954]

ADAMS, William Thomas. 155 Percy Road, London. S. of John Adams, Esq., of Oxted. B. 10 Sept. 1884; m. 27 Feb. 1908, Florence, d. of Richard Nightingale, Esq. Educ. at London School Board. A Clerk. Member of Hammersmith Borough Council 1934-37, Alderman 1938-45, Leader of Council 1944-45; J.P. 1940. A Labour Member. Unsuccessfully contested Hammersmith S. in 1935. Elected for Hammersmith S. in July 1945 and sat until his death on 9 Jan. 1949. [1949]

ADAMSON, Janet Laurel. 20 Woodcombe Crescent, Forest Hill, London. D. of Thomas Johnston, Esq., of Kirkcudbright. B. 9 May 1882; m. 1902, William Murdoch Adamson, Esq., MP for Cannock 1922-31 and 1935-45 (he died 25 Oct. 1945). Additional Parliamentary Private Secretary to Sir Walter Womersley, Minister of Pensions Sept. 1939. Parliamentary Secretary Ministry of Pensions Aug. 1945-May 1946. A Labour Member. Unsuccessfully contested Dartford in 1935. Sat for the Dartford division from 1938-45. Elected for the Bexley division of Kent in July 1945 and sat until May 1946 when she was appointed Dept. Chairman of Assistance Board. Member of London County Council 1928-31. Member of National Executive Committee of Labour Party 1927-47, Chairman 1935-36. Dept.

Chairman of Assistance Board 1946-48, of National Assistance Board 1948-53. Died 25 Apr. 1962.   [1946]

ADLEY, Robert James. Woodend House, Ridgeway Lane, Lymington, Hampshire. 128 King Henry's Road, London. Carlton, and Royal Lymington Yacht. S. of Harry Adley, Esq., Company Director. B. 2 Mar. 1935; m. 31 Aug. 1961, Jane Elizabeth, d. of Wilfrid Pople, Esq., of Somerset. Educ. at Falconbury and Uppingham. Director of Sales, May fair Hotel 1960-64; Marketing Director Commonwealth Holiday Inns of Canada Limited; member Slough Borough Council 1965-68; Chairman Sunningdale Conservative Association 1966-69. Vice-Chairman of Parliamentary Tourism Committee; Founder and first Chairman Brunel Society; Vice-Chairman Conservative Parliamentary Transport Committee; Vice-Chairman British-Chinese Parliamentary Group; Chairman British-Jordanian Parliamentary Group; National Council member, British Hotels, Restaurants and Caterers' Association. A Conservative. Unsuccessfully contested Birkenhead in 1966. Sat for the N.E. division of Bristol from 1970 to Feb. 1974 and for Christchurch and Lymington from Feb. 1974.*   [1979]

AGNEW, Commander Sir Peter Garnett, Bart., R.N. 2 Smith Square, London. Carlton. S. of C.L. Agnew, Esq., of Knutsford. B. 9 July 1900; m. 1928, Enid Frances, d. of Henry Boan, Esq., of Perth, Western Australia. Educ. at Repton, and R.N. Coll. Joined R.N. 1918; Aide-de-Camp to Gov. of Jamaica 1927-28; served in H.M. Yacht *Victoria and Albert* 1930; rejoined R.N. 1939; (despatches 1941). Parliamentary Private Secretary to Rt. Hon. Walter Runciman, President of the Board of Trade Dec. 1935-May 1937, and to Rt. Hon. Sir Philip Sassoon, First Commissioner of Works Oct. 1937-39. Assistant Government Whip May-July 1945. Conservative Whip Aug. 1945-Feb. 1950. Member of House of Laity, Church Assembly 1935-65. A Church Commissioner for England 1948-68. Led British Parliamentary Delegation to Iran 1956. Created 1st Bart. 1957. A Conservative. Sat for the Camborne division from 1931-50.

Unsuccessfully contested Falmouth and Camborne in 1950. Elected for S. Worcestershire in 1955, 1959 and 1964 and sat until he retired in 1966. President of European Centre of Documentation and Information 1974-76. Knight Grand Cross of Order of Civil Merit (Spain) 1977.* [1966]

AINSLEY, John William. House of Commons, London. S. of John George Ainsley, Esq. B. 30 June 1898; m.1924. Educ. at Elementary School, and Evening Classes. Member Durham County Council 1942-56, Alderman 1955-56 and Chairman 1953-55; Chairman County Education Committee and Northern Advisory Council for Further Education. Served with Durham Light Infantry in First World War. A Methodist Lay Preacher. A Labour Member. Elected for N.W. Durham in 1955 and sat until he retired in 1964. Died 1976.   [1964]

AITKEN, Group Capt. Hon. John William Maxwell, D.S.O., D.F.C. Wellbottom Cottage, Givons Grove, Leatherhead. S. of Baron Beaverbrook. B. 15 Feb. 1910; m. 1st, 25 Aug. 1939, Cynthia, d. of Col. H.G. Monteith, D.S.O., O.B.E. (marriage dissolved in 1943); 2ndly, 15 Aug. 1946, Jane, d. of Capt. Robert Kenyon-Slaney and Lady Mary Gilmour (marriage dissolved in 1950); 3rdly, 1951, Violet, d. of Sir Humphrey de Trafford. Educ. at Westminster, and Pembroke Coll., Cambridge. Commissioned A.A.F. 1935, served with R.A.F. 1939-45, Day Fighter Pilot Battle of Britain, subsequently Night Fighter Pilot, Group Commander Middle East 1942-44. A Conservative. Elected for Holborn in July 1945 and sat until he retired in 1950. Succeeded in 1964 to his father's peerage as Baron Beaverbrook, which he renounced, and to his baronetcy. D.F.C. 1940, D.S.O. 1942. Director of Associated Television Limited. Chairman of Beaverbrook Newspapers, later Express Newspapers 1968-77, President from 1977. Chancellor of University of New Brunswick from 1966, Hon. LL.D.*   [1950]

AITKEN, Jonathan William Patrick. 47 Phillimore Gardens, London. Turf, and Pratt's. S. of Sir William Aitken, K.B.E., MP.

B. 30 Aug. 1942; m. 1979, Lolicia Olivera, d. of O. Azucki, Esq. of Zurich. Educ. at Eton, and Christ Church, Oxford. Private Secretary to Rt. Hon. Selwyn Lloyd from 1964-66. A Journalist and Author of 4 books 1966-72. Managing Director of Slater Walker (Middle East) Limited from 1973-75. A Conservative. Unsuccessfully contested Meriden in 1966. Member for Thanet E. from Feb. 1974. Prospective candidate for Thirsk and Malton from Dec. 1967 until he resigned in May 1970 when he was accused of charges under the Official Secrets Act in connection with articles in *The Sunday Telegraph* on the war in Biafra; acquitted on all charges on 3 Feb. 1971. Chairman of R.H. Sanbar Consultants Ltd. from 1976.* [1979]

AITKEN, Sir William Traven, K.B.E. Playford Hall, Playford, Nr. Ipswich, Suffolk. S. of Joseph Mauns Aitken, Esq., of Toronto and nephew of Lord Beaverbrook. B. 10 June 1905; m. 28 Apr. 1938, Hon. Penelope Loader Maffey, d. of Lord Rugby, G.C.M.G., K.C.B., K.C.V.O., C.S.I., C.I.E. Educ. at Upper Canada Coll. and University of Toronto. A Journalist on the *Evening Standard*. Served with R.A.F. 1939-45. Managing Director of London Express News and Feature Services. A Conservative. Unsuccessfully contested W. Derbyshire in 1945. Elected for the Bury St. Edmunds division of Suffolk in 1950, 1951, 1955 and 1959 and sat until his death on 19 Jan. 1964. K.B.E. 1963. Died 19 Jan. 1964. [1964]

ALBU, Austen Harry. House of Commons, London. S. of Ferdinand Albu, Esq. B. 21 Sept. 1903; m. 1st, 14 Apr. 1929, Rose, d. of Simon Marks, Esq., of Newcastle (she died 1956); 2ndly, 26 Mar. 1958, Marie Jahoda, of New York. Educ. at Tonbridge School, and City and Guilds Coll. (Imperial Coll. of Science and Technology). An Engineer, B.Sc., F.C.G.I., M.I. Mech.E. Works Manager Aladdin Industries Limited 1930-46; Dept. President Governmental Sub-Commission of Control Commission for Germany 1946-47; Dept. Director British Institute of Management Feb.-Nov. 1948. Fellow of Imperial Coll. of Science and Technology. Doctor of University of Surrey (*h.c.*). Chairman Parliamentary and

Scientific Committee 1962-64. Minister of State, Department of Economic Affairs Jan. 1965-Jan. 1967. A Labour Member. Elected for Edmonton in Nov. 1948 and sat until he retired in Feb. 1974. Member of Select Committee on Estimates 1950-54, Nationalised Industries 1952-64 and Procedure 1967-68. Chairman, The Harvester Press Ltd., Publishers, 1970-73. Author of *The Anatomy of Private Industry* 1951, *Socialism and The Study of Man* 1951, *Management in Transition* 1942, and *The Young Man's Guide to Mechanical Engineering* 1962. Contributer to *New Fabian Essays* (ed. R.H.S. Crossman 1952), *Lessons of Public Enterprise* (ed. M. Shanks 1963), *Suicide of a Nation* (ed. A. Koestler 1963) and *Technical Innovation and British Industrial Performance* (ed. Keith Pavitt 1980).* [1974]

ALEXANDER, Rt. Hon. Albert Victor, C.H. Ministry of Defence, Storeys Gate, London. S. of Albert Alexander, Esq., Artisan Engineer. B. at Weston-super-Mare 1 May 1885; m. 6 June 1908, Esther Ellen, youngest d. of George Chapple, Esq., of Tiverton. Educ. at Barton Hill Elementary School, Bristol, and St. George Technical Classes, LL.D. 1945. Sheffield 1947 and Bristol. Secretary of the Parliamentary Committee of the Co-operative Congress 1920-45. On the staff of the Education Committee of the Somerset County Council from 1 Dec. 1903. For many years Baptist lay preacher. Served in the army; gazetted out with the honorary rank of Capt. Parliamentary Secretary Board of Trade Jan.-Nov. 1924; First Lord of the Admiralty June 1929-Aug. 1931, May 1940-May 1945 and July 1945-Oct. 1946; Minister Without Portfolio Oct.-Dec. 1946; Minister of Defence Dec. 1946-Feb. 1950; an Elder Brother of Trinity House 1941; Freeman of Weston-super-Mare and Sheffield. PC. 1929. C.H. 1941. Member Cabinet Mission to India and of British Delegation Paris Peace Conference 1946. A Labour Member. Sat for the Hillsborough division of Sheffield from 1922 to Oct. 1931 when he was defeated and from 1935 until Jan. 1950 when he was created Visct. Alexander of Hillsborough. Member of Executive Committee of P.L.P. Sept.-Oct. 1931 and 1935-40. Chancellor of Duchy of

3

Lancaster Feb. 1950-Oct. 1951. Leader of the Labour Party in the House of Lords 1955-64. President of U.K. Council of Protestant Churches 1956. Created Earl Alexander of Hillsborough in 1963. K.G. 1964. Died 11 Jan. 1965. [1950]

ALISON, Michael James Hugh. Moat Hall, Ouseburn, Yorkshire. Flat 7, 55 Barkston Gardens, London. S. of J.S.I. Alison, Esq. B. 1926; m. 1958, Sylvia, d. of Anthony Haigh, Esq., (2 s. 1 d.). Educ. at Eton, and Wadham College, Oxford (M.A. Hons). Served in the army 1944-48. Employed with Lazard Brothers, Merchant Bankers 1951-53. Member of Kensington Borough Council 1956-59; Dept. Chairman of N. Kensington Conservative Association 1961-62; Research Officer, Foreign Affairs Section of the Conservative Research Department 1958-63. Parliamentary Under-Secretary of State (Health) at the Department of Health and Social Security 1970-74. A Conservative. Sat for the Barkston Ash division of the W. Riding of Yorkshire from Oct. 1964. Theological student at Ridley Hall, Cambridge 1953-54. Member of General Advisory Council of Independent Television Authority 1969-70. An Opposition spokesman on Home Affairs 1975-77 and on the Environment 1977-79. Minister of State, Northern Ireland Office from May 1979.* [1979]

ALLAN, Commander Robert Alexander, D.S.O., O.B.E., R.N.V.R. 5 Campden House Terrace, London. S. of Claud A. Allan, Esq., V.L., J.P., Shipowner, of Kilmahew Castle, Cardross, Dunbartonshire. B. 11 July 1914; m. 23 July 1947, Maureen, eld. d. of Commander H. Stuart-Clark, of Singapore. Educ. at Harrow (Rothschild Scholar), Clare Coll., Cambridge (Mellon Fellow), and Yale University, U.S.A. Director of *Financial Times* and other companies. Commander R.N.V.R.; Senior Officer Inshore Squadron 1943-45; Dept. Chief of Naval Information, Washington 1945-46, D.S.O. 1944, O.B.E. 1942, despatches 5 times; Commander de la Légion d'Honneur, Croix de Guerre, Officer American Legion of Merit. Assistant Whip Nov. 1953-55; Parliamentary Private Secretary to Minister of State for the Colonies

1952-53; and to Prime Minister 1955-58; Parliamentary and Financial Secretary Admiralty Jan. 1958-Jan. 1959. Under-Secretary of State for Foreign Affairs Jan. 1959-Oct. 1960. Treasurer of Conservative and Unionist Party Oct. 1960-Nov. 1965. Chairman Conservative Central Board of Finance Nov. 1960. A Conservative. Unsuccessfully contested Dunbartonshire in 1945 and W. Dunbartonshire in Feb. and Apr. 1950. Elected for Paddington S. in Oct. 1951 and sat until he retired in 1966. Gov. of B.B.C. 1971-76. Created Baron Allan of Kilmahew (Life Peerage) 1973. Director of Pearson Longman and Longman Penguin. Chairman of Ladybird Books 1971-79. Died in Sydney 4 Apr. 1979. [1966]

ALLASON, James Harry, O.B.E. 82 Ebury Mews, London. Hillside Cottage, Markyate, St. Albans, Hertfordshire. S. of Brigadier-Gen. W. Allason, D.S.O. B. 6 Sept. 1912; m. 1946, Nuala, d. of J.A. McArevey, Esq. (marriage dissolved in 1973). Educ. at Haileybury, and Royal Military Academy, Woolwich. Commander R.A. 1932, transferred to 3DG 1937, Active Service, Burma 1944. Retired with rank Lieut.-Col. 1953. O.B.E. 1953. Member Kensington Borough Council 1956-65. Parliamentary Private Secretary to Rt. Hon. John Profumo, Secretary of State for War 1960-63, and to Rt. Hon. James Ramsden, Secretary of State for War 1963-64. Vice-Chairman Conservative Housing Parliamentary Committee 1964-70, Chairman 1970-74. Vice-Chairman Conservative Environment Parliamentary Committee 1974. A Conservative. Unsuccessfully contested Hackney Central in 1955. Elected for Hemel Hempstead in 1959 and sat until he was defeated in Oct. 1974.* [1974 2nd ed.]

ALLAUN, Frank Julian. 1 South Drive, Manchester. S. of Harry Allaun, Esq. B. 27 Feb. 1913; m. 1941, Lilian Ball, (1 s. 1 d.). Educ. at Manchester Grammar School. Took B. Com. degree by night study and is a Qualified Chartered Accountant (A.C.A.); member N.U.J. Former Northern Industrial Correspondent to *Daily Herald*. Vice-President Public Health Inspectors' Association. National Chairman Labour Action for

Peace. Broadcast frequently and is Author of *No Place Like Home, Heartbreak Housing, Stop the H-Bomb Race,* etc. Parliamentary Private Secretary to Rt. Hon. Anthony Greenwood, Secretary of State for the Colonies Oct. 1964-Mar. 1965. Elected to National Executive Labour Party Oct. 1967. Vice-Chairman of the Labour Party 1977-78, Chairman 1978-79. Chairman Labour Party Housing Committee. A Labour Member. Unsuccessfully contested the Moss Side division of Manchester in 1951. Sat for the E. division of Salford from 1955.* [1979]

ALLDRITT, Walter Harold. 104 Longmeadow Road, Knowsley, Prescot, Lancashire. S. of Henry Alldritt, Esq. B. 4 July 1918; m. 22 Aug. 1945, Mary-Teresa, d. of W.H. McGuinness, Esq. Educ. at St. Francis de Sales, and Liverpool University, W.E.A. Served with H.M. Forces 1939-46. Trade Union Officer. Councillor Sandhills Ward 1955-67. J.P. 1958. Youngest Past President Borough Labour Party and Trades Council. A Labour Member. Elected for the Scotland division of Liverpool in June 1964 and sat until he resigned in Feb. 1971. Regional Secretary of National Union of General and Municipal Workers in Liverpool, N. Wales and N. Ireland from 1970.* [1971]

ALLEN, Arthur Cecil. Nenehurst, Thrift Street, Higham Ferrers, Northamptonshire. S. of Charles Allen, Esq. B. 10 Jan. 1887; m. 1914, Polly Mary Bradshaw. Educ. at Elementary School, and Ruskin Coll. Oxford. An official of Boot Operatives Union. Parliamentary Private Secretary to Rt. Hon. Hugh Gaitskell, Chancellor of the Exchequer 1950-51. An Opposition Whip 1951-55. Parliamentary Private Secretary to the Rt. Hon. Hugh Gaitskell, Leader of the Opposition 1955-59. A Labour Member. Elected for the Bosworth division of Leicestershire in July 1945 and sat until he retired in 1959. Served 1914-18, Salonica. Alderman Northamptonshire County Council 1937-49.* [1959]

ALLEN, Sydney Scholefield, Q.C. 2 Romney Close, Hampstead Way, London. S. of Joseph Allen, Esq., of Birkenhead. B. 3 Jan. 1898; m. 25 Aug. 1928, F. Mona, d. of John Irving, Esq. Educ. at Birkenhead Institute,

and University of Liverpool, LL.B. (1st Class Hons.). Barrister-at-Law, Gray's Inn 1923. K.C. June 1945. Chairman of Liverpool Fabian Society 1934-40; President 1940-45. Chairman of Birkenhead Branch of League of Nations Union 1935-45. Served overseas with R.A. 1916-19. Member of Delegation to Poland June 1958; Rumania 1961; Greece 1963; Turkey 1966; Hungary 1970. Vice-Chairman of British Group of Inter-Parliamentary Union from 1962-67 and 1968-71; Parliamentary Delegation to Annual Meeting of Inter-Parliamentary Union, Rio de Janeiro July 1958, Brasilia 1962, Belgrade 1963, Copenhagen 1964, Canada 1965, and Teheran, Iran 1966. Member of the Council of the I.P.U. 1964 and 1965. Delegate to the Council of Europe 1958-61; member of Executive Committee of British Branch of the Commonwealth Parliamentary Association 1965-71. Honorary Treasurer British American Parliamentary Association 1965-71. Vice-Chairman of Legal Committee of Council of Europe 1959-61 and Western European Union 1958-61. Recorder of Blackburn 1947-Jan. 1970. J.P. 1947. Admitted Honorary Freeman of the Borough of Crewe Sept. 1967. A Labour Member. Elected for the Crewe division of Cheshire in July 1945 and sat until he retired in Feb. 1974. Died 26 Mar. 1974. [1974]

ALLEN, Lieut.-Col. Sir William James, K.B.E., D.S.O. 6 Cleaver Park, Belfast. S. of Joseph Allen, Esq. B. 15 Oct. 1866; m. 1st, 18 Mar. 1892, Maria, d. of John Ross, Esq. (she died 14 Nov. 1937); 2ndly, 1938, Lillah Ierne, d. of R. Hill Forsythe, Esq., of Lurgan. Educ. at Lurgan Coll. Honorary Secretary Ulster Unionist Council. Raised and served with Pioneer Battalion Royal Irish Rifles in France and Belgium, which regiment he commanded in 1918. Had Croix de Chevalier of Legion of Honour; D.S.O. 1918; K.B.E. 1921, on King's visit to open 1st Parliament of Northern Ireland. Dept.-Lieut. for Armagh. A Conservative. Elected for N. Armagh Nov. 1917 and Dec. 1918. Sat for Co. Armagh from Nov. 1922 until his death on 20 Dec. 1947 as a result of a road accident. [1948]

5

ALLIGHAN, Garry. Harvest Bank Cottage, West Wickham, Kent. S. of George Allighan, Esq. B. 16 Feb. 1900. Educ. at Enfield Grammar School. A Journalist and Author. Served in Royal Navy 1918. Assistant Editor of *John Bull* 1921-25, Feature Editor of *Toronto Evening Telegram* 1925-28, Feature Writer on *Daily Express* 1928-31, Radio Editor of *Evening Standard* 1931-39, War correspondent of *Toronto Star* 1939-41, News Editor of *Daily Mirror* 1941-44, Industrial Editor of *Daily Mail* 1944-46. Member of London County Council 1937-42. A Labour Member. Elected for the Gravesend division of Kent in July 1945 and sat until he was expelled on 30 Oct. 1947 'for his gross contempts of this House and for his misconduct' after the House had resolved that 'the article written by Mr. Allighan and published in *World's Press News* of 3 Apr. 1947 in its general tone and particularly by its unfounded imputations against unnamed members of insobriety in the precincts of this House, is an affront to this House.' Principal of Premier School of Journalism, Johannesburg 1963-73.* [1947]

ALPASS, Joseph Herbert. 37 Ormerod Road, Stoke Bishop, Bristol. S. of Thomas Alpass, Esq., of Berkeley. B. 1873; m. d. of John Neal. Educ. at Merchant Venturers' Coll., Bristol. Member Education Committee of Gloucestershire County Council and Labour Party Agricultural and Rural Advisory Committee. A Labour Member. Unsuccessfully contested the Cirencester and Tewkesbury division of Gloucestershire in 1918 and 1924 and the Thornbury division of Gloucestershire in 1922. Sat for Bristol Central from 1929 to 1931, when he was defeated, and for the Thornbury division from 1945 until he retired in 1950. C.B.E. 1951. Auctioneer and Estate Agent. Member of the Forestry Commission 1929-31. Died 31 May 1969. [1950]

ALPORT, Rt. Hon. Cuthbert James McCall. The Cross House, Layer de la Haye, Colchester. S. of Professor Arthur Cecil Alport. B. 22 Mar. 1912; m. 26 Oct. 1945, Rachel Cecilia, d. of Lieut.-Col. R.C. Bingham, C.V.O., D.S.O. Educ. at Haileybury, and Pembroke Coll., Cambridge. Barrister-at-Law, Middle Temple 1944. President of Cambridge Union 1935; Lieut.-Col. T.A. R.O. Assistant Postmaster-Gen. Dec. 1955-Jan. 1957; Parliamentary Under-Secretary of State for Commonwealth Relations Jan. 1957-Oct. 1959. Minister of State for Commonwealth Relations Oct. 1959-Feb. 1961. PC. 1960. A Conservative. Elected for the Colchester division of Essex in 1950, 1951, 1955 and 1959. Sat until Feb. 1961 when he was created Baron Alport (Life Peerage) and appointed High Commissioner in Rhodesia and Nyasaland. Tutor, Ashridge Coll. 1935-37. Director of Conservative Political Centre 1945-50. Chairman of Joint East and Central African Board 1953-55. Gov. of Charing Cross Hospital 1954-55. High Commissioner in Federation of Rhodesia and Nyasaland 1961-63. British Government Representative in Rhodesia in 1967. Dept. Speaker of House of Lords from 1971. Pro-Chancellor of City University 1972-79. Dept.-Lieut. of Essex 1974, High Steward of Colchester from 1967.* [1961]

ALTON, David Patrick. 45 Onslow Road, Liverpool. S. of Frederick Alton, Esq., Car Worker with Fords. B. 15 Mar. 1951. Unmarried. Educ. at Edmund Campion School, Hornchurch, and Christ's Coll. of Education, Liverpool. Elected as Britain's youngest ever City Councillor to Liverpool City Council 1972. Elected to Merseyside C.C. 1973; Dept. Leader of Liverpool City Council and Chairman of Housing Committee 1978. A Liberal. Unsuccessfully contested the Edge Hill division of Liverpool in Feb. and Oct. 1974. Sat for the Edge Hill division of Liverpool from Mar. 1979.* [1979 2nd ed.]

AMERY, Rt. Hon. (Harold) Julian. 112 Eaton Square, London. Bucks', Carlton, White's and Beefsteak. S. of the Rt. Hon. L.S. Amery, C.H., MP. (d. 1955). B. 27 Mar. 1919; m. 26 Jan. 1950, Catherine, d. of the Rt. Hon. Harold Macmillan and Lady Dorothy Macmillan, (1 s. 3 d.). Educ. at Eton. and Balliol College, Oxford. An Author. Attaché H.M. Legation Belgrade and on Special Missions to Turkey, Bulgaria, and Rumania 1939-40. Sergeant R.A.F. 1940-41. Transferred to army with rank of Capt. and served

in Middle East, Malta, and Yugoslavia 1941-44. Liaison Officer to Albanian Resistance Movement 1944; attached to Gen. Carton de Wiart, then Prime Minister's Personal Representative to Generalissimo Chiang Kai-Shek 1945. Under-Secretary of State for War Jan. 1957-Dec. 1958; Under-Secretary of State for the Colonies 1958-60; Secretary of State for Air 1960-62. Minister of Aviation 1962-64. Minister of Public Buildings and Works June 1970-Oct. 1970. Minister for Housing and Construction Oct. 1970-Nov. 1972. Minister of State for Foreign and Commonwealth Affairs Nov. 1972-Mar. 1974. PC. 1960. Opposition spokesman on the Colonies 1964-65. Biographer of Joseph Chamberlain. A Conservative. Unsuccessfully contested Preston in 1945. Member for Preston N. from 1950 to 1966, when he was defeated. Sat for the Pavilion division of Brighton from 27 Mar. 1969 (by-election).*
[1979]

AMORY, Rt. Hon. Derick Heathcoat. See HEATHCOAT-AMORY, Rt. Hon. Derick.

ANCRAM, Michael Andrew Foster Jude Kerr, Earl of. Monteviot, Jedburgh. House of Commons, London. Turf. S. of Marq. of Lothian. B. 7 July 1945; m. 1975, Lady Jane Fitzalan-Howard, d. of 16th Duke of Norfolk. Educ. at Ampleforth Coll., Yorkshire, and Christ Church, Oxford, M.A. Hons., and University of Edinburgh LL.B. Member Executive Scottish Conservative and Unionist Associations 1967. Founder and first Chairman Thistle Group 1967. Member Scottish Advisory Council of Shelter 1968-73. Advocate, Scottish bar 1970. Freelance Journalist to daily national newspapers and periodicals. A Conservative. Unsuccessfully contested West Lothian in 1970. Elected for Berwickshire and East Lothian in Feb. 1974 and sat until he was defeated in Oct. 1974. Elected for Edinburgh S. in May 1979. Vice-Chairman of Conservative Party in Scotland from 1975. A Roman Catholic.*
[1974 2nd ed.]

ANDERSON, Alexander. 31 Kenilworth Avenue, Wishaw, Lanarkshire. S. of Thomas Anderson, Esq., of Wick. B. 12 Apr. 1888; m. 1922, Margaret, d. of D. Sinclair, Esq. Educ.

at Wick, and Edinburgh University, M.A. Member of Motherwell and Wishaw Town Council 1929-45. A Teacher. A Labour Member. Unsuccessfully contested the Motherwell division of Lanarkshire in Apr. 1945. Returned for the same division in July 1945 and sat until his death on 11 Feb. 1954. Chairman of Estimates Committee 1950-51. Member of Nature Conservancy 1949-54. Died 11 Feb. 1954.
[1954]

ANDERSON, David Colville, Q.C. 8 Arboretum Road, Edinburgh. S. of J.L. Anderson, Esq., of Pittormie. B. 8 Sept. 1916; m. 1948, Juliet, d. of Lord Hill Watson, Senator of the Coll. of Justice. Educ. at Trinity Coll., Glenalmond, Pembroke Coll., Oxford, and Edinburgh University. Served with R.N.V.R. from 1935, Lieut.-Commander 1948, V.R.D. 1947. Advocate 1946, Q.C. (Scotland) 1957. Lecturer in Scots Law, Edinburgh University 1947-60. Standing Junior Counsel to Ministry of Works 1953-55, to War Office 1955-57. Commissioner for Northern Lighthouses 1960-64. Solicitor Gen. for Scotland May 1960-Mar. 1964. A Conservative. Unsuccessfully contested Coatbridge and Airdrie in 1955 and Dunbartonshire E. in 1959. Elected for Dumfriesshire at a by-election in Dec. 1963 and sat until he retired in Sept. 1964. Honorary Sheriff Substitute for Lothians and Peebles from 1965. Chairman of Industrial Tribunals, Scotland 1971-72. Chief Reporter for Public Inquiries and Under-Secretary, Scottish Office 1972-74.*
[1964]

ANDERSON, Donald. House of Commons, London. S. of David Robert Anderson, Esq., Fitter. B. 17 June 1939; m. 28 Sept. 1963, Dr. Dorothy Mary Trotman, eld. d. of Rev. Frank Trotman, (3 s.). Educ. at Swansea Grammar School, and University Coll., Swansea. A Methodist local preacher. H.M. Diplomatic Service 1960-64. Lecturer University Coll., Swansea 1964-66. A Barrister on the S.E. Circuit, Inner Temple, 1969. Parliamentary Private Secretary to Roy Hattersley, Minister of Defence Administration 1969-70. Councillor Royal Borough of Kensington and Chelsea 1971-75. Parliamentary Private Secretary to S.C. Silkin, Attorney Gen. 1974-79. Chairman of

Welsh Labour Group from 1977. A Labour Member. MP for Monmouth from 1966-70, when he was defeated. Elected for E. Swansea in Oct. 1974.* [1979]

ANDERSON, Frank. House of Commons, London. S. of Thomas Anderson, Esq., of Hercules Farm, Bury. B. 21 Nov. 1889; m. 10 July 1919, Mary Elizabeth Thompson. Educ. at Elementary School. A Railway Clerk. Labour Whip 1937-39. A Labour Member. Unsuccessfully contested the High Peak division in 1922 and 1923, and the Stretford division in 1929 and 1931. Elected for the Whitehaven division of Cumberland in Nov. 1935 and sat until his death on 25 Apr. 1959. [1959]

ANDERSON, Rt. Hon. Sir John, G.C.B., G.C.S.I., G.C.I.E., F.R.S. 4 Lord North Street, London. Athenaeum, and Brook's. S. of David Anderson, Esq., of Westland House, Midlothian. B. 8 July 1882; m. 1st, 1907, Christina, d. of Andrew Mackenzie, Esq., of Edinburgh (she died 1920); 2ndly, 1941, Ava, d. of J.E.C. Bodley, Esq., and widow of Ralph Wigram, Esq., C.M.G. Educ. at George Watson's Coll., Edinburgh University, M.A., B.Sc., and University of Leipzig. Honorary LL.D. Cambridge, Aberdeen, Edinburgh, St. Andrews, Liverpool, Leeds, Sheffield and Kingston, Ontario. Honorary D.C.L. Oxford. Honorary D.Sc. McGill. Secretary National Health Insurance Committee 1913; Secretary Ministry of Shipping 1917; 2nd Secretary Ministry of Health 1919; Chairman of Board of Inland Revenue 1919-22; Joint Under-Secretary to Lord-Lieut. of Ireland in 1920; Permanent Under-Secretary of State Home Department 1922-32; Gov. of Bengal 1932-37; Lord Privy Seal Oct. 1938-Sept. 1939. Secretary of State for Home Affairs and Minister of Home Security Sept. 1939-Oct. 1940; Lord President of the Council Oct. 1940-Sept. 1943; Chancellor of the Exchequer Sept. 1943-July 1945; Chairman of Port of London Authority from 1946; Honorary Fellow Gonville and Caius Coll., Cambridge; Commander of French Legion of Honour and of the Crown of Italy; had Russian Order of St. Anne; K. St. J., PC. (Ireland) 1920, (England) 1938; F.R.S. 1945. A National Member. Sat for the Scot-

tish Universities from Feb. 1938 until he retired in 1950. C.B. 1918, K.C.B. 1919, G.C.B. 1923, G.C.I.E. 1932, G.C.S.I. 1937. Created Visct. Waverley 1952. O.M. 1957. Died 4 Jan. 1958. [1950]

ANDERSON, Rt. Hon. Margaret Betty Harvie. See HARVIE ANDERSON, Rt. Hon. Margaret Betty.

ANSTRUTHER-GRAY, Maj. Rt. Hon. Sir William John St. Clair, Bart., M.C. Kilmany, Cupar, Fife. Brooks's, Carlton, Turf, and New (Edinburgh). S. of Col. Anstruther-Gray, of Kilmany, Fife, MP for St. Andrews Burghs from 1906-18. B. 1905; m. 1934, Monica, d. of Geoffrey Lambton, Esq. Educ. at Eton, and Christ Church, Oxford, M.A. Honours. Lieut. Coldstream Guards 1926-30; rejoined 1939-45; served in North Africa and N.W. Europe. M.C. 1943. Parliamentary Private Secretary to Rt. Hon. John Colville, MP, when Secretary to Department of Overseas Trade 1935, when Financial Secretary to the Treasury 1936, and when Secretary of State for Scotland 1938-39. Assistant Postmaster-Gen. May-July 1945. Lay member of General Medical Council from 1952-1965. Dept.-Lieut. for Fife 1953-74. Created 1st Bart. 1956. Dept. Chairman of Ways and Means Oct. 1959-Jan. 1962. Chairman of Ways and Means Jan. 1962-Oct. 1964. Elected Chairman of the 1922 Committee Nov. 1964. PC. 1962. A Conservative. Elected for Lanarkshire N. in 1931 and 1935, defeated 1945. Unsuccessfully contested Berwick and East Lothian in 1950. Elected for Berwick and East Lothian in Oct. 1951, 1955, 1959 and 1964. Sat until he was defeated in 1966. Created Baron Kilmany (Life Peerage) 1966. Member of National Hunt Committee 1948 and of Horserace Betting Levy Board 1966-74. Lord-Lieut. of Fife 1974-80.* [1966]

ARBUTHNOT, Sir John Sinclair-Wemyss, Bart., M.B.E., T.D. 7 Fairholt Street, London. Poulton Manor, Ash, Canterbury, Kent. Carlton, City of London, and M.C.C. S. of Maj. Kenneth Arbuthnot, The Seaforth Highlanders. B. 11 Feb. 1912; m. 3 July 1943, Margaret Jean youngest d. of A.G. Duff, Esq., (2 s. 3 d.). Educ. at Eton, and

Trinity Coll., Cambridge, M.A., Honours in Natural Sciences. Second Church Estates Commissioner from 1962-64. A Chairman of Standing Committees and temporary Chairman of the House from 1958. A Director of Tea and other companies. Member of Council of Ceylon Association 1953-62. Member of Committee of S. Indian Association 1954-62. Member of Lloyd's from 1937; Joint-Honorary Secretary Association of British Chambers of Commerce 1953-59. Served throughout 2nd World War R.A. Maj. T.A.R.O. 1948-62. Member Public Accounts Committee from 1955; Parliamentary Private Secretary to J.G. Smyth, Parliamentary Secretary, Ministry of Pensions 1952-53, to O. Peake, Minister of Pensions and National Insurance 1953-56; and to R.H. Turton, Minister of Health 1956-57. Member of House of Laity of Church Assembly and of Gen. Synod from 1955-75. Member of the Legislative Committee of Church Assembly from 1961. Member of Ecclesiastical Committee of Parliament from 1963. A Conservative. Unsuccessfully contested the Don Valley division of Yorkshire in 1935, and the Dover division of Kent in 1945. Elected for the Dover division of Kent in 1950, 1951, 1955 and 1959 and sat until he was defeated in 1964. Prospective candidate for Dunbartonshire 1936-45. Created Bart. Jan. 1964. M.B.E. 1944, T.D. 1951. Church Commissioner 1962-77. President of Trustee Savings Bank Association 1962-76. Chairman of Folkestone and District Water Company.*

ARCHER, Jeffrey Howard. 24A The Boltons, London. 27/31 Whitehall, London. Carlton, and M.C.C. S. of William Archer, Esq. B. 15 Apr. 1940; m. July 1966, Mary Weeden. Educ. at Wellington School, Somerset, and B.N.C., Oxford. Member of Greater London Council 1966-70 for Havering. International Athlete. A Conservative. Elected for the Louth division of Lincolnshire in Dec. 1969 and sat until he retired in Sept. 1974, after being declared bankrupt. Fellow of Royal Society of Arts. Author of *Not a penny more, not a penny less,* and *Shall we tell the President?** [1974 2nd ed.]

ARCHER, Rt. Hon. Peter Kingsley, Q.C. "Arvika", 44 Clements Road, Chorleywood, Hertfordshire. S. of Cyril Kingsley Archer, Esq., Toolsetter. B. 20 Nov. 1926; m. 7 Aug. 1954, Margaret Irene, d. of Sydney John Smith, Esq., (1 s.). Educ. at Wednesbury Boys' High School, London School of Economics, and University Coll., London. Called to the bar, Gray's Inn, 1952. Q.C. 1971. Author of *The Queen's Courts, Communism and the Law, Human Rights, Freedom at Stake* (co-Author), and *Purpose in Socialism.* Editor of *Social Welfare and the Citizens.* Chairman Amnesty International (British Section) 1971-74. Chairman Society of Labour Lawyers 1971-74. Solicitor-Gen. Mar. 1974-May 1979. A Labour Member. Unsuccessfully contested Hendon S. in 1959 and Brierley Hill in 1964. Member for Rowley Regis and Tipton Mar. 1966-Feb. 1974, and for the W. division of Warley from Feb. 1974. Parliamentary Private Secretary to Sir Elwyn Jones, Attorney-General, 1967-70. Chairman of Parliamentary Group for World Government 1970-74. Voted in favour of entry to E.E.C. on 28 Oct. 1971. Bencher of Gray's Inn 1974. PC. 1977. An Opposition spokesman on Legal Affairs from 1979.* [1979]

ARMSTRONG, Christopher Wyborne, O.B.E. House of Commons, London. United University. S. of the Rt. Hon. H.B. Armstrong, MP. B. 9 May 1899; m. Apr. 1956, Hilde, d. of Hans Kolz. Educ. at Winchester, and Trinity Coll., Cambridge. Served in France 1918 and 1940; with Burmah Oil Company in Burma 1922-39 and 1940-42; European Elected Member of House of Representatives, Burma 1942; Controller of Petroleum Industry, Burma 1942; M.E.L.F. Egypt A.Q.M.G. 1942-43; G.H.Q. India 1944-45; Commissioner Magwe Division Burma 1945-46; Farming in Kenya 1946-54 and from 1959; O.B.E. 1943. An Ulster Unionist Member. Elected for Armagh in Nov. 1954 and sat until he retired in 1959. Member of Council of Europe and Western European Union 1957-59.* [1959]

ARMSTRONG, Rt. Hon. Ernest. Penny Well, Witton-le-Wear, Co. Durham. S. of John Armstrong, Esq. B. 12 Jan. 1915; m. 1941, Hannah, d. of Thomas and Margaret

Jane Lamb of Sunderland. Educ. at Wolsingham Grammar School, and City of Leeds Teachers' Training Coll. A Schoolmaster. Member of Sunderland Town Council 1956-65; Chairman of Sunderland Borough Education Committee. Joined the Labour Party in 1931. Member of N.U.G.M.W. from 1951 and Fabian Society from 1948. Parliamentary Private Secretary to Rt. Hon. Anthony Greenwood, Colonial Secretary Mar. 1965 Chairman Education Group. Lord Commissioner H.M. Treasury Oct. 1969-June 1970. Opposition Whip July 1970-Dec. 1973. Parliamentary Under-Secretary Department of Education and Science 1974-75. Parliamentary Under-Secretary Department of Environment June 1975-May 1979. A Labour Member. Unsuccessfully contested Sunderland S. in the 1955 and 1959 general elections. Sat for Durham N.W. from Oct. 1964. Assistant Government Whip Jan. 1967-Oct. 1969. An Opposition spokesman on Education Dec. 1973-Mar. 1974. Vice-President of Methodist Conference 1974-75. PC. 1979.* [1979]

ARNOLD, Thomas Richard. 19 Sudbury Road, Hazel Grove, Stockport, Cheshire. Carlton. S. of Thomas Charles Arnold, Esq., Impresario. B. 25 Jan. 1947. Educ. at Bedales, Le Rosey (Geneva), and Pembroke Coll., Oxford. A Theatre Producer. Parliamentary Private Secretary to Rt. Hon. Humphrey Atkins, Secretary of State for N. Ireland from 1979. A Conservative. Unsuccessfully contested the Cheetham division of Manchester in 1970, and Hazel Grove in Feb. 1974. Elected for Hazel Grove in Oct. 1974.* [1979]

ASHLEY, Rt. Hon. John, C.H. House of Commons, London S. of John Ashley, Esq., Labourer. B. 6 Dec. 1922; m. 15 Dec. 1951, Pauline, d. of C.A. Crispin, Esq. Educ. at St. Patrick's Elementary School, Widnes, Ruskin Coll., Oxford, and Caius Coll., Cambridge. President of Cambridge Union. Formerly a Labourer, Crane Driver, and Shop Steward. A B.B.C. radio and television producer. Autobiography *Journey into Silence*. Companion of Honour 1975. A Labour Member. Unsuccessfully contested Finchley in 1951. Sat for Stoke-on-Trent S. from Mar.

1966. Member of Widnes Borough Council 1945-46. Member of General Advisory Council of B.B.C. 1967-69 and 1970-74. Parliamentary Private Secretary to Rt. Hon. Michael Stewart, Secretary of State for Economic Affairs and Foreign Secretary 1967-70 and to Rt. Hon. Barbara Castle, Secretary of State for Social Services 1974-76. Member of National Executive Committee of Labour Party 1976-78. PC. 1979.* [1979]

ASHTON, Sir Hubert, K.B.E., M.C. Wealdside, South Weald, Brentwood, Essex. City of London, Oriental, and Carlton. S. of Hubert S. Ashton, Esq., of Trueloves, Ingatestone, Essex. B. 1898; m. 1927, Dorothy, d. of Arthur Gaitskell, Esq., I.C.S., (2 s. 2 d.). Educ. at Winchester, and Trinity Coll., Cambridge, M.A. Served overseas 1916-19 with R.A. Served with Burmah Oil Company in Burma and London 1922-45. Dept-Lieut. 1942 and County Alderman 1950-61 for Essex, High Sheriff 1943. Elected Essex County Council 1946, Vice-Chairman Essex County Council 1949-51, Parliamentary Private Secretary to Rt. Hon. R.A. Butler when Chancellor of Exchequer, Lord Privy Seal and Home Secretary Oct. 1951-Oct. 1957, when appointed Second Church Estates Commissioner. Third Church Estates Commissioner 1962-72. President M.C.C. 1960-61. President Essex County Cricket Club, 1948-70. K.B.E. June 1959. A Conservative. Elected for the Chelmsford division of Essex in 1950, 1951, 1955 and 1959 and sat until he retired in 1964. Died 17 June, 1979. [1964]

ASHTON, Joseph William. 16 Ranmoor Park Road, Sheffield. S. of Arthur Ashton, Esq., Steelsmelter. B. 9 Oct. 1933; m. 24 Dec. 1957, Margaret, d. of George Lee, Esq., (1 d.). Educ. at High Storrs Grammar School, and Rotherham Technical Coll. City Councillor and Chief Whip in Sheffield 1962-68. Parliamentary Private Secretary to Denis Howell 1969-70 and Anthony Wedgwood Benn 1974-76. A Journalist, weekly column for *Labour Weekly*. Chairman E. Midlands group of Labour MPs. Chairman Back Bench Industry Group. A Labour Member. Elected for the Bassetlaw division of Nottinghamshire at a by-election in Oct.

1968. Assistant Government Whip Nov. 1976-Nov. 1977, when he resigned. An Opposition spokesman on Energy from 1979. Author of *Grass roots* (1977).*   [1979]

ASSHETON, Rt. Hon. Ralph. 45 Wilton Crescent, London. Downham Hall, Clitheroe, Lancashire. Carlton, and City of London. S. of Sir Ralph C. Assheton, Bart., of Downham Hall, Clitheroe. B. 24 Feb. 1901; m. 24 Jan. 1924, Hon. Sylvia Hotham, F.L.A.S., d. of 6th Baron Hotham. Educ. at Eton, and Christ Church, Oxford, M.A. Barrister-at-Law, Inner Temple 1925; Stock Exchange 1927-39; a landowner in Lancashire and Yorkshire; J.P. for lancashire; Director of National Provincial Bank and other companies. Fellow of Society of Antiquaries; represented Blackburn on National Assembly of Church of England 1930-50; Parliamentary Private Secretary to Rt. Hon. William Ormsby-Gore when First Commissioner of Works 1936 and when Secretary of State for the Colonies May 1936. Member of West Indies Royal Committee 1938-39. Parliamentary Secretary Ministry of Labour and National Service Sept. 1939-Feb. 1942. Parliamentary Secretary Ministry of Supply Feb. 1942-Feb. 1943. Financial Secretary to the Treasury Feb. 1943-Oct. 1944, Chairman of Conservative and Unionist Organisation Nov. 1944-July 1946 and of Public Accounts Committee House of Commons 1948-50. Chairman of Select Committee on Nationalised Industries 1951-53. PC. 1944. A Conservative. Sat for the Rushcliffe division from July 1934-July 1945 when he was defeated, for the City of London Oct. 1945-Feb. 1950. Elected for Blackburn W. in 1950 and 1951 and sat until he retired in 1955. Created Baron Clitheroe June 1955. Succeeded to his father's baronetcy Sept. 1955. Dept.-Lieut. for Lancashire 1955, Vice-Lieut. 1956-71, Lord-Lieut. 1971-76. High Steward of Westminster from 1962. Chairman of Mercantile Investment Trust Limited 1958-71. Member of Council of Duchy of Lancaster 1956-77. K.C.V.O. 1977.*   [1954]

ASTERLEY JONES, Philip. See JONES, Philip Asterley.

ASTOR, Hon. John. Kirby House, Inkpen, Nr. Newbury, Berkshire. Bucks, and Royal Yacht Squadron. 3rd s. of 1st Baron Astor of Hever. B. 1923; m. 1950, Diana Kathleen Drummond. Educ. at Summerfields, Hastings, and Eton. Flight-Lieut. R.A.F.V.R. 1942-46. Public Relations Department of B.O.A.C. 1946-48. Director of Universal Shipyards from 1946. County Councillor for Berkshire from 1953-1974; Alderman 1960. Vice-Chairman of the S. Berkshire Conservative Association from 1957. A Conservative. Elected for the Newbury division of Berkshire in Oct. 1964 and sat until he retired in Feb.1974. Parliamentary Private Secretary to Rt. Hon. Richard Wood, Minister for Overseas Development 1970-74.*   [1974]

ASTOR, Maj. Hon. John Jacob, M.B.E. Hatley Park, Gamlingay, Sandy, Bedfordshire. S. of 2nd Visct. Astor. B. 29 Aug. 1918; m. 1st, 23 Oct. 1944, Anna Inez, d. of Señor Don Miguel Carcano, former Argentine Ambassador in London (divorced 1972); 2ndly, 1976, Susan Sheppard, d. of Maj. M. Eveleigh. Educ. at Eton, and New Coll., Oxford. Joined Life Guards 1939 and served overseas 1939-45. Secretary to British Delegation to Commonwealth Conference in Canada 1949. Parliamentary Private Secretary to J. Boyd-Carpenter, Financial Secretary to Treasury 1951-53. A Conservative. Unsuccessfully contested the Sutton division of Plymouth in 1950. Elected for the Sutton division of Plymouth in Oct. 1951 and sat until he retired in 1959. M.B.E. 1945. Knighted 1978. Chairman of Agricultural Research Council 1968-78. Member of Horserace Totalisator Board 1962-68, of Horserace Betting Levy Board from 1976. Dept.-Lieut. for Cambridgeshire.*   [1959]

ASTOR, Hon. Michael Langhorne. 28 Mallord Street, London. Bruern Abbey, Churchill, Oxfordshire. S. of 2nd Visct. Astor. B. 10 Apr. 1916; m. 1st, 1942, Barbara, d. of Capt. R. McNeill (divorced 1961); 2ndly, 1961, Mrs. Pandora Jones, d. of Sir Bede Clifford (divorced 1968); 3rdly, 1970, Judy, d. of Paul Innes, Esq. Educ. at Eton, and New Coll., Oxford. Capt. R.A. (T.A.). A Conservative. Elected for E. Surrey in July

1945 and sat until he retired in 1951. Chairman of the London Library. Member of Arts Council 1968-71. Died 28 Feb. 1980.

[1951]

ASTOR, Hon. William Waldorf. 45 Upper Grosvenor Street, London. Carlton, Marlborough, Pratt's, and Buck's. S. of Waldorf, 2nd Visct. Astor and Nancy, Lady Astor, MP. B. 13 Aug. 1907; m. 1st, 1945, Hon. Sarah Norton, d. of 6th Baron Grantley (divorced 1953); 2ndly, 1955, Philippa Victoria, d. of Lieut.-Col. H.P. Hunloke, MP. (divorced 1960); 3rdly, 1960, Janet Bronwen, d. of Judge Sir Alun Pugh. Educ. at Eton, and New Coll., Oxford. On Staff of the Pilgrim Trust 1930-31, in Unemployment Department of National Council of Social Service 1933-34. Secretary to the Earl of Lytton on League of Nations Committee of Enquiry in Manchuria 1932; Parliamentary Private Secretary to Rt. Hon. Sir Samuel Hoare when 1st Lord of the Admiralty June 1936, and when Home Secretary May 1937-39; Lieut. R.N.V.R. 1939. A Conservative. Sat for Fulham E. from 1935-45 when he was defeated. Unsuccessfully contested the Wycombe division of Buckinghamshire in 1950 and sat for the same division from 1951 until he succeeded to the peerage as Visct. Astor on 30 Sept. 1952. Member of Executive Committee of U.K. Committee for World Refugee Year 1959-60. High Steward of Maidenhead. Grand Cross of Merit of the Order of Malta 1957. Died 8 Mar. 1966.

[1952]

ATKINS, Rt. Hon. Humphrey Edward Gregory. 3 North Court, Great Peter Street, London Brooks's. S. of Capt. E.D. Atkins, of Kenya. B. 12 Aug. 1922; m. 21 Jan. 1944, Margaret, d. of Sir Robert Spencer-Nairn, Bart., (1 s. 3 d.). Educ. at Wellington Coll. Special Entry Cadetship Royal Navy 1940; Lieut. R.N. 1943, resigned 1948. Parliamentary Private Secretary to C.I. Orr-Ewing, Civil Lord of the Admiralty 1959-62; Opposition Whip 1967-70. Treasurer of the Household and Government Dept. Chief Whip June 1970-Dec. 1973; Parliamentary Secretary to the Treasury and Chief Whip Dec. 1973-Mar. 1974. PC. 1973. Opposition Chief Whip 1974. A Conservative. Un-

successfully contested West Lothian in 1951. Member for Merton and Morden from 1955-70. Sat for the Spelthorne division of Surrey from June 1970. Secretary of State for N. Ireland from May 1979.* [1979]

ATKINS, Ronald Henry. House of Commons, London. S. of Frank Atkins, Esq., of Barry, Glamorgan. B. 13 June 1916; m. Jessie Hall, d. of Adam Scott, Esq. (3 s. 2 d.). Educ. at Elementary and County Schools and London University, (B.A. Hons.). Joined Labour Party 1934. A Teacher 1949-66. Lecturer, Accrington Coll. of Further Education 1970-74. Member of United Nations Association. Member of Fabian Society. Member of National Council on Inland Transport, Chairman of P.L.P. Transport Group. Member of Braintree Rural District Council 1952-61 and Preston District Council 1974-76. A Labour Member. Unsuccessfully contested Lowestoft in 1964. Member for Preston N. from 1966-70, when he was defeated and from Feb. 1974 to 1979, when he was again defeated.* [1979]

ATKINSON, David Anthony. House of Commons, London. S. of Arthur Joseph Atkinson, Esq. B. 1940; m. 1968, Susan Nicola Pilsworth. Educ. at St. George's Coll., Weybridge, Southend Coll. of Technology, and the Coll. of Automobile and Aeronautical Engineering, Chelsea. Member of Southend County Borough Council 1969-72. Elected to Essex County Council 1973 and re-elected 1977. Chairman National Young Conservatives 1970-71. Member of the Conservative Group for Europe. Travelled widely in 42 countries of Western and Communist Europe, Russia, America, the Middle East and N. Africa. A Conservative. Unsuccessfully contested Newham N.W. in Feb. 1974 and Basildon in Oct. 1974. Member for Bournemouth E. from Nov. 1977. Parliamentary Private Secretary to Paul Channon, Minister of State, Civil Service Department from 1979.* [1979]

ATKINSON, Norman. House of Commons, London. S. of George Atkinson, Esq. of Manchester. B. 25 Mar. 1923; m. 15 May 1948, Irene, d. of Mr. and Mrs. E. Parry of Manchester. Educ. at Technical Coll. Chief

Designer, Engineering Department, Member Manchester City Council 1945-49 University of Manchester 1957-64. Joined the Labour League of Youth in 1939. Member Section I.A.E.U. Governor Royal Coll. of Science and Technology. Elected National Treasurer Labour Party Oct. 1976. A Labour Member. Unsuccessfully contested Manchester Wythenshawe in 1955 and Altrincham and Sale in 1959. Member for Tottenham from Oct. 1964 to Feb. 1974 and for Tottenham division of Haringey from Feb. 1974.*

[1979]

ATTEWELL, Humphrey Cooper. 2 Willoughby Lane, Tottenham, London. S. of H.C. Attewell, Esq., of Northampton. B. 1894; m. 1915, Rose, d. of David Brazier, Esq. Educ. at Elementary School. Served overseas 1914-19. A Trades Union official. A Labour Member. Elected for the Harborough division of Leicestershire in July 1945 and sat until he was defeated in 1950. National Organiser of National Union of Boot and Shoe Operatives 1950-59. Member of Middlesex County Council 1940-49. Died 1972. [1950]

ATTLEE, Rt. Hon. Clement Richard, O.M., C.H., F.R.S. Cherry Cottage, Prestwood, Great Missenden, Buckinghamshire. S. of Henry Attlee, Esq., of Westcott, Putney. B. 3 Jan. 1883; m. 10 Jan. 1922, Violet Helen, d. of H.E. and Ada Millar (she died 1964). Educ. at Haileybury, and University Coll., Oxford, Hon. D.C.L. Oxford and Hon. LL.D. Cambridge, London, Wales and Glasgow, and D.Litt. Reading. Barrister-at-Law, Inner Temple 1905. Secretary of Toynbee Hall 1910. Lecturer at the London School of Economics 1913-23. Served in Gallipoli, Mesopotamia and France 1914-18; Maj. South Lancashire Regiment. Mayor of Stepney 1919-20; Alderman 1919-27. Chairman London Labour Mayors' Association 1919. Parliamentary Private Secretary to Rt. Hon. J.R. MacDonald 1922-24; Under-Secretary for War Jan.-Nov. 1924. Chancellor of the Duchy of Lancaster May 1930-Mar. 1931; Postmaster-Gen. Mar.-Aug. 1931. Member of Indian Statutory Commission 1927; Dept. Leader of the Labour Party in the House of Commons 1931-35; PC. 1935. Leader of the Opposition 1935-40, May-July 1945 and from Oct. 1951-Nov. 1955. Leader of Labour Party 1935-55. Lord Privy Seal in the War Cabinet May 1940-Feb. 1942. Secretary of State for the Dominions Feb. 1942-Sept. 1943. Lord President of the Council Sept. 1943-May 1945, Dept. Prime Minister 1942-45; C.H. 1945; O.M. 1951; Minister of Defence 1945-46. Prime Minister and First Lord of the Treasury 1945-51. A Labour Member. Sat for Limehouse from Nov. 1922-Feb. 1950. Sat for Walthamstow W. from Feb. 1950 to Nov. 1955 when he was created Earl Attlee. Member of National Executive Committee of Labour Party 1934-55. K.G. 1956. President of Association of Municipal Corporations 1961-64. Died 8 Oct. 1967. [1955]

AUSTICK, David. Clarence Place, Burley in Wharfdale. 29 Cookridge Street, Leeds, Yorkshire. National Liberal. S. of Bertie Lister Austick, Esq. B. 8 Mar. 1920; m. 9 Sept. 1945, Florence Elizabeth Lomath. Educ. at City of Leeds School. Partner Austicks Bookshops, Leeds 1946. Chairman Education Board Booksellers Association 1960-65. Leeds City Councillor 1969; District Councillor 1973; W. Yorkshire County Councillor 1973. A Liberal. Elected for Ripon in July 1973 and sat until he was defeated in Feb. 1974. Unsuccessfully contested Ripon in Oct. 1974 and Cheadle in 1979. Unsuccessfully contested Leeds for European Parliament in 1979.* [1974]

AUSTIN, Sub.-Lieut. Herschel Lewis, R.N. House of Commons, London. S. of Mark Austin, Esq., of Plymouth B. 22 Mar. 1911; m. 8 May 1944, Irene, d. of J. Raymond, Esq. Educ. at Elementary Schools. A Labour Member. Elected for the Stretford division of Lancashire in July 1945 and sat until he was defeated in 1950. Served in R.N. 1943-45. Died 8 Apr. 1974. [1950]

AWBERY, Stanley Stephen. 37 Woodlands Road, Barry, Glamorgan. B. 19 July 1888; m. 1911, Elizabeth Jane (she died Apr. 1969). Educ. at Evening Classes. Member of Barry Borough Council from 1931. Alderman 1939; Mayor of Barry 1941-42; Chairman of Swansea General and Eye Hospital 1921. Trades Union Official from

1920; Dept.-Lieut., and J.P. for Glamorgan; Port Labour Inspector South Wales 1941-42. Parliamentary Delegate to Malaya 1948; member Select Committee on Estimates 1950-51. Chairman of Magistrates, Glamorgan 1951. A Labour Member. Unsuccessfully contested Clitheroe in 1931 and 1935. Elected for the Central division of Bristol in July 1945 and sat until he retired in 1964. President of Welsh Division of Independent Labour Party 1928. A Baptist. Author and local historian. Died 7 May 1969.

[1964]

AWDRY, Daniel Edmund, T.D. Old Manor, Beanacre, Wiltshire. S. of Col. E.P. Awdry, M.C., T.D., D.L. B. 10 Sept. 1924; m. 30 Sept. 1950, Elizabeth Cattley, d. of Mr. and Mrs. Jack Cattley. Educ. at Winchester Coll. A Solicitor, qualified 1950. Mayor of Chippenham 1958-59. Served during the war with the 10th Hussars, and with the Royal Wilts Yeomanry 1947-61. Parliamentary Private Secretary to Edward du Cann, Minister of State, Board of Trade Jan.-Oct. 1964, and to Sir Michael Havers, Solicitor Gen. 1973-74. A Conservative. Sat for the Chippenham division of Wiltshire from Nov. 1962 until he retired in 1979. Director of BET Omnibus Services Ltd., Sheepbridge Engineering and Rediffusion Ltd. Dept.-Lieut. for Wiltshire 1979.*

[1979]

AYLES, Walter Henry. Brookwood, Kingussie, Inverness-shire. S. of Percy Walter Ayles, Esq., Railway Porter. B. 24 Mar. 1879; m. 1st, 1904, Bertha Winifred, d. of Abraham Batt, Esq. (she died 1942); 2ndly, 21 Oct. 1944, Jean, d. of William Middleton, Esq., of Stonehaven. Educ. at Elementary Schools. Engineer 1894; member of Aston Board of Guardians 1906; Bristol City Council 1911-25, and Orpington District Council 1937-43. A Labour Member. Unsuccessfully contested Bristol N. in 1922. Sat for Bristol N. from 1923-24, when he was defeated, re-elected in 1929 and sat until he was defeated in 1931, and unsuccessfully contested the seat again in 1935. Sat for Southall from 1945-50 and for Hayes and Harlington from 1950 until he resigned in Feb. 1953. Died 6 July 1953.

[1953]

BACON, Rt. Hon. Alice Martha, P.C., C.B.E. 3NB Artillery Mansions, London. 53 Snydale Road, Normanton, Yorkshire. D. of Benjamin Bacon, Miner, of Normanton. B. 1911. Educ. at Elementary Schools, Normanton Girls' High School, Stockwell Coll., and External London University. A Teacher. Member of National Executive Committee Labour Party from 1941-70. Chairman of Standing Joint Committee of Working Women's Organisations 1946-47; member of Consultative Assembly of Council of Europe 1950-53; Chairman of the Labour Party 1950 and of Labour Party Conference, Scarborough 1951. C.B.E. June 1953. Minister of State, Home Office Oct. 1964-Aug. 1967. PC. 1966. Minister of State Education and Science Aug. 1967-June 1970. A Labour Member. Sat for Leeds N.E. from 1945-1955 and for Leeds S.E. from 1955 until she retired in 1970. Created Baroness Bacon (Life Peerage) 1970. Dept.-Lieut. for W. Yorkshire 1974. An Opposition spokesman on Home Affairs 1959-64.*

[1970]

BAGIER, Gordon Alexander Thomas. "Rahana", Whickham Highway, Dunston, Gateshead. S. of Alexander Thomas Bagier, Esq. of Glasgow. B. 7 July 1924. m. 1949, Violet Sinclair. Educ. at Pendower Technical Secondary School, Newcastle-on-Tyne. District Signalman's Inspector, British Railways. Joined the Labour Party 1950. Member of the National Union of Railwaymen from 1950, held many official positions and in 1962 elected President of the Yorkshire District Council of the N.U.R. Member Keighley Borough Council 1956-60 and of Sowerby Bridge U.D.C. from 1962-65. A Labour Member. Sat for Sunderland S. from Oct. 1964. Parliamentary Private Secretary to Rt. Hon. James Callaghan, Home Secretary 1968-69.*

[1979]

BAIN, Margaret Anne. House of Commons, London. D. of John McAdam, Esq. B. Sept. 1945; m. 1968, Donald Straiton Bain, Esq. Educ. at Biggar High School, Glasgow University, Jordanhill Coll., Strathclyde University. A Teacher. Member of Scottish National Party National Executive. A Scottish National Party Member. Unsuccessfully contested Dunbartonshire E.

in Feb. 1974. Sat for Dunbartonshire E. from Oct. 1974 until 1979 when she was defeated.*

[1979]

BAIRD, John. 293 Green Lane, London. 7 Lyndhurst Gardens, London. S. of Alexander Baird, Esq., of Glasgow. B. 26 Sept. 1906; m. 22 June 1933, Agnes, d. of John Kerr, Esq. Educ. at Secondary School, and St. Mungo's Medical Coll. A Dental Surgeon. Capt. Army 1942-45. A Labour Member. Sat for Wolverhampton E. from July 1945 to Feb. 1950 and for Wolverhampton N.E. from Feb. 1950 until he retired in 1964, after the Constituency Labour Party had declined to re-adopt him as their candidate. Editor of *Free Algeria*. Died 21 Mar. 1965. [1964]

BAKER, Kenneth Wilfred. House of Commons, London. Carlton. S. of Wilfred Michael Baker, Esq., O.B.E. B. 3 Nov. 1934; m. 1963, Mary Elizabeth Gray-Muir, (1 s. 2 d.). Educ. at St. Paul's School, and Magdalen Coll., Oxford. National Service 1953-55 (Lieut. in Gunners). Oxford 1955-58 (Secretary of Union. Served Twickenham Borough Council 1960-62. Parliamentary Private Secretary to Paul Bryan, Minister of State, Department of Employment 1970-72. Parliamentary Secretary, Civil Service Department 1972-74. Member of Executive of 1922 Committee 1975. Chairman Hansard Society from 1978. Joint Parliamentary Private Secretary to Rt. Hon. Edward Heath, Leader of the Opposition, 1974-75. A Conservative. Unsuccessfully contested Poplar in 1964 and Acton in 1966. Member for Acton from Mar. 1968 to June 1970, when he was defeated, for St. Marylebone from Oct. 1970 to Feb. 1974, and for the City of Westminster, St. Marylebone division of the Cities of London and Westminster from Feb. 1974.* [1979]

BAKER, Peter Arthur David, M.C. Kensington Close, London. Brooke House, Pulham St. Mary, Diss, Norfolk. Junior Carlton, and Norfolk Country. S. of Maj. R.P. Baker, of Loddenden Manor, Staplehurst, Kent. B. 20 Apr. 1921; m. 5 June 1948, Gloria Mae, d. of Col. C.G.W.S. Heaton-Armstrong, O.B.E. Educ. at Eastbourne Coll. Director of The Falcon Press, W. and S. Strang Limited, Dunstead Trust Limited,

The Grey Walls Press, etc. Served overseas 1939-45. A Conservative. Elected for S. Norfolk in 1950 and 1951 and sat until he was expelled from the House on 16 Dec. 1954 after being convicted of forgery and sentenced to 7 years imprisonment. Bankruptcy discharged 1962. M.C. 1944. Died 14 Nov. 1966.

[1954]

BAKER, Willfred Harold Kerton. Eastertown of Mayen, Rothiemay, Banffshire. House of Commons, London. S. of W.H. Baker, Esq. B. 1920; m. 15 Mar. 1945, Kathleen Helen, eld. d. of Lieut.-Col. W.T. Murray Bisset, of Lessendrum. Educ. at Nottingham, Edinburgh and Cornell Universities. Served in Army 1939-45, Maj. A Conservative. Elected for Banffshire in Oct. 1964 and sat until he was defeated in Feb. 1974. Parliamentary Private Secretary to Paul Bryan, Minister of State, Department of Employment 1971-72.* [1974]

BALDOCK, John Markham. 57 St. George's Square, London. Hollycombe House, Liphook, Hampshire. Carlton, and Farmers'. S. of Capt. W.P. Baldock, of Frinsted, Kent. B. 19 Nov. 1915; m. 14 May 1949, Pauline Ruth Gauntlett. Educ. at Rugby, and Balliol Coll., Oxford. Lieut.-Commander R.N.V.R. attached to H.M.S. *President*. Parliamentary Private Secretary to John Foster, Under-Secretary for Commonwealth Relations 1952 and to Rt. Hon. D. Ormsby-Gore, Minister of State, Foreign Office 1957-59. A Conservative. Elected for the Harborough division of Leicestershire at 1950 and sat until he retired in 1959. V.R.D. 1949. Chairman of Lenscrete Limited.* [1959]

BALDWIN, Sir Archer Ernest, M.C. Underley, Tenbury Wells, Worcestershire. Empire, and Farmers'. S. of William Baldwin, Esq. B. 30 Dec. 1883 in Tennessee; m. 1911, Minnie Powell Baldwin. Educ. at Lucton School. Chairman of the firm of Russell, Baldwin and Bright Limited, Auctioneers, Hereford until 1965. Served with R.H.A. in France and Italy 1914-18. A Farmer and Auctioneer. Member Joint East and Central Africa Board from 1945; Council Three Counties' Show Southfield Club. Knight Bach. 1958. A Conservative. Elected for the Leominster division of Hereford in July 1945 and sat until he retired in 1959. Dept.-Lieut. for Herefordshire. Died 27 Mar. 1966. [1959]

BALDWIN, Oliver Ridsdale. See CORVEDALE, Maj. Oliver Ridsdale Baldwin, Visct.

BALFOUR, Alfred. 12 Union Grove, Aberdeen. S. of William Balfour, Esq., of Old Aberdeen. B. 7 Sept. 1885; m. 9 Jan. 1913, Margaret, d. of John Grant, Esq., of Aberdeen. Educ. at Elementary School. Member of Aberdeen Town Council 1941-42. A Railwayman. A Labour Member. Elected for the West Stirlingshire division of Stirling and Clackmannan in July 1945 and sat until he retired in 1959. Member of Executive of N.U.R. Died 26 Jan. 1963. [1959]

BALNIEL, Rt. Hon. Robert Alexander Lindsay, Lord. House of Commons, London. S. of the Earl of Crawford and Balcarres. B. 5 Mar. 1927; m. 1949, Ruth, d. of Leo Meyer, Esq., of Zürich. Educ. at Eton, and Trinity Coll., Cambridge. Served with Grenadier Guards 1945-48; Honorary Attache British Embassy, Paris 1950-51; Conservative Research Department 1951-55. Parliamentary Private Secretary to Henry Brooke, Financial Secretary, Treasury 1955-57, and Minister of Housing and Local Government 1957-59. Minister of State for Defence 1970-72. Minister of State for Foreign and Commonwealth Affairs 1972-74. PC. 1972. A Conservative. Sat for Hertford from 1955 to Feb. 1974 and for Welwyn and Hatfield from Feb. 1974 to Oct. 1974 when he was defeated. Styled Lord Balniel from 1940. Created Baron Balniel (Life Peerage) 1974. Succeeded his father as Earl of Crawford and Balcarres 1975. Opposition spokesman on Foreign Affairs 1965-67 and on Social Services 1967-70. Member of Shadow Cabinet 1967-70. President of Rural District Councils Association 1959-65. Chairman of National Association for Mental Health 1963-70. Chairman of Historic Buildings Council for Scotland. Chairman of Lombard North Central. First Crown Estate Commissioner from 1980.* [1974 2nd ed.]

BANKS, Col. Cyril, M.B.E. Springside, Otley, Yorkshire. S. of Edward Banks, Esq., of Sheffield. B. 12 Aug. 1901; m. Apr. 1930, Gladys Drackley. Educ. at Sheffield Council School, and University of Sheffield. A Mechanical Engineer. Member of Yorkshire West Riding County Council 1946-49. A Conservative. Elected for Pudsey in 1950 and sat until he retired in 1959 after his local association had declined to readopt him as their candidate. Chief Engineer of Madras Tramways 1926-29. Managing Director of Banks Equipment Limited 1935-39. Served with Ministry of Food 1939-43 and War Office 1943-45, M.B.E. 1942. Associate Member of Institution of Mechanical Engineers. Associate of Institute of Transport. Parliamentary Private Secretary to Rt. Hon. A.T. Lennox-Boyd, Minister of Transport 1952-53. He criticised the Government's Suez policy in 1956 and the Conservative Whip was withdrawn from him Nov. 1956-Dec. 1958. Died 23 Oct. 1969. [1959]

BANKS, Robert George. Bretteston Hall, Stanstead, Sudbury, Suffolk. Cow Myers, Galphay, Ripon, Yorkshire. S. of George Walmsley Banks, Esq., M.B.E. B. 18 Jan. 1937; m. 1967, Diana Margaret Payne Crawfurd, (4 s. 1 d.). Educ. at Haileybury. Lieut.-Commander R.N.R. Joint Founder Director Antocks Lairn Limited 1963-67. Partner Breckland Securities. Joint Secretary Conservative Party Defence Committee. Vice-Chairman Parliamentary Horticulture Committee. Secretary All-Party Tourism Group. Member Council of Europe 7 Apr. 1977, also of Western European Union. Parliamentary Private Secretary to Nicholas Ridley and Peter Blaker, Ministers of State, Foreign and Commonwealth Office, from 1979. A Conservative. Sat for Harrogate from Feb. 1974.* [1979]

BARBER, Rt. Hon. Anthony, P.C., T.D. 15 Montpelier Square, London. Wentbridge, Nr. Pontefract, Yorkshire. Carlton. S. of John Barber, Esq., C.B.E., Company Director. B. 4 July 1920; m. 5 Sept. 1950, Jean Patricia, d. of Milton Asquith, Esq. Educ. at Oriel Coll., Oxford. Called to the bar in 1948. Served 1939-45 (P.O.W.) Germany. Parliamentary

Private Secretary Air Ministry 1952; Government Whip 1955. Lord Commissioner of the Treasury 1957-58; Parliamentary Private Secretary to Rt. Hon. Harold Macmillan, Prime Minister 1958. Economic Secretary to the Treasury 1959-62. Financial Secretary to the Treasury 1962-63. Minister of Health Oct. 1963-Oct. 1964. Chairman Conservative Party Sept. 1967-June 1970. Chancellor of the Duchy of Lancaster and Member of the Cabinet June 1970. Chancellor for the Exchequer 1970-74. Member of Shadow Cabinet 1965-70 and Mar.-June 1974. Opposition spokesman on Trade, Feb. 1965-Feb. 1967, on Steel Aug. 1965-Feb. 1967, on Power Apr. 1966-Feb. 1967, and on Co-ordination of Home Policy from Feb. 1967. A Conservative. Unsuccessfully contested Doncaster in 1950. Sat for Doncaster from 1951 to 1964 when he was defeated, and for Altrincham and Sale from Feb. 1965 until he retired in Sept. 1974. Created Baron Barber (Life Peerage) 1974. Honorary Fellow of Oriel Coll. Oxford 1971. Chairman of Standard Chartered Bank Limited from 1974. Government-appointed Director of British Petroleum from 1979.

[1974 2nd ed.]

BARLOW, Sir John Denman, Bart. Bradwell Manor, Sandbach, Cheshire. S. of Sir John Barlow, 1st Bart. B. 15 June 1898; m. 27 June 1928, Hon. Diana Helen, d. of 1st Baron Rochdale. Educ. at Leighton Park School, Reading, and Haverford, U.S.A. Partner of Thomas Barlow Brothers; Director of Manchester Chamber of Commerce, of Barclays Bank, Manchester Board, and of Calico Printers' Association. J.P. for Cheshire. A Conservative. Unsuccessfully contested the Northwich division of Cheshire as a Liberal in 1929. Sat for the Eddisbury division of Cheshire as a Conservative from 1945 to 1950, when he unsuccessfully contested Walsall, and for Middleton and Prestwich from 1951 until he was defeated in 1966. Succeeded as Bart. 1932.*   [1966]

BARNES, Rt. Hon. Alfred John. Eastcliffe Hotel, Walton-on-Naze, Essex. S. of William Barnes, Esq., Docker of N. Woolwich. B. 1887. Educ. at Northampton Institute. A Modeller and Repoussé Worker. Chairman of Co-operative Party 1924-45. Parliamentary Private Secretary to William Graham, Financial Secretary to Treasury, 1924. A Labour Whip 1925-30. Junior Lord of the Treasury June 1929-Oct. 1930. Minister of Transport 1945-51. A Labour Member. Sat for East Ham S. Nov. 1922-Oct. 1931, when he was defeated, and from 1935 until he retired in 1955. PC. 1945. Died 26 Nov. 1974.   [1954]

BARNES, Michael Cecil John. 45 Ladbroke Grove, London. S. of Maj. C.H.R. Barnes, O.B.E. B. 22 Sept. 1932; m. 21 Apr. 1962. Anne, d. of Basil Mason, Esq. (1 s. 1 d.). Educ. at Malvern, and Corpus Christi Coll., Oxford. Marketing Consultant. Member of Public Accounts Committee from 1967. Joint Secretary Labour Committee for Europe 1969-71. Chairman Parliamentary Labour Party Social Security Group 1969-70. Opposition spokesman on Food and Food Prices 1970-71. Chairman Association of Scientific Technical and Management Staffs Parliamentary Committee 1970-71. Member of the Council of Management on War on Want 1971-77. A Labour Member. Unsuccessfully contested Wycombe in the general election of 1964. Elected for Brentford and Chiswick in Mar. 1966 and sat until Feb. 1974 when he unsuccessfully contested the Brentford and Isleworth division of Hounslow. Voted in favour of entry into E.E.C. 28 Oct. 1971. Member of National Consumer Council from 1975. Chairman of Electricity Consumers Council from 1977.*   [1974]

BARNETT, Rt. Hon. Joel. 10 Park Lane, Whitefield, Lancashire. S. of Louis Barnett, Esq. B. 14 Oct. 1923; m. 1949, Lilian Goldstone, (1 d.). Educ. at Elementary School, and Manchester Central High. An Accountant. Served with R.A.S.C. and British Military Government in Germany. Member of Fabian Society, at one time Hon. Treasurer, Manchester Branch. Prestwich Borough Council 1956-59. J.P. for Lancashire 1960. Member of Public Accounts Committee. Chairman Parliamentary Labour Party Economic, Finance and Taxation Group 1967-70 and 1972-74. Voted in favour of entry to E.E.C. on 28 Oct. 1971. Official Opposition spokesman on Financial and Economic matters 1970-74. Chief Secretary to the Treasury Mar. 1974-May 1979. PC. 1975. Member Select Committee Public Accounts. Member Public Expenditure Committee. Member of Cabinet Feb.1977-May 1979. Chairman of Public Accounts Committee from 1979. A Labour Member. Unsuccessfully contested Runcorn in 1959. Elected for the Heywood and Royton division of Lancashire in Oct. 1964.*   [1979]

BARNETT, Nicholas Guy. 32 Woolwich Road, London. Royal Commonwealth Society. S. of B.G. Barnett, Esq., Shipbroker. B. 23 Aug. 1928; m. 1967, Daphne Anne, d. of G.W. Hortin, Esq., J.P. (1 s. 1 d.). Educ. at Highgate, St. Edmund Hall, Oxford. Member of Society of Friends. A Teacher 1953-61. Staff of Voluntary Service Overseas 1966-69. Chief Education Officer, Commonwealth Institute 1966-71. Member Select Committee on Race Relations and Immigration 1972-74. Parliamentary Private Secretary to John Silkin, Minister for Planning and Local Government 1974-75. Member Committee Public Accounts 1974-75. Trustee National Maritime Museum 1974-76. Member European Assembly 1975-76. Under-Secretary of State Department of Environment Apr. 1976-May 1979. A Labour Member. Unsuccessfully contested Scarborough and Whitby in 1959. Sat for S. Dorset from Nov. 1962 to 1964, when he was defeated, for Greenwich from July 1971 to Feb. 1974 and for the Greenwich division of Greenwich from Feb. 1974. Member of General Advisory Council of B.B.C. 1973-76. Parliamentary Adviser, Society of Civil Servants 1973-76.*   [1979]

BARSTOW, Percy Gott. Vectis, Jason Hill, Chesham, Buckinghamshire. S. of William Henry Barstow, Esq. Engine Driver of Grove Town, Pontefract. B. 25 Oct. 1883; m. 8 Mar. 1923, Dorothy Frances, d. of W.H. Scrutton, Esq. Educ. at Leeds Higher Grade School. An Engine Driver 1898-1906; Clerk at Headquarters of N.U.R. 1906-13; Departmental Manager N.U.R. 1913-34, Office Manager 1934-41. A Socialist. Unsuccessfully contested Barrow-in-Furness 1935. Elected for the Pontefract division of the W. Riding of Yorkshire in July 1941 and sat until he retired in 1950. Died 2 Jan. 1969.
[1950]

BARTER, John Wilfred. House of Commons, London. S. of W.F. Barter, Esq. B. 6 Oct. 1917; m. 1st, 1941, Joan, d. of W.F. Mackay, Esq. (she died 1973); 2ndly, 1974, Jessica Crabtree. Educ. at Royal Commercial Travellers' School. Member Middlesex County Council from 1949-65, Leader 1962-63. Vice-Chairman 1963-64, Chairman 1964-65. County Alderman 1961-65; a Chartered Secretary; Commercial Consultant. Parliamentary Private Secretary to Rt. Hon. Dennis Vosper when Minister of Health 1957. Parliamentary Private Secretary to Sir Ian Horobin when Parliamentary Secretary Ministry of Power 1958-59. A Conservative. Unsuccessfully contested East Ham S. in 1951. Elected for Ealing N. in 1955 and sat until he was defeated in 1964. Unsuccessfully contested Ealing N. in 1966 and 1970. J.P. for Greater London 1974.*   [1964]

BARTLETT, (Charles) Vernon Oldfield. 6 Gower Street, London. Stone Cottage, Byworth, Petworth. Garrick. S. of T.O. Bartlett, Esq., of Swanage. B. 30 Apr. 1894; m. 1st Sept. 1917, Marguerite, d. of H. Van den Bemden of Antwerp (she died 1966); 2ndly, 1969, Eleanor Needham Ritchie. Educ. at Blundell's School, Tiverton. A Journalist and Author. An Independent Member. Elected for the Bridgwater division of Somerset in 1938 and sat until he retired in 1950. C.B.E. 1956. London Director of League of Nations 1922-32. On staff of *News Chronicle* 1934-54 and *Manchester Guardian* 1954-61.*   [1950]

BARTLEY, Patrick. 29 Oxford Avenue, Washington, Co. Durham. S. of James Bartley, Esq., a Miner, of Washington, Co. Durham. B. 24 Mar. 1909; m. 15 Jan. 1938, Edith, d. of Jake Wood, Esq. Educ. at St. Joseph's Elementary School, and Catholic Workers' Coll., Oxford. A Miner 1923-42; Assistant Labour Director Northern 'B' Region Ministry of Fuel and Power 1942-46; N.C.B. Conciliation Officer 1947-50. A Labour Member. Elected for the Chester-le-Street division of Durham in 1950 and sat until his death on 25 June 1956. Member of Washington Urban District Council 1934-37 and of Durham County Council 1937-49. Died 25 June 1956.   [1956]

BARTON, Clarence. 9 Bassingham Road, Wembley. S. of Frederick Barton, Esq., of Pudsey. B. 21 June 1892; m. 20 Jan. 1917, Jennie, d. of W.F. Blackett, Esq., of Bradford. Educ. at Pudsey Elementary School, and Hanson Memorial Secondary School, Bradford. A Railway Clerk in L.N.E.R. Member of Wembley Borough Council 1934-49; Alderman 1942-49; Mayor 1942-43, Dept. Mayor 1943-44; J.P. Middlesex. A Labour Member. Elected for Wembley S. in July 1945 and sat until he was defeated in 1950. President of Transport Salaried Staffs Association 1944. Died 15 Sept. 1957.

[1950]

BATES, Alfred. 5 Dunbar Close, Little Sutton, South Wirral. S. of Norman Bates, Esq. B. 8 June 1944. Educ. at Stretford Grammar School for Boys, Manchester University, Corpus Christi Coll., Cambridge. Lecturer in Maths, De La Salle Coll. of Education, Middleton 1967-74 Member Stretford Borough Council 1971-74. Parliamentary Private Secretary to Rt. Hon. Brian O'Malley 1975-76. Assistant Whip Mar. 1976-Jan. 1979. A Labour Member. Unsuccessfully contested Northwich in 1970. Sat for Bebington and Ellesmere Port from Feb. 1974 until 1979, when he was defeated. Lord Commissioner of Treasury Jan.-May 1979.*

[1979]

BATSFORD, Brian Caldwell Cook. 19 Norfolk Road, London. Carlton, St. James's, and Marylebone Cricket. S. of Arthur Caldwell Cook, Esq., Merchant. B. 18 Dec. 1910; m. 4 Sept. 1945, Joan, d. of Norman Cunliffe, Esq. Educ. at Repton. Joined B.T. Batsford Limited 1928; Chairman 1952-74, President 1974-77. Served 1941-46 with R.A.F. Lectured in Canada 1935 and 1936, and in Scandinavia and Baltic States 1940. F.R.S.A.; elected to Council 1967, Chairman 1973-75; F.S.I.A. 1971. Parliamentary Private Secretary to Lord John Hope, Minister of Works 1959-60. Assistant Government Whip 1962-64. Opposition Dept.-Chief Whip Nov. 1964-Apr. 67. Alderman Greater London Council 1967-70. Chairman House of Commons Library Sub-Committee. Chairman Advisory Committee in Works of Art in the House of Commons, member Post Office

Stamp Advisory Committee. A Conservative. Unsuccessfully contested Chelmsford as a National Government Member in Apr. 1945. Elected for S. Ealing in June 1958 and sat until he retired in Feb. 1974. Knighted 1974. Assumed surname Batsford in lieu of Cook in 1946.*

[1974]

BATTLEY, John Rose. 94 Clapham Park Road, London. Trade Union, and City Livery. S. of George Battley, Esq., B. 26 Nov. 1880; m. 7 Mar. 1932, Dorothy Sybil, d. of Stanley Allchurch, Esq. Educ. at Elementary School. J.P. 1940. Member of London County Council 1938-46. Governing Director of Battley Brothers Limited, Printers. A Socialist. Elected for the Clapham division of Wandsworth in 1945 and sat until he retired in 1950. A Baptist. Member of 'Fellowship of Reconciliation' and a conscientious objector in the First World War. Died 1 Nov. 1952.

[1950]

BAXTER, Sir Arthur Beverley. 19 Oakwood Court, London. Carlton, and Royal Canadian Yacht. S. of James Baxter, Esq., of Toronto. B. 8 Jan. 1891; m. 1924, Edith, d. of J.K.L. Letson, Esq., of Vancouver. Educ. in Canada. A Journalist and Novelist. Served with Canadian Army in France 1915-18. Editor in chief of the *Daily Express* 1929-33. Public Relations Counsel, Gaumont British Picture Corporation Ltd. 1933-35. Fellow of Royal Society of Literature. Joint subject of *Beverley and Brendan* 1944 by 'Cassius' (Michael Foot). Knight Bach. 1954. A Conservative. Sat for the Wood Green division from 1935-50. Elected for the Southgate division in 1950 and sat until his death on 26 Apr. 1964. Died 26 Apr. 1964.

[1964]

BAXTER, William. House of Commons, London. S. of William Baxter, Esq. of Kilsyth. B. 1911; m. 1938, Margaret, d. of Anthony Bassy Esq. Educ. at Banton Public School. Elected to Stirling County Council 1932-61. Founder member of Western Regional Hospital Board. Chairman many of Stirling County Council Committees. Dept. Chairman Stirling County Council 1957. Represents Stirling County Council of Scottish County Councils Association. A Labour

Member. Elected for Stirlingshire W. in 1959 and sat until he retired in Sept. 1974 after his Constituency Labour Party had declined to re-adopt him. Labour Whip withdrawn Mar. 1961-May 1963. Died 20 Apr. 1979.

[1974 2nd ed.]

BEACH, Maj. William Whitehead Hicks. Witcombe Park, Gloucester. S. of Ellis Hicks Beach, Esq. B. 23 Mar. 1907; m. 1939, Diana, d. of C.G. Hoare, Esq., of Holywell, Stamford. Educ. at Eton, and Magdalene Coll., Cambridge. Maj. Royal Gloucestershire Hussars. Admitted a Solicitor 1932. Partner in the firm of Payne, Hicks Beach and Company. A Head Office Director and Dept. Chairman of the General Accident, Fire and Life Assurance Corporation Limited and the Road Transport and General Insurance Company Limited, General Life Assurance Company and various other companies. A Conservative. Unsuccessfully contested Cheltenham in 1945. Elected for Cheltenham in 1950, and sat until he retired in 1964. Dept.-Lieut. for Gloucestershire. Died 1 Jan. 1975. [1964]

BEAMISH, Sir Tufton Victor Hamilton, M.C., D.L. 6 Eaton Terrace, London. Chelworth House, Chelwood Gate, Sussex. Brooks's, and White's. S. of Rear Admiral T.P.H. Beamish, C.B., D.L., MP. B. 27 Jan. 1917; m. 1st, 1950, Janet, d. of Andrew Stevenson, Esq., of New York (divorced 1973), (2 d.); 2ndly, 1975, Mrs. Pia McHenry. Educ. at Stowe, and Royal Military Coll., Sandhurst. Served with Royal Northumberland Fusiliers in Palestine 1938-39 and in France, Belgium, Far East, North Africa and Italy 1939-45 (wounded, despatches). M.C. 1940. Staff Coll. 1945. Honorary Col. 411 (Sussex) Coast Regiment R.A. (T.A.) 1951-58. Delegate to the Council of Europe and Chairman of the Special Committee to watch the interests of non-member countries 1951-54; Vice-Chairman British Group Inter-Parliamentary Union 1951-54; Vice-Chairman of 1922 Committee from 1958-1974. Chairman Conservative Foreign Affairs Committee 1960-64. Member of G.P. Committee and Executive of British Council of the European Movement. Chairman of the Conservative Group for Europe

1970-73. Member of the Monnet Action Committee. Director of companies. Gov. of Stowe School. President of the Royal Society for the Protection of Birds 1966-70 and Sussex Trust for Nature Conservation. Fellow of the Royal Society of Arts. Author of *Must Night Fall, Battle Royal* and *Half Marx*. Dept. Leader European Committee Group in European Parliament 1973-74. Dept.-Lieut. for Sussex 1970. A Conservative. Elected for the Lewes division of East Sussex in July 1945 and sat until he retired in Feb. 1974. Knighted 1961. Created Baron Chelwood (Life Peerage) 1974. An Opposition Defence spokesman 1965-67.* [1974]

BEAN, Robert Ernest. House of Commons, London. S. of Harold Bean, Esq., Dockyard Worker. B. Sept. 1935; m. 12 Aug. 1970, Hilary Wynne-Burch, (1 s. 1 d.). Educ. at Rochester Mathematical School, and Medway Coll. of Technology. Lecturer at a Polytechnic. Member Chatham Council 1958-74, Kent County Council 1973-75 and Medway Borough Council 1973-75. Member Fabian Society and Co-operative Party. Parliamentary Private Secretary to Rt. Hon. Reg Freeson, Minister for Housing and Construction 1976-77. A Labour Member. Unsuccessfully contested Gillingham in 1970 and Thanet E. in Feb. 1974. Sat for Rochester and Chatham from Oct. 1974 until 1979, when he was defeated.* [1979]

BEANEY, Alan. House of Commons, London. S. of John Beaney, Esq., of New Silksworth, Co. Durham. B. 1905; m. 1926, Mary Elizabeth, d. of W. Wass, Esq., of Durham, (1 s. 3 d.). Educ. at Elementary School, and National Council of Labour Colls. Member of Dearne Urban District Council 1938-52 and W. Riding of Yorkshire County Council 1949-52 and 1958-59. Member of Yorkshire Executive of National Union of Mineworkers. A Labour Member. Elected for Hemsworth, Yorkshire in 1959 and sat until he retired in Feb. 1974.* [1974]

BEATTIE, Charles. A Farmer and Auctioneer. Member of Omagh Rural District Council. An Ulster Unionist Member. Unsuccessfully contested Mid Ulster at the general election in May 1955 and after his opponent had been declared incapable of election, at the by-election in Aug. 1955. Declared elected by the Northern Ireland High Court on 7 Oct. 1955, after his opponent had again been declared incapable of election, and took his seat on 25 Oct. 1955. On 15 Dec. 1955 the House of Commons Select Committee on Elections recommended that his election be declared invalid because he held an office of profit under the Crown as a member of three Northern Ireland National Insurance and National Assistance Tribunals; this recommendation was accepted by the House on 7 Feb. 1956. A Bill was passed in Mar. 1956 indemnifying him from all the consequences of sitting and voting while disqualified but it did not validate his election; a new writ was moved on 19 Apr. 1956.* [1956]

BEATTIE, Francis. Auchans, Dundonald, Ayrshire. Carlton, Caledonian and Western. New, Art, and Conservative, Glasgow. S. of William Beattie, Esq., J.P., of Dineiddwg, Stirlingshire. B. 1885; m. 1922, Sarah Edith, d. of Henry Lewis-Thomas, Esq. Educ. at Whitehill School, Glasgow, Blairlodge, Stirlingshire, and the University of Glasgow. Chairman of William Beattie Limited, and various other Bread Bakeries in Scotland. Dept. Director of Emergency Bread Supplies and Trade Adviser on Bread Supplies for Scotland, Ministry of Food to 1942; member of Sea-Fish Commission 1933-36, of Market Supply Committee (Agricultural Marketing Act 1933) 1937-39, and of other Government Committees; of Committee of Enquiry on Rating and Valuation in Scotland 1943. Deacon Convener of the Trades of Glasgow 1933-35; Freeman and Liveryman of the City of London; Gov. of Royal Mechanical Coll., Glasgow; member of Board of Management of the Western Infirmary, Glasgow; Gen. Commissioner of Income Tax for Lower Ward of Lanark; Trustee of Savings Bank of Glasgow; Director of Merchants' House, Glasgow; member of Executive Committee of Scottish Development Council, of T.A. and A.F. Association of Glasgow, of Board of Trade local Price Regulation Committee for S.W. District of Scotland. Maj. 9th H.L.I., served in France 1914-18. Dept.-Lieut., and

J.P. for Glasgow. A National Unionist Member. Member for the Cathcart division of Glasgow from April 1942 until his death in a road accident on 28 December 1945. [1946]

BEATTIE, John. 83 High Street, Belfast. B. 1886. Member of Northern Ireland Labour Party until he was expelled in 1934; thereafter a member of Eire Labour Party. Northern Ireland organizer for Irish National Teachers Organization 1934-52. A Labour Member. Represented first E. Belfast 1925-29 and then Pottinger division of Belfast 1929-49 in the Northern Ireland Parliament. Elected to Westminster for W. Belfast in Feb. 1943 and sat until he was defeated in Feb. 1950; again defeated in Nov. 1950; re-elected in 1951 and sat until he was defeated in 1955. Died 9 Mar. 1960. [1954]

BEAUMONT, Hubert. Crows Nest, West Drayton. Trade Union, and Farmers. B. 1883. Educ. at Saltley Coll. School, Ruskin Coll., Oxford, and Central Labour Coll. Member of Derbyshire County Council 1914-25. Member of Yiewsley and W. Drayton Urban District Council 1934-39. Member of Luxmoore Commission on Agricultural Education 1943-44. Parliamentary Private Secretary to Tom Williams, Parliamentary Secretary Ministry of Agriculture June 1940-May 1945. Dept. Chairman of Ways and Means Aug. 1945-Oct. 1948. A Labour Member. Unsuccessfully contested the Aldershot division in 1924, Harrow in 1929, Peckham in 1931, and Colchester in 1935. Elected for Batley and Morley in Mar. 1939 and sat until his death on 2 Dec. 1948. Died 2 Dec. 1948. [1949]

BECHERVAISE, Albert Eric. 347 Cannhall Road, Leytonstone, London. S. of Richard Rundle Bechervaise, Esq. B. 15 July 1884; m. 7 Aug. 1911, Lilian Winifred, d. of James Lee, Esq. Educ. at Mayville Road School, Leytonstone. A Piano Worker 1900; London Co-operative Agent and Lecturer 1927. Member of Leyton Borough Council 1926-65, Alderman. Mayor 1930. Member of Leyton Urban District Council 1924-26. Member of Metropolitan Water Board 1954-60. A Labour Member. Unsuccessfully contested Southend in 1931 and Leyton E. in 1935. Elected for Leyton E. in July 1945 and sat until he retired in 1950. Died 20 Dec. 1966. [1950]

BEECHMAN, Nevil Alexander, M.C., K.C. Penquite, Lelant, Cornwall, S. of N.C. Beechman, Esq. B. 5 Aug. 1896; m. 1953 Mary Gwendolen, widow of Capt. Garth Caradoc Williams. Educ. at Westminster School (King's Scholar), and Balliol Coll., Oxford (Domus Exhibitioner in Classics, M.A.). Barrister-at-Law, Inner Temple 1923. Member of Select Committee on National Expenditure (Naval Services); Parliamentary Private Secretary to G.H. Shakespeare when Parliamentary Secretary of Overseas Trade Department Apr.-May 1940, and when Parliamentary Under-Secretary of State for Dominions May 1940-Feb. 1941, to Rt. Hon. Ernest Brown, Minister of Health Feb. 1941-Dec. 1942, Chief Liberal National Party Whip Dec. 1942-July 1945. A Lord Commissioner of the Treasury Sept. 1943-July 1945. A National Liberal Member. Elected for the St. Ives division of Cornwall in June 1937 and sat until he retired in 1950. Served with King's Royal Rifle Corps, Capt., M.C. 1917. K.C. 1947. Member of St. Ives Borough Council 1957-60. Died 6 Nov. 1965. [1950]

BEITH, Alan James. Overdale, Corchester Terrace, Corbridge, Northumberland. S. of James Beith Esq. B. 20 Apr. 1943; m. 1 Sept. 1965, Barbara Jean, d. of S.E. Ward, Esq. (1 s.). Educ. at King's School, Macclesfield, and Balliol and Nuffield Colls., Oxford, (B. Litt., M.A.). A Methodist local preacher. Lecturer in Politics, University of Newcastle-upon-Tyne 1966-73. Councillor Hexham R.D.C. 1969-74. Vice-President National Association of Local Councils. Joint Chairman Association of Councillors. Chief Whip of Liberal Party from Mar. 1976 and Liberal spokesman on Education from 1976. A Liberal. Unsuccessfully contested Berwick-upon-Tweed in 1970. Sat for Berwick-upon-Tweed from Nov. 1973. Member of N.E. Transport Users Consultative Committee 1970-74. Member of General Advisory Council of B.B.C. from 1974. Member of Tynedale District Council 1973-74. Liberal

spokesman on Home Affairs and N. Ireland 1974-76. Dept. Liberal Whip 1975-76.* [1979]

BELCHER, John William. 34 Sydney Road, Enfield. National Trades Union. S. of John Belcher, Esq. B. 2 Aug. 1905; m. 1927, Louise, d. of William Moody, Esq. Educ. at Latymer Upper School, and University of London. G.W.R. Clerk 1922; Ministry of Information Lecturer 1941-44; Railway Commercial Representative 1945. Parliamentary Secretary Board of Trade Jan. 1946-Dec. 1948 when he resigned. A Labour Member. Elected for the Sowerby division of the W. Riding of Yorkshire in July 1945 and sat until he resigned in Feb. 1949, as a result of the findings of the Lynskey Tribunal on Bribery of Ministers of the Crown. Employed by British Railways 1949-63. Fellow of Royal Economics Society. Died 26 Oct. 1964. [1949]

BELL, Philip Ingress, Q.C. 11 King's Bench Walk, Temple, London. S. of Geoffrey Vincent Bell, Esq., Sculptor. B. 10 Jan. 1900; m. 14 Sept. 1933, Agnes Mary, d. of Charles Eastwood, Esq., Late High Sheriff of Lancashire. Educ. at Stonyhurst, and Queen's Coll., Oxford. Barrister-at-Law, called Inner Temple Nov. 1925; B.A., B.C.L., Q.C. Apr. 1952; Midshipman R.N. 1918-20, Lieut. T.A. 1939 E. Lancashire Regiment, at Dunkirk 1940; J.A.G. Staff 1941-45, A/Maj. Normandy to Belsen; T.D. 1950. A Conservative. Unsuccessfully contested Bolton E. in 1950. Elected there in Oct. 1951 and sat until June 1960 when he was appointed a County Court Judge. County Court Judge 1960-71, Circuit Judge 1972-75.* [1960]

BELL, Sir Ronald McMillan, Q.C. 2 Mitre Court Buildings, Temple, London. First House, West Witheridge, Knotty Green, Beaconsfield, Buckinghamshire. S. of John Bell, Esq., of Cardiff. B. 1914; m. Apr. 1954, Elizabeth Audrey, d. of Kenneth Gossell, Esq. Educ. at Cardiff High School, and Magdalen Coll., Oxford. Served R.N.V.R. (Lieut.-Commander) 1939-45; Barrister-at-Law, Gray's Inn 1938. Q.C. 1966. A Conservative. Unsuccessfully contested Caerphilly in July 1939. Sat for Newport, Monmouthshire from May-July 1945, when he was defeated and for Buckinghamshire S. from 1950-Feb. 1974. Elected for Beaconsfield in Feb. 1974. Member of Paddingtton Borough Council 1947-49. An Opposition spokesman on Labour in 1965 and on Defence 1965-66. Voted against entry to E.E.C. on 28 Oct. 1971. Knighted 1980.* [1979]

BELLENGER, Rt. Hon. Frederick John. 198 Old Brompton Road, London. S. of Eugene Bernard Bellenger, Esq. B. 23 July 1894; m. 1922, Marion Theresa, d. of Generalkonsul Karl Stollwerck of Cologne. A Surveyor. Capt. R.A., served in France 1914-18, with Army of Occupation of the Rhine 1919 and Dunkirk 1940. Member of Fulham Borough Council, as a Conservative 1922-28. Financial Secretary to the War Office Aug. 1945-Oct. 1946. Secretary of State for War Oct. 1946-Oct. 1947. PC. 1946. A Labour Member . Elected for the Bassetlaw division of Nottinghamshire in 1935 and sat until his death on 11 May 1968. Died 11 May 1968. [1968]

BENCE, Cyril Raymond. 112 Mill Road, Clydebank, Glasgow. S. of Harris Bryant Bence, Esq., retired Meat Purveyor. B. 26 Nov. 1902; m. 1st, 5 Apr. 1926, Florence Maud Bowler (she died 1974); 2ndly, 1975, Mrs. I. N. Hall. Educ. at Newport, Monmouthshire High School. Engineer. Member of Birmingham Trades Council 1942-45. A Labour Member. Unsuccessfully contested the Handsworth division of Birmingham in 1945, Feb. 1950 and at a by-election in Nov. 1950. Elected for Dunbartonshire E. in Oct. 1951 and sat until he retired in 1970. Parliamentary Private Secretary to Rt. Hon. Anthony Crosland, Secretary of State for Education and Science 1965-67.* [1970]

BENDALL, Vivian Walter Hough. The Old House, Bletchingly, Surrey. 25 Brighton Road, South Croydon, Surrey. Carlton. S. of Cecil Aubrey Bendall, Esq. Chartered Auctioneer, Estate Agent and Surveyor. B. 14 Dec. 1938; m. Dec. 1969, Ann Rosalind, d. of H. Jarvis, Esq., of Ardingly. Educ. at Coombe Hill House, and Broad Green Coll., Croydon. Chartered Auctioneer, Estate Agent and Surveyor Councillor London Borough of Croydon 1964-78. Chairman Greater London Young Conservatives 1967-68. Member of Greater London Council from 1970-73. A Conservative. Unsuccessful Parliamentary Candidate for Hertford and Stevenage Feb. and Oct. 1974. Elected for Redbridge Ilford North in Mar. 1978.* [1979]

BENN, Rt. Hon. Anthony (Neil) Wedgwood. House of Commons, London. 2nd s. of William Wedgwood Benn, Labour MP for N. Aberdeen and Gorton, who later became Visct. Stansgate. B. 3 Apr. 1925; m. 17 June 1949, Caroline Middleton, d. of James Milton de Camp, (3 s. 1 d.). Educ. at Westminster and New Coll., Oxford. Pilot Officer, R.A.F.V.R. 1945. Postmaster-Gen. 1964-66. PC. 1964. Minister of Technology July 1966-June 1970. Opposition spokesman on Trade and Industry 1970-74. Chairman Labour Party 1971-72. Secretary of State for Industry and Minister of Posts and Telecommunications 1974-75. Secretary of State for Energy from June 1975 to May 1979. A Labour Member. Sat for Bristol S.E. from Nov. 1950 until he was disqualified on 21 Mar. 1961 as he had succeeded to the Peerage as Visct. Stansgate on his father's death on 17 Nov. 1960. Re-elected at a by-election on 4 May 1961 but his opponent was declared elected on 28 July 1961. Renounced his Peerage in Aug. 1963 and was re-elected for S.E. Bristol on 20 Aug. 1963. Member of National Executive Committee of Labour Party 1959-60 and from 1962. Opposition spokesman on Transport 1959-60. Member of Parliamentary Committee of P.L.P. 1970-74. Unsuccessful candidate for Dept.-Leadership of Labour Party 1971 and for Leadership 1976.* [1979]

BENNETT, Andrew Francis. House of Commons, London. B. Mar. 1939; m. Gillian. Educ. at Birmingham University. A Teacher. Member Oldham Borough Council 1964-74. A Labour Member. Unsuccessfully contested Knutsford in 1970. Member for Stockport N. from Feb. 1974.* [1979]

BENNETT, Sir Frederic Mackarness. 2 Stone Buildings, Lincoln's Inn, London.

Kingswear Castle, South Devon. Cwmllecoediog Aberangell, Nr. Machynlleth, Powys, Wales. Carlton. S. of Sir Ernest Bennett, MP. B. 2 Dec. 1918; m. 16 Feb. 1945, Marion Patricia, eld. d. of Maj. Cecil Burnham, F.R.C.S. Educ. at Westminster. Served with Middlesex Yeomanry and R.A. and in Petroleum Warfare Dept. 1939-46, Maj. Barrister-at-Law, Lincoln's Inn Nov. 1946; Advocate High Court, S. Rhodesia Mar. 1947; Diplomatic Correspondent *Birmingham Post* 1950-52. Parliamentary Private Secretary to Sir Hugh Lucas-Tooth, Under-Secretary at Home Office 1953-55. Parliamentary Private Secretary to Rt. Hon. R. Maudling in numerous appointments 1955-61. Lloyd's Underwriter. Member Council of Europe and Western European Union from 1974. Director various financial and industrial institutions in the U.K. and overseas. Knight Bach. 1964. A Conservative. Unsuccessfully contested the Burslem division of Stoke-on-Trent in 1945 and Birmingham, Ladywood division in 1950. Sat for Reading N. division from Oct. 1951-May 1955, when he unsuccessfully contested Reading. Sat for Torquay from Dec. 1955 to Feb. 1974 and for Torbay from Feb. 1974.* [1979]

BENNETT, James. 105 Boreland Drive, Glasgow. S. of Samuel Bennett, Esq. B. 1912; m. 1936, Dorothy Maclaren (1 s. 1 d.). Educ. at N. Kelvinside Secondary School, Glasgow. An ex-Railwayman. Formerly represented the Dalmarnock ward of Glasgow as a Councillor 1947-1962. Parliamentary Private Secretary to Rt. Hon. William Ross, Secretary of State for Scotland 1964-67. A Labour Member. Elected for the Bridgeton division of Glasgow in Nov. 1961 and sat until he retired in Feb. 1974.* [1974]

BENNETT, Sir Peter Frederick Blaker, O.B.E. 44 Park Street, London. Ardencote, Luttrell Road, Four Oaks, Warwickshire. Carlton, and R.A.C. S. of F.C. Bennett, Esq. B. 1880; m. 1905, Agnes, d. of Joseph Palmer, Esq. Educ. at King Edward's School, Birmingham. Joint Managing Director of Joseph Lucas Industries Limited; member of British Productivity Council and Director of Imperial Chemical Industries Limited, of Lloyds Bank Limited, and President of F.B.I.

and of Society of Motor Manufacturers and Traders; Gov. of Birmingham University; J.P. for Birmingham; Knight Bach. 1941; LL.D. Birmingham 1950. Parliamentary Secretary Ministry of Labour Nov. 1951-May 1952. A Conservative. Elected for the Edgbaston division of Birmingham in Dec. 1940 and sat until he resigned in June 1953. Created Baron Bennett of Edgbaston July 1953. O.B.E. 1918. Industrial Adviser to Ministry of Supply 1938-39. Director Gen. of Tanks and Transport 1939-40. Director Gen. of Emergency Services, Ministry of Aircraft Production 1940-41. Chairman of Automatic Gun Board 1941-44. A Methodist. Died 27 Sept. 1957. [1953]

BENNETT, Dr. Reginald Frederick Brittain. House of Commons, London. White's, Imperial Poona, and other Yacht Clubs. S. of Samuel Robert Bennett, Esq., M.A. B. 22 July 1911; m. 1947, Henrietta, d. of Capt. H.B. Crane, C.B.E., R.N., (1 s. 3 d.). Educ. at Winchester, and New Coll., Oxford. A Psychiatrist. V.R.D., M.A. (Oxon.). B.M., B.Ch., L.M.S.S.A., D.P.M. Grand Officer of the Italian Order of Merit 1977. R.N.V.R. 1935-46. R.A.F., Civil and Naval Air Pilot 1930-46. Chairman of the Catering S/Committee of the House of Commons Services Committee 1970-74. Vice-Chairman 1974-76. Parliamentary Private Secretary to Iain MacLeod 1955-63; previously to Sir David Maxwell Fyfe, Home Secretary 1951-54, to Geoffrey Lloyd, Minister of Fuel and Power 1954-55. Parliamentary Scientific Committee Chairman 1958-62 and Chairman Anglo-Italian Parliamentary Group from 1970. Member Executive Inter-Parliamentary Union from 1962. Vice-President Franco-British Parliamentary Committee from 1959. Member of Council International Institute of Human Nutrition 1975. Freeman of the City of London and Liveryman of the Society of Apothecaries 1956; Chevalier du Tastevin 1971, de St. Etienne (Alsace) 1972, de Bretvin (Muscadet) 1973. Commander de Bontemps-Medoc 1959; Galant de la Verte Marennes 1959; Honorary Lieut.-Col. Georgia (U.S.A.) Militia 1960; Honorary Citizen of Atlanta. Ga., 1960. Vice-Commodore of the House of Commons Yacht Club. Dept.

Chairman House of Commons Motor Club. A Conservative. Unsuccessfully contested Woolwich in 1945. Sat for Gosport and Fareham from 1950-Feb. 1974, and for Fareham from Feb. 1974 when he retired in 1979. Knighted June 1979.* [1979]

BENNETT, Sir William Gordon. House of Commons, London. Member of Glasgow Royal Exchange, Chamber of Commerce and Glasgow Trades House. Late President of Scottish Unionist Association. Served in the Tank Corps 1914-18. A Conservative. Unsuccessfully contested the Shettleston division of Glasgow in 1945. Elected for the Woodside division of Glasgow in 1950 and 1951 and sat until he retired in 1955. Knighted Jan. 1955.* [1954]

BENSON, Sir George. 6 Constable Drive, Littleover, Derby. S. of T.D. Benson, Esq., Estate Agent, and for many years Treasurer of the Independent Labour Party. B. 3 May 1889; m. 25 June 1919, Marjorie, d. of H.B. Lodge. Educ. at Manchester Grammar School. An Estate Agent. Treasurer of the Independent Labour Party from 1923-24. Chairman of Howard League for Penal Reform 1938-61. Member of Home Office Advisory Committee on Treatment of Offenders. A Labour Member. Unsuccessfully contested the Altrincham division of Cheshire in 1922 and Chesterfield in 1923 and 1924. Sat for Chesterfield from 1929 until Oct. 1931, when he was defeated. Re-elected for Chesterfield in 1935 and sat until he retired in 1964. Knighted 1958. Imprisoned as a conscientious objector during the First World War. Fellow of Auctioneers Institute. Parliamentary Private Secretary to F. Pethick-Lawrence, Financial Secretary to Treasury 1930-31. Died 17 Aug. 1973. [1964]

BENYON, William Richard, J.P., D.L. Englefield House, Nr. Reading, Berkshire. S. of Vice-Admiral Richard Benyon, C.B., C.B.E.B. 17 Jan. 1930; m. 1957, Elizabeth Ann, d. of Vice-Admiral Ronald Hallifax, C.B., C.B.E., (2 s. 3 d.). Educ. at Royal Naval Coll., Dartmouth. J.P. 1964; Royal Navy 1947-56; Courtaulds Limited 1956-64; Farmer and Landowner 1964. Member Council of Reading University, Royal

Agricultural Society of England and Council of Bradfield Coll. Gov. Dominion Students Hall Trust; member Berkshire County Council 1964-74. Dept.-Lieut. for Berkshire from 1970. President Berkshire Association of Parish Councils 1974 and Berkshire Blind Society. Parliamentary Private Secretary to Paul Channon, Minister for Housing and Construction 1972-74. Conservative Whip 1974-76. A Conservative. Sat for the Buckingham division of Buckinghamshire from June 1970.* [1979]

BERKELEY, Humphry John. 46 Redcliffe Road, London. Carlton, and Hurlingham. S. of Reginald Berkeley, Esq., MP., Playwright. B. 21 Feb. 1926. Educ. at Malvern, and Pembroke Coll., Cambridge. President of the Cambridge Union 1948. Conservative Political Centre 1948-57. A Conservative. Unsuccessfully contested Southall in 1951. Elected for Lancaster in Oct. 1959 and sat until he was defeated in 1966. Joined the Labour Party in July 1970 and unsuccessfully contested N. Fylde in Oct. 1974. Director Gen. of U.K. Council of European Movement 1956-57. Member of Council of Europe and Council of Western European Union 1963-66. Chairman of United Nations Association 1966-70. Hon. Treasurer of Howard League for Penal Reform 1965-71. Chief Diplomatic Adviser and Overseas Representative, Government of Transkei from 1978.* [1966]

BERRY, Hon. Anthony George. 1 Graham Terrace, London. White's, Portland and Cardiff and County S. of 1st Visct. Kemsley (d. 1968). B. 1925; m. 1st, 1954, Hon. Mary Roche, d. of 4th Baron Fermoy (d. 1955) (from whom he obtained a divorce 1965), (1 s. 3 d.); 2ndly, 5th Apr. 1966, Sarah Anne, d. of Raymond Clifford-Turner, (1 s. 1 d.). Educ. at Eton, and Christ Church, Oxford (M.A.). Served in Welsh Guards 1943-47, Lieut. F.R.S.A. Assistant Editor of *Sunday Times* 1952-54; Editor of *Sunday Chronicle* 1954; a Director of Kemsley newspapers Limited 1954-59. Commander of the Order of St. John; High Sherriff of Glamorgan 1962 and J.P. for Cardiff. Dept. Chairman of Leopold Joseph and Sons Limited, President Welsh Games Council. Vice-Chairman

Conservative Transport Committee 1969-70 and 1974-75. Parliamentary Private Secretary to Rt. Hon. Peter Walker, Minister of Housing and Local Government 1970, Secretary of State for Environment 1970-72, and Secretary of State for Trade and Industry 1972-74. Opposition Whip 1975-79. Vice-Chamberlain of H.M. Household from May 1979. A Conservative. Sat for Southgate from Oct. 1964 to Feb. 1974 and for the Southgate division of Enfield from Feb. 1974.* [1979]

BERRY, Henry. 10 Greenholm Road, Eltham, London. S. of Benjamin Berry, Esq., of Woolwich. B. 7 Jan. 1883; m. 2 June 1906, Mary, d. of John Startup, Esq., of Plumstead (she died 6 Dec. 1945). Educ. at Woolwich Polytechnic and Goldsmiths Coll. M.I.Mech.E., A.I.Struct.E. Mayor of Woolwich 1935-36. Member of London County Council from 1928 to 1955. Vice-Chairman 1940-44. Member of Metropolitan Water Board from 1923, Chairman 1940-46. Member of Thames Conservancy from 1940, of Central Water Advisory Committee 1946; President of International Allotments Federation from 1947 to 1949; Treasurer of National Allotments Society from 1923; President British Water Works Association 1948. A Labour Member. Elected for Woolwich W. in July 1945 and sat until he was defeated in 1950. C.B.E. 1951. Died 14 Feb. 1956. [1950]

BESSELL, Peter Joseph. 41 Pall Mall, London. Polrean, Sandplace, Nr. Looe, Cornwall. Reform, and National Liberal. S. of Joseph Edgar Bessell, Esq., of Ludlow. B. 24 Aug. 1921; m. 1st, 1942, Joyce Margaret Thomas (she died 1947); 2ndly, 1948, Pauline, d. of William Stimpson Colledge, Esq., (1 s. 1 d.). Educ. in Bath. A Director of a number of companies. Government Lecturer on Music to British and Allied Forces stationed in Great Britain during the War. Contributes articles on music and politics to a number of magazines and periodicals. Committee on Procedure 1964-65. Liberal Party spokesman on Transport. Member of Estimates Committee 1964-67. Member Agricultural Committee 1967. President of the Brotherhood 1967-68. Liberal Party spokesman on Transport and Board of

Trade. A Liberal. Unsuccessfully contested Torquay in the 1955 general election and in the subsequent by-election later that year, and Bodmin in 1959. Elected for the Bodmin division of Cornwall in Oct. 1964 and sat until he retired in 1970. Emigrated to California. Prosecution witness in the Jeremy Thorpe trial 1978-79.* [1970]

BESWICK, Frank. House of Commons, London. S. of Jesse Beswick, Esq., of Hucknall. B. 1912; m. 1936, Dora, d. of Edward Plumb, Esq., of Kettering. Parliamentary Private Secretary to Geoffrey de Freitas, Under-Secretary of State for Air May 1946-May 1949. Parliamentary Secretary Ministry of Civil Aviation 1950-51. Served in R.A.F. Transport Command 1940-46. British observer at the Bikini Atomic Bomb Tests 1946. Alternate delegate to United Nations Assembly 1946. Chairman of all-Party delegation studying refugee problems in Austria and Germany 1947. Chairman Parliamentary Labour Party Civil Aviation Committee and Co-operative Party Parliamentary Group 1956. A Co-operative and Labour Member. Elected for the Uxbridge division of Middlesex in July 1945 and sat until he was defeated in 1959. Created Baron Beswick (Life Peerage) 1964. Lord-in-Waiting and Government Whip in House of Lords Dec. 1964-Oct. 1965. Under-Secretary for Commonwealth Relations Oct. 1965-July 1967. Capt. of the Gentlemen-at-Arms and Government Chief Whip in House of Lords July 1967-June 1970. Opposition Chief Whip in House of Lords June 1970-Mar. 1974. Minister of State, Department of Industry and Dept. Leader of House of Lords Mar. 1974-Dec. 1975. PC. 1968. Chairman of British Aerospace 1977-80.* [1959]

BEVAN, Rt. Hon. Aneurin. House of Commons, London. S. of David Bevan, Esq., of Tredegar. B. 15 Nov. 1897; m. Oct. 1934, Jennie Lee (MP. 1929-31 and 1945-70). Educ. at Sirhowy Council School, Tredegar. A Miners' Agent. Member of Tredegar Urban District Council from 1922 and Monmouth County Council from 1928; Vice-President of Urban Council Association. Editor of *The Tribune* 1942-45. Minister of Health with a seat in the Cabinet July 1945-

Jan. 1951; Minister of Labour Jan.-Apr. 1951 when he resigned. PC. 1945. Dept. Leader of the Labour Party and of the Opposition 1959-60. A Labour Member. Elected for the Ebbw Vale division of Monmouthshire in May 1929 and sat until his death on 6 July 1960. Expelled from the Labour Party Mar.-Dec. 1939 for refusing to withdraw from Sir Stafford Cripps's campaign for a Popular Front Government. Member of Parliamentary Labour Party Parliamentary Committee Nov. 1952-Apr. 1954, when he resigned, and from June 1955. Labour Whip withdrawn Mar.-Apr. 1955. Member of National Executive Committee of Labour Party 1944-54 and 1956-60. Treasurer of Labour Party 1959-60. Opposition spokesman on Labour 1955-56, Colonial Affairs 1956, and on Foreign Affairs 1956-60. Died 6 July 1960.   [1960]

BEVIN, Rt. Hon. Ernest. Foreign Office, Whitehall, London. S. of Mercy Bevin, B. 1881; m. Florence Townley. Chairman of Trades Union Congress General Council 1937; Gen. Secretary of Transport and General Workers' Union Jan. 1922-May 1940. Minister of Labour and National Service May 1940-May 1945; Secretary of State for Foreign Affairs from July 1945-Mar. 1951; Member of War Cabinet Oct. 1940-May 1945. PC. 1940. A Labour Member. Unsuccessfully contested Bristol Central in 1918 and Gateshead in 1931. Sat for Central Wandsworth from June 1940-Feb. 1950 and for E. Woolwich from Feb. 1950 until his death on 14 Apr. 1951. Lord Privy Seal Mar.-Apr. 1951. Hon. Fellow of Magdalen Coll., Oxford. Hon. LL.D. Universities of Cambridge and Bristol. Died 14 Apr. 1951.
[1950]

BEVINS, Rt. Hon. (John) Reginald. 37 Queen's Drive, Liverpool. S. of John Milton Bevins, Esq., of Liverpool. B. 20 Aug. 1908; m. 1933, M. Leonora Jones. Educ. at Collegiate School, Liverpool. An Insurance Underwriter. Parliamentary Private Secretary to Rt. Hon. Harold Macmillan, Minister of Housing and Local Government 1951-53. Parliamentary Secretary Ministry of Works Nov. 1953-Jan. 1957. Parliamentary Secretary Ministry of Housing and Local Govern-

ment Jan. 1957-Oct. 1959. Postmaster-Gen. Oct. 1959-Oct. 1964. A Conservative. Unsuccessfully contested the W. Toxteth division of Liverpool in 1945 and the Edge Hill division of Liverpool in Sept. 1947. Elected for the Toxteth division of Liverpool in 1950 and sat until he was defeated in 1964. PC. 1959. Served in the Army 1939-45, Maj. R.A.S.C. Member of Liverpool City Council 1935-50. Author of *The Greasy Pole* 1965.*
[1964]

BIDGOOD, John Claude. Linton, Wetherby, Yorkshire. Flat 19, 36 Buckingham Gate, London. Royal Aero, Constitutional, and Leeds and County Conservative. S. of Edward Charles Bidgood, Esq. B. 12 May 1914; m. 17 Nov. 1945, Sheila Nancy, d. of Dr. and Mrs. J. Walker-Wood. Educ. at London Choir School, and Woodhouse Technical School. Member Leeds City Council 1947-55, and the W. Riding of Yorkshire Rating and Valuation Court; Vice-President Yorkshire Association for Disabled; member Leeds Council of Social Service. Director of Engineering companies and Middle East Merchant. Member of Institute of Export. R.A.F. pilot 1939. Parliamentary Private Secretary to Miss Edith Pitt and Hon. Richard Wood, Joint Parliamentary Secretaries Ministry of Pensions and National Insurance 1956-58. A Conservative. Unsuccessfully contested N.E. Leeds in 1950 and 1951. Elected for Bury and Radcliffe in 1955 and sat until he was defeated in 1964. Unsuccessfully contested Bury and Radcliffe in 1966. Member of Estimates Committee 1958-64. Chairman of Anglo-Dominion Finance Company Limited, Anglo-Dominion Construction Company Limited and Anglo-Dominion Trading Company Limited.*
[1964]

BIDWELL, Sydney James. House of Commons, London. S. of Herbert Emmett Bidwell, Esq. of Southall. B. 14 Jan. 1917; m. 1941, Daphne, d. of Robert Peart Esq., (1 s. 1 d.). Educ. in Trade Union movement and evening classes. Tutor/Organiser N.C.L.C. Joined Labour Party 1933; member N.U.R. from Jan. 1933. Member Co-operative Party. Member T and G.W.U. Southall Borough Councillor 1951-55. TUC Regional Education Officer, London, 1963-66. Race Relations Select Committee 1968-77. Member Tribune Group, Chairman 1975. A Labour Member. Unsuccessfully contested E. Hertfordshire in 1959 and S.W. Hertfordshire in 1964. Member for Southall from 1966-Feb. 1974. Elected for the Southall division of Ealing in Feb. 1974.* [1979]

BIFFEN, Rt. Hon. (William) John. House of Commons, London. S. of Victor W. Biffen, Esq. B. 1930; m. 1979, Mrs. Sarah Wood. Educ. at Dr. Morgan's Grammar School, Bridgwater, and Jesus Coll., Cambridge. Vice-Chairman of Federation of University Conservative and Unionist Associations. On Staff of Tube Investments Ltd. 1953-60 and Economist Intelligence Unit 1960-61. Opposition spokesman on Technology 1965-66, on Energy 1976, on Industry 1976-77 and on Small Businesses and the Self-employed 1978-79. Member of Shadow Cabinet Jan. 1976-Mar 1977 and Nov. 1978-May 1979. Member of Cabinet from May 1979. Chief Secretary to Treasury from May 1979. PC. 1979. Voted against entry to E.E.C. on 28 Oct. 1971. A Conservative. Unsuccessfully contested Coventry E. in 1959. Adopted as Conservative candidate in 1961 and won Oswestry in Nov. of that year.* [1979]

BIGGS-DAVISON, John Alec. 35 Hereford Square, London. Green Farn Cottage, Stapleford Tawney, Essex. S. of Maj. J.N. Biggs-Davison, R.G.A., (Retired). B. 7 June 1918; m. 27 Nov. 1948, Pamela, 2nd. d. of Ralph Hodder-Williams, M.C. Educ. at Clifton Coll., and Magdalen Coll., Oxford (M.A.). A Roman Catholic. Commissioned in R.M. 1939; Indian Civil Service (last British Officer appointed to Punjab Commission) 1942; Forward Liaison Officer Cox's Bazar 1943-44; Political Assistant and Commandant Border Military Police and later Dept. Commissioner Dera Ghazi Khan 1946-48; Conservative Research Department 1950-55; Secretary British Conservative Delegation to Council of Europe 1952 and 1953; Observer at Malta Referendum 1956; Secretary Parliamentary Delegation to W. Africa 1956; Parliamentary Delegation to Guernsey 1961, Austria 1964, France and Ottawa (Inter-Parliamentary Union) 1965,

Malawi 1968, Gibraltar 1969, Tunisia 1969, Zambia 1975. An Official Opposition spokesman on Northern Ireland (1976-78). Vice-President Franco-British Parliamentary Relations Committee. Author of *George Wyndham, Tory Lives, The Uncertain Ally, Walls of Europe, Portuguese Guinea, Africa-Hope Deferred, The Hand is Red* and *Nailing a Lie.* A Conservative. Unsuccessfully contested Coventry S. in 1951. Member for the Chigwell division of Essex from 1955-Feb. 1974 and for Epping Forest from Feb. 1974. Conservative whip withdrawn May 1957-July 1958.* [1979]

BING, Maj. Geoffrey Henry Cecil, Q.C. House of Commons, London. S. of Geoffrey Bing, Esq., Schoolmaster, of Craigavad. B. 24 July 1909; m. 1st, 1940, Christian Frances, d. of Sir Ralph Blois, Bart. (divorced 1955); 2ndly, 1956, Eileen Mary, d. of Alderman Frederick Cullen. Educ. at Tonbridge School, and Lincoln Coll., Oxford. Called to bar, English 1934, Gibraltar 1937, Gold Coast 1950 and Nigerian 1934. K.C. 1950. Served in Army 1941-45. Assistant Whip Aug. 1945-Nov. 1946. A Labour Member. Elected for Hornchurch in July 1945 and sat until he was defeated in 1955. Constitutional Adviser to Kwame Nkrumah, President of Ghana 1956-66. Attorney-Gen. of Ghana 1957-61. C.M.G. 1960. Consultant to Irish University Press 1970-77. Died 24 Apr. 1977. [1954]

BINGHAM, Richard Martin, Q.C. 2 Pump Court, Temple, London. R.A.C. S. of John Bingham, Esq. B. 26 Oct. 1915; m. 23 July 1949, Elinor Stephenson. Educ. at Harrow, and Clare Coll., Cambridge. Served with R.A. 1939-45 (Maj.). Barrister-at-Law, Inner Temple 1941, Benched 1964; Q.C. 1958. Member Liverpool City Council 1946-49. Appointed Recorder of Oldham 1960. A Conservative. Elected for the Garston division of Liverpool in Dec. 1957 and sat until he retired in 1966. Judge of Appeal Isle of Man 1965-72. Member of Departmental Committee on Coroners 1965 and Royal Commission on Assizes and Quarter Sessions 1966. Circuit Judge from 1972.* [1966]

BINNS, John. 18 Paget Street, Keighley, Yorkshire. B. 1914. Educ. at Holycroft School, N.C.L.C., and W.E.A. Courses. An Engineer. Joined the Labour Party in 1944. Member of Amalgamated Engineering Union. Member of Keighley Borough Council from 1945, Alderman 1954, Mayor 1958-59. A Labour Member. Elected for Keighley in Oct. 1964 and sat until he was defeated in 1970. Resigned from Labour Party and unsuccessfully contested Keighley as a Social Democratic candidate in Feb. 1974.* [1970]

BINNS, Joseph. 27 Halfway Street, Sidcup, Kent. S. of Alderman Joseph Binns, former Lord Mayor of Manchester. B. 19 Mar. 1900; m. 1924, Daisy Graham. Educ. at Elementary Schools, and Manchester Coll. of Technology. A Consulting Engineer. Member of Greenwich Borough Council 1932-49. Commissioner of Public Works Loan Board 1948. Parliamentary Private Secretary to the Rt. Hon. John Wilmot, Minister of Supply June 1946-Oct. 1947. Chairman of Metropolitan Standing Joint Committee 1945-49. A Labour Member. Elected for the Gillingham division of Rochester in July 1945 and sat until he was defeated in 1950. Dept.-Chairman of Public Works Loan Board 1958-70, Chairman 1970-72. C.B.E. 1961. Died 23 Apr. 1975. [1950]

BIRCH, Rt. Hon. (Evelyn) Nigel Chetwode, O.B.E. 73 Ashley Gardens, London. Holywell House, Swanmore, Hampshire. Brooks's, White's, and Pratt's. S. of Gen. Sir Noel Birch, G.B.E., K.C.B., K.C.M.G.B. 18 Nov. 1906; m. 1 Aug. 1950, Hon. Esme Glyn, d. of 4th Baron Wolverton. Educ. at Eton. Partner in Messrs. Cohen Laming Hoare to 1939. Served with K.R.R.C. and on General Staff in G.B. and Italy 1939-45; Lieut.-Col. 1944. Parliamentary Under-Secretary of State for Air 1951-52; Parliamentary Secretary to Ministry of Defence 1952-54; Minister of Works 1954-55; Secretary of State for Air Dec. 1955-Jan. 1957; Economics Secretary to the Treasury Jan. 1957, resigned Jan. 1958. PC. 1955. A Conservative. Sat for Flintshire from 1945 to 1950 and for W. Flintshire from 1950 until he retired in 1970. Created Baron Rhyl (Life Peerage) 1970. O.B.E. 1945. President of Johnson Society, Lichfield 1966.* [1970]

BISHOP, Rt. Hon. Edward Stanley. House of Commons, London. S. of Frank and Constance Bishop of Bristol. B. 3 Oct. 1920; m. 1945, Winifred Mary Bryant, J.P., (4 d.). Educ. at South Bristol Central School, and Merchant Venturers' Technical Coll., Extra Mural Studies at Bristol University. Joined Labour Party 1936. Fellow Ancient Monuments Society. Aeronautical Engineering Designer (T. Eng. (C.E.I.), A.M.R.Ae.S. and M.I.E.D.). J.P. from 1957. Member Archbishop's Commission on Organisation of the Church by Dioceses in London and S.E. England. An Assistant Government Whip Apr. 1966-Mar. 1967. For 17 years member Bristol City Council (former Dept. Leader and Chairman of Finance and General Purposes Committee). Former Chairman S.W. Regional Council of Labour Party; former President Bristol Borough Labour Party and former President Bristol S.E. Constituency Labour Party. Vice-President Rural District Councils Association 1965-74. Church Commissioner from 1968. Member of Redundant Churches Fund 1969-74. A U.K. Delegate to the North Atlantic Assembly from 1966. Chairman of its Economic Committee 1969-73. Opposition spokesman on Trade and Industry and Aerospace 1970-74. Opposition spokesman on Agriculture 1970. Member Council of Air League 1970-74. Chairman of the All-Party Parliamentary Equal Rights Group. Second Church Estates Commissioner 1974. Parliamentary Secretary Ministry of Agriculture, Fisheries and Food June-Oct. 1974. Minister of State Ministry of Agriculture, Fisheries and Food Oct. 1974-May 1979. A Labour Member. Unsuccessfully contested Bristol W. 1950, Exeter 1951 and S. Gloucestershire in 1955. Sat for the Newark division of Notthinghamshire from Oct. 1964 until 1979, when he was defeated. PC. 1977.* [1979]

BISHOP, Frank Patrick, M.B.E. House of Commons, London. S. of Henry James Bishop, Esq. B. 1900; m. 1st 1924, Vera Sophie Drew (she died 1953); 2ndly, 1955, Ella Mary Hunt. Educ. at Tottenham Grammar School, and Kings Coll., London. Director Rediffusion

Limited. Barrister-at-Law, Gray's Inn 1923; Assistant Manager of *The Times* 1937-45. Served with R.F.C. 1914-18 and in Home Guard 1939-45. Gen. Manager of Newsprint Supply Company 1947-57. Chairman of Morphy-Richards 1957-60. A Conservative. Elected for Harrow Central in 1950 and sat until he retired in 1964. M.B.E. 1945. Knighted 1964. Died 5 Oct. 1972. [1964]

BLACK, Sir Cyril Wilson. Rosewall, Calonne Road, Wimbledon. Carlton, City Livery, and London Magistrates. S. of Robert Wilson Black, Esq., Estate Agent. B. 8 Apr. 1902; m. 1930, Dorothy Joyce, d. of Thomas Birkett, Esq., of Leicester. Educ. at King's Coll. School, Wimbledon. A Chartered Surveyor, F.R.I.C.S. Chairman of various companies. Appointed Justice of the Peace for the County of London in 1942. Member of Wimbledon Borough Council 1942-65; Mayor 1945-47; member of Surrey County Council 1943-65; Vice-Chairman 1953-56; Chairman 1956-59. Member of Merton Borough Council 1965-78; Mayor of the Borough of Merton 1966-67. Chairman of the N.E. Surrey Divisional Executive 1945-65, and Gov. of various schools, including King's Coll., Wimbledon, The Ursuline Convent, Wimbledon, and Wimbledon Coll. Chairman of Wimbledon Community Association. Honorary Freeman of Borough of Wimbledon 1957. Appointed Dept.-Lieut. of Surrey July 1957-66. Appointed Dept.-Lieut. of Greater London 1966. Knighted 1959. A Conservative. Elected for Wimbledon in 1950 and sat until he retired in 1970. President of Baptist Union 1970-71.* [1970]

BLACKBURN, Capt. Albert Raymond. S. of Dr. Albert Edward Blackburn, of Bournemouth. B. 11 Mar. 1915; m. 1st, 1939, Barbara Mary, d. of Gerald Robison, Esq. (divorced 1954); 2ndly, 1956 (divorced 1959); 3rdly, 1959, Tessa, d. of Lieut.-Col. J.G. Hume. Educ. at Rugby and London University. Served with E. Yorkshire Regiment 1939-45. Solicitor. A Labour Member. Unsuccessfully contested the Watford division of Hertfordshire as a Common Wealth candidate in Feb. 1943. Member for King's Norton division of Birmingham July 1945-Feb. 1950. Elected for the Northfield division

of Birmingham in Feb. 1950 and sat until he retired in 1951. Resigned Labour Whip in Aug. 1950 and sat as an Independent. Author of *The element of the law of torts, I am an alcoholic, The erosion of freedom, The soldier's guide to his rights and duties* and, with F.J. Bellenger, *The ex-serviceman's problem.** [1951]

BLACKBURN, Fred. 114 Knutsford Road, Wilmslow, Cheshire. S. of Richley Blackburn, Esq. B. 29 July 1902; m. 31 July 1930, Marion, d. of Walter Wright Fildes, Esq., of Manchester. Educ. at Queen Elizabeth's Grammar School, Blackburn, St. John's Coll., Battersea, and Manchester University. A Teacher; Lancashire County Magistrate from 1942. Ten years experience of Local Government. A Labour Member. Unsuccessfully contested Macclesfield in 1950. Elected for the Stalybridge and Hyde division of Cheshire in Oct. 1951 and sat until he retired in 1970.* [1970]

BLAKER, Peter Allan Renshaw. House of Commons, London. S. of Cedric Blaker, Esq., C.B.E., M.C., E.D.B. 4 Oct. 1922; m. 24 Oct. 1953, Jennifer, d. of Sir Pierson Dixon, G.C.M.G., C.B. Educ. at Shrewsbury, Toronto University, and New Coll., Oxford. Served with the Canadian Infantry 1942-46; wounded in action. Admitted a Solicitor 1948; called to the bar at Lincoln's Inn 1952, Foreign Service 1953-64; served in Cambodia, Canada and London, Private Secretary to the Minister of State for Foreign Affairs 1962-64. Attended the signing of the Nuclear Test Ban Treaty, Moscow 1963. Joint Secretary Conservative Parliamentary Foreign Affairs Committee 1965-66. An Opposition Whip 1966-67. Joint Secretary Conservative Parliamentary Trade Committee 1967-70. Member of Executive Committee of 1922 Committee 1967-70. Parliamentary Private Secretary to Rt. Hon. Anthony Barber, Chancellor of Duchy of Lancaster 1970 and Chancellor of the Exchequer 1970-72. Parliamentary Under-Secretary of State for Defence (Army) Nov. 1972-Jan. 1974, and for Foreign and Commonwealth Office Jan.-Mar. 1974. Vice-Chairman Conservative Parliamentary Foreign Affairs Committee 1974. A Conservative. Sat for Blackpool S. from Oct. 1964.

Minister of State, Foreign and Commonwealth Office from May 1979. Member of Council of Chatham House from 1977.*
[1979]

BLENKINSOP, Arthur. 233 Wingrove Road, Newcastle-upon-Tyne. S. of John Matthewson Blenkinsop, Esq. B. 30 June 1911; m. 1939, Mary Norman, d. of Foster Harrold, Esq., of Newcastle-upon-Tyne. Educ. at Newcastle Royal Grammar School. University Research Fellow 1960-61. Parliamentary Secretary Ministry of Pensions May 1946-Feb. 1949; Ministry of Health Feb. 1949-Oct. 1951. Chairman Committee for Social and Health Questions of Council of Europe 1968-70. Former member Advisory Council on Drug Misuse. Chairman Labour Parliamentary Shipping Group. Chairman Council Town and Country Planning Association. Member Executive Committee National Trust. A Labour Member. Sat for Newcastle E. from 1945-59, when he was defeated, and for South Shields from 1964 until he retired in Apr. 1979. Lord Commissioner of Treasury Aug. 1945-May 1946. Opposition spokesman on Health until 1959. Voted in favour of entry to E.E.C. on 28 Oct. 1971. Died 23 Sept. 1979. [1979]

BLYTON, William Reid. 139 Brockley Avenue, South Shields. S. of Charles H. Blyton, Esq., of South Shields. B. 2 May 1899; m. 26 Dec. 1919, Jane, d. of Edward Ord, Esq. Educ. at Elementary School. Served in Royal Navy 1917-18. A Miner 1914-45. Official of Harton Miners' Lodge; member of Durham Miners' Executive Committee 1930-31, 1932-33, and 1942-43. Member of South Shields Town Council 1936-45; Parliamentary Private Secretary to G.S. Lindgren Parliamentary Secretary Ministry of Civil Aviation 1947-May 1949. Delegate to Council of Europe, Strasbourg 1949, 1950 and 1951. A Labour Member. Elected for the Houghton-le-Spring division of Durham in July 1945 and sat until he retired in 1964. Created Baron Blyton (Life Peerage) 1964.* [1964]

BOARDMAN, Harold. 18 Norris Road, Sale, Manchester. S. of Alfred Boardman, Esq., of Bolton. B. 1907; m. 1936, Winifred

May, d. of Jesse Thorlby, Esq. Educ. at Elementary Schools in Bolton and Derby. A Trades Union Official. President of Derby Labour Party. Member of Derby Town Council 1934-37. Parliamentary Private Secretary to the Rt. Hon. George Isaacs, Minister of Labour 1947-51. Delegate to Council of Europe 1960-61. A Labour Member. Sat for Leigh from July 1945 until he retired in 1979.* [1979]

BOARDMAN, Thomas Gray, M.C., T.D. The Manor House, Welford, Rugby. 9 Tufton Street, London. St. Stephen's, and Cavalry. S. of John Clayton Boardman, Esq. B. 12 Jan. 1919; m. 1948, Norah Mary Deirdre (née Gough), widow of John Henry Chaworth Musters, Esq. Educ. at Bromsgrove. Served Northamptonshire Yeomanry 1939-46. Admitted a Solicitor 1947. Minister for Industry Apr. 1972-Jan. 1974. Chief Secretary to the Treasury Jan.-Mar. 1974. A Conservative. Unsuccessfully contested Leicester S.W. in 1964 and 1966. Sat for Leicester S.W. from Nov. 1967-Feb. 1974 and for Leicester S. from Feb. 1974-Oct. 1974 when he was defeated. M.C. 1944, T.D. 1952. Chairman of Chamberlain Phipps Limited 1958-72, of Steetley Company Limited from 1978. Dept.-Lieut. for Northamptonshire 1977. Created Baron Boardman (Life Peerage) 1980.* [1974]

BODY, Richard Bernard Frank Stewart. Jewell's House, Stanford Dingley, Berkshire. Carlton. S. of Lieut.-Col. B.R. Body. B. 18 May 1927; m. 1959, Marion, d. of Maj. H. Graham, O.B.E., (1 s. 1 d.). Educ. at Reading School. Called to the bar of the Middle Temple 1949. A Farmer. Chairman Open Seas Forum 1970. Voted against entry to E.E.C. on 28 Oct. 1971. Joint Chairman Council of the Get Britian Out Referendum Campaign 1974. A Conservative. Unsuccessfully contested Rotherham in Feb. 1950, Abertillery Nov. 1950, and Leek in 1951. Sat for Billericay from 1955-59 when he retired, and for the Holland with Boston division of Lincolnshire from Mar. 1966.* [1979]

BOLES, Lieut.-Col. Dennis Coleridge. Barrow Court, Galhampton, Yeovil. Forsinard, Sutherland, Cavalry, Hurlingham, and Roehampton. S. of F.J. Coleridge Boles, Esq., of Exmouth. B. 4 June 1885; m. 21 Apr. 1921, Katherine Monica, d. of Col. J. Reid Walker, of Ruckley, Shifnal. Educ. at Eton, and Royal Military Coll., Sandhurst. Joined 17th Lancers 1906, Royal Horse Guards 1929; Lieut.-Col. Commanding R.H.G. 1930. A National Conservative Member. Elected for the Wells division of Somerset in Dec. 1939 and sat until he retired in 1951. Member of Somerset County Council 1952-58. Member of Church Assembly 1955-58. Died 25 Apr. 1958. [1951]

BONHAM CARTER, Mark Raymond. 42 Victoria Road, London. Brooks's, and Savile. S. of Sir Maurice Bonham Carter, K.C.B., K.C.V.O. and Lady Violet Bonham Carter (created Baroness Asquith of Yarnbury 1964). B. 11 Feb. 1922; m. 1955, Leslie, d. of Condé Nast. Educ. at Winchester, Balliol Coll., Oxford, and Chicago University. Served in World War II with Grenadier Guards in 8th Army in Africa and N.W. Europe (prisoner but escaped). Director Collins, Publishers until 1958, and Royal Opera House, Covent Garden from 1958; Gov. of Royal Ballet School. A Liberal. Unsuccessfully contested the Barnstaple division of Devon in 1945. Elected for the Torrington division of Devon in Mar. 1958 and sat until he was defeated in 1959. Unsuccessfully contested Torrington in 1964. Member of Council of Europe 1958-59. Chairman of Race Relations Board 1966-70, of Community Relations Commission 1971-77. Member of Council of Consumers Association 1966-71, Vice-President from 1972. Vice-Chairman of B.B.C. from 1975. Hon. LL.D. University of Dundee 1978. Chairman of Outer Circle Policy Unit from 1976. Styled 'The Honourable' after his mother's elevation to the Peerage in 1964.* [1959]

BOOTH, Rt. Hon. Albert Edward. House of Commons, London. S. of Albert Henry Booth, Esq. B. 28 May 1928; m. 23 Feb. 1957, d. of Josiah Amis. Educ. in London and Winchester. Tynemouth Borough Councillor 1962-65. Minister of State, Department of Employment Mar. 1974-Apr. 1976. Secretary of State for Employment Apr. 1976-May 1979. PC. 1976. A Labour Member. Un-successfully contested Tynemouth in 1964. Sat for Barrow-in-Furness from Mar. 1966. Chairman of Select Committee on Statutory Instruments 1970-74. Opposition spokesman on Trade and Industry Jan. 1972-Feb. 1973 and Dec. 1973-Mar. 1974. Member of Parliamentary Committee of P.L.P. from 1979. Opposition spokesman on Transport from 1979.* [1979]

BOOTH, Alfred. House of Commons, London. B. 24 Feb. 1893; m. 1927, Anne Webster. A Congregationalist Local Preacher. A Labour Member. Elected for Bolton E. in Feb. 1950 and sat until he was defeated in 1951. Unsuccessfully contested Bolton E. in 1955. Served with Lancashire Fusiliers 1914-18. Member of Bolton Borough Council from 1933, Alderman from 1945, Mayor 1941-42. Vice-President of Cremation Society. Chairman of Bolton National Savings Committee. President of Bolton Labour Party, Bolton Council of Christian Congregations, and Bolton Y.M.C.A. Executive. Died 19 Dec. 1965. [1951]

BOOTHBY, Sir Robert John Graham, K.B.E. 1 Eaton Square, London. White's, and Beefsteak. S. of Sir R.T. Boothby, K.B.E. B. 12 Feb. 1900; m. 1st, 21 Mar. 1935, Diana, d. of Lord Richard Cavendish (marriage dissolved 1937); 2ndly, 1967, Wanda, d. of Giuseppe Sanna, of Sardinia. Educ. at Eton, and Magdalen Coll., Oxford, B.A. 1921. Parliamentary Private Secretary to Rt. Hon. Winston Churchill, Chancellor of the Exchequer 1926-29. Parliamentary Secretary Ministry of Food May 1940-Jan. 1941. British Delegate to Council of Europe at Strasbourg 1949-55. Officer of the Legion of Honour 1950. Served with Scots Guards 1918 and R.A.F. 1941-42. K.B.E. 1953. A Conservative. Unsuccessfully contested Orkney and Shetland in 1923. Sat for the E. Aberdeenshire division of Aberdeen and Kincardine from Oct. 1924-50. Elected for Aberdeenshire E. in 1950 and sat until he was created Baron Boothby (Life Peerage) in July 1958. Rector of St. Andrews University 1958-61, Honorary. LL.D. 1959. Chairman of Royal Philharmonic Orchestra 1961-63. President of Anglo-Israel Association 1962-75.*

[1958]

BOOTHROYD, Betty. House of Commons, London. D. of Archibald and Mary Boothroyd. B. 8 Oct. 1929. Educ. at Dewsbury Coll. of Commerce and Art. Personal/Political Assistant to Labour Ministers. Accompanied Labour Party delegations to European conferences, Soviet Union, China and Vietnam. Chairman Parliamentary Staffs Trade Unions 1958-65. Legislative Assistant U.S. Congressman 1960-62. Councillor Hammersmith Borough Council 1965-68; Chairman Welfare Committee. Chairman Hammersmith Race Relations Employment Committee 1967-72. Chairman School Governors 1970-72. British Delegation to North Atlantic Assembly 1974. Delegate 20th Commonwealth Parliamentary Association Conference 1974. Member of European Parliament July 1975-Mar. 1977. Assistant Government Whip Oct. 1974-Nov. 1975. A Labour Member. Unsuccessfully contested S.E. Leicester at a by-election in 1957, Peterborough 1959, Nelson & Colne at a by-election in 1968, and Rossendale in 1970. Member for West Bromwich from May 1973-Feb. 1974 and for the W. division of West Bromwich from Feb. 1974. Member of Speaker's Panel of Chairmen from 1979.*

[1979]

BOSCAWEN, Hon. Robert Thomas, M.C. House of Commons, London. Pratt's, and Royal Yacht Squadron. S. of 8th Visct. Falmouth. B. 17 Mar. 1923; m. 19 Nov. 1949, Mary, eld. d. of Col. Sir Geoffrey Codrington, K.C.V.O., (1 s. 2 d.). Educ. at Eton, and Trinity Coll., Cambridge. Served with Coldstream Guards 1942-45, Capt., M.C. 1944. Member London Executive Council, National Health Service 1956-65; a Lloyds Underwriter. Vice-Chairman Conservative Parliamentary Health and Social Security Committee. Assistant Government Whip from May 1979. A Conservative. Unsuccessfully contested Falmouth and Camborne in 1964 and 1966. Member for the Wells division of Somerset from June 1970.*

[1979]

BOSSOM, Sir Alfred Charles, Bart. 5 Carlton Gardens, London. Stoneacre, Otham, Maidstone. Carlton, Garrick, and Kent County. S. of Alfred Henry Bossom, Esq. B. 16 Oct. 1881; m. 1st, 1910, Emily, d. of Samuel Bayne, Esq., President of Seaboard National Bank, New York (she died 27 July 1932); 2ndly, 1934, Elinor, d. of Samuel Dittenhofer, Esq. (marriage dissolved 1947). Educ. at St. Thomas, Charterhouse, and Royal Academy of Arts. Underwriter at Lloyds; Author, at one time an Architect with International Practice. F.R.I.B.A. Chairman Executive Committee American Mid-European Association, of Slum Clearance Committee 1930-34, of S.E. Provincial Area National Union of Conservative and Unionist Associations, and of St. George's Society; Vice-Chairman of London County Council Improvement Sub-Committee and of Housing Committee; member of Parliamentary Select Committee on National Expenditure 1939; member of British Building Mission to U.S.A. 1943; J.P. for Maidstone; President Anglo-Baltic Society; Alderman London County Council 1930-34; Secretary Home Guard Parliamentary Committee Lords and Commons 1942-44; Chairman Royal Society of Arts; Chairman Anglo-Belgian Section Inter-Parliamentary Union, Anglo-Iranian Group and Anglo-Belgian Union. President the Pitman Fellowship. Member of Paviors, Needlemakers (Senior Warden) and Armourers and Brasiers. London City Companies. Honorary Freeman of the Borough of Maidstone; member of Chapter-Gen. and K.St.J.; Officer of Legion of Honour, Real Academia de Nobles Artes de San Fernando, Spain; Order of the Crown of Italy, of the White Lion of Czechoslovakia, Commander of the Order of the Lithuania Grand Duke Gediminas, Eagle Cross of Estonia, Grand Commissioner of Latvian Order of Stars and Latvian Order of Merit; Commissioner of Finnish Order of the White Rose, and the Chilean Order of Merit; Diploma and Gold Medal of Les Invalides Preyvoyants (Belgium); Order of Christ of Portugal; Commissioner of Order of the Crown (Belgium); Grand Prior of Primrose League; President Association of Public Health Inspectors; membre d'Hon. La Federation Nat. des Sapeurs-Pompiers de France et de l'Union Francaise. Honorary Fellow, University Coll., London; Honorary LL.D. Pittsburgh University; Honorary Cit. Dallas and Texas; Honorary member

33

Flanders Fire Service. A Conservative. Unsuccessfully contested Hackney Central in 1929. Elected for the Maidstone division of Kent in Oct. 1931 and sat until he retired in 1959. Created Bart. 1953. Created Baron Bossom (Life Peerage) 1960. Died 4 Sept. 1965. [1959]

BOSSOM, Hon. Sir Clive, Bart. Parsons Orchard, Eastnor, Nr. Ledbury, Herefordshire. 3 Eaton Mansions, London. Carlton, and M.C.C.S. of Lord Bossom (Life Peer), Bart., F.R.I.B.A. (he died Sept. 1965). B. 4 Feb. 1918; m. 28 Sept. 1951, Lady Barbara North, d. of Maj. Lord North, (3 s. 1 d.). Educ. at Eton. Kt. Order of St. John. Fellow of the Royal Society of Arts. Maj., The Buffs, served in Europe and Far East 1939-48. Member Kent County Council 1949-51. President Anglo-Belgian Union 1970-73. President Industrial Fire Protection Association. Vice-President of Urban District Councils of England and Wales. National Vice-Chairman of Ex-Services War Disabled Help Committee. On Councils of Royal Society of Arts, Royal Geographical Society and Royal Automobile Club. Parliamentary Private Secretary to Joint Parliamentary Secretaries of Ministry of Pensions 1960-62. Parliamentary Private Secretary to Rt. Hon. Hugh Fraser, Secretary of State for Air 1962-64. Parliamentary Private Secretary to Rt. Hon. Reginald Maudling, Home Secretary 1970-72. A Conservative. Unsuccessfully contested Faversham division of Kent in 1951 and 1955. Elected for Leominster division of Herefordshire in 1959 and sat until he retired in Feb. 1974. Succeeded to his father's baronetcy in 1965. Chairman of Iran Society 1973-76.* [1974]

BOSTON, Terence George. 3 Manwood Close, Sittingbourne, Kent. S. of George Thomas Boston, Esq., Civil Servant. B. 21 Mar. 1930; m. 3 Apr. 1962, Margaret Joyce Head, eld. d. of R.H.J. Head, Esq., and of Mrs. E.M. Winters and step d. of H.F. Winters, all of Melbourne, Australia. Educ. at Woolwich Polytechnic School, and King's Coll., University of London. Commissioned in R.A.F. during national service 1950-52. Called to the bar at the Inner Temple 1960 and Gray's Inn 1973; B.B.C. News Sub-editor 1957-60; Senior Producer, Current Affairs 1960-64. Member National Committee Young Socialists (then Labour League of Youth) 1949-51; Executive Committee International Union of Socialist Youth 1950. Dept. President (for a time Acting President) University of London Union 1955-56. Member of the Fabian Society International Bureau N.U.J., N.U.G.M.W. Parliamentary Private Secretary to Rt. Hon. Charles Pannell, Minister of Public Building and Works 1964-66; to Rt. Hon. Richard Marsh, Minister of Power 1966-68 and Minister of Transport 1968-69. Member Speaker's Conference on Electoral Law 1965-68. Member Select Committee on Broadcasting (the Proceedings of the House of Commons) 1966. Founder Vice-Chairman G.B.-East Europe Centre 1967. Assistant Government Whip Oct. 1969-June 1970. A Labour Member. Unsuccessfully contested the Wokingham division of Berkshire in 1955 and 1959. Elected for the Faversham division of Kent in June 1964 and sat until he was defeated in 1970. Created Baron Boston of Faversham (Life Peerage) 1976. Minister of State, Home Office Jan.-May 1979.* [1970]

BOTTOMLEY, Rt. Hon. Arthur George, O.B.E. 19 Lichfield Road, Woodford Green, Essex. S. of George Howard Bottomley, Esq. B. 7 Feb. 1907; m. 25 July 1936, Bessie, D.B.E., d. of Edward Wiles, Esq. Educ. at Elementary School, and Toynbee Hall. Employed on L.M.S. Railway 1921-35. London Organiser, National Union of Public Employees 1935-41; Chairman of Emergency Committee and A.R.P. Controller for Walthamstow 1939-41; Dept.-Regional Commissioner for S.E. England 1941-45. Member of Walthamstow Borough Council 1929-49, Mayor of Walthamstow 1945-46. Parliamentary Under-Secretary of State for Dominions 1946-47; Secretary for Overseas Trade 1947-51. PC. 1951. Secretary of State for Commonwealth Relations Oct. 1964-Aug. 1966. Minister of Overseas Development Aug. 1966-Aug. 1967. Chairman Select Committee on Race Relations 1968-70. Dept.-Chairman C.P.A., U.K., B.C.H. Treasurer, Commonwealth Parliamentary Association. Governor Commonwealth Institute. Chairman Special Committee on House of Commons Services and Organisation 1975-76. Chairman Atlee Foundation. A Labour Member. Sat for the Chatham division of Rochester 1945-50, Rochester and Chatham from 1950-59, when he was defeated, for Middlesbrough E. from Mar. 1962-Feb. 1974 and for Teesside, Middlesbrough division from Feb. 1974. O.B.E. 1941. An Opposition spokesman on Trade and Treasury affairs to 1956, on Defence 1956-57, on Housing 1957-58, on Commonwealth Affairs 1957-59 and 1963-64. Member of Parliamentary Committee of P.L.P. 1957-59. Member of Cabinet Oct. 1964-Jan. 1967.   *[1979]

BOTTOMLEY, Peter James. 2 St. Barnabas Villas, London. T.G.W.U. S. of Sir James Bottomley, K.C.M.G., H.M. Diplomatic Service. B. 30 July 1944; m. 1967, Virginia, J.P., d. of W. John Garnett, Esq., C.B.E. of Sea View, Isle of Wight, (1 s. 1 d.). Educ. at Comprehensive School, Westminster School, and Trinity Coll., Cambridge. Worked in industrial relations and industrial economics. Chairman British Union of Family Organisations. President Conservative Trade Unionists. Contested Vauxhall in G.L.C. election in 1973. A Conservative. Unsuccessfully contested Woolwich W. in the general elections of Feb. and Oct. 1974. Member for the Woolwich W. division of Greenwich from June 1975 (by-election).*   [1979]

BOURNE-ARTON, Anthony Temple, M.B.E. Tanfield Lodge, Ripon. Army & Navy, Carlton, and Yorkshire (York). S. of W.R.T. Bourne, Esq., of Walker Hall, Winston, Co. Durham. B. 1 Mar. 1913; m. 16 July 1938, Elaine, d. of W.D. Arton, Esq., J.P., of Sleningford Park, Ripon. Educ. at Clifton. 2nd Lieut. R.A. 1935; Palestine 1936. War Service 1939-45, France, North Africa, Sicily, Italy. Mentioned in despatches 1940. M.B.E. 1944. Malaya 1947-48. Retired as Maj. 1948. Member North Riding County Council 1949-61; Bedale Rural District Council 1949-52. J.P. for the North Riding of Yorkshire 1950. Parliamentary Private Secretary to Rt. Hon. Henry Brooke, Home Secretary from 1962-64. A Conservative. Elected for

Darlington in 1959 and sat until he was defeated in 1964. Unsuccessfully contested Darlington in 1966 and 1970. Member of W. Riding County Council 1967-70. Chairman of Yorkshire Regional Land Drainage Committee from 1973. Assumed the surname Bourne-Arton in lieu of Bourne in 1950.*
[1964]

BOWDEN, Andrew, M.B.E. House of Commons, London. S. of W.V. Bowden, Esq., Solicitor. B. 8 Apr. 1930; m. 21 June 1970, Benita, d. of B. Napier, Esq., (1 s. 1 d.). Educ. at Ardingly Coll., Sussex. Member Wandsworth Borough Council 1956-62; National Chairman Young Conservative Movement 1960-61; Managing Director of Personal Assessments Limited 1969-71; and Haymarket Personnel Selection Limited 1969-71. Director Jenkin and Purser (Holdings) Limited 1973-77. Vice-President Council for International Contact. Member Select Committee on Expenditure 1973; Joint Chairman All-Party Parliamentary Group for Pensioners 1972; Chairman All-Party Parliamentary British Limbless Ex-Servicemens Group 1975; member Select Committee on Abortion 1975. National President Captive Animals Protection Society. M.B.E. 1961. A Conservative. Unsuccessfully contested N. Hammersmith in 1955, N. Kensington in 1964 and Brighton Kemptown in 1966. Member for the Kemptown division of Brighton from June 1970.*
[1979]

BOWDEN, Rt. Hon. Herbert William, C.B.E. House of Commons, London. S. of Herbert Henwood Bowden, Esq., of Cardiff. B. 20 Jan. 1905; m. 1928, Louise, d. of William Brown, Esq., of Cardiff, (1 d.). Educ. at Canton High School, Cardiff. President of Leicester Labour Party 1938. Member of Leicester City Council 1938-45. Member of Advisory Committee on Private Flying and Gliding, Ministry of Civil Aviation 1947. Parliamentary Private Secretary to the Rt. Hon. Wilfred Paling, Minister of Pensions Mar. 1947, and when Postmaster-Gen. May 1947-Feb. 1949; Assistant Whip Feb. 1949-Mar. 1950; Lord Commissioner of Treasury Mar. 1950-Oct. 1951. Dept. Chief Opposition Whip Oct. 1951; Chief Opposition Whip

35

1955-64. Lord President of the Council and Leader of the House of Commons Oct. 1964-Aug. 1966. Commonwealth Secretary Aug. 1966-Aug. 1967. A Labour Member. Sat for Leicester S. from 1945 to 1950 and for Leicester S.W. from 1950 until Aug. 1967 when he was created Baron Aylestone (Life Peerage) and appointed Chairman of Independent Television Authority. C.B.E. 1953. PC. 1962. C.H. 1975. Chairman of Independent Television Authority 1967-72, of Independent Broadcasting Authority 1972-75.*   [1967]

BOWEN, Evan Roderic, Q.C. Trem-y-Mor, Aberporth, Cardiganshire. S. of Evan Bowen, Esq. B. 6 Aug. 1913. Educ. at Cardigan School, University Coll., Aberystwyth, and St. John's Coll., Cambridge. Served in Army 1940-45 in ranks and on J.A.G. staff. Barrister-at-Law, Middle Temple 1937. Q.C. 1952. Dept. Chairman of Ways and Means from 1965-66. A Liberal. Elected for Cardigan in July 1945 and sat until he was defeated in 1966. Recorder of Carmarthen 1950-53, Merthyr Tydfil 1953-60, Swansea 1960-64 and Cardiff 1964-67. Chairman of Montgomeryshire Quarter Sessions 1959-71. President of St. David's University Coll., Lampeter from 1977. Honorary LL.D. University of Wales 1972. National Insurance Commissioner from 1967.*   [1966]

BOWER, Norman Adolph Henry. Carlton. S. of Waldemar Sophus Bower, Esq. B. 18 May 1907. Educ. at Rugby, and Wadham Coll., Oxford. Barrister-at-Law, Inner Temple 1935. A Conservative. Unsuccessfully contested W. Bermondsey in Oct. 1931 and N. Hammersmith in Nov. 1935. Sat for the Harrow division of Middlesex from Dec. 1941 to July 1945 and for Harrow W. from July 1945 until he resigned in Mar. 1951. Member of Westminster City Council 1937-45.*   [1950]

BOWLES, Francis George. 73 St. James's Street, London. S. of Horace Edgar Bowles, Esq., Analytical Chemist. B. 2 May 1902; m. 25 May 1950, Kay d. of E.H. Musgrove, Esq., and widow of Air Commodore E.D.M. Hopkins. Educ. at Highgate School, and University of London, LL.B., B.Sc. (Econ.).

Admitted Solicitor 1925. Vice-Chairman Parliamentary Labour Party 1946-48. Dept. Chairman of Ways and Means Oct. 1948-Mar. 1950. A Trustee of the House of Commons from 1952. A Labour Member. Unsuccessfully contested Hackney N. In 1929, 1931 and 1935, and Preston in 1936. Elected for the Nuneaton division of Warwickshire in Mar. 1942 and sat until Dec. 1964 when he was created Baron Bowles (Life Peerage). Capt. of Yeoman of the Guard and Government Dept. Chief Whip in House of Lords Dec. 1964-June 1970. Died 29 Dec. 1970.   [1964]

BOX, Donald Stewart. Laburnum Cottage, Sully Road, Penarth. 1 South Block, Artillery Mansions, Victoria Street, London. S. of Stanley Carter Box, Esq. B. 22 Nov. 1917; m. 1st 1940, Margaret, d. of Charles Bates, Esq., of Whitchurch, Cardiff (marriage dissolved in 1947); 2ndly, 1948, Peggy, d. of Henry Charles Gooding, Esq., of London (marriage dissolved in 1973); 3rdly, 1973, Margaret Rose Davies. Educ. at Llandaff Cathedral School, St. John's School, Pinner, Harrow County School. R.A.F. 1939-45. Member of Cardiff Stock Exchange 1945. A Conservative. Unsuccessfully contested Newport, Monmouthshire in 1955 and 1956. Elected for Cardiff N. in 1959 and sat until he was defeated in 1966. Partner in Lyddon and Company, Stockbrokers.*   [1966]

BOYD, (Thomas) Christopher. 22 Cheyne Gardens, Chelsea, London. Overseas League. S. of Canon W.G. Boyd. B. 1916; m. 1957, Anneliese, d. of Franz Bamback, of Icking, Bavaria. Educ. at Marlborough, and Hertford Coll., Oxford. Served as sapper 1940-41; Commission in Oxford and Bucks L.I. 1941; Staff Capt. G.H.Q. India 1942; D.A.Q.M.G. 1944; Loaned to Gov. of India as Under-Secretary 1944-46; Secretary to All-Party Parliamentary Delegation to India 1946; Senior Assistant to Secretary Building Apprenticeship and Training Council 1946-47; Economics, Foreign Trade and Prices Department of British Iron and Steel Federation 1948-51; served on Central Economic Planning Staff in Cabinet office and Treasury 1947-48; Chairman Chelsea Branch of United Nations Association and Chelsea

Labour Party; member Chelsea Borough Council from 1953 to 1959 and of N.W. London Rate Valuation Panel; Gov. United Westminster Schools; Freeman of the City of London; member of the Parliamentary Delegation to France 1957. A Labour Member. Unsuccessfully contested Isle of Thanet in 1945 and 1950 and Harborough division of Leicestershire in 1951. Elected for N.W. Bristol in 1955 and sat until he was defeated in 1959. Unsuccessfully contested Dumfriesshire in 1966.* [1959]

BOYD-CARPENTER, Rt. Hon. John Archibald. 12 Eaton Terrace, London. Carlton. S. of Sir Archibald Boyd-Carpenter, MP. B. 2 June 1908; m. 25 June 1937, Margaret, d. of Lieut.-Col. G.L. Hall, O.B.E., (1 s. 2 d.). Educ. at Stowe, and Balliol Coll., Oxford, Harmsworth Law Scholar 1932. Barrister-at-Law, Middle Temple 1934. President of Oxford Union Society 1930. Served with Scots Guards 1940-45. Maj. 1943. Financial Secretary to the Treasury Oct. 1951-July 1954. Minister of Transport and Civil Aviation July 1954-Dec. 1955; Minister of Pensions and National Insurance Dec. 1955-July 1962. Chief Secretary to the Treasury and Paymaster-Gen. July 1962-Oct. 1964. PC. 1954. Chairman Public Accounts Committee Nov. 1964-70. Chairman Conservative London Members. President Anglo-Polish Conservative Society 1971. A Conservative. Elected for Kingston-upon-Thames in July 1945 and sat until Mar. 1972 when he was created Baron Boyd-Carpenter (Life Peerage) and appointed Chairman of Civil Aviation Authority. Opposition spokesman on Housing and Land and Member of Shadow Cabinet 1964-66. Chairman of Civil Aviation Authority 1972-77. Chairman of Orion Insurance Company 1969-72, CLRP Investment Trust 1970-72, and Rugby Portland Cement from 1976. High Steward of Kingston-upon-Thames 1973. Dept.-Lieut. for Greater London 1973.* [1972]

BOYD-ORR, Sir John, D.S.O., M.C., F.R.S. Wardenhill, Bucksburn, Aberdeenshire. Newton of Stracathn, Brechin, Angus. Athenaeum. S. of R.C. Orr, Esq., of Holland Green, Kilmaurs. B 23 Sept. 1880; m. 1915, Elizabeth, d. of John Callum, Esq., of West Kilbride. Educ. at Glasgow University, M.A., M.D., D.Sc. Served with R.A.M.C. and in Royal Navy 1914-18; D.S.O. 1917, M.C. Director of Rowett Research Institute, Aberdeen University, and of Imperial Bureau of Animal Nutrition; member of Advisory Committee on Nutrition Ministry of Health. An Independent Member. Member for the Scottish Universities from Apr. 1945 until he resigned in Oct. 1946. F.R.S. 1932. Knighted 1935. Rector of Glasgow University 1945, Chancellor 1946-71. Professor of Agriculture, Aberdeen University 1942-45. Created Baron Boyd-Orr 1949. Nobel Peace Prize 1949. Companion of Honour 1968. Director General of United Nations Food and Agriculture Organisation 1945-48. Died 25 June 1971. [1946]

BOYDEN, Harold James, J.P. House of Commons, London. S. of Claude James Boyden, Esq. B. 19 Oct. 1910; m. 1935, Emily, d. of John Thomas Pemberton, Esq., of Warrington. Educ. at Elementary School, Tiffin Grammar, and King's Coll., London. A Teacher and Lecturer 1933-47. R.A.F. 1940-45. Called to the bar at Lincoln's Inn 1947. Director of Extra Mural Studies, Durham Colls. 1947-59. First Labour County Councillor, Durham City 1952. Chairman Durham County Education Committee 1959. Joint Parliamentary Under-Secretary of State for Education and Science Oct. 1964-Feb. 1965. Parliamentary Secretary Ministry of Public Building and Works Feb. 1965-Jan. 1967. Parliamentary Under-Secretary of State for Defence (Army) Jan. 1967-Oct. 1969. Fellow of King's Coll. 1969. Delegate to Council of Europe and Western European Union 1970-73. Chairman Expenditure Committee 1974-79. A Labour Member. Member for Bishop Auckland from 1959 until he retired in 1979.* [1979]

BOYLE, Rt. Hon. Sir Edward Charles Gurney, Bart. Ockham, Hurst Green, Sussex. Carlton, and Pratt's. S. of Sir Edward Boyle, Bart., Barrister. B. 31 Aug. 1923. Educ. at Eton, and Christ Church, Oxford. A Journalist. Formerly Assistant Editor of *The National and English Review*. President of the Oxford Union Society 1948. Parliamentary

Private Secretary to Nigel Birch when Parliamentary Under-Secretary of State for Air 1951-52, and as Parliamentary Secretary to Ministry of Defence 1952-54. Parliamentary Secretary Ministry of Supply Jan. 1954-Apr. 1955. Economic Secretary to the Treasury Apr. 1955-Nov. 1956 when he resigned. Parliamentary Secretary Ministry of Education Jan. 1957-Oct. 1959. Financial Secretary to the Treasury Oct. 1959-July 1962. Minister of Education July 1962-Apr. 1964. Minister of State, Department of Education and Science with a seat in the Cabinet Apr.-Oct. 1964. Honorary LL.D. (Leeds) May 1965; Honorary LL.D. (Southampton) July 1965. Pro-Chancellor, University of Sussex Dec. 1965-70. Member Fulton Committee on Civil Service 1966-68. A Trustee of The Winston Churchill Memorial Trust. Director of Penguin Books 1965. A Conservative. Unsuccessfully contested the Perry Barr division of Birmingham in Feb. 1950. Elected for the Handsworth division of Birmingham in Nov. 1950 and sat until he retired in 1970. Succeeded as Bart. 1945. PC. 1962. Opposition spokesman on Home Affairs 1964-65 and on Education and Science 1965-69. Member of Shadow Cabinet 1964-69. Created Baron Boyle of Handsworth (Life Peerage) 1970. Vice-Chancellor of Leeds University from 1970. Chairman of Top Salaries Review Body from 1971. President of Incorporated Society of Preparatory Schools 1970-74.* [1970]

BOYSON, Dr. Rhodes. Laneham, 71 Paines Lane, Pinner, Middlesex. St. Stephen's. S. of Alderman William Boyson, M.B.E., J.P.B. 11 May 1925; m. 1st, 1946, Violet Burletson (divorced) (2 d.). 2ndly, 1971, Florette MacFarlane. Educ. at Haslingden Grammar School, Manchester University, London School of Economics, and Corpus Christi Coll., Cambridge. A Methodist. Headmaster Lea Back School, Lancashire, Robert Montefiore School, London, and Highbury Grove School. Writer, Author, Publisher, and Broadcaster. Member of Haslingden Borough Council 1957-61 and Waltham Forest Borough Council 1968-74. Under-Secretary of State for Education and Science from May 1979. A Conservative. Unsuccessfully contested

Eccles in 1970. Member for Brent N. from Feb. 1974.* [1979]

BRACKEN, Rt. Hon. Brendan. 8 Lord North Street, London. Brooks's, and White's. S. of J.K.A. Bracken, Esq., of Ardvullen House, Kilmallock. B. Feb. 1901. Unmarried. Educ. in Australia, and at Sedbergh. A Newspaper Publisher. Parliamentary Private Secretary to the Rt. Hon. Winston Churchill, Prime Minister 1940-41; Minister of Information July 1941-May 1945; PC. 1940. A Conservative. Member for Paddington N. from 1929-45 when he was defeated, for Bournemouth from Nov. 1945-50. Returned for Bournemouth East and Christchurch in Feb. 1950 and sat until Jan. 1952 when he was created Visct. Bracken. First Lord of the Admiralty May-July 1945. Director of *The Economist* and *Financial News*. Chairman of Union Corporation and of *Financial Times*. Trustee of National Gallery 1955-58. Died 8 Aug. 1958. [1951]

BRADDOCK, Elizabeth Margaret. 2 Zig Zag Road, Liverpool. Transport House, 41 Islington, Liverpool. D. of Hugh Bamber, Esq. B. 24 Sept. 1899; m. 9 Feb. 1922, John Braddock (he died 12 Nov. 1963). Educ. at Liverpool Elementary Schools. A J.P. from 1946. A Labour Member. Elected for the Exchange division of Liverpool in July 1945 and sat until she retired in May 1970. Member of Communist Party until 1924. Member of Liverpool City Council from 1930-61, Alderman 1955-61. Member of National Executive Committee of Labour Party 1947-48 and 1958-69, Vice-Chairman 1968-69. Died 13 Nov. 1970. [1970]

BRADDOCK, Thomas. 25 Parkside, Wimbledon Common, London. 14 Great Smith Street, London. S. of Henry William Braddock, Esq., of Bolton B. 1887; m. 1912, Betty Houghton. Educ. at Rutlish School, Merton. An Architect. Member of Surrey County Council 1934-46 and of Wimbledon Borough Council 1936-1945. A Labour Member. Unsuccessfully contested Wimbledon in 1929, 1931 and 1935. Elected for Mitcham in July 1945 and sat until he was defeated in 1950. Unsuccessfully contested Kingston-on-Thames in 1959 and 1964, and

Wimbledon in 1966. Member of London County Council 1958-61. Fellow of Royal Institute of British Architects. Died 9 Dec. 1976. [1950]

BRADFORD, Rev. Robert John. House of Commons, London. B. 1941. Educ. at Queen's University. Methodist Minister. Member of Vanguard Unionist Progressive Party until 1975, when he joined the Official Unionists. Whip for the United Ulster Unionist Coalition 1974-75. An Ulster Unionist Member. Unsuccessfully contested S. Antrim in the N. Ireland Assembly election 1973. Sat for Belfast S. from Feb. 1974.* [1979]

BRADLEY, Thomas George. 111 London Road, Kettering, Northamptonshire. S. of George Henry Bradley, Esq. B. 13 Apr. 1926; m. 15 Aug. 1953, Joy Patricia Starmer, d. of George Starmer, Esq., of Kettering. Educ. at Kettering Central School. Member of Northamptonshire County Council 1952; County Alderman 1961-74. Treasurer of Transport Salaried Staffs' Association 1961-64, President from 1964. Parliamentary Private Secretary to Rt. Hon. Roy Jenkins, Minister of Aviation 1964-65, Home Secretary 1965-67 and Chancellor of Exchequer 1967-70. Elected Member of National Executive of Labour Party 1966. Vice-Chairman of Party 1974-75; Chairman 1975-76. A Labour Member. Unsuccessfully contested Rutland and Stamford in 1950, 1951 and 1955, and Preston S. in 1959. Sat for Leicester N.E. from July 1962-Feb. 1974, and for Leicester E. from Feb. 1974. Member of Kettering Borough Council 1957-61. An Opposition spokesman on Transport 1970-74. Voted in favour of entry to E.E.C. on 28 Oct. 1971. Chairman of Select Committee on Transport from 1979. Chairman of the European League for Economic Co-operation.* [1979]

BRAINE, Sir Bernard Richard. King's Wood, Rayleigh, Essex. Carlton, and Beefsteak. S. of Arthur Ernest Braine, Esq. B. 24 June 1914; m. 1935, Kathleen Mary, d. of H.W. Faun, Esq., of East Sheen, (3 s.). Educ. at Hendon County Grammar School. Joined N. Staffordshire Regiment 1940, Maj. 1943;

Staff Coll., Camberley 1944. Served in W. Africa, N.W. Europe and S.E. Asia; T. Lieut.-Col.; on staff of Admiral Lord Mountbatten. Parliamentary Private Secretary to Rt. Hon. A.T. Lennox-Boyd, Minister of Transport and Civil Aviation 1952-53. Chairman British Commonwealth Producers' Organisation 1958-60. Parliamentary Secretary Ministry of Pensions Oct. 1960-Feb. 1961. Under-Secretary of State Commonwealth Relations Feb. 1961-July 1962. Parliamentary Secretary to the Ministry of Health July 1962-Oct. 1964. Dept. Chairman of the U.K. branch of the Commonwealth Parliamentary Association 1964-65 and 1970-74, Treasurer 1965-70 and 1974-78. Leader of British Parliamentary Mission to India 1963, to Mauritius 1971, to Germany 1973. Opposition Front Bench spokesman on Commonwealth Affairs and Overseas Aid 1967-70. Chairman Select Committee on Overseas Aid 1970-71. Chairman Select Committee on Overseas Development 1973-74. Chairman Anglo-German Parliamentary Group. Chairman S.O.S. Childrens Villages. Chairman National Council on Alcoholism. Chairman Society for International Development (U.K. Chapter). Association Institute Development Studies Sussex University. A Gov. Commonwealth Institute, F.R.S.A. Knighted 1972. C. St. J. Grand Cross, German Order of Merit. Dept.-Lieut. Essex 1978. A Conservative. Unsuccessfully contested Leyton E. in 1945. Member for the Billericay division of Essex from 1950-55 and for S.E. Essex from 1955.* [1979]

BRAITHWAITE, Sir Albert Newby, D.S.O., M.C. Coxland, Ewhurst, Surrey. Carlton. S. of Albert Braithwaite, Esq., Lord Mayor of Leeds 1921, and Pattie, d. of Timothy Newby, Esq., of Harrogate. B. 2 Sept. 1893; m. 1st, 30 Mar. 1918, Anne, d. of Albert Anderson, Esq., of Augusta, Georgia, U.S.A. (she died Mar. 1950); 2ndly, Aug. 1950, Mrs. Joan Weiner. Educ. at Woodhouse Grove School, and Leeds University. Served with W. Yorkshire Regiment and Yorkshire Hussars 1914-18. D.S.O. 1918, M.C. An Engineer. Director of Sir Lindsay Parkinson and Company Limited, of Sterling Engineering Company Limited, of Guardian

39

Eastern Insurance Company Limited, of Dent Estates Limited, of Feltham Sand and Gravel Company Limited, of Skinner and Holford (Holdings) Limited, and of Russell Newbery and Company Limited. A Conservative. Unsuccessfully contested the Rothwell division in 1922, the Pontefract division in 1923, and the Elland division in 1924. Sat for the Buckrose division of the E. Riding of Yorkshire from May 1926 until July 1945, when he was defeated. Elected for W. Harrow in Apr. 1951 and sat until he committed suicide on 20 Oct. 1959. Knighted 1945. Died 20 Oct. 1959. [1959]

BRAITHWAITE, Lieut.-Commander Sir Joseph Gurney, Bart., R.N.V.R. 97 Hampstead Way, London. R.N.V.R., and Royal Aero. S. of Joseph Bevan Braithwaite, Esq. B. 24 May 1895; m. 1st, 13 Sept. 1919, Emma Louise Jeanne Teissère (marriage annulled 1932); 2ndly, 31 Dec. 1932, Emily Victoria, d. of A.M. Lomax, Esq., of Edinburgh. Educ. at Bootham School, Yorkshire. A Speaker in Hyde Park for 1912 Club 1927-31. Lieut. R.N.V.R., served in Dardanelles, Egypt and Palestine 1914-19; Resident Naval Officer at Port Said 1919; Lieut.-Commander R.N.V.R. Sept. 1939. Parliamentary Secretary Ministry of Transport and Civil Aviation Nov. 1951-Nov. 1953. Bart. 1954. A Conservative. Unsuccessfully contested Rotherhithe division of Bermondsey in May 1929. Elected for the Hillsborough division of Sheffield in Oct. 1931, defeated Nov. 1935. Sat for the Holderness division of E. Riding of Yorkshire from Feb. 1939 to Feb. 1950 and for N.W. Bristol from Feb. 1950 until May 1955 when he was defeated. Died 25 June 1958. [1954]

BRAMALL, Maj. Ernest Ashley. 5 Trafalgar Road, Twickenham. S. of Maj. E.H. Bramall. B. 6 Jan. 1916; m. 2 Sept. 1939, Margaret Elaine, d. of Raymond Taylor, Esq., of Teddington. Educ. at Westminster, Canford Schools, and Magdalen Coll., Oxford. A Secretary 1938-40. Served in the army 1940-46. A Labour Member. Unsuccessfully contested Fareham in 1945. Elected for the Bexley division of Kent in July 1946 and sat until he was defeated in 1950. Unsuccessfully contested Bexley in 1951 and 1959 and

Watford in 1955. Barrister-at-Law, Inner Temple 1949. Knighted 1975. Member of Westminster City Council 1959-68. Member of London County Council 1961-65, of Greater London Council from 1964. Chairman of Inner London Education Authority 1965-67, Leader from 1970. Leader of Burnham Committee Management Panel 1973-78.* [1950]

BRAY, Jeremy William. House of Commons, London. S. of the Rev. A.H. Bray. B. 29 June 1930; m. 26 Aug. 1953, Elizabeth Trowell, (4 d.). Educ. at Aberystwyth Grammar School, Kingswood School, and Jesus Coll., Cambridge, and Harvard University. Ph.D. 1957. A Methodist local preacher. Technical Officer I.C.I. Wilton 1956-62. Parliamentary Secretary Ministry of Power Apr. 1966-Jan. 1967 and Ministry of Technology Jan. 1967-Sept. 1969, when he resigned. Personnel and Consultancy Work 1970-73. Chairman Fabian Society 1971. Dept. Chairman Christian Aid 1972. A Labour Member. Unsuccessfully contested Thirsk and Malton in 1959. MP for Middlesbrough W. from June 1962 to 1970, when he was defeated. Sat for Motherwell and Wishaw from Oct. 1974. Parliamentary Private Secretary to Rt. Hon. George Brown, Secretary of State for Economic Affairs 1964-66. Author of *Decision in Government* (1970) and other works. Director of Mullard Ltd, 1970-73. Senior Research Fellow, University of Strathclyde 1974.* [1979]

BRAY, Ronald William Thomas. "Greenfield", Buckden, Nr. Skipton, Yorkshire. Constitutional. S. of William Ernest Bray, Esq., Mechanical Engineer and Company Director. B. 5 Jan. 1922; m. 30 Sept. 1944, Margaret Florence, d. of J.B. Parker, Esq. Educ. at Latymer Upper School, London. Mechanical Engineer. Underwriting member of Lloyd's. Entered family business in 1938; became Managing Director 1945. Developed various types British Construction Equipment; travelled extensively, Africa, U.S.A., Central and South America, Europe and Middle East developing exports. Member Woking Urban District Council 1959-62; commenced farming in 1962. A Vice-Chairman of the Association of Conservative Clubs 1972. A Conservative. Unsuccessfully contested Stockton-on-Tees in 1964. Elected for Rossendale in June 1970 and sat until he was defeated in Oct. 1974. Member of N. Yorkshire County Council from 1977.* [1974 2nd ed.]

BREWIS, Henry John Beverley. Ardwell, Stranraer, Wigtownshire. S. of Lieut.-Col. F.B. Brewis. B. 8 Apr. 1920; m. 1949, Faith, d. of Sir Edward O. Mactaggart-Stewart, Bart. Educ. at Eton, and New Coll., Oxford. Served R.A. 1940-46. Demobilized with rank of Maj. Mentioned in despatches twice. Called to the bar at the Middle Temple 1946. Member Wigtownshire County Council 1955-59 and Chairman of Finance Committee. Dept.-Lieut. for Wigtownshire 1966. Member U.K. Delegation to Council of Europe and Assembly of Western European Union 1966-69. Speaker's Panel of Chairmen 1965. Chairman Select Committee on Scottish Affairs 1971. Member British Delegation to European Parliament 1973. A Scottish Unionist Member. Elected for Galloway in Apr. 1959 and sat until he retired in Sept. 1974. Parliamentary Private Secretary to Rt. Hon. William Grant, Lord Advocate 1960-61. Chairman of Scottish Conservative Group for Europe 1973-76. Managing Director of Ardwell Estates, Stranraer. Director of Border Television Limited from 1977.*
[1974 2nd ed.]

BRINTON, Sir (Esme) Tatton Cecil. Kyrewood House, Tenbury Wells, Worcestershire. 34 De Vere Gardens, London. Bath, and Carlton, S. of Col. Cecil Charles Brinton. B. 1916; m. 1st, 1938, Mary Elizabeth, d. of Gibson Fahnestock, Esq., of U.S.A. (she died 1960), (4 s. 1 d.); 2ndly, 1961, Irene Sophie, d. of J. Heller, Esq., of London (she died 1978); 3rdly, 1979, Mary, widow of Commander N.L. Cappel. Educ. at Eton, and Caius Coll., Cambridge. Served in France, North Africa and Italy with the 12th Royal Lancers 1939-45. Chairman and Joint Managing Director of Brintons Limited, of Kidderminster, Carpet Manufacturers 1968. Mayor of Kidderminster 1953-54. Former Chairman and Treasurer of Kidderminster Conservative Association. Treasurer of the West Midlands Union of Conservative Associations 1958-61; Chairman 1962-64; President 1972. High Sheriff of Worcestershire 1961-62. Knighted in the 1964 New Year Honours List. Joint Treasurer Conservative Party 1966-74. Dept.-Lieut. for Worcestershire 1968. A Conservative. Unsuccessfully contested Dudley in 1945. Elected for the Kidderminster division of Worcestershire in Oct. 1964 and sat until he retired in Feb. 1974. President of Federation of British Carpet Manufacturers 1974-76. High Steward of Kidderminster 1978.* [1974]

BRITTAN, Leon. Lease Rigg Farm, Grosmont, Whitby, Yorkshire. 14 Ponsonby Terrace, London. Carlton, and M.C.C. S. of Dr. J. Brittan. B. 25 Sept. 1939. Educ. at Haberdashers Aske's School, Trinity Coll., Cambridge, and Yale University, U.S.A. President Cambridge Union 1960. Chairman Bow Group 1964-65. Opposition Front Bench spokesman on Devolution 1976-79 and on Employment 1978-79. Q.C. 1978. Minister of State, Home Office from May 1979. A Conservative. Unsuccessfully contested N. Kensington in 1966 and 1970. Member for Cleveland and Whitby from Feb. 1974.*
[1979]

BROADBRIDGE, Sir George Thomas, Bart., K.C.V.O. 27 Old Bond Street, London. Wargrave Place, Wargrave, Berkshire. Carlton. S. of Henry Broadbridge, Esq., of Brighton. B. 13 Feb. 1869; m. 1st, 1894, Fanny Kathleen, d. of Richard Brigden Esq., of Brighton (she died 8 Mar. 1928), 2ndly, 1929, Clara Maud, d. of John Swansbourne, Esq., of Bognor (she died 1949). Educ. at Brighton. Created Bart. in 1937; Knight Bach. 1929; K.C.V.O. 1937; F.I.C.S., F.R.G.S. Master of the Worshipful Company of Gardeners 1934; a Lieut. of the City of London; Sheriff 1933-34; Lord Mayor 1936-37. Alderman of the City of London for Ward of Candlewick from 1930; Master of the Worshipful Company of Lorimers. A Conservative. Elected for the City of London in Apr. 1938 and sat until Aug. 1945 when he was created Baron Broadbridge. Died 16 Apr. 1952. [1945]

BROCKLEBANK-FOWLER, Christopher. Long Cottage, Flitcham, King's

Lynn. Junior Carlton. S. of Sidney Stratton Brocklebank Fowler, Esq., M.A., LL.B., Solicitor. B. 13 Jan. 1934; m. 1st, 10 Aug. 1957, Joan (2 s.) (marriage dissolved 1975); 2ndly, 8 Aug. 1975, Mrs. Mary Berry. Educ. at Perse School, Cambridge. Five years farming as pupil and Manager in East Anglia and Kenya 1950-57; National Service, submarines Sub-Lieut. R.N.V.R. 1950-52. Management training Unilever 1957-59; Advertising Consultant 1960. Director Creative Consultants 1967. Member of Bow Group 1961, Secretary 1966-68, Chairman 1968-69; London Conciliation Committee 1966-67; Vice-Chairman Information panel National Committee for Commonwealth Immigrants 1966-67; Executive Committee Africa Bureau 1970-74. Joint Secretary United Nations Parliamentary Group 1972; Secretary Conservative Parliamentary Foreign and Commonwealth Affairs Committee 1974-76. Vice-Chairman Conservative Parliamentary Agriculture Committee 1974-75. Chairman Conservative Parliamentary Horticultural Committee 1972-74. Member Select Committee on Overseas Development 1973. Author of pamphlets and articles on race relations, African Affairs and Overseas Development. A Conservative. Unsuccessfully contested West Ham N. in 1964. Member for King's Lynn from 1970 to Feb. 1974 and for Norfolk N.W. division from Feb. 1974.* [1979]

BROCKWAY, Archibald Fenner. 273 East End Road, London. S. of the Rev. W.G. Brockway, Missionary in Calcutta. B. 1 Nov. 1888; m. 1st, 1914, Lilla, d. of Rev. W. Harvey-Smith (divorced 1946); 2ndly, 1946, Edith Violet, d. of A.H. King, Esq., of Catford. Educ. at Eltham Coll. A Journalist. Imprisoned as a conscientious objector during First World War. Secretary of No Conscription Fellowship 1917. Editor of *Labour Leader* 1912-17, of *New Leader* 1926-29, 1931-46, Secretary of ILP 1923, Chairman 1931, Gen. Secretary 1934-38. A Labour Member. Unsuccessfully contested Lancaster in 1922 and Westminster Abbey at the by-election in Mar. 1924. Sat for the E. Leyton division from 1929-31. Unsuccessfully contested, as the ILP candidate, E. Leyton in 1931, the Upton division of West Ham in May 1934, Norwich

in 1935, Lancaster in Oct. 1941 and E. Cardiff in Apr. 1942. Rejoined Labour Party in 1946. Elected for Eton and Slough in 1950 and sat until 1964 when he was defeated. Chairman of Congress of Peoples against Imperialism 1948. Chairman of Movement for Colonial Freedom 1954, British Asian and Overseas Socialist Fellowship 1959, Peace in Nigeria Committee 1967 and British Council for Peace in Vietnam 1965. Created Baron Brockway (Life Peerage) 1964.* [1964]

BROMLEY-DAVENPORT, Lieut.-Col. Sir Walter Henry. 39 Westminster Gardens, London. S. of Walter Arthur Bromley-Davenport, Esq., of Capesthorne, Macclesfield, Cheshire. B. 15 Sept. 1903; m. 3 Aug. 1933, Lenette, d. of Joseph Y. Jeanes, Esq., of Philadelphia. Educ. at Malvern. Lieut.-Col. late Grenadier Guards. Raised 5th Earl of Chester Battalion 1939. British Boxing Board of Control 1953. Conservative Whip 1948-51; Dept.-Lieut. for Cheshire 1949. Knighted 1961. A Conservative. Elected for the Knutsford division of Cheshire in July 1945 and sat until he retired in 1970.* [1970]

BROOK, Dryden. 85 Dunwell Lane, Halifax. S. of James Brook, Esq. B. 25 Aug. 1884; m. 1911, Louisa (she died 1968). Member of Halifax Borough Council 1940-68, Mayor 1958-59. A Wool Merchant. A Labour Member. Elected for Halifax in July 1945 and sat until he was defeated in 1955. Knighted 1965. Died 30 Jan. 1971. [1954]

BROOKE, Rt. Hon. Henry, C.H. 45 Redington Road, London. S. of L. Leslie Brooke, Esq. B. 9 Apr. 1903; m. 1933, Barbara, d. of Canon A.A. Mathews (created a Life Peeress as Baroness Brooke of Ystradfellte 1964.) Educ. at Marlborough, and Balliol Coll., Oxford. Member of London County Council 1945-55 and Hampstead Borough Council 1936-57. Financial Secretary to the Treasury 1954-57; Minister of Housing and Local Government and Minister for Welsh Affairs 1957-61; Chief Secretary to the Treasury and Paymaster-Gen. 1961-62. Home Secretary July 1962-Oct. 1964. PC. 1955. C.H. 1964. A Conservative. Sat for W. Lewisham from Nov. 1938 to July 1945 when he was defeated.

Elected for Hampstead in 1950 and sat until 1966 when he was defeated. Created Baron Brooke of Cumnor (Life Peerage) 1966. Dept.-Chairman of Southern Railway Company 1946-48. Member of Central Housing Advisory Committee 1944-54. Chairman of Joint Select Committee on Delegated Legislation 1971-73.*　　[1966]

BROOKE, Hon. Peter Leonard. 110A Ashley Gardens, London. Brooks's, City Livery, I Zingari, M.C.C., and St. Stephen's. S. of Lord Brooke of Cumnor and Baroness Brooke of Ystradfellte. B. 3 Mar. 1934; m. 1964, Joan Margaret, d. of Frederick Smith, Esq., (3 s. and 1 deceased). Educ. at Marlborough, and Balliol Coll., Oxford and Harvard Business School. Research Associate I.M.E.D.E., Lausanne and Swiss Correspondent for *Financial Times*. Spencer Stuart Management Consultants 1961. Served in New York 1969-71, Brussels 1971-72. Chairman from 1974. Assistant Government Whip from May 1979. A Conservative. Unsuccessfully contested Bedwellty in Oct. 1974. Member for the City of London and Westminster S. division of the Cities of London and Westminster from Feb. 1977.*　　[1979]

BROOKS, Edwin. 39 Waterpark Road, Prenton, Birkenhead, Cheshire. S. of Edwin Brooks, Esq., Railway Blacksmith. B. 1 Dec. 1929; m. 4 Apr. 1956, Winifred Hazel Soundie. Educ. at Barry Grammar School, and St. John's Coll., Cambridge, Ph.D. 1958. Birkenhead County Borough Councillor from 1958-67. A Labour Member. Unsuccessfully contested Bebington in the 1964 general election. Elected for Bebington in Mar. 1966 and sat until 1970 when he was defeated. Lecturer in Geography, University of Liverpool 1954-66 and 1970-72, Sen. lecturer 1972-77, Dean of Coll. Studies 1975-77. Dean of Business and Liberal Studies, Riverina Coll. of Advanced Education, Wagga Wagga, N.S.W. from 1977.*　　[1970]

BROOKS, Thomas Judson, M.B.E. 22 Leake Street, Castleford, Yorkshire. S. of William Brooks, Esq., of Thurgoland B. 1880; m. 1906, Annie, d. of G. H. Carver, Esq., of Finningley. A Coal Miner; Secretary of Glasshoughton Branch of Y.M.W.A. 1911-

42; member of Castleford Urban District Council 1914-42, and of W. Riding County Council 1925-42; Alderman 1940; Chairman of Wakefield and Pontefract War Pensions Committee from 1924; J.P. for the W. Riding of Yorkshire 1924. A Labour Member. Sat for the Rothwell division from Aug. 1942-Feb. 1950. Elected for the Normanton division of the W. Riding of Yorkshire in Feb. 1950 and sat until he retired in 1951. A Spiritualist. M.B.E. 1931. Died 15 Feb. 1958.　　[1951]

BROOMAN-WHITE, Richard Charles. 17 Cheyne Place, London. Pennymore, Furnace, Argyll. White's, and Conservative (Glasgow). S. of Maj. Charles James Brooman-White, C.B.E.B. 16 Feb. 1912; m. 1957, Rosalie Mary, d. of Maj.-Gen. T.W. Rees, of Abergavenny. Educ. at Eton, and Trinity Coll., Cambridge. A Journalist. War service in Intelligence Corps; Attaché British Embassy, Istanbul 1946-47. Lord Commissioner of Treasury Oct. 1957-June 1960. Vice-Chamberlain of H.M. Household June 1960-Oct. 1960. Parliamentary Private Secretary to J. Hutchison, Under-Secretary for War 1951-54, to A. Nutting, Minister of State at the Foreign Office 1954-55 and to Rt. Hon. James Stuart, Secretary of State for Scotland 1955-57. Assistant Whip (unpaid) 1957. Joint Parliamentary Under-Secretary of State Scottish Office Oct. 1960-Dec. 1963. A Conservative. Unsuccessfully contested the Bridgeton division of Glasgow in 1945 and the Rutherglen division of Lanarkshire in 1950. Elected for the Rutherglen division of Lanarkshire in Oct. 1951 and sat until his death on 25 Jan. 1964. Died 25 Jan. 1964.　　[1964]

BROTHERTON, Michael Lewis. House of Commons, London. S. of John Brotherton, Esq., Brewer. B. 26 May 1931; m. 1968, Julia, d. of A.G.C. King, Esq., of Bath. Educ. at Royal Naval Coll., Dartmouth. Royal Navy 1949-64. *Times* Newspaper 1966-74. A Conservative. Unsuccessfully contested Deptford in the 1970 general election. Member for Louth from Oct. 1974.*　　[1979]

BROUGHTON, Sir Alfred Davies Devonsher, D.L. Stockwell Shay Farm, Batley, West Yorkshire. S. of Dr. A.G.S.

Broughton, J.P., of Batley. B. 18 Oct. 1902; m. 1st, 1930, Dorothy, M.A., Ph.D., d. of Commander W.D. Parry Jones, R.D., R.N.R., (1 s. 1 d.) (divorced 1967); 2ndly, 1967, Joyce, d. of H.S. Denton, Esq. Educ. at Rossall School, Downing Coll., Cambridge, and The London Hospital, M.A., M.B., B. Chir., M.R.C.S., L.R.C.P., D.P.M., D.P.H., A Physician. Officer of Order of St. John. Honorary Freeman of the Borough of Morley (1972) and of Borough of Batley (1973). Squadron Leader R.A.F.V.R. 1940-45. Member of Batley Borough Council 1946-49. Opposition Whip 1960-64. Member of Speaker's Panel of Chairmen 1964-76. Vice-President Leeds Trustee Savings Bank 1974-78. U.K. Delegate to Council of Europe and to W.E.U. 1956-58. Honorary Treasurer Commonwealth Parliamentary Association 1969-70. Knighted 1969. Dept.-Lieut. W. Yorkshire 1971. A Labour Member. Member for Batley and Morley from Feb. 1949 until his death on 2 Apr. 1979. [1979]

BROWN, Alan Grahame. House of Commons, London. S. of Alexander Harris Brown, Esq., of Bedford. B. 1913; m. 1937, Joan Emily, (2 s.). Educ. at Bedford School, and London University. Served 1932-36 and 1940-44 Bedfordshire and Hertfordshire Regiment. Member of Middlesex County Council 1956-65. Specialised in Welfare, Children and Young Persons. Member Middlesex Approved Schools and Children's Committee. Introduced "Restriction Imprisonment Children" Bill 1960. Member of Council of Crusade of Rescue. Delivered the 1962 "Newman Address" (Juvenile Delinquency) to Oxford University. President Tottenham Old Age Pensioners' Federation, Vincent Road 1962. Elected for Tottenham as the Labour candidate in 1959, resigned the Labour Whip in Mar. 1961, sat as an Independent until May 1962 when he joined the Conservative Party and sat until 1964 when he unsuccessfully contested the constituency as a Conservative. Resigned from the Labour Party in Mar. 1962. Rejoined the Labour Party in Apr. 1966. A Pharmaceutical Chemist. Committed suicide 5 Jan. 1972. [1964]

BROWN, Rt. Hon. Douglas Clifton. See CLIFTON BROWN, Rt. Hon. Douglas

BROWN, Sir Edward Joseph, M.B.E., J.P. The Gatehouse, Bathwick Hill, Bath, Somerset. Junior Carlton, Bath and County, and Salisbury. S. of Edward Brown, Esq. B. 1913; m. 1940, Rosa Feldman, (1 s. 1 d.). Educ. at Greencoat Elementary School, Camberwell, and Morley Coll., Lambeth. Served with the R.A.F. as Leading Aircraftman. A Laboratory Technician, Repair and Maintenance of Industrial Instruments. Member A.S.S.E.T. Served on Tottenham Borough Council 1956-64. Chairman of the National Union of Conservative and Unionist Association 1959-60; member Executive Committee from 1953. M.B.E. 1958. Knighted 1961. J.P. for Middlesex 1963. A Conservative. Adopted for Stalybridge and Hyde in 1959, but unsuccessful in the 1959 general election. Member for Bath from Oct. 1964 until he retired in 1979.* [1979]

BROWN, Rt. Hon. George Alfred. 154 High Street, Newhall, Swadlincote, Burton-on-Trent. S. of George Brown, Esq. B. 2 Sept. 1914; m. 1937, Sophie Levene. A Trade Union Official. Parliamentary Private Secretary to the Rt. Hon. George Isaacs, Minister of Labour Aug. 1945, and to the Rt. Hon. Hugh Dalton, Chancellor of the Exchequer Apr. 1947. Joint Parliamentary Secretary Ministry of Agriculture Oct. 1947 to May 1951. Minister of Works May-Oct. 1951. PC. 1951. Dept. Leader of the Opposition 1960-64. First Secretary of State and Secretary of State for Economic Affairs Oct. 1964-Aug. 1966 Secretary of State for Foreign Affairs Aug. 1966-Mar. 1968, when he resigned. A Labour Member. Elected for the Belper division of Derbyshire in July 1945 and sat until he was defeated in 1970. Opposition spokesman on Agriculture 1955-56, on Labour 1956, on Supply 1955-59, on Defence 1956-61 and on Home Affairs 1961-64. Member of Parliamentary Committee of Parliamentary Labour Party 1955-58 and 1959-64. Dept.-Leader of the Labour Party 1960-70. Member of National Executive Committee of Labour Party 1960-70. Created Baron George-Brown (Life Peerage) 1970, and assumed the surname George-

Brown in lieu of Brown. Resigned from the Labour Party in Mar. 1976. Productivity Counsellor, Courtaulds Limited 1968-73. Dept.-Chairman of G.C. Turner and Company Limited from 1977. Director of Commercial Credit (Holdings) Limited from 1974. Director of British Northrop Limited from 1978.*   [1970]

BROWN, Hugh Dunbar. 29 Blackwood Road, Milngavie, Glasgow. S. of Neil Brown, Esq. B. 18 May 1919; m. 14 Feb. 1947, Mary Glen, d. of James Carmichael, Esq, MP. Educ. at Secondary School. Former Civil Servant Executive Officer. Joined the Labour Party in 1946. Member of the U.P.W. Indoor Postal Section, Glasgow branch 1937-47; Secretary to section 1946-47. Member of the Independent Labour Party 1939-46. Member Glasgow Corporation 1954-64. Magistrate from 1961. Parliamentary Under-Secretary of State for Home Affairs and Agriculture, Scottish Office June 1974-May 1979. A Labour Member. Sat for the Provan division of Glasgow from Oct. 1964.*   [1979]

BROWN, Robert Crofton. 82 Beckside Gardens, Newcastle-upon-Tyne. S. of William Brown, Esq., Engineer. B. 16 May 1921; m. 13 Oct. 1945, Marjorie, d. of Mrs. Anne Hogg of Slaithwaite, Yorkshire, (1 s. 1 d.). Educ. at Elementary and Technical Schools, and Rutherford Coll. Apprenticed as plumber to Newcastle Gas Company 1937; promoted to Inspector 1949. Served in Royal Signals 1942-46. Speakers Conference 1966-68. Select Committee Nationalised Industries 1966-68. Councillor Newcastle C.B.C. 1958-68; Chief Whip of Labour Group. Parliamentary Secretary Ministry of Transport Apr. 1968-June 1970. Vice-Chairman T.U. Group of MPs. 1970, Vice-Chairman P.L.P. Transport Group 1970. Parliamentary Under-Secretary of State, Department of Health and Social Security Mar.-Oct. 1974. Parliamentary Under-Secretary of State for Defence for the Army Oct. 1974-May 1979. Front Bench spokesman for the Environment 1973-74. A Labour Member. Sat for Newcastle-upon-Tyne W. division from 1966.*   [1979]

BROWN, Ronald William. 91 Gore Road, Hackney, London. S. of George Brown Esq. B. 7 Sept. 1921; m. 1944, Mary Munn. Educ. at Elementary School and Borough Polytechnic. Member Association of Teachers in Technical Institutes, and Hackney South and Shoreditch C.L.P. Member of Camberwell Borough Council 1956-65 and Southwark Borough Council 1964-71. J.P. for County of London. An Assistant Government Whip Apr. 1966-Jan. 1967. Senior Lecturer in Electrical Engineering, Principal of Industrial Training School, member of Council of Europe Assembly and Western European Union 1965-68. Member European Parliament Mar. 1977-May 1979. Chairman of Energy Commission and Rapporteur on Science Technology and Aerospace questions. Parliamentary Adviser to Furniture Timber and Allied Trade Union. Member British Institute of Management. Associate member of Institute of Engineering Designers. Member of Council of Europe from 1974. A Labour Member. Member for Shoreditch and Finsbury from 1964-Feb. 1974, and for Hackney, South and Shoreditch from Feb. 1974.*   [1979]

BROWN, Thomas James. 393 Leigh Road, Hindley Green, Wigan. S. of Thomas Brown, Esq. B. 12 Aug. 1886; m. 1912. Educ. at Brunswick School, and Leigh Technical School. A Coalminer 1898-1942. J.P. for Lancashire and member of Hindley Urban District Council from 1919, twice Chairman. Vice-President of Lancashire Miners' Federation; Miners' Agent 1937-42; Delegate to French Miners' Congress 1938; 40 years a County Magistrate. Retired from Active List. A Labour Member. Elected for the Ince Division of Lancashire in Oct. 1942 and sat until he retired in 1964. Died 10 Nov. 1970.   [1964]

BROWN, William John. 108 Cambridge Street, London. S. of Joseph Morris Brown, Esq. B. 13 Sept. 1894; m. 1917, Mabel, d. of H. Prickett, Esq., of Penge. Educ. at Salmestone Elementary School, Margate, and Sir Roger Manwood's Grammar School, Sandwich. Author and Journalist. Secretary Civil Service Clerical Association 1919-42. Unsuccessfully contested, as a Labour candidate, the Uxbridge division of Middlesex in 1922 and W. Wolverhampton in 1923 and 1924. Elected Labour Member for W. Wolverhampton in 1929, resigned the Labour Whip in Mar. 1931, was a Member of Sir Oswald Mosley's New Party for one day, and then sat as an Independent Labour Member until he was defeated in Oct. 1931. Unsuccessfully contested W. Wolverhampton as an Independent Labour candidate in 1935. Elected for the Rugby division of Warwickshire as an Independent in Apr. 1942 and sat until he was defeated in 1950. Unsuccessfully contested W. Fulham as an Independent, with unofficial Conservative support, in 1951. Died 3 Oct. 1960.   [1950]

BROWNE, Jack Nixon, C.B.E. St. Stephen's House, Westminster, London. 12 Renfield Street, Glasgow, Carlton. S. of Edwin Gilbert Izod, Esq., of Rugby and Johanesburg. Assumed the surname of Browne in lieu of Izod 1920. B. 3 Sept. 1904; m. 1st, 1936, Helen Anne, d. of G.J. Inglis, Esq., of Glasgow (divorced 1949); 2ndly, 1950, Eileen, d. of Henry Whitford Nolan, Esq. Educ. at Cheltenham. Served with R.A.F. 1939-45. Parliamentary Private Secretary to Rt. Hon. James Stuart, Secretary of State for Scotland 1952-55. Joint Under-Secretary of State for Scotland Apr. 1955-Oct. 1959. A Conservative. Unsuccessfully contested the Govan division of Glasgow in 1945. Sat for the Govan division of Glasgow from 1950-55. Elected for the Craigton division of Glasgow in 1955 and sat until he was defeated in 1959. C.B.E. 1944. Created Baron Craigton (Life Peerage) 1959. Minister of State for Scotland Oct. 1959-Oct. 1964. PC. 1961. President of City of Westminster Chamber of Commerce from 1966. Chairman of United Biscuits (Holdings) Limited 1967-72. Trustee of World Wildlife Fund from 1965. Vice-Chairman of Fauna Preservation Society from 1970. Chairman of Committee for Environmental Conservation from 1972.*   [1959]

BROWNE, Percy Basil. Torr House, Westleigh, Nr. Bideford, Devon. S. of W.P. Browne, Esq. B. 2 May 1923; m. Feb. 1953, Jenefer Mary, d. of Maj. and Lady Jeane Petherick. Educ. at The Downs, Colwall, and Eton Coll. A Farmer. Served with Royal Dragoons in Italy and N.W. Europe. Rode in the Grand National 1953. A Conservative. Elected for the Torrington division of Devon in 1959 and sat until he retired in 1964. Director of Appledore Shipbuilders Limited 1965-72. Member of North Devon District Council from 1974. Member of S.W. Regional Hospital Board 1967-70. High Sheriff of Devon 1978. Director of Western Counties Building Society from 1965.*   [1964]

BRUCE, Maj. Donald William Trevor. Westmead, Park Avenue, Chorleywood. S. of William Trevor Bruce, Esq., Insurance Broker, of Norbury. B. 3 Oct. 1912; m. 15 July 1939, Joan, d. of C.H. Butcher, Esq. Educ. at Donington Grammar School. A Chartered Accountant. Served with Middlesex Yeomanry 1931-33, with Royal Signals at home and in France 1939-45 (despatches). Parliamentary Private Secretary to the Rt. Hon. Aneurin Bevan, MP, Minister of Health 1945-50; member of Ministry of Health Delegation to Sweden and Denmark 1946 and of Select Committee on Public Accounts from 1947. A Labour Member. Elected for Portsmouth N. in July 1945 and sat until 1950 when he unsuccessully contested Portsmouth W. Unsuccessfully contested the Wrekin division of Shropshire in 1959 and 1964. Created Baron Bruce of Donington (Life Peerage) 1974. Member of European Parliament 1975-79. Opposition spokesman in House of Lords from 1979.*   [1950]

BRUCE-GARDYNE, John. 13 Kelso Place, London. South Eskill, by Forfar, Angus. S. of Capt. E. Bruce-Gardyne, D.S.O., R.N.B. 12 Apr. 1930; m. 1959, Sarah, d. of Sir John Maitland, MP., (2 s. 1 d.). Educ. at Winchester, and Magdalen Coll., Oxford. 2nd Lieut. Royal Dragoons 1949-50, Foreign Office 1953-54. Third Secretary, British Legation, Sofia 1954-56. *Financial Times* London 1956. Paris Correspondent *Financial Times* 1957-60. Dept. Editor of the *Statist* 1961. Member of Council Bow Group 1962. Parliamentary Private Secretary to Rt. Hon. Gordon Campbell, Secretary of State for Scotland 1970-72. Vice-Chairman Conservative Parliamentary Finance Committee 1972-74. A

Conservative. Elected for the S. Angus division of Angus and Kincardine in Oct. 1964 and sat until he was defeated in Oct. 1974. Elected for Knutsford at a by-election in Mar. 1979.*   [1974 2nd ed.]

BRYAN, Sir Paul Elmore Oliver, D.S.O., M.C. Park Farm, Sawdon, Scarborough. S. of Rev. Dr. J.I. Bryan, Ph.D. B. 3 Aug. 1913; m. 1st, 17 June 1939, Betty Mary, d. of J.C. Hoyle, Esq. (she died 1968); 2ndly, 5 May 1971, Mrs. Cynthia Duncan, widow of Patrick Duncan, Esq., and d. of Sir Patrick Ashley Cooper. Educ. at St. John's School, Leatherhead, and Caius Coll., Cambridge. Commissioned in Royal W. Kent Regiment 1940; Lieut.-Col. commanding R.W.K. Regiment in Africa, Sicily and Italy campaigns (D.S.O., M.C., Despatches) 1943; Commandant 164 Infantry O.C.T.U. 1944. Member of Sowerby Bridge Urban District Council 1947-50. Parliamentary Private Secretary to Sir Walter Monckton, Minister of Defence 1956; Assistant Government Whip 1956-58; Lord Commissioner of the Treasury 1958-61. Vice-Chairman of Conservative Party Organisation 1961-65. Opposition Front Bench spokesman on Post Office and Broadcasting 1965-70. Minister of State Department of Employment and Productivity 1970-72. Knighted 1972. Vice-Chairman of 1922 Committee from 1978. Director Granada T.V. Limited, Manchester Independent Radio Limited. A Conservative. Unsuccessfully contested Sowerby in 1949, 1950 and 1951. Sat for the Howden division of the E. Riding of Yorkshire from 1955.*
[1979]

BUCHAN, Norman Findlay. 72 Peel Street, Glasgow,. S. of John Buchan, Esq. of Fraserburgh. B. 27 Oct. 1922; m. 1945, Janey, d. of Joseph Kent, Esq., of Glasgow. Educ. at Kirkwall Grammar School and Glasgow University (Eng. Lit.). Served with Royal Tank Regiment 1942-45. Teacher (English and History). Joined the Labour Party in 1957. Regular contributor to *Tribune* and other publications. Joint Parliamentary Under-Secretary of State for Scotland Jan. 1967-June 1970. Minister of State, Ministry of Agriculture Mar. 1974, resigned Oct. 1974 over Common Market. Chairman Parlia-

mentary Labour Group Agricultural Committee. Vice-Chairman Scottish Labour Group of MPs. A Labour Member. Sat for the W. division of Renfrewshire from Oct. 1964. An Opposition spokesman on Scotland June 1970-Dec. 1972 and on Agriculture Jan. 1972-Mar. 1974, Principal Spokesman Feb. 1973-Mar. 1974. Chairman Edinburgh Folk Festival Society from 1979.*   [1979]

BUCHAN-HEPBURN, Rt. Hon. Patrick George Thomas. 76 Eaton Square, London. Carlton, Travellers', and New (Edinburgh). S. of Sir Archibald Buchan-Hepburn, 4th Bart. B. 2 Apr. 1901; m. 7 June 1945, Diana, d. of Brigadier-Gen. Hon. Charles Lambton, D.S.O., and widow of Maj. W.H. Williamson. Educ. at Harrow, and Trinity Coll., Cambridge. Attaché at H.B.M. Embassy, Constantinople 1925-27; member of London County Council 1930-31; Parliamentary Private Secretary to Rt. Hon. Oliver Stanley 1931-39; Assistant Government Whip June 1939; a Lord Commissioner of the Treasury Nov. 1939-June 1940 and Dec. 1944-July 1945. Served with 11th City of London Yeomanry L.A.A. Regiment A.A., and as G.S.O. and Brigade Maj. June 1940-43. Dept. Conservative Chief Whip July 1945; Conservative Chief Whip July 1948-Dec. 1955. Parliamentary Secretary to the Treasury and Government Chief Whip Nov. 1951-Dec. 1955; Minister of Works Dec. 1955-Jan. 1957. PC. 1951. A Conservative. Unsuccessfully contested E. Wolverhampton in 1929. Sat for E. Toxteth division of Liverpool from Feb. 1931-Feb. 1950. Elected for Beckenham in Feb. 1950 and sat until he was created Baron Hailes in Jan. 1957. Gov.-Gen. of the West Indies 1958-62. G.B.E. 1957. C.H. 1962. Chairman of Historic Buildings Council 1963-73. Knight of St. John of Jerusalem. Died 5 Nov. 1974.   [1956]

BUCHANAN, Rt. Hon. George. 16 Ardbeg Street, Glasgow. B. 1890; m. 19 June 1924, Annie, d. of G. McNee, Esq., of Glasgow. Three years member of United Patternmakers Society; Vice-Chairman of Glasgow Trades Council; represented Gorbals on the City Council 1919-23. Joint Parliamentary Under-Secretary of State for Scotland Aug. 1945-Oct. 1947. Minister of Pensions Oct.

1947-July 1948. PC. 1948. An Independent Labour Party Member for the Gorbals division from Nov. 1922. Joined the Labour Party in 1939 and sat until July 1948 when he resigned on appointment as Chairman of National Assistance Board. Chairman of United Patternmakers Association of Great Britain 1932-48. Chairman of National Assistance Board 1948-53, member 1953-55. Died 28 June 1955. [1948]

BUCHANAN, Richard. 18 Gargrave Avenue, Garrowhill, Glasgow. S. of Richard Buchanan, Esq. B. 1912; m. 1st, 1938, Margaret, younger d. of Mr. and Mrs. Edward McManus (she died 1963); 2ndly, 1971, Helen, only d. of John Duggan, Esq. Educ. at St. Mungo's Academy, and Royal Technical Coll., N.C.L.C. Tutor in Economics. Toolmaker. Member I.L.P. 1937-42. Joined the Labour Party in 1942. Member of N.U.R. from 1928 and Co-operative Party from 1940. Member Glasgow City Council 1949-64; Honorary Treasurer 1962-64. Director Glasgow Citizens Theatre. Chairman Scottish Central Library 1965-74. Chairman National Library of Scotland Advisory Council. Member Select Committee on Public Accounts; Services; Chairman House of Commons Library Committee. Honorary President Scottish Library Association. Secretary Scottish Labour MPs. 1965-72. Parliamentary Private Secretary to Treasury Ministers 1967-70. J.P. for Glasgow. Voted in favour of entry to E.E.C. on 28 Oct. 1971. A Labour Member. Sat for the Springburn division of Glasgow from Oct. 1964 until he retired in 1979.* [1979]

BUCHANAN-SMITH, Hon. Alick Laidlaw. House of Commons, London. S. of Lord Balerno, C.B.E. B. 8 Apr. 1932; m. 17 Aug. 1956, Janet, d. of Thomas Lawrie, Esq., C.B.E. Educ. at Edinburgh Academy, Trinity Coll., Glenalmond, Pembroke Coll., Cambridge, and Edinburgh University. Served with Gordon Highlanders. Capt. Joint Parliamentary Under-Secretary Scottish Office June 1970-Mar. 1974. A Conservative. Unsuccessfully contested W. Fife at the general election of 1959. Sat for the North Angus and Mearns division of Angus and Kincardine from Oct. 1964. Opposition spokesman on Scotland Oct. 1969-June 1970 and Mar. 1974-Dec. 1976. Member of Shadow Cabinet Mar. 1974-Dec. 1976, when he resigned. Minister of State, Ministry of Agriculture, Fisheries and Food from May 1979.* [1979]

BUCK, Philip Antony Fyson, Q.C. House of Commons, London. United Oxford and Cambridge. S. of A.F. Buck, Esq. B. 19 Dec. 1928; m. 1955, Judy Elaine, eld. d. of Dr. C.A. Grant, and Mrs. Grant, (1 d.). Educ. at King's School, Ely and Trinity Hall, Cambridge. Barrister, Inner Temple, 1954, Q.C. Mar. 1974. Legal Adviser to National Association of Parish Councils 1957-59, Vice-President 1970-74. Parliamentary Private Secretary to Sir John Hobson, Attorney Gen. Nov. 1963-Oct. 1964. Vice-Chairman Home Affairs Committee 1970-72; Chairman 1972. Member of the 1922 Committee Executive 1972 and from 1977. Parliamentary Under-Secretary of State for Defence (Royal Navy) Nov. 1972-Mar. 1974. An Opposition spokesman on Defence 1974-75. Sponsored 1963 Limitation Act. Member Parliamentary Assembly of the Council of Europe and the Western European Union 1975-77. Chairman Select Committee Parliamentary Commissioner for Administration (Ombudsman) from 1977. Chairman Cambridge University Conservative Association and Federation of University Conservative Associations. A Conservative. Sat for the Colchester division of Essex from Mar. 1961.* [1979]

BUDGEN, Nicholas William. House of Commons, London. S. of Capt. G.N. Budgen. B. 3 Nov. 1937; m. 14 Apr. 1964, Madeleine Elizabeth, d. of Col. Raymond Kittoe, O.B.E. (1 s. 1 d.). Educ. at St. Edward's School, Oxford, and Corpus Christi, Cambridge. Called to the bar, Gray's Inn 1962. A Conservative. Unsuccessfully contested the Small Heath division of Birmingham in 1970. Sat for S.W. Wolverhampton from Feb. 1974.* [1979]

BULLARD, Denys Gradwell. House of Commons, London. S. of John Henry Bullard, Esq. B. 1912; m. 1970 Diana Patricia Cox. Educ. at Wisbech Grammar School,

Fitzwilliam House, Cambridge, and Cambridge School of Agriculture. Parliamentary Private Secretary to Rt. Hon. Henry Brooke, Financial Secretary to Treasury 1955, Minister of Housing and Local Government 1959-61, Chief Secretary to Treasury 1961-62 and Home Secretary 1962. A Conservative. Unsuccessfully contested S.W. Norfolk in 1950. Elected for S.W. Norfolk in 1951 and sat until 1955, when he was defeated. Elected for the Kings Lynn division of Norfolk in 1959 and sat until he was defeated in 1964. Unsuccessfully contested Kings Lynn in 1966. Member of Anglian Water Authority and Chairman of Broads Committee from 1974.*
[1964]

BULLOCK, Capt. (Harold) Malcolm, M.B.E. Middlefield, Great Shelford, Cambridge. Turf, Bucks, and Allies, and Jockey, Paris. S. of F.M. Bullock, Esq., of Thursley. B. 10 July 1890; m. 10 June 1919, Lady Victoria Stanley, widow of Rt. Hon. Neil Primrose, MP, and d. of Edward, 17th Earl of Derby (she died 26 Nov. 1927). Educ. privately, in Paris, and Trinity Coll., Cambridge, M.A. Barrister-at-Law, Inner Temple 1918; Capt. Scots Guards 1914-20; Honorary Col. 136 Field Regiment R.A. 1940-50. Aide-de-Camp to F.M. Lord Methuen 1915-16; Foreign Office 1917-18; at the British Embassy at Paris 1918-21. M.B.E. 1918. Chevalier of the Legion of Honour; Officer 1951. Honorary Secretary Franco-British Society 1924-49; Chairman of Political Education Committee N.W. Area 1935-45, of N.W. Area of National Union of Conservative and Unionist Associations 1936 and 1937, of Anglo-French Inter-Parliamentary Committee 1950, and of Sadlers Wells Society 1930-44; Honorary Secretary University Conservative Associations 1948-50; Chairman of War Organisation of British Red Cross Hospital Library 1939-44. Member of Red Cross Commission with B.E.F. in France 1939-40. A Conservative. Sat for the Waterloo division of Lancashire from 1923-50. Elected for Crosby in 1950 and sat until he resigned in Oct. 1953. Created Bart. 1954. Chairman of Sadler's Wells Society 1930-46. Died 20 June 1966. [1953]

BULLUS, Wing-Commander Sir Eric Edward. Westway, Herne Bay, Kent. House of Commons, London. S. of Thomas Bullus, Esq., of Leeds. B. 20 Nov. 1906; m. 8 June 1949, Joan, d. of Capt. H.M. Denny, (2 d.). Educ. at Leeds Modern School, and University of Leeds. A Journalist. With *Yorkshire Post* 1923-46. Secretary of London Municipal Society 1946-50. Served in Air Ministry War Room 1940-43. Wing-Commander on Earl Mountbatten's Staff in S.E. Asia 1943-45. Member of Leeds County Borough Council 1930-40 and of Harrow Urban District Council 1947-50. Diocesan Lay Reader London, Canterbury and St. Albans. Member Central Reader's Board 1960-70; member of the House of Laity, Church Assembly 1960-7; Vice-President Association of Municipal Corporations 1953; Gov. Westfield Coll., University of London 1963-70, Leeds Modern School; Parliamentary Private Secretary to Rt. Hon. Peter Thorneycroft, Minister of Aviation 1960-62; Parliamentary Private Secretary to H. Mackeson, Secretary for Overseas Trade 1953; Parliamentary Private Secretary to T. Low, Minister of State, Board of Trade 1954-56; Parliamentary Private Secretary to Rt. Hon. Peter Thorneycroft, Secretary of State for Defence 1962-64. Knight Bach. 1964. Historian and Honorary Treasurer Lords and Commons Cricket. Member of M.C.C.A Conservative. Elected for Wembley N. in 1950 and sat until he retired in Feb. 1974. Fellow of Royal Geographical and Royal Statistical Societies.* [1974]

BULMER, (James) Esmond. The Old Rectory, Pudleston, Leominster, Herefordshire. Boodles. Eld. s. of E.C. Bulmer, Esq. B 19 May 1935; m. 4 July 1959, Morella Caroline Mary, d. of C.E. Kearton, Esq. Educ. at Rugby, and King's Coll., Cambridge. Commissioned Scots Guards 1954. H.P. Bulmer Limited 1959. Secretary of the Employment Committee 1974. Parliamentary Private Secretary to Timothy Raison and Leon Brittan, Ministers of State at the Home Office from 1979. A Conservative. Sat for Kidderminster from Feb. 1974.* [1979]

BULMER-THOMAS, Ivor. See THOMAS, Ivor.

BURDEN, Sir Frederick Frank Arthur. 291 Latymer Court, London. The Knapp, Portesham, Dorset. S. of A.F. Burden, Esq. of Bracknell. B. 27 Dec. 1905; m. Marjorie, d. of H.G. Greenwood, Esq. Educ. at Sloane School, Chelsea. Served with R.A.F. 1939-45 and on staff of Lord Louis Mountbatten. A Company Director. Chairman of Parliamentary Animal Welfare Group. Vice-Chairman of R.S.P.C.A. Made Freeman of the borough of Gillingham 1971. A Conservative. Unsuccessfully contested South Shields in 1935, Finsbury in 1945 and the Rotherhithe division of Bermondsey in Nov. 1946. Sat for Gillingham from Feb. 1950. Knighted 1980.*
[1979]

BURDEN, Thomas William, C.B.E. 27 Deycourt Gardens, Upminster, Essex. S. of Thomas Burden, Esq., Master Cooper. B. 29 Jan. 1885; m. 2 July 1910, Augusta, d. of David Sime, Esq. Educ. at Elementary School, and London School of Economics. A Railway Goods Agent. Member of East Ham Borough Council 1926, Alderman 1931-49. Mayor 1935; West Ham Guardian 1929-30. J.P. for Essex. A Church Estate Commissioner Aug. 1945-Jan. 1950. A Labour Member. Unsuccessfully contested East Ham N. in 1935. Sat for the Park division of Sheffield from Aug. 1942 until Jan. 1950 when he was created Baron Burden. Member of House of Laity of Church Assembly 1947-50. Lord-in-Waiting Mar. 1950-Oct. 1951. Opposition Whip in House of Lords 1951-64. C.B.E. 1948. Died 27 May 1970. [1950]

BURKE, Wilfrid Andrew. 79 Crow Hill, Middleton, Manchester. B. 23 Nov. 1889; m. 1920, Jean, d. of D. Flett, Esq., of Orkney. Educ. at Oulton Coll., Liverpool. Area organiser for Union of Shop, Distributive and Allied Workers 1919-54. Labour Whip 1941-43. Assistant Postmaster-Gen. Aug. 1945-Oct. 1947. Member of National Executive Committee of Labour Party 1944-56, Chairman 1953-54. A Labour Member. Unsuccessfully contested the Blackley division of Manchester in 1924, 1929 and 1931. Elected for Burnley in 1935 and sat until he retired in 1959. Died 18 July 1968. [1959]

BURTON, Elaine Frances. 47 Molyneux Street, London. D. of Leslie Burton, Esq., of Scarborough. B. 2 Mar. 1904. Educ. at Girls' Modern School, and Training Coll., Leeds. A Teacher 1924-35; Social Worker 1935-37; Organiser National Fitness Council 1937-39; Retail Trade Executive, John Lewis Partnership, 1940-45; Public Relations Consultant and Lecturer 1945-50. A Labour Member. Elected for Coventry S. in Feb. 1950 and sat until she was defeated in 1959. Created Baroness Burton of Coventry (Life Peerage) 1962. Chairman of Domestic Coal Consumers' Council 1962-65. Chairman of Council on Tribunals 1967-73. Member of Council for Industrial Design 1963-68. Member of Independent Television Authority 1964-69. Member of Sports Council 1965-71. Chairman of Mail Order Publishers Authority from 1970.* [1959]

BUTCHER, Sir Herbert Walter, Bart. 4 Furze Hill, Purley, Surrey. Carlton. S. of Herbert Butcher, Esq., of Bexhill. B. 12 June 1901; m. 31 Oct. 1935, Mary, d. of James Odom, Esq., of Peterborough. Educ. at Hastings Grammar School, and Coll. of Estate Management. A Surveyor and Land Agent. Gold Medal of Auctioneers Institute 1922. Member of Soke of Peterborough Council 1931-37. Parliamentary Private Secretary to R. Bernays, when Parliamentary Secretary Ministry of Health 1938-July 1939, and when Parliamentary Secretary Ministry of Transport July 1939-May 1940; member of Parliamentary Delegation to Australia and New Zealand 1944, and to Istanbul 1951; Lieut. R.N.V.R. 1941; Chief Whip National Liberal Party 1945-51; Temporary Chairman of Committees 1945-51 and 1959; a Lord Commissioner of the Treasury Nov. 1951-July 1953; Joint Dept. Government Chief Whip 1951-53; Chairman of Kitchen Committee, House of Commons 1959-64. Chairman British Group Inter Parliamentary Union 1962-65; Knight Bach. 1953. Created Bart. 1960. A National Liberal and Conservative Member. Elected for the Holland with Boston division of Lincolnshire in June 1937 and sat until he retired in Mar. 1966. Vice-Chairman of National Liberal Organisation 1952-62, Chairman of National Liberal Organisation 1952-62, Chairman 1962-66. Died 11 May 1966. [1966]

BUTLER, Hon. Adam Courtauld. House of Commons, London. S. of The Lord Butler of Saffron Walden. B. 11 Oct. 1931; m. 1955, Felicity, d. of K.M. St. Aubyn (2 s. 1 d.). Educ. at Eton, and Pembroke Coll., Cambridge, B.A. Economics and History 1954. National Service 2nd Lieut. K.R.R.C. 1949-51; Aide-de-Camp to Gov.-Gen. of Canada 1954-55; Courtaulds Limited 1955-73 holding various directorships of Couvtaulds subsidiaries; Director Capital and Counties Property Company. Member N.F.U. Member Public Expenditure Committee 1971. Parliamentary Private Secretary to Rt. Hon. Joseph Godber 1971-74. Assistant Government Whip Jan.-Mar. 1974. Opposition Whip 1974-75. Parliamentary Private Sectretary to Rt. Hon. Mrs. Margaret Thatcher, Leader of Opposition 1975-79. Minister of State, Department of Industry from May 1979. A Conservative. Sat for Bosworth division of Leicestershire from June 1970.*
[1979]

BUTLER, Herbert William, J.P. 214 Well Street, Hackney, London. S. of Frank Butler, Esq. B. 30 Jan. 1897; m. 18 Sept. 1926, Nellie Bingley (she died 1961). Educ. at London County Council Elementary School. Member of Hackney Borough Council 1928-61; Mayor of Hackney 1936-37. Parliamentary Private Secretary to Civil Lord and Parliamentary Secretary to The Admiralty 1950-51. Served in Royal Navy 1916-19. Member North East Metropolitan Regional Hospital Board. Chairman Hackney and Queen Elizabeth Hospital Group. Freeman, Borough of Hackney. A Labour Member. Sat for S. Hackney from 1945-55 and for the Central division of Hackney from 1955 until he retired in 1970. J.P. for London 1929. Died 16 Nov. 1971.
[1970]

BUTLER, Joyce Shore. House of Commons, London. D. of Arthur Wells, Esq. B. 1910; m. Victor Butler, Esq. Educ. at King Edward's High School, Birmingham. Vice-Chairman Labour Party Housing and Local Government Group 1959-64. Parliamentary Private Secretary to Rt. Hon. F. T. Willey, Minister of Land and Natural Resources 1965-67. Commons Chairman's Panel. Member of Commons Estimates Committee 1959-60. Member of Wood Green Council 1947-64. Leader of Wood Green Council 1954-55. Dept. Mayor 1962-63. First Chairman of new London borough of Haringey 1964-65, first Mayoress 1965-66, Alderman 1964-68. A Labour and Co-operative member. Sat for Wood Green from 1955-Feb. 1974 and for the Wood Green division of Haringey from Feb. 1974 until she retired in 1979.*
[1979]

BUTLER, Rt. Hon. Richard Austen, C.H. 3 Smith Square, London. Stanstead Hall, Halstead, Essex. Carlton, Beefsteak, and Farmers'. S. of Sir Montagu Butler, K.C.S.I., C.B., C.V.O., C.B.E. B. 9 Dec. 1902; m. 1st, 1926, Sydney, d. of Samuel Courtauld, Esq. (she died 9 Dec. 1954); 2ndly, Mollie, d. of F.D. Montgomerie, and widow of Augustine Courtauld. Educ. at Marlborough, and Pembroke Coll., Cambridge. President of Union 1924. Fellow, Corpus Christi Coll., Cambridge 1925-29, Honorary Fellow 1952; Honorary Fellow of Pembroke Coll., Cambridge 1942; Honorary Fellow of St. Anthony's Coll., Oxford 1957; member of Indian Franchise Committee 1931. President of Modern Language Association 1946; Chairman of Council of Royal India Society and Anglo-Netherlands Society 1946, President National Association for Mental Health 1946, of Royal Society of Literature 1951, and of British and Foreign Schools Societies 1945. Member of Privy Council Committee for Reform of Channel Islands Government 1946. Parliamentary Under-Secretary of State for India Sept. 1932-May 1937. Parliamentary Secretary Ministry of Labour May 1937-Feb. 1938. Parliamentary Under-Secretary of State for Foreign Affairs Feb. 1938-July 1941. President of Board of Education July 1941-Aug. 1944. PC. 1939. Minister of Education Aug. 1944-May 1945; Minister of Labour May-July 1945; Chancellor of the Exchequer (Cabinet) Oct. 1951-Dec. 1955; Lord Privy Seal Dec. 1955-Oct. 1959; Leader of the House Dec. 1955-Oct. 1961; Home Secretary Jan. 1957-July 1962; Minister responsible for Central African Federation Mar. 1962-Oct. 1963. First Secretary of State and Dept. Prime Minister July 1962-Oct. 1963. Secretary of State for Foreign Affairs Oct. 1963-Oct. 1964. Chairman of Conservative Party 1959-61. Chairman of National Union of Conservative and Unionist Associations 1945-46, President 1956. A Conservative. Elected for the Saffron Walden division of Essex in May 1929 and sat until Jan. 1965 when he was created Baron Butler of Saffron Walden (Life Peerage). Chairman of Conservative Research Department 1945-64. C.H. 1954. Father of the House of Commons Oct. 1964-Jan. 1965. Master of Trinity Coll., Cambridge 1965-78. High Steward of Cambridge University 1958-66, Dept. High Steward from 1978. High Steward of the City of Cambridge from 1963. Opposition spokesman on Foreign Affairs and Member of Shadow Cabinet 1964-65. K.G. 1971. Chairman of Home Office Committee on Mentally Abnormal Offenders 1972-75. Rector of Glasgow University 1956-59. Chancellor of Sheffield University 1960-78 and of Essex University from 1962.* [1965]

BUXTON, Ronald Carlile. 67 Ashley Gardens, London. S. of Murray Barclay Buxton, Esq. B. 1923; m. 20 June 1959, Phyllida Dorothy Roden Buxton, d. of Capt. R.H.V. Buxton, R.N. (retired), of Smallburgh Hall, Norwich, (2 s. 2 d.). Educ. at Eton, and Trinity Coll., Cambridge. A Director of H. Young and Company Limited, of London. Chartered Structural Engineer. A Farmer, farming 400 acres. A Conservative. Adopted as the Conservative candidate for Leyton in 1952. Unsuccessfully contested the 1955, 1959 and 1964 general elections. Elected for Leyton in Jan. 1965 and sat until he was defeated in Mar. 1966.* [1966]

BYERS, Lieut.-Col. Charles Frank. O.B.E. 18 Tite Street, London. S. of Charles Cecil Byers, Esq. B. 24 July 1915; m. 15 July 1939, Joan, d. of William Oliver, Esq. Educ. at Westminster, and Christ Church, Oxford. President of Oxford University Liberal Club 1937. Chairman of Liberal Association 1946-63 and Chief Whip 1946-50. Enlisted Sept. 1939, Commissioned 1940, served with H.Q. 8th Army and H.Q. 21st Army Group (despatches 3). Chevalier of Legion of Honour and Croix de Guerre avec Palmes. A Liberal. Elected for Dorset N. in July 1945 and sat until he was defeated in 1950. Unsuccessfully

contested Dorset N. in 1951 and Bolton E. in Nov. 1960. O.B.E. 1944. Fellow of British Institute of Management. Created Baron Byers (Life Peerage) 1964. Leader of the Liberal Party in the House of Lords from 1967. Chairman of the Liberal Party 1950-52 and 1965-67. PC. 1972. Director of Rio Tinto Company Limited and Rio Tinto-Zinc Corporation Limited 1951-73. Chairman of Company Pensions Information Centre from 1973. Dept.-Lieut. for Surrey 1974. *[1950]

CALLAGHAN, James. House of Commons, London. S. of James Callaghan, Esq. B. 1927. Educ. at Manchester and London Universities. A Roman Catholic. Lecturer, St. John's Coll., Manchester 1959-74. Art Lecturer at Manchester Coll. Member of Middleton Borough Council 1971-74. Parliamentary Private Secretary to Joel Barnett, Chief Secretary to Treasury, 1976-77. A Labour Member. Sat for Middleton and Prestwich from Feb. 1974.* [1979]

CALLAGHAN, Rt. Hon. (Leonard) James. 10 Downing Street, London. Athenaeum. S. of James Callaghan, Esq., R.N. B. 27 Mar. 1912; m. 1938, Audrey Elizabeth Moulton (1 s. 2 d.). Educ. at Portsmouth Northern Secondary School. Assistant Secretary Inland Revenue Staff Federation 1936-50 (serving with Royal Navy during World War II). Parliamentary Private Secretary to John Parker, Under-Secretary of State for the Dominions 1945-46. Parliamentary Secretary Ministry of Transport Oct. 1947-Mar. 1950. Parliamentary and Financial Secretary to the Admiralty Mar. 1950-Oct. 1951. Chancellor of the Exchequer Oct. 1964-Nov. 1967. Secretary of State for the Home Department from Nov. 1967-June 1970; Foreign and Commonwealth Secretary Mar. 1974-Apr. 1976. Prime Minister and First Lord of the Treasury Apr. 1976-May 1979. Opposition spokesman on the Admiralty and Fuel and Power to 1956, on the Colonies 1956-61, on Treasury Affairs 1961-64, on Trade 1961-62, on Home Affairs 1970-71, on Employment 1971-72 and on Foreign Affairs 1972-74. Unsuccessful candidate for Dept. Leadership of Labour Party 1960 and for Leadership 1963. Leader of Opposition from May 1979. PC. 1964. A Labour Member. Sat for S. Cardiff from 1945-Feb. 1950 and for S.E. division of Cardiff from Feb. 1950. Consultant to Police Federations of England, Wales and Scotland 1955-64. President United Kingdom Pilots Association 1963-76. Visiting Fellow, Nuffield Coll., Oxford 1956-67. Honorary Life Fellow 1967. President International Maritime Pilots Association 1971-76, Member of Parliamentary Committee of P.L.P. 1951-64 and 1970-74. Member of National Executive Labour Party 1957-62 and from 1963, Treasurer 1967-76, Chairman 1973-74. Honorary Freeman City of Cardiff 1975. Honorary Bencher, Inner Temple.* [1979]

CAMPBELL, Rt. Hon. Sir David Callender, K.B.E., C.M.G. 19 Adelaide Park, Belfast. S. of William H. Campbell, Esq. B. 29 Jan. 1891; m. 29 Nov. 1919, Ragnhild, d. of Hugo Gregersen, Esq. Educ. at Foyle Coll., Londonderry, and Edinburgh University. Interned in Hungary during First World War. Late of Colonial Civil Service. Lieut-Gov. Malta 1943-52. K.B.E. 1950; Kt. 1945; C.M.G. 1944. Honorary LL.D. Queen's University Belfast 1961. An Ulster Unionist member. Elected for S. Belfast in Nov. 1952 and sat until his death on 12 June 1963. PC. Jan. 1963. Chairman of Ulster Unionist group in the House of Commons from 1955. Dept.-Chief Secretary, Uganda 1936-42. Colonial Secretary, Gibraltar 1942-43. Died 12 June 1963. [1963]

CAMPBELL, Sir Edward Taswell, Bart. 52 Westmorland Road, Bromley, Kent. Carlton, I Zingari and M.C.C.S. of Col. Frederick Campbell, C.B., and grand-s. of Sir John Campbell, Bart., of Airds, Argyllshire. B. 9 Apr. 1879; m. 28 Jan. 1904, Edith, L. (G.) St.J., d. of A. J. Warren, Esq. Educ. at Dulwich Coll., later Gov. An East India Merchant. H.B.M. Vice-Consul in Java 1914-20. Chairman Anglo-Netherlands Society, of James Allens' Girls School, Dulwich, and of Royal Normal Coll. for the Blind. K. (G.) St. J., Member of London County Council 1922-25. Parliamentary Private Secretary to the Rt. Hon. Sir Kingsley Wood when Postmaster-Gen., Nov. 1931, when Minister of Health June 1935, when Secretary of State for Air May 1938, when Lord

Privy Seal Apr. 1940, when Chancellor of the Exchequer May 1940-Sept. 1943, and to the Rt. Hon. H.U. Willink when Minister of Health Nov. 1943. Created Knight Bach. 1933; Bart. 1939; J.P. for Kent. Commissioner of Staff of Metropolitan Special Constabulary. A Conservative. Unsuccessfully contested N.W. Camberwell in 1918. Elected for N.W. Camberwell in Oct. 1924, defeated May 1929. Sat for Bromley from Sep. 1930 until his death on 17 July 1945, after the completion of polling for the General Election but before the result was announced. He was subsequently returned at the head of the poll and a by-election was held. [1945]

CAMPBELL, Rt. Hon. Gordon Thomas Calthrop, M.C. Holme Rose, Nairnshire. Brooks', and Caledonian, Edinburgh. S. of Maj.-Gen. J.A. Campbell, D.S.O. B. 8 June 1921; m. 1949, Nicola, d. of G.S. Madan, Esq. Educ. at Wellington. Regular Army 1939-46. Maj. 1942 in 15th (Scottish) Division. M.C. 1944 and Bar 1945. Wounded and disabled in 1945. H.M. Foreign Service 1946-57. F.O. 1946-49; U.K. Permanent Mission U.N.O. 1949-52; Cabinet Office 1954-56; British Embassy, Vienna 1956-57; Assistant Government Whip 1961. A Lord Commissioner of the Treasury Sept. 1962-Dec. 1963, and Scottish Whip. Under-Secretary of State for Scotland Dec. 1963-Oct. 1964. Secretary of State for Scotland June 1970-Feb. 1974. A Scottish Unionist Member. Elected for Moray and Nairn in 1959 and sat until he was defeated in Feb. 1974. PC. 1970. Created Baron Campbell of Croy (Life Peerage) 1974. Opposition spokesman on Scotland 1965-70, Chief spokesman and Member of the Shadow Cabinet Jan. 1969-June 1670.* [1974]

CAMPBELL, Ian. 20 McGregor Drive, Dumbarton. S. of William Campbell, Esq. B. 26 Apr. 1926; m. 14 June 1950, Mary, d. of Alexander Millar, Esq., (2 s. 3 d.). Educ. at Dumbarton Academy, and Royal Technical Coll., Glasgow, C.Eng., M.I.Mech.E. Provost of Dumbarton 1962-70; J.P. Dunbartonshire; Electrical Power Engineer with South of Scotland Electric Board 1953-70. Parliamentary Private Secretary to Rt. Hon. Bruce Millan, Secretary of State for Scotland

1976-79. Secretary to Scottish Parliamentary Labour Group 1974-77. Chairman All-Party Scotch Whisky Industry Group 1976. A Labour Member. Sat for the W. division of Dunbartonshire from 1970.*　　　[1979]

CAMPBELL, Keith Bruce, Q.C. 3 Dr. Johnson's Buildings, Temple, London. 1 Hare Court, Temple, London. S. of Walter Henry Pearson Campbell, Esq., of Christchurch, New Zealand. B. 25 Oct. 1916; m. 1939, Betty, d. of F.A. Muffett, Esq., of London. Educ. in New Zealand, and London University. Served 1939-45 war. Commissioned 1941 R.A.S.C. and served N. Africa and Italy. Barrister, Inner Temple 1947; Q.C. 1964. A Conservative. Unsuccessfully contested the Gorton division of Manchester in 1955 and Oldham W. in 1966. Elected for Oldham W. in June 1968 and sat until he was defeated in 1970. Master of the Bench, Inner Temple 1970. Recorder of Crown Court 1972-76. Circuit Judge from 1976. Member of Gen. Council of Bar 1956-60, 1965-70 and 1973-74. Member of Senate of Inns of Court 1974-75.*　　　[1970]

CANAVAN, Dennis Andrew. 15 Margaret Road, Bannockburn, Stirlingshire. House of Commons, London. Bannockburn Miners' Welfare. S. of Thomas and Agnes Canavan. B. 8 Aug. 1942; m. 1964, Elnor, d. of Charles and Jessie Stewart, (3 s. 1 d.). Educ. at St. Columba's High School, Cowdenbeath, and Edinburgh University. B.Sc. (Hons.) 1967, and Dip.Ed. 1968. A Roman Catholic Principal Teacher of Mathematics St. Modan's High School, Stirling 1970-74. Assistant Head Master, Holy Rood High School, Edinburgh 1974. Stirling District Councillor 1973-74. A Labour Member. Sat for W. Stirlingshire from Oct. 1974.*
　　　[1979]

CANT, Robert Bowen. 119 Chell Green Avenue, Tunstall, Stoke-on-Trent, Staffordshire. S. of Robert Cant, Esq. B. 24 July 1915; m. 1940, Rebecca Harris Watt (1 s. 1 d.). Educ. at Middlesbrough High School, and London School of Economics. Lecturer in economics, University of Keele, 1962-66. Member of Association of University Teachers. Member of Stoke-on-Trent City

Council 1953-74, of Staffordshire County Council from 1973. A Labour Member. Unsuccessfully contested Shrewsbury in 1950 and 1951. Sat for the Central division of Stoke-on-Trent from Mar. 1966.*　　　[1979]

CARLISLE, Rt. Hon. Mark, Q.C. Newstead, Mobberley, Cheshire. 3 Kings Bench Walk, Temple, London. Garrick. S. of Philip Edmund Carlisle, Esq. B. 1929; m. 1959, Miss S.J. Des Voeux, (1 d.). Educ. at Radley, and Manchester University. Served as 2nd Lieut. Royal Army Education Corps 1948-50. Called to the bar by Gray's Inn 1953; Entrance Scholar Junior. Northern Circuit, practised in Manchester from Feb. 1954. Member of Bar Council 1966-70. Recorder 1976. Chairman Federation of University Conservative and Union Associations 1953-54. Joint Hon. Secretary Conservative Party Home Affairs Committee 1966-69. Member Home Office Advisory Council on the Penal System 1966-70. Under-Secretary of State, Home Office June 1970-Apr. 1972. Minister of State, Home Office Apr. 1972-Mar. 1974. Member B.B.C. Advisory Council 1975. Q.C. 1971. A Conservative. Adopted for the St. Helens division in Apr. 1958, but unsuccessful in the by-election of June 1958 and in the general election of 1959. Sat for the Runcorn division of Cheshire from Oct. 1964. Opposition spokesman on Affairs 1969-70 and on Education 1978-79. Member of Shadow Cabinet 1978-79. Secretary of State for Education and Science from May 1979. PC. 1979.*　　　[1979]

CARMICHAEL, James. 31 Sandyhill Place, Glasgow. B. 1894. Member Glasgow Town Council 1929-46; J.P. A Labour Member. Unsuccessfully contested the Tradeston division of Glasgow in 1935 and the Cathcart division of Glasgow in Apr. 1942 as an I.L.P. candidate. Elected for the Bridgeton division of Glasgow in Aug. 1946 as an I.L.P. member, joined the Labour Party in Nov. 1947 and sat until he resigned in June 1961. Member of National Union of Life Assurance Workers. Died 19 Jan. 1966.　　　[1961]

CARMICHAEL, Neil George. 53 Partickhill Road, Glasgow. S. of James Carmichael, Esq., MP. B. Oct. 1921; m. 1948, Catherine

McIntosh (Kay), d. of J.D. Rankin, Esq. Educ. at Estbank Academy and Royal Coll. of Science and Technology, Glasgow. Employed by the Gas Board in Planning Department. A City Councillor 1962-63. Joint Parliamentary Under-Secretary Ministry of Transport Aug. 1967-Oct. 1969. Parliamentary Private Secretary to Rt. Hon. Anthony Wedgwood Benn, Postmaster-General and Minister of Technology 1966-67. Joint Parliamentary Secretary Ministry of Technology Oct. 1969-June 1970. An Opposition spokesman on Scotland 1970-74. Under-Secretary of State, Department of Environment Mar. 1974-Dec. 1975; Under-Secretary of State, Department of Industry Dec. 1975-Apr. 1976; Member Select Committee on Nationalised Industries 1976. A Labour Member. Sat for Woodside division of Glasgow from Nov. 1962 to Feb. 1974, and for the Kelvingrove division of Glasgow from Feb. 1974.*　　　　　[1979]

CARR, Rt. Hon. (Leonard) Robert. Monkenholt, Hadley Green, Hertfordshire. Brooks's, and Carlton. S. of Ralph Edward Carr, Esq. B. 11 Nov. 1916; m. 1943, Joan Kathleen, d. of Dr. E.W. Twining, M.R.C.P. Educ. at Westminster School, Gonville and Caius Coll., Cambridge, M.A. Fellow Institute of Metallurgists 1957. Director of John Dale Limited 1948-55; Chairman 1958-63 and 1965-70. Dept. Chairman Metal Closures Group Limited 1960-63 and 1964-65; Director 1965-70. Member of London Board Scottish Union and National Insurance Company 1958-63. Norwich Union Insurance Group (London Advisory Board) 1965-70 and 1974. Director Securicor Limited and Security Services Limited 1961-63, 1965-70 and from 1974. Director of S. Hoffnung and Company 1958-63, 1965-70 and from 1974. Director S.G.B. Group Limited from 1974. Parliamentary Private Secretary to Rt. Hon. Anthony Eden as Secretary of State for Foreign Affairs 1951-55 and as Prime Minister 1955; Parliamentary Secretary Ministry of Labour Dec. 1955-Apr. 1958. Secretary for Technical Co-operation May 1963-Oct. 1964. Secretary of State for Employment June 1970-Apr. 1972. Lord President of the Council and Leader of the House of Commons Apr.-Nov. 1972. Home

Secretary July 1972-Mar. 1974. Gov. of St. Mary's Hospital 1954-55 and 1958-63; Gov. of Imperial Coll. of Science and Technology 1959-63. A Conservative. Sat for Mitcham from 1950-74. Elected for the Carshalton division of Sutton in Feb. 1974 and sat until he was created Baron Carr of Hadley (Life Peerage) in Dec. 1975. Opposition spokesman on Overseas Development 1964-65, on Aviation 1965-67, on Labour 1967-70 and on Treasury Affairs 1974-75. Member of the Shadow Cabinet Feb. 1967-June 1970 and Mar. 1974-Feb. 1975. PC. 1963. Director of Prudential Corporation from 1976, Chairman from 1980.*　　　　　[1976]

CARR, William Compton. 18 Ennismore Gardens Mews, London. Carlton, Hurlingham, and R.A.C. S. of Bernard Compton Carr, Esq., Solicitor. B. 10 July 1918; m. (divorced). Educ. at The Leys, Cambridge. Admitted a Solicitor in 1950. Member London County Council, Alderman 1956-58 and 1961. Parliamentary Private Secretary to Alan Green, Minister of State, Board of Trade 1963 and Financial Secretary to Treasury 1963-64. A Conservative. Elected for Barons Court in 1959 and sat until he was defeated in 1964. Unsuccessfully contested Barons Court in 1966.*　　　　　[1964]

CARSON, Hon. Edward. Millstream Cottage, Fox Corner, Worplesdon, Surrey. Cleve Court, Minster-in-Thanet. S. of Baron Carson, Lord of Appeal in Ordinary. B. 17 Feb. 1920; m. 2 Mar. 1943, Heather, d. of Capt. Frank Sclater. Educ. at Eton, and Trinity Hall, Cambridge. Lieut. Life Guards. A Conservative. Elected for the Isle of Thanet division of Kent in July 1945 and sat until he resigned in Feb. 1953.*　　　　　[1953]

CARSON, John. House of Commons, London. B. 1933. Member Belfast Corporation 1971. Supported the Labour Government in the vote of confidence on 28 Mar. 1979. An Ulster Unionist Member. Sat for Belfast N. from Feb. 1974 until he retired in 1979.*　　　　　[1979]

CARTER, Raymond John. 1 Lynwood Chase, Bracknell, Berkshire. S. of John Carter, Esq., Agricultural Worker. B. 17 Sept.

1935; m. 30 Mar. 1959, Jeanette, d. of William Hills, Esq. Educ. at Mortlake Secondary School, Reading Coll. of Technology, and Stafford Coll. of Technology. National Service–Army 1953-55. Technical Assistant Sperry Gyroscope Company 1956-65; Central Electricity Generating Board 1965-70; member of Public Accounts Committee 1973-74. Member of Easthampstead Rural District Council 1963-68. Member Select Committee Science and Technology 1974-76. Member Western European Union 1974-76. Member Council of Europe 1974-76. Member General Advisory Council, B.B.C. 1974-76. Promoter of Congenital Injuries (Civil Liabilities) Bill 1976. Parliamentary Under-Secretary of State Northern Ireland Office Apr. 1976-May 1979. A Labour Member. Unsuccessfully contested Wokingham in 1966 and Warwick and Leamington in Mar. 1968. Sat for the North-field division of Birmingham from June 1970 until 1979, when he was defeated.* [1979]

CARTER-JONES, Lewis. 5 Cefn Road, Rhosnesni, Wrexham, Denbighshire. S of Tom Jones, Esq. B. 17 Nov. 1920; m. 1945, Patricia Hilda, d. of Alfred Bastiman, Esq. of Scarborough. Educ. at Kenfig Hill Council School, Bridgend County School, and University Coll. of Wales, Aberystwyth, B.A. degree with honours in Economics, diploma in Education. Head of Business Studies Department, Yale Grammar-Technical School, Wrexham. Joined the Labour Party in 1940. Member T.G.W.U. Parliamentary Panel. Secretary Indo-British Parliamentary Group. Major interest-use of technology to aid severely disabled and aged. Industrial Training, Industrial Safety. Chairman Possum Charity Foundation. Chairman of the Committee for Research into Aids for Disabled organised by National Foundation for Crippling Diseases. Advisory member British Association for the Retarded. Chair-man Committee National Listening Library. A Labour Member. Unsuccessfully contested Chester in the 1956 by-election, and Chester in the 1959 general election. Sat for Eccles from Oct. 1964. Assumed the surname of Carter-Jones in lieu of Jones.* [1979]

CARTWRIGHT, John Cameron. 17 Commonwealth Way, London. S. of Aubrey John Randolph Cartwright, Esq., Technical Representative. B. 29 Nov. 1933; m. 23 Feb. 1959, Iris June, d. of Arthur Mark Tant, Esq., (1 s. 1 d.). Educ. at Woking County Gram-mar School. Executive Civil Servant 1952-55. Labour Party Agent 1955-67. Political Secretary RACS Limited 1967-72. RACS Limited full-time Director 1972 until his election as MP. Leader, London Borough of Greenwich Council 1971-74. Member Labour Party National Executive Committee 1971-75 and 1976-78. J.P. Inner London 1970. Parliamentary Private Secretary to Mrs. Shirley Williams 1976-78. Trustee of National Maritime Museum from 1976. A Labour Member. Unsuccessfully contested Bexley in 1970 and Bexleyheath in Feb. 1974. Sat for Greenwich, Woolwich East from Oct. 1974.* [1979]

CARY, Sir Robert Archibald, Bart. Wrotham Water, Wrotham, Kent. Turf, and Pratt's. S. of Robert Cary, Esq. B. 25 May 1898; m. 30 Apr. 1924, Hon. Rosamond Mary, d. of Col. Hon. Alfred Nathaniel Curzon, and sister of 2nd Visct. Scarsdale. Educ. at Ardingly Coll., and Royal Military Coll., Sandhurst. Served with 4th Dragoon Guards 1916-23; rejoined 4/7th Royal Dragoon Guards Sept. 1939. Parliamentary Private Secretary to the Rt. Hon. L.S. Amery, C.H., Secretary of State for India and Burma 1942-44; Assistant Government Whip Nov. 1944; Lord Commissioner of the Trea-sury May-July 1945. Knight Bach. Aug. 1945. Parliamentary Private Secretary to the Lord Privy Seal and Leader of the House, the Rt. Hon. H.F.C. Crookshank, C.H., Nov. 1951-Dec. 1955. Chairman of J. Compton, Sons and Webb Limited, and Director Lancashire United Transport Limited. Created Bart. 1955. A Conservative. Sat for Eccles from 1935-45 when he was defeated. Unsuccessfully contested Ashton-under-Lyne in a by-election in Oct. 1945 and Central Nottingham in the general election of Feb. 1950. Elected for the Withington division of Manchester in 1951 and sat until he retired in Feb. 1974. Parliamentary Private Secretary to A.U.M. Hudson, Civil Lord of the Admir-alty 1939-42. Died 1 Oct. 1979. [1974]

CASTLE, Rt. Hon. Barbara Anne. House of Commons, London. D. of Frank Betts, Esq. B. 6 Oct. 1911; m. 28 July 1944, Edward Castle, a Journalist, (created Baron Castle 1974 and died 1979). Educ. at Bradford Girls Grammar School, and St. Hugh's Coll., Oxford. Member of St. Pancras Borough Council 1937-45 and of Metropolitan Water Board 1940-45. Parliamentary Private Secretary to Rt. Hon. Sir Stafford Cripps 1945 and to Rt. Hon. J. H. Wilson, President of the Board of Trade 1947. Chairman of the Labour Party 1958-59; member of N.E.C. of Labour Party 1950-79. Minister of Overseas Development Oct. 1964-Dec. 1965. Minister of Transport from Dec. 1965-Apr. 1968. First Secretary and Secretary of State for Employment and Productivity Apr. 1968-June 1970. Secretary of State for Social Services Mar. 1974-Apr. 1976. PC. 1964. A Labour Member. Sat for Blackburn from 1945 to Feb. 1950, for E. Blackburn from Feb. 1950 to May 1955 and for Blackburn from May 1955 until she retired in 1979. Opposition spokesman on Works 1959-60, on Employment 1970-71 and on Social Services 1971-72. Unsuccessful candidate for Dept. Leadership of Labour Party 1961. Member of Parliamentary Committee of P.L.P. 1970-71 and May-Nov. 1972. Member of European Parliament for Greater Manchester N. from 1979; Leader of Labour Party delegation and Vice-Chairman of Socialist Group.* [1979]

CHALKER, Lynda. House of Commons, London. D. of Sidney Henry James Bates, Esq. B. Apr. 1942; m. 1967, Eric Robert Chalker, Esq. (divorced 1973). Educ. at Roedean, Heidelberg University, Westfield Coll., London University, and Cen. Polytechnic. Executive Director International Market Research Company. Member of National Young Conservatives Vice-Chairman 1970-71. Gov. Roedean School and Battersea County, General Advisory Council B.B.C. Honorary Parliamentary Adviser to British Ports Authority. Honorary Parliamentary Adviser to Market Research Society. An Opposition spokesman on Social Services 1976-79. Under-Secretary of State, Department of Health and Social Security from May 1979. A Conservative. Sat for Wallasey from Feb. 1974.* [1979]

CHALLEN, Charles. Hall Place, Lyndhurst Terrace, Hampstead, London. 11 Kings Bench Walk, Temple, London. Oxford & Cambridge. S. of Charles Hollis Challen, Esq. B. 15 Feb. 1894. Unmarried. Educ. at Merchant Taylors' School, and Jesus Coll., Cambridge. Barrister-at-Law, Gray's Inn, and Arden Prizeman 1922. Served overseas 1940-46; Flt.-Lieut. R.A.F. Member of Hampstead Borough Council 1931-45; Chairman of General Emergency Committee Sept. 1939-Nov. 1940. A Conservative. Elected for Hampstead in Nov. 1941 and sat until he retired in 1950 after the local association had declined to readopt him. Lieut. in R.F.A. 1914-18. Liveryman of Merchant Taylors' Company. Died 20 June 1960. [1950]

CHAMBERLAIN, Ronald Arthur. 18 Basing Hall, Golders Green, London. S. of James Arthur Chamberlain, Esq. B. 19 Apr. 1901; m. 1st, 1924, Joan, d. of Smith M'Neill, Esq., of Edinburgh (she died 1950); 2ndly, 1951, Florence Lilian Illingworth. Educ. at Owens School, Islington, and Gonville and Caius Coll., Cambridge, M.A. Secretary of National Federation of Housing Societies 1936-40; Chief Executive Officer of Miners Welfare Commission 1940-43; Assistant Administration Officer National Hostels Corporation 1944-45; Housing Consultant to Co-operative Movement 1945; Member of Middlesex County Council 1947-52; Parliamentary Private Secretary to Lewis Silkin, MP., Minister of Town and Country Planning Aug. 1945-Feb. 1948. A Labour Member. Elected for the Norwood division of Lambeth in July 1945 and sat until he was defeated in 1950. Unsuccessfully contested the Norwood division of Lambeth in 1951.* [1950]

CHAMPION, Arthur Joseph. 22 Laneley Terrace, Pontypridd, Glamorgan. S. of William Champion, Esq., of Glastonbury. B. 26 July 1897; m. 1930, Mary E. Williams, of Pontypridd. Educ. at St. John's School, Glastonbury. J.P. for Glamorgan. A Signalman. Served with Royal Welch Fusiliers 1914-18, 2nd Lieut. Parliamentary Private Secretary to Rt. Hon. E.J. Strachey, Minister of Food and Secretary of State for War June 1949 to Apr. 1951. Parliamentary Secretary to Ministry of Agriculture and Fisheries Apr.-Oct. 1951. A Labour Member. Member for Derbyshire S. July 1945 to Feb. 1950 and for Derbyshire S.E. from Feb. 1950 until he was defeated in 1959. Director of British Sugar Corporation 1960-64 and 1967-68. Created Baron Champion (Life Peerage) 1962. Minister without Portfolio and Dept.-Leader of House of Lords Oct. 1964-Jan. 1967. PC. 1967. A Dept.-Speaker of House of Lords from 1967. Representative of Labour Peers on Parliamentary Committee of Parliamentary Labour Party 1970-74. Honorary Associate of Royal College of Veterinary Surgeons.* [1959]

CHANNON, Sir Henry. 5 Belgrave Square, London. Kelvedon Hall, Brentwood, Essex. Carlton, Buck's, Pratt's, and R.A.C. S. of H. Channon, Esq. B. 7 Mar. 1897; m. 14 July 1933, Lady Honor Guinness, d. of Rupert, 2nd Earl of Iveagh (whom he divorced in 1945). Educ. at Christ Church, Oxford. Parliamentary Private Secretary to R.A. Butler, MP., when Parliamentary Under-Secretary of State for Foreign Affairs 1938-41. Knight Bach. 1957. A Conservative. Sat for Southend from 1935-50. Elected for Southend W. in Feb. 1950 and sat until his death on 7 Oct. 1958. [1958]

CHANNON, Rt. Hon. Henry Paul Guinness. Kelvedon Hall, Brentwood, Essex. 96 Cheyne Walk, London. White's, and Buck's. S. of Sir Henry Channon, MP. B. 1935; m. 1963, Ingrid Olivia Georgia Wyndham. Educ. Eton, and Christ Church, Oxford. Served in Royal Horse Guards 1955-56. Parliamentary Private Secretary to Rt. Hon. Richard Wood, Minister of Power, Nov. 1959-60; Parliamentary Private Secretary to Rt. Hon. R.A. Butler, Home Secretary Dec. 1960-62, First Secretary of State July 1962-Oct. 1963 and Foreign Secretary Oct. 1963-Oct. 1964. Opposition spokesman on Public Building and Works 1965-66 and Arts and Amenities 1967-70. Joint Parliamentary Secretary to Ministry of Housing and Local Government June-Oct. 1970. Joint Parliamentary Under-Secretary of State Department of the Environment Oct. 1970-Mar. 1972; Minister of State for Northern Ireland Mar.-Nov. 1972; Minister for Housing and Construction Nov. 1972-Mar. 1974. Opposition spokesman on Prices and Consumer Affairs Mar.-Nov. 1974. Opposition spokesman on the Environment Nov. 1974-Feb. 1975. Member of Shadow Cabinet June 1974-Feb. 1975. Minister of State, Civil Service Department from May 1979. Dept.-Leader Conservative Group on Council of Europe 1976-79. A Conservative. Sat for Southend W. from Jan. 1959. Member of General Advisory Council of Independent Television Authority 1964-66. PC. 1980.* [1979]

CHAPMAN, Sydney Brookes. 18 Wood Lane, Handsworth, Birmingham. S. of W.D. Chapman, Esq. B. 17 Oct. 1935; m. 1976, Claire Lesley McNab. Educ. at Rugby School, and Manchester University. Chartered Architect and Surveyor and Chartered Town Planner; Lecturer in Architecture and Planning at a Technical Coll. 1964-70. National Chairman of Young Conservatives 1964-66 and holds the distinction of having been Chairman and Vice-Chairman at every level of the movement; Sen. Elected Vice-Chairman of N.W. Area of the National Union of Conservative and Unionist Associations from 1966-70. Co-Author of *Blueprint for Britian, Social Security in the '70's*, and *Local Freedom*, a study in Local Government Reform 1968. Associate Partner, McDonald, Hamilton and Montefoire, Architects. Planning Consultant, House Builders Federation. Member of Council R.I.B.A. June 1972-77, Vice-President and Chairman of Public Affairs Board 1974-75. Instigator National Tree Planting Year 1973. Honorary Secretary All-Party Animal Welfare Group. Secretary Conservative MP.'s Local Government and Development Committee. A Conservative. Unsuccessfully contested Stalybridge and Hyde in 1964. Elected for the Handsworth division of Birmingham in June 1970 and sat until he was defeated in Feb. 1974. Elected for the Chipping Barnet division of Barnet in May 1979. Vice-President of Arboricultural Association.* [1974]

CHAPMAN, (William) Donald. 2 Crescent Place, Brighton. S. of William H. Chapman, Esq., of Barnsley. B. 25 Nov. 1923. Educ. at Barnsley Grammar School, and

Emmanuel Coll., Cambridge, M.A. Hons. Econ. General Secretary Fabian Society 1949-53; formerly Honorary Secretary of Cambridge Trades Council and Labour Party. City Councillor 1945-47. Research Secretary of Fabian Society 1948-49. Company Director. A Labour Member. Elected for the Northfield division of Birmingham in Oct. 1951 and sat until he retired in 1970. Created Baron Northfield (Life Peerage) 1975. Gwilym Gibbon Fellow of Nuffield Coll., Oxford 1971-73. Visiting Fellow, Centre for Contemporary European Studies, University of Sussex from 1973. Chairman of Development Commission from 1974. Chairman of Telford Development Corporation from 1975. Special adviser to E.E.C. Commission from 1978. Chairman of Inquiry into recent trends in acquisition and occupancy of agricultural land from 1977.* [1970]

CHATAWAY, Rt. Hon. Christopher John. 3 Lowndes Square, London. Lordington Mill, Chichester, Sussex. Carlton. S. of James Denys Percival Chataway, O.B.E. B. 31 Jan. 1931; m. 1st, 1959, Anna Maria, d. of Mrs. M. Lett (divorced 1975); m. 2ndly, 1976, Carola Walker. Educ. at Sherborne, and Magdalen Coll., Oxford, B.A. 1953. Olympic Athlete 1952 and 1956. Junior Executive, Arthur Guinness Son & Company Limited 1953-55 Television Reporter and Commentator 1955-59. Member of London County Council for N. Lewisham 1958-61, Alderman of G.L.C. 1967-70. Awarded Nansen Medal for work on World Refugee Year 1961. Parliamentary Private Secretary to Rt. Hon. Richard Wood, Minister of Power 1961-62. Parliamentary Secretary Ministry of Education July 1962-Apr. 1964. Under-Secretary of State, Department of Education and Science Apr.-Oct. 1964. Opposition spokesman Overseas Development 1965-66. Leader Inner London Education Authority 1967-69. Opposition spokesman on Environment 1969-70. Minister of Posts and Telecommunications June 1970-Apr. 1972. PC. 1970. Minister for Industrial Development Apr. 1972-Mar. 1974. A Conservative. Sat for N. Lewisham 1959-66, when he was defeated. Elected for the Chichester division of West Sussex at a by-election in May 1969 and sat until he retired in Sept. 1974. Managing Director of Orion Bank from 1974. Treasurer of National Committee for Electoral Reform from 1976. Chairman of British Telecommunications Systems from 1979.* [1974]

CHATER, Daniel. 41 Water Lane, Seven Kings, Essex. S. of Henry Chater, Esq., of Lambeth. B. 1870; m. 1894, Kate Wood (she died in 1939). Member of National Union of General and Municipal Workers. General Secretary of National Union of Allotment Holders. Member of Essex County Council 1919-22. Chairman of Political Committee of London Co-operative Society 1926. A Labour Member. Unsuccessfully contested Ilford in 1923 and 1924. Sat for Hammersmith S. May 1929-Oct. 1931, when he was defeated. Elected for N.E. Bethnal Green and sat until he retired in 1950. Died 25 May 1959. [1950]

CHETWYND, George Roland. 95 Croxted Road, London. S. of George Chetwynd, Esq. B. 14 May 1916; m. 1939, Teresa Reynolds Condon, (2 d.). Educ. at Queen Elizabeth Grammar School, Atherstone, Warwickshire, and King's Coll., London, B.A. a W.E.A. Lecturer. Chairman and Gov. of Queen Mary's Hospital, Roehampton. Served with R.A. and Army Education Corps 1940-45. Parliamentary Private Secretary to the Rt. Hon. Hugh Dalton, Chancellor of Duchy of Lancaster and Minister of Local Government and Planning 1948-51. Member of Nature Conservancy 1959-62. A Labour Member. Elected for Stockton-on-Tees in July 1945 and sat until he resigned in Jan. 1962 on appointment as Director of North East Development Council. Opposition spokesman on Aviation 1959-61. Director of North East Development Council 1962-67. Director of Northern and Tubes Group, British Steel Corporation 1968-70. Member of Board, British Steel Corporation 1970-76. Member of Northern Economic Planning Council from 1964. Member of Board of B.O.A.C. 1966-74. C.B.E. 1968. Member of Northern Industrial Development Board from 1972. Chairman of Northern Regional Health Authority from 1978.* [1962]

CHICHESTER-CLARK, Robert. Ross House, Kells, Co. Antrim, Northern Ireland. S. of Capt. J.L. Chichester-Clark, D.S.O., R.N.B. 10 Jan. 1928; m. 1st 6 Nov. 1953, Jane Helen, d. of Air Marshal Sir Victor Goddard, K.C.B., C.B.E. (marriage dissolved in 1972), (1 s. 2 d.); 2ndly, 1974, Caroline, d. of Anthony Bull, Esq. Educ. at Royal Naval Coll., Dartmouth, and Magdalene Coll., Cambridge (Honours degree in History and Law 1949). Journalist, Portsmouth Evening *News* 1950-51; P.R.O. Glyndebourne Opera 1952-53; Executive O.U.P. 1953-55. Parliamentary Private Secretary to J.E.S. Simon, Financial Secretary to the Treasury 1958; Assistant Government Whip 1958. Lord Commissioner of Treasury June 1960-Nov. 1961. Comptroller of the Household Nov. 1961-Oct. 1964. Ch. Opposition spokesman on Public Building and Works and on N. Ireland Affairs 1965-70 and on the Arts 1966-67. Director Institution of Works Managers 1968. Minister of State Department of Employment Apr. 1972-Mar. 1974. An Ulster Unionist Member. Elected for Londonderry in 1955 and sat until he retired in Feb. 1974. Kinghted 1974.*   [1974]

CHURCHILL, Rt. Hon. Sir Winston Leonard Spencer, K.G., O.M., C.H., F.R.S. 28 Hyde Park Gate, London. Chartwell, Westerham. Carlton, and Turf. S. of Rt. Hon. Lord Randolph Churchill, MP. B. 30 Nov. 1874; m. 12 Sept. 1908, Clementine, G.B.E., d. of Col. Sir Henry Hozier, K.C.B. Educ. at Harrow, and Sandhurst. Joined 4th Hussars 1895; served with Spanish forces in Cuba, with the Malakand field force, the Tirah Expedition, the Nile, in South African War, and with Royal Scots Fusiliers in France 1916. Under-Secretary of State for the Colonies 1905-08, President of the Board of Trade 1908-10, Home Secretary 1910-11, First Lord of the Admiralty 1911-15, Chancellor of Duchy of Lancaster 1915, Minister of Munitions 1917-19, Secretary of State for War and for Air 1919-21, Secretary of State for the Colonies 1921-22. Chancellor of the Exchequer Nov. 1924-June 1929. First Lord of the Admiralty and Member of War Cabinet Sept. 1939-May 1940. Prime Minister and Minister for Defence and First Lord of the Treasury May 1940-July

1945; Lord Warden of the Cinque Ports 1941-65. Grand Master of the Primrose League 1943. Prime Minister and First Lord of the Treasury 1951-55, Minister of Defence 1951-52. PC. 1907. K.G. 1953; C.H. 1922; O.M. 1946. Unsuccessfully contested Oldham as a Conservative in July 1899 and elected there in 1900. Joined the Liberal Party in 1904 and sat until Jan. 1906 when he was elected for N.W. Manchester. Unsuccessfully contested N.W. Manchester in Apr. 1908, on his appointment as President of Board of Trade, but elected for Dundee in May 1908 and sat until he was defeated in Nov. 1922. Unsuccessfully contested W. Leicester as a Liberal in Dec. 1923 and the Abbey division of Westminster as a Constitutionalist, in opposition to Conservative and Liberal candidates, in Mar. 1924. Elected for the Epping division of Essex in Oct. 1924 as a Constitutionalist, with Liberal but not Conservative opposition, took the Conservative Whip and sat until July 1945 when he was elected for Woodford. Sat for Woodford until he retired in 1964. Leader of the Conservative Party Oct. 1940-Apr. 1955. Father of the House of Commons 1959-64. Died 24 Jan. 1965.
          [1964]

CHURCHILL, Winston Spencer. House of Commons, London. White's, and Buck's. S. of the Hon. Randolph S. Churchill, M.B.E. B. 10 Oct. 1940; m. 1964, Minnie, d. of Sir Gerard d'Erlanger, (2 s. 2 d.). Educ. at Eton and Christ Church, Oxford, M.A. Oxon. Author, Journalist and Lecturer. A Trade Unionist (Institute of Journalists). Motor Vehicles Pass. Ins. Act. 1971. Published *First Journey* 1964, *Six Day War* 1967. Parliamentary Private Secretary to Rt. Hon. Julian Amery, Minister for Housing and Construction 1970-72 and Minister of State, Foreign and Commonwealth Office 1972-73. Gov. of English Speaking Union. Trustee of Winston Churchill Memorial Trust, Honorary Fellow of Churchill Coll., Cambridge. Trustee of the National Benevolent Fund for the Aged 1974. Secretary Conservative Foreign Affairs Committee 1974-76. Conservative Front Bench spokesman on Defence 1976-78, when he retired. A Conservative. Unsuccessfully contested Manchester, Gorton division in 1967. Sat for Stretford from June 1970.* [1979]

CHUTER EDE, Rt. Hon. James, C.H. See EDE, Rt. Hon. James Chuter, C.H.

CLARK, Hon. Alan Kenneth McKenzie. Town Farm, Bratton-Clovelly, Okehampton. Brooks's. Eld. s. of The Lord Clark, of Saltwood, O.M., K.C.B., C.H. B. 13 Apr. 1928; m. 31 July 1958, Caroline, d. of Col. L.B. Beuttler, (2 s.). Educ. at Eton, and Christ Church, Oxford. Served in Household Cavalry and Royal Auxiliary Air Force. Barrister-at-Law, Inner Temple 1955. Member of Institute for Strategic Studies and Royal United Services Institute for Defence Studies. An author and historian. A Conservative. Sat for the Sutton division of Plymouth from Feb. 1974.* [1979]

CLARK, David George. House of Commons, London. S. of George Clark, Esq. B. 19 Oct. 1939; m. 24 Mar. 1970, Christine, d. of Ronald Kirkby, Esq. (1 d.). Educ. at Windermere Grammar, and Manchester University. Laboratory Worker in Textile Mill 1957-59; Student Teacher in Salford 1959-60; Undergraduate Student Manchester University 1960-63; Post-graduate student at U.M.I.S.T. 1963-65, Lecturer in Public Administration, Salford University 1965-70; President University of Manchester Union 1963-64; Author of *Industrial Manager* 1966. A Labour Member. Unsuccessfully contested the Withington division of Manchester in 1966. Elected for the Colne Valley division of the W. Riding of Yorkshire in June 1970 and sat until Feb. 1974 when he was defeated. Unsuccessfully contested Colne Valley in Oct. 1974. Elected for South Shields in May 1979. Opposition spokesman on Agriculture and Food Prices 1973-74. Ph.D. Sheffield University 1978.* [1974]

CLARK, Henry Maitland. Rockwood, Upperlands, Co. Londonderry, Northern Ireland. 11 Chesham Place, London. Junior Carlton, Leander, University (Dublin), and Royal Portrush Golf. S. of Harry F. Clark, Esq., M.B.E., J.P.B. 11 Apr. 1929; m. 1972, Penelope Winifred Tindal. Educ. at Shrewsbury, Trinity Coll., Dublin, and Trinity Hall,

Cambridge. District Officer H.M. Colonial Service, Tanganyika 1951-59, resigned to enter Parliament. Chairman Conservative Eastern Central Africa Committee 1963-65. Member British Delegation to Council of Europe and Western European Union 1962-65. Leader British Parliamentary Delegation to Uganda 1965. Commonwealth Observer at Mauritius general election 1967. An Ulster Unionist Member. Elected for N. Antrim in 1959 and sat until he was defeated in 1970. A Wine Merchant 1972-76. Assistant Controller of Council for Small Industries in Rural Areas from 1977.* [1970]

CLARK, Sir William Gibson Haig. 3 Barton Street, London. The Clock House, Box End, Bedford. Buck's, and Carlton. S. of Hugh Clark, Esq. Merchant. B. 18 Oct. 1917; m. 28 Aug. 1944, Irene Dorothy, d. of F.D. Rands, Esq. Educ. at Secondary School in London. An Accountant. Served in Army 1941-45, Maj. Wandsworth Borough Councillor, Vice-Chairman Finance 1949-52; Chairman Clapham Conservative Association 1949-52; Chairman Mid Bedfordshire Conservative Association 1956-59. Front Bench spokesman on Trade, Finance and Economics 1964-66. National Director (Honorary) £2 million Carrington Appeal 1967. Voted against entry to E.E.C. on 28 Oct. 1971. Joint Treasurer Conservative Party 1974-75. Dept. Chairman Conservative Party Mar. 1975-Nov. 1977. A Conservative. Unsuccessfully contested Northampton in 1955. Sat for Nottingham S. from 1959-66, when he was defeated. Member for Surrey E. from 1970 to Feb. 1974, and for Croydon S. from Feb. 1974. Knighted 1980.* [1979]

CLARKE, Kenneth Harry. House of Commons, London. S. of Kenneth Clarke, Esq., Watchmaker and Jeweller. B. 2 July 1940; m. 7 Nov. 1964, Gillian Mary, d. of Bruce Edwards, Esq., of Kent, (1 s. 1 d.). Educ. at Nottingham High School, and Gonville and Caius Coll., Cambridge. Chairman Cambridge University Conservative Association 1961; President Cambridge Union 1963; Chairman Federation Conservative Students 1963-65. Called to the bar, Gray's Inn 1963; member of Midland Circuit, practising from Birmingham. Parliamentary Private

Secretary to Sir Geoffrey Howe, Solicitor-Gen. 1971-72. Assistant Government Whip 1972-74. Government Whip for Europe 1973-74. Lord Commissioner of the Treasury Jan.-Mar. 1974. Opposition spokesman on Social Services June 1974-Nov. 1976 and on Industry 1976-79. Parliamentary Secretary Dept. of Transport from May 1979. A Conservative. Unsuccessfully contested Mansfield, Nottinghamshire in 1964 and 1966. Sat for the Rushcliffe division of Nottinghamshire from June 1970.*　　　[1979]

CLARKE, Philip Christopher. B. 1933. A Civil Servant from Dublin. Served a sentence of 10 years' penal servitude in Belfast Gaol for taking part in the raid on the depot of the Royal Inniskilling Fusiliers on 17 Oct. 1954. A Sinn Fein Member. Elected for Fermanagh and S. Tyrone in May 1955 but was declared incapable of election on the grounds that he was a felon; a petition to unseat him was upheld by the Northern Ireland High Court on 2 Sept. 1955 and by the House of Commons on 25 Oct. 1955; his opponent was declared elected.*　　　[1955]

CLARKE, Col. Sir Ralph Stephenson, K.B.E. 27 Chapel Street, London. Borde Hill, Haywards Heath, Sussex. Carlton, and Junior Carlton. S. of Col. Stephenson R. Clarke, C.B., LL.D., of Borde Hill, Haywards Heath, and Edith Gertrude, d. of Joseph Godman, Esq., of Park Hatch, Surrey. B. 17 Aug. 1892; m. 1921, Rebekah Mary, d. of Gerald Buxton, Esq., of Birch Hall, Theydon Bois. Educ. at Eton, and King's Coll., Cambridge, Scholar, 1st Class Hons. in Nat. Science Tripos 1913. Joined Sussex Yeomanry 1914, served in Gallipoli, Egypt and Palestine. Rejoined R.A. 1939 as Lieut.-Col. Commanding Tr. Regiments 1939-41; 12th Finsbury Rifles L.A.A. Regiment 1941-44 in Iraq, Iran, Palestine and Sicily; Honorary Col. 344 (Sussex Yeomanry) L.A.A./S.L. Regiment R.A. (T.A.) from 1947. Dept.-Lieut. 1932 and County Councillor for East Sussex from 1934 to 1963. Alderman 1953. Parliamentary Private Secretary to Earl Winterton, Chancellor of the Duchy of Lancaster June 1938-Sept. 1939. A Conservative. Elected for the East Grinstead division of East Sussex in July 1936 and sat until he retired in

1955. K.B.E. Jan. 1955. Chairman of East Sussex County Council 1958-61. Member of Nature Conservancy Committee for England 1960-66. Director of Stephenson Clarke Limited. Died 9 May 1970.*　　　[1954]

CLARKE, Brigadier Terence Hugh, C.B.E. Hollybank, Emsworth, Hampshire. Constitutional. S. of Col. H. Clarke, of Ascot. B. 17 Feb. 1904; m. 1928, Eileen, d. of Mr. Armistead, of Woodville, New Zealand. Educ. at Temple Grove, Haileybury, and Sandhurst. Served with Gloucestershire Regiment and Royal Army Ordnance Corps in North Africa and in Normandy (despatches) 1939-45. A Conservative. Unsuccessfully contested the Pudsey and Otley division of the W. Riding of Yorkshire as a Liberal in 1945. Elected for Portsmouth W. in Feb. 1950 and sat until 1966 when he was defeated. Unsuccessfully contested Portsmouth W. in 1970. C.B.E. 1943.*　　　[1966]

CLEAVER, Leonard Harry, J.P. Brook House, Church Lane, Lapworth, Solihull, Warwickshire. S. of Harry Cleaver, Esq., O.B.E. B. 27 Oct. 1909; m. 1938, Mary, d. of Hettie and Frank Hart Matthews. Educ. at Bilton Grange, and Rugby. Chartered Accountant. Secretary and Chief Accountant Chance Brothers Limited 1935-51. Director of A.W. Phillips Limited, Yoxalls Limited and Nuneaton Timber Company Limited; Partner, Heathcote and Coleman 1951-59; Treasurer Deritend Division Unionist Association 1945-48, and Yardley Division Unionist Association 1949-52, Chairman 1952-57. City Magistrate 1954. A Conservative. Elected for the Yardley division of Birmingham in 1959 and sat until he was defeated in 1964. Unsuccessfully contested the Yardley division of Birmingham in 1966. Parliamentary Private Secretary to F.V. Corfield, Parliamentary Secretary to Minister of Housing and Local Government 1963-64. Member of Birmingham City Council 1966-70. Member of Central Council of Probation and After-Care Committees for England and Wales 1966-73.*　　　[1964]

CLEGG, Sir Walter. Beech House, Raikes Road, Thornton, Lancashire. Carlton, and Garrick. S. of Edwin Clegg, Esq., Hotel Man-

ager. B. 18 Apr. 1920; m. 2 Apr. 1951, Elise Margaret, d. of J. Hargreaves, Esq. Educ. at Bury Grammar School, Arnold School, and Manchester University Law School. Articled to Town Clerk, Barrow-in-Furness 1937. Served R.A. 1939-46; commissioned 1940. Qualified as a Solicitor 1947, and had a partnership in practice. Lancashire County Councillor 1955-61. Chairman North Fylde Conservative Association 1965-66. Opposition Whip 1969-70. Lord Commissioner of the Treasury June 1970-Apr. 1972. Vice-Chairman Association Conservative Clubs 1968-71. Joint Honorary Secretary Conservative Parliamentary Housing and Local Government Committee 1967-69. Vice-Chamberlain of the Royal Household Apr. 1972-Dec. 1973. Comptroller of H.M. Household Dec. 1973-Mar. 1974. Opposition Whip Mar.-Oct. 1974. Elected to Executive 1922 Committee 1975; Treasurer 1922 Committee 1976. President Association of Conservative Clubs 1977. A Conservative. Unsuccessfully contested the Ince division of Lancashire 1959. Sat for the North Fylde division of Lancashire from Mar. 1966 Knighted 1980.*
[1979]

CLEMITSON, Ivor Malcolm. 49 Marlborough Road, Luton, Bedfordshire. S. of Daniel Malcolm Clemitson, Esq. B. 8 Dec. 1931; m. 15 Oct. 1960, Janet, d. of Ronald Meeke, Esq., (1 s. 1 d.). Educ. at Luton Grammar School, London School of Economics, and Bishop's Theological Coll., Cheshunt. Curate, St. Mary's, Sheffield 1958-61, Christ Church, Luton 1962-64. Industrial Chaplain, Diocese of St. Albans 1964-69 Director Singapore Industrial Mission 1969-70. Research Officer, National Graphical Association 1971-74. Parliamentary Private Secretary to Rt. Hon. Albert Booth, Secretary of State for Employment, 1976-78. A Labour Member. Sat for Luton E. from Feb. 1974 until 1979, when he was defeated.*
[1979]

CLIFFE, Michael. 63 Hatfield House, Golden Lane Estate, London. B. 1904; m. 1932, Sophia Whitesman. Worked in the clothing industry; member of executive of National Union of Tailors and Garment Workers. Member of Finsbury Borough Council 1949-64, Alderman 1953-64, Mayor 1956-57. A Labour Member. Elected for Shoreditch and Finsbury in Nov. 1958 and sat until his death on 9 Aug. 1964. [1964]

CLIFTON BROWN, Rt. Hon. Douglas. Speaker's House, Palace of Westminster, London. Ruffside Hall, Shotley Bridge, Co. Durham. Travellers', and Oxford & Cambridge. S. of Col. J. Clifton Brown, MP., of Holmbush, Faygate. B. 16 Aug. 1879; m. 24 June 1907, Violet Cicely Kathleen, d. of F. Wollaston, Esq., of Shenton Hall, Nuneaton. Educ. at Cheam, Eton, and Trinity Coll., Cambridge, M.A. Served in 1st Dragoon Guards and Northland. Hussars Yeomanry. Parliamentary Private Secretary to Rt. Hon. J.I. Macpherson, Minister of Pensions 1920-22. Dept. Chairman of Ways and Means Jan. 1943. Elected Speaker 9 Mar. 1943. PC. 1941. A Conservative. Unsuccessfully contested St. George-in-the-East Dec. 1910. Sat for the Hexham division of Northumberland from Dec. 1918-Nov. 1923, defeated Dec. 1923. Re-elected for Hexham in Oct. 1924 and sat until he retired in 1951. Elected Speaker 9 Mar. 1943 and served until he retired in 1951. Created Visct. Ruffside 1951. High Steward of Cambridge University 1951-58. Dept.-Lieut. for Co. Durham. Died 5 May 1958.
[1951]

CLIFTON-BROWN, Lieut.-Col. Geoffrey Benedict. 4 White Horse Street, London. Flempton Hall, Bury St. Edmunds. Cavalry. S. of Edward Clifton Brown, Esq. B. 25 July 1899; m. 1927, Robina, d. of Rowland Sutton, Esq. Educ. at Eton, and Royal Military Coll., Sandhurst. Lieut.-Col. 12th Royal Lancers. A Conservative. Elected for the Bury St. Edmunds division of Suffolk in July 1945 and sat until he retired in 1950.*
[1950]

CLITHEROW, Dr. Richard. 79 Underley Street, Edge Hill, Liverpool. S. of John Clitherow, Esq., of Liverpool. B. 18 Jan. 1902; m. 4 Feb. 1930, Gladys, d. of John Arber and Mrs. Florence Dix. Educ. at Liverpool Schools and University, M.R.C.S., L.R.C.P., L.M.S.S.A. A Registered Medical Practitioner and Registered Pharmacist (C.M.P.S.). Served with North West

Mounted Police, Canada 1919-22 and with Liverpool City Police Force until 1927. Pharmacist in U.S.A. and China 1927-30. Member of Liverpool City Council 1937-45 as a Conservative until he joined the Labour Party in 1943. A Labour Member. Elected for the Edge Hill division of Liverpool in July 1945 and sat until his death on 3 June 1947.
[1947]

CLUNIE, James. House of Commons, London. S. of James Clunie, Esq., of Lower Largo. B. 1889; m. 1912, Elizabeth Stewart (she died 1965). A House Painter and Decorator. Police Magistrate from 1948. Late member of Executive Scottish Painters' Society and Chairman of local Trades and Labour Council from 1926. Member of Dunfermline Town Council 1933-50. A Labour Member. Elected for Dunfermline in Feb. 1950 and sat until he retired in 1959. Died 25 Feb. 1974.
[1959]

CLUSE, William Sampson. 18 Horsenden Lane, South Perivale, Middlesex. S. of Sampson Bakewell Cluse, Esq., of Islington. B. 20 Dec. 1875; m. 26 July 1903, Alice Louise, d. of W. Warner, Esq. Educ. at Council School. A Compositor. Member of Islington Borough Council 1919-25. Parliamentary Private Secretary to F. Montague, Parliamentary Secretary to Ministry of Transport May 1940-May 1941, and when Parliamentary Secretary Ministry of Aircraft Production May 1941-Mar. 1942. A Labour Member. Sat for S. Islington from Dec. 1923 until 1931, when he was defeated; re-elected for S. Islington in 1935 and sat until he retired in 1950. Served with R.A.M.C. 1914-18. Died 8 Sept. 1955.
[1950]

CLYDE, Rt. Hon. James Latham McDiarmid, Q.C. House of Commons, London, 14 Heriot Row, Edinburgh. S. of Rt. Hon. J.A. Clyde, M.P. (Lord President of Court of Session-Lord Clyde). B. 30 Oct. 1898; m. Aug. 1928, Margaret Letitia, d. of A.E. Du Buisson, Esq., of Hartley Wintney, Hampshire (she died 1974). Educ. at Edinburgh Academy, Trinity Coll., Oxford, and University of Edinburgh. Member of Scottish Bar 1924; K.C. 1936. A Unionist Member. Unsuccessfully contested Mid-

lothian S. and Peebles in 1945. Elected for N. Edinburgh in 1950 and sat until he was appointed Lord President of the Court of Session Dec. 1954. PC. 1951. Lord Advocate for Scotland Nov. 1951-Dec. 1954. Lord President of the Court of Session, with the judicial title of Lord Clyde, 1954-72. Dept. Lieut. for County of Kinross. Died 30 June 1975.
[1954]

COBB, Frederick Arthur. 40 Bloomsbury Street, London. S. of Frederick Cobb, Esq. B. 11 Feb. 1901. Educ. at Elementary School in Winchester. Late B.B.C. Engineer; Assistant Chief Engineer, Indian Broadcasting Company; Managing Director Electronic Tubes Limited. Served in the Merchant Navy 1918. A Labour Member. Elected for the Elland division of the W. Riding of Yorkshire in July 1945 and for Brighouse and Spenborough in Feb. 1950. Sat until his death on 27 Mar. 1950.
[1950]

COCKCROFT, John Hoyle. House of Commons, London. S. of Lionel Fielden Cockcroft, Esq. B. 6 July 1934; m. 29 Oct. 1971, Tessa Fay Shepley, (2 d.). Educ. at Oundle, and St. John's, Cambridge. President Cambridge Union 1958. Feature Writer, *Financial Times* 1959-61. Economic Advisor G.K.N. 1962-67. Seconded Treasury 1965-66. Economic Leader Writer, *Daily Telegraph* 1967-74. Economist with Duff Stoop & Co., stockbrokers from 1978. Director of RSJ Aviation from 1979. Author of *Why England Sleeps.* A Conservative. Sat for Nantwich from Feb. 1974. until he retired in 1979.*
[1979]

COCKERAM, Eric Paul, J.P. Woodstock, Burrell Road, Birkenhead, Cheshire. 15 Montpelier Square, London. S. of John W. Cockeram, Esq. B. 4 July 1924; m. 2 July 1949, Frances, youngest d. of Herbert Irving, Esq. Educ. at The Leys School, Cambridge. Chairman Watson Prickard Limited. J.P. of Liverpool 1960. President Men's Wear Association of Britain 1964-65; member Liverpool N.H.S. Executive Council 1958-70, Chairman 1969-70. Member of the Board of Governors, United Liverpool Hospitals 1965-74. Parliamentary Private Secretary to Sir John Eden, Minister for Industry 1971-72, and Minister of Posts and Telecommunications 1972. Parliamentary Private Secretary to Rt. Hon. Anthony Barber, Chancellor of the Exchequer 1972-74. Member Select Committee Corporation Tax 1972. A Conservative. Elected for Bebington in June 1970 and sat until Feb. 1974 when he unsuccessfully contested Bebington and Ellesmere Port. Unsuccessfully contested Bebington and Ellesmere Port again in Oct. 1974. Elected for the Ludlow division of Shropshire in 1979. Served with Gloucestershire Regiment 1942-46, Capt.*   [1974]

COCKS, Frederick Seymour, C.B.E. 8 Wykeham Mansions, Rosendale Road, London. S. of Frederick Augustus Cocks, Esq., Inspector of Machinery, R.N. of Plymouth, and Lucy Matilda, d. of Edwin Marcus Letcher, Esq., of Cinderford, Gloucestershire. B. 25 Oct. 1882; m. 1907, Hilda, d. of Charles Derry, Esq., of Plymouth, (1 s. 1 d.). Educ. at Plymouth Coll. An Author and Journalist. During First World War was London Secretary of the Union of Democratic Control and an official of the London Council for the Prevention of War. Member of Joint Select Committee on Indian Constitutional Reform 1933-34. Member of Select Committee on Parliamentary Procedure 1945-46; Chairman of Foreign Affairs Group of Parliamentary Labour Party 1945-47; led Parliamentary Delegation to Greece 1946; member of Parliamentary Delegation to Italy 1949, and of British Delegation to Consultative Assembly of Council of Europe 1949. C.B.E. 1950. A Labour Member. Unsuccessfully contested Maidstone in 1923 and 1924. Sat for the Broxtowe division of Nottinghamshire from May 1929 until his death on 29 May 1953.   [1953]

COCKS, Rt. Hon. Michael Francis Lovell. House of Commons, London. S. of Dr. H.F. Lovell Cocks. B. 19 Aug. 1929; m. 1954, Janet Macfarlane, (2 s. 2 d.). Educ. at Bristol University. President Bristol Borough Labour Party 1961-63. A Lecturer. Opposition Whip 1973-74. Assistant Government Whip Mar.-June 1974. Lord Commissioner of the Treasury June 1974-Apr. 1976. Parliamentary Secretary to H.M. Treasury (Chief Whip) Apr. 1976-May 1979. PC. 1976.

Opposition Chief Whip from 1979. A Labour Member. Unsuccessfully contested S. Gloucestershire in 1964 and 1966 and Bristol W. in 1959. Sat for Bristol S. from June 1970.*   [1979]

COE, Denis Walter. House of Commons, London. S. of James Coe, Esq., retired Schoolmaster. B. 5 June 1929; m. 15 Aug. 1953, Margaret Rae, d. of W. Chambers, Esq. Educ. at Tynemouth Grammar School, Bede Training Coll., Durham, and London School of Economics. Teachers Certificate 1952; B.Sc. (Econ.) 1960; M.Sc. (Econ.) 1966. Junior School Teacher 1952-54; Secondary School Teacher 1954-59. Dept. Headmaster 1959-61. Lecturer in Government at Manchester Coll. of Commerce 1961-66. A Labour Member. Unsuccessfully contested Macclesfield in the 1964 general election. Elected for the Middleton and Prestwich division of Lancashire in Mar. 1966 and sat until he was defeated in 1970. Parliamentary Private Secretary to David Ennals, Minister of State, Department of Health and Social Security 1968-70. Dean of Students, N.E. London Polytechnic 1970-74. Assistant Director of Middlesex Polytechnic from 1974. Chairman of National Bureau for Handicapped Students from 1975.*   [1970]

COHEN, Stanley. 164 Halton Ring Road, Leeds 15. S. of Thomas Cohen, Esq. B. 31 July 1927; m. 7 Aug. 1954, Brenda, d. of Alderman John Rafferty. Educ. at St. Patricks and St. Charles Elementary Schools, Leeds. Employed in the Clothing Industry 1941-45 and 1947-51. Served in the Royal Navy 1945-47. Employed in British Railways Estate Department 1951-70. Labour Parliamentary candidate in Barkston Ash County Constituency 1966; member of Leeds City Council from 1952; elected Alderman 1968; member of Duke of Edinburgh's Commonwealth Study Conference. Australia 1968; Parliamentary Private Secretary to Harold Walker, Minister of State for Employment 1976; Parliamentary Private Secretary to Gordon Oakes, Minister of State, Education 1977. A Labour Member. Sat for the S.E. division of Leeds from June 1970.*   [1979]

COLDRICK, William. 52 The Crescent, Sea Mills, Bristol. S. of Thomas Coldrick, Esq., of Abersychan. B. 19 Feb. 1894; m. Jessie, d. of James Ivory, Esq. Educ. at London Labour Coll. Organiser and Lecturer for National Council of Labour Coll.; Member of Monmouthshire County Council 1924-27. Chairman of National Committee of Co-operative Party until 1955; member of National Council of Labour. A Labour and Co-operative Member. Sat for Bristol N. from July 1945-Feb. 1950. Elected for Bristol N.E. in Feb 1950 and sat until he was defeated in 1959. Assistant Whip 1946-47. Sheriff of City and County of Bristol 1964. Died 15 Sept. 1975. [1959]

COLE, Norman John, V.R.D. House of Commons, London. S. of Walter John Cole., Esq. B. 1909, m. 1935 Margaret Grace, d. of Arthur Potter, Esq., of Buxton, Derbyshire (1 s. 1 d.). Educ. at St. John's Coll., Southsea. Enrolled with R.N.V.R. 1934; served as a Lieut. and Lieut. Commander R.N.V.R. with Royal Navy 1939-46, retired 1954. Member of Potters Bar Urban District Council 1947-48. A Conservative. Unsuccessfully contested Southall in 1950. Elected for Bedfordshire S. in Oct. 1951 and sat until he was defeated in 1966. Died 22 Jan. 1979. [1966]

COLE, Thomas Loftus. Elmfield House, Whiwell, Belfast. B. 1877. Educ. at Sullivan Upper School, Holywood. A Pharmaceutical Chemist and Estate Agent. Member of Lurgan Urban District Council 1911-17. Councillor of Belfast Corporation 1931-43, Dept. Lord Mayor 1937-39, Alderman 1943-61. An Ulster Unionist Member. Elected for Belfast E. in July 1945 and sat until he retired in 1950. Member of N. Ireland Parliament for Belfast Dock 1949-53. C.B.E. 1958. Died 7 Mar. 1961. [1950]

COLEGATE, Sir (William) Arthur. Artillery Mansions, Victoria Street, London. Hillgrove, Bembridge, Isle of Wight. Carlton. S. of Robert Colegate, Esq., of Sutton, Surrey. B. about 1884; m. 22 Nov. 1917, Winifred Mary, d. of Sir William Worsley, 3rd Bart., and widow of Capt. Francis PC. Pemberton, 2nd Life Guards (she died 1955).

Educ. at University Coll., London. Chairman of the Wright Saddle Company Limited, and Director of other companies. President of the Rural District Councils Association. Chairman of Industrial Property Committee of the International Chamber of Commerce Committee 1925-29; Vice-President of West Midland Conservative and Unionist Associations. Knight Bach. 1955. A Conservative. Unsuccessfully contested the Sowerby division of the W. Riding of Yorkshire in 1929. Prospective candidate for the Bassetlaw division of Nottinghamshire 1936-40. Sat for the Wrekin division from Sept. 1941-July 1945, when he was defeated. Elected for the Burton division of Staffordshire in 1950 and sat until he retired in 1955. Director of Brunner Mond and Company to 1927. Died 10 Sept. 1956. [1955]

COLEMAN, Donald Richard, C.B.E. Penderyn, 18 Penywern Road, Bryncoch, Neath, Glamorganshire. S. of Albert Archer Coleman, Esq. B. 19 Sept. 1925; m. 1st 1949, Phyllis Eileen William (1 s.) (she died 1963); 2ndly, Jan. 1966, Margaret Elizabeth Morgan, (1 d.). Educ. at Cadoxton Boys' School, Barry, Glamorgan, and Cardiff Technical Coll. A Metallurgist. Joined the Labour Party in Nov. 1948. Member of the Iron and steel Trades Confederation. Appointed Justice of the Peace for Swansea County Borough 1962. Assistant Opposition Whip July 1970-Mar. 1974. Lord Commissioner of the Treasury Mar. 1974-July 1978. Vice-Chamberlain, Royal Household July 1978-May 1979. A Labour Member. Sat for the Neath division of Glamorganshire from Oct. 1964. Former tenor soloist with Welsh National Opera. Parliamentary Private Secretary to Rt. Hon. George Thomas, Secretary of State for Wales 1968-70. C.B.E. 1979. Opposition Whip from 1979.* [1979]

COLLARD, Richard Charles Marler, D.S.O., D.F.C. 31 Lincoln House, Basil Street, London. Royal Automobile, and Royal Aero. S. of Charles John Collard, Esq., Stockbroker. B. 25 Aug. 1911; m. 1st 1938, Suzette, d. of Alfred W. White, Esq., of Spalding (she died 1958); 2ndly, 1961, Joan Putt. Educ. at Haileybury Coll. Commissioned service in R.A.F. 1930-53, retired at own request 1953. D.F.C. 1941, D.S.O. 1942. Retired from R.A.F. at rank of Group Capt. Joined Handley Page Limited, and became a Director in 1958. A Conservative and National Liberal Member. Elected for Central Norfolk in 1959 and sat until his death on 9 Aug. 1962. Died 9 Aug. 1962.   [1962]

COLLICK, Percy Henry. 142 Hendon Way, London. B. 1897. Assistant Gen. Secretary of Associated Society of Locomotive Engineers 1940-57. Member of General Purposes Committee T.U.C. 1930-34. Served in France 1914-18. Joint Parliamentary Secretary Ministry of Agriculture Sept. 1945-Oct. 1947. Member of Executive Committee of Labour Party 1943-44; member of Council of Royal Coll. of Veterinary Surgeons 1949-53. A Labour Member. Unsuccessfully contested Reigate as a Labour candidate in 1929 and 1931. Sat for W. Birkenhead from July 1945-50. Elected for Birkenhead in Feb. 1950 and sat until he retired in 1964.*   [1964]

COLLINDRIDGE, Frank. 14 Hemingfield Road, Wombwell, Barnsley. S. of John Collindridge, Esq. B. 1891; m. 1918, Rebecca, d. of J. Debney, Esq. A Miner. Member of Miners Federation of Great Britain; a delegate to U.S.S.R.1937 and to Australia and New Zealand 1944. Member of Wombwell Urban District Council 1920-39, Chairman 1931-32. Parliamentary Private Secretary to D.R. Grenfell, Secretary for Mines 1941-June 1942. A Lord Commissioner of The Treasury Aug. 1945-Dec. 1946. Comptroller of H.M. Household Dec. 1946-Oct. 1951. A Labour Member. Elected for Barnsley in June 1938 and sat until his death on 16 Oct. 1951 during the campaign for the general election at which he was a candidate. C.B.E. 1950. Died 16 Oct. 1951.   [1951]

COLLINS, Victor John, O.B.E. Cobham Lodge, Leigh Hill Road, Cobham, Surrey. 65-67 Kingsland Road, London. S. of Victor Collins, Esq., Manufacturer. B. 1 July 1903; m. 30 Apr. 1929, Mary, d. of T.E. Savage, Esq., of Wellington, Shropshire. Educ. at Regent Street Polytechnic, and London University. President Employers' Federation of Cane and Willow Workers' Associations 1932;

Chairman of National Basket and Willow Trades Advisory Committee 1942-64; O.B.E. 1946. Chairman Mental Health Committee of S.W. Regional Hospital Board 1950-54. A Labour Member. Sat for the Taunton division of Somerset from 1945-50 when he was defeated. Unsuccessfully contested Taunton in 1951. Elected for Shoreditch and Finsbury in Oct. 1954 and sat until July 1958 when he was created Baron Stonham (Life Peerage). Chairman of Standing Joint Council on Inland Transport 1962-64. President of Prison Reform Council. Under-Secretary at Home Office Oct. 1964-Aug. 1967. Minister of State, Home Office Aug. 1967-Oct. 1969. PC. 1969. Chairman of National Society for Mentally Handicapped Children 1963-64. Chairman of Advisory Council on Probation and After-Care 1970-71. Died 22 Dec. 1971.   [1958]

COLMAN, Grace Mary. 3 Avis Court, 50 Ladbroke Grove, London. 5 Kitchener Terrace, North Shields, Northumberland. D. of Canon F.S. Colman, Rector of Hanbury. B. 1892. Educ. at Newnham Coll., Cambridge, M.A. J.P. A Labour Member. Unsuccessfully contested the Hythe division in 1929 and 1931 and the Hallam division of Sheffield in 1935. Elected for Tynemouth in July 1945 and sat until she was defeated in 1950. Unsuccessfully contested Tynemouth in 1951. Tutor at Ruskin Coll. and Staff Tutor of London University. Died 7 July 1971.   [1950]

COLQUHOUN, Maureen Morfydd. House of Commons, London. B. Aug. 1928; m. 1949 Keith Colquhoun Esq. (divorced 1979). Educ. at Convent, Eastbourne, Brighton, and London School of Economics. Member of N.U.G.M.W. W. Sussex County Council 1975, member of Shoreham Council 1965-74, Adur District Council from 1973. A Labour Member. Unsuccessfully contested Tonbridge in 1970. Sat for Northampton N. from Feb. 1974 until 1979, when she was defeated.*   [1979]

COMYNS, Dr. Louis. 16 Hermit Road, Canning Town, London. B. in Glasgow 17 Aug. 1904; m. 1933. Local Doctor from 1932. Chairman West Ham (No. 9) Hospital

Management Committee; member of N.E. Metropolitan Regional Hospital Board and of Board of Governors Hammersmith, W. London and St. Mark's Hospitals. A Labour Member. Elected for the Silvertown division of West Ham in July 1945 and sat until he retired in 1950. L.R.C.P., L.R.C.S. (Edinburgh). Member of West Ham Borough Council, Alderman from 1954. Died 10 Feb. 1962. [1950]

CONANT, Maj. Sir Roger John Edward, Bart., C.V.O. 14a North Court, Great Peter Street, London. Lyndon Hall, Oakham. Carlton. S. of E.W.P. Conant, Esq., of Lyndon Hall, Oakham. B. 28 May 1899; m. 1st 9 Nov. 1920, Daphne, d. of A.E. Learoyd, Esq. (divorced), 2ndly 1972 Mrs. Mary Buchanan. Educ. at Eton, and Royal Military Coll., Sandhurst. Maj. Grenadier Guards. Conservative Whip 1946-51. Comptroller of the Household Nov. 1951-June 1954. Created 1st Bart. 1954. Parliamentary Private Secretary to Lord Stanley, Under-Secretary for India and Secretary of State for the Dominions 1938, to Sir John Simon, Chancellor of Exchequer 1939-40 and to R.S. Hudson, Minister of Agriculture 1943-45. C.V.O. 1953. A Conservative. Unsuccessfully contested Chesterfield in 1929. Sat for Chesterfield from 1931-35 when he was defeated and for Bewdley from June 1937-Feb. 1950. Elected for the Rutland and Stamford division of Lincolnshire in Feb. 1950 and sat until he retired in 1959. Died 30 Mar. 1973. [1959]

CONCANNON, Rt. Hon. John Dennis ('Don'). 69 Skegby Lane, Mansfield, Nottinghamshire. S. of James Dennis Concannon, Esq., Miner. B. 16 May 1930; m. 20 June 1953, Iris, d. of C. Wilson, Esq., (2 s. 2 d.). Educ. at Rossington Secondary School, and W.E.A. Served in Coldstream Guards 1947-53. Official of National Union of Mineworkers 1960-66. Member of Mansfield Borough Council 1962-66. Assistant Government Whip 1968-70; Opposition Whip 1970-74; Vice-Chamberlain H.M. Household Mar.-June 1974; Under-Secretary of State, Northern Ireland Office June 1974-Apr. 1976. Minister of State, Northern Ireland Office Apr. 1976-May 1979. PC. 1978. An

Opposition spokesman on Defence from 1979. A Labour Member. Sat for the Mansfield division of Nottinghamshire from Mar. 1966.* [1979]

CONLAN, Bernard. 33 Beccles Road, Sale, Cheshire. B. 24 Oct. 1923. Educ. at Manchester Primary and Secondary Schools. A Roman Catholic. City Councillor in Manchester from 1954 to 1966. An Engineer. Joined the Labour Party in 1942. Member of the A.E.U. from 1940 and Officer from 1943. A Labour Member. Unsuccessfully contested High Peak in 1959. Sat for Gateshead E. from Oct. 1964.* [1979]

COOK, Robert Finlayson. House of Commons, London. S. of Peter Cook, Esq. B. 28 Feb. 1946; m. 15 Sept. 1969, Margaret Whitmore, (2 s.). Educ. at Aberdeen Grammar School, Edinburgh Royal High School and University of Edinburgh. Tutor-Organiser with W.E.A. 1970-74. Member of Edinburgh Town Council 1971-74. Chairman Edinburgh Housing Committee 1973-74. A Labour Member. Unsuccessfully contested Edinburgh N. in 1970. Sat for the Central division of Edinburgh from Feb. 1974.* [1979]

COOK, Thomas Fotheringham. 13 Wardlaw Drive, Rutherglen, Glasgow. S. of Charles Cook, Esq., and Mary Fotheringham. B. 7 June 1908; m. 1929, Elizabeth Wallace. Educ. at Glasgow. An Electrician. Parliamentary Private Secretary to Rt. Hon. J.H. Wilson, President of Board of Trade 1947-50. Parliamentary Under-Secretary Colonial Office 1950-51. A Labour Member. Sat for Dundee from July 1945-50. Elected for E. Dundee in Feb. 1950 and sat until his death in a car accident on 31 May 1952. Lecturer in Economics for National Council of Labour Colleges. Died 31 May 1952. [1952]

COOKE, Robert Gordon. Athelhampton, Dorset. Carlton, Garrick, Pratt's, and M.C.C. Eld. s. of Robert V. Cooke, Esq., Ch.M., M.D., F.R.C.S. B. 29 May 1930; m. 30 July 1966, Jenifer P.E. King, d. of E.M. King, Esq., MP., (1 s. 1 d.). Educ. at Harrow, and Christ Church, Oxford. Member Bristol

City Council 1954-57. Parliamentary Private Secretary to David Renton, Under-Secretary of State, Home Office 1958-59; to Sir Derek Walker-Smith, Minister of Health 1959-60; to Lord John Hope, Minister of Works 1960-62. Foreign Leader Guest of State Department in U.S.A. Jan.-Mar. 1961. Introduced Fatal Accidents Act 1959, Historic Buildings Bill 1963. Member Mr. Speaker's Committee on Accommodation in Palace of Westminster 1960; Select Committee Palace of Westminster 1964; House of Commons Services Committee 1967. Chairman Administration Committee 1974. Chairman Conservative Arts and Heritage Committee. Vice-Chairman Conservative Media Committee 1976. Vice-Chairman Countryside Conservation Committee 1977. Director of Westward Television. Historic Houses Committee British Tourist Authority. Trustee Primrose League. Member Historic Buildings Council for England 1975. Knighted June 1979. Special Adviser to Secretary of State for the Environment on the Palace of Westminster from Dec. 1979. Member Select Committee on Wealth Tax (Chairman for National Heritage). Clerk Athelhampton Parish Meeting. A Conservative. Unsuccessfully contested S.E. division of Bristol in 1955. Sat for W. Bristol from Mar. 1957 until he retired in 1979.* [1979]

COOKE, Roger Gresham, C.B.E. Flat No. 36, 35 Buckingham Gate, London. Turgis Court, Stratfield Turgis, Basingstoke, Hampshire. R.A.C., and Carlton. S. of Arthur Cooke, Esq., F.R.C.S., of Cambridge. B. 26 Jan. 1907; m. 1 Sept. 1934, Anne, d. of Hugh Pinckney, Esq., C.B.E. Educ. at Winchester and New Coll., Oxford, and Trinity Coll., Cambridge. Barrister-at-Law, Inner Temple, 1930; Secretary British Road Federation 1935-38, of United Steel Company Limited 1938-46; Director Society of Motor Manufacturers and Traders 1946-55, and of Rootes Motors Overseas Limited 1955-67, and The Kerry Group Limited (Dept. Chairman). Dept.-Chairman of Wider Share Ownership Council 1950-68. President Institute of Road Transport Engineers 1962-64. Maj. Home Guard 1940-44; C.B.E. 1953; Chairman Wentworth, York Conservative Association 1945-46. Joint Secretary Conservative Parlia-

mentary Transport Committee 1955-58, Joint Chairman Conservative Parliamentary Transport Committee 1961. Parliamentary Private Secretary to Nigel Birch, Economic Secretary to Treasury 1957-58. Delegate, Council of Europe and W.E.U. 1963-65. A Manager, Royal Institution. President River Thames Society. A Conservative. Elected for Twickenham in Jan. 1955 and sat until his death on 22 Feb. 1970. Died 22 Feb. 1970. [1969]

COOMBS, Derek Michael. 14 Chester Street, London. Shottery Grange, Shottery, Stratford-on-Avon. S. of Clifford Coombs, Esq. B. 12 Aug. 1931; m. 1959, Patricia, d. of Patrick O'Toole, Esq. Educ. at Rydal School, and Bromsgrove. Director S. and U. Stores Limited 1960; Joint Managing Director S. and U. Stores Limited and 24 subsidiaries Mar. 1970-76, Chairman from 1976. A Conservative. Elected for the Yardley division of Birmingham in June 1970 and sat until Feb. 1974 when he was defeated. Unsuccessfully contested the Yardley division of Birmingham in Oct. 1974. Chairman of Hardanger Properties Limited and Bressel Properties Limited from 1976.* [1974]

COOPER, Albert Edward, M.B.E. House of Commons, London. S. of Albert Frederick Smith Cooper, Esq., Manufacturer. B. 23 Sept. 1910; m. 7 Sept. 1933, Emily Muriel, d. of William J. Nelder, Esq. Educ. in Australia and New Zealand. Served with R.A.F., demobilised with rank of Squadron Leader. Member of Ilford Borough Council 1935-52, Alderman 1947-52. Parliamentary Private Secretary to Rt. Hon. Peter Thorneycroft, President of Board of Trade 1953. Member Ilford Borough Council 1935-52. M.B.E. 1946. A Conservative. Unsuccessfully contested Dagenham in 1945. Sat for Ilford S. from 1950-66 when he was defeated and from June 1970 to Feb. 1974 when he unsuccessfully contested the Ilford S. division of Redbridge. Managing Director of Dispersions Limited.* [1974]

COOPER, Wing-Commander Geoffrey. 4 Morland Avenue, Leicester. S. of Albert Cooper, Esq. B. 18 Feb. 1907; m. 1951, Mrs. Tottie Resch, of Jersey. Educ. at

Wyggeston Grammar School, Leicester, and Royal Grammar School, Worcester. A.A.F. 1933. R.A.F. 1939-45; Pilot in Fighter Command 1939-40, Coastal Command 1943-45. Superintendent British Overseas Airways Corporation 1941-43. A Labour Member. Elected for Middlesbrough W. in July 1945 and sat until he retired in 1951. Emigrated to Bahamas. President of Raydel Limited, Estate Developers Limited, and Land Title Clearance Limited.* [1951]

COOPER, John. 11 Langley Avenue, Surbiton. S. of John Ainsworth Cooper, Esq., a Bricklayer. B. 7 June 1908; m. 1st, 11 Aug. 1934, Nelly Spencer (divorced 1969); 2ndly, 1969, Mrs. Joan Rogers. Educ. at Stockton Heath Council School, and Lymm Grammar School. A Trade Union Officer from 1928. Member for Manchester City Council 1936-42, of Metropolitan Water Board and of London County Council 1949-54, Alderman 1952-54. Parliamentary Private Secretary to Rt. Hon. Patrick Gordon Walker, Commonwealth Relations Secretary 1950-51. A Labour Member. Elected for Deptford in Feb. 1950 and sat until he retired in 1951. Member of National Executive Committee of Labour Party 1953-57, of T.U.C. General Council 1959-73, President of T.U.C. 1970-71. Created Baron Cooper of Stockton Heath (Life Peerage) 1966. Chairman of British Productivity Council 1965-66. Member of Thames Conservancy 1955-74. Secretary of Southern District of National Union of General and Municipal Workers 1944-61, Gen. Secretary and Treasurer of the Union 1962-73. Member of National Water Council 1973-77.* [1951]

COOPER-KEY, Sir Edmund McNeill ('Neill'). House of Commons, London. S. of Capt. E. Cooper-Key, C.B., M.V.O., R.N. B. 26 Apr. 1907; m. 11 Jan. 1941, Hon. Lorna Harmsworth, d. of 2nd Visct. Rothermere. Educ. at Royal Naval Coll., Dartmouth. Director of Associated Newspapers Limited 1944-72. Served with Irish Guards 1939-45. Director London and Aberdeen Investment Trust; Price Brothers (Canada). Chairman Transport Group (Holdings) Limited; Chairman Parliamentary Tourist and Resort Committee 1954-64. Member Committee of Management, R.N.L.I. 1957-67. Knighted 1960. A Conservative. Elected for Hastings in July 1945 and sat until he retired in 1970.* [1970]

COPE, John Ambrose. Bluegates, Berkeley, Gloucestershire. St. Stephen's, and Tudor House, Chipping Sodbury. S. of George Cope, Esq., M.C., F.R.I.B.A. B. 13 May 1937; m. 29 Mar. 1969, Djemila Payne, (2 d.). Educ. at Oakham School, Rutland. National Service (Commissioned R.A.) 1955-57. Chartered Accountant. Conservative Research Department, Westminster 1965-67. Assistant to Anthony Barber, Chairman Conservative Party 1967-70. Special Assistant Secretary of State at Department of Trade and Industry 1972-74. Assistant Government Whip from May 1979. Secretary Parliamentary Group for Concorde. Vice-Chairman Conservative Parliamentary Smaller Businesses Committee. Secretary Conservative Parliamentary Finance Committee. A Conservative. Unsuccessfully contested Woolwich E. in 1970. Sat for Gloucestershire S. from Feb. 1974.* [1979]

CORBET, Freda Künzlen. House of Commons, London. D. of James Mansell Esq. B. 1900; m. 1st, 1925, William, s. of William Corbet, Esq. (he died 1957); 2ndly 1962, Ian Campbell, Esq., (he died 1976). Educ. at Wimbledon County School, and University Coll., London. Barrister-at-Law, Inner Temple, 1932. Member of London County Council 1934-65. J.P. for County of London 1940. A Labour Member. Voted in favour of entry into E.E.C. 28 Oct. 1971. Unsuccessfully contested Lewisham E. in 1935. Sat for N.W. Camberwell from 1945-50. Elected for the Peckham division of Camberwell in 1950 and sat until she retired in Feb. 1974.* [1974]

CORBETT, Robin. 96 Piccotts End, Hemel Hempstead, Hertfordshire. S. of Thomas Corbett, Esq., Foundry Worker. B. 22 Dec. 1933; m. May 1970, Val Hudson, d. of Mr. and Mrs. Fred Jonas, of Cape Town. Educ. at Holly Lodge Grammar School, Staffordshire. A Newspaper and Magazine Journalist. Political Correspondent. Assistant Editor *Farmers Weekly* 1969. Senior Labour Adviser IPC

Magazines Limited 1972-74. Member National Executive Council, National Union of Journalists 1964-69. A Labour Member. Unsuccessfully contested Hemel Hempstead in 1966 and Feb. 1974 and W. Derbyshire in Nov. 1967. Sat for Hemel Hempstead, Hertfordshire from Oct. 1974 until 1979, when he was defeated.* [1979]

CORBETT, Lieut.-Col. Uvedale, D.S.O. Ox House, Shobdon, Leominster. Army & Navy. S. of Maj. C.U. Corbett, D.S.O. B. 12 Sept. 1909; m. 1st 1935, Veronica Marian, d. of Capt. L.D. Whitehead (divorced 1952); 2ndly, 1953 Mrs. Patricia Jane Walker. Educ. at Wellington, and Royal Military Academy, Woolwich. Served with Royal Artillery 1929-45. D.S.O. 1944. A Conservative. Elected for the Ludlow division of Shropshire in July 1945 and sat until he retired in 1951. Chairman of Sun Valley Poultry Limited from 1961.* [1951]

CORDEAUX, Lieut.-Col. John Kyme, C.B.E. 9 Strathray House, 30 Marylebone High Street, London. 1B Burns Street, Nottingham. M.C.C. S. of Col. E.K. Cordeaux, C.B.E. B. 23 July 1902; m. 1st, 1928, Norah Cleland, (2 s.) (marriage dissolved in 1953); 2ndly, 1953, Mildred Jessie Upcher. Educ. at Royal Naval Coll., Osborne and Dartmouth. Served R.N. 1916-23, transferred to R.M. (Lieut.) 1923; Staff Col. 1937; Naval Intelligence Division 1939-42; Maj. 1940; Acting Lieut.-Col. 1941; Temporary Col. 1942; Seconded to Foreign Office 1942-46; Lieut.-Col. 1946. Commander Order of Orange-Nassau (Netherlands) 1944, of Order of Dannebrog (Denmark) 1945, Haakon VII Liberty Cross (Norway) 1946; C.B.E. 1946. A Conservative. Unsuccessfully contested the Bolsover division of Derbyshire in 1950 and 1951. Prospective Conservative candidate for N. Norfolk 1952-53. Elected for Nottingham Central in 1955 and sat until 1964 when he was defeated.* [1964]

CORDLE, John Howard. Malmesbury House, The Close, Salisbury, Wiltshire. Carlton, National, English Speaking Union, and Royal Commonwealth Society. S. of Ernest William Cordle, Esq., retired. B. 11 Oct. 1912; m. 1st, 1938 (divorced 1956);

2ndly, 1957, Venetia Carolyn, d. of Col. Alister Maynard (divorced 1971). Educ. at City of London School. Served in R.A.F. as Flight Lieut. 1940-45. Member of Lloyds 1952. Member of the Archbishop of Canterbury's Commission on Evangelism 1945-46; member of Church Assembly 1946-53; Life Gov. St. Paul's and St. Mary's Coll., Cheltenham, and Epsom Coll. Member of the Founders Livery Company. Freeman of the City of London. Awarded Africa Star 1964. Member Court of Southampton University. Member Council of Europe, Strasbourg and U.K. Members Delegation to West Europe Union, Paris 1974-77. Chairman Anglo-Libyan Group, House of Commons Chairman West Africa Committee Commonwealth Conservative Council. A Conservative. Prospective candidate for N.E. Wolverhampton 1949. Unsuccessfully contested The Wrekin in 1951. Sat for Bournemouth E. and Christchurch from 1959 to Feb. 1974 and for Bournemouth E. from Feb. 1974 until July 1977, when he resigned after being criticised for contempt of the House as a result of his business links with John Poulson. Managing Director of E.W. Cordle & Son Limited 1946-68, Chairman from 1968.* [1977]

CORFIELD, Rt. Hon. Sir Frederick Vernon, Q.C. 9 Randolph Mews, London. Wordings Orchard, Sheepscombe, Stroud, Gloucestershire. United Service, and Royal Aero. S. of Brigadier F.A. Corfield, D.S.O., O.B.E. B. 1 June 1915; m. 1945, Elizabeth Mary Ruth, d. of E.C. Taylor, Esq., J.P. Educ. at Cheltenham Coll., and Royal Military Academy, Woolwich. Commissioned R.A. 1935; Field Artillery, India 1935-39, 3rd and 51st (H.) Division 1939 (despatches); P.O.W. 1940-45. Called to the bar by Middle Temple 1945; J.A.G.'s Branch at W.O. 1945-46. Retired 1946. Farmed until 1956; returned to the bar Oct. 1956. Parliamentary Private Secretary to R. Nugent and A. Neave, Parliamentary Secretaries Ministry of Transport Feb. 1957-Apr. 1958. Parliamentary Secretary Ministry of Housing and Local Government July 1962-Oct. 1964. Minister of State, Board of Trade June 1970-Oct. 1970. Minister of Aviation Supply Oct. 1970-Apr. 1971. Minister for Aerospace Apr. 1971-Apr. 1972. PC. 1970. A Conservative. Elected for S. Gloucestershire in 1955 and sat until he retired in Feb. 1974. Opposition spokesman on Land and Natural Resources 1964-65, on Trade 1966-67 and on Aviation 1967-70. Knighted 1972. Q.C. 1972. Member of British Waterways Board from 1974, Vice-Chairman from 1980. Chairman of London and Provincial Antique Dealers Association from 1975. Author of legal works on land and compensation. A Recorder of the Crown Court from 1979. Master of the Bench, Middle Temple 1980.* [1974]

CORLETT, John. 169 Hull Road, York. B. 1884; m. (she died 1961). Educ. at London University, B.Sc., Ph.D. Divisional Organiser of N.U.T. An Authority on Education and Economics. A Labour Member. Unsuccessfully contested the Stretford division of Lancashire in 1923. Elected for York in July 1945 and sat until he retired in 1950. J.P. for York. Died 18 Jan. 1968. [1950]

CORMACK, Patrick Thomas. The Cottage, Enville, Nr. Stourbridge, Staffordshire. Athenaeum. S. of Thomas C. Cormack, Esq., Local Government Officer. B. 18 May 1939; m. 18 Aug. 1967, Kathleen Mary, d. of W.E. Macdonald, Esq., of Grimsby, (2 s.). Educ. at Havelock School, Grimsby, and University of Hull. Second Master at St. James' Choir School, Grimsby 1961-66. Training and Education Officer, Ross Group Limited 1966-67. Assistant Housemaster Wrekin Coll., Shropshire 1967-69. Head of History, Brewood Grammar School, Staffordshire 1969-70. Member of Council of Historical Association 1963-66. Member of Grants Committee of Historic Churches Preservation Trust. Parliamentary Private Secretary to Michael Alison and Paul Dean, Joint Parliamentary Secretaries, Department of Health and Social Security 1970-73. Chairman All-Party Parliamentary Committee for Soviet Jews 1971-74. Chairman All-Party Committee for Widows and Single Parent Families Mar. 1974-77; Secretary All-Party Committee for the Heritage. Publication *Heritage in Danger* 1976. Associate Editor *Time and Tide* 1977. Elected Fellow of Society of Antiquaries 1978. A Conservative. Unsuccessfully contested Bolsover in 1964 and Grimsby in 1966. Sat for the Cannock division of

Staffordshire from 1970 to Feb. 1974 and for Staffordshire S.W. from Feb. 1974.* [1979]

CORRIE, John Alexander. Park of Tongland, Kirkcudbright. Carlung Farm, West Kilbride. 3 Morpeth Terrace, London. Beefsteak. S. of Jack Corrie, Esq. B. 29 July 1935; m. 25 Aug. 1965, Jean Sandra, d. of G.G. Haride, Esq., (2 d.). Educ. at Kirkcudbright Academy, George Watsons and Lincoln Agricultural Coll., New Zealand. A Farmer. National Chairman Scottish Young Conservatives 1964. Nuffield Scholar. District Rotary Officer. Education spokesman for Scotland Oct. 1974-Mar. 1975. Opposition Whip Nov. 1975-Dec. 1976. Member of European Parliament Mar. 1975-Dec. 1975. Re-elected Feb. 1977-May 1979. Vice-President E.E.C. Turkey Committee 1975. Member Agricultural Committee and Regional and Transport Committees; also of Fisheries Sub-Committee in European Assembly 1977. Rapporteur Common Fisheries Policy and for Problems of Peripheral Maritime Regions 1977-78. Parliamentary Private Secretary to Rt. Hon. George Younger, Secretary of State for Scotland from 1979. A Conservative. Unsuccessfully contested N. Lanark in 1964 and the Central division of Ayrshire in 1966. Elected for the North and Bute division of Ayrshire and Bute in Feb. 1974.* [1979]

CORVEDALE, Maj. Oliver Ridsdale Baldwin, Visct. Little Stoke House, North Stoke, Oxfordshire. Bath, Press, and Savage. S. of 1st Earl Baldwin of Bewdley. B. 1 Mar. 1899. Unmarried. Educ. at Eton. An Author and Journalist. Lieut. Irish Guards; served in France 1916-19; Maj. Intelligence Corps, served in Egypt, Palestine, Syria, Eritrea, and Algeria 1940-43. Parliamentary Private Secretary to Rt. Hon. John Lawson 1946 and to the Rt. Hon. F.J. Bellenger 1947, successively Secretaries of State for War. A Labour Member. Unsuccessfully contested Dudley in 1924. Sat for Dudley from 1929-31. Unsuccessfully contested Chatham 1931 and Paisley 1935. Elected for Paisley in Nov. 1945 and sat until he succeeded to the peerage as Earl Baldwin of Bewdley on 14 Dec. 1947. Resigned the Labour Whip in Feb. 1931 and joined Sir Oswald Mosley's New Party but resigned the following day and rejoined the Labour Party. Styled Visct. Corvedale from 1937, when his father was created an Earl, until 1947, when he succeeded to the Earldom. Gov. of Leeward Islands 1948-50. Fellow of Royal Geographical Society and of Geographical Society of America. Died 10 Aug. 1958.   [1948]

COSTAIN, Sir Albert Percy, F.I.O.B. House of Commons, London. Carlton, and House of Commons Yacht. S. of William Percy Costain, Esq., Director. B. 5 July 1910; m. 6 Dec. 1933, Joan Mary, d. of John William Whiter, Esq. Educ. at King James Grammar School, Knaresborough, and College of Estate Management, London. On leaving school studied as a Quantity Surveyor. Joined firm of Richard Costain as trainee foreman in 1928; became first Production Director on formation of Public Company in 1933; appointed Joint Managing Director 1945; Chairman 1966-69; Director 1969-72. Member of the original Opencast Coal Committee of the Federation of Civil Engineering contractors; a first Vice-President of the International Prestressed Concrete Development Group. Member of Lloyds. Parliamentary Private Secretary to Rt. Hon. Geoffrey Rippon, Minister of Public Building and Works from 1962-64. Author of Home Safety Act 1961 and Auctions (Bidding Agreements) Act 1969. Member Committee of Public Accounts 1961-64 and 1974-79. Member Estimates Committee 1960-61 and 1965-70. Joint Vice-Chairman Conservative Party Transport Committee 1964. Joint Secretary Conservative Party Housing and Local Government Committee 1964-65; Joint Vice-Chairman 1965; Vice-Chairman All-Party Tourists and Resorts Committee 1964-66. Joint Secretary Conservative Party Land and Natural Resources Committee 1965; Joint Vice-Chairman Arts, Public Building and Works Committee 1965-68; Chairman 1969. Parliamentary Private Secretary to Rt. Hon. Geoffrey Rippon, Chancellor of Duchy of Lancaster 1970-72, and Secretary of State for the Environment 1972-74. Member Chairman's Panel 1975. A Conservative. Sat for Folkestone and Hythe from 1959. Knighted 1980.*   [1979]

COULSON, James Michael. Knapton Hall, Malton, Yorkshire. 16 Embankment Gardens, London. 5 Kings Bench Walk, London Cavalry. S. of William Coulson, Esq., of Fulwith Grange, Harrogate. B. 23 Nov. 1927; m. 1st, 1955, Dilys Adair Jones (marriage dissolved); 2ndly, 1977, Barbara Elizabeth Islay, d. of Dr. Roland Chambers. Educ. at Fulneck School, Yorkshire, Merton Coll., Oxford, and Royal Agricultural Coll., Cirencester. Called to the bar, Middle Temple 1951. Served with E. Riding Yeomanry, Queen's Own Yorkshire Yeomanry (Maj.). Parliamentary Private Secretary to Sir Peter Rawlinson, Solicitor-Gen. 1962-64. A Conservative. Elected for Kingston-upon-Hull N. in 1959 and sat until 1964 when he was defeated. Member of Tadcaster Rural District Council. Assistant Recorder of Sheffield 1965-71. Dept.-Chairman of N. Riding of Yorkshire Quarter Sessions 1968-71. Dept.-Chairman of Northern Agricultural Land Tribunal from 1967. Chairman of Industrial Tribunals from 1968.*   [1964]

COURTNEY, Commander Anthony Tosswill, O.B.E., R.N. Pembroke House, Valley End, Chobham, Surrey. 95 Roebuck House, Palace Street, London. Carlton, and White's. S. of Basil Tosswill Courtney, Esq., Engineer. B. 16 May 1908; m. 1st, 16 Oct. 1938, Elizabeth Mary, d. of the Rev. H.C. Stokes (she died 1 Mar. 1961); 2ndly, 3 Mar. 1962, Elizabeth, widow of 1st Baron Trefgarne (divorced 1966); 3rdly, 1971, Mrs. Angela Bradford. Educ. at Royal Naval Colleges Dartmouth and Greenwich. Served Royal Navy 1922-53, retired with the rank of Commander. Specialist in Signals and W/T. Interpreter in French, German and Russian. O.B.E. 1949. Export Consultant, Writer, Lecturer and Broadcaster. Chairman Parliamentary Flying Club 1965. A Conservative. Unsuccessfully contested Hayes and Harlington 1955. Elected for Harrow E. In Mar. 1959 and sat until 1966 when he was defeated. Alleged victim of a plot by the Russian Intelligence Service 1965-66. Managing Director of New English Typewriting School Limited from 1969.*   [1966]

COUSINS, Rt. Hon. Frank. Ministry of Technology, Millbank Tower, Millbank, London. S. of Charles Fox Cousins, Esq. B. 8 Sept. 1904; m. 1930, Annie Elizabeth Judd. Educ. at King Edward School, Doncaster. Organiser, Road Transport Section Transport and General Workers Union 1938; Assistant General Secretary T.G.W.U. 1955; General Secretary from 1956-69. Member General Council of the T.U.C. 1956-69. Gov. of the National Institute of Economic and Social Research 1958. Privy Councillor 1964. Minister of Technology from Oct. 1964 to July 1966, when he resigned. A Labour Member. Elected for Nuneaton in Jan. 1965 and sat until he resigned in Nov. 1966. Member of National Executive Committee of Labour Party 1955-56. Member of Colonial Labour Advisory Committee 1957-62. President of International Transport Workers Federation 1958-60 and 1962-64. Member of National Freight Corporation 1968-73. Chairman of Community Relations Commission 1968-70.* [1966 2nd ed.]

COVE, William George. House of Commons, London. B. 21 May 1888 at Treherbert. Educ. at Elementary School and University Coll. of South West, Exeter. Worked in the mines as a boy. Became a Teacher, and in 1922 was President of the National Union of Teachers. A Labour Member. Sat for the Wellingborough division of Northamptonshire from 1923-29. Parliamentary Private Secretary to C. Ammon, Parliamentary and Financial Secretary to Admiralty 1924. Elected for the Aberavon division of Glamorganshire in 1929 and sat until he retired in 1959. Died 15 Mar. 1963. [1959]

COWANS, Harry Lowes. 4 Station Cottages, Elysium Lane, Bensham, Gateshead. S. of Henry Cowans, Esq. B. 19 Dec. 1932; m. 23 June 1956, Margaret, d. of Edward McGee, Esq., (1 s. 3 d.). Educ. at Atkinson Road Technical School, Newcastle-upon-Tyne. N.U.R. Shop Steward 1958-76, Branch Secretary 1968-76. Labour Party 1964. Political Agent Gateshead 1970-75. Executive Member Regional Labour Party 1970-76. Secretary Labour Group. Gateshead Metropolitan Council 1973-76. Elected to Gateshead Borough Council 1970.

Elected to Gateshead Metropolitan District Council 1973. Housing Chairman 1973-76. Elected to Tyne and Wear Metropolitan County Council 1973-77. A.M.A. Housing Committee 1973-76. Parliamentary Private Secretary to Rt. Hon. Charles Morris, Minister of State, Civil Service Department 1978-79. A Labour Member. Sat for the Central division of Newcastle-upon-Tyne from Nov. 1976.* [1979]

COX, Thomas Michael. House of Commons, London. B. 1930. Educ. at State Schools, and London School of Economics. A Roman Catholic. Alderman Fulham Borough Council 1962-64, E.T.U. Assistant Government Whip Mar. 1974-Jan 1977. Lord Commissioner of the Treasury Jan. 1977-May 1979. Opposition Whip from 1979. A Labour Member. Unsuccessfully contested Stroud in 1966. Sat for the Central division of Wandsworth from June 1970 to Feb. 1974 and for the Tooting division of Wandsworth from Feb. 1974.* [1979]

CRADDOCK, George. 25 High Trees, Dore, Sheffield. S. of Amos George Craddock, Esq., of Kettering. B. 26 Feb. 1897; m. 1st, 29 Apr. 1936, Doris, d. of Arthur Kimberley, Esq., of Staple Hill, Bristol (she died 1949); 2ndly, 14 July 1962, Margaret Morris, of Cardiff. Educ. at Elementary School, Northampton, Fircroft Coll., Bournville, and University of Birmingham. Political Agent 1929-36, Trades Union Official 1936-49. Member of Sheffield City Council and of Sheffield Employment Exchange Committee until 1950. A Labour Member. Elected for Bradford S. in Dec. 1949 and sat until he retired in 1970. Labour Whip withdrawn Nov. 1954-Apr. 1955. Area Organiser National Union of Distributive and Allied Workers. Died 28 Apr. 1974. [1970]

CRADDOCK, Sir (George) Beresford. 9 The Grove, Highgate Village, London. Carlton. B. 7 Oct. 1898; m. 1936, Ethel Martin Bradford. Educ. at St. Andrew's University. Barrister-at-Law, Gray's Inn 1947. Served with R.A. 1914-18, and later on Chemical Warfare Staff. Parliamentary Private Secretary to Rt. Hon. Harold Watkinson, Minister of Transport and Civil Aviation

1956-59. Parliamentary Private Secretary to Rt. Hon. Harold Watkinson, Minister of Defence 1959-62. Member of Speaker's Panel of Chairman from 1965. Unsuccessfully contested the Lichfield division of Staffordshire as a National Labour candidate in May 1938 and as a National candidate in 1945. Elected as a Conservative for the Spelthorne division of Middlesex in Feb. 1950 and sat until he retired in 1970. Associate of Royal Institute of Chemistry. Knighted 1960. Died 22 Sept. 1976. [1970]

CRAIG, Rt. Hon. William. House of Commons. London. S. of John Craig, Esq. B. 1924; m. 1960, Doris Hilgendorff. Educ. at Larne Grammar School and Queen's University, Belfast. Served in R.A.F. 1943-46. A Solicitor 1952. Member of N. Ireland Parliament for Larne 1960-72. Chief Whip in Government N. Ireland 1962-63, Minister of Home Affairs 1963-64 and 1966-68, Minister of Health and Local Government 1964-65, Minister of Development 1965-66. PC. (N. Ireland) 1963. Member of N. Ireland Assembly for N. Antrim 1973-75 and Constitutional Convention for Belfast E. 1975-76. Founder of Ulster Vanguard 1972, Leader of Vanguard Unionist Progressive Party 1973-77. Vice-Chairman of U.U.U.C. Group 1974. Rejoined the Official Unionists 1977. An Ulster Unionist Member. Sat for Belfast E. from Feb. 1974 until 1979, when he was defeated.* [1979]

CRAIGEN, James Mark. House of Commons, London. S. of James Craigen, Esq. B. 2 Aug. 1938; m. 1971, Sheena Millar. Educ. at Shawlands Academy, Glasgow, and Strathclyde and Heriot-Watt Universities, M. Litt. 1974. Compositor 1954-61. Industrial Relations Assistant 1954-61. Scottish Gas Board 1963-64. Head of Organisation and Social Services Scottish T.U.C. 1964-68. Assistant Secretary and Industrial Liaison Officer Scottish Business Education Council 1968-74. Glasgow City Councillor 1965-68, Magistrate 1966-68. Member Scottish Ambulance Service Board 1966-71. Parliamentary Private Secretary to Rt. Hon. William Ross, Secretary of State for Scotland Nov. 1974-Apr. 1976. Member Police Advisory Board for Scotland 1970-74. A Labour and Co-operative Member. Unsuccessfully contested Ayr in 1970. Sat for the Maryhill division of Glasgow from Feb. 1974. Delegate to Council of Europe from 1976.* [1979]

CRANBORNE, Robert Edward Peter Cecil, Visct. 25 Charles Street, London. The Lodge House, Hatfield, Hertfordshire. S. of 5th Marq. of Salisbury. B. 24 Oct. 1916; m. 18 Dec. 1945, Marjorie Olein, d. of Capt. Hon. Valentine Wyndham-Quin, R.N., of Swallet House, Christian Malford, Wiltshire. Educ. at Eton. Capt. Grenadier Guards. Served overseas 1939-45. A Conservative. Unsuccessfully contested the Ince division of Lancashire in 1945. Elected for Bournemouth W. in Feb. 1950 and sat until he resigned in Jan. 1954. Styled Visct. Cranborne from 1947, when his father succeeded to the Marquessate, until 1972, when he succeeded to the Peerage as 6th Marq. of Salisbury. High Steward of Hertford from 1972. Dept.-Lieut. for Dorset 1974. President of Monday Club from 1974.* [1954]

CRAWFORD, (George) Douglas. House of Commons, London. S. of Robert Crawford, Esq. B. 1939; m. 1964, Joan, d. of William Burnie, Esq., (1 s. 1 d.). Educ. at Glasgow Academy, and St. Catherine's Coll., Cambridge University. Managing Director of a Group of economic and development consultants. A Journalist. Vice-Chairman of the Scottish Nationalist Party and Director of Communications. A Scottish National Party Member. Unsuccessfully contested Perth and E. Perthshire in Feb. 1974. Sat for Perth and E. Perthshire from Oct. 1974 until 1979, when he was defeated.* [1979]

CRAWLEY, Aidan Merivale, M.B.E. 19 Chester Square, London. White's, M.C.C., and Queen's. S. of Canon A.S. Crawley, who died in 1948. B. 10 Apr. 1908; m. 30 July 1945, Virginia, d. of Dr. Edward Cowles, of New York. Educ. at Harrow, and Trinity Coll., Oxford. Journalist 1930-36, Education Film Producer 1936-39. Served in Royal Air Force during Second World War; P.O.W. 1941-45, retiring with the rank of Squadron-Leader. Labour Member for Buckingham from 1945-51 when he was defeated. Parliamentary Private Secretary to Rt. Hon. G.H. Hall and Rt. Hon. A Creech Jones, Secretary for the Colonies 1945-50. Parliamentary Under-Secretary for Air 1950-51. Resigned from the Labour Party in 1957. Elected as Conservative Member of Parliament for W. Derbyshire in June 1962 and sat until he resigned in Oct. 1967. Editor-in-Chief, Independent Television News 1955-56. Member of Monckton Commission on Rhodesia and Nyasaland 1960. President of London Weekend Television 1971-73, Chairman 1967-71. President of M.C.C. 1973. Author and Biographer of De Gaulle. M.B.E. 1947.*   [1967]

CRAWSHAW, Lieut.-Col. Richard, O.B.E., T.D., D.L. The Orchard, Aintree Lane, Liverpool. S. of Percy Eli Lee Crashaw, Esq. B. 25 Sept. 1917; m. 16 Apr. 1960, Audrey Frances, d. of Francis Augustine Lima, Esq. Educ. at Pendleton Grammar School, Salford, Pembroke Coll., Cambridge, and Inns of Court, M.A. Cantab. A theological student 1936-39. LL.B. Lond. A Barrister-at-Law, Inner Temple 1948. Joined the Labour Party in 1949. Served with R.A. and Parachute Regiment 1939-45 in the Middle East and Italy, commanded 12/13 Battalion. The Parachute Regiment T.A. 1954-57. Dept.-Lieut. for Merseyside 1970. Appointed to Chairmans Panel 1971. Councillor Dingle Ward, Liverpool 1957-65. A Labour Member. Sat for the Toxteth division of Liverpool from Oct. 1964. O.B.E. 1958. Voted in favour of entry to E.E.C. on 28 Oct. 1971. Second Deputy Chairman of Ways and Means from May 1979.*   [1979]

CRIPPS, Rt. Hon. Sir Richard Stafford, K.C., F.R.S. 11 Downing Street, London. Frith Hill, Stroud, Gloucestershire. S. of Charles, 1st Baron Parmoor, K.C.V.O. B. 24 Apr. 1889; m. 12 July 1911, Isobel, G.B.E., d. of Commander H.W. Swithinbank of Denham Court. Educ. at Winchester, and University Coll., London. Barrister-at-Law, Middle Temple 1913; K.C. 1927; Rector of University of Aberdeen Nov. 1942; Solicitor-Gen. Oct. 1930-Aug. 1931; Knight Bach. 1930. H.B.M. Ambassador to the Soviet Union June 1940-Jan. 1942; Lord Privy Seal in War Cabinet and Leader of the House of

Commons Feb.-Nov. 1942. Minister of Aircraft Production Nov. 1942-May 1945; President of Board of Trade July 1945-Sept. 1947. Minister of Economic Affairs Sept. 1947 and Chancellor of the Exchequer from Nov. 1947 to Oct. 1950. PC. 1941. A Labour Member. Sat for E. Bristol from Jan. 1931-Feb. 1950, and for Bristol S.E. from Feb. 1950 until he resigned in Oct. 1950. Member of National Executive of Labour Party 1934-35 and 1937-39. Expelled from Labour Party as a result of his advocacy of the Popular Front Government in Jan. 1939; re-admitted in 1945. F.R.S. 1948. Companion of Honour 1951. President of Fabian Society 1951. Died 21 Apr. 1952.   [1950]

CRITCHLEY, Julian Michael Gordon. House of Commons, London. S. of Dr. Macdonald Critchley. B. 8 Dec. 1930; m. 1st, 15 Oct. 1955, Paula, d. of Paul Baron, Esq., (2 d.) (marriage dissolved in 1965); 2ndly, Apr. 1965, Heather Goodrick, d. of Charlie Moores, Esq., (1 s. 1 d.). Educ. at Shrewsbury, Sorbonne, and Pembroke Coll., Oxford. Chairman Bow Group and of Crossbow 1966-67; President Atlantic Association of Young Political Leaders 1968; Chairman of the Defence Committee of the W.E.U. Assembly 1974-77; Chairman Conservative Backbench Media Committee; Vice-Chairman Backbench Defence Committee. Writer and Journalist. Author of a number of Bow Group pamphlets. A Conservative. Elected for Rochester and Chatham in 1959 and sat until he was defeated in 1964. Unsuccessfully contested Rochester and Chatham in 1966. Sat for Aldershot from June 1970.* [1979]

CRONIN, John Desmond. 14 Wimpole Street, London. Hurlingham. S. of J.P. Cronin, Esq., Company Director. B. 1 Mar. 1916; m. 1 Mar. 1941, Cora, d. of Rowland Mumby-Croft, Esq., (1 s. 2 d.). Educ. at London University, (M.B., B.S. (Lond.) 1940; F.R.C.S. (England) 1947). Surgeon E.M.S. Royal Free Hospital 1941-42; R.A.M.C. 1942-46, Acting Lieut.-Col. 1945; Assistant Orthopaedic Surgeon, Prince of Wales Hospital 1947-51; Orthopaedic Surgeon, French Hospital from 1948. Member of London County Council 1952-55; Adviser on 1952 Industrial Injuries to numerous Trade

Unions. Opposition Whip 1959-62. An Opposition spokesman on Aviation 1962-64. Chevalier Legion d'Honneur Apr. 1960; Officier from 1967. Voted in favour of entry to E.E.C. on 28 Oct. 1971. Director Racal Electronics Limited. A Labour Member. Sat for the Loughborough division of Leicestershire from 1955 until 1979, when he was defeated.* [1979]

CROOKSHANK. Capt. Rt. Hon. Harry Frederick Comfort, C.H. 51 Pont Street, London. Guards', Carlton, and Pratt's. S. of H.M. Crookshank, Esq., of Cairo. B. 27 May 1893. Educ. at Eton (K.S.), and Magdalen Coll., Oxford, M.A. Capt. Grenadier Guards S.R. Served in France 1915-16, and Salonika 1917-18. Appointed to Diplomatic Service 1919; served as Third Secretary in Foreign Office 1919-21; Second Secretary Constantinople 1921-23, and at Washington 1924. Had Order of the White Eagle and Serbian Gold Medal for Valour; K.St.J.; Parliamentary Under-Secretary of State Home Office June 1934-June 1935; Secretary Mines Department June 1935-Apr. 1939; Financial Secretary to the Treasury Apr. 1939-Feb. 1943; Postmaster-Gen. Feb. 1943-July 1945. Leader of the House of Commons Oct. 1951-Dec. 1955, and Minister of Health Oct. 1951-May 1952, and Lord Privy Seal May 1952. PC. 1939; C.H. 1955. A Conservative. Elected for the Gainsborough division of Lincolnshire in Oct. 1924 and sat until Jan. 1956 when he was created Visct. Crookshank. Chairman of Political Honours Scrutiny Committee 1959-61. High Steward of Westminster 1960. Honorary D.C.L. University of Oxford 1960. Died 17 Oct. 1961. [1955]

CROSLAND, Rt. Hon. Charles Anthony Raven. House of Commons, London. S. of J.B. Crosland, Esq., C.B. B. 29 Aug. 1918; m. 1st, 1952, Hilary Anne, d. of Henry Sarson, Esq., of Newbury, Berkshire (marriage dissolved in 1957); 2ndly, 1964, Susan Barnes Catling, d. of Mark Watson, Esq., of Baltimore, Maryland, U.S.A. Educ. at Highgate School, and Trinity Coll., Oxford. Served with Royal Welch Fusiliers and Parachute Regiment 1939-45, Capt. Fellow and Lecturer in Economics, Trinity Coll., Oxford 1947-50. Secretary to Independent

Commission of Enquiry into Co-operative Movement 1956-58. Economic Secretary to Treasury Oct.-Dec. 1964. Minister of State Department of Economic Affairs Dec. 1964-Jan. 1965. Secretary of State for Education and Science Jan. 1965-Aug. 1967. President Board of Trade from Aug. 1967-Oct. 1969. Secretary of State Local Government and Regional Planning Oct. 1969-June 1970. Shadow Minister of Housing 1970 and Shadow Secretary for the Environment 1970-74. Secretary of State for the Environment Feb. 1974-Apr. 1976. Secretary of State for Foreign and Commonwealth Affairs Apr. 1976-Feb. 1977. A Labour Member. Sat for Gloucestershire S. from 1950-55 when he unsuccessfully contested the Test division of Southampton. Elected for Grimsby in 1959 and sat until his death on 19 Feb. 1977. Chairman of Fabian Society 1961-62. PC. 1965. Member of Parliamentary Labour Party Parliamentary Committee 1970-74. Author of *The Future of Socialism* and other works. Died 19 Feb. 1977. [1977]

CROSS, Rt. Hon. Sir Ronald Hibbert, Bart. 7 Hay Hill, Berkeley Square, London. Carlton. S. of James Carlton Cross, Esq. B. 9 May 1896; m. 1925, Louise Marion, d. of W.G. Emmott, Esq., of Emmott Hall, Colne. Educ. at Eton. A Merchant Banker. Served with Duke of Lancaster's Own Yeomanry and R.F.C. 1914-19; Parliamentary Private Secretary to R.S. Hudson, Parliamentary Secretary to Minister of Labour Feb. 1932, and to Rt. Hon. Walter Eliot when Minister for Agriculture June-Dec. 1935. Assistant Whip Dec. 1935. A Junior Lord of the Treasury May-Oct 1937. Vice-Chamberlain of H.M. Household Oct. 1937-May 1938. Parliamentary Secretary Board of Trade May 1938-Sept. 1939. Minister of Economic Warfare Sept. 1939-May 1940; Minister of Shipping May 1940-May 1941; High Commissioner in Australia for H.M. Government in the U.K. May 1941-May 1945. Created Bart. 1941. PC. 1940. A Conservative. Sat for Rossendale from 1931-45, when he was defeated. Elected for the Ormskirk division of Lancashire in Feb. 1950 and sat until Feb. 1951 when he resigned on appointment as Gov. of Tasmania. Chairman of Public Accounts Committee 1950-51. K.C.V.O.

1954. K.C.M.G. 1955. Gov. of Tasmania 1951-58. Died 3 June 1968. [1950]

CROSSMAN, Rt. Hon. Richard Howard Stafford, O.B.E. 9 Vincent Square, London. Prescote Manor, Banbury. S. of Mr. Justice Crossman. B. 15 Dec. 1907; m. 1st, Erika (divorced); 2ndly, 1937, Inezita Hilda Baker (she died 1952); 3rdly, 3 June 1954, Anne Patricia, d. of A.P. McDougall, Esq., of Banbury. Educ. at Winchester, and New Coll., Oxford. Fellow and Tutor of New Coll., Oxford 1930-37. Assistant Editor of *The New Statesman and Nation* 1938-55. Lecturer for Oxford University Delegacy for Extra-Mural Studies and for W.E.A. 1938-40. Member of Oxford City Council and Leader of Labour Group 1934-40. Engaged as a German propaganda specialist in Special Operations 1940-41 and in the Political Warfare Executive 1941-43. Dept. Director of Psychological Warfare, Algiers 1943, Asst. Chief of Psychological Warfare, S.H.A.E.F. 1944-45. O.B.E. 1945. Member of Anglo-American Palestine Committee 1946, and of Malta Round Table Conference 1955. Minister of Housing and Local Government Oct. 1964-Aug. 1966. Lord President of the Council Aug. 1966-Oct. 1968, Leader of the House of Commons Aug. 1966-Apr. 1968. PC. 1964. Secretary of State for Social Services Oct. 1968-June 1970. Editor of *New Statesman* 1970-72. A Labour Member. Unsuccessfully contested W. Birmingham in 1937. Elected for E. Coventry in July 1945 and sat until he retired in Feb. 1974. Member of National Executive Committee of Labour Party 1952-67, Chairman 1960-61. Opposition spokesman on Pensions 1959-60 and on Science 1963-64. Member of Parliamentary Labour Party Parliamentary Committee Oct.-Nov. 1960. Author of political and philosophical works and of the posthumously-published political diaries. Died 4 Apr. 1974. [1974]

CROSTHWAITE-EYRE, Sir Oliver Eyre. 11 Lord North Street, London. Warrens, Bramshaw, Lyndhurst, Hampshire. Carlton, and Boodles. S. of Maj. J.S. Crosthwaite-Eyre. B. 14 Oct. 1913; m. 15 July 1939, Maria, d. of Baron Heinrich Puthon. Educ. at Downside, and Trinity Coll., Cambridge. Chairman of Eyre & Spottiswoode Limited 1961-73. Chairman Associated Book Publishers Limited. 1963-73. Served with Royal Marines 1939-45, Col. 1945. A Conservative. Sat for the New Forest and Christchurch division from 1945-50 and for the New Forest division of Hampshire from Feb. 1950 until he resigned in July 1968. Verderer of New Forest 1948-74. Knighted 1961. Chairman of 1900 Club 1960-73. Dept.-Lieut. for Hampshire. Died 3 Feb. 1978. [1968]

CROUCH, David Lance. Barton Manor, Westmarsh, Canterbury, Kent. 3 Tufton Court, Tufton Street, London. Athenaeum. S. of Stanley Crouch, Esq., Company Director. B. 23 June 1919; m. 5 July 1947, Margaret Maplesden, d. of Maj. Sydney Maplesden Noakes, D.S.O., (1 s. 1 d.). Educ. at University Coll. School. Served with City of London Yeomanry 1939-45; Maj. Staff Officer R.A.F. (G.S.O. 2) 1944-45. With I.C.I. 1951-62 (Publicity Manager); Director of Publicity, International Wool Secretariat 1962-64. Travelled in Europe. U.S.A., Russia, Middle East, Far East and Commonwealth. Director Burson-Marsteller Limited, Pfizer Limited, David Crouch and Company Limited, Director of Companies Marketing and Public Relations Consultants. Member Council University of Kent Canterbury; member Council Royal Society of Arts; member Select Committee on Nationalised Industries 1966-74; member Public Accounts Committee from 1974. Chairman All-Party Parliamentary Group for the Chemical Industry. Chairman of Anglo-Egyptian Parliamentary Group. Vice-Chairman Conservative Party Industry Committee 1972-75. Member S.E. Thames Regional Health Authority. A Conservative. Unsuccessfully contested W. Leeds in 1959. Sat for the Canterbury division of Kent from Mar. 1966.* *[1979]

CROUCH, Robert Fisher. Shroton Cottage, Blandford Forum, Dorset. S. of William Fisher Crouch, Esq., of Hammoon, Blandford, Dorset. B. 7 Feb. 1904; m. 7 Oct. 1939, Kathleen Mary, d. of George William Bastable, Esq. Educ. at Milton Abbas School, Blandford. A Farmer. Vice-Chairman Salisbury Conservative Association 1942-46. A

Conservative. Elected for N. Dorset in Feb. 1950 and sat until his death on 7 May 1657. Member of the New Varieties Cereal Committee of National Institute of Agricultural Botany 1947-57. Chairman of British Land Council. Died 7 May 1957.   [1957]

CROWDER, (Frederic) Peter, Q.C. Aston Dene, Aston, Nr. Stevenage, Hertfordshire. 8 King's Bench Walk, Temple, London. Turf, and Pratt's. S. of Sir John Crowder, MP. B. 18 July 1919; m. 12 July 1948, Hon. Patricia Stourton, d. of 25th Lord Mowbray and Stourton. Educ. at Eton, and Christ Church, Oxford. A Barrister-at-Law, Inner Temple 1948, Bencher 1970, on the S.E. Circuit. Maj. Coldstream Guards 1939-46. Served in N. Africa, Italy and Burma. Parliamentary Private Secretary to Sir Reginald Manningham-Buller. Solicitor-Gen. Jan. 1952-Oct. 1954 and Attorney-Gen. Oct. 1954-July 1972. Recorder of Gravesend 1960. Dept. Chairman of Hertfordshire Quarter Sessions 1959, Chairman 1963. Q.C. 1964. Recorder of Colchester 1967. A Conservative. Unsuccessfully contested N. Tottenham at a by-election in Dec. 1945. Sat for Ruislip-Northwood from 1950 to Feb. 1974 and for Hillingdon, Ruislip-Northwood from Feb 1974 until he retired in 1979.*   [1979]

CROWDER, Sir John Frederick Ellenborough. 116 Ashley Gardens, London. Charlestown, St. Austell, Cornwall. Carlton. S. of A.G. Crowder and Louisa, sister of Cecil, 6th Baron Ellenborough. B. 10 Nov. 1890; m. 1918, Florence, d. of Alfred R. Petre, Esq. Educ. at Eton, and Christ Church, Oxford. Member of Lloyds, of Hampshire County Council 1931-46, and of Fleet Urban District Council 1933-46; J.P. for Hampshire 1942-48. Served 1914-19 with Lincolnshire Yeomanry R.H.G. and on Personal Staff. Re-employed Nov. 1939. Army Welfare Officer, Aldershot Nov. 1940-45 (unpaid). Parliamentary Private Secretary to A.T. Lennox-Boyd, when Parliamentary Secretary to Ministry of Labour Nov. 1938-Sept. 1939, to Ministry of Home Security Sept. 1939-Oct. 1939 and to Ministry of Food Oct. 1939-Mar. 1940, to Ministry of Aircraft Production 1943-45, and to Rt. Hon. Sir John Simon, Chancellor of the Exchequer Mar.-May

1940. Second (Parliamentary) Church Estates Commissioner Dec. 1951-Sept. 1957; member of Church Assembly 1956-60. Knight Bach. July 1952. A Conservative. Elected for Finchley in 1935 and sat until he retired in 1959. Died 9 July 1961.   [1959]

CROWTHER, (Joseph) Stanley. 15 Clifton Crescent South, Rotherham. S. of Cyril Joseph Crowther, Esq. B. 30 May 1925; m. 14 Aug. 1948, Margaret, d. of Llewellyn and Lydia Royston, (2 s.). Educ. at Rotherham Grammar School, and Rotherham Coll. of Technology. Served in Royal Signals 1943-47. A Methodist. A Journalist. Member of Rotherham Borough Council 1958-59 and 1961-76. Chairman of Council Labour Group. Chairman Planning and Development Committee 1964-76. Mayor of Rotherham 1971-72 and 1975-76. Chairman Yorks and Humberside Development Association 1973-76. Parliamentary Private Secretary to Harold Walker, Minister of State, Department of Employment 1978-79. Member of Town and Country Planning Association. A Labour Member. Sat for Rotherham from June 1976.*   [1979]

CRYER, (George) Robert. "Holyoake", Providence Lane, Oakworth, Keighley, Yorkshire. S. of John Arthur Cryer, Esq. B. 3 Dec. 1934; m. Aug. 1963, Constance Ann, d. of Alan Place, Esq. Educ. at Salt High School, Shipley, and Hull University. A Lecturer Keighley Technical Coll. 1965-74. Member Keighley Borough Council 1971-74. Parliamentary Under-Secretary for Industrial Sept. 1976-Nov. 1978, when he resigned. Chairman of Select Committee on Statutory Instruments from 1979. A Labour Member. Unsuccessfully contested the Darwen division of Lancashire in 1964. Sat for Keighley from Feb. 1974.*   [1979]

CULLEN, Alice. 73 Glencoe Street, Glasgow. D. of John McLoughlin, Esq. B. 1892; m. 1st, 1920, Pearce Cullen (he died); 2ndly, 1950, William Reynolds, Esq., Headmaster (he died 1961). Member of Glasgow City Council from 1938. A Labour Member. Elected for the Gorbals division of Glasgow in Sept. 1948 and sat until her death on 31 May 1969. A Roman Catholic. Died 31 May 1969.   [1969]

CUNDIFF, Maj. Frederick William.
Easedale, Prestbury Lane, Butley, Maccles-
field. S. of Sir William Cundiff. B. 1895.
Served with R.A. and R.F.C. 1914-18. A
Director of National Gas and Oil Engine
Company. A Conservative. Sat for the
Rusholme division of Manchester from July
1944 until he was defeated in July 1945.
Elected for the Withington division of Man-
chester in Feb. 1950 and sat until he retired in
1951. Director of Chesters Brewery Company
Limited.* [1951]

CUNNINGHAM, George. 28 Manor
Gardens, Hampton, Middlesex. S. of Harry
Jackson Cunningham, Esq., of Dunfermline.
B. 10 June 1931; m. 1957, Mavis, d. of Harold
Walton, Esq., (1 s. 1 d.). Educ. at Dunfermline High School, Blackpool Grammar
School and Manchester and London Universities. Member of the Staff of the Commonwealth Relations Office 1956-63. 2nd Secretary (Political) British High Commission at
Ottawa 1958-60. Commonwealth Officer of
the Labour Party 1963-66. On staff of
Ministry of Overseas Development 1966-69
and Overseas Development Institute 1969-
70. Author of Fabian pamphlet *Rhodesia, the
last Chance* 1966 and *The Management of Aid
Agencies* 1974. Editor of *Britain and the World in
the Seventies* 1970. Member European Parliament 1978-79. A Labour Member. Unsuccessfully contested the Henley division of
Oxfordshire in 1966. Sat for the S.W. division
of Islington from 1970 to Feb. 1974, and for
the South and Finsbury division of Islington
from Feb. 1974. Parliamentary Private Secretary to Rt. Hon. R.E. Prentice, Secretary of
State for Education and Science 1974-75.
Leading opponent of devolution and mover
of the 40% 'Yes' vote amendments to the
Scotland Bill and to the Wales Bill 1978. An
Opposition spokesman on Home Affairs
from 1979.* [1979]

CUNNINGHAM, John Anderson. House
of Commons, London. S. of Andrew
Cunningham, Esq. B. Aug. 1939; m. 1964,
Maureen. Educ. at Jarrow Grammar School,
and Bede Coll., Durham University, B.Sc.,
Ph.D. Chemistry. Research Fellow Durham
University 1966-68. Full-time Officer
G.M.W.U. 1969-70. Parliamentary Private

Secretary to the Rt. Hon. James Callaghan,
MP., Foreign and Commonwealth Secretary
1974-76 and Prime Minister 1976. Member
Select Committee Science and Technology.
Parliamentary Under-Secretary for Energy
Sept. 1976-May 1979. An Opposition spokes-
man on Industry from 1979. A Labour
Member. Sat for Whitehaven from June
1970.* [1979]

CUNNINGHAM, Patrick. Strathroy,
Omagh, Co. Tyrone. B. 1878; m. 1918 (12
children). A Dairy Farmer. An Irish
Nationalist. An Independent Member. Elected for Fermanagh and Tyrone in 1935 and
sat until he retired in 1950. Did not take his
seat at Westminster until 1945. Died 2 Feb.
1960. [1950]

**CUNNINGHAM, Sir (Samuel) Knox,
Bart., Q.C.** Derhams House, Minchin-
hampton, Stroud, Gloucestershire. 2 Essex
Court, Temple, London. Carlton, St. Ste-
phen's, M.C.C., and Ulster (Belfast). S. of
the Rt. Hon. Samuel Cunningham. B. 3 Apr.
1909; m. 2 July 1935, Dorothy Enid, J.P., d.
of Edwin Riley, Esq. Educ. at Royal Belfast
Academical Institution, Fettes, and Clare
Coll., Cambridge. In business in Ulster 1931-
37; called to the bar by Middle Temple 1939;
Inn of Court of N. Ireland 1942; Queen's
Counsel 1959. Served with Scots Guards
1939-45 war. Chairman National Council of
Y.M.C.A. 1949-67. Member of World
Alliance of Y.M.C.A.s 1947-69. Member of
Orpington Urban District Council 1954-55.
Assistant of the Court of the Drapers Com-
pany, Master 1973-74. U.K. Delegate to
Council of Europe and W. European Union
1956-59; Parliamentary Private Secretary to
J.E.S. Simon, Financial Secretary to the
Treasury 1958-59. Parliamentary Private
Secretary to the Rt. Hon. Harold Macmillan,
Prime Minister 1959-63. Member Ulster
Unionist Council from 1943. Gov. of Queen
Mary Coll. Member National Executive of
the Conservative and Unionist Party 1959-
66. Bart. 1963. An Ulster Unionist Member.
Unsuccessfully contested W. Belfast as a
Unionist in 1943 and 1945. Elected for S.
Antrim in 1955 and sat until he retired in
1970. Died 29 July 1976. [1970]

CURRAN, (Leslie) Charles. 9 Stone Buildings, Lincoln's Inn, London. 70 Park Mansions, Knightsbridge, London. Press, Savage, and Carlton. S. of C.J. Curran, Esq. B. 1903; m. Mona Regan, (1 s.). Educ. at Cardiff High School, Stonyhurst. A Barrister-at-Law, Gray's Inn; Journalist. A Conservative. Unsuccessfully contested W. Walthamstow in 1945 and Uxbridge in 1951 and 1955. Sat for the Uxbridge division of Middlesex from 1959-66 when he was defeated and from June 1970 until his death on 16 Sept. 1972 in Cyprus. Assistant Editor of (London) *Evening News, Evening Standard* and *Daily Mirror*. Died 16 Sept. 1972. [1972]

CURRIE, George Boyle Hanna, M.B.E. Rathdune House, Downpatrick, Co. Down. 1 Pump Court, Temple, London. S. of the Very Rev. William John Currie, B.A., D.D., Moderator of Gen. Assembly of Presbyterian Church in Ireland 1938. B. 19 Dec. 1905; m. 1933, Stephanie Maud Evelyn, d. of J.H.S. Costello, Esq. Educ. at Campbell Coll., Belfast, and Trinity Coll., Dublin, M.A., LL.B. 1932. Called to the bar by Middle Temple 1932, member of the Northern Circuit. Served with R.A.F. 1940-45, Squadron Leader 1943. Member Wirral Urban District Council 1934-50, Chairman 1938. M.B.E. (Mil.) 1946. An Ulster Unionist Member. Unsuccessfully contested Flintshire E. as a Conservative in 1950 and 1951. Elected for Down N. in 1955 and sat until he retired in 1970. Member of Council for Arab-British Understanding 1970-71. Died 20 Jan. 1978. [1970]

CUTHBERT, William Nicolson. 51 St. James Square, London. Carlekemp, Bexhill, Sussex. East India, and Sports'. S. of William Cuthbert, Esq., of Edinburgh. B. 24 Aug. 1890; m. 1915, Bernice Gertrude, d. of Charles Bungey, Esq. Educ. at George Watson's Coll., Edinburgh. Served with E. Surrey Regiment and R.A.F. 1914-19. A Banker, Imperial Bank of Iran. Served in Persia 1910-31. J.P. for Sussex. Mayor of Bexhill 1936-42. County Councillor for E. Sussex 1937-45. A Freeman of Bexhill. A Conservative. Sat for the Rye division from July 1945-50. Elected for the Arundel and Shoreham division of West Sussex in Feb. 1950 and sat until he

resigned in Feb. 1954. Died 7 May 1960. [1954]

DAGGAR, George. 25 High Street, Six Bells, Abertillery. S. of Jesse Dagger, Esq., of Abertillery. His birth was registered under the surname Dagger but he always used the spelling Daggar. B. 1879; m. 1915, Rachel, d. of J. Smith, Esq., of Bradford. Educ. at Elementary School, and Labour Coll., London. A Coal-Miner; Miners' Agent for the Western Welsh Valleys; Member of Executive of S. Wales Miners' Federation. Vice-Chairman of Parliamentary Labour Party Dec. 1948-Oct. 1950. A Labour Member. Elected for the Abertillery division of Monmouthshire in May 1929 and sat until his death on 14 Oct. 1950. Died 14 Oct. 1950. [1950]

DAINES, Percy. House of Commons, London. B. 29 Nov. 1902. A Locomotive Fireman and employee of Co-operative Insurance Society. Member of National Union of Railwaymen and National Union of Distributive and Allied Workers. Served with Royal Engineers 1939-45. A Labour and Co-operative Member. Elected for East Ham N. in July 1945 and sat until his death on 3 Mar. 1957. Died 3 Mar. 1957. [1957]

DALKEITH, Walter Francis John Montagu-Douglas-Scott, Earl of. Eildon Hall, Melrose, Roxburghshire. 46 Bedford Gardens, London. White's. S. of The Duke of Buccleuch and Queensberry. B. 28 Sept. 1923; m. 10 Jan. 1953, Jane, D. of John McNeill, Esq., Q.C., of Appin, Argyll, (3 s. 1 d.). Educ. at Eton, and Christ Church, Oxford. Served R.N.V.R. 1942-46. V.R.D. 1959. Lieut. Royal Company of Archers. Chairman Roxburgh, Selkirk, Peebles Unionist Association 1958; Roxburgh County Council. Dept.-Lieut. for Selkirkshire 1955; Dept.-Lieut. for Midlothian 1960. Chairman Conservative Party Sub-Committee on Forestry from 1966. Parliamentary Private Secretary to W. Grant, Lord Advocate 1961; Parliamentary Private Secretary to M. Noble, Secretary of State for Scotland 1962-64. Dept.-Lieut. for Roxburghshire 1961. President Royal Highland and Agricultural Society of Scotland 1969-70. A Unionist Member.

Unsuccessfully contested E. Edinburgh in 1959. Elected for N. Edinburgh at a by-election in May 1960 and sat until he succeeded to the Peerage as Duke of Buccleuch and Queensberry on 4 Oct. 1973. Styled Earl of Dalkeith 1935-73. Lord-Lieut. of Roxburghshire 1974, of Ettrick and Lauderdale from 1975. K.T. 1978. [1973]

DALTON, Rt. Hon. Edward Hugh John Neale. 185a Ashley Gardens, London. S. of Rev. J.N. Dalton, Canon of St. George's, Windsor. B. 26 Aug. 1887; m. 1914. Ruth, d. of T.H. Fox, Esq. (She was MP for Bishop Auckland, 1929.) Educ. at Eton, King's Coll., Cambridge and London School of Economics, DSc. Barrister-at-Law 1914, and Honorary Bencher of Middle Temple 1946. Served in Army, France and Italy 1914-19. Reader in Economics, University of London 1920-35. Chairman of Labour Party National Executive 1936-37. Author of books on Politics and Economics. Under-Secretary of State for Foreign Affairs June 1929-Aug. 1931. Minister for Economic Warfare May 1940-Feb. 1942, and (secretly) Minister responsible for the Special Operation Executive. President of the Board of Trade Feb. 1942-May 1945, Chancellor of the Exchequer July 1945-Nov. 1947, when he resigned after a Budget leak; Chancellor of Duchy of Lancaster, with a seat in the Cabinet June 1948-Feb. 1950. Minister of Town and Country Planning Feb. 1950-1951; of Local Government and Planning Jan.-Oct. 1951. Member of Parliamentary Labour Party Parliamentary Committee 1925-29, Sept.-Oct. 1931, 1935-40 and 1951-55. Member of National Executive Committee of Labour Party 1926-27 and 1928-52. PC. 1940. A Labour Member. Unsuccessfully contested Cambridge in Mar. 1922, Maidstone in Nov. 1922, Cardiff E. in Dec. 1923, and the Holland with Boston division of Lincolnshire in July 1924. Sat for the Peckham division of Camberwell from Oct. 1924-May 1929. Sat for the Bishop Auckland division of Durham from May 1929-Oct. 1931 when he was defeated and from 1935 until he retired in 1959. Created Baron Dalton (Life Peerage) 1960. Died 13 Feb. 1962. [1959]

DALYELL, Tam. Binns, Linlithgow. S. of Gordon Dalyell, Esq., Indian Civil Servant. B. 9 Aug. 1932; m. Dec. 1963, Kathleen, only d. of Lord Wheatley, Lord Justice Clerk of Scotland, (1 s. 1 d.). Educ. at Eton, King's Coll., Cambridge, and Moray House, Edinburgh. Author of *Case for Ship-Schools, Ship-School*, and *Devolution: End of Britain* 1977. Dept.-Director of Studies on British India ship-school *Dunera* 1961-Apr. 1962. Member of Public Accounts Committee 1962-66. Secretary Labour Party Standing Group on the Sciences 1963-64. Chairman of Parliamentary Labour Party Education Group from 1964-66. Parliamentary Private Secretary to the Rt. Hon. Richard Crossman 1964-65 and 1967-70. Member of House of Commons Select Committee on Science and Technology 1967-69. Political Columnist New Scientist 1967. Member of Scottish Trade Delegation to China 1971. Voted in favour of entry to E.E.C. on 28 Oct. 1971. Chairman Parliamentary Labour Party Foreign Affairs Group 1974-76. Chairman Scottish Group of Labour MPs. 1973-75. Elected P.L.P. Liaison Committee 1974-76. Vice-Chairman Parliamentary Labour Party 1974-75; member European Parliament 1975-79; Socialist Bureau of the Parliamentary and Budget Committee member 1975. Vice-Chairman Control Committee on Budgets of European Parliament 1976. Leading opponent of the Scotland Bill 1978, which proposed devolution to Scotland. A Labour Member. Unsuccessfully contested Roxburgh, Selkirk, Peebles in 1959. Sat for W. Lothian from June 1962.* [1979]

DANCE, James Cyril George. Moreton House, Moreton Morrell, Warwickshire. 8 York House, Turks Row, London. M.C.C., and White's. S. of Sir George Dance, Playwright. B. 5 May 1907; m. 1st, Charlotte, d. of G.H. Strutt, Esq. (she died); 2ndly, 20 Sept. 1934, Anne, C.B.E., d. of Col. Arthur Travis Walker. Educ. at Eton. Served in France, Middle East, and Italy; Maj. Queen's Bays (2nd Dragoon Guards) 1940-45. Chairman Rugby Division Conservative Association 1946-48; E.R.D. 1954. Parliamentary Private Secretary to G.R. Ward, Parliamentary Secretary to the Admiralty and Secretary of State for Air 1956-60. A

Conservative. Unsuccessfully contested Rugby in 1950 and 1951. Elected for the Bromsgrove division of Worcestershire in 1955 and sat until his death on 16 Mar. 1971. An Underwriter at Lloyd's. Died 16 Mar. 1971. [1971]

DARLING, Rt. Hon. George. Medway, Amersham Road, Beaconsfield, Buckinghamshire. S. of F.W. Darling, Esq. B. 1905; m. 1932, Dorothy, d. of T.W. Hodge, Esq. Educ. at Elementary School, Crewe, and Universities of Liverpool and Cambridge. A Journalist. Formerly Locomotive Fitter. B.B.C. Industrial Correspondent until 1949. Minister of State at the Board of Trade Oct. 1964-Apr. 1968. A Labour and Co-operative Member. Unsuccessfully contested the Macclesfield division of Cheshire in 1935. Elected for the Hillsborough division of Sheffield in Feb. 1950 and sat until he retired in Feb. 1974. Parliamentary Private Secretary to Rt. Hon. George Strauss, Minister of Supply 1951. Opposition Whip 1959-60. Opposition spokesman on Agriculture 1960-64 and on Trade 1962-64. PC. 1966. President of Institute of Trading Standards Administration. Created Baron Darling of Hillsborough (Life Peerage) 1974. [1974]

DARLING, Sir William Young, C.B.E., M.C. 6 Rothesay Terrace, Edinburgh. S. of William Darling, Esq. B. 8 May 1885; m. 1914, Olive, d. of James Simpson, Esq. Dept.-Lieut. and J.P. for Edinburgh. Educ. at James Gillespie's School, Daniel Stewart's Coll., Heriot Watt Coll., and University of Edinburgh, LL.D. Chairman of Bruce Peebles and Company Limited. Director of the Royal Bank of Scotland, Scottish and Union National Insurance Company, A. & R. Scott Limited, John Inglis and Company Limited, and David Scougal Limited. Lord Provost of Edinburgh 1941-44. Maj. Black Watch, Royal Scots, Royal Munster Fusiliers and General Staff. Served in France, Egypt, Gallipoli and Salonica 1914-19. Served in Ireland 1920-22. Member of Edinburgh City Council from 1933, Treasurer 1937-40. Commissioner Civil Defence S.E. Scotland 1939-41. A Conservative. Prospective Conservative candidate for W. Lothian 1937. Elected for Edinburgh S. In

July 1945 and sat until he resigned in May 1957. Chairman of Scottish Council of Industry 1941-46; President Edinburgh Chamber of Commerce 1946-47. C.B.E. 1923. Knighted 1943. Fellow of Royal Society of Edinburgh. Author and Poet. Died 4 Feb. 1962. [1957]

DAVIDSON, Arthur, Q.C. House of Commons, London. S. of A. Davidson Esq. of Liverpool. B. 7 Nov. 1928. Educ. at King George V Grammar School, Southport, Liverpool Coll., and Trinity Coll., Cambridge (Editor *Granta*; member University Athletics Team). A Barrister, Middle Temple 1953. Member G. & M.W.U. Parliamentary Private Secretary to Sir Arthur Irvine, Solicitor Gen. 1967-70. Council member Consumers Association. Chairman Home Office Group Parliamentary Labour Party 1971-74. Chairman Prices and Consumer Affairs Group Parliamentary Labour Party 1974. Member Committee on Boards of Visitors 1974. Joint Chairman Working Group for the eradication of colour prejudice in education 1974. Member Labour Party N.E.C. Sub-Committee Human Affairs Group. Member Labour Party N.E.C. Sub-Committee Consumer Affairs Group. Parliamentary Private Secretary to S.C. Silkin, Attorney General Mar.-July 1974. Parliamentary Secretary to the Law Officers July 1974-May 1979. A Labour Member. Candidate for Preston N. in 1959, and Blackpool S. in 1955. Sat for Accrington from Mar. 1966. Q.C. 1978.* [1979]

DAVIDSON, Frances Joan Davidson, Viscountess, D.B.E. Norcott Court, Berkhampstead. D. of the 1st Baron Dickinson, K.B.E. B. 1894; m. 10 Apr. 1919 Rt. Hon. J.C.C. Davidson, (created Visct. Davidson 1937 and died 1970). A Conservative. Elected for the Hemel Hempstead division of Hertfordshire in June 1937 in succession to her husband and sat until she retired in 1959. O.B.E. 1920. D.B.E. 1952. Created Baroness Northchurch (Life Peerage) 1964.* [1959]

DAVIDSON, James Duncan Gordon, M.V.O. Tillychetly, Alford, Aberdeenshire. S. of Capt. Alastair G. Davidson, R.N., retired. B. 10 Jan. 1927; m. 1st, Catherine, d.

of William A. Jamieson, Esq., of Almonte, Ontario, (3 children); 2ndly, 1973, Janet Stafford. Educ. at Royal Naval Coll., Dartmouth, Downing Coll., Cambridge, and Paris (Language study). A Farmer. Served in the Royal Navy in North Atlantic until after D-Day and in the Pacific until the Japanese surrender. Has studied Russian, qualified as an interpreter. Assistant Naval Attache, Moscow and Helsinki 1952-54. Member of Area Executive N.F.U. M.V.O. 1947. A Liberal. Unsuccessfully contested Aberdeenshire W. in 1964. Elected for Aberdeenshire W. in Mar. 1966 and sat until he retired in 1970. Chief Executive Royal Highland and Agricultural Society of Scotland from 1970. [1970]

DAVIES, Albert Edward. 65 Victoria Road, Tunstall, Stoke-on-Trent. S. of Albert Davies, Esq. B. 30 May 1900; m. 1944, Margaret, d. of Thomas Batty, Esq. Educ. at Smallthorne Council School, Stoke-on-Trent Technical School, and Manchester Coll., Oxford. A Railwayman 1914-45. Member of Stoke-on-Trent City Council from 1943. Associate Member Institute of Transport 1932. A Labour Member. Sat for The Burslem division of Stoke-on-Trent from July 1945-50. Elected for the N. Division of Stoke-on-Trent in Feb. 1950 and sat until his death on 19 Jan. 1953. [1953]

DAVIES, Bryan. 28 Churchfields, Broxbourne, Hertfordshire. 3 River Front, Enfield, Middlesex. S. of George William Davies, Esq. B. 9 Nov. 1939; m. 1963, Monica, d. of J.R. Shearing, Esq., (1 s. 2 d.). Educ. at Redditch High School, University Coll., London, Institute of Education, London, and London School of Economics. History Master, Latymer School 1962-65. Principal Lecturer in Politics and Modern History, Enfield Coll. and Middlesex Polytechnic 1965-74. Parliamentary Private Secretary to Rt. Hon. Frederick Mulley, Secretary of State for Education and Science 1975. Joint Parliamentary Private Secretary to Rt. Hon. Edward Short, Lord President of Council 1975-76; Parliamentary Private Secretary to Rt. Hon. Joel Barnett, Chief Secretary to Treasury 1976-77. Member of Medical Research Council 1977-79. Assistant

Government Whip Jan.-May 1979. Secretary of Parliamentary Labour Party from 1979. A Labour Member. Unsuccessfully contested Norfolk Central in 1966. Sat for the N. division of Enfield from Feb. 1974 until 1979, when he was defeated.* [1979]

DAVIES, (Claude) Nigel Byam. 56 Curzon Street, London. Brewery House, Harlow, Essex. Guards'. S. of Col. Claude Martin Davies. B. 2 Sept. 1920. Unmarried. Educ. at Eton. A Company Director. Officer Grenadier Guards 1939-45. A Conservative. Elected for the Epping division of Essex in Feb. 1950 and sat until he retired in 1951. Ph.D. in archaeology, London University 1970. Author of *The Aztecs, a history* 1973, *The Toltecs* 1977, *Voyagers to the New World* 1979, and other works. Managing Director of Windolite Limited from 1947. [1951]

DAVIES, Rt. Hon. (David John) Denzil. House of Commons, London. S. of G. Davies, Esq. of Carmarthen. B. Oct. 1938; m. 1963, Mary Ann Finlay, of Illinois. Educ. at Carmarthen Grammar School, and Pembroke Coll., Oxford University, first class Hons. (Law). Lectured at Chicago and Leeds Universities. Member Select Committee on Corporation Tax 1971. A Barrister, Gray's Inn 1964. Parliamentary Private Secretary to Rt. Hon. John Morris, Secretary of State for Wales 1974-75. Minister of State, Treasury from June 1975-May 1979. PC. 1978. An Opposite spokesman on Treasury Affairs from 1979. A Labour Member. Sat for Llanelli from June 1970.* [1979]

DAVIES, Ernest Arthur. 48 Ashbourne Road, Stretford, Manchester. S. of Daniel Davies, Esq., Plaster-mould Maker. B. 25 Oct. 1926; m. 1st, 28 July 1956, Margaret, d. of H. Gatt, Esq., of Gamesley, near Glossop (marriage dissolved in 1967); 2ndly, 1972, Patricia, d. of S. Bates, Esq., of Radford, Coventry. Educ. at Westminster Training Coll., London, St. Salvators Coll., University of St. Andrews, and St. John's Coll., Cambridge. Research Scientist A.E.I. Limited 1957-63; Lecturer in physics, Faculty of Technology, University of Manchester 1963-66. B.Sc. (Hons.) of St. Andrews; Ph.D. (Cantab.); A. Inst. Physics.

Member of the Select Committee for Science and Technology 1966-67, 1967-68 and 1968-69. Co-Vice-Chairman P.L.P. Defence and Services Group 1968-69. Parliamentary Private Secretary to the Rt. Hon. Edward Short, MP (then Postmaster-Gen.) Nov. 1967-Dec. 1967; Rt. Hon. George Brown, MP. (then Foreign Secretary) Jan. 1968-Mar. 1968; Rt. Hon. Michael Stewart, MP. (Secretary of State for Foreign and Commonwealth Affairs) Apr. 1968-Oct. 1969. Parliamentary Member of U.K. Mission to the United Nations for General Assembly 1969. Councillor, Borough of Stretford 1961-66. J.P. for Lancashire 1962. Parliamentary Secretary Ministry of Technology Oct. 1969-June 1970. A Labour Member. Elected for Stretford in Mar. 1966 and sat until June 1970 when he was defeated. Councillor, London Borough of Southwark from 1974. A Management Selection Consultant. [1970]

DAVIES, Ernest Albert John. 6F, Observatory Gardens, Kensington, London. S. of Alderman A. Emil Davies. B. 18 May 1902; m. 1st, 1926, Natalie, d. of Alfred Rossin, Esq. (marriage dissolved in 1944); 2ndly, 1944, Peggy, d. of William Yeo, Esq., of Caegarw, Court Colman, Bridgend, Glamorgan (she died 1963). Educ. at Wycliffe Coll., and University of London. A Journalist and Author. Editor of *Clarion* 1929-32, Associate Editor of *New Clarion* 1932. Gov. of National Froebel Foundation 1938-40. On staff of B.B.C. 1940-45. Organiser of North American service 1944-45. Parliamentary Private Secretary to Rt. Hon. H. McNeil, Minister of State at Foreign Office 1946-50. Joint Parliamentary Under-Secretary Foreign Office 1950-51. Chairman Parliamentary Labour Party Inland Transport Committee 1945-50 and from 1951. A Labour Member. Unsuccessfully contested Peterborough in 1935. Sat for Enfield from July 1945-Feb. 1950 and for Enfield E. from Feb. 1950 until he retired in Oct. 1959. Chairman of British Yugoslav Society from 1957. Opposition spokesman on Transport to 1959. Managing Editor of *Traffic Engineering and Control* 1960-76. Managing Editor of *Antique Finder* 1962-72. [1959]

DAVIES, Rt. Hon. (Edward) Clement, Q.C. 31 Evelyn Mansions, London. Plas Dyffryn, Meifod, Montgomeryshire. Reform. S. of M. and L. Davies. B. 19 Feb. 1884; m. 20 Sept. 1913, Jano, d. of Dr. Morgan Davies, M.D., F.R.C.S. London. Educ. at Llanfyllin, and Trinity Hall, Cambridge. Barrister-at-Law, Lincoln's Inn 1909; K.C. 1926, PC. 1947. Secretary to President of Probate, Divorce and Admiralty division of High Court 1918-19 and to Master of Rolls 1919-23. Junior counsel to Treasury 1919-25. Chairman of Montgomeryshire Quarter Sessions 1935-62. Bencher 1953. Parliamentary Charity Commissioner 1936-37. Chairman of the 'All Party Action Group' which played a major role in the defeat of the Chamberlain government in May 1940, President of Welsh Liberal Federation 1945-48. Leader of Liberal Party 1945-56. Was offered the Cabinet post of Minister of Education in Oct. 1951 but declined it. President of Parliamentary Association for World Government 1951. Chairman of History and Parliament Trust. Member of Political Honours Scrutiny Committee 1961-62. Elected for Montgomeryshire as a Liberal in May 1929, joined the Liberal National group in 1931 but resigned the Liberal National whip in Dec. 1939 and rejoined the Liberal Party in Aug. 1942. Sat until his death on 23 Mar. 1962. Died 23 Mar. 1962. [1962]

DAVIES, (Gwilym) Ednyfed Hudson. House of Commons, London. S. of E. Curig Davies, Esq., Minister of Religion. B. 4 Dec. 1929; m. 1972, Amanda, d. of Peter Barker-Mill, Esq. Educ. at Dynevor Grammar School, Swansea, Swansea University Coll., and Balliol Coll., Oxford. Lecturer at University Coll., Aberystwyth 1957-61; Lecturer in Political Thought at Welsh Coll. of Advanced Technology 1961-66. A Labour Member. Elected for the Conway division of Caernarvonshire in Mar. 1966 and sat until he was defeated in June 1970. Elected for Caerphilly in May 1979. Television commentator and programme presenter 1962-66 and 1970-76. Barrister-at-Law, Gray's Inn 1975. Chairman of Wales Tourist Board 1976-78* [1970]

DAVIES, Gwilym Elfed. "Maes-y-Ffrwd", Ferndale Road, Tylorstown, Rhondda, Glamorgan. S. of David Davies, Esq. A Miner. B. 9 Oct. 1913; m. 16 Dec. 1940, Gwyneth, d. of Daniel Rees, Esq. Educ. at Tylorstown Rhondda Elementary School. Chairman Tylorstown Lodge N.U.M. 1934-40. Treasurer Tylorstown Lodge N.U.M. 1940-54; Secretary from 1954-1959. Chairman Aberdare and Rhondda District N.U.M. 1958-59. Member of Executive Committee Rhondda East Divisional Labour Party and Rhondda Borough Labour Party. Member Glammorgan County Council from 1954-61. Parliamentary Private Secretary to Rt. Hon. R.J. Gunter, Minister of Labour and Minister of Power from Nov. 1964-June 1968. A Labour Member. Elected for Rhondda E. in 1959 and sat until he retired in Feb. 1974. Created Baron Davies of Penrhys (Life Peerage) 1974. Member of S. Wales Electricity Board from 1974. Member of National Sports Council for Wales from 1978. [1974]

DAVIES, Rt. Hon. Harold. 36 Clevedon Mansions, Lissenden Gardens, London. 81 Trentham Road, Longton, Stoke-on-Trent. S. of William Davies, Esq. B. July 1904; m. 1925 Elizabeth Bateman. Educ. at Lewis Grammar School, Pengam. A Teacher and Lecturer to H.M. Forces 1939-45. President of Tutors' Association N. Staffordshire. Executive member of Labour Party Regional Council. Writer and Freelance Journalist. Author; Books and Pamphlets, Far East, S.E. Asia etc. Extensive traveller, Far East, U.S.A., Europe, Africa and Middle East. Parliamentary Secretary to the Ministry of Pensions and National Insurance Oct. 1964-Aug. 1966. PC. 1969. A Labour Member. Elected for the Leek division of Staffordshire in July 1945 and sat until June 1970 when he was defeated. Parliamentary Secretary to the Ministry of Social Security Aug. 1966-Jan. 1967. Parliamentary Private Secretary to Rt. Hon. Harold Wilson when Prime Minister Jan. 1967-June 1970. Prime Minister's Special Envoy to Hanoi 1965. PC. 1969. Created Baron Davies of Leek (Life Peerage) 1970. Member of Executive Committee of Inter-Parliamentary Union from 1975. [1970]

DAVIES, Haydn. 4 Delta Road, The Avenue, Worcester Park, Surrey. S. of A. Davies, Esq., of Abertysswg. B. 8 May 1905; m. 1936, Mary, d. of John Dodd, Esq., of Ealing. Educ. at Lewis Grammar School, Pengam, University, Coll. of Wales, Aberystwyth, and London School of Economics. A London Schoolmaster. Honorary Joint Secretary Inter-Parliamentary Union (British Group) 1948. Education Correspondent of *News Chronicle* and Industrial Correspondent of *The Star*. A Labour Member. Unsuccessfully contested St. Pancras S.W. in 1929. Elected for St. Pancras S.W. in July 1945 and sat until Feb. 1950 when he unsuccessfully contested York. In Ministry of Economic Warfare and Board of Trade 1939-45. Died 18 Apr. 1976. [1950]

DAVIES, Ifor. Ty Pentwyn, Three Crosses, Gower. S. of Jeffrey Davies, Esq. B. 9 June 1910; m. 15 Aug. 1950, Doreen, d. of William Griffiths, Esq. Educ. at Gowerton School, and Ruskin Coll., Oxford. A Congregationalist. An Accountant 1931-39. Personnel Officer I.C.I. 1942-47, Aluminium Wire and Cable Co. Ltd. 1948-59. Statistics Department, Ministry of Labour 1947-48. Member Glamorgan County Council 1958-61. Chairman Coll. Council Swansea University 1969. Member Wales Civic Trust Board. Opposition Whip 1961-64. A Lord Commissioner of the Treasury and Government Whip Oct. 1964-Apr. 1966. Parliamentary Under-Secretary of State for Wales from Apr. 1966-Oct. 1969. Chairman Welsh Grand Committee. Voted in favour of entry to E.E.C. on 28 Oct. 1971. A Labour Member. Sat for the Gower division of Glamorgan from 1959. Member of Chairman's Panel.* [1979]

DAVIES, Rt. Hon. John Emerson Harding, M.B.E. House of Commons, London. S. of Arnold Thomas Davies, Esq., Chartered Accountant. B. 8 Jan. 1916; m. 8 Jan. 1943, Vera Georgina, d. of George William Bates, Esq. Educ. at St. Edwards School, Oxford. Articled Clerk (Chartered Accountancy) 1934-39; Chartered Accountant 1939-40 (A.C.A. 1939, F.C.A. 1949, Hon. Dip. M.A. 1967). Honorary D. Univ. Essex, Hon. D. Tech. Loughborough. Served in the army

(Combined Operations G2 Tech.) 1940-46; British Petroleum (Final Appointment Director B.P. Trading) 1946-61; Shell-Mex and B.P. (Vice-Chairman and Managing Director) 1961-65; Confederation of British Industry (Director-Gen.) 1965-69; Director Hill Samuel Group 1969-70 and from 1974. M.B.E. 1946. Member of British Productivity Council 1965-69, British National Export Council 1966-69, Council of Industrial Design 1966-70 and Public Schools Commission 1966-68. PC. 1970. Minister of Technology July 1970-Oct. 1970. Secretary of State for Trade and Industry and President of the Board of Trade Oct. 1970-Nov. 1972. Chancellor of the Duchy of Lancaster Nov. 1972-Mar. 1974. Opposition spokesman on Foreign Affairs and Member of Shadow Cabinet Nov. 1976-Oct. 1978. A Conservative. Sat for the Knutsford division of Cheshire from June 1970 until he resigned in Nov. 1978. Awarded a Life Peerage in June 1979 but died on 4 July 1979 before the Peerage could be gazetted. [1979]

DAVIES, Rhys John. Manceinion, Newton, Porthcawl, Glamorgan. S. of Rees and Ann Davies, of Llangennech, Carmarthenshire. B. 15 Apr. 1877; m. 1902, Margaret Griffiths. Domestic Arts Teacher. Educ. at Elementary School. Farm Labourer for three years, Coal-Miner ten years, Co-operative employee four years. A Trade Union Official from 1907. Member of Manchester City Council 1913-23. President Manchester and Salford Labour Party 1917-20, and of its Trades Council 1920-22. Under-Secretary of State, Home Department Jan.-Nov. 1924. "Father" of the Parliamentary Labour Party. A Labour Member. Unsuccessfully contested W. Salford in Dec. 1918. Elected for the Westhoughton division of Lancashire in Oct. 1921 and sat until he resigned in May 1951. Member of Executive Committee of Parliamentary Labour Party 1923-24. Member of National Executive Committee of Labour Party 1921-27. Died 31 Oct. 1954. [1951]

DAVIES, Robert Malcolm Deryck. 43 Beaumont Road, Cambridge. S. of Rhys Wilshire Davies, Esq. Surveyor. B. 7 May 1918; m. 16 Aug. 1941, Katharine Mary, d. of the Rev. Sidney H. Wing. Educ. at

Reading School, London University, and Oxford University. Secretary University of Cambridge Department of Applied Economics 1949-66. Member of Cambridge City Council 1954-67; Alderman 1964. A Labour Member. Unsuccessfully contested Cambridge in the 1959 and 1964 general elections and Cambridgeshire at a by-election in 1961. Elected for Cambridge in Mar. 1966 and sat until his death on 16 June 1967. [1967]

DAVIES, Stephen Owen. Gwynfryn Park Terrace, Merthyr-Tydfil. S. of Thomas Davies, Esq. B. 8 Nov. 1886; m. 1934, Seph. Educ. at University Coll., Cardiff. A Coal Miner. Miners Agent S. Wales Miners Federation 1918-34, Vice-President 1924-33; Graduate of University of Wales; also Governor of same; and Mining Engineer. Elected Labour Member for the Merthyr division of Merthyr Tydfil in June 1934 and sat until Feb. 1950 when he was elected for Merthyr Tydfil. His constituency party declined to readopt him in 1970 but he stood as an Independent Labour candidate, was expelled from the Labour Party and defeated the official Labour candidate at the general election in June 1970. Sat until his death on 25 Feb. 1972. Labour Whip withdrawn Nov. 1954-Apr. 1955 and Mar. 1961-May 1963. Representative of S. Wales Miners on Miners Federation of Great Britain 1924-34. Member of Merthyr Tydfil Borough Council 1931-49, Mayor 1945-46. Died 25 Feb. 1972. [1972]

DAVIES, Dr. Wyndham Roy, L.R.C.P., M.B., Ch. B., D.P.H., D.I.H. 20 Spur Hill Avenue, Poole, Dorset. Flat 42, 24 John Islip Street, London. United Services, Royal Ocean Racing; British Schools Exploring Society. S. of George Edward Davies, Esq., of Llangadock. B. 1926. Educ. at King Edward's School, Birmingham, and Birmingham and London Universities. Held appointments in Birmingham Hospitals. Joined the Royal Navy, served for twelve years, retiring in 1963 with the rank of Surgeon Lieut.-Commander. Medical Adviser to the British Sub-Aqua Club 1959-66, and British Safety Council 1962-64. A Conservative. Elected for the Perry Barr division of Birmingham in Oct. 1964 and sat until

Mar. 1966 when he was defeated. Unsuccessfully contested the St. Marylebone division of Westminster in Feb. 1974 as an 'All-Party Alliance for Enoch Powell' candidate. Member of Executive Council of Monday Club 1965-69. Director of Medical Economic Research Institute 1968. In Bahamas with Ministry of Overseas Development 1969-72. Director of British Cellular Therapy Society from 1974. Editor of *Fellowship for Freedom in Medicine Bulletin* 1972-74. Gov. of Royal Humane Society from 1962.   [1966]

D'AVIGDOR-GOLDSMID, Maj. Sir Henry Joseph, Bart., D.S.O., M.C., T.D. Somerhill, Tonbridge, Kent. St. James's, White's, and Carlton. S. of Sir Osmond Elim D'Avigdor Goldsmid, 1st Bart. B. 1909; m. 1940, Rosemary Margaret Horlick, eld. d. of Lieut.-Col. C.R.I. Nicholl. Educ. at Harrow, and Balliol Coll., Oxford, M.A. Served with R.W.K. Regiment and R.A.C. (despatches twice). Freeman of City of London; member Kent County Council 1946-53; J.P., Dept.-Lieut. (1949) and High Sheriff (1953) of Kent. Succeeded his father as 2nd Bart. in 1940. D.S.O. 1945; M.C. 1945. A Conservative. Elected for Walsall S. in 1955 and sat until he retired in Feb. 1974. Parliamentary Private Secretary to Rt. Hon. Duncan Sandys, Minister of Housing 1955-56. Chairman of Anglo-Israel Bank 1961-76. Chairman of Pergamon Press Limited 1969-71. Chairman of Select Committee on Nationalized Industries 1970-72. Chairman of Select Committee on Public Expenditure 1972-74. Member of Horserace Totalisator Board 1973-76. Died 11 Dec. 1976.   [1974]

D'AVIGDOR-GOLDSMID, Maj.-Gen. James Arthur ('Jack'), C.B., O.B.E., M.C. 101 Mount Street, London. Cavalry, St. James's, Jockey, and Turf. S. of Sir Osmond D'Avigdor-Goldsmid, Bart. B. 19 Dec. 1912. Unmarried. Educ. at Harrow, and Royal Military Coll., Sandhurst. 2nd Lieut. 4/7 Royal Dragoon Guards 1932; wounded in active service 1939-45. M.C. 1944. Commanded 4/7 Royal Dragoon Guards 1950-53 and 20 Armoured Brigade Group 1958-61; Director Royal Armoured Corps 1962-65 and Territorial Army 1965-68. A Conservative. Elected for the Lichfield and Tamworth

division of Staffordshire in June 1970 and sat until Oct. 1974 when he was defeated. O.B.E. 1955. C.B. 1975. Succeeded his brother as 3rd Bart. in 1976. Chairman of Racecourse Security Services Limited. Member of Horserace Betting Levy Board 1974-1977.   [1974 2nd ed.]

DAVIS, Stanley Clinton. 354 Finchley Road, London. House of Commons, London. S. of Sidney Davis, Esq., Manufacturer. B.6 Dec. 1928; m. 1954, Frances Jane, d. of Dr. Marcus Gershon Lucas, of Birmingham, (1 s. 3 d.). Educ. at Hackney Downs School, Mercers' School, Kings Coll., London University. Chairman Kings Coll. London Labour Club 1948; member National Executive of National Association of Labour Students' Organisations 1949-50; Bachelor of Law (London) 1950; admitted as Solicitor 1953. Mayor of the London borough of Hackney 1968-69, Councillor from 1959; Joint Secretary All-Party Solicitors Group 1971-74; Secretary Parliamentary Labour Party Anglo-Chilean Group 1972-74; member of APEX. Vice-President Hackney Association for the Disabled. Parliamentary Under-Secretary State, Department of Trade, responsibilities Companies, Aviation and Shipping Mar. 1974-May 1979. An Opposition spokesman on Trade from 1979. A Labour Member. Unsuccessfully contested Portsmouth, Langstone in 1955, and Yarmouth, Norfolk in 1959 and 1964. Sat for the Central division of Hackney from June 1970.*   [1979]

DAVIS, Terence Anthony Gordon. House of Commons, London. S. of C.G. Davis, Esq. B. 5 Jan. 1938; m. 1963, Anne, d. of F.B. Cooper, Esq. Educ. at King Edward VI Grammar School, Stourbridge, University Coll., London, and University of Michigan, U.S.A. Member of Yeovil Rural District Council 1967-68. A Labour Member. Unsuccessfully contested Bromsgrove in June 1970. Elected for the Bromsgrove division of Worcestershire in May 1971 and sat until Feb. 1974 when he unsuccessfully contested Bromsgrove and Redditch, where he was defeated again in Oct. 1974. Unsuccessfully contested the Stechford division of Birmingham in Mar. 1977. Elected for the Stechford division of Birmingham in May 1979. Company Executive in the motor industry. Opposition Whip from Nov. 1979. [1974]

DAVISON, Sir William Henry, K.B.E. 14 Kensington Park Gardens, London Carlton, Athenaeum, and Oxford & Cambridge. S. of Richard Davison, Esq., of Ballymena, Co. Antrim. B. 1872; m. 1st, 4 June 1898, Beatrice Mary, d. of Sir Owen Roberts (m.dissolved in 1928); 2ndly, 6 June 1929, Constance, d. of Maj. Charles Marriott, 6th Dragoon Guards. Educ. at Shrewsbury, and Keble Coll., Oxford; M.A. 1898. Barrister-at-Law, Inner Temple 1895. K.B.E. 1918. Mayor of Kensington 1913-19. Raised and equipped the 22nd Battalion Royal Fusiliers in Sept. 1914. Dept.-Lieut. and J.P. for London. Fellow of Society of Antiquaries, and Vice-President Royal Society of Arts. Treasurer of Whitechapel Arts Gallery; Gov. of the Foundling Hospital; Chairman of Income Tax Payers Society; Master of the Worshipful Company of Cloth Workers 1941-43; a Freeman of the City of London. President of Kensington Chamber of Commerce; Chairman of Improved Industrial Dwellings Company Limited, of E. Surrey Water Company and Water Companies Association of Great Britain, of British Mutual Banking Company Limited, of N.S.W. Land and Agency Company Limited and of Met. Division National Union of Conservative Associations 1928-30; Co-opted member of London Education Committee 1908-10. A Conservative. MP. for S. Kensington from 1918 until August 1945 when he was created Baron Broughshane. Died 19 Jan. 1953. [1945]

DEAKINS, Eric Petro. House of Commons, London. S. of Edward Deakins, Esq., Carpenter. B. 7 Oct. 1932. Educ. at Bruce Grove Elementary School, Tottenham Grammar School, and London School of Economics, B.A. (Hons.) in History 1953. National Service 1953-55; Employee of F.M.C. (Meat) Limited 1956-71, General Managing of Pigs division 1969. Author of *A Faith to Fight For* Gollancz 1964. An Opposition spokesman on Europe 1973-74. Parliamentary Under-Secretary of State for Trade Mar. 1974-Apr. 1976. Parliamentary Under-Secretary of State for Health and Social Security

Apr. 1976-May 1979. A Labour Member. Unsuccessfully contested Finchley in 1959, Chigwell in 1966 and W. Walthamstow in Sept. 1967. Sat for the W. Division of Walthamstow from 1970-Feb. 1974 and for the Walthamstow division of Waltham Forest from Feb. 1974.* [1979]

DEAN, (Arthur) Paul. Richmonte Lodge, East Harptree, Nr. Bristol. S. of Arthur Percival Dean, Esq. B. 1924; m. 1957, Doris Ellen Webb (she died 1979). Educ. at Ellesmere Coll., Shropshire, and Exeter Coll., Oxford, (M.A., B. Litt.). Served with the Welsh Guards during World War II and attained the rank of Capt. Personal Assistant to the Commander, 1st British Corps in Germany for eighteen months. A Farmer 1950-56. Resident Tutor, Swinton Conservative Coll. 1956-57. Joined the Conservative Research Department in 1958, appointed Assistant Director 1962. Parliamentary Under-Secretary of State Department of Health and Social Security 1970-74. Director of Antony Gibbs Financial Services Limited and Charterhouse Pensions Limited. Gov. of British United Provident Association. Member Executive Committee Commonwealth Parliamentary Association. Chairman Conservative Watch-dog Group for the Self-Employed. An Opposition spokesman on Social Services 1969-70. Member of Speaker's Panel of Chairmen from 1979. A Conservative. Adopted for Pontefract in Dec. 1961 but unsuccessful in the by-election of Mar. 1962. Sat for the N. division of Somerset from Oct. 1964.* [1979]

DEAN, Joseph Jabez. House of Commons, London. B. 1923. Educ. at St. Anne's R.C. School, Ancoats, Manchester. Engineer. Member of Manchester City Council 1960-74, Leader of Council. Parliamentary Private Secretary to Charles Morris, Minister of State, Civil Service Department 1974-77. Secretary AUEW Group MPs. Member House of Commons Services Committee 1977 and Catering Sub-Committee 1977. Assistant Government Whip July 1978-May 1979. Opposition Whip from 1979. A Labour Member. Sat for Leeds W. from Feb. 1974.* [1979]

de CHAIR, Somerset Struben. Blickling Hall, Aylsham, Norfolk. Carlton. S. of Admiral Sir Dudley de Chair, K.C.B., K.C.M.G., M.V.O. B. 22 Aug. 1911; m. 1st, 1932, Thelma Arbuthnot (divorced 1950); 2ndly, 24 Aug. 1950, Carmen Appleton, d. of Alan Bowen, Esq., of Brabourne, Kent (divorced 1958); 3rdly, 1958, Margaret Patricia Manlove (divorced 1974); 4thly, 1974, Juliet, Marchioness of Bristol. Educ. in Australia and at Balliol Coll., Oxford. An Author and Novelist. Served with Household Cavalry Middle East 1940-41, and as Intelligence Officer in Palestine, Iraq and Syria 1941. Capt. G.S. M.I.2 1942. Parliamentary Private Secretary to the Rt. Hon. Oliver Lyttelton, Minister of Production 1942-44. A Gov. of Wye Agricultural Coll. 1946-48. Chairman of Kent Association of Boys' Clubs 1947-48. Member of Select Committee House of Commons Rebuilding 1933-44. A Conservative. Sat S.W. Norfolk from 1935-45, when he was defeated. Elected for S. Paddington in Feb. 1950 and sat until he retired in 1951. Member of National Executive of United Nations Association 1947-50. [1951]

DEEDES, Rt. Hon. William Francis 7 Eaton Terrace, London. New Hayters, Aldington, Ashford, Kent. Junior Carlton. S. of Herbert William Deedes, Esq. B.1 June 1913; m. 21 Nov. 1942, Evelyn Hilary, d. of Clive Branfoot, Esq. Educ. at Harrow. A Journalist. Joined The *Morning Post* 1931, Editorial Staff of The *Daily Telegraph* 1937. Served with K.R.R.C. 1939-45, Maj., M.C. Parliamentary Secretary Ministry of Housing and Local Government Oct. 1954-Dec. 1955; Parliamentary Under-Secretary of State Home Department Dec. 1955-Jan. 1957. Minister without Portfolio July 1962-Oct. 1964. A Conservative. Elected for the Ashford division of Kent in Feb. 1950 and sat until he retired in Sept. 1974. PC. 1962. Dept.-Lieut. for Kent 1962. Editor of The *Daily Telegraph* from 1974. [1974 2nd ed.]

DEER, George, O.B.E. 13 Hunsley Crescent, Grimsby. S. of T. Deer, Esq., of Grimsby. B. 29 Mar. 1890; m. 1916, Olive Stoakes (Chairman of London County Council 1962-63). Educ. at Elementary School. A Trade Union Official. Member of Lincoln City Council from 1922-38 and 1945-50. Mayor 1933-34 and Sheriff 1943-44 of Lincoln. O.B.E. 1944. Opposition Whip 1955-59. A Labour Member. Unsuccessfully contested the Gainsborough division of Lincolnshire in 1929 and 1931 and Lincoln in 1935. Sat for Lincoln July 1945-Feb. 1950. Elected for the Newark division of Nottinghamshire in Feb. 1950 and sat until he retired in 1964. Died 15 May 1974. [1964]

DE ERESBY, Gilbert James Heathcote-Drummond-Willoughby, Lord Willoughby. See WILLOUGHBY DE ERESBY, Gilbert James Heathcote-Drummond-Willoughby, Lord.

de FERRANTI, Basil Reginald Vincent Ziani. House of Commons, London. S. of Sir Vincent de Ferranti. B. 2 July 1930; m. 1st, 17 Dec. 1956, Susan Sara, d. of Christopher Gore and Lady Barbara Gore (from whom he obtained a divorce in 1963), (3 s.); 2ndly, 1964, Simone, d. of Col. H.J. Nangle; 3rdly, 1971, Jocelyn Hilary Mary, d. of Wing-Commander A.T. Laing. Educ. at Eton, and Trinity Coll., Cambridge, M.A. Commissioned in 4/7th Dragoon Guards and served N. Africa 1949-50. Vice-Chairman Wythenshawe Conservative Association 1956. Parliamentary Private Secretary to David Renton, Minister of State, Home Office 1960-62. Parliamentary Secretary Ministry of Aviation July-Oct. 1962. Dept. Managing Director, International Computers and Tabulators Limited. Director and Dept. Chairman of Ferranti Limited. Member of Council, Cheltenham Coll., Institution of Electrical Engineers. A Conservative. Unsuccessfully contested the Exchange division of Manchester in 1955. Elected for the Morecambe and Lonsdale division of Lancashire in Nov. 1958 and sat until he retired in 1964. Member of European Parliament for Hampshire W. from 1979. Vice-President of European Parliament and Vice-Chairman of European Democratic Group. Member of Economic and Social Committee of European Communities 1973-78, Chairman 1976-78. President of British Computer Society 1968-69. [1964]

de FREITAS, Rt. Hon. Sir Geoffrey Stanley, K.C.M.G., 11 Trumpington Road, Cambridge. S. of Sir Anthony de Freitas, O.B.E. and Maud, d. of Augustus Panton Short. B. 7 Apr. 1913; m. 1938, Helen Graham, d. of Laird Bell, K.B.E. (Hon.), LL.D. (Hon.) of U.S.A. Educ. at Haileybury, Clare Coll. (Hon. Fellow), Cambridge (President of the Union), and Yale University (Mellon Fellow). Left Parliament in 1961 to become British High Commissioner in Ghana, in Dec. 1963 designated High Commissioner to the East African Federation but when the countries did not federate became first High Commissioner in Kenya, 1963-64. Barrister-at-Law (Cholmeley Scholar) Lincoln's Inn 1937. Joined R.A. 1939. Served R.A.F. 1940-45. Parliamentary Private Secretary to Prime Minister 1945-46. Under-Secretary of State for Air 1946-50; Under-Secretary of State, Home Office 1950-51. Delegate to U.N. 1949 and 1965, to Council of Europe 1951-54 and 1965-70, Leader of U.K. Delegation, President of Assembly 1966-69, to North Atlantic Assembly 1955-60 and 1965-77, Leader of U.K. Delegation, President from 1976. Vice-President European Parliament 1975-79. Director Laporte Industries 1968-77. Opposition spokesman on Home Affairs 1955-56 and on Air 1956-60. Shadow Minister of Agriculture 1960-61. Select Committee on Privileges 1964-67. Chairman Select Committee on Overseas Development 1974-76. Voted in favour of entry to E.E.C. on 28 Oct. 1971. A Labour Member. Sat for Central Nottingham from 1945-50, and for Lincoln from 1950-61, when he resigned on appointment as British High Commissioner in Ghana. Sat for the Kettering division of Northamptonshire from Oct. 1964 until he retired in 1979. Member of Shoreditch Borough Council 1936-39. Chairman of Society of Labour Lawyers 1955-58, Labour Committee for Europe 1965-72, Gauche Européenne from 1966, Atlee Foundation 1967-76. K.C.M.G. 1961. PC. 1967.*
[1979]

De la BERE, Sir Rupert, Bart. Crowborough Place, Crowborough. Carlton. S. of Reginald De la Bère, of Addlestone, Surrey. B. 16 June 1893; m. 30 Apr. 1919, Marguerite, d. of Sir John Humphrey (she died 1969). Educ. at Tonbridge School. A Director of Hays Wharf. Alderman of the City of London for the Ward of Tower. Served overseas 1914-18 with East Surrey Regiment and with R.A.F. A Sheriff of the City of London 1941; Lord Mayor of London 1952. Knighted June 1952. K.C.V.O. June 1953. Bart. Nov. 1953. A Conservative. Sat for the Evesham division of Worcestershire from 1935-50. Elected for Worcestershire S. in Feb. 1950 and sat until he retired in 1955. Knight of the Orders of St. John of Jerusalem, the Dannebrog (Denmark), and the North Star (Sweden). Died 25 Feb. 1978.   [1954]

DELARGY, Hugh James. 15 Winchester Court, London. S. of Bernard Delargy, Esq., of Co. Antrim. B. 1908; m. 1952, Margaret Horan. Served with Royal Artillery 1939-45, Capt. Member of Manchester City Council 1937-46. A Vice-Chairman of the British Council from 1969; Chairman Committee of Selection House of Commons. Commanders Cross Polonia Restituta. A Labour Member. Sat for the Platting division of Manchester from 1945-50. Elected for the Thurrock division of Essex in Feb. 1950 and sat until his death on 4 May 1976. Assistant Whip 1950-51, Opposition Whip 1951-52. Died 4 May 1976.   [1976]

DELL, Rt. Hon. Edmund Emanuel. 4 Reynolds Close, London. S. of Reuben Dell, Esq. B. 15 Aug. 1921; m. 1963, Susanne Gottschalk. Educ. at Owen's School, London, and The Queen's Coll., Oxford. Served in R.A. 1941-45. Lecturer in Modern History, The Queen's Coll., Oxford 1947-49. Executive with I.C.I. 1949-63. Simon Research Fellow, Manchester University 1963-64. Joined the Labour Party in 1949. Member of A.S.T.M.S. and the Fabian Society. President Manchester and Salford Trades Council 1958-61. Member 1960-61 Executive Lancashire and Cheshire Regional Council of the Labour Party. Member of Manchester City Council 1953-60. Joint Parliamentary Secretary Ministry of Technology Apr. 1966-Aug. 1967. Joint Parliamentary Under-Secretary of State, Department of Economic Affairs Aug. 1967-Apr. 1968. Minister of State, Board of Trade Apr. 1968- Oct. 1969.

Minister of State, Department of Employment and Productivity Oct. 1969-June 1970. Chairman Public Accounts Committee 1972-74. Published *Political Responsibility and Industry* 1973. Paymaster-Gen. May 1974-Apr. 1976. Secretary of State for Trade Apr. 1976-Nov. 1978. Opposition spokesman on Trade 1970-72. Voted in favour of entry to E.E.C. on 28 Oct. 1971. PC. 1970. A Labour Member. Unsuccessfully contested Middleton and Prestwich in 1955. Sat for Birkenhead from Oct. 1964 until he retired in 1979. Dept. Chairman of Guinness Peat Mar.-Aug. 1979, Chairman and Chief Executive from Aug. 1979.*　　　　　　　　　[1979]

DEMPSEY, James. House of Commons, London. S. of James Dempsey, Esq. B. 1917; m. 1945, Jane, d. of John McCann, Esq. Educ. at Holy Family School, Mossend, and Co-operative Coll., Loughborough. A Roman Catholic. Served with Auxiliary Military Pioneer Corps 1939-45. Member of the Lanarkshire County Council from 1945. J.P. for Lanarkshire. A Labour Member. Sat for Coatbridge and Airdrie from 1959.*
　　　　　　　　　　　　　　　　[1979]

DEVLIN, (Josephine) Bernadette. See McALISKEY, (Josephine) Bernadette.

DEWAR, Donald Campbell. 23 Cleveland Road, Glasgow, Scotland. S. of Dr. Alasdair Dewar. B. 21 Aug. 1937; m. 1964, Alison McNair, (1 s. 1 d.), (marriage dissolved in 1973). Educ. at Glasgow Academy, and Glasgow University. A Solicitor. Joined the Labour Party in 1956. President Glasgow University Union 1961-62. Parliamentary Private Secretary to Rt. Hon. Anthony Crosland, President of the Board of Trade 1967-69. Chairman of Select Committee on Scottish Affairs from 1979. A Labour Member. Unsuccessfully contested Aberdeen S. in 1964. Sat for Aberdeen S. from 1966-70, when he was defeated, and for the Garscadden division of Glasgow from Apr. 1978.*
　　　　　　　　　　　　　　　　[1979]

DIAMOND, Rt. Hon. John. Flat 4, 15 Greycoat Place, London. S. of Solomon Diamond, Esq., a Minister. B. 30 Apr. 1907; m. 1st, 1932, Sadie, d. of M.L. Lyttleton,

Esq., of Leeds (2 s. 1 d.) (divorced 1947); m. 2ndly, 1948, Julie (1 d.); m. 3rdly, 1976, Mrs. Barbara Kagan. Educ. at Leeds Grammar School. Practised as Chartered Accountant from 1931-64. (F.C.A.). Member Gen. Nursing Council (Chairman of Finance and Gen. Purposes Committee) 1947-53; Honorary Treasurer Fabian Society 1950-64; Managing Director of Capital and Provincial News Theatres 1951-57; Director Sadlers Wells Trust from 1957-64. Parliamentary Private Secretary to Rt. Hon. C.W. Key, Minister of Works 1947. Chief Secretary to the Treasury Oct. 1964-June 1970. Member of Cabinet Nov. 1968-June 1970. PC. 1965. A Labour Member. Sat for the Blackley division of Manchester 1945-1951 when he was defeated. Unsuccessfully contested the Blackley division of Manchester in 1955. Elected for Gloucester in Sept. 1957 and sat until 1970 when he was defeated. Created Baron Diamond (Life Peerage) 1970. Dept. Chairman of Committees, House of Lords 1974. Chairman of Royal Commission on Distribution of Income and Wealth from 1974. Chairman of Industry and Parliament Trust from 1976.*
　　　　　　　　　　　　　　　　[1970]

DICKENS, James McCulloch York. House of Commons, London. S. of A.Y. Dickens, Esq., Tool Buyer. B. 4 Apr. 1931; m. 1st, 1955, M.J. Grieve (divorced 1965); 2ndly, 1969, Mrs. Carolyn Casey. Educ. at Shawlands Academy, Glasgow, Ruskin Coll., and St. Catherine's Coll., Oxford. Industrial Relations Officer, National Coal Board 1958-65. Management Consultant 1965. A Labour Member. Elected for Lewisham W. in Mar. 1966 and sat until 1970 when he was defeated. Prospective candidate for Newham N.E. 1978-79 but resigned his candidacy in Apr. 1979. Assistant Director of Manpower, National Freight Corporation 1970-76. Assistant Director (Industrial Relations), National Water Council from 1976.　　　　　　　　　[1970]

DIGBY, (Kenelm) Simon Digby Wingfield, T.D., D.L. Haydon Gate, Nr. Sherborne, Dorset. Coleshill House, Coleshill, Birmingham. Carlton. S. of Col. F. Wingfield Digby, D.S.O. B. 13 Feb. 1910; m. 1936, Kathleen, d. of Hon. Mr. Justice Courtney

Kingstone, of Toronto, Canada. Educ. at Harrow, and Trinity Coll., Cambridge. Served in U.K. and overseas 1939-45; Maj. 1943. T.D. 1946. Formerly on Staff of Royal Institute for International Affairs. Secretary Conservative Society Services Committee 1948. Inter Parliamentary Union Delegation to Chile 1962. A Conservative Whip 1948-51. Civil Lord of the Admiralty Nov. 1951-Jan. 1957. Dept.-Lieut. for Dorset 1953. Chairman Conservative Forestry Sub-Committee 1958-67; Chairman Shipping and Shipbuilding Sub-Committee 1964-74. Member Select Sub-Committee on Coastal Pollution 1967-68; Delegate Council of Europe and Western European Union 1967; Leader 1973-74. Member Select Committee on Procedure and Public Accounts Committee. Barrister-at-Law, Inner Temple 1939. A Landowner and Farmer, Breeder of Bloodstock. A Conservative. Elected for W. Dorset in June 1941 and sat until he retired in Feb, 1974. [1974]

DIXON, Piers John Shirley. Probus, Cornwall. 22 Ponsonby Terrace, London. Brook's, and City University. S. of Sir Pierson Dixon, British Ambassador in New York and Paris. B. 29 Dec. 1928; m. 1st, 22 Dec. 1960, Edwina, d. of Rt. Hon. Duncan Sandys, MP. (marriage dissolved in 1973); 2ndly, 1976, Janet, d. of R.D. Aiyar, Esq., and widow of 5th Earl Cowley. Educ. at Eton (scholar), Magdalene Coll., Cambridge (exhibitioner), and Harvard Business School. Grenadier Guards 1948; Calvin Bullock, Investment Bankers, New York and London 1954; Philip Hill, Higginson, Merchant Bankers 1958; S.G. Warburg and Company, Merchant Bankers 1961. Sheppards and Chase, Stockbrokers 1964, Partner 1966. Author of *Double Diploma*. A Conservative. Unsuccessfully contested the Brixton division of Lambeth in 1966. Elected for the Truro division of Cornwall in June 1970 and sat until Oct. 1974 when he was defeated. Member of Centre for Policy Studies from 1976. [1974 2nd ed.]

DOBBIE, William. Unity House, Euston Road, London. 157 Carr Lane, York. S. of Frank Dobbie, Esq., Blacksmith, of Maybole, Ayrshire. B, 28 Oct. 1878; m. Dec. 1902,

Winifred, d. of Charles Thomas, Esq., of Shrewsbury. Educ. at Elementary School. A Coachpainter in the London and North Eastern Railway Works, York. Lord Mayor of York 1924 and 1948. President of National Union of Railwaymen 1924-27 and 1931-33. Served overseas 1914-18. A Labour Member. Unsuccessfully contested the Barkston Ash division of the W. Riding of Yorkshire in Oct. 1924, the Clitheroe division of Lancashire in May 1929 and the Stalybridge and Hyde division of Cheshire in Oct. 1931. Sat for Rotherham from Feb. 1933 until his death on 19 Jan. 1950. Member of York City Council from 1911. C.B.E. 1947. Member of National Executive Committee of Labour Party 1932-35 and 1941-42. Died 19 Jan. 1950. [1950]

DOBBS, Alfred James. B. 1882 at Wellingborough; m. Emily. Member of Executive of Boot and Shoe Operatives Union. Member of Rushden Urban District Council 1906. Member of Leeds City Council from 1923, Alderman 1929-36. J.P. for Leeds. Member of National Executive Committee of Labour Party 1936-45, Chairman 1942-43. A Labour Member. Unsuccessfully contested the Altrincham division of Cheshire in 1929 and N.E. Leeds in 1931 and 1935. Elected for Smethwick in 1945 but was killed in a car accident on 27 July 1945, the day after the declaration of the poll.

DOBSON, Raymond Francis Harvey. Hunters Moon, Highlands Road, Long Ashton, Bristol. 37 Elms Road, London. 157 Fishponds Road, Bristol. S. of Tom Doel Dobson, Esq., retired Police Chief Superintendent. B. 26 Apr. 1925; m. 4 Mar. 1948, Vivienne Joyce Martin, eld. d. of Vice-Admiral Sir Benjamin Martin, K.B.E., D.S.O., R.N. 3 s. 1 d. Educ. at Purbrook Park School, near Portsmouth. Joined the Labour Party in 1947. Executive member Union of Post Office Workers. Parliamentary Private Secretary to Rt. Hon. Anthony Wedgwood Benn, Minister of Technology 1967-68. Assistant Whip Oct. 1969-June 1970. A Labour Member. Unsuccessfully contested Torrington in 1959, Tiverton in 1960 and Bristol N.E. in 1964. Elected for Bristol N.E. in Mar. 1966 and sat until 1970 when he was defeated. Director of Personnel, British Caledonian Airways from 1970. Member of Board of Gambia Airways 1974-77, of Sierra Leone Airways from 1974, and of Air Liberia from 1976. Member of Air Transport and Travel Industry Training Board from 1973.* [1970]

DODDS, Norman Noel. 20 Havelock Road, Dartford. S. of Ambrose Dodds, Esq., of Dunston-on-Tyne. B. 1903; m. 1931, Eva, d. of Frank Pratt, Esq. Educ. at Elementary School. A Publicity Manager. Served with R.A.F. A Labour Member. Member for Dartford 1945-55 and for Erith and Crayford from 1955 until his death on 22 Aug. 1965. Member of Central Advisory Committee, Ministry of Pensions 1950-51. Director of People's Entertainment Society 1945-65. Parliamentary Private Secretary to Rt. Hon. Alfred Robens, Minister of Labour in 1951 and to Rt. Hon. Arthur Bottomley, Secretary of State for Commonwealth Relations 1964-65. Hon. Secretary of Homeworkers Products Society. Died 22 Aug. 1965. [1965]

DODDS-PARKER, Sir Arthur Douglas. 9 North Court, Great Peter Street, London. Carlton. S. of A.P. Dodds-Parker, Esq., F.R.C.S. B. 5 July 1909; m. 1946, Aileen, d. of N.B. Coster, Esq. Educ. at Winchester, and Magdalen Coll., Oxford. Sudan Political Service 1930-39. Grenadier Guards 1939-45, Col. Chairman of Joint East and Central Africa Board 1947-50. Joint Parliamentary Under-Secretary of State for Foreign Affairs Nov. 1953-Oct. 1954; Parliamentary Under-Secretary of State for Commonwealth Relations Oct. 1954-Dec 1955; for Foreign Affairs Dec. 1955-Jan. 1957. Knight Bach. 1973. A Conservative. Sat for Banbury from 1945-59, when he did not contest the general election. Elected for Cheltenham in Oct. 1964 and sat until he retired in Sept. 1974. Chairman of Conservative Commonwealth Council 1960-64. Delegate to Council of Europe and Western European Union 1965-72. Member of European Parliament 1973-75.* [1974 2nd ed.]

DODSWORTH, Geoffrey Hugh, J.P. Woodcote, Frithsden Copse, Berkhampsted, Hertfordshire. Carlton. S. of Walter J.J.

Dodsworth, Esq. B. 7 June 1928; m. 1st, 1949, Isabel Neale (she died); 2ndly 30 Jan. 1971, Elizabeth, d. of Dr. Alan W. Beeston, (1 s. 2 d.). Educ. at St. Peter's School, York. Member of York City Council 1959-65. J.P. for York and Hertfordshire. Director of Grindlay's Bank Ltd. from 1976. A Conservative. Unsuccessfully contested Don Valley in 1959, and The Hartlepools in 1964. Sat for Hertfordshire S.W. from Feb. 1974 until he resigned in Oct. 1979.* [1979]

DOIG, Peter Muir. House of Commons, London. S. of James Doig, Esq. B. 1911; m. 1938, Emily Scott (2 s.). Educ. at Blackness Public School, Dundee, and at evening classes. Joined the Labour Party in 1930; member of the Transport and General Workers Union, also member of Dundee Town Council 1953-63, Treasurer 1959-63. Holder of many offices in Local Labour Party. Served with the R.A.F. during the Second World War. A Labour Member. Unsuccessful Labour candidate for S. Aberdeen in 1959. Sat for Dundee W. from Nov. 1963 until he retired in 1979.* [1979]

DONALDSON, Commander Charles Edward McArthur, V.R.D., R.C.N.(R.). 27 Roxburgh Street, Galashields. S. of Thomas M. Donaldson, Esq. B. 15 Mar. 1903; m. 26 Apr. 1958, Kathleen Bradley, of London, (1 d.). Educ. at Aberdeen, Dawson, and King George British High Schools, Vancouver, British Columbia, Canada. Joined R.C.N. (Reserve) 1926. Aide-de-Camp to Lieut.-Gov. of British Columbia 1939-41. Commander 1945. Dept. Head of Canadian Naval Mission. London 1946. Retired 31 Dec. 1946. Assistant Secretary Tourist Association of Scotland 1947-51. Parliamentary Private Secretary to J. Clyde and W. Milligan when Lord Advocate 1953-59. Member of the Speaker's Panel of Chairmen 1959. A Conservative. Unsuccessfully contested E. Edinburgh in 1950. Sat for Roxburgh and Selkirk from Oct. 1951 to May 1955, and for Roxburgh, Selkirk and Peebles from May 1955 until his death on 11 Dec. 1964. V.R.D. 1943. Died 11 Dec. 1964. [1964]

DONNELLY, Desmond Louis. Pant-y-Beudy, Nr. Goodwick, Pembrokeshire. Flat 16, 88 Portland Place, London. S. of L.J. Donnelly, Esq., Tea Planter, of Assam. B. 1920; m. 1947, Rosemary, d. of Dr. John Taggart, of Belfast, (1 s. 2 d.). Educ. at Bembridge, Isle of Wight. A Journalist and Industrialist. A Labour Member 1950-68 and a Member of the Democratic Party 1968-70. Unsuccessfully contested the Evesham division of Worcestershire as a Common Wealth candidate in 1945 and County Down in June 1946 as a Labour candidate. Elected for Pembrokeshire in Feb. 1950 and sat until June 1970 when he was defeated, standing as a candidate of the Democratic Party. Resigned the Labour Whip in Jan. 1968. Expelled from Labour Party in Mar. 1968. Joined Conservative Party in Apr. 1971. Served in R.A.F. 1940-46, Flight-Lieut. Director of Town and Country Planning Association 1948-50. Chairman of ICPS Limited 1972-74. Managing Director of Practical Europe Limited 1973-74. Died 4 Apr. 1974. [1970]

DONNER, Sir Patrick William. Hurstbourne Park, Whitchurch, Hampshire. S of Ossian Donner, Esq., Diplomat. B. 1904; m. 1st, 25 Apr. 1938, Hon. Angela Chatfield, d. of Admiral of the Fleet Lord Chatfield, G.C.B., O.M., K.C.M.G., C.V.O. (she died 19 Aug. 1943); 2ndly, 9 Apr. 1947, Pamela, d. of Rear-Admiral Sir H.A. Forster, of Spring Hill, St. Mary Bourne, Andover. Educ. at Exeter Coll., Oxford. Hon. Secretary of India Defence League 1933-35. Parliamentary Private Secretary to Rt. Hon. Sir Samuel Hoare when Secretary of State for Home Affairs 1939; Parliamentary Private Secretary to Col. Rt. Hon Oliver Stanley, Secretary of State for the Colonies 1944. Joined R.A.F.V.R. Sept. 1939. Squadron-Leader 1941. Member of Advisory Committee on Education in the Colonies 1939-41 and of Executive Council Joint E. African Board 1937-54. Director of National Review Limited 1933-47. Knight Bach. 1953. A Conservative. Sat for W. Islington from Oct. 1931-Nov. 1935. Elected for the Basingstoke division of Hampshire in Nov. 1935 and sat until he retired in 1955. Chairman of Executive Committee of Men of the Trees

1959-62. Member of Art Panel of Arts Council 1963-66. High Sheriff of Hampshire 1967-68, Dept.-Lieut. 1971. [1954]

DONOVAN, Terence Norbert, K.C. 3 Temple Gardens, Temple, London. S. of Timothy Donovan, Esq. B. 1898; m. 1925, Marjorie Florence, d. of Charles Murray, Esq., of Winchester. Served with Bedfordshire Regiment and R.A.F. in France 1917-18; in the Civil Service 1920-32. Barrister-at-Law, Middle Temple 1924, Southern Rhodesia 1937; K.C. 1945. J.P. for Hampshire 1946; Chairman of Winchester County Bench; Dept. Chairman Appeals Committee Hampshire Quarter Sessions; member of Denning Committee on Divorce Procedure, Louis Committee on Court Central System, and of Statute Land Law Revision Committee. Additional member General Council of the Bar. A Labour Member. Sat for Leicester E. from July 1945-Feb. 1950. Elected for the N.E. division of Leicester in Feb. 1950 and sat until July 1950 when he was appointed a High Court Judge. Judge of Queen's Bench Division 1950-60. Knighted 1950; PC. 1960. Lord Justice of Appeal 1960-63. Lord of Appeal in Ordinary 1963-71. Created Baron Donovan (Law Life Peerage) 1964. Chairman of Royal Commission on Trades Unions and Employers' Associations 1965-68. Died 12 Dec. 1971. [1950]

DORMAND, John Donkin. House of Commons, London. S. of Bernard Dormand, Esq. B. 27 Aug. 1919; m. 26 Dec. 1963, Doris, d. of Thomas Pearson, Esq. Educ. at Bede Coll., Durham, Loughborough Coll., St. Peter's Coll., Oxford University, and Harvard University. A Teacher 1940-48; Education Adviser 1948-52 and 1959-63; Education Officer N.C.B. 1957-59; Education Officer Easington Rural District Council 1963-70. A Lord Commissioner of H.M. Treasury Oct. 1974-May 1979. Assistant Government Whip Mar.-Oct. 1974. A Labour Member. Sat for the Easington division of Durham from June 1970.* [1979]

DOUGHTY, Charles John Addison, Q.C. The Mill House, Buckland Monachorum, South Devon. 2 Harcourt Buildings, Temple, London. S. of Sir Charles Doughty, Q.C. B.

95

21 Sept. 1902; m. 29 July 1931, Adelaide, d. of E.H. Shackell, Esq., of Melbourne, Australia (she was created D.B.E. 1971). Educ. at Eton, and Magdalen Coll., Oxford. Barrister-at-Law, Inner Temple Jan. 1926; Queen's Counsel 1954; Recorder of Brighton 1955-71. Served in Coldstream Guards 1940-45, North Africa and Italy; demobilized as Maj. A Conservative. Unsuccessfully contested the Aston division of Birmingham in Feb. 1950. Elected for E. Surrey in Oct. 1951 and sat until he retired in 1970. Died 10 July 1973. [1970]

DOUGLAS, Francis Campbell Ross. 8 Cambridge Road, London. Maxfield Manor, Guestling, Sussex. S. of Francis J.B. Douglas, Esq. B. in Manitoba 21 Oct. 1889; m. 1st, Minnie Findlay, d. of William Smith, Esq. (she died 1969); 2ndly, 1971, Adela Elizabeth, widow of Capt. George La Croix Baudains. Educ. at University of Glasgow, M.A., F.R.A.S. A Solicitor. Parliamentary Private Secretary to J.C. Ede, Parliamentary Secretary Board of Education May 1940-May 1945, and when Secretary of State for Home Affairs Aug. 1945-May 1946; Chairman of Finance Committee London County Council 1940-46; member of Public Works Loan Board 1936-46, of Railway Assessment Authority 1938-46, and of Anglo-Scottish Railway Assesment Authority 1941-46. A Labour Member. Unsuccessfully contested Yeovil in May 1929. Elected for Battersea N. division in Apr. 1940 and sat until May 1946 when he resigned on appointment as Gov. of Malta. Member of Battersea Borough Council 1919-45, Alderman, Mayor 1922-23. Member of London County Council 1934-46. Chairman of Estimates Committee 1945-46. Gov. and Commander-in-Chief of Malta 1946-49. K.C.M.G. 1947. Created Baron Douglas of Barloch 1950. Vice-Chairman of Corby Development Corporation 1950-62. Dept. Speaker of House of Lords from 1962. Died 31 Mar. 1980. [1946]

DOUGLAS, Richard Giles. Braehead House, High Street, Auchtermuchty, Fife. S. of William Giles Douglas, Esq. B. 4 Jan. 1932; m. 19 July 1954, Jean Gray, d. of Andrew Arnott, Esq. Educ. at Govan Secondary School, and University of Strathclyde, B.Sc.

(Econ.). Engineering Apprenticeship 1948-53; Marine Engineer Officer 1953-55; Scholarship at Co-operative Coll. 1955-57; Education Officer 1957-61; University of Strathclyde 1961-64; Lecturer in Economics at Dundee Coll. of Technology 1964-70. A Labour Co-operative Member. Unsuccessfully contested S. Angus in 1964, W. Edinburgh in 1966, and the Pollok division of Glasgow in Mar. 1967. Elected for the Clackmannan and E. Stirlingshire division of Stirlingshire and Clackmannanshire in June 1970 and sat until he was defeated in Feb. 1974. Unsuccessfully contested same seat in Oct. 1974. Elected for Dunfermline in May 1979. Voted in favour of entry into E.E.C. on 28 Oct. 1971. Director of Berry Wiggins 1975-77 and of Ferguson Brothers, Port Glasgow, from 1975.* [1974]

DOUGLAS-HAMILTON, Lord James Alexander. 3 Blackie House, Lady Stair's Close, Edinburgh. S. of 14th Duke of Hamilton. B. 31 July 1942; m. 26 Aug. 1974, Hon. Susan Buchan, d. of Lord and Lady Tweedsmuir. Educ. at Eton, Balliol Coll., Oxford, and Edinburgh University, M.A. Oxon, Mod. History, LL.B. Edin. Scots Law, Scots Advocate 1968. Oxford Boxing Blue 1961; President Oxford University Conservative Association; President Oxford Union Society 1963-64. Capt. Cameronians R.A.R.O.; Com. 1961. Honorary President Scottish Boxing Association. Councillor for Murrayfield-Cramond Ward, Edinburgh 1972-74. Murrayfield District Councillor, Edinburgh 1974. Author of *Motive for a Mission: The Story Behind Hess's Flight to Britain* 1971. Scottish Conservative Whip 1977-79. Lord Commissioner of the Treasury from May 1979. A Conservative. Unsuccessfully contested the Hamilton division of Lanarkshire in Feb. 1974. Sat for Edinburgh W. from Oct. 1974.* [1979]

DOUGLAS-HAMILTON, Lord Malcolm Avendale, O.B.E., D.F.C. 56 Eaton Square, London. Allt Dearg, Sligachan, Isle of Skye. R.A.F. S. of 13th Duke of Hamilton. B. 12 Nov. 1909; m. 1st, 1931, Clodagh Pamela, d. of Lieut.-Col. the Hon. Malcolm Bowes-Lyon (marriage dissolved 1952); 2ndly, Jan. 1953, Mrs Natalie Wales Paine,

C.B.E., of New York City, widow of Edward Bragg Paine, Esq., and d. of Maj. Nathaniel B. Wales of Braintree, Massachusetts. Educ. at Eton. Chairman of Charity Organisation Society 1938-46. O.B.E. 1943. D.F.C. 1944. Group Capt. R.A.F.R., served 1939-46; member of Royal Company of Archers (Queen's Body Guard for Scotland). Heir presumptive to the Earldom of Selkirk. A Conservative. Elected for Inverness in Feb. 1950 and sat until he resigned in Dec. 1954. Presumed killed on 21 July 1964 when his aircraft was lost on a flight from Liberia to Cameroon. His death was announced on 11 Mar. 1965. [1954]

DOUGLAS-HOME, Rt. Hon. Sir Alexander Frederick, K.T. The Hirsel, Coldstream, Berwickshire. Castlemains, Douglas, Lanarkshire. S. of the 13th Earl of Home. B. 2 July 1903; m. 3 Oct. 1936, Elizabeth Hester, d. of the Very Rev. C.A. Alington, late Dean of Durham, (1 s. 3 d.). Educ. at Eton, and Christ Church, Oxford. Styled Lord Dunglass 1918-51. Succeeded his father as the 14th Earl in 1951. Disclaimed his Earldom and other titles under the Peerage Act Oct. 1963. Maj. Lanarkshire Yeomanry. Parliamentary Private Secretary to Rt. Hon. Neville Chamberlain, Chancellor of Exchequer and Prime Minister, 1935-40. Joint Under-Secretary of State for Foreign Affairs May-July 1945. Minister of State Scottish Office 1951-55. Secretary of State for Commonwealth Relations Apr. 1955-July 1960. Lord President of the Council Mar.-Sept. 1957 and Oct. 1959-July 1960. Leader of House of Lords Mar. 1957-Sept. 1960. Secretary of State for Foreign Affairs July 1960-Oct. 1963 and June 1970-Mar. 1974. Prime Minister and First Lord of the Treasury Oct. 1963-Oct. 1964. Leader of Opposition Oct. 1964-July 1965. Opposition spokesman on External Affairs 1965-66, on Foreign Affairs 1966-70 and Mar.-Sept. 1974. Freeman of the Town of Coldstream 1972. A Conservative. Sat for the Lanark division 1931-45, when he was defeated, and Feb. 1950-July 1951 when he succeeded to the Earldom. Elected for Kinross and W. Perthshire in Nov. 1963 and sat until he retired in Sept. 1974. Created Baron Home of the Hirsel (Life Peerage) 1974. Dept. Lieut. for

Lanarkshire 1960. PC. 1951. K.T. 1962. Chancellor of Heriot-Watt University 1966-77; Pres. of M.C.C. 1966-67* [1974]

DOUGLAS-MANN, Bruce Leslie Home. 26 Queensdale Road, London. S. of Leslie John Douglas-Mann, M.C. B. 23 June 1927; m. 6 May 1955, Helen, d. of Edwin Tucker, Esq. Educ. at Upper Canada Coll., Toronto, Ontario, and Jesus Coll., Oxford. Royal Navy (Leading Seaman) 1945-48; London School of Economics 1948 and Jesus Coll., Oxford 1948-51; Solicitor's Articled Clerk 1951-54; Private Legal Practice 1954-70. Member of Kensington Borough Council 1962-65, Kensington and Chelsea Borough Council 1964-68. Chairman of Society of Labour Lawyers. President of Socialist Environment and Resources Association 1973-77. Member of Board of Shelter from 1974. Chairman of Select Committee on the Environment from 1979. A Labour Member. Unsuccessfully contested St. Albans in 1964 and Maldon in 1966. Sat for Kensington, N. division from 1970 to Feb. 1974 and for the Mitcham and Morden division of Merton from Feb. 1974.* [1979]

DOWER, Col. Alan Vincent Gandar. 35 Lowndes Street, London. High Head Castle, Cumberland. Carlton, Naval & Military, Ranelagh, Queen's, and Prince's S. of J.W.G. Dower and Mrs. Dower of Collingham Gardens, London. B. Mar. 1898; m. 11 Feb. 1928, Aymée Lavender, d. of Sir George Clerk, 9th Bart., of Penicuik, and the Hon. Lady Clerk, sister of 6th Baron Sherborne. Educ. at Royal Military Coll., Sandhurst, and Oxford. Capt. late 2nd Dragoon Guards R. of O. Served with B.E.F. 1916-17. Maj. 25th A.A. Battalion R.E. 1937. Lieut.-Col. Commanding 36th A.A. Battalion R.E. 1938-40; Lieut.-Col. Commanding 39th (Lancashire Fusiliers) S.L. Regiment 1940; Commanding 84th S.L. Regiment 1941; Military Member Middlesex T.A. Association; Honorary Col. 609 H.A.A. Regiment R.A. (T.A.) from 1947; member of Select Committee on Estimates 1938-39 and Select Committee on Public Accounts from 1945. A Conservative. Member for Stockport Oct. 1931-Nov. 1935 and for the Penrith and Cockermouth division of Cumberland from

Nov. 1935 until he retired in 1950. Member of Executive of Royal Society of St. George. Dept.-Lieut. for Middlesex 1961-65 and for Greater London from 1965. Knight of St. John of Jerusalem. Assumed the surname of Gander-Dower in lieu of Dower. Died 6 May 1980. [1950]

DOWER, Eric Leslie Gandar. 60 Haymarket, London. Aberdeen Air Port, Dyce, Aberdeenshire. S. of Joseph Wilson Dower, Esq., who assumed the surname of Gandar-Dower. B. 3 July 1894. Educ. at Brighton Coll., and Jesus Coll., Cambridge. Served as Flight-Lieut. 1940-45. A Pioneer of Civil Aviation in North of Scotland. A Conservative. Elected for Caithness and Sutherland in July 1945 and sat until he retired in 1950. During the 1945 election campaign he announced his intention to resign his seat and seek re-election after the defeat of Japan but, as a result of pressure from his constituency association, he failed to do this and in 1948 he resigned his candidature and the Conservative Whip and sat as an Independent until 1950. Trained for the stage at R.A.D.A. Assumed the surname of Gandar-Dower in lieu of Dower.* [1950]

DRAYSON, George Burnaby. Linton House, Linton, Skipton. North Yorkshire. 131A Hamilton Terrace, London. Royal Automobile. S. of Walter Drayson, Esq., of Stevenage B. 9 Mar. 1913; m. 1st; 1 Sept. 1939, Winifred, d. of Percy Heath, Esq., (1 d.), (marriage dissolved 1958); 2ndly, 1962, Barbara Maria Teresa Radonska Chrzanowska, of Warsaw. Educ. at Borlase School. Company Director. Member of the Stock Exchange 1935-54. Commissioned in Essex Yeomanry 1931. Capt. 1938. Served with RA. in Western Desert; Prisoner of War 1942; escaped from Italy 1943 (T.D., despatches). Member of Parliamentary Delegation to Turkey 1947 to Trinidad and Tobago 1967, Ceylon 1970 and to New Zealand 1974. Expenditure Committee 1970-74. Chairman Parliamentary All-Party East-West Trade Committee. A Conservative. Sat for the Skipton division of West Riding of Yorkshire from July 1945 until he retired in 1979 Chairman of British-Polish Parliamentary Group.* [1979]

DREWE, Sir Cedric, K.C.V.O. Broadhembury House, Nr. Honiton, Devon. Junior Carlton. S. of J.C. Drewe, Esq., of Castle Drogo, Drewsteignton. B. 26 May 1896; m. 1918, Beatrice Foster, d. of Campbell Newington, Esq., of Oakover, Ticehurst. Educ. at Eton, and Royal Military Academy, Woolwich. Served with R.F.A. 1914-19. Parliamentary Private Secretary to Rt. Hon. Sir R. Dorman-Smith, Minister of Agriculture Feb. 1939-May 1940, and to Rt. Hon. R.S. Hudson, Minister of Agriculture May 1940-Oct. 1943; Assistant Whip Oct. 1943; Dept. Chief Conservative Whip July 1948-May 1955. A Lord Commissioner of the Treasury July 1944-July 1945. Treasurer to the Royal Household Nov. 1951-May 1955. K.C.V.O. June 1953. A Conservative. Elected for the S. Molton division of Devon in Oct. 1924, defeated May 1929. Sat for the Honiton division of Devon from 1931 until he retired in 1955. Died 21 Jan. 1971. [1954]

DRIBERG, Thomas Edward Neil. House of Commons, London. S. of John James Street Driberg, Esq. B. 22 May 1905; m. 1951, Mrs. Ena Mary Binfield. Educ. at Lancing, and Christ Church, Oxford. N.E.C. of Labour Party 1949-72, Chairman 1957-58. A Labour Member. Elected for the Maldon division of Essex in June 1942 as an Independent, took the Labour whip in Jan. 1945 and sat until he retired in 1955. Sat for Barking from 1959 until he retired in Feb. 1974. A Journalist on the *Daily Express* 1928-43, also *Reynolds News* and *New Statesman*. Created Baron Bradwell (Life Peerage) 1975. Member of Church of England Central Board of Finance. Select Preacher, University of Oxford 1965. Member of Historic Buildings Council from 1966. Author of *Ruling Passions* (published posthumously) and other works. Died 12 Aug. 1976. [1974]

DU CANN, Col. Rt. Hon. Edward Dillon Lott. Cothay Barton, Greenham, Wellington, Somerset. Carlton, Pratt's, and Somerset County, Taunton. S. of C.G.L. du Cann, Barrister-at-Law. B. 28 May 1924; m. 1962, Sallie Innes, d. of James Murchie, Esq., of Caldy, (1 s. 2 d.). Educ. at Colet Court, Woodbridge School, and St. John's Coll., Oxford, M.A. (Law). Visiting Fellow

Business School, Lancaster University. Served 1943-46 with R.N.V.R.. Founder of Unicorn group of Unit Trusts 1957 and pioneer of Equity-Linked Life Assurance. Chairman Cannon Assurance Limited. Economic Secretary to the Treasury July 1962-Oct. 1963. Chairman Association of Unit Trust Managers 1961. Commodore House of Commons Yacht Club 1961, Admiral 1973. Member Select Committee House of Lords Reform 1962. Minister of State, Board of Trade Oct. 1963-Oct. 1964. Chief Opposition spokesman Trade and Shipping 1964-65. First Chairman House of Commons Select Committee on Expenditure 1971-73. Chairman Public Accounts Committee 1974-79. PC. 1964. Chairman of the Conservative Party Jan. 1965-Sept. 1967. Honorary Col. 155 Regiment R.C.T. (Wessex) Volunteers. Chairman 1922 Committee from 1972. Patron Association of Insurance Brokers 1975-78. Vice-President British Insurance Brokers Association 1978. A Conservative. Unsuccessfully contested W. Walthamstow in 1951 and Barrow-in-Furness in 1955. Sat for the Taunton division of Somerset from Feb. 1956. Chairman of Barclays Unicorn Ltd. 1957-62 and 1964-72. Chairman of Keyser Ullman Holdings Ltd. 1970-75. Chairman of Select Committee on the Treasury and Civil Service from 1979.*　　　　　　　　　[1979]

DUDLEY-WILLIAMS, Sir Rolf Dudley, Bart. Little Hayne, Plymtree, Nr. Cullompton, Devon. S. of Arthur Williams, Esq., of Plymouth. B. 1908; m. 1940, Margaret Helen, d. of F.F. Robinson, Esq., O.B.E. and Mrs. Robinson, 2 s. Educ. at Plymouth Coll., and R.A.F. Coll., Cranwell. A Pioneer of jet propulsion and Managing Director of Power Jets Limited. Served R.A.F. 1926-34. Formerly Parliamentary Private Secretary to Rt. Hon. Christopher Soames, MP., Secretary of State for War and Minister of Agriculture 1958-64. Created Bart. 1964. A Conservative. Unsuccessfully contested Brierley Hill in 1950. Elected for Exeter in 1951 and sat until 1966 when he was defeated. Assumed the surname Dudley-Williams in lieu of Williams 1964.*　　　　　　　　　　　[1966]

DUFFY, Albert Edward Patrick. 169 Bennetthorpe, Doncaster, Yorkshire. The Naval. S. of James Duffy, Esq., Coalminer. B. 17 June 1920. Educ. at London University (L.S.E.) Ph.D., and Columbia University, New York. Served in the Royal Navy (Fleet Air Arm) 1940-46; London School of Economics 1946-50; Columbia University, New York 1950-51; Lecturer Leeds University 1951-63. Chairman Parliamentary Labour Party Economic Affairs and Finance 1965-66 and 1974-76. Visiting Professor Drew University, New Jersey 1966-70. Parliamentary Private Secretary to Rt. Hon. Roy Mason, Secretary of State for Defence 1974-76. An Opposition spokesman on Defence from 1979. Chairman Trade and Industry Sub-Committee of Select Committee on Expenditure; Under-Secretary of State for Defence for the Royal Navy Apr. 1976-May 1979. A Labour Member. Unsuccessfully contested the Tiverton division of Devon in 1950, 1951 and 1955. Sat for Colne Valley from Mar. 1963-1966, when he was defeated. Member for the Attercliffe division of Sheffield from June 1970.*　　　[1979]

DUGDALE, Rt. Hon. John. 113 Church Road, Barnes, London. S. of Col. Arthur Dugdale, C.M.G., D.S.O. B. 16 Mar. 1905; m. 21 Dec. 1938, Irene, grand-d. of Rt. Hon. George Lansbury, MP., 2 s. Educ. at Wellington Coll., and Christ Church, Oxford. A Newspaper Correspondent and Lecturer; Attaché in Diplomatic Service, Peking 1926-27. Private Secretary to the Rt. Hon. C.R. Attlee 1931-39 and Parliamentary Private Secretary when Lord President of the Council Mar.-May 1945. Financial Secretary to the Admiralty Aug. 1945-Feb. 1950. Minister of State, Colonial Affairs Feb. 1950-Oct. 1951. Officer in H.M. Army 1940-41; PC. 1949. Chairman Commonwealth Society for the Deaf. Vice-President of the Association of Municipal Corporations. A Labour Member. Unsuccessfully contested S. Leicester in Oct. 1931, Cardiff Central in Nov. 1935 and York in May 1937. Elected for West Bromwich in Apr. 1941 and sat until his death on 12 Mar. 1963.　　　　　　　　　　　　　[1963]

DUGDALE, Maj. Rt. Hon. Sir Thomas Lionel, Bart., T.D. Crathorne Hall, Yarm, Yorkshire. Carlton, White's, and Jockey. S. of James Dugdale, Esq., Dept.-Lieut. and J.P.

B. 20 July 1897; m. 22 Sept. 1936, Nancy, d. of Sir Charles Tennant, Bart. (she died 1969). Educ. at Eton, and Royal Military Coll., Sandhurst. Served overseas with Royal Scots Greys 1917-18; Maj. Yorks Hussars Yeomanry, served in Middle East Jan. 1940-Feb. 1941; J.P. for the N. Riding of Yorkshire 1928; Dept.-Lieut. 1931, Vice-Lieut. 1957-77. Parliamentary Private Secretary to Sir Philip Cunliffe-Lister when President of the Board of Trade Sept.-Nov. 1931 and when Secretary of State for the Colonies Nov. 1931-June 1935, and when Secretary of State for Air June-Nov. 1935; Parliamentary Private Secretary to Rt. Hon. Stanley Baldwin, Prime Minister Nov. 1935-May 1937; a Lord Commissioner of the Treasury May 1937-Feb. 1940, and Feb. 1941-Feb. 1942; Dept. Chief Whip Feb. 1941-Feb. 1942. Minister of Agriculture and Fisheries Oct. 1951-July 1954, when he resigned as a result of the Crichel Dawn Affair. Member of Cabinet Sept. 1953-July 1954. PC. 1951. A Vice-Chairman of Conservative Party Organisation July 1941, Chairman Mar. 1942-Oct. 1944, Chairman of Yorkshire Area National Union of Conservative and Unionist Associations 1948-52 and President from 1952. Created Bart. 1945. A Conservative. Elected for the Richmond division of the N. Riding of Yorkshire in May 1929 and sat until he was created Baron Crathorne in June 1959. Chairman of Committee on the Law on Sunday Observance 1961-64. Chairman of Political Honours Scrutiny Committee 1961-76. Member of Horserace Betting Levy Board 1964-73. Died 26 Mar. 1977.   [1959]

DUMPLETON, Cyril Walter. 272 London Road, St. Albans. S. of Walter Dumpleton, Esq., of St. Albans. B. 25 June 1897; m. 1920, Louise, d. of Charles Lefevre, Esq., of Birmingham. Educ. at Elementary School. Manager of Printing and Publishing Business. Member of St. Albans City Council 1937-50; Mayor 1943-44; Alderman 1946. J.P. for Hertfordshire. A Labour Member. Elected for the St. Albans division of Hertfordshire in July 1945 and sat until 1950 when he was defeated. Served with R.N.A.S. and R.A.F. 1914-18. Public Relations Executive, Colonial Development Corporation 1950-62. Member of Society of Friends. Died 1 Oct. 1966. [1950]

DUNCAN, Sir Alan Gomme. See GOMME-DUNCAN, Sir Alan Gomme.

DUNCAN, Rt. Hon. Sir Andrew Rae. 11 Tothill Street, London. Dunure, Foxgrove Road, Beckenham, Kent. Caledonian, and Reform. S. of George Duncan, Esq. B. 1884; m. 1916, Annie, d. of Andrew Jordan, Esq. Educ. at Irvine Academy and University of Glasgow. Honorary LL.D. Glasgow and Dalhousie University, Halifax, N.S., M.A., LL.B. University of Glasgow. Barrister-at-Law, Bencher of Gray's Inn. One of H.M.'s Lieuts. for the City of London; High Sheriff of the County of London 1939-40; Coal Controller 1919-20; Vice-President of Ship Building Employers' Federation 1920-27; Honorary Fellow Society of Engineers. A Director of the Bank of England 1929-40, of Imperial Chemical Industries Limited, of Dunlop Rubber Company Limited, of Royal Exchange Assurance, and of North British Locomotive Company Limited; Chairman of Central Electricity Board 1927-35 (member 1936-40), of Executive Committee of British Iron and Steel Federation 1935-40, and from 1945 of American Iron and Steel Institute, of Advisory Committee on Coal Mines Department 1920-29, of Royal Committees to enquire into Coal Industry in Nova Scotia 1925 and 1932, of Royal Committee to enquire into grievances of Eastern Marytime Provinces of Canada 1926, and of Sea Fish Commission for the U.K. 1933-35; President of Board of Trade Jan.-Oct. 1940 and June 1941-Feb. 1942; Minister of Supply Oct. 1940-June 1941 and Feb. 1942-July 1945. Unsuccessfully contested the Cathcart division of Glasgow as a Lloyd George Liberal in 1922 and Dundee as a Liberal in 1924. Sat for the City of London as a National Member from Feb. 1940 until he retired in 1950. Knighted 1921; G.B.E. 1938; PC. 1940. Died 30 Mar. 1952. [1950]

DUNCAN, Capt. Sir James Alexander Lawson, Bart. Jordanstone, Perthshire. Carlton, Bath, and Guards'. S. of Alexander Duncan, Esq., of Jordanstone, Perthshire. B. 1899; m. 1st, Adrienne, d. of William St. Quintin (she died 1966); 2ndly, 1966, Beatrice Mary Moore, d. of Thomas O'Carroll, Esq., and Widow of Maj. Philip Blair-

Oliphant. Educ. at Marlborough. In the Scots Guards. Served in France 1917-19. Member of London County Council from 1925-28; Parliamentary Private Secretary to E.L. Burgin, Parliamentary Secretary Board of Trade Oct. 1932-May 1937, when Minister of Transport May 1937-Apr. 1939, and when Minister of Supply July 1939-May 1940. Rejoined Scots Guards June 1940. Created a Bart. 1957. Given freedom of Arbroath Oct. 1963. A Conservative and Liberal-Unionist Member. Unsuccessfully contested Caithness and Sutherland 1929. Sat for Kensington N. from Oct. 1931- July 1945, when he was defeated. Elected for the S. Angus division of Angus and Kincardine in Feb. 1950 and sat until he retired in 1964. Chairman of National Liberal Parliamentary Party 1956-59. Died 30 Sept. 1974. [1964]

DUNGLASS, Alexander Frederick Douglas-Home, Lord. See DOUGLAS-HOME, Rt. Hon. Sir Alexander Frederick, K.T.

DUNLOP, John. Manor House, Moneymore, Magherafelt, Co. Londonderry. S. of Martin Dunlop, Esq. B. 20 May 1910; m. 1st, 1936, Ruby Hunter; 2ndly, 21 May 1970, Joyce E. Campbell. Educ. at Belfast Technical Coll. Methodist local preacher. Ran own Catering and Restaurant business 1949-74. Member of Vanguard Unionist Progressive Party until Oct. 1975, when he resigned. Elected for Mid-Ulster N.I. Assembly 1973. An Ulster Unionist member. Sat for Mid Ulster from Feb. 1974.* [1979]

DUNN, James Anthony. 45 Lisburn Lane. Tuebrook, Kirkdale, Liverpool. S. of James Richard Dunn. Esq. B. 30 Jan. 1926; m. 20 Mar. 1954, Dorothy. d. of Arthur Larkey, Esq., (2 s. 2 d.). Educ. at St. Teresa's School, Liverpool, and evening institute. T. & G.W.U. Scholarship to the London School of Economics. An Engineer. Joined the Labour Party in 1946. National Union of Enginemen, Firemen, Mechanics and Electrical Workers; Power Workers Group of T. & G.W.U. Member of Liverpool City Council 1958-66. Member Episcopal Commission for International Justice and Peace 1966-74; member Council for Catholic Education 1966-76; member Council Catholic Union of Great

Britain. Opposition Whip 1971-74. Lord Commissioner of the Treasury and Government Whip for Merseyside and N.W. Region Mar. 1974-Apr. 1976; Chairman Catering Sub-Committee 1974-76; House of Commons Select Committee of Services 1968-76; Parliamentary Under-Secretary of State for Northern Ireland Apr. 1976-May 1979. Member of T. & G.W.U. Liverpool Society Co-operative Party; St. John's Youth Centre. Member Playgrounds' Committee (Liverpool) and International Playground Association. Member of the North Atlantic Assembly. Member House of Commons Services Committee. President Kirkdale Pensioners Bowling and Social Club, Vice-President The National Council for the Single Woman and her Dependents Limited (Merseyside Branch), Vice-President Liverpool Regional Fire Liaison Panel. Chairman St. Cecilia's R.C. Youth Centre. President Liverpool Association for Brain Injured Children. Patron British Institute for Achievement of Human Potential. A Labour Member. Sat for the Kirkdale division of Liverpool from Oct. 1964.* [1979]

DUNNETT, John Jacob. 59a Derby Road, Nottingham. B. 24 June 1922; m. Pamela Lucille 1951, (2 s. 3 d.). Assumed the surname of Dunnett in lieu of Dunitz. Educ. at Whitgift Middle School, Croydon, and Downing Coll., Cambridge University, (M.A., LL.B.). A Solicitor. Military Service from 1941-46. Capt. Cheshire Regiment. Joined the Labour Party in July 1949. Member of A.S.S.E.T. 1958-61. Member of the National Union of General and Municipal Workers from 1961. Member Middlesex County Council 1958-61; Enfield Borough Councillor 1958-61 and Alderman 1961-63; Greater London Councillor 1964-67. Council of Football Association; member of Football League Management Committee and Chairman Nottinghamshire County F.C. A Labour Member. Sat for Nottingham Central from 1964-to Feb. 1974 and for Nottingham E. from Feb. 1974. Parliamentary Private Secretary to Rt. Hon. F.W. Mulley, Minister for Defence for the Army, Minister of Aviation, Minister of State, Foreign Office and Minister of Transport 1964-70. Voted in favour of entry to E.E.C. on 28 Oct. 1971.* [1979]

DUNWOODY, Hon. Gwyneth Patricia. 113 Cromwell Tower, Beech Street, London. D. of Morgan Phillips, Esq., sometime General Secretary of the Labour Party, and Baroness Phillips. B. 12 Dec. 1930; m. 28 May 1954, Dr. John Elliott Orr Dunwoody, former Labour Member for Falmouth and Camborne, and s. of Dr. William Orr Dunwoody (2 s. 1 d.) (marriage dissolved in 1975). Educ. at Fulham County Secondary School. Parliamentary Secretary to Board of Trade Aug. 1967-June 1970. An Opposition spokesman on Foreign and Commonwealth Affairs from 1979. A Labour Member. Unsuccessfully contested Exeter in 1964. Sat for Exeter from Mar. 1966-70 when, she was defeated, and for Crewe from Feb. 1974. Director of Film Production Association of Great Britain 1970-74. Member of European Parliament 1975-79.* [1979]

DUNWOODY, John Elliot Orr. 214 Ashley Gardens, London. S. of Dr. William Orr Dunwoody. B. 3 June 1929; m. 28 May 1954, Hon. Gwyneth Patricia, Labour Member for Exeter 1966-70, and d. of Morgan Phillips and Baroness Phillips (divorced 1975). Educ. at St. Paul's School, London University (King's Coll.), and Westminster Hospital Medical School, M.B., B.S. (Lonon), M.R.C.S., L.R.C.P. Parliamentary Under-Secretary Department of Health and Social Security Oct. 1969-June 1970. A Labour Member. Unsuccessfully contested Tiverton in 1959 and Plymouth Sutton in 1964. Elected for the Falmouth and Camborne division of Cornwall in Mar. 1966 and sat until June 1970 when he was defeated. A General Practitioner. Vice-Chairman of Kensington, Chelsea and Westminster Area Health Authority (Teaching) 1974-77, Chairman from 1977. Honorary Director of Action on Smoking and Health.* [1970]

DURANT, (Robert) Anthony Bevis. Hill House, Surley Row, Caversham, Reading. S. of Robert Michael Durant, Esq. B. Jan. 1928; m. 7 June 1958, Audrey, d. of Fred Stoddart, Esq., (2 s. 1 d.). Educ. at Bryanston, Dorset. Served in R.N. 1945-47. Coutts Bank 1947-52. Conservative Agent 1952-62. National Organiser Young Conservatives 1962-67. Director British Industrial Scientific Film Association 1967-70. Member Woking Urban District Council 1968-74. Secretary and Gen. Managing Audio Visual Aid Company 1970. Secretary of Conservative Candidates Association 1972-74. Member Select Committee Parliamentary Commissioner. Member Commonwealth Parliamentary Association British Branch Executive. Secretary Back Bench Conservative Committee on Industry. Secretary All-Party Group on Inland Waterways. Chairman All-Party Group on Widows and Single Parent Families. A Conservative. Unsuccessfully contested Rother Valley in 1970. Sat for Reading N. from Feb. 1974.* [1979]

DURBIN, Evan Frank Mottram. 372 Fore Street, London. S. of the Rev. F. Durbin, Baptist Minister. B. 1 Mar. 1906; m. 1932, Alice Marjorie, d. of Ernest Green, Esq. Educ. at Elementary Schools, at Heles School, Exeter, Taunton, and at New Coll., Oxford. Lecturer in Economics London School of Economics. Member of Economic Section of War Cabinet Secretariat and Personal Assistant to the Dept. Prime Minister (Attlee). Parliamentary Private Secretary to Rt. Hon. H. Dalton, Chancellor of the Exchequer Aug. 1945-Oct. 1946. Parliamentary Secretary Ministry of Works Mar. 1947-Sept. 1948. A Labour Member. Unsuccessfully contested the East Grinstead division of E. Sussex in 1931 and the Gillingham division of Kent in 1935. Elected for Edmonton in July 1945 and sat until 3 Sept. 1948 when he was drowned while trying to rescue his children from the sea near Crackington Haven, Cornwall. Author of several books on economics and politics. Died 3 Sept. 1948. [1948]

DUTHIE, Sir William Smith, O.B.E. House of Commons, London. S. of Lewis Duthie, Esq., of Portessie, Banffshire. B. 1892; m. 1 Mar. 1921, Elizabeth, d. of W.J. Tyson, Esq., of Liverpool (she died 1977). Educ. at Rathven, and Buckie Schools. Served overseas with Gordon Highlanders and with Canadian army 1915-18. Chairman Royal National Mission to Deep Sea Fishermen 1954-71. Adviser to Food (Defence Plans) Department of Board of Trade on Bread Supplies 1938-39. Director of Emergency Bread Supplies,

Ministry of Food 1940-45. Dept. Chief Balkans Mission U.N.R.R.A. 1945. Knighted in Birthday Honours 1959 (Knight Bachelor). A Conservative. Elected for Banffshire in July 1945 and sat until he retired in 1964. O.B.E. 1943. Conservative Whip withdrawn Oct. 1961-Nov. 1963 after his opposition to the Sea Fish Industry Bill.*   [1964]

DYE, Sidney. Redcroft, Norwich Road, Swaffham, Norfolk. National Farmers', and Whitehall Court. S. of J.W. Dye, Esq. B. 1900; m. Dec. 1932, Grace Lilian Gidney. Educ. at Wells Elementary School, and Ruskin Coll. A Farmer from 1932. Member of Norfolk County Council from 1934, Alderman and Chairman of Welfare Committee; member Swaffham Rural District Council from 1935; J.P. from 1934. A Labour Member. Unsuccessfully contested S.W. Norfolk in 1935. Sat for S.W. Norfolk from 1945-51 when he was defeated. Reelected in 1955 and sat until his death in a car accident on 9 Dec. 1958.   [1958]

DYKES, Hugh John Maxwell. House of Commons, London. S. of Richard Dykes, Esq. B. 17 May 1939; m. 25 Sept. 1965, Susan, d. of E. Smith, Esq. Educ. at Weston-super-Mare Grammar School, and Pembroke Coll., Cambridge. Partner in a leading firm of London Stockbrokers; joined the firm in 1964, partner 1968. Research Secretary Bow Group 1966; Chairman Coningsby Club 1969-71; Parliamentary Private Secretary to Lord Lambton, Peter Kirk, Ian Gilmour and Geoffrey Johnson Smith, Under-Secretaries of State for Defence 1970-72 and to Geoffrey Johnson Smith, Parliamentary Secretary, Civil Service Department 1972-74. Chief Sponsor of the Heavy Commercial Vehicles Act (The "Dykes Act") 1973. Member European Parliament 1974-77. Chairman Conservative Group for Europe Apr. 1978. A Conservative. Unsuccessfully contested Tottenham in 1966. Sat for Harrow E. from June 1970.*   [1979]

EADIE, Alexander, J.P. House of Commons, London. S. of Robert Eadie, Esq. B. 23 June 1920, m. 1941, Jemima, d. of T. Ritchie, Esq. of Wemyss. Educ. at Buckhaven Senior Secondary School. A Miner's Agent; member N.U.M. Nine years member Executive Committee of Scottish Regional Council of Labour Party; 15 years West Fife Constituency Labour Party and former Chairman. Chairman Fife Fabian Society for 7 years. Executive Committee member N.U.M. Scottish Area. Served in local government for 20 years. J.P. From 1950 for Fife County. Awarded B.E.M. in 1961. Parliamentary Private Secretary to Rt. Hon. Margaret Herbison, MP., Minister of Social Security in 1967. Member of Parliamentary Select Committee on Scottish Affairs. Vice-Chairman of Parliamentary Trade Union Group. Chairman of Parliamentary "Power and Steel Group". Chairman Miners' Parliamentary Group. Member of Scottish Eastern Regional Hospital Board. Opposition spokesman on Energy 1973-74 and from 1979. Under-Secretary of State for Energy 1974-79. A Labour Member. Labour candidate in Ayr Parliamentary Election in 1959 and 1964. Sat for Midlothian from Mar. 1966*   [1979]

ECCLES, Rt. Hon. Sir David McAdam K.C.V.O. 6 Barton Street, London. Dean Farm, Chute, Andover. Brooks's. S. of William McAdam Eccles, Esq., F.R.C.S., M.S., and Anna, d. of E.B. Anstie, Esq., of Devizes. B. 18 Sept. 1904; m. 10 Oct. 1929, Hon. Sybil Frances Dawson, d. of Visct. Dawson of Penn (she died 1977). Educ. at Winchester, and New Coll., Oxford. Joined Ministry of Economic Warfare Sept. 1939; Economic Adviser to H.M. Ambassadors at Madrid and Lisbon 1940-42; transferred to Ministry of Production 1942. Minister of Works Nov. 1951-Oct. 1954. Minister of Education Oct. 1954-Jan. 1957; President of Board of Trade Jan. 1957-Oct. 1959; Minister of Education Oct. 1959-July 1962. Honorary Fellow R.I.B.A. 1955. PC. 1951. K.C.V.O. 1953. A Conservative. Elected for the Chippenham division of Wiltshire in Aug. 1943 and sat until July 1962 when he was created Baron Eccles. Created Visct. Eccles 1964. Director of Courtaulds 1962-70. Chairman of Anglo-Hellenic League 1967-70. Paymaster-Gen. ('Minister for the Arts') June 1970-Dec. 1973. Chairman of Trustees of British Museum 1968-70. Chairman of British Library Board 1973-78. President of World Crafts Council 1974-78.*   [1962]

EDE, Rt. Hon. James Chuter, C.H. 172 East Street, Epsom, Surrey. S. of James Ede, Esq., of Epsom. B. 11 Sept. 1882; m. 1917, Lilian Mary, d. of Richard Williams, Esq., of Plymouth (she died 1 July 1948). Educ. at Epsom National School, Dorking High School, Battersea P.T. Centre, and Christ's Coll., Cambridge. A School Master 1905-14; Secretary to Surrey County Teachers' Association 1919-45; member of Epsom Urban District Council 1908-27 and 1933-37, of Surrey County Council 1914-49; Vice-Chairman 1930-33, Chairman 1933-37; Honorary Freeman of Wimbledon 1937, of Epsom and Ewell 1939, of Mitcham 1945, and of South Shields 1950; Charter mayor of Epsom and Ewell 1937; President British Electrical Development Association 1937; member of London and Home Counties Joint Electricity Authority 1928-45, Chairman 1934-40. Dept.-Lieut. and J.P. for Surrey; Chairman of Surrey and Sussex Area Committee National Fitness Council 1937-39; President County Councils Association 1953-61; President Commons, Open Spaces and Footpaths Preservation Society 1955-61, and of International Association for Liberal Christianity and Religious Freedom 1955-58; M.A. (Honoris causa) Cambridge 1943 for services to Education; Parliamentary Secretary Board of Education May 1940-Aug. 1944, Ministry of Education Aug. 1944-May 1945; Leader of House of Commons Mar.-Oct. 1951. Home Secretary Aug. 1945-Oct. 1951. Honorary LL.D. (Bristol) 1951; Honorary D.C.L. (Durham) 1954. Honorary LL.D. (Sheffield) 1960. PC. 1944. C.H. 1953. A Labour Member. Unsuccessfully contested the Epsom division in 1918. Elected for Mitcham in Mar. 1923 and sat until he was defeated in Dec. 1923. Unsuccessfully contested Mitcham again in 1924. Elected for South Shields in May 1929 and sat until he was again defeated in Oct. 1931. Re-elected for South Shields in 1935 and sat until he retired in 1964. Served with E. Surrey Regiment and R.E. 1914-18. Member of Parliamentary Labour Party Parliamentary Committee 1951-55. Created Baron Chuter-Ede (Life Peerage) 1964. Trustee of British Museum 1951-63. Dept.-Chairman of B.B.C. Gen. Advisory Council 1952-59. Died 11 Nov. 1965.   [1964]

EDELMAN, Maurice. House of Commons, London. S. of S. Edelman, Esq., of Cardiff. B. 2 Mar. 1911; m. 1933, Matilda, d. of H. Yager, Esq. Educ. at Cardiff High School, and Trinity Coll., Cambridge, M.A. A Journalist and Author. War Correspondent in N. Africa and France. Vice-President Franco-British Parliamentary Committee; a member European Consultative Assembly 1949-51 and 1965-70. Vice-Chairman British Council 1950-67. Chevalier Légion d'Honneur 1954; Officer Légion d'Honneur 1960. President Alliance Française 1973. Director Gen. Franco-British Council. Chairman Socialist Group, Western European Union 1965-70. A Labour Member. Sat for Coventry W. from 1945-50, and for Coventry N. from 1950-74. Elected for Coventry N.W. in Feb. 1974 and sat until his death on 14 Dec. 1975. Voted in favour of entry to E.E.C. on 28 Oct. 1971. Member of Advisory Council on Public Records 1974-75. Died 14 Dec. 1975.   [1976]

EDEN, Rt. Hon. Sir John Benedict, Bart. 29 Eldon Road, London. S. of Sir Timothy Eden, Bart. B. 15 Sept. 1925; m. 1st, 28 Jan. 1958, Belinda Jane, d. of Sir John Pascoe (marriage dissolved in 1973); 2ndly, 1977, Margaret Ann, Viscountess Strathallan, d. of Mr. and Mrs. R. Gordon. Educ. at Eton, and St. Paul's School, U.S.A. Served with Rifle Brigade, Gurkha Rifles and Gilgit Scouts 1943-47. President Independent Schools Association 1969-71. Vice-President National Chamber of Trade 1968-70. Minister of State, Ministry of Technology June-Oct. 1970. Minister for Industry Oct. 1970-Apr. 1972. Minister of Posts and Telecommunications Apr. 1972-Mar. 1974. Vice-President of the Association of Conservative Clubs Limited. Member of the Trade and Industry Sub-Committee of the House of Commons Expenditure Committee 1974-76. President Wessex Area National Union of Conservative and Unionist Associations 1974-77. Chairman of House of Commons Select Committee European Legislation, etc. 1976-79. An Opposition spokesman on Defence 1965-66 and on Power 1968-70. PC. 1972. A Conservative. Unsuccessfully contested Paddington N. in Dec. 1953. Sat for Bournemouth W. from Feb. 1954. Delegate to Council of Europe and W.E.U. 1960-62. Succeeded to Baronetcy 1963.* [1979]

EDEN, Rt. Hon. Sir (Robert) Anthony, K.G., M.C. 10 Downing Street, London. Carlton. S. of Sir William Eden, 7th Bart. B. 12 June 1897; m. 1st, 5 Nov. 1923, Beatrice, d. of Hon. Sir Gervase Beckett, MP. (marriage dissolved 1950); 2ndly, 12 Aug. 1952, Clarissa Spencer-Churchill. Educ. at Eton, and Christ Church, Oxford, B.A., First Class Honours, Oriental languages. Served with K.R.R.C. in France and Flanders, and as G.S.O. and Brigade-Maj. 1915-19, M.C. 1917. J.P. for Durham. Parliamentary Private Secretary to G. Locker-Lampson, Under-Secretary of State for Home Affairs and Foreign Affairs 1924-26; to St. Austen Chamberlain, Secretary of State for Foreign Affairs July 1926-June 1929; Parliamentary Under-Secretary of State for Foreign Affairs Sept. 1931-Jan. 1934; Lord Privy Seal Jan. 1934-June 1935; Minister for the League of Nations, Foreign Office with a seat in the Cabinet June-Dec. 1935; Secretary of State for Foreign Affairs Dec. 1935-Feb. 1938 when he resigned; Secretary of State for the Dominions Affairs Sept. 1939-May 1940; Secretary of State for War May-Dec., 1940; Secretary of State for Foreign Affairs Dec. 1940-July 1945 and Oct. 1951-May 1955 (Cabinet). Leader of the House of Commons Nov. 1942-July 1945; Dept. Prime Minister Oct. 1951-May 1955. Chancellor of Birmingham University 1945-73. PC. 1934. K.G. 1954. Prime Minister and First Lord of the Treasury May 1955-Jan. 1957. A Conservative. Unsuccessfully contested the Spennymoor division of Durham in 1922. Elected for the Warwick and Leamington division of Warwickshire in Dec. 1923 and sat until he resigned in Jan. 1957. Trustee of National Gallery 1935-49, President of Royal Shakespeare Theatre 1958-66. Created Earl of Avon 1961. Author of three volumes of memoirs. Died 14 Jan. 1977. [1956]

EDGE, Geoffrey. 32 Warren Bank, Simpson, Milton Keynes, Buckinghamshire. S. of John Edge, Esq. B. 26 May 1943. Unmarried. Educ. at Rowley Regis Grammar School, London School of Economics, and Birmingham University, B.A. (Hons.). London, George & Hilda Ormsby Prize 1964. Assistant Lecturer in Geography Leicester University 1967-70. Lecturer in Geography Open University 1970-74. Chairman Planning Committee Bletchley Urban District Council 1972-73. Vice-Chairman Planning Committee Milton Keynes District Council 1973-75. Parliamentary Private Secretary to Gerald Fowler, Minister of State for Higher Education 1974, Minister of State, Privy Council Office (Minister responsible for devolution) 1974-76 and Minister of State for Higher Education 1976. A Labour Member. Sat for Aldridge-Brownhills from Feb. 1974 until 1979, when he was defeated.* [1979]

EDWARDS, Alfred. Hemble Hill Farm, Guisborough, Yorkshire. S. of Thomas Edwards, Esq., of Middlesbrough. B. 1888; m. 1917, Anne Raines, d. of Thomas Hoskison, Esq. Joined the Labour Party in 1931. Managing Director in the Foundry Trade; member of Middlesbrough Town Council 1932-35. A Socialist Member. Sat for Middlesbrough E. from 1935-1950. Expelled from the Labour Party in May 1948, as a result of his opposition to the nationalization of the Iron and Steel industry. Joined the Conservative Party in Aug. 1949. Unsuccessfully contested, as a Conservative, Middlesbrough E. in 1950 and Newcastle on Tyne E. in 1951. A Christian Scientist. Died 17 June 1958. [1950]

EDWARDS, Rt. Hon. Sir Charles, C.B.E. 5 Gelli Crescent, Risca, Monmouth. S. of John and Catherine Edwards. B. 19 Feb. 1867 at Llangunllo, Radnorshire; m. 1886, Margaret, d. of William Davies, Esq., of Sirhowy. Educ. at the National School, Llangunllo. Was Miners' Agent and member of South Wales Miners' Executive; J.P. and County Councillor for Monmouth; member of Risca Urban Council and of Monmouth County Council. Chief Whip of Labour Party 1931-42. A Lord Commissioner of the Treasury June 1929-Aug. 1931. Joint Parliamentary Secretary to the Treasury May 1940-Mar. 1942. PC. 1940. Knight Bach. 1935. A Labour Member. Sat for the Bedwellty division of Monmouthshire from Dec. 1918 until he retired in 1950. C.B.E. 1931. Died 15 June 1954. [1950]

EDWARDS, Rt. Hon. (Lewis) John, O.B.E. 103 Hampstead Way, London. Reform. S. of Lewis John Edwards, Esq., of Aylesbury. B. 27 May 1904; m. 1931, Dorothy May, d. of James Watson, Esq., of Ilkley. Educ. at Aylesbury Grammar School, and University of Leeds. Gen. Secretary of P.O. Engineering Union 1938-47. Member of Leeds City Council 1933-36 and of National Whitley Council for Civil Service 1938-45. Parliamentary Private Secretary to the Rt. Hon. Sir Stafford Cripps, President of the Board of Trade 1945-47. Parliamentary Secretary Ministry of Health Feb. 1947-Feb. 1949, Board of Trade Feb. 1949-Feb. 1950; Economic Secretary to Treasury Oct. 1950-Oct. 1951. Leader Argentine Economic Mission 1951. Chairman Public Accounts Committee 1951-52. Member Select Committee on Delegated Legislation 1953, of Parliamentary Delegation to Japan and Thailand 1954, and of Assembly of Council of Europe; Chairman Budget Committee of Western European Union 1955-58; Vice-President Assembly of Council of Europe 1957-59, President Apr.-Nov. 1959. PC. 1953. A Labour Member. Unsuccessfully contested Leeds N. in 1931 and 1935. Sat for Blackburn from July 1945-Feb. 1950 when he unsuccessfully contested W. Blackburn. Elected for Brighouse and Spenborough in May 1950 and sat until his death on 23 Nov. 1959. Theological Student at Coll. of Resurrection, Mirfield. Staff Tutor University of Leeds 1932-36; Secretary for Adult Education, University of Liverpool 1936-38. O.B.E. 1946. Opposition spokesman on Education 1955-56 and Treasury and Trade Matters 1958-59. Died 23 Nov. 1959.   [1960]

EDWARDS, Rt. Hon. Ness. Danycoed House, Caerphilly, Glamorgan. B. 5 Apr. 1897; m. 1925, Elvina Victoria. Educ. at Labour Coll., London. A Coal Miner. Parliamentary Secretary Ministry of Labour Aug. 1945-Mar. 1950. Postmaster-Gen. Mar. 1950-Oct. 1951. PC. 1947. A Labour Member. Elected for the Caerphilly division of Glamorganshire in July 1939 and sat until his death on 3 May 1968. Imprisoned as a conscientious objector during First World War. Miners' Agent for E. Glamorgan 1932, and representative of the South Wales Miners Federation on the National Executive of the Miners Federation of Great Britain. Member of Gelligaer Urban District Council 1923-35. Organised the escape of Sudeten miners from Czechoslovakia 1939. Opposition spokesman on Post Office Matters until 1960. Chairman of Parliamentary Labour Party Trade Union Group 1964-68. Author of historical works on the South Wales mining industry. Died 3 May 1968.   [1968]

EDWARDS, Robert. House of Commons, London. S. of Richard Edwards, Esq. of Liverpool. B. 1906; m. 1933, Edith May, d. of Elijah Sandham, Esq., MP. (she died 1970), (1 s.). Educ. at Council Schools, and Technical Coll. Member of Liverpool City Council 1929-32. National Chairman of I.L.P. 1943-48. General Secretary of Chemical Workers Union 1947-71. National Officer of Transport and General Workers' Union 1971-76. Leader Parliamentary Delegation North Atlantic Assembly 1968-70. Vice-President Assembly of the Council of Europe 1969-70. Member European Parliament 1977-79. Chairman Defence Committee W.E.U. 1966-70. A Labour and Co-operative Member. Unsuccessfully contested, as an I.L.P. candidate, Chorley in 1935, Stretford in 1939 and Newport in May 1945. Sat for Bilston from 1955-Feb. 1974 and for Wolverhampton S.E. from Feb. 1974. Chairman of Chemical Section of International Federation of Chemical and General Workers Unions from 1971.*   [1979]

EDWARDS, Rt. Hon. (Roger) Nicholas. 20 Chester Row, London. Peach House, Rhos, Nr. Haverfordwest. Pontesgob Mill Forest, Nr. Abergavenny. City University. S. of Ralph Edwards, Esq., C.B.E., F.S.A. B. 25 Feb. 1934; m. 1963, Ankaret, d. of W.J. Healing, Esq., (1 s. 2 d.). Educ. at Westminster School, and Trinity Coll., Cambridge. Director Globtik Tankers Limited and Associate Companies. Director PA International and Sturge Underwriting Agency Limited. Member of Lloyds from 1965. Member Shadow Cabinet 1975-79. Secretary of State for Wales from May 1979. PC. 1979. Conservative Front Bench spokesman for Welsh Affairs 1974-79. A Conservative. Sat for Pembroke from June 1970.*   [1979]

EDWARDS, Walter James. 11 Parry House, Wapping, London. S. of W.J. Edwards, Esq., of Limehouse. B. 1900; m. 1919, Catherine, d. of Daniel O'Brien. A Stoker in the Royal Navy. Civil Lord of the Admiralty Aug. 1945-Oct. 1951. A Labour Member. Sat for the Whitechapel and St. George's division of Stepney from Aug. 1942 to Feb. 1950 and for Stepney from Feb. 1950 until he retired in Sept. 1964. A Roman Catholic. Member of Stepney Borough Council 1934-59, Alderman, Mayor 1944. Dept.-Lieut. for County of London 1946. Died 15 Oct. 1964. [1964]

EDWARDS, William Henry. House of Commons, London. S. of Owen Henry Edwards, Esq. B. 6 Jan. 1938; m. 1961, Ann Rogers. Educ. at Sir Thomas Jones Comprehensive School, and Liverpool University. Part-time Lecturer in Mercantile Law at Liverpool Coll.of Commerce. A Solicitor. A Labour Member. Unsuccessfully contested W. Flintshire in 1964. Elected for Merionethshire in Mar. 1966 and sat until Feb. 1974 when he was defeated. Unsuccessfully contested Merionethshire again in Oct. 1974. Voted in favour of entry to E.E.C. on 28 Oct. 1971. Parliamentary Private Secretary to Rt. Hon. Cledwyn Hughes, Minister of Agriculture 1968-70. Member of Historic Buildings Council for Wales 1971-76. Editor of *Solicitors Diary*. Opposition spokesman on Welsh affairs 1970-72.* [1974]

ELLIOT, Capt. Walter, D.S.C. House of Commons, London. International Sportsmen's. S. of John White Elliot, Esq. B. Feb. 1910; m. June 1936, Thelma Pirie, d. of Admiral G.P. Thomson. Educ. on H.M.S. *Conway* and Royal Naval Coll. Capt. R.N. Distinguished Service Cross, 1944 B.Sc. (Economics) London University, 1958. Served all over world 1939-45 war, mostly in Aircraft Carriers. In Industry 1958-60. A Conservative. Elected for the Carshalton division of Surrey in Nov. 1960 and sat until he retired in Feb. 1974.* [1974]

ELLIOT, Rt. Hon. Walter Elliot, C.H., M.C., F.R.S. 17 Lord North Street, London. Harwood, Bonchester Bridge, Hawick. Carlton, and New, Edinburgh. S. of William Elliot, Esq., of Muirglen, Lanark. B. 19 Sept. 1888; m. 1st, 1919, Helen, d. of Lieut.-Col. D.L. Hamilton (she was killed in 1919); 2ndly, 2 Apr. 1934, Katharine, d. of Sir Charles Tennant, 1st Bart. (she was created Baroness Elliot of Harwood in 1958.). Educ. at Glasgow Academy and University. Served 1914-18 Royal Scots Greys, M.C. and bar. B.Sc. 1910; M.B., Ch.B. 1913; D.Sc. 1922; F.R.C.P. 1940; LL.D. Aberdeen, Leeds, Glasgow, Edinburgh, St. Andrews and Manchester Universities; D.Sc. University of South Africa 1929; Rector of Aberdeen University 1933-36; PC. 1932; F.R.S. 1935. Under-Secretary of Health for Scotland Jan. 1923-Jan. 1924, and Nov. 1924-July 1926; Under-Secretary of State for Scotland July 1926-June 1929. Financial Secretary to the Treasury Sept. 1931-Sept. 1932; Minister of Agriculture and Fisheries Sept. 1932-Oct. 1936; Secretary of State for Scotland Oct. 1936-May 1938; Minister of Health May 1938-May 1940. Director of Public Relations. War Office Jan. 1941-Jan. 1942; Chairman of Public Accounts Committee House of Commons 1942. A Freeman of the City of Edinburgh, Lanark and Hawick. Rector of University of Glasgow 1947-50. Fellow of Royal Coll. of Physicians 1947. C.H. 1952. Lord High Commissioner to General Assembly of Church of Scotland 1956 and 1957. A Conservative. Elected for the Lanark division of Lanarkshire in Dec. 1918 and Nov. 1922. Unsuccessfully contested the same division in Nov. 1923. Sat for the Kelvingrove division of Glasgow from May 1924-July 1945, when he was defeated and for Scottish Universities from Nov. 1946-Feb. 1950. Re-elected for the Kelvingrove division of Glasgow in Feb. 1950 and sat until his death on 8 Jan. 1958. Parliamentary Private Secretary to Sir John Pratt, Parliamentary Secretary for Health (Scotland) 1919-22. Died 8 Jan. 1958. [1957]

ELLIOT, Walter Travers Scott. See SCOTT-ELLIOT, Walter Travers.

ELLIOTT, Sir Robert William. Low Heighley, Morpeth, Northumberland. Northern Counties, Newcastle, and Carlton. S. of Richard Elliott, Esq. B. 11 Dec. 1920; m. 1956. Catherine Jane, d. of John Burton Morpeth

Esq., of Newcastle. Educ. at King Edward. Grammar School, Morpeth. A Farmer. Chairman, Vice-President and President Northern Area Y.C.'s 1948-55. Assistant Whip (unpaid) 1963-64. Opposition Whip Nov. 1964-June 1970. Comptroller to H.M. Household June-Sept. 1970. Vice-Chairman Conservative Party Organization 1970-74. Knighted 17 July 1974. Parliamentary Private Secretary to Richard Nugent and Airey Neave, Parliamentary Secretaries, Ministry of Transport 1958-59 and to Rt. Hon. D.F. Vosper, Under-Secretary and Minister of State at the Home Office and Secretary for Technical Co-operation 1959-63. Chairman of Select Committee on Agriculture from 1979. A Conservative. Unsuccessfully contested Morpeth in 1954 and 1955. Elected for Newcastle-upon-Tyne N. in Mar. 1957.* [1979]

ELLIS, John. 15 Churchlease, Shirehampton, Bristol. S. of George Ellis, Esq. B. 22 Oct. 1930; m. 1953, Rita Butters, (1 s. 2 d.). Educ. at Rastrick Grammar School. Joined the Labour Party in 1954. Member of T.G.W.U. Assistant Government Whip Oct. 1974-Nov. 1976. A Labour Member. Unsuccessfully contested Wokingham in 1964 general election. Sat for Bristol N.W. from Mar. 1966 to June 1970, when he was defeated, and for Brigg and Scunthorpe from Feb. 1974 until 1979, when he was defeated. Laboratory technician, Meteorological Office 1947-63. J.P. for N. Riding of Yorkshire 1960-61. Member of Easthampstead Rural District Council 1962-66 and of Bristol City Council from 1971.* [1979]

ELLIS, Robert Thomas. Whitehurst House, Whitehurst, Chirk, Wrexham. S. of Robert Ellis, Esq. B. 15 Mar. 1924; m. 22 Dec. 1949, Nona, d. of Vernon Harcourt Williams, Esq., of Penrhyndeudraeth. Educ. at Ruabon Grammar School, and Universities of Wales and Nottingham. Works Chemist I.C.I. 1944-46. Student 1947-48, and 1950-52. Coal Miner Greford Colliery 1948-50. Mining Engineer 1953-70. Member of Russell Committee on Adult Education 1969-73. Published *Mines and Men.* Parliamentary Private Secretary to William Rodgers, Minister of State for Defence 1974-75.

Member of European Parliament 1975-79. Voted in favour of entry to E.E.C. on 28 Oct. 1971. A Labour Member. Unsuccessfully contested W. Flintshire in 1966. Sat for the Wrexham division of Denbighshire from June 1970.* [1979]

EMERY, Peter Frank Hannibal. 15 Tufton Court, Tufton Street, London. Tytherleigh Manor, Nr. Axminster, Devon. Carlton. S. of F.G. Emery, Esq., Manufacturer. B. 27 Feb. 1926; m. 1st, 1954, Elizabeth, d. of F.P. Nicholson, Esq. (divorced); 2ndly, 15 Dec. 1972, Elizabeth, d. of G.J.R. Monnington, Esq., (2 s. 2 d.). Educ. at Scotch Plains, New Jersey, U.S.A., and Oriel Coll., Oxford. Served R.A.F. 1943-47. Member Hornsey Borough Council 1951-59. Joint Founder of Bow Group. Parliamentary Private Secretary to David Ormsby-Gore, Minister of State, Foreign Office 1960-61 and to J.B. Godber, Minister of State, Foreign Office 1961-63, Secretary of State for War 1963 and Minister of Labour 1963-64. Secretary 1922 Committee 1964-65. Opposition Front Bench spokesman on Trade, Treasury and Economic Affairs Feb. 1965-Mar. 1966. Chairman Conservative West Country Members; Vice-Chairman Conservative Parliamentary Finance Committee; Vice-Chairman Parliamentary Industry Committee 1967-70. Chairman Housing Committee 1974. Delegate to Council of Europe and Western European Union 1964-66 and 1970-72. Director Institute of Purchasing and Supply 1961-72, Fellow. Secretary-Gen. of the European Federation of Purchasing 1962-72. Chairman of the Consultative Council of Professional Management Organisations 1967-72. Director Phillips Petroleum U.K. 1964-72. Director Property Growth Assurance 1969-72. Chairman Shenley Trust Services Limited. Parliamentary Under-Secretary of State, Industry 1972-73; for Industry and Consumer Affairs 1973-74; for Energy Jan.-Mar. 1974. A Conservative. Unsuccessfully contested Poplar in 1951 and Lincoln in 1955. Member for Reading from 1959-66, when he was defeated. Sat for the Honiton division of Devon from Mar. 1967.* [1979]

EMMET, Hon. Evelyn Violet Elizabeth. 3 Grosvenor Cottages, Eaton Terrace,

London. Amberley Castle, Amberley, Sussex. D. of 1st Baron Rennell of Rodd. B. 18 Mar. 1899; m. 1923, T.A. Emmet, Esq. (he died 1934). Educ. abroad, St. Margaret's Bushey, and L.M.H. Oxford. Member London County Council 1925-34; member W. Sussex County Council 1946-67; Alderman 1954; J.P. 1936; U.K. Delegate to U.N. 1952-53. Chairman W.N.A.C. 1952-54, of National Union of Conservative and Unionist Associations in 1955. A Conservative. Elected for the East Grinstead division of East Sussex in 1955 and sat until Dec. 1964 when she was created Baroness Emmet of Amberley (Life Peerage). Chairman of Lord Chancellor's Legal Aid Advisory Committee 1966-72. A Dept. Speaker of House of Lords 1968-77. Dept.-Lieut. for W. Sussex 1977.*   [1964]

ENGLISH, Michael. House of Commons, London. S. of William Agnew English, Esq. B. 1930; m. 11 Sept. 1976, Carol Owen. Educ. at King George V Grammar School, Southport and Liverpool University, (LL.B.). Joined the Labour Party in 1949. Assistant Dept. Manager. Councillor, County Borough of Rochdale 1953-65; Chairman of Finance Committee until 1964. Member Select Committees on Procedure 1964-66; Publications and Debates 1964-65 and Broadcasting 1965-67. Parliamentary Privilege 1966-67 and 1969-70. House of Commons (Services) 1968-70. Expenditure Committee, General Sub-Committee 1970 and its Chairman 1974. Member Procedure Committee 1976-78. Member Chairmans Panel House of Commons 1974. Parliamentary Private Secretary to Rt. Hon. Douglas Jay, President of the Board of Trade 1966-67. A Labour Member. Unsuccessfully contested Shipley in 1959. Sat for Nottingham W. from Oct. 1964.*   [1979]

ENNALS, Rt. Hon. David Hedley. 8 St. Anne's Close, London. S. of A.F. Ennals, Esq. B. 19 Aug. 1922; m. 1st, 1950, Eleanor Maud Caddick (divorced 1977); 2ndly, 1977, Mrs Katherine Tranoy. Educ. at Queen Mary's Grammar School, Walsall, and Loomis Institute, Windsor, Connecticut, U.S.A. Joined the Labour Party in 1945; member of A.S.S.E.T. 1958; N.U.J. 1938-46. Served in Royal Armoured Corps 1941-46,

Capt. Secretary of Council for Education in World Citizenship 1947-52, of United Nations Association 1952-57. Overseas Secretary of the Labour Party 1957-64. President of Anti-Apartheid Movement and Vice-Chairman of United Nations Association. Chairman of British Overseas Socialist Fellowship and member Overseas Bureau of Fabian Society. Parliamentary Private Secretary to Rt. Hon. Barbara Castle, Minister of Overseas Development and Minister of Transport 1964-66. Parliamentary Under-Secretary of State for the Army, Apr. 1966-Jan. 1967; Parliamentary Under-Secretary of State, Home Office Jan. 1967-Nov. 1968; Minister of State, Department of Health and Social Security Nov. 1968-June 1970. Minister of State, Foreign and Commonwealth Office Mar. 1974.-Apr. 1976. Secretary of State for Social Services Apr. 1976-May 1979. A Labour Member. Unsuccessfully contested Richmond, Surrey in 1950 and 1951. Sat for Dover from Oct. 1964-June 1970, when he was defeated and for Norwich N. from Feb. 1974. PC. 1970. Campaign Director of National Association for Mental Health 1970-73. Chairman of Peter Bedford Housing Associations 1972-74, Campaign for the Homeless and Rootless 1972-74, Ockenden Venture 1972-76 and John Bellers Ltd. 1972-74.*   [1979]

ENSOR, (Alick Charles) David. St. Margarets Boxgrove, Chichester, Sussex. S. of Charles William Ensor, Esq., M.R.C.S., L.R.C.P. B. 27 Nov. 1906; m. 1st, 1932, Norah Russell (marriage dissolved), (1 s. 1 d.); 2ndly, 1944, Vivienne, d. of F.W. Mason, Esq., M.R.C.S., of Bromsgrove, Worcestershire. Educ. at Westminster. Qualified as a Solicitor in 1928, retired from the law in 1947. Farmer, Author and Journalist, radio and television. Joined the Labour Party in 1954. Member of the Transport and General Workers' Union and a member of Equity. Prosecuting Solicitor, Newcastle-on-Tyne and later New Scotland Yard. Author of many books and regular contributor to national and provincial press and radio programmes. Member Estimates Committee 1964-68. Chairman Catering Sub-Committee of Services Committee 1969. A Labour Member. Elected for Bury and Radcliffe in Oct. 1964 and sat until he retired in 1970. Joined the Liberal Party in Sept. 1972. Vice-President of Mark Twain Society of America from 1977.*

[1970]

ERRINGTON, Sir Eric, Bart. Yyns Dwna, Trearddur Bay, Isle of Anglesey. Lombard Chambers, Bixteth Street, Liverpool. United University. B. 17 Mar. 1900; m. 12 Sept. 1924, Marjorie Grant Bennett. Educ. at Mill Hill, Liverpool Coll., and Trinity Coll., Oxford, M.A. Barrister-at-Law, Inner Temple 1923. J.P. for Liverpool 1948; Chairman N.W. Area National Union 1946-51; Chairman Executive Committee of National Union of Conservative and Unionist Associations 1952-57; President Wessex Provincial Area 1962-65. Member of Council of Europe and of Western European Union from 1963-66. President National Federation of Property Owners 1956-59; President Hire Purchase Trade Association 1965. Chairman Estimates Sub-Commitee on Home Affairs from 1961. Knight Bach. 1952. Created a Bart. 1963. A Conservative. Unsuccessfully contested the Hanley division of Stoke-on-Trent in 1929 and the Scotland division of Liverpool in 1931. Sat for Bootle from 1935-45 when he was defeated. Unsuccessfully contested the Edge Hill division of Liverpool in 1950. Elected for the Aldershot division of Hampshire in Oct. 1954 and sat until he retired in 1970. Served with Gordon Highlanders 1918 and in R.A.F. 1939-45. Member of Liverpool City Council 1934-35. Died 3 June 1973.

[1970]

ERROLL, Rt. Hon. Frederick James. 21 Ilchester Place, London. Westholme, Belmont Road, Hale, Cheshire. Carlton, and Royal Thames Yacht. S. of George Murison Erroll, Esq., of Glasgow. B. 27 May 1914; m. Dec. 1950, Elizabeth, d. of Mr. and Mrs. Sowton Barrow, of Exmouth. Educ. at Oundle School, and Trinity Coll., Cambridge, (Hons.), M.I.E.E., M.I.Mech.E. Visited Africa, later assisted Lord Hailey's African Survey 1936. With Metropolitan Vickers Electrical Company Limited 1931-32 and 1936-37; with Evershed and Vignoles Limited, Electrical Engineers, Chiswick 1938-39. Commissioned in 4th County of London Yeomanry (T.A.) 1939,

transferred to Tank Division Ministry of Supply 1941; to Italy, India and Burma as Technical Adviser on Armoured Fighting Vehicles to 1945; Col. 1945; member of Parliamentary Delegation to West Africa Jan. 1947; to Burma 1950 and to Russia 1954. Vice-President Parliamentary Scientific Committee 1952; Director of Engineering and Mining Companies until Apr. 1955; Parliamentary Secretary Ministry of Supply Apr. 1955-Nov. 1956; Board of Trade Nov. 1956-Oct. 1958; Economic Secretary, Treasury Oct. 1958-Oct. 1959; Minister of State Board of Trade Oct. 1959-Oct. 1961; President of Board of Trade Oct. 1961-Oct. 1963. Minister of Power Oct. 1963-Oct. 1964. Member of National Economic Development Council 1962. A Conservative. Elected for Altrincham and Sale in July 1945 and sat until Dec. 1964 when he was created Baron Erroll of Hale. President of London Chamber of Commerce 1966-69, of Hispanic and Luso-Brazilian Councils 1969-73, of British Export Houses Association 1969-72 and of Electrical Research Association 1971-74. PC. 1960. Chairman of Consolidated Gold Fields Limited. Chairman of Bowater Corporation from 1973. Chairman of Council of Institute of Directors 1973-76. Chairman of Committee on Liquor Licensing 1971-72, Dept.-Chairman of Decimal Currency Board 1966-71. Chairman of Automobile Association from 1974.*

[1964]

EVANS, Albert. 7 Alsen Road, London. S. of Moses Richard Evans, Esq. B. 10 June 1903; m. 1929, Beatrice Joan, d. of L.W. Galton, Esq. Educ. at London County Council School, and Workers' Educational Association. A Master Engraver. Member of Islington Borough Council 1937-47 and of London County Council from 1946-49. A Labour Member. Sat for Islington W. from Sept. 1947-Feb. 1950 and for Islington S.W. from Feb. 1950 until he retired in 1970.*

[1970]

EVANS, Alfred Thomas. "Menai", Dilwyn Avenue, Hengoed, Glamorganshire. S. of Alfred Evans, Esq., a Miner. B. 1914; m. 13 Sept. 1939, Mary Katharine, d. of Joseph and Cecilia O'Marah. Educ. at Primary and Secondary Schools, Bargoed, Glamorgan, and University Coll. of Wales, Cardiff. Head of English Department at Bargoed Grammar School 1937-49. Headmaster, Bedlinog Secondary School 1949-66. Headmaster, Lewis Boys Grammer School, Pengam, Monmouthshire 1966-68. Agent to the Rt. Hon. Ness Edwards, MP. for Caerphilly. Councillor Gelligaer Urban District Council 1948-51. A Labour Member. Unsuccessfully contested the Leominster division of Herefordshire in 1955 and the Stroud division of Gloucestershire in 1959. Sat for the Caerphilly division of Glamorganshire from July 1968 until he retired in 1979.* [1979]

EVANS, Edward, C.B.E. 128 Waxwell Lane, Pinner. Savage. S. of Daniel Evans, Esq., of Manchester. B. 11 Jan. 1883; m. 13 Nov. 1915, Evelyn, d. of Robert Muir, Esq. (she died 1953). Educ. at Llanelly Science Schools, St. Paul's Coll., Cheltenham, and London University. Dept. Secretary National Institute for the Blind 1943-45; Chairman National Institute for the Deaf. Chairman Ministry of Health Advisory Committee for the Health and for Welfare of Handicapped Persons; President National Deaf-blind Helpers' League; Chairman Labour Party Fisheries Committee; Chairman All-Party Coast Defence Committee; Vice-Chairman All-Party Resorts and Tourist Committee; Parliamentary Delegate to Austria 1946, Iceland 1953, Denmark 1955; Internation Congress on Deaf-blind, New York 1957; Survey of Welfare Services in Germany 1946. Author of *A Manual Alphabet for the Deaf-blind*; Editor of *Braille School Magazine*; Head Master of E. Anglian Schools for Blind and Deaf Children; Vice-President of Coll. of Teachers of the Blind; Vice-President National Coll. of Teachers of the Deaf, and of Central Council for the Care of Cripples; Gov. Chalfont Epileptic Colony; Trustee and Gov. Mary Hare Grammar School for the Deaf; member of Great Yarmouth County Borough Council and Education Committee. A Labour Member. Elected for the Lowestoft division of Suffolk in July 1945 and sat until 1959 when he was defeated. C.B.E. 1949. Died 30 Mar. 1960. [1959]

EVANS, Emlyn Hugh Garner. Islwyn, Llangollen. National Liberal. S. of Henry Garner Evans, Esq., of Llangollen. B. 3 Sept. 1910. Educ. at Llangollen Grammar School, University Coll., Wales, Aberystwyth, and Caius Coll., Cambridge, M.A., LL.B. President of Union 1934. Barrister-at-Law, Gray's Inn. 1946. Editor of *New Commonwealth* 1935-50. Squadron-Leader R.A.F. Served overseas 1935-45. A Conservative and National Liberal Member. Unsuccessfully contested, as a Liberal, the City of Chester division of Cheshire in 1935 and the Denbigh division of Denbighshire in 1945. Elected for the Denbigh division in 1950 and sat until he retired in 1959. Died 11 Oct. 1963. [1959]

EVANS, Gwynfor Richard. House of Commons, London. S. of Dan Evans, Esq. B. Sept. 1912; m. 1941, Rhiannon Prys Thomas. Educ. at Barry County School, University Coll. of Wales, Aberystwyth, and St. Johns Coll., Oxford. A Farmer and Market Gardener. President Plaid Cymru from 1945. Member of Carmarthenshire County Council 1949-74. Hon. LL.D. University of Wales 1973. A Plaid Cymru Member. Unsuccessfully contested Merioneth in 1945, 1950, 1955 and 1959, and the Aberdare by-election in 1954. Unsuccessfully contested Carmarthen in 1964 and Mar. 1966, but elected for Carmarthen in July 1966 and sat until he was defeated in 1970. Unsuccessfully contested the seat again in Feb. 1974; re-elected for Carmarthen in Oct. 1974 and sat until 1979, when he was again defeated.* [1979]

EVANS, Ioan Lyonel. House of Commons, London. B. July 1927; m. 1949, Maria Griffiths. Educ. at Llanelli Grammar School, and Swansea University. Comptroller of the Household and Whip Feb. 1968-June 1970. Honorary Secretary Parliamentary Association for World Government 1974. Director International Defence and Aid Fund 1970-74. Chairman Justice for Rhodesia 1973. Chairman Parliamentary Labour Party Trade Group 1974. Vice-Chairman Parliamentary Labour Party Disabled Group 1974. Vice-Chairman Parliamentary Labour Party Prices and Consumer Protection Group 1974. Vice-Chairman Co-operative Parliamentary

Group 1974. Parliamentary Private Secretary to Rt. Hon. John Morris, Secretary of State for Wales 1975-76. Honorary Secretary Welsh Parliamentary Party 1974; Honorary Secretary Welsh Labour Members of Parliament. Chairman Prices and Consumer Protection Group. Parliamentary Private Secretary to Rt. Hon. Anthony Wedgwood Benn, Postmaster General 1964-66. Assistant Government Whip July 1966-Feb. 1968. A Labour and Co-operative Member. Sat for the Yardley division of Birmingham from 1964-70, when he was defeated. Elected for Aberdare in Feb. 1974. Member of Executive Committee of Christian Action Council. J.P. for Birmingham 1960-70, for Middlesex from 1970.*   [1979]

EVANS, John, O.B.E. 30 Garnwen Road, Nantyffyllon, Maesteg, Bridgend, Glamorganshire. S. of Thomas Evans, Esq., Coal Miner. B. Sept. 1875; m. 27 Sept. 1909, Ellen d. of John Parton, Esq., of Oxford. Educ. at Park Board School, and Ruskin Coll., Oxford. Worked as a Miner for 21 years. Trade Union Official from 1910. Member of Glamorgan County Council from 1913, Alderman 1925-55, Chairman 1939-40; J.P. for Glamorgan. Member of Royal Commission (National Health Insurance) 1924-25 and (Magistrates) 1946. A Labour Member. Unsuccessfully contested Montgomeryshire in 1929. Elected for the Ogmore division of Glamorganshire in June 1946 and sat until he retired in 1950. O.B.E. 1945. Member of Maesteg Urban District Council 1916-37, Chairman 1923-24 and 1933-34. Died 18 Apr. 1961.   [1950]

EVANS, John. 6 Kirkby Road, Culcheth, Warrington. House of Commons, London. S. of James Evans, Esq. B. 19 Oct. 1930; m. 6 June 1959, Joan, d. of Thomas Slater, Esq., (2 s. 1 d.). Educ. at Jarrow Central School. A Tyneside Shipyard Worker. Joined A.U.E.W. in 1951 and the Labour Party in 1954. Member Hebburn Urban District Council 1962-74; Chairman 1972-73; Leader 1969-74. Member South Tyneside M.D.C. 1973-74. U.K. Member European Parliament from 1975 to 1978. Chairman European Parliament Regional Policy and Transport Committee from Mar. 1976. Assis-

tant Government Whip Oct. 1978-May 1979. Opposition Whip from 1979. A Labour Member. Sat for Newton from Feb. 1974.*   [1979]

EVANS, Stanley Norman. 6 Serpentine Road, Birmingham. 75 Fellows Lane, Harborne, Birmingham. S. of F.J. Evans, Esq., of Harborne. B. 1 Feb. 1898; m. Muriel Kathleen, d. of William Birkett, Esq., of Keswick, Foundry Moulding Sand Supplier. Educ. at Elementary School. Chairman of Town Crier Publishing Society Limited, Birmingham, and of Anglo-South American All-Party Parliamentary Group. Served with Northumberland Hussars in France and Belgium 1915-18. Member of Parliamentary Delegation to Hungary 1946 and with Foreign Office Mission to South America 1947; leader of Delegation to N. and S. Rhodesia, Nyasaland, Mauritius and Malta 1951. Parliamentary Secretary Ministry of Food Mar.-Apr. 1950, when he resigned over the Government's agricultural policy; member of Parliamentary Delegation to Russia 1954. A Labour Member. Elected for Wednesbury in July 1945 and sat until he resigned in Nov. 1956 after disagreeing with official party policy on the Suez question. Died 25 June 1970.   [1956]

EWART, Richard. House of Commons, London. S. of Richard Ewart, Esq. B. 15 Sept. 1904. Unmarried. Educ. at St. Bede's, South Shields. Organiser for the National Union of General and Municipal Workers. A Labour Member. Sat for Sunderland from 1945-50, and for Sunderland S. from 1950 until his death on 8 Mar. 1953. Member of South Shields Borough Council 1932-43, and of N. Riding of Yorkshire County Council 1943-53. Parliamentary Private Secretary to Sir Hartley Shawcross, President of the Board of Trade 1951. A Roman Catholic. Died 8 Mar. 1953.   [1953]

EWING, Harry. House of Commons, London. S. of William Ewing, Esq., Miner. B. 20 Jan. 1931; m. 10 July 1954, Margaret, d. of John Greenhill, Esq. Educ. at Beath High School, Cowdenbeath. Held many local and national positions in the Co-operative Movement. Active Trade Unionist A.U.F.W.

Member No. 1 District Council 1958-61. Various appointments Union of Post Office Workers 1962-71. Parliamentary Under-Secretary of State at the Scottish Office (with special responsibility for Devolution matters) Oct. 1974-May 1979. An Opposition spokesman on Scotland from 1979. A Labour Member. Unsuccessfully contested East Fife in 1970. Sat for Stirling and Falkirk from Sept. 1971-Feb. 1974, and for Stirling, Falkirk and Grangemouth from Feb. 1974.*

[1979]

EWING, Winifred Margaret. 52 Queens Drive, Glasgow. House of Commons, London. D. of George Woodburn, Esq., Wholesale Stationer. B. 1929; m. 1956, Stewart Martin Ewing, Esq., M.A., C.A. Educ. at Queen's Park School, Glasgow, and Glasgow University. A Solicitor. M.A. 1949 Lecturer at Strathclyde University. Member of National Executive of Scottish National Party. Vice-President of Scottish National Party. Secretary of Glasgow Bar Association 1962-67, President 1970-71. President Glasgow (Central) Soroptimist Club 1965-66. Member European Parliament from 1975. A Scottish National Party Member. Sat for Hamilton from Nov. 1967 to 1970, when she was defeated, and for Moray and Nairn from Feb. 1974 until 1979, when she was defeated. Member of Executive Committee of Scottish Council for Development and Industry from 1972. Member of European Parliament for Highlands and Islands from 1979; Vice-Chairman of European Progressive Democrat Group.*

[1979]

EYRE, Reginald Edwin. House of Commons, London. S. of Edwin Eyre, Esq. B. 28 May 1924; m. 1978, Anne Clements. Educ. at King Edwards Camp Hill School, Birmingham, and Emmanuel Coll., Cambridge. Served in the Royal Navy 1941-45. M.A. (Cantab.) and admitted a Solicitor 1950. Chairman West Midlands Area C.P.C. Committee 1960-63; Chairman National Advisory Committee, Conservative Political Centre 1964-66. Opposition Whip 1966-70. Lord Commissioner of the Treasury June-Sept. 1970; Comptroller of H.M. Household Sept. 1970-Apr. 1972. Parliamentary Under-Secretary of State, Department of the Envi-

ronment (Housing and Construction) Apr. 1972-Mar. 1974. Vice-Chairman of the Conservative Party with special responsibility for the urban areas 1975-79. Under-Secretary of State for Trade from May 1979. A Conservative. Prospective Conservative Parliamentary Candidate for the Northfield division of Birmingham from 1956-59, defeated 1959. Elected for the Hall Green division of Birmingham at a by-election in May 1965.*

[1979]

FAIRBAIRN, Nicholas Hardwick, Baron of Fordell, Q.C. Fordell Castle, By Dunfermline. Beefsteak, and New. S. of Dr. William Ronald Dodds Fairbairn (Psychoanalyst), M.A., M.D., D. Psych. and Mary More Gordon, of Charlton and Kinnaber. B. 24 Dec. 1933; m. 29 Sept. 1962, Hon. Elizabeth Mackay, d. of Aeneas, Lord Reay and Charlotte, Lady Reay, (3 d.), (divorced 1979). Educ. at Loretto, and Edinburgh University. Called to the Scots bar in 1957. Chairman Edinburgh Brook Advisory Centre 1968-74; President 1974. Chairman Traverse Theatre 1964-72; President of Society for Preservation of Duddingston Village; President Dysart and Dundonald Pipe Band. An Author, Poet, Painter, Farmer, and Broadcaster. Member Council of Edinburgh Festival. Q.C. 1972. Solicitor General for Scotland from May 1979. A Conservative. Unsuccessfully contested Central Edinburgh in 1964 and 1966. Sat for Kinross and West Perthshire from Oct. 1974.*

[1979]

FAIRGRIEVE, (Thomas) Russell, C.B.E., T.D. Pankalan, Boleside, Galashiels. Carlton. S. of Alexander Fairgrieve, Esq., O.B.E., M.C., J.P. B. 5 May 1924; m. 1954, Millie Mitchell. Educ. at St. Mary School. Melrose, and Sedbergh School, Yorkshire. Maj. 8th Gurkha Rifles (Indian Army) 1946. Member of Selkirk County Council 1949-59 and Galashiels Town Council 1949-59. J.P. for Selkirkshire. Managing Director Laidlaw and Fairgrieve Limited 1958. Director Joseph Dawson (Holdings) Limited 1961. Director William Baird and Company Limited 1975. President Scottish Conservative Association 1965. Scottish Conservative Whip in 1975. Chairman Scottish Conservative Party 1975. Under-Secretary of State

for Scotland from May 1979. Conservative. Unsuccessfully contested Roxburgh, Selkirk and Peebles in 1970. Sat for Aberdeenshire W. from Feb. 1974. C.B.E. 1974.*
[1979]

FAIRHURST, Frank. 195 Beach Hill Avenue, Gidlow, Wigan. S. of Edward Fairhurst, Esq., of Pemberton, Wigan. B. 1892; m. 18 Sept. 1917, May, d. of Peter Smalley, Esq. Educ. at St. Paul's Church of England School. President of National Association of Power Loom Overlookers. A Labour Member. Sat for Oldham from July 1945-Feb. 1950. Elected for the E. division of Oldham in Feb. 1950 and sat until he retired in 1951. Member of Wigan Borough Council 1934-50. Died 30 Aug. 1953. [1951]

FAREY-JONES, Frederick William. House of Commons, London. S. of Evan Francis Jones, Esq. B. 1904; m. 1931, Lilian Ada Farey, and assumed the surname of Farey-Jones in lieu of Jones. Educ. at Queen Elizabeth's Grammar School, Carmarthen, and at Paris, Liège and Geneva. Founder of the Conference of International Air Traffic Control and of revived Air Transport Association. A Conservative. Unsuccessfully contested Goole in 1950 and Pembrokeshire in 1951. Elected for Watford in 1955 and sat until 1964 when he was defeated. Chairman of Farey-Jones (Insurance) Limited. Master of Worshipful Company of Horners 1970. Knight of Order of Civil Merit (Spain) 1958. Died 18 Feb. 1974. [1964]

FARR, John Arnold. 11 Vincent Square, London. Shortwood, Lamport, Northampton. Tanrago, Beltra, Co. Sligo. Boodle's, and M.C.C. S. of Capt. John Farr, J.P.B. 25 Sept. 1922; m. 1960, Susan Ann, youngest d. of Joan Lady Milburn, and Sir Leonard Milburn, Bart., (2 s.). Educ. at Harrow. Served in the Royal Navy 1940-46 in the Mediterranean and the South Atlantic; later Lieut.-Commander R.N.R. Member of Lloyd's. Executive Director Home Brewery Limited, and Apollo Productions Limited 1950-55. Secretary Conservative Parliamentary Agriculture Committee 1970-74. Member Executive Committee U.K. Branch Commonwealth Parliamentary Association 1972-74.

Vice-Chairman Conservative Parliamentary Northern Ireland Committee 1974. Member of U.K. delegation to Western European Union and The Council of Europe and Vice-Chairman Committee on Agriculture 1973. Chairman Anglo-Irish Parliamentary Group. Secretary Parliamentary Conservation Committee 1972. Chairman British Shooting Sports Council. Vice-President The Shooting Sports Trust 1972. Voted against entry to E.E.C. on 28 Oct. 1971. A Conservative. Unsuccessfully contested Ilkeston in 1955. Sat for Harborough from 1959.*
[1979]

FARTHING, Walter John. 21 Blacklands, Bridgwater. B. 4 July 1887; m. 1913. Educ. at Elementary School. Member of T.U.C. General Council 1935-44 and Executive member of Transport and General Workers' Union 1925-45. Mayor of Bridgwater 1939-40. A Labour Member. Elected for the Frome division of Somerset in July 1945 and sat until he retired in 1950. J.P. for Somerset. Died 29 Nov. 1954. [1950]

FAULDS, Andrew Matthew William. 14 Albemarle Street, London. S. of Matthew Faulds, Esq., Minister, Church of Scotland. B. 1 Mar. 1923 in Tanzania; m. Bunty, 1945, d. of George Whitfield,Esq., (1 d.). Educ. at George Watsons, Edinburgh, King Edward VI Grammar School, Louth, Daniel Stewarts, Edinburgh, Stirling High School, and Glasgow University. Actor, over thirty-five films, numerous television performances and broadcasts. Council member of British Actors' Equity 1966-69. Parliamentary Private Secretary to John Stonehouse, Minister of Aviation and Minister of State, Ministry of Technology 1967-68 and Postmaster Gen. 1968-69. Opposition spokesman for the Arts 1970-73 and from July 1979. Chairman British branch Parliamentary Association for Euro-Arab Co-operation. Executive Committee member Great Britain-China Centre and Franco-British Council. Chairman All-Party Heritage Group. Voted in favour of entry to E.E.C. on 28 Oct. 1971. A Labour Member. Unsuccessfully contested Stratford-upon-Avon at a by-election in 1963 and at the general election of 1964. Sat for Smethwick from 1966 to Feb. 1974, and for Warley E. from Feb. 1974.* [1979]

FELL, Anthony. 58 Park Street, London. S. of Commander David Mark Fell, R.N. B. 18 May 1914; m. 1939, Dorothy Jane Warwick. Educ. at Tauranga District High School, New Zealand and Bedford School. A Roman Catholic. Voted against entry to E.E.C. on 28 Oct. 1971. A Conservative. Unsuccessfully contested Brigg in 1948 and South Hammersmith in 1949 and 1950. Elected for the Yarmouth division of Norfolk in Oct. 1951 and sat until Mar. 1966, when he was defeated. Conservative Whip withdrawn May 1957-July 1958. Re-elected for the Yarmouth division of Norfolk in June 1970* [1979]

FENNER, Peggy Edith. House of Commons, London. 12 Star Hill, Rochester. B. 1922; m. 31 Dec. 1940, Bernard S. Fenner, Esq. Educ. at London County Council School, Brockley. Member Sevenoaks Urban District Council 1957-71; Chairman 1962-63. Parliamentary Secretary to Ministry of Agriculture, Fisheries and Food Ministry Nov. 1972-Mar. 1974. A Conservative. Unsuccessfully contested Newcastle-under-Lyme in 1966. Elected for Rochester and Chatham in June 1970 and sat until Oct. 1974 when she was defeated. Re-elected for Rochester and Chatham in May 1979. Member of W. Kent Divisional Education Committee 1963-72. Member of European Parliament 1974-75.* [1974 2nd ed.]

FERNYHOUGH, Rt. Hon. Ernest. House of Commons, London. S. of Harry Fernyhough, Esq., Coal Miner, of Wood Lane, Stoke-on-Trent. B. 24 Dec. 1908; m. 24 Feb. 1934, Ethel, d. of A. Edwards, Esq., of Stoke-on-Trent. Educ. at Wood Lane Elementary School. President of Newcastle, Staffordshire Trades Council 1935; Trades Union Official, U.S.D.A.W. to 1947. Labour Whip withdrawn Nov. 1954-Apr. 1955. Freedom of the borough of Jarrow. Parliamentary Secretary, Ministry of Labour Jan. 1967-Apr. 1968. Parliamentary Under-Secretary Department of Employment and Productivity Apr. 1968-Oct. 1969. PC. 1970. Parliamentary Private Secretary to the Prime Minister 1964-67. A Labour Member. Sat for Jarrow from May 1947 until he retired in 1979.* [1979]

FIDLER, Michael, J.P. "San Remo", Sedgley Park Road, Prestwich, Manchester. 51 Tavistock Court, Tavistock Square, London. House of Commons, London. S. of Louis Fidler, Esq., Clothing Manufacturer. B. 10 Feb. 1916; m. 27 Aug. 1939, Madie, d. of J. Davis, Esq. Educ. at Salford Grammar School, and Salford Royal Technical Coll. Clothing Advisory Committee, British Board of Trade 1942-49; President Federation of Jewish Youth Societies of Great Britain 1951. Joint Chairman National Joint Clothing Council of Great Britain 1953-57; Director Manchester Chamber of Commerce 1951-55; Councillor Borough of Prestwich 1951-63; J.P. for County of Lancaster 1958; Alderman of the Borough of Prestwich 1963-74; North Manchester Hospital Management Committee 1962-69; Mayor of Prestwich 1957-58; Dept. Mayor of Prestwich 1958-59; Vice-Chairman World Conference of Jewish Organisations 1967. President Board of Deputies of British Jews 1967-73. Chairman Foreign Affairs Committee 1973. Gov. Institute of Contemporary Jewry, Hebrew University of Jerusalem 1967-68; Patron the All-Party Committee for the Release of Soviet Jewry 1971. Treasurer Parliamentary Migraine Group 1971. F.R.G.S., F.R.A.S., F.R.Econ.S., F.I.A.I. A Conservative. Elected for Bury and Radcliffe in June 1970 and sat until Oct. 1974 when he was defeated.* [1974 2nd ed.]

FIELD, William James. 33 St. Peter's Square, London. S. of Frederick William Field, Esq., Solicitor. B. 22 May 1909. Unmarried. Educ. at Richmond County School, and University of London. Served in Intelligence and with R.A.S.C. 1939-45, Capt. Member of Hammersmith Borough Council 1945-53, Leader 1946-49, of Metropolitan Boroughs Standing Joint Committee, a Vice-President of the Association of Municipal Corporations, and member of Association of Scientific Workers. Parliamentary Private Secretary to Michael Stewart, Under-Secretary for War 1950-51 and to Rt. Hon. John Strachey, Secretary of State for War 1951. A Labour Member. Unsuccessfully contested Hampstead in 1945. Elected for Paddington N. in Nov. 1946 and sat until he resigned in Oct. 1953.* [1953]

FIENBURGH, Wilfred, M.B.E. Little Coxpond Farmhouse, Leverstock Green Road, Hemel Hempstead, Hertfordshire. S. of Harry Fienburgh, Esq., of Bradford, Yorkshire. B. Nov. 1919; m. 4 May 1940, Joan Valerie Hudson, d. of Capt. Thomas and Eva McDowell, of Belfast. Educ. at Belle Vue High School, Bradford. Author and Research Worker. War service with Rifle Brigade and as Maj. on General Staff; M.B.E. 1945. Assistant Secretary Civil Service Clerical Association 1946-47; Secretary Labour Party Policy Committee and member of T.U.C. Economic Committee 1948-51. A Labour Member. Unsuccessfully contested Pembrokeshire in 1945. Elected for N. Islington in Oct. 1951 and sat until his death on 3 Feb. 1958 as the result of a car accident. [1957]

FINCH, Harold Josiah. 56 Kenwyn Road, Clapham Common, London. S. of Josiah Finch. Esq., of Barry. B. 2 May 1898; m. Sept. 1922, Gladys, d. of Arthur Hinder, Esq., of Barry. Educ. at Barry Elementary School. Trades Union Official, National Union of Mine Workers. Parliamentary Under-Secretary of State, Welsh Office Oct. 1964-Apr. 1966. A Labour Member. Elected for the Bedwellty division of Monmouthshire in 1950 and sat until he retired in 1970. Member of Mynyddislwyn Urban District Council 1922-33, Chairman 1932. Secretary of S. Wales Miners Federation 1934-39. Opposition spokesman on Fuel and Power 1959-60. Knighted 1976. Author of works on industrial injuries and compensation.* [1970]

FINLAY, Graeme Bell, E.R.D. 3 Verulam Buildings, Gray's Inn, London. 2 Francis Taylor Buildings, Temple, London. Carlton. S. of James Bell Pettigrew Finlay, Esq., of Portskewett House, near Chepstow, Monmouthshire. B. 29 Oct. 1917; m. 22 May 1953, June Evangeline, d. of Col. Francis Drake, O.B.E., M.C., D.L., late 10th Royal Hussars, of Harlow, Essex, (2 d.). Educ. at Marlborough and University Coll., London. Barrister-at-Law, Gray's Inn 1946. War service with S. Wales Borderers and 5th Royal Gurkha Rifles (Frontier Force) 1939-46, Acting Maj. President of the Hardwicke Society 1950-51; presided over the first televised joint debate between the Oxford and Cambridge Union Societies. Parliamentary Private Secretary to Rt. Hon. Iain Macleod, Minister of Health May 1952. Assistant Government Whip May 1957. Lord Commissioner of the Treasury Jan. 1959-Oct. 1960. Vice-Chamberlain of the Household Oct. 1960-Oct. 1964. A Conservative. Unsuccessfully contested, against Mr. Aneurin Bevan, Ebbw Vale in 1950. Elected for the Epping division of Essex in Oct. 1951 and sat until 1964 when he was defeated. Created Bart. 1964. Dept. Judge of County Court 1967-72, Circuit Judge 1972. Sous Juge d'Instruction and Assistant Judge of Petty Debts Court for Jersey 1972-77. Dept. Chairman of Agricultural Land Tribunal, S.E. Region 1971-72.* [1964]

FINSBERG, Geoffrey, M.B.E., J.P. 80 Westbere Road, London. St. Stephen's. S. of Monte Finsberg, Esq., M.C. B. 13 June 1926; m. 10 Apr. 1969, Pamela, d. of R. Benbow Hill, Esq. Educ. at City of London School. Vice-Chairman of the Conservative Party from 1975; Hampstead Borough Councillor 1949-65; Camden Borough Councillor 1964-74; Leader of Camden Borough Council 1968-70. Dept. Chairman Association of Municipal Corporations 1969-71; member Trustee Savings Bank Parliamentary Committee; member of Post Office Users National Council 1969-77. Industrial Relations Adviser and Controller of Personnel, Great Universal Stores 1960. M.B.E. 1959; J.P. 1962. Member of Council of Confederation of British Industry. Gov. of the Polytechnic of North London. Vice-Chairman All-Party Retail Parliamentary Group. Member House of Commons Expenditure Committee. Opposition spokesman on London 1974-75. Under-Secretary of State for the Environment from May 1979. A Conservative. Unsuccessfully contested Islington E. in 1955. Member for Hampstead from June 1970 to Feb. 1974 and for the Hampstead division of Camden from Feb. 1974.* [1979]

FISHER, Doris Mary Gertrude, J.P. 36 Irwin Avenue, Rednal, Birmingham. D. of Frederick Satchwell, Esq. B. 13 Sept. 1919; m. 1 July 1939, Joseph Fisher, Esq. Educ. at Birmingham Schools, and Fircroft Coll.

Member of Birmingham City Council 1952-74; past Chairman of its Housing Committee. A Labour Member. Unsuccessfully contested the Ladywood division of Birmingham in June 1969. Elected for the Ladywood division of Birmingham in June 1970 and sat until she retired in Feb. 1974. J.P. for Birmingham 1961. Created Baroness Fisher of Rednal (Life Peerage) 1974. Member of Warrington New Town Development Corporation from 1974. Member of New Towns Staff Commission from 1976. Member of European Parliament 1975-79. Member of Gen. Medical Council from 1974.* [1974]

FISHER, Sir Nigel Thomas Loveridge, M.C. 16 Northcourt, Great Peter Street, London. Portavo Point, Donaghadee, Co. Down. St. George's Court, St. George's Bay, Malta. M.C.C. S. of Commander Sir Thomas Fisher, K.B.E., R.N. and step-s. of Sir Geoffrey Shakespeare, MP. B. 1913; m. 1st, 1935, Lady Gloria Malet, d. of 7th Earl of Lisburne, (1 s. 1 d.) (marriage dissolved in 1952); 2ndly, 1956, Patricia Ford, MP., Ulster Unionist Member for N. Down from 1953-55, and d. of Lieut.-Col. Sir Walter Smiles, C.I.E., D.S.O., D.L., MP. (he died 1953). Educ. at Eton, and Trinity Coll., Cambridge. Maj. Welsh Guards; served overseas 1939-45. Parliamentary Private Secretary to the Rt. Hon. G. Lloyd George, Minister of Food 1951-54, and as Home Secretary 1954-57. Parliamentary Under-Secretary of State for the Colonies from July 1962-Oct. 1963. Parliamentary Under-Secretary of State for Commonwealth Relations and for the Colonies Oct. 1963-Oct. 1964. Opposition Front Bench spokesman on Commonwealth and Colonial Affairs 1964-66. Member National Executive Committee of the Conservative Party 1945-47 and 1973. Member of the Executive of the 1922 Committee 1959-62 and 1969. Treasurer Commonwealth Parliamentary Association 1966-68 and Treasurer U.K. Branch 1977; Vice Chairman 1975-76. Published *Iain Macleod* 1973, and *The Tory Leaders* 1977. Knighted 1974. A Conservative. Unsuccessfully contested Chislehurst in 1945. Sat for the Hitchin division of Hertfordshire from Feb. 1950 to May 1955, for Surbiton from May 1955 to Feb. 1974 and for the Surbiton division of Kingston-upon-Thames from Feb. 1974.* [1979]

FITCH, (Ernest) Alan. 117 The Avenue, Leigh, Lancashire. R.A.C. S. of the Rev. Ernest W. Fitch, Methodist Minister. B. 10 Mar. 1915; m. 1950, Nancy Maude, youngest d. of R. Kennard Davis, Esq., (1 s. 1 d.). Educ. at Kingswood School, Bath. A Mineworker until 1958. Secretary Golborne Trades and Labour Council 1949-58; member of the Select Committee on the Nationalised Industries 1959-64. Chairman North West Regional Council of the Labour Party. Contested for seat on the Wardle Urban District Council when aged 21. Justice of the Peace Aug. 1958. Assistant Government Whip Nov. 1964-Apr. 1966; Lord Commissioner of the Treasury Apr. 1966-Oct. 1969. Whip to the Labour Party Delegation to the Council of Europe Jan. 1967-Oct. 1969. Vice-Chamberlain H.M. Household Oct. 1969-June 1970. Opposition Whip 1970-71. Member of Chairman's Panel 1972-78. Member of European Parliament Mar. 1978-May 1979. Honorary Freeman of County Borough of Wigan. A Labour Member. Sat for Wigan from June 1958.* [1979]

FITT, Gerard. 85 Antrim Road, Belfast, Northern Ireland. S. of George Fitt, Esq. B. 9 Apr. 1926; M. 5 Nov. 1947, Susan, d. of James Doherty, Esq. Educ. in Belfast. A Merchant Seaman 1941-53. Councillor, Dock Ward, Belfast Corporation from 1958. MP. for the Belfast Dock Constituency, in the N. Ireland Parliament, Stormont 1962-72. A Socialist Member. Sat for the W. division of Belfast from Mar. 1966. Member of N. Ireland Assembly for N. Belfast 1973-75 and of Constitutional Convention 1975-76. Dept. Chief Executive of N. Ireland Executive 1974. Founder and Leader of the Social Democratic and Labour Party from Aug. 1970, when he was expelled from the Republican Labour Party, until Nov. 1979, when he resigned. Sat as a Socialist from Nov. 1979.* [1979]

FLANNERY, Martin Henry. House of Commons, London. S. of Martin Flannery, Esq. of Sheffield. B. Mar. 1918. m. 1949, Blanche Mary. Educ. at Sheffield Teachers' Training Coll. Served with Royal Scots 1940-46. Headmaster 1969-74. A Labour Member. Sat for the Hillsborough division of Sheffield from Feb. 1974.*[1979]

FLEETWOOD-HESKETH, Roger Fleet-wood. See HESKETH, Roger Fleetwood.

FLEMING, Edward Lascelles, K.C. 109 Dorset House, Gloucester Place, London. B. about 1891; m. 1920, Rita, d. of J.A. Porritt, Esq., of Cheadle. Barrister-at-Law, Grays Inn 1921. Served with E. Lancashire Regiment 1917-19 and R.A.F.V.R. 1939-43, Squadron-Leader. K.C. 1932. A Conservative. Unsuccessfully contested the Ince division of Lancashire in 1922. Sat for the Withington division of Manchester from 1931 until his death on 17 Feb. 1950 during the campaign for the general election at which he was a candidate for the Moss Side division of Manchester. Author of *Nazi Shadows* (1935) and *Sheba's Ring* (1933). Died 17 Feb. 1950.
[1950]

FLETCHER, Alexander MacPherson. House of Commons, London. S. of Alexander Fletcher, Esq. B. Aug. 1929; m. 1950, Christine Anne Buchanan. Educ. at Greenock High School. A Chartered Accountant. Member of East Kilbride Development Corporation 1971-73. Member of European Parliament 1975-77. Front Bench spokesman on Scottish Affairs Feb. 1977-May 1979. Under-Secretary of State for Scotland from May 1979. A Conservative. Unsuccessfully contested W. Renfrewshire in 1970. Elected for Edinburgh N. at a by-election in Nov. 1973.*
[1979]

FLETCHER, Edward Joseph. House of Commons, London. B. 25 Feb. 1911; m. Constance Murial, d. of George Lee, Esq., of Whickham, Hampshire, (2 d.). Educ. at St. Mary's Church of England School, Handsworth, Birmingham, and Fircroft Coll., Bournville, Birmingham. A Trade Union Official. Member of the Labour Party from 1926. Joined A.E.U. in 1932, and was member of Birmingham District Committee. Held many offices in the Labour movement–Divisional Chairman, Parliamentary Agent, etc. Northern Area Secretary of Clerical and Administrative Workers Union 1949-64. Member of Newcastle City Council 1952-64. Chairman of North Eastern Association for the Arts 1961-65. A Labour Member. Unsuccessfully contested Middlesbrough W. in 1959. Sat for Darlington from Oct. 1964.*
[1979]

FLETCHER, Rt. Hon. Sir Eric George Molyneux. 9 Robin Grove, Highgate, London. 3 Gray's Inn Place, London. Athenaeum. S. of Clarence Fletcher, Esq. B. 26 Mar. 1903; m. 20 Apr. 1929, Bessie, d. of James Butt, Esq. Educ. at Radley Coll., and University of London, LL.D. Admitted a Solicitor 1924. Member of London County Council for South Islington from 1934-49; member from 1945, Chairman of Select Committee on Statutory Instruments 1952-64; Minister Without Portfolio Oct 1964-Apr. 1966. Dept. Speaker and Chairman of Ways and Means Apr. 1966-Oct. 1968. Knighted 1964. PC. 1967. A Labour Member. Elected for Islington E. in 1945 and sat until he retired in 1970. Created Baron Fletcher (Life Peerage) 1970. Opposition spokesman on Home Affairs 1959-64. President of British Archaeological Association 1960-63. Fellow of Society of Antiquaries and Royal Historical Society. Dept.-Chairman of Associated British Picture Corporation 1946-64. Commissioner for Public Works Loans 1946-55. Member of Senate of London University 1946-50 and 1956-74. President of Selden Society 1967-70. Member of Commission on Church and State 1951, Church Assembly 1962, Advisory Council on Public Records 1959-64, Royal Commission on Historical Manuscripts from 1966, Statute Law Committee 1951-76. Trustee of British Museum 1968-77. Chairman of Advisory Board for Redundant Churches 1969-74*
[1970]

FLETCHER, (Leopold) Raymond. 304 Frobisher House, Dolphin Square, London. 23 Ilkeston Road, Heanor, Derbyshire. S. of Leopold Raymond Fletcher, Esq., of Ruddington. B. 3 Dec. 1921; m. 1st, 1947, Johanna Klara, d. of Karl Ising, Esq. (she died 1973); 2ndly, 1977, Dr. Catherine M. Elliott. Served with Indian Army Ordnance Corps 1941-48. A Journalist. Member of Transport and General Workers' Union, Institute of Strategic Studies. Joined the Labour Party in 1937. *Times* Columnist and contributor to other journals at home and abroad. Founder of Airship Association. Chairman Parliamentary Airships Group.

Chairman Parliamentary Branch Labour Friends of Israel. Parliamentary Private Secretary to Roy Mason, Minister of Defence (Equipment) 1967. Leader U.K. Delegation to Council of Europe and Western European Union 1974-76. Chairman Aerospace Developments (London) Limited. A Labour Member. Unsuccessfully contested Wycombe in 1955. Sat for the Ilkeston division of Derbyshire from Oct. 1964.*   [1979]

FLETCHER, Sir Walter, C.B.E. 54 Albert Court, London. Bath, and Garrick. S. of Paul Fleischl, Esq., of Reigate. B. 8 Apr. 1892; m. 17 Jan. 1928, Esme, d. of J.L. Boyd, Esq. Educ. at Charterhouse, and University of Lausanne. Maj. R.A.O.C. 1914-18 in E. Africa (despatches and O.B.E. 1919). In business in E. Africa 1918-24. A Rubber Merchant. Chairman and Managing Director of Hacht, Levis and Kahn Limited (Rubber Merchants) from 1926. Exhibited paintings at the Royal Academy 1937 and 1938. Special Service in Far East 1939-46. C.B.E. 1947 Knight Bach 1953. A Conservative. Prospective Conservative candidate for E. Birkenhead in 1931 but stood down in favour of the Liberal candidate. Sat for Bury July 1945-Feb. 1950. Elected for Bury and Radcliffe in Feb. 1950 and sat until he retired in 1955. Died 6 Apr. 1956.   [1954]

FLETCHER-COOKE, Charles Fletcher, Q.C. 4 North Court, London. Garrick, and Pratt's. S. of Capt. C.A. Fletcher-Cooke. B. 5 May 1914; m. 1959, Diana, Lady Avebury (marriage dissolved in 1966). Educ. at Malvern Coll., and Peterhouse, Cambridge. A Barrister-at-Law, Lincoln's Inn 1938; Q.C. 1958, Bencher 1969. Served R.N.V.R. (Lieut.-Commander) 1940-46. Joint Under-Secretary Home Office June 1961-Feb. 1963, when he resigned. Member of European Parliament Mar. 1977-May 1979. Unsuccessfully contested Dorset E. as a Labour candidate in 1945. Resigned from Labour Party in 1947. A Conservative. Elected for the Darwen division of Lancashire in Oct. 1951. Delegate to Council of Europe 1954-55. Member of Statute Law Committee 1955-61 and from 1970. Member of Senate of Inns of Court 1970-74. Chairman of Select Committee on Parliamentary Commission for Administration 1974-77.*   [1979]

FLETCHER-COOKE, Sir John, C.M.G. "Salterns", Old Bursledon, Southampton. Travellers', and Royal Southampton Yacht. S. of Charles Arthur Fletcher-Cooke, Esq. B. 1911; m. 1st, Alice, d. of Dr. and Mrs. Russell Egner, of Washington, D.C., U.S.A. (divorced 1971), (2 s. 1 d.); 2ndly, 1977, Marie-Louise, widow of Louis, Vicomte Fournier de la Barre. Educ. at Malvern Coll. (Barham Scholar), University of Paris (Diploma), St. Edmund Hall (Senior Exhibitioner) Oxford, M.A. (First Class Honours, Politics, Philosophy and Economics). In 1934 obtained 2nd place in Home Civil Service competitive exam. (Administrative Grade). Appointed to Colonial Office and Served in West African, Pacific and Mediterranean Departments and as Private Secretary to Permanent Under-Secretary of State 1934-37. Transferred to Colonial Administrative Service; appointments in Malaya and Singapore 1937-42. Joined R.A.F. as Intelligence Officer 1942. Captured by Japanese in Java (P.O.W. in Java and Japan for $3\frac{1}{2}$ years). Special Duty Malta 1946. Dept. Financial Secretary, Palestine 1946-48. Adviser on Palestine, and subsequently Counsellor (Colonial Affairs) U.K. Mission to U.N., New York 1948-51. Represented U.K. at General Assembly Sessions and meetings of Trusteeship Council etc., in New York, Geneva and Paris. Colonial Secretary (and Acting Gov. on various occasions) Cyprus 1951-55. C.M.G. 1952. Represented Cyprus at H.M. Coronation 1953. Minister for Constitutional Affairs, Chief Secretary and Dept. Gov. (Acting Gov. on various occasions), Tanganyika 1956-61. Special Representative of Tanganyika on U.N. Trusteeship Council and at inaugural meeting of Economic Commission for Africa, Addis Ababa. Visiting Professor (African Affairs) University of Colorado, U.S.A. 1961-62. Member of Constituencies Delimitation Commission, Kenya 1962. Knighted 1962. Councillor, Royal Commonwealth Society; member Executive Committee Overseas Employers Federation 1963-67. A Conservative. Unsuccessfully contested Luton in Nov. 1963. Elected for the Test division of Southampton in Oct. 1964 and sat until 1966 when he was defeated. Director of Programmes in Diplomacy, Carnegie Endowment for International Peace 1967-69.*   [1966]

FLETCHER VANE, William Morgan. See VANE, William Morgan Fletcher.

FLOUD, Bernard Francis Castle. 89 Albert Street, London. Younger s. of Sir Francis Floud. B. 22 Mar. 1915; m. 1938, Ailsa, younger d. of Granville Craig, Esq., (1 s. 2 d.) (she died 1967). Educ. at Gresham's School, Holt, and Wadham Coll., Oxford. Army service 1939-42. Ministry of Information 1942-45; Board of Trade 1945-51; Farmer 1951-55. Television programme Company Executive (Granada Television Limited) from 1955. Joined the Labour Party in 1937. A Labour Member. Unsuccessfully contested Chelmsford in 1955 and Hemel Hempstead in 1959. Elected for Acton in Oct. 1964 and sat until he committed suicide on 10 Oct. 1967. Member of Kelvedon Hatch Parish Council 1952-61. Member of Ongar Rural District Council 1952-55. Chairman of Independent Television Labour Relations Committee 1963. Died 10 Oct. 1967. [1967]

FOLEY, Maurice Anthony. House of Commons, London. S. of Jermiah Foley Esq. B. 1925 at Durham; m. 1952 Catherine, d. of Patrick O'Riordan, Esq. Educ. at Elementary and Grammar Schools. Member of Transport and General Workers Union. Chairman International Committee National Council of Social Service. Parliamentary Under-Secretary of State in the Department of Economic Affairs Oct. 1964-Jan. 1966. Parliamentary Under-Secretary of State, Home Office Jan. 1966-Jan. 1967, for Defence for the Royal Navy Jan. 1967-July 1968, Foreign and Commonwealth Office July 1968-June 1970. Opposition spokesman on Foreign Affairs 1970-73. Voted in favour of entry to E.E.C. on 28 Oct. 1971. A Labour Member. Unsuccessfully contested Bedford in 1959. Elected for West Bromwich in July 1963 and sat until Jan. 1973 when he resigned on appointment as Dept.-Director General for Development of the Commission for the European Communities. A Roman Catholic.* [1973]

FOLLICK, Dr. Mont. 43 South Molton Street, London. B. at Cardiff 1887. Unmarried. Educ. at Sorbonne University, Paris, University of Halle, and Padua. Spoke many languages and dialects. Founder and Proprietor of the Regent School of Languages. Late Professor of English University of Madrid. Secretary to the Prime Minister of Queensland, to the late Emperor of Morocco. Doctor of Philosophy; F.R.G.S., F.R.S.A. A Labour Member. Unsuccessfully contested the Ashford division of Kent in 1929, E. Surrey in 1931 and W. Fulham in 1935. Elected for the Loughborough division of Leicestershire in July 1945 and sat until he retired in 1955. Advocate of spelling reform and decimal currency. Died 10 Dec. 1958. [1954]

FOOKES, Janet Evelyn. Delphia, 11 Branksome Road, St. Leonards-on-Sea, Sussex. Royal Overseas League. D. of Lewis Aylmer Fookes, Esq., Company Director. B. 21 Feb. 1936. Educ. at Hastings and St. Leonards Ladies' Coll., Hastings High School for Girls and Royal Holloway Coll., London University, B.A. (Hons.). A School Teacher 1958-70. Councillor, County Borough of Hastings 1960-61 and 1963-70; Chairman of Education Committee 1967-70. Member Councils of R.S.P.C.A. and National Canine Defence League. Secretary Parliamentary Animal Welfare Group. Member of Select Committee on Expenditure. Chairman of Education, Arts and Home Affairs Sub-Committee of Expenditure Committee. Member of Speakers Panel of Chairmen from 1976. A Conservative. Sat for Merton and Morden from 1970-Feb. 1974 and for the Drake division of Plymouth from Feb. 1974.* [1979]

FOOT, Rt. Hon. Sir Dingle Mackintosh, Q.C., P.C. 2 Paper Buildings, Temple, London. 76A Ashley Gardens, Thirleby Road, Westminster, London. Garrick, and Beefsteak. S. of the Rt. Hon. Isaac Foot, MP. B. 1905; m. 1933, Dorothy Mary, d. of Maj. William Rowley Elliston, T.D., of Ipswich. Educ. at Bembridge School, and Balliol Coll., Oxford. President of Oxford Union 1928. Barrister-at-Law, Gray's Inn 1930; Bencher 1952; Treasurer 1968. Royal Observer Corps 1939. Member British Delegation to San Francisco Conference 1945. Chairman *Observer* Trustees 1953-55. Parliamentary Secretary Ministry of Economic Warfare May

1940-May 1945. Chairman Society of Labour Lawyers 1960-64. Solicitor Gen. Oct. 1964-Aug. 1967. Knighted 1964. PC. 1967. Liberal Member for Dundee from 1931-45 when he was defeated. Unsuccessfully contested, as Liberal, the Tiverton division of Devon in 1929 and N. Cornwall in 1950 and 1951. Joined the Labour Party in July 1956. Elected for Ipswich in Oct. 1957 and sat until 1970 when he was defeated. Member of the Bar of Gold Coast 1948, Ceylon 1951, Nigeria 1955, Northern Rhodesia 1956, Sierra Leone 1959, India 1960, Bahrain 1962, Malaya 1964, Southern Rhodesia 1964 and Northern Ireland 1970. Q.C. 1954. Member of Royal Commission on Justices of the Peace 1946. Honorary LL.D. Dundee University 1974. President of Electoral Reform Society 1970-78. Died 18 June 1978. [1970]

FOOT, Rt. Hon. Michael Mackintosh. House of Commons, London. S. of the Rt. Hon. Isaac Foot, MP for Bodmin. B. 23 July 1913; m. 1949, Jill Craigie. Educ. at Leighton Park School, Reading, and Wadham Coll., Oxford. President of Oxford Union 1933. A Journalist, Editor of the *Evening Standard* 1942-43. Political Columnist *Daily Herald* 1944-64; Managing Director of *Tribune* until 1974. Secretary of State for Employment from Mar. 1974-Apr. 1976. Leader of the House of Commons and Lord President of the Council Apr. 1976-May 1979. Dept. Leader of Labour Party from Oct. 1976. Member of National Executive Committee of Labour Party 1948-50 and from 1972. Labour Whip withdrawn Mar. 1961-May 1963. Member of Parliamentary Committee of P.L.P. 1970-74. Opposition spokesman on Fuel and Power 1970-71, on House of Commons Affairs 1971-72 and on Europe 1972-74. Unsuccessful candidate for Dept. Leadership of Labour Party 1970, 1971, and 1972, and for the Leadership 1976. Dept. Leader of the Opposition from May 1979. PC. 1974. A Labour Member. Unsuccessfully contested Monmouth in 1935. Sat for Plymouth Devonport from 1945-55, when he was defeated. Unsuccessfully contested Plymouth Devonport in 1959. Member for the Ebbw Vale division of Monmouthshire from Nov. 1960. Biographer of Aneurin Bevan; co-author of *Guilty Men* (1940) and other pamphlets.*
[1979]

FORD, Benjamin Thomas. House of Commons, London. R.A.C., and Idle Working Men's. S. of Benjamin Charles Ford, Esq., Compositor. B. 1 Apr. 1925; m. 30 Dec. 1950, Vera, d. of H. Faucett, Esq., (2 s. 1 d.). Educ. at Rowan Road Central School, Surrey. An Electronic Fitter-wireman. Joined the Labour Party in June 1947. Member of London Society of Compositors 1941-48, Amalgamated Engineering Union 1950. Shop Stewards' Convenor. Served in the Royal Navy, Fleet Air Arm 1943-47. President Harwich Constituency Labour Party 1955-63. Served on Clacton Urban District Council from 1959-62, and Essex County Council from 1959-65 (Alderman). J.P. for Essex 1963-67. Chairman Inter-Parliamentary Union (U.K. Branch). Chairman British Latin American Parliamentary Group. Chairman Joint Select Committee on Sound Broadcasting. Chairman British-Brazilian and British-Portuguese Parliamentary Groups. Chairman W.A.G.B.I. Parliamentary Panel. Treasurer Parliamentary Labour Party Benevolent Fund. Voted in favour of entry to E.E.C. on 28 Oct. 1971. A Labour Member. Sat for Bradford N. from Oct. 1964.* [1979]

FORD, Patricia. 7 Russell Court, Cleveland Row, St. James, London. Portavo Point, Donaghadee, Co. Down, Northern Ireland. D. of Lieut.-Col. Sir W.D. Smiles, C.I.E., D.S.O., Dept.-Lieut., and MP. (drowned M.V. *Princes Victoria* 31 Jan. 1953). B. 5 Apr. 1921; m. 1st, 22 Feb. 1941, Neville M. Ford, s. of Dr. Lionel Ford, Dean of York, and Headmaster of Harrow (marriage dissolved 1956); 2ndly, 1956, Sir Nigel Fisher, MP. for Surbiton. Educ. at Bangor Collegiate School, Glendower School, London, and abroad. An Ulster Unionist and Conservative Member. Elected for Co. Down N. in Apr. 1953 in succession to her father and sat until she retired in 1955. Founder and Co-Chairman of Women Caring Trust.* [1954]

FORMAN, Francis Nigel. House of Commons, London. S. of Brigadier J.F.R. Forman. B. 25 Mar. 1943; m. 1971, Susan Orchard. Educ. at Dragon School, Oxford, Shrewsbury School, New Coll., Oxford, The Coll. of Europe, Bruges, Harvard University, and Sussex University, D. Phil. Information Officer, C.B.I. 1970-71. Head of External Affairs Section in the Conservative Research Department from May 1974-Sept. 1975. Assistant Director from Sept. 1975-Mar. 1976. Member of the Royal Institute of International Affairs, the International Institute for Strategic Studies and member of the London Library. Parliamentary Private Secretary to Lord Carrington, Secretary of State for Foreign and Commonwealth Affairs, and to Sir Ian Gilmour, Lord Privy Seal from 1979. A Conservative. Unsuccessfully contested Coventry N.E. in Feb. 1974. Sat for Sutton, Carshalton from Mar. 1976.* [1979]

FORMAN, John Calder. House of Commons, London. B. 1884. m. Barbara. An Insurance Agent. Member of Glasgow Corporation from 1928. A Labour and Co-operative Member. Elected for the Springburn division of Glasgow in July 1945 and sat until he retired in 1964. [1964]

FORREST, George. West Street, Stewartstown, Dungannon, Co. Tyrone, Northern Ireland. S. of Joseph Forrest, Esq. B. 26 Oct. 1921; m. 1946, Anna, d. of Richard Morgan, Esq., of Stewartstown, Co. Tyrone. Educ. at Donaghey Public School. Served 1941-46 with R.E. in Europe. An Auctioneer and Livestock Salesman. An Ulster Unionist Member. Elected for mid-Ulster in May 1956 as an Independent Unionist but later joined the Ulster Unionist Group and sat until his death on 10 Dec. 1968. [1968]

FORRESTER, John Stuart. House of Commons, London. S. of Harry Forrester, Esq. B. 1924; m. 1945, Gertrude H. Weaver. Educ. at Eastwood Council School. Stoke-on-Trent City School of Commerce and Alsager Teacher Training Coll. A Teacher. Member N.U.T. Member of Stoke-on-Trent City Council from 1970. Parliamentary Private Secretary to David Ennals, Minister of State, Department of Health and Social Security 1970. A Labour Member. Sat for Stoke-on-Trent N. from Mar. 1966.* [1979]

FORT, Richard. Ruscombe House, Twyford, Berkshire. Brooks's. S. of James Alfred Fort, Esq., of Harrington House, Bourton-on-the-Water, Gloucestershire. B. 8 Aug. 1907; m. 2ndly, 10 July 1943, Jean, d. of George Bentham Rae, Esq. Educ. at Eton, and New Coll., Oxford. A Chemist. Employed I.C.I. 1932. Ministry of Supply 1941-45; Director Atlas Electric and General Trust Limited, and Colonial Mutual Assurance Company. Parliamentary Private Secretary to Rt. Hon. Florence Horsbrugh, Minister of Education 1951-54. Lay member Medical Research Council; Chairman Parliamentary and Scientific Committee. A Conservative. Unsuccessfully contested the Clitheroe division of Lancashire in 1945. Elected for Clitheroe in 1950 and sat until his death in a car accident on 16 May 1959. [1959]

FORTESCUE, Trevor Victor Norman ('Tim'). Ruxbury House, St. Ann's Hill Road, Chertsey, Surrey. 7 Eton Court, Hornby Lane, Liverpool. Flat 8, 27 Cleveland Square, London. S. of Frank Fortescue, Esq. B. 28 Aug. 1916; m. 1st, 15 July 1939, Margery, d. of Dr. G.H. Hunt (divorced 1975); 2ndly, 1975, Anthea Maureen, d. of R.M. Higgins, Esq. Educ. at Uppingham School, and King's Coll., Cambridge. Col. Administrative Service Hong Kong 1939-47 (Japanese P.O.W. 1941-45); Kenya 1949-51. F.A.O. of U.N. Washington 1947-49 and Rome 1951-54. Chief Marketing Officer, Milk Marketing Board 1954-59. With Nestle Group of companies Vevey, Switzerland 1959-63 and London 1963-66. Assistant Whip June 1970-Nov. 1971. Lord Commissioner of the Treasury Nov. 1971-Sept. 1973. A Conservative. Elected for the Garston division of Liverpool in Mar. 1966 and sat until he retired in Feb. 1974. Secretary-Gen. of Food and Drink Industries Council from 1973.* [1974]

FOSTER, Sir John Galway, K.B.E., Q.C. Parsonage House, Stanton Harcourt, Oxford. All Souls' Coll, Oxford. Carlton, and Pratt's. S. of Gen. Hubert John Foster. B. 1904. Unmarried. Educ. at Eton, and New Coll., Oxford. Barrister-at-Law, Inner Temple 1927. Recorder of Oxford 1938-51 and 1956-64. First Secretary, British Embassy, Washington 1939. Brigadier 1944-45. K.C.

1950. Parliamentary Under-Secretary Commonwealth Relations Nov. 1951-Oct. 1954. Chairman Sir Isaac Pitman and Sons. A Conservative. Elected for the Northwich division of Cheshire in July 1945 and sat until he retired in Feb. 1974. K.B.E. 1964. Fellow of All Souls Coll., Oxford from 1924. Lecturer in Private International Law, Oxford 1934-39. Recorder of Dudley 1936-38.* [1974]

FOSTER, William. 21 Newton Road, St. Helens. S. of John Foster, Esq., of Wigan. B. 12 Jan. 1887; m. 1911, Jane Stringfellow, of Wigan (she died Jan. 1947). Vice-Chairman of National Board of Mining Examinations Ministry of Fuel 1944. Parliamentary Secretary Ministry of Fuel and Power Aug. 1945-May 1946. A Labour Member. Member for Wigan from Mar. 1942 until his death on 2 Dec. 1947. A Miner. Vice-President of Lancashire and Cheshire Miners' Federation 1932. Member of Executive of Miners Federation of Great Britain 1934 and 1939. Member of Abram Urban District Council, Chairman 1929-30. Member of St. Helens Borough Council 1935-42. J.P. for Wigan and St. Helens. Labour Party Agent for Ince 1929. Died 2 Dec. 1947. [1948]

FOWLER, Gerald Teasdale. 1 St. Chad's Close, Wellington, Shropshire. Flat 18, 36 Buckingham Gate, London. S. of James A. Fowler, Esq., of Long Buckby, Northamptonshire. B. 1 Jan. 1935; m. 1968, Julie, d. of Wilfred Brining, Esq. Educ. at Long Buckby, Northamptonshire Elementary School, Northampton Grammar School, Lincoln Coll., Oxford, and University of Frankfurt-am-Main. A Lecturer, Pembroke Coll., Oxford 1958-59, Hertford and Lincoln Colls., Oxford 1959-65, Lancaster University 1965-66. Oxford City Councillor 1960-64. Assistant Director Huddersfield Polytechnic 1970-72, Visiting Professor University of Strathclyde 1970-74. Professor of Educational Studies (Admin. & Man.), The Open University 1972-74. Associate Professor, Department of Government, Brunel University from 1977. President Association for Recurrent Education 1976-77. President Association for Liberal Education 1977. President Association for the Teaching of Social Sciences, 1976. Chairman Youthaid 1977; Vice-Chairman

Parliamentary Youth Lobby 1978. Leader of the Wrekin District Council 1973-74, Councillor 1973-76. Joint Parliamentary Secretary Ministry of Technology Sept. 1967-Oct. 1969. Minister of State Department of Education and Science Oct. 1969-June 1970 and Feb. 1974-Oct. 1974. Minister of State, Privy Council Office Oct. 1974-Jan. 1976. Minister of State, Education and Science Jan.-Sept. 1976. A Labour Member. Unsuccessfully contested the Banbury division of Oxfordshire in 1964. Sat for the Wrekin division of Shropshire from Mar. 1966-70, when he was defeated and from Feb. 1974-79, when he was again defeated.* [1979]

FOWLER, Rt. Hon. (Peter) Norman, M.A. Grounds Cottage, Oxleys Road, Wishaw, Sutton Coldfield. 27 Marsham Court, Marsham Street, London. S. of N.F. Fowler, Esq. B. 2 Feb. 1938; m. 1st, 17 Aug. 1968, Linda, d. of S. Christmas, Esq., 2ndly, 1979, Mrs Fiona Poole. Educ. at King Edward VI School, Chelmsford, and Trinity Hall, Cambridge. National Service, Essex Regiment 1956-58; Chairman Cambridge University Conservative Association 1960; Special Correspondent of *The Times* 1961-66; Home Affairs Correspondent of *The Times* 1966-70; Council member Bow Group 1967-69; on Editorial Board of Crossbow 1962-70; Vice-Chairman North Kensington Conservative Association 1967-68. Chairman East Midlands Conservative Political Centre 1970-73. Member Select Committee Immigration and Race Relations 1970-74. Secretary Conservative Parliamentary Party Home Affairs Committee 1971-72; Vice-Chairman 1974. Opposition spokesman Home Affairs Nov. 1974-75. Chief Opposition spokesman Social Services and Member of Shadow Cabinet 1975-76. Chief Opposition spokesman Transport 1976-79. Parliamentary Private Secretary to William van Straubenzee and David Howell, Ministers of State for Northern Ireland 1972-74. Minister of Transport from May 1979. PC. 1979. A Conservative. Sat for Nottingham S. division from 1970-Feb. 1974 and for Sutton Coldfield from Feb. 1974.* [1979]

FOX, Sir Gifford Wheaton Grey, Bart. 41 Eaton Mews North, London. Towersey Manor, Thame, Oxfordshire. Carlton. S. of Sir Gilbert Fox, 1st Bart. B. 2 Feb. 1903; m. 1st, 20 Oct. 1927, Hon. Myra Alice Newton, d. of Baron Eltisley (marriage dissolved in 1952); 2ndly, 1954. Mrs. Maryoth Trotter, d. of Lieut.-Col. Lord Edward Hay. Educ. at Eton, and Magdalen Coll., Oxford, M.A. 1929. Barrister-at-Law, Middle Temple 1926. Squadron Leader A.P.M., R.A.F.V.R. A Conservative. Member for the Henley division of Oxfordshire from Feb. 1932 until he retired in 1950 after his local association had declined to readopt him as their candidate. Succeeded as Bart. 1925. Died 11 Feb. 1959. [1950]

FOX, (John) Marcus, M.B.E. 10 Woodvale Crescent, Oakwood Park, Bingley, Yorkshire. House of Commons, London. S. of Alfred H. Fox, Esq. B. 11 June 1927; m. 9 Sept. 1954, Ann, d. of F.W.J. Tindall, Esq., (1 s. 1 d.). Educ. at Wheelwright Grammar School, Dewsbury. Served with Duke of Wellington's Regiment and the Green Howards 1945-48. National Vice-Chairman of the Young Conservatives, Area Chairman of the Yorkshire Young Conservatives and Chairman of Dewsbury Young Conservatives. Also Chairman of Yorkshire Area C.P.C. 1966-68; served on Dewsbury Council 1956-65. M.B.E. 1963. Assistant Government Whip Apr. 1972-Dec. 1973. Opposition Whip Mar.-June 1974. Lord Commissioner of the Treasury Dec. 1973-Mar. 1974. Opposition spokesman on Housing 1974-75 and on Transport 1975-76. Vice-Chairman of Conservative Party with Responsibility for Candidates 1976-79. Under-Secretary of State for the Environment from May 1979. A Conservative. Unsuccessfully contested Dewsbury in 1959 and Huddersfield W. in 1966. Sat for the Shipley division of the W. Riding of Yorkshire from June 1970.* [1979]

FRASER, Rt. Hon. Sir Hugh Charles Patrick Joseph, M.B.E. Eilean Aigas, Beauly, Inverness-shire. S. of 14th Baron Lovat. B. 23 Jan. 1918; m. Sept. 1956, Lady Antonia, d. of 7th Earl of Longford (marriage dissolved in 1977), (3 s. 3 d.). Educ. at Ampleforth, Sorbonne, and Balliol Coll.,

Oxford. President of Oxford Union. Maj. Lovat Scouts (T.A.) and S.A.S. Parliamentary Private Secretary to Rt. Hon. Oliver Lyttelton, Colonial Secretary 1951-54. Chairman West Midlands Conservative Union 1956-59. Financial Secretary War Office Nov. 1958-Oct. 1960. Parliamentary Under-Secretary of State for the Colonies Oct. 1960-July 1962. Secretary of State for Air July 1962-Apr. 1964. Minister of Defence for the Royal Air Force Apr.-Oct. 1964. President of W.M.C.A. 1968. Chairman Association of Conservative Clubs 1975-76. Voted against entry to the E.E.C. on 28 Oct. 1971. Unsuccessful candidate for the Leadership of the Conservative Party 1975. A Conservative. Sat for the Stone division of Staffordshire from 1945-Feb. 1950 and for the Stafford and Stone division of Staffordshire from Feb. 1950. PC. 1962.* [1979]

FRASER, Ian Montagu, M.C. How Hatch, Chipstead, Surrey. 5 Elliot Terrace, The Hoe, Plymouth. S. of Col. Herbert Cecil Fraser, D.S.O., O.B.E., T.D., M.I.E.E. B. 14 Oct. 1916; m. 1st, 21 Nov. 1945, Mary, d. of John Stanley, Esq., of Wigan (she died 1964); 2ndly, 1967, Angela Meston. Educ. at Shrewsbury, and Christ Church, Oxford. Commissioner U.L.I.A. 1939; 4th (Wilde's) Frontier Force Rifles 1940. Served Middle East and India; P.O.W. 1942-45; M.C. 1945, retired as Maj. 1948. R.A.R.O. The Rifle Brigade. Executive Guthrie and Company, East India Merchants 1948-55. Gen. Secretary The John Lewis Partnership 1956-59, and Consultant 1959-64. Parliamentary Private Secretary to Reginald Maudling, Secretary of State for the Colonies Dec. 1961-Apr. 1962. Assistant Government Whip from Apr. 1962-Oct. 1964. Opposition Whip 1964-66. A Conservative. Unsuccessfully contested Tottenham in 1955. Elected for the Sutton division of Plymouth in 1959 and sat until 1966 when he was defeated. On staff of Conservative Research Department 1966-67. Executive Director of G.U.S. Export Corporation 1967-70. Dept.-Secretary of The Buttle Trust from 1971* [1966]

FRASER, John Denis. 44 Pymers Mead, London. S. of Archibald Fraser, Esq., Fire Officer. B. 30 June 1934; m. 30 July 1960,

Ann, d. of George Hathaway, Esq., (2 s. 1 d.). Educ. at Sloane Grammar School. Qualified as a Solicitor (honours) 1960 Lewis Silkin and Partners. Lambeth Borough Councillor 1962-68. Parliamentary Private Secretary to the Rt. Hon. Barbara Castle, MP. Secretary of State for Employment and Productivity 1968-70. Opposition spokesman on Home Affairs 1972-74. Parliamentary Under-Secretary of State Department of Employment 1974-76. Minister of State Department of Prices and Consumer Protection 1976-79. An Opposition spokesman on Trade and Consumer Affairs from 1979. A Labour Member. Unsuccessfully contested Norwood division of Lambeth in the 1964 general election. Sat for the Norwood division of Lambeth from Mar. 1966. Member of General Advisory Council of Independent Television Authority 1973-74.*   [1979]

FRASER, Rt. Hon. Thomas. 15 Broompark Drive, Lesmahagow, Lanarkshire. S. of Thomas and Mary Fraser, of Blackwood, Lanarkshire. B. 18 Feb. 1911; m. 31 Dec. 1935, Janet, d. of James Scanlon, Esq., of Lesmahagow. Educ. at Blackwood School, and Lesmahagow Higher Grade School. A Miner from Dec. 1925, retired Jan. 1943. Secretary of Lanark Divisional Labour Party 1939-43; Secretary, then President of Coalburn Miners Lodge 1939-43. Parliamentary Private Secretary to Rt. Hon. Hugh Dalton, President of the Board of Trade Dec. 1944-May 1945. Joint Parliamentary Under-Secretary of State Scottish Office Aug. 1945-Oct. 1951. Minister of Transport Oct. 1964-Dec. 1965. A Labour Member. Elected for the Hamilton division of Lanarkshire in Jan. 1943 and sat until Sept. 1967 when he resigned on appointment as Chairman of N. of Scotland Hydro-Electricity Board. PC. 1964. Opposition spokesman on Scottish Affairs until 1961, on Power 1961-64. Member of Parliamentary Committee of Parliamentary Labour Party 1956-64. Member of Royal Commission on Local Government in Scotland 1966-69. Chairman of N. of Scotland Hydro-Electricity Board 1967-73. Member of S. of Scotland Electricity Board 1967-73. Member of Highlands and Islands Development Board 1967-70. Chairman of Scottish Local Government Staff Commission

1973-77. Chairman of Commission for Local Authority Accounts in Scotland from 1974. Chairman of Scottish Local Government Property Commission 1976-77.*   [1967]

FRASER, Sir (William Jocelyn) Ian, C.H., C.B.E. St. John's Lodge, Regent's Park, London. Bath. S. of W.P. Fraser, Esq., of Johannesburg. B. 30 Aug. 1897; m. 23 July 1918, Irene Gladys, d. of George Mace, Esq., of Chipping Norton. Educ. at Marlborough, and Royal Military Coll., Sandhurst. Late K.S.L.I.; served in France 1915-16, blinded in Battle of the Somme. Chairman of Executive Council of St. Dunstan's from 1921. Barrister-at-Law, Inner Temple, 1932. President of British Legion from June 1947-58; member of Council of Royal National Institute for the Blind; member of London County Council 1922-25. Knight Bach. 1934. A Gov. of B.B.C. 1937-39 and 1941-46. A Conservative. Elected for St. Pancras N. in Oct. 1924, defeated 1929. Re-elected in 1931 and 1935, resigned in Jan. 1937. Sat for the Lonsdale division of Lancashire Apr. 1940-Feb. 1950. Elected for the Morecambe and Lonsdale division of Lancashire in Feb. 1950 and sat until July 1958 when he was created Baron Fraser of Lonsdale (Life Peerage). C.B.E. 1922 C.H. 1953. President of International Congress of War Blinded 1973. Died 19 Dec. 1974.   [1958]

FREEMAN, John, M.B.E. House of Commons, London. S. of Horace Freeman, Esq., Barrister-at-Law. B. 19 Feb. 1915; m. 1st, 1938, Elizabeth Allen Johnston (marriage dissolved 1948); 2ndly, 1948, Margaret Ista Mabel Kerr (she died 1957); 3rdly, 1962, Catherine Dove (marriage dissolved 1976); 4thly, 1976, Judith Mitchell. Educ. at Westminster School, and Brasenose Coll., Oxford, Hon. Fellow 1968. Advertising Consultant 1937-40. On Active Service 1940-45. Parliamentary Private Secretary to Rt. Hon. J. Lawson, Secretary of State for War 1945-46; Financial Secretary to the War Office Oct. 1946, and Parliamentary Under-Secretary of State for War Apr.-Oct. 1947. Leader of U.K. Defence Mission to Burma 1947. Parliamentary Secretary Ministry of Supply Oct. 1947 until resignation Apr. 1951. Assistant Editor *New Statesman and Nation* from June

1951. A Labour Member. Elected for Watford in July 1945 and sat until he retired in 1955. Dept. Editor of *New Statesman* 1958-60, Editor 1961-65. M.B.E. 1943. High Commissioner in India 1965-68. Ambassador to United States 1969-71. PC. 1966. Chairman of London Weekend Television from 1971, and of Independent Television News from 1976.* [1954]

FREEMAN, Peter. 3 Rectory Road, Penarth, Glamorgan. S. of George Freeman, Esq., Tobacco Manufacturer. B. 19 Oct. 1888; m. 1914, Ella Drummond, d. of Sir Andrew Torrance, MP. Educ. at Haberdashers' School, London. Member of Penarth Urban District Council 1924-26 and of Cardiff City Council 1928-30 and Glamorgan County Council 1927-31. Chairman of International Council for Ethiopian Affairs 1945-55. A Labour Member. Sat for Brecon and Radnor from 1929-31 when he was defeated. Unsuccessfully contested Newport in 1935. Elected for Newport in July 1945 and sat until his death on 19 May 1956. Director and Manager of J.R. Freeman and Son Limited 1908-29. Member of Hoxton Board of Guardians 1910-12. Chairman of Vegetarian Catering Association. Secretary of Theosophical Society in Wales 1922-44. Died 19 May 1956. [1956]

FREESON, Rt. Hon. Reginald Yarnitz. 159 Chevening Road, London. B. 24 Feb. 1926. Educ. at Elementary School, Jewish Orphanage, W. Norwood and matriculated by private study. A Journalist. Joined the Labour Party in 1948. Member of N.A.T.S.O.P.A. (Later S.O.G.A.T.) 1942-53, N.U.J. from 1954 and Co-operative Party 1958. Chairman of Willesden Council of Social Service 1960-62, Founder-Chairman of Willesden Friendship Council (later Brent Community Relations Council) in 1959-63. Member of Willesden Borough Council 1952 and leader of Council 1958-65. Chairman of new Brent Borough Council (comprising Willesden and Wembley) 1964-65. Alderman of Willesden and Brent 1955-68. Parliamentary Private Secretary to Rt. Hon. Thomas Fraser and Rt. Hon. Barbara Castle, Ministers of Transport Nov. 1964-Jan. 1967. Parliamentary Secretary Ministry of Power from

Jan. 1967-Oct. 1969. Parliamentary Secretary Ministry of Housing and Local Government Oct. 1969-June 1970. Opposition spokesman on Housing July 1970-Mar. 1974. Minister for Housing and Construction, Department of Environment 1974-79. PC. 1976. An Opposition spokesman on Social Services from 1979. A Labour Member. Sat for Willesden E. from Oct. 1964 to Feb. 1974 and for Brent E. from Feb. 1974.* [1979]

FREETH, Denzil Kingson. 66a Warwick Way, London. Carlton. S. of Walter Kingson Freeth, Esq. B. 10 July 1924. Educ. at Sherborne School, and Trinity Hall, Cambridge, Scholar. Served with R.A.F. as pilot 1943-46 (Flying Officer), when invalided out. President Cambridge Union Society 1949; Chairman Cambridge University Conservative Association 1949. A Stockbroker. Member of Executive Committee of Conservative Party 1955-56; Parliamentary Private Secretary to Toby Low, Minister of State Board of Trade 1955 and to Sir David Eccles, President Board of Trade 1957-59. Parliamentary Private Secretary to Sir David Eccles, Minister of Education from Oct. 1959-Aug. 1960. Parliamentary Secretary to Minister for Science Feb. 1961-Oct. 1963. A Conservative. Elected for the Basingstoke division of Hampshire in 1955 and sat until he retired in 1964. Member of Stock Exchange 1959-61 and from 1965.* [1964]

FREUD, Clement Raphael. House of Commons, London. S. of Ernst Freud, Esq. B. Apr. 1924; m. 1950, Jill Raymond, (5 children). Educ. at Dartington Hall, and St. Pauls School. A Writer/Broadcaster. Member National Union of Journalists and Equity. Consultant and Director to Hotel and Restaurant Companies. Rector Dundee University 1974. Liberal spokesman on Education 1974-76, on N. Ireland 1976-79, on Price and Consumer Protection 1976-77, and on Broadcasting and the Arts from 1977. A Liberal Member. Sat for the Isle of Ely from July 1973.* [1979]

FRY, Peter Derek. "Chiltern Lodge", Poplars Farm Road, Barton Seagrave, Kettering, Northamptonshire. R.A.C. S. of Harry Walter Fry, Esq. B. 26 May 1931; m. 20 Feb. 1956, Edna, d. of John Bates Roberts, Esq., of Liverpool, (1 s. 1 d.). Educ. at Royal Grammar School, High Wycombe, and Worcester Coll., Oxford, M.A. Modern History. A Teacher, Buckinghamshire Education Committee 1956. Northern Assurance Group 1956-61. Political Education Officer, Conservative Central Office 1961-63. Own Insurance Broking Business 1963. Served on Buckinghamshire County Council from 1961-67. Vice-Chairman Conservative Transport Industries Committee, Joint Chairman All-Party Roads Study Group. Voted against entry to E.E.C. on 28 Oct. 1971. A Conservative. Unsuccessfully contested Nottingham N. in 1964 and E. Willesden in 1966. Sat for Wellingborough from Dec. 1969.* [1979]

FYFE, Rt. Hon. Sir David Patrick Maxwell, G.C.V.O., Q.C. See MAXWELL-FYFE, Rt. Hon. Sir David Patrick, G.C.V.O., Q.C.

GAGE, Conolly Hugh. The Malt House, Widdington, Newport, Essex. Carlton, and Ulster (Belfast). S. of William Charles Gage and Mary, d. of Rt. Hon. Lord Justice Hugh Holmes. B. 10 Nov. 1905; m. 1932, Elinor Nancy, d. of W.E. Martyn, Esq. Educ. at Repton, and Sidney Sussex Coll., Cambridge, Fellow Commoner 1962. Barrister-at-Law, Inner Temple 1930. Late Assistant Dept. Judge Advocate-Gen. with Canadian Forces in Belgium (despatches). Chancellor of the Diocese of Coventry 1948-76 and of Lichfield 1954-76. Recorder of Saffron Walden and Maldon 1950-52. An Ulster Unionist Member. Elected for Belfast S. in July 1945 and sat until he resigned in Oct. 1952. Member of Delegation to Council of Europe 1949-52. Dept.-Chairman of Essex Quarter Sessions 1955-71. Chairman of Huntingdon and Peterborough Quarter Sessions 1963-71. County Court Judge 1958-71, Circuit Judge from 1972.* [1952]

GAITSKELL, Rt. Hon. Hugh Todd Naylor, C.B.E. 18 Frognal Gardens, London. S. of Arthur Gaitskell, Esq., I.C.S. B. 9 Apr. 1906; m. 9 Apr. 1937, Anna Dora, d. of L. Creditor, Esq. (she was created Baroness

Gaitskell in 1964). Educ. at Winchester, and New Coll., Oxford. University Lecturer and Reader 1928-39; Civil Servant 1939-45. Parliamentary Secretary Ministry of Fuel and Power May 1946-Oct. 1947. Minister of Fuel and Power Oct. 1947-Feb. 1950. Minister of State for Economic Affairs Feb.-Oct. 1950. Chancellor of the Exchequer Oct. 1950-Oct. 1951; Leader of the Labour Party Dec. 1955-Jan. 1963. PC. 1947. A Labour Member. Unsuccessfully contested Chatham in 1935. Elected for S. Leeds in July 1945 and sat until his death on 18 Jan. 1963. Private Secretary to Hugh Dalton, Minister of Economic Warfare 1940-42. C.B.E. 1945. Member of Parliamentary Labour Party Parliamentary Committee 1951-55. Treasurer of Labour Party 1954-55. Vice-Chairman of National Executive of Labour Party 1962-63. Died 18 Jan. 1963. [1962]

GALBRAITH, Commander Rt. Hon. Thomas Dunlop, R.N. Barskimming, Mauchline, Ayrshire. S. of William Brodie Galbraith, Esq., of Glasgow, and Annie, d. of Thomas Dunlop, Esq. B 20 Mar. 1891; m. 2 Dec. 1915, Ida Jean, d. of Thomas Galloway, Esq., of Auchendrane, Ayrshire. Educ. at Glasgow Academy, R.N. Coll., Osborne, and at Dartmouth. Joined R.N. 1903, retired 1922. Rejoined 1939-42. A Chartered Accountant 1925. Member of Glasgow Town Council 1933-40; Magistrate Glasgow 1938-40. Joint Parliamentary Under-Secretary of State for Scotland May-July 1945 and Nov. 1951-Apr. 1955. A Conservative. Sat for the Pollok division of Glasgow from Apr. 1940 until Apr. 1955 when he was created Baron Strathclyde. PC. 1953. Minister of State, Scottish Office Apr. 1955-Oct. 1958. Chairman of North of Scotland Hydro-Electric Board 1959-67. Member of South of Scotland Electricity Board 1965-67. President of Electrical Research Association 1965-66.* [1954]

GALBRAITH, Hon. Thomas Galloway Dunlop. 2 Cowley Street, London. Barskimming, Mauchline, Ayrshire. Carlton, Conservative, Glasgow, and New, Edinburgh. S. of Rt. Hon. Thomas Dunlop Galbraith, MP., created Lord Stratchclyde. B. 10 Mar. 1917, m. 11 Apr. 1956, Simone, eld. d. of Jean du

Roy de Blicquy, Bois d'Hautmont, Brabant (marriage dissolved in 1974) (2 s. 1 d.). Educ. at Aytoun House, Glasgow, Wellington Coll., Christ Church, Oxford, (M.A.), and at Glasgow University, (LL.B.). Joined R.N.V.R. 1939; Lieut. 1942; specialised in Signals; on the staff of Commander-in-Chief Mediterranean 1944; demobilised 1946. Member of Queen's Bodyguard for Scotland (Royal Company of Archers). A Gov. of Wellington Coll. Assistant Conservative Whip 1950; Scottish Unionist Whip 1950-57; a Lord Commissioner of the Treasury 1951-54; Comptroller of H.M. Household 1954-55, Treasurer of H.M. Household 1955-57. Civil Lord of the Admiralty 1957-59. Joint Parliamentary Under-Secretary of State for Scotland Oct. 1959-Nov. 1962, when he resigned. Parliamentary Secretary Ministry of Transport May 1963-Oct. 1964. An Opposition spokesman on Transport in 1965. A Unionist Member. Unsuccessfully contested Paisley at the general election of 1945 and E. Edinburgh in Oct. 1945. Sat for the Hillhead division of Glasgow from Nov. 1948.* [1979]

GALLACHER, William. 16 King Street, London. S. of John Gallacher, Esq., of Paisley. B. 25 Dec. 1881; m. Jan. 1913, Jean Miller, d. of John Roy. Educ. at Elementary School. A Brass-fitter. A Communist. Unsuccessfully contested Dundee in 1922 and 1923, West Fife in May 1929 and Oct. 1931 and the Shipley division of the W. Riding of Yorkshire in Nov. 1930. Sat for West Fife from 1935 until 1950 when he was defeated. Member of Executive Committee of Communist International 1924 and 1935. President of British Communist Party 1956-63. Died 12 Aug. 1965. [1950]

GALPERN, Sir Myer. House of Commons, London. S. of Maurice Galpern, Esq. B. 1903; m. 1940, Alice, d. of Thomas Stewart, Educ. at Glasgow University. Elected Lord Provost of Glasgow in 1958; Lord-Lieut. of Glasgow 1958-60. Honorary LL.D. Glasgow University; Honorary F.E.I.S., J.P. Dept.-Lieut. Member of Glasgow Corporation from 1932-60, Chairman of Education Committee. Member of Glasgow University Court; member Chairman's Panel. Second Dept. Chair-

man of Ways and Means Nov. 1974-Feb. 1976, First Dept. Chairman Feb. 1976-Apr. 1979. A Labour Member. Sat for the Shettleston division of Glasgow from 1959 until he retired in 1979. Knighted 1960. Created Baron Galpern (Life Peerage) 1979.* [1979]

GAMMANS, (Ann) Muriel Gammans, Lady. 19 Buckingham Palace Mansions, London. Canhouse Farm, Milland, Liphook, Hampshire. D. of Frank Paul, Esq., of Warblington, Hampshire. B. 1898; m. 1917, Sir (Leonard) David Gammans, 1st and last Bart, MP. (he died 1957). Educ. at Portsmouth High School. A Conservative. Elected for Hornsey in May 1957 in succession to her late husband and sat until she retired in 1966.* [1966]

GAMMANS, Sir Leonard David, Bart. 19 Buckingham Palace Mansions, London. St. Stephens, Royal Automobile, and Royal Empire. S. of David Gammans, Esq., of East Court, East Cosham, Hampshire. B. 10 Nov. 1895; m. 21 Nov. 1917, Muriel, d. of Frank Paul, Esq., of Warblington, Hampshire (she succeeded him as MP. for Hornsey in 1957). Educ. at Portsmouth Grammar School, and London University. Served in France 1914-18, at Royal Military Coll., Canada 1918-20, in Colonial Service, British Malaya 1920-34, at British Embassy, Tokyo 1926-28. Director and Secretary of Land Settlement Association 1934-39. In Ministry of Information 1939-41. Member of Conference of Institute of Pacific Relations, Canada 1942 and Hot Springs, Virginia 1945 and of Parliamentary Delegation to the West Indies 1944, Sarawak 1946, and Ceylon 1949. Assistant Postmaster Gen. Nov. 1951-Dec. 1955. Created Bart. 1955. A Conservative. Elected for Hornsey in May 1941 and sat until his death on 8 Feb. 1957. [1957]

GANDAR DOWER, Col. Alan Vincent. See DOWER, Col. Alan Vincent Gandar.

GANDAR DOWER, Eric Leslie. See DOWER, Eric Leslie Gandar.

GANLEY, Caroline Selina. 5 Thirsk Road, London. D. of James Blumfield, Esq. B. 1879; m. 1901, James H.W. Ganley, Esq. Member of Battersea Borough Council 1919-25 and 1953-65 and of Price Regulation Committee London Region. A Labour Member. Unsuccessfully contested Paddington N. in 1935. Elected for Battersea S. in July 1945 and sat until 1951 when she was defeated. J.P. for County of London from 1920. Member of Board of London Co-operative Society 1921-46, President 1942-46. Member of London County Council 1925-28 and 1934-37. C.B.E. 1953. Died 31 Aug. 1966.   [1951]

GARDINER, George Arthur. House of Commons, London. S. of Stanley Gardiner, Esq. B. 3 Mar. 1935; m. 1961, Juliet Wells, (2 s. 1 d.). Educ. at Harvey Grammar School, Folkestone, and Balliol Coll., Oxford. Chief Political Correspondent Thomson Newspapers 1968-74. Author of *Margaret Thatcher: From Childhood to Leadership* 1975. Secretary Conservative European Affairs Committee 1976. A Conservative. Unsuccessfully contested Coventry S. in 1970. Sat for Reigate from Feb. 1974.*   [1979]

GARDNER, Antony John. 30 Brookside Avenue, East Leake, Loughborough. S. of David Gardner, Esq. B. 27 Dec. 1927; m. 22 Sept. 1956, Eveline, d. of Mrs. V.C. Burden, of Portsmouth. Educ. at Elementary School, Co-operative Coll., and Southampton University. Engineering Industry, National Service and Building Trade 1941-53. President Southampton University Union 1958-59. Education Officer Co-operative Union 1959-66. A Labour Member. Unsuccessfully contested S.W. Wolverhampton in 1964. Elected for the Rushcliffe division of Nottinghamshire in Mar. 1966 and sat until 1970 when he was defeated. Unsuccessfully contested Beeston in Feb. and Oct. 1974. Principal Information Officer, Central Council for Education and Training in Social Work from 1970.*   [1970]

GARDNER, Edward Lucas, Q.C. 4 Raymond Buildings, Gray's Inn, London. Outlane Head Cottage, Chipping, Preston, Lancashire. Garrick. S. of E.W. Gardner, Esq., Company Director. B. 10 May 1912; m. 1st, 1950, Noreen Margaret, d. of John Collins, Esq. (divorced 1962); 2ndly, 27 July 1963, Joan Elizabeth, d. of B.B. Belcher, Esq., (2 s. 2

d.). Educ. at Hutton Grammar School. During the war served in R.N.V.R. in cruisers; Commander R.N.V.R. Chief of Naval Information (East India) 1945. Called to the bar, Gray's Inn, 1947; appointed Q.C. 1960; elected Master of the Bench, Gray's Inn 1968. Dept. Chairman of E. Kent Quarter Sessions 1961-71. Essex Quarter Sessions 1968-71. A Recorder of the Crown Court from 1972. Parliamentary Private Secretary to Sir John Hobson, Attorney General 1962-63. A Conservative. Unsuccessfully contested Erith and Crayford in 1955. Sat for Billericay from 1959-66, when he was defeated and for Fylde S. from June 1970. Member of Commonwealth War Graves Commission from 1971.*   [1979]

GARNER EVANS, Emlyn Hugh. See EVANS, Emlyn Hugh Garner.

GARRETT, John Laurence. House of Commons, London. S. of Laurence Garrett, Esq. m. 1959, Wendy Ady. B. 8 Sept. 1931. Educ. at Sir George Monoux Grammar School, Walthamstow, University Coll., Oxford, (M.A., B.Litt), and University of California (King George VI Fellow). Labour Officer in chemical industry 1958-59. Head of market research in motor industry 1959-63. Management Consultant. T.G.W.U. Director of Public Services in management consultancy group 1963-74. Parliamentary Private Secretary to Robert Sheldon Minister of State, Civil Service Department and Minister of State, Treasury 1974 and to Rt. Hon. Stanley Orme, 1977. Minister of Social Security 1977. An Opposition spokesman on Treasury and Economic Affairs from 1979. Member Greenwich Council. A Labour Member. Sat for Norwich S. from Feb. 1974.*   [1979]

GARRETT, (William) Edward. 84 Broomhill Road, Prudhoe Station, Northumberland. S. of John Garrett, Esq. B. 21 Mar. 1920; m. May 1946, Beatrice, youngest d. of John and Mary Anne Kelly. Educ. at Elementary School, London School of Economics, and evening classes. An Engineer. Joined the Labour Party in 1939. Member of Northumberland County Council from 1954 to 1964 and member of Prudhoe Urban

District Council from 1948 to 1964. Parliamentary Adviser, Machine Tools Trades Association. A Labour Member. Unsuccessfully contested Hexham in 1955 and Doncaster in 1959. Sat for Wallsend from Oct. 1964.* [1979]

GARROW, Alexander. 45 Titwood Road, Glasgow. S. of William Garrow, Esq., of Glasgow. B. 12 Mar. 1923; m. 1955, Flora Wilson Mackay, d. of J.B. Mackay, Esq., of Paisley. Educ. at Queen's Park Secondary School, Glasgow and N.C.L.C. Insurance Agent (Co-operative Insurance Society). Joined the Labour Party in May 1946. Member of Glasgow City Council 1954-57 and 1960-66. Chairman Municipal Transport Committee, Glasgow. Branch Chairman of Union of Shop, Distributive and Allied Workers. Magistrate and J.P. of Glasgow from May 1960 until May 1963. A Labour Member. Elected for the Pollok division of Glasgow in Oct. 1964 and sat until his death on 16 Dec. 1966. [1966 2nd ed.]

GATES, Maj. Ernest Everard. 15 Grosvenor Square, London. Nore, Hascombe, Surrey. Calton, Portland, and St. James's. S. of Ernest Henry Gates, Esq., of Old Buckenham Hall, Norfolk. B. 29 May 1903; m. 1931, Stella, d. of Henry Knox Simms, Esq. Educ. at Repton School, and Corpus Christi Coll., Cambridge, M.A. Maj. R.A. (T.A.). Chairman and Joint Managing Director of Ernest H. Gates and Company Limited 1925-29; Director of Manchester Chamber of Commerce. A Conservative. Unsuccessfullly contested Deptford in 1929. Elected for the Middleton and Prestwich division of Lancashire in May 1940 and sat until he retired in 1951 after criticism from his local association.* [1951]

GEORGE, Bruce Thomas. 42 Wood End Road, Walsall, West Midlands. S. of Edgar Lewis George, Esq. B. 1 June 1942. Educ. at Mountain Ash Grammar School, University Coll. of Wales, Swansea and University of Warwick, B.A. (Wales), M.A. (Warwick). Assistant Lecturer in Politics Glamorgan Coll. of Technology 1964-66. A Lecturer in Politics Manchester Polytechnic 1968-70. Senior Lecturer in Politics Birmingham Polytechnic 1970-74. Tutor at Open University. Member of Select Committee on Violence in the family. A Labour Member. Unsuccessfully contested Southport in 1970. Sat for Walsall S. from Feb. 1974.* [1979]

GEORGE, Sir John Clarke, K.B.E. Seton Lodge, Ayr. Constitutional, and Conservative (Glasgow). S. of John Clarke George, Esq., a Miner. B. 16 Oct. 1901; m. 7 Aug. 1929, Euphamia, d. of Robert Donaldson, Esq. Educ. at Ballingry Public School, Fife. Entered coal mine aged 14. C.B.E. 1952. K.B.E. 1963. C.St. J. Parliamentary Secretary Ministry of Power Oct. 1959-June 1962. Chairman of the Unionist Party in Scotland 1963-65. A Conservative. Unsuccessfully contested S. Ayrshire in 1950. Elected for the Pollok division of Glasgow in 1955 and sat until he retired in 1964. Manager of New Cumnock Collieries 1938-46, of Alloa Glass Works 1946-55. Member of Alloa Town Council 1951-56 and Clackmannan County Council 1949-56. Chairman of Scottish Rexco Limited and Preswick Precision Products Limited. Died 14 Oct. 1972. [1964]

GIBBINS, Joseph. 8 Hargreaves Road, Liverpool. S. of George Gibbins, Esq., of Liverpool. B. 1888; m. 1912, Sarah Beatrice, d. of G.W. Hugill, Esq. Educ. at St. Thomas C. of E. Schools and evening classes at Liverpool University. Served with R.N.R. 1915-19. Secretary of Liverpool Boilermakers' Union. Served overseas 1914-19. A Labour Member. Unsuccessfully contested the West Toxteth division of Liverpool in 1922 and 1923. Elected there in May and Oct. 1924, and again in May 1929 and sat until Oct. 1931, when he was defeated. Re-elected for the West Toxteth division of Liverpool in July and Nov. 1935 and in July 1945 and sat until Feb. 1950 when he unsuccessfully contested the Toxteth division of Liverpool. J.P. for Liverpool from 1924. Died 26 Aug. 1965. [1950]

GIBSON, Charles William. 25 Dalmore Road, Dulwich, London. S. of Charles Gibson, Esq., of Little Dunmow. B. 1889; m. 1915, Jessie Davison. Educ. at Elementary School, and Morley Working Men's Coll. Vice-Chairman of London County Council

1941-42; Chairman of Housing Committee 1943-50; member of Central Housing Advisory Committee 1945-51; J.P. for London. An officer of Transport and General Workers' Union. A Labour Member. Unsuccessfully contested the Norwood division of Lambeth in 1935. Sat for the Kennington division of Lambeth from 1945-50. Elected for the Clapham division of Wandsworth in Feb. 1950 and sat until 1959 when he was defeated. Died 22 Mar. 1977. [1959]

GIBSON-WATT, Rt. Hon. (James) David, M.C. Doldowlod, Llandrindod Wells, Radnorshire. 64 Cadogan Place, London. Boodle's. S. of Maj. James Miller Gibson-Watt, D.L., J.P. B. 1918; m. 1942, Diana, d. of Sir Charles Hambro, K.B.E., M.C., (3 s. 2 d.). Educ. at Eton, and Trinity Coll., Cambridge. Maj. Welsh Guards in Second World War; M.C. and 2 bars. J.P. and County Councillor for Radnor 1946. Chairman Livestock Export Council 1962-64. Minister of State Welsh Office June 1970-Mar. 1974. Fellow Royal Agricultural Societies of England and Wales. A Conservative. Unsuccessfully contested Brecon and Radnor in 1950 and 1951. Elected for the Hereford division of Herefordshire in Feb. 1956 and sat until he retired in Sept. 1974. Assistant Whip 1957-59. Lord Commissioner of the Treasury Oct. 1959-Nov. 1961. Parliamentary Private Secretary to Rt. Hon. Reginald Maudling, Chancellor of Exchequer 1962-64. Opposition spokesman on Post Office and Broadcasting 1965-66 and on Welsh Affairs 1965-70. PC. 1974. Forestry Commissioner from 1976. Dept.-Lieut. for Radnorshire 1968-74, for Powys from 1974. Member of Historic Buildings Council for Wales from 1975. Created Baron Gibson-Watt (Life Peerage) 1979.* [1974 2nd ed.]

GILBERT, Rt. Hon. John William. House of Commons, London. Reform S. of Stanley Gilbert, Esq. B. 5 Apr. 1927; m. 2ndly, 1963, Jean Ross Skinner. Educ. at Merchant Taylors School, St. John's Coll., Oxford, and New York University, Ph.D. (New York). A Chartered Accountant (Canada). An Opposition spokesman on Treasury Affairs 1972-74. Financial Secretary to the Treasury Mar. 1974-June 1975. Minister for Transport June 1975-Sept. 1976. Minister of State for Defence Sept. 1976-May 1979. PC. 1978. A Labour Member. Unsuccessfully contested the Ludlow division of Shropshire in 1966 and Dudley in Mar. 1968. Sat for Dudley from 1970 to Feb. 1974, and for Dudley E. from Feb. 1974.* [1979]

GILES, Rear-Admiral Morgan Charles Morgan. See MORGAN-GILES, Rear-Admiral Morgan Charles.

GILMOUR, Rt. Hon. Sir Ian Hedworth John Little, Bart. House of Commons, London. S. of Sir John Little Gilmour, Bart. B. 1926; m. 1951, Lady Caroline Margaret Montagu-Douglas-Scott, youngest d. of the 8th Duke of Buccleuch and Queensberry, (4 s. 1 d.). Educ. at Eton, and Balliol Coll., Oxford. Served in the Grenadier Guards from 1944-47. Called to the bar, Inner Temple, 1952. Editor of the *Spectator* 1954-59. Parliamentary Private Secretary to the Rt. Hon. Quintin Hogg 1963-64. Parliamentary Under-Secretary of State for Defence for the Army June 1970-Apr. 1971. Minister of State for Defence Procurement Apr. 1971-Nov. 1972. Minister of State for Defence Nov. 1972-Jan. 1974. Secretary of State for Defence Jan.-Mar. 1974. PC. 1973. Chairman Conservative Research Department 1974-75. Opposition spokesman on Defence 1974, on N. Ireland 1974-75, on Home Affairs 1975-76 and on Defence 1976-79; member of Shadow Cabinet 1974-79. Lord Privy Seal and Principal spokesman for the Foreign and Commonwealth Office in the House of Commons from May 1979. A Conservative. Sat for Norfolk Central from Nov. 1962 to Feb. 1974, and for Chesham and Amersham from Feb. 1974 Author of *The Body Politic* and *Inside Right.* Succeeded as Bart. 1977.* [1979]

GILMOUR, Sir John Edward, Bart., D.S.O., T.D., D.L. Montrave, Leven, Fife. Cavalry, and Leander. S. of Col. Rt. Hon. Sir John Gilmour, Bart., G.C.V.O., D.S.O., MP. B. 24 Oct. 1912; m. 1941, Ursula Wills, d. of F.O. Wills, Esq., (2 s.). Educ. at Eton, and Trinity Hall, Cambridge. Served with Fife and Forfar Yeomanry 1939-45. D.S.O. 1945. Battalion Col. 1950. Succeeded his father as 3rd Baronet 1940. Dept.-Lieut. for Fife 1953, Lord Lieut. 1980. Member Fife County Council 1955-61. Lieut. Royal Company of Archers (Queen's Bodyguard for Scotland). Chairman Unionist Party in Scotland Apr. 1965-Jan. 1967. A Conservative. Unsuccessfully contested Clackmannan and E. Stirlingshire in 1945. Sat for E. Fife from Nov. 1961 until he retired in 1979.* [1979]

GILZEAN, Andrew, O.B.E. 4 Bernard Terrace, Edinburgh. S. of James Gilzean, Esq., of Edinburgh. B. 3 Dec. 1877; m. 1904, Annie Thomson. Educ. at St. Leonard's School, Edinburgh. Member of Edinburgh City Council 1924-45; Chairman of Scottish Labour Party 1935-36, of Scottish Socialist Party 1936-38 and of Edinburgh Trades and Labour Council 1929-32; Curator of Patronage University of Edinburgh 1934-45; Dept.-Lieut. and J.P. for Edinburgh. A Labour Member. Unsuccessfully contested the Central division of Edinburgh in 1935. Elected for the Central division of Edinburgh in July 1945 and sat until he retired in 1951. O.B.E. 1945. Served with Royal Artillery 1916-19. Died 6 July 1957. [1951]

GINSBURG, David. 3 Bell Moor, East Heath Road, London. Reform. S. of N. Ginsburg, Esq. B. 18 Mar. 1921; m. 3 Apr. 1954, Louise, eld. d. of S.P. Cassy, Esq. Educ. at University Coll. School, and Balliol Coll., Oxford. Commissioned Oxford-Bucks. Light Infantry 1942. Capt. Intelligence duties 1944-45. Senior Research Officer, Government Social Survey 1946-52. Secretary of the Research Department of the Labour Party and Secretary of the Home Policy Sub-Committee of the National Executive Committee 1952-59. Chairman Parliamentary and Scientific Committee Feb. 1968-71, subsequently Dept. Chairman and Vice-President. Member Select Committee on Science and Technology 1967. Economist and Market Research Consultant. Writer and Broadcaster. Parliamentary Private Secretary to Rt. Hon. Douglas Houghton, Chancellor of Duchy of Lancaster and Minister without Portfolio 1964-67. Voted in favour of entry to E.E.C. on 28 Oct. 1971. A Labour Member. Sat for Dewsbury from Oct. 1959.* [1979]

GLANVILLE, James Edward. 22 Gray Terrace, Oxhill, Stanley, Co. Durham. B. 1891. A Miner. A Labour Member. Elected for the Consett division of Durham in Nov. 1943 and sat until he retired in 1955. Member of Executive of Durham Miners Association. Died 18 Sept. 1958. [1954]

GLOSSOP, Clifford William Hudson. Bramwith Hall, Doncaster. Carlton, and Junior Carlton. S. of Maj. William Glossop. B. 30 June 1901. Unmarried. Educ. at Harrow. An Agriculturist. Director of Public Utility Companies; Chairman of Water Companies Association. J.P. West Riding of Yorkshire. Member of Council of R.A.S.E. N.E. Area Meat and Livestock Officer Ministry of Food 1940-44. Member of Empire Parliament delegation to Uganda and Tanganyika 1934. President of British Friesian Cattle Society 1947. A Conservative. MP. for Penistone division of the W. Riding of Yorkshire from 1931-35 when he was defeated, and for the Howdenshire division of the E. Riding of Yorkshire from July 1945 until he resigned in Oct. 1947. Prospective candidate for Berwick-on-Tweed 1936-38. Emigrated to South Africa. Died 4 July 1975. [1947]

GLOVER, Sir Douglas, T.D. Flat 5, 37 Smith Square, London. White Barn, Wilmslow, Cheshire. Carlton, and Constitutional. S. of S.B. Glover, Esq. B. 1908; m. 1st, 22 Feb. 1934, Agnes May, d. of William Brown, Esq., J.P. (she died 1976); 2ndly, 1976, Margaret Eleanor Hurlimann. Educ. at Giggleswick. Commanded 2nd Battalion P.L. Kensington Regiment in N.W. Europe 1945, 9th Battalion Manchester Regiment T.A. 1947-50. Col. T.A. 1950. T.D. 1945. Knight Officer Orange Nassau 1946. Vice-Chairman of National Union of Conservative and Unionist Associations 1958. Chairman 1961-62. Chairman N.W. Area Conservative Provincial Council 1956-60; National Executive Conservative Party from 1951-69 and Treasurer N.W. Area 1951-54. Delegate to United Nations 17th Assembly 1962. Member of Public Accounts Committee 1965-70 and Mr. Speaker's Conference on Electoral Reform 1964-66. President of Lancastrian Association 1966. Knighted Jan. 1960. Chairman of the Anti-Slavery Society of Great Britain 1965-73. A Conservative. Unsuccessfully contested Blackburn in 1945 and Stalybridge and Hyde in 1950 and 1951. Elected for the Ormskirk division of Lancashire in Nov. 1953 and sat until he retired in 1970. Member of Speaker's Panel of Chairmen 1961-70. Member of Council of National Federation of Housing Associations 1966-72.* [1970]

GLYN, Dr. Alan Jack, E.R.D. 17 Cadogan Place, London. Carlton. S. of John P. Glyn, Esq., Barrister-at-Law, Royal Horse Guards. B. 26 Sept. 1918; m. 4 Jan. 1962, The Lady Rosula Caroline Windsor Clive, youngest d. of 2nd Earl of Plymouth, PC., G.C.St.J., (2 d.). Educ. at Westminster, Caius Coll., Cambridge, St. Bartholomews, and St. Georges. Served in the 1939-45 war; Brigade Maj. 1946; Capt. (Hon. Maj.) Royal Horse Guards (E.R.) until 1967. Qualified Medical Practitioner 1948; Barrister, Middle Temple 1955; Co-opted member L.C.C. Education Committee 1956-58. Member No. 1 L.C.C. Divisional Health Committee 1959-61; member Inner London Medical Committee from 1967; member Chelsea Borough 1959-62; member governing body British Post Graduate Medical Federation (London University); member of Greater London Central Valuation Panel. Author of *Witness to Vietnam*. A Conservative. Sat for the Clapham division of Wandsworth from 1959-64, when he was defeated, and for the Windsor division of Berkshire from 1970 to Feb. 1974. Member for Windsor and Maidenhead from Feb. 1974.* [1979]

GLYN, Col. Sir Ralph George Campbell, Bart., M.C. Flat 12, 120 Wigmore Street, London. Marndhill, Ardington, Wantage. Farnborough Down Farms, Wantage. Carlton, Beefsteak, and United Service. S. of Rt. Rev. the Hon. Edward Carr Glyn, D.D., Bishop of Peterborough, and Lady Mary Campbell, d. of George, 8th Duke of Argyll. B. 3 Mar. 1884; m. 25 Apr. 1921, Hon. Sibell Johnstone, d. of Francis, 2nd Lord Derwent, and widow of Brigadier-Gen. Walter Long, C.M.G., D.S.O. (she died 1958). Educ. at Harrow, and Royal Military Coll., Sand-

hurst. High Steward of Wallingford from 1933; Dept.-Lieut. for Berkshire, Vice-Lieut. 1957-60. Joined Rifle Brigade 1906; served in France, Gallipoli, Balkans and Russia 1914-18. Director of J. Samuel White and Company, Ship Builders, Cowes, of L.M.S. Railway and of British Match Corporation; Chairman of Skefco Ball Bearing Company; Honorary Secretary Unionist Reorganization Committee 1911; Parliamentary Private Secretary to Rt. Hon. R. MacDonald, Prime Minister Aug. 1931-June 1935, and when Lord President of the Council June 1935-May 1937; member of Whitley Council 1926-29. Created Bart. Jan. 1934. A Conservative. Unsuccessfully contested Moray and Nairn in Jan. 1910, South Edinburgh in Apr. 1910, and the College division of Glasgow in Dec. 1910, and Abingdon in 1923. Sat for E. Stirling and Clackmannan from 1918-22 when he was defeated, and for Abingdon division of Berkshire from 1924 until June 1953 when he was created Baron Glyn. Died 1 May 1960. [1953]

GLYN, Sir Richard Hamilton, Bart., O.B.E., T.D., D.L. Knapp House, Gillingham, Dorset. Carlton and Kennel. S. of Sir Richard Fitzgerald Glyn, Bart. B. 12 Oct. 1907; m. 1st, 2 Nov. 1939, Lyndsay Mary, d. of T.H. Baker, Esq., of Stoneygate, Leicester (divorced 1969); 2ndly, 4 Feb. 1970, Mrs. Barbara Henwood. Educ. at Down House, and Worcester Coll., Oxford. A Barrister-at-Law, Lincoln's Inn 1935. Commanded Queen's Own Dorset Yeomanry Field Regiment R.A., T.A. 1944-45 and 1953-56; Honorary Col. 1959. Dept. Commander 128th Infantry Brigade T.A. 1956. Member Chelsea Borough Council 1948-50 and Shaftesbury and Gillingham Rural District Council 1957. Parliamentary Private Secretary to Sir D. Eccles President of the Board of Trade June-Oct. 1958. Dept.-Chairman Dorset Quarter Sessions 1952-57. A Conservative. Unsuccessfully contested N. Dorset in 1945. Elected for N. Dorset in June 1957 and sat until he retired in 1970. T.D. 1941. O.B.E. 1955. Succeeded as Bart. 1960. Dept.-Lieut. for Dorset 1960. Member of Commonwealth War Graves Commission 1965-70. Chairman of Kennel Club from 1973. Chairman of Canine Consultative

Council from 1974. Chairman of Crufts Dog Show 1963-73, President from 1976.*

[1970]

GODBER, Rt. Hon. Joseph Bradshaw. The Manor, Willington, Bedfordshire. Carlton. S. of Isaac Godber, Esq. B. 17 Mar. 1914; m. 17 Apr. 1936, Miriam, d. of Hayden Arnold Sanders, Esq., (2 s.). Educ. at Bedford School. County Councillor for Bedfordshire from 1946-52; Assistant Government Whip 1955-57; Joint Parliamentary Secretary to Ministry of Agriculture 1957-60. Parliamentary Under-Secretary of State, Foreign Office 1960-61. Minister of State, Foreign Office 1961-63. Secretary of State for War June-Oct. 1963. Minister of Labour Oct. 1963-Oct. 1964. Minister of State for Foreign and Commonwealth Affairs 1970-72. Minister of Agriculture, Fisheries and Food 1972-74. Parliamentary Private Secretary to H.A. Watkinson, Parliamentary Secretary to Ministry of Labour 1952-55. Member of Cabinet Oct. 1963-Oct. 1964 and Nov. 1972-Mar. 1974. Opposition spokesman on Labour 1964-65 and on Agriculture 1965-70. Member of Shadow Cabinet 1964-70. PC. 1963. Chairman S.C. Banks Limited 1974; Director Booker McConnell Limited 1974; Chairman Tricentrol Limited 1976; Consultant Beecham Foods Limited 1974; Chairman Retail Consortium 1976; Director British Home Stores 1977. A Conservative. Sat for the Grantham division of Lincolnshire from Oct. 1951 until he retired in 1979. Created Baron Godber of Willington (Life Peerage) 1979. Died 25 Aug. 1980. [1979]

GOLDING, John. 8 Ashbourne Drive, Silverdale, Newcastle-under-Lyme, Staffordshire. S. of Peter John Golding, Esq. B. 3 Mar. 1931; m. 24 May 1958, Thelma, d. of Sidney Gwillym, Esq. Educ. at City Grammar School, Chester, University of Keele, and London School of Economics. Office boy 1947. Clerical Officer, Ministry of National Insurance 1948-51. Assistant Research Officer, Education Officer, Political and Parliamentary Officer of Post Office Engineering Union from 1960. Parliamentary Private Secretary to Mr. E. Varley, Minister of State, Technology Feb. June 1970. Member Select Committee on Nationalised Industries. Opposition Whip July 1970-Mar. 1974. Lord Commissioner of the Treasury Mar.-Oct. 1974. Parliamentary Under-Secretary of State for Employment Apr. 1976-May 1979. Member of National Executive Committee of Labour Party from 1978. An Opposition spokesman on Employment from 1979. Chairman of Select Committee on Employment from 1979. A Labour Member. Sat for Newcastle-under-Lyme from Oct. 1969.* [1979]

GOMME-DUNCAN, Col. Sir Alan Gomme, M.C. House of Dunbarney, Bridge of Earn, Perthshire. United Service, Pratt's, and New (Edinburgh). S. of Alfred Edward Duncan, Esq. B. 5 July 1893; m. 2 Apr. 1919, Mary, d. of W.W. Bourne, Esq., of Garston Manor, Hertfordshire. Educ. at Merchant Taylors' School. H.M. Inspector of Prisons for Scotland 1938-39. Served with the London Scottish and Black Watch in France, Belgium and Germany 1914-18, at home and in India until 1937, and 1939-45. A Conservative. Sat for the Perth division of Perth and Kinross from July 1945-Feb. 1950. Elected for Perth and East Perthshire in Feb. 1950 and sat until he retired in 1959. Assumed the surname of Gomme-Duncan in lieu of Duncan 1938. Knighted 1956. Member of Royal Company of Archers. Fellow of Society of Antiquaries (Scotland). Died 13 Dec. 1963.

[1959]

GOOCH, Edwin George, C.B.E. Rydal Mount, Wymondham, Norfolk. S. of Simon Gooch, Esq., Master Blacksmith, of Wymondham. B. 15 Jan. 1889; m. 1st, 26 Dec. 1914, Ethel, d. of C.D. Banham, Esq. (she died 1953); 2ndly, 7 Apr. 1960, Mollie, d. of William Curl, Esq. A Journalist. Alderman Norfolk County Council and Vice-Chairman of Norfolk County Council and Education Committee; Member of National Executive Committee of Labour Party 1935-36 and 1946-61, Chairman 1955-56; President of National Union of Agricultural Workers 1928-61; President of International Landworkers' Federation. Member of Council, Royal Agricultural Society. President Royal Norfolk Agricultural Society. President Royal Norfolk Agricultural Association. C.B.E. 1944. A Labour Member. Unsuccessfully contested the Southern division of Norfolk in 1931. Elected for the Northern division of Norfolk in July 1945 and sat until his death on 2 Aug. 1964. [1964]

GOODHART, Philip Carter. 27 Phillimore Gardens, London. Whitebarn, Boars Hill, Oxford. Athenaeum, Beefsteak, Carlton, and Garrick. S. of Professor Arthur Lehman Goodhart, K.B.E. (hon.), Q.C. B. 3 Nov. 1925; m. 1950, Valerie Forbes, d. of Clinton Winant, Esq., of New York, U.S.A., (3 s. 4 d.). Educ. at Hotchkiss School, U.S.A., and Trinity Coll., Cambridge. Served 1943-47 with K.R.R.C. and 1st Parachute Brigade. On Editorial Staff of *Daily Telegraph* 1950-55 and of *Sunday Times* 1955-57. Member London County Council Education Committee 1956-57. Parliamentary Private Secretary to Julian Amery at the War Office and Colonial Office 1958-60; member of British Delegation to Council of Europe and W.E.U. 1961-63; British Delegation to U.N. General Assembly 1963; N.A.T.O. Parliamentary Assembly 1964 (Chairman Arms Standardisation Sub-Committee 1966-69). An Opposition spokesman on Home Affairs 1965-66. Joint Honorary Secretary 1922 Committee 1960. Secretary Conservative Parliamentary Defence Committee 1967-72, Chairman 1972-74, Vice-Chairman 1974. Member F.C.O. Advisory Panel on Arms Control and Disarmament Questions 1973 and member of Conservative Advisory Committee on Policy from 1973. Chairman Conservative Parliamentary Northern Ireland Committee 1976. Under-Secretary of State for N. Ireland from May 1979. Member of the Council, Consumers' Association 1959-68 and 1970; Advisory Council on Public Records 1970; Executive Committee British Council 1974; Council R.U.S.I. 1973-76. Published *The Hunt for Kimathi* (with Ian Henderson, G.M.) 1958, *In the Shadow of the Sword* 1964, *Fifty Ships that Saved the World* 1965 (with Christopher Chataway), *War Without Weapons* 1968, *Referendum* 1970 (with Ursula Branston), *The 1922: the history of the 1922 Committee* 1973, and *Full-Hearted Consent* 1975, and various pamphlets. Chairman Lords and Commons Ski Club 1971-73. A Conservative. Unsuccessfully contested the Consett division of Co. Durham at the general election 1950.

Sat for Beckenham from Mar. 1957 to Feb. 1974 and for the Beckenham division of Bromley from Feb. 1974.* [1979]

GOODHEW, Victor Henry. 100 Eaton Place, London. S. of Rudolph Victor Goodhew, Esq. B. 1919; m. 1st, 1940, Sylvia Johnson (marriage dissolved), (1 s. 1 d.); 2ndly, 1951, Suzanne, d. of Wing-Commander Cyril Gordon-Burge, O.B.E. (marriage dissolved in 1972); 3rdly, 3 Aug. 1972, Eva, d. of Eduard Wilhelm Rittinghausen. Educ. at King's Coll. School. Served R.A.F. 1939-46, Squadron-Leader. Commanded Airborne Radar Unit Attached to 6th Airborne Division. Member of Westminster City Council 1953-59. Member of London County Council (Cities of London and Westminster) 1958-61. Parliamentary Private Secretary to C.I. Orr-Ewing, Civil Lord of the Admiralty May 1962-May 1963. Parliamentary Private Secretary to T.G.D. Galbraith, Parliamentary Secretary to the Ministry of Transport June 1963-Oct. 1964. Vice-Chairman Conservative Defence Committee 1965-70 and 1974. Assistant Whip June-Oct. 1970. A Lord Commissioner H.M. Treasury Oct. 1970-Oct. 1973. Member of Speaker's Panel of Chairmen from 1975. A Conservative. Unsuccessfully contested Paddington N. in 1955. Sat for the St. Albans division of Hertfordshire from Oct. 1959.* [1959]

GOODLAD, Alastair Robertson. 70 Drayton Gardens, London. Brooks'. S. of Dr. John F.R. Goodlad. B. 4 July 1943; m. 7 Dec. 1968, Cecilia, d. of Col. R. Hurst. Educ. at Marlborough Coll., and King's Coll., Cambridge. A Conservative. Unsuccessfully contested Crewe in 1970. Sat for Northwich from Feb. 1974. Director of Bowater Overseas Holdings Ltd.* [1979]

GOODRICH, Henry Edwin. 257 Evering Road, Hackney, London. S. of Edward Goodrich, Esq. B. 6 Apr. 1887; m. 1911, Julia Murphy. Educ. at Balham Grammar School. Served in Royal Navy and in Metropolitan Police. Solicitor's Clerk. Friendly Society Executive Councillor. Member of Hackney Borough Council from 1925, Mayor 1935-36. A Labour Member. Elected for N. Hackney in July 1945 and sat until he retired in 1950. Member of London County Council 1934-45. Gen. Secretary of Association of Police Strikers 1919. Died 13 Apr. 1961. [1950]

GORDON WALKER, Rt. Hon. Patrick Chrestien, C.H. 22 South Square, London. S. of Judge A.L. Gordon Walker. B. 7 Apr. 1907; m. 1934, Audrey, d. of Norman Rudolf, Esq., of Jamaica. Educ. at Wellington, and Christ Church, Oxford. Formerly a Tutor at Christ Church, Oxford. Member of Staff of B.B.C. European Service broadcasting to German workers 1940-45. Chairman of Governors of British Film Institute. A Vice-Chairman of British Council 1946; Honorary Treasurer 1946. Chairman of the Book Development Council 1965-67. Adviser to Initial Teaching Alphabet Foundation 1965. Parliamentary Private Secretary to the Rt. Hon. Herbert Morrison, Lord President of the Council Oct. 1946-Oct. 1947. Under-Secretary of State for Commonwealth Relations Oct. 1947-Feb. 1950. Secretary of State for Commonwealth Relations Feb. 1950-Oct. 1951. Opposition spokesman on Commonwealth Affairs to 1956; on Treasury Affairs 1956-59; on Home Affairs 1957-61; on Defence 1961-63 and on Foreign Affairs 1963-64. Secretary of State for Foreign Affairs Oct. 1964-Jan. 1965, when he resigned after his defeat in the Leyton by-election. Minister without Portfolio Jan.-Aug. 1967. Secretary of State for Education and Science Aug. 1967-Apr. 1968. Member of Parliamentary Committee of P.L.P 1957-64. PC. 1950. C.H. 1968. Voted in favour of entry to E.E.C. on 28 Oct. 1971. A Labour Member. Unsuccessfully contested Oxford City in 1935. Elected for Smethwick in Oct. 1945 and sat until 1964 when he was defeated. Unsuccessfully contested Leyton in Jan. 1965. Elected for Leyton in 1966 and sat until he retired in Feb. 1974. Created Baron Gordon-Walker (Life Peerage) 1974. Member of European Parliament 1975-76.* [1974]

GORST, John Michael. House of Commons, London. Garrick. S. of Derek Charles Gorst, Esq. B. 28 June 1928; m. 23 July 1954, Noel Harington, d. of Austine Walker, Esq. Educ. at Ardingly, and Corpus Christi, Cambridge. Advertising and Public Relations

Manager, Pye Limited 1953-63; Public Relations Consultant 1964. Secretary and Founder Telephone Users Association 1964-70; Secretary and Founder, Local Radio Association 1964-71. A Conservative. Unsuccessfully contested Chester-le-Street in 1964 and Bodmin in 1966. Sat for Hendon N. from June 1970 to Feb. 1974 and for the Hendon N. division of Barnet from Feb. 1974.* [1979]

GOUGH, (Charles) Frederick Howard, M.C., T.D. House of Commons, London. S. of Lieut.-Col. C.H.H. Gough, Indian Army. B. 1901; m. 1929, Barbara May Pegler. Educ. at Cheam School, and Royal Naval Colls., Osborne and Dartmouth. Member of Lloyds and Company Director. Served in Royal Navy in first World War and with Airborne Forces in the second World War. A Conservative. Unsuccessfully contested S. Lewisham in 1950. Elected for the Horsham division of W. Sussex in 1951 and sat until he retired in 1964. President of Royal Aero Club 1958-68. M.C. 1943, T.D. 1948. Honorary Colonel, Sussex Yeomanry 1959-63. Prime Warden of Fishmongers Company 1971-72. Died 19 Sept. 1977. [1964]

GOULD, Barbara Bodichon Ayrton. 74 Philbeach Gardens, London. D. of Prof. W.E. Ayrton, F.R.S. B. about 1888; m. Gerald Gould, Esq. (he died 1936). Educ. at Notting Hill High School and University Coll., London. Publicity Manager of *Daily Herald* 1919-21. Organizing Secretary of National Society for Lunacy Reform until 1923. Member of National Executive of Labour Party 1926-27 and 1929-50, Chairman 1939-40. Member of Royal Commission on the Civil Service 1929-31. Vice-chairman of British Council 1948. A Labour Member. Unsuccessfully contested Lambeth N. in 1922, Northwich in 1924, 1929 and 1931, the Norwood division of Lambeth in Mar. 1935 and the Hulme division of Manchester in Nov. 1935. Elected for Hendon N. in July 1945 and sat until she was defeated in Feb. 1950. Member of Arts Council 1950. J.P. for St. Marylebone. Died 14 Oct. 1950. [1950]

GOULD, Bryan Charles. 10 Furzedown Road, Southampton. S. of C.T. Gould, Esq.

B. 11 Feb. 1939; m. 27 Dec. 1967, Gillian Anne, d. of W. Harrigan, Esq. Educ. in New Zealand, and Balliol Coll., Oxford. H.M. Diplomatic Service 1964-68. H.M. Embassy, Brussels 1966-68. Fellow and Tutor in Law, Worcester Coll., Oxford 1968-74. Parliamentary Private Secretary to Rt. Hon. Peter Shore, Secretary of State for Trade 1975-76 and Secretary of State for the Environment 1976-77. A Labour Member. Unsuccessfully contested the Test division of Southampton in Feb. 1974. Sat for the Test division of Southampton from Oct. 1974 until 1979, when he was defeated. Television current affairs programme presenter from 1979.* [1979]

GOURLAY, Harry Philp Heggie. House of Commons, London. S. of William Gourlay, Esq. B. 1916; m. 1942, Margaret McFarlane Ingram. Educ. at Kirkcaldy High School. A Coachbuilder and vehicle examiner. Member of Kirkcaldy Town Council 1946-60, Treasurer 1953-57. J.P. from 1951. Vice-Chairman Fife Education Committee 1958; and Gov. Dundee Coll. of Education 1958. Member of Estimates Committee 1959-64; Chairman Scottish Parliamentary Labour Group 1975-77. Dept. Speaker and Dept. Chairman Ways and Means Oct. 1968-June 1970. Assistant Government Whip Nov. 1964-July 1966. A Lord Commissioner H.M. Treasury July 1966-Oct. 1968. Member of Speaker's Panel of Chairmen. Dept. Lieut. for Fife 1978. A Labour Member. Unsuccessfully contested S. Angus in 1955. Sat for Kirkcaldy from 1959.* [1979]

GOW, Ian Reginald Edward, T.D. The Dog House, Hankham, Nr. Pevensey, Sussex. 120 Pavilion Road, London. Cavalry, and M.C.C. S. of Dr. Alexander Gow, M.D., F.R.C.P. B. 11 Feb. 1937; m. 10 Sept. 1966, Jane, d. of Maj. Charles Packe, (2 s.). Educ. at Winchester. National Service, Commissioned 15th/19th Hussars. A Solicitor. T.D. 1970. Parliamentary Private Secretary to Rt. Hon. Margaret Thatcher, Prime Minister, from 1979. A Conservative. Unsuccessfully contested Coventry E. in 1964 and the Clapham division of Wandsworth in 1966. Sat for Eastbourne from Feb. 1974.* [1979]

GOWER, Sir (Herbert) Raymond. Sully, South Glamorgan. Carlton, and Royal Overseas League. S. of Lawford R. Gower, Esq., Glamorgan County Architect, of Penylan. B. Aug. 1916; m. 1973, Cynthia, d. of James Hobbs, Esq. Educ. at Cardiff High School, University Coll., Cardiff, and Cardiff School of Law. A Solicitor Apr. 1944. A Journalist and Broadcaster. Honorary Secretary Friends of Wales Society (Cultural only). Parliamentary Private Secretary to R. Maudling, J. Profumo, J.G. Braithwaite and H. Molson, Parliamentary Secretaries, Ministry of Transport Nov. 1951-Jan. 1957 and also Parliamentary Secretaries, Civil Aviation Apr. 1952-Jan. 1957; Parliamentary Private Secretary to H. Molson Minister of Works Jan. 1957-Jan. 1960. Member Court of Governors, National Library of Wales 1952. Member of Court of Governors, National Museum of Wales 1953. Vice-President Cardiff Business Club from Aug. 1952 and of National Chamber of Trade from Dec. 1956; member Court of Governors University Coll., Cardiff from 1954. Political Columnist *Western Mail* 1951-64. Member Court of Governors, University Coll., Aberystwyth. Director Broughton and Company (Bristol) Limited; Joint Founder and Director, Management of Welsh Dragon Unit Trust 1963. Member Welsh Advisory Civil Aviation Council June 1959-Feb. 1961. Chairman Welsh Conservative Members' Group 1960-61. Treasurer Welsh Parliamentary Party from 1967. President Glamorgan Society of London 1968-70. A member of Mr. Speaker's Conference on Electoral Law and Reform 1967-69 and 1971-73. Member Select Committee on Expenditure 1971; member Education and Arts Sub-Committee of Select Committee 1971. A Conservative. Unsuccessfully contested the Ogmore division of Glamorganshire in 1950. Elected for the Barry division of Glamorganshire in Oct. 1951. Knighted 1974.* [1979]

GRAHAM, Sir (Frederick) Fergus, Bart., K.B.E. Netherby Longtown, Cumberland. Guards'. S. of Sir Richard Graham, 4th Bart., of Netherby. B. 10 Mar. 1893; m. 1 Jan. 1918, Mary Spencer Revell, d. of Maj.-Gen. Raymond Reade, C.B., C.M.G. Educ. at Eton, and Christ Church, Oxford. Capt. Late Irish

Guards (S.R.); served with B.E.F. 1914. Honorary Col. 4th Battalion The Border Regiment. Created K.B.E. 1956. A Conservative. Sat for the Northern division of Cumberland from Sept. 1926 to 1935, when he was defeated. Elected for Darlington in 1951 and sat until he retired in 1959. Succeeded as Bart. in 1932. Member of Cumberland County Council 1925-74. Alderman 1934-74. Lord-Lieut. of Cumberland 1958-68. Died 1 Aug. 1978 [1959]

GRAHAM, (Thomas) Edward. House of Commons, London. B. Mar. 1925; m. Margaret. Educ. at Co-operative Coll., W.E.A., and Open University. Labour Leader on Enfield Council, Chairman Housing and Redevelopment Committee 1961-68. Education Secretary, Enfield Highway Co-operative Society 1953-62. Secretary of Co-operative Union Southern Section 1962-67. National Secretary of Co-operative Party 1967-74. Parliamentary Private Secretary to A.J. Williams, Minister of State, Dept. of Prices and Consumer Protection 1974-76. Opposition Whip from 1979. Lord Commissioner to the Treasury Apr. 1976-May 1979. A Labour Member. Unsuccessfully contested Enfield W. in 1966. Sat for Enfield, Edmonton from Feb. 1974.*[1979]

GRAHAM-LITTLE, Sir Ernest Gorden Graham. 19 Upper Wimpole Street, London. Wimpole Lodge, Manor Green Road, Epsom. Athenaeum. S. of Michael Little, Esq., I.C.S. B. 1867; m. 1911, Sarah Helen, d. of Maurice Kendall, Esq. Educ. at South African Coll., at Cape University, B.A., Gold Medallist and Porter Scholar, at Guy's and St. George's Hospitals, and at the Universities of London and Paris. M.D., F.R.C.P. London, M.R.C.S. England. Member of Court 1909-47, and of Senate of University of London from 1906. Consulting Physician, Skin Department, St. Mary's Hospital 1902-34 and 1940-41, and E. London Hospital for Children. Consulting Dermatologist to Military Hospitals in London 1914-19; President Dermatological Sections of Royal Society of Medicine and British Medical Association; Honorary member of American Dermatological Association; member of Council London School of Hygiene and Tropical Medi-

cine, Royal Medical Coll.; Knight Bach. 1931. An Independent National Member. Elected for London University in Oct. 1924 and sat until he retired in Feb. 1950. Assumed the surname Graham-Little in lieu of Little in 1931. Died 6 Oct. 1950. [1950]

GRANT, George. 30 Sheepwash Bank, Choppington, Northumberland. S. of Joseph Henry Grant, Esq., Miner. B. 11 Oct. 1924; m. 6 Nov. 1948, Adeline, d. of Jacob Conroy, Esq., (1 s. 4 d.). Educ. at Bedlingtonshire North Schools. Member Bedlingtonshire Urban District Council 1959-70; Chairman and J.P. 1964-66; Chairman Ashington Branch N.U.M. 1959-66 and Compensation Secretary 1959-66; Conciliation Officer N.U.M. North area 1962-70. Parliamentary Private Secretary to the Rt. Hon. F. Peart, MP., Minister of Agriculture 1974-76. A Labour Member. Sat for the Morpeth division of Northumberland from June 1970.*
[1979]

GRANT, (John) Anthony. House of Commons, London. S. of Arthur Ernest Grant, Esq. B. 1925; m. 1953, Sonia Isobel, d. of G.H. Landen, Esq. Educ. at St. Paul's School, and Brasenose Coll., Oxford. Served in the 3rd Dragoon Guards during World War II (Capt.). Solicitor and Company Director. A Liverman of the Worshipful Company of Solicitors and a Senior Warden of the Guild of Freemen of the City of London. Opposition Whip Apr. 1966-June 1970; Parliamentary Secretary to the Board of Trade June-Oct. 1970. Parliamentary Under-Secretary of State for Industry Oct. 1970-Apr. 1972 and for Industrial Development Apr. 1972-Mar. 1974. Vice-Chairman Conservative Party Apr. 1974-76. Member of Council of Europe and Western European Union from 1977. A Conservative. Unsuccessfully contested Hayes and Harlington in 1959. Sat for the Central division of Harrow from Oct. 1964.* [1979]

GRANT, John Douglas. 16 Magpie Hall Lane, Bromley, Kent. S. of M. de Burgh Grant. B. 16 Oct. 1932; m. 28 Mar. 1955, Patricia Julia Ann Rush. Educ. at Stationers' Company's School, London. A Journalist on Provincial Newspapers and from 1955 on

Daily Express. Dept. Industrial Correspondent 1960-67; Chief Industrial Correspondent 1967-70. Chairman Labour and Industrial Correspondents' Group 1967. Labour Party Chairman, Bromley, Kent 1966-70. Opposition spokesman on Policy for Broadcasting and the Press 1973-74. Opposition spokesman on Employment 1974. Parliamentary Secretary Civil Service Department Mar.-Oct. 1974. Parliamentary Secretary of Ministry of Overseas Development Oct. 1974-Apr. 1976. Parliamentary Under-Secretary of State for Employment Apr. 1976-May 1979. Published *Member of Parliament* 1974. An Opposition spokesman on Employment from 1979. A Labour Member. Unsuccessfully contested the Beckenham division of Kent in 1966. Sat for Islington E. division from 1970 to Feb. 1974 and for the Central division of Islington from Feb. 1974.*

[1979]

GRANT OF MONYMUSK, Priscilla Jean Fortescue, Lady. See TWEEDSMUIR, Priscilla Jean Fortescue, The Lady.

GRANT, Rt. Hon. William, T.D., Q.C. 30 Moray Place, Edinburgh. Union, and New. S. of Edward Grant, Esq. B. 19 June 1909; m. 4 Apr. 1936, Margaret Katharine, d. of J.W. Milne, Esq., C.A. Educ. at Fettes, Oriel Coll., Oxford, and Edinburgh University. Advocate 1934. Served R.A. (T.A.) 1939-45, Maj. K.C. (Scotland) 1951; Solicitor-Gen. for Scotland Jan. 1955-Apr. 1960. Lord Advocate Apr. 1960-Aug. 1962. PC. 1958. A Unionist Member. Unsuccessfully contested E. Edinburgh in 1951 and Apr. 1954. Elected for the Woodside division of Glasgow in 1955 and sat until Aug. 1962 when he was appointed Lord Justice Clerk. Chairman of National Health Service (Scotland) Tribunal 1949-54. Lord Justice Clerk, with the judicial title of Lord Grant 1962-72. Chairman of Committee on the Sheriff Court 1963-67. Died 19 Nov. 1972 in a road accident.

[1962]

GRANT-FERRIS, Wing Commander Rt. Hon. Sir Robert Grant. 16 Stafford Place, London. 8 Dysart Buildings, Nantwich, Cheshire. S. of Dr. Robert Francis Ferris. B.

30 Dec. 1907; m. 30 July 1930, Florence, d. of William Brennan De Vine, M.C. Educ. at Douai School, Woolhampton, Berkshire. Barrister-at-Law, Inner Temple 1937; member Birmingham City Council 1933-36; Fighter Pilot R.A.F., Europe, Malta, Egypt, and India (Wing Commander) 1939-45; Air Efficiency Award 1942. Parliamentary Private Secretary to Rt. Hon. W.S. Morrison, Minister of Town and Country Planning 1944-45; Vice-Chairman London Conservative Union 1943-45; Knight of Malta 1949; Grand Cross 1959. Commander of the Order of Leopold (Belgium). President National Sheep Breeders of Great Britain 1956-58, also 1965-69. President Royal Smithfield Club 1969. Chairman Board of Management Hospital of St. John and Elizabeth, St. John's Wood, London 1963-70, now amalgamated and known as The Hospital of St. John and St. Andrew. Member panel of Chairmen of Standing Committees and a temporary Chairman of Commons from 1962. Knighted 1969. Elected Dept. Speaker and Chairman of Ways and Means by House of Commons after general election June 1970 and held this office until Feb. 1974. PC. 1971. A Conservative. Unsuccessfully contested Wigan in 1935. Sat for St. Pancras N. from Feb. 1937-July 1945. Unsuccessfully contested St. Pancras N. in 1945, and Wandsworth Central in 1950 and 1951. Elected for the Nantwich division of Cheshire in 1955 and sat until he retired in Feb. 1974. Assumed the surname of Grant-Ferris in lieu of Ferris. Created Baron Harvington (Life Peerage) 1974.*

[1974]

GRANVILLE, Edgar Louis. 31 Ashley Court, Morpeth Terrace, London. S. of Reginald Granville, Esq. B. 1898; m. 1st, Lulu, d. of P.T. Berry, Esq.; 2ndly, 11 Sept. 1943, Elizabeth, d. of the Rev. Hunter. Educ. at High Wycombe, London, and Australia. Served with A.I.F. in Gallipoli, Egypt and France 1914-18 and with R.A. 1939-40, Capt. Honorary Secretary Liberal Agricultural Group, House of Commons 1929-31; Honorary Secretary Foreign Affairs Group; Vice-President National League of Young Liberals 1949-50, and Chairman of Y.L. Manifesto Group. Parliamentary Private Secretary to the Rt. Hon. Sir Herbert

Samuel, Secretary of State Home Office Aug.-Oct. 1931, and to Sir John Simon, Secretary of State for Foreign Affairs Nov. 1931-May 1935, and when Home Secretary Nov. 1935-Nov. 1936. Elected as a Liberal for the Eye division of Suffolk in May 1929, joined the Liberal National group in 1931, but resigned the whip in Feb. 1942 and sat as an Independent until Apr. 1945 when he rejoined the Liberal Party. Joined the Labour Party in 1951 and unsuccessfully contested the Eye division of Suffolk as the Labour candidate in 1955 and 1959. Created Baron Granville of Eye (Life Peerage) 1967.*

[1951]

GRAY, Hugh, Ph.D. 22 Bridstow Place, London. S. of William Marshall Kemp Gray, Esq., Dental Surgeon. B. 19 Apr. 1916; m. 31 Oct. 1954, Edith, d. of Paul Rudinger, Esq. Educ. at Battersea Grammar School, and London School of Economics. Served in Army Intelligence Corps 1940-45. With U.N.R.R.A. International Refugees Association (Regional Welfare Officer) 1945-52. A Social Worker 1952-57. Student at London School of Economics 1957-60; University Teacher 1960-66 and from 1970. A Labour Member. Unsuccessfully contested Aylesbury in 1959 and Cheltenham in 1964. Elected for the Yarmouth division of Norfolk in Mar. 1966 and sat until 1970 when he was defeated. Unsuccessfully contested Cheltenham in Feb. 1974 and S. Norfolk in Oct. 1974. Unsuccessfully contested Norfolk for European Parliament in 1979. Lecturer in Sociology and Politics of South Asia.*

[1970]

GRAY, James Hector Northey (Hamish). The Cedars, Drummond Road, Inverness. S. of James Northey Gray, Esq. B. 28 June 1927; m. 11 Sept. 1953, Judith W. Brydon, B.Sc. Educ. at Inverness Royal Academy. Served Queens Own Cameron Highlanders 1945-48. Served Highland Chamber of Commerce 1963-70. Inverness Town Council 1965-70. Company Director. Assistant Government Whip 1971-73. Lord Commissioner to the Treasury 1973-74. Opposition Whip 1974-75; Front Bench spokesman on Energy Feb. 1975-May 1979. Minister of State, Department of Energy

from May 1979. Successfully piloted Education Scotland (Mentally Handicapped) Bill through Parliament. A Conservative. Sat for Ross and Cromarty from 1970.* [1979]

GREEN, Alan. The Stables, Sabden, Blackburn. 125 Whitehall Court, London. Carlton, Pratt's, and R.A.C. S. of Edward Green, Esq., Manufacturer. B. 29 Sept. 1911; m. 8 Jan. 1935, Hilda Mary, d. of John Wolstenholme, Esq., J.P. Educ. at Brighton Coll. Served in The Army 1940-45. A Schoolmaster 1931-35. Joined Scapa Dryers Limited, Blackburn 1935, Director 1945, Vice-Chairman 1956. Chairman of Walmsley Operating Companies 1954, of Walmsley (Bury) Group from 1970, and of Beloit Walmsley Limited. Parliamentary Secretary Ministry of Labour June 1961-July 1962; Minister of State, Board of Trade July 1962-Oct. 1963; Financial Secretary Treasury Oct. 1963-Oct. 1964. A Conservative. Unsuccessfully contested Nelson and Colne in 1950 and 1951. Elected for Preston S. in 1955 and sat until 1964 when he was defeated. Unsuccessfully contested Preston S. in 1966 and was re-elected there in 1970. Sat until he was defeated in Feb. 1974. Unsuccessfully contested Preston S. again in Oct. 1974. C.B.E. 1974* [1974]

GREENWOOD, Rt. Hon. Arthur, C.H. 8 Gainsborough Gardens, Hampstead, London. S. of William Greenwood Esq. of Leeds. B. 1880. m. 1904 Catherine Ainsworth Brown. Educ. at Leeds Higher Grade School and Leeds University. Lecturer in Economics in the University of Leeds. Honorary LL.D. Honorary Freeman of City of Leeds 1931. Secretary of Research and Information Department of the Labour Party 1920-22. Assistant Secretary to Ministry of Reconstruction and Joint Secretary of the Whitley Committee 1917-19. Parliamentary Ministry of Health Jan.-Nov. 1924; Minister of Health June 1929-Aug. 1931. PC. 1929. Vice-Chairman P.L.P. Dec. 1935, Dept.-Leader 1935-45. Minister without Portfolio and Member of the War Cabinet May 1940-Feb. 1942. Acting Leader of P.L.P. 1942-45. Treasurer 1943-54. Created C.H. 1945. Lord Privy Seal July 1945-Apr. 1947 and Paymaster-Gen. July 1946-Mar. 1947. Minister without Portfolio Apr.-Sept. 1947. A Labour Member. Unsuccessfully contested Southport in 1918. Sat for Nelson and Colne from Nov. 1922 to Oct. 1931 when he was defeated. Elected for Wakefield in Apr. 1932 and sat until his death on 9 June 1954. Chairman of National Executive Committee of Labour Party 1952-53. Member of Executive Committee of P.L.P. Sept.-Oct. 1931. Died 9 June 1954. [1954]

GREENWOOD, Rt. Hon. Arthur William James ('Anthony'). 38 Downshire Hill, London. Savile. S. of the Rt. Hon. Arthur Greenwood, C.H., MP. B. 14 Sept. 1911; m. 1 June 1940, Gillian, d. of Leslie C. Williams, Esq. Educ. at Merchant Taylor's School, and Balliol Coll., Oxford. President of Oxford Union 1933. Served in Ministry of Information 1939-42 and with R.A.F. 1942-46; member of Allied Reparations Commission, Moscow 1945, and of Allied Reparations Conference, Paris 1945; Vice-President Central Council for the Care of Cripples; Vice-President R.S.P.C.A.; Vice-President British Rheumatic Association; J.P. for London. Vice-Chairman P.L.P. 1950-51; member of Parliamentary Committee of Labour Party Nov. 1951-Nov. 1952 and 1955-60, when he resigned; National Executive Committee of Labour Party from 1954-70. Chairman 1963-64. Parliamentary Private Secretary to Rt. Hon. Wilfred Paling, Postmaster-Gen. 1949-50. Opposition spokesman on Works 1955-59, on Home Affairs 1956-59, and on Education 1959-60. Unsuccessful candidate for the Leadership of the Labour Party in 1961. Member of the Cabinet Oct. 1964-Oct. 1969. Secretary of State for the Colonies Oct. 1964-Dec. 1965. Minister of Overseas Development Dec. 1965-Aug. 1966. Minister of Housing and Local Government Aug. 1966-May 1970. PC. 1964. President Socialist Educational Association. A Labour Member. Sat for Heywood and Radcliffe from Feb. 1946-Feb. 1950. Elected for Rossendale in Feb. 1950 and sat until he retired in 1970. Chairman of Britannia Building Society 1974-76. Dept.-Lieut. for Essex 1974. Pro-Chancellor of Lancaster University from 1972. President of Socialist Educational Association 1963-72. Member of Hampstead Borough Council

1945-49. Member of Commonwealth Development Corporation 1970-78, Chairman-Designate May-July 1970. Member of Central Lancashire New Town Development Corporation 1971-76. Created Baron Greenwood of Rossendale (Life Peerage) 1970. Chairman of U.K. Housing Association from 1972. Chairman of Local Government Staff Commission 1972-76, of Local Government Training Board from 1975. Principal Dept. Chairman of Committees and Chairman of Select Committee on Europe, House of Lords 1977-80.* [1970]

GREGORY, Arnold. 6 Avalon Road, Orpington, Kent. 2nd s. of Samuel Gregory, Esq., of Salford, Lancashire. B. 14 Nov. 1924; m. 1945, Betty, d. of Albert E. Spooner, Esq., of Urmston, (1 d.). Educ. at Municipal Schools, Manchester Coll. of Technology, and extramural, University of Manchester. Contracts Manager (Textiles). Joined the Labour Party in 1944. Apprentice member of the A.E.U. 1941, Guild of Insurance Officials 1946. Clerical and Administrative Workers' Union 1950. Member of Co-operative Party (Manchester and Salford) from 1951. A Labour Member. Unsuccessfully contested Stafford and Stone in 1959. Elected for Stockport N. in Oct. 1964 and sat until 1970 when he was defeated. Lecturer and Tutor, National Council of Labour Colls. 1956-64. Died 30 July 1976. [1970]

GRENFELL, Rt. Hon. David Rhys, C.B.E. Ardwyn, Carnglas Road, Sketty, Swansea. S. of William and Ann Grenfell, of Penrheol. B. 27 June 1881; m. 1905, Beatrice Morgan. Educ. at Penrheol Elementary School, and Technical Classes. A Miner 1893-1916; Certified Mine Manager, Nova Scotia (2nd Class 1904), U.K. (1st Class) 1907; Miners' Agent 1916; taught Mining, Geology and Mathematics; J.P. 1922. Parliamentary Private Secretary to Maj. C.R. Attlee, Under-Secretary for War Jan.-Oct. 1924, to Morgan Jones, Parliamentary Secretary to Board of Education June 1929-Aug. 1931; Secretary for Mines May 1940-June 1942; Chairman of Welsh Tourist Holiday Board 1948-51. Forestry Commissioner 1929-42; Welsh Land Settlement Committee 1936-55; Royal Commission on Safety in Mines

141

1936-39. Member Anglo-Czech Relief Committee 1939-58. Visited New Zealand and Australia 1940 and Canada, U.S.A., New Zealand and Australia 1950-51 on behalf of Parliament. PC. 1951. Father of the House of Commons 1952-59. LL.D. University of Wales 1958. A Labour Member. Elected for the Gower division of Glamorgan in July 1922 and sat until he retired in 1959. C.B.E. 1935. Chevalier de la Légion d'Honneur 1953. Member of Executive Committee of P.L.P. 1931-40. Died 21 Nov. 1968. [1959]

GREY, Charles Frederick, C.B.E. 1A Moor House Gardens, Four Lane Ends, Hetton-le-Hole, Durham. S. of Thomas Grey, Esq. B. 1903; m. 1925, Margaret, d. of James Aspey, Esq. Educ. at Elementary School. A Miner. Member of Divisional Labour Executive. Northern Area Whip 1962-1969. Comptroller of H.M. Household Oct. 1964-July 1966. Treasurer H.M. Household July 1966-Oct. 1969. Independent Methodist Minister. C.B.E. 1966. A Labour Member. Elected for the Durham division of Co. Durham in July 1945 and sat until he retired in 1970. President of Independent Methodist Connexion 1971. Honorary D.C.L. Durham University 1976.* [1970]

GRIDLEY, Sir Arnold Babb, K.B.E. Culwood, Lye Green, Chesham, Buckinghamshire. Carlton, St. Stephen's, and Devonshire. S. of Edward Gridley, Esq., of Abbey Dore, Herefordshire. B. 1878; m. 10 Aug. 1905, Mabel, d. of Oliver Hudson, Esq., of Fakenham, Norfolk (she died 1955). Educ. at Bristol Grammar School, and University Coll., Bristol. A Consulting Engineer. M.I.E.E. Director of Electric Manufacturing and other Industrial Companies; Controller of Electric Power Supply 1916-18. Chairman of Conservative Members '1922' Committee 1945-51. President of Association of British Chambers of Commerce 1946-48. For six years on Evershed Committee examining High Court Practice and Procedure. Created K.B.E. 1920. A Conservative. Sat for Stockport from 1935-50. Elected for Stockport S. in Feb. 1950 and sat until Jan. 1955 when he was created Baron Gridley. Member of Pig Marketing Board. Died 27 July 1965. [1954]

GRIERSON, Edgar. 268 Warwick Road, Carlisle. S. of William Grierson, Esq. of Scotby, Carlisle. B. 6 Nov. 1882; m. 1906, Jane, d. of Thomas Ridley, Esq (she died) Educ. at Scotby Elementary School. Served in France with Border Regiment 1914-18. A Local Co-operator. Member of Carlisle City Council 1929-50. Mayor of Carlisle 1941-42, Dept. Mayor 1942-44; Alderman; J.P. A Labour Member. Elected for Carlisle in July 1945 and sat until he retired in 1950. Died 1 Mar. 1959. [1950]

GRIEVE, William Percival, Q.C. 32 Gunterstone Road, London. Royal Automobile, and Hurlingham. S. of 2nd Lieut. W.P. Grieve (killed in action 1915). B. 1915; m. 1949, Evelyn, d. of Commandant Hubert Mijouain of Paris, (1 s. 1 d., 1 s. deceased). Educ. privately, and at Trinity Hall, Cambridge. Served as Liaison Officer, British Embassy, Paris 1939-40; Ministry of Information 1940-41; attached to H.Q. Fighting France 1941-43; Executive Officer, S.H.A.E.F. Mission, Luxembourg 1944. Demobilised as Honorary Maj. Officer with Crown, Order of Adolphe of Nassau, Chevalier Order of Couronne de Chene, Croix de Guerre with palms (Luxembourg) and Bronze Star (U.S.A.); Chevalier de la Legion d'Honneur (France) 1974. Commandeur de l'order de Merite (Luxembourg) 1976. Called to the bar by the Middle Temple 1938, bencher 1969, took silk 1962. Recorder 1972 (Recorder of Northampton 1965-72). Assistant Recorder of Leicester 1956-65. Dept. Chairman Lincolnshire (Holland) Quarter Sessions 1962-71. Chairman Franco-British Parliamentary Relations Committee 1970. Honorary Vice-President Franco-British Parliamentary Relations Committee. Vice-Chairman Anglo-Benelux Group. Delegate to Council of Europe and Western European Union 1969. Chairman of Rules of Procedure Committee Council of Europe and of Rules of Procedure Committee of Western European Union. A Conservative. Adopted for Lincoln in Nov. 1961 but was unsuccessful in the by-election in Mar. 1962. Sat for the Solihull division of Warwickshire from Oct. 1964.* [1979]

GRIFFITHS, David. 6 Lincoln Gardens, Goldthorpe, Rotherham. B. 1896. Educ. at

Goldthorpe Elementary School. Started work at Hickleton Main Colliery at the age of 13. Served 1915-19. Member Bolton-on-Dearne Urban District Council 1924-37, Chairman 1935-36, Member Dearne Urban District Council 1937-46, Chairman 1941-42. Member Swinton and District Hospital Board for 20 years. Local Official Hickleton Main Branch N.U.M. for 20 years. Board of Guardians 1929-45; Vice-President of Urban District Councils Association for 18 years. Commonwealth War Graves Commissioner from 1962-70. Honours Medal for Public Work 1936. A Labour Member. Elected for the Rother Valley division of the W. Riding of Yorkshire in July 1945 and sat until he retired in 1970. Died 13 Jan. 1977.
[1970]

GRIFFITHS, Edward. Treuddyn House, 14, Mill View Road, Shotton, Deeside, Flintshire. S. of Robert Griffiths, Esq., J.P., of Treuddyn, near Mold, Flintshire. B. 7 Mar. 1929; m. 1954, Ella, d. of W.G. Griffiths, Esq., of Shotton. Educ. at Mold Grammar School, and University Coll. of North Wales, Bangor. An Industrial Chemist. Director of British Steel Corporation Mar.-June 1968. A Labour Member. Unsuccessfully contested the Denbigh division of Denbighshire in 1966. Elected for the Brightside division of Sheffield in June 1968 and sat until Oct. 1974 when, after failing to secure re-adoption by the Constituency Labour Party, he unsuccessfully contested the seat as an Independent Labour candidate. Member of Flintshire County Council 1964-67.*
[1974 2nd ed.]

GRIFFITHS, Eldon Wylie. Linton Cottage, Ixworth Thorpe, Bury St. Edmunds, Suffolk. 44 Carlisle Mansions, Carlisle Place, London. Carlton. S. of Thomas H.W. Griffiths, Esq. B. 25 May 1925; m. 1949, Sigrid Grante, (1 s. 1 d.). Educ. at Ashton Grammar School, Emmanuel Coll., Cambridge, and Yale University, M.A. (Cantab), M.A. (Yale). A Correspondent *Time* and *Life* magazines 1949-55; Editor *Newsweek* magazine 1956-63; Columnist *Washington Post* 1962-63. Conservative Research Department 1963-64. Consultant to Police Federation 1964-70.

Parliamentary Secretary Ministry of Housing and Local Government June 1970-Oct. 1970. Parliamentary Under-Secretary of State to Department of Environment Oct. 1970-Mar. 1974. 'Minister for Sport' 1970-74. Conservative spokesman on Industry 1974-75, on Foreign Affairs and Europe 1975-76. Chairman of Anglo-Iranian Parliamentary Group. Travelled extensively in America, Africa and Asia. A Conservative. Sat for the Bury St. Edmunds division of Suffolk from May 1964.*
[1979]

GRIFFITHS, George Arthur. 14 Park View, Royston, Nr. Barnsley. S. of William Griffiths, Esq., of Buckley, N. Wales. B. 7 May 1878; m. Sept. 1902, June, d. of John Cadman, Esq., of Beverley, Shropshire. Educ. at Buckley National School. A miner from the age of 12. Member of Royston U.D.C. from 1910 to 1941. Parliamentary Private Secretary to Wilfred Paling, Parliamentary Secretary Ministry of Pensions April 1941 and when Minister of Pensions Aug. 1945. A Labour Member. Sat for the Hemsworth division of Yorkshire from 1934 until his death on 15 Dec. 1945. Member of W. Riding County Council 1925-45. J.P. for W. Riding. Member of Salvation Army. Died 15 Dec. 1945.
[1946]

GRIFFITHS, Rt. Hon. James, C.H. House of Commons, London. S. of William Griffiths, Esq., of Betws. B. 1890; m. 1918, Winifred, d. of William Rutley, Esq., of Overton, Hampshire. Educ. at Elementary School, and Central Labour Coll., London. A Miners' Agent 1925-36; J.P. for Breconshire; President S. Wales Miners' Federation 1934-36; member of National Executive Labour Party 1939-40 and 1941-59. Secretary of Welsh Parliamentary Party 1942; Minister of National Insurance Aug. 1945-Feb. 1950; Secretary of State for the Colonies Feb. 1950-Oct. 1951. Chairman of Labour Party 1948. Dept. Leader of the Opposition 1956-59. Secretary of State for Wales Oct. 1964-Apr. 1966. C.H. 1966. A Labour Member. Elected for the Llanelli division of Carmarthenshire in Mar. 1936 and sat until he retired in 1970. PC. 1945. Member of B.B.C. Advisory Council 1952. Member of P.L.P. Parliamentary Committee 1951-59, Opposition spokesman

on Welsh Affairs 1959-64. Died 7 Aug. 1975.
[1970]

GRIFFITHS, Peter Harry Steve. 49 Pitcairn Road, Smethwick, Staffordshire. S. of W.L. Griffiths, Esq. of West Bromwich. B. 1928; m. 1962, Jeannette Christine Rubery. Educ. at West Bromwich Grammar School, the City of Leeds Training Coll., University of London, B.Sc. Econ., and University of Birmingham, M.Ed. A Teacher. Headmaster of Hall Green Road Junior School, West Bromwich 1962-64. Elected to Smethwick County Borough Council 1955. Chairman of the Smethwick Education Committee 1964; Alderman 1964. A Conservative. Adopted for Smethwick in Apr. 1957 but was unsuccessful in the general election of 1959. Elected for Smethwick in Oct. 1964 and sat until 1966 when he was defeated. Unsuccessfully contested Portsmouth N. in Feb. 1974. Elected for Portsmouth N. in May 1979. Senior Lecturer in Economics, Portsmouth Coll. of Technology, later Portsmouth Polytechnic 1967-79. Fulbright Exchange Professor of Economics, Pierce Coll., Los Angeles 1968-69. Author of *A Question of Colour.** [1966]

GRIFFITHS, William. 24 Onslow Avenue, Richmond, Surrey. 11 Crossgate Avenue, Manchester. S. of William Griffiths, Esq., of Manchester. B. 7 Apr. 1912; m. 1949, Decia, eld. d. of Noel Robinson, Esq., of Blackpool, Lancashire, (1 s. 1 d.). Educ. at Elementary Schools. An Ophthalmic Optician. Fellow of British Optical Association. Served in the Army 1940-45. Eighth Army, Alamein; Commissioned Middle East 1944. Parliamentary Private Secretary to Rt. Hon. Aneurin Bevan, Minister of Health 1950-51, and Minister of Labour Jan.-Apr. 1951. Chairman of Anglo-Iraqi Parliamentary Group. A Labour Member. Sat for the Moss Side division of Manchester from July 1945-Feb. 1950. Elected for the Exchange division of Manchester in Feb. 1950 and sat until his death on 14 Apr. 1973. [1973]

GRIMOND, Rt. Hon. Joseph. House of Commons, London. S. of Joseph Grimond, Esq., of St. Andrews, Fife. B. 29 July 1913; m. 1938, Hon. Laura, d. of Sir Maurice Bonham-Carter and Lady Asquith of Yarn-

bury, (2 s. 1 d.). Educ. at Eton, and Balliol Coll., Oxford. A Barrister-at-Law, Middle Temple 1937. Director of Personnel, European division U.N.R.R.A. 1945-47. Secretary of National Trust for Scotland 1947-49. Chief Liberal Whip 1950-56. Served with Fife and Forfar Yeomanry 1939-45, T.D. Leader Parliamentary Liberal Party 1956-67. Liberal spokesman on Energy, 1974 resigned Oct. 1977. Acting Leader Parliamentary Liberal Party May-July 1976. PC. Oct. 1961. Rector, Edinburgh University 1960-63, University of Aberdeen 1970-73. Chancellor, University of Kent from 1970. Honorary LL.D. Edinburgh, Aberdeen and Birmingham, Honorary D.C.L. Kent. Liberal spokesman on Scotland to 1975, Defence 1975-76 and on Foreign Affairs from 1979. A Liberal. Unsuccessfully contested Orkney and Shetland in 1945. Sat for Orkney and Shetland from Feb. 1950. Director of The Manchester Guardian and Evening News Ltd. from 1967.* [1979]

GRIMSTON, Hon. John. Gorhambury, St. Albans. S. of the 4th Earl of Verulam. B. 17 July 1912; m. 2 June 1938, Marjorie Ray, d. of Walter Duncan, Esq. Educ. at Oundle and Christ Church, Oxford. Flight-Lieut. A.A.F. Reserve. A Conservative. Sat for the St. Albans division of Hertfordshire from Oct. 1943-July 1945, when he was defeated, re-elected in Feb. 1950 and sat until he retired in 1959. Gen. Manager of Enfield Rolling Mills 1938-53, Managing Director 1953. Chairman of Delta Metal Company Limited 1968-72. Succeeded his brother as 6th Earl of Verulam in 1960. President of London Chamber of Commerce 1963-66. Dept.-Lieut. for Hertfordshire 1963. Died 15 Apr. 1973. [1959]

GRIMSTON, Sir Robert Villiers, Bart. 3 Lowndes Court, Lowndes Square, London. Carlton, and M.C.C. S. of the Rev. and Hon. Robert Grimston, Canon of St. Albans. B. 8 June 1897; m. 24 Oct. 1923, Sybil, d. of Sir Sigmund Neumann, Bart. (she died 1977). Educ. at Repton, City and Guilds Engineering Coll., and London University, B.Sc., A.C.G.I. Served in Salonica and Palestine as Lieut. R.G.A. 1916-19. Parliamentary Private Secretary to Rt. Hon. Douglas Hacking, when Parliamentary Under-Secretary of State, Home Office Mar. 1933-June 1934, when Financial Secretary to War Office June 1934-Nov. 1935 and when Under-Secretary for Dominions Nov. 1935-Mar. 1936; to H. Ramsbotham, Minister of Pensions July 1936; Assistant Whip May 1937; a Lord Commissioner of the Treasury Oct. 1937-May 1938; Vice-Chamberlain of H.M. Household May 1938-Nov. 1939; Treasurer Nov. 1939-Mar. 1942; Assistant Postmaster-Gen. Mar. 1942-May 1945. Parliamentary Secretary Ministry of Supply May-July 1945. President Urban District Councils Association from 1949-70. Created 1st Bart. 1952. Dept. Chairman of Ways and Means Jan. 1962-Sept. 1964. A National Conservative Member. Elected for the Westbury division of Wiltshire in 1931 and sat until he retired in 1964. Created Baron Grimston of Westbury 1964. Died 8 Dec. 1979.   [1964]

GRIST, Ian. 18 Tydfil Place, Roath, Cardiff. S. of B.W. Grist, Esq., M.B.E. B. 5 Dec. 1938; m. 24 Mar. 1966, Wendy White, (2 s.). Educ. at Repton, and Jesus Coll., Oxford. Southern Cameroons Plebiscite Officer, Colonial Office 1960-61. United Africa Company, Nigeria 1961-63. Conservative Central Office, Wales Area 1963-74. Conservative Research Department 1970-74. Parliamentary Private Secretary to Rt. Hon. Nicholas Edwards, Secretary of State for Wales from 1979. A Conservative. Unsuccessfully contested Aberavon in 1970. Sat for Cardiff N. from Feb. 1974.*   [1979]

GROCOTT, Bruce Joseph. House of Commons, London. S. of Reg. Grocott, Esq., Railwayman. B. 1 Nov. 1940; m. 17 July 1965, Sally, d. of Jim and Doris Ridgway, (2 s.). Educ. at State Schools, and Leicester and Manchester Universities. Administrative Officer, London County Council 1963-64. Lecturer Manchester University, Birmingham Polytechnic and North Staffordshire Polytechnic 1964-74. Chairman Finance and General Purposes Committee, Bromsgrove Urban District Council 1972-74. Parliamentary Private Secretary to the Rt. Hon. John Silkin July 1975-Nov. 1978. A Labour Member. Unsuccessfully contested S.W. Hertfordshire in 1970 and Lichfield and

Tamworth in Feb. 1974. Sat for Lichfield and Tamworth from Oct. 1974 until 1979, when he was defeated.*   [1979]

GROSVENOR, Lord Robert George, T.D., M.P. 68 Brook Street, London. Ely Lodge, Enniskillen, Co. Fermanagh, Northern Ireland. Turf, Buck's, Ulster (Belfast), Marylebone Cricket, Royal Ocean Racing, and Royal Yacht Squadron. S. of Capt. Lord Hugh William Grosvenor. B. 1910; m. 1946, Hon. Viola Maud Lyttelton, d. of 9th Visct. Cobham, K.C.B. (she died 1949). Educ. at Eton. 2nd Lieut. City of London Yeomanry 1938; served 1939-45 with R.A. (Middle East); Lieut.-Col. 1943; Maj. City of London Yeomanry 1946-49; Maj. North Irish Horse 1949; Lieut.-Col. 1953-56. Freeman The Goldsmiths' Company and City of London. Dept.-Lieut. 1953, J.P. 1950, High Sheriff for Co. Fermanagh 1952; Aide-de-Camp to Gov. of Northern Ireland 1953-55. Parliamentary Private Secretary to Rt. Hon. Selwyn Lloyd, Secretary of State for Foreign Affairs 1957-59. C.St.J. An Ulster Unionist Member. Contested Fermanagh and S. Tyrone in May 1955 and, after his opponent had been disqualified, was declared elected in Sept. 1955. Sat until he retired in 1964. Member of Northern Ireland Senate 1964-67. Granted the Precedence of a Duke's younger son in 1963. Succeeded his brother as Duke of Westminster in 1967. Dept.-Lieut. for Cheshire 1970. Chairman of Maritime Trust 1970-75. Lord-Lieut. of Co. Fermanagh 1977-79. Died 19 Feb. 1979.   [1964]

GRUFFYDD, Professor William John. House of Commons, London. Athenaeum. S. of John and Jane Gruffydd, of Llanddeiniolen, Caernarvonshire. B. 14 Feb. 1881; m. 16 Aug. 1909, Gwenda, d. of Rev. John Evans, of Abercarn. Educ. at Caernarvon School, and Jesus Coll., Oxford, M.A., Honorary D. Litt. (Wales), Honorary D. es L. (Rennes); Professor of Celtic, University Coll., Cardiff from 1918-46, later Emeritus Professor. Member of various Departmental Committees including the Fleming Committee on Public Schools 1942. An Author. Lieut. R.N.V.R. 1915-18. President of Council of National Eisteddfod of Wales. A Liberal. Elected for the University of Wales in

Jan. 1943 and sat until he retired in 1950. Editor of *Y Llenor* 1922-51. Died 29 Sept. 1954. [1950]

GRYLLS, (William) Michael John. Walcot House, 139 Kennington Road, London. Carlton. S. of Brigadier W.E.H. Grylls, O.B.E. B. 1934; m. May 1965, Sarah Ford, d. of Mr. Neville Ford and Lady Fisher (formerly Mrs Patricia Ford, MP.), (1 s. 1 d.). Educ. at Royal Naval Coll., Dartmouth, University of Paris, and University of Madrid. Elected member of St. Pancras Borough Council 1959-62 and was Vice-Chairman of Finance Committee and member of Housing Management Committee 1959; elected member of Greater London Council 1967-70. Dept. Leader of the I.L.E.A. 1969-70 and Chairman of the Further and Higher Education Sub-Committee 1968-70; member of the National Youth Employment Council 1968-70. Vice-Chairman Conservative Industry Committee. Member Select Committees Overseas Development and Expenditure. A Conservative. Unsuccessfully contested Fulham in 1964 and 1966. Sat for the Chertsey division of Surrey from 1970 to Feb. 1974 and for the N.W. division of Surrey from Feb. 1974.* [1979]

GUEST, Dr. Leslie Haden. See HADEN-GUEST, Dr. Leslie Haden.

GUMMER, John. Selwyn. House of Commons, London. S. of Rev. Canon Selwyn Gummer. B. Nov. 1939; m. 1977, Penelope Jane, d. of John P. Gardner, Esq. Educ. at King's School, Rochester, and Selwyn Coll., Cambridge. (President of the Union 1962). Chairman Federation of Conservative Students 1961. Member Inner London Education Authority 1967-70; Publisher and Journalist. Parliamentary Private Secretary to Rt. Hon. James Prior Minister of Agriculture, Fisheries and Food 1971-72. Vice-Chairman Conservative Party 1972-74. Publications: *When the Coloured People Come, The Permissive Society* and *The Christian Calendar*. A Conservative. Unsuccessfully contested Greenwich in 1964 and 1966. Elected for Lewisham W. in June 1970 and sat until Feb. 1974 when he was defeated. Elected for

the Eye division of Suffolk in May 1979. Editor, Business Publications 1962-64. Editor-in-Chief, Max Parrish and Oldbourne Press 1964-66. With BPC Publishing 1967-70. Managing Director of EP Group of Companies from 1975. Chairman of Selwyn Shandwick International from 1976.* [1974]

GUNTER, Rt. Hon. Raymond Jones. House of Commons, London. S. of Miles Gunter, Esq., of Abertillery, Miner. B. 30 Aug. 1909; m. 4 Aug. 1934, Elsie, d. of James Elkins, Esq., Coal Miner (she died 1971). Educ. at Elementary School. A Railway Clerk. Staff Capt. Royal Engineers 1940-45. President Transport Salaried Staff Association 1956-64. Member National Executive of the Labour Party 1955-66. Chairman of the Labour Party 1964-65. Minister of Labour Oct. 1964-Apr. 1968. Minister of Power Apr. 1968-June 1968. A Labour Member. Sat for S.E. Essex from 1945-50 and Doncaster from 1950-51 when he resigned. Unsuccessfully contested Doncaster again in 1955. Elected for Southwark in 1959 and sat until he resigned in Mar. 1972. Member of P.L.P. Parliamentary Committee 1960-64. Opposition spokesman on Power 1960-61, and on Labour 1961-64. Voted in favour of entry to E.E.C. on 28 Oct. 1971. Resigned the Labour Whip on 16 Feb. 1972. Died 12 Apr. 1977. [1972]

GURDEN, Harold Edward. 53 Sussex Street, London. S. of A.W. Gurden, Esq. B. 28 June 1903; m. 1st, 16 Apr. 1929, Lucy Isabella, d. of Henry A. Izon, Esq. (she died 1976); 2ndly, 1977, Elizabeth Joan, widow of Arthur Taylor, Esq. Educ. at Cambridge House School. Member Birmingham City Council 1946-56; President Birmingham and District Dairymen's Association 1947-50; President-elect of National Dairymen's Association 1951; Chairman Society of Dairy Technology, Midland division and of Northfield division Conservative Association 1950-52. Appointed Speakers Panel of Chairmen 1966, also Chairman of Committee of Selection 1970. President Birmingham R.S.P.C.A. Rector's Warden, St. Margarets Church, Westminster 1973-75. A Conservative. Elected for the Selly Oak division of

Birmingham in 1955 and sat until Oct. 1974 when he was defeated.* [1974 2nd ed]

GUY, William Henry. 128 Kerbey Street, Poplar, London. B. 1890. A Labour Member. Elected for Poplar S. in 1942 and sat until he retired in 1950. Served in Royal Navy and as Inspector of Armaments 1914-18. Member of London County Council 1934-65. Member of Poplar Borough Council 1945-65, Mayor 1953-54. Director of Amalgamated Tobacco Corporation. Died 1 Aug. 1968. [1950]

HADEN-GUEST, Dr. Leslie Haden, M.C. 44 Westminster Palace Gardens, London. Hitchcocks, Little Saling, Braintree, Essex. S. of Alexander Haden Guest, Esq., of Manchester. B. 10 Mar. 1877; m. 1st, 1898, Edith, d. of Max Low, Esq. (marriage dissolved 1909); m. 2ndly, 1910, Muriel Carmel, d. of Col. A. Goldsmid (she died 1943). m. 3rdly, 10 Jan. 1944, Edith, d. of George Macqueen, Esq., of Montrose, Angus. Educ. at William Hulme's Grammar School, Owens Coll., Manchester, and London Hospital. Served in South African War 1902 and in Red Cross and R.A.M.C. in France, Palestine and Egypt 1914-18. Member of London County Council for E. Woolwich 1919-22. Maj. R.A.M.C. 1940. A Labour Member. Unsuccessfully contested Southwark Central in 1918 and Southwark N. in 1922. Elected for Southwark N. in 1923 and sat until Feb. 1927 when he resigned his seat on leaving the Labour Party because he disagreed with its policy towards China. Unsuccessfully contested the by-election in Mar. 1927 as an Independent, with unofficial Conservative support, and Salford N. as a Conservative in 1929. Later rejoined the Labour Party and unsuccessfully contested the Wycombe division of Buckinghamshire in 1931 and Brecon and Radnor in 1935. Elected for Islington N. in Oct. 1937 and sat until Jan. 1950 when he was created Baron Haden-Guest. Lord-in-Waiting and Government Whip in House of Lords Feb.-Oct. 1951. Opposition Whip in House of Lords 1951-60. Died 20 Aug. 1960. [1950]

HAIRE, John Edwin. 3 Cheyne Gardens, London. The Platt, Bourne End, Buckinghamshire. S. of John Haire, Esq., of Portadown. B. 14 Nov. 1908; m. 30 June 1939, Suzanne, d. of Eugene Kemeny, Esq., of Hatvan. Educ. at Queen's University, Belfast, M.A. A School Teacher 1931, and Journalist. Senior History Master Bangor Grammar School 1933; M.O.I. and Forces Lecturer 1940. Joined R.A.F. 1941. Operations Officer Coastal Command on Staff of Air Officer Commanding Plymouth 1942, Air Liaison Officer Admiralty 1943, Air Historian Air Ministry 1945. Leader of Parliamentary Delegation to Hungary 1946. Parliamentary Private Secretary to Arthur Bottomley, Under-Secretary at the Dominions Office Oct. 1946-Nov. 1947. Parliamentary Private Secretary to Douglas Jay, Financial Secretary to the Treasury Apr. 1950-Oct. 1951. A Labour Member. Elected for the Wycombe division of Buckinghamshire in July 1945 and sat until 1951 when he was defeated. Unsuccessfully contested the Eastleigh division of Hampshire in 1955. Created Baron Haire of Whiteabbey (Life Peerage) 1965. Died 7 Oct. 1966 in New Brunswick, N.J. [1951]

HALE, Charles Leslie. 92 College Road, Dulwich, London. S. of Benjamin Hale, Esq. B. 13 July 1902; m. 1926, Dorothy Ann Latham (she died 1971). Educ. at Ashby-de-la-Zouch Grammar School. A Solicitor. A Labour Member. Unsuccessfully contested S. Nottingham as a Liberal in 1929. Sat for Oldham from July 1945-Feb. 1950 and for the W. division of Oldham from Feb. 1950 until he resigned in Jan. 1968. Member of Leicestershire County Council 1925-49. Author of *Thirty who were tried, John Philpot Curran, his life and times, Blood on the scales,* and *Hanging in the balance.* Created Baron Hale (Life Peerage) 1972.* [1968]

HALE, Joseph. 71 Park Avenue, Palmers Green, London. 30 Thorpe Street, Bolton, Lancashire. S. of Gordon Tyson Hale, Esq., of Waterloo, Lancashire. B. 28 Oct. 1913; m. 21 June 1939, Anne Irene, d. of Henry Woodruff Clowes, Esq. Educ. at Elementary School, and Secondary Technical School. An Engineer, in Merchant Marine 1933-39, Plastics 1939. Member of Bolton Borough Council 1946-50, and of A.E.U. District Committee 1943-50. Chairman of Bolton

West Labour Party. A Labour Member. Elected for Rochdale in Feb. 1950 and sat until 1951 when he was defeated.* [1951]

HALL, Rt. Hon. George Henry. 4 Harris View, Penrhiwceiber, Glamorgan. S. of George Hall, Esq. B. 31 Dec. 1881; m. 1st, 1910, Margaret, d. of William Jones, Esq. (she died May 1941); 2ndly, 1964, Alice Martha Walker. Educ. at Penrhiwceiber, Glamorgan. A Colliery Checkweighman 1911-22. J.P. Glamorganshire; Chairman of Mountain Ash Urban District Council and Education Committee; Gov. of Cardiff University. Civil Lord of the Admiralty June 1929-Aug. 1931. Parliamentary Under-Secretary of State for the Colonies May 1940-Feb. 1942. Financial Secretary to the Admiralty Feb. 1942-Sept. 1943; Parliamentary Under-Secretary of State for Foreign Affairs Sept. 1943-May 1945; Secretary of State for the Colonies and Member of the Cabinet July 1945-Oct. 1946. PC. 1942. A Labour Member. Member for the Aberdare division of Merthyr Tydfil from 1922 until Oct. 1946 when he was created Visct. Hall. Member of Executive Committee of P.L.P. 1939-40. First Lord of the Admiralty Oct. 1946-May 1951. Dept.-Leader of House of Lords 1947-51. Dept.-Lieut. for Glamorgan. Died 8 Nov. 1965. [1946]

HALL, Joan Valerie. Wheathead Cottage, Wheathead Lane, Keighley, Yorkshire. D. of Robert Percy Hall, Esq., retired. B. 31 Aug. 1935. Educ. at Queen Margaret's School, York, and Ashridge House of Citizenship. Parliamentary Private Secretary to J.A. Stodart, Minister of State, Ministry of Agriculture, Fisheries and Food 1972-74. A Conservative. Unsuccessfully contested Barnsley in 1964 and 1966. Elected for Keighley in June 1970 and sat until Feb. 1974 when she was defeated.* [1974]

HALL, Sir John, O.B.E. 41 Carlisle Mansions, Carlisle Place, London. Marsh, Great Kimble, Buckinghamshire. B. 21 Sept. 1911; m. 1935, Nancy, d. of W. Hearn Blake, Esq. President and Director of Companies concerned with Cellulose chemistry, Packaging and Brewing. Served in the war of 1939-45 R.A. and R.A.O.C. Staff Coll., Camberley

1941-42; various Staff appointments 1942-45, Lieut.-Col. O.B.E. (Mil.) 1945. T.D. 1946. Member Grimsby Borough Council from 1946-48. Parliamentary Private Secretary to Rt. Hon. Aubrey Jones, Minister of Fuel and Power 1956-57, and Minister of Supply 1957-59. Member Select Committee on Public Accounts 1958-64. Opposition spokesman on Treasury and Economic Affairs 1964-65. Vice-Chairman Conservative Parliamentary Trade and Industry Committee 1964-65, and of Finance Committee 1965-68 and 1969-72; Chairman Finance Committee 1973-74, Vice-Chairman 1974-78; Vice-Chairman 1922 Committee 1970-78; member of Select Committee on Expenditure. Chairman Sub-Committee on Environment and Home Office 1970-72. Dept.-President Inter-Parliamentary Union 1970-73. Chairman British Group I.P.U 1970-73. Chairman Select Committee on Nationalised Industries 1973-74. Created Knight Bachelor June 1973. Order of Diplomatic Merit 1975. A Conservative. Unsuccessfully contested Grimsby in 1950 and E. Fulham in 1951. Elected for the Wycombe division of Buckinghamshire in Nov. 1952 and sat until his death on 19 Jan. 1978. [1978]

HALL, John Thomas. House of Commons, London. S. of William Alfred Hall, Esq., of Philadelphia, Co. Durham. B. 9 Nov. 1896; m. 1927, Blanche Gardner. Educ. at Elementary School and Ruskin Coll., Served with 1st Life Guards 1914-18. Northern District Chairman National Union of General and Municipal Workers. Member Durham County Council 1934-50. J.P. for Durham Co. 1939. A Labour Member. Elected for Gateshead W. in Feb. 1950 and sat until his death on 11 Oct. 1955. [1955]

HALL, Rt. Hon. William George Glenvil. House of Commons, London. S. of W.G. Hall, Esq., of Almeley, Herefordshire. B. 1887; m. 1921, Rachel, d. of Late Rev. Robert Bury Sanderson (she died 1950). Educ. at Ellesmere Coll. Barrister-at-Law, Gray's Inn 1933. Served with The Buffs, Sherwood Foresters and Royal Tanks Corps 1914-19. Financial Secretary to the Treasury Aug. 1945-Mar. 1950. PC. 1947. Chairman of P.L.P. 1950-51. Member of P.L.P. Parliamentary Committee 1951-55. Member of Gen. Advisory Council of B.B.C. 1952. President of United Kingdom Alliance 1959. A Quaker. A Labour Member. Unsuccessfully contested the Isle of Ely in 1922, Bromley in 1923, and Portsmouth Central in 1924. Elected for Portsmouth Central in 1929 and sat until 1931, when he was defeated. Unsuccessfully contested Norwich in 1935. Elected for the Colne Valley division of the W. Riding of Yorkshire in July 1939 and sat until his death on 13 Oct. 1962.   [1962]

HALL-DAVIS, Alfred George Fletcher.
House of Commons, London. S. of George Hall-Davis, Esq., B.A., M.B. B. 21 June 1924; m. 1956, Margaret, d. of George Carr Rushworth, Esq., J.P., of Colne, Lancashire, (1 d.). Educ. at Clifton Coll., Bristol. Joined Massey's Burnley Brewery 1940; rejoined in 1944 after serving in the Royal Artillery. Appointed Joint Managing Director Jan. 1954, Chairman Oct. 1963. Director Charrington United Breweries Limited 1966; Director Bass Charrington Limited 1969. Vice-Chairman Young Conservative National Advisory Committee 1946-48. Parliamentary Private Secretary to Rt. Hon. Margaret Thatcher, Secretary of State for Education and Science 1970-73. Assistant Government Whip Oct. 1973-Mar. 1974. Opposition Whip Mar.-Oct. 1974. Knighted June 1979. A Conservative. Unsuccessfully contested St. Helens in 1950 and Chorley in 1951 and 1955. Sat for the Morecambe and Lonsdale division of Lancashire from Oct. 1964 until he retired in Apr. 1979. Died 20 Nov. 1979.   [1979]

HAMILTON, Hon. Archibald Gavin.
Danes Hole, Bramley, Surrey. 7 Portland Road, London. S. of the Lord Hamilton of Dalzell, M.C. B. 30 Dec. 1941; m. 14 Dec. 1968, Anne, d. of Commander Trevylyan Napier, D.S.O., (3 d.). Educ. at Eton. Lieut. Coldstream Guards 1960-62. Councillor for Royal Borough of Kensington and Chelsea 1968-71. Parliamentary Private Secretary to Rt. Hon. David Howell, Secretary of State for Energy from 1979. A Conservative. Parliamentary candidate for the Dagenham division of Barking in Feb. and Oct. 1974 elections. Sat for Epsom and Ewell from Apr. 1978.*   [1979]

HAMILTON, James. 12 Rosegreen Crescent, North Road, Bellshill, Lanarkshire. S. of George Hamilton Esq. B. 11 Mar. 1918; m. 1945, Agnes McGhee. Educ. at Secondary School, and N.C.L.C. postal courses. A Roman Catholic. Member of Lanarkshire 6th District Council 1955-58. Member of Lanarkshire County Council 1958-64, held offices on education, water and housing committees. Constructional Engineer. Joined the Labour Party in 1946. Member of Constructional Engineering Union from 1946. President of Constructional Engineering Union 1968-Oct. 1969. Assistant Government Whip Oct. 1969-June 1970. Opposition Whip 1970-74 and from 1979. Chairman of T.U. Group of P.L.P. 1969-70. Lord Commissioner of the Treasury Mar.-June 1974; Vice-Chamberlain of the Royal Household June 1974-July 1978; Comptroller of the Royal Household July 1978-May 1979. C.B.E. 1979. A Labour Member. Sat for the Bothwell division of Lanarkshire from Oct. 1964.*   [1979]

HAMILTON, James Hamilton, Marq. of. Barons Court, Newton Stewart, Co. Tyrone, Northern Ireland. 23 Eaton Place, London. S. of the 4th Duke of Abercorn. B. 4 July 1934; m. 20 Oct. 1966, Alexandra (Sacha), d. of Lieut.-Col. and Mrs. Harold Phillips, of Berkshire, (1 s.). Educ. at Eton, and Royal Agricultural Coll., Cirencester. Formerly a Lieut. in the Grenadier Guards. An Ulster Unionist Member. Elected for Fermanagh and S. Tyrone in Oct. 1964 and sat until 1970 when he was defeated. High Sheriff of Co. Tyrone 1970. Styled Marq. of Hamilton from 1953, when his father succeeded to the Dukedom of Abercorn, until 1979 when he became Duke of Abercorn on his father's death.*   [1970]

HAMILTON, Michael Aubrey. 27 Kylestrome House, Cundy Street, London. Lordington House, Chichester, Sussex. S. of the Rt. Rev. Eric Hamilton, K.C.V.O. B. 5 July 1918; m. 16 May 1947, Lavinia, 3rd d. of Col. Sir Charles Ponsonby, Bart., MP. Educ. at Radley, and University Coll., Oxford. Active service with 1st Battalion Coldstream Guards. Assistant Whip 1961-62. A Lord Commissioner of H.M. Treasury 1962-64. A

Conservative. Sat for Wellingborough from 1959-64 when he was defeated. Member for Salisbury from Feb. 1965.* [1979]

HAMILTON, Lieut.-Col. Roland, O.B.E. Maryfield, Haslemere. S. of Maj. Henry Hamilton. B. 23 Nov. 1886; m. 9 Sept. 1933, Sarah, d. of Dr. H.J. Campbell, of Dartmouth, and widow of T.H. Stern, Esq., M.C., B.Sc. Educ. at Cheltenham, and Royal Military Academy, Woolwich. Served with R.E. 1916-18 in Baluchistan, Persia, Mesopotamia, and Kurdistan 1923. O.B.E. 1924. A Labour Member. Elected for the Sudbury division of Suffolk in July 1945 and sat until 1950 when he unsuccessfully contested the Sudbury and Woodbridge division. Died 10 Feb. 1953. [1950]

HAMILTON, William Winter. House of Commons, London. S. of J. Hamilton, Esq. of Philadelphia, Co. Durham. B. 1917; m. 1944 Joan Callon (she died 1968). Educ. at Washington Grammar School, Co. Durham. A School Teacher. Sheffield University B.A. (Ecs. and History). Served overseas 1939-45. Capt. in R.A.E.C. Served in M.E. Chairman House of Commons Estimates Committee 1964-70. Vice-Chairman Labour Party 1966-70. Member of European Parliament 1975-79. A Labour Member. Unsuccessfully contested W. Fife in 1945. Sat for the West division of Fife from Feb. 1950 to Feb. 1974 and for the Central division of Fife from Feb. 1974.* [1979]

HAMLING, William. House of Commons, London. S. of William Hamling Esq. of Liverpool. B. 10 Aug. 1912; m. 1940, Olive Victoria, d. of William Fraser, Esq. Educ. at Church of England School, Liverpool Institute High School for Boys, and University of Liverpool. Commissioned in Royal Marines 1941; served in Commando Group as Signals Officer. A Lecturer. Joined the Labour Party in 1927. Member National Union of Teachers, Royal Arsenal Co-operative Society and Fabian Society. Justice of the Peace (Blackheath Division), formerly Justice of the Peace, Liverpool. Parliamentary Private Secretary to Rt. Hon. Kenneth Robinson, Minister of Health 1966-68, and Minister of Planning and Land 1968-69.

Trustee of National Maritime Museum 1967-75. Assistant Government Whip Oct. 1969-June 1970. Opposition Whip July 1970-72. Parliamentary Private Secretary to Prime Minister, Mr. Harold Wilson 1974-75. A Labour Member. Unsuccessfully contested Southport in 1945, the Wavertree division of Liverpool in 1950 and 1951, Woolwich W. in May 1955, Torquay in Dec. 1955, and Woolwich W. again in 1959. Sat for Woolwich W. from 1964 to Feb. 1974 and for the Woolwich W. division of Greenwich from Feb. 1974 until his death on 20 Mar. 1975. [1975]

HAMPSON, Keith. House of Commons, London. Carlton. S. of B. Hampson, Esq. B. 14 Aug. 1943; m. June 1975, Frances Pauline, d. of M.D. Einhorn, Esq., of Killinghall, Harrogate (she died Sept. 1975). Educ. at King James I Grammar School, Bishop Auckland, Bristol University, Ph.D. 1971, and Harvard University. Assistant to Rt. Hon. Edward Heath in the general election of 1966, in House of Commons 1968, and his representative at Bexley election 1970. Lecturer in History, University of Edinburgh 1968-74. Secretary to Sir Alec Douglas Home's Scottish Constitutional Committee 1968-70. Parliamentary Private Secretary to Rt. Hon. Tom King, Minister for Local Government from 1979. A Conservative. Unsuccessfully contested Ripon in July 1973. Sat for Ripon from Feb. 1974.* [1979]

HANNAM, John Gordon. Woodslea House, Brampford Speke, Nr. Exeter, Devon. 35 Tufton Court, London. All England, Wimbledon, International Law Tennis, and Royal London Yacht. S. of Thomas William Hannam, Esq. B. 2 Aug. 1929; m. 19 June 1956, Wendy, d. of Thomas Lamont Macartney, Esq. Educ. at Yeovil Grammar School. Studied agriculture from 1945-46. Served in 4th Royal Tank Regiment Middle East 1947-48 and 4th Battalion Somerset Light Infantry (T.A.) 1949-51. Director Hotels and Restaurant Company 1952-60; Managing Director two Motels' Companies 1961-72; Director 1972-75. President Exeter and District Chamber of Commerce and Trade 1972. Divisional Young Conservative Chairman 1950-51. Vice-Chairman Constituency Association 1967-68. Somerset County Councillor

1967-69. Chairman British Motels Federation 1967-72. President British Motels Limited 1973. Member Council British Travel Association 1968-69. Vice-President Disabled Drivers Association 1977. Secretary Conservative Party Trade Committee 1971-72. Parliamentary Private Secretary to Tom Boardman Minister for Industry 1972-74, and Chief Secretary to Treasury Jan.-Mar. 1974. Vice-Chairman Conservative Arts and Amenities Committee 1974. Vice-Chairman Conservative Energy Committee 1973. Secretary All-Party Disablement Committee 1973. Commodore House of Commons Yacht Club 1975. Capt. Lords and Commons Tennis Club 1975-77. Chairman Lords and Commons Ski Club 1977. Member Snowdon Working Party on Disabled 1976-77. A Conservative. Elected for Exeter in June 1970.*

[1979]

HANNAN, William. 23 Tamar House, Kennington Lane, London. Balmoral Drive, Bearsden, Dunbartonshire. S. of T. Hannan, Esq. B. 30 Aug. 1906; m. 18 Sept. 1930, Helen, d. of William Scott, Esq. Educ. at Maryhill School, and North Kelvinside Secondary School. Honorary Organiser Labour League, S. Glasgow Federation; Secretary Glasgow Federation Labour Parties. An Insurance Agent. Member of Glasgow Town Council 1941-45. Assistant Government Whip 1945-46. A Lord Commissioner of the Treasury May 1946-Oct. 1951. Opposition Whip 1951-53. Parliamentary Private Secretary to Rt. Hon. George Brown, Secretary of State for Economic Affairs and Foreign Secretary 1964-68. Voted in favour of entry to E.E.C. on 28 Oct. 1971. A Labour Member. Elected for the Maryhill division of Glasgow in July 1945 and sat until he retired in Feb. 1974.*

[1974]

HANNON, Sir Patrick Joseph Henry. 1 Westminster Gardens, London. 22 Northumberland Avenue, London. Magna Carta Island, Wraysbury, Buckinghamshire. Carlton, Constitutional, Union, Conservative, and Midland Conservative. S. of Mathew Hannon, Esq. B. 1874; m. 1st, 1894, Mary, d. of Thomas Wynne, Esq. (she died 5 Feb. 1928); 2ndly, 22 Aug. 1931, Amy Hilda Gordon, d. of James Barrett, Esq., of The Mount, Farnham Royal (she died 1960). Educ. at University Coll., Dublin, Royal Coll. of Science, Royal University of Ireland. Director of the British Commonwealth Union July 1918-28. Director of Agricultural Organization, South Africa 1904-09. Vice-President of Tariff Reform League 1910-14. Gen. Secretary of the Navy League 1911-18. Editor of *The Navy* 1912-18. Gen. Secretary of Comrades of the Great War. Chairman National Council of Inland Waterways; member of National Whitley Council of C.S. 1921-29; President of Central Chamber of Agriculture 1930-31; Honorary Secretary Empire Industries Association from 1925; President National Union of Manufacturers; Vice-President of F.B.I.; Knight Bach. 1936. Director of Companies. President of Institute of Export 1939-43, and of British and Latin American Chamber of Commerce. A Conservative. Unsuccessfully contested Bristol E. in Dec. 1910. Returned unopposed for the Moseley division of Birmingham in Mar. 1921 and Nov. 1922. Re-elected for the Moseley division of Birmingham in Dec. 1923 and sat until he retired in 1950. Master of Worshipful Company of Patternmakers 1930-32. Fellow of Statistical, Royal Geographical, Royal Economic and Royal Entomological Societies. A Roman Catholic. Died 10 Jan. 1963.

[1950]

HARDEN, Maj. James Richard Edwards, D.S.O., M.C. Harrybrook, Tandragee, Portadown, Co. Armagh. S. of Maj. J.E. Harden. B. 12 Dec. 1916; m. 27 July 1948, Ursula Joyce, d. of Gerald Strutt, Esq., of Newhouse, Terling, Chelmsford. Educ. at Bedford School, and Royal Military Coll., Sandhurst. A Farmer. M.C. 1944, D.S.O. 1945. Dept.-Lieut. for Armagh 1946. Maj. Late Royal Tank Regiment. Served on Staff in France 1940 and in Middle East and Western Europe 1939-45. An Ulster Unionist Member. Elected for Armagh in Mar. 1948 and sat until he resigned in Nov. 1954. J.P. for Armagh 1956, for Caernarvonshire 1971, for Gwynedd 1974. Dept.-Lieut. for Caernarvonshire 1968, for Gwynedd 1974. High Sheriff of Caernarvonshire 1971-72.*

[1954]

HARDMAN, David Rennie. Little Ote Hall, Burgess Hill, Sussex. Savile. S. of David Hardman, Esq. B. 18 Oct. 1901; m. 1st, 1928, Freda, d. of Edwin Riley, Esq.; 2ndly, 1946, Barbara, d. of Herbert Lambert, Esq. Educ. at Coleraine Academical Institution, Ulster, and Christ's Coll., Cambridge, M.A., LL.B. Lecturer and University Secretary from 1925. President of C.U. Union Society 1925; Chairman of Cambridgeshire Education Committee 1945; Leader of U.K. Unesco Delegations 1946-50; President of Shaw Society 1947-49; Parliamentary Secretary Ministry of Education from Oct. 1945 to Oct. 1951; member of Cambridge Borough Council and of Cambridgeshire County Council from 1937 to 1946. J.P. for Cambridge. An Author. A Labour Member. Unsuccessfully contested Cambridge in 1929. Elected for Darlington in July 1945 and sat until 1951 when he was defeated. Unsuccessfully contested the Rushcliffe division of Nottinghamshire in 1955. Parliamentary Private Secretary to Rt. Hon. Arthur Greenwood, Lord Privy Seal 1945. Secretary of Cassel Educational Trust from 1955. Secretary of Stafford Cripps Memorial Trustees from 1962. Visiting Professor of English Literature, Elmira, New York 1964-66. Barclay Acheson Professor of International Studies, Macalester Coll., St. Paul, Minn., 1967.* [1951]

HARDY, Edward Arthur. 38 Argyle Square, London. 19 Otranto Avenue, Salford. S. of George Ernest Hardy, Esq. B. 1884; m. 1907, Amy, d. of William Gormon, Esq. Educ. at St. Clements School, Salford. Member of Salford City Council from 1922. Mayor 1933-34. A Labour Member. Sat for Salford S. from July 1945-Feb. 1950. Elected for Salford E. in Feb. 1950 and sat until he retired in 1955. Area Secretary of Confederation of Health Service Employees. Freeman of City of Salford 1960. Died 4 Feb. 1960. [1954]

HARDY, Peter. 53 Sandygate, Wath-upon-Dearne, Rotherham, Yorkshire. S. of Lawrence Hardy, Esq., A Miner and Underground Official. B. 17 July 1931; m. 28 July 1954, Margaret Ann, d. of C.A. Brookes, Esq., of Canada, (2 s.). Educ. at Wath-upon-Dearne Grammar School, Westminster Coll., London, and Sheffield University. Served in R.A.F. 1949-51. A Teacher in South Yorkshire 1953-70, Head of Department 1960-70; Councillor Wath-upon-Dearne Urban District Council from 1960 to 1970, Chairman 1968-69. Sponsored The Badgers Act 1973, The Conservation of Wild Creatures and Wild Plants Act 1975, The Protection of Birds (Amendment) Act 1976, and the Education (Northern Ireland) Act 1978. Parliamentary Private Secretary to Rt. Hon. Anthony Crosland, Secretary of State for the Environment Mar. 1974-Apr. 1976, and Foreign and Commonwealth Secretary Apr. 1976-Feb. 1977. Member of U.K. Delegation to the Council of Europe 1976. Author of *A Lifetime of Badgers* 1975. A Labour Member. Parliamentary Candidate for Scarborough and Whitby in 1964 and the Hallam division of Sheffield in 1966. Elected for the Rother Valley division of the W. Riding of Yorkshire in June 1970.* [1979]

HARE, Rt. Hon. John Hugh, O.B.E. 1 Sussex Place, London. Cottage Farm, Little Blakenham, Ipswich. White's, and Buck's. S. of 4th Earl of Listowel. B. 22 Jan. 1911; m. 31 Jan. 1934, Hon. Beryl Nancy Pearson, d. of 2nd Visct. Cowdray. Educ. at Eton. Lieut-Col. Suffolk Yeomanry; served in North Africa and Italy 1939-45. Alderman London County Council 1937-52. Chairman London Municipal Society 1947-51. Vice-Chairman Conservative Party Dec. 1951-Sept. 1955; Minister of State for Colonial Affairs Dec. 1955-Oct. 1956; Secretary of State for War Oct. 1956-Jan. 1958. Minister of Agriculture Jan. 1958-July 1960. Minister of Labour July 1960-Oct. 1963. PC. 1955. A Conservative. Sat for Woodbridge division from July 1945-Feb. 1950. Elected for the Sudbury and Woodbridge division of Suffolk in Feb. 1950 and sat until Oct. 1963 when he was created Visct. Blakenham. Chancellor of Duchy of Lancaster and Dept.-Leader of House of Lords Oct. 1963-Oct. 1964. Chairman of Conservative Party Organisation 1963-65. Chairman of Council of Toynbee Hall from 1966. Chairman of Peabody Trust from 1967. Treasurer of Royal Horticultural Society from 1971. M.B.E. 1943, O.B.E. 1945. Dept.-Lieut. for Sufford 1968.* [1963]

HARGREAVES, Alfred. 48 Warmington Road, Liverpool 14. S. of Henry Hargreaves, Esq. B. 15 Feb. 1899. Educ. at Liverpool. A Railway Clerk. A Labour Member. Elected for Carlisle in Feb. 1950 and sat until 1955 when he was defeated. Unsuccessfully contested Carlisle in 1959. Member of Liverpool City Council 1928-50. President of Liverpool Trades Council and Labour Party 1945. Member of Mersey Docks and Harbour Board 1949.* [1954]

HARPER, Joseph. 11 Bedford Close, Purston, Featherstone, Yorkshire. S. of Henry Harper, Esq., Miner. B. 17 Mar. 1914; m. 8 Apr. 1939, Gwendoline, d. of Samuel Hughes, Esq. (2 s. 2 d.). Educ. at Featherstone Elementary School. Lodge Delegate N.U.M. (Yorkshire Area) 1943-62. Member of Yorkshire Exec. (N.U.M.) 1947-48 and 1950-52. Member of Featherstone Urban District Council 1949-63. Chairman of Featherstone Urban District Council 1955-56 and 1961-62. Chairman of Managers and Govs. Featherstone Education Committee 1956-62. Vice-Chairman of Pontefract Division ed. ex. 1954-62. Chairman South Featherstone Youth Club 1953-62. Justice of the Peace, Osgoldcross (West Riding) 1959. Member of Pontefract and Castleford Hospital Management Committee 1958. Assistant Government Whip Nov. 1964-Apr. 1966. Lord Commissioner to the Treasury Apr. 1966-June 1970. Comptroller of the Royal Household Mar. 1974-June 1978. A Labour Member. Sat for Pontefract from Mar. 1962 to Feb. 1974 and for Pontefract and Castleford from Feb. 1974 until his death on 24 June 1978. [1978]

HARRIS, Frederic Walter. Wood Rising, The Ridge, Woldingham, Surrey. S. of Walter Harris, Esq. B. 6 Mar. 1915; m. 1st, 23 Apr. 1939, Betty, d. of Walter W. Benson, Esq. (she died 1955); 2ndly, 1957, Joan Hope, d. of David N.K. Bagnall, Esq., of Overmist, Tadworth, Surrey. Educ. at Belmont Coll. A Director of Companies. A Conservative. Sat for N. Croydon from Mar. 1948 to May 1955 and for N.W. Croydon from May 1955 until he retired in 1970. Member of Surrey County Council 1946-48. C.B.E. 1972. Chairman of Marshall's Investments Limited. Managing Director of Marshall's Universal Limited 1945-75, Chairman 1964-75. Died in Nairobi 4 Jan. 1979. [1970]

HARRIS, Henry Wilson. 13 Park Village West, London. Foxholt, Abinger Common, Dorking. S. of Vigurs Harris, Esq., of Plymouth. B. 21 Sept. 1883; m. 7 May 1910, Florence, d. of Dr. A.N. Cash, of Torquay. Educ. at Plymouth Coll., and St. John's Coll., Cambridge. A Journalist and Author. Editor of the *Spectator* from 1932-53. An Independent Member. Elected for Cambridge University in July 1945 and sat until he retired in 1950. President of the Cambridge Union 1905. On the staff of the League of Nations Union 1923-32 and Editor of *Headway*. Died 11 Jan. 1955. [1950]

HARRIS, Richard Reader. 2 Carlyle Mansions, Cheyne Walk, London. R.A.C. S. of Richard Reader Harris, Esq. B. 4 June 1913; m. 1940, Pamela Rosemary Merrick Stephens. Educ. at St. Lawrence Coll., Ramsgate. A Barrister-at-Law, Gray's Inn 1941. Served in Fire Service 1939-45. Secretary of National Association of Fire Officers from 1944. A Conservative. Elected for Heston and Isleworth in Feb. 1950 and sat until he retired in 1970, after his local Conservative Association had declined to re-adopt him as their candidate. Member of Church Assembly 1951-60. Charged in Feb. 1968 with fraud in connection with Rolls Razor Limited, of which he was Chairman, and other companies; acquitted on all charges on 29 May 1970.* [1970]

HARRISON, Alastair Brian Clarke. Copford Hall, Colchester. S. of Brigadier E.F. Harrison. B. 3 Oct. 1921; m. 23 Feb. 1952, Elizabeth Hood, d. of R.M. Hardie, Esq., of New South Wales, Australia. Educ. at Geelong Grammar School, Australia, and Trinity Coll., Cambridge. Estate Manager. Served with A.I.F., Capt. 1939-45. Parliamentary Private Secretary to Rt. Hon. J.H. Hare, Minister of State for Colonial Affairs Feb.-Oct. 1956, Secretary of State for War Oct. 1956-Jan. 1958, and Minister of Agriculture, Fisheries and Food 1958-60. Chairman Eastern Sports Council 1965-67. Chairman of

St. Helena Group Hospital Management Committee Apr. 1967-71. Director Dalgety Limited and Commercial Bank of Australia Limited. A Conservative. Elected for Maldon, Essex in 1955 and sat until he retired in Feb. 1974. Director of Grindlay (Australia) Limited, Agricultural Investments Australia Limited and Commercial Bank of Australia Limited.* [1974]

HARRISON, James. 270 Breedon Street, Long Eaton, Nottingham. S. of George Harrison, Esq. B. 30 Aug. 1899; m. 1924, Mary Earnshaw. Educ. at Labour Coll., London. An Engine Driver, Trade Union Organiser and Lecturer. A Labour Member. Sat for Nottingham E. from July 1945 to May 1955 and for Nottingham N. from May 1955 until his death on 2 May 1959. [1959]

HARRISON, Sir (James) Harwood, Bart., T.D. Little Manor, Haseton, Woodbridge. Carlton, and Pratt's. S. of the Rev. Ernest W. Harrison. B. 6 June 1907; m. 16 Jan. 1932, Peggy Alberta Mary, d. of Lieut.-Col. V.D. Stenhouse. Educ. at Northampton Grammar School, and Trinity Coll., Oxford, M.A. T.D., J.P. A Merchant. Chairman of four private companies and director of six others. Commissioned 4th Suffolks T.A. July 1935; commanded 1947-51; Brevet Col. Sept. 1951; T.A.R.O. Dec. 1951. Prisoner-of-War in Singapore for 3½ years; T.D. and two bars. Parliamentary Private Secretary to Rt. Hon. Harold Macmillan 1953-54. President of Eastern Area Conservative Association 1963-66; Chairman 1956-59. Assistant Government Whip 1954-56; Lord Commissioner of the Treasury Apr. 1956-Jan. 1959; Comptroller H.Ms. Household Jan. 1959-Nov. 1961. Created Bart. 1961. Chairman of Unionist Club from 1966. Chairman Defence and Foreign Office Overseas Sub-Committee of Expenditure Committee 1971. Chairman Inter-Parliamentary Union 1973-74. Member Ipswich Borough Council 1935-46. A Conservative. Unsuccessfully contesed Eye division of Suffolk in 1950. Elected for the Eye division of Suffolk in Oct. 1951 and sat until he retired in 1979. Died 11 Sept. 1980. [1979]

HARRISON, Rt. Hon. Walter. 1 Milnthorpe Drive, Sandal, Wakefield, Yorkshire. S. of Henry Harrison, Esq. B. 2 Jan. 1921; m. 1948, Enid Mary Coleman, (1 s. 1 d.). Educ. at Secondary-Technical School and School of Art. An Installation Foreman (Electrical). Joined the Labour Party in 1946. Member of E.T.U. and held various offices. Labour Councillor, Castleford from 1952 to 1959 and W. Riding County Councillor from 1958 to 1964. Labour Alderman, Castleford from 1959 to 1966. J.P. from 1962. Regional Executive Member of the Labour Party 1954. Assistant Government Whip Apr. 1966-Oct. 1968. Lord-Commissioner of the Treasury Oct. 1968-June 1970. Opposition Dept. Chief Whip July 1970-Mar. 1974 and from 1979. Treasurer of the Household and Dept. Chief Whip of the Government Mar. 1974-May 1979. PC. 1977. A Labour Member. Sat for Wakefield from Oct. 1964.* [1979]

HART, Rt. Hon. Dame Judith Constance Mary, D.B.E. House of Commons, London. D. of H. Ridehalgh, Esq., Linotype Operator. B. 1924; M. 1946, Anthony Hart, (2 s.). Educ. at Elementary School, Clitheroe Royal Grammar School, and London University. A Lecturer and Research Worker in Sociology 1945-49, and 1955-57. Joint Under-Secretary of State for Scotland Oct. 1964-Apr. 1966. Minister of State for Commonwealth Relations from Apr. 1966-July 1967. Minister of Social Security July 1967-Nov. 1968. Paymaster-Gen. Nov. 1968-Oct. 1969. Member of National Executive of the Labour Party from 1969. Published *Aid and Liberation*. Member of the Cabinet Nov. 1968-Oct. 1969. Minister of Overseas Development Oct. 1969-June 1970 and June 1974-June 1975. Minister for Overseas Development (Foreign and Commonwealth Office) Mar.-June 1974. Minister for Overseas Development Feb. 1977-May 1979. Opposition spokesman on Overseas Development 1970-74 and from 1979. A Labour Member. Unsuccessfully contested Bournemouth W. in 1951 and Alberdeen S. in 1955. Elected for Lanark in 1959. PC. 1967. D.B.E. 1979.* [1979]

HARVEY, Sir Arthur Vere, C.B.E. House of Commons, London. Buck's, Carlton, and R.Y.S.S. of Arthur William Harvey, Esq. B. 31 Jan. 1906; m. 1st, 6 July 1940, Jacqueline, d. of W.H. Dunnett, Esq. (marriage dissolved in Mar. 1954); 2ndly, June 1955, Mrs. Hilary Williams (marriage dissolved in 1977); 3rdly, 1978, Mrs. Carol Cassar Torreggiani. Educ. at Framlingham Coll. Served with R.A.F. 1925-30. Director Mullard Limited; Director CIBA Limited, Basle; CIBA United Kingdom Limited; Chairman CIBA Laboratories Limited; CIBA Clayton Limited; CIBA (A.R.L.) Limited; Clayton Aniline Company Limited; Director Philips Electrical Industries Limited; Chairman Ilford Limited. Knighted 1957. Founded 615 County of Surrey Squadron A.A.F. 1937, Air Commodore 1944. Elected Chairman 1922 Committee May 1966-June 1970. Given Honorary Freedom of Borough of Macclesfield in Oct. 1969 and Honorary Freedom of Borough of Congleton in Mar. 1970. Decorated as a Commander of the Order of Orange Nassau in Oct. 1969. a Conservative. Elected for the Macclesfield division of Cheshire in July 1945 and sat until Apr. 1971 when he was created Baron Harvey of Prestbury (Life Peerage). Director of Far East Aviation Company Limited 1930-35, Adviser to Southern Chinese Air Forces 1932-35.*
[1971]

HARVEY, Ian Douglas, T.D. 19 Orchard Rise, Richmond, Surrey. Carlton. S. of Maj. Douglas Harvey, D.S.O. B. 25 Jan. 1914; m. 25 Nov. 1949, Clare, d. of Sir Basil Mayhew, K.B.E., of Felthorpe Hall, Norwich. Educ. at Fettes Coll., Edinburgh, and Christ Church, Oxford, M.A., President of Union 1936. A Director of W.S. Crawford Limited, Advertising Agents 1946-56. Served in A.A. Command, Brigade Maj. and G.S.O.2. and in N.W. Europe B.M. R.A. (A.A.) 1939-45; Staff Coll., Camberley, p.s.c. Lieut.-Col. commanding 566 LAA/SL Regiment R.A. (City of London Rifles), T.A. 1947-50; member of Kensington Borough Council 1947-51, and of London County Council 1949-52; Gov. of Birkbeck Coll. 1949-52. Member of County of London T.A. and Air Force Association 1949-52; Chairman Press Relations Committee, International Advertising Con-

ference 1951. Member Standing Committee of the National Society 1950-55; of Institute of Practitioners in Advertising and of Institute of Public Relations. Author. Parliamentary Secretary Ministry of Supply Nov. 1956-Jan. 1957. Joint Parliamentary Under-Secretary of State, Foreign Office Jan. 1957-Nov. 1958. A Conservative. Unsuccessfully contested Spelthorne in 1945. Elected for Harrow E. in Feb. 1950 and sat until Nov. 1958 when he resigned. Director of Colman, Prentis and Varley Ltd. 1962-63. Advertising Director, Yardley of London Ltd. 1964-66. Author of *Talk of Propaganda, The Technique of Persuasion, Arms and Tomorrow* and *To Fall like Lucifer*.*
[1958]

HARVEY, John Edgar. Colway, 87 Woodford Road, South Woodford, London. Carlton. S. of John Watt Harvey, Esq. B. 24 Apr. 1920; m. 17 Nov. 1945, Mary Joyce, d. of A.E. Lane, Esq., of Lyme Regis, Dorset. Educ. at Xaverian Coll., Bruges, and Lyme Regis Grammar School. Radio Officer, Merchant Navy 1939-45; Export representative 1946-53; Gen. Managing 1953-55, and Director from 1955 of firm of Lubricating Oil Distributors; Chairman of Woodford Conservative Association 1954-56; member National Executive Committee Conservative Party 1950-55. A Conservative. Unsuccessfully contested St. Pancras N. in 1950 and Walthamstow E. in 1951. Elected for Walthamstow E. in 1955 and sat until 1966 when he was defeated. Member of Central Executive Committee of N.S.P.C.C. 1963-68. Verderer of Epping Forest from 1970. Dept.-Chairman of Burmah Castrol Europe Limited from 1970. Director of Burmah Oil Trading Limited from 1974.*
[1966]

HARVIE ANDERSON, Rt. Hon. Margaret Betty. Quarter by Denny, Stirlingshire. Durrington Farmhouse, Worthing, Sussex. D. of Col. T.A. Harvie Anderson, C.B., T.D., D.L., of Quarter and Shirgarton, B. 1915; m. 1960, Dr. J.F.P. Skrimshire, M.D., F.R.C.P., Consultant Physician. Educ. at St. Leonard's School, St. Andrews. Ch. Commander (Lieut.-Col.) A.T.S. 1939-45, serving with M.H.A.A. Regiment R.A. Member Stirling County Council 1945-59 and Chairman Moderate Group 1952-59.

Chairman Scottish Association of Mixed and Girl's Clubs 1950-53. President Scottish Young Conservatives 1955-58. Member S. of S. for Scotland's Advisory Committee on Education 1956-59. Member of Royal Commission on Local Government (Scotland) 1966-69. Member of Historic Buildings Council for Scotland from 1966. Member of Executive Committee 1922 Committee 1962-70 and 1974-79. Secretary Conservative Arts and Public Buildings Committee 1965-69. Member Chairman's Panel 1966-70. Dept. Chairman of Ways and Means 1970-73, First Dept. Chairman 1971-73. O.B.E. 1955, T.D. 1959, Dept.-Lieut. for Stirlingshire 1973, PC. 1974. A Conservative. Unsuccessfully contested W. Stirlingshire in 1950 and 1951, and the Sowerby division of Yorkshire in 1955. Elected for E. Renfrewshire in 1959 and sat until she retired in Apr. 1979. Created Baroness Skrimshire of Quarter (Life Peerage) June 1979. Died 7 Nov. 1979. [1979]

HARVIE-WATT, Sir George Steven, Bart., Q.C. Earlsneuk, Elie, Fife. Carlton, Pratt's, and New (Edinburgh). S. of James McDougal Watt, Esq., of Armadale. B. 23 Aug. 1903; m. 4 June 1932, Bettie, d. of Paymaster-Capt. Archibald Taylor, R.N., O.B.E. Educ. at George Watson's Coll., Edinburgh, and at the Universities of Glasgow and Edinburgh. Barrister-at-Law, Inner Temple 1930; K.C. 1945. Dept.-Lieut. for Surrey 1942; J.P. for London 1944-56; Commanded 31st Battalion R.E. 1939-41; Commanded 6th A.A. Brigade 1941, and 63rd A.A. Brigade 1948-50; Honorary Col. 566 A.A.A. Regiment R.A.; T.A. from 1950; member of Queen's Bodyguard for Scotland (Royal Company of Archers); Aide-de-Camp to H.M. the King 1948-52 and to H.M. the Queen 1952-58; Parliamentary Private Secretary to Capt. Rt. Hon. D.E. Wallace, Parliamentary Secretary to the Board of Trade May 1937; Assistant Government Whip May 1938; Parliamentary Private Secretary to the Rt. Hon. Winston Spencer Churchill, Prime Minister July 1941-July 1945; Bart. 1945. A Conservative. Sat for the Keighley division from Oct. 1931-Nov. 1935 when he was defeated. Elected for Richmond (Surrey) in Feb. 1937 and sat until he retired in 1959. Member of Kensington

Borough Council 1934-45. T.D. 1942. Chief Executive of Consolidated Gold Fields Limited 1954-69, Chairman 1960-69, President from 1973. Dept.-Lieut. for Greater London 1966-78. Chairman of Monotype Corporation Limited. President of Printers Pension Corporation 1956-57.* [1959]

HASELDINE, Charles Norman. 115 Psalter Lane, Sheffield. S. of Charles Edward Haseldine, Esq., Insurance Agent. B. 25 Mar. 1922; m. 26 Sept. 1946, Georgette Bernard, d. of Monsieur Louis Bernard, of Marseille. Educ. at Nether Edge Grammar School, Sheffield. Sectional Secretary, British Federation of Young Co-operators 1940. Army service 1942-46; Sergeant R.A.O.C. Education Officer, Doncaster Co-operative Society 1947-57; member Doncaster Rural District Council 1952-58. Public Relations Officer, Sheffield and Ecclesall Co-operative Society 1957-66. Parliamentary Private Secretary to Rt. Hon. Roy Mason, Minister of Power July 1968-Oct. 1969 and President of Board of Trade Oct. 1969-June 1970. Member Select Committee Nationalised Industries Nov. 1967. A Labour and Co-operative Member. Unsuccessfully contested Bradford W. in 1964. Elected for Bradford W. in Mar. 1966 and sat until 1970 when he was defeated. Joint Managing Director of Linden Marketing and Communications Limited.* [1970]

HASELHURST, Alan Gordon Barraclough. House of Commons, London. M.C.C. S. of John Haselhurst, Esq. B. 23 June 1937; m. 16 Apr. 1977, Angela Margaret Bailey, d. of Mr. and Mrs. John Bailey. Educ. at King Edward VI School, Birmingham, Cheltenham Coll., and Oriel Coll., Oxford. President Oxford University Conservative Association 1958; Secretary, Treasurer, Librarian, Oxford Union Society 1959-60. National Chairman Young Conservative Movement 1966-68. Chairman Commonwealth Youth Exchange Council 1978. Parliamentary Private Secretary to Richard Sharples and Mark Carlisle, Ministers of State at Home Office 1970-74. Parliamentary Private Secretary to Rt. Hon. Mark Carlisle, Secretary of State for Education and Science from 1979. A Conservative. Adopted for

Middleton and Prestwich in Nov. 1967. Member for Middleton and Prestwich from June 1970 to Feb. 1974, when he was defeated. Elected for the Saffron Walden division of Essex in July 1977.* [1979]

HASTINGS, Somerville. Brackenfell, Kingwood, Henley-on-Thames. S. of Rev. H.G. Hastings, of Warminster. B. 1878; m. 1911, Bessie, d. of W.C. Tuke, Esq. (she died 1958). Educ. at Wycliffe Coll., Stonehouse, and Middlesex Hospital. Served with R.A.M.C. 1914-18, Capt. Consulting Aural Surgeon to the Middlesex Hospital. M.B., M.S., F.R.C.S. President of Socialist Medical Association; late member N.E. Metropolitan Regional Hospital Board. Member of London County Council from 1932-46, Chairman 1944-45. Alderman 1946-64. A Labour Member. Unsuccessfully contested Epsom in 1922. Sat for Reading from 1923-24, when he was defeated, and from 1929-31, when he was again defeated. Unsuccessfully contested Reading in 1935. Sat for Barking from 1945 until he retired in 1959. Parliamentary Private Secretary to Rt. Hon. C.P. Trevelyan, President of Board of Education 1924. President of Otological Section of Royal Society of Medicine. Author of works on medicine and botany. Died 7 July 1967. [1959]

HASTINGS, Stephen Lewis Edmonstone, M.C. 12a Ennismore Gardens, London. Buck's, and White's. S. of Lewis Aloysius Macdonald Hastings, Esq., M.C. B. 4 May 1921; m. 1st, 1948, Harriet Mary Elizabeth Tomlin (marriage dissolved in 1971), (1 s. 1 d.); 2ndly, 1975, The Hon. Lady Naylor-Leyland. Educ. at Eton, and Royal Military Coll. Gazetted Ensign Scots Guards 1939; served 2nd Battalion Western Desert 1941-43; S.A.S. Regiment 1943. M.C. 1944. Joined the Foreign Office in 1948. British Legation, Helsinki; British Embassy, Paris 1952-58. First Secretary Pol. Office M.E. Forces 1959-60. Chairman European Supersonic Aviation Limited. Director Oxley Development Limited and Dust Suppression Limited. Author of *The Murder of TSR2*. A Conservative. Elected for the mid division of Bedfordshire in Nov. 1960.* [1979]

HATTERSLEY, Rt. Hon. Roy Sydney George. House of Commons, London. 14 Gayfere Street, London. S. of Frederick Roy Hattersley, Esq. B. 28 Dec. 1932; m. 1956, Molly, d. of Michael Loughran, Esq. Educ. at Sheffield City Grammar School, and University of Hull, B.Sc. (Econ.). Joined the Labour Party in 1949. Member of A.S.T.M.S. Member Sheffield City Council 1957-65. Parliamentary Private Secretary to Rt. Hon. Margaret Herbison, Minister of Pensions Oct. 1964-Jan. 1967. Parliamentary Secretary Ministry of Labour Jan. 1967-Apr. 1968. Parliamentary Under-Secretary of State Department Employment and Productivity Apr. 1968-July 1969. Minister of Defence for Administration July 1969-June 1970. Opposition spokesman on Foreign Affairs 1970-72, on Defence 1972, on Education and Science 1972-74. Minister of State, Foreign and Commonwealth Affairs Mar. 1974-Sept. 1976. Secretary of State for Prices and Consumer Protection Sept. 1976-May 1979. Member of Parliamentary Committee of P.L.P. from 1979. Opposition spokesman on the Environment from 1979. PC. 1975. Voted in favour of entry to E.E.C. on 28 Oct. 1971. A Labour Member. Unsuccessfully contested Sutton Coldfield in 1959. Elected for the Sparkbrook division of Birmingham in Oct. 1964. Director of Campaign for a European Political Community 1966-67.* [1979]

HATTON Frank, J.P. 50 Merston Drive, East Didsbury, Manchester. S. of James Hatton, Esq. B. 25 Sept. 1921; m. 18 Aug. 1949, Olive, d. of Richard Kelly, Esq. Educ. at Manchester Central High School for Boys. Railway Clerk 1939-51. Personnel Officer, C.E.G.B. 1951-73. Member Manchester City Council 1954-74; Alderman 1971-74; Chairman of Education Committee 1962-67 and 1971-74. Member of Manchester District Council 1973-74. Chairman various education committees and of Manchester Polytechnic. Member of council of University of Manchester; Manchester Institute of Science and Technology and Open University. Gov. of several schools. J.P. 1965. Parliamentary Private Secretary to C.R. Morris, Minister of State, Civil Service Department 1977-78. A Labour Member. Unsuccessfully contested the Moss Side division of Manchester in 1970.

Sat for the Exchange division of Manchester from June 1973-Feb. 1974, and for the Moss Side division of Manchester from Feb. 1974 until his death on 16 May 1978.   [1978]

HAUGHTON, Maj. Samuel Gillmor. Red Cottage, Cullybackey, Co. Antrim. Broughan, Ballycastle, Co. Antrim. Junior Carlton. S. of T.W. Haughton, Esq. B. 1 Dec. 1889; m. 11 Sept. 1912, Dorothy, d. of M. Wilson, Esq., of Craigavad, Co. Down. Educ. at St. Edward's, Oxford. Managing Director of Frazer and Haughton Limited. Director of W.S. Moore Limited, Linen Merchants. Partner Circulating and Statistical Service, Branches in Dublin and Belfast; Vice-President Belfast Chamber of Commerce 1948. Served in Middle East with 26th Battery R.A. 1939-44; Honorary Col. 248 L.L.A. Regiment, R.A. (T.A.) from 1947. Chief A.A. Adviser to Egyptian Army 1942. Dept.-Lieut. Co. Antrim. An Ulster Unionist Member. Elected for Antrim in July 1945 and sat until he retired in 1950. High Sheriff of Co. Antrim 1955. Died 19 May 1959.   [1950]

HAVERS, Rt. Hon. Sir (Robert) Michael Oldfield, Q.C. White Shutters, Ousden, Newmarket. 6b Woodhayes Road, London. Garrick, R.A.C., Royal Wimbledon G.C., and Hurlingham. S. of Sir Cecil Havers, Retired High Court Judge. B. 10 Mar. 1923; m. 3 Sept. 1949, Carol, d. of Stuart Lay, Esq., (2 s.). Educ. at Westminster, and Corpus Christi Coll., Cambridge. R.N.V.R. 1941-46. Barrister, Inner Temple 1948. Dept. Chairman West Suffolk quarter sessions 1961-65, Chairman 1965-71. Recorder of Dover 1962-68; Recorder of Norwich 1968-71. Chancellor diocese of St. Edmundsbury and Ipswich from 1965-73; Q.C. 1964; Chancellor of diocese of Ely 1969-73. Knighted Nov. 1972. Solicitor General Nov. 1972-Mar. 1974. Legal Adviser to Shadow Cabinet and Front Bench spokesman on Legal Matters 1974-79. Privy Councillor, Jubilee Honours List June 1977. A Conservative. Member for Wimbledon from June 1970 to Feb. 1974 and for the Wimbledon division of Merton from Feb. 1974. Master of the Bench, Inner Temple, 1971. Attorney General from May 1979.*
        [1979]

HAWKINS, Paul Lancelot, T.D., F.R.I.C.S. Stables, Downham Market, Norfolk. S. of Lance Hawkins, Esq., J.P., F.R.I.C.S. B. 1912; m. May 1937, Joan, d. of Ralph Snow, Esq., (2 s. 1 d.). Educ. at Cheltenham Coll. Joined the Royal Norfolk Regiment (T.A.) in 1933; served in World War II (Prisoner-of-War Germany). A Chartered Surveyor and Auctioneer and Valuer in agricultural practice. With family firm 1930; partner 1946. On Norfolk County Council 1949-70, Alderman 1968-70. Vice-Chairman of the S.W. Norfolk Conservative Association 1948-50. Chairman (seven years in all). Assistant Whip July 1970-Jan. 1971. Opposition Whip Mar.-Oct. 1974. Lord Commissioner of the Treasury Jan. 1971-Dec. 1973. Vice-Chamberlain of the Household Dec. 1973-Mar. 1974. Wealth Tax Select Committee 1975. Member Delegation to Council of Europe and Western European Union, 1976. A Conservative. Elected for Norfolk S.W. in Oct. 1964.*   [1979]

HAWORTH, James. 34 Sydney Road, Enfield. S. of Mark Haworth, Esq., of Accrington. B. 1896; m. 1st, 1919, Cassie, d. of Richard Thomas, Esq. (she died June 1946); 2ndly, 1973, Louisa Belcher. A Railway Clerk; National Treasurer Railway Clerk's Association. Member of Bootle Borough Council 1924-30, Alderman 1930-41. J.P. 1928-41. A Labour Member. Unsuccessfully contested the W. Derby division of Liverpool in 1935. Elected for the Walton division of Liverpool in July 1945 and sat until 1950, when he was defeated. Unsuccessfully contested the Chelmsford division of Essex in 1951 and Bolton W. in 1955. President of Transport Salaried Staffs Association 1953-56. Member of National Executive Committee of Labour Party 1953-55. Honorary Treasurer of National Federation of Professional Workers 1949-56. Member of British Railways London Midland Region Board 1956-67. Died 16 Dec. 1976. [1950]

HAY, John Albert. Walport Limited, 14 Soho Square, London. S. of Alderman J.E. Hay, of Brighton. B. 24 Nov. 1919; m. 1st, 12 Sept. 1947, Beryl Joan, d. of Commander H.C. Found, R.N. (divorced 1973); 2ndly, 1974, Janet May, d. of A.C. Spruce, Esq.

Educ. at Brighton, Hove and Sussex Grammar School. Admitted a Solicitor May 1945. National Chairman Young Conservative and Unionist Organisation 1947-49. Served with R.N.V.R. 1940-44 (invalided out). Parliamentary Private Secretary to Rt. Hon. Peter Thorneycroft, President of Board of Trade Nov. 1951-Jan. 1956; Chairman Conservative Party Housing and Local Government Committee Jan. 1956-Jan. 1959; U.K. Delegate Council of Europe and Assembly, Western European Union 1957-59. Director of London Municipal Society 1956-59. Vice-President Urban District Councils Association 1957. Chairman British Section Council of European Municipalities 1971-76, President from 1977 . Member of Court of Reading University 1969. Joint Parliamentary Secretary Ministry of Transport and Civil Aviation Jan.-Oct. 1959. Parliamentary Secretary Ministry of Transport Oct. 1959-May 1963. Civil Lord of the Admiralty May 1963-Mar. 1964. Parliamentary Under-Secretary of State for Defence for the Royal Navy Apr.-Oct. 1964. A Conservative. Elected for the Henley division of Oxfordshire in Feb. 1950 and sat until he retired in Feb. 1974. Honorary Secretary, U.K. Council of European Movement 1965-66. Fellow of Royal Philharmonic Society. Managing Director of Walport Group from 1968.*
[1974]

HAYHOE, Bernard John ('Barney'). 20 Wool Road, London. S. of Frank S. Hayhoe, Esq., Retired Schoolmaster. B. 8 Aug. 1925; m. 1962, Ann Gascoigne, d. of Bernard W. Thornton, Esq. Educ. at State Schools, Croydon, and Borough Polytechnic. A Tool Room Apprentice 1941-44; A Roman Catholic. Technical and Engineering appointment in Ministry of Supply and Ministry of Aviation 1944-63. Associate Director Ariel Foundation 1963-65; Conservative Research Dept. Head of Research Section 1965-70. Honorary Secretary Conservative Parliamentary Employment Committee 1970-71, Vice-Chairman 1974. Joint Secretary Conservative Group for Europe 1970, Vice-Chairman 1973-76. An Opposition spokesman on Employment June 1974-May 1979. Parliamentary Private Secretary to Rt. Hon. James Prior Lord President and

Leader of the House of Commons 1972-74. Gov. of Birkbeck Coll. 1976. Under-Secretary of State for Defence for the Army from May 1979. A Conservative. Unsuccessfully contested Lewisham S. in 1964. Sat for Heston and Isleworth from 1970 to Feb. 1974. Elected for the Brentford and Isleworth division of Hounslow in Feb. 1974.* [1979]

HAYMAN, Frank Harold. 8 West Park, Redruth, Cornwall. S. of Frank Edward Hayman, Esq., of Truro. B. 12 Dec. 1894; m. 1920, Amelia Vaughan, d. of George Turner, Esq., of Newquay, Cornwall. Educ. at Fairmantle Street C.E. School, Truro, and Truro Technical School. District Education Officer, Redruth from 1920. Parliamentary Private Secretary to Hugh Gaitskell 1959-63. Delegate to I.P.U. Annual Conference to Berne 1952. C.P.A. Delegate to Jersey 1956. Member of Parliamentary Delegation to Western Germany 1955. Member of Court of Referees and of Standing Orders Committee for Private Bills, House of Commons. I.P.U. Delegate to Finland 1961. A Labour Member. Unsuccessfully contested the Camborne division of Cornwall in 1945. Elected for the Falmouth and Camborne division of Cornwall in Feb. 1950 and sat until his death on 4 Feb. 1966. [1966]

HAYMAN, Helene Valerie. House of Commons, London. D. of Maurice Joseph Middleweek, Esq. B. 26 Mar. 1949; m. 30 Aug. 1974, Martin Heathcote Hayman, Esq., s. of Ronald and Rosemary Hayman, (1 s.). Educ. at Wolverhampton Girls High School, and Newnham Coll., Cambridge. President of Cambridge Union 1969. Dept. Director, National Council for One-Parent Families 1974. A Labour Member. Unsuccessfully contested Wolverhampton S.W. in Feb. 1974. Elected for Welwyn and Hatfield in Oct. 1974 and sat until 1979, when she was defeated.* [1979]

HAZELL, Bertie, C.B.E. 42 Felbrook Avenue Beckfield Lane, Acomb, York. S. of John Hazell, Esq. B. 18 Apr. 1907; m. 15 Aug. 1936, Dora Anna, d. of Frederick and Anna Barham, of Wymondham, Norfolk, (1 d.). Educ. at various Elementary Schools in Norfolk. Trade Union Organiser, National

Union of Agricultural Workers. Joined the Labour Party in 1927. Member of N.U.A.W. from 1923. South Norfolk C.L.P. from 1927. Joined staff of N.U.A.W. in May 1937. Secretary and organiser of E. Norfolk Constituency Labour Party from 1933 to 1937. Labour agent to N.R. Tillett, Parliamentary candidate in E. Norfolk in the 1935 general election. In 1947 appointed by Sir Stafford Cripps, Chancellor of the Exchequer, to the East and West Ridings Regional Board for Industry. Appointed in 1954, Chairman of the Board to Oct. 1964. Appointed 1946 to E. Riding of Yorkshire Agricultural Executive Committee. Appointed member of Leeds Regional Hospital Board 1947; Vice-Chairman May 1967. Member Agricultural Wages Board 1946. Created M.B.E. in 1946 and C.B.E. in Jan. 1962. Magistrate in the City of York 1952. Elected President of the National Union of Agricultural Workers May 1966-78. A Labour Member. Unsuccessfully contested Barkston Ash in 1945 and 1950. Member for N. Norfolk from Oct. 1964. Re-elected Mar. 1966 and sat until 1970, when he was defeated. Member of Potato Marketing Board from 1970. Vice-Chairman of Agricultural, Horticultural and Forestry Training Board 1972-74. Chairman of N. Yorkshire Area Health Authority from 1974. Chairman of N. Yorkshire Special Programme Board of Manpower Services Commission from 1978.* [1970]

HEAD, Rt. Hon. Antony Henry, C.B.E., M.C. 17 Cowley Street, London. S. of Geoffrey Head, Esq. B. 1906; m. 1935, Lady Dorothea Louise Ashley-Cooper, d. of 9th Earl of Shaftesbury. Educ. at Eton, and Royal Military Coll., Sandhurst. Late Life Guards 1939-45. B.M. 20th Guards Brigade. Assistant Secretary War Cabinet Office Combined Operations. Representative Joint Planning Staff. Retired as Brigadier. Secretary of State for War Nov. 1951-Oct. 1956. PC. 1951. Minister of Defence Oct. 1956-Jan 1957. A Conservative. Elected for the Carshalton division of Surrey in July 1945 and sat until July 1960 when he was created Visct. Head, M.C. 1940, C.B.E. 1946, K.C.M.G. 1961, G.C.M.G. 1963. High Commissioner to Federation of Nigeria 1960-63. High Commissioner to Federation of

Malaysia 1963-66. Trustee of Thomson Foundation 1967-75. Chairman of Royal National Institute for the Blind 1968-75, President from 1975. Chairman of Wessex Region, National Trust 1970-76.* [1960]

HEADLAM, Lieut.-Col. Rt. Hon. Sir Cuthbert Morley, Bart., D.S.O., O.B.E., T.D. Holywell Hall, Furham, Durham. Brandon Colliery, Durham. Travellers'. S. of Francis John Headlam, Esq. B. 27 Apr. 1876; m. 22 Mar. 1904, Beatrice, C.B.E., d. of George Baden Crawley, Esq. Educ. at King's School, Canterbury, and Magdalen Coll., Oxford. Clerk in the House of Lords 1897-1924; Barrister-at-Law, Inner Temple 1906; Created Bart. 1935. Dept.-Lieut. and J.P. for Durham. Joined Bedfordshire Yeomanry 1910; served overseas 1914-18; Lieut.-Col. Gen. Staff 1918; Member of Durham County Council 1931-39; Chairman of National Union Conservative and Unionist Associations, Northern Area 1937-46, and of National Union of Conservative and Unionist Associations 1941. Parliamentary Secretary to the Admiralty Dec. 1926-June 1929, to Ministry of Pensions Nov. 1931-Sept. 1932, to Ministry of Transport Sept. 1932-July 1934. PC. 1945. A Conservative. Sat for the Barnard Castle division from 1924-29 when he was defeated and 1931-35 when he was again defeated. Unsuccessfully contested Gateshead in June 1931. Elected for Newcastle-on-Tyne N. in June 1940 and sat until he retired in 1951. D.S.O. 1918, O.B.E. 1919, T.D. 1926. Editor of *Army Quarterly* 1921-26. Died 27 Feb. 1964. [1951]

HEALD, Rt. Hon. Sir Lionel Frederick, Q.C. Queen Elizabeth Buildings, Temple, London. Chilworth Manor, Guildford. Garrick. S. of James Heald, Esq., of Parrs Wood, Didsbury. B. 7 Aug. 1897; m. 1st, 1923, Flavia, d. of Lieut.-Col. J.S. Forbes (divorced 1928, she died 1959); 2ndly, 1929, Daphne Constance, d. of Montague Price, Esq. Educ. at Charterhouse, and Christ Church, Oxford. Barrister-at-Law, Middle Temple 1923; K.C. 1937; Bencher 1946; Junior Counsel Board of Trade 1931-37; member of St. Pancras Borough Council 1934-37. Served as Lieut. R. Monmouthshire R.E. 1916-19; R.A.F.V.R. 1939-45, Air

Commodore. Attorney-Gen. Oct. 1951-Oct. 1954. Member of the Monckton Commission on future of Central Africa 1960. PC. 1954. A Conservative. Unsuccessfully contested S.W. St. Pancras in 1945. Elected for the Chertsey division of Surrey in Feb. 1950 and sat until he retired in 1970. Knighted 1951. J.P. for Surrey.*   [1970]

HEALEY, Rt. Hon. Denis Winston, C.H. House of Commons, London. S. of William Healey, Esq. B. 30 Aug. 1917; m. 21 Dec. 1945, Edna May Edmunds, of Coleford, Gloucestershire. Educ. at Bradford Grammar School, and Balliol Coll., Oxford. Secretary International Department Labour Party 1945-52. Served in Army 1940-45, Maj., mentioned in despatches 1944. M.B.E. 1945. Secretary of State for Defence Oct. 1964-June 1970. Foreign Affairs spokesman in Labour Shadow Cabinet June 1970-Apr. 1972. PC. 1964. Economics spokesman Apr. 1972-Mar. 1974. Chancellor of the Exchequer Mar. 1974-May 1979. Delegate to W.E.U. and Council of Europe 1953-55. Opposition spokesman on Foreign Affairs 1959-61, on Colonial and Commonwealth Affairs 1961-63 and on Defence 1963-64. Member of Parliamentary Committee of P.L.P. 1959-64, 1970-74 and from 1979. Member of National Executive of Labour Party 1970-75. Unsuccessful candidate for Leadership of Labour Party 1976. Opposition spokesman on Treasury and Economic Affairs from 1979. A Labour Member. Unsuccessfully contested Pudsey and Otley in 1945. Sat for S.E. Leeds from Feb. 1952-May 1955 and for E. Leeds from May 1955. C.H. 1979. Hon. Fellow of Balliol Coll., Oxford 1979.*   [1979]

HEALY, Cahir. Enniskillen, Ireland. S. of Patrick Healy, Esq., of Mountcharles, Co. Donegal. B. 1877 in Co. Donegal; m. 1897, Catherine (she died 1940). A retired Insurance Official. Member of Fermanagh Health and Welfare Committee, Regional Education Committee, and of Fermanagh County Hospital and Erne Hospital. Member of Northern Ireland Parliament for Fermanagh and Tyrone 1925-29 and for Fermanagh S. 1929-65. An Irish Nationalist Member. Sat for Fermanagh and Tyrone from 1922 until he retired in 1924, from Mar. 1931 until he retired in 1935, and for Fermanagh and S. Tyrone from 1950 until he retired in 1955. Interned from 1922 to 1924 and from 1941 to 1942. Died 8 Feb. 1970.   [1954]

HEATH, Rt. Hon. Edward Richard George, M.B.E. House of Commons, London. S. of William George Heath, Esq. B. 9 July 1916; Unmarried. Educ. at Chatham House Grammar School and Balliol Coll., Oxford. President of the Oxford University Conservative Association 1937, President of Union 1939. Chairman Federation of University Conservative Association 1938. Served with R.A. overseas 1940-46. Commanded 2nd Regiment H.A.C. 1947-51. Master Gunner within the Tower of London 1951-54. Opposition Whip Feb. 1951. A Lord Commissioner of the Treasury Nov. 1951-Dec. 1955 Joint Dept. Government Chief Whip May 1952-July 1953. Dept. Government Chief Whip July 1953-Dec. 1955. Parliamentary Secretary to the Treasury and Government Chief Whip Dec. 1955-Oct. 1959. Minister of Labour Oct. 1959-July 1960. Lord Privy Seal July 1960-Oct. 1963. Secretary of State for Industry, Trade and Regional Development, and President of the Board of Trade Oct. 1963-Oct. 1964. Elected Leader of the Conservative and Unionist Party and Leader of the Opposition July 1965, failed to secure re-election Feb. 1975. PC. 1955. Opposition spokesman on Economics Affairs 1964-65 and on Treasury and Economic Affairs Feb.-July 1965. Leader of Opposition July 1965-June 1970 and Mar. 1974-Feb. 1975. Prime Minister, First Lord of the Treasury and Minister for the Civil Service June 1970-Mar. 1974. A Conservative. Sat for Bexley from 1950 to Feb. 1974. Elected for the Sidcup division of Bexley in Feb. 1974. M.B.E. 1946. Member of Council of Royal Coll. of Music 1961-70. Visiting Fellow, Nuffield Coll., Oxford 1962-70, Honorary Fellow 1970.*   [1979]

HEATHCOAT-AMORY, Rt. Hon. Derick. Chevithorne Barton, Tiverton. 150 Marsham Court, London. Brooke's S. of Sir Ian Heathcoat-Amory, 2nd Bart. B. 26 Dec. 1899. Unmarried. Educ. at Eton, and Christ Church, Oxford. Lieut.-Col. R.A. (T.A.), retired, T.D. Minister of Pensions Nov. 1951-Sept. 1953. Minister of State, Board of Trade

Sept. 1953-July 1954; Minister of Agriculture and Fisheries July-Oct. 1954; Minister of Agriculture and Fisheries and Minister of Food Oct. 1954-Apr. 1955; and Minister of Agriculture, Fisheries and Food Apr. 1955-Jan. 1958. Chancellor of the Exchequer Jan. 1958-July 1960. Member of the Cabinet 1954-60. PC. 1953. A Conservative. Elected for the Tiverton division of Devon in July 1945 and sat until July 1960 when he was created Visct. Amory. Dept.-Lieut. for Devon 1962. High Steward of South Molton 1960-74. Member of Devon County Council 1932-51. Director of Lloyds Bank 1948-51 and 1964-70. Chairman of Medical Research Council 1960-61 and 1965-69. High Commissioner in Canada 1961-63. G.C.M.G. 1961. Chairman of Voluntary Service Overseas 1964-75. K.G. 1968. Succeeded his brother as Bart. 1972. Chancellor of Exeter University from 1972. Gov. of Hudson's Bay Company 1965-70. Chairman of John Heathcoat and Company 1966-72. Director of I.C.I. 1964-70. President of County Councils Association 1961-74, of Association of County Councils 1974-79* [1960]

HEFFER, Eric Samuel. House of Commons, London. S. of William George Heffer, Esq. B. 12 Jan. 1922; m. Dec. 1945, Doris Murray, d. of Herbert and Janetta Murray, of Liverpool. Educ. at Elementary School. A Carpenter and Joiner. Joined the Labour Party in 1939. Served in R.A.F. 1942-45. Member of Amalgamated Society of Woodworkers from 1938, Chairman of Local Branch. President of Liverpool Trades Council and Labour Party. City Councillor 1960-66. Member of North West Regional Council of the Labour Party and of the Lancashire Federation of Trades Councils. Co-author of books published in America, *The Agreeable Autocrats*, and Author of *The Class Struggle in Parliament*. Regular Contributor to foreign and British Socialist journals also to various other foreign and British Newspapers. Visited U.S. on English Speaking Scholarship 1959. Member of Council of Europe and Western European Union 1965-68. Member of Political and Social Committees. Member Select Committee of Procedure. The Select Committee of Race Relations and The Select Committee of the House of Commons

Standing Orders. Opposition spokesman on Industrial Relations 1970-73. Minister of State, Department of Industry Mar. 1974-Apr. 1975, when he resigned. Member of National Executive of Labour Party from 1975. A Labour Member. Elected for the Walton division of Liverpool in Oct. 1964.* [1979]

HENDERSON, Rt. Hon. Arthur, Q.C. 710 Hood House, Dolphin Square, London. S. of the Rt. Hon. Arthur Henderson, MP. B. 27 Aug. 1893; m. 1958, Mary Elizabeth Gliksten, of Miami, widow of Harold Gliksten, Esq. Educ. at Central School, Darlington, Queen's Coll., Taunton, and Trinity Hall, Cambridge, M.A., LL.B. Parliamentary Private Secretary to Rt. Hon. Sir William Jowitt when Attorney-Gen. 1929-31. Served 1914-18 in France and Belgium, and in World War II; and Maj. on Gen. Staff 1939-Mar. 1942; Joint Parliamentary Under-Secretary of State for War Mar. 1942-Feb. 1943. Financial Secretary to the War Office Feb. 1943-May 1945; Parliamentary Under-Secretary of State for India and Burma Aug. 1945-Aug. 1947. Minister of State Commonwealth Relations Aug.-Oct. 1947. Secretary of State for Air Oct. 1947-Oct. 1951. PC. 1947. Dept.-Lieut. for the County of London. Vice-President Council of Europe Assembly 1961-62. Vice-President Parliamentary Group for World Government; Chairman U.N. Parliamentary Group. A Labour Member. Unsuccessfully contested Portsmouth N. in 1922. Sat for Cardiff S. from 1923-24 when he was defeated, and from 1929-31 when he was again defeated, and for Kingswinford from 1935-Feb. 1950. Elected for Rowley Regis and Tipton in Feb. 1950 and sat until he retired in 1966. Secretary of University Labour Federation 1921-24. Barrister-at-Law, Middle Temple 1921. K.C. 1939. Created Baron Rowley (Life Peerage) 1966. Died 28 Aug. 1968. [1966]

HENDERSON, Douglas. House of Commons, London. B. July 1935. Educ. at Royal High School, and Edinburgh University. Senior Vice-Chairman Scottish National Party until 1972 and from 1979. S.N.P. Whip in House of Commons 1974-76. A Scottish National Party Member. Elected for Aberdeenshire E. in Feb. 1974 and sat until 1979, when he was defeated.*   [1979]

HENDERSON, (James Stewart), Barry. Millersneuk Cottage, Lenzie, Kirkintilloch, Glasgow. St. Stephen's. S. of James Henderson, Esq., C.B.E. B. 29 Apr. 1936; m. 12 Aug. 1961, Janet, d. of Col. D.K. Todd, D.S.O., C.D. (2 s.). Educ. at Lathallan School, and Stowe School. National Service 1954-56. Active Young Conservative. Business career in computer industry 1956-66 and 1970-74. Information Officer at Scottish Conservative Central Office 1966-70. A Conservative. Unsuccessfully contested Edinburgh E. in 1966 and Dunbartonshire E. in 1970. Elected for Dunbartonshire E. in Feb. 1974 and sat until Oct. 1974 when he was defeated. Elected for Fife E. in May 1979. Management Consultant.*   [1974 2nd ed.]

HENDERSON, Sir John. Dundrennan, 658 Clarkston Road, Netherlee, Glasgow. S. of John Henderson, Esq., of Glasgow. B. 12 July 1888; m. 19 Dec. 1918, Nessie, d. of George Brander, Esq., of Crosshill, Glasgow. Educ. at Martyrs School, Glasgow. Chairman of J. Henderson Limited, Produce Importers. Member of Glasgow Corporation 1926-46. J.P. for Police Judge, Glasgow; Master of Works, Glasgow; Chairman Scottish Committee Fact and Faith Films Society; Chairman Houses of Parliament Christian Fellowship; Dept.-Lieut. for the Co. and City of Glasgow. A Conservative. Elected for the Cathcart division of Glasgow in Feb. 1946 and sat until he retired in 1964, after his local association had declined to readopt him as their candidate. Knighted June 1964. Died 1975.   [1964]

HENDERSON, Joseph. Rowanby, Eskdale Avenue, Morton Park, Carlisle. B. 1884; m. 1908, Janet Glendenning, d. of James Byers, Esq., of Dumfriesshire. Mayor of Carlisle 1927-28, Alderman until 1931. Served on Executive Committee of N.U.R., President 1933-36; a Lord Commissioner of the Treasury Aug. 1945-Jan. 1950. Member of National Executive Committee of Labour Party 1935-40. Labour Whip 1943-50. A Labour Member. Unsuccessfully contested the Lonsdale division of Lancashire in 1929. Sat for the Ardwick division of Manchester from June to Oct. 1931, when he was defeated, and from 1935 until Jan. 1950, when he was created Baron Henderson of Ardwick. Died 26 Feb. 1950.   [1950]

HENDERSON-STEWART, Sir James Henderson, Bart. 10 Edwardes Square, London. Shielhill House, Forfar, Angus. National Liberal, R. & A., St. Andrews, and New Club, Edinburgh. S. of Matthew Deas Stewart, Esq., of Crieff. B. 6 Dec. 1897; m. 25 July 1940, Anna Margaret, d. of Sir Bernard Greenwell, Bart., of Marden Park, Godstone. Educ. at Morrison's Academy, and University of Edinburgh, M.A. (Hons. Econ.), B. Com. Capt. R.A. (T.A.), retired. Served with B.E.F. 1917-19; re-employed R.A. 1940-41. Chairman of Liberal National Parliamentary Party 1945-46 and 1959-61; Vice-President Trustee Savings Banks Association; member of Management Committee of Shipwrecked Fishermen and Mariners' Royal Benevolent Society. Joint Parliamentary Under-Secretary of State for Scotland Feb. 1952-Jan. 1957. Assumed the surname of Henderson-Stewart in lieu of Stewart in 1957. Created Bart. 1957. A Conservative and Liberal Unionist Member. Unsuccessfully contested, as a Liberal, E. Leicester in 1923, Derby in 1924 and Dundee in 1929. Elected for E. Fife in Feb. 1933 and sat until his death on 3 Sept. 1961.   [1961]

HENDRY, Alexander Forbes, O.B.E., M.C., T.D., D.L. Denny, Stirlingshire. Headinch House, Dinnet, Aberdeenshire. S. of Alexander Hendry. Esq., Solicitor. B. Oct. 1908; m. 12 Sept. 1938, Margaret, d. of George Whitehead, Esq. Educ. at Stirling High School, and Glasgow University. Solicitor 1932. Dean of the Faculty of Solicitors and Procurators of Stirling 1963. Town Clerk of Denny and Dunipace 1934-59. Served with 7th Argyll and Sutherland Highlanders (T.A.) from 1934-56. Lieut.-Col. 1953. Dept.-Lieut. for Stirlingshire 1965. Executive Committee British Group, Inter-Parliamentary Union 1963. Chairman Anglo-Tunisian Parliamentary Group 1963. A Unionist Member. Unsuccessfully contested Lanarkshire N. in 1955. Elected for Aberdeenshire W. in 1959 and sat until 1966, when he was defeated. M.C. 1940; T.D. 1947; O.B.E. 1957. President of Scottish Conservative and Unionist Association 1974-75. Chairman and Managing Director of Cannerton Brick Company Limited. Provost of Denny and Dunipace 1971-74. J.P. for Stirlingshire 1971. Honorary Sheriff of Tayside, Central and Fife 1976.* [1966]

HENIG, Stanley. 29 Whinfell Drive, Lancaster, Lancashire. S. of Sir Mark Henig. B. 7 July 1939; m. 27 Mar. 1966, Ruth, d. of Kurt Munzer, Esq., of Leicester. Educ. at Wyggeston Grammar School, Leicester, and Corpus Christi Coll., Oxford. Teaching Assistant in Department of Political Science, University of Minnesota, U.S.A. 1961-62. Research Student at Nuffield Coll., Oxford 1962-64. Lecturer in Department of Politics at Lancaster University 1964-66. M.A. Oxford. Editor *European Political Parties* and Author of *External Relations of the European Community.* A Labour Member. Elected for Lancaster in Mar. 1966 and sat until 1970, when he was defeated. Lecturer in Politics, Warwick University 1970-71. Lecturer, Civil Service Coll. 1972-75. Head of Division of Political Science, Preston Polytechnic from 1976. Gov. of British Institute of Recorded Sound from 1975. Assistant Editor of *Journal of Common Market Studies* 1964-72, Editor 1973-76.* [1970]

HERBERT, Sir Alan Patrick. 12 Hammersmith Terrace, London. Pratt's, Savage, and Beefsteak. S. of P.H. Herbert, Esq., India Office. B. 24 Sept. 1890; m. 1914, Gwendolen, d. of Harry Quilter, Esq. Educ. at Winchester, and New Coll., Oxford. Author and Barrister-at-Law, Inner Temple. Served with R.N.D. Gallipoli and France 1914-17, and with R.E.S. and R.N.A.P. (Thames Patrol) Sept. 1939-45. A Thames Conservator 1940. Trustee of National Maritime Museum 1947-53. Knight Bach. 1945. An Independent Member. Elected for Oxford University in 1935 and sat until he retired in 1950. Private Secretary to Sir Leslie Scott. MP. in 1922. Companion of Honour 1970. Honorary LL.D. Queen's University, Kingston, Ontario 1957; Honorary D.C.L. Oxford 1958. President of Society of Authors and Inland Waterways Association. Chairman of British Copyright Council. Journalist, Novelist and Writer of musical revues. Contributor to *Punch* from 1910. Died 11 Nov. 1971. [1950]

HERBISON, Rt. Hon. Margaret McCrorie. 18 Tamar House, Kennington, London. 61 Shotts Kirk Road, Shotts, Lanarkshire. D. of John Herbison, Esq., of Shotts. B. 12 Mar. 1907. Educ. at Bellshill Academy, and University of Glasgow. A Teacher in Glasgow Secondary School. Tutor for National Council Labour Colls. Member National Executive Committee Labour Party from 1948-60 and 1961-68; Chairman Labour Party 1956-57; member Women's Consultative Committee of Ministry of Labour. Joint Parliamentary Under-Secretary of State Scottish Office Mar. 1950-Oct. 1951. Minister of Pensions and National Insurance Oct. 1964-Aug. 1966. Minister of Social Security Aug. 1966-July 1967. Opposition spokesman on Scotland until 1956, on Education 1956-59, on Pensions 1958-59 and 1962-64 and on Scotland again 1959-62. PC. 1964. A Labour Member. Elected for Lanarkshire N. in July 1945 and sat until she retired in 1970. Chairman of Select Committee on Overseas Aid 1969-70. Lord High Commissioner of the Church of Scotland 1970. Member of Royal Commission on Standards of Conduct in Public Life from 1974. Honorary LL.D. University of Glasgow 1970.* [1970]

HESELTINE, Rt. Hon. Michael Ray Dibdin. 39 Connaught Square, London. S. of Col. R.D. Heseltine, of Swansea. B. Mar. 1933; m. 1962, Anne Williams, (1 s. 2 d.). Educ. at Shrewsbury School, and Pembroke Coll., Oxford, (President of the Union). Opposition spokesman on Transport 1969-70. Chairman Haymarket Press (Magazine Publishers) 1964-70 and 1974-79. Parliamentary Secretary Ministry of Transport June 1970-Oct. 1970. Parliamentary Under-Secretary of State to Minister for Local Government and Development, Department of the Environment Oct. 1970-Apr. 1972. Minister for Aerospace Apr.-Nov. 1972, Minister for Aerospace and Shipping, Department of Trade and Industry Nov. 1972-Mar. 1974. Opposition spokesman on Trade Mar.-June

1974, on Trade and Industry June 1974-Feb. 1975, on Industry Feb. 1975-Nov. 1976 and on the Environment Nov. 1976-May 1979. Member of Shadow Cabinet June 1974-May 1979. Secretary of State for the Environment from May 1979. PC. 1979. A Conservative. Unsuccessfully contested the Gower in 1959 and Coventry N. in 1964. Sat for Tavistock from 1966-Feb. 1974. Elected for Henley in Feb. 1974.* [1979]

HESKETH, Roger Fleetwood, T.D., D.L. Meols Hall, Southport, Lancashire. H4 Albany, Piccadilly, London. Travellers', Carlton, and Pratt's. S. of C.H. Fleetwood-Hesketh, Esq., Dept.-Lieut. Assumed the surname of Hesketh in lieu of Fleetwood-Hesketh in 1956. B. 28 July 1902; m. 23 Aug. 1952, Lady Mary Lumley, d. of 11th Earl of Scarbrough, K.G. Educ. at Eton, and Christ Church, Oxford, B.A. 1928; called to the bar, Inner Temple 1928; High Sheriff Lancashire 1947; Mayor of Southport 1950; Councillor Southport County Borough 1938-53; J.P. for the County of Lancashire and County Borough of Southport; Dept.-Lieut. for Lancashire 1950, Vice-Lieut. 1972-77. Served Duke of Lancaster's Own Yeomanry 1922-39 and in Second World War (despatches); Lieut.-Col. 1944; Honorary Col. Duke of Lancaster's Own Yeomanry 1956; T.D. 1942, Bronze Star Medal (U.S.A.). A Conservative. Elected for Southport in Feb. 1952 and sat until he retired in 1959. Chairman of Lancashire Agricultural Executive Committee 1965-72. O.B.E. 1970.* [1959]

HEWITSON, Capt. Mark. House of Commons, London. B. 15 Dec. 1897; m. 1927, Gwynneth, d. of James Wicks, Esq., of Sunningwell, Berkshire. Educ. at Consett Council School, and Ruskin Coll., Oxford. Trade Union Official 1927. Served with Northumberland Fusiliers West Yorkshire Regiment 1916-20 and Pioneer Corps 1940-42. Member of Durham County Council 1930-40; President Public and Civil Service International 1937-40; President General Factory Workers International 1945-50. A Labour Member. Sat for Kingston-upon-Hull Central from July 1945 to May 1955 and for Kingston-upon-Hull W. from May 1955 until he retired in 1964. Member of National

Executive Committee of Labour Party 1939-40 and 1947-53. National Industrial Officer of General and Municipal Workers Union to 1964. Died 27 Feb. 1973. [1964]

HICKS, (Ernest) George, C.B.E. Bransby, St. Leonard's Road, Thames Ditton. Parliamentary Labour, and National Trades Union. S. of William Hicks, Esq., Builder, of Vernham Dean, Hampshire. B. 13 May 1879; m. 1st, 29 Aug. 1897, Kate Louise, d. of William Bennett, Esq. (she died 24 June 1934); 2ndly, 1 Oct. 1938, Mrs. Emma Ellen Ellis. Educ. at National Schools, and at Polytechnic. Gen. Secretary of Amalgamated Union of Building Trade Workers 1921-41. President of Trades Union Congress 1927; President of National Federation of Building Trade Operatives 1919-37; member of Central Housing Advisory Committee, Housing Act 1935, and of Holidays with Pay Committee; Honorary A.R.I.B.A. A Freeman of the City of London. Parliamentary Secretary Ministry of Works Nov. 1940-May 1945. A Labour Member. Elected for E. Woolwich in Apr. 1931 and sat until he retired in 1950. Member of Executive Committee of P.L.P. 1931-35. C.B.E. 1946. Died 19 July 1954. [1950]

HICKS, Robert Adrian. Parkwood, St. Keyne, Liskeard, Cornwall. S. of W.H. Hicks, Esq., Electrical Engineer. B. 18 Jan. 1938; m. 1962, Maria, d. of Robert W. Gwyther, Esq., (2 d.). Educ. at Queen Elizabeth Grammar School, Crediton, University Coll., London, and University of Exeter. A Lecturer Weston-Super-Mare Technical Coll. 1964-70. Assistant Government Whip Oct. 1973-Mar. 1974. Vice-Chairman Conservative Parliamentary Agricultural Committee 1972-73, and from Nov. 1974. Member Select Committee on European Secondary Legislation 1973 and from 1976. Chairman W. County Group of Conservative MPs. 1976-77. A Conservative. Unsuccessfully contested Aberavon in 1966. Sat for Bodmin from 1970-Feb. 1974, when he was defeated, and again from Oct. 1974.* [1979]

HICKS-BEACH, Maj. W.W. See BEACH, Maj. W.W.H.

HIGGINS, Rt. Hon. Terence Langley. 18 Hallgate, Blackheath Park, London. Hawk's, Cambridge, and Yale of London. S. of Reginald Higgins, Esq. B. 18 Jan. 1928; m. 30 Sept. 1961, Professor Rosalyn Higgins, M.A., LL.B. (Cantab.), J.S.D. (Yale), d. of Lewis Cohen, Esq., (1 s. 1 d.). Educ. at Alleyn's School, Dulwich, Gonville and Caius Coll., Cambridge, and Yale University, U.S.A. An Associate of the Institute of Chartered Shipbrokers. Employed New Zealand Shipping Company, in U.K. and New Zealand 1948-55. Economic Specialist, Unilever Limited 1958-64. Served in the R.A.F. 1946-48. President Cambridge Union 1958 and Treasurer of the Cambridge University Conservative Association. British Olympic Team 1948 and 1952. Commonwealth Games Team 1950. Secretary Conservative Parliamentary Finance Committee 1965-67. Conservative Opposition Front Bench spokesman on Treasury and Economic Affairs 1967-70. Minister of State, Treasury June 1970-Apr. 1972. Financial Secretary Treasury Apr. 1927-Mar. 1974. Opposition spokesman on Treasury and Economic Affairs 1974. Opposition spokesman on Trade 1974-76. A Conservative. Elected for Worthing in Oct. 1964, Director of Warne Wright Group from 1976 PC. 1979.*   [1979]

HIGGS, John Michael Clifford. Flat 109, Nell Gwynn House, Sloane Avenue, London. Greenbanks, West Hagley, Worcestershire. S. of Albert W. Higgs, Esq., Solicitor, of Lye, Worcestershire. B. 30 May 1912; m. 1st, 2 May 1936, Diana Louise, d. of Harry Jerrams, Esq., of Springfield Clent (she died 7 Oct. 1950); 2ndly, 28 June 1952, Rachel Mary, d. of William Jones, Esq., of Pedmore, Stourbridge. Educ. at Shrewsbury School, and University of Birmingham, LL.B. Admitted Solicitor 1934. Served with R.A. 1939-42. Member of Judge Advocate-General's Staff 1942-46, of Staffordshire County Council 1946-49, and Worcestershire County Council Mar. 1953-73, Chairman 1959-73. A Conservative. Elected for the Bromsgrove division of Worcestershire in Feb. 1950 and sat until he retired in 1955. Knighted 1969. Chairman of Hereford and Worcester County Council 1973-77. Member of W. Midlands Economic Planning Council from 1965.*   [1954]

HILEY, Joseph. "Elmaran", Layton Road, Horsforth, Leeds, Yorkshire. Constitutional, Leeds, and Leeds and County Conservative. S. of Frank Hiley, Esq., Merchant. B. 18 Aug. 1902, m. Sept. 1932, Mary, d. of Dr. William Boyd. Educ. at West Leeds High School, and Leeds University. Leeds City Council 1930-39, 1947-60; elected Alderman 1949. President West Leeds Conservative Association. Lord Mayor Leeds 1957-58. Past President Leeds Chamber of Commerce. Past President Handknitting Association. Member of Lloyds. Dept.-Lieut. for the W. Riding of Yorkshire. Elected Honorary Alderman of Leeds. A Conservative. Unsuccessfully contested W. division of Leeds in 1955. Elected for Pudsey in 1959 and sat until he retired in Feb. 1974. Managing Director of J.B. Battye and Company Limited 1927-59. Director of Irish Spinners Limited 1952-74. Member of Lloyd's from 1966. Dept.-Lieut. for W. Yorkshire 1971.*   [1974]

HILL, Rt. Hon. Dr. Charles. House of Commons, London. S. of Charles Hill, Esq. B. 1904; m. 1931 Marion Spencer Wallace. Educ. at St. Olave's School, Trinity Coll., Cambridge, and London Hospital. Vice-President and at one time Chairman, Central Council for Health Education; Secretary of British Medical Association 1944-50; President of World Medical Association 1949-50. Parliamentary Secretary Ministry of Food Nov. 1951-Apr. 1955; Postmaster-Gen. Apr. 1955-Jan. 1957; PC. 1955. Chancellor of the Duchy of Lancaster Jan. 1957-Oct. 1961. Minister of Housing and Local Government and Minister for Welsh Affairs Oct. 1961-July 1962. A Liberal and Conservative Member. Unsuccessfully contested Cambridge University as an Independent in 1945. Elected for Luton in Feb. 1950 and sat until June 1963 when he was created Baron Hill of Luton (Life Peerage). Dept. Medical Officer of Health for Oxford. Member of Cabinet 1957-62. Chairman of Independent Television Authority 1963-67. Chairman of Governors of B.B.C. 1967-72. Chairman of Laporte Industries Limited 1965-70, of Abbey National Building Society 1976-78. Chairman of National Joint Council for Local Authorities' Administrative, Professional, Technical and Clerical Services 1963-78.*   [1963]

HILL, Eveline. Grand Hotel, Southampton Row, London. Glenavon, 115 Styal Road, Gatley, Cheadle, Cheshire. D. of Richard Ridyard, Esq., of Manchester. B. 16 Apr. 1898; m. 26 Apr. 1922, John Stanley Hill, Esq. (he died 1947). W.V.S. Organiser in Manchester 1943-50. J.P. for Manchester 1945; member of Manchester City Council from 1936-66, Alderman 1957-66. A Conservative. Elected for the Wythenshawe division of Manchester in Feb. 1950 and sat until 1964 when she was defeated. Died 22 Sept. 1973.

[1964]

HILL, James Meechan. House of Commons, London. B. 1899. Educ. at Bellshill Public School. A Miner. Elected to Musselburgh Town Council 1945 and to Midlothian County Council 1946. A Labour Member. Elected for Midlothian in Oct. 1959 and sat until he retired in Mar. 1966. Died 22 Dec. 1966.

[1966]

HILL. John Edward Bernard. Watermill Farm, Wenhaston, Halesworth, Suffolk. Garrick, and Marylebone Cricket. S. of Capt. R.W. Hill. B. 13 Nov. 1912; m. July 1944, Edith, 5th d. of John Maxwell, Esq., and widow of Commander R.A.E. Luard, R.N.V.R. Educ. at Charterhouse, and Merton Coll., Oxford. Barrister-at-Law, Inner Temple 1938; served with R.A. (T.A.) 1939-45. A Farmer. Assistant Government Whip Jan. 1959. Lord Commissioner of the Treasury Oct. 1960-Oct. 1964. Member of European Parliament 1973-74. A Conservative. Elected for Norfolk S. in Jan. 1955 and sat until he retired in Feb. 1974. Delegate to Council of Europe and W. European Union 1970-72. Opposition Whip 1964-65. Opposition spokesman on Education 1965-66.*

[1974]

HILL, Stanley James Allen. House of Commons, London. Royal Aero, Constitutional, and Royal Southampton Yacht. S. of James Hill, Esq. B. 21 Dec. 1924; m. 1958, Ruby Evelyn Ralph (5 children). Educ. at Regents Park School, and Southampton University. Served in Royal Fleet Auxiliaries 1941-46; served with B.O.A.C. 1947-58. Southampton City Councillor 1966-70 and 1976-78, Chairman Housing Committee 1968-70 and 1976-78; member of Southampton Airport Consultative Committee, South Hampshire Plan Advisory Committee, and The United Nations Association; President of British Legion Southampton Club; Trustee of Taunton, D'Aussey and Hammond Charities; member of European Parliament 1973-75; member Committee on Transport. Chairman Regional Policy and Transport Committee (Europe) 1973. Member Inter-Parliamentary Union, British-American Parliamentary Group, British-Yugoslavia Parliamentary Group. A Conservative. Elected for the Test division of Southampton in June 1970 and sat until Oct. 1974 when he was defeated. Re-elected for the Test division of Southampton in May 1979.*

[1974 2nd ed.]

HILTON, Albert Victor. House of Commons, London. S. of Thomas Hilton, Esq. B. 1908; m. 1944, Nelly Simmons (she died 1976). Educ. at Elementary School. Member of Norfolk County Council from 1952-70. Labour Party Agent, E. Norfolk 1936-45. Official of National Union of Agricultural Workers 1946-59, President 1964-66. J.P. for Norfolk. Member of National Executive Committee of Labour Party 1961-66. A Labour Member. Elected for S.W. Norfolk at a by-election in Mar. 1959 and sat until 1964 when he was defeated. Created Baron Hilton of Upton (Life Peerage) 1965. Lord-in-Waiting and Government Whip in House of Lords Apr. 1966-June 1970. Chairman of National Brotherhood Movement 1967. Methodist Lay Preacher. Died 3 May 1977.   [1964]

HILTON, William Samuel. House of Commons, London. S. of William Hilton, Esq., of Saltcoats. B. 21 Mar. 1926; m. 1948, Agnes Aitken Orr. Educ. at Ardrossan Academy, Ayrshire. Trade Union Research Officer with National Federation of Building Trades Operatives 1952-66. Parliamentary Private Secretary to Rt. Hon. Robert Mellish, Minister of Public Building and Works 1968-69. A Labour Member. Unsuccessfully contested E. Hertfordshire in 1955 and Ealing N. in 1959. Elected for Bethnal Green in Mar. 1966 and sat until he retired in Feb. 1974. A Railway Fireman until 1949. Labour Party Agent for Dunbartonshire E. 1949-52.

Editor of *Builders Standard* 1954-66. Member of Economic Development Council for the Building Industry 1964-66. Director of Master Builders Federation from 1969. National Director of Federation of Master Builders from 1970. Managing Director of Trade Press Limited from 1972.* [1974]

HINCHINGBROOKE, Alexander Victor Edward Paulet Montagu, Visct. 17 Great College Street, London. Mapperton, Beaminster, Dorset. Brooks's, and Carlton. S. of 9th Earl of Sandwich. B. 22 May 1906; m. 1st, 27 July 1934, Rosemary, d. of Maj. Ralph Harding Peto (from whom he obtained a divorce in 1958); 2ndly, 1962, Lady Anne, d. of 9th Duke of Devonshire. Educ. at Eton, and Trinity Coll., Cambridge, Natural Sciences M.A. Served in France 1940 with the Northamptonshire Regiment and subsequently on the General Staff. Private Secretary to Rt. Hon. Stanley Baldwin, MP. 1932-34; Treasurer Junior Imperial and Constitutional League 1934-35; Chairman of Tory Reform Committee 1943-44; Director of Northern Assurance Company. A Conservative. Member for S. Dorset from Feb. 1941 (sat as Independent Conservative from May 1957-July 1958) until June 1962 when he succeeded his father as Earl of Sandwich. Unsuccessfully contested Accrington in 1964. Styled Visct. Hinchingbrooke from 1916 until 1962. Renounced the Earldom in 1964 and became known as Mr. Victor Montagu. President of Anti-Common Market League from 1962. Chairman of Conservative Trident Group from 1973.* [1962]

HIRST, Geoffrey Audus Nicholson. Bramhope Manor, Bramhope, Nr. Leeds. Boodle's. S. of Col. E. Hirst, C.M.G., T.D., of Ingmanthorpe Hall, Wetherby, Yorkshire. B. 14 Dec. 1904. Educ. at Charterhouse, and St. John's Coll., Cambridge. Served in T.A. 1924-32 and with R.A. 1939-45, T.D. 1945. A Company Director. Past President Leeds Chamber of Commerce; past Chairman E. and W. Ridings Yorkshire Regional Council Federation of British Industries. Member of Council Economic Committee and E. and W. Ridings of Yorkshire Regional Council of Confederation of British Industries. Former Chairman Conservative Parliamentary Trade and Industry Committee. A Conservative. Elected for the Shipley division of the W. Riding of Yorkshire in Feb. 1950 and sat until he retired in 1970. Resigned the Conservative Whip in July 1966 and sat as an Independent Conservative until his retirement. Vice-President of Urban District Councils Association 1951-70.* [1970]

HOBDEN, Dennis Harry. 3 Queens Park Terrace, Brighton. S. of Charles Hobden, Esq. B. 1920; m. 1st, 1950, Kathleen Mary Holman (divorced 1970); 2ndly, 1977, Sheila Tugwell. Elementary education. Postal and Telegraph Officer, G.P.O. Served R.A.F. Air Crew, World War II; Flight-Lieut. Joined the Labour Party in 1944. Member of Union of Post Office Workers and Co-operative Party. Member of Brighton Borough Council 1956-67 and 1968-74, and of Brighton District Council from 1973. A Labour Member. Elected for the Kemptown division of Brighton in Oct. 1964 and sat until 1970, when he was defeated. Unsuccessfully contested the Kemptown division of Brighton in Feb. and Oct. 1974.* [1970]

HOBSON, Charles Rider. 115 Dewsbury Road, London. S. of Edwin Hobson Esq., of Leeds. B. 1904; m. 1933, Doris Mary. d. of F. Spink, Esq. Educ. at Leeds Elementary School. A Power Station Engineer. Member of Amagamated Engineering Union; member of Willesden Borough Council from 1931-45. Assistant Postmaster-Gen. Oct. 1947-Oct. 1951. A Labour Member. Sat for N. Wembley from July 1945-Feb. 1950. Elected for Keighley in Feb. 1950 and sat until 1959, when he was defeated. Opposition spokesman on Post Office matters until 1959. Vice-Chairman of Joint East Africa Board 1955-58 and 1964-65. Created Baron Hobson (Life Peerage) 1964. Lord-in-Waiting and Government Whip in House of Lords Oct. 1964-Feb. 1966. Died 17 Feb. 1966. [1959]

HOBSON, Rt. Hon. Sir John Gardiner Sumner, O.B.E., T.D., Q.C. 1 Harcourt Buildings, Temple, London. 28 Hereford Square, London. S. of Lieut.-Col. G.W. Hobson, C.M.G., D.S.O. B. 1912; m. 1939, Beryl Marjorie, d. of A. Stuart Johnson, Esq., of Henshall Hall, Congleton, Cheshire. Educ.

at Harrow, and B.N.C., Oxford. Served 1939-45 with Northamptonshire Yeomanry, IX Corps, A.F.H.Q. and 21 Army Group; Lieut.-Col. 1943. Barrister-at-Law, Inner Temple 1938; Q.C. 1957; Chairman Rutland Quarter Sessions 1954-62 and Chairman Bedfordshire Quarter Sessions 1957-62; Recorder of Northampton 1958-62. Parliamentary Private Secretary to C.J.M. Alport, Minister of State for Commonwealth Relations 1960-61. Solicitor-Gen. Feb.-July 1962; Attorney-Gen. July 1962-Oct. 1964. PC. 1963. A Conservative. Elected for the Warwick and Leamington division of Warwickshire in Mar. 1957 and sat until his death on 4 Dec. 1967. O.B.E. 1945. Knighted 1962. Member of Royal Commission of the Police 1960. T.D. 1948. Opposition spokesman on Legal Affairs 1964-67. Died 4 Dec. 1967.

[1967]

HOCKING, Philip Norman. Tudor Grange, Warwick Road, Coventry. Junior Carlton. S. of Fred Hocking, Esq. B. Oct. 1925; m. 1950, Joan Jackson, d. of Horace E. Jackson, Esq., C.B.E. Educ. at King Henry VIII School, Coventry, and Birmingham School of Architecture. Elected Chairman of Conservative Housing and Local Government Committee 1962 and appointed Parliamentary Private Secretary to Peter Thomas, Minister of State, Foreign Office in 1963. A Conservative. Elected for Coventry S. in 1959 and sat until 1964, when he was defeated. Unsuccessfully contested Coventry S. in 1966. Member of Coventry City Council 1955-60.*

[1964]

HODGSON, Robin Granville. 144 Campden Hill Road, London. Astley Abbotts, Bridgnorth, Shropshire. S. of Henry Edward Hodgson, Esq. B. 25 Apr. 1942. Educ. at Shrewsbury School, St. Peter's Coll., Oxford University, Wharton School of Finance, and University of Pennsylvania. A Banker in New York and Montreal 1964-67. Director Engineering Company, W. Midlands 1969-72. Director M.J.H. Nightingale and Company Limited, Investment Bankers 1972, Managing Director from 1979. A Conservative. Unsuccessfully contested Walsall N. in Feb. and Oct. 1974. Elected for Walsall N. in Nov. 1976 and sat until 1979, when he was defeated.*

[1979]

HOGG, Rt. Hon. Quintin McGarel, Q.C. S. of 1st Visct. Hailsham, whom he succeeded in 1950. Renounced the Viscountcy and Barony of Hailsham in Nov. 1963 under the provision of the Peerage Act 1963. B. 9 Oct. 1907; m. 18 Apr. 1944, Mary Evelyn, d. of Richard Martin, Esq., of Ross (she died 1978). Educ. at Eton and Christ Church, Oxford, M.A. President of Union Society 1929; Fellow of All Souls 1931-38 and from 1961. Barrister-at-Law, Lincoln's Inn 1932. Served overseas with the Rifle Brigade 1939-45. Bencher of Lincoln's Inn 1956, Treasurer 1975. Rector of Glasgow University 1959-62. Editor of *Halsbury's Laws of England* from 1972. Joint Parliamentary Under-Secretary of State for Air Apr.-July 1945. First Lord of the Admiralty Sept. 1956-Jan. 1957. Minister of Education Jan.-Sept. 1957. Chairman of Conservative Party Sept. 1957-Oct. 1959. Lord President of the Council Sept. 1957-Oct. 1959 and July 1960-Oct. 1964. Lord Privy Seal Oct. 1959-July 1960. Minister for Science Oct. 1959-Apr. 1964. Leader of House of Lords Sept. 1960-Oct. 1963. Secretary of State for Education and Science Apr.-Oct. 1964. Opposition spokesman on Education 1964-65; on Home Affairs 1966-70; Member of Shadow Cabinet 1964-70 and 1974-79. Lord Chancellor June 1970-Mar. 1974 and from May 1979. Q.C. 1953. PC. 1956 C.H. 1974. A Conservative. Sat for Oxford City from Oct. 1938 until Aug. 1950 when he succeeded to the Peerage. Elected for St. Marylebone in Dec. 1963 and sat until June 1970 when he was appointed Lord Chancellor and created Baron Hailsham of St. Marylebone (Life Peerage).*

[1970]

HOLLAND, Philip Welsby. 2 Holland Park Mansions, Holland Park Gardens, London. S. of John Holland, Esq. B. 1917; m. 1943, Josephine, d. of Arthur Hudson, Esq., of Plymouth. Educ. at Sir John Deane's Grammar School, Northwich. Served with R.A.F. 1936-46. Member Kensington Borough Council 1955-59. Parliamentary Private Secretary to Rt. Hon. John Boyd Carpenter, Minister of Pensions and National Insurance 1961-62 and Chief Secretary to the Treasury 1962-64. Joint Secretary Conservative Parliamentary Labour Committee Nov. 1967-May 1970. Vice-Chairman from

July 1970. Parliamentary Private Secretary to Rt. Hon. F.V. Corfield, Minister of Aviation Supply and Minister for Aerospace from Oct. 1970-Apr. 1972 and to Rt. Hon. Michael Noble, Minister for Trade Apr.-Nov. 1972. President Conservative Trade Union National Advisory Committee 1971-73. A Conservative. Unsuccessfully contested the Yardley division of Birmingham in 1955. Sat for Acton from 1959 until he was defeated in 1964. Elected for the Carlton division of Nottinghamshire in Mar. 1966. Personnel Manager, Ultra Electronics Group of Companies 1964-66. Personnel Consultant to Standard Telephones and Cables Ltd. from 1969. Chairman of Committee of Selection from 1979.* [1979]

HOLLAND-MARTIN, Christopher John. 28 Kinnerton Street, London. Old Colwall, Nr. Malvern, Worcestershire. S. of Robert Holland-Martin, Esq., of Overbury Court, Tewkesbury. B. 1910; m. 1949, Lady Anne Cavendish, d. of 9th Duke of Devonshire (she m. 1st Lieut.-Col. Henry Hunloke, MP., and obtained a divorce in 1945). Educ. at Eton, and Balliol Coll., Oxford. Served with Royal Fusiliers 1939. Military Secretary to Gov.-Gen. of New Zealand 1942-44 and to Gov. of Kenya 1945. Director of Martin's Bank; Joint Honorary Treasurer Conservative and Unionist Party 1947-60. A Conservative. Elected for the Ludlow division of Shorpshire in 1951 and sat until his death on 5 Apr. 1960. [1960]

HOLLINGWORTH, John Harold. House of Commons, London. S. of Harold Hollingworth, Esq. B. 1930; m. 1968, Susan Barbara, d. of J.H. Walters, Esq., of the Isle of Man. Educ. at Chigwell House School, and King Edward School, Birmingham. A Conservative. Elected for the All Saints division of Birmingham in 1959 and sat until 1964, when he was defeated. Unsuccessfully contested the All Saints division of Birmingham in 1966 and 1970.* [1964]

HOLLIS, (Maurice) Chirstopher. c/o, Hollis and Carter Limited, 25 Ashley Place, London. S. of the Rt. Rev. George Hollis, Bishop of Taunton. B. 29 Mar. 1902; m. 25 Aug. 1929, Margaret, d. of the Rev. W.R.C.

King of Cholderton, Wiltshire. Educ. at Eton, and Balliol Coll., Oxford. Assistant Master at Stonyhurst Coll. 1925-35. Served in Intelligence Branch of R.A.F. 1939-45. An Author and Publisher. A Conservative. Elected for the Devizes division of Wiltshire in July 1945 and sat until he retired in 1955. A Roman Catholic. Joined the Liberal Party in Aug. 1974. Died 5 May 1977. [1954]

HOLMAN, Percy. 3 Arundel Court, Raymond Road, Wimbledon, London. S. of Sidney Herbert Holman, Esq. B. 5 Apr. 1891; m. 10 May 1918, Dorothy Mary, d. of George Anderson, Esq. (she died 1976). Educ. at Mill Hill School, and London School of Economics, University of London. A Paper Merchant. Served in France with British Red Cross Society 1915-18. A Co-operative and Labour Member. Unsuccessfully contested the Twickenham division of Middlesex in 1931, Sept. 1932, June 1934 and 1935. Sat for S.W. Bethnal Green from July 1945-Feb. 1950. Elected for Bethnal Green in Feb. 1950 and sat until he retired in 1966. Member of Middlesex County Council 1928-31 and of Teddington Urban District Council 1928-34. Died 9 June 1978. [1966]

HOLMES, Horace Edwin, D.C.M. 16 Park Avenue, Lakeside Estate, Hartesholme, Lincoln. S. of William Holmes, Esq., Millwright, of Weston, Nottinghamshire. B. 30 Mar. 1888; m. 20 May 1912, Nellie Florence, d. of Thomas Marshall, Esq., of Royston. Educ. at Elementary and Technical Schools, and W.E.A. Classes. Late Coal Miner; for 23 years Trade Union Official; Sergeant Leeds Rifles 1914-18; awarded D.C.M. Trades Union Branch Secretary 1923-46; member of Joint Conciliation Board 1935 and Advisory Committee on Training, Safety, Further Education in Mining to 1946. J.P. for the W. Riding of Yorkshire. Parliamentary Private Secretary to Rt. Hon. H.T.N. Gaitskell, Minister of Fuel and Power 1947-50, and to Rt. Hon. P. Noel-Baker, Minister of Fuel and Power 1950-51. Labour Whip (Yorkshire) Nov. 1951-Sept. 1959. Member of Royston Urban District Council for 23 years and West Riding County Council for 11 years. A Labour Member. Elected for the Hemsworth division of the W. Riding of Yorkshire in Feb.

1946 and sat until he retired in 1959. Knighted 1966. Died 9 Sept. 1971.   [1959]

HOLMES, Sir (Joseph) Stanley. 15 Grosvenor Square, London. 68 Pall Mall, London. Reform, M.C.C., Roehampton, and Portland. S. of Horace Holmes, Esq., F.C.A. B. 31 Oct. 1878; m. Apr. 1905, Eva, d. of Thomas Bowley, Esq. Educ. at City of London School. A Chartered Accountant (Hon. 1901); Chairman of Beecham Group Limited, of North West Building Society; Director of Philip Hill Investment Trust Limited; Vice-President Building Societies Association; Senior Trustee of the Portland Club; member of Order of Merit of Chile; member of London County Council for Hoxton 1910-19; Knight Bach. 1945. A National Liberal and Conservative Member. Sat for N.E. Derbyshire as a Liberal from 1918 to 1922, when he was defeated. Unsuccessfully contested, as a Liberal, Dunbartonshire in 1923 and Cheltenham in 1924. Elected for the Harwich division of Essex in Nov. 1935 and sat until Jan. 1954 when he was created Baron Dovercourt. Died 22 Apr. 1961.   [1953]

HOLT, Arthur Frederick. House of Commons, London. Reform. S. of Alfred Ernest Holt, Esq., J.P. B. 8 Aug. 1914; m. 1939, Kathleen Mary, d. of Arnold Openshaw, Esq., of Turton, near Bolton. Educ. at Mill Hill School, and Manchester University. Served in T.A. 1939-45, prisoner-of-war, Singapore 1942-45. Hosiery Manufacturer, family business. A Liberal. Unsuccessfully contested Bolton E. in Feb. 1950. Elected for Bolton W. in Oct. 1951 and sat until 1964, when he was defeated. Liberal Whip 1962-63. Chairman of Holt Hosiery Company Limited 1971-73. President of Liberal Party 1974-75.*   [1964]

HOLT, Mary. House of Commons, London. D. of Henry James Holt, Esq., Solicitor. B. 1924. Educ. at Park School, Preston, and Girton Coll., Cambridge. Former Vice-Chairman Preston North Conservative Association; member National Executive Council and of Women's National Advisory Committee 1969-70. A Barrister, Gray's Inn 1949. A Conservative. Elected for Preston N. in June 1970 and sat until Feb. 1974, when she was defeated. Unsuccessfully contested Preston N.

in Oct. 1974. A Circuit Judge from 1977.*   [1974]

HOME ROBERTSON, John David. Paxton South Mains, Berwick-on-Tweed. Farmers. S. of Lieut.-Col. J.W. Home Robertson. B. 5 Dec. 1948; m. 1977, Catherine Brewster, of Glamis, Angus. Educ. at Ampleforth Coll., and West of Scotland Agricultural Coll. A Farmer. A Roman Catholic. Member of Berwickshire District Council 1974-78. Member of Borders Health Board 1975-78. A Labour Member. Sat for Berwick and East Lothian from Oct. 1978.*   [1979 2nd ed.]

HOOLEY, Frank Oswald. House of Commons, London. S. of Malcolm Oswald Hooley, Esq. B. 30 Nov. 1923; m. 1945, Doris Irene Snook, (2 d.). Educ. at Elementary School, King Edward's High School, Birmingham, and Birmingham University. Administrative Assistant Birmingham University 1948-52; Assistant Registrar, Sheffield University 1952-65; Senior Assistant Registrar 1965-66; Registrar, Fourah Bay Coll., Freetown, Sierra Leone (secondment from Sheffield) 1960-62. Senior Administrative Assistant Manchester Polytechnic 1970-71. Chief Administrative Officer, Sheffield City Coll. of Education 1971-74. A Labour Member. Unsuccessfully contested the Skipton division of the W. Riding of Yorkshire in 1959 and the Heeley division of Sheffield in 1964. Sat for the Heeley division of Sheffield from Mar.1966-June 1970, when he was defeated, and from Feb. 1974.*   [1979]

HOOSON, Hugh Emlyn. 1 Dr. Johnson's Buildings, Temple, London. Summerfield Park, Llanidloes, Monmouthshire. S. of Hugh Hooson, Esq., Farmer. B. 26 Mar. 1925; m. 1950, Shirley Margaret Wynne, d. of Sir George and Lady Hamer, (2 d.). Educ. at Denbigh Grammar School, University Coll. of Wales, Aberystwyth, and Gray's Inn. Called to the bar 1949, Q.C. 1960. Dept. Chairman of Flintshire Quarter Sessions 1960-71. Chairman of Merioneth Quarter Sessions 1967-71, Dept. Chairman 1960-67. Bencher of Gray's Inn 1968. Recorder of Merthyr Tydfil Apr. 1971; Recorder of Swansea July 1971. Elected Leader of Wales and Chester Circuit May 1971, resigned Dec. 1974. Honorary Professorial Fellow in

Law of University of Wales 1971. Leader of Welsh Liberal Party 1966. Vice-Chairman of Political Committee of North Atlantic Assembly from 1975. Liberal spokesman on Wales to 1974, on Law, on Agriculture 1974-76, on Home Affairs 1976-77 and on Defence 1976-79. Voted against entry to E.E.C. on 28 Oct. 1971. A Liberal Member. Unsuccessfully contested the Conway division of Caernarvonshire in 1950 and 1951. Elected for Montgomeryshire in May 1962 and sat until 1979, when he was defeated. Member of General Advisory Committee of Independent Television Authority to 1966. Created Baron Hooson (Life Peerage) 1979.*   [1979]

HOPE, Rt. Hon. Lord John Adrian. 46 Chelsea Square, London. S. of 2nd Marq. of Linlithgow. B. 7 Apr. 1912; m. 1948, Elizabeth, d. of Somerset Maugham, Esq. Educ. at Eton, and Christ Church, Oxford, B.A. 1936. Served with Scots Guards 1939-45. Joint Under-Secretary of State Foreign Affairs Oct. 1954-Nov. 1956; Under-Secretary of State for Commonwealth Relations Nov. 1956-Jan. 1957; Under-Secretary of State for Scotland Jan. 1957-Oct. 1959. Minister of Works Oct. 1959-July 1962. PC. 1959. A Conservative. Sat for the N. Midlothian division of Midlothian and Peebles from July 1945 to Feb. 1950 and for the Pentlands division of Edinburgh from Feb. 1950 to June 1964 when he was created Baron Glendevon. Chairman of Royal Commonwealth Society 1963-66. Dept.-Chairman of Ciba-Geigy (UK) Limited 1971-78. Chairman of Historic Buildings Council for England 1973-75. Fellow of Eton Coll. 1956-67.*   [1964]

HOPKINS, Alan Cripps Nind. 46 Egerton Crescent, London. Upway, Barrack Lane, Aldwick, Sussex. Brooks's. S. of the Rt. Hon. Sir Richard Hopkins, G.C.B. B. 27 Oct. 1926; m. 1st, Mar. 1954, Margaret, d. of E.C. Bolton, Esq., of Waco, Texas, U.S.A. (marriage dissolved in 1962); 2ndly, Sept. 1962, Venetia, d. of Sir Edward Wills, Bart. Educ. at Winchester, King's Coll., Cambridge, and Yale University Law School, U.S.A. called to the bar by Inner Temple 1948. Councillor St. Marylebone Borough Council 1949-51. Co-opted Member of Education Committee of London County Council 1949-51. Free-

man of the City of London, Liveryman of Fishmongers Company. Parliamentary Private Secretary to Sir Edward Boyle, Financial Secretary to Treasury 1960-62. A Conservative and National Liberal Member. Elected for N.E. Bristol in 1959 and sat until 1966, when he was defeated. Chairman of Wellman Engineering Corporation.*   [1966]

HOPKINSON, Rt. Hon. Henry Lennox d'Aubigné, C.M.G. 27 Smith Terrace, London. Netherton Hall, Colyton, Devon. White's, and Buck's. S. of Sir Henry Lennox Hopkinson, K.C.V.O. B. 3 Jan. 1902; m. 1st, 10 Nov. 1927, Alice, d. of Henry Lane Eno, Esq., of Princeton, New Jersey, U.S.A. (she died Apr. 1953); 2ndly, 1956, Mrs. Barbara Addams, d. of Stephen Barb, Esq., of New York. Educ. at Eton, and Trinity Coll., Cambridge. Joined Diplomatic Service 1924, served in Washington, Stockholm, Cairo, Athens and Foreign Office; H.M. Minister Lisbon 1943; Dept. High Commissioner Italy 1944-46. C.M.G. 1944 Secretary for Overseas Trade Oct. 1951-May 1952. Minister of State for Colonial Affairs May 1952-Dec. 1955. PC. 1952. A Conservative and Unionist Member. Elected for the Taunton division of Somerset in Feb. 1950 and sat until Jan. 1956 when he was created Baron Colyton. Joint Director of Conservative Research Department 1946-50. Chairman of Anglo-Egyptian Resettlement Board 1957-60. Chairman of Joint East and Central Africa Board 1960-65. Chairman of Tanganyika Concessions Limited 1966-72.*   [1955]

HORABIN, Thomas Lewis. House of Commons, London. B. 1896; m. 1920, d. of Dr. Cargil Martin. Educ. at Cardiff High School. Served with the Cameron Highlanders 1914-18. A Business Consultant. Chief Liberal Party Whip Aug. 1945-Oct. 1946 Elected for N. Cornwall in July 1939 as a Liberal; resigned the Liberal Whip in Oct. 1946, sat as an Independent until Nov. 1947 when he accepted the Labour Whip, and sat as a Labour Member until Feb. 1950, when he unsuccessfully contested Exeter. Died 26 Apr. 1956.   [1950]

HORAM, John Rhodes. 19 West Street, Kings Cliffe, Peterborough. 21 Valley Gardens, Gateshead. S. of Sydney Horam, Esq., Fitter. B. 7 Mar. 1939; m. 12 Apr. 1977, Iris Crawley. Educ. at Silcoates School, Wakefield, and St. Catherine's Coll., Cambridge University. A Market Research Officer, Rowntree and Company 1960-62; Feature and Leader Writer, *Financial Times* 1962-65, *The Economist* 1965-68 and contributor to *Tribune* 1966-68. Managing Director Commodities Research Unit Limited 1968-70. Parliamentary Under-Secretary of State for Transport Sept. 1976-May 1979. A Labour Member. Unsuccessfully contested Folkestone and Hythe in 1966. Elected for Gateshead W. in June 1970.* [1979]

HORDERN, Peter Maudslay. 55 Cadogan Street, London. S. of Capt. C.H. Hordern, M.B.E., Company Director. B. 18 Apr. 1929; m. 25 July 1964, Susan, d. of Denys Chataway, Esq., (2 s. 1 d.). Educ. at Geelong Grammar School, Australia, and Christ Church, Oxford, (M.A.). A Company Director. Vice-Chairman Conservative Parliamentary Finance Committee. Member of 1922 Executive Committee. Member of Stock Exchange 1957-74. A Conservative. Sat for Horsham from Oct. 1964-Feb. 1974 and for Horsham and Crawley from Feb. 1974.* [1979]

HORNBY, Richard Phipps. 10 Hereford Square, London. S. of Rt. Rev. H.L. Hornby, Suffragan Bishop of Hulme. B. 20 June 1922; m. 7 Apr. 1951, Stella, d. of W.L. Hichens, Esq., and Mrs. Hichens, of North Aston Hall, Oxford. Educ. at Winchester, and Trinity Coll., Oxford, M.A. Served 1941-45 with K.R.R.C. Taught at Eton Coll. 1948-50; with Unilever Limited 1951-52, then with J. Walter Thompson Company Limited 1952-63 and again from Nov. 1964. Parliamentary Private Secretary to Rt. Hon. Duncan Sandys, Minister of Aviation 1959-60, and Secretary of State for Commonwealth Relations from 1960-63. Parliamentary Under-Secretary of State for Commonwealth Relations and Colonies Oct. 1963-Oct. 1964. Member of General Advisory Council of the B.B.C. 1969-74. Member of Home Office Committee on Privacy 1970-72. Member of Executive Committee of British Council 1971-74. A Conservative. Unsuccessfully con-

tested W. Walthamstow in 1955 and Mar. 1956. Elected for the Tonbridge division of Kent in June 1956 and sat until he retired in Feb. 1974. Director of J. Walter Thompson Company Limited from 1974 and of Halifax Building Society from 1976.* [1974]

HORNER, (Frederick) John. Yew Tree, Howle Hill, Ross-on-Wye, Herefordshire. S. of Ernest Charles Horner, Esq. B. 5 Nov. 1911; m. 1936, Patricia, d. of Geoffrey Palmer, Esq. Educ. at Elementary School, then by scholarship to Sir George Monoux Grammar School. Served in the Merchant Navy and London Fire Brigade. Gen. Secretary of Fire Brigades Union 1939-64. A Labour Member. Elected for Oldbury and Halesowen in Oct. 1964 and sat until 1970 when he was defeated.* [1970]

HORNSBY-SMITH, Rt. Hon. Dame Margaret Patricia, D.B.E. 31 Stafford Mansions, Stafford Place, London. Constitutional, Special Forces, and Cowdrey. D. of Frederick Charles Hornsby-Smith, Esq. B. 17 Mar. 1914. Educ. at Richmond County School. In Ministry of Economic Warfare 1941-45. Member of Barnes Borough Council 1945-49. Parliamentary Secretary Ministry of Health Nov. 1951-Jan. 1957; Joint Under-Secretary of State Home Office Jan. 1957-Oct. 1959; Joint Parliamentary Secretary Ministry of Pensions and National Insurance Oct. 1959-Aug. 1961; Delegate to U.N. 1958; PC. 1959; D.B.E. 1961; led Parliamentary Delegation to Australasia 1962; Kenya 1972. A Conservative. Sat for the Chislehurst division of Kent from 1950-66, when she was defeated, and from June 1970-Feb. 1974, when she unsuccessfully contested Aldridge-Brownhills. Created Baroness Hornsby-Smith (Life Peerage) 1974. President of Electrical Association for Women from 1975.* [1974]

HOROBIN, Sir Ian Macdonald. House of Commons, London. Reform. S. of Principal J.C. Horobin, M.A., of Cambridge. B. 1899. Unmarried. Educ. at Highgate, and Sidney Sussex Coll., Cambridge. A Social Worker. Warden of the Mansfield House University Settlement, Albert Dock, London, which he

refounded in 1923. Served R.N.V.R. and
R.A.F. 1918 and R.A.F. 1939-45 (Japanese
P.O.W.). Knight Bach. 1955. Parliamentary
Secretary Ministry of Power Jan. 1958-Oct.
1959. A Conservative. Sat for Southwark
Central from 1931-35 when he retired. Unsuccessfully contested Oldham W. in 1950.
Elected for Oldham E. in 1951 and sat until
1959, when he was defeated. Included in list
of new life Peers on 29 Mar. 1962 but
withdrew his acceptance on 13 Apr. Arrested
on charges of indecency in May 1962 and
sentenced to 4 years imprisonment on 17 July
1962. Author of *Pleasures of Planning* and 3
volumes of verse. Died in Tangier 5 June
1976. [1959]

**HORSBRUGH, Rt. Hon. Dame Florence
Gertrude, G.B.E.** 21 Marsham Street, Lon-
don. 18 East Camus Place, Edinburgh. D. of
Henry Moncrieff Horsbrugh, C.A., of Edin-
burgh. B. 1889. Educ. at Lansdowne House,
Edinburgh, and St. Hilda's, Folkestone. Par-
liamentary Secretary Ministry of Health July
1939-May 1945, and to Ministry of Food
May-July 1945; PC. 1945; Honorary Fellow
Royal Coll. of Surgeons, Edinburgh 1946.
Honorary LL.D. Edinburgh University.
Minister of Education Nov. 1951-Oct. 1954.
G.B.E. 1954. Member of Cabinet Sept. 1953-
Oct. 1954. A Conservative. Elected for
Dundee in Oct. 1931 and sat until July 1945,
when she was defeated. Unsuccessfully con-
tested Midlothian and Peebles in Feb. 1950.
Elected for the Moss Side division of Man-
chester in Mar. 1950 (where the poll had been
delayed owing to the death of the previous
Conservative candidate) and sat until she
retired in 1959. Created Baroness Horsbrugh
(Life Peerage) 1959. M.B.E. 1920; C.B.E.
1939. Died 6 Dec. 1969. [1959]

**HOUGHTON, Rt. Hon. (Arthur Leslie
Noel) Douglas, C.H.** 110 Marsham Court,
London. Becks Cottage, Bletchingley, Sur-
rey. S. of John Houghton, Esq. B. 11 Aug.
1898 at Long Eaton, Derbyshire; m. 1939,
Vera Travis. Alderman London County
Council 1947-49; Secretary Inland Revenue
Staff Federation 1922-60; member of Civil
Service National Whitley Council 1923-58;
Chairman (Staff Side) 1956-58. Member
General Council Trades Union Congress

1952-60. Chairman of Public Accounts Committee 1963-64. Chancellor of the Duchy of
Lancaster Oct. 1964-Apr. 1966. Minister
without Portfolio Apr. 1966-Jan. 1967. Privy
Councillor 1964. Chairman P.L.P. Apr. 1967-
June 1970 and Nov. 1970-Feb. 1974. Chairman Commonwealth Scholarships Commission 1967-68. C.H. 1967. Opposition spokesman on Pensions 1959-63 and on Treasury
Affairs 1963-64. Member of Parliamentary
Committee of P.L.P. 1960-64 and 1970.
Member of Cabinet 1964-67. Voted in favour
of entry to E.E.C. on 28 Oct. 1971. A Labour
Member. Elected for the Sowerby division of
the W. Riding of Yorkshire in Mar. 1949 and
sat until he retired in Feb. 1974. Created
Baron Houghton of Sowerby (Life Peerage)
1974. Member of Commission on the Constitution 1969-73. Member of Royal Com-
mission on Standards of Conduct in Public
Life from 1974. Chairman of Commonwealth
Scholarships Commission 1967-68, of Young
Volunteer Force Foundation 1967-70, of
Teachers Pay Inquiry 1974, of Committee on
Aid to Political Parties 1975-76 and of Committee on Security of Cabinet Papers 1976.*
[1974]

HOUSE, George. Wrythe Green, Carshalton, Surrey. S. of Robert House, Esq., of
Bristol. B. 7 Mar. 1892; m. 1921. Educ. at
Queen Elizabeth Hospital, Bristol. Secretary
of Constructional Engineering Union 1924-
41. Member of London County Council from
1937. A Labour Member. Elected for St.
Pancras N. in July 1945 and sat until his
death on 8 Feb. 1949. [1949]

**HOWARD, Hon. Arthur Jared Palmer,
C.V.O.** 60 Park Lane, Flat 50, London.
Wappingthorn, Steyning, Sussex. Junior
Carlton, and Guards'. S. of Margaret,
Baroness Strathcona and Robert Howard,
Esq. B. 1896; m. 20 June 1922, Lady Lorna
Baldwin, d. of 1st Earl Baldwin of Bewdley.
Fellow of King's Coll., University of London.
Capt. Scots Guards, served in France 1914-17
(wounded, Croix de Guerre). Principal War-
den, London C.D. Region 1939-42; Joint
Treasurer of St. Thomas's Hospital 1943-64.
J.P. for Sussex, Dept.-Lieut. for London.
Mayor of Westminster 1937. Vice-Chairman
of British Council. A Conservative. Elected

for the St. George's division of Westminster in July 1945 and sat until he retired in 1950. C.V.O. 1937. K.B.E. 1953. Chairman of Teaching Hospital Association. Member of South Eastern Electricity Board 1953-64. Died 25 Apr. 1971. [1950]

HOWARD, Hon. Greville Reginald Charles. Treskello, Marazion, Cornwall. White's, R.N.V.R., Royal Photographic Society, and Royal Cornwall Yacht. S. of 19th Earl of Suffolk. B. 7 Sept. 1909; m. 24 Nov. 1945, Mary, d. of W.S. Ridehalgh, Esq., of Broughton Lodge, Cartmel, Lancashire. Educ. at Eton, and Sandhurst. Lieut. K.S.L.I. Lieut.-Commander R.N.V.R.; served at sea in destroyers throughout war, including Command 1939-45. Mayor of Westminster 1946-47. Director Colour Processing Laboratories Limited. A National Liberal and Conservative Member. Unsuccessfully contested N. Portsmouth in 1945. Elected for the St. Ives division of Cornwall in Feb. 1950 and sat until he retired in 1966. President of National Association of Inshore Fishermen.* [1966]

HOWARD, John Melbourne. House of Commons, London. S. of Harry Howard, Esq., of Warlingham. B. 1913; m. 1948, Maisie Alexandra, d. of Alexander Bartlett Gilbert, Esq. Educ. at Whitgift School. Served with Royal Navy 1941-46; member of London County Council from 1949-52, Alderman 1952-54. A Chartered Accountant. Parliamentary Private Secretary to Enoch Powell, Financial Secretary to the Treasury 1957-58, to R.A. Allan, Parliamentary Secretary to Admiralty and T.G.D. Galbraith, Civil Lord of Admiralty 1958-59, and to Rt. Hon. Edward Heath, Minister of Labour 1959-60 and Lord Privy Seal 1960-63. A Conservative. Unsuccessfully contested Croydon N. as a Liberal in 1945, and Hammersmith N. as a Conservative in 1951. Elected for the Test division of Southampton in 1955 and sat until he retired in 1964. Partner in John Howard and Company and in A.J. Pickard and Company, Chartered Accountants.* [1964]

HOWARD, Stephen Gerald, Q.C. 9 Carlyle Square, London. The Moat, Upend,
Kirtling, Newmarket. Oxford & Cambridge, and Lansdowne. S. of Maj. S.G. Howard, C.B.E., MP., of The Moat, Upend, Kirtling, Newmarket. B. 7 June 1896; m. 1934, Claudia Primrose, d. of Graves Stoker, Esq., M.D., F.R.C.S. Educ. at Harrow, and Balliol Coll., Oxford. Served with R.F.C. and R.A.F. 1916-18. Barrister-at-Law, Loncoln's Inn 1924, Bencher 1942; K.C. 1950. Recorder of Bury St. Edmunds 1942-47, of Ipswich 1947-58 and Southend from 1958-61; J.P. for Cambridgeshire. High Sheriff of Cambridgeshire and Huntingdonshire 1945. Chairman of Quarter Sessions for Cambridgeshire 1947-52 and for E. and W. Suffolk 1952-61. A Conservative. Unsuccessfully contested the Eye division of Suffolk, as a Lloyd George Liberal with Conservative support in 1922 and Cambridgeshire as a Conservative in 1945. Elected for Cambridgeshire in Feb. 1950 and sat until Jan. 1961, when he was appointed a High Court Judge. Knighted 1961. Judge of Queen's Bench Division 1961-71 Died 25 June 1973. [1961]

HOWARTH, Harry. 2 Kenwood Drive, Rickmansworth, Hertfordshire. S. of Robert Howarth. Esq. B. 3 Aug. 1916; m. Dec. 1945, Kathleen Marion, d. of Herbert Charles Rayner, Esq., of London. Educ. at Crompton House School, Shaw, Lancashire. Railway Clerk. Served with R.A.F. 1939-45. Joined the Labour Party in 1950. Member of T.S.S.A. from 1934. National Executive Committee member from 1954-60. Justice of the Peace for the Gore Division of the Middlesex area of Greater London from 1957. Member of Wembley Borough Council from 1953-56 and from 1957-60. A Labour Member. Elected for the Wellingborough division of Northamptonshire in Oct. 1964 and sat until his death on 8 Aug. 1969. [1969]

HOWARTH, Robert Lever. 11 Kinloch Drive, Bolton, Lancashire. S. of James Howarth, Esq. B, 31 July 1927; m. 1952, Josephine, d. of Joseph and Margaret Doyle, (1 s. 1 d.). Educ. at Bolton County Grammar School, and Bolton Technical Coll. Draughtsman. Joined the Labour Party in 1945. Member of D.A.T.A. from 1946; served on N.E.C. 1960-63. Member of A.E.U.

1943-45. Past President of Bolton Borough Labour Party. School and Technical Coll. Gov. from 1955. Served on Bolton Town Council 1958-60. While on Council, member of Education Committee and Vice-Chairman Housing Committee. Re-elected to Town Council 1963-66, Vice-Chairman Planning Committee. Chairman P.L.P. Aviation Committee. A Labour Member. Unsuccessfully contested Bolton E. in 1960 by-election. Elected for Bolton E. in Oct. 1964 and sat until 1970, when he was defeated. Leader of Labour group, Bolton Metropolitan Borough Council from 1975. Lecturer in Liberal studies, Leigh Technical Coll. 1970-76. Senior Lecturer in General Studies, Wigan Coll. of Technology from 1977.*   [1970]

HOWE, Rt. Hon. Sir (Richard Edward) Geoffrey, Q.C. 61 Fentiman Road, London. S. of Benjamin Edward Howe, Esq. B. 20 Dec. 1926; m. 29 Aug. 1953, Elspeth Rosamund, d. of Philip Morton Shand, Esq. Educ. at Wincester Coll., and Trinity Hall, Cambridge. Barrister-at-Law, Middle Temple, 1952. Appointed Q.C. Apr. 1965. Represented Britain's Young Barristers' Committee at the Washington Convention of the American Bar Association 1960; Chairman Cambridge University Conservative Association; Chairman of the Bow Group and Editor for two years of the paper *Crossbow*. Elected Secretary of the Conservative Parliamentary Committee on Health and Social Security Session 1964-65. Elected Bencher of the Middle Temple Dec. 1969. Dept. Chairman of Glamorgan Quarter Sessions 1966-70; Solicitor Gen. June 1970-Nov. 1972. Knighted 1970. Minister for Trade and Consumer Affairs and Member of the Cabinet Nov. 1972-Mar. 1974. Director A.G.B. Research Group 1974; Sun Alliance and London Insurance Group 1974; E.M.I. Limited 1976. PC. 1972. An Opposition spokesman on Labour and Social Services 1965-66. Opposition spokesman on Social Services 1974-75; Opposition spokesman on Treasury and Economic Affairs 1975-79. Member of Shadow Cabinet 1974-79. Chancellor of the Exchequer from May 1979. A Conservative. Unsuccessfully contested Aberavon in 1955 and 1959. MP. for Bebington from 1964-66, when he was defeated. Sat for Reigate from 1970 to Feb. 1974 and for Surrey E. division from Feb. 1974. Member of General Council of the Bar 1957-61, Member of Council of Justice 1963-70.*   [1979]

HOWELL, Charles Alfred. 36 Cardigan Street, Derby. S. of Charles Howell, Esq., a Brewer's Miller. B. 22 Oct. 1905; m. 24 Dec. 1927, Ivy Jeanette, d. of Arthur Silvester, Esq. Educ. at Winshill School, Burton-on-Trent. Member Derby Town Council 1943-54; Chairman Derby Labour Party 1950; member of N.U.R. Executive Committee 1951, 1952 and 1953; President Midland District Council of N.U.R. 1950; member L.M.S. Sectional Council No. 3 1945-55, Local Valuation Tribunal 1948-58, and Derby No. 2 Hospital Management Committee 1948; Chairman Derwent Hospital (Derby) 1948. Secretary Trades Council (Derby) 1945-55; N.U.R. Branch Secretary 1939-55. Appointed Opposition Whip Oct. 1959. A Labour Member. Elected for the Perry Barr division of Birmingham in 1955 and sat until 1964, when he was defeated. O.B.E. 1965. Secretary of Derby Area Trades Union Council from 1966 and N. Midlands Federation of Trades Councils from 1973. Died 26 Oct. 1974.   [1964]

HOWELL, Rt. Hon. David Arthur Russell. House of Commons, London. Buck's. S. of Arthur Howell, Esq., retired Army Officer and Businessman. B. 18 Jan. 1936; m. 10 Aug. 1967, Miss Davina Wallace, (1 s. 2 d.). Educ. at Eton, and King's Coll., Cambridge. Graduated First Class Honours from Cambridge 1959. Treasury 1959-60. Leader Writer on *Daily Telegraph* 1960-64. Chairman of Bow Group 1962; Editor of *Crossbow* 1962-64; Director of Conservative Political Centre 1964-66. Travelled extensively in Africa and America. Trustee of the Federal Trust for Education and Research. Lord Commissioner of the Treasury June 1970-Jan. 1971; Parliamentary Secretary Civil Service Department June 1970-Mar. 1972. Under-Secretary in Department of Employment Jan. 1971-Mar. 1972. Parliamentary Under-Secretary for Northern Ireland Mar.-Nov. 1972. Minister of State for Northern Ireland Nov. 1972-Jan. 1974. Minister of State, Department of Energy Jan.-Mar.

1974. An Opposition spokesman on Energy Mar.-June 1974, on Treasury Affairs June 1974-Nov. 1977 and on Home Affairs Nov. 1977-May 1979. Secretary of State for Energy from May 1979. PC. 1979. A Conservative. Unsuccessfully contested Dudley in 1964. Sat for the Guildford division of Surrey from Mar. 1966.* [1979]

HOWELL, Rt. Hon. Denis Herbert. 33 Moor Green, Moseley, Birmingham. S. of Herbert Howell, Esq. B. 1923; m. 1955, Brenda Willson, d. of Stephen Willson, Esq., (3 s. 1 d.). Educ. at Gower Street Elementary School, and Handsworth Grammar School. Member Birmingham City Council 1946-56. Honorary Secretary City Council Labour Group 1949-55. West Midlands Regional Council of Labour E.C. 1948-54. Parliamentary Under-Secretary for Education and Science Oct. 1964-Oct. 1969. Minister of State, Ministry of Housing and Local Government Oct. 1969-June 1970. 'Minister for Sport' 1964-70. Opposition spokesman on Local Government and Sport 1970-74. President Apex Association of Professional, Clerical and Computer Staff 1970. Chairman Central Council of Physical Recreation 1973-74. Minister of State, Department of Environment, responsible for sport and re-creation, countryside, environment policy, water resources, and Property Services Agency Mar. 1974-May 1979. Opposition spokesman on Local Government and Sport from 1979. PC. 1976. Voted in favour of entry to E.E.C. on 28 Oct. 1971. A Labour Member. Unsuccessfully contested the Kings Norton division of Birmingham in 1951. Sat for the All Saints division of Birmingham from 1955-59, when he was defeated. Elected for the Small Heath division of Birmingham in Mar. 1961. A Football League Referee 1956-70. Opposition spokesman on Local Government and Sport from 1979.* [1979]

HOWELL, Ralph Frederick. Wendling Grange, Dereham, Norfolk. Carlton, and Farmers'. S. of Walter Howell, Esq. B. 25 May 1923; m. Apr. 1950, Margaret, d. of Walter Bone, Esq., (2 s. 1 d.). Educ. at Diss Grammar School. Served in R.A.F. Bomb-aimer/Navigator 1941-46; farming in mid-Norfolk 1946; Director Mid-Norfolk Farmers

Trading Group from 1963. Member European Parliament 1974-79. A Conservative. Unsuccessfully contested the North division of Norfolk in 1966. Elected for the North division of Norfolk in June 1970.* [1979]

HOWELLS, Geraint Wyn. Glennydd, Ponterwyd. S. of D. J. Howells, Esq. B. 15 Apr. 1925; m. 7 Sept. 1957, Mary Olwen Hughes, d. of M. A. Griffiths, Esq., (2 d.). Educ. at Ardwyn Grammar School. Liberal spokesman on Wales from 1974 and Agriculture from 1976. A Liberal. Unsuccessfully contested Brecon and Radnor in 1970. Sat for Cardigan from Feb. 1974. Vice-Chairman of British Wool Marketing Board from 1971. Managing Director of Wilkinson and Stanier Ltd., Meat Wholesalers.* [1979]

HOWIE, William. 34 Temple Fortune Lane, London. S. of Peter Howie, Esq. B. 1924; m. 1951, Mairi Margaret, d. of John Sanderson, Esq., (2 s. 2 d.). Graduated B.Sc. (Eng.) from the Royal Technical Coll., Glasgow. A Civil Engineer. Member of the Labour Party from 1950 and also a member of the Parliamentary Labour Association. Vice-Chairman of P.L.P. 1968-70. Member of Council of Institution of Civil Engineers 1964-67. Gov. of Imperial Coll. of Science 1965-67. Member of Council of City University 1968. Assistant Government Whip Nov. 1964-66. A Lord Commissioner of the Treasury Apr. 1966-Mar. 1967. Comptroller of Royal Household Mar. 1967-Feb.1968, when he resigned. A Labour Member. Unsuccessfully contested the Cities of London and Westminster at the 1959 general election. Elected for Luton in Nov. 1963 and sat until 1970, when he was defeated. Gen. Manager of *New Civil Engineer*. Member of Committee of Inquiry into the Engineering Profession from 1977. Created Baron Howie of Troon (Life Peerage) 1978.* [1970]

HOY, Rt. Hon. James Hutchison. House of Commons, London. 77 Orchard Road, Edinburgh. S. of William Hoy. Esq., of Edinburgh. B. 21 Jan. 1909; m. 11 Mar. 1942, Nancy, d. of John McArthur, Esq., of Edinburgh. Educ. at Public Schools in Edinburgh. An Interior Decorator. Parliamentary Private Secretary to John Freeman, Under-

Secretary of State for War Apr. 1947, and to the Rt. Hon. Arthur Woodburn, Secretary of State for Scotland 1947-50. Parliamentary Secretary Ministry of Agriculture, Fisheries and Food Oct. 1964-June 1970. PC. 1969. A Labour Member. Sat for Leith from 1945 to 1950 and for the Leith division of Edinburgh from 1950, until he retired in 1970. Gov. of British Film Institute 1947. President of National Association of Inshore Fishermen 1963. Dept.-Lieut. City of Edinburgh from 1958. Opposition spokesman on Scotland 1961-64. Created Baron Hoy (Life Peerage) 1970. Died 7 Aug. 1976.   [1970]

HOYLE, Eric Douglas Harvey, J.P. 30 Ashfield Road, Anderton, Nr. Chorley, Lancashire. Wig and Pen. S. of William Hoyle, Esq., Shop Assistant. B. 17 Feb. 1930; m. 20 Dec. 1952, Pauline, d. of William and Martha Ann Spencer, (1 s.). Educ. at Adlington School, and Horwich Technical Coll. British Rail 1944-51. A.E.I. 1951-53. C. Weston Limited, Salford Sales Engineer 1953-74. Vice-President A.S.T.M.S. 1972-74; President May 1977. Chairman A.S.T.M.S. Parliamentary Committee. A Labour Member. Unsuccessful Parliamentary Candidate for Clitheroe in 1964 and Nelson and Colne in 1970 and Feb. 1974. Sat for Nelson and Colne from Oct. 1974 until 1979, when he was defeated. J.P. 1958. Member of North Western Regional Health Authority 1974-75. Member of National Executive Committee of Labour Party from 1978.*   [1979]

HUBBARD, Thomas Frederick. 25 Kennedy Crescent, Kirkcaldy, Fife. S. of F. J. Hubbard, Esq., of Kirkcaldy. B. 1898; m. 1922, Jessie, d. of T. Cooper, Esq., of Dysart. A Miner. Air-raid Shelter Superintendent at Kirkcaldy. Served in R.N. 1914-18. Member of Kirkcaldy Town Council from 1936. Parliamentary Private Secretary to Rt. Hon. Joseph Westwood, Secretary of State for Scotland 1946-47. A Labour Member. Elected for Kirkcaldy Burghs in Feb. 1944 and sat until he retired in 1959. Died 7 Jan. 1961.   [1959]

HUCKFIELD, Leslie John. House of Commons, London. S. of Ernest L. Huckfield, Esq. B. 7 Apr. 1942; m. 20 May 1976, Karolyn

Celia, d. of Albert Shindler, Esq. Educ. at Prince Henry's Grammar School, Evesham, Keble Coll., Oxford, and University of Birmingham. Lecturer City of Birmingham Coll. of Commerce 1963-67. Member Birmingham Regional Hospital Board 1970-72. Parliamentary Private Secretary to Rt. Hon. John Silkin, Minister of Public Building and Works 1969-70. Parliamentary Under-Secretary of State, Department of Industry Apr. 1976-May 1979. An Opposition spokesman on Industry from 1979. A Labour Member. Unsuccessfully contested Warwick and Leamington in 1966. Elected for Nuneaton in Mar. 1967. Member of National Executive Committee of Labour Party from 1978.*   [1979]

HUDSON, Sir Austin Uvedale Morgan, Bart. 28 Essex Street, London. 141 Marsham Court, Marsham Street, London. Carlton, United Service, and Buck's. S. of Leopold Hudson, Esq., F.R.C.S. B. 6 Feb. 1897; m. 14 July 1930, Peggy, d. of Harold Broadbent, Esq. Educ. at Eton, and Royal Military Coll., Sandhurst. Conservative Whip June 1931 and Assistant Whip in National Government Aug.-Nov. 1931. A Lord Commissioner of the Treasury Nov. 1931-Apr. 1935; Parliamentary Secretary Ministry of Transport Apr. 1935-July 1939. Civil Lord of the Admiralty July 1939-Mar. 1942. Parliamentary Secretary Ministry of Fuel and Power May-July 1945. Director of Morgan Brothers, Publishers. Created Bart. 1942. A Conservative. Sat for Islington E. from 1922-23, when he was defeated, and for Hackney N. from 1924-45, when he was again defeated. Elected for Lewisham N. in Feb. 1950 and sat until his death on 29 Nov. 1956. Served with Royal Berkshire Regiment and Guards Machine Gun Regiment 1915-18 and 1st County of London Home Guard 1939-45. Chairman of National Union of Conservative and Unionist Associations, Metropolitan Area 1932-34. Died 29 Nov. 1956.   [1956]

HUDSON, James Hindle. 14c The Oval, London. S. of James Hudson, Esq., Schoolmaster of Flixton. B. 27 Sept. 1881; m. 23 July 1913, Nancy Horsfield, of Barnoldswick (she died 1958). Educ. at Elementary School, and University of Manchester. Teacher in Elementary Schools 1903-07. Master at Salford Secondary School for Boys 1907-16. Imprisoned as a conscientious objector during First World War. Parliamentary Private Secretary to Rt. Hon. Philip Snowden, Chancellor of the Exchequer 1924 and 1929-31, and to Rt. Hon. Sir Hartley Shawcross, President of Board of Trade June 1951. A Labour Member. Unsuccessfully contested Huddersfield in 1922. Sat for Huddersfield from 1923 to 1931, when he was defeated. Unsuccessfully contested the Altrincham division of Cheshire in 1933 and Stockport in 1935. Sat for Ealing W. from July 1945 to Feb. 1950 and for Ealing N. from Feb. 1950 until he was defeated in 1955. Methodist local preacher. Member of National Temperance Federation. Died 10 Jan. 1962.   [1954]

HUDSON, Rt. Hon. Robert Spear, C.H. 18 Cowley Street, London. Fyfield Manor, Pewsey, Wiltshire. Carlton, Athenaeum, and R.Y.S. S. of Robert William Hudson, Esq. B. 15 Dec. 1886; m. 1918, Hannah, d. of P.S.P. Randolph, Esq., of Philadelphia. Educ. at Eton, and Magdalen Coll., Oxford. Late Diplomatic Service. Served in St. Petersburg, Washington, Athens and Paris. Attaché 1911. First Secretary 1920. Parliamentary Secretary Ministry of Labour Nov. 1931-June 1935. Minister of Pensions June 1935-July 1936; Parliamentary Secretary Ministry of Health July 1936-May 1937; Secretary of Overseas Trade Department May 1937-Apr. 1940; Minister of Shipping Apr.-May 1940; Minister of Agriculture and Fisheries May 1940-July 1945. PC. 1938. C.H. 1944. A Conservative. Unsuccessfully contested Whitehaven in 1923. Sat for Whitehaven from 1924-29, when he was defeated. Elected for Southport in 1931 and sat until Jan. 1952, when he was created Visct. Hudson. Vice-President of Royal Agricultural Society. Died 2 Feb. 1957 in Southern Rhodesia. [1951]

HUDSON, Walter Richard Austen. Flat 19, 36 Buckingham Gate, London. Wyton Lodge, Wyton, Hull, Yorkshire. S. of Walter Hudson, Esq. B. 8 Dec. 1894, at Leeds; m. 1917, Marion Hyde. Educ. at Hymers Coll., Hull and Ashville Coll., Harrogate. Served with E. Yorkshire Regiment and R.A.S.C. 1914-17. Sheriff of Kingston-upon-Hull

1946-47. A Conservative. Elected for the North division of Kingston-upon-Hull in Feb. 1950 and sat until he retired in 1959. Chairman of Conservative Agriculture and Food Committee 1951-55. C.B.E. 1962. Died 21 Aug. 1970.   [1959]

HUGHES, Rt. Hon. Cledwyn, C.H. Swynol Le, Trearddur, Holyhead, Gwynedd. Travellers'. S. of the Rev. Henry David Hughes, Presbyterian Minister. B. 14 Sept. 1916; m. 19 June 1949, Jean Beatrice, only d. of Capt. Jesse Hughes, of Holyhead, (1 s. 1 d.). Educ. at Holyhead Grammar School, University Coll. of Wales, Aberystwyth, and Law Society. A Solicitor, qualified 1940 admitted Jan. 1946. Served in R.A.F. (Flight-Lieut.) 1940-45. Acting Clerk Holyhead Urban District Council to 1949; Anglesey County Council 1946-53. Member of the Labour Party from 1938. Opposition spokesman on Housing and Local Government 1959-64. Minister of State, Commonwealth Relations Oct. 1964-Apr. 1966. Secretary of State for Wales Apr. 1966-Apr. 1968. Minister of Agriculture, Fisheries and Food Apr. 1968-June 1970. Opposition spokesman on Agriculture June 1970-Jan. 1972. Honorary LL.D. University of Wales 1970. Honorary Freeman of the borough of Beaumaris 1972. Alderman, Anglesey County Council 1973. Honorary Freeman Isle of Anglesey 1976. Vice-Chairman P.L.P. 1974; Chairman 1974-79. President University Coll. of Wales 1976. PC. 1966. C.H. 1977. A Labour Member. Unsuccessfully contested Anglesey in 1945 and 1950. Elected for Anglesey in Oct. 1951 and sat until he retired in 1979. Created Baron Cledwyn of Penrhos (Life Peerage) 1979.*   [1979]

HUGHES, Emrys. Lochnorris, Cumnock, Ayrshire. S. of the Rev. J.R. Hughes, of Tonypandy. B. 10 July 1894; m. 1st, 1924, Nan. d. of Keir Hardie, Esq., MP. (she died 1947); 2ndly, 1949, Martha, d. of P.M. Cleland, Esq., of Glasgow. Educ. at Mountain Ash School, and City of Leeds Training Coll. A Teacher, Journalist and Author, late Editor of *Forward*, Glasgow. A Labour Member. Unsuccessfully contested the Bosworth division of Leicestershire in 1923. Elected for the S. Ayrshire division of Ayrshire and Bute in Feb. 1946 and sat until his death on 18 Oct. 1969. Labour Whip withdrawn Nov. 1954-Apr. 1955 and Mar. 1961-May 1963. Died 18 Oct. 1969. [1969]

HUGHES, Hector Samuel James, Q.C. 1 Garden Court, Temple, London. Devonshire. S. of Alexander Hughes, Esq., of Dublin. B. 1887; m. 2ndly, Oct. 1966, Mrs. Elsa Lilian Riley. Educ. at Diocesan School, St. Andrews' Coll., and University of Dublin. A Barrister-at-Law, Irish Bar 1915, English Bar, Gray's Inn 1923; Middle Temple 1932; Ghana Bar 1952; K.C. Irish Bar, Kings Inn 1927; K.C. English Bar 1932. A Gov. of Queen Anne's Bounty. Board member of Church Army. Author of eight law books, poems, and numerous articles. A Labour Member. Unsuccessfully contested Camberwell N.W. in 1931 and 1935. Elected for Aberdeen N. in July 1945 and sat until he retired in May 1970. President of National Council for Promotion of Education in Swimming. Died 23 June 1970. [1970]

HUGHES, Herbert Delauney. 25 Canonbury Park North, London. National Trades Union. S. of Arthur Percy Hughes, Esq., Schoolmaster. B. 7 Sept. 1914; m. 25 Sept. 1937, Beryl, d. of H.A.M. Parker, Esq., of Bristol. Educ. at Cheadle Hulme School, and Balliol Coll., Oxford. Organising Secretary Fabian Society 1939-42. Member of Fabian Executive 1946, Chairman 1959-60. Lieut. R.A. 1943-45. Parliamentary Private Secretary to the Rt. Hon. Ellen Wilkinson, Minister of Education 1945-47, and to Michael Stewart, Esq., Under-Secretary of State for War 1948-50; Gov. of Educational Foundation for Visual Aids 1948. A Labour Member. Elected for Wolverhampton W. in July 1945 and sat until Feb. 1950, when he unsuccessfully contested Wolverhampton S.W. Member of Lambeth Borough Council 1937-42. Principal of Ruskin Coll., Oxford 1950-79. Gov. of Educational Foundation for Visual Aids 1948-56. Member of Civil Service Arbitration Tribunal from 1955. Member of Commonwealth Scholarship Commission 1968-74. Member of Committee on Adult Education 1969-73, of Advisory Council on Adult and Continuing Education from 1978. President of Workers Educational Associa-

tion from 1971. Chairman of Adult Literacy Resource Agency from 1975.* [1950]

HUGHES, Robert. House of Commons, London. B. Jan. 1932; m. 1957, Ina Margaret Miller (2 s. 3 d.). Educ. at Robert Gordon's Coll., Aberdeen, Benoni High School, Transvaal, and Pietermaritzburgh Technical Coll., Natal. A Draughtsman. Member Aberdeen Town Council from 1962-1970. Chairman Aberdeen City Labour Party 1963-69. Member N.E. Scotland Regional Hospital Board. Member General Medical Council from 1976. Founder member C.N.D. An Opposition spokesman on Scottish Affairs 1973-74. Parliamentary Under-Secretary of State Scottish Office Mar. 1974 to July 1975, when he resigned. Member A.E.F.; Vice-Chairman Anti-Apartheid Movement 1976; Chairman 1977. Piloted the Rating (Disabled Persons) Act 1978 to Statute as Private Members Bill. A Labour Member. Unsuccessfully contested N. Angus and Mearns in 1959. Elected for Aberdeen N. division in June 1970.* [1979]

HUGHES, Ronw Moelwyn, K.C. 2 Paper Buildings, Temple, London. 9 Greenaway Gardens, London. Oxford & Cambridge. S. of the Rev. J.G. Moelwyn Hughes of Cardigan. B. 6 Oct. 1897; m. 11 May 1929, Hon. Louisa Mary Greer, d. of Lord Fairfield. Educ. at Cardigan Council and County Schools, University Coll. of Wales, Aberystwyth, and Downing Coll., Cambridge. Barrister-at-Law, Inner Temple 1922, on the Northern Circuit, Bencher 1950. Served with West Yorkshire Regiment R.F.C. and R.A.F. 1915-19. Parliamentary Private Secretary to Maj. Rt. Hon. G. Lloyd George, Parliamentary Secretary Ministry of Food Mar. 1942 and when Minister of Fuel and Power June 1942-June 1944. Member of Select Committee on Rules and Orders and of Lord Chancellor's Committee Legal Aid. K.C. 1943. Recorder of Bolton 1946-53. Chairman of Cotton Manufacturing Commission 1947-49, and of Catering Wages Board 1946-50. Joined the Labour Party in 1934. Unsuccessfully contested Rhondda W. in 1929 and Southport in 1931 as a Liberal, and Cardiganshire as a Labour candidate in

1935. Returned unopposed for Carmarthen Mar. 1941 and sat until he was defeated in 1945. Elected for Islington N. in Feb. 1950 and sat until he retired in 1951. Member of Birkenhead Borough Council and Ealing Borough Council. Chairman of Greater London Water Inquiry 1947. Died 1 Nov. 1955. [1951]

HUGHES, Royston John. 34 St. Kingsmark Avenue, Chepstow, Monmouthshire. S. of John Hughes, Esq., Miner. B. 9 June 1925; m. 10 June 1957, Marion, d. of John Appleyard, Esq., of Scarborough, (3 d.). Educ. at Pontllanfraith County Grammar School and Ruskin Coll., Oxford. Coventry City Councillor 1962-66. Secretary Coventry Borough Labour Party 1962-66. Held numerous offices in T. & G.W.U. from 1959. Chairman Welsh Parliamentary Party 1969-70. Chairman Parliamentary Group T. & G.W.U. 1968-69. Vice-Chairman Labour Middle East Council 1973. Chairman P.L.P. Sports Group 1974. Chairman P.L.P. Steel Group 1977. Parliamentary Private Secretary to Rt. Hon. F.W. Mulley, Minister for Transport 1974-75. A Labour Member. Sat for Newport from Mar. 1966. Administrative Officer, Standard Motor Company Ltd. 1958-66.* [1979]

HUGHES, William Mark. "Grimsdyke", Vicarage Road, Potten End, Berkhamsted, Hertfordshire. S. of Professor Edward Hughes. B. 18 Dec. 1932; m. 1958, Jennifer, d. of Dr. G.H. Boobyer. Educ. at Durham School, and Balliol Coll., Oxford. Ph.D., University of Newcastle 1963. Sir James Knott Research Fellow, Newcastle-upon-Tyne 1958-60; Extra Mural Tutor, N.W. Derbyshire, Manchester University 1960-64; Lecturer in Economic History, Durham University 1964-70. Parliamentary Private Secretary to Joel Barnett, Chief Secretary to the Treasury 1974-75. Member Select Committee on Parliamentary Commissioner 1970. Member European Parliament July 1975-May 1979; Chairman European Parliament Fisheries Sub-Committee 1977. Member of Executive of British Council 1975, Vice-Chairman 1978 and of General Advisory Council of the B.B.C. 1976. A Labour Member. Sat for the Durham division of County Durham from June 1970.* [1979]

HUGHES-HALLETT, Vice Admiral John, C.B., D.S.O. House of Commons, London. Travellers'. S. of Col. Wyndham Hughes-Hallett. B. 1 Dec. 1901. Unmarried. Educ. at Bedford School, Osborne, Dartmouth, Gonville and Caius Coll., Cambridge. Went to sea 1918 and specialised in Torpedos and Electrical Engineering. Dept. Director Local Defence 1940-41; Commanded Channel Assault Force 1942-43; Naval Chief of Staff for planning "Overland" 1943; Naval Commander of the raid on Dieppe; D.S.O. 1942; C.B. 1945; Vice-Controller of Navy 1950-52; Flag Officer commanding Heavy Squadron 1952-54. Retired in Sept. 1954 on being elected Member from Croydon E. Parliamentary Secretary to Ministry of Transport with special responsibilities for shipping and shipbuilding from Apr. 1961-Oct. 1964. A Conservative. Sat for Croydon E. from Sept. 1954 to May 1955 and for Croydon N.E. from May 1955 until he retired in 1964. Consultant Director of British Shippers Council 1964-69. Gov. of Westminster Hospital 1957-60. Member of W. Sussex County Council 1969-70. Died 5 Apr. 1972. [1964]

HUGHES-YOUNG, Michael Henry Colin, M.C. House of Commons, London. S. of Brigadier-Gen. H.G. Young. B. 1912; m. 1939, Elizabeth Agnes, d. of Capt. Richard Blakiston-Houston (she died 1956). Educ. at Harrow, and Royal Military Coll., Sandhurst. Commissioned in Black Watch, retired as Lieut.-Col. 1948, twice wounded in Second World War, M.C. 1944. Staff of Publicity Department, Conservative Central Office. Parliamentary Private Secretary to Rt. Hon. Toby Low, Minister of State, Board of Trade Mar.-Apr. 1956; Assistant Government Whip Apr. 1956; Lord Commissioner of the Treasury Oct. 1958-Mar. 1962. Government Dept. Chief Whip Oct. 1959-Oct. 1964. Treasurer of H.M. Household Mar. 1962-Oct. 1964. A Conservative. Unsuccessfully contested St. Helens in 1951. Elected for the Central division of Wandsworth in 1955 and sat until 1964, when he was defeated. Created Baron St. Helens 1964. Assumed the surname of Hughes-Young in lieu of Young.* [1964]

HULBERT, Sir Norman John. 28 Bryanston Court, George Street, London.

Carlton, and Royal Automobile. S. of Norman Hulbert, Esq., Ship Broker. B. 5 June 1903; m. 1st, 1938, Dr. Eileen Pearl Gretton-Watson, M.B., B.Chir, J.P. (marriage dissolved in 1960); 2ndly, 1962, Mrs. Betty Joyce Bullock (marriage annulled 1966); 3rdly, 1966, Eliette, d. of Baron F.G. von Tschirschky und Boegendorff. Educ. at Tonbridge. A Director of Public Companies. A Freeman of the City of London. A Gov. of King's Coll. Hospital. Dept.-Lieut. County of Middlesex 1952-65 and County of London 1965-72. Served with R.A.F. 1939-43. British Liaison Officer, Polish Forces 1943-45. Vice-Chairman of Middlesex T. and A. Auxiliary Association; Honorary Col. 461 (Middlesex) H.A.A. Regiment R.A. (T.A.). Member of London County Council for East Islington 1934-37. Parliamentary Private Secretary to Rt. Hon. Oliver Lyttelton when Minister of Production and President of Board of Trade 1944-July 1945. Temporary Chairman of the House of Commons and Chairman of Standing Committees from 1950. Knight Bach. 1955. A Conservative. Sat for Stockport from 1935-50, and for the N. division of Stockport from Feb. 1950 until 1964, when he was defeated. Died 1 June 1972.   [1964]

HUNT, David James Fletcher. House of Commons, London. S. of Alan Nathaniel Hunt, Esq., O.B.E., Shipping Agent. B. 21 May 1942; m. 2 June 1973, Patricia, d. of Roger and Margery Orchard, (1 s. 1 d.). Educ. at Liverpool Coll., Montpellier University, France, Bristol University, and the Guildford Coll. of Law. A Solicitor. Chairman of Bristol University Conservative Association 1964-65. National Vice-Chairman of Federation of Conservative Students 1965-66. Chairman of Bristol City C.P.C. 1965-68. Chairman of Bristol Federation of Young Conservatives and Vice-Chairman of Bristol Conservative Association 1970. National Young Conservative Chairman 1972-73. Vice-Chairman of National Union 1974, and member of General Purposes Committee and the National Union Executive 1967-76. member of Government Advisory Committee on Pop Festivals. Chairman of British Youth Council 1971-74. Gov. of European Youth Foundation at Strasbourg 1972-75. Vice-President of European Con-

servative and Christian Democratic Youth Community and Chairman of National Youth Study Group on "Young People and Politics." Parliamentary Private Secretary to Rt. Hon. John Nott, Secretary of State for Trade from 1979. A Conservative. Unsuccessfully contested Bristol S. in 1970 and Kingswood in Oct. 1974. Sat for the Wirral from Mar. 1976. Member of South Western Economic Planning Council 1972-76. M.B.E. 1973.*   [1979]

HUNT, John Leonard. Basings, Westerham Road, Keston, Kent. 94 Park West, Marble Arch, London. S. of William John Hunt, Esq. B. 1929; unmarried. Educ. at Dulwich Coll. Served in the Intelligence Corps, National Service. A Stockbroker. Member Bromley Borough Council 1953-65; Alderman 1961-65. Chairman of Town Planning and Public Library Committees. Mayor of Bromley 1963-64, the second youngest in the history of the Borough. Chairman S. Lewisham Young Conservatives 1953-56. Member of Stock Exchange 1958-70. Joint Chairman British Caribbean Association 1967-76, later Vice-President. Vice-Chairman Indo-British Parliamentary Group. Chairman All-Party Committee on U.K. Citizenship. Member U.K. Delegation to the Council of Europe and Western European Union 1973-77. Member General Advisory Council of B.B.C. from 1975. A Conservative. Unsuccessfully contested S. Lewisham in 1959 general election. Sat for Bromley from 1964 to Feb. 1974, and for the Ravensbourne division of Bromley from Feb. 1974.*   [1979]

HUNTER, Adam. 1 Whitegates Terrace, Kelty, Fife. B. 11 Nov. 1908. Educ. at Kelty Public School (Elementary). A Miner. Joined the Labour Party in 1933. Member of Lochgelly District Council 1948-52, and Fife County Council 1961-64. Member Executive Committee N.U.M. (Scottish area). A Labour Member. Sat for Dunfermline Burghs from Oct. 1964 until he retired in 1979.*   [1979]

HUNTER, Albert Edward. House of Commons, London. S. of Alfred Hunter, Esq. B. 1900. Served in Army 1918. Joined Labour

Party in 1919; Holborn Board of Guardians 1925-30; member Holborn Borough Council 1928-34, St. Pancras Borough Council 1945-53; Alderman 1949-53; J.P. for London 1951. President National Union of Shop Assistants 1937, National Treasurer 1939-44, later U.S.D.A.W. A Labour Member. Unsuccessfully contested Spelthorne in 1951. Elected for Feltham in 1955 and sat until he retired in 1966. Died 6 Apr. 1969.   [1966]

HURD, Sir Anthony Richard. Winterbourne Holt, Newbury. United University, and Carlton. S. of Sir Percy Hurd, MP. B. 2 May 1901; m. 26 Sept. 1928, Stephanie, d. of E.M. Corner, Esq., F.R.C.S. Educ. at Marlborough, and Pembroke Coll., Cambridge. A Farmer and Company Director. Chairman of Conservative Parliamentary Agriculture and Food Committee from 1951. Knight Bach. 1959. A Conservative. Elected for the Newbury division of Berkshire in July 1945 and sat until Aug. 1964 when he was created Baron Hurd (Life Peerage). Agricultural correspondent of *The Times* 1932-58. Died 12 Feb. 1966 in Antigua.   [1964]

HURD, Hon. Douglas Richard, C.B.E. 2 Mitford Cottages, Westwell, Burford, Oxfordshire. Travellers'. S. of Lord Hurd. B. 8 Mar. 1930; m. 10 Nov. 1960, Tatiana, d. of Arthur Benedict Eyre (3 s.). Educ. at Eton, and Trinity Coll., Cambridge. H.M. Foreign Service, Peking, U.N., and Rome 1952-66. Conservative Research Department 1966-68. Political Secretary to the Rt. Hon. Edward Heath 1968-74, Opposition spokesman on Europe 1976-79. Author of several thrillers. Minister of State, Foreign and Commonwealth Office from May 1979. A Conservative. Sat for mid Oxfordshire from Feb. 1974. C.B.E. 1974. Visiting Fellow, Nuffield Coll., Oxford 1978.*   [1979]

HUTCHINSON, Sir Geoffrey Clegg, Q.C., M.C., T.D. 2 Paper Buildings, Temple, London. Carlton. S. of Maj. Henry Ormerod Hutchinson, V.D., of Prestwich. B. 14 Oct. 1893; m. 1919, Janet Bidlake, d. of H.F. Keep, Esq., of Edgbaston. Educ. at Cheltenham, and Clare Coll., Cambridge, Scholar 1912, M.A. 1919. Called to the bar by Inner Temple 1920. K.C. 1939. Master of

Bench 1946. Served with Lancashire Fusiliers 1914-18, Capt., M.C., and 1939-42 Maj., T.D. Honorary Col. 5th Lancashire Fusiliers 1948-54. Member of Select Committee on National Expenditure; member of Speaker's Conference on Electoral Reform 1944. Chairman of Home Counties, North Area, National Union of Conservative and Unionist Associations 1946-47. Knighted 1952. A Conservative. Unsuccessfully contested the Gower division of Glamorgan in 1935. Sat for Ilford from June 1937 to 1945, when he unsuccessfully contested Ilford N., and for Ilford N. from Feb. 1950 until Jan. 1954 when he was appointed Chairman of National Assistance Board. Chairman of National Assistance Board 1954-64. Created Baron Ilford (Life Peerage) 1962. President of Association of Municipal Corporations 1964-68. President of British Waterworks Association 1947 and of Water Companies Association 1951-54. Member of Hampstead Borough Council 1931-37 and of London County Council 1944-52. Died 20 Aug. 1974.

[1954]

HUTCHINSON, Hugh Lester. 8 Ladybarn Crescent, Fallowfield, Manchester. S. of Richard Hutchinson, Esq. B. 13 Dec. 1904. Educ. at Bootham School, York, and Universities of Neuchâtel, Geneva, and Edinburgh. Member of Fulham Borough Council 1937-40. Served in R.N. 1942-44. A Journalist and Author. Elected for the Rusholme division of Manchester in July 1945 as a Labour candidate and sat until 1950 when he unsuccessfully contested Walthamstow E. as an Independent Labour candidate in opposition to Mr. Attlee. Expelled from Labour Party in July 1949 and was a member of the Labour Independent Group.   [1950]

HUTCHISON, (Alan) Michael Clark. 19 Newington Road, Edinburgh. Wellcroft End, Chapel Row, Bucklebury, Reading. New, Edinburgh. Youngest s. of Sir George A. Clark Hutchison, K.C., MP. B. 26 Feb. 1914; m. 1937, Anne, d. of Rev. A.R. Taylor, D.D., of Aberdeen. Educ. at Eton, and Trinity Coll., Cambridge. Served with Australian Imperial Forces 1939-46 (despatches). Barrister-at-Law, Gray's Inn 1937. With Colonial Administrative Service

(Palestine and Aden) 1946-55. Joint Secretary Scottish Unionist Members' Committee 1958, Vice-Chairman 1965-66 and 1967-68, Chairman 1970. Parliamentary Private Secretary to C.I. Orr-Ewing, Parliamentary and Financial Secretary to Admiralty and to T.G.D. Galbraith, Civil Lord Feb. 1959; Parliamentary Private Secretary to W.R. Milligan, Lord Advocate 1959-60; Parliamentary Private Secretary to J.S.Maclay, Secretary of State for Scotland 1960-62. Honorary National President Scottish Young Unionists 1960. Director Westclox (U.K.) Limited. Voted against entry to E.E.C. on 28 Oct. 1971. A Unionist Member. Unsuccessfully contested Motherwell in 1955. Elected for Edinburgh S. in May 1957 and sat until he retired in 1979.*   [1979]

HUTCHISON, Lieut.-Commander Sir George Ian Clark, R.N. 16 Wester Coates Gardens, Edinburgh. Carlton. S. of Sir George Clark Hutchison, K.C., MP., of Eriska, Argyllshire. B. 4 Jan. 1903; m. 20 Apr. 1926. Sheena, d. of A.B. Campbell, Esq., W.S., of Mylne and Campbell, W.S. (she died 1966). Educ. at Edinburgh Academy, and at Royal Naval Colls., Osborne and Dartmouth. Joined R.N. 1916, specialised in Torpedoes, retired 1931; rejoined Sept. 1939 and served in Naval Ordnance Inspection Department 1939-43. Member of Edinburgh Town Council 1935-41, Chairman of Public Assistance Committee 1937-39. Member of National Executive Council of British Legion (Scotland) 1943-51; Life Gov. of Donaldson's School for the Deaf, Edinburgh. Member of Committee on Electoral Representation 1945. Member Scottish Leases Committee Nov. 1951. Dept.-Lieut. for Edinburgh 1958. Knight Bach. 1954. A Conservative. Unsuccessfully contested the Maryhill division of Glasgow in 1935. Sat for Edinburgh W. from July 1941 until he retired in 1959. Member of Royal Company of Archers.*   [1959]

HUTCHISON, Col. Sir James Riley Holt, Bart., D.S.O., T.D. Rossie, Forgandenny, Perthshire. Cavalry, New (Edinburgh), and Western (Glasgow). S. of Thomas Holt Hutchison, Esq., Shipowner, of Glasgow. B. 1893; m. 31 July 1928, Winefryde, d. of the Rev. R.A. Craft, of Ford, Shropshire. Educ. at Harrow. Director of Companies. Glasgow

Representative to Chamber of Shipping 1933-35. Vice-President Associated British Chambers of Commerce 1958, President 1960-62 National President Incorporated Sales Managers' Association 1949-51. Parliamentary Chairman Dock and Harbour Authorities' Association 1951, and of Defence Committee Western European Union 1956. Served with Lanark Yeomanry and 17th Cavalry, I.A. 1914-18, and in France, N. Africa and on the Staff 1939-45. J.P. for Perthshire. D.S.O. 1945. Parliamentary Under-Secretary of State and Financial Secretary War Office Nov. 1951-Oct. 1954; President Western European Union Assembly 1957-59. Croix de Guerre; Chevalier of Legion of Honour 1945. A Conservative. Sat for Glasgow Central from 1945-Feb. 1950 when he was defeated. Elected for the Scotstoun division of Glasgow in Oct. 1950 and sat until he retired in 1959. President of U.K. Council of European Movement 1955. Created Bart. 1956. Died 24 Feb. 1979.   [1959]

HYDE, Harford Montgomery. 42 Wilton Place, London. 4 Brick Court, Temple, London. Bertha House, Malone Road, Belfast. Athenaeum, and Garrick. S. of James Johnstone Hyde, Esq., J.P., of Belfast. B. 14 Aug. 1907; m. 1st, 15 Apr. 1939, Dorothy Mabel, d. of Murray Crofts, Esq., C.B.E., of Disley, Cheshire (divorced 1952); 2ndly, 1955, Mary Eleanor, d. of Col. L.G. Fischer (divorced 1966); 3rdly, 1966, Rosalind Roberts, d. of Commander J.F.W. Dimond. Educ. at Sedbergh, Queen's University, Belfast, D.Lit., and Magdalen Coll., Oxford, M.A. Barrister-at-Law, Middle Temple 1934. An Author. Private Secretary to the Marq. of Londonderry 1935-39. Commissioned in Intelligence Corps 1940; Lieut.-Col. 1945. Assistant Editor Law Reports 1946-47. Legal Adviser Alexander Korda Group of Film Companies 1947-49. An Ulster Unionist Member. Elected for Belfast N. in Feb. 1950 and sat until he retired in 1959 after his local association had declined to readopt him. Delegate to Council of Europe 1952-55. Professor of History and Political Science, University of the Punjab 1959-61. Biographer of Stanley Baldwin, Neville Chamberlain, Lord Reading, Lord Birkett, Lord Nathan, Lord Carson, Oscar Wilde and Judge Jeffreys.*   [1959]

HYLTON-FOSTER, Rt. Hon. Sir Harry Braustyn Hylton, Q.C. Speaker's House, London. S. of H.B.H. Hylton-Foster, Esq., of Ewell, Surrey. B. 10 Apr. 1905; m. 22 Dec. 1931, Audrey, d. of the Rt. Hon. Visct. Ruffside, Speaker of House of Commons 1943-51 (she was created Baroness Hylton Foster 1965). Educ. at Eton, and Magdalen Coll., Oxford. Barrister-at-Law 1928. K.C. 1947. Recorder of Richmond 1940-44, of Huddersfield 1944-50, of Hull 1950-54; Chancellor of the Diocese of Ripon 1947-54, and of Durham 1948-54. Intelligence R.A.F.V.R. 1940; Dept. Judge Advocate N. Africa and Italy 1942-45. Solicitor-Gen. Oct. 1954-Oct. 1959. Elected Speaker 21 Oct. 1959 and again in Oct. 1964. Knight Bach. 1954. PC. 1957. A Conservative. Unsuccessfully contested the Shipley division of W. Riding of Yorkshire in 1945. Sat for York from 1950-59. Elected for the Cities of London and Westminster in Oct. 1959 and sat until his death on 2 Sept. 1965.   [1965]

HYND, Henry. 31 Alford House, Stanhope Road, London. S. of Henry Hynd, Esq. B. 4 July 1900; m. 1st, 1925, Phyllis Jarman (divorced 1971); 2ndly, 1971, Mrs Anne Nadine Scott. Educ. at Perth Academy. A Railway Clerk 1915-20. Trade Union Official Railway Clerks' Association 1920-45. J.P. for Middlesex. Member House of Commons Chairmen's Panel. Parliamentary Private Secretary to Rt. Hon. A.V. Alexander when 1st Lord of the Admiralty Jan.-Oct. 1946, and when Minister of Defence Dec. 1946-Jan. 1950. Chairman Parliamentary Branch B.-P. Scout Guild. Commander Order of the Crown (Belgium) and Officer of Order of the Oak Crown (Luxembourg). A Labour Member. Sat for Hackney Central from 1945-50. Elected for Accrington in Feb. 1950 and sat until he retired in 1966. Member of Hornsey Borough Council 1939-52.*   [1966]

HYND, John Burns. 18 Lakeside, Enfield, Middlesex. S. of Henry Hynd, Esq., Painter and Decorator, of Perth. B. 4 Apr. 1902; m. 25 June 1927, Elsie Margaret, d. of Albert Charles Doran, Esq. Educ. at St. Ninian's Cathedral School, and Caledonian Road School, Perth. A Railway Clerk 1916-25; Trades Union Clerk (N.U.R.) 1925-62.

Member of Gen. Medical Council 1951-55; West German G.C. of the Order of Merit, with Star 1958; Legion of Honour (Chevalier) 1960; Austrian Golden Cross of Merit, with Star 1961. Chancellor of the Duchy of Lancaster and Minister for German and Austrian Affairs July 1945-Apr. 1947. Minister of Pensions Apr.-Oct. 1947. A Labour Member. Elected for the Attercliffe division of Sheffield in Feb. 1944 and sat until he retired in 1970. Member of Colonial Economic and Development Council. Author of *Willy Brandt, a pictorial biography.* Died 8 Nov. 1971.   [1970]

IREMONGER, Thomas Lascelles Isa Shandon Valiant. 34 Cheyne Row, London. Carlton. S. of Lieut.-Col. H.E.W. Iremonger, D.S.O. B. 14 Mar. 1916; m. Lucille d'Oyen (Author and Broadcaster, and London County Council member for Norwood, Lambeth), eld. d. of Basil Parks, Esq., J.P. Educ. at Oriel Coll., Oxford. Sailed for Oxford against Cambridge; District Officer H.M. Overseas Service, Western Pacific 1938-46; Lieut. R.N.V.R. Member of Inner Temple; member Chelsea Borough Council 1953-56. Parliamentary Private Secretary to Sir Fitzroy Maclean when Under-Secretary of State for War 1954-57. Member of Royal Commission on the Penal System, of the Home Secretary's Advisory Council on the Employment of Prisoners and of Council of Institute for Study and Treatment of Delinquency. Underwriting member of Lloyd's. Publications: *Disturbers of the Peace* (1962), and *Money, Politics and You* (1963). A Conservative. Unsuccessfully contested the Northfield division of Birmingham in 1950. Sat for Ilford N. from Feb. 1954 to Feb. 1974 and for the Ilford N. division of Redbridge from Feb. 1974 to Oct. 1974, when he was defeated. Unsuccessfully contested Ilford N. in Mar. 1978 and in 1979 as an Independent Conservative in opposition to the official Conservative candidate.*   [1974 2nd ed.]

IRVINE, Rt. Hon. Sir Arthur James, Q.C. 20 Wellington Square, London. S. of J.M. Irvine, Esq., K.C. B. 14 July 1909; m. 2 Oct. 1937, Eleanor, d. of E.E.T. Morris, Esq., of Petersfield, Hampshire. Educ. at Edinburgh Academy and University, (M.A.), and at Oriel Coll., Oxford, (M.A.). President of the Oxford Union 1932. A Barrister-at-Law, Middle Temple 1935, and Inner Temple 1954. Secretary to the Rt. Hon. Lord Hewart, Lord Chief Justice of England 1935-40. Served in the Army 1940-45. D.A.A.G., H.Q. Eastern Command and D.A.M.S., H.Q. Land Forces, Greece. Q.C. 1958. Recorder of Colchester 1965-67; Bencher Middle Temple 1965. Solicitor General Aug. 1967-June 1970. Kt. 1967; PC. 1970. Honorary Fellow Oriel Coll.1969. Joined Labour Party 1943. Chairman of Select Committee on Procedure 1964-65. A Labour Member. Unsuccessfully contested Kincardine and W. Aberdenshire in 1935 and Mar. 1939 as a Liberal, Twickenham in 1945 and S. Aberdeen in Nov. 1946. Elected for the Edge Hill division of Liverpool in Sept. 1947 and sat until his death on 15 Dec. 1978. Edge Hill Constituency Labour Party declined to re-adopt him as their candidate in 1977. Died 15 Dec. 1978.

[1979]

IRVINE, Bryant Godman. Great Ote Hall, Burgess Hill, Sussex. S. of W. Henry Irvine, Esq. B. 1909. m. 1945, Valborg Cecilie, d. of P.F. Carslund, Esq. Educ. at St. Paul's School, and Magdalen Coll., Oxford. Secretary Oxford Union Society. Called to the bar at the Inner Temple 1932; R.N.V.R. 1939-45. Lieut.-Commander; Chairman N.F.U. Branch; Chairman Agricultural Land Tribunal S.E. Province 1954-55. Had farms in Sussex. Parliamentary Private Secretary to Rt. Hon. Geoffrey Lloyd, Minister of Education 1957-59; to Sir Edward Boyle, Financial Secretary to the Treasury 1959-60. Chairman Parliamentary Horticulture Sub-Committee 1960-62; Vice-Chairman Parliamentary Agriculture Committee 1964-70. Honorary Treasurer 1922 Committee 1974-76, Joint Secretary 1965-68. Secretary or Vice-Chairman Parliamentary Commonwealth Affairs Committee 1957-66 and 1967-68. Vice-Chairman Parliamentary Foreign and Commonwealth Committee 1969-76. Chairman Canadian Parliamentary Group and member Executive Committee U.K. Branch. Commonwealth Parliamentary Association 1964-76, co-opted 1978. General Councillor Commonwealth Parliamentary Association 1969-73. Treasurer Common-

wealth Parliamentary Association 1970-73. Chairman All-Party Tourist and Resorts Committee 1964-66. President British Resorts Association 1964. Speakers Panel of Chairman of the House of Commons and of Standing Committees 1965-76. Second Dept. Chairman Ways and Means and Dept. Speaker Feb. 1976-May 1979, First Dept. Chairman from May 1979. A Conservative. Unsuccessfully contested Wood Green in 1951. Elected for the Rye division of East Sussex in 1955.*

[1979]

IRVING, Charles Graham. Drake House, Malvern Road, Cheltenham. Constitutional. S. of Charles Irving, Esq. B. 1926; unmarried Educ. at Glengarth School, Cheltenham, and Lucton School, Herefordshire. Member of the Gloucestershire County Council 1948-74. Member of Cheltenham Borough Council 1947-74 and of Cheltenham District Council from 1973. Dept. Mayor of Cheltenham 1959-63 and 1972-73. Mayor of Cheltenham 1958-60 and 1971-72. Alderman Cheltenham Borough Council 1959-74. Elected an Alderman of the county 1965-74. Member of the National Council for the Care and Resettlement of Offenders. Chairman of the N.A.C.R.O. Regional Council for South Wales and South-West. Founder and Chairman of the National Victims Association 1973. Chairman of the South-West Midlands Housing Association Limited. Chairman of the Cheltenham and District Housing Association Limited 1972. Director of Public Relations for the Dowty Group Limited. Chairman Gloucestershire Social Security Committee. Member of the National Union of Journalists. Founder member of the University Committee for Gloucestershire. A Conservative. Unsuccessfully contested the Bilston division of Staffordshire in 1970 and Kingswood in Feb. 1974. Elected for Cheltenham in Oct. 1974.*

[1979]

IRVING, Rt. Hon. Sydney. 10 Tynedale Close, Dartford, Kent. S. of Sydney Irving, Esq. of Newcastle-upon-Tyne. B. 1918; m. 1942, Mildred, d. of Chariton Weedy, Esq. Educ. at Pendower School, Newcastle-upon-Tyne, and London School of Economics, University of London, B.Sc. (Econ.), Dip.Ed. Served with W. Yorkshire Regiment 1939-46,

Maj. Member Dartford Borough Council 1952-74. Member N.W. Kent Divisional Executive of Kent Education Committee 1952-74, Chairman 1971-74, and Dartford District Council from 1973, Chairman 1973-74. Vice-Chairman Kent County Joint Committee 1973. President Thames-side Association of Teachers (N.U.T.) 1955; member Minister of Education's Advisory Committee on Handicapped Children 1958-65. A Dept. Pro-chancellor of University of Kent 1968-71 and Director of the Foundation Fund 1971-74. Chairman of the Dartford and Darenth Hospital Management Committee 1971-73. Opposition Whip for South and South West Oct. 1959-Oct. 1964. Dept. Chief Government Whip and Treasurer of H.M. Household Oct. 1964-Apr. 1966. Dept. Chairman of Committee of Ways and Means Apr. 1966-Oct. 1968. Dept. Speaker and Chairman of Ways and Means Oct. 1968-June 1970. Member Commonwealth Parliamentary Association Delegation to Hong Kong and Ceylon 1958. Delegate to British-American Parliamentary Conference, Bermuda 1965; Leader All-Party Delegations to Malta 1965 and Israel 1975. Delegate Council of Europe and Western European Union Assemblies 1963-64. PC. 1969. Member Committee of Privileges and Select Committees on Members Interests (Declaration) 1974 and on the Rt. Hon. Member for Walsall (North) 1975. Chairman of the Sessional Committees on Procedure 1974-76 and Direct Elections to The European Assembly 1976. Member of the Parliamentary Group to advise on a Register of the Dependents of Immigrants 1976. Chairman of the Manifesto Group 1976-77 and member of Liaison Committee of the P.L.P. 1975. Dept.-Lieut. for Kent 1976. A Labour and Co-operative Member. Sat for the Dartford division of Kent from 1955-70, when he was defeated, and from Feb. 1974 until 1979, when he was again defeated. Chairman of Southern Regional Council of Labour Party 1965-67. Member of Executive Committee of Council of European Municipalities 1972-77. Created Baron Irving of Dartford (Life Peerage) 1979.* [1979]

IRVING, William John. 18 Kimberley Road, London. S. of Robert Irving, Esq., Railway Worker of Carlisle. B. 1 Apr. 1892; m. 17 Apr. 1917, Martha Cowley, d. of Albert Strong, Esq. Educ. at Workington Secondary School. A Political Organiser 1922-45. J.P. and County Councillor for Middlesex 1936; Chairman 1948, and of Lee Conservancy Catchment Board 1948. A Co-operative and Labour Member. Sat for Tottenham N. from Dec. 1945 to Feb. 1950 and for Wood Green from Feb. 1950 until he retired in 1955. Died 15 Mar. 1967. [1954]

ISAACS, Rt. Hon. George Alfred. House of Commons, London. Berryvil, Wolsey Road, East Molesey. S. of Alfred Isaacs, Esq., Printer. B. 28 May 1883; m. 1905, Flora, d. of R. Beasley, Esq. Educ. at Wesleyan Elementary School. Mayor of Southwark 1919-21; late Alderman of Southwark; Dept.-Lieut. and J.P. for Surrey; late Chairman of Kingston Bench. Liveryman of the Worshipful Company of Stationers; Gen. Secretary of National Society of Operative Printers and Assistants 1909-49; late President of Printing and Kindred Trades Federation; late member of Trades Union Congress Gen. Council; Parliamentary Private Secretary to Rt. Hon. J.H. Thomas when Secretary of State for the Colonies 1924 and when Secretary of State for the Dominions 1929-31, and to the Rt. Hon. A.V. Alexander, 1st Lord of the Admiralty Jan. 1942-45; Minister of Labour and National Service July 1945-Jan. 1951; Minister of Pensions Jan.-Oct. 1951. PC. 1945. A Labour Member. Unsuccessfully contested Gravesend in 1922. Sat for Gravesend from Dec. 1923 until Oct. 1924, when he was defeated. Sat for Southwark N. from May 1929 until Oct. 1931, when he was again defeated. Unsuccessfully contested Southwark N. in Mar. 1927 and 1935. Re-elected for Southwark N. in May 1939 and sat until 1950. Elected for Southwark in Feb. 1950 and sat until he retired in 1959. Member of Royal Commission on Workmen's Compensation 1938-44. President of World Trade Union Conference 1945. Died 26 Apr. 1979. [1959]

JACKSON, Frank Lawson John, O.B.E., T.D. 1 Hamilton Road, Burton-on-Trent. Public Schools. S. of S.V. Jackson, Esq. B. 12 June 1919; m. 1st, 1950, Jane Grizelda, d. of Col. L.M. Robinson (marriage annulled

1961); 2ndly, 1963, Pamela Marion, d. of W. Fergusson Wood, Esq. Educ. at Oundle. A. Barley Merchant. Commissioned 6th Battalion N. Staffordshire Regiment T.A. 1938. War service 1939-46. Commanded Battalion 1954-58. Honorary Col. 1959. Burton-on-Trent County Borough Council 1950-54. A Conservative. Unsuccessfully contested S.E. Derbyshire in 1955. Elected for S.E. Derbyshire in 1959 and sat until he retired in 1964. O.B.E. 1959. Died 29 Mar. 1976.   [1964]

JACKSON, George Colin. House of Commons, London. S. of George Hutton Jackson, Esq. B. 6 Dec. 1921. Educ. at Tewkesbury Grammar School, St. Johns Coll., Oxford University, and Gray's Inn, London. A Lecturer, Writer and Broadcaster. Joined the Labour Party in 1939. Member of the National Union of Journalists and the Co-operative movement. Chairman of Oxford University Labour Party Group debating tour to S. Africa 1948 and India 1949. Called to the Bar 1950. Chairman of Council for Advancement of Arab-British understanding. Vice-Chairman of the Arab-British Centre. Chairman P.L.P. Foreign Affairs Group. A Labour Member. Unsuccessfully contested Newbury in 1950 and 1951, Kings Lynn in 1959 and Brighouse and Spenborough at a by-election in 1960. Sat for Brighouse and Spenborough from Oct. 1964 to 1970, when he was defeated, and from Feb. 1974 until he retired in 1979.*   [1979]

JACKSON, Margaret Mary. Department of Education and Science, Elizabeth House, York Road, London. B. 15 Jan. 1943; m. 1979, Lionel A. Beckett, Esq. Educ. at St. Mary's R.C. Primary School, Ashton-under-Lyne, and Notre Dame High School, Norwich. Student apprentice in Metallurgy, A.E.I. Manchester 1961-66. Experimental Officer, Department of Metallurgy, University of Manchester 1966-70. Research Assistant Labour Party 1970-74. Political Adviser, Ministry of Overseas Development Feb.-Oct. 1974. Parliamentary Private Secretary to Rt. Hon. Mrs. Judith Hart, MP. 1974-Jan. 1975. Assistant Government Whip Jan. 1975-Mar. 1976. Parliamentary Under-Secretary of State, Department of Education and

Science Mar. 1976-May 1979. A Labour Member. Unsuccessfully contested Lincoln in Feb. 1974. Elected for Lincoln in Oct. 1974 and sat until 1979, when she was defeated. Current Affairs researcher, Granada Television from 1979.*   [1979]

JACKSON, Peter Michael. Cobb Barn, Smalldale, Bradwell, Derbyshire. S. of Leonard Patterson Jackson, Esq. B. 14 Oct. 1928; m. 1961, Christine Thomas. Educ. at University of Durham, and University Coll., Leicester. Lecturer in the Department of Sociology, University of Hull 1964-Mar. 1966. A Labour Member. Elected for the High Peak division of Derbyshire in Mar. 1966 and sat until 1970 when he was defeated. Unsuccessfully contested High Peak again in Feb. 1974. Unsuccessfully contested Birmingham N. for European Parliament 1979. Fellow University of Hull 1970-72. Tutor, Open University 1972-74. Senior Planning Officer, S. Yorkshire County Council from 1974.*   [1970]

JAMES, David Pelham, M.B.E., D.S.C. House of Commons, London. S. of Sir Archibald James, K.B.E., MP. B. Dec. 1919; m. 1950, Hon. Jaquetta Digby, d. of 11th Baron Digby, K.G. Educ. at Eton, and Balliol Coll., Oxford. Served with R.N.V.R. 1939-45, Prisoner of war 1943-44. M.B.E. 1944. D.S.C. 1944. Member 1945-46 Antarctic Expedition; Polar Adviser for film *Scott of the Antarctic*. Member of Outward Bound Trust from 1948 to 1972; Trustee National Maritime Museum 1953-65. A Conservative. Sat for the Kemp Town division of Brighton from 1959-64, when he was defeated. Elected for Dorset N. in June 1970 and sat until he retired in 1979.*   [1979]

JAMES, Robert Vidal Rhodes. See RHODES JAMES, Robert Vidal.

JANNER, Sir Barnett. 69 Albert Hall Mansions, London. Victoria House, Bloomsbury Square, London. The Jungle, Broadstairs. S. of Joseph Janner, Esq., of Barry. B. 1892; m. 12 July 1927, Elsie Sybil, C.B.E., J.P., d. of Joseph Cohen, Esq. Educ. at Barry County School, University of South Wales and Monmouth (Cardiff Coll.), B.A.; President Students' Representative Council;

Honorary LL.D. University of Leeds 1957. Admitted a Solicitor 1919. World War I, served in France and Belgium with R.G.A. A.R.P. Warden in London 1940-45. Commander of the Order of Leopold II of Belgium 1963. Knighted 1961. A Labour Member. Unsuccessfully contested as a Liberal Cardiff Central in 1929 and the Whitechapel and St. Georges division of Stepney in 1930. Liberal Member for Whitechapel and St. Georges from 1931-35, when he was defeated. Labour Member for W. Leicester from July 1945-50 and for N.W. Leicester from Feb. 1950 until he retired in 1970. Joined the Labour Party in 1936. President of Board of Deputies of British Jews 1955-64. President of Zionist Federation of Great Britain and Ireland. Created Baron Janner (Life Peerage) 1970.* [1970]

JANNER, Hon. Greville Ewan, Q.C. 2 Linnell Drive, Hampstead Garden Sub., London. Chambers, 1 Garden Court, London. S. of Lord Janner, of the city of Leicester. B. 11 July 1928; m. 6 July 1955, Myra Sheink, of Australia, (1 s. 2 d.). Educ. at St. Paul's School, Trinity Hall, Cambridge, and Harvard Post-Graduate Law School, U.S.A. President Cambridge Union; Chairman Cambridge University Labour Club; International Section National Association of Labour Students 1952; President Trinity Hall Athletic Club 1952. A Barrister-at-Law, Middle Temple 1954; Legal Correspondent of various journals and Author of 24 books. Member N.U.J. (London Freelance Branch). Vice-President Association of Jewish Ex-Servicemen, Board of Deputies of British Jews and of Association for Jewish Youth. Member All-Party Parliamentary Committee with Concern for Homeless and Rootless People (C.H.A.R.). Vice-Chairman All-Party Parliamentary Committee for release of Soviet Jewry. Honorary Secretary All-Party Parliamentary Retirement Group. Q.C. 1971. A Labour Member. Unsuccessfully contested Wimbledon in 1955. Sat for Leicester N.W. division in succession to his father from 1970 to Feb. 1974 and for Leicester W. division from Feb. 1974.* [1979]

JARVIS, Col. Sir (Joseph) John, Bart. Hascombe Court, Godalming. Carlton. S. of Joseph Charles Jarvis, Esq., of Harpenden. B. 25 Mar. 1876; m. 10 Sept. 1901, Bessie, d. of Edwin Woodfield, Esq., of Foretrees, Enfield. Honorary D.C.L. Durham; Dept.-Lieut., and High Sheriff of Surrey 1934-35; Honorary Col. R.A.M.C. Dec. 1939. A National Conservative Member. Elected for the Guildford division of Surrey in 1935 and sat until he retired in Feb. 1950. Chairman of J. & A. Churchill Limited (Publishers) and Armstrong Whitworth (Ironfounders) Limited. Created Bart. 1922. Inaugurator of 'The Surrey Fund' which was used to provide economic assistance for Tyneside. Died 3 Oct. 1950. [1950]

JAY, Rt. Hon. Douglas Patrick Thomas. House of Commons, London. S. of Edward Aubrey Hastings Jay, Esq., of Woolwich. B. 23 Mar. 1907; m. 1st, 30 Sept. 1933, Peggy Garnett (marriage dissolved 1972); 2ndly, 27 May 1972, Mary Lavinia Thomas. Educ. at Winchester, and New Coll., Oxford. Fellow of All Souls 1930-37 and from 1968. A Journalist on the staff of *The Times* 1929-33, *The Economist* 1933-37, and *Daily Herald* 1937-40. Assistant Secretary Ministry of Supply 1940-43; Principal Assistant Secretary of Board of Trade 1943-45; Personal Assistant to the Prime Minister 1945-46. Parliamentary Private Secretary to Rt. Hon. Hugh Dalton, Chancellor of the Exchequer Oct. 1947; Economic Secretary to the Treasury Dec. 1947-Feb. 1950; Financial Secretary to the Treasury Feb. 1950-Oct. 1951. President of the Board of Trade Oct. 1964-Aug. 1967. Director Courtaulds 1967-70. Chairman London Motorway Action Group 1968. Chairman Common Market Safeguards Campaign 1970-76. Director Trades Union Unit Trust 1967. Published *The Socialist Case* 1937, *Socialism in the New Society* 1962, and *After the Common Market* 1968. PC. 1951. An Opposition spokesman on Trade and Treasury Affairs until 1962, Principal spokesman on Trade 1962-64. Member of Parliamentary Committee of P.L.P. Feb. 1963-Oct. 1964. A Labour Member. Sat for Battersea North from July 1946 to Feb. 1974 and for the Battersea North division of Wandsworth from Feb. 1974.* [1979]

JEFFREYS, Gen. Sir George Darell, K.C.B., K.C.V.O., C.M.G. Burkham House, Alton, Hampshire. Carlton, and Guards'. S. of Rt. Hon. Arthur Frederick Jeffreys, MP., of Burkham, Hampshire. B. 8 Mar. 1878; m. 28 Feb. 1905, Dorothy, d. of John Postle Heseltine, Esq., of Walhampton, Lymington, and widow of Lionel, Visct. Cantelupe (she died 1953). Educ. at Eton, and Royal Military Coll., Sandhurst. Joined Grenadier Guards 1897. Served with Nile Expedition 1898, in South African War 1899-1902. Commanding Guards Depot 1911-14, 2nd Battalion Grenadier Guards 57th and 58th Infantry Brigades, 1st Guards Brigade and 19th Division 1915-19; commanding Light Division of the Army of the Rhine 1919, London District 1920-24, Wessex Area and Wessex Division 1926-30; Commander-in-Chief Southern Command India 1932-36. Gen. 1935. Aide-de-Camp Gen. to H.M. The King 1936-38. Retired 1938. Dept.-Lieut., J.P. and County Alderman for Hampshire. Col. Royal Hampshire Regiment 1945-48; Col. Grenadier Guards from 1952; Chairman of Hampshire and Isle of Wight T.A. Association 1938-48; Grand Officer of the Belgian Order of Leopold; Order of the Crown of Belgium; Commander of the Legion of Honour; of the Order of St. Olaf of Norway; the Russian Order of St. Stanislas; the Order of the Rising Sun of Japan; Grand Cross of the Order of the Crown of Rumania; and the Croix de Guerre France and Belgium. A Conservative. Elected for the Petersfield division of Hampshire in Feb. 1941 and sat until he retired in 1951. C.M.B. 1916; C.B. 1918; K.C.V.O. 1924; K.C.B. 1932. Created Baron Jeffreys 1952. Died 19 Dec. 1960. [1951]

JEGER, George. 2 Parkfields, Putney, London. B. 19 Mar. 1903; m. 1950. Sybil, d. of Abraham Prinsky, Esq. Educ. at Elementary School and evening classes at the London School of Economics. Mayor of Shoreditch 1937-38; member of Shoreditch Borough Council 1926-40. J.P. for London. Secretary of Spanish Medical Aid Committee 1936-40. Served in the Army 1940-45. Member of Parliamentary Delegations to Pakistan, Germany. Holland, Eire, Northern Ireland, and Gibraltar. Commander of the Spanish Order of Liberation. Grand Decoration of Honour in Gold (Commander 1st Class) of Austria. Former Delegate to the Council of Europe and to Western European Union. Chairman Anglo-Austrian Society. Chairman Spanish Democrats' Defence Committee. Parliamentary Chairman of Docks and Harbours Authorities Association. Gen. Manager of Whitehall Theatre. A Labour Member. Unsuccessfully contested S.W. Bethnal Green in 1935 and Walsall in Nov. 1938. Sat for Winchester from July 1945 to Feb. 1950. Elected for the Goole division of the W. Riding of Yorkshire in Feb. 1950 and sat until his death on 6 Jan. 1971. [1971]

JEGER, Lena May. 9 Cumberland Terrace, Regents Park, London. D. of Charles Chivers, Esq. of Yorkley, Gloucestershire. B. 1915; Widow of the former Labour Member for Holborn and St. Pancras S. Dr. Santo Jeger (he died 1953). Educ. at Southgate County School. B.A. (London). Labour Representative of Holborn and St. Pancras S. on the London County Council 1951-54. Formerly employed at the Ministry of Information and Foreign Office. Assistant Editor in Moscow of *British Ally,* a newspaper published by the British Government for issue in the Soviet Union. Staff Writer on *The Guardian* 1959-64. Member National Executive Committee of the Labour Party 1960-61 and from 1968, Chairman 1979-80. U.K. Representative on the Status of Women Commission of U.N. 1967. Chairman of the Government's Working Party on Sewage Disposal 1969-70. Member of the Consultative Assembly of the Council of Europe and Western European Union 1969-71. Member of St. Pancras Borough Council 1945-59 and of London County Council 1952-55. Member of Speaker's Panel of Chairmen 1971-79. A Labour Member. Sat for Holborn and St. Pancras S. from Nov. 1953 to 1959, when she was defeated, and from 1964 to Feb. 1974. Elected for the Holborn and St. Pancras S. division of Camden in Feb. 1974 and sat until she retired in 1979. Created Baroness Jeger (Life Peerage) 1979.* [1979]

JEGER, Dr. Santo Wayburn. 31 Nottingham Place, London. B. 20 May 1898; m. 1948, Lena May, d. of Charles Chivers, Esq. (she was MP. for Holborn and St.

Pancras S. 1953-59 and 1964-79 and was created Baroness Jeger 1979). Educ. at University Coll., Cardiff, and London and St. Mary's Hospitals, M.R.C.S., L.R.C.P. Mayor of Shoreditch 1930. Member of London County Council 1931-46. Founder of Socialist Medical Association. A Labour Member. Unsuccessfully contested S.E. St. Pancras in 1935. Sat for S.E. St. Pancras from July 1945 to Feb. 1950. Elected for Holborn and St. Pancras S. in Feb. 1950 and sat until his death on 24 Sept. 1953.   [1953]

JENKIN, Rt. Hon. (Charles) Patrick Fleeming. 9 Hurst Avenue, Highgate, London. S. of C.O.F. Jenkin, Esq., Industrial Chemist. B. 1926; m. 1952, Alison Monica, d. of Capt. P.S. Graham, R.N., (2 s. 2 d.). Educ. at Clifton Coll., and Jesus Coll., Cambridge. Went to the Middle Temple as a Harmsworth Scholar, called to the bar 1952. Served in the Cameron Highlanders, including service abroad 1945-48. A Barrister, Practised at the bar 1952-57. Employed by The Distillers Company Limited 1957-70. Member of the Hornsey Borough Council 1960-63. Member of the Bow Group from 1951. Member London Council of Social Service from 1963-67. Gov. of Westfield Coll. (London University) 1964-70. Opposition spokesman on Treasury, Trade and Economic Affairs Oct. 1965-June 1970. Vice-Chairman Conservative Parliamentary Trade and Power Committee 1966. President Conservative Greater London Area Education Committee 1967. President Dundee University Conservative Association 1967. Financial Secretary to the Treasury June 1970-Apr. 1972. Chief Secretary to the Treasury Apr. 1972-Jan. 1974. Minister for Energy Jan.-Mar. 1974. Member of Shadow Cabinet 1974-79 and Opposition spokesman on Energy 1974-76, and on Social Services 1976-79. Secretary of State for Social Services from May 1979. Non-Executive Director Tilbury Contracting Group Limited 1974, Royal Worcester Limited and Continental and Industrial Trust Limited 1975. PC. 1973. A Conservative. Sat for Wanstead and Woodford from Oct. 1964 to Feb. 1974 and for the Wanstead and Woodford division of Redbridge from Feb. 1974.*   [1979]

JENKINS, Arthur. Greenlands, Pontypool, Monmouth. B. 1884; m. Hattie Harris. Educ. at Varleg Council School, Ruskin Coll., Oxford, and in France. Member of Monmouth County Council 1919-46, Chairman 1932-33, Alderman. Late Vice-President of S. Wales Miners Federation. A Miner. Member of National Executive Committee of Labour Party 1925-29, 1931-32, Nov. 1932-1933 and 1935-37. Parliamentary Private Secretary to The Rt. Hon. C.R. Attlee when Lord Privy Seal, Dominions Secretary and Lord President May 1941-Mar. 1945. Parliamentary Secretary Ministry of Town and Country Planning Mar.-May 1945; Parliamentary Secretary Ministry of Education Aug.-Oct. 1945. A Labour Member. Elected for the Pontypool division of Monmouthshire in 1935 and sat until his death on 25 Apr. 1946.   [1946]

JENKINS, Hugh Gater. 75 Kenilworth Court, Lower Richmond Road, London. S. of Joseph Walter Jenkins, Esq., Dairyman. B. 27 July 1908; m. 1936, Marie, d. of Squadron-Leader E. Crosbie. Educ. at Enfield Grammar School. R.A.F. Flight-Lieut. Served with R.A.F. during World War II. Joined the Labour Party in 1933. A Trade Unionist from 1930. A Writer and Broadcaster on various subjects. Under-Secretary of State for Education and Science ('Minister for the Arts') Mar. 1974-Apr. 1976. Assistant Gen. Secretary of Actors' Equity to 1964 and Chairman of Theatres Advisory Council to 1974. Chairman Arts Amenities Sub-Committee of P.L.P. Dept. Chairman Theatres Trust. Member Board of National Theatre and of Public Accounts Committee. Member of London County Council 1958-65. Member of Arts Council 1968-71. Opposition spokesman on the Arts 1973-74. A Labour Member. Unsuccessfully contested Enfield W. in 1950 and Mitcham in 1955. Sat for the Putney division of Wandsworth from Oct. 1964 until 1979, when he was defeated.*   [1979]

JENKINS, Robert Christmas Dewar. 57 Campden Hill Court, London. Carlton, and Junior Carlton. S. of John Hamilton Jenkins, Esq. B. 1900; m. 1927, Marjorie, d. of George Houstoun, Esq. Educ. at Latymer Upper

School. Served with Inns of Court O.T.C. and with K.R.R.C. Director of Hamilton and Dewar Properties Limited, and other companies. Member of London County Council 1934-49. Member of Kensington Borough Council 1927-68, Mayor, 1939-45, Leader of Conservative Group 1945-53. J.P. for London. A Conservative. Unsuccessfully contested the Dulwich division of Camberwell in 1950. Elected for Dulwich in Oct. 1951 and sat until he retired in 1964. Died 25 June 1978. [1964]

JENKINS, Rt. Hon. Roy Harris. 33 Ladbroke Square, London. S. of Arthur Jenkins, Esq., MP. for Pontypool from 1935-46. B. 11 Nov. 1920; m. 1945, Mary Jennifer d. of Sir Parker Morris. Educ. at Abersychan Grammar School, and Balliol Coll., Oxford. Secretary and Librarian of Oxford Union Society. Served in the Army 1942-46; on Staff of Industrial and Commercial Finance Corporation 1946-48. Parliamentary Private Secretary to Rt. Hon. P.J. Noel-Baker, Secretary of State for Commonwealth Relations 1949-50. An Opposition spokesman on Treasury Matters 1959-62, 1970-72 and on Home Affairs 1973-74. Minister of Aviation Oct. 1964-Dec. 1965. Home Secretary Dec. 1965-Nov. 1967. Chancellor of the Exchequer from Nov. 1967-June 1970. Dept. Leader Labour Party July 1970-Apr. 1972, when he resigned. Home Secretary Mar. 1974-Sept. 1976. Member of Cabinet 1965-70 and 1974-76. Unsuccessful candidate for Leadership of Labour Party 1976. PC. 1964. Voted in favour of entry to E.E.C. on 28 Oct. 1971. A Labour Member. Unsuccessfully contested Solihull in 1945. Sat for Southwark Central from Apr. 1948-Feb. 1950. Elected for the Stechford division of Birmingham in Feb. 1950 and sat until Jan. 1977, when he resigned on appointment as President of the Commission of the European Communities. Member of National Executive Committee of Labour Party 1970-72. Chairman of Fabian Society 1957-58. Member of Committee of Management of Society of Authors 1956-60. Director of Financial Operations, John Lewis Partnership 1962-64. Member of Parliamentary Committee of P.L.P. 1973-74. Biographer of Attlee, Asquith and Dilke and author of political and historical works.* [1976]

JENNINGS, John Charles. House of Commons, London. S. of Josiah Jennings, Esq. of Seaham. B. 1903; m. 1927, Berta Nicholson. Educ. at Grammar School, Bede Coll., Durham, and King's Coll., Durham University. Member of Seaham Urban District Council 1936-44. A Headmaster. Former Chairman Parliamentary Education Committee. Member of Mr. Speaker's Panel of Chairmen 1964. Voted against entry to E.E.C. on 28 Oct. 1971. A Conservative. Unsuccessfully contested S.E. Derbyshire in 1950 and 1951. Elected for the Burton division of Staffordshire in 1955 and sat until he retired in Feb. 1974. Chairman of Select Committee on Public Petitions 1970-74.* [1974]

JENNINGS, Sir Roland. 167-170 Fleet Street, London. Hill House, Whitburn, Co. Durham. S. of Cornelius Jennings, Esq., of Sunderland. B. 1894; m. 1919, Hannah, d. of John T. Peacock, Esq., of Sunderland. A Chartered Accountant. Served with Durham Light Infantry 1914-18. Knight Bach. 1954. A Conservative-Liberal Member. Sat for the Sedgefield division of Durham from 1931-35 when he was defeated. Unsuccessfully contested Wandsworth Central in Apr. 1937. Elected for the Hallam division of Sheffield in May 1939 and sat until he retired in 1959. J.P. for County Durham. Died 5 Dec. 1968. [1959]

JESSEL, Thomas Francis Henry ('Toby'). Old Court House, Hampton Court, East Molesey, Surrey. Garrick, and Hurlingham. S. of Commander Richard F. Jessel, D.S.O., O.B.E., D.S.C., R.N. (Retired). B. 11 July 1934; m. 29 July 1967, Philippa, d. of Henry C. Jephcott (marriage dissolved in 1973). Educ. at Royal Naval Coll., Dartmouth, and Balliol Coll., Oxford, M.A. (Oxon) 1961. Councillor Borough of Southwark 1964-65, Greater London Council member for Richmond-upon-Thames 1967-73; member Metropolitan Water Board 1967-70. Voted against entry to E.E.C. on 28 Oct. 1971. A Conservative. Unsuccessfully contested Peckham in 1964, and N. Hull at a by-election in Jan. 1966 and at the general election of Mar. 1966. Sat for Twickenham from June 1970 to Feb. 1974 and for the

Twickenham division of Richmond-on-Thames from Feb. 1974. Delegate to Council of Europe and W.E.U. 1976.*   [1979]

JOHN, Brynmor Thomas. "Yalehaven", Church Village, Glamorganshire. S. of William Henry John, Esq. B. 18 Apr. 1934; m. 6 Aug. 1960, Ann Pryce, d. of David L. Hughes, Esq. Educ.at Wood Road Junior, Pontypridd Grammar School, and University Coll., London. LL.B. 1954. Articled Clerk 1954-57; qualified as a Solicitor 1957. National Service 1958-60. Partner in a firm of Solicitors 1960-70. Parliamentary Under-Secretary of State for Defence for Royal Air Force Mar. 1974-Apr. 1976. Minister of State, Home Office Apr. 1976-May 1979. Chief Opposition spokesman on N. Ireland from 1979. A Labour Member. Sat for the Pontypridd division of Glamorganshire from June 1970.*   [1979]

JOHN, William. Gelli-deg, Tonypandy. S. of Evan and Rachel John. B. at Cockett, near Swansea 6 Oct. 1878; m. 1908, Anna, d. of George and Catherine Brooks (she died 1950). Educ. at Cockett National School. Entered the mines at the age of 13; Checkweigher Glamorgan Collieries 1909; Financial Secretary Rhondda Miners 1910; Miners' Agent for Rhondda 1912. Member of Rhondda War Pensions Committee; Secretary Rhondda Belgian Relief Committee; member of South Wales Miners' Federation Executive Council from 1912. Secretary Tonypandy Baptist Church from 1902. Parliamentary Private Secretary to J.J. Lawson, Parliamentary Secretary to Ministry of Labour June 1929-Aug. 1931. Welsh Whip Nov. 1931. Comptroller of H.M. Household and Dept. Chief Whip of P.L.P. Mar. 1942-Oct. 1944; a Lord Commissioner of the Treasury Oct. 1944-May 1945. A Labour Member. Elected for Rhondda W. in Dec. 1920 and sat until he retired in 1950. President of Welsh Baptist Union. Imprisoned after the Tonypandy riots in 1911. Died 27 Aug. 1955.   [1950]

JOHNSON, Carol Alfred, C.B.E. 19 Melior Court, Shepherds Hill, London. B. 1903. Educ. at Law Society's School of Law, and London School of Economics. Solicitor (Hons.) 1933 originally in private practice in City of London, subsequently in Local Government Service (Assistant Town Clerk). Secretary to P.L.P. 1943-59. Alderman Lambeth Borough Council 1937-49. Chairman History of Parliament Trust and on Chairmen's Panel of House of Commons, member Executive Committee Inter-Parliamentary Union (British Branch); Chairman Anglo-Tunisian Parliamentary Group and Vice-Chairman Anglo-Italian Parliamentary Group. Joint Honorary Secretary British Council of European Movement and member Council of European Municipalities. Chairman Commons Open Spaces and Footpaths Preservation Society. President Southern Area Ramblers' Association; member Standing Committee on National Parks. Commendatore dell'Ordine al Merito della Repubblica Italiana. Voted in favour of entry to E.E.C. on 28 Oct. 1971. A Labour Member. Elected for Lewisham S. in 1959 and sat until he retired in Feb. 1974. C.B.E. 1951.*   [1974]

JOHNSON, Dr. Donald McIntosh. House of Commons, London. S. of Isaac Wellwood Johnson, Esq. B. 1903; m. 1st, 1928, Christiane Coussaert (she died); 2ndly, 1947, Betty Plaisted. Educ. at Cheltenham Coll., and Caius Coll., Cambridge. Medical Officer, Cambridge University East Greenland Expedition 1926 and Grenfell Mission 1928-29. Served with R.A.M.C. 1939-45. Barrister, Gray's Inn 1930. Demonstrator in Anatomy, Oxford University 1937-39. A Conservative. Unsuccessfully contested Bury in 1935 and Bewdley in 1937 as a Liberal. Unsuccessfully contested Chippenham as an Independent in 1943 and as a Liberal in 1945. Elected as Conservative Member for Carlisle in 1955 and sat until 1964 when he unsuccessfully contested the seat as an Independent Conservative. Resigned the Conservative Whip in Jan. 1964. Author of works on medicine and politics. Founder of Independent Publishers Guild. Member of Sutton and Cheam Borough Council 1951-56. Died 5 Nov. 1978.   [1964]

JOHNSON, Eric Seymour Thewlis, M.C. Ashton Heys, Chester. Cavalry. S. of Ernest Johnson, Esq. B. 8 Sept. 1897. Educ. at

Winchester Coll., and Royal Military Coll., Sandhurst. Served in 16th Lancers 1916-20; awarded M.C. 1918; served in R.A.C. 1940-45. Engaged in cattle ranching in British Columbia 1923-30. Trained racehorses in Cheshire 1931-40. A Conservative. Unsuccessfully contested Lancaster in 1945 as a Liberal, and Droylsden in 1950 as a Conservative. Elected as Conservative Member for the Blackley division of Manchester in Oct. 1951 and sat until 1964, when he was defeated. Died 22 July 1978.   [1964]

JOHNSON, Howard Sydney. Valetta, Dyke Road Avenue, Hove, Sussex. S. of Sydney Thomas Johnson, Esq. B. 25 Dec. 1911; m. 6 July 1939, Betty, d. of Harry Frankiss, Esq. Educ. at Brighton Coll. Preparatory School, and Highgate School. Admitted a Solicitor 1931. Maj. R.A. (T.A.). Spent some years in Gambia, Sierra Leone, Gold Coast and Nigeria. A Conservative. Elected for the Kemptown division of Brighton in Feb. 1950 and sat until he retired in 1959. Member of Brighton Borough Council 1945-50. Director of Alliance Building Society from 1970.*   [1959]

JOHNSON, James. 70 Home Park Road, Wimbledon Park, London. S. of James Johnson, Esq. B. 16 Sept. 1908; m. 1937, Gladys Evelyn, d. of Percy Ellison Green, Esq., of Wanstead, (1 d.). Educ. at Elementary School, Duke's School, Alnwick, Scholarships to Leeds University (B.A. 1st class hons.), London University (diploma in public administration and diploma in education). A Teacher. Fellow of Royal Geographical Society Lecturer, Coventry Technical Coll. 1948-50. Student adviser to Republic of Liberia 1960-64. Member of the Labour Party from 1935. Member N.U.G.M.W., former overseas officer, Kenya. Fabian Society; Co-operative Party. Coventry City Councillor (co-opted member Education Committee). Opposition Whip 1952-54. Parliamentary Private Secretary to Rt. Hon. F.T. Willey, Minister of Land and Natural Resources 1964-65. A Labour Member. Sat for Rugby from 1950-59, when he was defeated. Elected for Kingston-upon-Hull W. division in Oct. 1964.*   [1979]

JOHNSON, Walter Hamlet. Walkden House, 10 Melton Street, London. S. of Jack Johnson, Esq., Aircraft Engineer. B. 21 Nov. 1917; m. 1945. Educ. at Devon House School, Margate. National Treasurer of T.S.S.A. and N.F.P.W. from 1965, Gov. of Ruskin Coll., Oxford. Staff Training Executive, London Transport. Assistant Government Whip June 1974-Jan. 1975. President of T.S.S.A. from 1977. A Labour Member. Unsuccessfully contested Bristol W. in 1955, South Bedfordshire in 1959 and Acton in Mar. 1968. Elected for the S. division of Derby in June 1970.*   [1979]

JOHNSON SMITH, Geoffrey. House of Commons, London. S. of J. Johnson Smith, Esq. B. 16 Apr. 1924; m. 21 July 1951, Jeanne, d. of F.K. Pomeroy, Esq., M.D., of California, U.S.A., (2 s. 1 d.). Educ. at Charterhouse, and Lincoln Coll., Oxford. Army service 1942-47. Capt. R.A. Oxford 1947-49. Information Officer, British Con.-General, San Francisco 1950-52. Member Production Staff, Talks Department B.B.C. T.V. 1953-54. Interviewer-Reporter with B.B.C. T.V. 1954-59. Member I.B.A. General Advisory Council 1976. London County Councillor member for Putney 1955-58. Parliamentary Private Secretary to Niall Macpherson, Parliamentary Secretary Board of Trade 1960-62 and Minister of Pensions July 1962-Oct. 1963. Secretary Conservative Party Parliamentary Education Committee 1963-64. Opposition Whip Feb.-July 1965. Vice-Chairman Conservative Party 1965-71. Under-Secretary of State for Defence (Army) Apr. 1971-Nov. 1972. Parliamentary Secretary Civil Service Department Nov. 1972-Mar. 1974. A Conservative. Sat for Holborn and St. Pancras S. from 1959-64, when he was defeated. Elected for the East Grinstead division of East Sussex in Feb. 1965.*   [1979]

JOHNSTON, (David) Russell. Drummond Tower, Dores Road, Inverness. S. of David Knox Johnston, Esq. B. July 1932; m. 1967, Joan Graham Menzies (2 s.). Educ. at Carbost Public School, Isle of Skye, Portree Secondary School, Skye, and Edinburgh University, (M.A. (Hons.) History). A History Teacher at Liberton Secondary

School, Edinburgh 1961-63. President of Edinburgh University Liberal Club 1956-57; Vice-President from 1960-61. Member of the Scottish Liberal Party Executive from 1961. A Research Assistant with the Scottish Liberal Party from Sept. 1963. Vice-Chairman Scottish Liberal Party 1965-70. Chairman Scottish Liberal Party 1970-74. Member Royal Commission on Local Government in Scotland 1966-69. Leader Scottish Liberal Party from 1974. Member of U.K. Delegation to European Parliament Jan. 1973-July 1975 and Oct. 1976-May 1979. Liberal spokesman on Foreign Affairs and Defence to 1975 and on Scotland from 1975. A Liberal. Sat for the Inverness division of Inverness and Ross and Cromarty from Oct. 1964. Unsuccessfully contested Highlands and Islands for European Parliament 1979.*

[1979]

JOHNSTON, Douglas Harold, Q.C. Dunosdale, Cammo Crescent, Barnton, Edinburgh. Caledonian. S. of Joseph Johnston, Esq., Advocate of Aberdeen. B. 1 Feb. 1907; m. 4 Apr. 1936, Doris, d. of James Kidd, Esq., Conservative MP. for Linlithgowshire from 1918-22 and 1924-28. Educ. at Aberdeen Grammar School, St. John's Coll., Oxford, and Edinburgh University. Served with R.A. 1939-45, Lieut.-Col., T.D. Barrister-at-Law, Inner Temple 1931; Advocate 1932; K.C. (Scotland) 1947. Solicitor Gen. for Scotland Oct. 1947-Oct. 1951. A Labour Member. Elected for Paisley in Feb. 1948 and sat until Jan. 1961 when he was appointed a Judge of the Court of Session, with the judicial title of Lord Johnston. Judge of Court of Session 1961-78.* [1961]

JONES, (Albert) Arthur. House of Commons, London. S. of Frederick Henry Jones, Esq. B. 1915; m. 1939, Miss Joyce Wingate, (1 s. 1 d.). Educ. at Bedford Modern School. Joined the Bedfordshire Yeomanry, Territorial R.A. in 1938, commissioned in the Royal Artillery in 1940. Went to the Middle East with the 1st Armoured Division 1941, captured at Alamein, escaped from Italy in 1943. Surveyor and Company Director. Member of Bedford Rural District Council 1946-49. Member of Bedford Borough Council 1949-74. Alderman 1957-74. Mayor of Bedford 1957-58 and 1958-59. Member of the Bedfordshire County Council 1956-67. Vice-President of the Association of District Councils. Member of the Central Housing Advisory Committee 1959-62. Member of Select Committee on Race Relations and Immigration 1968-70. Expenditure 1970. Chairman of Environment Sub-Committee 1974. Member of Speakers Panel of Chairmen 1974-79. Representative of U.K. (Conservative) to the Consultative Assembly of the Council of Europe and a member of the U.K. Delegation to the Assembly of the Western European Union 1971-72. Chairman Local Government National Advisory Committee to Conservative Central Office 1963-73. Honorary Treasurer Town and Country Planning Association. Chairman, Estates Committee of the Harpur Charity. Member of the Management Committee, United Kingdom Housing Association. Vice-President Inland Waterways Association. A Conservative. Adopted as candidate for Wellingborough in 1953, but unsuccessful in the general election of 1955. Sat for South Northamptonshire division from Nov. 1962 to Feb. 1974. Elected for Daventry in Feb. 1974 and sat until he retired in 1979.*

[1979]

JONES, Rt. Hon. Arthur Creech. 3 Stirling Mansions, London. S. of Joseph Jones, Esq. B. in Bristol 1891; m. 1920, Violet May Tidman. National Secretary Transport and General Workers' Union 1919-29; Gov. of Ruskin Coll., Oxford; Vice-President of Workers' Educational Association; Vice-President of Anti-Slavery Society and Royal Commonwealth Society; Chairman Fabian Commonwealth Bureau, Executive member of Africa Bureau; Honorary Treasurer Workers' Travel Association and Pit Ponies Protection Society; member of Colonial Office Education Advisory Committee; Chairman of Labour Party Imperial Advisory Committee; Vice-Chairman of Higher Education Committee to W. Africa 1942-43; Chairman of International Pacific Relations. Executive Member of U.K. Branch. Member of Metropolitan Water Board, of Southern Electricity Board and Executive member of Royal Institute of International Affairs, of British Council and of Travel Association of Great Britain; Executive London Labour Party, and of National Film Council; Organising Secretary Workers' Travel Association 1930-40. Responsible for Access to Mountains Act 1939. Trustee of Municipal Mutual Insurance Limited; Director Solway Chemicals Limited, and Marchon Products Limited. Author of *Trade Unionism Today, African Challenge, Fabian Colonial Essays*, etc. Parliamentary Private Secretary to Rt. Hon. Ernest Bevin, Minister of Labour May 1940-June 1944. Parliamentary Under-Secretary of State for the Colonies Aug. 1945-Oct. 1946. Secretary of State for the Colonies Oct. 1946-Feb. 1950. PC. 1946. A Labour Member. Unsuccessfully contested the Heywood and Radcliffe division in May 1929. Sat for the Shipley division of the W. Riding of Yorkshire from 1935-50, when he was defeated. Unsuccessfully contested Romford in 1951. Elected for Wakefield in Oct. 1954 and sat until he retired in Sept. 1964. Imprisoned as a conscientious objector during First World War. Opposition spokesman on Commonwealth and Colonial Affairs until 1964. Died 23 Oct. 1964. [1964]

JONES, Rt. Hon. Aubrey. 116 Oakwood Court, London. S. of Evan Jones, Esq., Coal Miner. B. 20 Nov. 1911 at Merthyr Tydfil; m. 7 Sept. 1948, Joan, d. of G. Godfrey Isaacs, Esq., (2 s.). Educ. at Cyfarthfa Castle Secondary School, Merthyr Tydfil, and London School of Economics. Journalist on *The Times* 1937-39 and 1947-48. Served in Army 1939-46. Parliamentary Private Secretary to Sir Arthur Salter, Minister for Economic Affairs and Minister of Materials 1952-53. Gen. Director of British Iron and Steel Federation June-Dec. 1955; Minister of Fuel and Power Dec. 1955-Jan. 1957; Minister of Supply Jan. 1957-Oct. 1959. Director Guest Keen and Nettlefolds Steel Company Limited 1960-65, Staveley Industries Limited 1962-65, Chairman 1964-65. PC. 1955. Director of Courtaulds Limited 1960-63. A Unionist Member. Unsuccessfully contested S.E. Essex in 1945 and Heywood and Radcliffe in Feb. 1946. Elected for the Hall Green division of Birmingham in Feb. 1950 and sat until Mar. 1965 when he resigned on appointment as Chairman of the National Board for Prices and Incomes. Chairman of National Board for Prices and Incomes 1965-70. Chairman of Laporte Industries Limited 1970-72. Chairman of Cornhill Insurance Company Limited 1971-74, Director from 1971. Director of Thomas Tilling Limited, Inbucon International Limited, and Black and Decker. Joined Liberal Party June 1980.* [1965]

JONES, Daniel, B.E.M. House of Commons, London. S. of Daniel Jones, Esq., of Porth, Rhondda. B. 1908; m. 1932, Phyllis, d. of John Williams, Esq., of Maesteg. Educ. at Ynyshir (Rhondda) School, and National Council of Labour Colls. A Miner 1920-32. Awarded B.E.M. 1946 for services in the Aircraft Industry 1939-45. Lectured for N.C.L.C. Parliamentary Private Secretary to Rt. Hon. Douglas Jay, President of the Board of Trade 1964-67. 20 years part and full time official of A.E.U., later A.U.E.W. A Labour Member. Unsuccessfully contested Barry in 1955. Elected for Burnley in 1959.* [1979]

JONES, David Thomas. House of Commons, London. B. 17 Oct. 1899 at Pontypridd. A Railway Signalman. Member of Pontypridd Urban District Council 1934-45. Parliamentary Private Secretary to Rt. Hon. A. Barnes, Minister of Transport Jan. 1948-Oct. 1951. A Labour Member. Elected for The Hartlepools in July 1945 and sat until 1959, when he was defeated. Chairman of South Wales Advisory Planning Committee 1942-45. Member of Council of Europe 1955-57 and of Assembly of Western European Union 1956-57. Died 4 Apr. 1963. [1959]

JONES, Rt. Hon. Sir Frederick Elwyn. 5 Gray's Inn Square, London. S. of Frederick Jones, Esq., of Llanelli. B. 24 Oct. 1909; m. 1937, Pearl Binder. Educ. at Llanelli County School, U.C.W. Aberystwyth, and Gonville and Caius Coll., Cambridge. President of Cambridge Union, M.A. (Cantab.). Barrister-at-Law, Gray's Inn 1935. Queen's Counsel 1953 and Q.C. (Northern Ireland) 1958. Bencher of Gray's Inn 1960. Maj. R.A. (T.A.) and Dept. Judge Advocate. Member of British War Crimes Executive 1945. Parliamentary Private Secretary to the Attorney-Gen. (Sir Hartley Shawcross and Sir Frank Soskice) 1946-Oct. 1951. Recorder of

Merthyr Tydfil 1949, of Swansea 1953, of Cardiff 1960-64, and of Kingston-on-Thames 1966. Member General Council of the Bar 1956-59. Attorney-Gen. Oct. 1964-June 1970. Knighted 1964. President Cardiff University Coll., Honorary LL.D. University of Wales. Fellow of King's Coll., London. A Labour Member. Sat for the Plaistow division of West Ham from 1945-Feb. 1950; sat for S. West Ham from Feb. 1950 to Feb. 1974 and for S. Newham from Feb. 1974 to Mar. 1974, when he was appointed Lord Chancellor and created Baron Elwyn-Jones (Life Peerage). PC. 1964. Lord Chancellor from Mar. 1974 to May 1979. C.H. 1976.* [1974]

JONES, Gwynoro Glyndwr. 15 Glyndern, Tanerdy, Carmarthen. Labour Party Office, 116a Priory Street, Carmarthen. S. of John Ellis Jones, Esq., Colliery Carpenter. B. 21 Nov. 1942; m. 19 Aug. 1967, Annie Laura, d. of N.R. Miles, Esq., (1 s. 1 d.). Educ. at Gwendraeth Grammar School, and Cardiff University. Attained B.Sc. (Hons.) Politics and Economics 1965; Market Research Officer 1965-67; Economist Department of Wales Gas Board 1967-69; Public Relations Office Labour Party in Wales Mar. 1969-June 1970; member H.O.C. Expenditure Committee and Standing Orders. Publication: *Labour's Record in Wales 1964-70*. Parliamentary Private Secretary to Rt. Hon. Roy Jenkins, Home Secretary 1974. A Labour Member. Elected for Carmarthen in 1970 and sat until Oct. 1974 when he was defeated. Director of Research, W. Glamorgan County Council 1974-77, Assistant Education Officer for Development Forward Planning from 1977. Member of Council of Europe Municipalities from 1977. President of National Eisteddfod 1974.* [1974 2nd ed.]

JONES, James Idwal. House of Commons, London. S. of James Jones, Esq. B. 1900; m. 1931, Catherine Humphreys. Educ. at Ruabon Grammar School, Normal Coll., Bangor, and London University. Headmaster of Rhosllanerchrugog Secondary Modern School 1938; published books in Welsh and English on the History and Geography of Wales. Publications: *Geographical Atlas of Wales, Historical Atlas of Wales, J.R. Jones, Ramoth.* Member Circle of Bards, National Eisteddfod. A Labour Member. Unsuccessfully contested Denbigh in 1951. Elected for the Wrexham division of Denbighshire in Mar. 1955 and sat until he retired in 1970.* [1970]

JONES, John Henry. Braemar, 17 Holcroft Lane, Culcheth, Warrington. S. of J.W. Jones, Esq., of Rotherham. B. 26 Oct. 1894; m. 1st, 1919, Olive Archer (she died 1957); 2ndly, 1958, Mabel Graham. Educ. at Port Talbot School, Elementary School, Rotherham, and Bangor University. A Steel Smelter. Served in Middle East with E. Riding of Yorkshire Yeomanry 1914-18. Parliamentary Private Secretary to Lord Pakenham, Chancellor of Duchy of Lancaster, and to C.P. Mayhew, Under-Secretary for Foreign Affairs, May-Oct. 1947. Joint Parliamentary Secretary Ministry of Supply Oct. 1947-Feb. 1950. A Labour Member. Sat for Bolton from 1945-50. Elected for Rotherham in Feb. 1950 and sat until he was killed in a car accident on 31 Oct. 1962. [1962]

JONES, Philip Asterley. 73 Valley Road, Welwyn Garden City. S. of Leonard Jones, Esq., of St. Albans. B. 21 June 1914; m. 3 Oct. 1941, Ruth, d. of Wilfrid Davis, Esq., of Duffield. Educ. at Tonbridge School, and Law Societys School. Member of St. Albans City Council 1938-40. Served with R.A.S.C., Driver 1939, 2nd Lieut. 1940, Major 1943. A Labour Member. Elected for the Hitchin division of Hertfordshire in July 1945 and sat until 1950, when he was defeated. A Solicitor, admitted 1937. Editor of *Local Government Chronicle* 1950-63 and of *Solicitors Journal* 1956-68. Law Society Lecturer in law 1945-51. Head of Department of Law, City of Birmingham Polytechnic 1975-77. Died 23 Oct. 1978. [1950]

JONES, (Stephen) Barry. 30 Paper Mill Lane, Oakenholt, Flintshire. S. of Stephen Jones, Esq., Steelworker. B. 1938; m. Janet, d. of Mr. and Mrs. Davies, (1 s.). Educ. at Hawarden Grammar School, and Normal Coll., Bangor, B.Sc. (Econ.). Head of English Department Deeside Secondary School, Flintshire. Regional Officer National Union of Teachers. Honorary Secretary, Atlantic Union Movement (U.K.). Member Delegation of Council of Europe, Western European Union. Parliamentary Under-Secretary of State for Wales Mar. 1974-May 1979. A Labour Member. Unsuccessfully contested the Northwich division of Cheshire in 1966. Elected for the East division of Flintshire in June 1970.* [1979]

JONES, (Trevor) Alec. 58 Kenry Street, Tonypandy, Rhondda, Glamorganshire. S. of Alexander Jones, Esq. B. 12 Aug. 1924; m. 12 Aug. 1950, Mildred, d. of William T. Evans, Esq., (1 s.). Educ. at Porth Grammar School, and Bangor Normal Training Coll. A Teacher. Sponsored Divorce Reform Act 1969. Parliamentary Under-Secretary of State for Health and Social Security Oct. 1974-June 1975. Under-Secretary at the Welsh Office June 1975-May 1979. Parliamentary Private Secretary to John Morris, Minister for Defence Equipment 1968-70, and to Brian O'Malley, Minister of State, Department of Health and Social Security 1974. PC. 1979. Principal Opposition spokesman on Welsh Affairs from 1979. A Labour Member. Sat for Rhondda W. from Mar. 1967-Feb. 1974. Elected for Rhondda in Feb. 1974.* [1979]

JONES, Thomas William. Bro Hedd, Clarke Street, Poncian, Wrexham. S. of James Jones, Esq. B. 10 Feb. 1898; m. 1 Jan. 1928, Flossy, d. of Jonathan Thomas, Esq. Educ. at Poncian Boys' School, and Bangor Normal Training Coll. A School Teacher; former Welfare and P.R.O. to Merseyside and North Wales El. Board; Chairman Ruabon Bench of Magistrates. A Labour Member. Unsuccessfully contested Merionethshire in 1935. Elected for Merionethshire in 1951 and sat until he retired in 1966. Created Baron Maelor (Life Peerage) 1966.* [1966]

JONES, William Elwyn Edwards. Bryn Llinos, Bangor. S. of the Rev. R.W. Jones, of Bootle. B. 4 Jan. 1904; m. 1936, Dydd, d. of the Rev. E. Tegla Davies. Educ. at Bootle Secondary School, Festiniog Grammar School, and University Coll., Bangor. Admitted Solicitor 1927. Town Clerk of Bangor 1939-69; member of Caernarvonshire County Council from 1945-69; Clerk to Ban-

gor Justices. Member of Council of University Coll. of N. Wales. A Labour Member. Unsuccessfully contested Caernarvonshire in 1935 and the Caernarvon Boroughs in 1945. Elected for the Conway division of Caernarvonshire in Feb. 1950 and sat until he was defeated in 1951. Defeated again contesting the same seat in 1955. Member of National Parks Commission 1966-68. Member of Countryside Commission 1968-71. Knighted 1978.* [1951]

JOPLING, Rt. Hon. (Thomas) Michael. Ainderby Hall, Thirsk, Yorkshire. Pine Rigg, Windermere, Westmorland. Beefsteak. S. of Mark Bellerby Jopling, Esq. B. 1930; m. Apr. 1958, Gail, d. of Ernest Dickinson, Esq., of Harrogate, (2 s.). Educ. at Cheltenham Coll., and King's Coll., Newcastle-upon-Tyne, (B.Sc. Agric.). A Farmer, with 500 acres. Formerly member of the N.F.U. North Riding and South Durham Branch, Executive Committee. Formerly member National Council of N.F.U. Member Thirsk Rural District Council 1958-64. Joint Secretary Conservative Parliamentary Agricultural Committee from 1966-70. Joint Secretary House of Commons Motor Club 1968-71. Parliamentary Private Secretary to Rt. Hon. James Prior, Minister of Agriculture, Fisheries and Food June 1970-Nov. 1971. Assistant Whip Nov. 1971-Oct. 1973. Lord Commissioner of the Treasury Oct. 1973-Mar. 1974. Executive Committee U.K. Branch of C.P.A. 1974, Vice-Chairman 1977-78. Sponsored Bill which gave added power to Parish Councils. Opposition Whip Mar.-June 1974. Front Bench spokesman on Agriculture June 1974-May 1979. Shadow Cabinet Apr. 1975-Jan. 1976. Parliamentary Secretary to Treasury and Government Chief Whip from May 1979. PC. 1979. A Conservative. Unsuccessfully contested Wakefield at the general election of 1959. Elected for Westmorland in Oct. 1964.* [1979]

JOSEPH, Rt. Hon. Sir Keith Sinjohn, Bart. 23 Mulberry Walk, London. Carlton. S. of Sir Samuel Joseph, Bart. B. 17 Jan. 1918; m. 1951, Hellen Louise, youngest d. of Sigmar Guggenheimer, Esq., of New York, (1 s. 3 d.). Educ. at Harrow, and Magdalen Coll., Oxford, Fellow of All Souls Coll., Oxford

1946-60 and from 1972. Capt. R.A. (despatches, wounded). Barrister-at-Law, Middle Temple 1946; Common Councilman, then Alderman, Portsoken Ward of the City of London 1946-49. Director Bovis Holdings Limited 1951-59, Chairman of Bovis Limited 1958-59; Director of Gilbert Ash Limited 1949-58. Co-founder and Chairman of the Foundation for Management Education 1958. Parliamentary Private Secretary to C.J.M. Alport, Parliamentary Under-Secretary of State, C.R.O. 1957-59; Parliamentary Secretary Ministry of Housing and Local Government 1959-61; Minister of State, Board of Trade 1961-62; Minister of Housing and Local Government and Minister for Welsh Affairs July 1962-Oct. 1964. Opposition spokesman on Social Services 1964-66, on Labour 1965-67, on Trade and Steel 1967-70, on Home Affairs June 1974-Feb. 1975 and on Industry 1977-79. Spokesman without specific subject responsibilities Mar.-June 1974 and 1975-77. Member of Shadow Cabinet 1964-70 and 1974-79. Secretary of State for Industry from May 1979. PC. 1962. Dept. Chairman Bovis Holdings Limited Oct. 1964-June 1970. Founder Mulberry Housing Trust 1965, Chairman to Dec. 1969. Secretary of State for Social Services June 1970-Mar. 1974. Founder and Chairman of Management Committee of Centre for Policy Studies Limited 1974. Conservative spokesman with overall responsibility for policy and research from 1975. A Conservative. Unsuccessfully contested Barons Court in 1955, defeated by 125 votes. Elected for Leeds N.E. division in Mar.-Feb. 1956. Succeeded to Baronetcy in 1944.* [1979]

JOWITT, Rt. Hon. Sir William Allen, K.C. 61 Marsham Court, London. S. of the Rev. William Jowitt, Rector of Stevenage. B. 1885; m. 19 Dec. 1913, Lesley, d. of J.P. M'Intyre, Esq. Educ. at Marlborough, and New Coll., Oxford. Barrister-at-Law, Middle Temple 1909; K.C. 1922. Served with R.N.A.S. 1914-18. Attorney-Gen. June 1929-Jan. 1932; Solicitor Gen. May 1940-Mar. 1942; Paymaster Gen. Mar.-Dec. 1942; Minister without Portfolio Dec. 1942; Minister of Social Insurance Oct.-Nov. 1944; Minister of National Insurance Nov. 1944-

May 1945. Elected for Hartlepools Nov. 1922 and Dec. 1923; defeated in 1924. Elected for Preston as a Liberal in May 1929, joined the Labour Party June 1929 and was re-elected in July 1929. Unsuccessfully contested the Combined English Universities in Oct. 1931. Elected for Ashton-under-Lyne Oct. 1939 and sat until he was appointed Lord Chancellor in July 1945. A Liberal until June 1929 when he joined the Labour Party; joined the National Labour Party in Aug. 1931 but rejoined the Labour Party in 1936. Knighted 1929. PC. 1931. Created Baron Jowitt 1945, Visct. Jowitt 1947, and Earl Jowitt 1951. Lord Chancellor July 1945-Oct. 1951. Treasurer of Middle Temple 1951. Trustee of National Gallery 1946-53 and of Tate Gallery 1947-53, Chairman 1951-53. Leader of Opposition in the House of Lords 1952-55. President of British Travel and Holidays Association. Died 16 Aug. 1957. [1945]

JOYNSON-HICKS, Hon. Sir Lancelot William, Bart. Newick Park, Newick, Sussex. S. of 1st Visct. Brentford. B. 10 Apr. 1902; m. 15 July 1931, Phyllis, d. of Maj. Herbert Cyril Allfrey, of Newnton House, Tetbury. Educ. at Winchester, and Trinity Coll., Oxford, M.A. A Solicitor 1926. Member of National Assembly of Church of England 1934-70. Served with R.N. 1940-45. Created 1st Bart. 1956. Parliamentary Secretary Ministry of Fuel and Power Oct. 1951-Dec. 1955. A Conservative. Elected for the Chichester division of W. Sussex in May 1942 and sat until June 1958 when he succeeded his brother as Visct. Brentford. Chairman of Automobile Association 1956-74. Dept.-Lieut. for E. Sussex 1977.* [1958]

JUDD, Frank Ashcroft. 84 Kingston Crescent, Portsmouth, Hampshire. S. of Charles and Helen Judd. B. 28 Mar. 1935; m. 26 Aug. 1961, Christine Elizabeth Louise, d. of F.W. Willington, Esq., (2 d.). Educ. at City of London School, and London School of Economics. Secretary Gen. International Voluntary Service from 1960-66. Parliamentary Private Secretary to the Rt. Hon. Harold Wilson, Leader of the Opposition 1970-72. Member of the British Delegation to the Council of European and Western European Union 1970-73. Chairman of the Fabian

Society 1973-74. Published *Radical Future, Fabian International Essays* 1970 and *Purpose in Socialism.* Member A.S.T.M.S. and G.M.W.U. Parliamentary Private Secretary to Rt. Hon. Anthony Greenwood, Minister of Housing and Local Government 1968-70. An Opposition Defence spokesman 1972-74. Under-Secretary of State for Defence for Royal Navy Mar. 1974-Apr. 1976. Parliamentary Secretary, Ministry of Overseas Development Apr.-Dec. 1976. Minister for Overseas Development Dec. 1976-Feb. 1977. Minister of State Foreign and Commonwealth Office Feb. 1977-May 1979. A Labour Member. Unsuccessfully contested Sutton and Cheam in 1959 and Portsmouth W. in 1964. Sat for Portsmouth W. from 1966 to Feb. 1974, and for the North division of Portsmouth from Feb. 1974 until 1979, when he was defeated. Associate Director of International Defence and Aid Fund for Southern Africa from 1979. Director of Voluntary Service Overseas from 1980.*
[1979]

KABERRY, Sir Donald, Bart. Beckfield, East Keswick, Leeds. Carlton, and Constitutional. S. of Abraham Kaberry, Esq. B. 18 Aug. 1907; m. 3 Sept. 1940, Lily Margaret, d. of E. Scott, Esq. Educ. at Leeds Grammar School. Admitted a Solicitor 1930. Member of Leeds City Council 1930-50, Honorary Alderman of Leeds, Dept. Lord Mayor of Leeds 1946-47. Served R.A. (T.A.) 1939-45, Dunkirk 1940, France, Belgium and Germany. Lieut.-Col. (despatches twice). T.D. 1946. Assistant Government Whip 1952-55. Chairman Yorkshire Prov. Area Council Conservative Association 1951-55. Dept. President 1955-66, later President. Parliamentary Secretary Board of Trade Apr.-Oct. 1955; Vice-Chairman Conservative Party Organisation Oct. 1955-Feb. 1961. Member Select Committee on Nationalised Industries 1960 and Chairman Sub-Committee 'C' 1974. Created Bart. Jan. 1960. Dept.-Lieut. W. Yorkshire 1974. Chairman W.H. Baxter Limited and E. Walker and Company Limited. Chairman Association of Conservative Clubs June 1961. Chairman Board of Govs. United Leeds Hospitals 1961-74. Chairman Special Trustees Leeds A.H.A.(T.) 1974. Member of Speaker's Panel of Chairmen

from 1974. Chairman of Select Committee on Industry and Trade from 1979. Voted against E.E.C. on 28 Oct. 1971. A Conservative. Elected for Leeds N.W. in Feb. 1950. Chairman of Yorkshire Chemicals Ltd. 1964-77.*
[1979]

KAUFMAN, Rt. Hon. Gerald Bernard. 87 Charlbert Court, Eamont Street, London. S. of Louis Kaufman, Esq. B. 21 June 1930. Educ. at Leeds Council Schools, Leeds Grammar School, and The Queen's Coll., Oxford. Assistant Gen. Secretary, Fabian Society 1954-55. On Political Staff of *Daily Mirror* 1955-64; Political Correspondent *New Statesman* 1964-65; Parliamentary Press Liaison Officer Labour Party 1965-70. Under-Secretary of State for the Environment Mar. 1974-June 1975; Under-Secretary Department of Industry June-Dec. 1975. Minister of State, Department of Industry Dec. 1975-May 1979. PC. 1978. An Opposition spokesman on the Environment from 1979. A Labour Member. Unsuccessfully contested Bromley in 1955 and Gillingham in 1959. Elected for the Ardwick division of Manchester in June 1970.*
[1979]

KEEGAN, Denis Michael. 77 London Road, Redhill, Surrey. S. of Denis Francis Keegan, Esq., Indian Civil Servant, retired. B. 26 Jan. 1924; m. 1st, 28 May 1951, Pamela Barbara, younger d. of Percy Bryan, Esq. (divorced), (1 s.); 2ndly, 1961, Marie Patricia, d. of Harold Jennings, Esq. (divorced); 3rdly, 1973, Ann Irene, d. of Norman Morris, Esq. Educ. at Oundle School, and Queen's University, Kingston, Ontario. Petty Officer Pilot in Fleet Air Arm 1944-46. Called to the bar by Gray's Inn 1950. Member of Nottingham City Council 1953-55. A Conservative. Elected for Nottingham S. in 1955 and sat until he retired in 1959. Director of Radio and Television Retailers Association. Gen. Manager of Mercantile Credit Company Limited.*
[1959]

KEELING, Sir Edward Herbert, M.C. 20 Wilton Street, Grosvenor Place, London. Brooks's, and Beefsteak. S. of the Rev. William Hulton Keeling. B. 1888; m. 1929, Martha Ann, d. of Henry Dougherty, Esq. of New York. Educ. at Bradford Grammar

School, and University Coll., Oxford, M.A. Barrister-at-Law. Dept.-Lieut. for Co. of London. Member of Lloyds. Served in Mesopotamia, Russia and Syria 1915-18. M.C. 1918. General Manager of Turkish Petroleum Company Limited. Honorary Secretary British School of Archaeology in Iraq. Mayor of Westminster 1945-46; Chairman of Greater London Council for Smoke Abatement. F.S.A. Member of Statute Law Committee, and of Executive Committee, National Trust; C.P.R.E. Parliamentary Private Secretary to Lieut.-Col. A.J. Muirhead when Parliamentary Secretary Ministry of Labour Feb. 1937, when Under-Secretary of State for Air May 1937, and when Under-Secretary of State for India and Burma May 1938-Sept. 1939. Joined R.A.F. Aug. 1939. Chairman Commonwealth Affairs Cons. Committee 1954. A Conservative. Unsuccessfully contested Southwark Central in 1929. Elected for Twickenham in 1935 and sat until his death on 23 Nov. 1954. Knighted 1952. Chairman of Income Tax Payers Society 1953-54. Died 23 Nov. 1954.   [1954]

KEENAN, William, O.B.E. 7 Worcester Road, Bootle, Liverpool. S. of William Keenan, Esq., of Bootle. B. 1889; m. 8 Sept. 1937, Catherine, d. of Alfred Barker, Esq. Educ. at Elementary School, Bootle. Trade Union Official from 1923. Member of Bootle Town Council from 1925. Alderman 1933-45. Mayor of Bootle 1944. O.B.E. 1946. Official of Transport and General Workers' Union. A Socialist. Elected for the Kirkdale division of Liverpool in July 1945 and sat until May 1955, when he was defeated. Died 15 Dec. 1955.   [1954]

KELLETT, (Mary) Elaine. See KELLETT-BOWMAN, (Mary) Elaine.

KELLETT-BOWMAN, (Mary) Elaine. The Beeches, 42 Schoolhouse Lane, Halton, Nr. Lancaster. E.S.U., and Farmers'. D. of Walter Kay, Esq. Assumed the surname of Kellett-Bowman in lieu of Kellett on her second marriage in 1971. B. 8 July 1924; m. 1st, 15 Sept. 1945, Charles Norman, s. of John Kellett, Esq. (he died 1959), (3 s. 1 d.); 2ndly, 1971, Edward Bowman, Esq. Educ. at Queen Mary School, Lytham, The Mount,

York, and St. Anne's Coll., Oxford, Post-Graduate Distinction, Social Studies, Barnet House, Oxford. Barrister, Middle Temple 1964. J.P., Welfare Work Liverpool and London. Delegate to Luxemburg 1956. Lay member Press Council 1964-68. Alderman Camden borough 1968-74. Select Committee Tax Credits 1973. A Conservative. Unsuccessfully contested Nelson and Colne in 1955, S.W. Norfolk in Mar. and Oct. 1959 and Buckingham in 1964 and 1966. Elected for Lancaster in June 1970. Member of European Parliament from Mar. 1975. Member of European Parliament for Cumbria from 1979.*   [1979]

KELLEY, Richard. House of Commons, London. B. 1904; m. 1924. Educated at Elementary School. Served on Thorne Rural District Council for 25 years. Full time Trade Union Secretary for 10 years. National Union of Mineworkers. War service for $5\frac{1}{2}$ years, R.A.S.C. Served on the W. Riding Council 1949-59. A Labour Member. Elected for the Don Valley division of the W. Riding of Yorkshire in 1959 and sat until he retired in 1979.*   [1979]

KENDALL, William Denis. Brusa, Belton Lane, Grantham. National Liberal, and International Sportsmen's. S. of J.W. Kendall, Esq., of Halifax. B. 27 May 1903; m. 1952, Margaret Hilda Irene Burden. Educ. at Halifax Technical Coll. M.I.Mech.E., M.I.A.E., M.I.P.E. A Chartered Engineer. Member of Automatic Gun Bd. 1941-45. A Freeman of the City of London. Chevalier de l'Ordre du Ouissam Alouite Cherifien. An Independent Member. Elected for the Grantham division of Lincolnshire in Mar. 1942, re-elected as an Independent in 1945 and sat until he was defeated, standing as an Independent in 1950. Unsuccessfully contested Grantham as a Liberal in 1951. Member of Society of Friends. Director of Manufacturing, Citroen Motor Company, Paris 1929-38. Managing Director of British Manufacture and Research Company, Grantham 1938-45. Executive Vice-President of Brunswick Ordnance Corporation, New Jersey 1952-55. President of American MARC Inc. 1955-61. President of Dynapower Systems Corporation, California 1961-

73. President of Kendall Medical International, Los Angeles from 1973.* [1950]

KENYON, Clifford. Scarr Barn Farm, Crawshawbooth, Rossendale. S. of John H. Kenyon, Esq., Farmer, of Rossendale. B. 11 Aug. 1896; m. 16 Dec. 1922, Doris, d. of Pemberton Lewis, Esq., of Herne Hill. Educ. at Elementary School, Brighton Grove Coll., and University of Manchester. A Farmer. Mayor of Rawtenstall 1938-42, Councillor 1923-45. A Labour Member. Elected for the Chorley division of Lancashire in July 1945 and sat until he retired in 1970. Joined the Labour Party in 1922. J.P. for Lancashire 1941. C.B.E. 1966.* [1970]

KERANS, Commander John Simon, D.S.O., R.N. House of Commons, London. S. of Maj. E.T.J. Kerans, D.S.O., of Birr, Ireland. B. 1915; m. Jan. 1946, Stephanie Campbell Shires, (2 d.). Educ. at Royal Naval Coll., Dartmouth. Served in Royal Navy 1932-58. D.S.O. 1949. British Naval Attaché, Bangkok, Phnom Penh, Vientiane, Saigon, and Rangoon 1954-55. A Conservative. Elected for Hartlepools in 1959 and sat until he retired in 1964. On staff of Pensions Appeal Tribunals from 1969.* [1964]

KERBY, Capt. Henry Briton. Hobbs Farm House, Yapton, Arundel, Sussex. S. of Henry Kerby, Esq. B. in Russia 11 Dec. 1914; m. 1947, Enid, d. of Judge Philip Herchenroder, C.M.G., C.B.E., (2 d.). Educ. at Highgate School. Served in Regular Army 1933-39; Honorary Attaché H.M. Diplomatic Service 1939-40; specially employed by War Office 1941-45; Acting Consul at Malmö, Sweden 1940. Holds Knight's Cross of Order of White Rose (Finland); Commander Order of Polonia Restituta (Poland); Cross of Haakon VII (Norway); Christian X Pro Dania Medal (Denmark); Commander Royal Order of St. Sava (Jugoslavia); member Parliamentary Delegation to Denmark 1955, to Israel 1957, and to the U.S.S.R. 1957 and 1959, and to Nationalist China (Formosa) 1958, to Federation of Rhodesia and Nyasaland 1959, to Rhodesia 1967. Member Southampton University Court 1960-64 and Sussex University Court 1961-68. F.R.G.S. 1962. A Conservative. Unsuccessfully contested, as a Liberal, the Spelthorne division of Middlesex in 1945 and, as a Conservative, Swansea W. in 1951. Sat for the Arundel and Shoreham division of W. Sussex from Mar. 1954 until his death on 4 Jan. 1971. [1971]

KERR, Anne Patricia. 37 Pope's Avenue, Twickenham Green, London. D. of Arnold Bersey, Esq. B. 24 Mar. 1925; m. 1st, 6 May 1944, Lieut. James E.D. Clark, Royal Marines, (1 s.); 2ndly, 29 Apr. 1960, Russell Whiston Kerr, Labour MP. for Feltham from Mar. 1966. Educ. at St. Paul's Girls' School, Hammersmith. Served W.R.N.S. 1943-45. Member of British Actors Equity Association from 1951. Member of the Labour Party from 1953. Elected to London County Council for Putney in 1958. Re-elected to London County Council in 1961. Member of the Co-operative Party, Council of Christian Action, R.S.P.C.A., Amnesty, Anti-Apartheid Movement, Howard League for Penal Reform. A Labour Member. Unsuccessfully contested Twickenham in the 1959 general election, and the Wandsworth Borough Council (Putney Ward) in 1956. Elected Member for Rochester and Chatham in Oct. 1964; re-elected Mar. 1966 and sat until 1970 when she was defeated. Chairman of Women Against the Common Market. Died 29 July 1973. [1970]

KERR, Dr. David Leigh. 222 Norbury Avenue, Thornton Heath, Surrey. S. of Myer Woolf Kerr, Esq. B. 25 Mar. 1923; m. 1st, 1944, Aileen Saddington (divorced 1969); 2ndly, 3 Apr. 1970, Miss Margaret Dunlop. Educ. at Norbury Manor Primary School, Scholarship to Whitgift School 1933, Macloghlen Scholar, Royal Coll. of Surgeons 1941, and Middlesex Hospital Medical School (London University) 1941-46. A Family Doctor. Joined the Labour Party in 1956. Member of Socialist Medical Association from 1944. Parliamentary Private Secretary to Rt. Hon. Judith Hart, Minister of State, Commonwealth Office 1966-67 and Minister of Social Security 1967-68. Honorary Secretary Socialist Medical Association 1957-62; Honorary Vice-President 1962. Elected member of London County Council for Wandsworth Central 1958 (held the seat 1961). Gov. British Film Institute 1966. A

Labour Member. Unsuccessfully contested the Streatham division of Wandsworth in 1959. Elected for Wandsworth Central in Oct. 1964 and sat until he retired in 1970. Member of London Borough of Wandsworth Council 1964-68. Gov. of British Film Institute 1966-71. Director of War on Want 1970-77.* [1970]

KERR, Sir Hamilton William, Bart. 71 Westminster Gardens, Marsham Street, London. The Mill House, Whittlesford, Cambridge. S. of Henry S. Kerr, Esq., of Long Island, New York. B. 1 Aug. 1903. Unmarried. Educ. at Eton, and Balliol Coll., Oxford. A Journalist; worked on *Daily Mail* and *Daily Telegraph* 1927-30. Parliamentary Private Secretary to Rt. Hon. A. Duff Cooper, MP. when Financial Secretary to War Office 1933-July 1934, when Financial Secretary to the Treasury July 1934-Nov. 1935, when Secretary of State for War Nov. 1935-May 1937, and when First Lord of the Admiralty May 1937-Oct. 1938; to the Rt. Hon. Harold Balfour, Under-Secretary of State for Air Feb. 1942-Nov. 1944; Parliamentary Secretary to the Ministry of Health May-July 1945. Joined A.A.F. Feb. 1939; member of Speaker's Conference on Electoral Reform 1944. A delegate to Consultative Assembly of the Council of Europe 1952; Parliamentary Private Secretary to the Rt. Hon. Harold Macmillan, Minister of Defence 1954-55, when Secretary of State for Foreign Affairs 1955, and when Chancellor of the Exchequer 1955-57. Created Bart. 1957. Chevalier of the Legion of Honour 1959. Chancellor, The Primrose League 1961-63. A Conservative. Elected for Oldham in Oct. 1931 and sat until 1945, when he was defeated. Elected for Cambridge in Feb. 1950 and sat until he retired in 1966. Honorary LL.D. Cambridge 1972. Bequeathed to the Fitzwilliam Museum, Cambridge his house at Whittlesford, now the Hamilton Kerr Institute. Died 26 Dec. 1974. [1966]

KERR, Sir John Graham, F.R.S. Dalny Veed, Barley, Royston, Hertfordshire. Athenaeum. S. of James Kerr, Esq., Principal of Hoogly Coll., Calcutta, and Sybella, d. of John Graham, Esq. B. 18 Sept. 1869; m. 1st, 7 July 1903, Elizabeth, d. of Thomas Kerr,

Esq., W.S. (she died 1934); 2ndly, 2 Apr. 1936, Isobel Dunn Macindoe, widow of Alan E. Clapperton, Esq. Educ. at Royal High School, Edinburgh, and Universities of Edinburgh and Cambridge. A Biologist. Demonstrator in Animal Morphology, University of Cambridge 1897-1902; Regius Professor of Zoology, University of Glasgow 1902-35; Honorary LL.D. Edinburgh and St. Andrews; Honorary Fellow of Christ's Coll., Cambridge; Associate of Royal Academy of Belgium; Knight Bach. 1939. A National Conservative Member. Elected for the Scottish Universities in June 1935 and sat until he retired in 1950. F.R.S. 1909. President of Royal Philosophical Society of Glasgow 1925-28. President of Scottish Unionist Association 1934-35. Chairman of Advisory Committee on Fishery Research 1941-49. Died 21 Apr. 1957. [1950]

KERR, Russell Whiston. House of Commons, London. S. of Ivo W. Kerr, Esq. B. Feb. 1921; m. 1st, 1946, Shirley Huie; 2ndly, 29 Apr. 1960, Mrs. Anne Kerr (Labour MP. for Rochester and Chatham 1964-70), who died in 1973. Educ. in Sydney, Australia, Graduate in Economics Sydney University. An Air Charter Executive. Former R.A.F. Pathfinder Officer. National Executive member of Association of Scientific Technical and Managerial Staffs from 1964. Joined Labour Party in 1950. Previously member Australian Labour Party from 1938. Chairman of "Tribune" Group of Labour MPs. 1969-70. Director (unpaid) of *Tribune* Publications Limited from Jan. 1969. Chairman of Select Committee on Nationalised Industries 1974-79. A Labour Member. Unsuccessfully contested Horsham in 1951, Merton and Morden in 1959 and Preston N. in 1964. Sat for Feltham from 1966 to Feb. 1974. Elected for the Hounslow, Feltham and Heston division in Feb. 1974.* [1979]

KERSHAW, (John) Anthony, M.C. The Tithe Barn, Didmarton, Badminton, Gloucestershire. White's. S. of Judge J.F. Kershaw. B. 14 Dec. 1915; m. June 1939, Barbara, d. of Harry Crookenden, Esq. Educ. at Eton, and Balliol Coll., Oxford. A Barrister-at-Law, Inner Temple 1939. Served with 16th/5th Lancers and Staff in Africa, France and Germany 1939-46. M.C. 1943. Member London County Council 1946-49, and Westminster City Council 1947-48. Parliamentary Private Secretary to Sir David Eccles, President of Board of Trade 1957-59, to Rt. Hon. John Boyd-Carpenter, Minister of Pensions 1959-61 and to Rt. Hon. Edward Heath, President of Board of Trade 1963-64. Parliamentary Private Secretary to Rt. Hon. Edward Heath, Leader of the Opposition 1967-70. Parliamentary Secretary Ministry of Public Buildings and Works June 1970-Oct. 1970. Parliamentary Under-Secretary of State Foreign and Commonwealth Office, with responsibility for Overseas Development Oct. 1970-June 1973. Under-Secretary of State for Defence (R.A.F.) June 1973-Jan. 1974. Vice-Chairman British Council 1975. Chairman of Select Committee on Foreign and Commonwealth Affairs from 1979. Vice-Chairman Great Britain and East Europe Centre 1975. A Conservative. Unsuccessfully contested Gloucester in 1950 and 1951. Elected for the Stroud division of Gloucestershire in 1955.*　　　　　　　　　[1979]

KEY, Rt. Hon. Charles William. Little Chantry, Bull Lane, Gerrards Cross, Buckinghamshire. S. of Charles Key, Esq., of Chalfont St. Giles. B. 8 Aug. 1883; m. 1917, Florence, d. of Frank Thomas Adams, Esq. Educ. at Chalfont Village School, and Borough Road Training Coll. A Schoolmaster. Member of Poplar Borough Council from 1919, Mayor 1923, 1926 and 1932; Chairman of Metropolitan Boroughs Standing Joint Committee 1934. A Regional Commissioner for London Civil Defence Region Jan. 1941. Parliamentary Secretary Ministry of Health Aug. 1945-Feb. 1947; Minister of Works Feb. 1947-Feb. 1950. PC. 1947. A Labour Member. Sat for the Bow and Bromley division of Poplar from June 1940-Feb. 1950. Elected for Poplar in Feb. 1950 and sat until he retired in Sept. 1964. Died 6 Dec. 1964.　　　　　　　　　[1964]

KILFEDDER, James Alexander. Eastonville, Donaghadee Road, Millisle, Co. Down. 7 Gray's Inn Square, London. House of Commons, London. S. of Robert Kilfedder, Esq. B. 16 July 1928; unmarried. Educ. at Portora Royal School, Enniskillen, and Dublin University, B.A. A Barrister-at-Law, Gray's Inn 1958 and King's Inn, Dublin. Former Auditor of the Coll. Historical Society, Trinity Coll., Dublin. Former President Cromac Young Unionists. Member Trustee Savings Bank Parliamentary Committee. Member of the Northern Ireland Assembly for N. Down 1973. Member of the Northern Ireland Convention for N. Down 1975. An Independent Ulster Unionist Member. Sat for W. Belfast from 1964-66, when he was defeated. Elected for N. Down in June 1970. Chief Whip of Ulster Unionist Party to 1974. Resigned from the Ulster Unionist Party on 11 Feb. 1979 and sat as Independent Unionist. Founder of Ulster Progressive Unionist Party in Jan. 1980. Unsuccessfully contested N. Ireland for European Parliament 1979.*　　　　[1979]

KILROY-SILK, Robert Michael. House of Commons, London. S. of William Silk, Esq. Adopted his step-father's surname of Kilroy in addition to Silk. B. 19 May 1942; m. 1 Mar. 1963, Jan, d. of William Beech, Esq., (1 s. 1 d.). Educ. at Secondary Modern School, Saltley Grammar School, Birmingham, and London School of Economics, B.Sc. (Econ.) 1964. A Lecturer, Liverpool University 1966-74. Author of *Socialism Since Marx*. Parliamentary Private Secretary to Hugh Jenkins, 'Minister for the Arts' 1974-75. Member Select Committee on Public Accounts June 1975-77. Gov. of the National Chest Hospitals 1974-77. Patron of *Apex*. Vice-Chairman of P.L.P. Home Affairs Group 1976. A Labour Member. Unsuccessfully contested Ormskirk in 1970. Sat for Ormskirk from Feb. 1974.*　　　[1979]

KIMBALL, Marcus Richard. 70 Cranmer Court, Sloane Avenue, London. Great Easton Manor, Market Harborough, Leicestershire. Altnaharra, Lairg, Sutherland. White's, and Pratt's. S. of Maj. Lawrence Kimball, MP. B. 18 Oct. 1928; m. 15 Mar. 1956, June Mary, only d. of Montagu Fenwick, Esq., of Great Stukeley Hall, Huntingdon. Educ. at Eton, and Trinity Coll., Cambridge. Capt. Leicestershire and Derbyshire Yeomanry (T.A.). Member Rutland County Council 1955-64. Chairman E. Midlands Area Young Conservatives 1954-58. Privy Council Rep. Royal Coll. of Veterinary Surgeons 1969. Chairman British Field Sports Society 1966. Director The Royal Trust Company of Canada 1970. A Conservative. Unsuccessfully contested Derby S. in 1955. Sat for the Gainsborough division of Lincolnshire from Feb. 1956*   [1979]

KING, Evelyn Mansfield. 11 Barton Street, London. Embley Manor, Romsey, Hampshire. S. of Harry Percy King, Esq. B. 1907; m. 1935, Hermione, d. of Commander A.F. Crutchley, D.S.O., R.N. Educ. at Cheltenham Coll., King's Coll., Cambridge, M.A., and the Inner Temple. A Farmer. Member of the N.U.T. Headmaster of Clayesmore School 1935-40. Co-author (with J.C. Trewin) of *Printer to the House*, the biography of Luke Hansard. During the war served with the Gloucestershire Regiment attaining the rank of acting Lieut.-Col. Parliamentary Secretary Ministry of Town and Country Planning Oct. 1947-Mar. 1950. A Conservative. Sat as Labour Member for Penryn and Falmouth from 1945-50, when he unsuccessfully contested Poole. Joined Conservative Party in 1951. Unsuccessfully contested the Itchen division of Southampton as a Conservative in the general election of 1959. Conservative Member for Dorset S. from Oct. 1964 until he retired in 1979.* [1979]

KING, Rt. Hon. Horace Maybray, Ph.D. The Speaker's House, Palace of Westminster, London. 37 Manor Farm Road, Southampton. S. of John William King, Esq., of Grangetown-on-Tees. B. 25 May 1901; m. 1st, 21 Dec. 1924, Victoria Florence, d. of George Harris, Esq. (she died 31 May 1966); 2ndly, July 1967, Una, d. of W.H. Porter, Esq. (she died 1978). Educ. at Stockton Secondary School, and King's Coll., University of London. Senior English Master Taunton School 1924-46. Headmaster of Regent's Park Secondary School, Southampton 1946-50, B.A. 1st Class Hons. 1921, Dr. of Philosophy 1940, Honorary D.C.L. Durham, Honorary LL.D. London, Southampton and Bath, Honorary D.Litt. Loughborough. Fellow of King's Coll., London 1966. Honorary Alderman of Hampshire County Council 1966. Freeman of the City of Southampton 1966. Freeman of Stockton-on-Tees 1968. Member of Speaker's Panel and Chairman from 1953. Elected Chairman of Ways and Means and Dept. Speaker Nov. 1964. Privy Councillor 1965. Elected Speaker of the House of Commons from Oct. 1965. A Labour Member. Unsuccessfully contested New Forest and Christchurch in 1945. Sat for the Test division of Southampton from 1950 to 1955 and for the Itchen division of Southampton from 1955 until he retired as Speaker in Jan. 1971. Created Baron Maybray-King (Life Peerage) 1971, when he assumed the surname of Maybray-King in lieu of King. Dept.-Speaker of House of Lords from 1971. Member of B.B.C. Complaints Commission 1971-74. Honorary Treasurer of Help the Aged from 1972. President of Spina Bifida Association from 1971. Dept.-Lieut. for Hampshire 1975.*   [1971]

KING, Rt. Hon. Thomas Jeremy. House of Commons, London. S. of J.H. King, Esq., J.P., Company Director. B. 13 June 1933; m. 20 Jan. 1960, Jane, d. of Robert Tilney, Esq., C.B.E., D.S.O., T.D., D.L., (1 s. 1 d.). Educ. at Rugby, and Emmanuel Coll., Cambridge. Commissioned Somerset Light Infantry 1952 (N.S.); Seconded to K.A.R.; served Tanganyika and Kenya, Acting Capt. 1953. Cambridge 1953-56. Joined E.S. and A, Robinson Limited, Bristol 1956; various positions up to Divisional General Manager 1964-69; resigned on adoption for Bridgwater. Chairman Sale, Tilney and Company Limited 1971-79. Parliamentary Private Secretary to Christopher Chataway, Minister of Posts and Telecommunications 1970-72 and Minister for Industrial Development 1972-74. Vice-Chairman Conservative Parliamentary Backbenchers Industry Committee 1974-75. Opposition Front Bench spokesman for Industry 1975-76. Shadow spokesman for Energy 1976-79. Minister of State (Minister for Local Government and Environmental Services) Department of the Environment from May 1979. A Conservative. Elected for the Bridgwater division of Somerset in Mar. 1970. PC. 1979.*   [1979]

KINGHORN, Squadron-Leader Ernest. Field House, Collingham Bridge, Leeds. S. of A. Kinghorn, Esq., of Leeds. B. 1 Nov. 1907; m. 1942, Eileen Mary Lambert Russell. Educ. at Leeds, Basle and Lille

Universities. A Teacher. Served in Intelligence Branch of R.A.F. Staff Officer on Control Commission in Germany 1945. A Labour Member. Unsuccessfully contested the Hexham division of Northumberland in 1935. Sat for Great Yarmouth from 1945-50. Elected for the Yarmouth division of Norfolk in Feb. 1950 and sat until 1951 when he was defeated. Unsuccessfully contested the Yarmouth division of Norfolk in 1955.* [1951]

KINGSMILL, Lieut.-Col. William Henry, D.S.O., M.C. 18 Hertford Street, London. Dores Hill, North Sydmonton, Newbury, Guards'. S. of Lieut.-Col. Andrew de Portal Kingsmill, D.S.O., O.B.E., M.C., of Sydmonton, Hampshire. B. 1 Dec. 1905; m. 1st, 1929, Aileen Kyrle Smith (marriage dissolved); 2ndly, 29 June 1939, Diana Ivy, d. of Col. J. Rowan Robinson, and widow of Lieut.-Col. Guy Olliver. Educ. at Eton, and Royal Military Coll., Sandhurst. Joined Grenadier Guards 1925, retired 1929. Company Director 1929-39. Rejoined 1939 with 3rd Division at Dunkirk and later with 8th Army and 1st Army, M.C. 1940, D.S.O. 1943. A Conservative. Elected for the Yeovil division of Somerset in July 1945 and sat until he retired in 1951. Chairman and Managing Director of Taylor Walker brewing group. Chairman of Brewers' Society. Died 3 June 1971. [1951]

KINLEY, John. 32 Merton Road, Bootle, Lancashire. B. 1878. A Labour Member. Unsuccessfully contested Bootle in 1923 and 1924. Sat for Bootle from 1929 until 1931, when he was defeated. Unsuccessfully contested Bootle in 1935. Re-elected for Bootle in July 1945 and sat until he retired in 1955. A Hairdresser. Member of Bootle Borough Council 1925-49, Alderman 1935-49. Died 13 Jan. 1957. [1954]

KINNOCK, Neil Gordon. House of Commons, London. S. of Gordon H. Kinnock, Esq., Labourer. B. 28 Mar. 1942; m. 25 Mar. 1967, Glenys Elizabeth, d. of Cyril Parry, Esq., Railway Porter. Educ. at Lewis School, Pengam 1953-61, and University Coll., Cardiff 1961-66. President Socialist Society U.C. Cardiff 1963-65; President of Union U.C. Cardiff 1965-66. N.E.C. member

Anti-Apartheid Movement. Director *Tribune* Publications and Editorial Board Member Labour Research Department (both unpaid). Sponsored from 1970 by T.G.W.U. Parliamentary Private Secretary to Rt. Hon. Michael Foot, Secretary of State for Employment 1974-75. Member of National Executive Committee of Labour Party from 1978. Principal Opposition spokesman on Education from 1979. A Labour Member. Elected for the Bedwellty division of Monmouthshire in June 1970. W.E.A. Tutor 1966-70.* [1979]

KINSEY, Joseph Ronald. 147 Grange Road, Birmingham. S. of Walter Kinsey, Esq., Licensee. B. 28 Aug. 1921; m. 19 Sept. 1953, Joan Elizabeth, d. of Arthur Walters, Esq. Educ. at Birmingham Elementary and Church of England Schools. Served with R.A.F. 1940-47. A Telephone Engineer 1947-57. A Florist and Fruiterer from 1957. Chairman Aston division Y.C.S. 1949; Vice-Chairman Birmingham City Y.C.S. 1952; Councillor Perry Barr Ward Birmingham 1955; Secretary Perry Barr division Conservative Association 1956-69; J.P. for City of Birmingham 1962. Alderman Birmingham 1969. A Conservative. Unsuccessfully contested the Aston division of Birmingham in 1966. Elected for the Perry Barr division of Birmingham in June 1970 and sat until Feb. 1974 when he was defeated. Unsuccessfully contested the Perry Barr division of Birmingham in Oct. 1974 and 1979.* [1974]

KIRBY, Capt. Bertie Victor, C.B.E., D.C.M. 710 Queen's Drive, Stoneycroft, Liverpool. S. of Henry Kirby, Esq., of Cheltenham. B. 2 May 1887; m. 12 Jan. 1916, Alice Elizabeth, d. of Henry Richmond, Esq. Educ. at the Abbey School, Tewkesbury. Member of Liverpool City Council and Elective Auditor City of Liverpool 1924, later Alderman. J.P. 1929; member of Select Committee on National Expenditure 1941-45, and of Public Accounts 1946-49. Chairman of Select Committee on Estimates 1946-49. Served in R.H.A. in France and Belgium 1914-18, D.C.M. 1917, and in R.A. (A.A. Home Defence 1939-41). C.B.E. 1947. A Labour Member. Elected for the Everton division of Liverpool in 1935 and sat until

1950, when he unsuccessfully contested the W. Derby division of Liverpool. Died 1 Sept. 1953. [1950]

KIRK, Sir Peter Michael. House of Commons, London. Brooks's. S. of Dr. Kenneth Escott Kirk, 37th Bishop of Oxford. B. 18 May 1928; m. 26 Aug. 1950, Elizabeth Mary, d. of R.B. Graham, Esq., (3 s.). Educ. at Marlborough, Trinity Coll., Oxford, and University of Zürich. President Oxford Union Society 1949. Editorial Staff Glasgow *Daily Record* and *Evening News* 1949-51; Diplomatic Correspondent Kemsley Newspapers 1951-53 and 1954-55; Foreign Editor *Sunday Chronicle* Mar.-Nov. 1954. Member Carshalton Urban District Council 1952-55. Member of U.K. delegation to Council of Europe 1956-63 and 1966-70. Parliamentary Under-Secretary of State for War Oct. 1963-Apr. 1964, and for Defence for the Army Apr.-Oct. 1964. Parliamentary Under-Secretary of State for Defence for the Royal Navy June 1970-Nov. 1972. Chairman European Conservative Group in European Parliament Nov. 1972-Apr. 1977. Knight Bachelor 1976. A Conservative. Sat for Gravesend from 1955-64, when he was defeated. Elected for the Saffron Walden division of Essex in Mar. 1965 and sat until his death on 17 Apr. 1977. [1977]

KIRKWOOD, Rt. Hon. David. Karleen, Roman Road, Bearsden, Dunbartonshire. S. of John Kirkwood, Esq., of Glasgow, B. at Parkhead, Glasgow 1872; m. 1899, Elizabeth, d. of Robert Smith, Esq., of Parkhead. Educ. at Parkhead Public School. An Engineer. For many years member of Glasgow Town Council; J.P. for Glasgow; for over 12 years on the National Administrative Council I.L.P., and for 50 years active member of the A.E.U. Chief Shop Steward of the Beardmore Works 1914-15, and Treasurer of the Clyde Workers' Committee. Deported in 1916. PC. 1948. A Labour Member. Unsuccessfully contested Dumbarton Burghs in 1918. Sat for Dumbarton Burghs from Nov. 1922 to Feb. 1950. Elected for the E. division of Dunbartonshire in Feb. 1950 and sat until he retired in 1951. Secretary of Scottish Labour Housing Association. Elected as an I.L.P. Member in 1931 but rejoined the Labour Party in Aug. 1933.

Created Baron Kirkwood 1951. Died 16 Apr. 1955. [1951]

KITSON, Sir Timothy Peter Geoffrey. Leases Hall, Leeming Bar. S. of Col. Geoffrey H. Kitson, O.B.E. B. 28 Jan. 1931; m. Sept. 1959, Diana Mary, d. of Edward W. Fattorini, Esq. Educ. at Charterhouse. A Roman Catholic. Farmed in Australia 1950-51. Royal Agricultural Coll., Cirencester 1951-53. Member Thirsk Rural District Council 1954-57. Member North Riding County Council 1957-61. Parliamentary Private Secretary to the Parliamentary Secretaries, Ministry of Agriculture 1960-64. Opposition Whips Office 1967-70. Parliamentary Private Secretary to Rt. Hon. Edward Heath, Prime Minister 1970-74, and Leader of the Opposition 1974-75. Knighted 1974. A Conservative. Elected for the Richmond division of the N. Riding of Yorkshire in 1959.* [1979]

KNIGHT, (Joan Christabel) Jill, M.B.E. 6 Iris Close, Northfield, Birmingham. Holmwood, Collingtree, Northampton. D. of A.E. Christie, Esq. B. 1923; m. 14 June 1947, James Montague Knight. Educ. at King Edward Grammar School, Birmingham. Member of Northampton County Borough Council 1956-66. M.B.E. (New Year's Honours) 1964. A Conservative. Unsuccessfully contested Northampton in 1959 and 1964. Elected for the Edgbaston division of Birmingham in Mar. 1966.* [1979]

KNOX, David Laidlaw. House of Commons, London. S. of John McGlasson Knox, Esq., Printer and Publisher. B. 30 May 1933. Educ. at Lockerbie Academy, Dumfries Academy, and London University. Printing Management Trainee 1953-56; Printing Executive 1956-62; O. and M. Specialist 1962-70. Chairman West Midlands Area Young Conservatives 1963-64; Chairman West Midlands Area C.P.C. 1966-69; Secretary Conservative Finance Committee 1972-73. Parliamentary Private Secretary to Rt. Hon. Ian Gilmour, Minister of State for Defence 1973-74, and Secretary of State for Defence 1974. Vice-Chairman Conservative Party 1974-75. Secretary Conservative Employment Committee 1976-78. A Conservative. Unsuccessfully contested the Stechford division of Birmingham in 1964 and 1966, and Nuneaton in Mar. 1967. Elected for the Leek division of Staffordshire in June 1970.* [1979]

LAGDEN, Godfrey William. St. Austell, Southend Arterial Road, Harold Wood, Hornchurch, Essex. Constitutional. S. of Augustine William Lagden, Esq. B. 12 Apr. 1906; m. 1935, Dorothy Blanche, d. of C.M.P. Wheeler, Esq. Educ. at Richmond Hill School. Member Hornchurch Urban District Council 1948-54; member Essex County Council from 1949, re-elected 1955; Alderman 1955. A Conservative. Unsuccessfully contested Thurrock in 1951. Elected for Hornchurch in 1955 and sat until 1966 when he was defeated. Director of Elm Park Petrol and Oil Supplies Limited from 1958.* [1966]

LAMBERT, Hon. George, T.D. 35 Millbank, London. Spreyton, Crediton, Devon. Eld. s. of Visct. Lambert. B. 27 Nov. 1909; m. 16 Sept. 1939, Patricia Quinn. Educ. at Summer Fields, Oxford, Harrow, and New Coll., Oxford. Served with T.A. 1939-45, Lieut.-Col., T.D. Gov. of Seale Hayne Agricultural Coll.; member Council of Royal Agricultural Society. A National Liberal and Conservative Member. Sat for S. Molton division from 1945-Feb. 1950. Elected for the Torrington division of Devon in Feb. 1950 and sat until Feb. 1958 when he succeeded to the Peerage as Visct. Lambert. Chairman of Devon and Exeter Savings Bank 1958-70. Dept.-Lieut. for Devon 1969-70.* [1957]

LAMBIE, David. 11 Ivanhoe Drive, Saltcoats, Ayrshire. S. of Robert Lambie, Esq. B. 13 July 1925; m. 10 July 1954, Netta May Merrie. Educ. at Kyleshill School, Ardrossan Academy, Glasgow, and Geneva Universities. A Teacher in Glasgow 1950-70. Chairman of Labour Party in Scotland 1964. A Labour Member. Unsuccessfully contested Bute and North Ayrshire in 1955, 1959, 1964 and 1966. Sat for the Central division of Ayrshire from June 1970.* [1979]

LAMBORN, Harry George. 53 Farne Close, Hailsham, E. Sussex. S. of Cecil Lamborn, Esq. B. 1 May 1915; m. 5 June 1938,

Lilian Ruth, d. of J. Smith, Esq., (2 s. 1 d.). Educ. at London County Council Secondary School. Member Camberwell Borough Council 1953-65. Mayor 1963-64. Member London County Council 1958-65. Member Greater London Council 1964-73; Dept. Chairman 1971-72. Member of Central Health Services Council 1963-68. Director Royal Arsenal Co-operative Society 1965-72. Parliamentary Private Secretary to Rt. Hon. Denis Healey, Chancellor of the Exchequer from Mar. 1974 to May 1979. A Labour Member. Sat for Southwark from May 1972 to Feb. 1974 and for the Peckham division of Southwark from Feb. 1974.* [1979]

LAMBTON, Antony Claud Frederick. Biddick Hall, Lambton Park, Chester-le-Street, Co. Durham. S. of 5th Earl of Durham who died in Feb. 1970 and whose title he disclaimed in Feb. 1970. B. 10 July 1922; m. 1942, Belinda, d. of Maj. Douglas Holden Blew-Jones, of Westward Ho! Educ. at Harrow. Parliamentary Under-Secretary of State for Defence for the Royal Air Force June 1970-May 1973, when he resigned. Parliamentary Private Secretary to Rt. Hon. Selwyn Lloyd, Foreign Secretary, 1955-57. A Conservative. Unsuccessfully contested Chester-le-Street in 1945 and Bishop Auckland in 1950. Elected for the Berwick-upon-Tweed division of Northumberland in Oct. 1951 and sat until May 1973 when he resigned after publicity had been given to his casual acquaintance with a call girl. Styled Visct. Lambton from the death of his elder brother in 1941 until Feb. 1970, when he succeeded his father as Earl of Durham.* [1973]

LAMOND, James Alexander. 15 Belvidere Street, Aberdeen. S. of Alexander Lamond, Esq., Railway Porter. B. 29 Nov. 1928; m. 1954, June Rose, d. of Joseph Wellburn, Esq. Educ. at Burrelton and Coupar Angus Schools and Kings Coll., Newcastle. An Engineering Draughtsman 1944-70. City Councillor, Aberdeen from May 1959 to 1971. Chairman Transport Committee 1964-67; Chairman Finance Committee 1967-70; Leader, Aberdeen Labour Group 1967-70. J.P. 1967; Lord Provost 1970-71; Lord-Lieut., Aberdeen

1970-71. Parliamentary Private Secretary to Rt. Hon. Stanley Orme, Minister of State for N. Ireland 1974-76 and Minister of State, Health and Social Security 1976. Member of Speaker's Panel of Chairmen. A Labour Member. Elected for Oldham E. in June 1970.* [1979]

LAMONT, Norman Stewart Hughson. House of Commons, London. Carlton. S. of Daniel Lamont, Esq. B. 1942; m. 18 Sept. 1971, Rosemary, d. of Lieut.-Col. Peter White, (1 s.). Educ. at Loretto School, and Fitzwilliam House, Cambridge, B.A. 1965. Chairman Cambridge University Conservative Association 1963. President Cambridge Union 1964. A Merchant Banker. Conservative Research Department 1966-68. Chairman Bow Group 1971-72. Parliamentary Private Secretary to Norman St. John-Stevas, 'Minister for Arts' 1974. Secretary Conservative Parliamentary Finance Committee 1974. Opposition spokesman on Prices and Consumer Affairs 1975-76. Opposition spokesman on Industry 1976-79. Under-Secretary of State for Energy from May 1979. A Conservative. Unsuccessfully contested East Hull in 1970. Sat for Kingston-upon-Thames from May 1972 to Feb. 1974 and for the Kingston division of Kingston-upon-Thames from Feb. 1974.* [1979]

LANCASTER, Claude Granville. 11 St. Leonards Terrace, London. Langford Grove, Maldon, Essex. Kelmarsh Hall, Northamptonshire. B. 30 Aug. 1899. Educ. at Eton, and Royal Military Coll., Sandhurst. Capt. late Royal Horse Guards 1918, Col. Sherwood Foresters 1939-43. Chairman of B.A. Collieries Limited until 1946. Chairman and Managing Director of the Bestwood Company Limited. A Director of other commercial undertakings. A Conservative. Sat for the Fylde division of Lancashire from Nov. 1938 to Feb. 1950 and for the S. Fylde division of Lancashire from Feb. 1950 until he retired in 1970. Died 25 July 1977. [1970]

LANE, David William Stennis Stuart. 40 Chepstow Place, London. 5 Spinney Drive, Great Shelford, Cambridge. Junior Carlton. S. of Hubert Samuel Lane, Esq., M.C., Barrister-at-Law. B. 24 Sept. 1922; m. 23 July 1955, Lesley Anne, d. of Sir Gerard and Lady Clauson. Educ. at Eton, Trinity Coll., Cambridge, and Yale University, U.S.A. M.A. (Cantab.). Barrister-at-Law, Middle Temple 1955. Served in the navy in Second World War. Joined British Iron and Steel Federation 1948, and appointed Secretary in 1956. With Shell International Petroleum Company 1959-67. Parliamentary Private Secretary to Rt. Hon. Robert Carr, Secretary of State for Employment 1970-72. Parliamentary Under-Secretary of State for the Home Office Apr. 1972-Mar. 1974. A Conservative. Unsuccessfully contested the Vauxhall division of Lambeth in 1964 and Cambridge in 1966. Elected for Cambridge in Sept. 1967 and sat until he resigned in Nov. 1976 on appointment as Chairman-designate of Commission for Racial Equality. Opposition spokesman on Home Affairs 1974-75. Chairman of Commission for Racial Equality from 1977.* [1976]

LANG, Rev. Gordon. Wycliffe, Chepstow, Monmouth. National Labour, and Authors'. S. of T.W. Lang, Esq., of Monmouth. B. 25 Feb. 1893; m. 12 Sept. 1916, Emily, d. of J.W. Evans, Esq. Educ. at Monmouth Grammar School, and Cheshunt Coll. A Nonconformist Minister. Lecturer in adult education to H.M. Forces 1940-45. Honorary Chaplain Showmen's Guild of Great Britain and Ireland from 1930; Chairman Federal Union of Proportional Representation Society 1947-51; Joint Secretary United Europe Movement. A Labour Member. Sat for Oldham from 1929-31, when he was defeated. Unsuccessfully contested Oldham in 1935 and Stalybridge and Hyde in Apr. 1937. Elected for the Stalybridge and Hyde division of Cheshire in July 1945 and sat until he retired in 1951. Vice-President of International Youth Bureau 1946-56. Member of Cwmbran New Town Corporation 1955-64. Minister of Peny-waun Church, Cwmbran 1956-77.* [1951]

LANGFORD-HOLT, Sir John Anthony. House of Commons, London. S. of Ernest Langford-Holt, Esq. B. 30 June 1916; m. 1st, 1953, Flora Evelyn Innes Stuart (divorced 1969); 2ndly, 1971, Maxine Veale, (1 s. 1 d.). Educ. at Shrewsbury School. Lieut.-

Commander R.N. (F.A.A.) June 1939. Director Siebe Gorman Holdings Limited and Authority Investments Limited. Former Director Tretol Limited. Freeman and Liveryman of the City of London. Chairman of Select Committee on Defence from 1979. A Conservative. Sat for the Shrewsbury division of Shropshire from July 1945. Knighted 1962.* [1979]

LATHAM, Arthur Charles. House of Commons, London. S. of Arthur Frederick Latham, Esq. B. 14 Aug. 1930; m. 6 Oct. 1951, Margaret, d. of E. Green, Esq., (1 s. 1 d.). Educ. at Clockhouse Lane, Romford, Royal Liberty, Romford, and Garnett Coll. of Education. Teacher's Certificate. Councillor for Romford at the age of 21. Member of N.E. Metropolitan Hospital Board 1966-72. Lecturer in Government, English and Liberal Studies at Southgate Technical Coll. from 1967. Alderman London Borough of Havering 1964-78, Leader of Labour Group 1964-70. Chairman Greater London Labour Party 1977. Joint Chairman and Founder All-Party Parliamentary Group for Pensioners 1971. Chairman Tribune Group of MPs. 1975-76. A Labour Member. Unsuccessfully contested Woodford in opposition to Sir Winston Churchill, in 1959 and Rushcliffe, in opposition to Martin Redmayne, in 1964. Sat for Paddington N. from Oct. 1969-Feb. 1974. Elected for the Paddington division of Cities of London and Westminster, City of Westminster in Feb. 1974 and sat until 1979, when he was defeated.* [1979]

LATHAM, Michael Anthony. House of Commons, London. Carlton. S. of Wing-Commander S.H. Latham. B. 20 Nov. 1942; m. 29 Nov. 1969, Caroline, d. of Maj. A. Terry, (1 s.). Educ. at Marlborough Coll., King's Coll., Cambridge, and New Coll., Oxford. Housing Officer Conservative Research Department 1965-67. Parliamentary Officer, National Federation of Building Trades Employers 1967-73. Member of Westminster City Council 1968-71. Director The House Builders' Federation 1971-73. Member Ecclesiastical Committee of Parliament 1974. Director Lovell Homes Limited 1975. Member Expenditure Committee 1974, and

Joint Committee on Statutory Instruments 1974-75; Vice-Chairman Conservative Parliamentary Housing Committee 1974-76. Secretary Conservative Parliamentary Countryside Conservation Committee 1977. A Conservative. Unsuccessfully contested the West Derby division of Liverpool in 1970. Elected for Melton in Feb. 1974.* [1979]

LAVERS, Sydney Charles Robert. Gosforth, Newcastle-on-Tyne. S. of Charles Lavers, Esq., of Plymouth. B. 4 June 1890; m. 18 Aug. 1915, Ellen, d. of Frank Elliott, Esq. Educ. at Plymouth Board School. Served overseas 1914-19. Organiser of National Union of General and Municipal Workers. Member of Chester-le-Street Rural District Council 1927-46, Chairman 1940-41. Member of Durham County Council 1934-45. A Socialist. Elected for the Barnard Castle division of Durham in July 1945 and sat until he retired in 1950. Died 9 Apr. 1972. [1950]

LAW, Rt. Hon. Richard Kidston. 43B, Sloane Street, London. Travellers'. S. of the Rt. Hon. Andrew Bonar Law, MP. B. 27 Feb. 1901; m. 1929, Mary Virginia, d. of A.F. Nellis, Esq., of Rochester, New York (she died 1978). Educ. at Shrewsbury, and St. John's Coll., Oxford. A Journalist. Member of Medical Research Council 1936-40. Financial Secretary to War Office May 1940-July 1941; Parliamentary Under-Secretary of State Foreign Office July 1941-Sept. 1943; Minister of State Sept. 1943-May 1945; Minister of Education May-July 1945. Head of United Kingdom Delegation to Conference of Foodstuffs in U.S.A. 1943. PC. 1943. A Conservative. Sat for S.W. Hull from Oct. 1931-July 1945, when he was defeated, for Kensington S. from Nov. 1945-Feb. 1950. Elected for the Haltemprice division of Kingston-upon-Hull in Feb. 1950 and sat until Jan. 1954 when he was created Baron Coleraine. High Steward of Kingston-upon-Hull. Chairman of National Youth Employment Council 1955-62. Chairman of Central Transport Consultative Committee 1955-58. Chairman of Mansfield House University Settlement 1953-66. Chairman of Standing Advisory Committee on Pay of Higher Civil Service 1957-61. Chairman of Council of

British Societies for Relief Abroad 1945, 1949 and 1954.* [1953]

LAWLER, Wallace Leslie. 39 Tenbury Road, Birmingham. National Liberal. S. of Stephen Lawler, Esq., Musician. B. 15 Mar. 1912; m. 23 Sept. 1941, Catherine, d. of Thomas Durcan, Esq. Educ. at St. Paul's, Worcester, and privately. Elected Birmingham City Council 1962. Leader Liberal Group City Council 1965. Chairman A.B.C.D. (Plastics) Limited 1947. Chairman Citizens Services Limited 1970 and Wallace Lawler Friendship Trust 1969. Liberal Party spokesman, Housing, Home Office. A Liberal. Unsuccessfully contested Dudley in 1955, the Perry Barr division of Birmingham in 1959, the Handsworth division of Birmingham in 1964 and the Ladywood division of Birmingham in 1966. Elected for Birmingham Ladywood in June 1969 and sat until June 1970 when he was defeated. Served with the Worcester Regiment 1939-45. Vice-Chairman of Liberal Party 1967, Vice-President 1968. Died 28 Sept. 1972. [1970]

LAWRENCE, Ivan John. Dunally Cottage, Lower Halliford Green, Walton Lane, Shepperton, Middlesex. Grove Farm, Drakelow, Burton-on-Trent. 1 Essex Court, Temple, London. S. of Leslie Lawrence, Esq. B. 24 Dec. 1936; m. 3 Apr. 1966, Gloria Helene, d. of Charles Crankshaw, Esq., (1 d.). Educ. at Brighton, Hove and Sussex Grammar School, and Christ Church, Oxford. Called to the bar, Inner Temple 1962. Practised at the Criminal bar. Secretary Conservative Parliamentary Legal Committee. Member Social Services and Employment Sub-Committee of Select Committee on Expenditure. President of National Association of Approved Driving Instructors. A Conservative. Unsuccessfully contested Peckham in 1966 and 1970. Elected for Burton in Feb. 1974.* [1979]

LAWSON, George McArthur. 37 Burnblea Street, Hamilton, S. of Alexander Lawson, Esq. B. 11 July 1906; m. 10 July 1939, Margaret Robertson, d. of George and Cicely Munro. Educ. at St. Bernard's, and North Merchiston Schools, Edinburgh. Staff Tutor and Organiser National Council of Labour Colls. 1937-50; full-time Secretary Edinburgh Trades Council 1950-54. A Lord Commissioner of the Treasury Oct. 1964-Mar. 1967. Dept. Government Chief Whip from Apr. 1966-Mar. 1967. Opposition Whip 1959-64. Voted in favour of entry to E.E.C. on 28 Oct. 1971. A Labour Member. Sat for the Motherwell division of Lanarkshire from Apr. 1954-Feb. 1974. Elected for Motherwell and Wishaw in Feb. 1974 and sat until he retired in Sept. 1974. Campaign Director of Scotland is British Campaign. Died 3 July 1978. [1974 2nd ed.]

LAWSON, Rt. Hon. John James. 7 Woodside, Beamish, Co. Durham. S. of John and Elizabeth Lawson, of Whitehaven. B. 1881; m. 1906, Isabella Scott. Educ. at Board School, and Ruskin Coll., Oxford. Active Trade Union leader. Durham County Councillor 1913. Served with Royal Artillery 1914-18. Alderman 1919. Financial Secretary to the War Office Jan.-Nov. 1924; Parliamentary Secretary Ministry of Labour June 1929-Aug. 1931. Dept. Commissioner Civil Defence N. Region 1939-44. Secretary of State for War July 1945-Oct. 1946; PC. 1945; Lord Lieut. 1949-58, and Dept.-Lieut. for the County of Durham. A Labour Member. Unsuccessfully contested the Seaham division of Durham in 1918. Elected for the Chester-le-Street division of Durham in Nov. 1919 and sat until Dec. 1949 when he resigned on appointment as Vice-Chairman of National Parks Commission. Created Baron Lawson 1950. Member of Executive Committee of P.L.P. 1939-40. Vice-Chairman of National Parks Commission 1949-57. Honorary D.C.L. Durham University. Vice-Chairman of British Council 1944. Member of Imperial War Graves Commission 1930-47. Died 3 Aug. 1965. [1950]

LAWSON, Nigel. The Old Rectory, Stoney Stanton, Leicestershire. 39 Tedworth Square, London. Garrick. S. of Ralph Lawson, Esq. B. 11 Mar. 1932; m. 1955, Vanessa Mary Addison, d. of F.A. Salmon, Esq., (1 s. 3 d.). Educ. at Westminster School, and Christ Church, Oxford. R.N. 1954-56. A Journalist. Member Editorial Staff *Financial Times* 1956-60. City Editor *Sunday Telegraph* 1961-63. Special Assistant to Sir Alec Douglas-Home, then Prime Minister 1963-64. Editor of *The*

Spectator 1966-70. Fellow of Nuffield Coll., Oxford 1972-73. An Opposition Whip 1976-77. Special Political Adviser, Conservative Party Headquarters 1973-74. Opposition spokesman on Treasury and Economic Affairs 1977-79. Financial Secretary to the Treasury from 1979. A Conservative. Unsuccessfully contested Eton and Slough in 1970. Sat for Blaby from Feb. 1974.*

[1979]

LEADBITTER, Edward. 30 Hylton Road, Hartlepool, Co. Durham. House of Commons, London. S. of Edward Leadbitter, Esq. B. 18 June 1919; m. 1940, Phyllis Irene Mellin, (1 s. 1 d.). Educ. at State Schools, and Teachers' Training Coll. A Teacher. Joined the Labour Party in 1938. Formerly member of N.U.G.M.W. and now member of N.U.P.E. Commissioned Royal Artillery 1941. War Office Commissioned Instructor in Gunnery. Organiser of the Exhibition on the History of Labour Movement 1941. Member of West Hartlepool Borough Council 1954-67. Chairman of various Local Government Committees. President Hartlepool Constituency Labour Party 1956-58. Member of Estimates Committee, House of Commons 1966-69. Member of Select Committee House of Commons on Science and Technology 1969-73. Chairman P.L.P. Ports Committee 1974. Vice-Chairman P.L.P. Transport Group. Education Officer, Hartlepools and leader of Labour Group 1961 and 1962. Member of Speaker's Panel of Chairmen. A Labour Member. Sat for Hartlepools from Oct. 1964.*

[1979]

LEATHER, Sir Edwin Hartley Cameron. Eden Park, Batheaston, Somerset. 97 Roebuck House, Palace Street, London. S. of Harold H. Leather, Esq., M.B.E., of Hamilton, Ontario. B. 22 May 1919; m. 9 Mar. 1940, Sheila, d. of Maj. A.H. Greenlees, of Hamilton, Ontario. Educ. at Trinity Coll. School, Port Hope, Ontario, and Royal Military Coll., Kingston, Ontario. Served with Canadian Army 1940-45. An Insurance Broker from 1946. Knighted June 1962. A Conservative. Unsuccessfully contested Bristol S. in 1945. Elected for Somerset N. in 1950 and sat until he retired in 1964. Gov. and Commander-in-Chief of Bermuda 1973-

77. K.C.M.G. 1974. K.C.V.O. 1975. Honorary LL.D. University of Bath 1975. Director of Credit Insurance Association Limited 1950-64, of Hogg Robinson and Capel-Cure Limited 1952-64, of William Baird Limited 1966-73, of Hill Samuel and Company Limited 1969-73. Chairman of National Union of Conservative and Unionist Associations 1969-70. President of Institute of Marketing 1963-67. Dept.-Chairman of English Speaking Union 1973.*

[1964]

LEAVEY, John Anthony. Carlton. S. of George Edwin Leavey, Esq. B. 3 Mar. 1915; m. 28 Apr. 1952, Lesley Doreen, d. of Lord Justice Ormerod. Educ. at Mill Hill School, and Trinity Hall, Cambridge. Served with 5th Royal Inniskilling Dragoon Guards 1939-46. A Conservative. Unsuccessfully contested Blackburn E. in 1950 and 1951. Elected for the Heywood and Royton division of Lancashire in 1955 and sat until 1964 when he was defeated. Chairman of Wilson Connolly Holdings Limited. Director of Smith and Nephew Associated Companies Limited.*

[1964]

LEBURN, (William) Gilmour. House of Commons, London. S. of George Cheape Leburn, Esq. B. 1913; m. 1944, Agnes Barbara, d. of A.J. May, Esq., of Reading. Educ. at Gateside School, and Strathallan School, Perthshire. Served in 51st Highland Division 1939-42, at Staff Coll., Camberley 1944-45. Member of Fife County Council 1948-55. Parliamentary Private Secretary to Rt. Hon. J.S. Maclay, Secretary of State for Scotland 1957-59. Joint Under-Secretary of State for Scotland Oct. 1959-Aug. 1963. A Unionist Member. Elected for Kinross and West Perthshire in 1955 and sat until his death on 15 Aug. 1963.

[1963]

LEDGER, Ronald Joseph. House of Commons, London. S. of Arthur Ledger, Esq. B. 1920; m. 1946, Madeleine Odette de Villeneuve. Educ. at Skinner's Grammar School, and Nottingham University. Served with R.A.F. 1942-47. Founded Nottingham University Labour Club and was first Chairman 1948-49; member of A.S.S.E.T. Director London Co-operative Society from 1961. A Labour and Co-operative Member. Unsuccessfully contested Rushcliffe in 1951. Elected for Romford in 1955 and sat until he retired in 1970. Member of Hertfordshire County Council 1952-54. Chairman of Hairdressing Council from 1966. A Casino Proprietor.* [1970]

LEE, Rt. Hon. Frederick. 52 Ashton Road, Newton-le-Willows, Lancashire. S. of Joseph Lee, Esq. B. 3 Aug. 1906; m. 1938, Amelia, d. of William Shay, Esq. Educ. at Salford. Member of Salford City Council. Chairman of Metropolitan Vickers Works Committee. Member of Executive Committee of Salford Labour Party. Parliamentary Private Secretary to H.A. Marquand when Paymaster-Gen. Mar.-Oct. 1947, to Rt. Hon. Sir Stafford Cripps, Minister of Economic Affairs Oct. 1947, and when Chancellor of the Exchequer 1947-50. Parliamentary Secretary Ministry of Labour and National Service Mar. 1950-Oct. 51. Minister of Power Oct. 1964-Apr. 1966. Secretary of State for the Colonies from Apr. 1966-Jan. 1967. PC. 1964. Chancellor of the Duchy of Lancaster Jan. 1967-Oct. 1969. A Labour Member. Sat for the Hulme division of Manchester from 1945-50. Elected for the Newton division of Lancashire in Feb. 1950 and sat until he retired in Feb. 1974. Member of Parliamentary Committee of P.L.P. 1959-64 and of the Cabinet 1964-67. Created Baron Lee of Newton (Life Peerage) 1974. Opposition spokesman on Labour until 1959, on Fuel and Power 1959-60, on Labour 1960-61 and on Aviation 1961-64. Unsuccessful candidate for Dept. Leadership of Labour Party 1960. Member of Salford City Council 1941-45. Representative of Labour Peers on the Parliamentary Committee of P.L.P. from 1979.* [1974]

LEE, Rt. Hon. Jennie. House of Commons, London. D. of James Lee, Esq., of Lochgelly. B. 3 Nov. 1904; m. Oct. 1934, Rt. Hon. Aneurin Bevan, MP. (he died July 1960). Educ. at Cowdenbeath Secondary School, Moray House Coll., Edinburgh, and Edinburgh University, M.A., LL.B. A Writer and Lecturer. Director of *The Tribune*. Parliamentary Secretary to the Ministry of Public Building and Works Oct. 1964-Feb. 1965. Parliamentary Under-Secretary of State,

Department of Education and Science Feb. 1965-Feb. 1967. Minister of State, Department of Education and Science Feb. 1967-June 1970. Minister for the Arts 1964-70. PC. 1966. A Labour Member. Sat for N. Lanarkshire from Mar. 1929-1931 when she was defeated. Unsuccessfully contested N. Lanarkshire as an I.L.P. candidate in 1935 and Bristol Central in Feb. 1943, as an Independent Labour candidate, with the support of Common Wealth. Elected for the Cannock division of Staffordshire in July 1945 and sat until 1970 when she was defeated. Member of Central Advisory Committee on Housing. Member of National Executive Committee of Labour Party 1958-70, Chairman 1967-68. Created Baroness Lee of Asheridge (Life Peerage) 1970. Honorary LL.D. Cambridge University 1974.* [1970]

LEE, John Michael Hubert. House of Commons, London. S. of Victor Lee, Esq. B. 13 Aug. 1927; m. 1960, Margaret Ann, d. of James Russell, Esq. Educ. at Reading School, Christ's Coll., Cambridge, and School of Oriental and African Studies, London University. A Barrister, Middle Temple 1960. Joined the Labour Party in 1955. Member T. and G.W.U. Member of Overseas Civil Service (Colonial Service) in Gold Coast (Ghana) 1951-58. Member Tribune Group. Chairman West Midlands Group of Labour MPs. Nov. 1974-75. A Labour Member. Unsuccessfully contested Reading in 1964. Sat for Reading from Mar. 1966-1970, when he was defeated. Elected for the Handsworth division of Birmingham in Feb. 1974 and sat until he retired in 1979. Dept. Circuit Judge from 1978.* [1979]

LEGGE-BOURKE, Sir (Edward Alexander) Henry, K.B.E., D.L. 9 Wilbraham Place, London. S. of N.W.H. Legge-Bourke, Esq., and Lady Victoria Forester. B. 16 May 1914; m. 10 June 1938, Catherine, d. of Col. Sir Arthur Grant, D.S.O., 10th Bart. of Monymusk. Educ. at Eton, and Royal Military Coll., Sandhurst. Chairman Grant Production Company Limited; 2nd Lieut. Royal Horse Guards 1934; served in Greece 1941 (wounded) and Western Desert 1942. Aide-de-Camp to British Ambassador in Cairo 1941-42. Chairman Conservative

Party Science and Technology Committee 1961-64 and Vice-Chairman 1964-70. Chairman 1922 Committee from July 1970-Nov. 1972. K.B.E. 1960. Chairman Parliamentary and Scientific Committee from 1971. A Conservative. Elected for the Isle of Ely in July 1945 and sat until his death on 21 May 1973. Dept.-Lieut. for Cambridgeshire. Resigned Conservative Whip July-Oct. 1954 in disagreement with the Government's Egyptian policy. Died 21 May 1973.   [1973]

LEGH, Hon. Peter Richard. Vernon Hill House, Bishops Waltham, Hampshire. S. of 3rd Baron Newton. B. 6 Apr. 1915; m. 6 July 1948, Priscilla, d. of Capt. John Egerton-Warburton, and widow of Visct. Wolmer. Educ. at Eton, and Christ Church, Oxford. Formerly Maj. in Grenadier Guards, served 1939-45. J.P. for Hampshire. Member of Hampshire County Council 1949-52 and 1954-55. Parliamentary Private Secretary to Rt. Hon. John Boyd-Carpenter, MP. when Financial Secretary to Treasury 1952-53. Assistant Whip Nov. 1953. Lord Commissioner of the Treasury June 1955-Sept. 1957. Vice-Chamberlain of the Household Sept. 1957-Jan. 1959; Treasurer of the Household Jan. 1959-June 1960. A Conservative. Elected for the Petersfield division of Hampshire in Oct. 1951 and sat until June 1960 when he succeeded to the Peerage as Baron Newton. Capt. of the Yeoman of the Guard and Dept. Chief Whip in House of Lords Oct. 1960-Sept. 1962. Parliamentary Secretary to Ministry of Health Sept. 1962-Apr. 1964. Minister of State, Department of Education and Science Apr.-Oct. 1964.*
          [1960]

LE MARCHANT, Spencer. Hillside, Whitehough, Chinley, via Stockport, Cheshire. 41 Rivermill, Grosvenor Road, London. White's. S. of A. G. Le Marchant, Esq. B. 15 Jan. 1931; m. 5 May 1955, Lucinda Gaye, d. of Brigadier H.N. Leveson Gower. Educ. at Eton. National Service and Territorial Commissions, Sherwood Foresters 1949-54. Member of The Stock Exchange 1954. Partner L. Messel and Company 1961. Member Westminster City Council 1956-71. Parliamentary Private Secretary to Patrick Jenkin, Chief Secretary to the Treasury 1972-74, and

Minister for Energy 1974. Opposition Whip 1974-79. Secretary Party Energy Committee 1974. A Conservative. Unsucceessfully contested the Vauxhall division of Lambeth in 1966. Elected for the High Peak division of Derbyshire in June 1970. Comptroller of the Royal Household from May 1979.* [1979]

LENNOX-BOYD, Rt. Hon. Alan Tindal, C.H. 5 Eaton Close, London. The Old Rectory, Upper Stondon, Henlow, Bedfordshire. Carlton. S. of Alan Walter Lennox-Boyd, Esq. B. 18 Nov. 1904; m. 29 Dec. 1938, Lady Patricia Guinness, d. of Rupert, 2nd Earl of Iveagh. Educ. at Sherborne School, and Christ Church, Oxford, Scholar, Beit Prize, President of the Union. Parliamentary Secretary Ministry of Labour Feb. 1938-Sept. 1939; Parliamentary Secretary Ministry of Home Security Sept.-Oct. 1939; Parliamentary Secretary Ministry of Food Oct. 1939-May 1940. Lieut. R.N.V.R. May 1940-43. Parliamentary Secretary Ministry of Aircraft Production Nov. 1943-July 1945. Minister of State for Colonial Affairs Nov. 1951-May 1952. PC. 1951. Minister of Transport and Civil Aviation May 1952-July 1954. Secretary of State for the Colonies July 1954-Oct. 1959. A Conservative. Unsuccessfully contested the Gower division of Glamorgan in 1929. Elected for Mid-Bedfordshire in 1931 and sat until July 1960 when he was created Visct. Boyd of Merton. Barrister-at-Law, Inner Temple 1941. C.H. Jan. 1960. Dept.-Lieut. for Bedfordshire 1954-61, for Cornwall from 1965. Managing Director of Arthur Guinness, Son and Company Limited 1960-67, Joint Vice-Chairman from 1967. Director of I.C.I. 1967-75, of Tate and Lyle 1966-74 and of Royal Exchange 1962-70. Chairman of Royal Commonwealth Society 1961-64, Voluntary Service Overseas 1962-64. Trustee of British Museum 1962-78, of Natural History Museum 1963-76. Leader of Conservative Party delegation to observe the Rhodesian elections 1979.* [1960]

LEONARD, Richard Lawrence. 16 Albert Street, London. S. of Cyril Leonard, Esq. B. 12 Dec. 1930; m. 29 Mar. 1963, Irene, d. of Dr. Ernest Heidelberger, of France. Educ. at Ealing Grammar School, London University Institute of Education, and Essex University,

M.A. A School Teacher 1953-55; Dept. Gen. Secretary Fabian Society 1955-60; Journalist and Broadcaster 1960-68; Sen. Research Fellow, Essex University 1968-70. Parliamentary Private Secretary to Anthony Crosland from 1970 to 1974. Author of *Guide to the General Election* 1964, and *Elections in Britain* 1968. Co-Author of *Backbencher and Parliament* 1972. Voted in favour of entry to E.E.C. on 28 Oct. 1971. A Labour Member. Unsuccessfully contested Harrow W. in 1955. Elected for Romford in June 1970 and sat until he retired in Feb. 1974. Assistant Editor of *The Economist* from 1974. Chairman of Fabian Society 1977-78. Chairman of Library Advisory Council for England from 1978.*　　　　[1974]

LEONARD, William. 2 Lochview Road, Bearsden, Glasgow. S. of James Leonard, Esq., of Glasgow and Vancouver. B. 14 Feb. 1887; m. 1915, Mary Dunlop, d. of John Boyd, Esq., of Glasgow. Educ. at Board Schools in Glasgow and Manchester. Journeyman Cabinet Maker 1907-13 Canada; Financial Secretary Woodworkers' Union, Vancouver; Trade Union Organizer from 1921; National Secretary Scottish Labour Coll. 1917-20. Member of Glasgow Corporation. Parliamentary Private Secretary to Rt. Hon. Sir Andrew Duncan, when President of Board of Trade July-Oct. 1940 and July 1941-Feb. 1942 and when Minister of Supply Oct. 1940-July 1941 and Feb. 1942-May 1945. Member of Waste Food Board Jan. 1944. Parliamentary Secretary to Ministry of Supply Aug. 1945-Oct. 1947. A Labour Member. Unsuccessfully contested Greenock in 1929. Elected for the St. Rollox division of Glasgow in May 1931 and sat until 1950 when he unsuccessfully contested the Woodside division of Glasgow. President of Scottish T.U.C. 1925 and 1931-32. Member of N. of Scotland Hydro-Electricity Board 1950-55. Member of National Assistance Board 1955-60. Died 14 Oct. 1969.　[1950]

LESLIE, John Robert. 46 Grosvenor Road, Muswell Hill, London. S. of John Leslie, Esq., of Lerwick. B. 3 Nov. 1873; m. 16 Aug. 1899, Alice, d. of Robert McQueen, Esq. (she died Oct. 1936). Educ. at Anderson Institute, Lerwick. Gen. Secretary National Amalgamated Union of Shop Assistants, etc. from 1924. J.P. for London. Member of Finchley Borough Council. A Labour Member. Unsuccessfully contested the Finchley division of Middlesex in 1918. Elected for the Sedgefield division of Durham in 1935 and sat until he retired in 1950. Member of the Labour Advisory Committee of the League of Nations Union. Died 12 Jan. 1955.　　[1950]

LESTER, James Theodore. House of Commons, London. S. of A.E. Lester, Esq. B. 23 May 1932; m. 1953, Iris Yvonne, d. of J.T. Whitby, Esq., (2 s.). Educ. at Nottingham High School. Member of Bingham Rural District Council 1964-70. Member Nottinghamshire County Council 1967-75. Chairman Finance Committee 1969-74. Appointed to Opposition Whips Office Dec. 1975. Under-Secretary of State for Employment from May 1979. A Conservative. Unsuccessfully contested Bassetlaw in Oct. 1968 and 1970. Elected for Beeston in Feb. 1974.*
　　　　　　　　　　　　[1979]

LESTOR, Joan. House of Commons, London. B. 13 Nov. 1931; (1 s. 1 d. adopted). Educ. in London and South Wales, and London University. A Nursery School Teacher, member G. & M.W.U. Joined the Labour Party in 1956. Parliamentary Under-Secretary Department of Education and Science Oct. 1969-June 1970. Under-Secretary Foreign and Commonwealth Office Mar. 1974-June 1975; Under-Secretary Department of Education and Science June 1975-Feb. 1976, when she resigned. Member Labour Party National Executive from 1967. Labour Party Chairman 1977-78. A Labour Member. Unsuccessfully contested West Lewisham, 1964. Sat for Eton and Slough from Mar. 1966. Member of Wandsworth Borough Council 1958-68 and of London County Council 1962-64. An Opposition spokesman on Education 1970-74.*　[1979]

LEVER, Leslie Maurice. 27 Pine Road, Didsbury, Manchester. S. of Bernard Lever, Esq., of Manchester. B. 29 Apr. 1905; m. 7 Sept. 1939, Ray Rosalia, J.P. for Lancashire, and d. of Dr. L. Levene of Leicester. Educ. at Manchester Grammar School, and Leeds University. LL.B. (Hons.) 1925; Solicitor (Hons.) 1927; member of Manchester City

Council from 1932; F.R.S.A. 1935; Associate Serving Brother, Order of St. John; Alderman Feb. 1951; Lord Mayor 1957-58. Gov. of University of Manchester. Gov. of Manchester Grammar School. Knight Grand Cross of Order of St. Gregory the Great with Silver Star; G.C.S.G. 1968. LL.D. (Honorary) Leeds University 1963. A Labour Member. Unsuccessfully contested the Moss Side division of Manchester in 1935. Elected for the Ardwick division of Manchester in Feb. 1950 and sat until he retired in 1970. Knighted 1970. Created Baron Lever (Life Peerage) 1975. Died 26 July 1977. [1970]

LEVER, Rt. Hon. (Norman) Harold. House of Commons, London. S. of Bernard Lever, Esq., of Manchester. B. 1914; m. 1st, 1945, Billie, d. of M. Woolf, Esq. (she died in 1948), (1 d.); 2ndly, 1962, Mrs. Diana Zilkha, d. of Saleh Bashi of Geneva, (3 d.). Educ. Manchester Grammar School and Manchester University. A Barrister, Middle Temple 1935. Parliamentary Under-Secretary of State Department of Economic Affairs Jan.-Aug. 1967. PC. 1969. Financial Secretary to the Treasury Aug. 1967-Oct. 1969. Paymaster-Gen. Oct. 1969-June 1970; Chancellor of the Duchy of Lancaster from Mar. 1974 to May 1979. Chairman of the Committee of Public Accounts July 1970-73. Member of Cabinet 1969-70 and 1974-79. Member of Parliamentary Committee of P.L.P. July 1970-Apr. 1972, when he resigned, and Dec. 1972-Mar. 1974. Opposition spokesman on Europe July 1970-Dec. 1971, on Power, Steel and Trade Dec. 1971-Apr. 1972 and on Trade Dec. 1972-Mar. 1974. Voted in favour of entry to E.E.C. on 28 Oct. 1971. A Labour Member. Sat for the Exchange division of Manchester from 1945-50 and for the Cheetham division of Manchester from 1950-74. Elected for the Central division of Manchester in Feb. 1974 and sat until June 1979 when he was created Baron Lever of Manchester (Life Peerage).* [1979]

LEVY, Benn Wolfe, M.B.E. 66 Old Church Street, London. Garrick, and Queen's. S. of Octave Levy, Esq. B. 7 Mar. 1900; m. 1933, Constance Cummings, Actress, d. of Dallas Halverstadt, Esq. Educ. at Repton, and University Coll., Oxford. A Dramatist and

Director. Served with R.A.F. 1918, R.N. 1942-45. A Labour Member. Elected for the Eton and Slough division of Buckinghamshire in July 1945 and sat until he retired in 1950. Arts Council Executive 1953-61. Died 7 Dec. 1973. [1950]

LEWIS, Arthur William John. 1 Doveridge Gardens, Palmers Green, London. S. of James Lewis, Esq. B. 21 Feb. 1917; m. 20 Apr. 1940, Lucy, d. of John Clack, Esq. Educ. at Elementary School, and at Borough Polytechnic. Served in the Army 1940-42. Ex-Trade Union Official. Member of Ministry of Labour Appeal Board 1942-45. Formerly member of London Labour Party Executive Committee; Chairman Eastern Regional Group of Labour MPs.; member Executive Committee E. Regional Council of Labour Party. Ex-Member of Licensed and Unlicensed Residential Hotel and Restaurant Wages Board. A Labour Member. Sat for Upton division of West Ham 1945-50 and for West Ham North division 1950-Feb. 1974. Sat for Newham N.W. from Feb. 1974.* [1979]

LEWIS, John. 4 Abbey Lodge, Hanover Gate, Regent's Park, London. Royal Automobile, and City Livery. S. of Leon Lewis, Esq. B. 14 Dec. 1912; m. 1st, 17 Feb. 1948, Joy Jocille Fletcher (divorced 1954); 2ndly, 1968, Stella. Educ. at Grocers School, and City of London Coll. A Rubber Technologist and Company Director. Parliamentary Private Secretary to Rt. Hon. Ness Edwards, Postmaster Gen. Apr.-July 1950. A Labour Member. Sat for Bolton from July 1945-Feb. 1950. Elected for the W. division of Bolton in Feb. 1950 and sat until 1951 when he was defeated. Steward of British Boxing Board of Control from 1949. Died 14 June 1969. [1951]

LEWIS, Kenneth. 96 Green Lane, Northwood, Middlesex. Preston, Rutland. 114 Grand Buildings, Trafalgar Square, London. Carlton, M.C.C., Pathfinder, and St. Stephen's. S. of William Lewis, Esq. B. 1 July 1916; m. 1948, Jane, d. of Samuel Pearson, Esq., (1 s. 1 d.). Educ. at Jarrow, and Edinburgh University. War Service R.A.F. Chairman of travel business. Dept.-Lieut. for

Rutland 1973. Member Middlesex County Council 1949-51. Member of N.W. Metropolitan Hospital Management Committee 1949-62. Chairman Conservative Parliamentary Labour Committee 1961-64. A Conservative. Unsuccessfully contested the Newton division of Lancashire in 1945 and 1950, and Ashton-under-Lyne in 1951. Elected for Rutland and Stamford in 1959.* [1979]

LEWIS, Ronald Howard. 22 Alandale Avenue, Langwith Junction, Mansfield, Nottinghamshire. S. of Oliver Lewis, Esq. B. 16 July 1909; m. 1937, Edna Cooke (she died 1976), (2 s.). Educ. at Elementary and Secondary Schools and at Cliff Methodist Coll. British Railways Fitter's Assistant. Joined the Labour Party in 1928. Member of the N.U.R. Former President Pleasley Cooperative Society Limited (now merged with Mansfield Society). Member Derbyshire County Council from 1949 to 1974 and member Blackwell Rural District Council from 1940 to 1974, Chairman 1964-65. Local Methodist Preacher. Secretary to the N.U.R. Group in the House of Commons. A Labour Member. Unsuccessfully contested Rugby in 1945, Crosby in 1950, W. Derbyshire in 1951, S. Northamptonshire in 1955 and Darlington in 1959 general elections. Elected for Carlisle in Oct. 1964.* [1979]

LEWIS, Thomas. 8 Brighton Road, The Avenue, Southampton. S. of John Lewis, Esq. B. 12 Dec. 1873. Unmarried. Educ. at Eastern District School. Member of Southampton Borough Council from 1901, Alderman from 1929; retired 1961. Chairman of Southampton Harbour Board. A Labour Member. Unsuccessfully contested Southampton in 1918, 1922, 1923 and 1924. Sat for Southampton from 1929-31 when he was defeated. Unsuccessfully contested Southampton again in 1931 and 1935. Sat again for Southampton from July 1945 until he retired in 1950. J.P. for Hampshire 1920. President of National Conference of Friendly Societies 1920-21. C.B.E. 1950. Honorary LL.D. Southampton University 1955. Died 28 Feb. 1962. [1950]

LILLEY, Francis James Patrick. House of Commons, London. S. of Francis John Charles Lilley, Esq. B. 1907; m. 1937, Agnes Crossley Mackay. Educ. at Bellahouston Academy. Served with Argyll and Sutherland Highlanders 1934-40 and Home Guard 1941-45, Lieut.-Col. Elected to Glasgow Corporation 1957. Parliamentary Private Secretary to Rt. Hon. Richard Wood, when Minister of Power 1960-63 and when Minister of Pensions and National Insurance Oct. 1963-Oct. 1964. A Conservative. Elected for the Kelvingrove division of Glasgow in 1959 and sat until 1964 when he was defeated. Chairman of F.J.C. Lilley group of companies, Civil Engineering Contractors. Died 21 Aug. 1971. [1964]

LINDGREN, George Samuel. Attimore Close, Welwyn Garden City, Hertfordshire. S. of George William Lindgren, Esq. B. 11 Nov. 1900; m. 10 July 1926, Elsie, d. of Frank Reed, Esq., of Christhill, Hertfordshire. Educ. at London County Council Elementary School. A Railway Clerk. Member of Welwyn Garden City Urban District Council 1927-46, of Hertfordshire County Council 1931-49. Re-elected member of Hertfordshire County Council in 1952. Dept. Regional Commissioner for Civil Defence, Midland Region 1942-45. Parliamentary Secretary Ministry of National Insurance Aug. 1945-Oct. 1946. Parliamentary Secretary Ministry of Civil Aviation Oct. 1946-Mar. 1950. Parliamentary Secretary Ministry of Town and Country Planning Mar. 1950-Jan. 1951; Parliamentary Secretary Ministry of Local Government and Planning Jan.-Oct. 1951. A Labour Member. Unsuccessfully contested the Hitchin division of Hertfordshire in 1935. Elected for the Wellingborough division of Northamptonshire and Soke of Peterborough in July 1945 and sat until 1959 when he was defeated. Chairman of London Trades Council 1938-42. Treasurer of Transport Salaried Staffs Association 1956-61. Created Baron Lindgren (Life Peerage) 1961. Parliamentary Secretary to Ministry of Transport Oct. 1964-Jan. 1966, and to Ministry of Power Jan.-Apr. 1966. J.P. and Dept.-Lieut. for Hertfordshire. Died 8 Sept. 1971 in Majorca. [1959]

LINDSAY, Hon. James Louis. House of Commons, London. S. of 27th Earl of Crawford and Balcarres. B. 16 Dec. 1906; m. 26 Apr. 1933, Hon. Bronwen Mary Scott-Ellis, d. of 8th Lord Howard de Walden. Educ. at Eton, and Magdalen Coll., Oxford. Farmed in South Africa before the Second World War; served with K.R.R.C. and Commando Groups (Maj.); invalided 1944. With Foreign Office until 1945; Honorary Attaché Rome and Insurance Broker at Lloyd's. A Conservative. Unsuccessfully contested S.E. Bristol in Nov. 1950 and 1951. Elected for N. Devon in 1955 and sat until 1959 when he was defeated.* [1959]

LINDSAY, Kenneth Martin. 39 Hill Street, London. Athenaeum. S. of George Lindsay, Esq. B. 16 Sept. 1897. Unmarried. Educ. at St. Olave's School, and Worcester Coll., Oxford; President of Union 1921. Member of Stepney Borough Council 1922-25. Served with Honourable Artillery Company 1916-18. Director of Voluntary Migration Societies, Dominions Office 1929-31. Gen. Secretary of Political and Economic Planning 1931-35. Civil Lord of the Admiralty June 1935-May 1937; Parliamentary Secretary to Board of Education May 1937-May 1940. Unsuccessfully contested, as a Labour candidate, Oxford in June 1924, the Harrow division of Middlesex in Oct. 1924 and Worcester in 1929. Sat for Kilmarnock from Nov. 1933-1945 and for the Combined English Universities from 1945 until he retired in 1950. Sat as a National Labour Member until Feb. 1942, afterwards as a National Independent. Director of Anglo-Israel Association 1962-73. An Author.* [1950]

LINDSAY, Sir Martin Alexander, Bart., C.B.E., D.S.O. House of Commons, London. S. of Lieut.-Col. A.B. Lindsay. B. 22 Aug. 1905; m. 1st, 15 Dec. 1932, Joyce, d. of Maj. Hon. R.H. Lindsay (divorced 1967); 2ndly, 1969, Loelia, Duchess of Westminster, d. of 1st Baron Sysonby. Educ. at Wellington Coll. Served in the Army 1925-36 and 1939-45 (despatches, twice wounded), demobilised as Lieut.-Col.; member of British Arctic Air Route Expedition 1930-31 and leader of British Trans-Greenland Expedition 1934; member of the Queen's Body Guard for Scotland (Royal Company of

Archers). Chairman W. Midlands Area of Conservative Associations 1949-52. An Author and Company Director. A Conservative. Elected for the Solihull division of Warwickshire in July 1945 and sat until he retired in 1964. D.S.O. 1945. C.B.E. 1952. Created Bart. 1962. Dept.-Lieut. for Lincolnshire 1938-45.* [1964]

LINSTEAD, Sir Hugh Nicholas. 17 Bloomsbury Square, London. Athenaeum. S. of Edward Flatman Linstead, Esq. B. 3 Feb. 1901; m. 1928, Alice Winifred, d. of Cecil Henry Freke, Esq. (she died 1978). Educ. at City of London School, Birkbeck Coll., and at Pharmaceutical Society's School, London. F.P.S., LL.D., British Columbia 1956, Toronto 1963. Barrister-at-Law, Middle Temple 1929; Secretary of Pharmaceutical Society of Great Britain 1926-64; member of Poisons Board (Home Office 1933-57); member Medical Research Council 1956-64; Chairman Parliamentary and Scientific Committee 1955-57, and Franco-British Parliamentary Group 1956-60; Parliamentary Charity Commissioner 1956-60. Knight Bach. 1953. Commander of Légion d'Honneur. A Conservative. Elected for the Putney division of Wandsworth in May 1942 and sat until 1964 when he was defeated. Unsuccessfully contested the Putney division of Wandsworth in 1966. O.B.E. 1937. President of International Pharmaceutical Federation 1953-65. Chairman of Farriers Registration Council from 1976. Chairman of Macarthys Pharmaceuticals Limited.* [1964]

LIPSON, Daniel Leopold. 103 Old Bath Road, Cheltenham. S. of H.R. Lipson, Esq., of Sheffield. B. 26 Mar. 1886; m. 1914, Juliet Lyon, d. of D. Barnett, Esq., of Brighton. Educ. at Sheffield Royal Grammar School, and Corpus Christi Coll., Cambridge. Housemaster at Cheltenham Coll. 1914-23, Head Master of Corinth Coll., Cheltenham 1923-35: Mayor of Cheltenham 1935-37; member of Gloucestershire County Council from 1925 and of Cheltenham Town Council from 1929. An Independent Member. Elected for Cheltenham in June 1937 and sat until 1950 when he was defeated. Died 14 Apr. 1963. [1950]

LIPTON, Marcus, C.B.E. 3 Wellington Court, Shelton Street, London. S. of Benjamin Lipton, Esq. B. 29 Oct. 1900. Educ. at Council School, Bede Grammar School, Sunderland, and at Merton Coll., Oxford, M.A. Barrister-at-Law, Gray's Inn 1926; J.P. for London, Member of Stepney Borough Council 1934-37, Alderman Lambeth Borough Council 1937-56. Private (T.A.) 1939. Lieut.-Col. 1944. O.B.E. 1949, C.B.E. 1965. Member Parliamentary Delegation to Denmark 1949, Belgium 1956 and Hungary 1965. Delegate Inter-Parliamentary Union Conference, Belgrade 1963 and Sofia 1977. Leader Parliamentary Delegation to Sierra Leone 1969. Chairman Anglo-Nepalese Parliamentary Group; Chairman Anglo-Bulgarian Parliamentary Group. Parish Councillor of Binfield 1955-59. Freeman of Lambeth 1974. A Labour Member. Unsuccessfully contested the Brixton division of Lambeth in 1935. Sat for the Brixton division of Lambeth from 1945-Feb. 1974, and the Central division of Lambeth from Feb. 1974 until his death on 22 Feb. 1978.   [1978]

LITCHFIELD, Capt. John Shirley Sandys. House of Commons, London. S. of Rear-Admiral F.S. Litchfield-Speer. B. 1903; m. 1939, Margaret, d. of Sir Bertram and Hon. Lady Portal, of Overton, Hampshire, (1 s. 2 d.). Educ. at Royal Naval Colls. Osborne and Dartmouth, R.N. Staff Coll., Imperial Defence Coll., and National War Coll., U.S.A. O.B.E. 1943. Dept. Director of Naval Intelligence 1949-50. Director of Operations, Admiralty 1953-54. Retired from R.N. as Capt. 1955. Member of Kent County Council 1955-58. A Conservative. Elected for Chelsea in 1959 and sat until he retired in 1966.*   [1966]

LITTERICK, Thomas. House of Commons, London. S. of William Litterick, Esq., Engineer Fitter. B. 25 May 1929; m. 30 Mar. 1957, Jane Ellen, eld. d. of Charles Birkenhead, Esq. Educ. at Dundee School of Economics, and Warwick University. Senior Lecturer, Management Studies, Lanchester Polytechnic 1961-67. Lecturer, Industrial Relations, Aston University, Birmingham 1967-74. Chairman Kenilworth Labour Party 1969-70. Political Education Officer Warwick and Leamington C.L.P. 1969-70. Chairman Warwick and Leamington C.L.P. 1970-72. Member Kenilworth Urban District Council 1970-74. A Labour Member. Unsuccessfully contested the Selly Oak division of Birmingham in Feb. 1974. Elected for Selly Oak in Oct. 1974 and sat until 1979, when he was defeated. Lecturer, Management Centre, Aston University from 1979.*   [1979]

LITTLE, Sir Ernest Gordon Graham. See GRAHAM-LITTLE, Sir Ernest Gordon Graham.

LITTLE, Rev. Dr. James. Castlereagh Manse, Belfast. Seaforth, Whitehead, Co. Antrim. Constitutional. S. of Francis Little, Esq., of Ouley House, Co. Down. B. Oct. 1868; m. 9 Sept. 1903, Jane Graham, d. of the Rev. Hugh Hastings. Educ. at Rathfriland Class. School, University Classes, Belfast, Queen's University, Belfast, Royal University, Dublin, and at Presbyterian Coll., Belfast. Doctor's degree in Theology 1910; Minister of Dundrod Presbyterian Church 1900-10, of Knoxland Parish, Dumbarton 1910-15, and of Castlereagh Presbyterian Church, Belfast from 1915. Life Gov. of Royal Victoria Hospital, Belfast; Grand Chaplain of Loyal Orange Order in Ireland. Member of Dumbarton School Board 1911-14. A Conservative. Elected for Co. Down in May 1939. Resigned from the Conservative Party in May 1945, after a disagreement over his renomination, contested the general election in July 1945 as an Independent Unionist and defeated the official candidate. Sat until his death on 31 Mar. 1946.   [1946]

LLEWELLYN, David Treharne. House of Commons, London. S. of Sir David Llewellyn, 1st Bart. B. 17 Jan. 1916; m. 18 Feb. 1950, Joan Anne, O.B.E., d. of R.H. Williams, of Bonvilston House, Bonvilston, Cardiff, (2 s. 1 d.). Educ. at Eton, and Trinity Coll., Cambridge. Private Royal Fusiliers and Capt. Welsh Guards; served in N.W. Europe 1939-45. Parliamentary Under-Secretary of State, Home Office Nov. 1951-Oct. 1952, resigned through ill health. Member of Institute of Journalists. A Conservative. Unsuccessfully contested Aberavon in 1945.

Elected for Cardiff N. in Feb. 1950 and sat until he retired in 1959. Knighted 1960. Author of *Nye, the Beloved Patrician* and *The Adventures of Arthur Artfully.** [1959]

LLOYD, Maj. Sir (Ernest) Guy (Richard), D.S.O., D.L. Hazelwood House, Rhu, Dunbartonshire. Carlton. S. of Maj. Ernest Thomas Lloyd, Bengal C.S., and Ethel Mary, d. of Sir Richard Green-Price, Bart. B. 7 Aug. 1890; m. 5 Mar. 1918, Helen Kynaston, d. of Col. E.W. Greg, C.B., of Norcliffe Hall, Styal, Cheshire. Educ. at Rossall School, and Keble Coll., Oxford, M.A. Capt. 1st K.S.L.I. 1914, Capt. Res. of O. (R.A.) 1919-30; Maj. (T.A.) 1930, Royal Warwickshire Regiment 1940. Administrator J.P. Coats Limited, Paisley and Glasgow, retired 1938. Knighted 1953. A Conservative. Elected for Renfrewshire E. in May 1940 and sat until he retired in 1959. D.S.O. 1917. Dept.-Lieut. for Dunbartonshire 1953. Created Bart. 1960.* [1959]

LLOYD, Rt. Hon. Geoffrey William. 77 Chester Square, London. Brooks's, Carlton, and Pratt's. S. of G.W.A. Lloyd, Esq., of Andover House, Newbury. B. 17 Jan. 1902. Unmarried. Educ. at Harrow, and Trinity Coll., Cambridge; President of Union 1924. Private Secretary to Rt. Hon. S. Hoare, Secretary of State for Air 1926-29; to Rt. Hon. Stanley Baldwin 1929-31, and Parliamentary Private Secretary to him when Lord President of the Council Nov. 1931-June 1935, and when Prime Minister June-Nov. 1935; Parliamentary Under-Secretary of State Home Office Nov. 1935-Apr. 1939; Secretary for Mines Apr. 1939-May 1940; Secretary for Petroleum May 1940-June 1942; Parliamentary Secretary for Petroleum, Ministry of Fuel and Power June 1942-May 1945; Chairman Oil Control Board 1939-45; Minister in charge of Petroleum Warfare Department 1940-45; Minister of Information May-July 1945. Gov. of B.B.C. 1946-49; PC. 1943; Minister of Fuel and Power Nov. 1951-Dec. 1955; Minister of Education Sept. 1957-Oct. 1959. President Birmingham Conservative and Unionist Association 1946-76. A Conservative. Unsuccessfully contested S.E. Southwark in 1924 and the Ladywood division of Birmingham in

1929. Sat for the Ladywood division of Birmingham from Oct. 1931-July 1945 when he was defeated, and for the King's Norton division of Birmingham from Feb. 1950-May 1955. Elected for Sutton Coldfield in May 1955 and sat until he retired in Feb. 1974. Created Baron Geoffrey-Lloyd (Life Peerage) 1974, when he assumed the surname of Geoffrey-Lloyd in lieu of Lloyd. Chairman of Leeds Castle Foundation from 1974.* [1974]

LLOYD, Ian Stewart. Bakers House, Prior Dean, Nr. Petersfield, Hampshire. Brook's, and Royal Yacht Squadron. S. of W.J. Lloyd, Esq. B. 30 May 1921; m. 1951, Frances Dorward, d. of the Hon. W. Addison, C.M.G., O.B.E., D.C.M., M.C., (3 s.). Educ. at Michaelhouse, (Natal), Witwatersrand University, and King's Coll., Cambridge, (M.A., M.Sc.). Director Bricomin Limited. Economic Adviser to the British and Commonwealth Shipping Group. Formerly an adviser to the Minister of Transport on Maritime Research Policy. Economic Adviser to the Central Mining and Investment Corporation 1949-53. Led the U.K. Delegations to the 5th and 6th biennial International Conferences of the International Cargo Handling Co-ordination Association Sept. 1961 and Oct. 1963. British Delegation, Council of Europe and Western European Union 1968-72. Member Select Committee on Science and Technology 1971. Chairman Select Sub-Committee on Science 1975, on Technological Innovation 1976, and on Energy from 1979. A Conservative. Sat for the Langstone division of Portsmouth from 1964 to Feb. 1974. Elected for Havant and Waterloo in Feb. 1974.* [1979]

LLOYD, Rt. Hon. John Selwyn Brooke, C.H., C.B.E., T.D., D.L., Q.C. Speaker's House, House of Commons, London. Hilbre House, Macdona Drive, West Kirby, Wirral, Merseyside. S. of J.W. Lloyd, Esq., M.R.C.S., L.R.C.P. B. 28 July 1904; m. 1951, Elizabeth, d. of Roland Marshall, Esq., of W. Kirby (divorced 1957). Educ. at Fettes Coll., and Magdalene Coll., Cambridge. President of Cambridge Union 1927. Barrister-at-Law, Gray's Inn 1930, Bencher 1951. Served overseas 1939-45. Brigadier Gen.

Staff, H. Q. 2nd Army, B.L.A. Recorder of Wigan 1948-51. Minister of State Foreign Office Nov. 1951-Oct. 1954. Minister of Supply Oct. 1954-Apr. 1955; Minister of Defence Apr.-Dec. 1955; Secretary of State for Foreign Affairs Dec. 1955-July 1960. Chancellor of the Exchequer July 1960 to July 1962. Lord Privy Seal and Leader of the House of Commons Oct. 1963-Oct. 1964. PC. 1951. Has U.S. Order of Legion of Merit. Honorary Freeman Ellesmere Port. Elected Speaker of the House of Commons in Jan. 1971. A Conservative. Unsuccessfully contested Macclesfield as a Liberal in 1929. Elected for Wirral in July 1945 and sat until he retired as Speaker of the House in Feb. 1976. Member of Hoylake Urban District Council. K.C. 1947. O.B.E. 1943, C.B.E. 1945. Companion of Honour 1962. Member of Shadow Cabinet 1964-66; Opposition spokesman on Commonwealth Affairs 1965-66. Member of Commission on the Constitution 1969-71. Created Baron Selwyn-Lloyd (Life Peerage) 1976. Dept. High Steward of Cambridge University 1971-78. Dept. Lieut. for Cheshire. Died 17 May 1978. [1976]

LLOYD GEORGE, Maj. Rt. Hon. Gwilym, T.D. 231 St. James's Court, Buckingham Gate, London. The Lordship, Cottered, Buntingford, Hertfordshire. Reform, and Boodle's. S. of Rt. Hon. Earl Lloyd George, of Dwyfor, O.M. B. 4 Dec. 1894; m. 1921, Edna, d. of David Jones, Esq., of Denbigh. Educ. at Eastbourne Coll., and Jesus Coll., Cambridge, Honorary Fellow 1953. Served with R.A. (T.) in France, etc. 1914-18. Liberal Whip 1924. Parliamentary Secretary to Board of Trade Aug.-Oct. 1931 and Sept. 1939-Feb. 1941. Parliamentary Secretary Ministry of Food Oct. 1940-June 1942. Minister of Fuel and Power June 1942-July 1945. Minister of Food Nov. 1951-Oct. 1954. Secretary of State for Home Affairs and Minister for Welsh Affairs Oct. 1954-Jan. 1957. PC. 1941. A Liberal. Sat for Pembrokeshire from 1922-24, when he was defeated and 1929-50, when he was again defeated. Sat as a Liberal until Oct. 1931, as a member of the Independent Liberal Group 1931-35, as a Liberal from 1935 until he joined the Government in Sept. 1939; allied with the Conservatives from 1939. Elected for Newcastle-upon-Tyne N. in Oct. 1951 as a National Liberal and Conservative and sat until Jan. 1957 when he was created Visct. Tenby. Member of the Cabinet Sept. 1953-Jan. 1957. Chairman of the Council on Tribunals 1961-67. T.D. 1952. Died 14 Feb. 1967. [1956]

LLOYD GEORGE, Lady Megan Arfon. Brynawelon, Criccieth, North Wales. D. of the Rt. Hon. David Lloyd George, O.M., and Dame Margaret Lloyd George, G.B.E., J.P. B. 22 Apr. 1902. Educ. at Garratt's Hall, Banstead, and in Paris. J.P. for Co. Caernarvon. Chairman of the P.L.P. Agricultural Committee. A Liberal Member 1929-51, a Labour Member 1957-66. Sat for Anglesey from 1929 until 1951, when she was defeated. Joined the Labour Party 1955. Labour Member for the Carmarthen division of Carmarthenshire from Feb. 1957 until her death on 14 May 1966. Styled Lady Megan Lloyd George from 1945 when her father was created Earl Lloyd George of Dwyfor. Dept.-Leader of Liberal Party 1949-51. Honorary LL.D. University of Wales 1949. Companion of Honour May 1966. Died 14 May 1966. [1966]

LOCKWOOD, Lieut.-Col. John Cutts, T.D. Bishop's Hall, Romford, Essex. S. of Col. John Lockwood. B. 1889. Educ. at Chigwell School. A Barrister-at-Law, Middle Temple 1921. A Conservative. Sat for Hackney Central from 1931-35, when he was defeated. Unsuccessfully contested Bexley in 1945 and July 1946. Elected for Romford in Feb. 1950 and sat until he retired in 1955. Served with Essex Regiment and Coldstream Guards 1914-18, with Essex Territorials, J.A.G. Department and with S.H.A.E.F. in Denmark 1939-45, Lieut.-Col. J.P. for Essex. C.B.E. 1960. Member of Essex County Council 1949-52 and 1955-70, Alderman 1962-70. Chairman of R.S.P.C.A. Member of House of Laity of Church Assembly.* [1954]

LOFTHOUSE, Geoffrey. House of Commons, London. S. of Ernest Lofthouse, Esq. B. 18 Dec. 1925; m. 1952, Sarah Lofthouse, (1 d.). Educ. at Featherstone Primary and Secondary Schools. A Personnel Manager, NCB Fryston 1970-78. A Labour Member. Sat for Pontefract and Castleford from Oct. 1978. Member of Wakefield Metropolitan District Council from 1974.* [1979 2nd ed.]

LOGAN, David Gilbert, C.B.E. 362 Scotland Road, Liverpool. S. of Thomas Logan, Esq. B. in Liverpool 22 Nov. 1871; m. 1896, Susan Georgina, d. of G.H.S. Gains, Esq. Educ. at St. Anthony's and St. Sylvester's Schools, and privately. J.P. and City Alderman, Liverpool. A Labour Member. Elected for the Scotland division of Liverpool in Dec. 1929 and sat until his death on 25 Feb. 1964. Gen. Secretary of National Pawnbrokers Assistants Approved Society. C.B.E. 1949. Knight of Order of St. Gregory. Died 25 Feb. 1964.   [1964]

LOMAS, Kenneth. House of Commons, London. S. of George Lomas, Esq. B. 16 Nov. 1922; m. 1945, Helen, d. of William Henry Wilson, Esq., (3 children). Former employee of Manchester Regional Hospital Board. Member of the Labour Party from 1947. Member of the I.L.P. before 1947. Justice of the Peace, County of Chester from 1960, Huddersfield from 1972 Chairman Anglo-South Pacific Group. Treasurer Anglo-Icelandic Group. Former Group. Rapporteur North Atlantic Committee Education/Culture. Chairman Migraine Group. Secretary Ex-Royal Marine Group. Secretary Friends of Cycling Group. Chairman All-Party Humane Research Group. Vice-Chairman Animal Welfare Group. Vice-President National Anti-Vivisection Society. Secretary National Union of Public Employees MPs. Group. Central Office, Union of Shop, Distributive and Allied Workers 1937-55. Assistant Regional Organiser, Blood Transfusion Service 1955-64. Voted in favour of entry to E.E.C. on 28 Oct. 1971. Parliamentary Private Secretary to Rt. Hon. Anthony Wedgwood Benn, Minister of Technology Jan. 1969-June 1970. A Labour Member. Unsuccessfully contested Blackpool S. in 1951, and Macclesfield in 1955. Elected for Huddersfield W. in Oct. 1964 and sat until he retired in 1979.*   [1979]

LONGBOTTOM, Charles Brooke. 46 Bootham, York. 34 Bryanston Square, London. Carlton. S. of William Ewart Longbottom, Esq. B. 22 July 1930; m. 1962, Anita, d. of Mr Giulio Trapani and Mrs. Basil Mavroleon, (1 d.). Educ. at Uppingham. Called to the bar, Inner Temple 1958. Director of firm of Insurance Brokers. Chairman of the Ariel Foundation. Parliamentary Private Secretary to Mr. Iain Macleod, Chancellor of the Duchy of Lancaster and Leader of the House 1961-63. A Conservative. Unsuccessfully contested Stockton-on-Tees in 1955. Elected for York in 1959 and sat until 1966, when he was defeated. Chairman of Austin and Pickersgill, Shipbuilders 1966-72. Chairman of A. and P. Appledore International Limited, Seascope Holdings Limited and Seascope Shipbrokers Limited. Member of Gen. Advisory Council of B.B.C. 1965-75. Member of Community Relations Commission 1968-70*   [1966]

LONGDEN, Fred. 58 Ansell Road, Erdington, Birmingham. S. of Harry Longden, Esq. B. 23 Feb. 1886; m. 1914, Alice Sherlock. Educ. at Elementary School, W.E.A., and Ruskin Coll., Oxford, (Dip. (Dist.) Econ. Pol. Sci.). Member of Union of Democratic Control and Conscientious objector during First World War; imprisoned for 2 years. A Lecturer and Author. A Labour Member. Unsuccessfully contested the Deritend division of Birmingham in 1922, 1923, 1924. Sat for the Deritend division of Birmingham from 1929-31 when he was defeated. Unsuccessfully contested the same seat in 1935. Sat again for the Deritend division of Birmingham from July 1945-Feb. 1950. Elected for the Small Heath division of Birmingham in Feb. 1950 and sat until his death on 5 Oct. 1952.
                                                          [1952]

LONGDEN, Sir Gilbert James Morley, M.B.E. 89 Cornwall Gardens, London. S. of Lieut.-Col. James Morley Longden, of Castle Eden, Co. Durham. B. 16 Apr. 1902. Unmarried. Educ. at Haileybury, and Emmanuel Coll., Cambridge. Admitted a Solicitor 1927. Secretary of I.C.I. (India) Limited 1930-37; University of Paris 1938. Commissioned into Durham Light Infantry and served with 2nd and 36th Division overseas 1940-45. M.B.E. 1944. U.K. Delegate to Council of Europe 1954-56 and to XII and XIII Sessions of the United Nations. Vice-Chairman of the British Council. Executive Committee of 1922 Committee. Chairman of Great Britain/East Europe Centre. Vice-President of the British Atlantic Committee. Honorary Secretary Conservative National Advisory Council on

Education. Knighted 1972. A Conservative. Unsuccessfully contested Morpeth in 1945. Elected for S.W. Hertfordshire in Feb. 1950 and sat until he retired in Feb. 1974.* [1974]

LOUGHLIN, Charles William. House of Commons, London. Staunton, Nr. Coleford, Gloucestershire. S. of Charles Loughlin Esq. of Grimsby. B. 1914; m. 19 Dec. 1945, May, d. of Arthur Dunderdale, Esq., (1 s.). Educ. at St. Mary's School, Grimsby, and National Council of Labour Colls. Parliamentary Secretary Ministry of Health Feb. 1965-Jan. 1967; Joint Parliamentary Secretary Ministry of Social Security Jan. 1967-Nov. 1968; Under-Secretary of State for Health and Social Security Nov. 1968. Parliamentary Secretary Ministry of Public Building and Works Nov. 1968-June 1970. A Labour Member. Elected for Gloucestershire W. in 1959 and sat until he retired in Sept. 1974. Area Organiser, Union of Shop, Distributive and Allied Workers 1945-74.*
[1974 2nd ed.]

LOVERIDGE, John Warren, J.P. House of Commons, London. Carlton, and Hurlingham. S. of C.W. Loveridge, Esq., and Emily (Mickie), d. of John Malone, Esq. B. 9 Sept. 1925; m. 1954, Jean Marguerite (J.P. for S. Westminster), d. of E.J. Chivers, Esq., (3 s. 2 d.). Educ. at St. John's Coll., Cambridge, (M.A.). Principal of St. Godric's Coll. from 1954. A Farmer. Contested (C) Aberavon in 1951 and Brixton in the London County Council elections, 1952. Member Hampstead Borough Council 1953-59. Treasurer/Trustee Hampstead Conservative Association 1959-74. Freeman of the City of London and Liveryman of Girdlers Company. Served Select Committees, Procedure and Expenditure. Vice-Chairman Conservative Parliamentary Smaller Business Committee. J.P. West Central Division 1963. F.R.A.S., M.R.I.I.A. A Conservative. Sat for Hornchurch from 1970 to Feb. 1974. Elected for the Upminster division of Havering in Feb. 1974.* [1979]

LOVEYS, Walter Harris. Bonhams, Flansham, Bognor Regis, Sussex. R.A.C., Lansdowne, and Carlton. S. of Walter Loveys, Esq. B. 2 Nov. 1920; m. 28 Nov. 1944, Muriel, d. of Commander Redvers Prior, MP. Educ. at Lancing. Chairman Chichester Conservative Association 1953-58 and of Agricultural Education Committee West Sussex County Council; member West Sussex County Council from 1953. Honorary Secretary Conservative Parliamentary Horticulture Committee; Honorary Secretary House of Commons Motor Club. Member Chichester Group Hospital Management Committee. Farms about 500 acres. A Conservative. Elected for the Chichester division of West Sussex in Nov. 1958 and sat until his death on 7 Mar. 1969. [1968]

LOW, Rt. Hon. Sir Austin Richard William ('Toby'), K.C.M.G., C.B.E., D.S.O., T.D. 4 Eaton Terrace, London. The Knoll Farm, Aldington, Kent. Carlton, and Brooks's. S. of Col. S. Low, B. 25 May 1914; m. 10 Apr. 1947, Araminta, d. of Sir Harold MacMichael, of Nouds, Teynham, Kent, (1 s. 2 d.). Educ. at Winchester, and New Coll., Oxford. Barrister-at-Law, Middle Temple 1939. War Service 1939-45, Brigadier 1944-45, Honorary Col. 288 L.A.A. Regiment, T.A. 1946-51, and 337 L.A.A. Regiment, T.A. 1951-59. Parliamentary Secretary Ministry of Supply Nov. 1951-July 1954. Minister of State, Board of Trade July 1954-Jan. 1957; PC. 1954. Dept. Chairman of the Conservative Party Organisation 1959-63. A Conservative. Elected for Blackpool N. in July 1945 and sat until Jan. 1962 whe he was created Baron Aldington. D.S.O. 1941, M.B.E. 1944, C.B.E. 1945, T.D. 1950, K.C.M.G. 1957. Chairman of Grindlay's Bank Limited 1964-76, of Port of London Authority 1971-77. Dept. Chairman of G.E.C. Limited. Chairman of Sun Alliance and London Insurance Limited, of National Nuclear Corporation and Westland Aircraft Limited. Dept.-Lieut. for Kent. 1973. Fellow of Winchester Coll.* [1962]

LOYDEN, Edward. House of Commons, London. S. of Patrick Loyden, Esq. B. 3 May 1923; m. 12 Feb. 1944, Rose, d. of Hugh Boyle, Esq., (1 s. 2 d.). Educ. at Friary School, Liverpool. A Port Worker, Mersey Docks and Harbour Board 1946-74. Liverpool City Councillor, Gillmoss 1960-64 and 1970-73, Old Swan 1964-70. District Councillor Gillmoss 1973. Metropolitan County Councillor Merseyside 1973. President Liverpool Trade Council. Regional Advisory Committee (Education) T.U.C. 1965-72. Chairman Liverpool Borough Labour Party 1966-68. Transport and General Workers Union—District and National Committee, member of Docks and Waterways Section 1967-75. Mental Health Review Tribunal—Sup. Benefits Appeal Tribunal. Vice-Chairman T.G.W.U. Parliamentary Group. A Labour Member. Sat for the Garston division of Liverpool from Feb. 1974 until 1979, when he was defeated.*   [1979]

LUARD, David Evan Trant. St. Antony's College, Oxford. S. of Col. T.B. Luard, D.S.O., R.M. B. 31 Oct. 1926. Educ. at Felsted, and King's Coll., Cambridge. In the Diplomatic Service 1950-56. Fellow St. Antony's Coll., Oxford from 1957. Member of Oxford City Council 1958-61. Parliamentary Under-Secretary F.C.O. 1969-70 and 1976-79. Visiting Professor, New York State University 1971-72. Author of several books on International Affairs. A Labour Member. Unsuccessfully contested Oxford in 1964. Sat for Oxford from 1966 to 1970, when he was defeated. Unsuccessfully contested Oxford again in Feb. 1974. Re-elected for Oxford in Oct. 1974 and sat until 1979, when he was defeated.*   [1979]

LUBBOCK, Eric Reginald. High Elms Farms, Downe, Orpington, Kent. National Liberal. S. of Hon. Maurice F.P. Lubbock, Company Director. B. 29 Sept. 1928; m. 1953, Kina-Maria, d. of Count J. O'Kelly de Gallagh, K.M., of 10 Sloane Gardens, London. Educ. at Upper Canada Coll., Harrow, and Balliol Coll. With Rolls-Royce (Aero-engine division) 1951-55; Production Engineering Limited (Management Consultant) 1955-60. Charterhouse Group 1960-64. Liberal Whip 1963-70. A Liberal. Elected for Orpington in Mar. 1962 and sat until 1970 when he was defeated. Member of Institution of Mechanical Engineers. Served with Welsh Guards 1949-51, 2nd Lieut. Consultant, Morgan-Grampian Limited from 1970. Succeeded to the Peerage as Baron Avebury 1971. Member of Gen. Advisory Council of Independent Television Authority

1972-73. President of Data Processing Management Association 1972-75. President of Fluoridation Society from 1972, of Conservation Society from 1973. Member of Council of Institute of Race Relations 1972-74 and of Royal Commission on Standards of Conduct in Public Life 1974-76.*   [1970]

LUCAS, Sir Jocelyn Morton, Bart., K.B.E., M.C. House of Commons, London. 65 Chester Row, London. Blickling Hall, Norfolk. Carlton, Bath, and Kennel. S. of Sir Edward Lucas, 3rd Bart. B. 27 Aug. 1889; m. 1st, 20 Dec. 1933, Edith, d. of the Very Rev. David Barrie Cameron, M.A., D.D., J.P., and widow of Sir Trehawke Kekewich, 1st Bart (she died 1956); 2ndly, 18 Oct. 1960, Mrs. Thelma de Chair (she died 1974). Educ. at Eton, and Royal Military Coll., Sandhurst. Maj. late 4th Royal Warwickshire Regiment. Served overseas 1914-19 (wounded, prisoner). President Immortal 7th Division Survivors Association Ypres 1914. Liaison Officer (Welfare) Dominion Forces in London 1940-50; served with A.F.S. (London) and N.F.S. 1938-42, Section Leader, twice wounded. Vice-Chairman of Royal Overseas League; Chairman of Hospitality Committee from 1938. Founder and Chairman of Allies Welcome Committee 1940-50, and of Returned P.O.W. Advice Committee 1944-48; Chairman Empire War Memorial Fund, St. Paul's Cathedral; Chairman British Sportsmen's Club. A Conservative. Elected for Portsmouth S. in July 1939 and sat until he retired in 1966. Member of Council of Royal Veterinary Coll. A Dog Breeder. Succeeded as Bart. 1936. K.B.E. 1959. Died 2 May 1980.   [1966]

LUCAS, Percy Belgrave, D.S.O., D.F.C. 20 Berkeley Square, London. Bath. S. of P.M. Lucas, Esq., of Sandwich. B. 1915; m. 22 May 1946, Jill Addison. Educ. at Stowe, and Pembroke Coll., Cambridge. A Journalist, later Managing Director Greyhound Racing Association Trust Limited, and Associated Companies. Served with R.A.F. 1939-46; demobilized as Wing-Commander. Awarded D.S.O. 1943 and Bar 1945, D.F.C. 1942 and Croix de Guerre. A Conservative. Unsuccessfully contested W. Fulham in 1945. Elected for Brentford and Chiswick in Feb. 1950 and sat until he retired in 1959. An International Golfer. Managing Director of G.R.A. Property Trust Limited 1957-65, Chairman 1965-75. Member of Sports Council from 1971.*　　　　　　　　　　　　[1959]

LUCAS-TOOTH, Sir Hugh Vere Huntly Duff, Bart. See MUNRO-LUCAS-TOOTH, Sir Hugh Vere Huntly Duff, Bart.

LUCE, Richard Napier. House of Commons, London. S. of Sir William Luce, G.B.E., K.C.M.G. B. 14 Oct. 1936; m. 5 Apr. 1961, Rose, d. of Sir Godfrey Nicholson, MP. (2 s.). Educ. at Wellington Coll., and Christ's Coll., Cambridge. Overseas Civil Service (Kenya) 1960-62. Brand Manager Gallaher Limited 1963-65. Marketing Manager Spirella 1965-68. Chairman National Innovations Centre 1968-71. Chairman Selanex Limited 1973. Parliamentary Private Secretary to Sir Geoffrey Howe, Minister for Trade and Consumer Affairs 1972-74. Opposition Whip 1974-75. Vice-President Institute of Patentees and Inventors 1974. Member European Advisory Board Corning Glass International S.A. Chairman Courtenay Stewart Int. Limited 1975. Secretary Conservative Parliamentary Foreign Affairs Committee 1975-77. Opposition spokesman for Foreign and Commonwealth Affairs Nov. 1977-May 1979. Under-Secretary of State, Foreign and Commonwealth Office from May 1979. A Conservative. Unsuccessfully contested Hitchin in 1970. Sat for Arundel and Shoreham division of W. Sussex from Apr. 1971-Feb. 1974. Elected for the Shoreham division of W. Sussex in Feb. 1974.*　　　　　　　　　　　　[1979]

LYLE, Sir Charles Ernest Leonard, Bart. 52 Cadogan Square, London. Grey-stoke, Canford Cliffs, Bournemouth. Carlton, and Bath. S. of Charles Lyle, Esq., of Brooke Hall, Norwich. B. 22 July 1882; m. 14 July 1904, Edith Louise, d. of John Levy, Esq., of Rochester (she died 22 Dec. 1942). Educ. at Harrow, and Trinity Hall, Cambridge. President of Tate and Lyle Limited. Knight Bach. 1923; Bart. 1932; Chairman of East Dorset Conservative Association 1932-40, and of Queen Mary's Hospital for the East End 1916-23; J.P. for West Ham; Parlia-mentary Private Secretary to the Rt. Hon. Charles McCurdy when Food Controller Mar. 1920-Mar. 1921. A Director of Lloyds Bank. A Conservative. MP. for the Stratford division of West Ham from Dec. 1918-Nov. 1922 when he was defeated. Sat for the Epping division of Essex from 1923 until he retired in Oct. 1924. Returned unopposed for Bournemouth in June 1940 and sat until Aug. 1945 when he was created Baron Lyle of Westbourne. Died 6 Mar. 1954.　　　　　　　　　　　　[1945]

LYNE, Arthur William, O.B.E. 52 Greenfield Road, Northampton. S. of William Lyne, Esq., of Finedon, Northants. B. 21 July 1882; m. 8 Apr. 1931, Beatrice Henman. A Boot and Shoe Operative. Served with Northamptonshire Regiment 1914-18; Sergeant Executive Officer Boot and Shoe Operatives Union. J.P. for Northampton 1923-64, and Borough Councillor 1920-64; Mayor 1938-39, Chairman of Housing and Town Planning Committee from 1930. O.B.E. 1939. A Labour Member. Elected for the Burton division of Staffordshire in July 1945 and sat until 1950 when he was defeated. Died 30 Dec. 1971.　　　　　　　　　　　　[1950]

LYON, Alexander Ward. House of Commons, London. S. of Alexander Pirie Lyon, Esq. B. 15 Oct. 1931; m. 7 July 1951, Hilda Arandall, Educ. at West Leeds High School, and University Coll., London. A Barrister-at-Law, Inner Temple 1954. Member of Select Committee on Overseas Aid. Member of Younger Committee on Privacy. Parliamentary Private Secretary to Roy Jenkins and Harold Lever 1968-70. Opposition spokesman on Foreign Affairs 1970-72, and Home Affairs 1972-74. Minister of State, Home Office Mar. 1974-Apr. 1976. Methodist Local Preacher. A Labour Member. Unsuccessfully contested York in 1964. Sat for York from Mar. 1966. Vice-Chairman of British Council of Churches Board for Social Responsibility 1970-74. Voted in favour of entry to E.E.C. on 28 Oct. 1971. Chairman of U.K. Immigrants Advisory Service from 1978.* [1979]

LYONS, Edward. House of Commons, London. S. of Albert Lyons, Esq. B. 17 May 1926; m. 4 Sept. 1955, Barbara, d. of Alfred

Katz, Esq., (1 s. 1 d.). Educ. at Elementary and Secondary Schools in Leeds, and Leeds University. Served Royal Artillery 1944-48 (including period at Cambridge University studying Russian). Interpreter in Russian attached to British Control Commission in Germany 1946-48. LL.B. (Hons.) degree 1951. Called to the bar, Lincoln's Inn 1952. Practised at bar on North-Eastern Circuit from 1952 and in London from 1974. Member Select Committee on Race Relations and Immigration 1968-70. Parliamentary Private Secretary to Dick Taverne and William Rodgers, Treasury Ministers Oct. 1969-June 1970. Dept. Chairman P.L.P. Home Office Group 1970-74, Chairman 1974. Voted in favour of entry to E.E.C. on 28 Oct. 1971. Member Executive of Justice 1975. Member Select Committee European Secondary Legislation 1974. Recorder from Jan. 1972. Queen's Counsel 1974. Chairman P.L.P. Legal and Judicial Group 1974-77. A Labour Member. Unsuccessfully contested Harrogate in 1964. Sat for Bradford E. from 1966-Feb. 1974, and for Bradford W. from Feb. 1974.*   [1979]

LYTTELTON, Capt. Rt. Hon. Oliver, D.S.O., M.C. 14 Upper Belgrave Street, London. Trafalgar House, Salisbury. St. James's, and Turf. S. of Rt. Hon. Alfred Lyttelton, K.C., MP. B. 15 Mar. 1893; m. 30 Jan. 1920, Lady Moira Godolphin Osborne, d. of the 10th Duke of Leeds. Educ. at Eton and Trinity Coll., Cambridge. Capt. Grenadier Guards, served overseas 1914-18; Brigade Maj. 1918. PC. 1940. President of Board of Trade Oct. 1940-June 1941. Minister of State Resident in Cairo July 1941-Feb. 1942, with a seat in War Cabinet July 1941-May 1945; Minister of State with responsibility for war production Feb.-Mar. 1942, Minister of Production Mar. 1942-July 1945 and also President of Board of Trade May-July 1945. Secretary of State for the Colonies Nov. 1951-July 1954. Member of Cabinet 1945 and 1951-54. Had Soviet Order of Suvorov, 1st Class. A Conservative. Elected for the Aldershot division of Hampshire in Nov. 1940 and sat until Aug. 1954 when he was created Visct. Chandos. D.S.O. 1916, M.C. 1918. President of Institute of Directors 1948-51 and 1954-63. Managing Director of

British Metal Corporation. Controller of Non-Ferrous Metals 1939-40. Chairman of Associated Electrical Industries 1945-51 and 1954-63. K.G. 1970. Chairman of National Theatre Board 1962-71, Life President 1971. Trustee of Churchill Coll., Cambridge and of National Gallery. Died 21 Jan. 1972.   [1954]

MABON, Rt. Hon. (Jesse) Dickson. House of Commons, London. S. of Jesse Dickson Mabon, Esq. B. 1 Nov. 1925; m. 6 Jan. 1970, Miss Elizabeth Zinn, (1 s.). Educ. at Possilpark School, Cumbrae, North Kelvinside Schools, and University of Glasgow, M.B. and Ch.B.1954. D.H.M.S.A. 1974, F. Inst. Pet., F.R.S.A. Served in the mines, W.O. in Army. President Glasgow Union 1951-52 and of Scottish Union of Students 1954-55. Physician and Journalist. Political Columnist *Scottish Daily Record* 1955-64. Freeman of the City of London 1972. Minister of State Scottish Office Jan. 1967-June 1970. Joint Parliamentary Under-Secretary of State, Scottish Office Oct. 1964-Jan. 1967. Member U.K. Delegation to Council of Europe and Assembly of Western European Union 1970-72 and 1974-76. Chairman Manifesto Group of P.L.P. 1974-76. Minister of State for Energy Apr. 1976-May 1979. PC. Jan. 1977. Voted in favour of entry to E.E.C. on 28 Oct. 1971. An Opposition spokesman on Scottish Affairs 1970-72. A Labour and Co-operative Member. Unsuccessfully contested Bute and North Ayrshire in 1951, and W. Renfrewshire in 1955. Sat for Greenock from Dec. 1955 to Feb. 1974 and for Greenock and Port Glasgow from Feb. 1974. Chairman of U.K. Labour Committee for Europe 1974-76. President of European Movement 1975-76.*   [1979]

McADAM, William. 16 Overdale Gardens, Langside, Glasgow. S. of Robert McAdam, Esq. B. 7 Aug. 1886; m. 20 June 1913, Helen, d. of John MacFarlane, Esq. Educ. at Hoddom Public School, Ecclefechan. A Railway Worker from 1904. A soldier. Branch Secretary National Executive Committee and District Auditor of N.U.R. A Labour Member. Unsuccessfully contested Edinburgh W. in May 1935 and Salford N. in Nov. 1935. Elected for Salford N. in July 1945 and sat until he retired in 1950. Member of Scottish

Executive of Labour Party. Died 22 Apr. 1952. [1950]

McADDEN, Sir Stephen James, C.B.E. 552 Woodgrange Drive, Thorpe Bay, Southend-on-Sea, Essex. S. of William John McAdden, Esq., of Ilford, B. 3 Nov. 1907; m. 4 Jan. 1951, Doris Hearle, of Thorpe Bay. Educ. at Salesian School, Battersea. An Export Sales Manager. Member of Hackney Borough Council 1937-45, Woodford Borough Council 1945-48 and Essex County Council 1947-48. Voted against entry to E.E.C. on 28 Oct. 1971. A Conservative. Elected for Southend E. in Feb. 1950 and sat until his death on 26 Dec. 1979. Director of Butlins Construction Co. Ltd. C.B.E. 1959. Knighted 1962. Member of Speaker's Panel of Chairmen from 1966. Died 26 Dec. 1979. [1979]

McALISKEY, (Josephine) Bernadette. House of Commons, London. D. of John James Devlin, Esq. B. 23 Apr. 1947; m. 23 Apr. 1973, Michael McAliskey, Esq. Educ. at Queen's University Belfast. Youngest Member of Parliament. An Independent Unity Member. Elected for Mid-Ulster in Apr. 1969 and sat until Feb. 1974 when she was defeated. Founder Member of Irish Republican Socialist Party 1975. Unsuccessfully contested Northern Ireland for European Parliament 1979.* [1974]

McALISTER, Mary Agnes. House of Commons, London. D. of Charles McMackin, Esq. M. 1927, J. Alexander McAlister, Esq. Educ. at Franciscan Convent, Glasgow. Served with Civil Nursing Reserve and in Postal Censorship 1939-45. A Nurse. Member of Glasgow City Council 1945-58, J.P. 1947-51. A Labour Member. Member from 1958, winning Kelvingrove division of Glasgow from the Conservatives in a by-election on 13 Mar. 1958. Sat until 1959 when she was defeated. C.B.E. 1968. Member of National Assistance Board 1961-66, of Supplementary Benefits Commission 1966-67, Dept. Chairman 1967. Died 26 Feb. 1976. [1959]

McALLISTER, Gilbert. 1 The Grove, Highgate Village, London. 55 Kenilworth Avenue, Wishaw, Lanarkshire. Travellers',

R.A.C., and Press. S. of Archibald McAllister, Esq., J.P. of Wishaw. B. 26 Mar. 1906; m. 1937, Elizabeth, d. of William Glen, Esq., of Saltcoats. Educ. at Wishaw High School, and Glasgow University. Editor of *Merchant Navy Journal* 1943-46, Feature Writer *Daily Herald* from 1945. Secretary of Town and Country Planning Association 1936-42; member of Lord Reith's Reconstruction Group, Ministry of Works, and of Empire Delegation to East Africa 1948. A Labour Member. Unsuccessfully contested N. Lanark in 1935 and the Hillhead division of Glasgow in 1937. Elected for the Rutherglen division of Lanarkshire in July 1945 and sat until 1951 when he was defeated. Unsuccessfully contested Rutherglen in 1955. Secretary of Scottish P.L.P. 1948-50. Chairman of Parliamentary Group for World Government 1950-51. Gen. Administrator of National Music Council of Great Britain 1959-64. Director of Gilbert McAllister and Partners, Public Relations Consultants. Died 27 May 1964 at Monte Carlo. [1951]

MacANDREW, Col. Rt. Hon. Sir Charles Glen. St. John's House, Smith Square, London. The White House, Monkton, Ayrshire. Carlton, R.Y.S., and Royal & Ancient. S. of Francis Glen MacAndrew, Esq., of Knock Castle, Largs. B. 13 Jan. 1888; m. 1st, 7 Feb. 1918, d. of J.P. Curran, Esq., of St. Andrews (marriage dissolved in 1938); 2ndly, 20 Feb. 1941, Mona, d. of J.A. Ralston Mitchell, Esq., of Perceton House, Irvine. Educ. at Uppingham, and Trinity Coll., Cambridge, LL.D. St. Andrews. Honorary Col. Ayrshire Yeomanry 1951-55. Member of Racecourse Betting Control Board from 1938-1961. Created Kinght Bach. 1935. PC. 1952. J.P. and Dept.-Lieut. for Ayrshire. Temporary Chairman of Committees 1934. Dept. Chairman of Ways and Means May-July 1945 and Mar. 1950-Oct. 1951. Chairman of Ways and Means from Nov. 1951-Sept. 1959. A Conservative. Sat for the Kilmarnock division of Ayrshire from Oct. 1924-May 1929, when he was defeated. Unsuccessfully contested Kilmarnock again in Nov. 1929. Sat for the Partick division of Glasgow from 1931-35. Elected for the Bute and N. Ayrshire division of Ayrshire and Bute in 1935 and sat until he retired in 1959. Created Baron MacAndrew 1959. Died 11 Jan. 1979. [1959]

MacARTHUR, Ian. Tayfletts House, Perth. Naval, and New (Edinburgh). S. of Lieut.-Gen. Sir William MacArthur, K.C.B., D.S.O., F.R.C.P. B. 17 May 1925; m. 21 Mar. 1957, Judith Mary, d. of Francis Gavin Douglas Miller, Esq., (3 s. 3 d.). Educ. at Cheltenham Coll., and The Queen's Coll., Oxford. Served R.N. and R.N.V.R. 1943-46. Honorary President Scottish Young Unionists 1962-65. Assistant Government Whip 1962-63; Lord Commissioner of the Treasury Dec. 1963-Oct. 1964; Opposition Whip 1964-Oct. 1965. Vice-Chairman of Conservative Party in Scotland 1972-75. Chairman Scottish Conservative Members Committee 1972-73. A Conservative. Unsuccessfully contested Greenock in May 1955 and a by-election in Dec. 1955. Elected for Perth and E. Perthshire in 1959 and sat until Oct. 1974 when he was defeated. Director of Administration J. Walter Thompson Company Limited. Opposition spokesman on Scottish Affairs 1965-70. Director of British Textile Confederation from 1977.*

[1974 2nd ed.]

McBRIDE, Neil. 116 Eaton Road, Brynn-fryd, Swansea, Glamorgan. S. of Neil McBride, Esq. B. 13 Apr. 1910 at Neilston, Renfrewshire; m. 12 June 1937, Delia, 4th d. of James Maloney, Esq., of Paisley. Educ. at Elementary School, and continuation classes. Secretary P.L.P. Trade Union Group 1964-66. Alternate Delegate, Assembly of W.E.U. and Council of Europe 1964-66. Joined the Labour Party in 1940. Member of the Amalgamated Engineering Union from 1937. Member of the Co-operative Party, Paisley Co-operative Manufacturing Society for 17 years. Member of the A.E.U. Parliamentary Panel from 1950. Chairman of Paisley C.L.P. 1950-62. Alternate Delegate W.E.U. and Cncl. of Europe 1965. Visited Europe, Africa, South America and Middle East. Patron Welsh Boxing Club. Vice-President Clydach and Gendros Amateur Operatic Societies. Welsh Whip 1966-70. Assistant Government Whip Apr. 1966-Oct. 1969. Lord Commissioner H.M. Treasury Oct. 1969-June 1970. Chairman Welsh Labour Parliamentary Group 1972-73. A Roman Catholic. A Labour Member. Unsuccessfully contested Perth and

E. Perthshire in 1951 and the High Peak division of Derbyshire in 1955. Elected for Swansea E. at a by-election in Mar. 1963 and sat until his death on 9 Sept. 1974.

[1974 2nd ed.]

McCALLUM, Maj. Sir Duncan, M.C. 1 Cranmer Court, Sloane Avenue, London. Ardanaiseig, Kilchrenan, By Taynuilt, Argyll. S. of Colin Whitton McCallum, Esq., the music-hall artist Charles Coborn. B. 24 Nov. 1888; m. 1925, Violet Mary, d. of J.L.A. Hope, Esq., of Whitney Court Hereford, and widow of Capt. E.A. Hume. Educ. at Filey, Christ's Hospital, and Military Staff Course, Caius Coll., Cambridge. Late E. Yorkshire Regiment. Served in West Africa 1907-14, and Cameroons, France, Belgium and Germany 1914-19. Liaison Officer with French Army in Syria 1920-24. Commandant British Legation Guard Peking 1926-27. Honorary Attaché British Legation, Bulgaria 1932-34; in Cairo 1934-38; G.S.O.I. G.H.Q. Middle East Cairo 1939-40; member of Highlands and Islands Advisory Panel from 1947. Knight Bach. 1955. Fellow of Zoological Society and Royal Geographical Society. A Conservative. Elected for Argyllshire in Apr. 1940 and sat until his death on 10 May 1958.

[1958]

McCANN, John, C.B.E. House of Commons, London. S. of John McCann, Esq. B. 1910; m. 1939, Alice Nolan, (1 s. 1 d.). Educ. at Elementary School. Councillor Eccles Borough 1945, Alderman 1952, Mayor 1955-56. Member Select Committee of Estimates. Opposition Whip 1961-64. Government Whip 1964-69. A Lord Commissioner of the Treasury Oct. 1964-Apr. 1966. C.B.E. 1966. Vice-Chamberlain of H.M. Household from Apr. 1966-July 1967. A Lord Commissioner of the Treasury from July 1967-Oct. 1969. A Labour Member. Unsuccessfully contested Rochdale in 1955. Elected for Rochdale in 1958, winning the seat from the Conservatives in a by-election in Feb. and sat until his death on 16 July 1972. [1972]

McCARTNEY, Hugh. House of Commons, London. S. of John McCartney, Esq. B. Jan. 1920; m. 1949, Margaret, d. of F. Macdonald, Esq. of Kirkintilloch. Educ. at John

Street Secondary School, and Royal Technical Coll., Glasgow. Member Dunbarton County Council 1965-70; Member Kirkintilloch Town Council 1955-70. Magistrate for 5 years. Opposition Whip from 1979. A Labour Member. Sat for Dunbartonshire East division from June 1970 to Feb. 1974 and for Dunbartonshire Central division from Feb. 1974.* [1979]

MacCOLL, James Eugene. 21 Randolph Road, London. S. of Hugo MacColl, Esq., of Suderland. B. 27 June 1908. Educ. at Sedbergh School, Balliol Coll., Oxford and University of Chicago. Conscientious Objector 1939-45, served with Civil Defence. Barrister-at-Law, Inner Temple 1933. Mayor of Paddington 1947-49. Opposition spokesman on Local Government 1959-64. Joint Parliamentary Secretary Ministry of Housing and Local Government Oct. 1964-Oct. 1969. A Labour Member. Elected for the Widnes division of Lancashire in Feb. 1950 and sat until his death on 17 June 1971. Co-opted member of London County Council Education Committee 1936-46. Member of Paddington Borough Council from 1934-1965, Mayor 1947-49. J.P. for County of London. Research Assistant, Political and Economic Planning Trust 1945-50. Member of Hemel Hempstead New Town Corporation 1946-50. Member of Domestic Coal Consumers Council 1947-50. Author of *British Local Government* and other works. Died 17 June 1971. [1971]

MACCORMICK, Iain Somerled Mac-Donald. House of Commons, London. S. of Dr. John MacDonald MacCormick. B. 1939; m. 1964, Micky Trefusis Elsom. Educ. at High School and Glasgow University. Served in Queen's Own Lowland Yeomanry 1957-67, Capt. A Scottish Nationalist Member. Unsuccessfully contested Argyll in 1970. Elected for Argyll in Feb. 1974 and sat until 1979, when he was defeated. Member of Argyll and Bute District Council from 1979.* [1979]

McCORQUODALE, Rt. Hon. Malcolm Stewart. 6 West Eaton Place, London. 15 King Street, London. Balcombe House, Balcombe, Sussex. S. of Norman McCorquodale, Esq., of Winslow Hall, Buckinghamshire. B. 29 Mar. 1901; m. 1st, 6 Oct. 1931, Winifred, d. of J.O.M. Clark, Esq. (she died 1960); 2ndly, 1962, Hon. Daisy Pearson, d. of 2nd Visct. Cowdray, widow of Hon. Robin Gurdon and of Lieut.-Col. Alastair Gibb. Educ. at Harrow, and Christ Church, Oxford. Chairman of various Printing Companies. Parliamentary Private Secretary to G.H. Shakespeare when Financial Secretary to the Admiralty 1939-40, to Rt. Hon. Sir Andrew Duncan when President of Board of Trade. Joint Parliamentary Secretary Ministry of Labour Feb. 1942-July 1945. Pilot Officer R.A.F.V.R. 1940; Flight-Lieut. Nov. 1940. PC. 1945. A Conservative. Unsuccessfully contested West Willesden in May 1929. Sat for Sowerby from 1931 until 1945, when he was defeated. Elected for the Epsom division of Surrey in Dec. 1947 and sat until he retired in 1955. Created Baron McCorquodale of Newton 1955. Chairman of Governors of Harrow School. K.C.V.O. 1965. President of British Employers' Confederation 1960. Died 25 Sept. 1971. [1954]

McCRINDLE, Robert Arthur. 26 Ashburnham Gardens, Upminster, Essex. S. of Thomas McCrindle, Esq. B. 19 Sept. 1929; m. 3 Oct. 1953, Myra, d. of J.P. Anderson, Esq. Educ. at Allen Glens Coll., Glasgow. Parliamentary Private Secretary to Mark Carlisle, Minister of State, Home Office 1974. A Conservative. Unsuccessfully contested Dundee E. in 1959 and Thurrock in 1964. Sat for Billericay from 1970 to Feb. 1974 and for Brentwood and Ongar from Feb. 1974. Vice-President of Corporation of Mortgage Brokers 1970-76. Vice-Chairman of Sausmarez, Carey and Harris, Financial Consultants 1972-75.* [1979]

McCUSKER, James Harold. House of Commons, London. Portadown. S. of James Harold McCusker, Esq. B. 7 Feb. 1940. m. 1965, Jennifer Leslie Mills. Educ. at Lurgan Coll. A Schoolmaster 1961-68. Personnel Officer 1968-72. Production Manager 1972-74. U.U.U.C. Chief Whip 1975-76. Supported the Labour Government in vote of confidence on 28 Mar. 1979. An Ulster Unionist Member. Elected for Armagh in Feb. 1974.* [1979]

MacDERMOT, Niall, O.B.E., Q.C. House of Commons, London. S. of Henry MacDermot, Esq., K.C. B. 10 Sept. 1916; m. 1st, 1940, Violet Denise Maxwell (divorced); 2ndly, 6 Aug. 1966, Ludmila Benvenuto. Educ. at Rugby School, Corpus Christi Coll., Cambridge, and Balliol Coll., Oxford. Served with Intelligence Corps 1939-46. Member Executive Committee London Labour Party 1958-62. Honorary Treasurer of "Justice", British Section of the International Commission of Jurists from 1968-70. Dept. Chairman Bedfordshire Quarter Sessions 1961-63, and from 1969-72. Trustee of the Tate Gallery from 1969-76. Recorder of Newark 1963-64. Financial Secretary to the Treasury Oct. 1964-Aug. 1967. Minister of State, Ministry of Housing and Local Government Aug. 1967-Sept. 1968. A Labour Member. Sat for Lewisham N. from Feb. 1957 to 1959 when he was defeated. Elected for Derby N. in Apr. 1962 and sat until he retired in 1970. O.B.E. 1944. Barrister-at-Law, Inner Temple 1946, Bencher 1970. Q.C. 1963. Secretary-Gen. of International Commission of Jurists from 1970. Recorder of Crown Court 1972-74.* [1970]

MACDONALD, Alistair Huistean. 79 Oakdene Avenue, Chislehurst, Kent. S. of John Hendry Macdonald, Esq. B. 18 May 1925. Educ. at Dulwich Coll., Enfield Technical Coll., and Corpus Christi Coll., Cambridge. Councillor, Chislehurst and Sidcup Urban District Council 1958-62; Alderman, London Borough of Bromley 1964-68, Councillor from 1971. A Labour Member. Unsuccessfully contested Beckenham in 1964. Elected for the Chislehurst division of Kent in Mar. 1966 and sat until he was defeated in 1970. Unsuccessfully contested the Chislehurst division of Bromley in Feb. and Oct. 1974.* [1970]

MACDONALD, Archibald James Florence. 22 Heath Drive, Hampstead, London. Fairnilee House, Galashiels, Scotland. Reform. S. of Dr. G.B.D. Macdonald, of Uniondale, South Africa. B. 2 May 1904; m. 12 Sept. 1945, Hon. Elspeth Shaw, d. of 2nd Lord Craigmyle. Educ. at Chatswood Grammar School, Australia, and Royal Australian Naval Coll. Joint Chief Executive, Management Research Groups, London 1937-40. Secretary of Paint Industry Export Group 1940-49. A Director of Robert Bowran and Company Limited 1949-53. A Liberal. Unsuccessfully contested Roxburgh and Selkirk in 1945. Elected for Roxburgh and Selkirk in Feb. 1950 and sat until 1951 when he was defeated. Vice-Chairman of Joseph Freeman Sons and Company Limited 1954-66. Joined the Conservative Party in Mar. 1971. J.P. for County of London. Member of Hampstead Borough Council 1962-65, and Camden Borough Council 1971-76.* [1951]

MacDONALD, Margo. 115 Bardykes Road, High Blantyre, Glasgow. D. of Robert Aitken, Esq. B. 19 Apr. 1944; m. 1965, Peter MacDonald, Esq. Educ. at Hamilton Academy and Dunfermline Coll. A Scottish National Party Member. Unsuccessfully contested Paisley in 1970. Elected for the Govan division of Glasgow at a by-election in Nov. 1973 and sat until Feb. 1974 when she was defeated. Unsuccessfully contested the Govan division of Glasgow in Oct. 1974 and Hamilton in May 1978. Vice-Chairman of S.N.P. 1972-79. Scottish Director of Shelter from 1978.* [1974]

MACDONALD, Sir Murdoch, K.C.M.G., C.B. 72 Victoria Street, London. St. James's. S. of Roderick Macdonald, Esq. B. at Inverness 6 May 1866; m. 21 Nov. 1899, Margaret, d. of Alexander Munro, Esq., of Balmacarra (she died 1956). Educ. at Farraline Park Institution, Inverness. A Consulting Civil Engineer; President of Institution of Civil Engineers. 1932; Adviser and Under-Secretary of State for Public Works in Egypt. K.C.M.G. 1914, C.B. 1916, C.M.G. 1910. Elected for the Inverness division of Inverness-shire and Ross and Cromarty in Mar. 1922 and sat until he retired in 1950. Elected as a Lloyd George Liberal in 1922, sat as a Liberal until 1931, and as a Liberal National from 1931 until he resigned the Whip in Feb. 1942. Elected as an Independent Liberal National Member in 1945, with Liberal but not Conservative opposition. Described as 'an Independent Member' in Dod 1950. Died 24 Apr. 1957. [1950]

McDONALD, Dr. Oonagh Anne. House of Commons, London. D. of Dr. H.D. McDonald, Baptist Minister. B. 1938; m. 1965, Richard Whitehouse, Esq. Educ. at East Barnet Grammar School, and King's Coll., London B.D. 1959, Ph.D. 1974. A Lecturer in Philosophy, Bristol University 1965-76. Parliamentary Labour Candidate for South Gloucestershire Feb. and Oct. 1974. Member of Industrial Policy Sub-Committee and Finance and Economic Affairs Sub-Committee for Labour Party's National Executive Committee. Member A.S.T.M.S. Parliamentary Private Secretary to Rt. Hon. Joel Barnett, Chief Secretary to the Treasury 1977-79. A Labour Member. Sat for the Thurrock division of Essex from July 1976.* [1979]

MACDONALD, Capt. Sir Peter Drummond, K.B.E. 4/1 Princess Row, London. Ningwood Manor, Isle of Wight. Carlton. S. of Ronald A. MacDonald, Esq., of Nova Scotia. B. 1895; m. 1st, Dec. 1933, Lady Jean Cochrane, d. of Douglas, 12th Earl of Dundonald (she died 1955); 2ndly, May 1956, Dr. Phoebe Napier Harvey. Educ. at Dalhousie Coll., Canada, and Trinity Hall, Cambridge. Served in France 1915-18; Joined R.A.F. Sept. 1939. Retired with rank of Squadron Leader 1943. Parliamentary Private Secretary to Sir Philip Cunliffe Lister when President of the Board of Trade June 1928-June 1929. Created K.B.E. 1945. A Conservative. Unsuccessfully contested the Isle of Wight in 1923. Elected for the Isle of Wight in 1924 and sat until he retired in 1959. Chairman of Conservative Parliamentary Imperial Affairs Committee. Fellow of Royal Society of Arts. Died 2 Dec. 1961. [1959]

McELHONE, Francis Patrick. 22 Windlaw Road, Carmunnock, Glasgow. S. of Thomas Joseph McElhone, Esq. B. 5 Apr. 1929; m. 13 Nov. 1958, Helen Margaret, d. of John Brown, Esq. Educ. at St. Bonaventure's Secondary School. A Roman Catholic. J.P., elected Councillor for Hutcheson Town Ward, Glasgow Corporation 1963. Appointed Bailie of the River and Firth of Clyde 1965. Appointed Magistrate of the City of Glasgow 1966. Appointed Senior Magistrate of Glasgow 1968-69. Parliamentary Private Secretary to Secretary of State for Industry, A.W. Benn 1974-75. Under-Secretary of State, Scottish Office Sept. 1975-May 1979. An Opposition spokesman on Overseas Development from 1979. A Labour Member. Sat for the Gorbals division of Glasgow from Oct. 1969-Feb. 1974. Elected for the Queens Park division of Glasgow in Feb. 1974.* [1979]

McENTEE, Valentine La Touche, C.B.E. 57 Hillcrest Road, Walthamstow, London. S. of Dr. W.C. McEntee, of Kingstown, Co. Dublin. B. 16 Jan. 1871; m. 1st, 1890, Elizabeth, d. of Edward Crawford, Esq. (she died); 2ndly, 5 June 1920, Catherine Windsor. Educ. at an Elementary School, and private tuition. A Woodworker. Member of Walthamstow Borough Council and 1st Mayor 1929-30 and again 1950-51. Parliamentary Private Secretary to G. Hicks, Parliamentary Secretary Ministry of Works and Planning Jan. 1942-May 1945. Freeman of Borough of Walthamstow 1948. A Labour Member. Unsuccessfully contested Walthamstow W. in 1918. Elected for Walthamstow W. in 1922 and again in 1923 and sat until 1924 when he was defeated. Re-elected for Walthamstow W. in May 1929 and sat until he retired in 1950. C.B.E. 1948. Created Baron McEntee 1951. Died 11 Feb. 1953. [1950]

McFARLANE, Charles Stuart. Cairnyard, Lochanhead, Dumfries. S. of Charles McFarlane, Esq., of Glasgow. B. at Glasgow 10 Oct. 1895; m. 20 Sept. 1924, Jean Hart Kerr. Educ. at Glasgow. Served with R.F.C. 1914-18. Director of J. and A. McFarlane, Hardware Manufacturers, Glasgow. A Conservative. Unsuccessfully contested the Camlachie division of Glasgow in 1945. Elected for the Camlachie division of Glasgow in Jan. 1948 and sat until 1950 when he was defeated. Unsuccessfully contested the Camlachie division of Glasgow in 1951 and the Provan division of Glasgow in 1955. O.B.E. 1936. Knighted 1955. President of Scottish Unionist Association 1954-55. Died 4 Feb. 1958. [1950]

MACFARLANE, (David) Neil. House of Commons, London. Caledonian, M.C.C., and Surrey C.C. S. of Robert Macfarlane, Esq. B. 7 May 1936; m. 7 Jan. 1961, June King. Educ. at St. Aubyns, and Bancrofts, Woodford Wells. An Oil Executive and Company Director. Dept. Chairman Wycombe Association 1970. Served in Essex Regiment 1955-57 and R.A. (T.A.) 1958-64. Vice-Chairman Wessex Area C.P.C. 1970-72. Executive member International Parliamentary Union. Secretary Greater London Conservative MPs. Secretary Conservative Sports Committee. Member Select Committee on Science and Technology Mar. 1974. Joint Secretary Conservative Energy Committee. Under-Secretary of State for Education and Science from May 1979. A Conservative. Unsuccessfully contested East Ham N. in 1970 and Sutton and Cheam in Dec. 1972. Elected for the Sutton and Cheam division of Sutton in Feb. 1974.* [1979]

MacFARQUHAR, Roderick Lemond. House of Commons, London. S. of Sir Alexander MacFarquhar, K.B.E., C.I.E. B. 2 Dec. 1930; m. 23 Dec. 1964, Emily, d. of Dr. P. Cohen, (1 s. 1 d.). Educ. at Fettes Coll., Keble Coll., Oxford, and Harvard, U.S.A. Parliamentary Private Secretary to David Ennals Minister of State, F.C.O. 1974-75 and 1975-76. Member North Atlantic Assembly 1974. Parliamentary Private Secretary to David Ennals Secretary of State for Social Services. 1976-78. Member Select Committee on Science and Technology 1976. A Labour Member. Unsuccessfully contested Ealing S. in 1966 and the Meriden division of Warwickshire in Mar. 1968. Sat for Belper from Feb. 1974 until 1979, when he was defeated. Author of works on China. Editor of *China Quarterly* 1959-68. Contributor to *Daily Telegraph* and *Sunday Telegraph*. Television Reporter and Programme Presenter. Associate Fellow of St. Antony's Coll., Oxford 1965-68. Senior Research Fellow, Columbia University 1969 and Royal Institute of International Affairs 1971-74. Governor of School of Oriental and African Studies from 1978.*
[1979]

McGHEE, Henry George. 29 Burghley Avenue, New Malden, Surrey. 284 Millhouses Lane, Sheffield. S. of Richard McGhee, Esq., MP. B. 3 July 1898; m. 1927, Edith Shelmerdine. Educ. at Lurgan, and Glasgow. A Dentist. Member of National Union of General and Municipal Workers. Parliamentary Private Secretary to the Rt. Hon. R. Stokes, Minister of Works 1950-51 and Lord Privy Seal 1951. A Labour Member. Unsuccessfully contested the Hallam division of Sheffield in 1931. Elected for the Penistone division of the W. Riding of Yorkshire in 1935 and sat until his death on 6 Feb. 1959.
[1958]

McGOVERN, John. 416 Amulree Street, Sandyhills, Tollcross, Glasgow. S. of Thomas McGovern, Esq., Steelworker, of Glasgow. B. 13 Dec. 1887; m. 1909, Mary Fenton (she died 1963). Member of Glasgow City Council 1929-31. A Roman Catholic and supporter of Moral Re-armament. A Labour Member. Elected for the Shettleston division of Glasgow in June 1930 and sat until he retired in 1959. Elected as an I.L.P. Member in 1931 and sat as an I.L.P. Member until he joined the Labour Party in Mar. 1947. Labour Whip withdrawn Nov. 1954-Mar. 1955. Supported Conservative Party in 1964. Died 14 Feb. 1968.
[1959]

MacGREGOR, John Roddick Russell, O.B.E. House of Commons, London. S. of Dr. N.S.R. MacGregor. B. 14 Feb. 1937; m. 22 Sept. 1962, Jean Mary Elizabeth, d. of L.U.E. Dungey, (1 s. 2 d.). Educ. at Merchiston Castle School, Edinburgh, St. Andrew's University, and King's Coll., London University. Administrator, London University 1961-62. Editorial Staff, *New Society* 1962-63. Special Assistant to Rt. Hon. Sir Alec Douglas Home, Prime Minister 1963-64. Conservative Research Department 1964-65. Head of Private Office of Rt. Hon. Edward Heath 1965-68. Member Public Accounts and Expenditure Committees 1974-75 and 1975-77. Conservative Opposition Whip 1977-79. Business Executive in City 1968. Director Hill Samuel and Company Limited and Hill Samuel Registrars Limited. Former Chairman Bow Group and Young Conservatives. External Relations Committee. First President Conservative and Christian Democratic Youth Community. A Conservative. Sat for Norfolk S. from Feb. 1974. O.B.E. 1971. Lord Commissioner of the Treasury from May 1979.* [1979]

McGUIRE, Michael Thomas Francis. 8 Elm Grove, Eccleston Park, Prescot, Lancashire. House of Commons, London. S. of Hugh McGuire, Esq. B. 3 May 1926; m. 1954, Marie Murphy. Educ. at Elementary School. A Roman Catholic. Full-time Branch Secretary National Union Mineworkers, Sutton Manor Branch, St. Helens 1957-64. Joined the Labour Party in 1951. Member of St. Helens Co-operative Society from 1954. Member Select Committee on Nationalised Industries. Parliamentary Private Secretary to Denis Howell, Minister for Sport and Recreation from Mar. 1974 to 1977. Delegate to Council of Europe and W.E.U. from 1977. A Labour Member. Sat for the Ince division of Lancashire from Oct. 1964.* [1979]

MACHIN, George. 246 Blackstone Road, Sheffield. S. of Edwin Machin, Esq. B. 30 Dec. 1922; m. 2 Apr. 1949, Margaret Ena, d. of Maj. Heard. Educ. at Marlcliffe School, Sheffield. Served with R.A.F. 1943-47. Engineering Inspector until Mar. 1973. A Labour Member. Elected for Dundee E. in Mar. 1973 and sat until Feb. 1974 when he was defeated. Unsuccessfully contested Dundee E. in Oct. 1964. Member of Sheffield City Council 1967-74.* [1974]

McINNES, James, M.B.E. 94 Bellahouston Drive, Glasgow. S. of James William McInnes, Esq., of Newry. B. 17 May 1901; m. 26 Dec. 1926, Elizabeth Hislop Cowie (she died 1963). Educ. at Glasgow Secondary School. A Railway Clerk 1916-44. Chairman Scottish Council Labour Party 1938; member of Glasgow Town Council 1933-50, Leader of Labour Group 1949-50; J.P. for Glasgow 1942. A Labour Member. Unsuccessfully contested the Pollok division of Glasgow in 1935 and Glasgow Central in 1945. Elected for Glasgow Central in Feb. 1950 and sat until he retired in 1966. M.B.E. 1941. Member of Fire Service Commission 1941. Chairman of Scottish Housing and Town Planning Council 1948. Died 14 Apr. 1974. [1966]

MACK, John David. Eaton House, Upper Grosvenor Street, London. 16 Belvedere Road, Liverpool 8. B. about 1899; m. 2 Dec. 1943, Adele Cywan. A Lecturer. Member of Liverpool City Council 1928-46. Political Representative of National Amalgamated Union of Life Assurance Workers. Lecturer of Council of Labour Coll. National Propagandist for Labour Party. A Labour Member. Unsuccessfully contested Wallasey in 1929 and 1931. Elected for Newcastle-under-Lyme in Mar. 1942 and sat until 1951 when he retired. Died 9 Feb. 1957. [1951]

McKAY, Allen. 24 Springwood Road, Hoyland Common, Barnsley, South Yorkshire. S. of Fred McKay, Esq. B. 1927; m., 1949, June Simpson, (1 s.). Educ. at Secondary Modern School and Sheffield University Department of Extra-Mural Studies. Worked in steel works and mining industry. Later Assistant Manpower Officer with N.C.B. Member of a Trade Union for 37 years. Member of Hoyland Nether Urban District Council 1965-74, Chairman 1973-74. J.P. 1971. Vice-Chairman Housing Committee Barnsley Metropolitan District Council, Councillor 1974-78. Chairman St. Peter's Ward; Secretary Hoyland District Labour Party and former Secretary/Agent Penistone C.L.P. A Labour Member. Elected for the Penistone division of the W. Riding of Yorkshire at a by-election in July 1978.* [1979]

MACKAY, Andrew James. House of Commons, London. S. of Robert James Mackay, Esq. B. 27 Aug. 1949; m. 15 June 1974, Diana Joy, d. of Leslie Kinchin, Esq., (1 s.). Educ. at Solihull. Chairman Solihull Young Conservatives 1971-74. Vice-Chairman Solihull Conservatives Association 1971-74. Chairman of "Britain in Europe" Meriden Branch (1975 Referendum). Partner, Jones Mackay and Croxford, Estate Agents. A Conservative. Prospective Parliamentary Candidate for Stechford division of Birmingham 1975-77. Elected for the Stechford division of Birmingham in Mar. 1977 and sat until 1979, when he was defeated.* [1979]

McKAY, John. 351 West Road, Newcastle-on-Tyne. S. of Peter McKay, Esq. B. 1885; m. Mary, d. of Thomas Hamilton, Esq. Educ. at Backworth Elementary School, and Ruskin Coll., Oxford. A Checkweighman and Gen. Secretary Montagu Mines, Newcastle-on-Tyne for 30 years. Member of Newcastle

City Council 1924-27. A Labour Member. Elected for Wallsend in July 1945 and sat until he retired in Sept. 1964. Died 4 Oct. 1964. [1964]

McKAY, Margaret. 8A Dalebury Road, London. D. of Mr. McCarthy, B. 22 Jan. 1911; m. Mr. McKay Public Relations Consultant. Joined the Labour Party in 1932. Sponsored by T.G.W.U. Joined T.U. movement in 1924. Held every position up to Chief Woman Officer, T.U.C. Member of Co-operative Society from 1928. Author of *Generation in Revolt, Women in Trade Union History* and works on the Middle East. A Labour Member. Unsuccessfully contested Walthamstow E. in 1959. Elected for the Clapham division of Wandsworth in Oct. 1964 and sat until she retired in 1970 after conflicts with Clapham Constituency Labour Party over her pro-Arab attitudes and other policies. Commander of the Order of the Cedar of Lebanon. Emigrated to Abu Dhabi.* [1970]

MACKAY, Ronald William Gordon. 14 Elmtree Road, St. John's Wood, London. Reform. S. of Alexander Mackay, Esq., of Bathurst. B. 3 Sept. 1902; m. 15 Aug. 1946, Doreen M. Armstrong, of Linden Lodge, Frome. Educ. at Sydney Grammar School and University. Admitted Solicitor N.S.W. 1926, London 1934. A Labour Member. Unsuccessfully contested the Frome division of Somerset in 1935 and, as an Independent Labour candidate, Llandaff and Barry in 1942. Sat for Hull N.W. from July 1945-Feb. 1950. Elected for Reading N. in Feb. 1950 and sat until 1951 when he was defeated. Member of Common Wealth until Jan. 1945 when he rejoined the Labour Party. Arthur of *Federal Europe* and other works. Delegate to Council of Europe. Died 15 Jan. 1960. [1951]

MACKENZIE, Alasdair Roderick. Heathmount, Tain, Ross-shire. S. of Roderick Mackenzie, Esq., of Fearn, Ross-shire. B. 3 Aug. 1903; m. 2 Sept. 1948, Anne, d. of Duncan Mackay, of Dingwall, Ross-shire. Educ. at Broadford Junior Secondary School, Skye. A Farmer. Member of the National Farmers Union; President of the East Ross branch for two years. Member of the Crofters Commission 1955-60 and of Ross-shire County Council 1935-55. Opponent of entry to E.E.C. A Liberal. Elected for Ross and Cromarty in Oct. 1964 and sat until June 1970 when he was defeated. Member of Scottish Agricultural Advisory Committee. Died 8 Nov. 1970. [1970]

MACKENZIE, Rt. Hon. (James) Gregor. 19 Stewarton Drive, Cambuslang, Glasgow. 7 Carrick Court, Kennington Park Road, London. S. of James MacKenzie, Esq. B. 15 Nov. 1927; m. 1958, Joan S. Provan, eld. d. of John C. Provan, Esq., (1 s. 1 d.). Educ. at Queens Park Secondary School, and Glasgow University, (School of Social Studies). Member and Magistrate Glasgow Corporation 1952-55 and 1956-64. J.P. for Glasgow 1962. Chairman of Scottish Labour League of Youth 1948. Parliamentary Private Secretary to Rt. Hon. James Callaghan, Chancellor of Exchequer and Home Secretary 1966-70. Opposition spokesman on Posts and Telecommunications 1970-74. Parliamentary Under-Secretary of State for Industry Mar. 1974-June 1975. Minister of State for Industry June 1975-Apr. 1976. Minister of State for Scotland Apr. 1976-May 1979. PC. 1977. A Labour Member. Unsuccessfully contested E. Aberdeenshire in 1950 and W. Perthshire and Kinross in 1959. Elected for Rutherglen in May 1964.* [1979]

MACKESON, Brigadier Sir Harry Ripley, Bart. Little Manor, Barham, Kent. S. of Harry Mackeson, Esq., Littlebourne House, Littlebourne. B. 25 May 1905; m. 22 Feb. 1940, Alethea, d. of Commander R. Talbot, R.N. Educ. at Lockers Park, Hemel Hempstead, and Rugby. Lieut.-Col. Royal Scots Greys 1940, served in India 1925, psc 1937; Brigade Maj. 1938-40 in Egypt. B.G.S. H.Q. Royal Armoured Corps 1942 and Brigade Commander U.K., France and Belgium 1943-44. Conservative Whip Dec. 1947; Joint Dept. Chief Whip Feb. 1950-May 1952; a Lord Commissioner of the Treasury Nov. 1951-May 1952. Secretary for Overseas Trade May 1952-Sept. 1953. Created Bart. 1954. A Conservative. Sat for Hythe from July 1945 to Sept. 1953. Elected for the Folkestone and Hythe division of Kent in Feb. 1950 and sat until he retired in 1959. Director of Mackeson and Company Limited. Chairman of Dosco Overseas Engineering Company. President of Kent Football Association 1949, and Kent County Cricket Club 1951. Died 25 Jan. 1964. [1959]

McKIBBIN, Alan John, O.B.E. 26 Chiltern Court, Baker Street, London. 22 Corporation Street, Belfast. S. of John McKibbin, Esq., of Belfast. B. 2 Feb. 1892; m. 1922, Kathleen Laura, d. of Alexander Brennan, Esq., of Ballycarry. Educ. at Campbell Coll., Belfast. Served in Army 1914-18. J.P. and Dept.-Lieut. for Belfast from 1955. Managing Director of John McKibbin and Sons Limited. Chairman of Northern Ireland Army Cadet Force Association. O.B.E. 1949. A Unionist and Conservative member. Elected for E. Belfast in Feb. 1950 and sat until his death on 2 Dec. 1958. [1958]

MACKIE, George Yull. Ballinshoe, Kirriemuir, Angus. S. of Dr. Maitland Mackie. B. 10 July 1919; m. 1944, Lindsay Lyall, d. of Alexander Sharp, Esq., Advocate, Aberdeen and Baillie Mrs. Sharp, O.B.E., (3 d.). Educ. at Aberdeen Grammar School, and Aberdeen University. A Farmer. Served with R.A.F. during the war attaining the rank of Squadron Leader. Awarded the D.S.O. and D.F.C. 1944. Chairman of the Scottish Liberal Party 1965-70. A Liberal. Unsuccessfully contested S. Angus in the 1959 general election. Elected for Caithness and Sutherland in Oct. 1964 and sat until 1966 when he was defeated. Unsuccessfully contested Caithness and Sutherland in 1970. Chairman of Caithness Glass Limited from 1966. Chairman of Caithness Pottery Company Limited and Benshie Cattle Company Limited. C.B.E. 1971. Created Baron Mackie of Benshie (Life Peerage) 1974. Liberal Party spokesman in House of Lords. Unsuccessfully contested N.E. Scotland for European Parliament in 1979.* [1966]

MACKIE, John. Bent, Laurencekirk, Kincardineshire. Harold's Park Farm, Nazeing, Essex. S. of Maitland Mackie, Esq., Farmer. B. 24 Nov. 1909; m. 6 June 1934, Jeannie Inglis, d. of Mrs. Milne, of Carcary, Brechin, Angus. Educ. at Aberdeen Grammar School.

A Farmer. Parliamentary Secretary Ministry of Agriculture, Fisheries and Food Oct. 1964-June 1970. Voted in favour of entry to E.E.C. on 28 Oct. 1971. A Labour Member. Unsuccessfully contested N. Angus and Mearns in 1951 and the Lanark division of Lanarkshire in 1955. Elected for Enfield E. in 1959 and sat until he retired in Feb. 1974. Chairman of Forestry Commission from 1976.* [1974]

MACKIE, John Hamilton. Auchencairn House, Castle Douglas, Kirkcudbrightshire. Carlton, and New (Edinburgh). S. of W.M. Mackie, Esq., of Ernespie. B. 8 Jan. 1898. Educ. at Harrow, and Christ Church, Oxford. A Conservative. Unsuccessfully contested Edinburgh Central in May 1929. Elected for the Galloway division of Kirkcudbrightshire and Wigtownshire in Oct. 1931 and sat until his death on 29 Dec. 1958. He was refused readoption by his local association in 1945 but contested the seat as an Independent Conservative and defeated the official candidate. The Conservative Whip was restored in Mar. 1948. Died 29 Dec. 1958. [1958]

M'KINLAY, Adam Storey. 49 Kestrel Road, Glasgow. B. 1887; m. Eliza Wilson. A Woodworker. Member of Glasgow City Council 1932-37 and 1938-45. J.P. for Glasgow. A Labour Member. Sat for the Partick division of Glasgow from 1929 to 1931 when he was defeated. Unsuccessfully contested the Perth division of Perthshire and Kinross-shire in Apr. 1935 and the Partick division of Glasgow in Nov. 1935. Sat for Dunbartonshire from Feb. 1941 to Feb. 1950. Elected for W. Dunbartonshire in Feb. 1950 and sat until his death on 17 Mar. 1950. [1950]

MACKINTOSH, John Pitcairn. House of Commons, London. S. of Colin M. Mackintosh, Esq. B. 24 Aug. 1929; m. 1st, 1957, Janette M. Robertson (divorced 1963), (1 s. 1 d.); m. 2ndly, 1963, Catherine Margaret Una Maclean. (1 s. 1 d.). Educ. at Melville Coll., Edinburgh, Edinburgh University, Balliol Coll., Oxford, and Princeton University, New Jersey. Professor of Politics, University of Strathclyde 1965-66. Appointed Professor and Head of Department of Politics, Edinburgh University 1977. Joined the

Labour Party in 1948. Assistant Lecturer, University of Glasgow 1953-54, Lecturer, University of Edinburgh 1954-61. Senior Lecturer in Government University Coll., Ibadan, Nigeria 1961-63. Senior Lecturer in Politics, University of Glasgow 1963-65. Awarded D. Litt. by Edinburgh University 1967. Author of *The British Cabinet* (1962), *Nigerian Government and Politics* (1966), *The Devolution of Power* (1968), and *The Government and Politics of Britain.* Chairman of The Hansard Society 1974. Joint Editor of *The Political Quarterly* July 1975. A Labour Member. Unsuccessfully contested Edinburgh Pentlands in 1959 and Berwick and East Lothian in 1964. Sat for Berwick and East Lothian from Mar. 1966 to Feb. 1974, when he was defeated and again from Oct. 1974 until his death on 30 July 1978. Member of General Advisory Council of Independent Television Authority 1968-73. Voted in favour of entry to E.E.C. on 28 Oct. 1971. Died 30 July 1978.

[1978]

McLAREN, Martin John. House of Commons, London. S. of Hon. Francis McLaren, MP. B. 11 Jan. 1914; m. 18 Sept. 1943, Nancy, d. of Gordon Ralston, Esq. Educ. at Eton Coll., New Coll., Oxford, and Harvard, U.S.A. Assistant Principal, Home Office 1938-39. Grenadier Guards 1939-45. Principal, Home Office 1945-47. Barrister-at-Law, Middle Temple 1948. Assistant Government Whip 1961-63. A Lord Commissioner of the Treasury Nov. 1963-Oct. 1964. Opposition Whip 1964-66. Parliamentary Private Secretary to Sir Alec Douglas-Home 1970-74. A Conservative. Sat for the N.W. division of Bristol from 1959-66 when he was defeated, and from June 1970 to Oct. 1974 when he was again defeated. Director of English China Clays Limited and Archway Unit Trust Managers Limited 1973-79. Died 27 July 1979. [1974 2nd ed.]

McLAUGHLIN, (Florence) Patricia Alice. House of Commons, London. D. of Canon F.B. Aldwell. B. 23 June 1916; m. 1937, Henry, s. of Maj. W. McLaughlin. Educ. in Belfast, and Trinity Coll., Dublin. Member of Executive Committee of Ulster Women's Unionist Council. Member Executive Committee National Union. British Delegate to Conservative Assembly Council of Europe. British Delegate to Western European Union. Gen. Secretary of London Foundation for Marriage Education. An Ulster Unionist Member. Elected for Belfast W. in 1955 and sat until she retired in 1964. Unsuccessfully contested Wandsworth Central in 1970. O.B.E. 1975.* [1964]

MACLAY, Rt. Hon. John Scott, C.H., C.M.G. 9 Mount Row, London. Knapps, Kilmacolm, Renfrewshire. Turf, and Western (Glasgow). S. of the Rt. Hon. Lord Maclay. B. 26 Oct. 1905; m. 16 Oct. 1930, Betty L'Estrange, d. of Maj. Delaval Astley, of Wroxham, Norfolk (she died 1974). Educ. at Winchester, and Trinity Coll., Cambridge. Honorary LL.D. Universities of Edinburgh, Glasgow and Strathclyde. A Shipowner; Head of British Merchant Shipping Mission to the U.S.A. 1944. Parliamentary Secretary Ministry of Production May-July 1945. Minister of Transport and Civil Aviation Nov. 1951-May 1952. President Assembly of Western European Union 1955-56; Minister of State Colonial Office Oct. 1956-Jan. 1957; Secretary of State for Scotland Jan. 1957-July 1962. PC. 1952. A National Liberal and Conservative Member. Sat for Montrose Burghs from July 1940 to Feb. 1950. Elected for Renfrewshire W. in Feb. 1950 and sat until June 1964 when he was created Visct. Muirshiel. C.M.G. 1944. Companion of Honour 1962. President of National Liberal Council 1957-67. Chairman of Joint Exchequer Board for Northern Ireland 1965-72. Lord-Lieut. of Renfrewshire from 1967. K.T. 1973. Director of Clydesdale Bank from 1970.* [1964]

MACLEAN, Sir Fitzroy Hew Royle, Bart., C.B.E. Strachur House, Argyll. 42 Lowndes Square, London. White's, and Pratt's. S. of Maj. Charles Maclean, D.S.O., Cameron Highlanders. B. 11 Mar. 1911; m. 12 Jan. 1946, Hon. Veronica Fraser, d. of 14th Baron Lovat and widow of Lieut. Alan Phipps, R.N. Educ. at Eton, and King's Coll., Cambridge, Hon. LL.D. (Glasgow) 1969, (Dalhousie 1971); D. Lit. (University of Acadia) 1970. Joined Diplomatic Service 1933; 3rd Secretary Paris 1934-37, 2nd Secretary Moscow 1937-39; Foreign Office 1939-41; Joined Cameron Highlanders and

Special Air Service Regiment 1941; Brigadier 1943. Created Bart. 1957. Under-Secretary and Financial Secretary War Office Oct. 1954-Jan. 1957. A Conservative. Sat for the Lancaster division of Lancashire from Oct. 1941-59. Elected for Bute and N. Ayrshire in 1959 and sat until he retired in Feb. 1974. Sent to Yugoslavia in 1943 as Churchill's personal representative at Tito's Partisan H.Q. and commanding officer of S.O.E. missions working with the Yugoslavia Partisans. C.B.E. 1944. Member of Council of Europe and Western European Union 1972-74. Lees Knowles Lecturer, University of Cambridge 1953. Author of *Eastern Approaches* and *Disputed Barricade.** [1974]

MACLEAN, Neil. 759 Mosspark Drive, Glasgow. S. of Neil Maclean, Esq., of Mull. B. 1875; m. 1900, Laura, eld. d. of George Archibald, Esq., of Glasgow. Active member of Socialist movement from 1893. Worked at his trade as a mechanic until 1912 when he was appointed organizer for Co-operative movement under Scottish Co-operative Wholesale Society. A Labour Whip Jan. 1919-Nov. 1921 and Nov. 1922-Dec. 1923. Member of National Executive Labour Party 1920-22, Chairman of P.L.P. 1945-46. Delegate from British Trade Union Congress to Canada 1921. A Labour Member. Elected for the Govan division of Glasgow in Dec. 1918 and sat until he retired in 1950 after his constituency party had declined to readopt him. Expelled from the Workers Union 1927 and brought an unsuccessful lawsuit against them in 1929. Elected as a Independent Labour candidate in 1929 as a result of the adoption of another official candidate, who subsequently withdrew before the poll. C.B.E. 1946. Member of Executive Committee of P.L.P. 1931-36. Died 12 Sept. 1953. [1950]

McLEAN, Lieut.-Col. Neil Loudon Desmond, D.S.O. 17 Eaton Square, London. Dunachton, Kingcraig, Inverness-shire. Buck's, Pratt's, White's, Cavalry, and Highland (Inverness). S. of Neil G. McLean, Esq. B. 28 Nov. 1918; m. Nov. 1949, Daska Kennedy, formerly Ivanović-Banac, of Dubrovnik, Jugoslavia. Educ. at Eton, and Royal Military Coll., Sandhurst. 2nd Lieut.

Royal Scots Greys Sept. 1938; Palestine Campaign 1939; served Middle East and Balkans 1939-44; Ethiopia 1941; awarded Ethiopian Distinguished Service Order by H.I.M. Haile Selassie; Albania 1943-44, Lieut.-Col. and D.S.O. 1943; served China and Far East 1945-47. Member of Highlands and Islands Advisory Panel 1955; and of Queen's Bodyguard for Scotland (Royal Company of Archers). A Conservative. Unsuccessfully contested Preston S. in 1950 and 1951. Elected for the Inverness division of Inverness and Ross and Cromarty in Dec. 1954 and sat until 1964 when he was defeated.* [1964]

McLEAVY, Frank. 9 Sheridan Terrace, Whitton Avenue, Greenford, Middlesex. S. of John McLeavy, Esq. B. 1 Jan. 1899; m. 3 Sept. 1924, d. of George Waring, Esq. Educ. at Elementary and Evening Schools. Road Passenger Transport Officer. Alderman Cheshire County Council and J.P. 1938-50. J.P. for Middlesex 1951. Chairman of the All-Party Committee which organised the Parliamentary Presentation to Sir Winston Churchill on his eightieth birthday. Mayor of Bebington 1939-41. A Labour Member. Elected for Bradford E. in July 1945 and sat until he retired in 1966. Created Baron McLeavy (Life Peerage) 1967. Died 1 Oct. 1976. [1966]

MACLENNAN, Robert Adam Ross. House of Commons, London. S. of Sir Hector Maclennan. B. 26 June 1936; m. Aug. 1968, Mrs. Helen Noyce, (1 s. 1 d. and 1 step-s.). Educ. at Glasgow Academy, Balliol Coll., Oxford, Trinity Coll., Cambridge, and Columbia University, New York. A Barrister, Gray's Inn 1962. Member Society of Labour Lawyers. Member of House of Commons Select Committee on Estimates. Parliamentary Private Secretary to Rt. Hon. George Thomson, MP., Commonwealth Secretary 1967-68, Minister without Portfolio 1968-69 and Chancellor of the Duchy of Lancaster 1969-70. Member of Latey Committee on Age and Majority, 1968. Additional Opposition spokesman on Scottish Affairs 1970-72. Voted in favour of entry to E.E.C. on 28 Oct. 1971. Additional Opposition spokesman on Defence Jan.-Apr. 1972.

Member G.M.W.U. Parliamentary Under-Secretary of State, Department of Prices and Consumer Protection Mar. 1974-May 1979. A Labour Member. Sat for Caithness and Sutherland from Mar. 1966.*　　[1979]

MACLEOD, Rt. Hon. Iain Norman. The White Cottage, Potters Bar. White's, and M.C.C. S. of Dr. Norman Macleod, of Skipton. B. 11 Nov. 1913; m. 25 Jan. 1941, Evelyn Hester, d. of the Rev. Gervase Blois, and the Hon. Mrs. Blois (she was created Baroness Macleod of Borve in 1971). Educ. at Fettes Coll., Gonville and Caius Coll., Cambridge. Author. Minister of Health May 1952-Dec. 1955. Minister of Labour and National Service Dec. 1955-Oct. 1959. Secretary of State for the Colonies Oct. 1959-Oct. 1961. Chancellor of the Duchy of Lancaster, Leader of the House and Chairman of the Conservative and Unionist Party Oct. 1961-Oct. 1963. Editor of *The Spectator* Dec. 1963-Dec. 1965. A Conservative. Unsuccessfully contested the Western Isles in 1945. Elected for Enfield W. in Feb. 1950 and sat until his death on 20 July 1970. Served in Army, France and Norway 1939-45. Head of Home Affairs Conservative Research Department 1948-50. PC. 1952. Declined to serve under Sir Alec Douglas-Home 1963. Member of Shadow Cabinet 1964-70; Opposition spokesman on Steel 1964-65 and on Treasury Affairs 1965-70. Chancellor of the Exchequer June-July 1970. Died 20 July 1970.　　[1970]

MacLEOD, Sir John. Culloden House, Inverness-shire. Naval & Military, and Highland, Inverness. S. of Duncan MacLeod, Esq., C.B.E., of Skeabost, Isle of Skye. B. 1913; m. 1938, Rosemary, d. of Noel Hamilton Wills, Esq., of Stroud, Gloucestershire. Educ. at Fettes Coll. Joined Cameron Highlanders 1935; served overseas 1939-45, T.D.. Member of Highlands and Islands Advisory Panel. Knight Bach. 1963. A Conservative and National Liberal. Elected for Ross and Cromarty in July 1945 and sat until 1964 when he was defeated.*　　[1964]

MacMANAWAY, Rev. James Godfrey, M.B.E. House of Commons, London. S. of Rt. Rev. James MacManaway, Bishop of Clogher. B. 1898; m. 1926, Catherine, d. of Sir Thomas Lecky (she died in Jan. 1951). Educ. at Campbell Coll., Belfast, and Trinity Coll., Dublin. Was in Church of Ireland Ministry. Rector of Christ Church, Londonderry 1930-47. Served in Royal Flying Corps 1915-18, and as Chaplain to Forces 1939-45. An Ulster Unionist Member. Elected for W. Belfast in Feb. 1950 but in Oct. 1950 was disqualified as a Clergyman of the Church of Ireland. Member of Northern Ireland Parliament for City of Londonderry from June 1947 until he resigned in Jan. 1951. M.B.E. 1945. Died 3 Nov. 1951.　　[1950]

MCMANUS, Francis Joseph. House of Commons, London. S. of Patrick McManus, Esq. B. 16 Aug. 1942; m. 1971, Carmel V. Doherty, of Lisnaskea. Educ. at Queen's University, Belfast. Chairman Fermanagh Civil Rights Movement. A Teacher and Solicitor. A Unity Member. Elected for Fermanagh and S. Tyrone in June 1970 and sat until Feb. 1974 when he was defeated. Founder member of Irish Independence Party 1977.*　　[1974]

McMASTER, Stanley Raymond. House of Commons, London. S. of F.R. McMaster, Esq. B. 23 Sept. 1926; m. 1959, Verda Ruth Tynan. Educ. at Campbell Coll., Belfast, and Trinity Coll., Dublin, (M.A. Economics and Political Science) B. Comm. Barrister-at-Law, called to the bar at Lincoln's Inn May 1953. Member Council of Belfast Chamber of Commerce and Association of British Chambers of Commerce from 1959. An Ulster Unionist Member. Elected for E. Belfast at a by-election in Mar. 1959 and sat until Feb. 1974 when he was defeated. Unsuccessfully contested S. Belfast in Oct. 1974. Lecturer in Company Law, Regent Street Polytechnic 1954-59.*　　[1974]

MACMILLAN, Malcolm Kenneth. 60 Bellshill Road, Uddingston, Lanarkshire. S. of Kenneth Macmillan, Esq., Mining Engineer. B. 21 Aug. 1913; m. 1936, Nancy Noreen Stirling. Educ. at Nicolson Institute, Stornoway and Edinburgh University. A Journalist. Served in Army 1939-45. Chairman of Government Advisory Panel on the Highlands and Islands 1947-54, and of Scottish P.L.P. 1946-51. Chairman Parliamentary East-West Trade Committee 1965-68. A Labour Member. Elected for the Western Isles in 1935 and sat until he was defeated in 1970. Expelled from the Labour Party in 1972 after a disagreement over the Western Isles candidacy and unsuccessfully contested the seat in Feb. 1974 as a United Labour Party candidate. Died 17 Nov. 1978. [1970]

MACMILLAN, Rt. Hon. (Maurice) Harold. Birch Grove House, Chelwood Gate, Haywards Heath. Turf, Carlton, Pratt's, and Beefsteak. S. of Maurice Crawford Macmillan, Esq. B. 10 Feb. 1894; m. 21 Apr. 1920, Lady Dorothy Cavendish, d. of Victor, 9th Duke of Devonshire, K.G. (she died 1966) Educ. at Eton, and Balliol Coll., Oxford, Exhibitioner. Served with Grenadier Guards 1914-20 (three times wounded). Aide-de-Camp to the Duke of Devonshire when Gov.-Gen. of Canada 1919-20. Parliamentary Secretary Ministry of Supply May 1940-Feb. 1942. Parliamentary Under-Secretary of State for the Colonies Feb.-Dec. 1942. PC. 1942. Minister Resident at Allied Force Headquarters, Mediterranean Theatre Dec. 1942-May 1945 and Acting President of Allied Commission in Italy 1944. Secretary of State for Air May-July 1945. Minister of Housing and Local Government (Cabinet) Oct. 1951-Oct. 1954. Minister of Defence Oct. 1954-Apr. 1955; Foreign Secretary Apr.-Dec. 1955; Chancellor of the Exchequer Dec. 1955-Jan. 1957; Prime Minister and First Lord of the Treasury Jan. 1957-Oct. 1963. A Conservative. Unsuccessfully contested Stockton-on-Tees in 1923. Sat for Stockton-on-Tees from 1924 to 1929, when he was defeated, and from 1931 to July 1945 when he was again defeated. Elected for Bromley in Nov. 1945 and sat until he retired in 1964. Conservative Whip withdrawn June 1936-July 1937. Honorary D.C.L. Oxford University, Honorary LL.D. Cambridge and Sussex. Honorary Fellow of Balliol Coll., Oxford 1957. Chancellor of Oxford University from 1960. Chairman of Macmillan Limited 1963-74, President from 1974. O.M. 1976.* [1964]

MACMILLAN, Rt. Hon. Maurice Victor. 9 Warwick Square, London. Turf, Garrick, Beefsteak, Carlton, and Pratt's. S. of Rt. Hon.

Harold Macmillan, O.M., MP. B. 1921; m. 1942, Hon. Katharine Margaret Alice Ormsby-Gore, d. of the 4th Baron Harlech, (3 s. 1 d.). Educ. at Eton, and Balliol Coll., Oxford. Served with Sussex Yeomanry and as Military Assistant to Adjutant-Gen. 1939-45. A Publisher and Chairman of Macmillan Limited. PC. 1972. Member Kensington Borough Council 1948-51. Founder-Chairman Wider Share Ownership Council 1957. Delegate to Council of Europe 1960-63 and Political Committee Rapporteur 1962-63. Economic Secretary, Treasury Oct. 1963-Oct. 1964. Chief Secretary Treasury June 1970-Apr. 1972. Secretary of State for Employment Apr. 1972-Dec. 1973; thereafter Paymaster Gen. (Treasury) Dec. 1973-Mar. 1974. Opposition spokesman on Health 1967-70. Member of Cabinet 1972-74. An Opposition spokesman on Economic Affairs and Member of Shadow Cabinet Mar.-June 1974. A Conservative. Unsuccessfully contested Seaham in 1945, Lincoln in 1951 and Wakefield in Oct. 1954. Sat for Halifax from 1955-64, when he was defeated. Elected for the Farnham division of Surrey in Mar. 1966.* [1979]

McMILLAN, Thomas McLellan. House of Commons, London. S. of James McMillan, Esq., of Glasgow. B. 12 Feb. 1919; m. 1946, Mary Elizabeth Conway, (1 s. 1 d.). Educ. at Secondary School. Formerly a Wood-Machinist with British Rail. Glasgow City Councillor 1962-66; Magistrate 1964. Former Secretary Glasgow Central Constituency Labour Party. A Labour Member. Elected for the Central division of Galsgow in Mar. 1966 and sat until his death on 30 Apr. 1980. [1979]

McNAIR-WILSON, Patrick Michael Ernest David. 5 Kelso Place, London. Godfreys Farm, Beaulieu, Hampshire. S. of Dr. Robert McNair-Wilson. B. 28 May 1929; m. 1953, Diana Evelyn Kitty, d. of Hon. Laurence Methuen-Campbell, (1 s. 4 d.). Educ. at Hall School, Hampstead, and Eton. Served with Coldstream Guards 1946-52. Conservative Central Office 1954-58, Conservative Political Centre 1958-61. Director of London Municipal Society 1961-63. Public Relations Executive, British Iron and Steel

Federation 1963-64. Vice-Chairman Conservative London Members Committee 1965. Front Bench spokesman on Fuel and Power 1965-66. Vice-Chairman Conservative Fuel and Power Committee 1969. Member Select Committee on Science and Technology 1968-70. Parliamentary Private Secretary to Rt. Hon. John Peyton Minister of Transport 1970-74. Opposition Front Bench spokesman on Energy 1974-76. A Conservative. Sat for Lewisham W. from 1964-66, when he was defeated. Elected for the New Forest at a by-election in Nov. 1968.*   [1979]

McNAIR-WILSON, (Robert) Michael Conal. House of Commons, London. S. of Dr. Robert McNair-Wilson. B. 12 Oct. 1930; m. 20 Nov. 1974, Mrs. Deirdre Granville, (1 d.). Educ. at Eton. 2nd Lieut. Royal Irish Fusiliers during National Service 1948-50. A Journalist 1953-55. Joined Sidney-Barton Limited 1955 and later became Director. Parliamentary Private Secretary to Rt. Hon. Peter Walker, Minister of Agriculture from 1979. A Conservative. Unsuccessfully contested Lincoln in 1964. Sat for Walthamstow E. from Mar. 1969 to Feb. 1974. Elected for Newbury in Feb. 1974.*   [1979]

McNAMARA, (Joseph) Kevin. 128 Cranbrook Avenue, Hull. S. of Patrick McNamara, Esq. B. 5 Sept. 1934; m. 4 Aug. 1960, Nora, d. of J.W. Jones, Esq., of Warrington, (4 s. 1 d.). Educ. at St. Mary's Coll., Crosby, and Hull University. A Roman Catholic. Secretary of National Association of Labour Student Organisations 1956-57. Head of History Department, St. Mary's Grammar School, Hull 1958-64. Secretary Parliamentary Group T. and G.W.U. Member British Delegation Council of Europe. Chairman Select Committee on Overseas Development 1978-79. A Lecturer in Law, Hull Coll. of Commerce 1964-66. Parliamentary Private Secretary to Rt. Hon. Peter Shore, Secretary of State for Economic Affairs 1967-69 and Minister without Portfolio 1969-70. A Labour Member. Unsuccessfully contested Bridlington in 1964. Sat for Kingston-upon-Hull N. from Jan. 1966 to Feb. 1974. Elected for the Central division of Kingston-upon-Hull in Feb. 1974.*   [1979]

McNEIL, Rt. Hon. Hector. 64 St. John's Wood Court, London. 5 Orchy Street, Cathcart, Glasgow. Press. S. of Donald McNeil, Esq., of Garelochhead, Dumbartonshire. B. 1907; m. 29 Apr. 1939, Sheila, d. of Dr. James Craig. Educ. at Woodside School, Glasgow, and Glasgow University. A Journalist. Member of Glasgow Corporation 1932-38. Magistrate Glasgow 1937-38. Member of Empire Parliamentary Delegation to Central and South Africa 1944. Parliamentary Private Secretary to Philip Noel-Baker, Joint Parliamentary Secretary Ministry of War Transport Apr. 1942-May 1945. Parliamentary Under-Secretary of State for Foreign Affairs Aug. 1945-Oct. 1946. Minister of State Oct. 1946-Feb. 1950. PC. 1946. Member of British Delegation Paris Peace Conference 1946. Secretary of State for Scotland with a seat in the Cabinet Feb. 1950-Oct. 1951. A Labour Member. Unsuccessfully contested the Kelvingrove division of Glasgow in 1935 and Ross and Cromarty in Feb. 1936. Elected for Greenock in July 1941 and sat until his death in New York on 11 Oct. 1955.   [1955]

MacPHERSON, Malcolm. Airlie Mount, Alyth, Perthshire. S. of John MacPherson. Esq., of Ardnamurchan, Argyll. B. 18 Aug. 1904; m. 1929, Janet Elspeth, d. of William MacKay, Esq. (she died 2 Feb. 1961). Educ. at Trinity Academy, and University of Edinburgh. Lecturer University of New Brunswick, Canada 1928-38; University Coll., Exeter 1938-40. In Canadian Army 1940-45. A Vice-Chairman of the P.L.P. 1964-67. A Labour Member. Unsuccessfully contested the Yeovil division of Somerset in 1945. Elected for Stirling and Falkirk in Oct. 1948 and sat until his death on 24 May 1971. Parliamentary Private Secretary to Rt. Hon. Hector McNeil, Secretary of State for Scotland, 1950-51. M.B.E. 1945. Died 24 May 1971.   [1971]

MACPHERSON, Rt. Hon. Niall Malcolm Stewart. High Larch, Iver Heath, Buckinghamshire. S. of Sir T. Stewart Macpherson, I.C.S., C.I.E., of Newtonmore, Inverness-shire. B. 3 Aug. 1908; m. 1937, Margaret Phyllis, d. of J.J. Runge, Esq. and Mrs. N.C. Runge, MP. (she died 1979). Educ. at Edinburgh Academy, Fettes, and

Trinity Coll., Oxford. Business experience in Great Britain, France and Turkey. Served with Q.O. Cameron Highlanders 1939-45, Maj. Chairman British Commonwealth Producers' Organisation 1952-55, President 1967-70. General Advisory Council of B.B.C. 1951-55. Honorary Secretary and Treasurer Franco-British Parliamentary Committee 1947-55; member Parliamentary Delegation to Belgium 1946, Turkey 1947 and Malaya 1950. Scottish Whip (National Liberal) 1945-55; Joint Under-Secretary of State for Scotland June 1955-Oct. 1960. Parliamentary Secretary Board of Trade Oct. 1960-July 1962. Minister of Pensions and National Insurance July 1962-Oct. 1963. PC. 1962. A National Liberal and Conservative Member. Elected for Dumfriesshire in July 1945 and sat until Oct. 1963 when he was created Baron Drumalbyn. Minister of State, Board of Trade Oct. 1963-Oct. 1964. Chairman of Advertising Standards Authority 1965-70 and 1974-77. Minister without Portfolio Oct. 1970-Jan. 1974. K.B.E. 1974.*
[1963]

MACPHERSON, Thomas. Fairstead, Great Warley, Essex. S. of James Macpherson, Esq. B. 9 July 1888; m. Lucy, d. of Arthur Butcher, Esq., of Maldon. Educ. at St. George's Road School, Glasgow. Served in H.L.I. 1914-18. Foreign and Colonial Produce Importer and Exporter. Regional Port Director for Scotland 1942-45; Chairman of London Provision Exchange 1941; Chairman Thames Passenger Services Interest Committee 1948; member of Committee Organisation of Domestic Food Producers 1948, and of Port of London Authority 1949-65. Had Medal of Freedom U.S.A., Officer of the Order of Orange Nassau (Netherlands) 1948. A Farmer and Breeder of Ayrshire Cattle. A Labour Member. Elected for Romford in July 1945 and sat until 1950, when he was defeated. Created Baron Macpherson of Drumochter 1951. Chairman of the Council of Scottish Clan Societies 1952-56. Member of Essex River Board from 1956. Member of Romford Urban District Council 1924-27. President of Domestic Poultry Keepers Council of England and Wales from 1953. Died 11 June 1965.
[1950]

MADDAN, (William Francis) Martin. House of Commons, London. S. of James G. Madden, Esq., C.B.E. B. 4 Oct. 1920; m. Apr. 1958, Susanne, d. of R.C. Huband, Esq., (2 s. 2 d.). Educ. at Fettes, and Brasenose Coll., Oxford. Served with Royal Marines 1939-46, Maj. Chairman AGB Research Limited 1962-73. Member Market Research Society from 1953. Joint Honorary Treasurer European Movement from 1956 (earlier Britain in Europe). U.K. sponsor, Declaration of Atlantic Unity from 1958. Council Oxford and Bermondsey Club from 1952. Fellow St. Michael's Coll., Tenbury from 1964. Parliamentary Private Secretary to Rt. Hon. Enoch Powell, Minister of Health 1961-63. A Conservative. Unsuccessfully contested N. Battersea in 1950. Sat for Hitchin from 1955-64 when he was defeated. Elected for Hove in July 1965 and sat until his death on 22 Aug. 1973.
[1973]

MADDEN, Maxwell Francis. House of Commons, London. S. of George Francis Leonard Madden, Esq. B. 29 Oct. 1941; m. 15 Jan. 1972, Sheelagh, d. of M. Howard, Esq. Educ. at Lascelles Secondary Modern School, South Harrow, and Pinner Grammar School. A Reporter, *East Essex Gazette, Tribune, The Sun,* and *The Scotsman* (London). Press and Information Officer, British Gas Corporation. Member Wandsworth Borough Council 1971-74. A Labour Member. Unsuccessfully contested Sudbury and Woodbridge in 1966. Sat for Sowerby from Feb. 1974 until 1979, when he was defeated. Director of Publicity, Labour Party from 1979. *[1979]

MADEL, William David. House of Commons, London. Junior Carlton. S. of William Madel, Esq. B. 6 Aug. 1938; m. 16 Oct. 1971, Susan Catherine, d. of Lieut.-Commander and Mrs. Carew, (1 d.). Educ. at Uppingham School, and Keble Coll., Oxford, M.A. Oxford, 1965. Advertising Executive, Thomson Organisation 1964-70. Parliamentary Private Secretary to Anthony Buck, Lord Lambton, Anthony Kershaw, Peter Blaker and Dudley Smith, Under-Secretaries of State for Defence 1973-74. A Conservative. Unsuccessfully contested Erith and Crayford in Nov. 1965 and Mar. 1966. Elected for Bedfordshire S. division in June 1970.*
[1979]

MAGEE, Bryan Edgar. 12 Falkland House, London. Garrick, Reform, and Savile. S. of Frederick Magee, Esq. B. 12 Apr. 1930; m. 1954, Ingrid Söderlund (marriage dissolved), (1 d.). Educ. at Christ's Hospital, Lycée Hoche (Versailles), Keble Coll., Oxford, (M.A. Oxford), and Yale. Elected Lecturer in Philosophy, Balliol Coll., Oxford 1970. Visiting Fellow of All Souls 1973-74. Author of 13 books. Member of the Critics' Circle. Several own T.V. and Radio series. Regular columnist on *The Times* 1974-76. A Labour Member. Unsuccessfully contested Mid Bedfordshire in 1959 and Nov. 1960. Elected for the Leyton division of Waltham Forest in Feb. 1974.* [1979]

MAGINNIS, John Edward, J.P. Mandeville Hall, Mullahead, Tandragee, Portadown, Co. Armagh, Northern Ireland. Queensway Court Hotel, 36 Queensway, London. Ulster (London). S. of Edward Maginnis, Esq., Farmer. B. 7 Mar. 1919; m. 22 Apr. 1944, Dorothy, d. of R.J. Rusk, Esq., J.P., of Cavanaleck, Fivemiletown, Co. Tyrone, (1 s. 4 d.). Educ. at Moyallon P.E. School, and Portadown Technical Coll. Served with Royal Ulster Constabulary 1939-45. Group Secretary North Armagh Group Ulster Farmer's Union 1956-59. Vice-President Portadown Football Club. J.P. for Co. Armagh 1956. An Ulster Unionist Member. Elected for Armagh in 1959 and sat until he retired in Feb. 1974. Unsuccessful candidate for the N. Ireland Constitutional Convention in Armagh for the Unionist Party of N. Ireland 1975.* [1974]

MAGUIRE, Meredith Francis. House of Commons, London. B. 1929; m. Philomena. Educ. at St. Mary's Marist Brothers School, Athlone. A Roman Catholic. A Publican in Lisnaskea. An Independent Member. Elected for Fermanagh and South Tyrone in Oct. 1974.* [1979]

MAHON, Peter. 2 Radnor Drive, Bootle, Lancashire. S. of Alderman Simon Mahon of Bootle. B. 4 May 1909; m. 24 June 1935, Margaret, d. of Patrick Hannon, Esq. Educ. at St. James Elementary School, and St. Edwards Coll. Representative in family business. Member of the Labour Party from 1924-71. Member of Bootle Council from 1933-70. Mayor of Bootle 1954. J.P. from 1954. A Labour Member. Parliamentary candidate for Blackburn W. from 1954-55 until constituency went out on redistribution. Elected for Preston S. in Oct. 1964 and sat until 1970 when he was defeated. Expelled from the Labour Party in Mar. 1971 and unsuccessfully contested the Scotland division of Liverpool in Apr. 1971 as an Independent Labour and Anti-Abortion candidate. Joined Liberal Party 1973. Member of Liverpool City Council 1970-74 and of Liverpool Metropolitan District Council from 1973.* [1970]

MAHON, Simon. House of Commons, London. S. of Alderman Simon Mahon, of Bootle. B. 1914; m. 1941, Veronica, eld. d. of H. Robertshaw, Esq., of Crosby, Liverpool. Educ. at St. James Elementary School, and St. Joseph's Coll. Served with R.E. and Indian Army in the Far East in the Second World War. Trustee of Far Eastern Prisoners of War Fund. Member of Labour Party from boyhood. Alderman Bootle Borough Council, Mayor of Bootle 1962-63; Opposition Whip 1959-61. Member of Transport and General Workers' Union. A Ship Repairer and Contractor. Created Knight Commander Order of St. Gregory the Great by Pope Paul VI 1969. Honorary Freeman County Borough of Bootle. A Labour Member. Sat for Bootle from 1955 until he retired in 1979.* [1979]

MAINWARING, William Henry. 11 Aubrey Road, Pen-y-Graig, Rhondda, Glamorgan. S. of William Mainwaring, Esq., of Swansea. B. 1884; m. 1914, Jessie, d. of Thomas Hazell, Esq., of Oxford. Educ. at Swansea, and Labour Coll., London. A Miner; Lecturer at Labour Coll. 1919-24; Miners' Agent Rhondda district 1924-33. A Labour Member. Elected for Rhondda E. in Mar. 1933 and sat until he retired in 1959. Died 18 May 1971. [1959]

MAITLAND, Commander Sir John Francis Whitaker, R.N. Harrington Hall, Spilsby, Lincolnshire. Carlton. S. of William Whitaker Maitland, Esq., C.V.O., O.B.E., of Loughton Hall, Essex. B. 24 Mar. 1903; m. 1930, Bridget, d. of Edward Denny, Esq., of Staplefield Place, Sussex. Educ. at Royal

Naval Colls. Osborne and Dartmouth. Lieut.-Commander retired 1934, recalled 1939; Commander retired 1943. Gunnery Officer on Staff of Admiral Commanding Submarines. Dept.-Lieut. and J.P. for Essex 1935-45. Dept.-Lieut. for Lincolnshire 1957. Verderer of Epping Forest 1937-45. Knight Bach. June 1960. A Conservative. Elected for the Horncastle division of Lincolnshire— Parts of Lindsey in July 1945 and sat until he retired in 1966. Fellow of Royal Society of Arts. President of Institute of Patentees and Inventors 1966-75. Member of Lindsey County Council 1967. Died 17 Nov. 1977.

[1966]

MAITLAND, Hon. Patrick Francis, The Master of Lauderdale. 10 Ovington Square, London. Damhill Lodge, Corehouse, Lanark. Travellers', St. Stephen's and Conservative (Glasgow). S. of the Rev. Hon. Sydney G.W. Maitland, Clerk in Holy Orders. B. 17 Mar. 1911; m. 1936, Stanka, d. of Professor Milivoje Lozanich, University of Belgrade, Yugoslavia. Educ. at Lancing Coll., and Brasenose Coll., Oxford, B.A. Hons. 1933. Founder of The Fleet Street Letter Limited, an agency for political and diplomatic news, and Editor of The Whitehall Letter. A Journalist from 1933, served *The Times* and other newspapers as a foreign and war correspondent in Europe, America and Pacific 1936-43. Joined Political Intelligence Department, Foreign Office 1943. Member of Coll. of Guardians of the Shrine of Our Lady of Walsingham; President of Church Union 1956-61. Chairman The Expanding Commonwealth Group; Author of *Task for Giants*. A Conservative. Elected for the Lanark division of Lanarkshire in Oct. 1951 and sat until 1959 when he was defeated. Unsuccessfully contested Caithness and Sutherland in 1964. Conservative Whip withdrawn May-Dec. 1957. Succeeded to the Peerage as Earl of Lauderdale 1968.*

[1959]

MALLALIEU, Edward Lancelot, Q.C. 40 Westminster Gardens, London. Royal Cruising. S. of County Alderman F.W. Mallalieu, M.P., of Delph, Yorkshire. B. 14 Mar. 1905; m. 1934, Betty Margaret Oxley, d. of the Rev. J.A. Pride, LL.D. Educ. at Dragon School,

Oxford, Cheltenham Coll., and Trinity Coll., Oxford, M.A. 1930. Called to the bar at the Inner Temple 1928. K.C. 1951. Parliamentary Private Secretary to Rt. Hon. Sir Donald Maclean, President of Board of Education 1931-32. Sometime Chairman British Branch of the Inter-Parliamentary Union and member of the Executive Committee of the Union at Geneva. Chairman of Franco-British Parliamentary Relations Committee (now Honorary Vice-Chairman). Chairman Parliamentary Group for World Government (now Honorary Vice-President). Secretary General World Association of World Federalists at the Hague (now Parliamentary Adviser). Commodore of the House of Commons Yacht Club. A Gov. of the Royal Agricultural Society of England. Chev. Legion of Honour. Second Church Estates Commissioner 1964-70. Member of the Chairman's Panel from 1964. Second Dept. Chairman of Ways and Means 1971-73, First Dept. Chairman 1973-74. Voted in favour of entry to E.E.C. on 28 Oct. 1971. Sat for the Colne Valley division of the W.Riding of Yorkshire as a Liberal from 1931-35 when he was defeated. Unsuccessfully contested Colne Valley as a Liberal in July 1939. Elected for the Brigg division of Lincolnshire, Parts of Lindsey as a Labour Member in Mar. 1948 and sat until he retired in Feb. 1974. Knighted 1974. President of Electoral Reform Society 1978-79. Died 11 Nov. 1979. [1974]

MALLALIEU, Joseph Percival William. The Village Farm, Boarstall, Brill, Buckinghamshire. S. of F.W. Mallalieu, Esq., MP. B. 18 June 1908; m. 13 Feb. 1945, Harriet Tinn. Educ. at Cheltenham, Trinity Coll., Oxford, and Chicago University. A Journalist and Author. Parliamentary Private Secretary to Rt. Hon. John Strachey when Under-Secretary of State for Air Aug. 1945 and when Minister of Food May 1946-May 1949. Parliamentary Under-Secretary of State for the Royal Navy Oct. 1964-Feb. 1966. Minister of Defence for the Royal Navy Feb. 1966-Jan. 1967. Minister of State, Board of Trade Jan. 1967-June 1968. Minister of State, Ministry of Technology June 1968-Oct. 1969. Knighted June 1979. A Labour Member. Sat for Huddersfield from July 1945 to Feb. 1950 and for the E. division of Huddersfield from Feb. 1950 until he retired in 1979. Died 13 Mar. 1980. [1979]

MANN, Jean, J.P. Redcliffe, 18 Albert Road, Gourock, Renfrewshire. D. of William Stewart, Esq., of Polmadie, Lanarkshire. B. 1889; m. William Lawrence Mann. (he died 1958). Educ. at Kinning Park, and Bellahouston Academy. Publications: Rent Restriction Acts, Town Planning, and Scots Town and County Councillor. Vice-President Royal Society for the Prevention of Accidents, Town and Country Planning Association (Scotland). A Labour Member. Unsuccessfully contested Renfrewshire W. in 1931 and 1935. Sat for Coatbridge 1945-50. Elected for Coatbridge and Airdrie in Feb. 1950 and sat until she retired in 1959. Member of National Executive Committee of Labour Party 1953-58. Member of Glasgow City Council. Vice President of Haemophilia Society. Died 21 Mar. 1964. [1959]

MANNING, Cecil Aubrey Gwynne. 2 Menthing Road, Nunhead, London. Draycott Hill, Shepton Mallet, Somerset. S. of Charles Walter Manning, Esq., of Draycote Hall, Shepton Mallet. B. 23 May 1892; m. 1st, 1915, d. of William Twitchett, Esq.; 2ndly, 17 July 1940, Maryanne Johnson, d. of J. Green, Esq., of Seghill, Northumberland. Educ. at Board School, and London County Council Elementary School. Served with The Queen's Westminsters and The Rangers 1914-18. Member of Wandsworth Borough Council 1919-22, of London County Council 1922-32, and from 1937-49, Dept. Chairman 1930-31; Member of Camberwell Borough Council 1931-53, Mayor 1951-53. Dept.-Lieut. and J.P. for London. A Labour Member. Elected for N. Camberwell in Mar. 1944 and sat until he retired in 1950. Member of Shepton Mallet Urban District Council 1954-68, Chairman 1967-68.* [1950]

MANNING, (Elizabeth) Leah. 9 Red Lion Square, London. Willow Cottage, Hatfield Broad Oak, Bishops Stortford. D. of Charles Perrett, Esq., of Rockford, Illinois. B. 1886; m. 1915, William Henry Manning, Esq., of Cambridge (he died 1951). Educ. at St. John's School, Bridgwater, and Homerton Coll., Cambridge. President of National Union of Teachers 1930. A Labour Member. Sat for E. Islington from Feb.-Oct. 1931 when she was defeated. Unsuccessfully contested Sunderland in 1935. Elected for the Epping division of Essex in 1945 and sat until 1950 when she was defeated. Unsuccessfully contested Epping again in 1951 and 1955. Member of National Executive Committee of Labour Party 1931-32. D.B.E. 1966. Died 15 Sept. 1977. [1950]

MANNINGHAM-BULLER, Rt. Hon. Sir Reginald Edward, Bart., Q.C. Green's Norton Court, Towester, Northamptonshire. Carlton, and Buck's. S. of Sir Mervyn Manningham-Buller, 3rd Bart. B. 1 Aug. 1905; m. 18 Dec. 1930, Lady Mary Lilian Lindsay, d. of 27th Earl of Crawford and Balcarres, K.T. Educ. at Eton, and Magdalen Coll., Oxford. Barrister-at-Law, Inner Temple 1927. K.C. 1946. Joined the Army Oct. 1939; Maj. 1940. Member of Parliamentary Mission to U.S.S.R. 1945, of Anglo-American Committee of Enquiry on Palestine and Problem of European Jewry 1946. Member of Legal Aid Committee. Parliamentary Secretary Ministry of Works May-July 1945. Solicitor-Gen. Oct. 1951-Oct. 1954. Attorney-Gen. Oct. 1954-July 1962. PC. 1954. A National Conservative Member. Sat for Daventry from Apr. 1943 to Feb. 1950. Elected for the South division of Northamptonshire and the Soke of Peterborough in Feb. 1950 and sat until July 1962 when he was appointed Lord Chancellor and created Baron Dilhorne. Knighted 1951; succeeded to Baronetcy 1956. Lord Chancellor July 1962-Oct. 1964. Created Visct. Dilhorne 1964. Dept.-Lieut. for Northamptonshire 1967. Lord of Appeal in Ordinary from 1969. Recorder of Kingston-upon-Thames Jan.-July 1962. Died 7 Sept. 1980. [1962]

MANUEL, Archibald Clark. House of Commons, London. B. 1901. Educ. at Elementary School, and National Council of Labour classes. Past member of Ardrossan Town Council, Ayr County Council, Western Regional Hospital Board, and Ayrshire Executive Council of the Health Service. A Labour Member. Sat for the Central Ayrshire division of Ayrshire and Bute from

1950-55 when he was defeated. Re-elected in 1959 and sat until he retired in 1970. An Engine Driver and member of A.S.L.E.F. Died 10 Oct. 1976. [1970]

MAPP, Charles. House of Commons, London. S. of Albert Mapp, Esq. B. 1903; m. 1927, Amy Bourden. Educ. at Elementary and Grammar Schools. A Railway Goods Agent. Member of Sale Borough Council 1932-35 and 1945-46. J.P. A Labour Member. Unsuccessfully contested Northwich in 1950, Stretford in 1951 and Oldham E. in 1955. Elected for Oldham E. in 1959 and sat until he retired in 1970. Died 3 May 1978. [1970]

MARKHAM, Maj. Sir (Sydney) Frank. House of Commons, London. Constitutional. S. of William James Markham, Esq. B. 19 Oct. 1897; m. 1928, Frances, d. of S.F. Lawman, Esq., of Newport Pagnell. Educ. at Elementary School, and Wadham Coll., Oxford. A Company Director. Parliamentary Private Secretary to Rt. Hon. Ramsay Macdonald, when Prime Minister Aug.-Oct. 1931 and when Lord President of the Council 1936-37; Chairman Parliamentary Scientific Committee 1938-41; President Museums Association 1938-42. Knighted 1953. Leader of Parliamentary Delegations to Kenya 1961, and Malta 1963. Member Select Committee on Estimates 1953-63. Unsuccessfully contested Guildford as a Labour candidate in 1924. Elected for the Chatham division of Rochester as a Labour Member in 1929, joined the National Labour Party in Aug. 1931 and sat until he retired in Oct. 1931. Unsuccessfully contested, as a National Labour candidate, N. Lambeth in Oct. 1934. Sat as National Labour Member for S. Nottingham from 1935 until 1945, when he unsuccessfully contested the seat as a National candidate with Conservative support. Unsuccessfully contested the Buckingham division of Buckinghamshire as a Conservative in 1950 and sat for Buckingham from 1951 until he retired in 1964. Served in France, India and Mesopotamia 1915-19. Private Secretary to Sir Sydney Lee, biographer of King George V to 1926. Secretary of Museums Association 1929-32, of its Empire Surrey 1932-36. Author of works on mu-

seums, the history of Buckinghamshire and climatology. Member of Buckingham County Council 1928-31, and Bedfordshire County Council 1965-74. Dept.-Lieut. for Bedfordshire 1966. Died 13 Oct. 1975. [1964]

MARKS, Kenneth. 1 Epping Road, Denton, Manchester. S. of Robert P. Marks, Esq., Electrical Engineer. B. 15 June 1920; m. 1944, Kathleen, d. of John Lynch, Esq. Educ. at Peacock Street School, Gorton, Central High School, Manchester, and Didsbury Coll. of Education. Offices of L.N.E.R. 1936-40. Served in ranks of Grenadier Guards and as Officer in the Cheshire Regiment in the Middle East, Malta, and N.W. Europe 1940-46. Holds honorary rank of Capt. A Teacher in Manchester schools 1946-67; Headmaster of Clough Top Secondary School 1964-67. Parliamentary Private Secretary to Rt. Hon. A. Crosland, Secretary of State for Local Government and Regional Planning from Nov. 1969 to June 1970. Opposition Whip July 1970-June 1971. Vice-Chairman P.L.P. Education Group 1971. Chairman P.L.P. Education and Science Group 1972. Chairman P.L.P. N.W. Regional Group Feb. 1974. Parliamentary Private Secretary to Roy Hattersley (Foreign Office) 1974-75; Parliamentary Private Secretary to Rt. Hon. Harold Wilson, Prime Minister Apr.-Dec. 1975. Executive C.P.A. U.K. Branch. Under-Secretary of State, Department of Environment (Transport) Dec. 1975-May 1979. A Labour Member. Unsuccessfully contested the Moss Side division of Manchester in 1955. Sat for the Gorton division of Manchester from Nov. 1967.* [1979]

MARLOWE, Anthony Alfred Harmsworth, Q.C. 3 Hare Court, Temple, London. Mill House, Wimbourne-St.-Giles, Dorset. Brooks's. S. of Thomas Marlowe, Esq., Chairman of Associated Newspapers Limited. B. 25 Oct. 1904; m. 1st, 1929, Patricia Mary, d. of Sir Patrick Hastings, K.C., MP. (marriage dissolved in 1955); 2ndly, 1956, Marion Slater, d. of Commander R. Tennant-Park, O.B.E., R.N.R. Educ. at Marlborough, and Trinity Coll., Cambridge. Barrister-at-Law, Inner Temple 1928. K.C. 1945. Master of the

Bench, Inner Temple, 1953. Served in the Army 1939-45; Lieut.-Col. 1942. A Conservative. Sat for Brighton from Nov. 1941 to Feb. 1950. Elected for Hove in Feb. 1950 and sat until he resigned in June 1965. Died 8 Sept. 1965. [1965]

MARPLES, Rt. Hon. (Alfred) Ernest. House of Commons, London. Carlton. S. of Alfred Marples, Esq. B. 9 Dec. 1907; m. 1st, 1937, Edna Harwood (divorced 1945); 2ndly, 1956, Ruth, d. of F.W. Dobson, Esq. Educ. at Stretford Grammar School. A Chartered Accountant. Joined London Scottish 1939. 2nd Lieut. R.A. 1941, served until 1944 with rank of Capt. Parliamentary Secretary Ministry of Housing and Local Government Nov. 1951-Oct. 1954, Joint Parliamentary Secretary, Ministry of Pensions and National Insurance Oct. 1954-Dec. 1955. Postmaster Gen. Jan. 1957-Oct. 1959. Minister of Transport Oct. 1959-Oct. 1964. Shadow Minister of Technology 1964-66. Sponsor Conservative Party Public Sector Research Unit 1967-70. Honorary Freeman of the Borough of Wallasey July 1970. International Director Purolator Services Inc. (U.S.A.). Director Purolator Services Inc. (U.K.). A Conservative. Elected for Wallasey in July 1945 and sat until he retired in Feb. 1974. PC. 1957. Created Baron Marples (Life Peerage) 1974. Died in Monte Carlo 6 July 1978. [1974]

MARQUAND, David Ian. House of Commons, London. S. of the Rt. Hon. Hilary Marquand, MP. B. 20 Sept. 1934; m. 12 Dec. 1959, Judith, d. of Dr. M. Reed. Educ. at Emanuel School, Magdalen Coll., Oxford, St. Antony's Coll., Oxford, and University of California, M.A. Leader Writer for *The Guardian* 1959-62; Research Fellow St. Anthony's Coll., Oxford 1962-64. Lecturer in school of social studies, University of Sussex 1964-66. Parliamentary Private Secretary to Rt. Hon. R.E. Prentice, Minister of Overseas Development 1967-69. Opposition spokesman on Treasury Affairs 1970-72. Voted in favour of entry to E.E.C. on 28 Oct. 1971. A Labour Member. Unsuccessfully contested the Barry division of Glamorgan in 1964. Elected for the Ashfield division of Nottinghamshire in Mar. 1966 and sat until Apr. 1977 when he

resigned on appointment to a post with the European Commission. Chief Adviser to Secretariat-General of European Commission 1977-78. Professor of Contemporary History and Politics, University of Salford from 1978. Biographer of Ramsey Macdonald.* [1977]

MARQUAND, Rt. Hon. Hilary Adair. House of Commons, London. S. of Alfred Marquand, Esq. B. 24 Dec. 1901; m. 1929, Rachel Eluned, d. of D.J. Rees, Esq., of Ystalyfera. Educ. at Cardiff High School, and University Coll., Cardiff, M.A., D.Sc., and at American Universities. Professor of Industrial Relations at University Coll., Cardiff 1930-45. Rockefeller Fellow in Social Sciences in U.S.A. 1925-26 and 1932-33; Visiting Professor University of Wisconsin 1938-39. Member Assemblies of Council of Europe and W.E.U. 1957-59. Lecturer in Economics University of Birmingham 1926-30; Director of Industrial Surveys, South Wales. Temporary Civil Servant, Board of Trade, Ministry of Labour and Ministry of Production (Labour Adviser). Member of Labour Party from 1920 and of Fabian Society from 1936. Secretary for Overseas Trade Aug. 1945-Mar. 1947; Paymaster-Gen. Mar. 1947-July 1948; Minister of Pensions July 1948-Jan. 1951; Minister of Health Jan.-Oct. 1951. Opposition spokesman on Pensions until 1959 and on Commonwealth Affairs 1959-61. PC. 1949. Member of National Union of Teachers and National Union of Blastfurnacemen. A Labour Member. Elected for Cardiff E. in July 1945 and for Middlesbrough E. in Feb. 1950. Sat until he resigned in Nov. 1961. Director of International Institute for Labour Studies at Geneva 1961-65. Dept. Chairman of National Board for Prices and Incomes 1965-68. Died 6 Nov. 1972. [1962]

MARSDEN, Capt. Arthur, R.N. Eastfield, Virginia Water. Carlton, and United Service. S. of Edmund Marsden, Esq. B. 1883; m. 6 Aug. 1921, Rachel Cecilia, d. of L.T. Saunderson, Esq., and widow of Brigadier-Gen. R.C. Gore. Educ. at Cheltenham and in H.M.S. *Britannia*. Joined R.N. 1898, retired 1921. Rejoined R.N. 1939. Commanded H.M.S. *Ardent* at the Battle of Jutland 1916. A Conservative. Unsuccessfully contested

Battersea N. in May 1929. Elected for Battersea N. in Oct. 1931 and sat until he was defeated in Nov. 1935. Elected for the Chertsey division of Surrey in July 1937 and sat until he retired in 1950 after his local association had declined to readopt him as their candidate. Chairman of Shipwrecked Fishermen and Mariners' Royal Benevolent Society from 1952. C.B.E. 1960. Died 26 Nov. 1960.
[1950]

MARSDEN, Frank. 2 Thunderbolt Cottage, 6 Alder Lane, Knowsley, Liverpool. S. of Sidney Marsden, Esq., Postman. B. 15 Oct. 1923; m. 15 May 1943, Muriel, d. of Harold Lightfoot, Esq. Educ. at Ranworth Square School, and Abbotsford Road School, Liverpool. Served with R.A.F. Bomber Command 1941-46. Member Liverpool City Council 1964-67 and 1969-72. Chairman Liverpool Markets Committee 1964-67. Justice of the Peace City of Liverpool 1970. A Labour Member. Elected for the Scotland division of Liverpool in Apr. 1971 and sat until he retired in Feb. 1974. Member of Knowsley Metropolitan District Council from 1976.*
[1974]

MARSH, Rt. Hon. Richard William. House of Commons, London. S. of William Marsh, Esq. B. 14 Mar. 1928; m. 1st, 1950, Evelyn, d. of Frederick Andrews, Esq., of Southampton (divorced 1973); 2ndly, 1973, Caroline Dutton (she died 1975); 3rdly, 1979, Felicity, d. of Sir Frank McFadzean. Educ. at Jennings School, Woolwich Polytechnic, and Ruskin Coll., Oxford. Health Services Officer National Union Public Employees 1951-59; member Whitley Council for N.H.S. 1951-59; member Select Committee Estimates 1961; member Executive Labour Parliamentary Committee 1960. Member of the National Executive of the Fabian Society 1963-64; Parliamentary Secretary Ministry of Labour Oct. 1964-Oct. 1965. Joint Parliamentary Secretary Ministry of Technology Oct. 1965-Apr. 1966. Minister of Power Apr. 1966-Apr. 1968. Minister of Transport Apr. 1968-Oct. 1969. Member Executive P.E.P. and Council Foundation Management Education. Director of several companies. PC. 1966. A Labour Member. Unsuccessfully contested the Hertford division of

Hertfordshire in 1951. Elected for Greenwich in 1959 and sat until May 1971 when he resigned on appointment as Dept. Chairman and Chairman-designate of British Railways Board. Opposition spokesman on Housing 1970-71. Chairman of British Railways Board 1971-76. Chairman of Michael Saunders Management Services 1970-71. Knighted 1976. Chairman of Newspaper Publishers Association from 1976. Chairman of British Iron & Steel Consumers Council from 1977. Chairman of Allied Investments Ltd. from 1977. Declared his intention to vote Conservative in 1979.*
[1971]

MARSHALL, Commander Sir Douglas, R.N.V.R. Hatt House, Saltash, Cornwall. Naval & Military, Carlton, R.N.V.R., Fowey Yacht, and M.C.C. S. of Capt. William Marshall. B. 2 Oct. 1906; m. 1st, 20 June 1929, Joan, d. of N. Sherry, Esq., (1 d.) (she died 1952); 2ndly, 19 Dec. 1953, Suzanne, d. of P. Haynes, Esq. and widow of Peter Symons, Esq., (1 d.). Educ. at Plymouth Coll. Joined Admiralty 1939; served with Royal Navy until 1945. Director of Friends Provident and Century Insurance Company Limited, and other companies. A Conservative. Elected for the Bodmin division of Cornwall in July 1945 and sat until 1964 when he was defeated. Knighted 1963. Leader of Parliamentary delegation to West Indies 1953 and 1963, and to Basutoland, Bechuanaland and Swaziland in 1964. Died 24 Aug. 1976.
[1964]

MARSHALL, Dr. Edmund Ian. House of Commons, London. Reform. S. of Harry Marshall, Esq. B. 31 May 1940; m. 19 Apr. 1969, Margaret Pamela, d. of John Antill, Esq., (1 d.). Educ. at Clee Humberstone Foundation School, and Magdalen Coll., Oxford, M.A. Oxford, 1965, Ph.D. Liverpool, 1965. A University Lecturer in Pure Mathematics (Liverpool and Hull) 1962-66. Operational Research Scientist in Industry 1967-71. Member of Wallasey Borough Council 1963-65. Joined Labour Party 1967. Member of the Methodist Conference 1969-72 and of World Methodist Conference 1971. Member of British Council of Churches 1972-78. Parliamentary Private Secretary to Rt. Hon. Merlyn Rees, Secretary of State for

Northern Ireland Apr. 1974-Sept. 1976 and Home Secretary Sept. 1976-May 1979. Unsuccessfully contested the Louth Division of Lincolnshire as a Liberal in 1964 and 1966. Sat as a Labour Member for the Goole division of W. Yorkshire from May 1971.*
[1979]

MARSHALL, Fred. 159 Abbey Lane, Sheffield. S. of John Marshall, Esq., of South Anston, Yorkshire. B. 1883; m. 1912, Florence, d. of Samuel Whitworth, Esq. Educ. at South Anston Elementary School. J.P. Member of Sheffield City Council 1919, Alderman 1926-38, Lord Mayor 1933-34. Parliamentary Secretary Ministry of Town and Country Planning Aug. 1945-Oct. 1947. A Labour Member. Sat for the Brightside division of Sheffield Feb. 1930-31, when he was defeated, and from 1935 until he retired in 1950. Died Nov. 1962.   [1950]

MARSHALL, James. House of Commons, London. S. of Fred Marshall, Esq. B. 13 Mar. 1941; m. 9 June 1962, Shirley, d. of W. Ellis Violet Ellis, of Sheffield. Educ. at Sheffield City Grammar School, and Leeds University, Ph.D. 1968. Research Scientist, Wool Industries Research Association 1963-67. Lecturer, Leicester Polytechnic 1968-74. Leeds City Councillor 1965-68. Leicester City Councillor 1971-76. Chairman Finance Committee 1972-74. Leader City Council 1974. Labour Leader, Association of District Councils 1974. Assistant Government Whip Nov. 1977-May 1979. A Labour Member. Unsuccessfully contested the Harborough division of Leicestershire in 1970 and Leicester S. in Feb. 1974. Sat for Leicester S. from Oct. 1974.*   [1979]

MARSHALL, (Robert) Michael. Old Inn House, Slindon, Nr. Arundel, Sussex. Garrick, and M.C.C. S. of Robert Ernest Marshall, Esq. B. 21 June 1930; m. 26 May 1972, Caroline Victoria Oliphant, d. of A.O. Hutchison, Esq. Educ. at Bradfield Coll., Harvard (M.B.A. 1960), and Stanford University. United Steel Companies Limited 1951-66. Calcutta Branch Manager and subsequently Managing Director United Steel (India) Limited 1953-64. Commercial Director Workington Iron and Steel Company

Limited 1964-66. Managing Director The Head Wrightson Export Company Limited 1967-69. Management Consultant with Urwick Orr and Partners Limited 1969-74. Founder of English Speaking Union, Bombay Branch. Advisory Committee of Business Graduates Association. Former B.B.C. Cricket Commentator. Vice-Chairman of Conservative Party Parliamentary Industry Committee; Vice-Chairman All-Party Group on Management, Executive Committee British American Parliamentary Group. Joint Chairman British-Burmese Parliamentary Group. Secretary British-American University Group. Under-Secretary of State for Industry from May 1979. A Conservative. Unsuccessfully contested The Hartlepools in 1970. Sat for Arundel from Feb. 1974.*
[1979]

MARSHALL, Sir Sidney Horatio. 56 The Crescent, Belmont, Surrey. Headley Grove Farm, Epsom. Constitutional. S. of William Marshall, Esq. B. 17 July 1882. Unmarried. Educ. at Elementary Schools. Member of Sutton and Cheam Urban District Council 1928; Charter-Mayor of Sutton and Cheam 1934; Alderman 1934; Mayor 1936-37; member of Surrey County Council 1931; Vice-Chairman 1944-47; Chairman 1947-50; Alderman 1941; Chairman Education Committee 1942-47; J.P. 1937; Dept.-Lieut. 1950; Honorary Freeman Sutton and Cheam 1949; member Agricultural Wages Committee Surrey 1945; member Reynolds Committee on Approved Schools; member of Educational Trust for Visual Aids; member of London Tribunal for hearing Conscientious Objectors. In Food, Chemical and Dye Industry. Created Knight Bach. 1952. A Conservative. Elected for Sutton and Cheam in July 1945 and sat until he resigned in Oct. 1954. Died 28 Mar. 1973.   [1954]

MARTEN, (Harry) Neil. Swalcliffe House, Nr. Banbury, Oxfordshire. Pratt's. S. of F.W. Marten, Esq. B. 3 Dec. 1916; m. 1944, Joan Olive, d. of Vice-Admiral Walter John C. Lake, C.B.E., (1 s. 2 d.). Educ. at Rossall School. Admitted a Solicitor 1939. Served 1939-45 Northamptonshire Yeomanry and with Special Forces (Middle East, France and Norway). Foreign Office 1947-57. Parliamentary Private Secretary to Rt. Hon. F.J. Erroll, Minister of State Board of Trade May 1960-Oct. 1961 and President of Board of Trade Oct. 1961-Dec. 1962. Parliamentary Secretary, Ministry of Aviation Dec. 1962-Oct. 1964. Chairman Conservative Party Space Committee 1965; Vice-Chairman Conservative Party Foreign Affairs Committee 1922 Committee. Executive Chairman Anglo-Norwegian Parliamentary Group. Select Committee European Legislative Executive, Commonwealth Parliamentary Association, Treasurer British-American Parliamentary Association. Voted against entry to E.E.C. on 28 Oct. 1971. Minister of State, Foreign and Commonwealth Office, with responsibility for Overseas Development, from May 1979. A Conservative. Sat for the Banbury division of Oxfordshire from 1959.* [1979]

MARTIN, John Hanbury. 24 Chester Street, London. S. of Waldyve Martin, Esq., of Ledbury, Herefordshire. B. 1890. m. 1st. 1934, Avice Blaneid, d. of Herbert Trench, Esq. (divorced 1938); 2ndly, 1951. Dorothy Helen, d. of E. Lloyd Jones, Esq. Educ. at Wellington and Brasenose Coll., Oxford. An Author and Journalist. Capt. Queen's Westminsters, served 1914-19. A Labour Member. Unsuccessfully contested Great Yarmouth in 1931. Sat for the Central division of Southwark from Feb. 1940 until he resigned in Apr. 1948. Member of Southwark Borough Council 1934-49. Member of London Insurance Committee 1936-45.* [1948]

MASON, Rt. Hon. Roy. 12 Victoria Avenue, Barnsley. S. of Joseph Mason, Esq., Miner. B. 18 Apr. 1924; m. 20 Oct. 1945, Marjorie, d. of Ernest Sowden, Esq., (2 d.). Educ. at Carlton and Royston Elementary Schools, and London School of Economics (T.U.C. Scholarship). A Miner 1938-53; Yorkshire Miners' Council 1949-53. Opposition spokesman on Defence and Post Office Affairs 1960-64. Minister of State (Shipping) Board of Trade Oct. 1964-Jan. 1967. Minister of Defence (Equipment) Jan. 1967-Apr. 1968. Postmaster-Gen. Apr. June 1968. Minister of Power July 1968-Oct. 1969. President Board of Trade Oct. 1969-June 1970. Opposition spokesman on Civil Aviation,

Shipping, Tourism, Films and Trade Matters 1970-74. Chairman Yorkshire Group of Labour MPs. Vice-Chairman Miners Group of MPs. Member Council of Europe and Western European Union 1973. Secretary of State for Defence Mar. 1974-Sept. 1976. Secretary of State for Northern Ireland Sept. 1976-May 1979. Chairman Yorkshire Group of Labour MPs. 1971-73. Chairman Miners Group of MPs. 1973-74. Voted in favour of entry to E.E.C. on 28 Oct. 1971. Member of Cabinet 1968-70 and 1974-79. Member of Parliamentary Committee of P.L.P. from 1979. Opposition spokesman on Agriculture from 1979. A Labour Member. Prospective candidate for Bridlington 1951-53. Elected for Barnsley in Mar. 1953. PC. 1968.* [1979]

MASON-MACFARLANE, Lieut.-Gen. Sir (Frank) Noel, K.C.B., D.S.O., M.C. 23 Westminster Gardens, London. S. of Lieut.-Col. D.J. Mason-MacFarlane, C.M.G., C.B., M.D., of Turin House, Angus. B. 23 Oct. 1889; m. 14 Sept. 1918, Islay, d. of F.I. Pitman, Esq., of Scarlets, Twyford, Berkshire (she died 1947). Educ. at Rugby, and at Royal Military Academy, Woolwich. Joined R.A. 1909, Lieut.-Gen. 1943. Military Attaché in Berlin 1937-39. Served with B.E.F. 1939-40. Gov. and C.-in-C. Gibraltar 1942-44. Head of Military Mission to Moscow 1941-42. Chief Commissioner A.C.C. Italy 1944. Had French Croix de Guerre, Grand Cross Polonia Restituta and Grand Cross Ouissam Alaouite. A Labour Member. Elected for the N. division of Paddington in July 1945 and sat until he resigned in Oct. 1946. C.B. 1939, K.C.B. 1943. Died 12 Aug. 1953. [1946]

MATES, Michael John. House of Commons, London. S. of Claude John Mates, Esq. B. 9 June 1934; m. 1959, Mary Rosamund Paton, d. of Brigadier J.A. Paton, O.B.E., (2 s. 2 d.). Educ. at Blundell's School, and King's Coll., Cambridge. Joined the Army in 1954; 2nd Lieut., R.U.R. 1955; Queen's Dragoon Guards, R.A.C. 1961; Maj. 1967; Lieut.-Col. 1973; resigned commission 1974. Secretary Conservative Northern Ireland Committee 1974. A Conservative. Elected for Petersfield in Oct. 1974.* [1979]

MATHER, Lieut.-Col. David Carol Mac-Donell, M.C. Brookfield, Horton, Slough. Brooks's. S. of Loris Emerson Mather, Esq., C.B.E. B. 3 Jan. 1919; m. 1951, Hon. Philippa Selina Bewicke-Copley, d. of 5th Baron Cromwell, D.S.O., (1 s. 3 d.). Educ. at Harrow, and Trinity Coll., Cambridge. Served with Welsh Guards 1940-62; M.C. 1944; Palestine Campaign 1946-48; A.M.A. British Embassy, Athens 1953-56; War Office 1958-61. A.M.S. to G.O.C. in C. Eastern Command 1961-62. Conservative Research Department 1962-70. Rural District Council 1965-66. Joint Secretary Conservative Parliamentary Foreign Affairs Committee and Northern Ireland Committee 1972-74. Opposition Whip 1975-79. Lord Commissioner of the Treasury from May 1979. Voted against entry to E.E.C. on 28 Oct. 1971. A Conservative. Unsuccessfully contested Leicester N.W. in 1966. Sat for the Esher division of Surrey from June 1970.*   [1979]

MATHERS, Rt. Hon. George. 2 Corrennie Gardens, Edinburgh. S. of George Mathers, Esq., J.P., of Newtown St. Boswells. B. 28 Feb. 1886; m. 1st, 6 June 1916, Edith Mary, d. of William Robinson, Esq., of Carlisle (she died 5 June 1938); 2ndly, 31 Jan. 1940, Jessie Newton, d. of George Graham, Esq., J.P., of Peebles. Educ. at Board School. Member of Railway Clerks' Association from 1908, and of Carlisle City Council 1919-21. Parliamentary Private Secretary to Dr. Drummond Shiels, Under-Secretary for India June 1929, and when Under-Secretary for the Colonies Nov. 1929-Aug. 1931. Scottish Whip Nov. 1935-June 1945. Comptroller of H.M.'s Household Oct. 1944-May 1945; Treasurer of H.M.'s Household and Dept. Chief Whip Aug. 1945-Mar. 1946. Lord High Commissioner to the General Assembly of the Church of Scotland 1946-48 and 1951. Dept.-Lieut. for Edinburgh. PC. 1947. Chairman British Group, Inter-Parliamentary Union 1950-51; President Edinburgh Y.M.C.A. from 1947; Chairman Committee of Selection House of Commons 1946-51; and on Speaker's Panel of Temporary Chairman of Committees from 1947. A Labour Member. Unsuccessfully contested W. Edinburgh in 1923 and 1924. Sat for W. Edinburgh from 1929-31 when he was defeated, for Linlithgow (later W.

Lothian) from 1935-50. Re-elected for W. Lothian in Feb. 1950 and sat until he retired in 1951. President of National Temperance Federation from 1950. Chairman of S.E. Scotland Regional Board 1951-54. Created Baron Mathers 1951. K.T. 1956. Died 26 Sept. 1965.   [1951]

MATHEW, Robert, T.D. House of Commons, London. Brooks's, Pratt's, and M.C.C. S. of Maj.-Gen. Sir Charles M. Mathew, K.C.M.G., C.B., D.S.O. B. 9 May 1911; m. 26 Feb. 1944, Joan Leslie, only d. of John Synnot Bruce, Esq. Educ. at Eton, and Trinity Coll., Cambridge, M.A. Called to the bar by Lincoln's Inn 1937. Served with K.R.R.C. (T.A.), Staff Coll., Italy and Greece 1939-45; Lieut.-Col. 1944. Member of Chelsea Borough Council 1945-49. Parliamentary Private Secretary to Rt. Hon. D. Walker-Smith, Minister of Health 1957-60, Parliamentary Under-Secretary of State for Foreign Affairs Jan.-Oct. 1964. A Conservative. Unsuccessfully contested S. Ayrshire in 1945 and 1946 and Rochester and Chatham in 1950 and 1951. Elected for the Honiton division of Devonshire in 1955 and sat until his death on 8 Dec. 1966.   [1966 2nd ed.]

MATTHEWS, Gordon Richards. Medford House, Mickleton, Chipping Campden, Gloucestershire. S. of Frank H. Matthews, Esq. B. 16 Dec. 1908; m. 6 Oct. 1934, Ruth, youngest d. of Sir David Brooks, G.B.E. Educ. at Repton School. Honorary Secretary Birmingham Unionist Association 1948-53. Executive Area Chairman Birmingham Y.M.C.A. 1951-59. Chartered Accountant. Gov. of Birmingham University. President of City of Birmingham Friendly Society 1957-64. Wide experience of Retail Trade. National President of Appeal Drapers' Cottage Homes 1954-55. Parliamentary Private Secretary to Rt. Hon. J.R. Bevins, Postmaster-Gen. Oct. 1961-Oct. 1964. A Conservative. Unsuccessfully contested the Deritend division of Birmingham in 1945 and the Yardley division of Birmingham in 1950. Elected for Meriden in 1959 and sat until 1964 when he was defeated. Chairman of West Midlands Conservative Council 1970-73. C.B.E. 1974. Chairman of Oxford Branch of Council for the Protection of Rural England from 1978.*   [1964]

MAUDE, Rt. Hon. Angus Edmund Upton. House of Commons, London. S. of Col. Alan Hamer Maude, D.S.O., C.M.G. B. 8 Sept. 1912; m. 1946, Barbara Elizabeth Earnshaw, only d. of J.E. Sutcliffe, Esq., of Bushey, (2 s. 2 d.). Educ. at Rugby, and Oriel Coll., Oxford. An Author and Journalist. Served with R.A.S.C. 1939-45 (prisoner $3\frac{1}{2}$ years). Editor of *Sydney Morning Herald* 1958-61. A Dept. Chairman of the Conservative Party and Chairman Conservative Research Department 1975-79. Director of Conservative Political Centre 1951-55. Conservative Whip withdrawn May 1957-Apr. 1958. Opposition spokesman on Aviation 1964-65, and on Colonies from 1965 until he resigned in Jan. 1966. Voted against entry to E.E.C. on 28 Oct. 1971. Member of Shadow Cabinet 1975-79. Paymaster General, with a seat in the Cabinet, from May 1979. A Conservative. Sat for S. Ealing from 1950 to Apr. 1958, when he resigned. Unsuccessfully contested S. Dorset in Nov. 1962. Elected for Stratford-on-Avon in Aug. 1963. PC. 1979.* [1979]

MAUDE, John Cyril, K.C. 5 Dunraven Street, London. Beefsteak, and Garrick. S. of Cyril Maude, Esq., Actor. B. 3 Apr. 1901; m. 1st, 13 June 1927, Rosamond, d. of Dr. T. Murray of Boston, U.S.A. (divorced 1955). 2ndly, 1955, Mrs. Maureen Constance Buchanan, d. of Hon. Arthur Guinness and widow of 4th Marquis of Dufferin and Ava. Educ. at Eton, and Christ Church, Oxford. Barrister-at-Law, Middle Temple 1925, Bencher 1951. Recorder of Plymouth from 1944-54, of Devizes 1939-44; Counsel to the Post Office at Central Criminal Court 1935-42; Junior Counsel to the Treasury 1942-43; Temporary Civil Assistant War Office 1939; Military Intelligence Corps with rank of Maj. 1940; Offices of War Cabinet 1942; Chancellor of the Diocese of Bristol 1948-50. A Conservative. Elected for Exeter in July 1945 and sat until he retired in 1951. K.C. 1943. Additional Judge, City of London Court 1954-65. Additional Judge, Central Criminal Court 1965-68. Director of Old Vic Trust Ltd. 1951-54, Chairman of British Drama League 1952-54.* [1951]

MAUDLING, Rt. Hon. Reginald. Bedwell Lodge, Essendon, Hertfordshire. Carlton, and Garrick. S. of Reginald George Maudling, Esq. B. in London 7 Mar. 1917; m. 1939, Beryl, d. of E. Laverick, Esq. Educ. at Merchant Taylor's School, and Merton Coll., Oxford. Barrister, Middle Temple 1940. Economic Secretary to the Treasury Nov. 1952-Apr. 1955. Parliamentary Secretary, Ministry of Civil Aviation Apr.-Nov. 1952. PC. 1955. Minister of Supply Apr. 1955-Jan. 1957; Paymaster-Gen. Jan. 1957-Oct. 1959. President of the Board of Trade Oct. 1959-Oct. 1961. Secretary of State for the Colonies Oct. 1961-July 1962. Chancellor of the Exchequer July 1962-Oct. 1964. Opposition spokesman on Treasury Affairs 1964-65, on Foreign Affairs 1965, on Commonwealth Affairs and Overseas Development 1966-68, and on Defence Apr.-Nov. 1968. Dept. Leader of Opposition 1965-70. Home Secretary June 1970-July 1972, when he resigned. Conservative spokesman on Foreign and Commonwealth Affairs 1975-76. A Conservative. Unsuccessfully contested Heston and Isleworth in 1945. Sat for Barnet from 1950 to Feb. 1974 and for the Chipping Barnet division of Barnet from Feb. 1974 until his death on 14 Feb. 1979. Unsuccessful candidate for Leadership of Conservative Party 1965. Criticised by the House of Commons Select Committee on the Conduct of Members on 14 July 1977 for 'conduct inconsistent with the standards which the House is entitled to expect from its members' as a result of his business contacts with John Poulson. An attempt to expel him was defeated by 331 votes to 11 on 26 July 1977. Died 14 Feb. 1979. [1979]

MAWBY, Raymond Llewellyn. 29 Applegarth Avenue, Newton Abbot, South Devon. House of Commons, London. S. of J.H. Mawby, Esq. B. 6 Feb. 1922; m. 7 Oct. 1944, C.S. Aldwinckle, (1 d.). Educ. at Long Lawford Council School. Contested seat in Rugby Borough Council, successful at the fifth attempt, resigned on leaving Rugby. Past President Rugby Branch of the Electrical T.U. Parliamentary Private Secretary to Rt. Hon. Reginald Bevins, Postmaster General 1959-61. Assistant Postmaster-General Mar. 1963-Oct. 1964. A Conservative. Sat for the Totnes division of Devonshire from 1955.* [1979]

MAXTON, James. Beechwood, Barrhead, Glasgow. S. of a Schoolmaster at Glasgow. B. 1885; m. 1st, July 1919, S.W. McCallum (she died 1922); 2ndly, 14 Mar. 1935, Madeleine, d. of G.H. Brougham Glasier, Esq. Educ. at Glasgow University, M.A. Was for some years a teacher. Organizing Secretary of the Glasgow Federation of the ILP; National Chairman ILP 1926-31; Chairman of ILP 1933-39; member of the Glasgow Education Authority 1919-22. An Independent Labour Party Member. Unsuccessfully contested the Bridgeton division of Glasgow in 1918. Member for the Bridgeton division of Glasgow from Nov. 1922 until his death on 23 July 1946. Member of National Executive Committee of Labour Party 1918-19. Member of Executive Committee of P.L.P. 1924-25. Died 23 July 1946. [1946]

MAXWELL, Ian Robert, M.C. 4 Fitzroy Square, London. Headington Hill Hall, Oxford. S. of Michael Hoch, Esq. B. 10 June 1923 in Czechoslovakia; m. 15 Mar. 1945, Elisabeth, d. of Paul Louis Meynard, Esq. Self-educ. Scientific Publisher, Editor and Film Producer. Joined the Labour Party in 1958. Member of A.S.S.E.T. and the Fabian Society. Speaks fluently nine languages including Russian. A Labour Member. Previous Parliamentary Candidate for Buckingham in 1959. Elected for the Buckingham division of Buckinghamshire in Oct. 1964 and sat until 1970 when he was defeated. Unsuccessfully contested Buckingham in Feb. 1974 and Oct. 1974. Served with Queen's Royal Regiment, M.C. Head of Press Section, Berlin in Foreign Office German Department 1945-47. Chairman of Robert Maxwell & Co. Ltd. from 1948. Chairman of International Learning Systems Corporation Ltd. 1968-69. Founder of Pergamon Press. Treasurer of Round House Trust Ltd. from 1965.* [1970]

MAXWELL FYFE, Rt. Hon. Sir David Patrick, G.C.V.O., Q.C. 2 Raymond Buildings, Gray's Inn, London. Athenaeum, Carlton, 1900, and Garrick. S. of W.T. Fyfe, Esq., Author, and Isabella, d. of David Campbell, Esq. B. 29 May 1900; m. 15 Apr. 1925, Sylvia, d. of W.R. Harrison, Esq., of Liverpool. Educ. at George Watson's Coll., and Balliol Coll., Oxford. Served with Scots Guards 1918. A Barrister-at-Law, Gray's Inn 1922; K.C. 1934, Bencher 1936; Recorder of Oldham 1936-42; Maj., Dept.-Judge Advocate, Staff Officer of the Judge Advocate-Gen. Jan. 1940. Solicitor Gen. Mar. 1942-May 1945; Attorney-Gen. May-July 1945; Home Secretary and Minister for Welsh Affairs (Cabinet) Oct. 1951-Oct. 1954. Knight Bach. 1942, PC. 1945. Dept. Chairman of Conservative Party Post-War Problems Committee 1941, Chairman 1943. A National Conservative member. Unsuccessfully contested Wigan in 1924. Sat for the W. Derby division of Liverpool from July 1935 until Oct. 1954 when he was appointed Lord Chancellor and created Visct. Kilmuir. Author of *Political Adventure* (1964). Dept. Chief Prosecutor at Nuremberg 1945-46. Chairman of National Union of Conservative and Unionist Associations 1950. G.C.V.O. 1953. Prospective candidate for Epsom in 1954 until his appointment as Lord Chancellor. Lord Chancellor Oct. 1954-July 1962. Created Earl of Kilmuir 1962. Chairman of Thomson Foundation 1962-67 and Plessey Company 1962-67. President of British Standards Institution 1963-67 and Electrical Development Association 1963-64. Died 27 Jan. 1967. [1954]

MAXWELL-HYSLOP, Robert John (Robin). 4 Tiverton Road, Silverton, Exeter, Devon. S. of Capt. A.H. Maxwell-Hyslop, G.C., R.N., retired. B. 6 June 1931; m. 1968, Joanna Margaret, eld. d. of Thomas McCosh, Esq., of Pitcon, Dalry, Ayrshire, (2 d.). Educ. at Stowe, and Christ Church, Oxford, (M.A.). Rolls-Royce Aero Engine Division 1954-60. Vice-Chairman Anglo-Brazilian Parliamentary Group. Secretary Conservative Parliamentary Aviation Committee. Member Select Committee of Public Expenditure (Trade and Industry Sub-Committee). Member Standing Orders Committee. A Conservative. Unsuccessfully contested Derby N. at the general election of 1959. Elected for the Tiverton division of Devonshire at a by-election in Nov. 1960.* [1979]

MAYDON, Lieut.-Commander Stephen Lynch Conway, D.S.O., D.S.C., R.N. Bruin

Wood, Wraxall, Nr. Bristol. Army & Navy. S. of John George Maydon, Esq., former member of Natal Legislative Assembly. B. 15 Dec. 1913; m. 26 Apr. 1938, Joan Mary Doligny, d. of C.V. Baker, Esq., of Betchworth, Surrey. Educ. at Twyford School, near Winchester, and Royal Naval Coll., Dartmouth. Served in the Royal Navy 1931-49; commanded H.M. Submarines L26, P35 and Tradewind 1941-45. Awarded D.S.O. 1942, bar to D.S.O. 1943, and D.S.C. 1945. Chairman of the Conservative Parliamentary Party Defence Committee Nov. 1959-Nov. 1961. Parliamentary Private Sec. to Rt. Hon. P. Thorneycroft, Pres. of Board of Trade 1952-53. Joint Parliamentary Secretary Ministry of Pensions and National Insurance July 1962-Oct. 1964. A Conservative. Unsuccessfully contested Bristol S. in 1950. Elected for the Wells division of Somerset in 1951 and sat until he retired in 1970. Died 2 Mar. 1971.
[1970]

MAYHEW, Christopher Paget. 39 Wool Road Wimbledon, London. S. of Sir Basil Mayhew, K.B.E. B. 12 June 1915; m. 1949, Cicely Elizabeth, d. of G.S. Ludham, Esq., (2 s. 2 d.). Educ. at Haileybury (Scholar), and Christ Church, Oxford (Open Exhibitioner). Broadcaster and Writer. Served in Surrey Yeomanry B.E.F., Phantom Regiment B.N.A.F. and Special Forces, B.L.A. (Maj., despatches). Publications: *Men Seeking God, Those in Favour, Co-existence Plus, Britain's Role Tomorrow*, and *Party Games*. Parliamentary Under-Secretary of State for Foreign Affairs Oct. 1946-Mar. 1950. Minister of Defence for the Royal Navy Oct. 1964-Feb. 1966 (resigned). Chairman MIND (National Association for Mental Health). Chairman Labour Campaign for Mental Health. Chairman Labour Middle East Council. Chairman Middle East International Publishers Limited. Chairman ANAF Foundation. Joint Chairman Parliamentary Association for Euro-Arab Co-operation. Parliamentary Private Sec. to Rt. Hon. Herbert Morrison, Leader of the House of Commons, 1945-64. Voted in favour of entry to E.E.C. on 28 Oct. 1971. A Labour Member, who joined the Liberal Party in July 1974. Sat for S. Norfolk from 1945-50 when he was defeated. Sat for Woolwich E. from June 1951 to Feb. 1974

and for the Woolwich E. division of Greenwich from Feb. 1974 to Oct. 1974, when he unsuccessfully contested Bath as a Liberal. Opposition spokesman on Broadcasting 1959-62, on War 1960-61, on Foreign Affairs 1961-64. Unsuccessfully contested Bath again in 1979. Unsuccessfully contested for European Parliament Surrey in June 1979 and London S.W. in Sept. 1979.*
[1974 2nd ed.]

MAYHEW, Patrick Barnabas Burke, Q.C. House of Commons, London. S. of A.G.H. Mayhew, Esq., M.C. B. 11 Sept. 1929; m. 15 Apr. 1963, Jean Elizabeth, 2nd d. of John Gurney, Esq., (4 s.). Educ. at Tonbridge, and Balliol Coll., Oxford. Q.C. 1972. Served in 4th/7th Royal Dragoon Guards National Service and A.E.R. Capt. Called to the bar by Middle Temple 1955. Vice-Chairman Conservative Home Affairs Committee 1976. Executive of 1922 Committee 1976-79. Under-Secretary for Employment from May 1979. A Conservative. Unsuccessfully contested the Dulwich division of Camberwell in 1970. Elected for Royal Tunbridge Wells in Feb. 1974.*
[1979]

MAYNARD, (Vera) Joan, J.P. House of Commons, London. D. of Mathew Maynard, Esq., Farmer. B. 1921. Educ. at Ampleforth, North Yorkshire and University Coll. of N. Wales. A Member of National Executive Committee of the Labour Party from 1972. National Vice-President National Union of Agriculture and Allied Workers 1966-72. Now Yorkshire County Secretary. A Labour Member. Sat for the Brightside division of Sheffield from Oct. 1974.*
[1979]

MEACHER, Michael Hugh. 45 Cholmeley Park, Highgate, London. S. of George H. Meacher, Esq. B. 4 Nov. 1939; m. 11 Aug. 1962, Molly Christine, d. of W.F. Reid, Esq., (4 children). Educ. at Berkhamsted School, Hertfordshire, and New Coll., Oxford. Secretary of the Danilo Dolci Trust 1964; Sembal Research Fellow in Social Gerontology at University of Essex 1965-66; Lecturer in Social Administration at University of York 1966-69; Lecturer in Social Administration at London School of Economics 1970. Author of *The Care of Old People* Fabian Society 1969,

Taken For A Ride, Special Residential Homes for the Elderly Infirm, A Study of Separatism in Social Policy 1972, and numerous articles and pamphlets on social and economic policy. Parliamentary Under-Secretary of State at the Department of Industry Mar. 1974-June 1975. Under-Secretary Department of Health and Social Security June 1975-Apr. 1976. Parliamentary Under-Secretary of State, Department of Trade Apr. 1976-May 1979. A Labour Member. Unsuccessfully contested Colchester in 1966 and Oldham W. in June 1968. Elected for Oldham W. in June 1970.* [1979]

MEDLAND, Hubert Moses. 44 Quarry Park Road, Peverell, Plymouth. S. of Alderman Charles Medland of Okehampton. B. 1 July 1881; m. 1906, Mary Ellen Smith of Newark. Educ. at Elementary School, and Tavistock Grammar School. Retired Civil Servant. Member of Plymouth City Council 1923, Lord Mayor 1935. President of British Waterworks Association 1938. Civil Defence Regional Commissioner for South-West. A Labour Member. Unsuccessfully contested Torquay in 1929 and 1931. Elected for the Drake division of Plymouth in July 1945 and sat until he retired in 1950. Member of South-West Electricity Board and South-West Regional Hospital Board from 1950. Died 11 Dec. 1964. [1950]

MEDLICOTT, Sir Frank. C.B.E. Carlton House, Lower Regent Street, London. Royal Empire Society. S. of John James Medlicott. Esq., of Taunton. B. 10 Nov. 1903; m. 6 June 1931, Helen Elizabeth, d. of the Rev. Walter Penny, (2 s.). Educ. at Huish's Grammar School, Taunton. Admitted a Solicitor 1925. Served with R.A. 1939. Brigadier on Staff 21st Army Group 1943-45 (despatches); had U.S.A. Bronze Star. Parliamentary Private Secretary to Rt. Hon. Ernest Brown, Minister of Health Jan.-Oct. 1943. Knight Bach. 1955. A Liberal National and Conservative Member. Unsuccessfully contested, as a Liberal, the Acton division of Middlesex in 1929. Sat for E. Norfolk from Jan. 1939-Feb. 1950. Elected for the Central division of Norfolk in Feb. 1950 and sat until he retired in 1959. Treasurer of U.K. Band of Hope Union. C.B.E. 1945. Conservative Whip withdrawn

Nov. 1957-Nov. 1958. Member of Norfolk County Council 1942-46 and 1950-58. Rejoined the Liberal Party in 1962. Treasurer of Liberal Party 1969-71. Died 9 Jan. 1972. [1959]

MELLISH, Rt. Hon. Robert Joseph. House of Commons, London. S. of John Mellish, Esq. B. 3 Mar. 1913; m. 15 Oct. 1938., Ann d. of George Warner Esq., Educ. at St. Joseph's School, Deptford. A Roman Catholic. A Trade Union Official. Served in R.E. 1939-45, Capt. Parliamentary Private Secretary to John Dugdale, Parliamentary Secretary, to Walter Edwards, Civil Lord of the Admiralty, 1947-49, to George Strauss, Minister of Supply, 1950-51, and to Rt. Hon. George Isaacs, Minister of Pensions 1951. An Opposition spokesman on Transport 1959-64. Parliamentary Secretary Ministry of Housing and Local Government Oct. 1964-Aug. 1967. PC. 1967. Minister of Public Buildings and Works, Aug. 1967-Apr. 1969. Government Chief Whip Apr. 1969-May 1970. Minister of Housing and Local Government May-June 1970. Opposition Chief Whip July 1970-Mar. 1974. Government Chief Whip Mar. 1974-Apr. 1976. Member of Cabinet July 1964-Apr. 1976. A Labour Member. Sat for the Rotherhithe division of Bermondsey from Nov. 1946 to Feb. 1950, for Bermondsey from Feb. 1950 to Feb. 1974 and for the Bermondsey division of Southwark from Feb. 1974. Dept. Chairman of London Docklands Urban Development Corporation from 1980.* [1979]

MELLOR, Sir John Serocold Paget, Bart. 67 Ennismore Gardens, London. Carlton. S. of Sir John Mellor, 1st Bart., K.C.B. B. 6 July 1893; m. 1st, 24 May 1922, Rachel Margaret, d. of Sir Herbert Cook, 3rd Bart. (marriage dissolved 1937); 2ndly, 23 Dec. 1937, Mrs. Raie Mendes (she died 1965); 3rdly, 1971, Mrs. Jessica de Pass, d. of Clarence de Sola, Esq. of Montreal. Educ. at Eton, and New Coll., Oxford, B.A. Barrister-at-Law, Inner Temple 1920; Capt. Somerset L.I., T.A.; served in Mesopotamia 1914-15 (wounded, prisoner); rejoined Sept. 1939. Director of Prudential Assurance Company Limited 1946-72, Chairman 1965-70. A Conservative. Unsuccessfully contested Workington division of Cumberland in May 1929. Member for the Tamworth division of Warwickshire from May 1935 to July 1945. Elected for the Sutton Coldfield division of Warwickshire in July 1945 and sat until he retired in 1955. Succeeded to Baronetcy in 1929. Prospective Conservative candidate for Luton 1931 but withdrew in favour of the Liberal National Conservative Whip withdrawn June-July 1954.* [1954]

MENDELSON John Jakob. 407 Fulwood Road, Sheffield. Flat 15A Dunrobin Court, Finchley Road, London. S. of J.C. Mendelson, Esq. B. 1917. Educ. at London University. Served in Army 1939-45. Capt. Lecturer in Political Science, Department of Extra-Mural Studies, Sheffield University 1949-59 and for W.E.A. Former Vice-President of the Sheffield Trades and Labour Council. Member of Public Accounts Committee 1964-66. Joint Author of *A History of The Sheffield Trades Council* and *The Growth of Parliamentary Scrutiny*, Pergamon Press, published 1970. Member of Speaker's Conference on Electoral Law 1973. Member of Consultative Assembly of the Council of Europe 1973-77. A Labour Member. Elected for the Penistone division of the West Riding of Yorkshire in June 1959 and sat until his death on 20 May 1978. [1978]

MESSER, Sir Frederick, C.B.E. 7 Kingsdown Avenue, Croydon, Surrey. S. of Robert Messer, Esq., Poor Law Officer. B. 12 May 1886; m. 1 Aug. 1908, Edith Beatrice, d. of Alfred Chapman, Esq., Educ. at Thornhill Board School, Islington. Apprenticed as a French polisher, Treasurer of French Polishers Union 1917-21. Member Middlesex County Council 1925-38, Alderman 1938-52, Vice-Chairman 1946, Chairman 1947. J.P. for Middlesex; Chairman of N.W. Metropolitan Regional Hospital Board until 1953, and of Central Health Services Council 1948-57; of King Edward's Hospital Fund for London of Nuffield Trust, of Medical School Royal Free Hospital School of Medicine. O.St.J.; Chairman of Ministry of Education Advisory Committee on handicapped children 1944-56; Parliamentary Private Secretary to the Rt. Hon. Ernest Bevin, Minister of Labour June 1944-May 1945. Knight Bach. 1953. A Labour and Co-operative Member.

Sat for S. Tottenham May 1929-Oct. 1931 when he was defeated and 1935-50. Elected for Tottenham in Feb. 1950 and sat until he retired in 1959. National Organizer of Industrial Orthopaedic Society. C.B.E. 1949. Died 8 May 1971. [1959]

MEYER, Sir Anthony John Charles, Bart. Cottage Place, Brompton Square, London. Rhewl House, Axton, Holywell, Flintshire. Beefsteak. S. of Sir Frank Meyer, 2nd Bart., MP. B. 1920; m. 1941, Barbadee Violet, d. of A.C. Knight, Esq., J.P. Educ. at Eton, and New Coll., Oxford. Succeeded his father in 1935. Served Scots Guards 1941-45 (wounded in North France 1944). Entered H.M. Treasury 1946; passed to Foreign Office 1947, in London until 1951; 1st Secretary H.M. Embassy, Paris 1951-56; H.M. Embassy Moscow 1956-58; Foreign Office again 1958-62. An Underwriter at Lloyds. Treasurer South Battersea Constituency 1963. A Trustee of the Shakespeare Memorial National Theatre. Founder and Editor of Political Journal *Solon*. Parliamentary Private Secretary to Rt. Hon. Maurice Macmillan, Chief Secretary to Treasury July 1970-Apr. 1972, and Secretary of State for Employment 1972-73. Vice-Chairman Franco-British Parliamentary Group. Member Select Committee on Expenditure. A Conservative. Sat for Eton and Slough from 1964-66, when he was defeated. Elected for the West division of Flintshire in June 1970.* [1979]

MIDDLETON, Lucy Annie. 7 Princes Road, Wimbledon, London. D. of Sidney Cox, Esq. B. 9 May 1894; m. 1 May 1936, J.S. Middleton, Esq., Gen. Sec. of Labour Party 1935-44. (He died 1962). Educ. at Elementary School, Colston's Girls High School, and Bristol University. A Teacher and Lecturer. A Labour Member. Unsuccessfully contested S. Paddington in 1931 and Pudsey and Otley in 1935. Elected for the Sutton division of Plymouth in July 1945 and sat until 1951 when she was defeated. Unsuccessfully contested the Sutton division of Plymouth in 1955. Director and Foundation Chairman of War on Want 1958-68. Vice-President of Trade Union, Labour and Co-operative Democratic History Society from 1969. Author of *Women in the Labour Movement.** [1951]

255

MIDDLEWEEK, Helene Valerie. See HAYMAN, Helene Valerie.

MIKARDO, Ian. House of Commons, London. S. of Morris Mikardo, Esq. B. 9 July 1908; m. 1932, Mary, d. of Benjamin Rosette, Esq. Educ. at Portsmouth Southern Secondary School for Boys, and Portsmouth Municipal Coll. Commercial and Industrial Consultant. Joined the Labour Party in 1930. Member Association of Scientific, Technical and Managerial Staffs, joined 1942; Member of National Executive Council 1945-77; President 1968-73. Poale Zion (Jewish Labour Party), Labour Friends of Israel. Author of many publications on social solutions to economic and industrial problems, frequent contributor to *Tribune* and other journals. Member of National Executive Committee of the Labour Party 1950-59 and 1960-78; Vice-Chairman of the Labour Party 1958-59 and 1969-70; Chairman of the Labour Party 1970-71; Chairman Select Committee on Nationalised Industries 1966-70. Chairman International Committee of the Labour Party 1972. Chairman P.L.P. Mar.-Oct. 1974. A Labour Member. Sat for Reading from 1945-50 and 1955-59, when he was defeated, and for Reading S. from 1950 to 1955. Sat for Poplar from 1964 to Feb. 1974. Elected for the Bethnal Green and Bow division of Tower Hamlets in Feb. 1974.* [1979]

MILLAN, Rt. Hon. Bruce. 46 Hardy Road, London. Son of David Millan, Esq. B. 5 Oct. 1927; m. 22 Aug. 1953, Gwen, d. of R.J. Fairey, Esq. Educ. at Harris Academy, Dundee. A Chartered Accountant. Chairman of Scottish Labour Youth Council 1949-50. An Opposition spokesman in Industry and Aviation 1970-73 and on Scottish Affairs 1973-74. Principal Opposition spokesman on Scottish Affairs from 1979. Parliamentary Under-Secretary of State for Defence for the Royal Air Force Oct. 1964-Apr. 1966. Parliamentary Under-Secretary of State, Scottish Office Apr. 1966-June 1970. Minister of State, Scottish Office Mar. 1974-Apr. 1976. Secretary of State for Scotland Apr. 1976-May 1979. PC. 1975. A Labour Member. Unsuccessfully contested Renfrewshire W. in 1951 and the Craigton division of Glasgow in 1955. Elected

for the Craigton division of Glasgow in 1959.* [1979]

MILLER, Hilary Duppa. House of Commons, London. S. of Lieut.-Commander J.B.P. Duppa-Miller. B. Mar. 1929; m. 1st 1956, Fiona Margaret McDermid: 2ndly, 1976, Jacqueline Roe. Educ. at Eton, Merton Coll., Oxford and London University. Colonial Services 1955-68. Fellow of the Institute of Economic Dev. World Bank. Delegate to Council of Europe 1974-76. Parliamentary Private Secretary to Rt. Hon. Francis Pym, Secretary of State for Defence from 1979. A Conservative. Unsuccessfully contested Barrow-in-Furness in 1970 and Bromsgrove in the by-election of 1971. Elected for Bromsgrove and Redditch in Feb. 1974.* [1979]

MILLER, Dr. Maurice Solomon. 82 Springkell Avenue, Glasgow. S. of David Miller, Esq. B. 16 Aug. 1920; m. 1944, Renée, d. of Joseph Modlin, Esq. Educ. at Shawlands Academy, Glasgow, and Glasgow University, (M.B., Ch. B.). Medical Practitioner and Medical Adviser to British Commonwealth Shipping Company in Port of Glasgow. Joined the Labour Party in 1947. Member of Medical Practitioners' Union. Chairman of Glasgow and West of Scotland branch of Socialist Medical Association. Justice of the Peace for City of Glasgow. Member of Glasgow Town Council from 1950. Parliamentary Private Secretary to George Thomas, Minister of State for Commonwealth Affairs 1967-68. Assistant Government Whip Oct. 1968-Oct. 1969. Parliamentary Private Secretary to Rt. Hon. Judith Hart, Minister of Overseas Development 1970. Parliamentary Private Secretary to Rt. Hon. Edward Short, Leader of House of Commons 1974-76. A Labour Member. Sat for the Kelvingrove division of Glasgow from 1964 to Feb. 1974 and for East Kilbride from Feb. 1974.* [1979]

MILLER, Mrs. Millie. House of Commons, London. 105 Highgate West Hill, London. N. 6 B. Apr. 1923. Educ. at Dame Alice Owen's School. Mayor of Stoke Newington 1957-58; Camden 1967-68. Leader of Camden Council 1971-73. Parliamentary Private Sec. to J.D. Fraser, Minister of State for Prices and Consumer Protection 1976-77. A Labour

Member. Unsuccessfully contested the Ilford N. division of Redbridge in Feb. 1974. Elected for the Ilford N. division of Redbridge in Oct. 1974 and sat until her death on 29 Oct. 1977. Died 29 Oct. 1977. [1978]

MILLIGAN, Rt. Hon. William Rankine. 38 India Street, Edinburgh. Union. S. of the Very Rev. George Milligan, D.D., Moderator of Gen. Assembly of Church of Scotland 1923. B. 12 Dec. 1898; m. 21 Dec. 1925, Muriel Jean, d. of James MacLehose, Esq., LL.D. Educ. at Sherborne School, University Coll., Oxford, and Glasgow University. Served in Highland Light Infantry 1917-19. Member of Scottish bar 1925; K.C. 1945; Solicitor-Gen. for Scotland Nov. 1951-Dec. 1954; Lord Advocate Dec. 1954-Apr. 1960; PC. 1955. A Conservative. Unsuccessfully contested Ayrshire Central in 1950 and 1951. Elected for Edinburgh N. in Jan. 1955 and sat until Apr. 1960 when he was appointed a Judge of the Court of Session, with the judicial title of Lord Milligan. Member of Royal Company of Archers. Judge of the Court of Sessions 1960-73. Died 28 July 1975. [1960]

MILLINGTON, Wing-Commander Ernest Rogers. 4 Gower Street, London. The Chestnuts, Boreham, Essex. S. of Edmund Rogers Millington, Esq., of Rumney. B. 15 Feb. 1916; m. 1st, 1937, Gwendolyn, d. of Sydney Pickard, Esq. (divorced (1974). 2ndly, 1975, Ivy Mary Robinson. Educ. at Chigwell, Coll. of St. Mark and St. John and Birkbeck Coll., London. Served with Lancaster Squad R.A.F. 1940-41. A Labour Member. Sat as Common Wealth MP. for the Chelmsford division of Essex Apr. 1945-Apr. 1946, when he joined the Labour Party, and as Labour MP. until 1950 when he was defeated, D.F.C. 1945. Rejoined R.A.F. 1954-57. Head of Social Education, Shoreditch Comprehensive School 1965-67. In charge of Teachers Centre. London Borough of Newnham from 1967.* [1950]

MILLS, Peter McLay. House of Commons, London. S. of L.H. Mills, Esq. of Exeter. B. 1921; m. 1948, Joan, d. of Arthur Weatherley, Esq. Educ. at Epsom Coll., and Wye Coll.

An Agricultural Student on various farms in Southern England for four years. Former member of the Gen. Synod. Member of General Advisory Committee of Independent Television Authority to 1969. Parliamentary Secretary to the Ministry of Agriculture Apr.-Nov. 1972. Parliamentary Under-Secretary of State for Northern Ireland Nov. 1972-Mar. 1974. Member European Legislation Committee 1974. Member Executive Commonwealth Parliamentary Association. A Conservative. Sat for Torrington 1964-Feb. 1974. Elected for the W. division of Devonshire in Feb. 1974.* [1979]

MILLS, (William) Stratton. 17 Malone Park, Belfast. Junior Carlton, and Ulster. Only s. of Dr. J.V.S. Mills, C.B.E., Resident Magistrate, Belfast. B. 1 July 1932; m. 7 Aug. 1959, Merriel, only d. of Mr. and Mrs. R.J. Whitla, of Belfast, (3 s.). Educ. at Campbell Coll., Belfast, and Queen's University, Belfast. Vice-Chairman Federation of University Conservative and Unionist Associations 1952-53, 1954-55. Parliamentary Private Secretary to Vice-Admiral John Hughes-Hallett, Joint Parliamentary Secretary Ministry of Transport May 1961-Oct. 1964. Gov. British Society for International Understanding. Honorary Secretary Conservative Broadcasting Committee 1962-70. Chairman 1970-73. Joint Chairman Europe-Africa Parliamentary Group. Member Estimates Committee House of Commons 1964-70. Member of Mr. Speaker's Conference on Electoral Law 1967. Member of Executive Committee of 1922 Committee 1967-70 and 1972-73. Solicitor and Company Director. Vice-Chairman of Conservative Committee on Northern Ireland 1972. Resigned from Ulster Unionist Party in Dec. 1972 but continued to take the Conservative Whip until he joined Alliance Party in Apr. 1973. An Alliance Party Member. Elected for Belfast N. in 1959 and sat until he retired in Feb. 1974.* [1974]

MILNE, Edward James. Strathearn, Alston Grove, Seaton Sluice, Northumberland. S. of Edward Milne, Esq., of Aberdeen. B. 18 Oct. 1915; m. 1939, Emily, d. of Robert Constable, Esq. Educ. at Kittybrewster Primary School, Sunnybank Int. School, and

Robert Gordon's Coll., Aberdeen. Lecturer National Council of Labour Colls. (West Midland) 1942-49; Area Organiser (Central Scotland) Union of Shop Distributive and Allied Workers 1951-60. Parliamentary Private Secretary to Sir Frank Soskice, Home Secretary 1964-65. Vice-Chairman P.L.P. 1967-68. Visited Liberia as member of Inter-Parliamentary Union Delegation 1963; Bulgaria I.P.U. Delegation 1970. Secretary Anglo-Norwegian Parliamentary Group. Secretary Anglo-Swedish Parliamentary Group. Visited India as member of Commonwealth Parliamentary Association Delegation 1965. Awarded Grand Order of the Star of Africa (Gold Band) 1964. A Labour Member until Feb. 1974, thereafter an Independent Labour Member. Unsuccessfully contested Rutherglen in 1959. Elected for Blyth at a by-election in Nov. 1960 and sat until he was defeated in Oct. 1974. Contested Blyth as an Independent Labour candidate in Feb. 1974 and defeated the official Labour candidate but in Oct. 1974 was defeated by the official candidate. Unsuccessfully contested Blyth again as an Independent Labour candidate in 1979. Member of Blyth Valley District Council from 1976. Author of *No Shining Armour* (1976).* [1974 2nd ed.]

MILNER, Maj. Rt. Hon. James, M.C., T.D. 95 Whitehall Court, London. 34 and 35 Norfolk Street, London. Albion Walk Chambers, Leeds. Summer Hill, Roundhay, Leeds. United Sports, and R.A.C. S. of J.H. Milner, Esq., of Alwoodley, Leeds. B. 12 Aug. 1889; m. 10 Feb. 1917, Lois Tinsdale, d. of Thomas Brown, Esq., of Roundhay, Leeds. Educ. at Easingwold, and Leeds University, LL.B. Admitted a Solicitor 1911. Commissioner of Oaths; member of the firm of J.H. Milner and Son, Leeds and London; President of Leeds Law Society 1936; member of Council London Law Society and of Court and Council Leeds University; member of Leeds City Council 1923-29; Chairman of Improvements Committee; Dept. Lord Mayor 1928-29. Served overseas 1914-18. M.C. and Bar. Parliamentary Private Secretary to Rt. Hon. C. Addison, Minister of Agriculture 1930-31; Temporary Chairman House of Commons and Chairman of Standing Committees 1935-43; Dept. Chairman of Ways and Means Jan.-Mar. 1943; Chairman of Ways and Means and Dept. Speaker Mar. 1943-May 1945, and Sept. 1945-Oct. 1951; Chairman of Select Committee on Revision of Standing Orders on Private Bills 1945, and of Committee on Standing Orders on Public Bills 1948; Acting Chairman History of Parliament Trust; member of Select Committee on Capital Punishment 1931, of Indian Franchise Committee 1932, of Council International Parliamentary Union, Geneva, of British Delegation to The Hague 1938, Oslo 1939, Cairo 1947 and Rome 1948; Trustee of British Legion Haig Memorial Homes; Vice-President of Association of Municipal Corporations and of Building Societies Association; Dept.-Lieut. for the W. Riding of Yorkshire; PC. 1945. A Labour Member. Elected for S. E. Leeds in Aug. 1929 and sat until Nov. 1951 when he was created Baron Milner of Leeds. Unsuccessful candidate for the Speakership of the House of Commons Nov. 1951. Dept. Speaker of House of Lords. Died 16 July 1967. [1951]

MISCAMPBELL, Norman Alexander. 7 Abbey Road, West Kirby, Lancashire. S. of Alexander Miscampbell, Esq. B. 1925; m. 1961, Miss Margaret Kendall. Educ. at St. Edward's School and Trinity Coll., Oxford. M.A. degree. Barrister-at-Law, Inner Temple, 1952. Member of Hoylake Urban District Council 1956-61. Q.C. 1974. A Recorder of the Crown Court from 1977. A Conservative. Adopted for the Newton division of Lancashire in 1954, but unsuccessful in the general elections of 1955 and 1959. Elected for Blackpool N. in Mar. 1962.* [1979]

MITCHELL, Austin Vernon. 1 Abbey Park Road, Grimsby. S. of Richard Vernon Mitchell, Esq., Dyer. B. 19 Sept. 1934; m. 1st, Patricia Dorothy Jackson (marriage dissolved), (2 d.); 2ndly, Linda Mary McDougall, (1 s. 1 d.). Educ. at Woodbottom Council School, Bingley Grammar School, Manchester University, and Nuffield Coll., Oxford, D. Phil. 1964. A Lecturer in History, Otago University, Dunedin, New Zealand 1959-63. Sen. Lecturer in Politics, University of Canterbury, Christchurch 1963-67.

Official Fellow of Nuffield Coll., Oxford 1967-69. Journalist with Yorkshire Television 1969-71, B.B.C. 1972 and Yorkshire Television 1973. Author of *Whigs in Opposition, 1815-30*, and *Politics and People in New Zealand*. Parliamentary Private Secretary to J.D. Fraser, Minister of State for Prices and Consumer Protection Nov. 1977-May 1979. Opposition Whip from Nov. 1979. A Labour Member. Elected for Grimsby in Apr. 1977.* [1979]

MITCHELL, Lieut.-Col. Colin Campbell. Leith Hall, Huntly, Aberdeenshire. Caledonian, Garrick, Lansdowne, and Public Schools. S. of Colin Mitchell, Esq., M.C. B. 17 Nov. 1925; m. 31 Mar. 1956, Jean Hamilton Susan, d. of Wing-Commander Stephen Phillips, M.C. Educ. at Whitgift. Served with Argyll and Sutherland Highlanders 1944-68. Parliamentary Private Secretary to Rt. Hon. Gorden Campbell, Secretary of State for Scotland 1972-73. Voted against entry to E.E.C. on 28 Oct. 1971. A Conservative. Elected for Aberdeenshire W. in June 1970 and sat until he retired in Feb. 1974.* [1974]

MITCHELL, David Bower. 46 Eaton Terrace, London. 1 Hare Place, London. Berry Horn Cottage, Odiham, Hampshire. S. of James Mitchell, Esq. B. 1928; m. 1954, Pamela Elaine, d. of Dr. Haward, (2 s. 1 d.). Educ. at Aldenham. Pursued a farming career for six years. A Wine Shipper and Director of a firm of wine merchants; a Liveryman of the Vintners' Company. Served on St. Pancras Borough Council 1956-59. Appointed an Opposition Whip Oct. 1965, resigned Nov. 1967. Secretary Conservative Parliamentary Labour Committee 1968-70. Parliamentary Private Secretary to Rt. Hon. Sir Keith Joseph, MP., Secretary of State for Social Services July 1970-Mar. 1974. Chairman Conservative Smaller Business Committee 1974. Under-Secretary of State for Industry from May 1979. A Conservative. Unsuccessfully contested the St. Pancras N. division in the 1959 general election. Sat for the Basingstoke division of Hampshire from 1964.* [1979]

MITCHELL, Richard Charles. 49 Devonshire Road, Polygon, Southampton, Hamp-

shire. S. of Charles Mitchell, Esq. B. 22 Aug. 1927; m. 27 May 1950, Doreen Lilian, d. of Albert Gregory, Esq., (1 s. 1 d.). Educ. at Tauntons School, Southampton, Godalming Grammar School, and Southampton University, B.Sc. (Economics) Hons. A Teacher; Dept. Headmaster of Bartley Secondary School 1965-66. Member Southampton City Council 1955-67. Parliamentary Private Secretary to Rt. Hon. Patrick Gordon Walker, Secretary of State for Education 1967-68. Chairman Education Group, P.L.P. 1968-70. Parliamentary Private Secretary to Rt. Hon. Shirley Williams, Secretary of State for Prices and Consumer Protection 1974-76. Member Labour Delegation to European Parliament 1975-79. Member Bureau Socialist Group of European Parliament. Member of Speaker's Panel of Chairmen. A Labour Member. Unsuccessfully contested the New Forest in 1959, and the Test division of Southampton in 1964. Sat for the Test division of Southampton from 1966-70, when he was defeated. Elected for the Itchen division of Southampton in May 1971.* [1979]

MITCHELL, Thomas James. B. in Cork 1931. A Building Inspector. Served a sentence of 10 years' penal servitude in Belfast Gaol for taking part in the raid on the depot of the Royal Inniskilling Fusiliers on 17 Oct. 1954. A Sinn Fein Member. Elected for Mid Ulster in May 1955 but was declared incapable of election on 18 July 1955, when a new writ was moved. Again elected at the by-election on 11 Aug. 1955 but a petition to unseat him on the grounds that he was a felon was upheld by the Northern Ireland High Court on 7 Oct. 1955 and by the House of Commons on 25 Oct. 1955; his opponent was declared elected. Unsuccessfully contested Mid Ulster again at a by-election in May 1956 and in 1959, 1964 and 1966.* [1955]

MITCHISON, Gilbert Richard, C.B.E., Q.C. 2 Harcourt Buildings, Temple, London. Carradale House, Carradale, Campbeltown, Argyllshire. Athenaeum. S. of A.M. Mitchison, Esq. B. 23 Mar. 1890; m. 1916, Naomi, d. of Dr. J.S. Haldane, C.H., F.R.S. Educ. at Eton, and New Coll., Oxford. Barrister-at-Law, Inner Temple 1917. K.C. 1946. Served with Queen's Bays (S.R.) 1914-18. Maj. G.S.O. 2 British Mission to French Forces in Italy 1915. Had French Croix de Guerre. Member of P.L.P. Parliamentary Committee 1955-64. Opposition spokesman on Housing and Local Government 1955-59, on Treasury and Trade Affairs 1959-61, on Science 1961-63, on Works 1962-63, on Treasury Affairs 1962-63, and on Pensions 1963-64. Parliamentary Secretary to Ministry of Land and Natural Resources Oct. 1964-Apr. 1966. A Labour Member. Unsuccessfully contested the Kings Norton division of Birmingham in 1931 and 1935. Elected for the Kettering division of Northamptonshire and the Soke of Peterborough in July 1945 and sat until Aug. 1964 when he was created Baron Mitchison (Life Peerage). C.B.E. 1953. Member of Harlow Development Corporation 1966-70. Died 14 Feb. 1970.   [1964]

MOATE, Roger Denis. 23 Ponsonby Terrace, London. Brownings, Stockers Hill, Rodmersham Green, Sittingbourne, Kent. St. Stephen's, and Constitutional. S. of H.S. Moate, Esq., Accountant. B. 12 May 1938; m. Dec. 1960, Hazel, d. of F.J. Skinner, Esq., (1 s. 1 d.). Educ. at Latymer Upper School. Director of Lloyds Brokers, Alexander Howden Insurance Brokers Limited. Vice-Chairman of Greater London Young Conservatives 1964-65 and member of the Young Conservative National Advisory Committee 1963-66. Honorary Secretary British American Parliamentary Group. Voted against entry to E.E.C. on 28 Oct. 1971. A Conservative. Unsuccessfully contested the Faversham division of Kent in 1966. Elected for the Faversham division of Kent in June 1970.*   [1979]

MOERAN, Edward Warner. House of Commons, London. S. of E.J. Moeran, Esq. B. 1903. Educ. at Christ's Coll., Finchley, and University of London. A Solicitor. Member of the Society of Labour Lawyers and of Atomic Scientists' Association. A Labour Member. Unsuccessfully contested, as a Common Wealth candidate, the Newark division of Nottinghamshire in June 1943, and, as a Labour candidate, the Thirsk and Malton division of the N. Riding of Yorkshire in 1945. Elected for S. Bedfordshire in Feb. 1950 and

sat until 1951 when he was defeated. Unsuccessfully contested S. Bedfordshire in 1955. President of W. London Law Society 1970-71. Chairman of Solicitors' Ecology Group 1972-74. Author of works on conveyancing and social welfare law.*   [1951]

MOLLOY, William John. 2A Uneeda Drive, Greenford, Middlesex. B. 26 Oct. 1918; m. Eva Lewis, (1 d.). Educ. at St. Thomas Elementary School, Swansea, and University Coll., Swansea, extra mural, political economy. Secretary. Member of T. & G.W.U. 1938. U.S.D.A.W. 1952, C.S.U. and I.P.C.S. 1946-52 and Co-operative Party 1952. "Civil Service Staff Side" lecturer on "British Trade Union Movement" and "Whitleyism" 1947-52. Chairman Foreign Office Departmental Whitley Council Germany and Austria Sections 1949-52. Member Fulham Borough Council 1956-64; Chairman Libraries Committee 1959-60; Leader of the Council 1960-63. Gov. Holland Park Co-ed Comp. School 1958-64. Editor *Civil Service Review* 1949-52. Fellow Royal Geographical Society and member of Council. Member of the Court, Reading University. Parliamentary Private Secretary to Rt. Hon. John Stonehouse, Minister of Posts and Telecommunications 1969-70. Vice-Chairman P.L.P. European Affairs Group. Member Commons Estimates Committee 1968-70. Member Assemblies Council of Europe and Western European Union 1969-73. Parliamentary Adviser London Trades Council Transport Committee. Member of European Parliament May 1976-Mar. 1977. Parliamentary Adviser to Civil Service Union. Parliamentary Adviser to Confederation of Health Service Employees. A Labour Member. Elected for Ealing N. in Oct. 1964 and sat until 1979, when he was defeated.*   [1979]

MOLSON, Rt. Hon. Arthur Hugh Elsdale. White Hall, Chinley, via Stockport. Cherrytrees, Kelso, Roxburghshire. 6 Lowndes Court, Lowndes Square, London. Athenaeum, and Carlton. S. of Maj. J.E. Molson, MP. for Gainsborough. B. 29 June 1903; m. 1949, Nancy, d. of W.H. Astington, Esq., of Bramhall, Cheshire. Educ. at Royal Naval Coll., Osborne and Dartmouth, at

Lancing and New Coll., Oxford. 1st Class Hons. in Jurisprudence. President of the Union 1925; Barrister-at-Law, Inner Temple 1931; Political Secretary Association of Chambers of Commerce of India 1926-29. Served with 36th Searchlight Regiment 1939-41, Staff Capt. 11 A.A. division 1941-42. Member of Central Housing Advisory Committee 1943-51. Parliamentary Secretary Ministry of Works Nov. 1951-Nov. 1953. Joint Parliamentary Secretary Ministry of Transport and Civil Aviation Nov. 1953-Jan. 1957; Minister of Works Jan. 1957-Oct. 1959. PC. 1956. Member of Monckton Commission on the Constitution of Rhodesia and Nyasaland 1960. A Conservative. Unsuccessfully contested the Aberdare division of Merthyr Tydfil in 1929. Sat for the Doncaster division from Oct. 1931 to 1935 when he was defeated. Elected for the High Peak division of Derbyshire in Oct. 1939 and sat until Jan. 1961 when he was created Baron Molson (Life Peerage). Member of Monckton Commission on Rhodesia and Nyasaland 1960. Chairman of Council for Protection of Rural England 1968-71, President from 1971.*   [1961]

MOLYNEAUX, James Henry. House of Commons, London. S. of William Molyneaux, Esq., of Seacash, Killead, Co. Antrim. B. 27 Aug. 1920; unmarried. Educ. at Aldergrove School, Co. Antrim. R.A.F. 1941-46. Vice-Chairman Eastern Special Care Hospital Committee 1966-73. Chairman Antrim Mental Health Branch 1967-70. Honorary Secretary S. Antrim Unionist Association 1964-70. Chairman Antrim division Unionist Association. J.P. for Co. Antrim from 1957. Antrim County Councillor 1964-73. Chairman Crumlin Branch British Legion. Sovereign Grand Master of British Commonwealth Royal Black Institution. Vice-President Ulster Unionist Council. Leader U.U.U.C. in House of Commons from Oct. 1974 and of Ulster Unionist Group from May 1977. An Ulster Unionist Member. Sat for Antrim S. from June 1970. Resigned Ulster Unionist Whip 24 Mar. 1972. Whip to U.U.U.C. Mar.-Oct. 1974. Leader of Official Unionist Party from Sept. 1979.*   [1979]

MONCKTON, Rt. Hon. Sir Walter, K.C.M.G., K.C.V.O., Q.C., M.C. 2 Harcourt Buildings, Temple, London. Brooks's, and Pratt's. S. of Frank W. Monckton, Esq., of Ightham Warren, Kent. B. 17 Jan. 1891; m. 1st, 1914, Mary Adelaide, d. of Sir T. Colyer Fergusson (divorced 1947); 2ndly, 1947, Hon. Bridget Helen Ruthven, C.B.E., d. of 9th Baron Ruthven (she succeeded as Baroness Ruthven of Freeland in 1956). Educ. at Harrow, and Balliol Coll., Oxford. K.C. 1930 Called to the Inner Temple 15 May 1919. Served with Royal W. Kent Regiment 1914-18, Capt., M.C. 1919. Recorder of Hythe 1930-37. K.C.V.O. 1937 for services to the Royal Family during the Abdication crisis; K.C.M.G. 1945; G.C.V.O. 1964. Solicitor-Gen. May-July 1945; Attorney-Gen. to Duchy of Cornwall 1932-47, and 1948-51. Director-Gen. of Press and Censorship Bureau 1939-40. Dept. Director-Gen. Ministry of Information and additional Dept. Under-Secretary of State for Foreign Affairs 1940. Director-Gen. 1940-41. Chairman of St. George's Hospital 1945-51. Director-Gen. of British Propaganda and Information Services, Cairo 1941-42. Minister of Labour and National Service (Cabinet) Oct. 1951-Dec. 1955; Minister of Defence Dec. 1955-Oct. 1956. Paymaster General, with a seat in the Cabinet, Oct. 1956-Jan. 1957. PC. 1951. Honorary D.C.L. (Oxon.) 1952; Honorary LL.D. (Bristol) 1954. Honorary LL.D. (Sussex) 1963. U.K. Delegate on Allied Reparations Commission, Moscow 1945. A Conservative. Elected for Bristol W. in Feb. 1951 and sat until Jan. 1957 when he was created Visct. Monckton of Brenchley. Chancellor of University of Sussex 1961-65. Chairman of Midland Bank 1957-64, of Iraq Petroleum Company 1958. Chairman of Advisory Commission on Central Africa 1960. Visitor of Balliol Coll., Oxford 1957-65. President of M.C.C. 1956-57, of British Bankers' Association 1962. Died 9 Jan. 1965.   [1956]

MONEY, Ernle David Drummond. High House, Rendlesham, Nr. Woodbridge, Suffolk. 5 Paper Buildings, Temple, London. Carlton. S. of Lieut-Col. E.F.D. Money, D.S.O. B. 17 Feb. 1931; m. 21 July 1960, Susan Barbara, d. of Lieut.-Col. Dudley Lister, M.C. Educ. at Marlborough Coll., and Oriel Coll., Oxford. Served in Suffolk

Regiment 1949-51; 4th Battalion Suffolk Regiment T.A. 1951-56; Tutor and Lecturer Swinton Conservative Coll. 1955; called to the bar by Lincoln's Inn 1958; in practice thereafter on S.E. Circuit. Secretary to Conservative Parliamentary Arts and Amenities Committee 1970-73; Vice-Chairman 1974. A Co-opted member of the Greater London Council Arts Committee 1972-73. Member of the General Council of the Bar 1962-66. Secretary to All-Party Parliamentary Committee for the Homeless and Rootless and the All-Party Parliamentary Association Football Committee. Member of the Court of the University of East Anglia 1970. Member of the Committee of Gainsborough's Birthplace, Sudbury 1968. Member of Government Advisory Committee on Theatres. Secretary East Anglian Conservative Members Committee. Opposition spokesman on the Arts June-Oct. 1974. A Conservative. Elected for Ipswich in June 1970 and sat until Oct. 1974 when he was defeated.*   [1974 2nd ed.]

MONKS, Constance Mary. House of Commons, London. D. of Ellis Green, Esq. B. May 1911; m. 1937, Jack Monks, Esq. Educ. at Chorley Grammar School, and City of Leeds Training Coll. Chorley Borough Councillor 1947-67; Alderman 1967-74; Mayor 1959-60. Member of Lancashire County Council 1961-64. A Teacher. A Conservative. Unsuccessfully contested Chorley in 1966. Elected for Chorley in June 1970 and sat until Feb. 1974 when she was defeated. O.B.E. 1962. J.P. for Chorley.*   [1974]

MONRO, Hector Seymour Peter, A.E.M., J.P., D.L. Williamwood, Kirtlebridge, Lockerbie, Dumfriesshire. Caledonian, and M.C.C. S. of Capt. Alastair Monro, Queens Own Cameron Highlanders. B. 4 Oct. 1922; m. 4 Mar. 1949. Elizabeth Anne Welch, d. of Maj. H. Welch, (2 s.). Educ. at Canford School, and King's Coll., Cambridge. Served R.A.F. 1941-46; R. Auxiliary A.F. 1947-54, A.E.M. 1953. Chairman Dumfriesshire Conservative Association 1958-63. Member Dumfries County Council 1952-67. Chairman Dumfries and Galloway Police Committee. Area Executive N.F.U. Member Queens Bodyguard for Scotland, Royal Company of Archers. Member Scot-

tish Rugby Union 1957-77; Vice-President 1975; President 1976-77. Conservative Whip Jan. 1967-June 1970. Lord-Commissioner of Treasury and Government Whip June 1970-July 1971. Under-Secretary of State for Scotland July 1971-Mar. 1974. Opposition spokesman on Scottish Affairs 1974-75. Opposition spokesman on Sport 1974-79. Dept.-Lieut. for Dumfriesshire from 1973. Under-Secretary of State for the Environment and 'Minister for Sport' from May 1979. A Conservative. Sat for Dumfriesshire from Oct. 1964.*   [1979]

MONSLOW, Walter. Ashleigh, 100 Crouch Hill, Hornsey, London. B. 1895; m. 2ndly, 1960, Jean Baird, d. of Rev. Angus Macdonald. Organising Secretary of Associated Society of Locomotive Engineers and Firemen. Parliamentary Private Secretary to G.S. Lindgren, Parliamentary Secretary Ministry of Civil Aviation 1949-50 and to Rt. Hon. Maurice Webb, Minister of Food 1950-51. A Labour Member. Unsuccessfully contested Newcastle upon Tyne Central in 1935. Elected for Barrow-in-Furness in July 1945 and sat until he retired in Mar. 1966. Member of Wrexham Rural District Council to 1937. Created Baron Monslow (Life Peerage) May 1966. Died 12 Oct. 1966.   [1966]

MONTAGU, Alexander Victor Edward Paulet. See HINCHINGBROOKE, Alexander Victor Edward Paulet Montagu, Visct.

MONTAGU-DOUGLAS-SCOTT, Lord William Walter, M.C. 21 Eaton Square, London. Eildon Hall, St. Boswells. S. of 7th Duke of Buccleuch. B. 17 Jan. 1896; m. 27 Apr. 1937, Lady Rachel Douglas-Home, d. of Charles, 13th Earl of Home. Educ. at Eton and Royal Military Coll., Sandhurst. Lieut.-Col. 10th Hussars; served 1914-18 and 1940-45; Aide-de-Camp to Gov.-Gen. of Canada 1925-26; Military Secretary to Field-Marshal Viscount Alexander of Tunis 1943-44. Member of King's Bodyguard for Scotland (Royal Company of Archers). A Conservative. Elected for Roxburgh and Selkirk in 1935 and sat until 1950, when he was defeated. Dept.-Lieut. and J.P. for Roxburghshire. Died 30 Jan. 1958.   [1950]

MONTAGUE, Frederick, C.B.E. 68 Camrose Avenue, Edgware. S. of John Montague, Esq. B. 1876; m. 1911, Constance Craig of Runcorn (she died 1964). Served in France, Belgium, Egypt and Palestine with 18th (S.) Battalion K.R.R.C. 1915-19; Member of Islington Borough Council, Alderman 1919-25. Under-Secretary of State for Air June 1929-Aug. 1931. Parliamentary Secretary Ministry of Transport May 1940-May 1941, of Aircraft Production May 1941-Mar. 1942. A Labour Member. Sat for W. Islington from Dec. 1923-Oct. 1931 when he was defeated and from 1935 until June 1947 when he was created Baron Amwell. C.B.E. 1946. Resigned Labour Whip in House of Lords Dec. 1955. Vice-President of Institute of Magicians. Died 15 Oct. 1966.   [1947]

MONTGOMERY, (William) Fergus. House of Commons, London. S. of William Montgomery, Esq., of Hebburn. B. 25 Nov. 1927; m. Joyce, d. of George Riddle, Esq., of Jarrow. Educ. at Jarrow Grammar School, and Bede Coll., Durham. Served in R.N. 1946-48. Member Hebburn Urban District Council 1950-58. Chairman Young Conservatives 1957-58. Finance Company Director and former Teacher. Parliamentary Private Secretary to Rt. Hon. Margaret Thatcher, Secretary of State for Education and Science 1973-74 and Leader of Opposition 1975-76. A Conservative. Sat for Newcastle E. from 1959-64, when he was defeated. Unsuccessfully contested Consett in 1955. MP. for Brierley Hill from Apr. 1967-Feb. 1974, when he unsuccessfully contested Dudley W. Elected for Altrincham and Sale in Oct. 1974.*   [1979]

MOODY, Arthur Seymour. 150 Boothferry Road, Hull. S. of William Henry Moody, Esq. B. 6 June 1891; m. 1937 Edith Mary Coney. Educ. at Council School, and Technical Coll., Hull. A Joiner. Member of Hull City Council 1934-37. Member of National Executive Committee of Labour Party 1942-46. A Labour Member. Unsuccessfully contested the Fairfield division of Liverpool in 1935. Sat for the Fairfield division of Liverpool from July 1945 to Feb. 1950. Elected for E. Gateshead in Feb. 1950 and sat until he retired in 1964. Died 12 Dec. 1971.   [1964]

MOONMAN, Eric. House of Commons, London. S. of Borach Moonman, Esq., Dairyman. B. 29 Apr. 1929; m. 1962, Jane (2 s. 1 d.). Educ. at Elementary School, and Manchester University, M.Sc. (Manchester). Sen. Research Fellow, University of Manchester 1964-66. Human Relations Adviser, British Institute of Management 1956-62. Senior Lecturer in Industrial Relations, S.W. Essex Technical Coll. 1962-64. Member of Stepney Borough Council 1961-65, Leader 1964-65, and of Tower Hamlets Borough Council 1964-67. European Director Scholastic International 1971-73. Author of *Manager and The Organisation* 1961, *Employee Security* 1963, and Editor of *European Science and Technology*, 1968, *Communications in an Expanding Organization* 1970, *Reluctant Partnership* 1970. Editor of *British Computers and Industrial Innovation* 1971. F.R.S.A. Chairman All-Party Management Affairs Committee. Chairman Parliamentary Mental Health Unit. Parliamentary Private Secretary to Rt. Hon. Patrick Gordon Walker, Secretary of State for Education and Science 1967, previously Minister without Portfolio 1967. A Labour Member. Unsuccessfully contested Chigwell in 1964. Sat for Billericay from Mar. 1966-June 1970, when he was defeated. Elected for Basildon in Feb. 1974 and sat until 1979, when he was defeated. Chairman of Zionist Federation 1975. Director of Group Relations Educational Trust from 1979.*   [1979]

MOORE, John Edward Michael. House of Commons, London. S of Edward O. Moore, Esq. B. 26 Nov. 1937; m. 23 June 1963, Sheila Sarah Tillotson, (2 s. 1 d.). Educ. at Licensed Victuallers' School, Slough, and London School of Economics. Chairman Conservative Association at London School of Economics 1958. President Student Union London School of Economics 1959-60. Lived in U.S.A. from 1960-65. Democratic Precinct Capt. 1962 Ward Chairman, Evanston, Illinois 1964. Director of Dean Witter (International) Ltd. 1968-79, Chairman 1975-79. Member of Lloyd's from 1978. Chairman Stepney Green Conservative Association 1968. Vice-Chairman Conservative Party with Responsibility for Youth 1975-79. Member Merton Borough Council 1971-74.

Under-Secretary of State for Energy from May 1979. A Conservative. Sat for Croydon Central from Feb. 1974.* [1979]

MOORE, Lieut.-Col. Sir Thomas Cecil Russell, Bart., C.B.E. 87 Harley House, Regent's Park, London. Ladykirk, Monkton, Ayrshire. Carlton, Garrick, St. James's, Conservative (Glasgow), and Ayr Town & County. S. of John Watt Moore, Esq., of Fintona, Co. Tyrone, and Mary, d. of Alexander Kirkpatrick, Esq., of Closeburn Castle, Dumfriesshire. B. 16 Sept. 1888. M. 1st, 19 Feb. 1925, Jean, d. of William Gemmill, Esq., and widow of J.H. Pettigrew, Esq., of Glasgow (she died 6 Feb. 1945); 2ndly, 26 Sept. 1950, Penelope, widow of Robert Angus, Esq., of Ladykirk, Monkton, Ayrshire. Educ. at Portora, Enniskillen, and Trinity Coll., Dublin. Lieut.-Col. Reserve of Officers. Served in France, Ireland and Russia 1914-19 (despatches twice) O.B.E. 1918, C.B.E. 1920; Food Controller in Russia 1918-19; attached to Ministry of Home Affairs, Ulster 1923-24, from W.O. Had Orders of the White Eagle of Serbia and of St. Vladimir and of St. Anne of Russia and Order of Merit, Hungary. Honorary Associate R.I.B.A.; F.R.G.S.; a Freeman of the City of London; Past Master Needlemakers' Company. Knight Bach. 1937. Chairman of Eastwoods Limited, of International League for the Protection of Horses, Anglo-Italian Society for the Protection of Animals and British Hungarian Cultural Fellowship; Fellow Royal Incorp. of Scottish Architects. Director Gen. Accident Assurance Corporation. On Council of R.S.P.C.A. A Conservative. Unsuccessfully contested Coatbridge in 1924. Sat for the Ayr Burghs from June 1925 to Feb. 1950 and for the Ayr division of Ayrshire and Bute from Feb. 1950 until he retired in 1964. Created Bart. 1956. Died 9 Apr. 1971.

[1964]

MORE, Jasper, J.P., D.L. Linley Hall, Bishop's Castle, Shropshire. Travellers', and Brooks's. S. of Thomas Jasper Mytton More, Esq. B. July 1907; m. Feb. 1944, Clare Mary Hope-Edwardes. Educ. at Eton, and King's Coll., Cambridge. A Landowner and Farmer. Barrister of Lincoln's Inn 1930 and Middle Temple 1931. Practised 1930-39.

Served 1939-42 with Ministry of Economic Warfare, Ministry of Aircraft Production and Light Metals Control. Commissioned 1943 and served as Legal Officer in Italy with Allied Commission, 8th Army and 5th Army 1944-45. Legal Adviser British Military Administration, Dodecanese M.E.F. 1946. Vice-Chairman Shrewsbury Conservative Association 1951-57. Vice-Chairman Ludlow Conservative Association 1957-60. J.P. for Shropshire 1951, Dept.-Lieut. Shropshire 1955. Member Shropshire County Council 1958-70, and from 1973. Assistant Government Whip Feb. 1964; Opposition Whip 1964-70. Vice-Chamberlain of H.M. Household June 1970-Oct. 1971, when he resigned. Voted against entry to E.E.C. on 28 Oct. 1971. Knighted June 1979. A Conservative. Elected for the Ludlow division of Shropshire at a by-election in 1960 and sat until he retired in 1979.* [1979]

MORGAN, (Dafydd) Elystan. Dolau, Llandre, Cardiganshire. S. of Dewi Morgan, Esq., Journalist. B. 7 Dec. 1932; m. 14 Nov. 1959, Alwen, d. of William Roberts, Esq., (1 s. 1 d.). Educ. at Ardwyn Grammar School, and University of Wales, Aberystwyth. LL.B. (Hons.). Former Partner in North Wales firm of Solicitors 1958-68. Barrister-at-Law, Gray's Inn 1971. Joint Under-Secretary of State Home Office Apr. 1968-June 1970. President Association of Welsh Local Authorities 1967-73. Chairman Welsh Parliamentary Party 1967-68 and 1971. Dept. Opposition spokesman Home Affairs 1970-72 and Welsh Affairs 1972-74. Unsuccessfully contested, as a Plaid Cymru candidate, the Wrexham division of Denbighshire in Mar. and May 1955 and 1959, and Merionethshire in 1964. A Labour Member. Elected for Cardiganshire in Mar. 1966 and sat until Feb. 1974 when he was defeated. Unsuccessfully contested Cardiganshire again in Oct. 1974 and Anglesey in 1979.* [1974]

MORGAN, Dr. Hyacinth Bernard Wenceslaus. 26 Hampstead Lane, London. S. of Leo F. Morgan, Esq., Accountant. B. 11 Sept. 1885 in West Indies; m. 1930 Mary, d. of David Powell, Esq. Educ. at Grenada Grammar School, and Glasgow University, graduated in Medicine M.B., Ch.B. 1909,

M.D. 1914, finally Surgical Specialist 1917-18. Served overseas 1914-19. Medical Adviser and Consultant Specialist on Industrial Diseases to T.U.C. General Council from 1933; Physician Manor House Hospital, London. Chief Medical Adviser, Union of Post Office Workers and of Federation of Post Office Supervisors; Late member of Greenwich and Paddington Borough Councils. A Labour Member. Unsuccessfully contested Camberwell N.W. in 1922, 1923 and 1924. Sat for Camberwell N.W. from May 1929-Oct. 1931 when he retired and for Rochdale from July 1940-Feb. 1950. Elected for Warrington in Feb. 1950 and sat until he retired in 1955. Member of Council of British Medical Association. A Roman Catholic. Died 7 May 1956. [1954]

MORGAN, William Geraint Oliver, Q.C. House of Commons, London. B. 1920; m. 1957. Educ. at University Coll. of Wales, Aberystwyth, and Trinity Hall, Cambridge. Served with Royal Marines 1939-46, Maj, Barrister-at-Law, Gray's Inn 1947, Q.C. 1971. A Recorder of the Crown Court from 1972. Voted against entry to E.E.C. on 28 Oct. 1971. A Conservative. Unsuccessfully contested Merioneth in 1951 and Huyton in 1955. Elected for the Denbigh division of Denbighshire in 1959.* [1979]

MORGAN-GILES, Rear-Admiral Morgan Charles, D.S.O., O.B.E., G.M. Upton Park, Alresford, Hampshire. Carlton, and Australian (Sydney). S. of F.C. Morgan Giles, Esq., O.B.E., M.R.I.N.A. B. 19 June 1914; m. 1st, 1946 Pamela Bushell, of Australia (she died 2 June 1966), (2 s. 4 d.); 2ndly, 1968, Mrs. Marigold Steel. Educ. at Clifton Coll., and in Royal Navy. Joined the Royal Navy in 1932 as a Public School entry, serving on the China Station and in destroyers. Served in H.M.S. *Emerald* on Trans-Atlantic convoys and in H.M.S. *Arethusa* during the Norwegian campaign and in the Mediterranean. With Coastal Forces, Malta 1943; Senior Naval Officer in the Adriatic and Jugoslavia 1944. G.M. 1941. M.B.E. 1942, O.B.E. 1943, D.S.O. 1944.Combined operations with the Army and Royal Marine Commandoes and liaison with Marshal Tito's Partisan Forces. Capt. of H.M.S.

Vernon 1959-60, and of H.M.S. *Belfast*, Flag ship of the Far East Fleet 1961-62. Promoted Rear-Admiral in Oct. 1962. President Royal Naval Coll., Greenwich 1962-64. Retired at own request in order to become Member for Winchester division in May 1964. Vice-Chairman Conservative Party Defence Committee 1965. Chairman H.M.S. Belfast Trust 1961. Chairman Anzac Group Conservative Commonwealth and Overseas Council. A Conservative. Sat for Winchester from May 1964 until he retired in 1979.* [1979]

MORLEY, Ralph. 40 Athelstan Road, Southampton. S. of Thomas Walter Morley, Esq. B. 25 Oct. 1882. Unmarried. Educ. at Modern School, Chichester, and University Coll., Southampton, M.A. A School Master. J.P. for Southampton; President of National Union of Teachers 1946-47 and of National Federation of Class Teachers 1928, Gen. Secretary 1937-42; Chairman Itchen Urban District Council 1920-21. A Labour Member. Unsuccessfully contested Southampton in 1935. Sat for Southampton from 1929-31 when he was defeated and from July 1945-Feb. 1950. Elected for the Itchen division of Southampton in Feb. 1950 and sat until he retired in May 1955. Secretary of Southampton branch of Social Democratic Federation 1907-11. Served in France 1915-19. Died 14 June 1955. [1954]

MORRIS, Rt. Hon. Alfred. 83 Mayow Road, London. S. of George Henry Morris, Esq. B. 23 Mar. 1928; m. 1950, Irene Jones. Educ. at Manchester Elementary Schools, and matriculated by means of Evening School tuition. Ruskin Coll., Oxford 1949-50, St. Catherine's Coll., University of Oxford 1950-53; Department of Education, University of Manchester 1953-54, M.A. (Oxon.) and Dip.Ed. (Manchester). National Officer (Industrial Relations) Electricity Supply Industry. Joined the Labour Party in 1944. Former National Chairman of the Labour League of Youth. Parliamentary Private Secretary to Rt. Hon. T.F. Peart, Minister of Agriculture, Fisheries and Food Oct. 1964-May 1967 and Lord President of the Council and Leader of the House of Commons 1968-70. Chairman Parliamentary Co-operative Group 1970-71. Opposition Front Bench spokesman on the Social Services 1970-74. Parliamentary Under-Secretary of State, Department of Health and Social Security with special responsibility for the Disabled Mar. 1974-May 1979. Promoted three Acts of Parliament as Private Member; the Chronically Sick and Disabled Persons Act 1970, the Food and Drugs (Milk) Act 1970, and the Police Act 1972. Parliamentary Adviser to the Police Federation 1971-74. Treasurer and member of Executive Committee British Group of Inter-Parliamentary Union 1971-74. Member of General Advisory Council B.B.C. 1968-74. Privy Council Representative on Council of Royal Coll. of Veterinary Surgeons 1969-74. First-ever recipient of Field Marshal Lord Harding Award for outstanding services to the disabled 1971, and Louis Braille Memorial Award of the National League for the Blind for distinguished services to the blind 1971. An Opposition spokesman on Social Services from 1979. PC. 1979. A Labour Member. Unsuccessfully contested the Wythenshawe division of Manchester in 1959 and the Garston division of Liverpool in 1951. Elected for the Wythenshawe division of Manchester in Oct. 1964.* [1979]

MORRIS, Rt. Hon. Charles Richard. House of Commons, London. S. of George Henry Morris, Esq. B. 1926; m. 1950, Pauline, d. of Albert Dunn, Esq., (2 d.). Postal and Telegraph Officer. Member Manchester City Council 1954-63. Chairman Manchester Corporation Transport Committee 1959-62. Member National Executive Council Union of Post Office Workers 1959-63. In 1963 was awarded Ford Foundation/English Speaking Union Travel Grant tenable in the United States. Parliamentary Private Secretary to Rt. Hon. Anthony Wedgwood Benn, Postmaster-Gen. Oct. 1964-Jan. 1966. Assistant Government Whip Jan. 1966-July 1967. Vice-Chamberlain to Royal Household July 1967-Oct. 1969. Treasurer H.M. Household (Dept. Chief Whip) Oct. 1969-June 1970. Parliamentary Private Secretary to the Rt. Hon. Harold Wilson, Leader of the Opposition July 1970-Mar. 1974. Minister of State for Urban Affairs Mar.-Oct. 1974. Minister of State, Civil Service Department Oct. 1974-May 1979. Appointed a PC. Jan. 1978. A

Labour Member. Unsuccessfully contested the Cheadle division in 1959. Elected for the Openshaw division of Manchester in Dec. 1963.* [1979]

MORRIS, Harry. 4 Kenwood Avenue, Sheffield 7. S. of Jacob Morris, Esq., of Sheffield. B. 7 Oct. 1893; m. 11 June 1924, Florence, d. of Henry Isaacs, Esq., of Leeds. Educ. privately and at Tivoli House School, Gravesend. A Solicitor 1920-36, Barrister-at-Law, Gray's Inn 1936. Member of Sheffield City Council 1920-26 and 1929-37. Served in the Army 1914-18 and 1940-45. A Labour Member. Sat for the Central division of Sheffield from July 1945-Feb. 1950 and for the Neepsend division of Sheffield from Feb. 1950 until he resigned in Mar. 1950. Created Baron Morris of Kenwood June 1950. Died 1 July 1954. [1950]

MORRIS, Rt. Hon. John, Q.C. House of Commons, London. S. of D.W. Morris, Esq. of Talybont, Cardiganshire. B. 1931; m. Margaret, 1959, d. of Edward Lewis, Esq., O.B.E., J.P., of Llandysul, (3 d.). Educ. at University Coll. of Wales, Aberystwyth, and Gonville and Caius Coll., Cambridge. Holker Senior Exhibitioner of Gray's Inn. Barrister-at-Law, Gray's Inn 1954. Member U.K. Delegation Consultative Assemblies Council of Europe and Western European Union 1963-64. Parliamentary Secretary to the Ministry of Power Oct. 1964-Jan. 1966. Joint Parliamentary Secretary Ministry of Transport from Jan. 1966-Apr. 1968. Chairman National Road Safety Advisory Council 1967-68. Chairman Joint Review of British Railways 1966-67. Member U.K. Delegates North Atlantic Assembly 1970. Minister of Defence for Equipment Apr. 1968-June 1970. PC. 1970. An Opposition spokesman on Defence 1970-74. Opposition spokesman on Legal Affairs from 1979. Secretary of State for Wales Mar. 1974-May 1979. A Labour Member. Elected for the Aberavon division of Glamorgan in 1959. Q.C. 1973.* [1979]

MORRIS, Michael Wolfgang Laurence. Caesar's Camp, Sandy, Bedfordshire. Carlton, Wellington and Northampton Town, and Country. S. of C.L. Morris, Esq., F.R.I.B.A. B. 25 Nov. 1936; m. 3 Sept. 1960,

Ann, d. of Percy Appleby, Esq., (2 s. 1 d.). Educ. at Bedford School, and St. Catharine's Coll., Cambridge, M.A. (Cantab.) 1960. Marketing Manager Reckitt and Colman Group 1960-64. Director Service Advertising 1964-71. Director Benton and Bowles Limited 1971. Chairman Roy Friedlander and Partners 1976. Councillor London Borough of Islington 1968-74, Leader 1969-71, Alderman 1971-74. Secretary Conservative Environment Committee. Secretary Anglo-Sri Lanka Committee. Parliamentary Private Secretary to Michael Alison and Hugh Rossi, Ministers of State for N. Ireland from 1979. A Conservative. Unsuccessfully contested Islington N. in 1966. Elected for Northampton S. in Feb. 1974.*   [1979]

MORRIS, Percy. 30 Lon Cedwyn, Cwngwyn, Swansea. Reform, and London Welsh. S. of Thomas Morris, Esq., of Swansea. B. 6 Oct. 1893; m. 1st, 7 June 1920, Elizabeth, d. of William Davis, Esq. (she died); 2ndly, 1956, Catherine Evans. Educ. at Swansea Secondary School. President of Railway Clerks Association of Great Britain and Ireland, later Transport Salaried Staffs Association 1943-53. Member of Swansea Borough Council, Alderman 1927. J.P. Dept. Mayor 1944-45, Mayor 1955-56, Freeman July 1958. Treasurer Railway Clerks Association 1937-43. Dept. Regional Commissioner Civil Defence, Wales 1941-45. A Labour Member. Unsuccessfully contested Swansea W. in 1935. Elected for Swansea W. in July 1945 and sat until 1959, when he was defeated. Member of National Assistance Board 1961-65, Dept. Chairman 1965-66; Dept. Chairman of Supplementary Benefits Commission 1966-67. Member of Western Area Board of British Transport Commission 1960-62. C.B.E. 1963. Died 7 Mar. 1967.
[1959]

MORRIS, Sir Rhys Hopkin, M.B.E., Q.C. 1 Brick Court, Temple, London. 16 Hatherley Crescent, Sidcup, Kent. S. of Rev. John Morris, Congregational minister, of Maesteg. B. 1888; m. 1918, Gladys Perrie Williams. Educ. at University Coll. of N. Wales, Bangor and University of London. A Barrister-at-Law, Middle Temple, 1919. Police Court Magistrate 1932-36. B.B.C. Regional

Director for Wales 1936-45; Dept. Chairman of Ways and Means Nov. 1951-Nov. 1956. Served with Royal Welch Fusiliers 1914-18, M.B.E. (Mil.) 1919. Knight Bach. 1954. A Liberal. Unsuccessfully contested Cardiganshire as an Asquithian Liberal in 1922. Elected for Cardiganshire as an Independent Liberal, defeating the official candidate, in 1923 and sat as a Liberal until Aug. 1932 when he resigned on appointment as a Metropolitan Police Magistrate. Elected for Carmarthen in July 1945 and sat until his death on 22 Nov. 1956. M.B.E. 1919; K.C. 1946. Died 22 Nov. 1956.   [1956]

MORRIS-JONES, Sir (John) Henry, M.C. The Shrubbery, Royston, Hertfordshire. Reform. S. of Capt. Morris-Jones. B. 2 Nov. 1884; m. 30 June 1931, Leila Augusta Paget, widow of J.I. Marsland, Esq., of Latchford, Ware. Educ. at Menai Bridge Grammar School, and St. Mungo's Coll., Glasgow. J.P. for Denbighshire; Dept.-Lieut.; member of Board of Governors Welsh National Library, and of National Museum of Wales; Honorary Capt. R.A.M.C.; served with 2nd Battalion Worcester Regiment overseas 1914-18; practised at Colwyn Bay for 20 years; Consulting Physician West Denbighshire Hospital; F.R.S.A. Assistant Whip Sept. 1932-May 1937; a Junior Lord of the Treasury Dec. 1935-May 1937. Member of Parliamentary Delegation to Australia 1938 and to Buchenwald Concentration Camp 1945. Chairman of Welsh Parliamentary Party 1941-42. Knight Bach. 1937. A National Liberal Member. Elected for the Denbigh division of Denbighshire in May 1929 as a Liberal, joined the National Liberal group in 1931, and sat until he retired in 1950. Member of Colwyn Bay Urban District Council and Denbighshire County Council. Liberal National Whip withdrawn Feb. 1942-May 1943. Member of Governing Body of Church in Wales 1950-62. Chairman of Executive of National Liberal Party 1953-54. Died 9 July 1972.   [1950]

MORRISON, Hon. Charles Andrew. Upper Farm, Milton Lilbourne, Pewsey, Wiltshire. 45 Westminster Gardens, Marsham Street, London. S. of 1st Baron Margadale. B. 25 June 1932; m. 28 Oct.

1954, Hon. Sara Long, d. of 2nd Visct. Long of Wraxall. Educ. at Eton, and Royal Agricultural Coll., Cirencester. Served in Life Guards 1950-52 and with Royal Wiltshire Yeomanry 1952-66. County Councillor, Wiltshire 1958-64. Chairman Wiltshire County Education Committee 1963-64. Chairman S.W. Regional Sports Council 1966-67. Opposition spokesman on Sport 1967-70. Chairman Young Volunteer Force Foundation 1971-74. Chairman British Trust for Conservation Volunteers 1972-78, President 1978. Vice-Chairman 1922 Committee from 1974. A Conservative. Elected for the Devizes division of Wiltshire in May 1964.*
[1979]

MORRISON, Rt. Hon. Herbert Stanley. House of Commons, London. S. of Henry Morrison, Esq., Metropolitan Police Constable. B. 3 Jan. 1888; m. 1st Mar. 1919, Margaret, d. of Howard Kent, Esq. (she died 1953); 2ndly, 1955, Edith Meadowcroft. Educ. at Elementary Schools. Secretary to London Labour Party 1915-47. Mayor of Hackney 1920-21; Alderman Hackney Council 1921-25; member of London County Council 1922-45 (Leader 1934-40); J.P. for County of London; member of Metropolitan Water Board 1925-28; London and Home Counties Joint Electricity Authority 1925-29; Joint Town Planning Advisory Committee for London Traffic Area 1927-28; Standing Joint Committee of Quarter Sessions and the London County Council 1922; Greater London Regional Planning Committee 1936; National Service Committee for London 1939-40; London Regional Council for Civil Defence 1939-40; Chairman of Labour Party National Executive Committee 1928-29; Author of *Socialisation and Transport, How London is Governed, Looking Ahead, Peaceful Revolution, Government and Parliament.* PC. 1931. Minister of Transport June 1929-Aug. 1931; Minister of Supply May-Oct. 1940; Secretary of State for Home Affairs and Minister of Home Security Oct. 1940-May 1945; member of the War Cabinet 1942-45; Lord President of the Council and Leader of the House of Commons July 1945 to Mar. 1951. Secretary of State for Foreign Affairs Mar.-Oct. 1951. C.H. 1951. LL.D. (Hon.), London University 1951, Cambridge University

1954, Leicester University 1960 and Maine (U.S.A.) 1956; D.C.L. (Hon.) Oxford University 1953. A Labour Member. Sat for South Hackney from 1923-24 when he was defeated, 1929-31, when he was again defeated and 1935-45. Sat for Lewisham E. from 1945-50. Elected for Lewisham S. in 1950 and sat until he retired in 1959. Member of National Executive Committee of Labour Party 1920-21, 1922-43, 1944-52 and 1953-56. Member of Executive Committee of P.L.P. 1935-40. Dept. Leader of Labour Party 1945-55. President of Workers Travel Association 1951. Created Baron Morrison of Lambeth (Life Peerage) 1959. President of British Board of Film Censors 1960-65. High Steward of Kingston upon Hull 1956. President of Association of Municipal Corporations 1958-61. Honorary Fellow of Nuffield Coll. Oxford. Died 6 Mar. 1965. [1958]

MORRISON, John Granville, T.D., D.L., J.P. 55 Eaton Place, London. Basildon House, Moorgate, London. Fonthill House, Tisbury, Wiltshire. Islay House, Bridgend, Argyllshire. S. of Hugh Morrison, Esq. MP. of Fonthill House, Tisbury, and Lady Mary Morrison. B. 16 Dec. 1906; m. 16 Oct. 1928. Hon. Margaret Esther Lucie Smith, d. of 2nd Visct. Hambledon (she died 1980). Educ. at Eton and Magdalene Coll. Cambridge. Honorary Col. Royal Wiltshire Yeomanry. Served in Middle East 1940-42. Gen. Staff 1942-44. Chairman of Salisbury division Conservative Association 1939. J.P. and High Sheriff of Wiltshire 1938, and J.P. for Argyll. Parliamentary Charity Commissioner 1951-55; Chairman 1922 Committee 1955-64; President Wessex Young Conservatives 1953-55; President of Wessex Area 1956-59. A Conservative. Elected for the Salisbury division of Wiltshire in July 1942 and sat until Dec. 1964 when he was created Baron Margadale. Member of Royal Company of Archers. Chairman of Yeomanry Association 1965-71. Dept.-Lieut. for Wiltshire 1950-69, Lord Lieut. from 1969.* [1964]

MORRISON, Hon. Peter Hugh. 81 Cambridge Street, London. Turf, White's, and Pratt's. S. of 1st Baron Margadale. B. 2 June 1944. Educ. at Eton, and Keble Coll., Oxford. Secretary of Conservative N.W. Members' Group 1974-76. Joint Secretary of Conservative Smaller Businesses Committee 1974-76. Personal Assistant to Rt. Hon. Peter Walker 1966-67. Investment Manager with Slater Walker 1968-70. Lord Commissioner of the Treasury from May 1979. Opposition Whip Nov. 1976-May 1979. A Conservative. Elected for the City of Chester in Feb. 1974.*

[1979]

MORRISON, Robert Craigmyle. 41 Talbot Road, Tottenham, London. S. of James Morrison, Esq. B. 29 Oct. 1881 in Aberdeen; m. 1910, Grace, d. of Thomas Glossop, Esq. Chairman of Waste Food Board, Ministry of Supply from 1941. Member of Metropolitan Water Board 1937-47; Alderman Tottenham Borough Council from 1934; J.P. for Middlesex. A Co-op and Labour Member. Sat for N. Tottenham from Nov. 1922-Oct. 1931, when he was defeated, re-elected for N. Tottenham in Nov. 1935 and sat until Oct. 1945 when he was created Baron Morrison. Member of Wood Green Urban District Council 1914-19, of Middlesex County Council 1919-25. Lord-in-Waiting to the King and Government spokesman in the House of Lords Jan. 1947-Sept. 1948. Parliamentary Secretary to Ministry of Works Sept. 1948-Oct. 1951. PC. 1949. Dept.-Lieut. for Middlesex. Parliamentary Private Secretary to H. Gosling when Minister of Transport in 1924. Joint Parliamentary Private Secretary to Ramsay MacDonald when Prime Minister June 1929-Aug. 1931. Died 25 Dec. 1953.   [1945]

MORRISON, Rt. Hon. William Shepherd, M.C., Q.C. (The Speaker). Speaker's House, Westminster, London. The Manor House, Withington, Gloucestershire. S. of John Morrison, Esq., of Torinturk. Argyll. B. 10 Aug. 1893; m. 22 Apr. 1924, Catherine Allison, d. of Rev. W. Swan, D.D. Educ. at George Watson's Coll., Edinburgh and Edinburgh University, M.A., LL.D. President University Union and Senior President Students' Representative Council 1920-21. Capt. R.F.A. Served in France R.F.A. 1914-18; M.C. 1915. Barrister-at-Law, Inner Temple 1923, (Bencher 1951). Recorder of Walsall 1935. K.C. 1934. Private Secretary to

Solicitor General 1922-23 and 1924-27, to Attorney-Gen. 1927-28. Chairman of Conservative Private Members' Committee 1932-35; Financial Secretary to the Treasury Nov. 1935-Oct. 1936; Minister of Agriculture Oct. 1936-Jan. 1939, Chancellor of Duchy of Lancaster (Assisting Minister for Co-ordination of Defence) Jan.-Sept. 1939, and Minister of Food Sept. 1939-Apr. 1940; Postmaster-Gen. Apr. 1940-Feb. 1943; Minister of Town and Country Planning Feb. 1943-July 1945; PC. 1936. Elected Speaker 31 Oct. 1951. Re-elected in 1955 and served until he retired in Sept. 1959. A Conservative. Unsuccessfully contested the Western Isles in 1923 and 1924. Elected for the Cirencester and Tewkesbury division of Gloucestershire in May 1929 and sat until he retired in 1959. Created Visct. Dunrossil 1959. Governor General of Australia 1959-61. G.C.M.G. 1959. Died 3 Feb. 1961.   [1959]

MORT, David Llewellyn. Celtic Hotel, 62 Guildford Street, London. Plas Gwyn, Caereithin, Swansea. S. of H. Mort, Esq., of Briton Ferry, South Wales. B. 25 Mar. 1888; m. 1st, 2 Aug. 1912, Hannah, d. of Thomas Perrett Esq. (she died Nov. 1947); 2ndly, 10 Nov. 1949, Mrs. W.J. Davies. Educ. at Vernon Place Elementary School, Briton Ferry. Congregational Preacher. Steelworker. Secretary of S. Wales Branch of Iron and Steel Trades Confederation from 1915. Member of Briton Ferry Urban District Council to 1922 and Neath Borough Council 1925-29. Parliamentary Private Secretary to Rt. Hon. Sir William Jowitt, K.C. Paymaster-Gen. Mar.-Dec. 1942, and when Minister without Portfolio 1943. Member of Select Committee on National Expenditure. A Labour Member. Elected for Eccles in 1929 and sat until 1931 when he was defeated. Unsuccessfully contested the Bilston division of Wolverhampton in 1935. Elected for E. Swansea in Feb. 1940 and sat until his death on 1 Jan. 1963.   [1962]

MORTON, George Martin. 40 Aylesby Court, 487 Wilbraham Road, Manchester. S. of Rev. T. Ralph Morton, D.D. B. 11 Feb. 1940; unmarried. Educ. at Fettes Coll., Edinburgh, Edinburgh Coll. of Art, and Glasgow University. Member Manchester City Council 1971-74. Member Greater Manchester Council 1973-77. Opposition Whip from 1979. A Labour Member. Elected for the Moss Side division of Manchester at a by-election in July 1978.* [1979]

MOSS, Reginald. House of Commons, London. S. of J.H. Moss, Esq., of Audley, Staffs. B. 1913; m. 1940, Marjorie Clara, d. of Sydney Knapper, Esq. Educ. at Wolstanton County Grammar School, and Birmingham, and London Universities. A Schoolmaster. A Labour Member. Unsuccessfully contested Hemel Hempstead in 1950. Elected for the Meriden division of Warwickshire in 1955 and sat until 1959 when he was defeated.* [1959]

MOTT-RADCLYFFE, Sir Charles Edward. Barningham Hall, Matlaske, Norwich. 38 Cadogan Square, London. Carlton, Turf, and M.C.C. S. of Lieut.-Col. C.E. Radclyffe, D.S.O., Rifle Brigade, of Little Park, Wickham, Hampshire, and Theresa Caroline, only child of John Stanley Mott, Esq., of Barningham Hall, Norfolk. B. 25 Dec. 1911; m. 1st, 1940, Diana, d. of Lieut.-Col. W. Gibbs, C.V.O., 7th Hussars of Severalls, Hatherop, Gloucestershire (she died 1955); 2ndly, 1956, Stella, d. of Lionel Harrisson, Esq., of Caynham Cottage, Ludlow. Educ. at Eton, and Balliol Coll., Oxford. Attaché Diplomatic Service at H.M. Legation, Athens, and H.M. Embassy, Rome 1936-38. Served on Military Mission to Greece and as Liaison Officer in Syria 1940-41, and with Rifle Brigade in Egypt and Italy 1943-44. Parliamentary Private Secretary to Rt. Hon. L.S. Amery, Secretary of State for India Dec. 1944-May 1945; a Lord Commissioner of the Treasury May-July 1945. Conservative Whip Aug. 1945-Mar. 1946. Chairman Conservative Parliamentary Foreign Affairs Committee 1951-59. Member of Historic Buildings Council for England 1962-70. A Vice-Chairman of the British Council. Vice-Chairman 1922 (Conservative Members) Committee 1957-66. Member of the Joint Committee on Lords Reform 1962-63; member of the Plowden Overseas Representational Services Commission 1962-63. Knight Bach. 1957. A Conservative. Elected for the Windsor division of Berkshire in June 1942

and sat until he retired in 1970. High Sheriff of Norfolk 1974, Dept.-Lieut. from 1977.* [1970]

MOYLE, Arthur, C.B.E. House of Commons, London. S. of David Moyle, Esq. B. 1894; m. 1st, 1921, Elizabeth Evans (she died 1949); 2ndly, 1951, Lena Bassett. Educ. at Elementary School, Llanidloes and Fircroft Coll., Birmingham. Trades Union Official. Magistrate for the Co. of London. Parliamentary Private Secretary to the Rt. Hon. Clement Attlee when Prime Minister May 1946-Oct. 1951 and reappointed 1951-55; Chairman of National Joint Council for Local Authorities Non-Trading Services (Manual Workers) 1937-38 and member 1938-45; member of National Joint Council for Local Authorities Administrative, Professional, Technical and Clerical Staffs. Gov. Birmingham University. Vice-President Association Drainage Authorities and Poultry Association. Vice-President Public Health Inspectors' Association. Gov. Birmingham University. C.B.E. 1951. A Labour Member. Unsuccessfully contested Torquay in 1924. Sat for Stourbridge from 1945-50. Elected for Oldbury and Halesowen in Feb. 1950 and sat until he retired in 1964. Created Baron Moyle (Life Peerage) 1966. Died 23 Dec. 1974. [1964]

MOYLE, Rt. Hon. Roland Dunstan. House of Commons, London. S. of Lord Moyle, of Llanidloes, former MP. 1945-64. B. 12 Mar. 1928; m. 1956, Shelagh, d. of Bernard Hogan, Esq. Educ. at Llanidloes County School, University Coll. of Wales, Trinity Hall, Cambridge, and Gray's Inn. National Service 1949-51; commanded Royal Welch Fusiliers. Legal Assistant Wales Gas Board 1953-56. Chairman Cambridge University Labour Club 1953. Called to the bar, Gray's Inn 1954. Industrial Relations Executive Gas Council 1956-62 and Electricity Council 1962-66. Councillor London Borough of Greenwich 1964-66. Member of Select Committee on Race Relations and Immigration 1968-72. Vice-Chairman P.L.P. Defence Group 1968-72. Parliamentary Private Secretary to Rt. Hon. John Diamond, Chief Secretary to the Treasury Dec. 1966-Jan. 1969 and Parliamentary Private Secretary to Rt. Hon. James Callaghan Home Secretary from Jan. 1969-June 1970. Honorary Secretary British-American Parliamentary Group 1971-74. The Opposition spokesman on Higher Education and Science 1972-74. Parliamentary Secretary to the Ministry of Agriculture, Fisheries and Food Mar.-June 1974. Minister of State Northern Ireland Office June 1974-Sept. 1976, with responsibilities for Education; Environment July-Nov. 1974, Health and Social Services Nov. 1974-Mar. 1976 and for Commerce and Manpower Services Apr.-Sept. 1976. Minister of State for Health and Social Security Sept. 1976-May 1979. PC. 1978. An Opposition spokesman on Health and Social Security from 1979. A Labour Member. Sat for Lewisham N. from 1966-Feb. 1974 and for Lewisham E. from Feb. 1974.*   [1979]

MUDD, (William) David. Field End, South Tehidy, Camborne, Cornwall. Athenaeum, Falmouth. S. of Capt. William N. Mudd. B. 2 June 1933; m. 2 Nov. 1965, Helyn, d. of Capt. William Smith, Royal Artillery. Educ. at Truro Cathedral School, Cornwall. A Methodist Editor *Cornish Echo* 1950-52; Editorial Staff *Western Morning News* 1953-54 and 1959-61. Cornwall County Council Weights and Measures Department 1955; Merchant Navy Officer 1956-59. Freelance Journalist and T.V. Commentator 1961-70. Member Tavistock Urban District Council 1963-65. Voted against entry to E.E.C. on 28 Oct. 1971. Author of works on Cornwall. Secretary Conservative West Country Members Club Committee 1973-76. A Conservative. Sat for Falmouth and Camborne from June 1970.*   [1979]

MULLAN, Lieut.-Commander Charles Heron, R.N.V.R. Cairn Hill, Newry, Co. Down. S. of Frederick Heron Mullan, Esq., Solicitor, of Newry. B. 17 Feb. 1912; m. 6 Sept. 1940, Marcella Elizabeth, d. of J.A. McCullagh, Esq., of Ballycastle, Co. Antrim. Educ. at Castle Park, Dalkey, Rossall School, and Clare Coll., Cambridge, M.A. A Solicitor 1948. Served with R.N.V.R. 1936-51. An Ulster Unionist Member. Unsuccessfully contested S. Down, Northern Ireland Parliament in 1945. Elected for

Co. Down in June 1946 and sat until he retired in 1950. J.P. and Resident Magistrate 1960, Chairman of Belfast Juvenile Courts 1964. Dept.-Lieut for Co. Down 1974.*
                                       [1950]

MULLEY, Rt. Hon. Frederick William. 192 Southerland Avenue, London. S. of W.J. Mulley, Esq., of Leamington Spa. B. 3 July 1918; m. Dec. 1948, Joan, d. of A.M. Phillips, Esq., (2 d.). Educ. at Church of England School, Leamington, Warwick School, and Christ Church, Oxford on Adult Scholarship 1945; Fellow of St. Catharine's Coll., Cambridge (Economics) 1948-50. 1st Class Hons. Philosophy, Politics and Economics 1947. Student of Nuffield Coll., 1948. Barrister-at-Law, Inner Temple 1954. Served with Worcestershire Regiment 1939 (Prisoner of War in Germany 1940-45). Parliamentary Private Secretary to Rt. Hon. George Brown, Minister of Works 1951 and member of Select Committee on Estimates 1951-61; Delegate to Council of Europe and Western European Union 1958-61. National Executive Committee of the Labour Party 1957-58, 1960-64 and from 1965, Vice-Chairman Labour Party 1973-74, Chairman Labour Party 1974-75. Council of Institute for Strategic Studies 1961-64. Author of *Politics and Western Defence* 1962. Dept. Secretary of State for Defence and Minister of Defence for the Army 1964-65. Minister of Aviation 1965-67. Minister of State, Foreign Office from Jan. 1967 to Oct. 1969. Minister of Transport 1969-70 and Minister for Transport in the Department of the Environment 1974-75. Opposition spokesman on Air and R.A.F. 1959-64 and on Transport 1970-74. Member of Cabinet 1975-79. Secretary of State for Education and Science 1975-76. Secretary of State for Defence Sept. 1976-May 1979. PC. 1964. A Labour Member. Elected for the Park division of Sheffield in Feb. 1950.*
                                       [1979]

MULVEY, Anthony J. Derry Road, Omagh, Co. Tyrone. S. of Gerald Mulvey, Esq., of Ballinaglera, Co. Leitrim. B. 1882; m. 1921 Kathleen, d. of Thomas Tiernan, Esq., of Ballinamore. Editor of *Ulster Herald*. An Irish Nationalist. An Independent Member. Sat for Fermanagh and Tyrone from 1935-

50. Did not take his seat at Westminster until 1945. Elected for Mid-Ulster in Feb. 1950 and sat until he retired in 1951. Died 11 Jan. 1957.   [1951]

MUNRO-LUCAS-TOOTH, Sir Hugh Vere Huntly Duff, Bart. Burgate Court, Fordingbridge, Hampshire. S. of Maj. Hugh Munro Warrand and Beatrice, d. of Sir Robert Lucas-Tooth. B. 13 Jan. 1903; m. to Sept. 1925, Laetitia, d. of Sir John Findlay, Bart. (she died 1978). Educ. at Eton, and Balliol Coll., Oxford, B.A. 1924. Barrister-at-Law, Lincoln's Inn 1933. Lieut.-Col. Cameron Highlanders. Parliamentary Under-Secretary of State, Home Office Feb. 1952-Dec. 1955. A Conservative. Sat for the Isle of Ely from 1924 to 1929, when he was defeated. Elected for Hendon S. in 1945 and sat until he retired in 1970. Chairman of Select Committee on Parliamentary Commissioner for Administration 1967-70. Member of National Water Council 1973-76. Adopted the surname Lucas-Tooth in lieu of Warrand in 1920 when his maternal grandfather's Baronetcy was recreated in his favour. Adopted the surname Munro-Lucas-Tooth in 1965 on becoming Laird of Teaninich and inheriting a legacy from a cousin.*   [1970]

MURRAY, Albert James. 233 Upper Wrotham Road, Gravesend, Kent. S. of Frederick Clifton Murray, Esq. B. 9 Jan. 1930; m. 2 Apr. 1960, Margaret Anne, d. of Frederick Charles Wakeford, Esq. Educ. at Elementary School. Printer's Assistant. Joined the Labour Party in 1946. Member of SOGAT (Society of Graphical and Allied Trades) from 1954. Member Royal Arsenal Co-operative Society from 1950. Member of Southwark Borough Council 1953-59 and of London County Council (Dulwich) 1958-65. Parliamentary Private Secretary to J.P.W. Mallalieu, MP. Minister of Defence (Navy) May 1966-Jan. 1967. Minister of State, Board of Trade 1967-68 and Minister of State, Ministry of Technology 1968-69. Parliamentary Secretary Ministry of Transport Oct. 1969-June 1970. Private Secretary to Rt. Hon. Harold Wilson when Prime Minister 1974-76. A Labour Member. Unsuccessfully contested Bromley at the 1959 general election. Sat for the Gravesend division of Kent

from Oct. 1964 until 1970 when he was defeated. Created Baron Murrey of Gravesend (Life Peerage) 1976. Member of European Parliament Oct. 1976-Feb. 1978 and July 1978-1979. Died 10 Feb. 1980.   [1970]

MURRAY, James Dixon. 11 Frederick Street North, Meadowfield, Co. Durham. S. of William Murray, Esq. B. 17 Sept. 1887; m. 8 Feb. 1908, Elizabeth Hannah, d. of Thomas Robson, Esq. Educ. at East Knowle Elementary School, and Workers Educational Association Coll. Summer Schools. A Miner. Mines Assistant Checkweigher and Assistant Miners Secretary 1914; Checkweigher 1927. President of Spennymoor divisional Labour Party 1925-45. Member of Durham County Council 1925; County Alderman 1937; member of Executive Committee of Miners Federation of Great Britain 1936, of Deputation to U.S.S.R. A Labour Member. Sat for the Spennymoor division of County Durham July 1942-Feb. 1950. Elected for Durham N.W. in Feb. 1950 and sat until he retired in 1955. An Independent Methodist minister. Died 24 Jan. 1965.   [1954]

MURRAY, Rt. Hon. Ronald King, Q.C. 31 Boswall Road, Edinburgh. S. of James King Murray, Esq., M.I.E.E. B. 15 June 1922; m. 1 Apr. 1950, Sheila, d. of S.T. Gamlin, Esq., of Bristol. Educ. at George Watson's, Edinburgh, University of Edinburgh and Jesus Coll., Oxford. Served in Army 1941-46, R.E.M.E. and S.E.A.C. Called to the Scottish bar 1953; Q.C. 1967; Advocate-depute 1964-70; Senior Advocate-depute 1967-70; Lord Advocate Mar. 1974-May 1979. PC. 1974. A Labour Member. Unsuccessfully contested Caithness and Sutherland in 1959, Edinburgh N. in May 1960 and Roxburgh, Selkirk and Peebles in 1964 and Mar. 1965. Sat for the Leith division of Edinburgh from June 1970 until he retired in 1979. Judge of Court of Session, with the judicial title of Lord Murray, from 1979.*   [1979]

MURTON, Rt. Hon. (Henry) Oscar, O.B.E., T.D., J.P. 343 Cromwell Tower, Barbican, London. Flat 5, Seaview Court, North Road, Parkstone, Poole, Dorset. S. of

H.E.C. Murton, Esq., of Hexham, Northumberland. B. 1914; m. May 1939, Constance Frances, eld. d. of F.O. Connell, Esq., of Low Fell, Co. Durham (she died 1977). Educ. at Uppingham. Joined T.A. in 1934 with a Commission in the Royal Northumberland Fusiliers on active service 1939-46. Continuously on General Staff for seven years. A Lieut.-Col. O.B.E. 1946. Formerly Dept. Secretary of the Northern Divisional Board of the National Coal Board. Managing Director of a Private Limited Company with Departmental Stores in North-East England 1949-57. Member Poole Borough Council 1961-64. Member of Poole and East Dorset Water Board 1961-64 and of Bournemouth (Hurn) Airport Committee 1961-64. Member Herrison (Dorchester) Hospital Management Committee until 1974. J.P. for the borough of Poole. Introduced Highways (Amendment) Act 1965. Secretary Conservative Parliamentary Committee for Housing and Local Government and Land 1964-67, Vice-Chairman 1967-70. Chairman Conservative Parliamentary Committee for Public Building and Works 1970. Parliamentary Private Secretary to R.G. Page, Minister for Local Government and Development 1970-71. Member of Panel of Chairmen of Standing Committees 1970-71. Member Executive Committee Inter-Parliamentary Union (British Group) 1970-71. Assistant Government Whip 1971-72. Lord Commissioner of Treasury 1972-73. Second Dept. Chairman of Ways and Means 1973-74, Dept. Chairman Mar.-Oct. 1974. First Dept. Chairman Oct. 1974-Feb. 1976. Dept. Speaker and Chairman of Ways and Means Feb. 1976-Apr. 1979. PC. 1976. Freeman of the City of London. Member Guild of Freemen. A Conservative. Member for Poole from Oct. 1964 until he retired in 1979. Created Baron Murton of Lindisfarne (Life Peerage) 1970.*
[1979]

NABARRO, Sir Gerald David Nunes.
House of Commons, London. The Orchard House, Broadway, Worcestershire. Carlton, Eccentric, and Army & Navy. S. of S.N. Nabarro, Esq. B. 29 June 1913; m. 1943, Joan, d. of Col. B.B. von B. in Thurn, D.S.O., M.C., of Dawn House, Winchester. Educ. at London County Council School. Regular Army 1930-37; Commissioned in R.A.T.A. 1938-43. T.A.R.O. 1943-63. Worked in Engineering, Road Transport, and Saw-milling concerns, now Chairman and Managing Director of Companies. Broadcaster, Televiser and Journalist. Chairman Young Conservative Organisation West Midlands 1946-48; President 1948-50. Author of Clean Air Legislation 1955-56; the Coroners' Act 1953; the Thermal Insulation (Industrial Buildings) Act 1957 and the Oil Burners (Standard) Act 1960. A Gov. of the University of Birmingham. Member of Convocation of University of Aston. Chairman Council for Independent Education. Member of the Institute of Fuel. Fellow of the Royal Society of Arts. Member of Society of Authors. Chairman of House of Commons Motor Club 1966-68 and from 1969. Chairman of the Trustees of the Elgar Birthplace Trust, Chairman of Directors of the Elgar Foundation. Parliamentary Adviser and Consultant to the National Tyre Distributors Association. Member of American Federation of Television and Radio Artists. President International Coil Winders Association. Knighted 1963. Voted against entry to E.E.C. on 28 Oct. 1971. A Conservative. Unsuccessfully contested West Bromwich in 1945. Sat for Kidderminster from 1950-64, when he did not seek re-election owing to ill-health. Elected for S. Worcestershire in Mar. 1966 and sat until his death on 18 Nov. 1973.   [1974]

NAIRN, Douglas Leslie Spencer. See SPENCER-NAIRN, Douglas Leslie Spencer.

NALLY, Will. Meads, Croft Hill Road, Moston, Manchester. S. of Tom Nally, Esq., Coal Miner. B. 13 Dec. 1914; m. 1937, Hilda, d. of Joseph Clarkson, Esq., of Manchester. Educ. at Elementary School. A Journalist. President of Manchester District Labour League of Youth Federation 1930-34; Secretary Parliamentary Labour Commonwealth Group; member of British Delegation to Consultative Assembly of Council of Europe 1949. Served as Gunner, R.A., and later as War Correspondent in Europe. Parliamentary Private Secretary to Rt. Hon. L. Silkin, Minister of Town and Country Planning 1948-50. A Labour Member. Sat for the

Bilston division of Wolverhampton from July 1945 to Feb. 1950 and for Bilston from Feb. 1950 until May 1955 when he retired. Died 4 Aug. 1965. [1954]

NAYLOR, Thomas Ellis. 10 Thornton Road, Wimbledon, London. S. of George Ellis Naylor, Esq., and Mary Ann Lancaster. B. in London 5 Mar. 1868; m. 9 Sept. 1899, Emily Fawcett. Educ. in London Board School. Secretary London Society of Compositors Mar. 1906-Mar. 1938; Chairman London Labour Party 1918-33. J.P. for County of London. A Labour Member. Unsuccessfully contested S.E. Southwark in 1918. Sat for S.E. Southwark from Dec. 1921 to 1922 when he was defeated, 1923-31 when he was again defeated and from 1935 to 1950 when he retired. Editor of *London Typographical Journal* 1906-38. Chairman of Joint Industrial Council for the Printing Industry 1934-35. Member of Royal Commission on Civil Service 1929. Died 24 Dec. 1958. [1950]

NEAL, Harold. "Riseholme", 94 Aldreds Lane, Langley, Heanor, Derbyshire. S. of Joseph Neal, Esq., of Langley Mill, Derbyshire. B. 3 July 1897. Educ. at Langley Mill School. Checkweigher, Shipley Collieries 1928-44. Vice-President Derbyshire Miners' Association 1942-44; member of Heanor Urban District Council 1930-44, Chairman 1939-40. Parliamentary Secretary Ministry of Fuel and Power Apr.-Oct. 1951. Member of Imperial War Graves Commission Feb. 1947-May 1951. Widely travelled in Europe and the Middle East. A Labour Member. Sat for the Clay Cross division of Derbyshire from Apr. 1944-Feb. 1950. Elected for the Bolsover division of Derbyshire in Feb. 1950 and sat until he retired in 1970. Opposition spokesman on Fuel and Power until 1959. Died 24 Aug. 1972. [1970]

NEAVE, Airey Middleton Sheffield. D.S.O., O.B.E., M.C., T.D. c/o Northern Engineering Industries Limited, Tavistock House East, Woburn Walk, London. S. of Dr. Sheffield Neave, C.M.G., O.B.E., D.Sc. of Mill Green Park, Ingatestone, Essex. B. 23 Jan. 1916; m. 29 Dec. 1942, Diana Josceline Barbara, d. of Thomas A.W. Giffard, Esq., M.B.E., of Chillington Hall, Wolverhampton

(she was created Baroness Airey of Abingdon 1979). Educ. at Eton, and Merton Coll., Oxford, B.A. (Hons Jurisprudence) 1938, M.A. 1955. Director of Clarke Chapman Services Limited. Served in Oxford and Bucks. Light Infantry (T.A.) and R.A. (T.A.) 1935-51. Wounded and Prisoner of War 1940, escaped 1942. M.C. 1942. M. 19, 1942/4 G.S.O. 21st Army Group 1944-45. T.D. 1945. D.S.O. 1945. Barrister, Middle Temple 1943. Assistant Secretary International Military Tribunal, Nuremburg, and Commander for Criminal Organisations 1945-46. O.B.E. 1947. An Author. Officer, Order of Orange of Nassau of Holland, Despatches, French Croix de Guerre, American Bronze Star. Commander 1971 and Knight 1977 Order Polonia Restituta. Lieut.-Col. (T.A.R.O.). Parliamentary Private Secretary to Rt. Hon. Alan Lennox-Boyd, Minister of Transport and Civil Aviation Feb. 1954, and as Secretary of State for the Colonies Aug. 1954-July 1956. Joint Parliamentary Secretary to Ministry of Transport and Civil Aviation Jan. 1957-Jan. 1959. Parliamentary Under-Secretary of State for Air Jan. 1959-Oct. 1959. Gov. Imperial Coll. of Science and Technology 1963-71. Chairman Select Committee on Science and Technology 1970-74. Chairman Sub-Committee on Computer Industry 1970-75. U.K. member Executive Committee of United Nations High Commissioner for Refugees 1970-75. Chairman Standing Conference of British Organisations for Aid to Refugees 1972-74. Member of Shadow Cabinet 1975-79. Opposition spokesman on Northern Ireland 1975-79. Head of the Leader of the Opposition's Private Office 1975-79. A Conservative. Unsuccessfully contested Thurrock in 1950 and Ealing N. in 1951. Elected for the Abingdon division of Berkshire in June 1953 and sat until 30 Mar. 1979 until his assassination by Irish terrorists. [1979]

NEILL, Sir William Frederick. Killeen, Fortwilliam Park, Belfast. The Links, Portrush Road, Port Stewart, Co. Londonderry. Constitutional. S. of John Neill, Esq., of Belfast. B. 8 May 1889; m. 1st, 27 Nov. 1912, Margaret, d. of Matthew Marshall, Esq., of Limavady, Co. Derry (she died 1957); 2ndly, 1957, Rhoda, d. of G.A.

Kinning, Esq. Educ. at Belfast Model School. An Estate Agent 1909. Alderman of Belfast Corporation from 1938; Chairman of Belfast Water Commissioners 1939-42; President of Belfast Section British Red Cross; Dept.-Lieut. and J.P. for Belfast; Lord Mayor from 1946-49; member of Harbour Commissioners and of Senate of Northern Ireland; Knight Bach. 1948. An Ulster Unionist Member. Elected for Belfast N. in July 1945 and sat until he retired in 1950. Pres. of British Waterworks Association 1951, Chairman of Water Research Association from 1953. High Sheriff of Belfast 1954, Dept.-Lieut. from 1949. Fellow of Auctioneers Institute and Royal Institute and Royal Institute of Chartered Surveyors. Died 3 Jan. 1960 at sea on return voyage from South Africa. [1950]

NELSON, (Richard) Anthony. The Old Vicarage, Easebourne, Midhurst, Sussex. S. of Group Capt. R.G. Nelson, B.Sc. B. 11 June 1948; m. 20 Apr. 1974, Caroline, d. of Mr. and Mrs. B.A. Butler. Educ. at Harrow, and Christ's Coll. Cambridge. A Merchant Banker 1969-75. Member Select Committee on Science and Technology 1975; Secretary Conservative Industry Committee 1975-77. Member of Council of Howard League for Penal Reform from 1977. Secretary All-Party Dental Health Committee. Chairman Parliamentary Penal Affairs Group. Secretary British Jordanian Parliamentary Group. A Conservative. Unsuccessfully contested E. Leeds in Feb. 1974. Sat for Chichester from Oct. 1974. Parliamentary Private Secretary to John Stanley, Minister of Housing from 1979.* [1979]

NEUBERT, Michael Jon. 12 Greatwood, Chislehurst, Kent. S. of Frederick Henry Neubert, Esq. B. 3 Sept. 1933; m. 22 Aug. 1959, Sally Felicity Bilger. Educ. at Bromley Grammar School, Royal Coll. of Music London, and Downing Coll., Cambridge. Councillor Bromley Borough Council 1960-63. Councillor London Borough of Bromley 1964-68, Alderman 1968-74. Leader of Council 1967-70. Mayor 1972-73. Chairman Bromley Conservative Association 1968-69. Author of *Running Your Own Society*. A Conservative. Unsuccessfully contested N. Hammersmith in 1966 and Romford in 1970. Elected for the

Romford division of Havering in Feb. 1974 Parliamentary Private Secretary to Rt. Hon. R.E. Prentice, Minister for Social Security from 1980.* [1979]

NEVEN-SPENCE, Maj. Sir Basil Hamilton Hebden. 15 Ashley Place, London. Hall of Uyea, Uyeasound, Lerwick, Shetland. Carlton, and Caledonian. S. of T.W.L. Spence, C.B., of Uyea, Shetland and Henrietta Fanny, d. of R.J. Hebden, Esq., of Eday, Orkney. B. 12 June 1888; m. 1st, 1917, Margaret Alice, d. of George Hunter Mackenzie, Esq., M.D., of Edinburgh (she died 1961); 2ndly, 1963, Constance Huddleston (she died 1967) Educ. at Edinburgh Academy and University, M.B., Ch. B. 1911; M.D., M.R.C.P. (Ed.) 1924, F.R.C.P. (Ed.) 1928, R.A.M.C. 1911-29. Secretary to Egyptian Army and to Sudan Government 1914-24; served in Darfur and Palestine; Vice-Convener of Shetland 1934-35, Dept.-Lieut. 1936, Lord-Lieut. 1952-63. Parliamentary Private Secretary to Rt. Hon. Walter Elliot, Minister of Health Nov. 1938-May 1940. Knight Bach. 1945. A Conservative. Unsuccessfully contested Orkney and Shetland in 1929. Elected for Orkney and Shetland in 1935 and sat until 1950, when he was defeated. Member of Nature Conservancy 1955-62. Fellow of Royal Geographical Society. Assumed the surname of Neven-Spence in lieu of Spence in 1925. Died 13 Sept. 1974. [1950]

NEWENS, Arthur Stanley. The Leys, 18 Park Hill, Harlow, Essex. S. of Arthur Ernest Newens, Esq. B. 4 Feb. 1930; m. 1st, 1954, Ann Sherratt (she died 1962); 2ndly, Feb. 1966, Sandra Frith, (4 d.). Educ. at Elementary and Grammar Schools, and University Coll., London (B.A. Hons in History). A Schoolteacher. Joined the Labour Party in 1949. Member National Union of Mineworkers 1952-55, holding various local offices. Member National Union of Teachers from 1956, holding various local offices. Chairman Liberation (formerly Movement for Colonial Freedom). N.U.T. Supported member from Oct. 1966-70. Member of Board, London Co-operative Society from Oct. 1971. President L.C.S. May 1977. Member of Central Executive, Co-operative Union. Vice-Chairman

E. Regional Council of Labour Party. A Labour and Co-operative Member. Sat for Epping from Oct. 1964-June 1970, when he was defeated. Elected for Harlow in Feb. 1974.* [1979]

NEWTON, Antony Harold., O.B.E. House of Commons, London. St. Stephen's Constitutional. S. of Harold Newton, Esq. B. 29 Aug. 1937; m. 25 Aug. 1962, Janet, d. of Phillip Huxley, Esq. Educ. at Friends' School, Saffron Walden, and Trinity Coll., Oxford. President Oxford University Conservative Association 1958. President Oxford Union Society 1959, debating tour in U.S. 1960. Secretary/Research Secretary Bow Group 1962-64. Conservative Research Department 1961-74. Head of Economic Section 1965-70. Assistant Director 1970-74. O.B.E. 1972. Secretary Conservative Health and Social Services Committee 1977. A Conservative. Unsuccessfully contested the Brightside division of Sheffield in 1970. Elected for Braintree in Feb. 1974. Assistant Government Whip from May 1979.* [1979]

NICHOL, Muriel Edith. 8 Elmwood, Welwyn Garden City, Hertfordshire. D. of Richard Wallhead, Esq., MP. for Merthyr Tydfil 1922-34. B. 1893; m. 1920, James Nichol, Esq. (he died 1976). Member of Welwyn Garden City Urban District Council 1937-45, Chairman 1943-44. A Lecturer to the Forces. J.P. for Hertfordshire. A Labour Member. Unsuccessfully contested Bradford N. 1935. Elected for Bradford N. in July 1945 and sat until 1950, when she was defeated. Unsuccessfully contested Stockport N. 1955.* [1950]

NICHOLLS, Sir Harmar, Bart. House of Commons, London. St. Stephen's, and Constitutional. S. of Charles E.C. Nicholls, Esq. B. 1 Nov. 1912; m. 1940, Dorothy Elsie, d. of James Edwards, Esq. Educ. at Queen Mary's Grammar School. Walsall. Lieut. R.E. with service on India and Burma. Director J. and H. Nicholls Limited, Paint Distributors; Nicholls and Hennessy Hotels Limited. Director Winkfields Estates Limited, Lloyd's Underwriter. Director Radio Luxembourg Limited, A.D.H. Limited (Associated Development), Cannon Insurance Company Limited. Chairman Malvern Festival Theatre Trust Limited. Chairman London Housing Association. Chairman of Pleasurama Limited. Parliamentary Private Secretary to D. Gammans, Assistant Postmaster-Gen. Oct. 1951-Apr. 1955; Parliamentary Secretary Ministry of Agriculture, Fisheries and Food Apr. 1955-Jan. 1957. Parliamentary Secretary Ministry of Works Jan. 1957-Oct. 1960. J.P. for Staffordshire 1946. A Conservative. Unsuccessfully contested Nelson and Colne in 1945 and Preston S. in Jan. 1946. Elected for the Peterborough division of Northamptonshire and Soke of Peterborough in Feb. 1950 and sat until Oct. 1974 when he was defeated. Member of Darlaston Urban District Council 1940-52, Chairman 1949-50. Created Bart. 1960. Voted against entry to E.E.C. on 28 Oct. 1971. Created Baron Harmar-Nicholls (Life Peerage) 1974, when he assumed the surname of Harmar-Nicholls in lieu of Nicholls. Member of European Parliament for Greater Manchester W. from 1979.* [1974]

NICHOLLS, Henry Richard. 35 Water Lane, London. B. about 1893. A Coach Painter in the L.N.E. Railway. A Trade Union Official. Member of West Ham Town Council 1929-32 and 1942-62. A Labour Member. Elected for the Stratford division of West Ham in July 1945 and sat until he retired in 1950. Died 5 Dec. 1962. [1950]

NICHOLSON, Sir Godfrey, Bart., F.S.A. Windsor House, 83 Kingsway, London. Bussock Hill House, Newbury. S. of Richard Francis Nicholson, Esq., Distiller. B. 9 Dec. 1901; m. 30 June 1936, Lady Katharine Lindsay, d. of David, 27th Earl of Crawford and Balcarres, K.T. (she died 1972). Educ. at Winchester, and Christ Church, Oxford. Royal Fusiliers 1939-42. Chairman Estimates Committee. 1961-64. Created Bart. 1958. A Conservative. Sat for Morpeth from Oct. 1931-Nov. 1935 when he was defeated. Elected for the Farnham division of Surrey in Mar. 1937 and sat until he retired in 1966. Parliamentary Private Sec. to Rt. Hon. Ralph Assheton, Financial Sec. to Treasury 1943-44. Fellow of Society of Antiquaries. Pres. of British Association of Parascending Clubs from 1973.* [1966]

NICHOLSON, Nigel. C. 1 Albany, Piccadilly, London. Shirley House. Bransgore, Nr. Christchurch, Hampshire. Travellers'. S. of Hon. Sir Harold Nicholson, C.M.G. and Victoria Sackville-West, C.H. B. 19 Jan. 1917; m. 1953, Philippa Janet, d. of Sir Gervais Tennyson d'Eyncourt, Bart. (divorced 1970) Educ. at Eton, and Balliol Coll., Oxford. A Publisher and Author. Director of Weidenfeld and Nicolson Limited, Contact Publications Limited from 1947. A Conservative. Unsuccessfully contested N.W. Leicester in 1950 and Falmouth and Camborne m. 1951. Elected for Bournemouth E. and Christchurch in Feb. 1952 and sat until he retired in 1959, after failing to gain renomination by his local constituency association, which had passed a vote of no confidence in him in Dec. 1956 as a result of his failure to support the Government's Suez policy. In a secret ballot of all party members in the constituency in Feb. 1959 Nicholson was defeated by 3762 votes to 3671 and resigned his candidacy. Served with Grenadier Guards 1939-45, Capt. M.B.E. 1945. Chairman of Executive Committee & United Nations Association 1961-1966.*

[1959]

NIELD, Basil, M.B.E., Q.C. 56 Cadogan Place, London. Upton Grange, Chester. 2 Essex Court, Temple, London. Carlton, Brooks's, St. Stephen's, and Junior Carlton. S. of Charles E. Nield, Esq., Registrar Liverpool County Court. B. 7 May 1903. Educ. at Harrow, and Magdalen Coll., Oxford, M.A. Barrister-at-Law, Inner Temple 1925. Master of the Bench of the Inner Temple 1952, Treasurer 1977. Chairman of Chester Conservative and Unionist Association 1930-40. Served in Middle East 1941-43, Lieut.-Col. (despatches), President of Palestine Military Courts 1941, with B.L.A. 1944-45. Vice-President National Chamber of Trade 1948-56. Parliamentary Chairman Dock and Harbour Authorities Association 1944-51; Chancellor of the Diocese of Liverpool 1948-56; member of General Council of the Bar 1951 and of Special Committee under reorganisation Areas Mission 1944 for the Province of York, and Hon. Standing Counsel Social Hygiene Committee; Recorder of Salford 1948-56; member Magistrates Courts

Rules Committee 1952-56; Advisory Council English-Speaking Union. A Conservative. Elected for the Chester division of Cheshire in Mar. 1940 and sat until Oct. 1956, when he was appointed Recorder of Manchester. Recorder of Manchester and Judge of the Crown Court 1956-60 M.B.E. 1945, C.B.E. 1956. Knighted 1957. Judge of Queen's Bench Division 1960-78. K.C. 1945. Dept.-Lieut. for Cheshire 1962.*　　[1956]

NOBLE, Commander Rt. Hon. Sir Allan Herbert Percy, K.C.M.G., D.S.O., D.S.C., R.N. 45 Chelsea Square, London. White's, and M.C.C. S. of Admiral Sir Percy Noble, G.B.E., K.C.B., C.V.O. B. 2 May 1908; m. 9 Apr. 1938, Barbara, d. of Brigadier Kenneth Gabbett. Educ. at Radley Coll. Joined R.N. 1926; Aide-de-Camp to The Marq. of Linlithgow, Viceroy of India 1936-38; served at sea 1939-45 (despatches), retired 1946. Government Observer, Bikini Atomic Bomb Tests 1946. Parliamentary Private Secretary to Mr. Eden 1947-51. Parliamentary and Financial Secretary to the Admiralty Nov. 1951-Dec. 1955; Parliamentary Under-Secretary of State for Commonwealth Relations Dec. 1955-Nov. 1956; Minister of State for Foreign Affairs Nov. 1956-Jan. 1959; PC. 1956. A Conservative. Elected for Chelsea in July 1945 and sat until he retired in 1959. D.S.C. 1941, D.S.O. 1943. K.C.M.G. June 1959. Director and Chairman of Tollemache Cobbold Breweries Ltd. 1960-73. Dept. Lieut. for Suffolk 1973.*

[1959]

NOBLE, Michael. Alfred. House of Commons, London. S. of Alfred Noble Esq. B. Mar. 1935; m. 1956 Brenda Kathleen Peak. Educ. at Hull Grammar School, and Sheffield and Hull Universities. Secondary school teacher 1959-63. W.E.A. tutor in Industrial Relations 1963-73. Consultant in Industrial Relations 1973-74. Parliamentary Private Secretary to Rt. Hon. Roy Hattersley, Secretary of State for Prices and Consumer Protection 1976. A Labour Member. Unsuccessfully contested the Withington division of Manchester in 1970 and Rossendale in Feb. 1974. Elected for Rossendale in Oct. 1974 and sat until 1979, when he was defeated.*

[1979]

NOBLE, Rt. Hon. Michael Antony Christobal. Strone, Cairndown, Argyllshire. Boodle's, and New (Edinburgh). S. of Sir John Noble, Bart. B. 13 Mar. 1913; m. 1940, Anne, d. of Sir Neville Pearson, 2nd Bart., (4 d.). Educ. at Eton, and Magdalen Coll., Oxford. Served with R.A.F.V.R. 1941-45, Squadron Leader 1943. Scottish Whip 1960-62. Lord Commissioner of Treasury Nov. 1961- July 1962. Secretary of State for Scotland July 1962-Oct. 1964. President of the Board of Trade June-Oct. 1970. Minister for Trade Oct. 1970-Nov. 1972. Opposition spokesman on Scotland and Member of Shadow Cabinet Nov. 1964-Jan. 1969. PC. 1962. A Conservative. Elected for Argyllshire in June 1958 and sat until he retired in Feb. 1974. Member of Argyll County Council 1949-51. Chairman of Associated Fisheries 1966-70, of Glendevon Farms 1969-70. Created Baron Glenkinglas (Life Peerage) 1974. Chairman of British Agricultural Export Council 1973-77. Director of John Brown Engineering Ltd. 1973-77 and of Monteith Holdings Ltd. from 1974.*

[1974]

NOEL-BAKER, Francis Edward. House of Commons, London. Travellers'. S. of the Rt. Hon. Philip Noel-Baker, MP. (Created Baron Noel-Baker 1977) B. 7 Jan. 1920; m. 1957 Barbara Christina, d. of Joseph Sonander, Esq., of Norrköping, Sweden, (4 s. 1 d.). Educ. at Westminster School, and King's Coll., Cambridge (Exhibitioner). Trooper R.T.R.. rising to Capt. Despatches 1940-45. Parliamentary Private Secretary to Walter Edwards, Civil Lord of the Admiralty 1949-50. A Labour Member. Sat for Brentford and Chiswick from 1945-50, when he was defeated. Elected for Swindon in 1955 and sat until he resigned in Mar. 1969. Secretary of United Nations Parliamentary Committee 1955-64, Chairman 1964-68. Chairman of Advertising Inquiry Council 1951-68. Director of North European Enterprises Ltd. from 1973, of Fini Fisheries, Cyprus, from 1976. Styled 'The Honourable' after his father's elevation to the Peerage in 1977.*

[1968]

NOEL-BAKER, Rt. Hon. Philip John. 16 South Eaton Place, London. S. of Joseph Allen Baker, Esq., MP. for East Finsbury. B. 1 Nov. 1889; m. June 1915, Irene, d. of Frank Noel, Esq., of Euboea, (1 s.). Francis Noel-Baker, MP. (she died 1956). Educ. at Bootham, Haverford Coll., and King's Coll., Cambridge. Served with Ambulance Units 1914-18. Cassell Professor of International Relations, University of London 1924-29; member of British Delegation at Peace Conference, Paris 1919, League of Nations Secretariat 1919-22; Personal Assistant to British Delegate, League of Nations Assembly 1923-24; Parliamentary Private Secretary to Rt. Hon. Arthur Henderson when Secretary of State for Foreign Affairs 1929-31. Parliamentary Secretary Ministry of War Transport Feb. 1942-May 1945; Minister of State July 1945-Oct. 1946. PC. 1945. Secretary of State for Air Oct. 1946-Oct. 1947. Secretary of State for Commonwealth Relations with a seat in the Cabinet Oct. 1947-Feb. 1950. Minister of Fuel and Power Feb. 1950-Oct. 1951. Nobel Peace Prize 1959. Labour Front Bench spokesman on U.N. and Disarmament Affairs 1952-64. Chairman P.L.P. Foreign Affairs Group 1964-70. President International Council on Sport and Physical Education (UNESCO). A Labour Member. Unsuccessfully contested the Handsworth division of Birmingham in 1924. Sat for Coventry from May 1929-31 when he was defeated. Unsuccessfully contested Coventry in 1935. Sat for Derby from July 1936 to Feb. 1950. Elected for S. Derby in Feb. 1950 and sat until he retired in 1970. Fellow of King's Coll. Cambridge 1915-25, Hon. Fellow from 1961. Assumed the surname Noel-Baker in lieu of Baker 1923. Member of Parliamentary Committee of P.L.P. 1936-40 and 1951-59. Member of National Executive Committee of Labour Party 1937-48, Chairman 1946-47. Created Baron Noel-Baker (Life Peerage) 1977.*

[1970]

NOEL-BUXTON, Lucy Edith Pelham Baroness. 11 Wilton Place, London. D. of Maj. Henry Pelham Burn. B. 1888; m. 30 Apr. 1914, Noel Edward Buxton, MP., 1st Baron Noel-Buxton (created 1930) (he died 1948). A Labour Member. Elected for N. Norfolk in July 1930, in succession to her husband, and sat until 1931,when she was defeated. Unsuccessfully contested N. Norfolk in 1935. Sat for Norwich from 1945 until she retired in 1950. Died 9 Dec. 1960. [1950]

NORMANTON, Tom, T.D. Bollin Court, Macclesfield Road, Wilmslow, Cheshire. St. James's (Manchester), and Beefsteak. S. of Tom O. Normanton, Esq., Textile Manufacturer. B. 12 Mar. 1917; m. 24 Oct. 1942, Annabel, d. of Dr. F. Yates, of Manchester, (2 s. 1 d.). Educ. at Malsis Hall Preparatory School, Manchester Grammar School, and Manchester University, (B.A. Com). Commissioned T.A. 1937. Served in the Army (General Staff) in Europe and North Africa 1939-46. Member of Rochdale Borough Council 1950-53. Council member Confederation of British Industry 1964-76. Vice-Chairman U.K. Automation Council 1969. President British Textile Employers Association 1970-72. Chairman European Textile Employers (I.F.C.A.T.I.) 1971-76. Vice-President International Federation of Textile Industries 1972-76, President 1976. Member European Parliament from 1973. A Conservative. Unsuccessfully contested Rochdale in 1959 and 1964. Elected for the Cheadle division of Cheshire in June 1970. Member of European Parliament for Cheshire E. from 1979.* [1979]

NORWOOD, Christopher Bonnewell Burton. House of Commons, London. S. of Harold Norwood, Esq. B. 17 Dec. 1932; m. 1955, Beryl Fleur, d. of Louis Goldwyn, Esq. (1 s.). Educ. at Elementary School, Whitgift School, Croydon, and Gonville and Caius Coll., Cambridge (open major scholarship). Commercial Officer. Joined the Labour Party in 1950. Member of Union of Shop Distributive and Allied Workers. Successfully contested Paddington Borough Council elections 1959. A Labour Member. Unsuccessfully contested Sutton Coldfield in the general election of 1955, and Bromsgrove in 1959. Elected for Norwich S. in Oct. 1964 and sat until he retired in 1970. Member of economic projection section of Central Electricity Generating Board 1960-64. Died 14 Nov. 1972. [1970]

NOTT, Rt. Hon. John William Frederic. 5 John Spencer Square, London. Trewinnard Manor, St. Erth, Hayle, Cornwall. S. of Richard Nott, Esq. B. 1 Feb. 1932; m. 2 Apr. 1959 Miloska Sekol, of Maribor, Yugoslavia. Educ. at Bradfield Coll., and Trinity Coll., Cambridge. Regular Officer 2nd Gurkha Rifles 1953-57. Cambridge (Hons in Law and Economics) 1957-59. President of the Cambridge Union 1959. Barrister-at-Law, Inner Temple 1959. Merchant Banker S.G. Warburg and Company Limited 1959-67. Chairman Imperial-Eastman (U.K.) Limited. Director Clarkson International Tools Limited. Minister of State, Treasury Apr. 1972-Mar. 1974. A Conservative. Sat for the St. Ives division of Cornwall from Mar. 1966. An Opposition spokesman on Treasury Affairs 1975-76 and on Trade 1976-79. Member of Shadow Cabinet Dec. 1976-May 1979. PC. 1979.* [1979]

NUGENT, Rt. Hon. Sir (George) Richard Hodges, Bart. Blacknest Farm, Dunsfold, Surrey. 13 Tufton Court, Tufton Street, London. Athenaeum, and Farmers'. S. of Col. George H. Nugent, R.A., of Churt, Surrey. B. 6 June 1907; m. July 1937, Ruth, d. of Hugh G. Stafford, Esq., of Tilford, Surrey. Educ. at Imperial Service Coll., Windsor, and Royal Military Academy, Woolwich. Commissioned R.A. 1926-29. J.P. for Surrey. Chairman of Thames Conservancy 1960-74. Past Alderman of Surrey County Council. Parliamentary Secretary Ministry of Agriculture, Fisheries and Food Nov. 1951-Jan. 1957. Parliamentary Secretary Ministry of Transport and Civil Aviation Jan. 1957-Oct. 1959. Chairman Select Committee for Nationalised Industries 1961-64. Chairman Agricultural Market Dev. Committee 1962. Chairman Standing Conference on London Regional Planning 1962-68. Chairman Animal Virus Research Institute 1964-77. President Association of River Authorities 1965-74. Created Bart. 1960. PC. 1962. A Conservative. Elected for the Guildford division of Surrey in Feb. 1950 and sat until he retired in 1966. Created Baron Nugent of Guildford (Life Peerage) 1966. A Dept. Speaker of House of Lords. Chairman of National Water Council 1973-78. Honorary D. Univ., Surrey University 1968.* [1966]

NUTTING, Rt. Hon. (Harold) Anthony. 6 Chester Square, London. Quenby Hall, Leicestershire. S. of Sir Harold Nutting, 2nd Bart. B. 11 Jan. 1920; m. 1st, 1941, Gillian, d. of Edward Strutt, Esq., of The Wick, Hatfield Peverel, Essex (divorced 1959); 2ndly, 1961, Anne Gunning Parker. Educ. at Eton, and Trinity Coll., Cambridge. Served with Leicestershire Yeomanry 1939; (invalided out) and in Embassies in France, Spain and Italy and at the Foreign Office 1940-45; Private Secretary to the Rt. Hon. Anthony Eden, Foreign Secretary 1942; National Chairman of Young Conservative Movement 1946-47; Chairman of National Union of Conservative and Unionist Associations 1950-51; Chairman of Executive Committee of National Union 1951-52. Parliamentary Under-Secretary of State for Foreign Affairs Nov. 1951-Oct. 1954. Minister of State for Foreign Affairs Oct. 1954-Nov. 1956 when he resigned. PC. 1954. A Conservative. Elected for the Melton division of Leicestershire in July 1945 and sat until Nov. 1956, when he resigned after leaving the Government over its Suez policy. Unsuccessfully contested Oldham E. in 1964. Succeeded to Baronetcy 1972. Author and biographer of Lawrence of Arabia and Nasser.* [1956]

OAKES, Rt. Hon. Gordon James. The Bridle Path, Upton, Widnes, Lancashire. S. of James Oakes, Esq. B. 1931; m. 11 Sept. 1952, Esther O'Neill, (3 s.). Educ. at Wade Deacon Grammar School, Widnes, and Liverpool University. A Solicitor. Chairman Widnes Labour Party 1952-59. Mayor of Widnes 1964-65. Parliamentary Private Secretary to Rt. Hon. Roy Jenkins, Home Secretary 1966-67 and Chancellor of Exchequer 1967-68 and to Rt. Hon. Edward Short, Secretary of State for Education and Science 1968-70. Delegate to NATO 1966-70. Vice-President Rural District Councils Association. Vice-President Institute of Public Health Inspectors. Opposition spokesman on Local Government 1973-74. Under-Secretary of State, Department of the Environment Mar. 1974-Apr. 1976. Under-Secretary of State Department of Energy Apr.-Sept. 1976. Minister of State for Education Sept. 1976-May 1979. Opposition spokesman on Local Government from 1979.

PC. 1979. A Labour Member. Unsuccessfully contested Bebington in 1959, and the Moss Side division of Manchester in 1961. Sat for Bolton W. from 1964-70, when he was defeated. Elected for the Widnes division of Lancashire from Sept. 1971.* [1979]

OAKSHOTT, Sir Hendrie Dudley, Bart., M.B.E. The Mount, Broxton, Nr. Chester. Pratt's, and Turf. S. of Arthur John Oakshott, Esq., of Bebington. B. 8 Nov. 1904; m. 4 Jan. 1928, Joan, d. of Marsden Withington, Esq. Educ. at Rugby, and Trinity Coll., Cambridge. Parliamentary Private Secretary to Rt. Hon. Duncan Sandys, Minister of Supply Nov. 1951. Assistant Government Whip Nov. 1951. Lord Commissioner of the Treasury May 1952-June 1955; Comptroller of the Household June 1955-Jan. 1957; Treasurer of the Household Jan. 1957-Jan. 1959. Parliamentary Private Secretary to Rt. Hon. Selwyn Lloyd, as Secretary of State for Foreign Affairs 1959-60, and as Chancellor of the Exchequer 1960-62. Created Bart. June 1959. A Conservative. Elected for Bebington in Feb. 1950 and sat until Aug. 1964 when he was created Baron Oakshott (Life Peerage). Served in Middle East and Italy 1940-44. Lieut.-Col., M.B.E. 1942. Delegate to Council of Europe 1952-58. Member of Totalisator Board 1964-73. Dept. Chairman of Committees, House of Lords 1967-68. Honorary Fellow of of Institute of Building. Died 1 Feb. 1975. [1964]

O'BRIEN, Sir Tom. 57 Parliament Hill, London. S. of John O'Brien, Esq., of Llanelly. B. 17 Aug. 1900; m. 27 May 1922, Josephine, d. of John McKelvie, Esq. Educ. at St. Mary's School, Llanelly. Served in Dardanelles Expedition 1915. Gen. Secretary National Association of Theatrical and Kine Employees 1932-70 and member of Trade Union Congress Gen. Council from 1940. President T.U.C. Sept. 1952-53, and Vice-President 1954-55; represented Britain T.U. Movement at Conferences throughout Europe, Canada, U.S.A. and Africa; member of International Federation of Trade Unions and President Federation of Theatre Unions and of Federation of Film Unions. A Labour Member. Sat for the W. division of Nottingham July 1945-Feb. 1950, for the

N.W. division Feb. 1950-May 1955. Elected for West Nottingham in May 1955 and sat until 1959 when he was defeated. Knighted 1956. Died 5 May 1970.   [1959]

ODEY, George William, C.B.E. Keldgate Manor, Beverley, Yorkshire. S. of George William Odey, Esq. B. 21 Apr. 1900; m. 1st, 15 Sept. 1926, Dorothy Christian, d. of James Frederick Moir, Esq. (she died 1975); 2ndly, 1976, Mrs. Doris Harrison-Broadley. Educ. at Faversham Grammar School, and University Coll., London, (Fellow 1953). Honorary Air Commodore No. 3505 Fighter Control Unit R.A.F. Assistant Secretary, University of London Appointments Board 1922-25. Managing Director of Barrow, Hepburn and Gale Limited 1931; Chairman 1937-74; Chairman of Leather, Footwear and Allied Industries Export Corporation 1940-46, and President from 1947. Chairman of United Tanners' Federation 1951, and of Board of Governors of National Leathersellers' Coll. from 1951. President of Glue and Gelatine Research Association from 1951. A Conservative. Elected for the Howdenshire division of the E. Riding of Yorkshire in Nov. 1947 and sat until Feb. 1950. Sat for the Beverley division of the E. Riding of Yorkshire from Feb. 1950 until he retired in 1955. C.B.E. 1945. Member of Western Hemisphere Export Council 1960-64. Member of E. Riding of Yorkshire County Council 1964-74, Dept.-Lieut. for Humberside 1977.*
                                        [1954]

OGDEN, Eric. House of Commons, London. S. of Robert Ogden, Esq. B. 23 Aug. 1923; m. 1st, 1945, Patricia, d. of George Aitken, Esq., divorced (1 s.); 2ndly, Marjorie, d. of Percival Smith, Esq. (2 s. 2 step d.). Educ. at Queen Elizabeth's Grammar School, Middleton, Leigh Technical Coll., and Wigan Mining Coll. A Coalminer. Joined the Labour Party in 1955. Member of the National Union of Mineworkers from 1951, but first union membership Radio Officers' Union (Merchant Navy) 1942. Member Middleton Borough Council 1958-65. Parliamentary Private Secretary Board of Trade 1968-70. Honorary Chairman Parliamentary Channel Tunnel Group. Honorary Vice-President Socialist Medical Association. Parliamentary Adviser Council of Pharma-

ceutical Society. Member P.O. Stamps Advisory Committee. War service in Merchant Navy, first with Blue Funnel Line of Liverpool, later with Dutch Merchant ship, independent, and with Allied task forces in Pacific. A Methodist. A Labour Member. Sat for the W. Derby division of Liverpool from 1964.*   [1979]

O'HALLORAN, Michael Joseph. 40 Tytherton Road, Islington, London. Irish, and Challoner. S. of Martin O'Halloran, Esq. B. 20 Aug. 1929; m. 1956, Stella Beatrice, d. of Mr. McDonald, (3 d.). Educ. at Clohanes National School, Co. Clare, Eire. Former Railway and Building Worker. Member of the Labour Party for 30 years. Member of Islington Borough Council 1968-71. Sponsored by N.U.R. A Roman Catholic. A Labour Member. Sat for Islington N. from Oct. 1969.*   [1979]

OLDFIELD, William Henry. 266 Dickinson Road, Manchester. S. of William Henry Oldfield, Esq. B. 9 June 1881; m. 1st, 10 Apr. 1909, Edith, d. of Levi Town, Esq.; 2ndly, 5 July 1950, E.M. Fraser. Educ. at Wesleyan School, Sowerby Bridge. A Cotton Worker, Doubler. Labour Organiser and Agent, Gorton 1923; Alderman Manchester City Council, J.P. A Labour Member. Elected for the Gorton division of Manchester in Mar. 1942 and sat until he retired in 1955. Secretary of Gorton Trade and Labour Council. Parliamentary Private Secretary to Rt. Hon. Ellen Wilkinson and Rt. Hon. George Tomlinson, when Ministers of Education 1945-51. Died 16 Nov. 1961.   [1954]

OLIVER, George Harold, Q.C. Crimbles Court, Scalby, Scarborough. B. 24 Nov. 1888; m. Sept. 1910, Ellen Christina, d. of James Bennett, Esq., of Bolton (she died 1974). Educ. at Holy Trinity School, Bolton. Barrister-at-Law, Middle Temple 1927. K.C. 1949. Parliamentary Under-Secretary of State Home Office Aug. 1945-Oct. 1947; elected to the Derby Town Council. A Labour Member. Unsuccessfully contested the Ilkeston division of Derbyshire in 1918. Sat for the Ilkeston division of Derbyshire from Nov. 1922-Oct. 1931, when he was defeated and from 1935 to 1964 when he retired.
                                        [1964]

O'MALLEY, Rt. Hon. Brian Kevin. 29 Hall Avenue, Mexborough, Yorkshire. S. of Frank O'Malley, Esq. B. 22 Jan. 1930; m. July 1959, Kathleen Sylvia Curtiss. Educ. at Mexborough Grammar School, and Manchester University. B.A. (Hons.) History, W.E.A. Lecturer, Schoolmaster. Branch Secretary of Musicians' Union. Assistant Government Whip Nov. 1964-Apr. 1967. Government Dept. Ch. Whip July 1967-Oct. 1969. Lord Commissioner of the Treasury Apr. 1967-Oct. 1969. Parliamentary Under-Secretary Department of Health and Social Security Oct. 1969-June 1970. Opposition spokesman on Pensions and Social Security 1970-74. Minister of State Department of Health and Social Security Mar. 1974-Apr. 1976. PC. 1975. A Labour Member. Elected for Rotherham in Mar. 1963 and sat until his death on 6 Apr. 1976. Died 6 Apr. 1976. [1976]

O'NEILL, Michael. Kildrum, Dromore, Tyrone. S. of Michael O'Neill, Esq. B. 7 Oct. 1910; m. 23 Sept. 1936, Kathleen, d. of James O'Connor, Esq., of Brackernagh, Ballinasloe, Galway Educ. at Dromore Boys' National School, and Bellisle Academy. Member of Tyrone County Council 1950-57; Honorary Treasurer of the Gaelic Athletic Association and executive of the Irish Anti-Partition League. Member of Omagh Rural District Council 1939-49. An Irish Republican. Elected for mid-Ulster in Oct. 1951 and sat until he retired in 1955. Unsuccessfully contested mid-Ulster at a by-election in May 1956 as an Anti-Partition candidate. Entertainments Officer, Tyrone and Fermanagh Hospital, 1960-74. [1954]

O'NEILL, Hon. Phelim Robert Hugh. House of Commons, London. S. of Rt. Hon. Sir Hugh O'Neill, MP., created Lord Rathcavan 1953. B. 2 Nov. 1909; m. 1st, 1934, Clare Désirée, d. of Detmar Blow (from whom he obtained a divorce in 1944); 2ndly, June 1953, Bridget, d. of Hon. Richard Coke. Educ. at Eton. An Insurance Broker at Lloyd's. An Ulster Unionist Member. Elected for N. Antrim in succession to his father Oct. 1952 and sat until he retired in 1959. Member of N. Ireland Parliament for N. Antrim 1958-72. N. Ireland Minister of Education 1969 and Minister of Agriculture 1969-71. PC. (N. Ireland) 1969. Joined Alliance Party Feb. 1972. Unsuccessful Alliance Party candidate for N. Ireland Assembly in N. Antrim 1973.* [1959]

O'NEILL, Rt. Hon. Sir (Robert William) Hugh, Bart. 28 Queen's Gate Gardens, London. Cleggan Lodge, Ballymena, Co. Antrim. Carlton, and Ulster (Belfast). S. of Edward, 2nd Baron O'Neill. B. 8 June 1883; m. 11 Feb. 1909, Sylvia Irene, d. of Walter A. Sandeman, Esq. (she died 1942). Educ. at Eton, and New Coll., Oxford, B.A. Barrister-at-Law, Inner Temple 1909, N.E. Circuit. 2nd Lieut. N. of Ireland Yeomanry 1902-07; Capt. R. Irish Rifles 1914-16; Capt. Gen. List 1917, and Maj. 1918. Served in France 1915-17, and as D.J.A.G. in Palestine 1918. Dept. Lieut. for Co. Antrim; Honorary LL.D. and former Pro-Chancellor of Belfast University. Sat for Co. Antrim, Northern Ireland Parliament May 1921 to May 1929; Speaker of House of Commons of Northern Ireland June 1921-May 1929. PC. (Ireland) Aug. 1921; PC. (G.B.) 1937. Created Bart. May 1929. Chairman of Conservative Party Members' "1922" Committee 1935-39. Parliamentary Under-Secretary for India and Burma Sept. 1939-May 1940. An Ulster Unionist. Unsuccessfully contested Stockport in 1906. Elected for mid Antrim Feb. 1915 and Dec. 1918. Member for Co. Antrim Nov. 1922-Feb. 1950, and for the N. division from Feb. 1950 until he resigned in Oct. 1952. Father of the House of Commons 1951-52. Created Baron Rathcavan 1953. Lord-Lieut. of Co. Antrim 1949-59.* [1952]

ONSLOW, Cranley Gordon Douglas. Chobham Park House, Chobham, Woking, Surrey. S. of F.R.D. Onslow, Esq. B. 8 June 1926; m. 7 May 1955, Lady June Hay, d. of 14th Earl of Kinnoull, (1 s. 3 d.). Educ. at Harrow, Oriel Coll., Oxford, and Geneva University. Served Royal Armoured Corps (Lieut. 7th Hussars) 1944-48. H.M. Foreign Service 1951-60. Member of Dartford Rural District Council 1960-62 and Kent County Council 1961-64. Parliamentary Under-Secretary of State for Aerospace, Department of Trade and Industry. Apr. 1972-Mar. 1974. A

Conservative. Sat for the Woking division of Surrey from Oct. 1964. An Opposition spokesman on Defence 1974-75 and Defence 1975-76. Delegate to Council of Europe and W.E.U. 1977-78.* [1979]

OPPENHEIM, Rt. Hon. Sally. 1 Ardmore Close, Tuffley, Gloucestershire. House of Commons, London. D. of Mark Viner, Esq. B. 26 July 1930; m. 1949, Henry, s. of A.L. Oppenheim, Esq. (1 s. 2 d.) (he died 1980). Educ. at Sheffield High School, Lowther Coll. North Wales and Royal Academy of Dramatic Art. Chairman Conservative Parliamentary Committee on Consumer Protection. Vice-President South Wales and West Fire Liaison Panel. President of Conservative Club of Gloucester 1970. Front Bench spokesman on Prices and Consumer Protection Nov. 1974-May 1979. Member of Shadow Cabinet Feb. 1975-May 1979. Former National Vice-President of the National Mobile Home Residents Association. President of the Union of Townswoman's Guilds. Member of the Society of Conservative Lawyers. Vice-President Wester Centre of Public Health Inspectors. Voted against entry to E.E.C on 28 Oct. 1971. Member of B.B.C. General Advisory Council 1971-74. Minister of State (Minister for Consumer Affairs) Department of Trade from 1979. PC. 1979. A Conservative. Sat for Gloucester from June 1970.* [1979]

ORAM, Albert Edward. 19 Ridgeside Avenue, Patcham, Brighton. S. of Henry Oram, Esq. B. 13 Aug. 1913; m. Mar. 1956, Frances Joan, d. of Charles and Dorothy Barber, of Lewes, Sussex. Educ. at Brighton Grammar School, and London School of Economics. Served in R.A. for three years when Teacher at Reading 1936-46. Research Officer, Co-operative Party 1946-55. Parliamentary Secretary Ministry of Overseas Development Oct. 1964-Oct. 1969. Co-ordinator of Development Programmes International Co-operative Alliance 1970-73. A Labour and Co-operative Member. Unsuccessfully contested the Lewes division of Sussex in 1945 and the Billericay division of Essex in 1950. Elected for East Ham S. in 1955 and sat until he retired in Feb. 1974. Voted in favour of entry to E.E.C. on 28 Oct.

1971. Created Baron Oram (Life Peerage) 1975. Lord-in-Waiting and Government Whip in House of Lords Feb. 1976-Mar. 1978. Member of Commonwealth Development Corporation 1975-76. Chairman of Commonwealth Development Agency from 1978.* [1974]

ORBACH, Maurice. 76 Eton Hall, London. S. of Hiam M. Orbach, Esq. B. 13 July 1902; m. 1935 Ruth Beatrice Huebsch Educ. at Cardiff and New York. Honorary Director Trades Advisory Council. Member of the Labour Party from 1918. Vice-President Socialist Medical Association. Member of London County Council 1937-45. St Pancras Board of Guardians 1924. A Labour Member. Unsuccessfully contested Willesden E. in 1935 and July 1938. Sat for Willesden E. from 1945-59, when he was defeated. Elected for Stockport S. in Oct. 1964 and sat until he retired on 7 Apr. 1979. Died 24 Apr. 1979. [1979]

ORME, Rt. Hon. Stanley. 47 Hope Road, Sale, Cheshire. S. of Sherwood Orme, Esq. of Sale. B. 5 Apr. 1923; m. 1951 Irene Mary, d. of Vernon F. Harris, Esq. Educ. at Elementary School, part-time technical, N.C.L.C., and W.E.A. Joined the Labour Party in 1944. Member of Amalgamated Engineering Union. Served in the R.A.F. 1942-47, Warrant Officer, Air-Bomber Navigator. Member of Sale Borough Council 1958-1965. An Opposition spokesman on Northern Ireland 1973-74. Minister of State for Northern Ireland Mar. 1974-Apr. 1976. Member of Cabinet Sept. 1976-May 1979. Minister of State, Department of Health and Social Security Apr.-Sept. 1976. Minister for Social Security Sept. 1976-May 1979. Member of Parliamentary Committee of P.L.P. from 1979. Opposition spokesman on Social Services from 1979. Chairman A.U.E.W. Parliamentary Group of Labour Members. PC. 1974. A Labour Member. Unsuccessful. Candidate for Stockport S. in 1959. Elected for Salford W. in Oct. 1964.* [1979]

ORMSBY-GORE, Maj. Rt. Hon. William David. Woodhill, Oswestry, Shropshire. S. of 4th Lord Harlech, K.G., P.C., G.C.M.G. B. 20 May 1918; m. 1st 9 Feb. 1940, Sylvia, d. of

Hugh Lloyd Thomas, Esq., of Compton Beauchamp, Shrivenham (she died 1967); 2ndly, 1969, Pamela, d. of Ralph Colin, Esq. of New York. Educ. at Eton, and New Coll., Oxford. Maj Berkshire Yeomanry and Gen. Staff 1939-46. Parliamentary Private Secretary to Selwyn Lloyd, Minister of State, Foreign Office 1951-54. Under-Secretary of State for Foreign Affairs Nov. 1956-Jan. 1957. Minister of State for Foreign Affairs Jan. 1957-June 1961. A Conservative. Elected for the Oswestry division of Shropshire in Feb. 1950 and sat until he resigned in June 1961 on appointment as Ambassador-designate in Washington. Ambassador to United States Oct. 1961-Feb. 1965. Dept. Chairman of Pearce Commission on Rhodesia 1971-72. Dept. Leader of Opposition in House of Lords 1966-67. Chairman of National Committee for Electoral Reform 1976. PC. 1957. K.C.M.G. 1961. Dept.-Lieut. for Shropshire 1961. President of British Board of Film Censors from 1965. Chairman of European Movement 1969-75, of Pilgrim Trust 1974-79, of Royal Institute of International Affairs from 1978. Prime Minister's Special Envoy in Southern Africa, 1979. Succeeded to Peerage as Baron Harlech 1964.*   [1961]

ORR, Sir John Boyd. See BOYD-ORR, Sir John.

ORR, Lawrence Percy Story. House of Commons, London. Garrick. S. of the Very Rev. W.R.M. Orr, former Dean of Dromore, Rector of Gilford, Co. Down. B. 16 Sept. 1918; m. 1939, Jean Mary, d. of F.C. Hughes, Esq. (divorced 1976). Educ. at Campbell Coll., Belfast, and Trinity Coll., Dublin. Capt. The Life Guards, Army Service 1939-46. Chairman Ulster Unionist Parliamentary Party 1964-74. Vice-President Ulster Unionist Council. Imperial Grand Master Loyal Orange Order. An Ulster Unionist Member. Elected for Down S. in Feb. 1950 and sat until he retired in Sept. 1974. Director of Associated Leisure Ltd. from 1972.*
[1974 2nd ed.]

ORR-EWING, Sir (Charles) Ian, Bart., O.B.E. 9 Eaton Mansions, London. Old Manor, Little Berkhamsted. Carlton, and

M.C.C. S. of Archibald Ian Orr-Ewing, Esq. B. 10 Feb. 1912; m. 2 Sept. 1939, Joan, d. of W.G. McMinnies, Esq., of Old Rowleys, Stoke Orchard, Cheltenham. Educ. at Harrow, and Trinity Coll., Oxford, M.A. (Physics). Chartered Engineer and Company Director. Fellow Institute of Electrical Engineers. B.B.C. Television Service 1938-49; R.A.F.V.R. 1939-46; Chief Radar Officer S.H.A.E.F. 1945. O.B.E. 1945. Parliamentary Private Secretary to the Rt. Hon. Sir Walter Monckton, Minister of Labour and National Service Nov. 1951-Dec. 1955. Gov. of Imperial College of Science 1951-57. Joint Secretary 1922 Committee 1956. Parliamentary Under-Secretary of State for Air Jan. 1957-Jan. 1959; Parliamentary and Financial Secretary to Admiralty Jan.-Oct. 1959. Civil Lord of the Admiralty Oct. 1959 to May 1963. Created Bart. 1963, 1922 Executive 1964. Vice-Chairman from 1966. Member Select Committee on Science and Technology 1967. A Conservative. Elected for Hendon N. in Feb. 1950 and sat until he retired in 1970. President and Chairman of Electronic Engineering Association 1969-70. Created Baron Orr-Ewing (Life Peerage) 1971. Dept. Chairman of Metrication Board 1971-72, Chairman 1972-77. President of National Ski Federation of Great Britain 1972-76. Member of Royal Commission on Standards of Conduct in Public Life 1975-76.*   [1970]

ORR-EWING, Sir Ian Leslie. 24 Roland Gardens, London. Carlton, M.C.C., and Royal Highland Yacht. S. of Charles Orr-Ewing, Esq., MP. for Ayr Burghs 1895-1903. B. 4 June 1893; m. 24 Jan. 1917, Helen, d. of Hon. Henry Gibbs. Educ. at Harrow, and Trinity Coll., Oxford. Lieut. Late Scots Guards and Royal Scots Fusiliers, served with B.E.F. 1914-18. Parliamentary Private Secretary to W.S. Morrison when Financial Secretary to the Treasury Dec. 1935, when Minister of Agriculture May 1937, when Chancellor of Duchy of Lancaster Jan. 1939, when Minister of Food Sept. 1939, and when Postmaster-Gen. 1940, to Rt. Hon. William Mabane, Parliamentary Secretary, Ministry of Food June 1942-43. Member of Rhodesia and Nyasaland Royal Commission 1938. F.R.S.A., Knight Bach. 1953. National President of Rural District Councils Association from 1957. A Conservative. Unsuccessfully contested Gateshead in 1929. Prospective candidate for St. Ives in 1931 but stood down in favour of the National Liberal candidate. Elected for the Weston-super-Mare division of Somerset in June 1934 and sat until his death on 27 Apr. 1958. [1958]

OSBORN, John Holbrook. Folds Head Close, Calver, Sheffield. Flat 13, 102 Rochester Row, London. Carlton. S. of S.E. Osborn Esq. B. 14 Dec. 1922; m. 1st, 12 Jan. 1952, Molly Suzanne (marriage dissolved in 1974), (2 d.); 2ndly, 6 Feb. 1976, Joan Mary MacDermot, d. of Mr. and Mrs. Wilkinson, of Buenos Aires. Educ. at Rugby School, and Trinity Hall, Cambridge. Served in the Army (Royal Signals) 1943-47. R.A. (T.A.) 1947-54. Director of Samuel Osborn and Company Limited, Sheffield. Parliamentary Private Secretary to Rt. Hon. Duncan Sandys, Commonwealth and Colonial Secretary 1963-64. Delegate to Council of Europe and W.E.U. 1972-75. Member of European Parliament 1975-79. A Conservative. Elected for the Hallam division of Sheffield in 1959.* [1979]

OSBORNE, Sir Cyril. Kinchley House, Rothley, Leicestershire. S. of Thomas Osborne, Esq., of Nottingham. B. 19 June 1898; m. 1935, Joyce Lawrence Feibusch, of Wolverhampton. Educ. at University Coll., Nottingham. Stockbroker and Company Director. Served with Royal Field Artillery 1914-18. Knighted 1961. A Conservative. Elected for the Louth division of Lincolnshire in July 1945 and sat until his death on 31 Aug. 1969. J.P. for Leicestershire. Chairman of Leicester Chamber of Commerce. Hon. Treasurer of British Group of Inter-Parliamentary Union 1964-67. Chairman of Anglo-Soviet Parliamentary Group. Master of Worshipful Company of Framework Knitters. Died 31 Aug. 1969. [1969]

OSWALD, Thomas. 28 Seaview Terrace, Joppa, Edinburgh. S. of John Oswald, Esq., of Leith. B. 1 May 1904; m. July 1933, Colina MacAskill, d. of Archibald MacAlpine, Esq., of Ballachulish, Argyllshire. Educ. at Yardheads, and Bonnington Elementary Schools,

Leith. Official of Transport and General Workers' Union; appointed Secretary Scottish Regional Trade Group 1941. Appointed Secretary Scottish Parliamentary Labour Group 1953; Secretary Members' Parliamentary Committee 1956-66. Parliamentary Private Secretary to Rt. Hon. William Ross, Secretary of State for Scotland 1968-70. A Labour Member. Unsuccessfully contested W. Aberdeenshire in Feb. 1950. Elected for Edinburgh Central in Oct. 1951 and sat until he retired in Feb. 1974. President of Scottish Old Age Pensions Association.* [1974]

OVENDEN, John Frederick. House of Commons, London. S. of Richard Ovenden, Esq. B. Aug. 1942; m. 1963 Maureen White. Educ. at Chatham House Grammar School Ramsgate. Post Office Engineer 1961-74. A Gillingham Councillor 1966-69 and 1972-74. A Labour Member. Unsuccessfully contested Sevenoaks in 1970. Elected for Gravesend in 1974 and sat until 1979, when he was defeated.* [1979]

OWEN, Rt. Hon. Dr. David Anthony Llewellyn. Castlehayes, Plympton, St. Maurice, Plymouth. 78 Narrow Street, Limehouse, London. S. of Dr. J.W.M. Owen, General Practitioner. B. 2 July 1938; m. 1968, Deborah, d. of Kyril Schabert, Esq., of New York, U.S.A., (2 s.). Educ. at Bradfield Coll., Sidney Sussex Coll., Cambridge, and St. Thomas's Hospital, London, M.A., M.B., B. Chir. (Cantab.). Late Research Fellow, Medical Unit, St. Thomas's Hospital. Member A.S.T.M.S. Parliamentary Private Secretary to Gerald Reynolds, Minister of Defence (Administration) from Apr. 1967-July 1968. Parliamentary Under-Secretary of State Ministry of Defence for the Royal Navy July 1968-June 1970. Opposition Defence spokesman 1970-72. Parliamentary Under-Secretary of State for Health and Social Security Mar.-July 1974. Minister of State Health and Social Security July 1974-Sept. 1976. Minister of State, Foreign and Commonwealth Office Sept. 1976-Feb. 77. Secretary of State for Foreign and Commonwealth Affairs Feb. 1977-Mar 1979. Member of Parliamentary Committee of P.L.P. from 1979. Opposition spokesman on Energy from 1979. Patron Disablement Income Group 1968. Published

A United Health Service 1968, *The Politics of Defence* 1972, *In Sickness and in Health* 1976, and *Human Rights* 1978. PC. 1976. Voted in favour of entry to E.E.C. on 28 Oct. 1971. A Labour Member. Unsuccessfully contested Torrington in the general election of 1964. Sat for the Sutton division of Plymouth from 1966 to Feb. 1974. Elected for the Devonport division of Plymouth in Feb. 1974.* [1979]

OWEN, Idris Wyn., J.P. Gawsworth Old Rectory, Cheshire. B. 1912. Educ. at Stockport School and Coll. of Technology, and Manchester School of Commerce. Member of Stockport Borough Council from 1946, Mayor 1962-63, Vice-President of National Federation of Building Trades Employers 1965. A Company Director in the construction industry. Fellow of the Institute of Building. A Conservative. Unsuccessfully contested Manchester Exchange in 1951, Stalybridge and Hyde in 1955, and Stockport N. in 1966. Elected for Stockport N. in June 1970 and sat until Feb. 1974, when he was defeated. Unsuccessfully contested Stockport N. in Oct. 1974.* [1974]

OWEN, William James. 18A Woodstock Road, Carshalton, Surrey. S. of W.E. Owen, Esq., a Miner. B. 18 Feb. 1901; m. 1 Sept. 1930, Ann, d. of Thomas Smith, Esq. (1 s. 1 d.). Educ. at Blaina Boys' Central School, and London Labour Coll. A Miner 1914-20. National Council of Labour Colleges Tutor Organiser 1923-30; member Blaina Urban District Council 1923-27; Secretary Leicester ILP 1930-34; member Leicester City Council 1932-37; of Education and Management Committee Leicester Co-operative Society 1932-38; Education Office Burslem Co-operative 1938-40; London Co-operative 1940-44 and Bristol Co-operative 1944-48. Community Office N.C.B. 1948-59; member Southern Sectional Board Co-operative Union. President of South Surburban Co-operative Society. Gen. Secretary Association of Clothing Contractors 1960-70. A Labour and Co-operative Member. Unsuccessfully contested the Dover division of Kent in 1950 and 1951. Elected for the Morpeth division of Northumberland in Nov. 1954 and sat until Apr. 1970 when he resigned after being charged under the Official Secrets Act of communicating information to Czechoslovak intelligence agents. Acquitted on all charges on 6 May 1970. Chairman of Sutton and Carshalton Constituency Labour Party from 1974.* [1970]

PADLEY, Walter Ernest. 73 Priory Gardens, Highgate, London. S. of Ernest Padley, Esq., of Chipping Norton. B. 24 July 1916; m. 7 Nov. 1942, Sylvia Wilson. Educ. at Chipping Norton Grammar School, and Ruskin Coll., Oxford. Member of National Council of I.L.P. 1940-46. President of Union of Shop, Distributive and Allied Workers 1948-64. Member National Executive Committee of Labour Party from 1956 to 1978 and Chairman of its International Committee 1963-71. Chairman Labour Party 1965-66. Minister of State Foreign Office Oct. 1964-Jan. 1967. Unsuccessfully contested the Acton division of Middlesex as I.L.P. candidate in Dec. 1943. A Labour Member. Sat for the Ogmore division of Glamorgan from 1950 until he retired in 1979.* [1979]

PAGE, (Arthur) John. Hitcham Lodge, Taplow, Buckinghamshire. Brooks's, and M.C.C. S. of Sir Arthur Page, Q.C. B. 16 Sept. 1919; m. 1950, Anne, d. of Charles Micklem, Esq., D.S.O., D.L., J.P., of Longcross, Surrey. Educ. at Harrow, and Magdalene Coll., Cambridge. Joined Royal Artillery 1939, served Europe, Middle East (wounded), demobilised as Maj. Norfolk Yeomanry. Chairman Bethnal Green and East London Housing Association 1952-62. Member Commonwealth Migration Council. President Conservative Trade Unionists' National Advisory Committee 1967-69. Parliamentary Private Secretary to Charles Fletcher-Cooke, C.M. Woodhouse and Mervyn Pike, Under-Secretaries of State, Home Office 1961-64. Vice-Chairman of Conservative Party Labour Affairs Committee 1964-70, Chairman 1970-74. President of the Independent Schools' Association 1971. Member of Executive Inter-Parliamentary Union British Group 1970. Treasurer 1974-76. Chairman of Council for Independent Education from 1974. Joint Secretary Conservative Broadcasting and Communications Committee 1974-76. British delegate to Council of Europe and Western European Union from 1972. Chairman Health and Social Affairs Committee Council of Europe 1976. Vice-Chairman Inter-Parliamentary Union British Group 1976. A Conservative. Unsuccessfully contested Eton and Slough in 1959 general election. Elected for Harrow W. at a by-election in Mar. 1960.*   [1979]

PAGE, John Derek. The Vicarage, Whaddon, Royston, Hertfordshire. S. of John Page, Esq.; m. 1948, Catherine Audrey Halls. B. 14 Aug. 1927. Educ. at Elementary Schools, then by scholarship to St. Bede's Coll., Manchester, (B.Sc. Sociology) London External. Gen. Sales Manager Chemical Company. Export Consultant in the chemical industry. Director Cambridge Chemical Company Limited. Joined the Labour Party in 1945. Member of Chemical Workers' Union. Member of Transport and General Workers Union. Private Pilot, member of Cambridge Aero Club. Member of Lymm (Cheshire) Urban District Council 1954-57. A Labour Member. Unsuccessfully contested Northwich in the 1955 general election, and the Isle of Ely in 1959. Elected for the Kings Lynn division of Norfolk in Oct. 1964 and sat until 1970, when he was defeated. Unsuccessfully contested N.W. Norfolk in Feb. 1974. Member of Council for Small Industries in Rural Areas. Created Baron Whaddon (Life Peerage) 1978.*   [1970]

PAGE, Rt. Hon. Sir (Rodney) Graham, M.B.E. 21 Cholmeley Lodge, Cholmeley Park, London. S. of Lieut.-Col. Frank Page, D.S.O. and Bar., of Hertford. B. 30 June 1911; m. 8 Feb. 1934, Hilda, d. of Edgar Dixon, Esq., (1 s. 1 d.). Educ. at Magdalen Coll. School, Oxford, and London University. A Privy Council Appeal Agent and a Solicitor. Admitted 1934. LL.B. Served with R.A.F.V.R. 1939-45, Flight-Lieut. M.B.E. 1944. Honorary Fellow Institute of Practitioners in Advertising. Honorary Fellow of Institute of Practitioners in Work Study Organisation and Methods. Honorary Fellow of Institute of Chartered Secretaries and Administrators. An Opposition spokesman on Local Government Housing and Land 1965-70. Minister of State, Housing and Local Government June-Oct. 1970. Minister for Local Government and Development Oct. 1970-Mar. 74. Chairman of the Select Committee of Lords and Commons on Statutory Instruments 1964-70 and 1974-79. PC. 1972. Chairman of Select Committee on Home Affairs from 1979. Knighted 1980. A Conservative. Unsuccessfully contested N. Islington in 1950 and 1951. Elected for Crosby in Nov. 1953.*   [1979]

PAGE, Richard Lewis. Brook Cottage, Gomshall, Surrey. S. of Victor Charles Page, Esq. B. 22 Feb. 1941; m. 3 Oct. 1964, Madeleine Ann Brown, (1 s. 1 d.). Educ. at Hurstpierpoint Coll., and Luton Technical Coll. Councillor, Banstead Urban District Council 1968-71. A Conservative. Parliamentary candidate for Workington 1971. Unsuccessfully contested Workington in Feb. and Oct. 1974. Sat for Workington from Nov. 1976 until May 1979, when he was defeated. Elected for Hertfordshire S.W. at a by-election in Dec. 1979.*   [1979]

PAGET, Reginald Thomas, Q.C. Lubenham Lodge, Market Harborough. 9 Grosvenor Cottages, London. S. of Guy Paget, Esq. B. 2 Sept. 1908; m. 28 Aug. 1931, Sybil Gibbons. Educ. at Eton, and Trinity Coll., Cambridge. Barrister-at-Law, Gray's Inn, 1934; Lieut. R.N.V.R. 1940. A Labour Member. Unsuccessfully contested Northampton in 1935. Elected for Northampton in July 1945 and sat until he retired in Feb. 1974. K.C. 1947. Secretary of U.K. Council of European Movement 1954. Opposition spokesman on Admiralty affairs 1960-61 and on War Office affairs 1961-64. Resigned Labour Whip Dec. 1966-June 1967 over the Government's Rhodesia policy. Created Baron Paget of Northampton (Life Peerage) 1974. Master of Pytchley Hounds 1958-71.*   [1974]

PAISLEY, Rev. Ian Richard Kyle. The Parsonage, 17 Cyprus Avenue, Belfast, Northern Ireland. S. of Rev. J. Kyle Paisley B. 1926; m. 1956 Eileen Emily Cassells. Educ. at Ballymena Model School and Technical High School, S. Wales Bible Coll. and Reformed Presbyterian Theological Coll., Belfast. Founder of the Protestant Unionist Party and of the Free Presbyterian Church. Minister of Martyrs Memorial Free Presbyterian Church, Belfast from 1946. Moderator of Free Presbyterian Church of Ulster 1951. Member of Northern Ireland Parliament for Bann Side 1970-72. Founder of Democratic Unionist Party 1972. Member of Northern Ireland Assembly for N. Antrim 1973-75. Vice-Chairman of United Ulster Unionist Coalition 1974. Member of Constitutional Convention for N. Antrim 1975-76. Member of European Parliament for Northern Ireland from 1979. Hon. D.D. Bob Jones University, South Carolina. A Democratic Unionist Member. Sat for Antrim N. from June 1970.* [1979]

PALING, Rt. Hon. Wilfred. Wayside, Scawthorpe, Doncaster. S. of George Thomas Paling, Esq., of Marehay, Ripley. B. 7 Apr. 1883; m. 28 Sept. 1903, Elizabeth, d. of John Hunt, Esq., of Huthwaite. Educ. at Ripley Elementary School. A Coal Miner and Checkweighman. Member of Bentley Urban District Council and of West Riding County Council 1919; Trustee of Yorkshire Mineworkers' Association. Parliamentary Private Secretary to Rt. Hon. Margaret Bondfield when Parliamentary Secretary to Ministry of Labour Jan.-Oct. 1924. An Opposition Whip Jan.-May 1929 and Aug.-Oct. 1931. A Lord Commissioner of the Treasury and Labour Whip June 1929-Aug. 1931 and May 1940-Feb. 1941. Dept. Chief Whip Nov. 1935-Feb. 1941; Parliamentary Secretary Ministry of Pensions Feb. 1941-May 1945; Minister of Pensions July 1945-Apr. 1947. Postmaster-Gen. Apr. 1947-Feb. 1950. PC. 1944. A Labour Member. Sat for the Doncaster division of the W. Riding of Yorkshire from Nov. 1922-Oct. 1931 when he was defeated, and for the Wentworth division of the W. Riding of Yorkshire Dec. 1933-Feb. 1950. Elected for the Dearne Valley Division of the W. Riding of Yorkshire in Feb. 1950 and sat until he retired in 1959. Died 17 Apr. 1971. [1959]

PALING, William Thomas. Sherwood, 22 Goose Lane, Wickersley, Rotherham. S. of George Thomas Paling, Esq. B. 28 Oct. 1892; m. 1919, Gladys Nellie, M.B.E., J.P., d. of William Frith, Esq., of Nuncar Gate, Not-tinghamshire. A Checkweighman. Member of the West Riding County Council. A Labour Member. Unsuccessfully contested the Burton division of Staffordshire in 1929 and 1931. Elected for Dewsbury in July 1945 and sat until he retired in 1959.* [1959]

PALMER, Arthur Montague Frank. 14 Lavington Court, London. Hill Cottage, Charlcutt, Nr. Calne, Wiltshire. Athenaeum. S. of Frank Palmer, Esq., of Northam, Devon. B. 4 Aug. 1912; m. 1939, Marion, d. of Frank Woollaston, Esq., of Chiswick, (2 s.). Educ. at Ashford Grammar School, and Brunel University. Student Engineer at Metropolitan Electric Supply Company Limited, London. Chartered Engineer. National Officer Electrical Power Engineers' Association. Town Councillor Brentford and Chiswick 1937-45. Former Chairman Parliamentary and Scientific Committee. Chairman Select Committee on Science and Technology 1966-70 and 1974-79. Voted in favour at entry to E.E.C. on 28 Oct. 1971. A Labour and Co-operative Member. Sat for Wimbledon from 1945 to 1950, when he unsuccessfully contested Merton and Morden. Unsuccessfully contested Merton and Morden again in 1951. Elected for the Cleveland division of N. Riding of Yorkshire in Oct. 1952 and sat until 1959, when he was defeated. Sat for Bristol Central from 1964 to Feb. 1974 and for Bristol N.E. from 1974.* [1979]

PANNELL, Norman Alfred. Thaxted, Mill Lane, Heswall, Cheshire. S. of Arthur Harry Pannell, Esq. B. 17 Apr. 1901; m. 1932, Isabel Morris. Educ. at Sir George Monoux Grammar School, London, F.C.I.S. 1937. Engaged in commerce in West Africa 1930-45. Member Nigeria Legislative Council 1944-45; member Liverpool City Council 1952-57 and 1967-70. Director of Ashanti Goldfields Corporation 1958. A Conservative. Unsuccessfully contested the Scotland division of Liverpool in 1951. Elected for the Kirkdale division of Liverpool in 1955 and sat until 1964, when he was defeated. Unsuccessfully contested the Kirkdale division again in 1966. Member of Cheshire County Council 1970-74 and Merseyside County Council 1973-76. Died 8 Mar. 1976. [1964]

PANNELL, Rt. Hon. (Thomas) Charles.
159 Glenview, Abbey Wood, London. S. of
James William Pannell, Esq. B. 10 Sept.
1902; m. 1929, Lilian Maud Frailing. Member A.E.U. 1918; Honorary Secretary T.U. Group P.L.P. 1953-64; member of Walthamstow Borough Council 1929-36; Erith Borough Council 1938-55.
Leader of Council and Chairman of Finance
and General Purposes Committee until 1949;
Alderman 1944-54; responsible Chairman
during whole of War of 1939-45 for post-blitz
services; Mayor 1945-46. Chairman of N.W.
Kent Division Executive for Education 1944-55; member and Dept. Leader Kent County
Council Labour Group 1946-49; Vice-President Association of Municipal Corporations.
Member Labour Party 1918; Member Select
Committee on Accommodation 1953, on
Procedure 1958-59, on House of Lords Reform 1962, on the Law of Privilege 1967, and
on Civil List; a Delegate to the N.A.T.O.
Parliamentary Conference 1955, 1956 and
1957; Delegate to the Commonwealth Party
Association Conference, Ottawa 1966; Leader Delegation to Singapore 1966; Delegate
to Poland 1958; Leader Delegation to United
Arab Republic 1973. Opposition Front Bench
spokesman for Ministry of Public Building
and Works 1963-64; Minister of Public Building and Works Oct. 1964-Apr. 1966; PC.
1964. A Labour Member. Elected for Leeds
W. in July 1949 and sat until he retired in
Feb. 1974. Voted in favour of entry to E.E.C.
on 28 Oct. 1971. Created Baron Pannell (Life
Peerage) 1974. Hon. LL.D. University of
Leeds 1975. Died 23 Mar. 1980.   [1974]

PARDOE, John Wentworth. House of
Commons, London. S. of Cuthbert B. Pardoe, Esq. B. 27 July 1934; m. 1958, Joy, d. of
Alfred Pearman, Esq., (2 s. 1 d.). Educ. at
Sherborne School, and Corpus Christi Coll.,
Cambridge. On Staff of Television Audience
Measurement Limited 1958-60, Osborne
Peacock and Company Limited 1960-61,
Liberal News 1961-66. Honorary Treasurer of
Liberal Party 1969. Member of General
Advisory Council of I.B.A. 1973-78. Dept.
Liberal Whip Nov. 1973-Mar. 1974. Liberal
spokesman on Economic Affairs 1974-79.
Dept. Leader of Liberal Party in House of
Commons 1976-79. A Liberal. Unsuccessfully

contested Finchley in the 1964 general election. Elected for Cornwall N. in Mar. 1966
and sat until 1979, when he was defeated.
Television programme presenter, London
Weekend Television, from 1979. Senior Research Fellow of Policy Studies Institute from
1979. Joint Managing Director of Sight and
Sound Education Limited from 1979. Member of London Metal Exchange.*   [1979]

PARGITER, George Albert, C.B.E. 190
Whyteleafe Road, Caterham, Surrey. S. of
William Pargiter, Esq., of Greens Norton. B.
16 Mar. 1897; m. 1919, Dorothy Woods.
Educ. at Towcester Grammar School. Served
in Gallipoli 1914-16. Member of Middlesex
County Council 1934-65, Alderman 1946.
Mayor of Southall 1938, 1939 and 1940.
Dept.-Lieut. for Middlesex, for County of
London and for Greater London 1953-76.
Chairman of Middlesex County Council
1959-60. Chairman of the Executive of the
County Councils Association 1963. A Labour
Member. Sat for the Spelthorne division of
Middlesex July 1945-Feb. 1950. Elected for
Southall in Feb. 1950 and sat until he retired
in 1966. C.B.E. 1961. Created Baron Pargiter
(Life Peerage) 1966.*   [1966]

PARK, George Maclean, J.P. 170 Binley
Road, Coventry. S. of James Park, Esq. B. 27
Sept. 1914; m. 1941 Joyce, d. of Robert Holt
Stead, Esq. Educ. at Onslow Drive and
Whitehill Grammar Schools, Glasgow and
Coventry Technical Coll. Senior A.U.E.W.
Shop Steward Chrysler U.K. Limited, Ryton
1962-72. Coventry City Councillor 1961-74,
Leader of Labour Group 1967-74, Leader of
Council 1972-74. Justice of the Peace from
1961. West Midlands Metropolitan County
Council 1973-77. Parliamentary Private Secretary to John Gilbert, Minister for Transport 1975-76. Parliamentary Private Secretary to Rt. Hon. Eric Varley, Secretary of
State for Industry 1976-79. Chairman West
Midlands Group of Labour MPs 1976. A
Labour Member. Sat for Coventry N.E. from
Feb. 1974.*   [1979]

PARK, (Joseph) Trevor. House of Commons, London. S. of Stephen Clifford Park,
Esq. B. 12 Dec. 1927; m. 1953, Barbara
Black. Educ. at Bury Grammar School, and

Manchester University (M.A. Degree in History). Lecturer, Extramural Department University of Sheffield 1960-64. A Schoolmaster from 1949-56. Joined the Labour Party in 1945. Member of T.G.W.U. Tutor at a number of Trade Union and Co-operative Residential Summer Schools. W.E.A. Tutor and Organiser 1956-60 and 1970-72. President of Bury and Radcliffe C.L.P. 1960. Member of Select Committee on Nationalized Ind. 1966-68. Member of Select Committee on Education and Science from 1968. A Labour Member. Unsuccessfully contested Altrincham and Sale in 1955 and Darwen in 1959 general elections. Elected for Derbyshire S.E. in Oct. 1964 and sat until he retired in 1970. Lecturer in Industrial Relations, Department of Adult Education and Extramural Studies, University of Leeds from 1972. Chairman of Association of Tutors in Adult Education 1972-75. Member of Yorkshire and Humberside Economic Planning Council from 1977.*   [1970]

PARKER, (Herbert) John Harvey, C.B.E. 4 Essex Court, Temple, London. S. of Capt. H.A.M. Parker. B. 15 July 1906; m. 20 Feb. 1943, Zena, d. of Clement Mimardiere, Esq., (1 s.). Educ. at Marlborough, and St. John's Coll., Oxford. An Author. Member of Executive London Labour Party 1942-47, and of National Executive Committee of Labour Party 1943-44; Gen. Secretary Fabian Research Bureau 1933-39, and of Fabian Society 1939-45, Vice-Chairman 1946-50, Chairman 1950-53, Honorary Secretary 1953-72, Vice-President 1972 Honorary Secretary Webb Trustees. Gov. of London School of Economics 1949. Member Essex University Court. Member of Staff of Social Survey of Merseyside (Liverpool University) 1929-32. Chairman Oxford University Labour Club 1929. Parliamentary Private Secretary to Miss Ellen Wilkinson, Parliamentary Secretary Ministry of Home Security 1940-42. Member of Speakers' Conference 1944, 1965 and 1973-74, and of Parliamentary Delegations to U.S.S.R. 1945, Italy 1957, and Ethiopia 1964. Leader Parliamentary Delegation Windward Islands 1965, and Forestry Delegation to Yugoslavia 1971. Parliamentary Under-Secretary of State for Dominions Aug. 1945-May 1946. Member Select Committee

Parliamentary Disqualifications 1956. C.B.E. 1965. Member Parliamentary Procedure Committee 1967-74. E.C. National Trust 1969. Member Historic Buildings Council 1974. Member Inland Waterways Amenity Council 1968. Chairman British Yugoslav Parliamentary Group 1964. Father of House of Commons from 1979. A Labour Member. Unsuccessfully contested Holland-with-Boston in 1931. Sat for Romford from Nov. 1935 to July 1945, for Dagenham from July 1945 to Feb. 1974 and for the Dagenham division of Barking from Feb. 1974.*   [1979]

PARKIN, Benjamin Theaker. 75A Winchester Street, London. S. of Capt. B.D. Parkin, of Leyton. B. 21 Apr. 1906; m. 1st, 1929, Phyllis Lunt (divorced 1957); 2ndly, 1957, Pamela Coates. Educ. at Wycliffe Coll., Lincoln Coll., Oxford, and Strasbourg University. Ex-teacher. R.A.F. 1941-45, Flight-Lieut. A Labour Member. Sat for Stroud from 1945-50. Unsuccessfully contested the Stroud and Thornbury division of Gloucestershire in 1950 and 1951. Elected for Paddington N. in Dec. 1953 and sat until his death on 3 June 1969.   [1969]

PARKINSON, Cecil Edward. House of Commons, London. Hawks (Cambridge). S. of Sidney Parkinson, Esq. B. 1 Sept. 1931; m. 1957, Ann Mary Jarvis, (3 d.). Educ. at Royal Grammar School, Lancaster, and Emmanuel Coll., Cambridge, (M.A.). A Chartered Accountant. Secretary Conservative Parliamentary Finance Committee 1971-72. Parliamentary Private Secretary to Michael Heseltine, Minister for Aerospace 1972-74. Assistant Government Whip Jan.-Mar. 1974, Opposition Whip 1974-76. Opposition spokesman on Trade 1976-79. Minister of State, Department of Trade from May 1979. Chairman Anglo-Swiss Parliamentary Group. Leader Institute of Directors Parliamentary Panel. A Conservative. Unsuccessfully contested Northampton in June 1970. Sat for Enfield W. from Nov. 1970 to Feb. 1974. Elected for Hertfordshire S. in Feb. 1974.*   [1979]

PARKYN, Brian Stewart. Mwnwg, Harrold, Bedford. Chemical. S. of Leslie Parkyn, Esq., Nurseryman. B. 28 Apr. 1923; m. 1951,

Janet, d. of C.H. Stormer, Esq., of Eastbourne. Educ. at King Edward VI Grammar School, Chelmsford. Joined Scott Bader and Company Limited as Plastics Chemist 1947; appointed Director 1953. Chairman of Reinforced Plastics Federation 1961-63. Travelled in China. Fellow of the Plastics Institute; Fellow of the Royal Society of Arts. Member of Select Committee on Science and Technology. A Labour Member. Unsuccessfully contested Bedford in 1964 general election. Elected for Bedford in Mar. 1966 and sat until 1970 when he was defeated. Unsuccessfully contested Bedford in Oct. 1974. Principal of Glacier Institute of Management from 1976.* [1970]

PARRY, Robert. House of Commons, London. S. of Robert Parry, Esq. B. Jan. 1933; m. 1956 Marie Hesdon. Educ. at Bishop Goss R.C. School, Liverpool. Member Liverpool City Council from 1963 to 1974. Member T. & G.W.U. A Building Trade Worker and former full-time Organiser for N.U.P.E. A Labour Member. Sat for the Exchange division of Liverspool from June 1970 to Feb. 1974 and for Scotland Exchange division of Liverpool from Feb. 1974.* [1979]

PARTRIDGE, Ernest, C.B.E. 4 Elm Bank Mansions, Barnes, London. St. Stephen's. S. of William Thomas Partridge, Esq., Doctor of Medicine. B. 10 Aug. 1895; m. 12 Feb. 1927, Sarah Millicent, d. of Sinclair Orr Langtry, Esq., of Co. Armagh. Educ. at Wilson's Grammar School, Camberwell. Served in Royal Fusiliers and Durham Light Infantry 1914-18, Capt.; and in Argyll and Sutherland Highlanders 1942-44. Director of Joshua Bigwood and Son Limited, Wolverhampton. Chairman Lloyds Permanent Building Society, London. C.B.E. 1954. Parliamentary Private Secretary to J. Hay, Parliamentary Secretary to Ministry of Transport and Civil Lord of the Admiralty 1960-64. A Conservative. Unsuccessfully contested Battersea S. in 1945 and 1950. Elected there in Oct. 1951 and sat until 1964 when he was defeated. Died 20 Apr. 1974. [1964]

PATON, Florence Beatrice. 63 Valley Road, Welwyn Garden City, Hertfordshire. D. of George Widdowson, Esq. B. 1 June 1891; m. 5 Apr. 1930, John Paton, MP. Educ. privately. A Labour Member. Unsuccessfully contested Cheltenham in Sept. 1928 and the Rushcliffe division of Nottinghamshire in 1929 and 1931. Elected for the Rushcliffe division of Nottinghamshire in July 1945 and sat until 1950 when she unsuccessfully contested the Carlton division of Nottinghamshire. Chairman of Committees 1947-50, first woman to preside over the whole House in Committee. Unsuccessfully contested the Carlton division of Nottinghamshire in 1951 and 1955. Member of the Royal Commission on Common Land 1955-58. Died 12 Oct. 1976. [1950]

PATON, John. 63 Valley, Road, Welwyn Garden City, Hertfordshire. S. of James Paton, Esq. B. in Aberdeen 8 Aug. 1886; m. 5 Apr. 1930, Florence Beatrice Widdowson, MP. for Rushcliffe 1945-50 (she died 12 Oct. 1976). Educ. at Elementary School. A Secretary and Lecturer. General Secretary of Independent Labour Party 1927-33. Editor of *New Leader* and *Penal Reformer*. A Labour Member. Unsuccessfully contested the Bute and N. Ayrshire division of Ayrshire and Bute in 1922 and S. Aberdeen in 1923. Sat for Norwich July 1945-Feb. 1950. Elected for the N. division of Norwich in Feb. 1950 and sat until he retired in 1964. Died 14 Dec. 1976. [1964]

PATTIE, Geoffrey Edwin. Terrington House, 15 College Road, Dulwich Village, London. St. Stephen's, Royal Green Jackets, and Marylebone Cricket. S. of A. Pattie, Esq., L.D.S. B. 17 Jan. 1936; m. 1 Oct. 1960, Tuëma Caroline, d. of C. Eyre-Maunsell, Esq., (1 s. 1 d.). Educ. at Durham School, and St. Catharines Coll., Cambridge, B.A. 1959, M.A. 1963. Barrister-at-Law, Gray's Inn 1964. Director Collett, Dickenson, Pearce International 1966; Joint Managing Director 1969-73. Greater London Council member, Lambeth 1967-70. Chairman Finance Committee I.L.E.A. 1968-70. Chairman London Coll. of Printing 1968-69. Secretary Conservative Parliamentary Aviation Committee 1974. Secretary Conservative Parliamentary Defence Committee 1975. Secretary Aviation Committee 1974-76, Vice-Chairman 1976. Secretary Defence

Committee 1975-76. Public Accounts Committee 1976. Vice-Chairman All-Party Committee on Mental Health. Member General Synod Church of England 1970-75. Under-Secretary of State for R.A.F. from May 1979. A Conservative. Unsuccessfully contested Barking in 1966 and 1970. Sat for Chertsey and Walton from Feb. 1974.*

[1979]

PAVITT, Laurence Anstice. House of Commons, London. Harlesden Labour. S. of George Pavitt, Esq., Railwayman. B. 1 Feb. 1914; m. 12 June 1937, Rosina, d. of Norman Walton, Esq. Educ. at Elementary School, and Co-operative Adult Education. National Secretary British Federation of Young Co-operators 1941-46. General Secretary Anglo-Chinese Development Society 1946-52. Education Officer Co-operative Union 1947-52. Expert Asian Co-operative Field Mission, Lahore 1952-55. National Organiser Medical Practitioners Union 1956-59. Member Medical Research Council 1969-72. Member Hearing Aid Council 1968-74. Member Select Committee Overseas Aid. Parliamentary Private Secretary to Rt. Hon. Michael Stewart, Secretary of State for Education 1964-65, Foreign Secretary 1965-66 and First Secretary of State and Secretary of State for Economic Affairs 1966-67. Chairman P.L.P's Health Group. Member Executive Committee U.K. Inter-Parliamentary Union and Commonwealth Parliamentary Association. Chairman British Chinese Parliamentary Group. Chairman All-Party Parliamentary Group on Smoking and Health. Assistant Government Whip Mar. 1974-Feb. 1976. A Co-operative and Labour Member. Sat for W. Willesden from 1959 to Feb. 1974. Elected for Brent S. in Feb. 1974.*

[1979]

PEAKE, Rt. Hon. Osbert. 36 Kingston House, Prince's Gate, London. S. of Maj. Herbert Peake, of Bawtry Hall, Yorkshire. B. 30 Dec. 1897; m. 19 June 1922, Lady Joan Capell, d. of George, 7th Earl of Essex. Educ. at Eton, Royal Military Coll., Sandhurst, and Christ Church, Oxford. Maj. Nottinghamshire Yeomanry and Lieut. Coldstream Guards R. of O. Barrister-at-Law, Inner Temple 1923. Parliamentary Under-Secretary of State for Home Affairs Apr. 1939-

Oct. 1944; Financial Secretary to the Treasury Oct. 1944-July 1945. Minister of National Insurance Nov. 1951-Sept. 1953. Chairman of Public Accounts Committee 1945-48. Minister of Pensions and National Insurance Sept. 1953-Dec. 1955. PC. 1943. A Conservative. Unsuccessfully contested Dewsbury in 1922. Sat for Leeds N. May 1929-May 1955 and for Leeds N.E. May 1955-Jan. 1956 when he was created Visct. Ingleby. Member of Cabinet Oct. 1954-Dec. 1955. Chairman of Airedale Collieries Limited. Died 11 Oct. 1966.

[1955]

PEARSON, Arthur, C.B.E. 24 The Avenue, Pontypridd, Glamorgan. S. of William Pearson, Esq., of Pontypridd. B. 1897. Educ. at Pontypridd Elementary School. J.P. for Glamorgan. Member of Glamorgan County Council 1928-46. Labour Whip 1939-59. Comptroller of H.M. Household Aug. 1945-Mar. 1946. Treasurer to H.M. Household Mar. 1946-Oct. 1951. A Labour Member. Elected for the Pontypridd division of Glamorganshire in Feb. 1938 and sat until he retired in 1970. C.B.E. 1949.*

[1970]

PEARSON, Sir Francis Fenwick, Bart., M.B.E., J.P. Gressingham Hall, Hornby. Carlton. S. of Frank Pearson, Esq., Solicitor. B. 13 June 1911; m. 1938, Katharine Mary, d. of the Rev. D. Denholm Fraser. Educ. at Uppingham, and Trinity Hall, Cambridge. 1st Gurkha Rifles 1931-32. Aide-de-Camp to Viceroy of India 1933-34. Indian Political Service 1933-47. M.B.E. 1945. Chief Minister of Manipur State 1945-47. Farming and Local Government 1947-58. J.P. for Lancashire 1952. Assistant Government Whip 1960-63. Lord Commissioner of Treasury Mar. 1962-Oct. 1963. Parliamentary Private Secretary to Sir Alec Douglas-Home, K.T., MP., Prime Minister and First Lord of the Treasury, 1963-64. Created Bart. Dec. 1964. Dept. Lieut. of Lancashire 1971. Chairman of Central Lancashire New Town Development Corporation from 1971. A Conservative. Elected for Clitheroe in 1959 and sat until he retired in 1970.*

[1970]

PEART, Rt. Hon. Thomas Frederick. House of Commons, London. S. of Emerson Featherstone Peart, Esq., of Durham. B. 30

Apr. 1914; m. 1945, Sarah Elizabeth Lewis. Educ. at Durham University, B.Sc., and Inns of Court (Inner Temple). A Schoolmaster, President of Durham University Union. Member of Easington Rural District Council 1937-40. Served in Italy and N. Africa with Anti-Aircraft Battery 1942-45, Lieut. R.A. Parliamentary Private Secretary to Rt. Hon. Tom Williams, Minister of Agriculture 1945-51. Delegate Council of Europe 1952-55; Privy Council Representative Council of the Royal Coll. of Veterinary Surgeons 1953-64. Opposition spokesman on Agriculture 1959-60 and 1961-64 and on Science 1960-61. Member Nature Conservancy 1961-64. PC. Oct. 1964. Minister of Agriculture, Fisheries and Food Oct. 1964-Apr. 1968. Lord Privy Seal and Leader of House of Commons Apr.-Oct. 1968. Lord President of the Council and Leader of the House of Commons Oct. 1968-June 1970. Opposition spokesman for Agriculture, Fisheries and Food 1971-73; Defence 1972-74. Leader Labour Delegation to the Council of Europe 1973-74, and Western European Assembly; Vice-President Council of Europe 1973-74. Minister of Agriculture, Fisheries and Food Mar. 1974-Sept. 1976. Unsuccessful candidate for Dept. Leadership of Labour Party 1970. Opposition spokesman on House of Commons affairs 1970-71. Member of Parliamentary Committee of P.L.P. 1970-73. A Labour Member. Elected for the Workington division of Cumberland in 1945 and sat until Sept. 1976 when he was created Baron Peart (Life Peerage). Lord Privy Seal and Leader of House of Lords Sept. 1976-May 1979. Leader of Opposition in House of Lords from 1979.*
[1976]

PEEL, Sir William John. 51 Cambridge Street, London. Carlton, and Leicestershire. S. of Sir William Peel, K.C.M.G., K.B.E. B. 16 June 1912; m. 1936, Rosemary, d. of Robert Readhead, Esq., of Hambledon, Surrey. Educ. at Wellington Coll., and Queens' Coll., Cambridge. Joined Colonial Service in Malaya 1934, Capt.; P.O.W.. 1942-45. British Resident, Brunei 1946-48; Resident Commissioner Gilbert and Ellice Islands 1949-51; retired 1951. Parliamentary Private Secretary to F.J. Erroll, Economic Secretary

to Treasury 1958-59 and Minister of State, Board of Trade 1959-60. Assistant Government Whip 1960-61. Lord Commissioner of the Treasury Nov. 1961-Oct. 1964. A Conservative. Unsuccessfully contested the Meriden division of Warwickshire in 1955. Elected for Leicester S.E. in Nov. 1957 and sat until he retired in Feb. 1974. President Assembly of Western European Union 1972. President North Atlantic Assembly 1972-73. Knight Bach. 1973. Member of European Parliament 1973-74. Hon. Director of Conservative Party International Office 1975-76.*
[1974]

PENDRY, Thomas. Chapel House, Gorsey Brow, Broadbottom, Hyde, Cheshire. Reform. S. of Leonard E. Pendry, Esq., Coach-builder. B. 10 June 1934; m. 19 Feb. 1966, Moira Anne Smith (1 d.). Educ. at St. Augustines School, Ramsgate and Plater Hall, Oxford. Member of Paddington Council 1962-65. Middleweight Colonial Champion, Hong Kong 1957; boxed for Oxford University 1957-59. Official of National Union of Public Employees 1960-70. Chairman Derby Labour Party 1966. Opposition Whip 1971-74. Member Council of Europe and Western European Union 1973-75. Lord Commissioner to the Treasury Mar. 1974-Jan. 1977, when he resigned. Under-Secretary of State for Northern Ireland Nov. 1978-May 1979. An Opposition spokesman on Northern Ireland from 1979. A Roman Catholic. A Labour Member. Sat for the Stalybridge and Hyde division of Cheshire from June 1970.*
[1979]

PENHALIGON, David Charles. 7 Fore Street, Chacewater, Truro. National Liberal. S. of Robert Charles Penhaligon, Esq. B. 6 June 1944; m. 6 Jan. 1968, Annette, d. of Owen Lidgey, Esq., (1 s. 1 d.). Educ. at Truro School, and Cornwall Technical Coll. A Chartered Mechanical Engineer. Member Liberal Party Council 1968. Liberal Party spokesman on Health and Social Services Oct. 1974-July 1976; spokesman on Employment July 1976-Mar. 1977; spokesman on Energy and Transport from 1977 and on Environment 1977-79. A Liberal. Unsuccessfully contested Totnes in 1970 and Truro in Feb. 1974. Elected for Truro in Oct. 1974.*
[1979]

PENTLAND, Norman. 10 Sandbach, Great Lumley. Chester-le-Street, Durham. S. of William Henry Pentland, Esq., retired Miner. B. 9 Sept. 1912; m. 21 Aug. 1937. Ethel Maude, d. of Charles Coates, Esq. Educ. at Fatfield County School. Worked as a Miner at Harraton Colliery, Co. Durham 1926-49, when elected Checkweighman. Chairman Chester-le-Street Rural District Council 1952-53. Member Durham Miners' Executive Committee 1952-53. Parliamentary Secretary Ministry of Pensions and National Insurance Oct. 1964-Aug. 1966 and to Ministry of Social Security Aug. 1966-Nov. 1968. Under-Secretary of State Department of Health and Social Security Oct. 1968-Oct. 1969. Parliamentary Secretary Ministry of Posts and Telecommunications Oct. 1969-June 1970. Opposition spokesman on Posts and Telecommunications July-Dec. 1970. A Labour Member. Elected for the Chester-le-Street division of Durham in Sept. 1956 and sat until his death on 28 Oct. 1972. Unsuccessful candidate for Chairmanship of P.L.P. 1971 and 1972. Died 28 Oct. 1972.

[1973]

PERCIVAL, Sir (Walter) Ian, Q.C. House of Commons, London. S. of S. Eldon Percival, Esq. B. 11 May 1921; m. 14 Feb. 1942, Madeline, d. of A.Cooke, Esq., (1 s. 1 d.). Educ. at Latymer, and St. Catharine's, Cambridge. Served in the Army, Maj. 2nd Buffs 1940-46. Barrister from 1948. Q.C. 1963. Bencher of the Inner Temple 1970. Member of Council of Royal Borough of Kensington 1952-59. Chairman of Committees etc. Fellow of the Institute of Taxation. Chairman of the Parliamentary Committee of the Institute 1966-71. Member Royal Economic Society. Member of the Inns of Court Conservative and Unionist Society and Director of Research 1963-65. Secretary of the Conservative Party's Parliamentary Legal Committee from Oct. 1964, Vice-Chairman 1968-70, Chairman 1970-74. Shadow Solicitor-Gen. Jan. 1976. Recorder of Deal July 1971. Solicitor General from May 1979. Knighted 1979. A Conservative. Unsuccessfully contested Battersea N. in 1951 and 1955. Elected for Southport in 1959.*

[1979]

PERKINS, Sir (Walter) Robert Dempster. Rookwoods Farm, Oakridge, Gloucestershire. Carlton. S. of Walter Frank Perkins, Esq., MP. for the New Forest division of Hampshire 1910-22. B. 1903; m. 6 Oct. 1944, Patricia Moyra, d. of Lieut.-Col. J.H.A. Annesley, C.M.G., D.S.O., and widow of Air Commander Sir Nigel Norman, 2nd Bart. Educ. at Eton, and Trinity Coll., Cambridge. An Engineer. Joined R.A.F. Sept. 1938. Parliamentary Secretary to Ministry of Civil Aviation Mar.-July 1945. A Conservative. Sat for Stroud from May 1931-July 1945, when he was defeated. Elected for the Stroud and Thornbury division of Gloucestershire in Feb. 1950 and sat until he retired in 1955. Knight Bach. 1954.* [1954]

PERRINS, Wesley. 39 Woodfield Avenue, Wollescote, Stourbridge. S. of Councillor Amos Perrins, of Stourbridge. B. 21 Sept. 1905; m. 30 July 1932, Mary, d. of Charles Evans, Esq. Educ. at Wollescote Council School, and Upper Standard School, Lye. Trade Union Official from 1935. Member of Lye and Wollescote Urban District Council 1928-33, and of Stourbridge Urban District Council 1933-36. A Socialist. Elected for the Yardley division of Birmingham in July 1945 and sat until he retired in 1950. M.B.E. 1952. Birmingham and District Secretary of General and Municipal Workers Union. Member of W. Midlands Economic Planning Council. Member of Worcestershire County Council 1955-74. Member of National Executive Committee of Labour Party 1963-65.*

[1950]

PERRY, Ernest George. 30 Old Park Avenue, Balham, London. B. 25 Apr. 1908; m. 1950 Edna Joyce Perks-Mankelow Educ. at London County Council School evening institutes, and N.C.L.C. correspondence courses. An Insurance Contractor. Joined the Labour Party in Mar. 1925. Member of the N.U.G.M.W. from 1926, L.C.S. from May 1926, and R.A.C.S. from 1933. War Service, R.A. 1940-46; Far East Indian Army 1942-46. President of the Battersea Labour Party and Trades Council. Mayor of Battersea 1955-56. Lord Commissioner, H.M. Treasury Oct. 1969-June 1970. Unsuccessfully contested Battersea municipal election in

1931, member from 1934 to 1965. Assistant Government Whip Feb. 1968-Oct. 1969, and Mar.-Oct. 1974. Alderman, London Borough of Wandsworth 1964-72. Opposition Whip 1970-74. A Labour Member. Sat for Battersea S. from 1964 to Feb. 1974 and for the Battersea S. division of Wandsworth from Feb. 1974 until he retired in 1979.* [1979]

PERRY, George Henry. 123 Hawthorn Street, Derby. S. of Arthur Perry, Esq. B. 24 Aug. 1920; m. 4 Apr. 1944, Mrs. Ida Lilian Garner, d. of Timothy Atkins, Esq. Educ. at St. Dunstan's Elementary School, Derby, and Derby Technical Coll. Served in R.N. 1941-46. A Railway Fitter 1946-66. Derby Town Councillor from 1955-66. Secretary Derby Trades Council 1961-66; Chairman Derby Labour Party 1961-62. Chairman S. Derbyshire Water Board 1961-66. Vice-Chairman Midland Regional Committee, B.W.A. 1963; Chairman Trent Catchment Area Committee, B.W.A. 1963. A Labour Member. Unsuccessfully contested Harborough in the 1964 general election. Elected for Nottingham S. in Mar. 1966 and sat until 1970 when he was defeated.* [1970]

PETHICK-LAWRENCE, Rt. Hon. Fredrick William. 11 Old Square, Lincoln's Inn, London. Fourways, Gomshall, Surrey. Royal Aero, and Queen's. S. of Alfred Lawrence, Esq. B. 28 Dec. 1871; m. 1st, 1901, Emmeline, d. of Henry Pethick, Esq., of Weston-super-Mare (she died 1954); 2ndly, 1957, Helen Millar, d. of Sir John Craggs, and widow of D. McCombie, Esq. Educ. at Eton, and Trinity Coll., Cambridge. Barrister-at-Law, Inner Temple 1898. Editor of *London Echo, Labour Record and Review* and *Votes for Women*. Financial Secretary to the Treasury June 1929-Aug. 1931. PC. 1937. Vice-Chairman of P.L.P. 1942. A Labour Member. Unsuccessfully contested S. Aberdeen in Apr. 1917 as a Peace candidate. and S. Islington in 1922. Sat for Leicester W. from Dec. 1923-Oct. 1931, when he was defeated. Elected for Edinburgh E. in Nov. 1935 and sat until Aug. 1945 when he was created Baron Pethick-Lawrence. Fellow of Trinity Coll., Cambridge 1897. A prominent supporter of women's suffrage, imprisoned for conspiracy

for nine months in 1912. Member of Union for Democratic Control, Treasurer 1916. Assumed the additional surname of Pethick 1901. Secretary of State for India and Burma Aug. 1945-Apr. 1947. Member of Political Honours Scrutiny Committee 1949-61. Died 10 Sept. 1961. [1945]

PETO, Brigadier Christopher Henry Maxwell, D.S.O. Kenwith Castle, Bideford, N. Devon S. of Sir Basil Peto, 1st Bart. MP., of Barnstaple. B. 19 Feb. 1897; m. 3 Oct. 1935, Barbara, d. of E.T. Close, Esq., of Woodcote, Camberley. Educ. at Harrow. Brigadier Late 9th Lancers; served in France and Flanders 1914-18 (wounded, despatches) and overseas 1939-45 (wounded, despatches). D.S.O. 1945. Had Legion of Honour, Croix de Guerre and Order of Leopold. Dept.-Lieut. for County of Devon 1950-55, for Wiltshire from 1956. Col. 9th Lancers Sept. 1950. A Conservative. Sat for the Barnstaple division from July 1945-Feb. 1950. Elected for N. Devon in Feb. 1950 and sat until he retired in 1955. High Sheriff of Wiltshire 1966. Succeeded his brother as Bart. 1971. Died 19 May 1980. [1954]

PEYTON, Rt. Hon. John Wynne William. 6 Temple West Mews, West Square, London. The Old Malt House, Hinton St. George, Somerset. S. of I.E. Peyton, Esq. B. 13 Feb. 1919; m. 1st, 1947, Diana, d. of Douglas Clinch, Esq. (marriage dissolved 1966); 2ndly, 27 July 1966, Mrs Mary Cobbold, d. of Col. Hon. Humphrey Wyndham. Educ. at Eton, and Trinity Coll., Oxford. A Barrister-at-Law, Inner Temple, called June 1945. Served 1939-45 with 15/19 Hussars (Prisoner-of-War in Germany). Parliamentary Private Secretary to Rt. Hon. Nigel Birch 1953-56. Parliamentary Secretary to Ministry of Power June 1962-Oct. 1964. Opposition spokesman on Power 1964-66, on House of Commons Affairs Oct. 1974-Nov. 1976 and on Agriculture Nov. 1976-May 1979. Member of Shadow Cabinet Oct. 1974-May 1979. Unsuccessful candidate for Leadership of Conservative Party 1975. Minister of Transport June-Oct. 1970; Minister for Transport Industries Oct. 1970-Mar. 1974. PC. 1970. A Conservative. Unsuccessfully contested Bristol Central in 1950.

Elected for the Yeovil division of Somerset in Oct. 1951. Chairman of Texas Instruments Limited from 1974.* [1979]

PHIPPS, Dr. Colin Barry, J.P. Mathon Court, Mathon, Malvern. Reform. S. of Edgar Reeves Phipps, Esq. B. 23 July 1934; m. 15 Sept. 1956, Marion Mary, d. of Clifford H. Lawrey, Esq., (2 s. 2 d.). Educ. at Acton County School, Bishop Gore School, Swansea, University Coll., London, and Birmingham University. B.Sc. (First Class Honours) 1955, F.G.S. 1956, Ph.D. 1957, F. Inst. Pet. 1972. J.P. 1973. Petroleum Geologist with Shell in Holland, Venezuela and U.S.A. 1957-64. Consultant to Oil Industry and Chairman Dr. Colin Phipps and Partners Limited. A Labour Member. Unsuccessfully contested Walthamstow E. in Mar. 1969. Elected for Dudley W. in Feb. 1974 and sat until he retired in 1979.* [1979]

PICKTHORN, Rt. Hon. Sir Kenneth William Murray, Bart. 15a Ashley Place, London. Carlton. S. of Charles Wright Pickthorn, Esq. B. 23 Apr. 1892; m. 1924, Nancy Catherine, d. of Lewis Richards, Esq. Educ. at Aldenham School, and Trinity Coll., Cambridge, Litt. D. Fellow of Corpus Christi Coll., Cambridge 1914-75. Served overseas with 15th London Regiment and R.A.F. Parliamentary Secretary Ministry of Education 1951-54. Created Bart. 1959. PC. 1964. A Conservative. Sat for Cambridge University from Feb. 1935-Feb. 1950. Elected for the Carlton division of Nottinghamshire in Feb. 1950 and sat until he retired in 1966. Died 12 Nov. 1975. [1966]

PIKE, (Irene) Mervyn Parnicott. West Eaton House, 15/17 West Eaton Place, London. Cold Overton, Nr. Oakham, Rutland. D. of Ivan Samuel Pike, Esq., Company Director. B. 16 Sept. 1918. Educ. at Hummanby Hall, and Reading University. Served in W.A.A.F. 1941-46. Member of W. Riding County Council 1955-57. Parliamentary Private Secretary to Patricia Hornsby-Smith, Parliamentary Under-Secretary of State for Home Affairs 1957-59. Assistant Postmaster-Gen. Oct. 1959-Mar. 1963. Parliamentary Under-Secretary of State for Home Affairs Mar. 1963-Oct. 1964. Opposition spokesman on Post Office affairs in Nov. 1964 and on Social Services 1966-67. Member of Shadow Cabinet 1966-67. A Conservative. Unsuccessfully contested Pontefract, Yorkshire in 1951, and Leek, Staffordshire in 1955. Elected for the Melton division of Leicestershire in Dec. 1956 and sat until she retired in Feb. 1974. Created Baroness Pike (Life Peerage) 1974. Chairman of Economic Models Limited. Chairman of Women's Royal Voluntary Service from 1974. Chairman of Independent Broadcasting Authority General Advisory Council from 1974.* [1974]

PILKINGTON, Sir Richard Antony, K.B.E., M.C. 14 Grove End Road, London. S. of Arthur Richard Pilkington, Esq., Chairman of Pilkington Brothers Limited. B. 10 May 1908; m. 1 Aug. 1946, Rosemary de Villeneuve, d. of Capt. Frederick Russell-Roberts, M.C. Educ. at Charterhouse, and Christ Church, Oxford. Served in Coldstream Guards 1930-35 and 1939-42. M.C. 1940. Parliamentary Private Secretary to Mr. Oliver Stanley at Board of Trade 1938-39; Civil Lord of the Admiralty Mar. 1942-July 1945. A Conservative. Sat for Widnes from 1935-45, when he was defeated. Unsuccessfully contested Widnes again in 1950. Elected for Poole in Oct. 1951 and sat until he retired in 1964. K.B.E. 1961. Died 9 Dec. 1976. [1964]

PINK, Ralph Bonner, C.B.E., V.R.D., J.P. House of Commons, London. S. of Frank Pink, Esq., Company Director. B. 30 Sept. 1912; m. 3 June 1939, Marguerite Nora Banner-Martin, V.R.D. 1951, C.B.E. 1961. Educ. at Oundle. Member Portsmouth Borough Council from 1948. Lord Mayor 1961-62. Member of Speakers Panel of Chairmen. A Knight of the Order of Dannebrog (Denmark). A Conservative. Sat for Portsmouth S. from Mar. 1966.* [1979]

PIRATIN, Philip. 35 Ashfield Road, Acton, London. 16 King Street, London. S. of Abraham Piratin, Esq. B. 15 May 1907; m. 1929, Celia, d. of P. Fund. Esq. Educ. at London County Council Elementary School, and Davenant Foundation. A Political Worker. Member of Stepney Borough Council

1937-45. A Communist. Elected for the Mile End division of Stepney in July 1945 and sat until 1950 when he unsuccessfully contested Stepney.* [1960]

PITMAN, Sir Isaac James, K.B.E. 58 Chelsea Park Gardens, London. Holme Wood, Marlow, Buckinghamshire. Carlton. Eld. s. of Ernest Pitman, Esq. B. 14 Aug. 1901; m. 28 Apr. 1927, Hon. Margaret Lawson-Johnston, d. of 1st Baron Luke. Educ. at Eton, and Christ Church, Oxford. Chairman and Managing Director of Sir Isaac Pitman and Sons Limited; a Director of the Bank of England 1940-45. Director of Organisation and Methods at H.M. Treasury 1943-45. A Conservative. Elected for Bath in July 1945 and sat until he retired in 1964. K.B.E. 1961. Chairman of Council of Initial Teaching Alphabet Foundation. Pro-Chancellor of University of Bath.* [1964]

PITT, Dame Edith Maud, D.B.E. 44 Westminster Gardens, London. 20 Blakesley Road, Yardley, Birmingham. D. of E.G. Pitt, Esq., of Birmingham. B. 14 Oct.1906. Educ. at Bordesley Green Council School, and Evening Institute. Industrial Welfare Officer from 1943. City Councillor for Birmingham 1941-45 and 1947-54. O.B.E. 1952. D.B.E. 1962. Joint Parliamentary Secretary Ministry of Pensions and National Insurance Dec. 1955 to Oct. 1959. Parliamentary Secretary Ministry of Health Oct. 1959 to July 1962. A Conservative. Unsuccessfully contested the Stechford division of Birmingham in 1950 and 1951 and the Small Heath division of Birmingham in Nov. 1952. Elected for the Edgbaston division of Birmingham in July 1953 and sat until her death on 27 Jan. 1966. [1966]

PLATTS-MILLS, John Faithful Fortescue. 1 Mitre Court Buildings, Temple, London. S. of J.F.W. Mills, Esq. B. 4 Oct. 1906 at Karori, New Zealand; m. 31 May 1936, Janet, d. of Richard Cree, Esq. Educ. at Nelson Coll., Victoria University (New Zealand), and Balliol Coll., Oxford, LL.M. (N.Z.), M.A., B.C.L. Barrister-at-Law, New Zealand 1928; London, Inner Temple, 1932; Uganda and Guyana. Served in R.A.F. 1940, Pilot Officer. A 'Bevin boy' 1944-45. Member

of Finsbury Borough Council 1945-53. A Labour Independent Member. Elected for Finsbury in July 1945 as a Labour Member and sat until 1950 when he unsuccessfully contested Shoreditch and Finsbury as an Independent Labour candidate. Expelled from Labour Party Apr. 1948. Member of Labour Independent Group 1949-50. Q.C. 1964. Bencher of Inner Temple 1970.* [1950]

PLUMMER, Sir Leslie Arthur. Berwick Hall, Toppesfield, Halstead, Essex. S. of George Henry Plummer, Esq., of Demerara, British Guiana. B. 1901; m. 1923, Beatrice Lapsker, created Baroness Plummer 1965. Educ. at Tottenham Grammar School. Chairman of Overseas Food Corporation 1948-50. Knight Bach. 1949. General Manager of *New Leader*. A Labour Member. Elected for Deptford in Oct. 1951 and sat until his death in New York on 15 Apr. 1963. [1963]

PONSONBY, Col. Charles Edward, T.D. 6 Eresby House, Rutland Gate, London. Woodleys, Woodstock. Brooks's. S. of Hon. Edwin Ponsonby, of Woodleys, Woodstock. B. 2 Sept. 1879; m. 23 July 1912, Hon. Winifred Gibbs, d. of 1st, Baron Hunsdon of Hunsdon. Educ. at Eton, and Balliol Coll., Oxford, B.A. 1901. A Solicitor. Dept.-Lieut. for Oxfordshire. Member of Council of Joint East African Board; President of Glass Manufacturers Federation; Vice-President of Royal Empire Society, of British Empire Produce Organisation, and of Royal African Society. Served with W. Kent (Q.O.) Yeomanry 1914-19 in Gallipoli, Egypt, Palestine and France; had Croix de Guerre avec Palmes. Col. Commanding 97th Kent Yeomanry Brigade R.A. (T.) 1930-36; Honorary Col. 297 Lt. A.A. Regiment. Parliamentary Private Secretary to Rt. Hon. Anthony Eden, when Secretary of State for War May-Dec. 1940 and when Secretary of State for Foreign Affairs Jan. 1941-July 1945. A Conservative. Elected for the Sevenaoks division of Kent in July 1935 and sat until he retired in 1950. Chairman of Council of Royal Empire Society 1954-57. Created Bart. 1956. President of Royal African Society 1962-71. Died 28 Jan. 1976. [1950]

POOLE, Cecil Charles. The Bungalow, Crown Lane, Four Oaks, Sutton Coldfield. S. of Alexander Poole, Esq., of Wellington, Shropshire. B. 1902; m. 1925, Gertrude, d. of J.H. Carter, Esq., of Blackwood. Educ. at Ludlow Grammar School. Maj. R.E. Jan. 1939. Member of Walsall Borough Council 1931-38. A Labour Member. Unsuccessfully contested the Shrewsbury division of Shropshire in 1935 and Cheltenham in June 1937. Sat for Lichfield from May 1938-Feb. 1950. Elected for the Perry Barr division of Birmingham in Feb. 1950 and sat until he retired in 1955. Parliamentary Private Secretary to Rt. Hon. Harold Wilson, President of the Board of Trade 1951. Died 2 Feb. 1956.
[1954]

POOLE, Oliver Brian Sanderson, C.B.E. Trawscoed House, Guilsfield, Welshpool. Buck's, and R.Y.S. S. of Donald Louis Poole, Esq. B. 11 Aug. 1911; m. 1st, 6 Sept. 1933, Betty, d. of Capt. D.S. Gilkison (divorced 1951); 2ndly, 1952, Mrs. Daphne Heber Percy (divorced 1965); 3rdly, 1966, Barbara Ann Taylor. Educ. at Eton, and Christ Church, Oxford. A member of Lloyds. Served in Life Guards 1932-33 and with Warwickshire Yeomanry from 1934. M.B.E. and O.B.E. 1943. C.B.E. 1945. A Conservative. Elected for the Oswestry division of Shropshire in July 1945 and sat until he retired in 1950. Governor of Old Vic 1945-63. Joint Treasurer of Conservative Party Organisation 1952-55, Chairman 1955-57, Dept.-Chairman 1957-59, Joint Chairman 1963, Vice-Chairman 1963-64. Created Baron Poole 1958. PC. 1963. Trustee of National Gallery from 1973.*
[1950]

POPPLEWELL, Ernest, C.B.E. North View, Moor Lane, Sherburn-in-Elmet, South Milford, Yorkshire. S. of J.W. Popplewell, Esq., of Selby. B. 10 Dec. 1899; m. 1922, Lavinia Rainbow. Educ. at Elementary School. A Railway Signalman. J.P. for the W. Riding of Yorkshire. Served in Royal Artillery 1914-18, holder of Belgian Croix de Guerre. Assistant Government Whip May 1946; Labour Whip 1946-59; Vice-Chamberlain of H.M. Household Oct. 1947-Oct. 1951. Dept. Chief Opposition Whip 1955-59. Chairman of Labour Parliamentary Transport Group 1959-65. Chairman of Select Committee on Nationalised Industries 1964-66. A Labour Member. Elected for Newcastle-upon-Tyne W. in July 1945 and sat until he retired in 1966. C.B.E. 1951. Created Baron Popplewell (Life Peerage) 1966. Died 11 Aug. 1977.
[1966]

PORTER, Edward. 313 Preston Old Road, Feniscliffe, Blackburn. S. of Richard Porter, Esq. B. 28 July 1880; m. 12 Sept. 1912, Mary Edith, d. of George Hindle, Esq. (she died 1948). Educ. at Elementary School. J.P. for Blackburn and County of Lancaster. Chairman of Blackburn Corporation Electricity Department; member of Incorporated Municipal Electrical Association. Alderman of Blackburn Borough Council, Mayor 1940-41 and part of 1942. A Labour Member. Unsuccessfully contested Blackburn in 1922 and 1923, Preston in 1931, and Warrington in 1935. Elected for Warrington in July 1945 and sat until he retired in 1950. National Organiser of General and Municipal Workers Union. Died 31 Aug. 1960.
[1950]

PORTER, George. 61 Stockbridge Lane, Huyton, Liverpool. S. of George Porter, Esq., of Liverpool. B. 29 July 1884; m. 18 July 1914, Florence, d. of Willouby Pickburn, Esq. Educ. at Windsor Wesleyan School. A Builder. Member of Amalgamated Society of Woodworkers. Member of Huyton Urban District Council 1941-46; J.P. for Liverpool. A Labour Member. Unsuccessfully contested the Fairfield division of Liverpool in 1918 and 1922. Elected for Leeds Central in July 1945 and sat until he retired in 1955. Died 25 Sept. 1973.
[1954]

POTT, Henry Percivall. House of Commons, London. S. of H.P. Pott, Esq, of Upham, Hants. B. 1908; m. 1946, Mary Vera, d. of F.B. Larkworthy, Esq. Educ. at Oundle School. Served in R.A.F. 1941-46, Squadron-Leader. Member Hampshire County Council 1949-64; served on Executive Committee of National Farmers' Union in Hampshire and Northamptonshire and on Estate Management Committee of Hampshire Agricultural Executive Committee. A Company Director and Farmer. A Conservative. Elected for the Devizes division of Wiltshire in 1955 and sat until his death on 17 Jan. 1964. Chairman of Wey Valley Water Company. J.P. for Hampshire. Died 17 Jan. 1964. [1964]

POUNDER, Rafton John. House of Commons, London. S. of Cuthbert Coulson Pounder, Esq., of Belfast. B. 13 May 1933; m. 26 Dec. 1959, Valerie Isobel, d. of Robert Stewart, Esq., of Belfast, (1 s. 1 d.). Educ. at Charterhouse, and Christ's Coll., Cambridge. A Chartered Accountant. Chairman Cambridge University Conservative and Unionist Association 1954; Ulster representative on Young Conservative and Unionist National Advisory Committee 1960-63; Honorary member of Ulster Young Unionist Council 1963. Secretary Ulster Unionist Parliamentary Party Apr. 1964-Nov. 1967. Member of the British Delegation to the Consultative Assembly of the Council of Europe and W.E.U. May 1965-Apr. 1968. Honorary Secretary Conservative Party Power Committee Nov. 1969-70. Vice-Chairman Conservative Party Technology Committee 1970. Member Select Committee on Public Accounts 1970-72. Parliamentary Private Secretary to Minister for Industry 1970-71. Member U.K. Delegation to European Parliament 1973. An Ulster Unionist Member. Elected for Belfast S. in Oct. 1963 and sat until Feb. 1974 when he was defeated. President of Ulster Society for Prevention of Cruelty to Animals, 1968-74. Director of Progressive Building Society, 1968-77. Secretary of N. Ireland Bankers' Association from 1977. Member of General Synod of Church of Ireland from 1966.* [1974]

POWELL, Rt. Hon. John Enoch, M.B.E. 33 South Eaton Place, London. S. of Albert Enoch Powell, Esq., of Stechford. B. 16 June 1912; m. 2 Jan. 1952, Margaret Pamela, d. of Lieut. -Col. L.E. Wilson (I.A. retired), (2d.). Educ. at King Edward's High School, Birmingham, and Trinity Coll., Cambridge. Fellow of Trinity Coll. 1934-38. Professor of Greek, University of Sydney 1938-39. Served 1939-46 with R. Warwicks Regiment and Gen. Staff, Brigg. 1944. Director London Municipal Society 1952-55. Parliamentary Secretary Ministry of Housing and Local Government Dec. 1955-Jan. 1957; Financial

Secretary to the Treasury Jan. 1957-Jan. 1958, when he resigned. Minister of Health July 1960-Oct. 1963, when he declined to serve under Sir Alec Douglas-Home. Member of Cabinet July 1962-Oct. 1963. Opposition spokesman on Transport 1964-65 and on Defence 1965-68. Member of Shadow Cabinet Nov. 1964 to Apr. 1968, when he was dismissed. Voted against entry to E.E.C. on 28 Oct. 1971. M.B.E. 1943. PC. 1960. Unsuccessfully contested Normanton in Feb. 1947. Sat as Conservative Member for Wolverhampton S.W. from Feb. 1950-Feb. 1974 when he retired. Elected as Ulster Unionist Member for Down S. in Oct. 1974.* [1979]

PRENTICE, Rt. Hon. Reginald Ernest. 5 Hollingsworth Road, Croydon, Reform. S. of Ernest G. Prentice, Esq., Scientific Instrument Maker. B. 16 July 1923; m. 8 Aug. 1948, Joan, d. of Mrs. R. Godwin, (1 d.). Educ. at Whitgift School and London School of Economics (B.Sc. Econ). Served 1942-46 with R.A. Member Croydon Borough Council 1949-55. J.P. Borough of Croydon from Mar. 1961. Assistant to Legal Secretary in charge of Advice and Service Bureau of T.G.W.U. 1950-57. Minister of State, Department of Education and Science Oct. 1964-Apr. 1966. Minister of Public Building and Works Apr. 1966-Aug. 1967. PC. 1966. Minister of Overseas Development Aug. 1967-Oct. 1969. Minister of State, Ministry of Technology from 6 Oct. to 10 Oct. 1969, when he resigned. Alderman, Greater London Council 1970-71. An Opposition spokesman on Employment Jan. 1972-Mar. 1974. Member of Parliamentary Committee of P.L.P Apr. 1972-Mar. 1974. Member of Cabinet Mar. 1974-Dec. 1976. Secretary of State for Education and Science Mar. 1974-June 1975. Minister for Overseas Development June 1975-Dec. 1976, when he resigned. Minister of State (Minister for Social Security) Department of Health and Social Security from May 1979. Unsuccessfully contested Croydon N. as a Labour candidate in 1950 and 1951 and the Streatham division of Wandsworth in 1955. Sat as a Labour Member for East Ham N. from May 1957 to Feb. 1974 and for Newham N.E. from Feb. 1974 to May 1979. Resigned from the Labour Party and joined the Conservatives on 8 Oct. 1977.

Elected as a Conservative for the Daventry division of Northampton in May 1979.*

[1979]

PRESCOTT, John Leslie. 365 Salthouse Road, Sutton, Hull. S. of John Herbert Prescott, Esq., Railway Controller. B. 31 May 1936; m. 11 Nov. 1961, Pauline, d. of E. Tilston, Esq. Educ. at Ellesmere Port Secondary Modern School, Ruskin Coll., Oxford, and Hull University. A Steward in the Merchant Navy 1955-63. T.U. Official National Union Seamen 1968-70. Member Select Committee Nationalised Industries 1973. Council of Europe 1972-75. Delegate European Parliament 1975-79. Parliamentary Private Secretary to Rt. Hon. Peter Shore, Secretary of State for Trade 1974-75. Leader of Labour Group in European Parliament 1976-79. An Opposition spokesman on Transport from 1979. A Labour Member. Unsuccessfully contested Southport in 1966. Elected for Kingston-upon-Hull E. in June 1970.* [1979]

PRESCOTT, (William Robert) Stanley. 1 Brick Court, Temple, London. 53 Campden Hill Court, London. City Livery, Constitutional, and Devonshire. S. of Col. Sir William Prescott, Bart., C.B.E., MP. B. 25 Apr. 1912; m. 1st, 9 Sept. 1939, Gwendolen Hylda, d. of Leonard Aldridge, Esq., C.B.E., of 31 Queen's Gate Gardens, London (divorced 1951); m. 2ndly, 1951 Sheila, d. of Surgeon Rear-Admiral D.W. Hewitt. Educ. at St. John's Coll., Cambridge. Barrister-at-Law, Gray's Inn 1935. Member of Court of Common Council 1945-51 and a Freeman of the City of London, Trustee of Sir Rowland Hill Trust for Post Office Workers; Vice-President of National Chamber of Trade and of Association of Municipal Corporations; Director of Manchester Chamber of Commerce; member of City of London Territorial and Air Force Association. Maj. Royal Corps of Signals 1939-43. A Conservative. Elected for the Darwen division of Lancashire in Dec. 1943 and sat until he retired in 1951. Committed suicide 6 June 1962. [1951]

PRICE, Christopher. House of Commons, London. S. of Stanley Price, Esq. B. 26 Jan. 1932; m. June 1956, Anne Grierson, d. of James Ross, Esq. Educ. at Leeds Grammar School, and Queen's Coll., Oxford. Chairman of National Association of Labour Student Organisations 1956. Sheffield City Councillor 1962-66; Dept. Chairman Sheffield Education Committee 1963. Parliamentary Private Secretary to Mr. Anthony Crosland, Secretary of State for Education and Science 1966-67. Editor of *New Education* 1967-68; Education Correspondent *New Statesman* 1968-74. Member Select Commitee on Education and Science 1968-70. Expenditure Committee 1974. Joint Parliamentary Private Secretary to Rt. Hon. F. W. Mulley, Secretary of State for Education and Science 1975-76. Member European Parliament 1977-78. Chairman National Youth Bureau 1977-80. Chairman of Select Committee on Education, Science and the Arts from 1979. A Labour Member. Unsuccessfully contested Shipley in 1964 general election. Sat for the Perry Barr division of Birmingham from Mar. 1966 to June 1970, when he was defeated, and for Lewisham W. from Feb. 1974.* [1979]

PRICE, Sir David Ernest Campbell. 36 Sloane Court West, London. Lepe House, Exbury, Southampton. Beefsteak. S. of Maj. V.M. Price. B. 20 Nov. 1924; m. 1960, Rosemary, d. of Cyril Johnston, Esq., O.B.E., (1 d.). Educ. at Eton, Trinity Coll., Cambridge, and Yale University. Capt. Scots Guards 1942-46. President Cambridge Union Society 1948; Honorary Fellow Yale 1948-49. Held various appointments with I.C.I. Limited 1949-62. Delegate to Council of Europe 1958-61. Industrial Consultant 1964-70 and 1972. Director Association British Maltsters Limited 1966-70. Parliamentary Secretary Board of Trade July 1962-Oct. 1964. Opposition spokesman on Aviation, 1965; on Science 1965-66 and on Technology 1966-70. Joint Parliamentary Secretary Ministry of Technology June 1970-Oct. 1970. Parliamentary Secretary to Ministry of Aviation Supply Oct. 1970-Apr. 1971. Parliamentary Under-Secretary of State for Aerospace, Department of Trade and Industry Apr. 1971-Apr. 1972. Chairman Parliamentary Scientific Committee 1973-75. Gen. Consultant to the Institute of Works Managers 1973. Consultant to Union International Company Limited 1973. Member of the

Public Accounts Committee 1974-75. A Roman Catholic. A Conservative. Sat for the Eastleigh division of Hampshire from 1955. Knighted 1980.* [1979]

PRICE, Henry Alfred, C.B.E. 22 Cator Road, London. S. of James William Price, Esq., a Builder's Labourer. B. 3 Jan. 1911; m. 27 Aug. 1938, Ivy, d. of George Trimmer, Esq. Educ. at Hungerford Road London County Council School, and Holloway County School. Managing Director of Price, Topley and Company Limited, Paper Merchants. Member of Lewisham Borough Council 1944-49 and London County Council 1946-52. Parliamentary Private Secretary to Rt. Hon. Geoffrey Lloyd, Minister of Fuel and Power 1951-54. A Conservative. Elected for Lewisham W. in Feb. 1950 and sat until he retired in 1964. C.B.E. 1962. Managing Director of Grove Paper Company Limited.* [1964]

PRICE, (Joseph) Thomas. House of Commons, London. S. of William Price, Esq., of Pendlebury. B. 1902; m. 1933, Muriel Anna Wilcock. Educ. at Salford Grammar School. Chief Legal Officer of Union of Shop, Distributive and Allied Workers. A Labour Member. Elected for the Westhoughton division of Lancashire in June 1951 and sat until his death on 1 Feb. 1973. Opposition Whip 1954-59. Died 1 Feb. 1973. [1973]

PRICE, Morgan Philips. The Grove, Taynton, Nr. Gloucester. Reform. S. of Maj. William Price, MP. of Tewkesbury. B. 29 Jan. 1885. m. 1 Aug. 1919, Elise, d. of Wilhelm Balster. Educ. at Harrow, and Trinity Coll. Cambridge, graduated in Natural Science and Agriculture 1907. A Landowner, Farmer and Author. J.P. for Gloucestershire. Parliamentary Private Secretary to Rt. Hon. Sir Charles Trevelyan, President of the Board of Education 1929-31. Forestry Commission 1942-45. Correspondent for *Manchester Guardian* in Russia 1917, and for *Daily Herald* in Germany 1919-23. Parliamentary Charity Commissioner Aug. 1945-Oct. 1951. Prospective Liberal candidate for Gloucester 1911-14. Founder member of Union of Democratic Control; joined Labour Party in 1919. A Labour Member. Unsuccessfully contested Gloucester in 1922, 1923 and 1924. Sat for the Whitehaven division from 1929-31, when he was defeated, and the Forest of Dean division from 1935-50. Elected for Gloucestershire W. in 1950 and sat until he retired in 1959. Died 23 Sept. 1973. [1959]

PRICE, William George. The Old Oak House, Flecknoe, Rugby, Warwickshire. S. of George Price, Esq. B. 15 June 1934; m. 1963 Joy Thomas. Educ. at Gloucester Technical Coll. A Journalist. Member of N.U.J. Joined the Labour Party in 1954. Parliamentary Private Secretary to Rt. Hon. Edward Short, Minister of Education 1968-70. Voted in favour of entry to E.E.C. on 28 Oct. 1971. Parliamentary Private Secretary to Rt. Hon. Edward Short, Dept. Leader of the Labour Party 1972-74. Under-Secretary of State for Overseas Development, Foreign and Commonwealth Office Mar.-June 1974. Parliamentary Secretary to Ministry of Overseas Development June-Oct. 1974. Parliamentary Secretary to Privy Council Office Oct. 1974-May 1979. A Labour Member. Sat for the Rugby division of Warwickshire from Mar. 1966 until 1979, when he was defeated. Consultant to National Union of Licensed Victuallers from 1979.* [1979]

PRICE-WHITE, Lieut.-Col. David Archibald. Netherwood, Bangor. Carlton, and Constitutional. S. of Price Foulkes White, Esq. B. 5 Sept. 1906; m. 29 Aug. 1934, Gwyneth, d. of James Lewis Harris, Esq., of Caernarvon. Educ. at Friars School, and University Coll. of North Wales. Admitted Solicitor 1932. Served in France, Middle East, Italy, and E. Africa 1939-45. T.D. 1945. A Conservative. Elected for Caernarvon Boroughs in July 1945 and sat until 1950 when he unsuccessfully contested the Conway division of Caernarvonshire. Died 6 Mar. 1978. [1950]

PRIOR, Rt. Hon. James Michael Leathes. Old Hall, Brampton, Beccles, Suffolk. S. of C.B.L. Prior, Esq., J.P. B. 11 Oct. 1927; m. 30 Jan. 1954, Jane Primrose, d. of A. Vice-Marshal O.G.W.G. Lywood, C.B., C.B.E., (3 s. 1 d.). Educ. at Charterhouse, and Pembroke Coll., Cambridge. Commissioned in army 1946. Served in India and

Germany. Chartered Surveyor and Land Agent 1950. Parliamentary Private Secretary to Rt. Hon. F.J. Erroll, President of the Board of Trade 1962-63 and Minister of Power 1963-64. Parliamentary Private Secretary to Rt. Hon. Edward Heath, Leader of the Opposition 1965-70. Vice-Chairman Conservative Party in 1965. Minister of Agriculture, Fisheries and Food June 1970-Nov. 1972. Lord President and Leader of the House of Commons Nov. 1972-Mar. 1974. Dept. Chairman Conservative Party 1972-74. Opposition spokesman on Home Affairs Mar.-June 1974 and on Employment June 1974-May 1979. Member of Shadow Cabinet Mar. 1974-May 1979. Secretary of State for Employment from May 1979. PC. 1970. A Conservative. Sat for Lowestoft from 1959. Chairman of Aston Boats Limited 1968-70.* [1979]

PRIOR-PALMER, Brigadier Sir Otho Leslie, D.S.O. West Broyle House, Chichester. House of Commons, London. R.Y.S.S. of Spunner Prior-Palmer, Esq., of Merion Square, Dublin. B. 28 Oct. 1897; m. 1st, 1926, Hon. Barbara Mary, d. of Sir Frederik Frankland, Bart. and of Baroness Zouche (divorced 1937); 2ndly, 11 May 1940, Sheila, d. of Edward Halifax Weller-Poley (divorced 1964); 3rdly, 1964, Elizabeth, d. of Harold Henderson, Esq. Educ. at Wellington, and Royal Military Coll., Sandhurst. Joined 9th Lancers 1916. Commanded Northamptonshire Yeomanry 1940 and 29th and 30th Armoured Brigade in England 1942-43 and 7th Armoured Brigade in Italy 1944-45. D.S.O. 1945. A Conservative. Elected for Worthing in July 1945 and sat until he retired in 1964. Knighted 1959.* [1964]

PRITT, Denis Nowell. 174 Uxbridge Road, London. 4 Essex Court, Temple, London. S. of Harry Walter Pritt, Esq. B. at Harlesden 22 Sept. 1887; m. 27 July 1914, Marie Frances Gough. Educ. at Winchester, and London University. Barrister-at-Law, Middle Temple 1909; K.C. 1927. A Labour (Independent) Member. Unsuccessfully contested Sunderland in 1931. Elected for Hammersmith N. in 1935 as a Labour candidate, was expelled from the Labour Party in Mar. 1940, after defending the Russian

invasion of Finland, defeated the official candidate in 1945 and sat until 1950 when he unsuccessfully contested the seat as an Independent Labour candidate. Member of Executive Committee of P.L.P. 1936-37. Member of National Executive Committee of Labour Party 1937-40. Chairman of Labour Independent Group 1949-50. Chairman of Howard League for Penal Reform. Winner of Stalin Peace Prize 1954. Professor of Law, University of Ghana 1965-66. Died 23 May 1972. [1950]

PROBERT, Arthur Reginald. Allt Fedw, Abernant, Aberdare, Glamorganshire. S. of Albert John Probert, Esq., of Aberdare. B. 1909; m. 1938, Muriel, d. of William Taylor, Esq. Educ. at Aberdare Grammar School. A Local Government Officer in Aberdare. Served with R.A.F.V.R. 1941-46. Secretary of Aberdare Trades and Labour Council 1949-54 and of Glamorgan Federation of Trades Councils 1951-54. Opposition Whip 1959-60. Parliamentary Private Secretary to Rt. Hon. Frank Cousins, Minister of Technology 1965-66. Member of the Speaker's Panel of Chairmen 1966-74. A Labour Member. Elected for Aberdare in Oct. 1954 and sat until he retired in Feb. 1974. Died 14 Feb. 1975. [1974]

PROCTOR, William Thomas. 198 Knollys Road, Streatham, London. Crown Cottage, Longtown, Abergavenny. S. of William Proctor, Esq., of Longtown, Herefordshire. B. 1896; m. 1930, Lucy, d. of D. Playsted, Esq. Educ. at Elementary School. A Railway Guard. Parliamentary Private Secretary to Rt. Hon. James Griffiths, Secretary of State for the Colonies 1950-51. Member of Monmouthshire County Council 1937-49. A Labour Member. Elected for Eccles in July 1945 and sat until he retired in 1964. Died 13 Jan. 1967. [1964]

PROFUMO, Rt. Hon. John Dennis, O.B.E. House of Commons, London. Boodle's. 5th Baron of the late Kingdom of Sardinia and 3rd Baron of the United Kingdom of Italy. S. of Baron Profumo, K.C.B. 30 Jan. 1915; m. 31 Dec. 1954, Miss Valerie Hobson. Educ. at Harrow, and Brasenose Coll., Oxford, M.A. Chairman of Fulham Conservative and Unionist Association 1938 and of West Midlands Federation Junior Imperial League 1939. 2nd Lieut. 1st Northamptonshire Yeomanry 1939; Lieut. - Col. G. (Air) C.M.F. Brigadier. Chief of Staff, British Military Mission to Japan 1945. Parliamentary Secretary to Ministry of Civil Aviation Nov. 1952-Nov. 1953. Joint Parliamentary Secretary Ministry of Transport and Civil Aviation Nov. 1953-Jan. 1957; Parliamentary Under-Secretary of State for the Colonies Jan. 1957-Nov. 1958; Parliamentary Under-Secretary of State, Foreign Office Nov. 1958-Jan. 1959; Minister of State for Foreign Affairs Jan. 1959-July 1960. O.B.E. 1944. PC. 1960. Secretary of State for War July. 1960-June 1963. A Conservative. Sat for the Kettering division from Mar. 1940 to 1945, when he was defeated. Elected for the Stratford division of Warwickshire in Feb. 1950 and sat until June 1963 when he resigned after admitting that on 22 Mar. 1963 he had been guilty of a grave misdemeanour in deceiving the House of Commons about the nature of his relationship with Miss Christine Keeler. Resigned from Privy Council on 26 June 1963. Director of Provident Life Association of London from 1975. C.B.E. 1975.*

[1963]

PROUDFOOT, George Wilfred. 278 Sealby Road, Scarborough. Constitutional. S. of Frank Proudfoot, Esq. B. 19 Dec. 1921; m. 4 Nov. 1950, Margaret Mary, d. of Percy B. Jackson, Esq. Educ. at Crook Council School, and Scarborough Coll. Served in R.A.F. 1941-46 as Air Frame Fitter. Vice-Chairman Yorkshire Young Conservatives 1950-51. Chairman Health Committee, Scarborough Town Council 1950-58. Parliamentary Private Secretary to Minister of Housing and later to Minister of State, Board of Trade. Parliamentary Private Secretary to Paul Bryan, Minister of State, Department of Employment 1970. Own Supermarket and Wholesale Operation. A Conservative. Unsuccessfully contested Hemsworth in 1951 and Cleveland in 1955. Sat for the Cleveland division 1959-64 when he was defeated. Unsuccessfully contested Cleveland again in 1966. Elected for Brighouse and Spenborough in June 1970 and sat until Feb. 1974 when he was defeated. Unsuccessfully con-

tested Brighouse and Spenborough again in Oct. 1974. Managing Director of Radio 270 from 1965.*

[1974]

PRYDE, David Johnstone. 66 Dobbies Road, Bonnyrigg, Midlothian. S. of Matthew Maitland Pryde, Esq., of Gorebridge. B. 3 Mar. 1890; m. 30 June 1916, Marion, d. of Henry Grandison, Esq. (she died 1958). Educ. at Lasswade Secondary School, and Scottish Labour Coll. A Miner. T.U. Official 1921-33. Organiser of Lothian Miners 1927-29; Vice-President of Lothian Miners 1927-32. J.P. for Midlothian 1933. Member of Bonnyrigg Town Council 1938. A Labour Member. Unsuccessfully contested Peebles and S. Midlothian in 1935. Sat for Peebles and S. Midlothian July 1945-Feb. 1950, for Midlothian and Peebles Feb. 1950-May 1955, and for Midlothian from May 1955 until his death on 2 Aug. 1959. [1959]

PURSEY, Commander Harry, R.N. 43 Farnaby Road, Bromley, Kent. S. of G. Pursey, Esq., of Sidmouth. B. 1891. Educ. at Elementary School, and Royal Hospital School, Greenwich. A Journalist and Lecturer. Joined R.N. in 1907; served 1914-18, Turkey, Somaliland and Mesopotamia 1919-20; retired 1936, Commander. Press Correspondent in Spain 1937. A Labour Member. Elected for Kingston-upon-Hull E. in July 1945 and sat until he retired in 1970.*

[1970]

PYM, Rt. Hon. Francis Leslie, M.C., D.L. Everton Park, Sandy, Bedfordshire. Buck's, and Cavalry. S. of Leslie Ruthven Pym, Esq., J.P., MP. B. 13 Feb. 1922; m. 25 June 1949, Valerie Fortune, d. of F.J.H. Daglish, Esq., (2 s. 2 d.). Educ. at Eton, and Magdalene Coll., Cambridge. Capt. 9th Lancers, served in Africa and Italy, M.C. 1945. Member Liverpool University Council 1949-53. Member Herefordshire County Council 1958-61. Parliamentary Private Secretary to Rt. Hon. Reginald Maudling, Colonial Secretary and Chancellor of the Exchequer 1962. Assistant Government Whip 1962-64. Opposition Whip 1964-70. Dept. Chief Whip for the Opposition 1967-70. Parliamentary Secretary to the Treasury and Government Chief Whip June 1970-Dec. 1973. Dept.-Lieut. for

Cambridgeshire 1973. Secretary of State for Northern Ireland Dec. 1973-Mar. 1974. Opposition spokesman on Northern Ireland Mar.-June 1974 and on Agriculture Mar. 1974-Apr. 1975 and Jan.-Nov. 1976. Opposition spokesman on House of Commons Affairs and on Devolution Nov. 1976-Nov. 1978. Opposition spokesman on Foreign and Commonwealth Affairs Oct. 1978-May 1979. Member of Shadow Cabinet. Mar. 1974 Apr. 1975 and Jan. 1976-May 1979. Secretary of State for Defence from May 1979. PC. 1970. A Conservative. Unsuccessfully contested Rhondda W. in 1959. Elected for Cambridgeshire in Mar. 1961.*   [1979]

PYM, Leslie Ruthven. 2 Halkin Place, London. Penpergwn Lodge, Abergavenny. Carlton, and Travellers'. S. of the Rt. Rev. Walter Ruthven Pym, Bishop of Bombay. B. 24 May 1884; m. 1 Jan. 1914, Iris, d. of Charles Orde, Esq., of Hopton House, Great Yarmouth. Educ. at Bedford, and Magdalene Coll., Cambridge. President of Land Agent's Society 1936. Parliamentary Private Secretary to A.T. Lennox-Boyd, later to Robert Boothby, and to Maj. Rt. Hon. G. Lloyd George, Parliamentary Secretary to Ministry of Food 1940-42. A Lord Commissioner of the Treasury Mar. 1942-May 1945. J.P. and Dept.-Lieut. for Monmouthshire. Comptroller of H.M. Household May-July 1945. A Conservative. Elected for the Monmouth division of Monmouthshire in July 1939 and sat until his death on 17 July 1945, after the completion of polling for the General Election but before the result was announced. He was posthumously returned at the head of the poll.   [1945]

QUENNELL, Joan Mary, M.B.E. House of Commons, London. D. of Walter Quennell, Esq., of Dangstein, Rogate. B. 23 Dec. 1923. Educ. at Bedales. Served with Women's Land Army and British Red Cross. Member of West Sussex County Council from 1951 to 1961. Gov. Crawley Coll. of Further Education 1956-69. Member Southern Region Council for Further Education 1959-61; member Regional Advisory Council Technological Education (London and Home Counties) 1959-61. J.P. for West Sussex 1959. Divisional Chairman Horsham Conservative

Association 1957-60. M.B.E. 1958. Parliamentary Private Secretary to Rt. Hon. Ernest Marples, Minister of Transport 1962-64. Member Speakers Conference on Electoral Reform 1965-67, Committee of Public Accounts 1970-74, House of Commons Committee of Selection 1970, Speaker's Panel of Temporary Chairmen 1970-74, Select Committee on European Secondary Legislation 1972-74. A Conservative. Elected for the Petersfield division of Hampshire in Nov. 1960 and sat until she retired in Sept. 1974.*   [1974]

RADICE, Giles Heneage. House of Commons, London. S. of L.W. Radice, Esq. B. 4 Oct. 1936; m. 4 Mar. 1971, Lisanne, d. of Adam Koch, Esq. Educ. at Winchester and Magdalen Coll., Oxford. A Research Officer G.M.W.U. 1966-73. Parliamentary Private Secretary to Mrs. Williams, Secretary of State for Education and Science Jan. 1978-May 1979. A Labour Member. Unsuccessfully contested the Chippenham division of Wiltshire in 1964 and 1966. Sat for the Chester-le-Street division of Durham from Mar. 1973.*   [1979]

RAIKES, Sir Henry Victor Alpin MacKinnon, K.B.E. 22 Queen's Gardens, London. Llwynegrin Cottage, Mold, Flintshire. Carlton, and M.C.C. S. of H. St. John Raikes, Esq., K.C., C.B.E. B. Jan. 1901; m. 10 Aug. 1940, Audrey Elizabeth Joyce, d. of A.P. Wilson, Esq., of Repton, Derbyshire. Educ. at Westminster School, and Trinity Coll., Cambridge, B.A. Honours in History 1922. Flight-Lieut. R.A.F.V.R. May 1940. Barrister-at-Law, Inner Temple 1924. J.P. for Derbyshire. A Conservative. Unsuccessfully contested the Ilkeston division of Derbyshire in 1924 and 1929. Sat for S.E. Essex from 1931 to July 1945 and for the Wavertree division of Liverpool July 1945-Feb. 1950. Elected for the Garston division of Liverpool in Feb. 1950 and sat until he resigned in Nov. 1957. K.B.E. 1953. Conservative Whip withdrawn May-Nov. 1957. Chairman of Monday Club 1975-78.*   [1957]

RAISON, Timothy Hugh Francis. 66 Riverview Gardens, London. Beefsteak, and M.C.C. S. of Maxwell Raison, Esq. B. 3 Nov.

1929; m. 11 Aug. 1956, Veldes, d. of J.A.P. Charrington, Esq. Educ. at Eton, and Christ Church, Oxford. A Journalist and Magazine Publisher, Editor, *New Society* 1962-68. Member of Youth Service Development Council 1960-63, Central Advisory Council for Education 1963-66, Advisory Committee on Drug Dependence 1966-70, Home Office Advisory Council on the Penal System 1970-74, Inner London Education Authority 1967-70 and Richmond-on-Thames Borough Council 1967-71. Parliamentary Private Secretary to Rt. Hon. William Whitelaw, Secretary of State for Northern Ireland 1972-73. Parliamentary Under-Secretary of State for Education Dec. 1973-Mar. 1974. An Opposition spokesman on Social Services 1974, on Consumer Affairs 1974-75, and on Environment 1975-76. Member of Shadow Cabinet Oct. 1974-Nov. 1976. Minister of State, Home Office from 1979. A Conservative. Sat for the Aylesbury division of Buckinghamshire from June 1970.* [1979]

RAMSAY, Maj. Hon. Simon, M.C. 40 North Audley Street, London. Logie, Kirriemuir, Angus. White's, and Buck's. S. of 14th Earl of Dalhousie. B. 17 Oct. 1914; m. 26 June 1940, Margaret, d. of Brigadier-Gen. Archibald Stirling of Keir. Educ. at Eton, and Christ Church, Oxford. Maj. 4th/5th Black Watch (T.A.). Served overseas 1939-45. M.C. 1944. A Conservative. Elected for Forfarshire in July 1945 and sat until he retired in Feb. 1950. Conservative Whip Oct. 1946-Nov. 1948. Succeeded to the Peerage as Earl of Dalhousie in May 1950 on the death of his elder brother. Gov.-Gen. of Federation of Rhodesia and Nyasaland 1957-63. G.B.E. 1957. Lord Chamberlain to the Queen Mother from 1965. Lord Lieut. of Angus from 1967. K.T. 1971. Chancellor of Dundee University from 1977. G.C.V.O. 1979.* [1950]

RAMSDEN, Rt. Hon. James Edward. Old Sleningford Hall, Ripon. 10 Cleaver Square, London. S. of Capt. E. Ramsden, M.C.B. 1 Nov. 1923; m. 25 June 1949, Juliet, Youngest d. of Sir Charles Ponsonby, MP. and the Hon. Lady Ponsonby. Educ. at Eton, and Trinity Coll., Oxford. Commissioned K.R.R.C. 1942; served with Rifle Brigade N.W. Europe 1944-45. Director Prudential

Assurance Company Limited, Standing Telephones and Cables Limited and London Clinic. Parliamentary Private Secretary to Rt. Hon. R.A. Butler, Home Secretary, 1959-60. Parliamentary Under-Secretary of State and Financial Secretary, War Office Oct. 1960-Oct. 1963. Secretary of State for War Oct. 1963-Apr. 1964. Minister of Defence for the Army Apr.-Oct. 1964. Opposition spokesman on Public Building and Works 1964-65 and on Defence 1967-70. PC. 1963. A Conservative. Unsuccessfully contested Dewsbury in 1950 and 1951. Elected for the Harrogate division of the W. Riding of Yorkshire in Mar. 1954 and sat until he retired in Feb. 1974.* [1974]

RANDALL, Harry Enos. Hillside, Arundel Road, Newhaven, Sussex. S. of Henry Randall, Esq., Agricultural Worker. B. 31 Dec. 1899; m. 28 Nov. 1925, Rose Nellie, d. of Joseph Henry Nicholson, Esq. Educ. at Melvin Road Elementary School, Penge, London. 8th City of London Post Office Rifles 1918. Branch Secretary Union of Post Office Workers 1928; Executive Council Union 1935-40 and National Organising Secretary 1940-55; Chairman Post Office Relief Fund Committee 1949-55, on Council from 1937; Vice-Chairman 2nd Post Office Relief Fund 1939-55. Labour Whip 1950; U.K. Delegate to Council of Europe and W.E.U. 1958-60. Member of Standing Conference of British Organisations for Aid for Refugees 1960. Chairman of European Committee 1970-73. Appointed Representative of H.M. Government on the Executive Council of U.N. High Commissioner for Refugees 1964. Member of Select Committee on Nationalised Industries 1965. A Labour Member. Sat for Clitheroe from 1945-50 when he was defeated. Unsuccessfully contested Mitcham in 1951. Elected for Gateshead W. in Dec. 1955 and sat until he retired in 1970. O.B.E. 1972. Died 28 Aug. 1976. [1970]

RANGER, James. 100 Grand Drive, London. S. of Richard Ranger, Esq., Bookbinder. B. 1889; m. 1915, Mabel Thorogood. Educ. at Council School, Plaistow. A Company Secretary. A Labour Member. Unsuccessfully contested the Epping division of Essex in 1931 and 1935. Elected for Ilford S. in July

1945 and sat until he was defeated in 1950. Unsuccessfully contested Ilford S. again in 1951 and 1955. Died Apr. 1975.   [1950]

RANKIN, Jon. 55 Holeburn Road, Glasgow. S. of George Rankin, Esq., of Dalry. B. 1 Feb. 1890; m. 1st, Jessie, d. of Adam Turnbull, Esq., of Barrhead (she died 1965); 2ndly, 1968, Mary Christina Parsons. Educ. at Allan Glen School, Glasgow, and University of Glasgow. Teacher and Lecturer in Economics and Industrial History. Former member of Eastwood Parish Council. Chairman Labour Party Parliamentary Aviation Group. Former member of Glasgow and District Co-operative Association. Chairman of Glasgow Independent Labour Party 1925-28. Voted in favour of entry to E.E.C. on 28 Oct. 1971. A Co-operative and Labour Member. Unsuccessfully contested the Pollok division of Glasgow in 1923, 1924 and 1931. Sat for the Tradeston division of Glasgow from 1945-55. Elected for the Govan division of Glasgow in 1955 and sat until his death on 8 Oct. 1973. Died 8 Oct. 1973.   [1973]

RATHBONE, Eleanor Florence. 26 Hampstead Lane, Highgate, London. D. of William Rathbone, Esq., MP. from 1868-95. B. 1872. Educ. at Kensington High School, and at Universities of Liverpool and Oxford. M.A., LL.D. (Liverpool); Honorary M.A. Durham; Honorary D.C.L. Oxford; Fellow of Somerville Coll., Oxford; a Writer on Economic, Sociological and Industrial Questions. Member of Liverpool City Council 1909-35. President of National Union of Societies for Equal Citizenship 1919-29. Fellow of Royal Statistical Society. An Independent Member. Unsuccessfully contested the E. Toxteth division of Liverpool in 1922. Member for Combined English Universities from May 1929 until her death on 2 Jan. 1946.   [1946]

RATHBONE, John Rankin (Tim). 30 Farringdon Street, London. Brooks's. S. of John R. Rathbone, Esq., MP. and Mrs B.F. Wright, MP. B. 17 Mar. 1933; m. 1960, Margarita Sanchez y Sanchez, (2 s. 1 d.). Educ. at Eton, Christ Church, Oxford, and Harvard Business School. Served 2nd Lieut. K.R.R.C. 1951-53. Trainee to Vice-Presi-

dent Ogilvy and Mather Inc. N.Y. 1958-66. Chief Publicity and Public Relations Officer Conservative Central Office 1966-68. Director Charles Barker A.B.H. International, Dept. Chairman Ayer Barker Hegemann 1968. Member of National Committee for Electoral Reform. Parliamentary Private Secretary to Dr. Gerard Vaughan, Minister for Health, from 1979. A Conservative. Sat for Lewes from Feb. 1974.*   [1979]

RAWLINSON, Rt. Hon. Sir Peter Anthony Grayson. 12 King's Bench Walk, Temple, London. M.C.C., and White's. S. of A.R. Rawlinson, Esq., O.B.E. (Lieut.-Col. retired), Author and Dramatist. B. 26 June 1919; m. 1st, 1940, Haidee Kavanagh (marriage annulled 1954); 2ndly, 1954, Elaine, d. of Vincent Dominguez, Esq., of the U.S.A. Educ. at Downside School, and Christ's Coll., Cambridge (Exhibitioner). Served with Irish Guards (Despatches), Maj. 1939-46. Called to the bar by the Inner Temple, 1946. Bencher 1962. Queen's Counsel 1959. Recorder of Salisbury 1961-62. Solicitor-Gen. July 1962-Oct. 1964. Attorney-Gen. June 1970-Mar. 1974 and Attorney-Gen. for N. Ireland 1972-74. Recorder Kingston-upon-Thames 1975. Chairman of the bar 1975. Vice-Chairman Senate and Bar Council 1974. A Conservative. Unsuccessfully contested Hackney S. in 1951. Sat for Epsom 1955-Feb. 1974 and for Epsom and Ewell Feb. 1974-Mar. 1978 when he was created Baron Rawlinson of Ewell (Life Peerage). Knighted 1962. PC. 1964. Opposition spokesman on Law 1964-65 and 1967-70 and on Broadcasting in 1965. Leader of Western Circuit from 1975.*   [1978]

RAYNER, Brigadier Ralph Herbert. 3 Trevor Square, London. Ashcombe Tower, Dawlish. Carlton, Pratt's, and Devon & Exeter. S. of the Rev. George Rayner, of Bradshaw, Yorkshire. B. 13 Jan. 1897; m. 1931, Elizabeth, d. of S.A. Courtauld, Esq. Served in France 1915-17, Afghanistan 1918-19 (despatches); British Mission to Kabul 1920; Waziristan 1924, with B.E.F. 1939-40 (despatches); Dept. Chief Signal Officer, 21 Army Group 1944. Aide-de-Camp to Gov.-Gen. of Canada 1928-30. Parliamentary Private Secretary to Sir Walter Womersley Assistant Postmaster-Gen. 1938 and to

Minister of Pensions 1939. Dept.-Lieut. for the County of Devon. High Sheriff 1958. A Conservative. Elected for the Totnes division of Devon in 1935 and sat until he retired in 1955. Chairman of Royal Society of St. George 1954-64. Knighted 1956. Member of Devon County Council 1964-73. Died 17 July 1977. [1954]

REDHEAD, Edward Charles. 2 Mapperley Drive, Oak Hill, Woodford Green, Essex. S. of Robert Charles Redhead, Esq. B. 8 Apr. 1902; m. 1 Sept. 1928, Gladys Mary, d. of James William Pannell, Esq. Educ. at Walthamstow Higher Elementary School, and privately. Boy Clerk in Post Office 1917-19; Customs and Excise, finishing as Higher Executive Officer 1919-48; Gen. Secretary Society of Civil Servants 1948-56. Walthamstow Borough Councillor 1929, Alderman 1945-65, Mayor 1949-50 and 1961-62. J.P. 1946. Minister of State, Board of Trade Oct. 1964-Oct. 1965. Minister of State, Department of Education and Science Oct. 1965-Jan. 1967. A Labour Member. Unsuccessfully contested Gillingham in 1951. Elected for Walthamstow W. in Mar. 1956 and sat until his death on 15 Apr. 1967. Opposition Whip 1959-64. Died 15 Apr. 1967. [1966]

REDMAYNE, Rt. Hon. Sir Martin, Bart., D.S.O. 39 Hans Place, London. S. of Leonard Redmayne, Esq. B. 16 Nov. 1910; m. 6 May 1932, Anne Griffiths. Educ. at Radley. Commanded 66th Infantry Brigade 1944-45. Honorary Brigadier 1945. J.P. for Nottinghamshire 1946. Assistant Government Whip 1951. Lord Commissioner of the Treasury July 1953-Oct. 1959. Dept.-Lieut. for Nottinghamshire 1954. Dept. Chief Whip 1956-59. Parliamentary Secretary to the Treasury and Government Chief Whip Oct. 1959-Oct. 1964. Opposition Chief Whip Oct.-Nov. 1964. Created Bart. Dec. 1964. A Conservative. Elected for the Rushcliffe division of Nottinghamshire in Feb. 1950 and sat until 1966 when he was defeated. Opposition spokesman on Post Office Affairs 1964-65, on Agriculture 1965 and on Transport 1965-66. Member of Shadow Cabinet Feb. 1965-Apr. 1966. Chairman of Retail Consortium 1971-76, Dept. Chairman 1976-77. Chairman of N. American Advisory Group, British Overseas Trade Board 1972-76. Dept. Chairman of House of Fraser Limited 1972-78. Created Baron Red mayne (Life Peerage) 1966. D.S.O. 1944. PC. 1959.* [1966]

REDMOND, Robert Spencer, T.D. Ballytrent, Horseshoe Lane, Alderley Edge, Cheshire. Special Forces. S. of Frederick Redmond, Esq. B. 10 Sept. 1919; m. 19 May 1949, Marjorie Helen, d. of Vincent Heyes, Esq. Educ. at Liverpool Coll. Served in war as Maj. 1939-46. Conservative Agent 1947-56. Managing Director Heyes and Company Limited 1956-66. Chairman of Northwest Export Club 1958-60. Director Ashley Associates Limited 1966-71. Secretary Conservative Employment Committee 1971-72, Vice-Chairman 1972-74. Member of Select Committee on Nationalised Industries 1972-74, on Statutory Instruments 1974. A Conservative. Elected for Bolton W. in June 1970 and sat until Oct. 1974 when he was defeated. T.D. 1953. Director and Chief Executive of National Federation of Clay Industries from 1976.* [1974]

REED, David. 26 New End, Hampstead, London. S. of Wilfred Reed, Esq., Engineer. B. 24 Apr. 1945; m. 1973, Susan Garrett. Educ. at West Hartlepool Grammar School. A Journalist 1964-66. P.R.O. N.E. Development Council 1966-68. P.R.O. Vickers Limited 1968-70. A Labour Member. Elected for the Sedgefield division of Durham in June 1970 and sat until he retired in Feb. 1974. Public Affairs Manager, Hawlett-Packard from 1975.* [1974]

REED, Sir (Herbert) Stanley, K.B.E. 30 Kingston House, Princes Gate, London. Athenaeum. B. 28 Jan. 1872; m. 20 Nov. 1901, Lilian, d. of John Humphrey, Esq. (she died Feb. 1947). Editor of *The Times of India* 1907-23. Lieut.-Col. commanding 4th Bombay Light Horse, Indian Defence Force 1914-19; Vice-President Central Publicity Board India. Special Correspondent *Daily Chronicle* and other papers during famines in India 1899. Founder and former Editor of *The Indian Year Book*. Honorary LL.D. Glasgow. Created Knight Bach. 1916; K.B.E. 1919. A Conservative. Unsuccessfully contested the

Stourbridge division of Worcestershire in 1929. Elected for the Aylesbury division of Buckinghamshire in May 1938 and sat until he retired in 1950. Died 17 Jan. 1969.

[1950]

REED, Laurance Douglas. House of Commons, London. St. Stephen's, and Carlton. S. of Douglas A. Reed, Esq., Draper. B. 4 Dec. 1937. Educ. at Gresham's School, and University Coll., Oxford. National Service Royal Navy 1956-58. Oxford University (law) 1960-63. Worked and studied on the Continent 1963-66. Public Sector Research Unit 1967-69. Member of the Bow Group, the Society of Underwater Technology, and British Council on the European Movement. Director of the Association Européenne Océanique. Joint Secretary Parliamentary and Scientific Committee. Member Select Comittee on Science and Technology. Author of *Europe in the Shrinking World, An Ocean of Waste* and *The Political Consequences of North Sea Oil.* Parliamentary Private Secretary to Rt. Hon. John Davies, Chancellor of Duchy of Lancaster 1973-74. A Conservative. Elected for Bolton E. in June 1970 and sat until Feb. 1974 when he was defeated.*

[1974]

REES, Dorothy Mary. House of Commons, London. B. 1898. m. David Rees (he died 1938). Late School Teacher and member of Barry Borough Council. Alderman Glamorgan County Council. Parliamentary Private Secretary to Rt. Hon. Edith Summerskill, Minister of National Insurance 1950-51. A Labour Member. Elected for the Barry division of Glamorganshire in Feb. 1950 and sat until 1951 when she was defeated. Member of Central Training Council in Child Care 1964-67. C.B.E. 1964. D.B.E. 1975.*

[1951]

REES, John Edward Hugh. Summerland House, Caswell, Swansea. S. of David Emlyn Rees, Esq., of Swansea. B. 1928; m. 1961, Jill Dian Milo-Jones. Educ. at Parc Wern School, Glanmor School, Swansea, and Bromsgrove School. Fellow of the Royal Institution of Chartered Surveyors; Fellow of the Chartered Auctioneers and Estate Agents' Institute. Parliamentary Private Secretary to

Sir Keith Joseph 1961-62. Assistant Government Whip 1962-64. A Conservative. Elected for Swansea W. in 1959 and sat until 1964 when he was defeated. Unsuccessfully contested Swansea W. in 1966 and 1970. Gov. of National Museum of Wales. Director of Abbey National Building Society. U.K. Representative on Economic and Social Committee of E.E.C. from 1973.*

[1964]

REES, Rt. Hon. Merlyn. House of Commons, London. Reform. S. of L.D. Rees, Esq. B. 18 Dec. 1920; m. 26 Dec. 1949, Colleen Faith, d. of H.F. Cleveley, Esq., of Kenton, (3 s.). Educ. at Elementary Schools, South Wales, Harrow Weald Grammar School, Goldsmiths' Coll., and London School of Economics. President of Students Union, Goldsmith's Coll. 1940. Served in the R.A.F. 1941-46, demobilised as Squadron Leader. Taught Economics and History at Harrow Weald Grammar School 1949-60. Organised Festival of Labour 1960-62. Lecturer in Economics at Luton Coll. of Technology 1962-63. Parliamentary Private Secretary to Rt. Hon. James Callaghan, Chancellor of the Exchequer 1964-65. Parliamentary Under-Secretary for the Army Dec. 1965-Apr. 1966. Parliamentary Under-Secretary of State for the Royal Air Forces Apr. 1966-Nov. 1968. Under-Secretary of State Home Office Nov. 1968-June 1970. An Opposition spokesman on Home Affairs June 1970-Apr. 1972. Member of the Departmental Committee on Section 2 of the Official Secrets Act. Front Bench Opposition spokesman for Northern Ireland Apr. 1972-Mar. 1974. Member of Parliamentary Committee of P.L.P. from Dec. 1972-Mar. 1974 and from 1979. Secretary of State for Northern Ireland Mar. 1974-Sept. 1976. Home Secretary Sept. 1976-May 1979. Opposition spokesman on Home Affairs from 1979. PC. 1974. A Labour Member. Labour candidate at Harrow E. in the general elections of 1955 and 1959. Unsuccessfully contested Harrow E. at a by-election in Mar. 1959. Elected for Leeds S. in June 1963.*

[1979]

REES, Peter Wynford Innes, Q.C. 39 Headford Place, London. Goytre Hall, Abergavenny, Monmouthshire. 5 Church Street, St. Clements, Sandwich, Kent. Boodle's. S. of

Maj.-Gen. T.W. Rees. B. 9 Dec. 1926; m. 15 Dec. 1969, Mrs. Anthea Wendell, d. of Maj. J.M. Hyslop. Educ. at Stowe, and Christ Church, Oxford. Served with Scots Guards 1945-48. Called to the bar Inner Temple, 1953, practised Oxford Circuit. Q.C. 1969. Parliamentary Private Secretary to Sir Geoffrey Howe and Sir Michael Havers. Solicitors Gen. 1972-73. Bencher of Inner Temple 1976. An Opposition spokesman on Treasury Affairs from Nov. 1977 to May 1979. Minister of State at the Treasury from May 1979. A Conservative. Unsuccessfully contested Abertillery in 1964 and 1965 and the W. Derby division of Liverpool in 1966. Sat for the Dover division from 1970 to Feb. 1974. Elected for Dover and Deal in Feb. 1974.*

[1979]

REES-DAVIES, William Rupert, Q.C. 6 Victoria Square, London. M.C.C. S. of Sir William Rees Davies, MP., K.C., J.P., D.L.B. 19 Nov. 1916; m. July 1959, Jane, d. of Henry Mander, Esq., (1 d.) divorced 1979. Educ. at Eton, and Trinity Coll., Cambridge (cricket eleven 1938). A Barrister-at-Law, Inner Temple Nov. 1939, called to the bar. Q.C. 1973. Commissioned Welsh Guards 1939. Practises Common Law and Criminal bar. Chairman British-Greek Parliamentary Group. A Conservative. Unsuccessfully contested S. Nottingham in 1950 and 1951. Sat for the Isle of Thanet from Mar. 1953 to Feb. 1974. Elected for Thanet W. in Feb. 1974.*

[1979]

REES-WILLIAMS, Lieut.-Col. David Rees, T.D. 15a Chichester Road, Croydon. S. of W. Rees-Williams, Esq. B. 22 Nov. 1903; m. 30 July 1930. Constance, d. of Alderman W.R. Wills. Educ. at Mill Hill School, and University of Wales. Admitted a Solicitor 1929. A Senior Tutor to Law Society 1945-46. Clerk to Cardiff Assessment Committee 1935-45. Lieut.-Col. R.A. Staff Officer 1st Grade. Chief Legal Officer, Military Government, Greater Berlin Area. Member of Straits Settlements Bar. Member of Government Mission to Sarawak 1946 and Chairman of Burma Frontier Areas Committee of Inquiry 1947. Parliamentary Under-Secretary of State for the Colonies Oct. 1947-Mar. 1950. A Labour Member. Elected for S. Croydon in July 1945 and sat until Feb. 1950 when he unsuccessfully contested W. Croydon. Created Baron Ogmore 1950. Parliamentary Under-Secretary of State for Commonwealth Relations July 1950-June 1951. Minister of Civil Aviation June-Oct. 1951. PC. 1951. Joined Liberal Party 1959. President of Liberal Party 1963-64. Died 30 Aug. 1976.

[1950]

REEVES, Joseph. 5 Russell Hill, Purley, Surrey. S. of Walter Cookson, Esq. B. 28 Jan. 1888; m. 14 Sept. 1940, Gladys, d. of Enos Holdup, Esq. Educ. at London County Council School. Education Secretary Royal Arsenal Co-operative Society 1918-38. Member of Deptford Borough Council 1920-49. Secretary and Manager of Workers, Film Association 1938-45. Member of the National Executive Committee of the Labour Party 1946-53, member of B.B.C. Enquiry Committee. An Author. A Labour Member. Unsuccessfully contested Woolwich W. in 1931 and Greenwich in 1935. Elected for Greenwich in July 1945 and sat until he retired in 1959. Pres. of International Cremation Federation. Vice-Chairman of Cremation Society. Died 8 Mar. 1969. [1959]

REID, George Newlands. 11 Drysdale Street, Alloa, Clackmannanshire. Caledonian. S. of George Reid, Esq. B. 4 June 1939; m. 1968 Daphne, d. of Calum MacColl., Esq., (2 d.). Educ. at Tullibody School, Dollar Academy, and St. Andrew's University (1st Class Hons. M.A.). A Reporter, Beaverbrook Newspapers. A Commentator, Scottish Television. A Producer and Presenter, Granada Television. Head of News and Current Affairs, Scottish Television. Freelance Broadcaster and Writer. Director Scottish Research Institute 1974-77. S.N.P. Parliamentary spokesman on Constitutional and E.E.C. Affairs. Member British Delegation to Council of Europe and Western European Union 1977-79. A Scottish Nationalist Party Member. Sat for East Stirlingshire and Clackmannan from Feb. 1974 until 1979 when he was defeated.* [1979]

REID, Rt. Hon. James Scott Cumberland, K.C. 46 Northumberland Street, Edinburgh. Carlton. S. of James Reid, Esq.,

Writer to the Signet, of Drem, E. Lothian. B. 30 July 1890; m. 1933, Esther May, d. of C.B. Nelson, Esq., and widow of G.F. Brierley, Esq., of Madras and Bombay. Educ. at Edinburgh Academy, and Jesus Coll., Cambridge. Admitted Advocate 1914. K.C. 1932. Solicitor-Gen. for Scotland June 1936-June 1941; Lord Advocate June 1941-July 1945 PC. 1941. Served with 8th Royal Scots and overseas with M.G.C. 1914-18. A Unionist. Sat for Stirling and Falkirk from Oct. 1931-Nov. 1935, when he was defeated, and for the Hillhead division of Glasgow June 1937-Sept. 1948 when he was created Baron Reid (Law Life Peerage) and appointed Lord of Appeal in Ordinary. Dean of Facuty of Advocates 1945-48. Lord of Appeal in Ordinary Sept. 1948-Jan. 1975. Chairman of Malayan Constitutional Commission 1956-57. Companion of Honour 1967. Hon. Fellow of Jesus Coll., Cambridge. Hon. Bencher of Gray's Inn. Hon. D.C.L. University of Oxford 1971. Died 29 Mar. 1975. [1948]

REID, Thomas, C.M.G. 15a Tring Avenue, Ealing Common, London. S. of John Reid, Esq. of Co. Carlow. B. 26 Dec. 1881; m. 1912, Brenda, d. of W. Broadway, Esq. Educ. at Queen's Coll., Cork, and Royal University, Dublin, B.A. In Ceylon C.S. 1905-31; Mayor and Chief Executive Officer Colombo; member of Ceylon Legislature in Charge of Labour. C.M.G. 1931. Financial Commissioner Seychelles 1933; member of the Palestine Partition Commission 1938; President League of Nations Commission on Sanjak of Alexandretta 1937-38. Fellow of Royal Empire Society. A Labour Member. Unsuccessfully contested the Northwich division of Cheshire in 1935. Elected for Swindon in July 1945 and sat until he retired in 1955. Died 28 Jan. 1963. [1954]

REID, William, J.P. House of Commons, London. S. of Hill Reid, Esq., of Glasgow. B. 6 Nov. 1889. Educ. at Whitehill Secondary School. Merchant and Manufacturer. Entered Glasgow Town Council 1920; Magistrate 1927-30. J.P. 1930. Police Judge 1930-50. Chairman Glasgow Corporation Transport Committee 1936-39, Public Health Committee 1946-49. Member of Scottish Western Regional Hospital Board. A

Labour Member. Unsuccessfully contested the Camlachie division of Glasgow in 1935. Sat for the Camlachie division of Glasgow 1950-55 and for the Provan division of Glasgow from 1955 until he retired in 1964. Died 16 July 1965. [1964]

REMNANT, Lieut.-Col. Hon. Peter Farquharson. 5 Harrington Court, London. Ipsden House, Ipsden, Oxfordshire. Constitutional. S. of Sir James Remnant, Bart., MP., 1st Lord Remnant. B. 21 Sept. 1897; m. 24 Nov. 1923, Elizabeth, d. of W.G. Tanner, Esq., of Frenchay, Gloucestershire (she died 1965). Educ. at Eton, and Magdalen Coll., Oxford. Served with R.G.A. 1916-19 and with R.A. (A.A.) and on Staff 1939-45. Chairman Assam Company Limited, and Director of other companies. A Conservative. Elected for the Wokingham division of Berkshire in Feb. 1950 and sat until he retired in 1959. Died 31 Jan. 1968. [1959]

RENTON, Rt. Hon. Sir David Lockhart-Mure, K.B.E., T.D., Q.C., D.L. 22 Old Buildings, Lincoln's Inn, London. Moat House, Abbots Ripton, Huntingdon. Carlton, and Pratt's. S. of Maurice Renton, Esq., M.D., C.M., D.P.H. B. 12 Aug. 1908; m. 17 July 1947, Claire Cicely, d. of Walter Duncan, Esq., (3 d.). Educ. at Oundle, and University Coll., Oxford, M.A., B.C.L. A Barrister-at-Law, Lincoln's Inn 1933. Q.C. 1954. President of Oxford University Liberal Club 1930-31. Member of Bar Council 1939. Bencher of Lincoln's Inn, 1962. Maj. R.A. Served 1939-45, overseas 1942-45. T.D. Parliamentary Secretary Ministry of Fuel and Power Dec. 1955-Jan. 1957; Parliamentary Secretary Minister of Power Jan. 1957-Jan. 1958; Joint Parliamentary Under-Secretary of State at the Home Office Jan. 1958-June 1961. Minister of State at the Home Office June 1961-July 1962. PC. 1962. Dept.-Lieut. for Huntingdonshire 1962, for Huntingdon and Peterborough 1964 and for Cambridgeshire 1974. K.B.E. 1964. Recorder of Rochester 1964-68 and of Guildford 1968-71. Royal Commission on the Constitution 1971-73. President Conservation Society 1971-72. Chairman Standing Orders Revision Committee 1963 and 1970. Chairman Committee on Preparation of Legislation 1973-75. Chairman National Society for Mentally Handicapped Children from 1978. A Conservative. Sat for Huntingdonshire from July 1945 until he retired in 1979. Created Baron Renton (Life Peerage) 1979.* [1979]

RENTON, Ronald Timothy. 8 Eaton Row, Hobart Place, London. Mount Harry House, Lewes, Sussex. Brooks's, and Coningsby. S. of R.K.D. Renton, Esq., C.B.E. B. 28 May 1932; m. 2 Apr. 1960, Alice, d. of Sir James Fergusson, Bart., of Kilkerran, (2 s. 3 d.). Educ. at Eton, and Magdalen Coll., Oxford. Worked for C. Tennant Sons and Company Limited, Canada 1957-62. Managing Director Tennant Trading Limited 1964-71. Director Silvermines Limited 1966. Director A.N.Z. Banking Group Limited 1969-76. J.H. Vavasseur and Company Limited 1971-74. Member of Select Committee on Nationalised Industries from Nov. 1974. Vice-Chairman of Conservative Parliamentary Trade Committee from Nov. 1974. Fellowship: Industry and Parliament Trust 1977-78. Parliamentary Private Secretary to Rt. Hon. John Biffen, Chief Secretary to Treasury from 1979. Articles in *The Statist, Financial Times, Banker's Magazine.* A Conservative. Unsuccessfully contested Sheffield Park in 1970. Elected for Sussex Mid division in Feb. 1974.* [1979]

REYNOLDS, Rt. Hon. Gerald William. House of Commons, London. S. of Arthur Reynolds, Esq. B. 17 July 1927; m. 1949, Dorothy, d. of Capt. E.V. Budd, of Acton. Educ. at Acton County Grammar School. Member of Acton Borough Council 1949-65, Mayor 1961-62. Local Government Officer to National Executive Committee of the Labour Party 1952-58. Parliamentary Under-Secretary of State for Defence for the Army Oct. 1964-Dec. 1965. Minister of Defence for the Army Dec. 1965-Jan. 1967. Minister of Defence for Administration Jan. 1967-June 1969. PC. 1968. A Labour Member. Unsuccessfully contested Worthing in 1951. Elected for Islington N. in May 1958 and sat until his death on 7 June 1969. Chairman of London Borough of Ealing 1964-65. Died 7 June 1969. [1969]

RHODES, Geoffrey William. 46 Cartington Terrace, Newcastle-upon-Tyne. S. of Harold Rhodes, Esq. of Leeds. B. 7 Nov. 1928; m. 1954, Marise Wiseman. Educ. at Elementary and Grammar Schools, and Leeds University, B.A. (Hons.), M.A., F.C.C.S., A.M.B.I.M. Head of Department of Business. Studies, Leigh Technical Coll. until 1964. Joined the Labour Party in 1944. Member of the National Union of Teachers from 1953. Fabian Society 1952, Co-operative Party 1955; Chairman Leeds Co-operative Party 1956-57. Chairman Huyton Co-operative Party 1960-64. Parliamentary Private Secretary to Rt. Hon. Richard Crossman Minister of Housing and Local Government 1965-66 and Leader of House of Commons 1966-67. Member of Council of Europe 1967-70. Chairman Labour Party National Working Group on Higher Education 1968-72. Successfully contested municipal elections Bramley Ward, Leeds in 1954 and 1957. A Labour and Co-operative Member. Unsuccessfully contested Parliamentary elections at Barkston Ash in 1955 and Battersea S. in 1959. Elected for Newcastle-upon-Tyne E. in Oct. 1964 and sat until his death on 22 June 1974. [1974 2nd ed.]

RHODES, Hervey, D.F.C. Cribbstones, Delph, Nr. Oldham. S. of John Eastwood Rhodes, Esq., of Greenfield. B. 12 Aug. 1895; m. 12 Aug. 1925, Ann, d. of John Bradbury, Esq. Educ. at Greenfield Elementary School, and Huddersfield Technical Coll. A Woollen Manufacturer. Served with R.F.C. 1914-18 (D.F.C. and Bar). Member of Saddleworth Urban District Council 1938-45, Chairman 1944-45. Commanded 36th Battalion W.R. H.G. 1940-45. Parliamentary Private Secretary to H.A. Marquand, Paymaster-Gen. Jan. 1948, and when Minister of Pensions July 1948-Mar. 1950. Parliamentary Secretary Board of Trade Mar. 1950-Oct. 1951. A Labour Member. Unsuccessfully contested the Royton division of Lancashire in July 1945. Elected for Ashton-under-Lyne in Oct. 1945 and sat until Aug. 1964 when he was created Baron Rhodes (Life Peerage). Parliamentary Secretary, Board of Trade for a second time Oct. 1964-Jan. 1967. Lord Lieut. of Lancashire 1968-71, Dept.-Lieut. from 1971. PC. 1969. K.G. 1972.* [1964]

RHODES JAMES, Robert Vidal. The Store House, Great Gransden, Nr. Sandy, Bedfordshire. Travellers'. S. of Lieut.-Col. W. Rhodes James, O.B.E., M.C. B. 10 Apr. 1933; m. 18 Aug. 1956, Angela Margaret, d. of R.M. Robertson, Esq., (4 d.). Educ. at Sedbergh School, Yorkshire, and Worcester Coll., Oxford. Junior Clerk, House of Commons 1955-61, Senior Clerk, House of Commons 1961-64. Fellow of All Souls Coll., Oxford 1964-68 and from 1979. Director of Institute for the Study of International Organization, University of Sussex 1968-73. Kratter Professor of European History, Stanford University 1968. Principal Officer, Executive Office of the Secretary General of the United Nations 1973-76. Parliamentary Private Secretary to Nicholas Ridley and Neil Marten, Ministers of State, Foreign and Commonwealth Office from 1979. Biographer of Lord Randolph Churchill 1959, Lord Rosebery 1961, Victor Cazalet 1976, and historian of Gallipoli Campaign 1963, etc. Editor of diaries of Sir Henry Channon, MP. and memoirs of J.C.C. Davidson, MP. Author of *The British Revolution 1880-1939*. A Conservative. Sat for Cambridge from Dec. 1976.* [1979]

RHYS-WILLIAMS, Sir Brandon Meredith, Bart. 32 Rawlings Street, London. White's, and Pratt's. S. of Sir Rhys Williams, Bart., D.S.O., Q.C., MP. B. 14 Nov. 1927; m. 1961, Caroline, d. of L.A. Foster, Esq., (1 s. 2 d.). Assumed the name of Rhys-Williams in lieu of Williams in 1938. Succeeded to Baronetcy in 1955. Educ. at Eton. Served in the Welsh Guards 1946-48. Assistant Director of Spastics Society 1962-63. Consultant, Management Selection Limited 1963-71. Author of *The New Social Contract* 1967. Member British Delegation to Council of Europe 1970-72 and to European Parliament from 1973 (Vice-Chairman Economic and Monetary Affairs Committee). Member of European Parliament for London S.E. from 1979. A Conservative. Unsuccessfully contested Pontypridd in 1959, Ebbw Vale in 1960, and again in 1964. Sat for Kensington S. from Mar. 1968 to Feb. 1974. Elected for the Kensington division of Kensington and Chelsea in Feb. 1974.* [1979]

RICHARD, Ivor Seward, Q.C. 47 Burntwood Grange Road, London. S. of Seward Thomas Richard, Esq. B. 30 May 1932; m. 9 June 1962, Alison Mary, d. of J. Imrie, Esq. Educ. at St. Michael's School, Llanelly, Scholarship Cheltenham Coll., Scholarship to Pembroke Coll., Oxford, B.A. Barrister-at-Law, Inner Temple, 1955. Q.C. 1971. Joined the Labour Party in 1953. Member Society of Labour Lawyers, Fabian Society. Member U.K. Delegation, Council of Europe and W.E.U. Parliamentary Private Secretary to Rt. Hon. Denis Healey, Minister of Defence 1966-69. Parliamentary Under-Secretary Ministry of Defence (Army) Oct. 1969-June 1970. Opposition spokesman on Broadcasting, Posts and Telecommunications 1970-72, and on Foreign Affairs 1972-74. Voted in favour of entry to E.E.C. on 28 Oct. 1971. A Labour Member. Unsuccessfully contested S. Kensington in 1959. Sat for Barons Court from Oct. 1964 until Feb. 1974 when he unsuccessfully contested Blyth, as the official Labour candidate in opposition to Edward Milne, the sitting Member, who was re-elected as an Independent Labour candidate. Permanent Representative to the United Nations 1974-79. Chairman of Rhodesia Conference in Geneva 1976.* [1974]

RICHARDS, Robert. Ambassadors Hotel, Woburn Place, London. Llangynog, Oswestry. S. of John Richards, Esq., a Mineworker. B. 1884; m. 1918, Mary Myfanwy, d. of Thomas Owen, Esq. (she died 1950). Educ. at Elementary School, University Coll. of Wales, Aberystwyth and St. John's Coll., Cambridge. Assistant Lecturer at Glasgow University, later Head of Economics Department of Bangor University. Tutor in economics and political science at Coleg Harlech. Civil Defence Commissioner for Wales. Under-Secretary for India Jan.-Nov. 1924. A Labour Member. Sat for the Wrexham division of Denbighshire 1922-24, when he was defeated, 1929-31, when he was again defeated, and from Nov. 1935 until his death on 22 Dec. 1954. [1954]

RICHARDSON, Josephine. House of Commons, London. D. of J.J. Richardson, Esq. B. 28 Aug. 1923. Educ. at Southend-on-Sea High School for Girls. Hornsey

Borough Councillor 4 years, Alderman 6 years, Hammersmith Borough Councillor 3 years. Secretary of the Keep Left Group, Bevan Group and Tribune Group from 1948. Chairman Parliamentary Committee of A.S.T.M.S. Vice-Chairman of C.N.D. Member of Executive Committee N.C.C.L. Member of National Executive Committee of Labour Party from 1979. A Labour Member. Unsuccessfully contested Monmouth in 1951 and 1955, Hornchurch in 1959 and Harrow E. in 1964. Elected for the Barking division of Barking in Feb. 1974.* [1979]

RIDEALGH, Mabel. 72 Hazlewood Road, Bush Hill Park, Enfield, Middlesex. D. of Mark Jewitt, Esq., Butcher, of Wallsend. B. 11 Aug. 1898; m. 14 June 1919, Leonard Ridealgh, Esq. National President Women's Co-op Guild 1941-42. Honorary Regional Organiser Board of Trade 1942-44. A Labour Member. Elected for N. Ilford in July 1945 and sat until 1950 when she was defeated. Unsuccessfully contested N. Ilford in 1951. Member of Women's Advisory Committee of British Standards Institute 1953-63. General Secretary of Women's Co-op Guild 1953-63.* [1950]

RIDLEY, Hon. Nicholas. House of Commons, London. 2nd s. of 3rd Visct. Ridley, C.B.E. B. 17 Feb. 1929; m. 1st, 1950, Hon. Clayre Campbell, d. of Lord Stratheden (divorced 1974), (3 d.). 2ndly, 1979 Judy Kendall. Educ. at Eton, and Balliol Coll., Oxford. A Civil Engineering Contractor. Executive Committee National Trust 1962-70. Parliamentary Private Secretary to Sir Edward Boyle, Minister of Education 1962-64. Member of U.K. Delegation to Council of Europe and Western European Union 1962-66. An Opposition spokesman on Power 1965 and on Defence 1965-66. Member of Royal Commission on Historical Manuscripts from 1967. Opposition Front Bench spokesman on Trade and Technology from Oct. 1969 to June 1970. Parliamentary Secretary to Ministry of Technology June 1970-Oct. 1970. Parliamentary Under-Secretary of State at Department of Trade and Industry Oct. 1970-Apr. 1972. Minister of State, Foreign and Commonwealth Office from 1979. Director A.F.I. Group Limited and Marshall Andrew Limited. Consultant to Univac Limited and Tate and Lyle Limited. A Conservative. Unsuccessfully contested Blyth in 1955. Elected for Cirencester and Tewkesbury in 1959.* [1979]

RIDSDALE, Julian Errington. 12 The Boltons, London. Fiddam, St. Osyth, Essex. Carlton. S. of Julian Ridsdale, Esq. B. 8 June 1915; m. 19 Sept. 1942, Patricia, d. of Col. J. Bennett. Educ. at Tonbridge School, Sandhurst, and Oriental School of Languages, London University. Served with Royal Norfolk Regiment from 1935, later with Royal Scots and Somerset Light Infantry, Tokyo 1938-39, Washington 1944-45, retired 1946, Maj. Chairman British Japanese Parliamentary Group. Vice-Chairman Parliamentary U.N. Association. Unsuccessful L.C.C. candidate for S.W. Islington 1949. Unsuccessful candidate for N. Paddington 1951. Parliamentary Private Secretary to J.D. Profumo, Under-Secretary of State for Colonial Affairs 1957-58 and Minister of State for Foreign Affairs 1958-60. Parliamentary Under-Secretary of State, Air Ministry July 1962-Apr. 1964. Parliamentary Under-Secretary of State for Defence for the Royal Air Force Apr.-Oct. 1964. Master of Skinners Company 1970-71. Member Select Committee of Public Accounts 1970-74. Leader Parliamentary Delegations to Japan 1973, 1975, 1977 and 1978. European member of the Trilateral Commission for Europe, U.S.A. and Japan. Chairman of the Japan Society of London 1976. C.B.E. 1977, Order of Sacred Treasure (Japan). A Conservative. Elected for the Harwich division of Essex in Feb. 1954.* [1979]

RIFKIND, Malcolm Leslie. 8 Old Church Lane, Duddingston Village, Edinburgh. S. of E. Rifkind, Esq. B. 21 June 1946; m. 24 May 1970, Edith, d. of Joseph Steinberg, Esq., of Rhodesia. Educ. at George Watsons Coll., Edinburgh University. Lecturer University Coll. of Rhodesia 1967-68. Called to the Scottish bar 1970. Honorary President Scottish Young Conservatives 1976-77. Honorary Secretary Federation of Conservative Students 1977. Opposition Front Bench spokesman on Scottish Affairs 1975-76, when he resigned. Member Select Committee on

European Sec. Legislation 1976-77. Honorary Secretary Parliamentary Group of Conservative Friends of Israel 1976. Joint Secretary Conservative Foreign and Commonwealth Affairs Committee 1977. Member Select Committee on Overseas Development 1978. Under-Secretary of State for Scotland from May 1979. A Conservative. Unsuccessfully contested Edinburgh Central in 1970. Elected for the Pentlands division of Edinburgh in Feb. 1974.* [1979]

RIPPON, Rt. Hon. (Aubrey) Geoffrey Frederick, Q.C. Ellwood House, Barrasford, Hexham, Northumberland. 37 Cadogan Square, London. White's, Carlton, M.C.C., and Pratt's. S. of A.E.S. Rippon, Esq. B. 28 May 1924; m. 1946, Ann Leyland, d. of Donald Yorke, Esq. Educ. at King's Coll., Taunton, and Brasenose Coll., Oxford, (Honorary Fellow 1972). PC. 1962. Barrister-at-Law, Middle Temple, 1948, Q.C. 1964, Bencher, 1979. Secretary and Librarian, Oxford Union Society 1943; President Oxford University Conservative Association 1943; Chairman Federation of University Conservative Associations 1943-44. Member of Surbiton Borough Council 1945-54; Alderman 1949-54; Mayor 1951-52. Member London County Council (now Greater London Council) from 1952 to 1961, Group Leader of Conservative Party 1957-59. Parliamentary Private Secretary to Rt. Hon. Duncan Sandys, Minister of Housing and Local Government 1956-57 and Minister of Defence 1957-59. Parliamentary Secretary Ministry of Aviation 1959-61; Joint Parliamentary Secretary Ministry of Housing and Local Government 1961-62. Minister of Public Building and Works 1962-64. Member of Cabinet 1963-64. Member of Shadow Cabinet 1966-70 and 1974-75. Chief Opposition spokesman on Housing and Local Government 1966-68 and on Defence 1968-70. Leader Conservative Delegation to Council of Europe and Western European Union 1968-70. Minister of Technology June-July 1970. Chancellor of the Duchy of Lancaster July 1970-Nov. 1972. Secretary of State for the Environment Nov. 1972-Mar. 1974. Chief Opposition spokesman on European Affairs Mar. 1974-Oct. 1974, and on Foreign and Commonwealth Affairs Oct. 1974-Mar.

1975. Leader of Conservative Group in European Parliament 1977-79. Admiral of the Manx Herring Fleet 1971-74. Chairman British Section European League for Economic Co-operation 1967-70. President 1970. Chairman of Holland, Hannen and Cubitts, Dun and Bradstreet Limited and Britannia Arrow Holdings. A Conservative. Unsuccessfully contested Shoreditch and Finsbury 1950 and 1951. Sat for Norwich S. from 1955 to 1964. Elected for the Hexham division of Northumberland in Mar. 1966.* [1979]

ROBENS, Rt. Hon. Alfred. Butlers Dene, Butlers Dene Road, Woldingham, Surrey. S. of George Robens, Esq. B. 18 Dec. 1910; m. 9 Sept. 1936, Eva, d. of Fred Powell, Esq. Educ. at Elementary and Secondary Schools, Manchester. Member of Manchester City Council 1941-45; Trade Union Official 1935. Parliamentary Private Secretary to Rt. Hon. Alfred Barners, Minister of Transport 1946; Parliamentary Secretary Ministry of Fuel and Power Oct. 1947-Apr. 1951. Minister of Labour Apr.-Oct. 1951. PC. 1951. A Labour Member. Sat for the Wansbeck division of Northumberland July 1945-Feb. 1950 and for Blyth from Feb. 1950 until Oct. 1960 when he resigned on appointment as Dept. Chairman and Chairman designate of National Coal Board. Member of Parliamentary Committee of P.L.P. 1951-60. Opposition spokesman on Foreign Affairs 1955-56, on Fuel and Power 1956-59 and on Labour 1956-60. Chairman of National Coal Board 1961-71. Created Baron Robens of Woldingham (Life Peerage) 1961. Chairman of Foundation on Automation and employment 1962. President of Advertising Association 1963-68. Member of Royal Commission on Trade Unions and employers Associations 1965-68. Director of Bank of England from 1966, of Times Newspapers Limited from 1967 and of Trust Houses Forte Limited from 1971. Chancellor of University of Surrey 1966-77. Chairman of Vickers Limited from 1971, of M.L.H. Consultants from 1971, of Johnson Matthey & Company Limited from 1971, of St. Regis International from 1976. Chairman of Engineering Industries Council from 1976.* [1960]

ROBERTS, Albert. House of Commons, London. S. of Albert Roberts, Esq. B. 14 May 1908; m. 26 Nov. 1932, Alice, d. of George Ashton, Esq., (1 s. 1 d.). Educ. at Woodlesford, Normanton, Castleford, and Whitwood Coll. A Trade Union Secretary (Mines) 1935-41. Mines Inspector from Dec. 1941. Elected to the Rothwell Urban District Council Yorkshire 1937. Chairman 1948-49. J.P. for the W. Riding of Yorkshire from 1946. Dept.-Lieut of the W. Riding of Yorkshire 1967. Criticised by the House of Commons Select Committee on the Conduct of Members on 14 July 1977 for 'conduct inconsistent with the standards which the House is entitled to expect from its members' as a result of his business contacts with John Poulson. An attempt to expel him was defeated by 353 votes to 11 on 26 July 1977. Executive member Inter-Parliamentary Union, British Group. Awarded Encomienda de Numero de Isabel la Catolica by Head of the Spanish State. A Labour Member. Elected for the Normanton division of the W. Riding of Yorkshire in Oct. 1951.* [1979]

ROBERTS, Emrys Owain, M.B.E. Court House, Basil Street, London. Bryn, Dedwydd, Dolgelly. Farmers'. S. of Owen Owens Roberts, Esq. B. 22 Sept. 1910; m. 1948, Anna Elisabeth Tudor. Educ. at Caernarvon Schools, University of Wales, Aberystwyth, Gonville and Caius Coll., Cambridge, and Geneva School of International Studies, M.A., LL.B., Double First Class Hons., Cambridge and Wales Law Societies Gold Medallist. Barrister-at-Law, Gray's Inn 1944. President National League of Young Liberals 1946-48, and of Liberal Party of Wales 1949-51; member of Parliamentary Delegations to Germany, Yugoslavia, Roumania and Sweden. Served with R.A.F. 1941-45; Squadron-Leader. A Liberal. Elected for Merionethshire in July 1945 and sat until 1951 when he was defeated. Director of Tootal Broadhurst Lee Company Limited, English Sewing Limited, English Calico Limited and Tootal Limited 1958-75. Chairman of Council of National Eisteddfod of Wales 1964-67. Chairman of Mid-Wales Development Corporation 1968-77. Director of Cambrian & General Securities Limited and Filtrasol Limited from 1974. M.B.E. 1946.

C.B.E. 1976. Chairman of Development Board for Rural Wales from 1977. Member of Welsh Development Agency from 1977. Director of Development Corporation of Wales from 1978.* [1951]

ROBERTS, Rt. Hon. Goronwy Owen. House of Commons, London. S. of Edward Roberts, Esq., of Bethesda. B. 20 Sept. 1913; m. 1942, Marian, d. of David Evans, Esq., of Aberdare. Educ. at Ogwen Grammar School, University of Wales, M.A. and Fellow, and London University. Lecturer 1944. Member of Court of Governors University Coll. of Wales and National Library of Wales. Broadcaster on Literary and Political subjects. Served with Infantry and Army Reserve 1941. Member Speaker's Panel of Chairmen 1963-64. Chairman Welsh Economic Planning Council 1964-66. F.R.S.A. 1967. Minister of State, Welsh Office Oct. 1964-Apr. 1966. Minister of State for Education and Science Apr. 1966-Aug. 1967. Minister of State for Foreign Affairs Aug. 1967-Oct. 69. Minister of State, Board of Trade Oct. 1969-June 1970. An Opposition spokesman on Foreign Affairs 1970-74. PC. 1968. Freeman of Caernarvon 1972. A Labour Member. Sat for Caernarvonshire July 1945-Feb. 1950 and for the Caernarvon division of Caernarvonshire from Feb. 1950 until Feb. 1974, when he was defeated. Created Baron Goronwy-Roberts (Life Peerage) 1974, when he assumed the surname of Goronwy-Roberts in lieu of Roberts. Under-Secretary of State for Foreign and Commonwealth Affairs Mar. 1974-Dec. 1975, Minister of State Dec. 1975-May 1979. Dept. Leader of House of Lords 1975-79. Dept. Leader of Opposition in House of Lords from 1979.* [1974]

ROBERTS, Gwilym Edffrwd. 60 Swasedale Road, Luton. 8 Main Road, Brereton, Rugeley. S. of William Roberts, Esq. B. 7 Aug. 1928; m. Apr. 1954, Mair Griffiths. Educ. at Brynrefail Grammar School and University of Wales. J.P. for Luton. Principal Lecturer Industrial Consultant on Computer Methods, Market and Operational Research. Vice-President Institute of Statisticians. Parliamentary Private Secretary to Alan J. Williams, Minister of State, Department of

Industry 1976-78. A Labour Member. Unsuccessfully contested Ormskirk in 1959 and Conway in 1964. Sat for Bedfordshire S. from Mar. 1966 to June 1970, when he was defeated. Elected for Cannock in Feb. 1974.*

[1979]

ROBERTS, Harold. The Cottage, Rose Hill, Rednal, Worcestershire. 106 Colmore Row, Birmingham. S. of William Roberts, Esq., of Bridgwater. B. 23 Aug. 1884; m. 29 Jan. 1913, Ann, d. of George Pettifor, Esq., of Anstey. Educ. privately. Admitted a Solicitor 1906, LL.B. London 1907; member of Birmingham City Council from 1922, Alderman 1936, Lord Mayor 1936. Chairman of W. Midlands Joint Industrial Council for Non-Trading Services 1943-45. A Unionist. Elected for the Handsworth division of Birmingham in July 1945 and sat until his death on 28 Sept. 1950. [1950]

ROBERTS, Ieuan Wyn Pritchard. Tan y Gwalia, Conway. Savile. S. of the Rev. Evan Pritchard Roberts. B. 10 July 1930; m. 1956, Enid Grace Williams. Educ. at Beaumaris County School, Harrow, and University Coll., Oxford. Sub-Editor *Liverpool Daily Post* 1952-54; News Assistant B.B.C. 1954-57. Executive T.W.W. Limited 1957-68; Executive Harlech T.V. Limited 1968-69. Member Court of Governors of National Museum of Wales and National Library of Wales. Member of Royal National Eisteddfod Gorsedd of Bards. Vice-President Association of District Councils. Parliamentary Private Secretary to Rt. Hon. Peter Thomas, Secretary of State for Wales 1970-74. Conservative spokesman on Welsh Affairs 1974-79. Under-Secretary of State for Wales from May 1979. A Conservative. Sat for the Conway division of Caernarvonshire from June 1970.* [1979]

ROBERTS, Michael Hilary Arthur. Ashgrove Farm, Whitchurch, Cardiff. S. of the Rev. T.A. Roberts. B. 6 May 1927; m. 4 Aug. 1952, Mrs. Eileen Evans, d. of C.H. Billing, Esq. Educ. at Neath Grammar School, and University Coll., Cardiff. Headmaster Bishop of Llandaff High School 1963-70. Member of Council of Europe and Western European Union 1973-74. Member

Opposition Whips' Office July 1974-May 1979. Under-Secretary of State for Wales from May 1979. A Conservative. Unsuccessfully contested Aberdare in 1954 and Cardiff S.E. in 1955 and 1959. Sat for Cardiff N. from 1970 to Feb. 1974. Elected for Cardiff N.W. in Feb. 1974.* [1979]

ROBERTS, Sir Peter Geoffrey, Bart. 11 Mount Street, London. Redholme, Sandygate Road, Sheffield. Carlton, and Brooks's. S. of Sir Samuel Roberts, 2nd Bart., MP. B. 23 June 1912; m. 5 Dec. 1939, Judith, d. of Randell Hempson, Esq. Educ. at Harrow, and Trinity Coll., Cambridge. Barrister-at-Law, Inner Temple 1935. Maj. Coldstream Guards. Succeeded his father as 3rd Bart. (created 1919) Dec. 1955. A Unionist Member. Sat for the Ecclesall division of Sheffield from July 1945 to Feb. 1950. Elected for the Heeley division of Sheffield in Feb. 1950 and sat until he retired in 1966. Director of Wellman Engineering Corporation Limited, Chairman 1952-72. Chairman of Newton Chambers & Company Limited 1954-72, Hadfields Limited 1961-67, Curzonia Knitwear Limited and Wombwell Investment Company Limited. Director of Guardian Royal Exchange Assurance Limited, Williams & Glyn's Bank Limited and National and Commercial Banking Group. Master Cutler 1957. High Sheriff of Hallamshire 1970-71.* [1966]

ROBERTS, Wilfrid Hugh Wace. Boothby House, Brampton, Cumberland. S. of Charles Roberts, MP. and Lady Cecilia Howard, d. of 9th Earl of Carlisle. B. 28 Aug. 1900; m. 4 June 1928, Anne, d. of George Jennings, Esq., C.I.E. Educ. at Gresham School, and Balliol Coll., Oxford. Liberal Assistant Whip 1940. Parliamentary Private Secretary to the Rt. Hon. Sir Archibald Sinclair, Secretary of State for Air Aug. 1941-Mar. 1942. A Liberal. Unsuccessfully contested N. Cumberland in 1931. Elected for N. Cumberland in 1935 and sat until 1950 when he unsuccessfully contested the Penrith and Border division of Cumberland. Joined Labour Party in 1956 and unsuccessfully contested the Hexham division of Northumberland in 1959.* [1950]

ROBERTSON, Sir David. 39 Hyde Park Gate, London. Royal Scottish Automobile, and Caledonian. S. of John Robertson, Esq., Chief Inspector G.P.O. Glasgow. B. 19 Jan. 1890; m. 1912, May, d. of Robert Weir Ritchie, Esq., of Prestwick, Ayrshire. Educ. at Woodside School, Allan Glens School, and Glasgow University. Managing Director of Cold Storage Companies. Capt. Argyll and Sutherland Highlanders, served in France, First World War. Knight Bach. 1945. An Independent Member. Sat for the Streatham division of Wandsworth as a Conservative Dec. 1939-Feb. 1950. Elected for Caithness and Sutherland in Feb. 1950 as a Conservative, resigned the whip in Jan. 1959, re-elected in Oct. 1959 as an Independent, but without Conservative opposition, and sat until he retired in 1964. Died 3 June 1970. [1964]

ROBERTSON, George Islay Macneill. House of Commons, London. S. of George P. Robertson, Esq., Police Inspector. B. 12 Apr. 1946; m. 1 June 1970, Sandra, d. of James V. Wallace, Esq., (2 s.). Educ. at Dunoon Grammar School, Argyll, and University of Dundee, (M.A. Honours 1968). Research Assistant Tayside Study, Economics Group 1968-69. Scottish Research Officer, G.M.W.U. 1969-70. Scottish Organiser G.M.W.U. 1970-78. Member Labour Party Scottish Executive 1973. Board member Scottish Tourist Board 1974-76. Member of Police Advisory Board for Scotland 1974-78. Governor Scottish Police Coll. 1974-78. Board Member Scottish Development Agency 1976-78. Chairman Labour Party Scottish Council 1977-78. Member of Council of National Trust for Scotland from 1977. A Labour Member. Sat for the Hamilton division of Lanarkshire from May 1978.* [1979]

ROBERTSON, John. House of Commons, London. S. of William Archibald Robertson, Esq. B. 3 Feb. 1913; m. 1st, 1939, Marion, d. of William Struthers, Esq. (Marriage dissolved in July 1977), (2 s. 2 d.); 2ndly, July 1977, June, d. of George Tyas., Esq., (she died Feb. 1978); 3rdly, 1979, Mrs Sheena Lynch. Educ. at Elementary School, and Secondary Schools. Member of the Labour Party from 1943. Councillor for Motherwell and Wishaw from 1946-51. Member of Lanarkshire County Council 1946-51. District Secretary of the A.E.U., Secretary of the Scottish Iron and Steel Trades Joint Committee. A Lanark County Councillor and member of the Hospital Management Board. A Scottish Labour Party Member. Unsuccessfully contested the Scotstoun division of Glasgow in 1951. Elected for Paisley at a by-election in Apr. 1961 and sat until he retired in 1979. Resigned the Labour Whip in July 1976 and thereafter sat as a member of the Scottish Labour Party.* [1979]

ROBERTSON, John David Home. See HOME-ROBERTSON, John David.

ROBERTSON, John James. Dunalastair, Eastfield Gardens, Joppa, Edinburgh. B. in Shetland Islands 23 May 1898; m. 1924, Agnes, d. of William Leslie, Esq. Educ. at Elementary School. Joined R.N. 1914; served until 1919, and 1939-40. Served in Merchant Navy 1919-34. Retail Fruiterer in Edinburgh from 1934. Sales representative for Scottish Housing Group. Lecturer for Minister of Information 1940-45. Chief Labour Officer Ministry of Supply 1941-45; Commissioner of Leith Docks. Gov. of Leith Nautical Coll. Member of Edinburgh Town Council 1937-45. Lay member of Gen. Medical Council 1946-49. Chairman of Commonwealth Group; Joint Parliamentary Under-Secretary of State for Scotland Oct. 1947-Mar. 1950. A Socialist. Sat for Berwick and Haddington from July 1945 to Feb. 1950. Elected for Berwick and East Lothian in Feb. 1950 and sat until 1951, when he was defeated. Died 6 Oct. 1955. [1951]

ROBINSON, Geoffrey. House of Commons, London,. S. of Robert Norman Robinson, Esq. B. 25 May 1939; m. 1967, Marie Elena Giorgio, (1 s. 1 d.). Educ. at Emanuel School, London, Clare Coll., Cambridge, and Yale University, U.S.A., (M.A. History/Economics). Labour Party Research Assistant 1965-68. Senior Executive Industrial Reorganisation Corporation 1968-70. Financial Controller, British Leyland 1970-72; Managing Director Leyland Innocenti

1972-73. Chief Executive Jaguar Cars, Coventry 1974-75. A Labour Member. Elected for Conventry N.W. at a by-election in Mar. 1976.* [1979]

ROBINSON, Rt. Hon. Sir (John) Roland. 24 Carlton House Terrace, London. Carlton, and Junior Carlton. S. of Roland Walkden Robinson, Esq., Solicitor, of Blackpool. B. 22 Feb. 1907; m. 9 July 1930, Maysie, d. of Clarence Warren Gasque, Esq. Educ. at Trinity Hall, Cambridge, M.A., LL.B. Barrister-at-Law, Lincoln's Inn, 1929. Chairman Conservative Commonwealth Affairs Committee; Chairman Gen. Council Commonwealth Parliamentary Association 1960-61. Past President of Residential Hotels Association of Great Britain, and of Royal Lancashire Agricultural Society; President of Association of Health and Pleasure Resorts. Wing-Commander R.A.F.V.R. 1943; Officer of the Legion of Merit, U.S.A. Knighted. 1954. PC. 1962. A Conservative. Sat for the Widnes division from Oct. 1931-Nov. 1935, for Blackpool Nov. 1935-July 1945, and for Blackpool S. from July 1945 to May 1964 when he was created Baron Martonmere. Gov. and Commander-in-Chief of Bermuda 1964-72. K.C.M.G. 1966. G.B.E. 1973.* [1964]

ROBINSON, Rt. Hon. Kenneth. 12 Grove Terrace, London. S. of Clarence Robinson, Esq., Physician and Surgeon, of Warrington. B. 19 Mar. 1911; m. 18 Apr. 1941, Helen Elizabeth, d. of F.H. Edwards, Esq. Educ. at Oundle School. Insurance Broker 1927-40; Secretary of Company 1946-49. Srerved in Royal Navy 1941-46, Lieut.-Commander R.N.V.R. Assistant Whip Apr. 1950-Oct. 1951. Opposition Whip 1951-54. Opposition spokesman on Health 1959-64. Minister of Health Oct. 1964-Oct. 1968. Minister for Planning and Land Nov. 1968-Oct. 1969. A Labour Member. Elected for St. Pancras N. in Mar. 1949 and sat until he retired in 1970. PC. 1964. Director of Social Policy, British Steel Corporation 1970-72. Managing Director, Personnel and Social Policy Division 1972-74. Chairman of English National Opera 1972-77. Chairman of London Transport Executive 1975-78. Chairman of Arts Council from 1977.

Biographer of Wilkie Collins and author of works on mental health.* [1970]

ROBINSON, William Oscar James. 120 Eastern Avenue, Wanstead, London. S. of Walter George Edwin Robinson, Esq., Engineer. B. 20 Mar. 1909; m. 9 Oct. 1949, Florence Anne, d. of Charles Highton Minot, Esq. Educ. at Elementary and Secondary Schools, Leyton, and London University. Legal and Administrative Officer, Harlow Development Corporation 1947-49. Secretary of Overseas Food Corporation 1949-51. Member of Leyton Borough Council 1949-52; of Wanstead and Woodford Borough Council 1952-65, Mayor 1962-63. J.P. 1953. A Solicitor 1947. A Labour Member. Unsuccessfully contested Windsor in 1955, Harwich in 1959 and Walthamstow E. in 1964. Elected for Walthamstow E. in Mar. 1966 and sat until his death on 18 Oct. 1968. [1968]

ROBSON-BROWN, Sir William. House of Commons, London. S. of John Brown, Esq. B. 1900; m. 1st 1922, Elsie Irene Thomas (she died 1968); 2ndly, 1969., Mrs. Kay Sanders. Educ. at Armstrong Coll., Newcastle-upon-Tyne. Member of Institute of Mechanical Engineers; served with R.F.C. 1914-18; closely associated with the Steel Industry. President The Marlow Conference. Member of Surrey County Council 1945-49. President Society of Commercial Accountants 1959-70. Author of *Management and Society*, and *Industrial Democracy in Action*. A Conservative. Elected for the Esher division of Surrey in Feb. 1950 and sat until he retired in 1970. Knighted 1957. Assumed the surname of Robson-Brown in lieu of Brown. Died 25 Feb. 1975. [1970]

RODERICK, Caerwyn Eifion. House of Commons, London. S. of David M. Roderick, Esq. B. 15 July 1927; m. 31 July 1952, Eirlys Mary Lewis. Educ. at University Coll. of North Wales. Assistant Master at Caterham School 1949-52; Senior Master at Chartesley School, London County Council 1952-54; Senior Master at Boys' Grammar School, Brecon 1954-57. Method Study Engineer National Coal Board 1957-60. Senior Master Hartridge High, Newport 1960-69; Lecturer

Coll. of Education. Cardiff 1969-70. Parliamentary Private Secretary to Michael Foot 1975-79. Member of Royal Council of Royal Coll. of Veterinary Surgeons. A Labour Member. Sat for Brecon and Radnor from June 1970 until 1979, when he was defeated.*

[1979]

RODGERS, George. 32 Willoughby Road, Liverpool. S. of George Rodgers, Esq. B. 7 Nov. 1925; m. Aug. 1952, Joan, d. of J.P. Graham, Esq., (1 s. 2 d.). Educ. at National Council of Labour Colls. Served in Royal Navy 1943-46. Employed as Industrial Welder B.I.C.C. 21 years. Councillor Huyton and Roby Urban District Council 1963-74, Chairman 1973-74. Member Liverpool Regional Hospital Board 1968-74. Chairman N.W. Group of Labour MPs. A Labour Member. Sat for Chorley from Feb. 1974 until 1979, when he was defeated.* [1979]

RODGERS, Sir John Charles, Bart., D.L. 72 Berkeley House, Hay Hill, London. The Dower House, Groombridge, Kent. Brooks's, Pratt's, and Royal Thames Yacht. S. of Charles Rodgers, Esq. B. 5 Oct. 1906; m. 1930, Betsy, d. of Francis Aikin-Sneath, Esq., (2 s.). Educ. at St. Peter's, York, in France, and at Keble Coll., Oxford. Sub.-Warden of Mary Ward Settlement 1929. Administrative Assistant, University Coll., Hull 1930. Served in Foreign Office 1939 and 1944-45, Ministry of Information 1939-41, Department of Overseas Trade 1941-42 and Ministry of Production 1942-44. Member of B.B.C. Gen. Advisory Council 1946-52. Council Institute of Directors 1954-58. U.K. Delegate I.P.U. Confederation, Washington 1953. Chairman of British Market Research Bureau Limited 1933-54. C.P.A. Delegate to Trinidad and Tobago Independence Celebrations 1962; to Bostwana and Lesotho 1966, and to Guyana and British Honduras 1969. President Parliamentary Library to St. Vincent 1971. U.K. Observer to the Caribbean Regional Conference, St. Lucia 1972. C.P.A. Delegate to the British Virgin Isles, Antigua and St. Lucia 1977. Honorary Secretary Gen. Smuts Memorial Committee 1953. Chairman Committee on Litter in Royal Parks 1954. Member Tucker Committee on Proceedings before Examining Justices 1957 and Executive Committee British Council 1957-58; Gov. of British Film Institute 1958. Foundation Gov. Administrative Staff Coll. Council Foundation for Management Education from 1959. Vice-Chairman of Executive P.E.P. 1958-68. F.B.I.M., F.R.S.A. U.K. Delegate and Conservative Leader to Parliamentary Assembly Council of Europe. President Political Affairs Commission and Chairman Group of Independent Representatives. Vice-President of Parliamentary Assembly Western European Union 1969. Honorary Treasurer European Atlantic Group and Vice-President European League for Economic Co-operation. Parliamentary Private Secretary to Rt. Hon. David Eccles 1951-57. Parliamentary Secretary to Board of Trade with responsibility for Regional Development and Employment Oct. 1958-Oct. 1960. Council British Institute of Management 1965-69. Council Royal Coll. of Art 1968. Created a Bart. 1964. Member Public Accounts Committee 1969-74. Estimates Committee 1974. Dept.-Lieut. County of Kent 1973. Dept. Chairman of J. Walter Thompson Company Limited. A Conservative. Elected for the Sevenoaks division of Kent in Feb. 1950 and sat until he retired in 1979.*

[1979]

RODGERS, Rt. Hon. William Thomas. 48 Patshull Road, London. S. of William Arthur Rodgers, Esq. B. 28 Oct. 1928; m. 22 Oct. 1955, Silvia Szulman, (3 d.). Educ. at Sudley Road Council School, Quarry Bank High School, Liverpool, and Magdalen Coll., Oxford. Gen. Secretary, The Fabian Society 1953-60. Borough Councillor, St. Marylebone 1958-62. Parliamentary Under-Secretary of State, Department of Economic Affairs 1964-67. Parliamentary Under-Secretary Foreign Office 1967-68. Minister of State Board of Trade 1968-69. Minister of State, Treasury Oct. 1969-June 1970. Leader U.K. Delegation to the Council of Europe 1967-68. Opposition spokesman on Aviation Supply 1970-72. Chairman Expenditure Sub-committee on Trade and Industry 1971-74. Voted in favour of entry to E.E.C. on 28 Oct. 1971. Minister of State for Defence Mar. 1974-Sept. 1976. Secretary of State for Transport Sept. 1976-May 1979. Member of Parliamentary Committee of P.L.P from 1979.

Opposition spokesman on Defence from 1979. PC. 1975. A Labour Member. Unsuccessfully contested Bristol W. at a by-election in 1957. Sat for Stockton-on-Tees from Apr. 1962 to Feb. 1974. Elected for the Stockton division of Teesside in Feb. 1974.*

[1979]

ROEBUCK, Roy Delville. 15 Old Forge Close, Stanmore, Middlesex. B. 1929; m. 1957, Dr. Mary Ogilvy Adams. Educ. at State Schools, and on various newspapers. National Service, R.A.F. 1948-50. A Journalist. Joined the Labour Party in 1945. Member of Fabian Society, Co-operative Party, N.U.J. and G. and M.W. A Labour Member. Unsuccessfully contested Altrincham and Sale in 1964 and in the by-election of 1965. Elected for Harrow E. in Mar. 1966 and sat until 1970, when he was defeated. Unsuccessfully contested Leek in Feb. 1974. Barrister-at-Law, Gray's Inn, 1974.*

[1970]

ROGERS, George Henry Roland, C.B.E. 92 Ladbroke Grove, London. S. of George Rogers, Esq. of Princes Risborough. B. 9 Dec. 1906; m., (1 s. 1 d.). Educ. at Willesden Elementary School, and Middlesex County School. Member of Wembley Borough Council 1937-41; Chairman of London Group, P.L.P. 1949-54; Honorary Secretary Parliamentary Painting Group 1950-70. Parliamentary Private Secretary to Rt. Hon. George Strauss, Minister of Supply 1947-49, and to the Hon. Kenneth Younger, Minister of State 1950-51; Delegate to United Nations 1950-51; Opposition Whip 1954-64. A Railway Clerk. Corporal Royal Signals. Delegate to Council of Europe and W.E.U. 1961-63. Member of the Commons Chairman's Panel, 1952-54 and 1966. Artist (R.A. Exhibitor). A Lord Commissioner of the Treasury and Government Whip Oct. 1964-Jan. 1966. A Labour Member. Unsuccessfully contested Richmond, Surrey, in Feb. 1937. Elected for Kensington N. in July 1945 and sat until he retired in 1970. C.B.E. 1965.*

[1970]

ROOKER, Jeffrey, William. House of Commons, London. B. June 1941; m. 1972 Angela. Educ. at Handsworth Technical Coll., and Warwick University. A Chartered Engineer. Member Birmingham Education Committee 1972. Lecturer at Lanchester Polytechnic, Coventry 1972-74. Member of Council of Institution of Production Engineers from 1975. Parliamentary Private Secretary to Peter Archer, Solicitor General 1947-77. An Opposition spokesman on Social Sciences from 1979. A Labour Member. Sat for Birmingham, Perry Barr from Feb. 1974.*

[1979]

ROOTS, William Lloyd, T.D., Q.C.. 2 Mitre Court Buildings, Temple, London. 6 Kensington Gate, London. Carlton. S. of Neville Roots, Esq. B. 10 Sept. 1911; m. 30 Dec. 1939, Elizabeth Colquhoun Gow Gray. Educ. at Tonbridge School, and Brasenose Coll., Oxford. Barrister-at-Law, Middle Temple, 1933. Served Surrey and Sussex Yeomanry, East Africa, Western Desert, War Office. Dept. Chairman Dorset Quarter Sessions from 1960. Chairman Fulham and Kensington Hospital Management Committee 1952-55. Alderman Kensington Borough Council 1953-59. A Conservative. Unsuccessfully contested the Brixton division of Lambeth in 1955. Elected for S. Kensington in 1959 and sat until he resigned in Sept. 1967. Q.C. 1959. Master of the Bench, Middle Temple, 1965. Opposition spokesman on Legal Affairs in 1965. Died 14 Aug. 1971.

[1968]

ROPER, Sir Harold, C.B.E., M.C. Gorse Hill, Marine Drive, Torquay. S. of Arthur Charles Roper, Esq., F.R.C.S., M.R.C.P., of Exeter. B. 2 Sept. 1891; m. 1929, Norah, d. of William Keys, Esq., of Edinburgh. Educ. at Blundells School, and Sidney Sussex Coll., Cambridge. Gen. Manager of Burmah Oil Company Limited 1936-45. Member of Burma Legislative Council 1935-36 and Burma Senate 1937-42. Chairman of Burma Chamber of Commerce 1940. Served overseas with Devonshire Regiment 1915-19, M.C.; mentioned in despatches as a civilian 1942. Knight Bach. 1945. A Conservative. Elected for N. Cornwall in Feb. 1950 and sat until he retired in 1959. Member of Devon County Council 1961-68. Died 20 Aug. 1971.

[1959]

ROPER, John Francis Hodgess. House of Commons, London. S. of the Rev. F.M. Hodgess Roper. B. 10 Sept. 1935; m. 9 Aug. 1959, Valerie Hope, d. of the Rt. Hon. L. John Edwards MP., (1 d.). Educ. at William Hulme's Grammar School, Manchester, Reading School, Magdalen Coll., Oxford, and University of Chicago. A former University Lecturer in Economics. Director of Co-operative Wholesale Society 1969-74 and Co-operative Insurance Society 1973-74. Voted in favour of entry to E.E.C. on 28 Oct. 1971. President of General Council of United Nations Association 1972-78. Consultative Assembly Council of Europe 1973. Western European Union Assembly 1973. Member of General Council of I.B.A. from 1974. Chairman of Western European Union Defence and Armaments Committee from 1977. Chairman British-Atlantic Group of Young Politicians 1974-75. Chairman Atlantic Association of Young Political Leaders 1974-77. Honorary Secretary, British Council, of the European Movement 1973-76. Vice-Chairman Anglo-German Parliamentary Group 1974. Trustee, History of Parliament Trust 1974. Chairman Labour Committee for Europe 1976. Honorary Treasurer, Fabian Society 1976. Parliamentary Private Secretary to Rt. Hon. Alan Williams, Minister of State, Department of Industry July 1978-May 1979. An Opposition Defence spokesman from 1979. A Labour and Co-operative Member. Unsuccessfully contested High Peak in 1964. Elected for the Farnworth division of Lancashire in June 1970.*

[1979]

ROPNER, Col. Sir Leonard, Bart., M.C., T.D., D.L. Thorp Perrow, Bedale, Yorkshire. Carlton, Bath, Bucks', and Durham County. S. of W. Ropner, Esq., of Thorp Perrow, Bedale, and West Hartlepool. B. 26 Feb. 1895; m. 23 June 1932, Esmé, d. of Bruce Robertson, Esq. Educ. at Harrow, and Clare Coll., Cambridge, Scholar. Served in France 1914-18 with Royal Artillery; commanded Durham Heavy Brigade Royal Artillery T.A. 1919-28; Honorary Col. 426 Coast Regiment R.A., T.A. 1928-56; Honorary Col. 132 Corps Engineer Regiment, T.A. 1956-58. Military member Durham County T. and A.F.A. 1920-61, Vice-Chairman 1948-52;

rejoined R.A. as 2nd Lieut. 1941; later Lieut.-Col. Commanding Regiment R.A., and Col. H.Q. 21st Army Group, Belgium and Germany; T.D. Honorary Treasurer Conservative and Unionist Films Association 1930-47; Chairman of Conservative and Unionist Films Association 1947-59. Chairman Conservative Shipping and Shipbuilding Committee from 1946. Chairman Conservative Films Committee 1952-57. Director of Sir R. Ropner and Company Limited, The Rank Organisation Limited, Odeon Associated Theatres Limited, and other Companies. Dept.-Lieut. and J.P. for Durham; Chairman of Hartlepools Conservative Association 1920-23; Treasurer of Sedgfield division Conservative and Unionist Association 1919-23; member of English Consultative Committee under Forestry Acts 1923-36; a Forestry Commissioner 1936-45; Parliamentary Private Secretary (unpaid) to Sir Laming Worthington-Evans, Secretary of State for War 1924-Apr. 1928; Controller Timber Supply, Ministry of Supply Sept. 1939; Timber Supply Department of Forestry Commission Jan. 1940; Dept. Director Home Grown Timber Production, Ministry of Supply Feb. 1941; Temporary Chairman of Committees 1945-58. Knight of the Order of St. John; County Commissioner St. John Ambulance Brigade for N. Riding of Yorkshire 1950. Created Bart., New Years Honours 1952. Honorary Treasurer Primrose League 1952-64. A Conservative. Sat for the Sedgefield division of Durham Dec. 1923-May 1929, when he was defeated. Elected for the Barkston Ash division of the W. Riding of Yorkshire in Oct. 1931 and sat until he retired in 1964. Died 12 Oct. 1977. [1964]

ROSE, Paul Bernard. 47 Lindsay Drive, Kenton, Middlesex. S. of Arthur Rose, Esq. B. 26 Dec. 1935; m. 13 Sept. 1957, Eve Marie-Thérèse, d. of Jean and Anna Lapu, (2 s. 1 d). Educ. at Elementary School, Bury Grammar School, and Manchester University. Grays Inn, LL.B. (Hons.). Member. South Eastern Circuit. Barrister-at-Law 1957 Dep. Circuit Judge Association of Institute of Linguists. Joined the Labour Party in 1952. A regular contributor to various legal and political periodicals. Author of Legal and Historical books including *The Manchester*

Martyrs published July 1970. Formerly employed in the legal department of the Co-operative Union Limited, and formerly Lecturer in the Department of Liberal Studies, University of Salford. Chairman Labour Party Home Affairs Group 1969-71. Former Chairman N.W. Sports Council 1966-69. Joint Secretary Anglo-Irish Parliamentary Group Until 1972, Anglo-Mauritian Parliamentary Group and Anglo-Ethiopian Parliamentary Group. Parliamentary Private Secretary to Rt. Hon. Barbara Castle, Minister of Transport and Secretary of State for Employment and Productivity 1966-68. Member of British Delegation to Council of Europe and Western European Union 1968-69. Chairman Campaign for Democracy in Ulster 1965-73. Voted in favour of entry to E.E.C. on 28 Oct. 1971. Vice-Chairman Labour Committee for Europe 1974-77. Executive League for Democracy in Greece and Labour friends for Israel. N.C.C.L. member. Opposition Front Bench spokesman Department of Aviation Supply 1970 and on Employment 1970-72. Chairman P.L.P. Employment Group 1972-74. Member of Committee on Electoral Reform from 1975. Member West Indies Committee. Chairman Family Action Information and Rescue. A Labour Member. Elected for the Blackley division of Manchester in Oct. 1964 and sat until he retired in 1979 in protest at the impotence and ineffectuality of Parliament.*   [1979]

ROSS, Sir Ronald Deane, Bart., M.C. 49 Morpeth Mansions, Morpeth Terrace, London. 2 Paper Buildings, Temple, London. Dunmoyle, Six Mile Cross, Co. Tyrone. Carlton, and Northern Counties. S. of the Rt. Hon. Sir John Ross, 1st Bart., of Dunmoyle (MP. for Londonderry 1892-95). B. 13 July 1888; m. 31 Mar. 1921, Dorothy, d. of Rev. Algernon Dudley Ryder, Rector of Maresfield, Sussex. Educ. at Eton, and Trinity Coll., Cambridge, B.A. Barrister-at-Law, Inner Temple, 1913. Served in France, etc. 1914-18, with North Irish Horse and 36th Ulster Division. Rejoined North Irish Horse 1939, and served throughout the war; retired as Lieut.-Col. Had French Croix de Guerre. Parliamentary Private Secretary to Sir Bolton Eyres Monsell (Later Visct. Monsell),

First Lord of the Admiralty Nov. 1931-Nov. 1935. Succeeded as Bart, 1935. Recorder of Sunderland 1936-51; Dept.-Lieut. for Co. Tyrone 1937; Chairman of Ulster Unionist Parliamentary Party 1939-41; member of Council of Europe 1949. A Conservative. Unsuccessfully contested the Seaham division of Durham in 1923 and 1924. Elected for Londonderry in Jan. 1929 and sat until Mar. 1951 when he resigned on appointment as Northern Ireland Government Agent in London. Northern Ireland Government Agent in London Mar. 1951-Aug. 1957. Died 31 Jan. 1968.   [1951]

ROSS, Stephen Sherlock. 47 Quay Street, Newport, Isle of Wight. Isle of Wight County. S. of Reginald Sherlock Ross, Esq., M.C. B. 6 July 1926; m. 8 Oct. 1949, Brenda Marie, d. of Arthur Ivor Hughes, Esq. Educ. at Bedford School. Fellow of Royal Institution of Chartered Surveyors. Served in the Royal Navy 1944-48. Articled Nock and Jossland Kidderminster 1948-51. Assistant Heywood and Sons Stone 1951-53. Sen. Assistant Sir Francis Pittis and Son, Isle of Wight 1953-57, Partner 1958-73. Isle of Wight County Councillor 1967-74. Chairman Policy and Resources Committee 1973-74. Liberal spokesman on Local Government 1974-79, on the Environment 1974-77, on Housing 1977-79 and on Defence and Northern Ireland from 1979. A Liberal. Unsuccessfully contested the Isle of Wight in 1966 and 1970. Sat for the Isle of Wight from Feb. 1974.*
                                              [1979]

ROSS, Rt. Hon. William, M.B.E. 10 Chapelpark Road, Ayr. S. of W. Ross, Esq. of Ayr. B. 7 Apr. 1911; m. 1948 Elizabeth Aitkenhead (2 d.). Educ. at Ayr Academy, and University of Glasgow, (M.A.). A School Master. Maj. H.L.I. and Royal Signals. Secretary of State for Scotland Oct. 1964-June 1970 and Mar. 1974-Apr. 1976. Opposition spokesman on Scotland Dec. 1962-Oct. 1964 and June 1970-Mar. 1974. Member of Parliamentary Committee of P.L.P. 1970-74. Lord High Commissioner to General Assembly of Church of Scotland 1978 and 1979. M.B.E. (Mil.) 1945. PC. 1964. Honorary LL.D. Universities of St. Andrews, Strathclyde and Glasgow. Created Baron Ross of

Marnock (Life Peerage) 1979. A Labour Member. Unsuccessfully contested the Ayr Burghs in 1945. Sat for the Kilmarnock division of Ayrshire and Bute from Dec. 1946 until he retired in 1979.*　　　　[1979]

ROSS, William. Turmeel, Dungiven, Co. Londonderry. S. of Leslie Alexander Ross, Esq. B. 4 Feb. 1936; m. 1974, Christine, d. of George Haslett, Esq. (1 s. 1 d.). Educ. at Dungiven Primary School. A Farmer. Former Secretary of Mid Londonderry Unionist Party, (N.I. Constituency) and former Secretary Londonderry Constituency Unionist Party. An Ulster Unionist Member. Sat for Londonderry from Feb. 1974.*　[1979]

ROSSI, Hugh Alexis Louis. 24 Wilton Place, London. 20 Buckingham Lodge, London. B. 21 June 1927; m. 23 Apr. 1955, Philomena Elizabeth Jennings. Educ. at Finchley Catholic Grammar School, and King's Coll., University of London. Hornsey Borough Councillor 1956-65; Chairman of Housing and Redevelopment Committees; Dept. Leader of Council and Dept. Mayor 1964-65. Middlesex County Councillor 1961-65. Chairman Building Committee London Borough of Haringey 1964, Councillor 1964-68; leader of Minority Party until Parliamentary Election. Secretary Conservative Parliamentary Housing Land and Local Government Committee 1968-70. Vice-Chairman Conservative Parliamentary Legal Committee 1970. LL.B. London 1947, Solicitors Honours 1950. A Knight of the Holy Sepulchre 1966. Assistant Government Whip Oct. 1970-Apr. 1972. Government Whip for Europe 1971-73. Lord Commissioner, Treasury Apr. 1972-Jan. 1974. Dept. Leader Delegation to Council of Europe and Western European Union 1972-74. Parliamentary Under-Secretary of State for the Environment Jan.-Mar. 1974. Opposition spokesman on the Environment (Housing and Land) 1974-79. Minister of State for Northern Ireland from May 1979. A Conservative. Sat for Hornsey from Mar. 1966 to Feb. 1974 and for the Hornsey division of Haringey from Feb. 1974.*　　　　　　　　　　　　　[1979]

ROST, Peter Lewis. Norcott Court, Berkhamsted, Hertfordshire. S. of F.H. Rosenstiel, Esq., Merchant Banker. B. 19 Sept. 1930; m. 9 Sept. 1961, Hilary, d. of A.W. Mayo, Esq., Banker, (2 s. 2 d.). Assumed the surname of Rost in lieu of Rosenstiel. Educ. at Aylesbury Grammar School, and Birmingham University. Former Financial Journalist. Member of Stock Exchange 1962-77. Vice-Chairman Conservative Trade and Industry Committee 1972-73. Secretary Conservative Energy Committee 1974. Select Committee, Science and Technology, Energy Resources. Honorary Treasurer British-German Parliamentary Group. A Conservative. Unsuccessfully contested Sunderland N. in 1966. Elected for Derbyshire S.E. in June 1970.*　　[1979]

ROWLAND, Christopher John Salter. 12 Blackheath Park, London. S. of Tom Rowland, Esq. B. 26 Sept. 1929; m. 2 Apr. 1955, Leslie, d. of Claude and Ethel Branch. Educ. at Chesterfield Grammar School, London School of Economics, B.Sc. Econ., and Corpus Christi Coll., Oxford, B.Phil. Commonwealth Fund Fellowship to U.S.A. Executive. Joined the Labour Party in 1946. Member of N.U.J.; N.U.G.M.W. Institute of Public Relations, and Fabian Society, Treasurer of the Africa Bureau; Council of Institute of Race Relations. Chairman of London School of Economics Labour Society 1952. Chairman of National Association of Labour Student Organisations 1953-54. Talks Producer B.B.C. Overseas service 1954-58. Information Officer for the Booker Group 1960-64. Parliamentary Private Secretary to Ministers of State at the Foreign Office 1964-67. A Labour Member. Unsuccessfully contested the Eastleigh division of Hampshire in 1959. Elected for the Meriden division of Warwickshire in Oct. 1964 and sat until his death on 5 Nov. 1967.　　　　　　　　[1967]

ROWLANDS, Edward. 4 St. Michael's Road, Porthcawl, Glamorgan. S. of William Samuel Rowlands, Esq., Clerk of Works. B. 23 Jan. 1940; m. 1968 Janice Williams. Educ. at Rhondda Grammar School, Wirral Grammar School, Cheshire, and King's Coll., London, B.A. (Hons.) History 1962. Research Student 1962; Research Assistant

323

History of Parliament Trust 1963-65. Lecturer, Modern History and Government Welsh C.A.T. 1965. Parliamentary Under-Secretary Welsh Office Oct. 1969-June 1970. Joint Parliamentary Under-Secretary Welsh Office Mar. 1974-June 1975. Under-Secretary Foreign and Commonwealth Office June 1975-Apr. 76. Minister of State for Foreign and Commonwealth Affairs Apr. 1976-May 1979. An Opposition spokesman on Commonwealth Affairs from 1979. A Labour Member. Sat for Cardiff N. from 1966-70, when he was defeated. Elected for Merthyr Tydfil in Apr. 1972.* [1979]

ROYLE, Sir Anthony Henry Fanshawe, K.C.M.G. The Chapter Manor, South Cerney, Gloucestershire. 47 Cadogan Place, London. White's, and Pratt's. S. of Sir Lancelot Royle. B. 27 Mar. 1927; m. 1957, Shirley, d. of J.R. Worthington, Esq. Educ. at Harrow. Capt. in The Life Guards 1945-48; 21st Special Air Service Regiment (T.A.) 1948-51. Parliamentary Private Secretary to Rt. Hon. Julian Amery Secretary of State for Air 1960-62, and Minister of Aviation 1962-64. Member of U.K. Delegation to Council of Europe and Western European Union 1965. Vice-Chairman of Conservative Foreign Affairs Committee 1965-67. Opposition Whip 1967-70. Parliamentary Under-Secretary of State for Foreign and Commonwealth Affairs June 1970-Jan. 1974. K.C.M.G. 1974. Vice-Chairman of Conservative Party from 1979. A Conservative. Unsuccessfully contested St. Pancras N. in 1955 and Torrington in 1958. Sat for Richmond from 1959 to Feb. 1974 and for the Richmond division of Richmond-on-Thames from Feb. 1974.* [1979]

ROYLE, Charles. Shepherds Cottage, Rottingdean, Brighton. S. of Alderman Charles Royle, MP., of Stockport. B. 23 Jan. 1896; m. 2 June 1919, Florence, d. of Henry Smith, Esq. Educ. at Stockport Grammar School. A Master Butcher from 1912. J.P. for Stockport and Brighton. Late President Manchester and Salford Meat Traders Association. Past Chairman of Stockport Labour Party. Dept. Chairman Magistrates' Association. Member of Stockport Borough Council 1929-35. Meat Agent, Ministry of Food 1939-45. Lord Commissioner of the Treasury Apr. 1950-Oct.

1951. Opposition Whip Nov. 1951-54. Co-Chairman British-Caribbean Association. Director and Chairman of Alliance Building Society. A Labour Member. Unsuccessfully contested the Lancaster division of Lancashire in 1935. Elected for Salford W. in July 1945 and sat until Aug. 1964 when he was created Baron Royle (Life Peerage). Died 30 Sept. 1975. [1964]

RUSSELL, Sir Ronald (Stanley). 29 Acacia Road, London. Carlton, Constitutional, and Press. S. of J. Stanley Russell, Esq., of Seahouses, Northumberland. B. 1904; m. Ena Glendenning, d. of Alfred Forrester, Esq., F.R.I.B.A., of Grove Hill, Middlesbrough (1 s. 1 d.). Educ. at Haileybury, and Caius Coll., Cambridge, M.A. 1929. An Author and Journalist. Member of Institute of Journalists. Chairman Commonwealth Producers' Organisation 1960-63 and from 1964. Dept. Chairman of Gen. Optical Council from 1959. Member of London County Council 1946-52. Parliamentary Private Secretary to Rt. Hon. Duncan Sandys, Minister of Supply 1951-54 and Minister of Housing and Local Government 1954-55. Member of U.K. Delegation to Council of Europe and Western European Union 1957-66. Member of the Chairman's Panel of the House of Commons 1959-74. Honorary Secretary All-Party Animal Welfare Group 1969-71. Joint Honorary Secretary Conservative Private Members Committee 1957-61; Honorary Treasurer from 1961. Knight Bach. 1964. Voted against entry to E.E.C. on 28 Oct. 1971. A Conservative. Unsuccessfully contested the Shettleston division of Glasgow in 1935 and the Coatbridge division of Lanarkshire in 1945. Elected for Wembley S. in Feb. 1950 and sat until he retired in Feb. 1974. Died 6 Apr. 1974. [1974]

RYAN, John. 77 Randolph Avenue, London. B. 30 Apr. 1940; m. 1964 Eunice Ann Edmonds. Educ. at Lanark Grammar School, and Glasgow University (Hons. degree in Econ. History). A Publishing Executive. Joined the Labour Party in 1958. Associate member Market Research Society. A Labour Member. Unsuccessfully contested Buckinghamshire S. in 1964. Elected for the Uxbridge division of Middlesex in Mar. 1966 and sat until 1970 when he was defeated. Management Consultant and Lecturer. Director of Tribune Publications Limited from 1969.* [1970]

RYDER, Capt. Robert Edward Dudley, V.C., R.N. House of Commons, London. S. of Col. C.H. Dudley Ryder, C.B., C.I.E., D.S.O. B. 1908; M. 1941, Hilaré, d. of the Rev. L.C. Green-Wilkinson, of Lovel Hill, Windsor Forest. Educ. at Hazelhurst, Frant, and Cheltenham Coll. Joined R.N. 1927; Capt. 1948. Commanded Naval Force at St. Nazaire 1942; V.C. 1942. British Graham Land Expedition 1934-37. Had Polar Medal; Naval Attache, Oslo 1948-50. A Conservative. Elected for Merton and Morden in Feb. 1950 and sat until he retired in 1955.* [1954]

RYMAN, John. House of Commons, London. B. 7 Nov. 1930; m. 1957 Shirley Summerskill, MP. for Halifax from 1964 (divorced 1971). Educ. at Leighton Park, and Pembroke Coll., Oxford. A Barrister, Middle Temple 1957. Member Executive Council Association of the Clergy. Inns of Court Regiment (T.A.) Committed for Trial on 10 Apr. 1976 on a charge of making a false declaration regarding the return of election expenses; acquitted on 7 Oct. 1976. A Labour Member. Unsuccessfully contested Gillingham in 1964 and Derbyshire S.E. in 1970. Elected for Blyth in Oct. 1974.* [1979]

SAINSBURY, Hon. Timothy Alan Davan. House of Commons, London. Boodle's. S. of Baron Sainsbury, Life Peer 1962. B. 11 June 1932; m. 1961, Susan Mary, d. of Brigadier J.A.H. Mitchell, C.B.E., D.S.O., (2 s. 2 d.). Educ. at Eton, and Worcester Coll., Oxford. National Service, Commissioned in the Life Guards 1951-52. J. Sainsbury Limited 1956, Director 1962. Chairman Council of Unit for Retail Planning Information 1974. Member Southern Sports Council 1966-68. Political Officer, Bow Group 1967-68. Member Environmental Planning Committee Greater London Council 1969-71. Member S.E. Economic Planning Council 1972-74. Part-time member Business Team, Civil Service Department 1971-72. Parliamentary Private Secretary to Rt. Hon.

Michael Heseltine, Secretary of State for the Environment from 1979. Member Expenditure Committee. Joint Honorary Treasurer, Conservative Friends of Israel; and Chairman All-Party Parliamentary Committee for the Release of Soviet Jewry. A Conservative. Sat for Hove from Nov. 1973.* [1979]

ST. CLAIR, Malcolm Archibald James. Optow House, Tetbury, Gloucestershire. 28 Chesham Place, London. Cavalry. S. of Maj.-Gen. G.P. St. Clair, C.B., C.B.E., D.S.O. B. 16 Feb. 1927; m. June 1955, Mary Jean Rosalie Alice, d. of Wing-Commander C.L. Hargreaves. Educ. at Eton. Lieut. Royal Scots Greys 1945-48. Maj. Royal Gloucestershire Hussars (T.A.), Lieut.-Col. 1967-69. A Farmer. Honorary Secretary to Winston Churchill 1948-50. A Conservative. Unsuccessfully contested Bristol S.E. in 1959. Contested the Bristol S.E. by-election on 4 May 1961 and was declared elected on 28 July 1961 after Anthony Wedgwood Benn (Visct. Stansgate) had been declared incapable of election. Sat until 1 Aug. 1963 when he resigned after the passing of the Peerage Act which allowed Visct. Stansgate to renounce his Peerage and again contest Bristol S.E. High Sheriff of Gloucestershire 1972.* [1963]

ST. JOHN-STEVAS, Rt. Hon. Norman Antony Francis. 34 Montpelier Square, London. Garrick, and Pratt's. S. of Stephen Stevas. B. 1929. Unmarried. Assumed the surname of St. John-Stevas in lieu of Stevas. Educ. at Ratcliffe, Fitzwilliam Coll., Cambridge, Christ Church, Oxford, and Yale. An Author, Barrister, and Journalist. President Cambridge Union 1950. 1st Class Hons Law 1950. Barrister, Middle Temple 1952; Blackstone and Harmsworth Scholar 1952. Tutored in jurisprudence King's Coll., London, Christ Church, and Merton, Oxford 1953-57. Ph.D. London University 1957. Yorke Prize, Cambridge 1957. Fellow, Yale Law School 1960. Political Correspondent, *The Economist* 1959. Editor of the *Dublin Review* 1961. Fellow Royal Society of Literature 1966. Publications include *Obscenity and the Law* 1956, *The Collected Works of Walter Bagehot* 1959, *Life, Death and the Law* 1961, *The Right to Life* 1963, *The Literary Works of Walter*

Bagehot Vols, I and II 1966, *The Historic Works Vols III and IV* 1968, and *The Agonizing Choice* 1971. Under-Secretary of State for Education and Science Nov. 1972-Dec. 1973. Minister of State, Department of Education and Science and 'Minister for the Arts' Dec. 1973-Mar. 1974. Opposition spokesman on the Arts May-June 1974 and Nov. 1974-May 1979. Opposition spokesman on Education and Science June 1974-Nov. 1978. Opposition spokesman on House of Commons Affairs Nov. 1978-May 1979. Member of Shadow Cabinet June 1974-May 1979. Chancellor of Duchy of Lancaster and Leader of House of Commons from May 1979. Minister responsible for the Office of Arts and Libraries, 'Minister for the Arts', from May 1979. PC. 1979. A Conservative. Unsuccessfully contested Dagenham at the general election of 1951. Elected for the Chelsford division of Essex in Oct. 1964.* [1979]

SALTER, Rt. Hon. Sir (James) Arthur, G.B.E., K.C.B. West House, 35 Glebe Place, London. S. of James Edward Salter, Esq., of Isis House, Oxford. B. 15 Mar. 1881; m. 15 June 1940, Widow of Arthur Bullard, Esq., of Washington, D.C. (she died 1969). Educ. at Brasenose Coll., B.A. Honorary Fellow 1931; Fellow of All Souls; Honorary LL.D. Manchester; Honorary D.C.L. Oxford. Appointed to Admiralty, Transport Department 1904, National Health Insurance Commission 1911-15, Assistant Director 1915, Director of Ship Requisitioning 1917, and of Economic and Finance Section League of Nations 1919-20 and 1922-30; Secretary Gen. of Reparation Commission 1920-22; Chairman of Advisory Council of International Bank for Reconstruction and Development 1947. Gladstone Professor of Political Theory and Institutions, University of Oxford 1934-44. Senior Dept. Director General of UNRRA 1944. Parliamentary Secretary Ministry of Shipping Nov. 1939-June 1941. Joint Parliamentary Secretary Ministry of War Transport June 1941-Dec. 1943 and U.K. Representative in Washington on Combined Shipping Adjustment Board Jan. 1942-Dec. 1943. Chancellor of the Duchy of Lancaster May-July 1945. Minister for Economic Affairs Oct. 1951-Nov. 1952. Minister of Materials Nov. 1952-Sept. 1953. C.B. 1918;

K.C.B. 1922; PC. 1941; G.B.E. 1944. A Conservative. Sat for Oxford University as an Independent Member from Feb. 1937 to Feb. 1950, when he retired. Elected for the Ormskirk division of Lancashire in Apr. 1951 and sat until Sept. 1953 when he was created Baron Salter. Died 27 June 1975. [1953]

SANDELSON, Neville Devonshire. 9 Kings Bench Walk, Temple, London. House of Commons, London. Reform. S. of David Sandelson, Esq., O.B.E., Solicitor. B. 27 Nov. 1923; m. 27 Aug. 1959, Nana, d. of M.J. Karlinski, of Neuilly S/Seine, (1 s. 2 d.). Educ. at Westminster School, and Trinity Coll., Cambridge. Called to the Bar (Inner Temple) 1946. Director of book publishing companies and a Television Producer 1948-64. Member of London County Council 1952-58. Voted in favour of entry to E.E.C. on 28 Oct. 1971. Promoted Matrimonial Proceedings (Polygamous Marriages) Act 1972 as a Private Members Bill. A Labour Member. Unsuccessfully contested the Ashford division of Kent in 1950, 1951 and 1955, Beckenham in 1957, the Rushcliffe division of Nottinghamshire in 1959, Heston and Isleworth in 1966, S.W. Leicester in 1967, and Chichester in 1970. Sat for Hayes and Harlington from June 1971 to Feb. 1974 and for the Hays and Harlinton division of Hillingdon from Feb. 1974.* [1979]

SANDERSON, Sir Frank Bernard, Bart. 48 Grosvenor Square, London. Malling Deanery, Lewes, Sussex. Carlton, and 1900. S. of John Sanderson, Esq., of Hull. B. 4 Oct. 1880; m. 1st, 8 Sept. 1904, Army Edith, d. of David Wing, Esq. (she died 1949); 2ndly 1951, Joan, D. of H. Cubberley, Esq. Chairman of Salts (Saltaire) Limited, of J.J. Crombie Limited, and of Aberdeen and Humber Fishing Company Limited. Controller of Trench Warfare National Filling Factories and Stores, Ministry of Munitions 1915-19, and of Aircraft and Chemical Ammunition Filling 1916-19. A Trustee of Stowe School; President of King Edward VII Memorial Hospital, Ealing. Member of Parliamentary Delegation to Poland 1925 and Canada 1928, and of I.P.U. Conference at The Hague 1938, and Cairo 1947; Vice-Chairman 1948; Member of Public Accounts Committee,

House of Commons from 1942. Created Bart. 1920. A Conservative. Sat for the Darwen division of Lancashire from Nov. 1922 to Dec. 1923, when he was defeated and from Oct. 1924 to may 1929, when he was defeated. Sat for Ealing from 1931 to 1945 and for Ealing E. from 1945 to 1950 when he retired. Chairman of Anglo-Egyptian Chamber of Commerce 1949-54. Died 18 July 1965. [1950]

SANDYS, Rt. Hon. Duncan Edwin, C.H. 8 Vincent Square, London. Carlton. S. of Capt. George Sandys, MP. for the Wells division of Somerset 1910-18. B. 24 Jan. 1908; m. 1st, 1935, Diana, d. of Rt. Hon. Sir Winston Churchill, K.G., MP. (marriage dissolved in 1960); 2ndly, 1962, Marie-Claire, d. of Adrien Schmitt, Esq., (1 s., 3 d.) Educ. at Eton, and Magdalen Coll., Oxford, M.A. Entered Diplomatic Service 1930; served at Foreign Office and in Berlin. Political Columnist *Sunday Chronicle* 1937-39. Commissioned in T.A. (R.A.) 1937. Member National Executive Conservative Party 1938-39. Served with Expeditionary Force, Norway 1940. Lieut.-Col. 1941. Disabled on active service 1941. Financial secretary to War Office and Finance Member of Army Council July 1941-Feb. 1943; Parliamentary Secretary Ministry of Supply Feb. 1943-Nov. 1944. Chairman War Cabinet Committee for defence against German flying Bombs and rockets 1943-45. Minister of Works Nov. 1944-July 1945. PC. 1944. Founder of the European Movement 1947. Chairman International Executive until 1950. Member European Consultative Assembly 1950-51 and from 1965. Leader of British Delegation to Assembly of Council of Europe and Assembly of Western European Union 1970-72. Member of General Advisory Council of B.B.C. 1947-51. Director Ashanti Goldfields Corporation 1947-51 and 1966-72. Minister of Supply Nov. 1951-Oct. 1954. Minister of Housing and Local Government Oct. 1954-Jan. 1957. Minister of Defence Jan. 1957-Oct. 1959. Minister of Aviation Oct. 1959-July 1960. Secretary of State for Commonwealth Relations July 1960-Oct. 1964, also Secretary of State for the Colonies 1962-64. Member of Cabinet 1954-64. Opposition spokesman on Commonwealth and Colonial Affairs 1964-65. Member of Shadow Cabinet

1964-66. President of the Civic Trust, which he founded in 1956. President of Europa Nostra from 1969. Chairman Lonrho Limited 1972. Chairman International Organising Committee for European Architectural Heritage Year. Honorary member Royal Town Planning Institute 1956. Order of Merit of Italy (1st class). Honorary Fellow of R.I.B.A. 1968. Companion of Honour 1973. A Conservative. Sat for The Norwood division of Lambeth from Mar. 1935 to July 1945, when he was defeated. Elected for the Streatham division of Wandsworth in Feb. 1950 and sat until he retired in Feb. 1974. Created Baron Duncan-Sandys (Life Peerage) 1974, when he assumed the surname of Duncan-Sandys in lieu of Sandys.* [1974]

SARGOOD, Richard. 138 Mulgrave Road, Cheam, Surrey. S. of Richard Sargood, Esq. of Lambeth. B. 31 July 1888; m. 25 Jan. 1919, Sarah Deane. Educ. at London County Council School. Trade Union Official. Member of Camberwell Borough Council 1923-29. J.P. for London 1930; Vice-Chairman of National Joint Council for Fire Services of England and Wales and of Peckham Labour Party. Member of London County Council 1934-65, Vice-Chairman 1951-52. A Labour Member. Elected for W. Bermondsey in July 1945 and sat until he retired in 1950. Died 27 Mar. 1979. [1950]

SAVORY, Professor Sir Douglas Lloyd. 33 Knockbreda Park, Belfast. Athenaeum, Authors', and Ulster, (Belfast), 2nd s. of the Rev. Ernest Lloyd Savory, Rector of Palgrave, Suffolk. B. 17 Aug. 1878; m. 1918, Madeline, d. of J.H. Clendinning, Esq., of Lurgan. Educ. at Marlborough, St. John's Coll., Oxford, M.A. Oxon and T.C.D., and at the Universitites of Paris, Berne, Lausanne and Marburg. Professor of French and of Romance Philology, Queen's University 1909-40. Professor Emeritus 1941; President of Huguenot Society 1945-48. Lieut. R.N.V.R. Naval Staff, Admiralty 1914-18; Secretary to H.M. Minister at Stockholm 1918-19; Commissioner for Intermediate Education for Ireland 1919-22. Knighted 1952. Officier d'Académie, Officier de l'Instruction Publique, Chevalier de la Légion d'Honneur. Chairman of Ulster Unionist

Parliamentary Party 1953-55. An Ulster Unionist Member. Sat for Queen's University from Nov. 1940 to Feb. 1950. Elected for Antrim S. in Feb. 1950 and sat until he retired in 1955. Died 5 Oct. 1969.   [1954]

SCHOFIELD, Sidney. House of Commons, London. S. of Sidney Schofield, Esq. of Castleford. B. 1911; m. 1934 Alice, d. of E. Ward, Esq. of Normanton. Educ. at Elementary School and Whitworth Technical Coll. Served with R.E. 1939-45, Sgt. Member of Castleford Urban District Council 1946-51. A Labour Member. Elected for Barnsley on 8 Nov. 1951 (the General Election had been postponed because of the death of the former Labour candidate) and sat until he resigned in Jan. 1953. N.U.M. Compensation agent, Yorkshire Area 1959-64. Yorkshire Area Secretary, N.U.M. 1964. Vice-President of N.U.M. 1968.*   [1953]

SCHOFIELD, Lieut.-Col. Wentworth. 2 Park Avenue, Southport. S. of Edwin James Schofield, Esq. of Failsworth. B. 17 Apr. 1891; m. 1st, 14 Oct. 1915, Sarah, d. of Joseph Twyerould, Esq., 2ndly 1957, Mrs Olga L. Stacey, of Sydney, N.S.W. Served in Manchester Regiment 1914-18, Capt. and in T.A., Lieut.-Col. 1939. Company Director; member Management Committee Oldham Master Cotton Spinners Association; The Federation of Master Cotton Spinners Association; Executive Committee British Empire Chamber of Commerce and British National Committee International Chamber of Commerce; Senior Vice-President of the Oldham Chamber of Commerce. A Conservative. Unsuccessfully contested Rochdale in 1950. Elected for Rochdale in 1951 and sat until his death on 16 Dec. 1957.   [1957]

SCOLLAN, Thomas. 9 Barlogan Avenue, Glasgow. B. 1882. An Engineer. Trade Union Organiser for Distributive Workers. President of Scottish T.U.C. 1934. A Labour Member. Elected for the Western division of Renfrewshire in July 1945 and sat until 1950, when he was defeated. Died about 1974.   [1950]

SCOTT, Nicholas Paul, M.B.E. J.P. House of Commons, London. Turf, Buck's, and M.C.C. S. of John Scott, Esq. B. 5 Aug. 1933; m. 1st, Elizabeth Rosemary, d. of Robert Robinson, Esq., (marriage dissolved 1976), (1 s. 2 d.).; 2ndly, 1979, Hon. Cecilia Hawke, d. of 9th Baron Hawke and former wife of Peter Tapsell, Esq. MP. Educ. at Clapham Coll. Member of Holborn Borough Council 1956-59 and 1962-65. National Chairman of Young Conservatives 1963. M.B.E. 1964. Managing Director of E. Allom and Company 1968-70. Parliamentary Private Secretary to Rt. Hon. Iain Macleod, Chancellor of the Exchequer 1970 and to Rt. Hon. Robert Carr, Leader of the House 1972 and Home Secretary 1972-74. Parliamentary Under-Secretary of State at Department of Employment Jan.-Mar. 1974. Shadow Minister for Housing and Member of Shadow Cabinet Nov. 1974-Feb. 1975. 1922 Executive 1978. A Conservative. Unsuccessfully contested S.W. Islington in 1959 and 1964. Sat for S. Paddington from 1966 to Feb. 1974, when he unsuccessfully contested the Paddington division of Westminster. Sat for the Chelsea division of Kensington and Chelsea from Oct. 1974.*   [1979]

SCOTT, Sir Robert Donald. Caistron, Thropton, Morpeth. Constitutional. S. of William Scott, Esq., Timber Importer of Newcastle-upon-Tyne. B. 1901; m. 1930, Olive Anna Daphne, d. of J.T. Russell, Esq., of Ballygasson House, Co. Louth. Educ. at Mill Hill School, and Magdalene Coll., Cambridge. A Landowner and Farmer. Joint Parliamentary Secretary Ministry of Agriculture and Fisheries May-July 1945. A Conservative. Sat for the Wansbeck division of Northumberland from July 1940 to July 1945, when he was defeated. Elected for the Penrith and the Border division of Cumberland in Feb. 1950 and sat until he retired in 1955. Knighted Jan. 1955. Member of Northumberland Rivers Catchment Board 1942-46. Chairman of Conservative Political Education Committee 1949-50. Member of Royal Commission on Common Land 1955-58. Died 18 June 1974.   [1954]

SCOTT, Lord William Walter Montagu Douglas. See MONTAGU-DOUGLAS-SCOTT Lord William Walter.

SCOTT-ELLIOT, Walter Travers. 35 Trevor Square, London. Arkleton, Langholm, Scotland. Guards. S. of William Scott.-Elliot, Esq., of Arkleton. B. 9 Oct. 1895; m. 1st, 1939, Maria, d. of Capt. Alexander Reichrilter von Groeller, former Austro-Hungarian Navy (annulled 1948); 2ndly, 31 Mar. 1948, Dorothy Alice, d. of William Nunn, Esq., of Calcutta. Educ. at Eton. Served with Coldstream Guards 1914-19. Joined Bombay Company Limited, East India Merchants, Managing Director 1927. Served on Headquarters Ministry of Labour 1941-45; Parliamentary Private Secretary to Frederick Bellenger and John Freeman, Financial Secretaries to War Office Mar. 1946-Mar. 1947. A Labour Member. Elected for Accrington in July 1945 and sat until he retired in 1950. Murdered on 14 Dec. 1977, along with his wife. His body was found at Guisachen, near Inverness, on 18 Jan. 1978.
[1950]

SCOTT-HOPKINS, James Sidney Rawdon. 602 Nelson House, Dolphin Square, London. Edensor House, Edensor, Nr. Bakewell, Derbyshire. S. of Lieut.-Col. R. Scott-Hopkins, D.S.O., M.C.B. 29 Nov. 1921; m. 1946, Geraldine Elizabeth Hargreaves, (3 s. 1 d.). Educ. at Eton, and New Coll., Oxford. Served Second World War with Gurkha Rifles 1946-50; K.O.Y.L.I., Maj. Parliamentary Private Secretary to Bernard Brain, Joint Parliamentary Under-Secretary of State Commonwealth Relations Office 1961-62; Joint Parliamentary Secretary, Ministry of Agriculture, Fisheries and Food 1962-64. Member European Parliament Jan. 1973; Vice-President European Parliament 1976-79. Dept. Leader European Conservative Group and spokesman on Agriculture to 1979. Member of European Parliament for Hereford and Worcester from 1979. Leader of Conservative Delegation and Chairman of European Democratic Group. A Conservative. Unsuccessfully contested Bedwellty in 1955. Sat for Cornwall N. from 1959 to 1966, when he was defeated. Elected for Derbyshire W. in Nov. 1967 and sat until he retired in 1979.*
[1979]

SCOTT-MILLER, Commander Ronald, V.R.D., R.N.V.R. Balsham Manor, Cambridgeshire. Carlton. S. of Col. Walter Scott-Miller, D.L. B. 1 Nov. 1904; m. 14 Apr. 1932, Stella, widow of Thomas Fraser, Esq., of Forfarshire and d. of Farquhar Deuchar, of Shortridge, Warkworth, Northumberland. Educ. at Aldro School, Eastbourne, and Uppingham. Served 25 years in London division R.N.V.R.; U.S. Legion of Merit, mentioned in despatches; V.R.D. 1942; Freeman of City of London; member of Executive Committee Metropolitan Drinking Fountain and Cattle Trough Association; Trustee of Uppingham School; Parliamentary Private Secretary to J.A. Boyd-Carpenter when Financial Secretary to the Treasury Dec. 1953-July 1954, when Minister of Transport July 1954-Dec. 1955, and when Minister of Pensions and National Insurance Dec. 1955-Oct. 1959. A Conservative. Unsuccessfully contested the King's Lynn division of Norfolk in Feb. 1950. Elected there in Oct 1951 and sat until he retired in 1959.*
[1959]

SEDGEMORE, Brian Charles John. 28 Studley Road, Luton, Bedfordshire. Flat 57, Belvedere Court, Upper Richmond Road, Putney, London. S. of Charles John Sedgemore, Esq. B. 17 Mar. 1937; m. 19 Dec. 1964, Mary Audrey, d. of Juby Reece, Esq., Q.C. Educ. at Corpus Christi Coll., Oxford University. Ministry of Housing and Local Government Principal 1962-66. Private Secretary to R.J. Mellish (then Jun. Minister) 1964-66. Barrister, Middle Temple 1966-74. Wandsworth Councillor 1971-74. Chairman Wandsworth Council for Community Relations 1971-74. Parliamentary Private Secretary to Rt. Hon. Anthony Wedgwood-Benn, Secretary of State for Energy 1976-78. A Labour Member. Elected for Luton W. in Feb. 1974 and sat until 1979, when he was defeated.*
[1979]

SEGAL, Squadron-Leader Samuel. 10 Vincent Square Mansions, London. S. of Professor M.H. Segal. B. 2 Apr. 1902; m. 18 Mar. 1934, Molly, d. of Robert Rolo, Esq., O.B.E., of Alexandria. Educ. at Elementary Schools, Royal Grammar School, New Castle-upon-Tyne, Jesus Coll., Oxford, B.A. (Hons.), M.A., M.R.C.S., M.R.C.P., and Westminster Hospital. Served on staffs of

Westminster Hospital and Hospital for Sick Children, Great Ormond Street; member of various London County Council Hospital Committees. Joined R.A.F. Medical Branch, Squadron-Leader 1942; served in Aden 1940, Western Desert 1941, Syrian Campaign attached Fleet Air Arm 1941; Royal Hellenic Air Force 1942; Chief Medical Officer R.A.F. Naval Co-operation Group Mediterranean 1942-43; on Headquarters Staff Medical Branch R.A.F., Middle East, Cairo 1943-44; Air Ministry 1944; member of Parliamentary Delegation to West Africa 1947, and delegations to Egypt and Persia. A Labour Member. Unsuccessfully contested Tynemouth in 1935 and the Aston division of Birmingham in May 1939. Elected for Preston in July 1945 and sat until 1950, when he unsuccessfully contested Preston N. Regional Medical Officer, Ministry of Health 1951-62. Chairman of National Society for Mentally Handicapped children 1965-78. Created Baron Segal (Life Peerage) 1964. A Dept. Speaker of House of Lords from 1973. Honorary Fellow of Jesus Coll., Oxford.*   [1950]

SELBY, Harry. 363 Paisley Road, Glasgow. S. of Max Soldberg, Esq. B. 18 May 1913; m. 20 May 1937, Jeannie, d. of William Reid, Esq. Assumed the surname of Selby in lieu of Soldberg. Educ. at Queen's Park Senior Secondary School. A Hairdresser. Served in Highland Light Infantry and Royal Corps of Signals 1940-45. City of Glasgow Councillor 1972-74. Active Labour Party Member. A Labour Member. Unsuccessfully contested the Govan division of Glasgow in Nov. 1973. Sat for the Govan division of Glasgow from Feb. 1974 until he retired in 1979.* [1979]

SEVER, Eric John, J.P. Flat 14, 25 Brookfield Precinct. Birmingham. S. of Eric Sever, Esq. B. 1 Apr. 1943. Educ. at Secondary School, and Sparkhill Commercial School. Birmingham City Councillor from 1970. Justice of the Peace. A Travel Executive. Gov. St. Thomas's School, Ladywood. Parliamentary Private Secretary to Rt. Hon. Peter Archer, Solicitor General 1978-79. A Labour Member. Unsuccessfully contested the Edgbaston division of Birmingham in 1970. Elected for the Ladywood division of Birmingham in Aug. 1977.*   [1979]

SEYMOUR, Leslie George, J.P. House of Commons, London. S. of George Seymour, Esq. B. 1900; m. 1941 Dorothy, d. of J. Murdoch, Esq., of Redditch. Educ. at Solihull Grammar School. A Conservative. Unsuccessfully contested the Ladywood division of Birmingham in 1951. Elected for the Sparkbrook division of Birmingham in 1959 and sat until 1964, when he was defeated. Unsuccessfully contested the Sparkbrook division of Birmingham in 1966. Managing Director of Improved Metallic Appliances Limited. Member of Birmingham City Council 1937-46 and 1947-53, Honorary Alderman 1974. J.P. for Birmingham. Died 15 Apr. 1976.   [1964]

SHACKLETON, Wing-Commander Edward Arthur Alexander, O.B.E., R.A.F.V.R. Four Acres, Burley, Ringwood. Bath. S. of Sir Ernest Shackleton, C.V.O., O.B.E. B. 15 July 1911; m. 27 Apr. 1938, Betty Marguerite, d. of Capt. Charles Homan. Educ. at Radley Coll., and Magdalen Coll., Oxford. A Lecturer and Author. Member of Oxford University Expedition to Sarawak 1932; Organiser and Surveyor Oxford University Expedition to Ellesmere Land 1934-35; B.B.C. and Ministry of Information 1938-40. Served with R.A.F. (Coastal Command) 1940-45 and R.A.F. (Intelligence) 1945; O.B.E. 1945; Parliamentary Private Secretary to Rt. Hon. G.R. Strauss, Minister of Supply 1949-50, and to the Rt. Hon. Herbert Morrison 1950-51. A Socialist Member. Unsuccessfully contested Epsom in July 1945 and Bournemouth in Nov. 1945. Sat for Preston from Feb. 1946 to Feb. 1950, and for Preston S. from Feb. 1950 until 1955, when he was defeated. Created Baron Shackleton (Life Peerage) 1958. Minister of Defence for R.A.F. Oct. 1964-Jan. 1967. PC. 1966. Minister without Portfolio and Dept. Leader of House of Lords Jan. 1967-Jan. 1968. Leader of House of Lords Jan. 1968-June 1970. Lord Privy Seal Jan.-Apr. 1968 and Oct. 1968-June 1970. Paymaster Gen. Apr.-Oct. 1968. Leader of Opposition in House of Lords 1970-74. K.G. 1974. President of Royal Geographical Society 1971-74. Dept. Chairman of R.T.Z. Corporation from 1975. Chairman of Political Honours Scrutiny Committee from 1976.

Chairman of British Standards Institute from 1977.* [1954]

SHARP, Lieut. -Col. Granville Maynard. Kirklands, Cleckheaton, Yorkshire. S. of Walter Sharp, Esq. B. 5 Jan. 1906; m. 11 Sept. 1935. Margaret, d. of Dr. J.H. Vincent of Wembley Hill. Educ. at Cleckheaton Grammar School, Ashville Coll., Harrogate, and St. John's Coll., Cambridge, M.A. Hons. Partner of Walter Sharp and Son. Outfitters. Economics Lecturer W.R. Technical Institute 1928-34; Chairman of Spenborough Housing and Town Planning Committee 1935-40; Battery Capt. 68th Anti-Tank Regiment R.A. 1939-42; Staff Capt. and D.A.Q.M.G. Northern Ireland 1942-43; Senior British Staff Officer, Economic Section Allied Control Commission Italy 1943-44; Chief Economics and Supply Officer Military Government Austria 1944-45. Parliamentary Private Secretary to the Rt. Hon. Lord Winster. Minister of Civil Aviation 1946, and to Rt. Hon. Charles Key, Minister of Works Dec. 1947-Feb. 1950. Chairman of Select Committee of Estimates Sub-Committee 1945-47. A Labour Member. Elected for the Spen Valley division of the W. Riding of Yorkshire in July 1945 and sat until he retired in 1950. Member of E. Sussex County Council 1970-74, of W. Sussex County Council from 1973 and of Mid-Sussex District Council 1973-76.* [1950]

SHARPLES, Richard Christopher, O.B.E., M.C. 20 Rivermill, Glosbery Road, London. Southfield Farm, Chawton, Nr. Alton, Hampshire. Turf, and Pratt's. S. of Richard William Sharples, Esq., O.B.E. B. 6 August 1916; m. July 1946, Pamela, d. of Lieut.-Commander Keith Newall, R.N., and of Lady Claud Hamilton (she was created Baroness Sharples 1973). Educ. at Eton, and Royal Military Coll., Sandhurst. Commissioned in Welsh Guards 1936; served at Boulogne (M.C.) 1940; Brigade Maj. 17th Infantry Brigade Italy 1943 (despatches); wounded in Italy 1944 (American Silver Star Medal); R.N. Staff Coll. 1948; Military Assistant to F.M. Viscount Montgomery of Alamein 1951-53; with local rank of Lieut. -Col.; worked in economic section of Conservative Research Department 1953-54. O.B.E.

1953. Parliamentary Private Secretary to Rt. Hon. Anthony Nutting, Minister of State for Foreign Affairs 1955-56, and to Rt. Hon. R.A. Butler, Home Secretary and Lord Privy Seal from 1957 to 1959. Assistant Government Whip Oct. 1959-60. Joint Parliamentary Secretary Ministry of Pensions and National Insurance Feb. 1961-July 1962. Parliamentary Secretary to Ministry of Public Building and Works July 1962-Oct. 1964. Opposition spokesman on Home Affairs 1965. Vice-Chairman Conservative Party Organisation 1967-70. Minister of State Home Office June 1970-Apr. 1972. A Conservative. Elected for Sutton and Cheam in Nov. 1954 and sat until Oct.1972, when he resigned on appointment as Governor of Bermuda. K.C.M.G. 1972. Governor of Bermuda from Oct. 1972 until 10 Mar. 1973, when he was assassinated in Bermuda. [1972]

SHAW, Arnold John. House of Commons, London. S. of Solomon Shaw, Esq. B. 12 July 1909; m. 25 Dec. 1935 Elizabeth Solomons. Educ. at Coopers' Company's School, London, and University Coll., Southampton, (B.A. Hons. London). A Schoolmaster 1932-66. Councillor, Stepney Borough Council 1934-48. Councillor, Ilford Borough Council 1952-64; Alderman 1963-64. Councillor, London Borough of Redbridge 1964-68 and 1971-74. Parliamentary Private Secretary to Reg Freeson, Minister for Housing and Construction 1977-79. A Labour Member. Unsuccessfully contested Ilford S. in 1964. Sat for Ilford S. from 1966 to 1970, when he was defeated, and for the Ilford S. division of Redbridge from Feb. 1974 until 1979, when he was again defeated.* [1979]

SHAW, Clarice Marion McNab. 36 Titchfield Road, Troon, Ayrshire. D. of Bailie Thomas Charles McNab of Leith; m. Ben Shaw, Esq. Chairman of Scottish Labour Party. Member of Leith Burgh Council 1913. Member of Ayrshire County Council 1932-46. A Labour Member. Unsuccessfully contested the Ayr Burghs in 1929 and 1931. Elected for the Kilmarnock division of Ayr and Bute in July 1945 and sat until she resigned on 4 Oct. 1946. Died 27 Oct. 1946. [1946]

SHAW, (John) Giles Dunkerley. 36 Marsham Court, Marsham Street, London. Grove Cottage, Hampsthwaite, Harrogate, Yorkshire. S. of Hugh D. Shaw, Esq., F.I.M.T. B. 16 Nov. 1931; m. 3 Mar. 1962, Dione, d. of Professor Mervyn Ellison, (1 s. 2 d.). Educ. at Sedbergh School, and St. John's, Cambridge. President Cambridge Union 1954. Joined Rowntree and Company Limited 1955; Member of Flaxton Rural District Council 1957-64. Marketing Director Rowntree Mackintosh Limited 1969-74. Vice-Chairman of the Conservative Committee for Prices and Consumer Affairs Mar. 1975. Member Select Committee on Nationalised Industries May 1976. Under-Secretary of State for Northern Ireland from May 1979, A Conservative. Unsuccessfully contested Hull W. in 1966. Elected for Pudsey in Feb. 1974.*
[1979]

SHAW, Michael Norman. Duxbury Hall, Liversedge, Yorkshire. Carlton. S. of Norman Shaw, Esq., F.C.A. B. 9 Oct. 1920; m. 25 Apr. 1951, Joan Mary Louise, d. of Sir Alfred Mowat, 2nd Bart., (3 s.). Educ. at Sedbergh. A.C.A. 1945, F.C.A. 1952, J.P. 1953., Dept. - Lieut. for W. Yorkshire 1977. Parliamentary Private Secretary to Rt. Hon. John Hare, Minister of Labour 1962-63 and to Rt. Hon. John Davies, Minister of Technology, Secretary of State for Trade and Industry and Chancellor of Duchy of Lancaster 1970-74. Member of European Parliament 1974-79. Member of Speaker's Panel of Chairmen. A Conservative. Unsuccessfully contested Dewsbury in 1955 and Brighouse and Spenborough in 1959. Sat for Brighouse and Spenborough from a by-election in Mar. 1960 to 1964, when he was defeated. Member for Scarborough and Whitby from 1966 to Feb. 1974. Elected for the Scarborough division of the N. Riding of Yorkshire in Feb. 1974.*
[1979]

SHAWCROSS, Christopher Nyholm, K.C. 5 Paper Buildings, Temple, London. 30 Tufton Court, London. S. of John Shawcross, Esq. B. 20 June 1905; m. 1st, 1932, Doreen, d. of Richard Burrows, Esq. (divorced 1949); 2ndly, 17 Aug. 1949. Maridel, d. of Dr. Maxwell Chance. Educ. at Dulwich, and University Coll., Oxford. Barrister-at-Law

Gray's Inn 1931, Bencher 1954. Joined R.N.V.R. 1940. A Labour Member. Elected for the Widnes division of Lancashire in July 1945 and sat until he retired in 1950. K.C. 1949. Recorder of Nottingham 1950-61. Chairman of International Space Law Committee 1959. Died 18 Aug. 1973. [1950]

SHAWCROSS, Rt. Hon. Sir Hartley William, Q.C. 201 Beatty House, Dolphin Square, London. 1 Harcourt Buildings, Temple, London. Peckhams, Halland, Sussex. S. of John Shawcross, Esq. B. 4 Feb. 1902; m. 1st, 24 May 1929, Alberta, d. of W. Shyvers, Esq. (she died 1943); 2ndly, 21 Sept. 1944, Joan, d. of Hume Mather, Esq. (she died 1974). Educ. at Dulwich, and Geneva. Barrister-at-Law, Gray's Inn 1925, K.C. 1939; Bencher 1939. Chairman of Enemy Aliens Tribunal 1939-40; Dept. Regional Commissioner S.E. Region 1940-41. Senior Regional Commissioner N.W. Region 1942-45. Recorder of Salford 1942-45. J.P. for Sussex. Assistant Chairman E. Sussex Quarter Sessions 1942-45; Chairman of Catering Wages Commission 1943-45. Attorney-Gen. Aug. 1945-Apr. 1951. President of Board of Trade Apr.-Oct. 1951 with Cabinet rank. Knight Bach. 1945; PC. 1946. Recorder of Kingston-on-Thames 1947-61. Chairman Bar Council 1952-57; President London Police Court Mission, later Rainer Foundation 1951-71; Chairman Sussex Prisoners' Aid Society. Honorary member of New York Bar Association. Chairman Friends of Atlantic Union; British member of the Permanent Court of Arbitration at The Hague 1950-67. A Labour Member. Elected for St. Helens in July 1945 and sat until he resigned in Apr. 1958. Chairman of Justice 1956-72. President of British Hotels and Restaurants Association 1959-71. Created Baron Shawcross (Life Peerage) 1959. Chairman of Royal Commission on the Press 1961-62, of Medical Research Council 1961-65, Thames Television Limited 1969-74, Birmingham Small Arms Company Limited 1971-73 and Press Council 1974-78. G.B.E. 1974. Chancellor of Sussex University from 1965. Chairman of Panel on Take-Overs and Mergers from 1969, of London and Continental Bankers from 1974, of International Chamber of Commerce Commission on Unethical Practices from 1976.* [1958]

SHELDON, Rt. Hon. Robert Edward. 27 Darley Avenue, West Didsbury, Manchester. 2 Ryder Street, London. B. 13 Sept. 1923; m. 1st, 1945 Eileen Shamash (she died 1969), (1 s. 1 d.); 2ndly, 1971, Mary Shield. Educ. at Elementary, Grammar and Technical Schools, served an Engineering Apprenticeship (qualified Engineer, external graduate of London University). Opposition Front Bench spokesman on Civil Service, Treasury Matters and Machinery of Government 1970-74. Chairman Northwest Group Labour MPs 1970-74. Chairman Gen. Sub-Committee of Expenditure Committee 1972-74. Member Fulton Committee on the Civil Service 1966-68. Chairman Economic Affairs and Finance Group 1966-67. Member Public Accounts Committee 1965-70. Vice-Chairman Lancashire and Cheshire Group of the P.L.P. 1968-70. Voted in favour of entry to E.E.C. on 28 Oct. 1971. Minister of State Civil Service Department Mar.-Oct. 1974. Minister of State at the Treasury Oct. 1974-June 1975. Financial Secretary to the Treasury June 1975-May 1979. PC. 1977. A Labour Member. Unsuccessfully contested the Withington division of Manchester at the general election of 1959. Elected for Ashton-under-Lyne in Oct. 1964.* [1979]

SHELTON, William Jeremy Masefield. 27 Ponsonby Terrace, London. S. of Lieut.-Col. Richard C.M. Shelton, O.B.E. B. 30 Oct. 1929; m. 1960, Anne Patricia, d. of John Warder, Esq., C.B.E. Educ. at Radley Coll., Worcester Coll., Oxford, M.A. (Oxon.) and University of Texas at Austin. With Colman, Prentis and Varley Limited 1952-55. In Venezuela 1955-60 and Colombia 1960-64. Greater London County Councillor Wnadsworth 1967-70; Chief Whip Inner London Education Authority 1968-70. Parliamentary Private Secretary to Sir John Eden, Minister of Posts and Telecommunications 1972-74. Chairman of Fletcher, Shelton, Delaney and Reynolds Limited from 1974. Vice-Chairman Conservative Education Committee 1974-75. Joint Secretary Conservative Greater London Members Committee 1974-75. Secretary Latin-American Parliamentary Group. Joint Parliamentary Private Secretary to Rt. Hon. Margaret Thatcher, MP., Leader of the Opposition in 1975. A Conservative. Sat for the Clapham division of Wandsworth from 1970 to Feb 74. Elected for the Streatham division of Lambeth in Feb. 1974.* [1979]

SHEPHARD, Sidney, M.C. Elston Hall, Newark. Inchnadamph Lodge, Lairg, Sutherland. Carlton, Bath, Lansdowne, and Nottinghamshire. S. of C.H. Shephard, Esq., of Lenton, Nottinghamshire. B. 29 Mar. 1894; m. 3 Feb. 1923, Lily Jane Alexander, d. of A.T. Shannon, Esq., of Darjeeling. An Industrialist. Founder of Bairns-Wear Limited. High Sheriff of Nottinghamshire 1940-41; member of Council of Industrial Welfare Society; member of Nottinghamshire T.A. Association. Served with Sherwood Foresters 1914-18; Military Welfare Officer (Maj.) 1939-46; Commanded Home Guard Battalion 1940-43. Lieut.-Col. A Conservative. Elected for the Newark division of Nottinghamshire in June 1943 and sat until 1950, when he was defeated. Unsuccessfully contested Nottingham E. in 1951. Died 25 Nov. 1953. [1950]

SHEPHERD, Colin Ryley. Manor House, Ganarew, Nr. Monmouth, Herefordshire. Naval. S. of T.C.R. Shepherd, Esq., M.B.E. B. 13 Jan. 1938; m. 26 Mar. 1966, Louise, d. of Lieut.-Col. E.A.M. Cleveland, M.C., (3 s.). Educ. at Oundle, Caius Coll., Cambridge and McGill University. Resigned from Royal Canadian Navy 1963. Joined Haigh Engineering Company Limited, Marketing Director 1963. A Conservative. Elected for Hereford in Oct. 1974.* [1979]

SHEPHERD, William Stanley. 33 Queen's Grove, London. S. of W.D. Shepherd, Esq. B. 1912; m. 1942, Betty, d. of T.F. Howard, Esq., MP. for Islington South from 1931-35. Educ. at Edleston School, Crewe. Served in the Army 1939-45 war. Joint Honorary Secretary Conservative Committee on Trade and Industry 1945-51. Managing Director of a number of companies and a Director Manchester Chamber of Commerce. Member Select Committee of Estimates. A Conservative. Sat for Bucklow from July 1945 to Feb. 1950. Elected for the Cheadle division of Cheshire in Feb. 1950 and sat until 1966 when he was defeated.* [1966]

SHERSBY, (Julian) Michael. House of Commons, London. Conservative (Uxbridge). S. of William Henry Shersby, Esq. B. 17 Feb. 1933; m. 31 May 1958, Barbara, d. of J.H. Barrow, Esq., (1 s. 1 d.). Educ. at John Lyon School, Harrow-on-the-Hill. Member Paddington Borough Council 1959-64 and of Westminster City Council 1964-71. Director of British Industrial Film Association 1962-66. Chairman Childrens Committee 1964-67. Dept. Lord Mayor of Westminster 1967-68. Chief Whip 1969-71. Gov. of Eton End P.N.E.U. School, Datchet, Buckinghamshire. Director British Sugar Bureau 1966-77, Director Gen. 1977. Secretary U.K. Sugar Industry Association 1978. Member of the Court, Brunel University 1975. Member Commonwealth Parliamentary Association Delegation to Caribbean 1975. Joint Secretary Conservative Party Industry Committee 1973-74. Parliamentary Private Secretary to Michael Heseltine, Minister for Aerospace and Shipping 1974. Chairman Conservative Party Trade Committee 1974-76. Vice-Chairman 1977. Joint Secretary Scientific Committee 1977. Promoted as a Private Member: Town and Country Amenities Act 1974; Parks Regulation Amendment Act 1974; Stock Exchange (Completion of Bargains) Act 1976. A Conservative. Sat for Uxbridge from Dec. 1972 to Feb. 1974 and for the Uxbridge division of Hillingdon from Feb. 1974.*   [1979]

SHINWELL, Rt. Hon. Emanuel, C.H. 33 Erskine Hill, London. S. of Samuel Shinwell, Esq. B. 18 Oct. 1884 in London; m. 1st, 1903, Fay Freeman (she died 1954); 2ndly, 1956, Dinah Meyer (she died 1971); 3rdly, 1972, Mrs. Sarah Hurst (she died 1977). Parliamentary Secretary Board of Trade, Mines Department Jan.-Nov. 1924. Member of Parliamentary Committee of P.L.P. 1923-24, Sept.-Oct. 1931, 1937-40 and 1951-55. Parliamentary and Financial Secretary War Office June 1929-June 1930. Secretary for Mines June 1930-Aug. 1931; Minister of Fuel and Power July 1945-Oct. 1947; was Member of the Cabinet 1945 until Oct. 1947. Secretary of State for War Oct. 1947-Feb. 1950; PC. 1945. Minister of Defence in Cabinet Feb. 1950-Oct. 1951. Member of National Executive Committee of Labour Party 1940-51. Chairman National Executive Labour Party 1947-48. Chairman P.L.P. Nov. 1964-Mar. 1967. C.H. 1965. Publications: *The Britain I Want, When the Men Come Home, Conflict without Malice, I've Lived through It All* and *The Labour Story.* A Labour Member. Unsuccessfully contested Linlithgow 1918. Sat for Linlithgow from 1922-24, when he was defeated, and Apr. 1928-Oct. 1931, when he was again defeated. Sat for the Seaham division of Durham from Nov. 1935-Feb. 1950 and for the Easington division of Durham from Feb. 1950 until he retired in 1970. Honorary D.C.L. Durham University 1969. Created Baron Shinwell (Life Peerage) 1970.*   [1970]

SHORE, Rt. Hon. Peter David. 23 Dryburgh Road, London. S. of Capt. R.N. Shore. B. 20 May 1924; m. 1948 Elizabeth Catherine, d. of Edward Murray Wrong, Esq. Educ. at Quarry Bank High School, Liverpool, and King's Coll., Cambridge. A Political Economist. Joined the Labour Party in 1948. Member T. and G.W.U. and Fabian Society. Head of Research Department of Labour Party 1959-64. Parliamentary Private Secretary to Rt. Hon. Harold Wilson, Prime Minister Mar. 1965-Mar. 1966; Joint Parliamentary Secretary Ministry of Technology Apr. 1966-Jan. 1967. Joint Parliamentary Under-Secretary Department of Economic Affairs Jan.-Aug 1967. PC. 1967. Secretary of State for Economic Affairs Aug. 1967-Oct. 1969. Minister without Portfolio Oct. 1969-June 1970. Dept. Leader of the House of Commons Nov. 1969-June 1970. Member of Parliamentary Committee of P.L.P. and Opposition spokesman on Europe 1971-74. Secretary of State for Trade Mar. 1974-Apr. 1976. Secretary of State for the Environment Apr. 1976-May 1979. Opposition spokesman on Foreign and Commonwealth Affairs and member of Parliamentary Committe of P.L.P. from 1979. Author of *Entitled to Know.* A Labour Member. Unsuccessfully contested the St. Ives division of Cornwall in 1950 and Halifax in 1959. Sat for Stepney from 1964-Feb. 1974. Elected for the Stepney and Poplar division of Tower Hamlets in Feb. 1974.*   [1979]

SHORT, Rt. Hon. Edward Watson, C.H.
House of Commons, London. S. of Charles
Short, Esq., of Warcop, Westmorland. B. 17
Dec. 1912; m. 1941, Jennie, d. of Thomas
Sewell, Esq., of Newcastle-upon-Tyne. Educ.
at Bede Coll., Durham. Capt. D.L.I. Head-
master of Princes Louise County Secondary
School, Blyth, 1947-51. Member Newcastle
City Council and leader of Labour Group
1948; President North Newcastle Labour
Party 1946; Secretary of South Northum-
berland Branch of N.U.T. 1950. Opposition
Assistant Whip 1955. Dept. Opposition Chief
Whip 1962-64. Parliamentary Secretary to
the Treasury and Chief Whip Oct. 1964-July
1966. Postmaster-Gen. July 1966-Apr. 1968.
PC. 1964. Secretary of State for Education
and Science Apr. 1968-June 1970. Opposi-
tion spokesman on Education 1970-72. Mem-
ber of Parliamentary Committee of P.L.P.
1970-74. Opposition spokesman on Educa-
tion and Science 1970-72 and on House of
Commons Affairs 1972-74. Member of
National Executive Committee of Labour
Party 1972-76. Dept. Leader of the Labour
Party Apr. 1972-Oct. 1976. Lord President of
the Council and Leader of the House of
Commons Mar. 1974-Apr. 1976. A Labour
Member. Elected for the Central division of
Newcastle-upon-Tyne in 1951 and sat until
Oct. 1976, when he resigned on appoint-
ment as Chairman of Cable and Wireless.
Chairman of Cable and Wireless Limited
from 1976. C.H. May 1976. Created Baron
Glenamara (Life Peerage) 1977.*   [1976]

SHORT, Renee. House of Commons, London. B. 1919; M. Dr. Andrew Short. Educ. at
Nottingham County Grammar School and
Manchester University. A Freelance Journalist. Member of the Labour Party from 1948.
Member of N.U.J. and T. and G.W.U.,
active Co-operator, member of Women's Co-
operative Guild for 18 years. Member Hertfordshire County Council 1952-67 and Watford Rural District Council 1952-64. Widely
travelled in Scandinavia, Soviet Union,
Hungary and member of British Delegation
to Cuba in 1963. Chairman Parliamentary
Anglo-German Democratic Republic Group.
Secretary Anglo-Soviet Parliamentary
Group. Vice-Chairman All-Party East-West
Trade Group. Member of National Exe-

cutive Committee of Labour Party from
1970. Chairman Sub-Committee Parliamen-
tary Expenditure Committee. Member Dele-
gation to Council of Europe and Western
European Union 1964-68. Chairman of
Select Committee on Social Service from
1979. National President Nursery Schools
Association and Campaign for Nursery
Education. Gov. Roundhouse Theatre.
Member Executive St. George's Theatre
Trust and Chairman Theatres Advisory
Council. A Labour Member. Unsuccessfully
contested St. Albans in 1955 and Watford at
the 1959 general elections. Elected for N.E.
Wolverhampton in Oct. 1964.*   [1979]

SHURMER, Percy Lionel Edward. 140
Belgrave Road, Birmingham. S. of Edward
Shurmer, Esq., Master Tailor, of Chelten-
ham. B. 1888; m. 1908, Maude, d. of A.
Taylor, Esq., of Newport, Monmouthshire.
Educ. at Council Schools. Served with Bir-
mingham Territorial Artillery 1914-18.
Member of Birmingham City Council 1921,
Alderman 1934. Worked for Post Office Tele-
phone Service in Birmingham until the Gen-
eral Strike in 1926, when he was arrested and
dismissed. On the Staff of Birmingham Co-
operative Society 1926-45. J.P.; awarded
National Commendation for Rescue Work in
Air Raids. A Labour Member. Elected for the
Sparkbrook division of Birmingham in July
1945 and sat until his death on 29 May 1959.
Served in Merchant Navy. Supporter of
Salvation Army. Died 29 May 1959. [1959]

SILKIN, Rt. Hon. John Ernest. House of
Commons, London. S. of 1st Baron Silkin. B.
1923; m. 1950, Rosamund John. Educ. at
Dulwich Coll., and Trinity Hall, Cambridge.
A Solicitor. Joined the Labour Party in
1939. During the war served in R.N.V.R.
Member of the T. and G.W.U. and the Co-
operative Society. Government Pairing Whip
Nov. 1964. Assistant Government Whip Nov.
1964-Jan. 1966. Lord Commissioner of the
Treasury Jan. to Apr. 1966; Treasurer of the
Household and Dept. Chief Whip. Apr. -July
1966. Government Chief Whip July 1966-
Apr. 1969. Parliamentary Secretary to the
Treasury 1966-69. Dept. Leader of the House
1968-69. Minister of Public Building and
Works Apr. 1969-June 1970. Minister for

Planning and Local Government Mar. 1974-Sept. 1976. Opposition spokesman on Local Government 1970-Dec. 1972 and on Health and Social Security Dec. 1972-Mar. 1974. Member of Parliamentary Committee of P.L.P. Apr.-Dec. 1972 and from 1979. Member of Cabinet Oct. 1974-May 1979. Minister of Agriculture, Fisheries and Food Sept. 1976-May 1979. Opposition spokesman on Industry from 1979. PC. 1966. A Labour Member. Unsuccessfully contested St. Marylebone in 1950. Woolwich W. in 1951, and Nottingham S. in 1959. Sat for Deptford from July 1963 to Feb. 1974 and for the Deptford division of Lewisham from Feb. 1974.* [1979]

SILKIN, Rt. Hon. Lewis, C.H. 32 St. James's Square, London. B. 1889; m. 1st, 1915, Rosa Neft (she died 29 Dec. 1947); 2ndly, 1948, Mrs. Freda Johnson, d. of Canon Pilling (she died 1963); 3rdly, 1964, Marguerite Schlageter. Educ. at Elementary and Secondary Schools, and University of London. Admitted a Solicitor 1920; Member of London County Council 1925-45; Chairman of Housing and Public Health Committee London County Council 1934-40, and Chairman of Town Planning Committee 1940-45; Minister of Town and Country Planning July 1945-Feb. 1950. PC. 1945. Member of Select Committee on National Expenditure. A Labour Member. Unsuccessfully contested the Central division of Wandsworth in 1922, Stoke Newington in 1924 and the Peckham division of Camberwell in 1935. Elected for the Peckham division of Camberwell in May 1936 and sat until he retired in 1950. Created Baron Silkin 1950. Dept. Leader of Labour Party in House of Lords 1955-64. C.H. 1965. Died 11 May 1972. [1950]

SILKIN, Rt. Hon. Samuel Charles, Q.C. Lamb Building, Temple, London. S. of 1st Baron Silkin. B. 6 Mar. 1918; m. 1941, Elaine, d. of Arthur Stamp, Esq. Educ. at Dulwich Coll., (Open Scholar) 1930-36, and Trinity Hall, Cambridge, (Open Maj. Scholar) 1936-39. B.A. (1st Class Hons. Parts I and II of Law Tripos, awarded Pro Hac Vice Law Studentship by Trinity Hall 1939). A Barrister-at-Law 1941 (1st Class Hons. Bar

Final), Harmsworth Law Scholar of Middle Temple 1946; Q.C. 1963; Recorder of Bedford 1966-70; Bencher of Middle Temple 1970. Served in the Royal Artillery 1940-46 (U.K., Europe and Singapore); mentioned in despatches 1945; Lieut.Col. 1946. Joined the Labour Party in 1946. Member of Society of Labour Lawyers from foundation, and Chairman 1964-71, Vice-President 1971. Member of Camberwell Borough Council 1953-59; Dept.-Leader and Vice-Chairman Finance Committee 1953-57; Chairman Planning Committee 1954-58. Member of Royal Commission on Penal System 1965-66. Member Public Accounts Committee 1964-65; Chairman Select Committee on Parliamentary Privilege 1966-67. Chairman P.L.P.'s European Affairs and Common Market Group 1966-70. Member of Assemblies of Council of Europe and Western European Union 1966-70, Leader of the British Delegation 1968-70. Chairman Legal Affairs Committee Council of Europe 1967-70. Gov. of Maudsley and Royal Bethlem Hospitals 1969-74. Opposition Front Bench spokesman on Legal Questions (Shadow Solicitor-Gen.) 1970-74. Voted in favour of entry to E.E.C. on 28 Oct. 1971. Attorney-Gen. Mar. 1974-May 1979. President Alcohol Education Council 1973. PC. 1974. A Labour Member. Sat for the Dulwich division of Camberwell from 1964 to Feb. 74. Elected for the Dulwich division of Southwark in Feb. 1974.* [1979]

SILLARS, James. 167 Glencairn Road, Ayr. S. of Matthew Sillars Esq., Locomotive Driver. B. 4 Oct. 1937; m. 7 June 1956, Ann, d. of John O'Farrell, Esq. Educ. at Ayr Academy. A Radio Operator Royal Navy. Lay Trade Union Official F.B.U. Full-time Agent Ayr Labour Party. Head of Organization Department Scottish T.U.C. 1968-70. Director of Scottish Federation of Housing Associations from 1979. Resigned the Labour Whip in July 1976 and Thereafter sat as a member of the Scottish Labour Party of which he was a founder and leader. Joined Scottish National Party May 1980. Sat for Ayrshire S. from Mar. 1970 until 1979 when he was defeated by the Labour candidate.* [1979]

SILVERMAN, Julius. House of Commons, London. S. of Nathan Silverman, Esq. B. 8 Dec. 1905; m. 25 May 1959, Eva O. Price. Educ. at Central High School, Leeds A Barrister-at-Law, Grays Inn 1931. Member of Birmingham City Council 1934-45. A Labour Member. Unsuccessfully contested the Moseley division of Brimingham in 1935. Sat for the Aston division of Birmingham from 1955 to Feb. 1974. Sat for the Erdington division of Birmingham from 1945-55 and again from Feb. 1974.* [1979]

SILVERMAN, Samuel Sydney. 10 Hamilton House, St. John's Wood, London. 4 Essex Court, Middle Temple, London. S. of Meyer Silverman, Esq., of Liverpool. B. 1895; m. 1933, Nancy, d. of L. Rubenstein, Esq., of Liverpool, (3 s.). Educ. at University of Liverpool, B.A., LL.B. Admitted a Solicitor 1928; member of Liverpool City Council 1932-38. Lecturer in English Lit. University of Finland, Helsingfors 1920-24. A Labour Member. Unsuccessfully contested the Exchange division of Liverpool in Jan. 1933. Elected for Nelson and Colne in 1935 and sat until his death on 9 Feb. 1968. Labour Whip withdrawn Nov. 1954-Apr. 1955 and Mar. 1961-May 1963. Member of National Executive Committee of Labour Party 1956-57. Advocate of abolition of capital punishment and sponsor of Murder (Abolition of Death Penalty) Act 1965. Died 9 Feb. 1968. [1967]

SILVESTER, Frederick John. House of Commons, London. S. of William Silvester, Esq. B. 1933; m. 1971, Victoria, d. of James H. Lloyd Davies, Esq., (2 d.). Educ. at Sir George Monoux Grammar School, Walthamstow and Sidney Sussex Coll., Cambridge. A Teacher 1955-57. Barrister, Grays Inn, 1957. Education Officer with Conservative Party 1957-60. With J. Walter Thompson Company Limited from 1960. A Councillor, Walthamstow 1960-64. Vice-Chairman Conservative Committee on Prices and Consumer Protection 1974. Opposition Whip 1974-76. Vice-Chairman Conservative Employment Committee 1976. Parliamentary Private Secretary to Rt. Hon. James Prior, Secretary of State for Employment from 1979. A Conservative. Sat for Walthamstow W. from

Sept. 1967 to June 1970, when he was defeated. Unsuccessfully contested Walthamstow W. in 1966. Elected for the Withington division of Manchester in Feb. 1974.* [1979]

SIMEONS, Charles Fitzmaurice Creighton. 21 Ludlow Avenue, Luton. Public Schools, and St. Stephen's. S. of Charles Albert Simeons, Esq., Merchant. B. 22 Sept. 1921; m. 10 Mar. 1945, Rosemary, d. of Ashley Tabrum, Esq. Educ. at Oundle, and Queens' Coll., Cambridge. Maj. R.A. 8th Indian Division 1942-46; Photographic Gelatin Manufacturer 1946-70; President Luton, Dunstable and District Chamber of Commerce 1967-68; Gov. Rotary International 1967-68. Justice of Peace County Borough of Luton 1959; Liveryman of the Worshipful Company of Feltmakers and Guild of the Freeman of the City of London. Vice-President of the Association of Joint Sewerage Boards, and member of Water Pollution Control Federation of America. Consultant Photographic Gelatine, Effluent Treatment Kodak Limited and Br. Leather Federation. Director Environmental Services Limited. A Conservative. Unsuccessfully contested Luton in 1964 and 1966. Elected for Luton in June 1970 and sat until Feb. 1974, when he unsuccessfully contested Luton E.* [1974]

SIMMONS, Charles James. 20 Slack Lane, Handsworth, Birmingham. S. of James Simmons, Esq. B. 9 Apr. 1893; m. 1st, 19 Aug. 1915, Beatrice, d. of Matthew Roberts, Esq. (she died 1972); 2ndly, 1972, Kate Showell. Educ. at Elementary Schools, Birmingham. A Political Lecturer and Organiser and Journalist; member of Birmingham City Council 1921-31 and 1942-45; Secretary of Borough Labour Party 1942-45. Editor of Birmingham Town Crier 1940-45; Chairman West Midland Group of Labour MPs. 1954 and 1955 sessions. Served in France, Egypt and Gallipoli 1914-17. Assistant Whip Aug. 1945. A Lord Commissioner of the Treasury Mar. 1946-Feb. 1949; Parliamentary Secretary Ministry of Pensions Feb. 1949-Oct. 1951. Opposition Whip from 1956. A Labour Member. Unsuccessfully contested the Erdington division of Birmingham in 1924, 1931, 1935 and Oct. 1936. Sat for the Erdington division of Birmingham from 1929-31 and for Birmingham W. from 1945-50. Elected for the Brierley Hill division of Staffordshire in Feb. 1950 and sat until 1959, when he was defeated. President of Birmingham Temperance Society and Birmingham Christian Socialist Movement. Died 11 Aug. 1975. [1959]

SIMON, Rt. Hon. Sir Jocelyn Edward Salis, Q.C. 22 Campden Hill Square, London. Carlton, and Beefsteak. S. of Frank Cecil Simon, Esq., Stock and Share Broker. B. 15 Jan. 1911; m. 1st, 1934, Gwendolen Helen, d. of Edwyn J. Evans, Esq., of London (she died 1938); 2ndly, 1948, Fay Elizabeth, d. of Brigadier H.G.A. Pearson, of Jersey, C.I., (3 s.). Educ. at Gresham's School, Holt and Trinity Hall, Cambridge. Barrister-at-Law, Middle Temple 1934; K.C. 1951; Assistant Recorder of Birmingham 1955-57. Served R.T.R. 1939-45, Lieut.-Col. Parliamentary Private Secretary to Sir Lionel Heald, Attorney-Gen. 1951-54. Joint Parliamentary Under-Secretary for Home Affairs Jan. 1957-Jan. 1958; Financial Secretary to the Treasury Jan. 1958-Oct. 1959. Solicitor-Gen. Oct. 1959-Feb. 1962. PC. 1961. A Conservative. Elected for Middlesbrough W. in Oct. 1951 sat until Feb. 1962, when he was appointed President of the Probate, Divorce and Admiralty Division of the High Court. Member of Royal Commission on the Law relating to Mental Illness and Mental Deficiency 1954-57. Knighted 1959. President of the Probate, Divorce and Admiralty Division of the High Court 1962-71. Created Baron Simon of Glaisdale (Life Peerage) 1971. Lord of Appeal in Ordinary 1971-77. Elder Brother of Trinity House. Honorary Fellow of Trinity Hall, Cambridge. Dept. Lieut. for N. Riding of Yorkshire 1973, for N. Yorkshire 1974.* [1962]

SIMS, Roger Edward., J.P. 68 Towncourt Crescent, Petts Wood, Orpington, Kent. Dodwell and Company Limited, 18 Finsbury Circus, London. S. of Herbert W. Sims, Esq. B. 27 Jan. 1930; m. 15 June 1957, Angela, d. of John R. Mathews, Esq., (2 s. 1 d.). Educ. at

City Boys' Grammar School, Leicester, and St. Olave's G.S. London. With Coutts and Company 1950-51 and Campbell Booker Carter Ltd. 1953-62. J.P. for Bromley 1960-72. Member Chislehurst and Sidcup Urban District Council 1956-62. Export Manager, Dodwell and Company Limited 1962. Parliamentary Private Secretary to Rt. Hon. William Whitelaw, Home Secretary from 1979. A Conservative. Unsuccessfully contested Shoreditch and Finsbury in 1966 and 1970. Elected for the Chislehurst division of Bromley in Feb. 1974.* [1979]

SINCLAIR, Sir George Evelyn, C.M.G., O.B.E. South Minack, Porthcurno, Cornwall. Carlton, Rookery, Saxmundham, Suffolk, Athenaeum, and Royal Commonwealth Society. S. of Francis Sinclair, Esq. B. 6 Nov. 1912; m. 1941, Katharine, d. of Beaufort Burdekin, Esq., of Sydney, Australia (she died 1971); 2ndly, 26 Apr. 1972, Violet, widow of G.L. Sawday, Esq. Educ. at Abingdon School, and Pembroke Coll., Oxford. Entered Colonial Service, Gold Coast 1936. Served R.W.A.F.F. in West Africa 1940-43. Colonial Office 1943-45; Secretary Commission on Higher Education in West Africa; Gold Coast 1945-55; Regional Officer Transvolta-Togoland 1952-55. Dept. Gov. of Cyprus 1955-60. Member Wimbledon Borough Council 1962-65. Member Council on Overseas Services Resettlement Bureau. Knighted 1960. Joint Secretary Conservative Party Commonwealth Affairs Committee 1966-68. Member Select Committee on Race Relations 1968-74. Member Select Committee on Overseas Aid 1969-71. Vice-Chairman Conservative Party Parliamentary Committee on Education 1974-76, Trustee Runnymede Trust 1969-75, and Human Rights Trust 1971-74. Physically Handicapped and Able Bodied (P.H.A.B.) 1973. Member Council of Christian Aid. Vice-President Intermediate Technology Development Group. Member Governing Bodies Association for Public Schools from 1973, Chairman from 1979. Chairman Governors Abingdon School. Member Direct Grants Joint Committee. O.B.E. 1950. C.M.G. 1956. A Conservative. Elected for the Dorking division of Surrey in Oct. 1964 and sat until he retired in 1979.* [1979]

SKEET, Trevor Herbert Harry. House of Commons, London. S. of H.M. Skeet, Esq., of New Zealand. B. 28 Jan. 1918; m. 3 May 1951, Margaret, d. of H.M. Gilling, Esq., of Devon (she died 1973). Educ. at King's Coll., Auckland, and University of New Zealand. LL.B., Barrister, Inner Temple 1947 and in New Zealand. Served with N.Z. Armed Forces 1939-45. Consultant and Writer. Chairman of the Conservative Trade Committee. Secretary of All-Party Committee on Airships. Secretary of All-Party Group on Minerals Vice-Chairman Conservative Energy Committee 1974-77. Chairman Conservative Middle East Committee. Secretary of All-Party British-Japanese and British-Brazilian Groups. A Conservative. Unsuccessfully contested Stoke Newington and Hackney N. in 1951 and Llanelli in 1955. Sat for Willesden E. from 1959 to 1964, when he was defeated. Elected for Bedford in June 1970.* [1979]

SKEFFINGTON, Arthur Massey. 2 Harcourt Buildings, Temple, London. The Old Vicarage, Meopham, Kent. S. of Arthur James and Edith Skeffington. B. 4 Sept. 1909; m. 4 Sept. 1952, Sheila, d. of Thomas C. McKenzie, Esq., of Birmingham. Educ. at Streatham Grammar School, and University of London, B.Sc. (Econ. Hons.) Economist and Barrister, Middle Temple 1951. Served in Board of Trade and Ministry of Supply 1941-45. Parliamentary Private Secretary to J.B. Hynd, Chancellor of Duchy of Lancaster and Minister of Pensions 1945-47 and to G. Buchanan, Minister of Pensions 1947-48. Visited E. Africa 1948 and 1957, U.S.A. 1949, 1958, 1965 and 1967, India 1961, and Australia 1966. Member of Fabian Society Executive from 1942, Chairman 1957. Member of L.C.C. for Peckham 1950-58. Labour Party Executive from 1953 to 1958 and 1959 to 1971. Chairman Labour Party 1969-70. Civil Service Tribunal (Staff Side). Joint President British Section of Council of European Municipalities and Council of Commonwealth Municipalities. President of the Arboricultural Society. Author of *Leasehold Enfranchisement* and *Tanganyika in Transition*. Introduced Enforcement of Contracts Act 1954. Parliamentary Secretary Ministry of Land and Natural Resources Oct. 1964- Feb. 1967. Joint Parliamentary Secretary Ministry of Housing and Local Government Feb. 1967-June 1970. Chairman of the Committee which produced the Government Report *People and Planning*. Freeman of the City of London. A Labour Member. Unsuccessfully contested the Streatham division of Wandsworth in 1935 and Lewisham W. in Nov. 1938. Sat for Lewisham W. from 1945, when he was defeated. Unsuccessfully contested Lewisham W. in 1951. Elected for Hayes and Harlington in Apr. 1953 and sat until his death on 18 Feb. 1971. Fellow of Royal Geographical and Royal Economic Societies. Died 18 Feb. 1971. [1971]

SKEFFINGTON-LODGE, Thomas Cecil. 17 Chatsworth Court, London. 3 Lewes Crescent, Brighton. Savile. S. of Thomas Lodge, Esq. B. 15 Jan. 1905. Unmarried. Educ. at Giggleswick School, and Westminster School. Occupied in Public Relations work in Coal Trade. Served with R.N.V.R. 1940-45. Member of Council for the Preservation of Rural England, of Central Council Socialist Christian League, of Labour Party, 25 years, and of Fabian Society; member of U.S.D.A.W. President of Pudsey and Otley division Labour Party 1935-39. A Labour Member. Elected for the Bedford division of Bedfordshire in July 1945 and sat until 1950, when he was defeated. Unsuccessfully contested York in 1951, Mid-Bedfordshire in 1955, the Grantham division of Lincolnshire in 1959 and the Pavilion division of Brighton in Mar. 1969. Personal Assistant to Chairman of Colonial Development Corporation 1950-52.* [1950]

SKINNARD, Frederick William. 1 Oakfield Avenue, Kenton, Harrow. S. of F.W. Skinnard, Esq., Engraver, of Plymouth. B. 8 Mar. 1902; m. 2 Apr. 1931, Muriel, d. of George Lightfoot, Esq. (she died 1959); 2ndly, 1960, Greta Cory Anthony. Educ. at Devonport High School, and Borough Road Training Coll. for Teachers. A Schoolmaster under London County Council and Willesden Local Education Authorities 1922-45; member of Labour Party's Advisory Committee on Imperial Affairs and of Fabian Colonial Bureau Committee and of Central Executive Committee N.S.P.C.C. A Labour

Member. Elected for Harrow E. in July 1945 and sat until 1950, when he was defeated. Registrar and External Director of Examinations, Institute of Optical Science, 1951-59.* [1950]

SKINNER, Dennis Edward. 86 Thanet Street, Clay Cross, Nr. Chesterfield, Derbyshire. S. of Edward Skinner, Esq. B. 11 Feb. 1932; m. 12 Mar. 1960, Mary, d. of James Parker, Esq. Educ. at Tupton Hall Grammar School, and Ruskin Coll. A Miner 1949-70. Member Clay Cross Urban District Council 1960-70, County Councillor for Derbyshire 1964-70. President Derbyshire Miners 1966, Sports Council 1966, Scarsdale Valuation Panel, President of Derbyshire Urban District Council Association. Member of National Executive Committee of Labour Party from 1978. A Labour Member. Elected for the Bolsover division of Derbyshire in June 1970.* [1979]

SLATER, Harriet. House of Commons, London. D. of John Edward Evans, Esq. B. 1903 in Tunstall; m. 1931, Frederick Slater, Esq. Educ. at Elementary Schools, Hanley High School, and Dudley Teachers' Training Coll. Elected to Stoke-on-Trent City Council 1933; made an Alderman in 1949; Chairman of Education Committee 1952-65. National Organiser for Co-operative Party 1942-53. A Lord Commissioner of the Treasury and Government Whip Oct. 1964-Apr. 1966. A Labour and Co-operative Member. Elected for Stoke-on-Trent N. in March 1953 and sat until she retired in 1966. C.B.E. 1965. Died 12 Oct. 1976. [1966]

SLATER, Joseph, B.E.M. House of Commons, London. S. of William Slater, Esq. B. 1904; m. 1928, Hilda Clement. A Miner. Member of Durham County Council 1944-50 and formerly of Sedgefield Rural District Council. A Trades Union Official for 20 years. Awarded B.E.M. 1949. Methodist Local Preacher from 1932. Parliamentary Private Secretary to the Rt. Hon. Hugh Gaitskell, MP., and the Rt. Hon. Harold Wilson, MP. when Leader of the Opposition 1960-64. Assistant Postmaster Gen. Oct. 1964-Oct. 1969. Parliamentary Secretary to Ministry of Posts and Telecommunications in

Oct. 1969. A Labour Member. Elected for the Sedgefield division of Durham in Feb. 1950 and sat until he retired in 1970. Created Baron Slater (Life Peerage) 1970. Died 21 Apr. 1977. [1970]

SLOAN, Alexander. Kerse Cottage, Rankinston, Ayrshire. S. of John Sloan, Esq., Ironstone Miner, of Rankinston, Ayrshire. B. 2 Nov. 1879. Conscientious objector in First World War. Member of Ayrshire. County Council 1919. Secretary of Ayrshire Miners' Union and from 1936 to 1940 of National Union of Scottish Mineworkers. A Labour Member. Unsuccessfully contested Ayrshire N. and Bute in May 1929 and Oct. 1931. Elected for S. Ayrshire 20 Apr. 1939 and sat until his death on 16 Nov. 1945. [1945]

SMALL, William Watson. House of Commons, London. S. of Edward Small, Esq., of Lochee. B. 1909; m. 18 July 1941, Isobel, d. of Matthew Murphy, Esq., of Stevenston, Ayrshire. Educ. at Elementary School. Member of Ayr County Council from 1945-51. J.P. 1950. Parliamentary Private Secretary to Rt. Hon. F. Lee, Minister of Power 1964-66, Secretary of State for the Colonies 1966-67, and to Chancellor of Duchy of Lancaster 1967-Oct. 1969. A Labour Member. Sat for the Scotstoun division of Glasgow from 1959 to Feb. 1974. Elected for the Garscadden division of Glasgow in Feb. 1974 and sat until his death on 18 Jan. 1978. [1978]

SMILES, Lieut.-Col. Sir Walter Dorling, C.I.E., D.S.O. Portavo, Donaghadee, Co. Down. Carlton. S. of William Holmes Smiles, Esq., of Belfast. B. 8 Nov. 1883; m. 1 Oct. 1917, Margaret, d. of George Heighway, Esq., of Manchester. Educ. at Rossall School. Commander late R.N.V.R. and Lieut.-Col. Machine Gun Corps, served overseas 1915-19 D.S.O. 1916. M.L.C. Assam 1922-30; Chairman of Assam branch of Indian Tea Association 1923-28, of Moran Tea Company and of other Companies. President of Belfast Chamber of Commerce 1945. C.I.E. 1925. Knight Bach 1930; Parliamentary Private Secretary to Sir Hugh O'Neill, Parliamentary Under-Secretary of State for India and Burma Sept. 1939-May 1940, and to Rt. Hon. L.S. Amery, Secretary of State for India and Burma June-Dec. 1940; Chairman of Area Board Northern Ireland 1941; High Sheriff 1943 and Dept.-Lieut. Co. Down 1946. Member of Parliamentary Delegation to South Africa 1944, and to Roumania 1947. Had Order of the Crown of Roumania and other foreign decorations. An Ulster Unionist Member. Sat for Blackburn as a Conservative from 1931-45 and for Co. Down from 1945-50. Elected for the N. division of Co. Down in Feb. 1950 and sat until 31 Jan. 1953, when he was drowned in the sinking of M.V. *Princess Victoria*. Chairman of Ulster Unionist Parliamentary Party 1952-53. Succeeded as Member for N.Down by his daughter, Mrs Patricia Ford. Died 31 Jan. 1953.   [1953]

SMITH, The Rt. Hon. Sir Benjamin, K.B.E. Transport House, Smith Square, London. S. of Richard Smith, Esq. B. 29 Jan. 1878; m. 1st, 1899, Mildred Ellen, d. of C. Edison, Esq., of Peckham (she died 1959); 2ndly, 1961, Gertrude Elizabeth, d. E.A. Lacey, Esq. Member of Middlesex County Council 1918-22. Gen. Organiser of the Transport and General Workers' Union; member of London Traffic Advisory Committee; Vice-Chairman of Roads Safety Committee; Alderman of Bermondsey Borough Council 1926-43; a Labour Whip June 1925. Treasurer of Royal Household June 1929-Aug. 1931. Parliamentary Secretary Ministry of Aircraft Production Mar. 1942-Nov. 1943; Minister of Food July 1945-May 1946. Minister resident in Washington Nov. 1943-May 1945. PC. 1943; K.B.E. 1945. A Labour Member. Member for Rotherhithe division of Bermondsey from 1923-31, when he was defeated, and from 1935 until Sept. 1946, when he resigned on appointment as Chairman of the W. Midlands Coal Board (retired 1950). Died 5 May 1964.   [1946]

SMITH, Capt. Charles George Percy. 33 Brookfield, West Hill, London. S. of Charles Smith, Esq., Wine Merchant, of Windsor. B. 25 Apr. 1917; m. 26 Dec. 1939, Margaret, d. of Frederick Hando, Esq., of Newport, Monmouth (she was created

Baroness Delacourt-Smith of Alteryn 1974). Educ. at Windsor County Boys School, and Wadham Coll., Oxford. A Trade Union Officer. Served in R.E. and R.A.S.C. 1939-45, mentioned in despatches. Assistant Secretary of Civil Service Clerical Association 1939-53. Parliamentary Private Secretary to Rt. Hon. P. Noel-Baker, Secretary of State for Commonwealth Relations Nov. 1947-Feb. 1949. A Labour Member. Elected for the Colchester division of Essex in July 1945 and sat until 1950, when he was defeated. General Secretary of Post Office Engineering Union 1953-69 and 1970-72. Chairman of Staffside of Civil Service National Whitley Council 1962-64. Member of British Airports Authority 1965-69. Created Baron Delacourt-Smith (Life Peerage) 1967. Minister of State, Ministry of Technology Oct. 1969-June 1970. PC. 1969. President of Postal Telegraph and Telephone Workers' International 1969. Adviser to Prison Officers Asociation 1956-69. J.P. for County of London. Died 2 Aug. 1972.   [1950]

SMITH, Cyril. 14 Emma Street, Rochdale Lancashire. National Liberal. S. of Eva Smith. B. 28 June 1928. Unmarried. Educ. at Rochdale Grammar School. In the Civil Service 1945-50. Liberal Party Agent, Stockport 1948-50. Labour Party Agent Ashton-under-Lyne and Heywood and Royton 1950-54. Member of Rochdale Borough Council 1952-74 and Rochdale Metropolitan District Council 1973-75. Newsagent 1954-58. Production Manager 1958-63. Managing Director Smith Springs (Rochdale) Limited 1963. Mayor of Rochdale 1966-67. Rejoined Liberal Party 1967. Formerly Chief Whip of the Liberal Party, resigned Mar. 1976. Liberal spokesman on Employment 1976, Mar.-Oct. 1977 and from 1978. M.B.E. 1966. A Unitarian. Dept. Liberal Whip 1974-75, Chief Whip 1975-76. Liberal spokesman on Social Services 1976-77 and on Industry from 1979. Author of *Big Cyril* and *Industrial Participation*. A Unitarian. A Liberal. Unsuccessfully contested Rochdale in 1970. Sat for Rochdale from Oct. 1972.*   [1979]

SMITH, Dudley Gordon. Hunningham Hill, Hunningham, Nr. Leamington Spa,

Warwickshire. S. of Hugh William Smith, Esq., Business Manager. B. 14 Nov. 1926; m. 1st, 1958, Anthea Higgins (marriage dissolved in 1974), (1 s. 2 d.); 2ndly, 1976, Catherine, d. of Mr. and Mrs. Thomas Amos. Educ. at Chichester High School. A Management Consultant. Divisional Director Beecham Group Limited 1966-70. First biographer of Harold Wilson 1964. Assistant News Editor *Sunday Express* 1953-59. Member Middlesex County Council 1958-65; Chief Whip of Majority Party 1961-63. Vice-Chairman Southgate Conservative Association 1958-59. Gov. of Mill Hill and North London Collegiate Schools. Parliamentary Private Secretary to Robert Carr, Secretary for Technical Co-operation 1963-64. Formerly Secretary Conservative Parliamentary Labour Committee. An Opposition Whip 1965-66. An Opposition Front Bench spokesman on Employment and Productivity 1969-70. Under-Secretary of State Department of Employment June 1970-Jan. 1974. Under-Secretary of State for Defence for Army Jan.-Mar. 1974. Promoted Town and Country Planning (Amendment) Act 1977. Vice-Chairman Parliamentary Select Committee on Race Relations and Immigration. Chairman United and Cecil Club 1975. A Conservative. Unsuccessfully contested Peckham in 1955. Sat for Brentford and Chiswick division from 1959 until he was defeated in 1966. Elected for the Warwick and Leamington division of Warwickshire at a by-election in Mar. 1968.* [1979]

SMITH, Edward Percy. Rysings, Stone-in-Oxney, Tenterden, Kent. Garrick, and Constitutional. S. of Benjamin Figgis Smith, Esq., Miller and Corn Merchant. B. 5 Jan. 1891; m. 1st, 1918, Gertrude Ethel, d. of Sir Richard Glazebrook, K.C.B., K.C.V.O. (divorced 1951); 2ndly, 1951, Mrs. Lilian Mary Denham. Educ. at Haileybury Coll., and in France. An East Indian and Colonial Broker 1910-30, a Miller and Corn Merchant from 1927. A Dramatist and Writer under the pen name of Edward Percy. Served in R.N.V.R. 1914-18. Vice-President 1923 and President 1924 of General Produce Brokers Association of London. A Conservative. Elected for the Ashford division of Kent in Feb. 1943 and sat until he retired in 1950. Died 27 May 1968. [1950 2nd ed.]

SMITH, Ellis. House of Commons, London. B. at Eccles 4 Nov. 1896; m. 1922, Edith Thornley. Educ. at Council Schools, and Labour Coll. Served in 1st World War in S. Lancashire, M.G. Corps and Tank Corps. President of Lancashire and Cheshire Trades Councils 1930-63. J.P. for Lancashire; Secretary of Eccles Trades Council 1925-35. Parliamentary Secretary Board of Trade Aug. 1945-Jan. 1946; Gen. President United Patternmakers' Association 1946-63. A Labour Member. Unsuccessfully contested the Stoke division of Stoke-on-Trent in 1931. Sat for the Stoke division of Stoke-on-Trent from 1935-50 and for the S. division of Stoke-on-Trent from Feb. 1950 until he retired in 1966. Died 7 Nov. 1969. [1966]

SMITH, Eric Martin. 65 Cornhill, London. Codicote Lodge, Hitchin. S. of Everard Martin Smith, Esq. B. 28 Dec. 1908; m. 1st, 1931, Joan, d. of J. Surtees, Esq. (she died 1937); 2ndly, 4 May 1940, Elizabeth, d. of Maj. A. Morrison. Educ. at Eton, and Pembroke Coll., Cambridge. Amateur golf champion of England 1931. Served with 4th County of London Yeomanry 1939-41. A Private Banker and Discount Agent. Director of Smith, St. Aubyn and Company Limited, and British Continental Banking Company Limited. A Conservative. Elected for the Grantham division of Lincolnshire, Parts of Kesteven and Ruthlandshire in Feb. 1950 and sat until his death on 13 Aug. 1951. [1951]

SMITH, Geoffrey Johnson. See JOHNSON SMITH, Geoffrey.

SMITH, Henry Norman. 10 Kennington Palace Court, Sancroft Street, London. S. of Enoch Smith, Esq., of Swindon. B. 31 Jan. 1890; m. 14 Feb. 1922, Clare, d. of Joseph Ody, Esq., of Eastcourt, Wiltshire. Educ. at Swindon High School, and Coll. Served in France with B.E.F. 1914-18. A Journalist. With *The Daily Herald* 1919-30 and 1944-45. Co-operative Press 1930-44. Author of *The Politics of Plenty*. A Co-operative and Labour Member. Unsuccessfully contested the Faversham division of Kent in 1931 and 1935. Elected for Nottingham S. in July 1945 and sat until 1955, when he was defeated. Died 21 Dec. 1962. [1954]

SMITH, Rt. Hon. John. 21 Cluny Drive, Edinburgh. S. of Archibald L. Smith, Esq., Headmaster. B. 13 Sept. 1938; m. 5 July 1967, Elizabeth Margaret, d. of Frederick Bennett, Esq., (3 d.). Educ. at Dunoon Grammar School, and Glasgow University. Graduated M.A. and LL.B. Glasgow University. A Solicitor in Glasgow for three years. Called to the Scottish bar in 1967. Chairman Glasgow University Labour Club 1960. Winner, Observer Mace National Debating Tournament 1962. Voted in favour of entry to E.E.C. on 28 Oct. 1971. Parliamentary Private Secretary to Rt. Hon. William Ross, Secretary of State for Scotland Mar. 1974-Oct. 1974. Parliamentary Under-Secretary of State, Department of Energy Oct. 1974-Dec. 1975. Minister of State, Department of Energy Dec. 1975-Apr. 1976. Minister of State, Privy Council Office Apr. 1976-Nov. 1978. PC. 1978. Secretary of State for Trade Nov. 1978-May 1979. Member of Parliamentary Committee of P.L.P. from 1979. Opposition spokesman on Trade, Prices and Consumer Protection from 1979. A Labour Member. Unsuccessfully contested E. Fife in 1961 and 1964. Elected for Lanarkshire N. in June 1970.* [1979]

SMITH, John Lindsay Eric. 1 Smith Square, London. Pratt's, Beefsteak, and Brooks's. S. of Capt. E.C.E. Smith, LL.D., M.C. B. 3 Apr. 1923; m. 5 Jan. 1952 Christian, d. of Col. U.E.C. Carnegy, D.S.O., M.C. Educ. at Eton, and New Coll., Oxford. Served with R.N.V.R. 1942-46. A Director of Coutts and Company, of Rolls-Royce Limited, and S. Pearson Publishers Limited. Member National Trust Executive from 1952; member Standing Commission on Museums and Galleries 1957-65. J.P. for Berkshire 1964. A Conservative. Elected for the Cities of London and Westminster at a by-election in Nov. 1965 and sat until he retired in 1970. Dept. Governor of Royal Exchange Assurance 1961-66. High Steward of Maidenhead 1966-75. Member of Historic Buildings Council 1971-78 and Redundant Churches Fund 1972-74. Fellow of Eton Coll. from 1974. C.B.E. 1975. Lord-Lieut. of Berkshire 1975-78, Dept. Lieut. from 1978, Fellow of Society of Antiquaries. Honorary Fellow of Royal Institute of British Architects.* [1970]

SMITH, Sydney Herbert. 757 Hessle Road, Hull. S. of Charles Edward Smith, Esq., of Woodbridge, Suffolk. Educ. at Ruskin Coll. Oxford and St. Catherine's Society, University of Oxford. Hons. Graduate Oxford, M.A. A Newsagent, Stationer and Bookseller. Member of Hull City Council from 1923 to 1970; Lord Mayor of Hull 1940-41. Oxford University Representative on Hymers Coll. Hull Governors: Representative Gov. of Sheffield University and Hull U. Coll. Director of *National Newsagent*. A Labour Member. Elected for Hull S.W. in July 1945 and sat until he retired in 1950. Honorary LL.D. University of Hull 1967.* [1950]

SMITH, Timothy John. 19 Albany Mansions, Albert Bridge Road, London. S. of Capt. N.W. Smith, C.B.E. B. 5 Oct. 1947. Educ. at Harrow, and St. Peter's Coll., Oxford. President Oxford University Conservative Association 1968. A Chartered Accountant. Secretary for Coubro and Scrutton (Holdings) Limited. Secretary Conservative Prices and Consumer Protection Committee 1977-78. Chairman Coningsby Club 1977-78. A Conservative. Elected for Ashfield in Apr. 1977 and Sat until 1979, when he was defeated.* [1979]

SMITH, Tom. 16 Marlborough Road, Doncaster. S. of Samuel Smith, Esq., of Sheffield. B. 24 Apr. 1886; m. 27 Mar. 1920, Lily, d. of Tom Ryder, Esq., of Balfour Road, Sheffield. A Miners' Checkweighman from 1916. Member of Sheffield Board of Guardians for 10 years. Assistant Secretary Yorkshire Miners' Association 1925-29; Parliamentary Private Secretary to Ben Turner June 1929, to E. Shinwell 1924 and 1930, and to David Grenfell June 1940-41, successfully Parliamentary Secretaries for Mines. Joint Parliamentary Secretary Ministry of Fuel and Power June 1942-May 1945. A Labour Member. Elected for Pontefract division from Nov. 1922 to Oct. 1924, when he was defeated, and May 1929-Oct. 1931, when he was again defeated. Member for the Normanton division of Yorkshire from May 1933 until Oct. 1946, when he was appointed Labour Director of N.E. Coal Board. C.B.E. 1946. Labour Director of North Eastern division of National Coal Board 1946-53. Died 27 Feb. 1953. [1946]

SMITHERS, Lieut.-Commander Peter Henry Berry Otway, R.N.V.R., V.R.D., D.Phil. Colebrook House, Winchester. Carlton. S. of Lieut.-Col. H.O. Smithers, of Itchen Stoke House, Hampshire. B. 9 Dec. 1913; m. 8 June 1943, Dojean, d. of Thomas M. Sayman, Esq., of St. Louis, Missouri. Educ. at Harrow, and Magdalen Coll., Oxford, (Demyship and 1st Class Honours), D.Phil. Barrister-at-Law, Inner Temple, 1936. London Division R.N.V.R. 1937-58. V.R.D. with clasp. Assistant Naval Attaché, British Embassy, Washington; Acting Naval Attaché, Mexico, and British Legations, Central American Republics and Panama. Winchester Rural District Council 1946-49; Parliamentary Private Secretary to Rt. Hon Henry Hopkinson, Minister of State for the Colonies 1952-55 and to Rt. Hon. Alan Lennox-Boyd, Secretary of State for the Colonies 1956-59. Delegate Council of Europe 1952-56 and 1960-61. Delegate General Assembly United Nations 1960-62. Chairman Conservative Overseas Bureau 1956-60. Joint Vice-Chairman Conservative Parliamentary Foreign Affairs Committee 1959-62. Chev. Legion of Honour 1957. Parliamentary Under-Secretary of State, Foreign Office July 1962-Jan. 1964. A Conservative. Elected for the Winchester division of Hampshire in Feb. 1950 and sat until Jan. 1964, when he resigned on appointment as Secretary-Gen. of the Council of Europe, 1964-69. Senior Research Fellow, U.N. Institute for Training and Research 1969-72. Knighted 1970. General Rapporteur, European Conference of Parliamentarians and Scientists from 1970, Biographer of Joseph Addison.* [1964]

SMITHERS, Sir Waldron. Shelleys, Knockholt, Kent. S. of Sir Alfred Waldron Smithers, MP. for Chislehurst 1918-22. B. 5 Oct. 1880; m. 17 Sept. 1904, Marjory Prudence, d. of Rev. F. Page Roberts, Rector of Strathfieldsaye. Educ. at Arlington, Brighton, and Charterhouse. Served in Cavalry 1914-18. J.P. for Kent. Member of London Stock Exchange. Knight Bach. 1934. A Conservative. Sat for the Chislehurst division of Kent from 1924 to 1945. Elected for the Orpington division of Kent in July 1945 and sat until his death on 9 Dec. 1954. [1954]

SMYTH, Brigadier Rt. Hon. Sir John George, Bart., V.C., M.C. 807 Nelson House, Dolphin Square, London. S. of W.J. Smyth, Esq., I.C.S., of Teignmouth. B. 24 Oct. 1893; m. 1st, 1920, Margaret, d. of Charles Dundas, Esq; I.C.S. (divorced 1940); 2ndly, 1940, Frances Read, d. of Lieut.-Col. R.A. Chambers, O.B.E. Educ. at Repton, and Sandhurst. Author and Journalist. Served in both World Wars and in several campaigns on the Indian Frontier. V.C. 1915, M.C. 1920. Holds Russian Order of St. George and was six times mentioned in depatches. In 1939-45 War, commanded a Brigade at Dunkirk, raised 19th (Dagger) Division and commanded 17th Division against the Japanese in Burma. Comptroller Royal Alexandra and Albert School for Orphans and Necessitous Children 1946-63. Had been Military Correspondent to several national newspapers. Lawn Tennis Correspondent *Sunday Times* 1946-51, and of *News of the World* 1956-57. First Chairman V.C. Association 1956. President D.C.M. League 1958. Honorary Vice-President Far Eastern P.O.W. Federation 1960. Master Worshipful Company of Farriers 1961-62. Parliamentary Secretary Ministry of Pensions Nov. 1951 to the closing of the Ministry in Aug. 1953. Parliamentary Secretary Ministry of Pensions and National Insurance Sept. 1953-Dec. 1955. A Conservative. Unsuccessfully contested Wandsworth Central in 1945. Elected for the Norwood division of Lambeth in Feb. 1950 and sat until he retired in 1966. Created Bart. 1955. PC. 1962.* [1966]

SNADDEN, William McNair. The Coldoch, Blair Drummond, by Stirling. Carlton, New (Edinburgh), and Royal & Ancient. S. of the Rev. James Snadden, M.A., of Newcastleton, Roxburghshire. B. 15 Jan. 1896; m. 27 Mar. 1919, Lesley, d. of Thomas Henderson, Esq., of Argaty, Doune, Perthshire. Educ. at Dollar Academy. J.P. for Perthshire. Served overseas 1915-17 with 51st Division. Vice-Chairman Conservative Party Agricultural Committee 1945-51; Parliamentary Private Secretary to Capt. John McEwen, Sept. 1939-May 1940, and to Capt. H.J. Scrymgeour-Wedderburn Feb. 1941-Mar. 1942, when Parliamentary Under-Secretaries of State for Scotland. Joint Parliamentary Under-Secretary of State for Scotland Nov. 1951-June 1955. A Conservative. Elected for the Kinross and West Perthshire division of Perthshire and Kinross-shire in Dec. 1938 and sat until he retired in 1955. Created Bart. June 1955. Chairman of Scottish Food Hygiene Council. Died 23 Nov. 1959. [1954]

SNAPE, Peter Charles. House of Commons, London. S. of Thomas Snape, Esq. B. Feb. 1942; m. 1963, Winifred, d. of Evelyn Grimshaw, Esq., (2 d.). Educ. at St. Joseph's School, Stockport. A Railwayman 1957-60. Regular Soldier R.E. and R.C.T. 1960-66. Goods Guard British Railways 1966-70; Clerical Officer British Railways 1970-74. Member Bredbury and Romiley Urban District Council 1971-74, and Chairman Finance Committee. Assistant Government Whip Nov. 1975-Nov. 1977. Delegate to Council of Europe and W.E.U. May-Nov. 1975. Lord Commissioner of Treasury Nov. 1977-May 1979. An Opposition spokesman on Defence from 1979. A Roman Catholic. A Labour Member. Elected for West Bromwich E. in Feb. 1974.* [1979]

SNOW, Julian Ward. House of Commons, London. S. of H.M. Snow, Esq., C.V.O., of Chislehurst. B. 24 Feb. 1910; m. 1948, Flavia, d. of Sir Ralph Blois, 9th Bart., of Cockfield Hall, Yoxford, Surfolk (she died 1980). Educ. at Haileybury, and La Sorbonne. With Dunlop Rubber Company Limited in India and E. Africa 1930-37; with John Lewis and Company 1937-39. Served with R.A. 1939-45. Member of Union of Shop, Distributive and Allied Workers; a member of the National Union of Agricultural Workers. Vice-Chamberlain of the Household Aug. 1945-Dec. 1946; a Lord Commissioner of the Treasury Dec. 1946-Mar. 1950; Government Whip 1945-50; Vice-President of the British-Japanese Parliamentary Group. Parliamentary Secretary Ministry of Aviation from Apr. 1966-Jan. 1967. Parliamentary Secretary Ministry of Health from Jan. 1967-Nov. 1968. Under-Secretary of State, Department of Health and Social Security Nov. 1968-Oct. 1969. A Labour Member. Sat for Central Portsmouth from July 1945 to Feb. 1950. Elected for the Lichfield and Tamworth

division of Staffordshire in Feb. 1950 and sat until he retired in 1970. Created Baron Burntwood (Life Peerage) 1970.* [1970]

SOAMES, Rt. Hon. (Arthur) Christopher John, C.B.E. Hamsell Manor, Eridge, Nr. Tunbridge Wells, Kent. Carlton, and White's. S. of Capt. A.G. Soames, O.B.E., of Sheffield Park, Uckfield, Sussex. B. 1920; m. 11 Feb. 1947, Mary, d. of Rt. Hon. Sir Winston Churchill, K.G., O.M., C.H., MP. Educ. at Eton, and Royal Military Coll., Sandhurst. Capt. Coldstream Guards. Served in France, Italy and Middle East 1939-45. Assistant Military Attache, Paris 1946-47. Has French Croix de Guerre. Parliamentary Private Secretary to the Prime Minister 1952-55; Parliamentary Under-Secretary of State Air Ministry Dec. 1955-Jan. 1957; Parliamentary and Financial Secretary to the Admiralty Jan. 1957-Jan. 1958; Secretary of State for War Jan. 1958-July 1960; Minister of Agriculture July 1960-Oct. 1964. Opposition spokesman on Agriculture 1964-65, on Defence 1965 and on Foreign Affairs 1965-66. Member of Shadow Cabinet 1964-66. C.B.E. 1955; PC. 1958. A Conservative. Elected for the Bedford division of Bedfordshire in Feb. 1950 and sat until 1966, when he was defeated. Director of Decca Ltd. and James Hole & Co. Ltd. 1964-68. Ambassador to France 1968-72. G.C.V.O. 1972. G.C.M.G. 1972. Vice President of the Commission of the European Communities 1973-77. Director of N.M. Rothschild & Sons Ltd. 1977-79 and National Westminster Bank 1978-79. Created Baron Soames (Life Peerage) 1978. Lord President of the Council and Leader of House of Lords from May 1979. Governor of Southern Rhodesia Dec. 1979-Apr. 1980. C.H. 1980.* [1966]

SOLLEY, Leslie Judah. 30 Heathcroft, Hampstead Way, London. 6 Pump Court, Temple, London. S. of Emmanuel Solley, Esq. B. 15 Dec. 1905; m. 12 Mar. 1944, Jose Olga, d. of Leopold Fisher, Esq. (divorced 1964). Educ. at London County Council Elementary School, and University of London, B.Sc. Barrister-at-Law, Inner Temple, 1934. Originally a Research Physicist. Honorary Treasurer of League for Democracy in Greece. An Independent Labour Party

Member. Elected for the Thurrock division of Essex in July 1945 as a Labour Member and sat until 1950, when he unsuccessfully contested the seat as an Independent Labour candidate. Expelled from the Labour Party in May 1949. Member of the Labour Independent Group 1949-50. Subsequently, re-admitted to the Labour Party. Vice-President of Songwriters Guild of Great Britain. Died 8 Jan. 1968. [1950]

SOLOMONS, Henry. 9 Flanchford Road, Stamford Brook, London. S. of Benjamin Solomons, Esq. B. 7 Nov. 1902; m. 1939, Anne, d. of Nathan Bass, Esq. Educ. at Secondary School. Sales Office Manager. Member of the Labour Party from 1932. Chairman of London Divisional Council U.S.D.A.W. (joined 1932). Member of London Co-operative Party from 1932. Member Fabian Society. Former Executive member London Labour Party, and London Trades Council 1952-60. Member Stepney Borough Council 1934-39. Served in the Army 1939-45. Organising Secretary, Union of Liberal and Progressive Synagogues 1946-54. Member Hammersmith Borough Council 1953-64. Officer of U.S.D.A.W. 1954-64. A Labour Member. Elected for Kingston-upon-Hull N. in Oct. 1964 and sat until his death on 7 Nov. 1965. [1965]

SOREF, Harold Benjamin. 125 Beaufort Mansions, London. 35 Chiswell Street, London. Carlton, Reform, 1900, and P.E.N. S. of Paul Soref, Merchant Shipper. B. 18 Dec. 1916. Educ. at St. Paul's School, and The Queen's Coll., Oxford. Elected Delegate first and only All-British Africa Conference to form Africa Defence Federation 1937; served in Royal Scots and Intelligence Corps 1940-46; founder member Conservative Commonwealth Council; Council Anglo-Rhodesian Society and Anglo-Zanzibar Society: Executive Council Monday Club; Managing Director Soref Brothers Limited 1959, Chairman 1976. Author of *The Puppeteers*, and part Author of *The War of 1939*. Voted against entry to E.E.C. on 28 Oct. 1971. A Conservative. Unsuccessfully contested Dudley in 1951 and Rugby in 1955. Elected for the Ormskirk division of Lancashire in June 1970 and sat until Feb. 1974, when he was defeated.* [1974]

SORENSEN, Reginald William. 38 Woodside Park Avenue, Walthamstow, London. S. of William James Sorensen, Esq., of Highbury, London. B. 19 June 1891; m. 1916, Muriel, d. of Rev. W. Harvey Smith. Ex-Minister of Free Christian Church, Walthamstow. Member of Walthamston Urban District Council 1921-24. Essex County Councillor 1924-45; Freeman of Leyton 1958. Chairman National Peace Council, United World Trust, India League, World Congress of Faiths, Gandhi Memorial Fund, Tagore India Centre. President London Brahmo-Somaj; Vice-President International Friendship League; Treasurer of Indo-British and British-U.A.R. Parliamentary Groups. A Labour Member. Unsuccessfully contested Southampton in 1923 and 1924. Sat for Leyton W. from 1929 to 1931, when he was defeated, and from 1935 to 1950. Unsuccessfully contested the Lowestoft division of Suffock in Feb. 1934. Sat for Leyton from 1950 until Dec. 1964, when he was created Baron Sorensen (Life Peerage). Lord-in-Waiting and Government Whip in House of Lords Dec. 1964-Apr. 1968. Treasurer of Help the Aged. Died 8 Oct. 1971. [1964]

SOSKICE, Rt. Hon. Sir Frank, Q.C. 1 Harcourt Buildings, Temple, London. Garrick. S. of David Soskice, Esq. B. 23 July 1902; m. 1940, Susan, d. of William Hunter, Esq. Educ. at St. Paul's School, and Balliol Coll., Oxford. Served 1940-45 with Army. Barrister-at-Law, Inner Temple, 1926; K.C. 1945. Knight Bach. 1945. Solicitor Gen. Aug. 1945-Apr. 1951. PC. 1948. Attorney Gen. Apr.-Oct. 1951. Member of P.L.P. Parliamentary Committee 1952-55 and 1956-64. Opposition spokesman on Legal Affairs 1957-64. Home Secretary Oct. 1964-Dec. 1965. Lord Privy Seal Dec. 1965-Apr. 1966. A Labour Member. Sat for Birkenhead E. from July 1945 to Feb. 1950, when he unsuccessfully contested Bebington. Sat for the Neepsend division of Sheffield from Apr. 1950 to May 1955, when he retired after failing to gain the nomination for the Gorton division of Manchester. Elected for Newport in July 1956 and sat until he retired in 1966. Created Baron Stow Hill (Life Peerage) 1966. Treasurer of Inner Temple 1968. Died 1 Jan. 1979. [1966]

SOUTHBY, Commander Sir Archibald Richard James, Bart., R.N. Burford Priory, Oxfordshire. Carlton, and R.Y.S. S. of Richard Southby, Esq., of Hodcott, and Chieveley, Berkshire, and Hon. Isabella Hewitt, d. of James, 4th Visct. Lifford. B. 8 July 1886; m. 1st, 20 July 1909, Phyllis Mary, d. of Charles H. Garton, Esq., of Banstead Wood, Surrey (divorced 1962); 2ndly, 1962, Norean Vera, d. of B. Compton Simm, Esq. Educ. at Brandon House School, Cheltenham, and H.M.S. *Britannia.* Joined R.N. 1901, Commander 1919, retired 1920. Served as Flag Lieut. to Admiral Hon. Sir Alexander Bethell on E. Indies Station 1912-13, as Flag Lieut. and Flag Lieut.-Commander to Sir Montague Browning, Home Fleet, Grand Fleet and N. America and W. Indies Station 1913-18, and on Allied Naval Armistice Commission and Naval Inter-allied Commission of Control 1918-20; Chevalier of Legion of Honour. Assistant Government Whip Nov. 1931; a Junior Lord of the Treasury Apr. 1935-May 1937. Bart. 1937. A Conservative. MP. for the Epsom division of Surrey from July 1928 until he resigned in Nov. 1947. Dept.-Lieut. for Surrey. J.P. Surrey and Oxfordshire. Died 30 Oct. 1969.

[1947]

SPARKS, Joseph Alfred. 10 Emanuel Avenue, Acton, London. S. of Samuel Sparks, Esq. B. 30 Sept. 1901; m. 1928, Dora Brent. Educ. at Central Labour Coll. A Railway Clerk. Alderman Acton Borough Council and Mayor 1957-58. President London District Council National Union of Railwaymen 1935-45. Alderman Middlesex County Council; Labour Whip 1950-51. A Labour Member. Unsuccessfully contested Taunton in 1929, Chelmsford in 1931 and Buckingham in 1935. Elected for Acton in July 1945 and sat until 1959, when he was defeated.* [1959]

SPEARING, Nigel John. House of Commons, London. S. of Austen Spearing, Esq. B. 8 Oct. 1930; m. 1956, Wendy, d. of Percy and Molly Newman, of Newport, (1 s. 2 d.). Educ. at Latymer Upper School, Hammersmith, and St. Catharine's Coll, Cambridge. Served in Royal Signals 1950-52. A Teacher LCC-ILEA 1957-70. Co-opted member Greater London Council Committees 1966-73. Secretary P.L.P. Education Group and All-Party Waterways Group 1970-74. Member Select Committee on Overseas Development 1973-74 and 1977. Select Committee on Members' Interests 1974-75. Select Committee on Procedure 1975-78. Chairman Safeguard Britain Campaign 1977. A Labour Member. Unsuccessfully contested Warwick and Leamington in 1964. Sat for Acton from 1970 to Feb. 1974, when he unsuccessfully contested the Acton division of Ealing. Elected for Newham S. in May 1974.* [1979]

SPEARMAN, Sir Alexander Cadwallader Mainwaring. 32 Queen Anne's Gate, London. Fealar, Enochdhu, Blairgowrie. S. of Commander A.Y.C.M. Spearman, R.N. B. 2 Mar. 1901; m. 1st, 11 Aug. 1928, Diana Violet Edith Constance, d. of Col. Sir Arthur Doyle, 4th Bart. (marriage dissolved 1951); 2ndly, 27 Apr. 1951 Diana Josephine, d. of Sir Lambert Ward, Bart., MP. Educ. at Repton and Hertford Coll., Oxford. Joint Parliamentary Private Secretary to the Rt. Hon. Peter Thorneycroft, President of the Board of Trade 1951-52. Knight Bach. 1956. A Conservative. Unsuccessfully contested the Mansfield division of Nottinghamshire in Nov. 1935 and the Gorton division of Manchester in Feb. 1937. Elected for the Scarborough and Whitby division of the N. Riding of Yorkshire in Sept. 1941 and sat until he retired in 1966.* [1966]

SPEED, (Herbert) Keith. Strood House, Rolvenden, Cranbrook, Kent. St. Stephen's. S. of Herbert Victor Speed, Esq., Director. B. 11 Mar. 1934; m. 14 Oct. 1961, Peggy Voss Clarke, (3 s. 1 deceased 1 d.). Educ. at Greenhill, Evesham, Bedford Modern, and Royal Naval Colls., Dartmouth and Greenwich. Officer Royal Navy 1947-56. Administrative Assistant H.J. Heinz and Company 1956-57; Marketing Manager 1957-65. Conservative Research Department 1965-68. Assistant Government Whip June 1970-Nov. 1971. Lord Commissioner of Treasury Nov. 1971-Apr. 1972. Under-Secretary of State, Department of the Environment Apr. 1972-Mar. 1974. Opposition spokesman on Local Government Feb. 1975-Nov. 1977 and on

Home Affairs Nov. 1977-May 1979. Under-Secretary of State for Defence for Royal Navy from May 1979. Consultant, Rank-Hovis-McDougall Limited. A Conservative. Sat for Meriden from Mar. 1968 to Feb. 1974, when he was defeated. Elected for Ashford in Oct. 1974.* [1979]

SPEIR, Sir Rupert Malise. 240 Cranmer Court, Sloane Avenue, London. Birtley Hall, Wark, Nr. Hexham, Northumberland. Brooks's. S. of Lieut.-Col. Guy Thomas Speir. B. 10 Sept. 1910. Educ. at Eton, and Pembroke Coll., Cambridge. Solicitor 1936; served in the Army (Lieut.-Col.). Parliamentary Private Secretary to A. Noble, Parliamentary and Financial Secretary and to S. Wingfield Digby, Civil Lord, Admiralty 1952-56; Parliamentary Private Secretary to A Noble, Under-Secretary Commonwealth Relations Office to Nov. 1956, and when Minister of State for Foreign Affairs Nov. 1956-Jan. 1959. Sponsor of The Litter Act 1958, The Noise Abatement Act 1960, The Diesel Fumes Bill 1962 and The Local Government (Financial Provisions) Act 1963. Chairman Crossley Building Products Limited 1953; Director Venner Limited, Matthew Hall Limited, Hellenic and General Trust, U.K. Provident Association, Smith's Potato Crisps Limited and William France, Fenwick and Company Limited. Special member of Hops Marketing Board from June 1958. Knight Bach. 1964. A Conservative. Unsuccessfully contested Linlithgow in 1945 and Leek in 1950. Elected for the Hexham division of Northumberland in Oct. 1951 and sat until he retired in 1966.* [1966]

SPENCE, Maj. Henry Reginald, O.B.E. 81 Gordon Street, Huntly, Aberdeenshire. Carlton. S. of James Henry Easton Spence, Esq. B. 22 June 1897; m. 1939, Eileen Walter. Principal of a Woollen Manufacturers firm. Served in R.F.C. and R.A.F. 1915-18. Area Commandant of A.T.C. for N.E. Scotland. A Conservative. Sat for Aberdeenshire Central from July 1945 to Feb. 1950 and for Aberdeenshire W. from Feb. 1950 until he retired in 1959.* [1959]

SPENCE, John Deane. House of Commons, London. Greystones, Maltongate, Thornton

Dale, Nr. Pickering, Yorkshire. Constitutional, Carlton, and Royal Automobile. S. of George Spence, Esq., Civil Servant. B. 7 Dec. 1920; m. 1944, Hester, d. of H. Nicholson. Esq. Educ. at Queen's University, Belfast. A Building and Civil Engineering Contractor; Director of various companies associated with the construction industry. Past National President of the United Kingdom Commercial Travellers' Association; Honorary Secretary Yorkshire Conservative Members Group; Honorary Secretary Back Bench Industry Committee 1971-72. Parliamentary Private Secretary to Rt. Hon. Graham Page, Minister for Local Government and Development 1971-74. Member Select Committee on Nationalised Industries 1974. Member of National Farmers' Union; Country Landowners Association, Yorkshire; Derwent Trust; and Anglo-Israel Friendship Society. Joint Secretary Conservative Back Bench Agriculture Committee 1974-75. Mr. Speaker's Panel of Chairman 1974. A Conservative. Unsuccessfully contested Wakefield in 1964 and the Heeley division of Sheffield in 1966. Sat for the Heeley division of Sheffield from 1970 to Feb. 1974. Elected for Thirsk and Malton in Feb. 1974.* [1979]

SPENCER-NAIRN, Douglas Leslie Spencer. House of Commons, London. S. of Sir Robert Spencer Nairn, 1st Bart. Assumed the surname of Spencer-Nairn in lieu of Nairn 1928. B. 1906; m. 1st, 1931 Elizabeth Livingston, d. of A.J. Henderson, Esq. (divorced 1946); 2ndly 1947 Louise, d. of Frederick Vester, Esq. Educ. at Shrewsbury and Trinity Hall, Cambridge. Commissioned in Black Watch and served as Staff Officer in the Middle East in the Second World War. Farmed in S. Rhodesia after the war, returning in 1954. Member of Fife County Council 1934-39. Parliamentary Private Secretary to J.C. Rodgers, Parliamentary Secretary to Board of Trade 1958-59. A Conservative. Elected for the Central Ayrshire division of Ayrshire and Bute in 1955 and sat until 1959, when he was defeated. Succeeded as Bart. 1960. Died 8 Nov. 1970. [1959]

SPENS, Rt. Hon. Sir William Patrick, K.B.E., Q.C. 12 King's Bench Walk, Temple, London. Carlton. S. of Nathaniel Spens, Esq. B. 9 Aug. 1885; m. 1st, 15 Sept. 1913, Hilda Mary, d. of Lieut.-Col. W.G. Bowyer, of Weston Manor, Olney, Buckinghamshire (she died 1962); 2ndly, 1963, Kathleen Annie Fedden, d. of Roger Dodds, Esq. Educ. at Rugby, and New Coll., Oxford. Barrister-at-Law, Inner Temple, 1911; K.C. 1925; Master of the Bench 1933, Treasurer 1958; Capt. and Adjutant Queen's Royal Regiment, served in India and Mesopotamia 1914-18; O.B.E. (Mil.) 1918; a Director of Southern Railway 1938-43, and of Prudential Assurance Company 1949-61; member of London Committee, The Bank of Scotland; Chief Justice of India 1943-47; Chairman Arbitration Tribunal India 1947-48; member Imperial War Graves Commission 1931-43 and 1949-65. K.St.J. of J. PC. 1953. A Conservative. Unsuccessfully contested St. Pancras S.W. in 1929. Sat for the Ashford division of Kent from Mar. 1933 to Jan. 1943, when he resigned on appointment as Chief Justice of India. Elected for Kensington S. in Feb. 1950 and sat until June 1959, when he was created Baron Spens. Knighted 1943. K.B.E. 1948. Died 15 Nov. 1973.   [1959]

SPICER, James Wilton. Whatley, Beaminster, Dorset. 12 Mary-le-Park Court, Albert Bridge Road, London. Naval and Military. S. of James Spicer, Esq. B. 4 Oct. 1925; m. 30 Jan. 1954, Winifred, d. of Douglas Shanks, Esq. Educ. at Latymer. Served in Royal Fusiliers, King's African Rifles and Parachute Regiment 1943-57, Maj. Member of European Parliament from 1975. Chairman of Conservative Group for Europe 1975-78. Member of European Parliament for Wessex from 1979 and Whip to European Democrat Group. A Conservative. Unsuccessfully contested the Itchen division of Southampton in May 1971. Sat for Dorset W. from Feb. 1974.*   [1979]

SPICER, William Michael Hardy. House of Commons, London. S. of Brigadier L.H. Spicer. B. 22 Jan. 1943; m. 7 Apr. 1967, Patricia Ann, d. of P.S. Hunter, Esq., (1 s. 2 d.). Educ. at Sacre Coeur Vienna, Gaunts House Preparatory School, Wellington Coll., and Emmanuel Coll., Cambridge. Assistant to Editor of The Statist 1964-66. Conservative

Research Department 1966-68. Director Conservative Systems Research Centre 1968-70. Managing Director Economic Models Limited 1970. Parliamentary Private Secretary to Sally Oppenheim and Cecil Parkinson, Minister of State, Department of Trade from 1979. A Conservative. Unsuccessfully contested Easington in 1966 and 1970. Sat for Worcestershire S. from Feb. 1974.*   [1979]

SPRIGGS, Leslie. 38 Knowle Avenue, Thornton Cleveleys, Lancashire. S. of William Spriggs, Esq. B. 22 Apr. 1910; m. 1931 Elfrida Mary Brindle Parkinson. Educ. at Bolton, and the National Council of Labour Colls. Secretary North Fylde Labour Party from 1948. A Merchant Seaman and Railwayman. Official of N.U.R.J.P. for N. Fylde 1955. A Labour Member. Unsuccessfully contested N. Fylde in 1955. Sat for St. Helens from June 1958.*   [1979]

SPROAT, Iain MacDonald. Dhualt House, Nr. Banchory, Kincardineshire. S. of William Sproat, Esq. B. 8 Nov. 1938; m. Judith Kernot. Educ. at Winchester, and Magdalen Coll., Oxford. Chairman of Sproat Group of Companies. A Conservative. Unsuccessfully contested Rutherglen in May and Oct. 1964. Sat for Aberdeen S. from June 1970.*   [1979]

STAINTON, Keith Monin. House of Commons, London. S. of Thomas Stainton, Esq. of Kendal B. 1921; m. 1st, 1946 Vanessa Ann Heald (divorced) (6 children); m. 2ndly, 1980, Frances, d. of Brig. G.L. Easton. Educ. at Kendal School, and Manchester University. (B.A. Commerce). Left school at 14. An Insurance Clerk 1935-39; joined the Royal Navy 1940, commissioned R.N.V.R. in submarines. Awarded the Legion d'Honneur, Croix de Guerre avec Palme and Order de l'Armee in connection with torpedo actions in the Mediterranean. Leader Writer on the Financial Times 1949-52; for three years a member of the National Union of Journalists. An Industrial Consultant 1952-56; from 1956 a Director of various public companies. Chairman of Manchester University Conservative Association, and a founder member of the Bow Group. Member Estimates

Committee, Select Committee on Science and Technology and Expenditure Select Committee 1965. Conservative spokesman on Aviation 1965-66. A Conservative. Sat for the Sudbury and Woodbridge division of Suffolk from Dec. 1963.*   [1979]

STALLARD, Albert William ('Jock'). House of Commons, London. S. of Frederick Stallard, Esq. of Tottenham B. Nov. 1921; m. 1944, Julie, d. of W.C. Murphy, Esq. of Co. Kerry. Educ. at Low Waters School, and Hamilton Academy. An Engineer 1937-65. Member St. Pancras Borough Council 1953-65 and Camden Council from 1965. Member A.U.E.W.; Chairman Camden Town Disablement Committee and Mental Health Association. Alderman Camden Borough Council May 1971. A Technical Training Officer, made full member of Institute of Training Officers 1971. Parliamentary Private Secretary to Norman Buchan, Minister of State, Ministry of Agriculture 1974 and to Reg. Freeson, Minister for Housing and Construction 1975-76. An Assistant Government Whip Feb. 1976-July 1978. Lord Commissioner, Treasury July 1978-Jan. 1979, when he resigned. A Roman Catholic. A Labour Member. Sat for St. Pancras N. from June 1970 to Feb. 1974 and for the St. Pancras N. division of Camden from Feb. 1974.*   [1979]

STAMFORD, Thomas William. 108 Durham Road, Bradford. S. of Thomas Stamford, Esq., of Cambridge. B. 20 Dec. 1882; m. 17 Dec. 1911, Florence, d. of Thomas Wadsworth, Esq. Educ. at Dunstable Ashton School. A Book Binder, President of Bradford Trades Council 1921-24, of City of Bradford Labour Party 1935-44; member of Bradford City Council 1912-22. A Labour Member. Unsuccessfully contested W. Leeds in 1922 and 1935. Represented W. Leeds from 1923 to 1931, when he was defeated, and from July 1945 until he committed suicide on 30 May 1949.   [1949]

STANBROOK, Ivor Robert. House of Commons, London. S. of Arthur William Stanbrook, Esq. B. 13 Jan. 1924; m. 17 Apr. 1946, Joan, d. of George Henry Clement, Esq., (2 s.). Educ. at State Schools, University Coll., London and Pembroke Coll., Oxford. Colonial Administrative Service, Nigeria 1950-60. Called to the bar Inner Temple 1960; practising Barrister. A Conservative. Unsuccessfully contested East Ham S. in 1966. Sat for Orpington from June 1970 to Feb. 1974 and for the Orpington division of Bromley from Feb. 1974.*   [1979]

STANLEY, John Paul. House of Commons, London. S. of H. Stanley, Esq. B. 19 Jan. 1942; m. 21 Dec. 1968, Susan Elizabeth, d. of Leslie A.D. Giles, Esq., (1 s. 1d.). Educ. at Repton School, and Lincoln Coll., Oxford. Conservative Research Department 1967-68. Research Associate of Institute for Strategic Studies 1968-69. Rio Tinto-Zinc Corporation Limited 1969-74. Joint Parliamentary Private Secretary to Rt. Hon. Margaret Thatcher, Leader of the Opposition Jan. 1976-May 1979. Minister of State (Minister for Housing and Construction) Department of the Environment from May 1979. Author of *The International Trade in Arms* (1972). A Conservative. Unsuccessfully contested Newton in 1970. Elected for Tonbridge and Malling in Feb. 1974.*   [1979]

STANLEY, Rt. Hon. Oliver Frederick George, M.C. Folly Farm, Sulhampstead, Reading. Turf. S. of Edward, 17th Earl of Derby, K.G. B. 4 May 1896; m. 4 Nov. 1920, Lady Maureen Vane-Tempest-Stewart, d. of Charles, 7th Marq. of Londonderry, K.G. (she died 1942). Educ. at Eton. Lieut.-Col. late R.F.A. and Lancashire Hussars (Yeomanry). Barrister-at-Law, Gray's Inn, 1919. Stockbroker 1924. Parliamentary Private Secretary to Lord Eustace Percy, President of Board of Education Nov. 1924-June 1929. Parliamentary Under-Secretary of State, Home Office Aug. 1931-Feb. 1933; Minister of Transport Feb. 1933-June 1934; Minister of Labour June 1934-June 1935; President of Board of Education June 1935-May 1937, of Board of Trade May 1937-Jan. 1940; Secretary of State for War Jan.-May 1940. Rejoined R.F.A. 1940. Secretary of State for the Colonies Nov. 1942-July 1945. President of Conservative and Unionist Association May 1946; Chancellor of Liverpool University 1948. PC. 1934. A Conservative. Unsuccessfully contested the Edge Hill division of

Liverpool in 1923. Sat for Westmorland from Oct. 1924-July 1945 and for Bristol W. from July 1945 until his death on 10 Dec. 1950.
[1950]

STANLEY, Capt. Hon. Richard Oliver. 14 Hyde Park Gardens, London. New England House, Newmarket. S. of Rt. Hon. Lord Stanley, MP., PC., M.C. and grandson of 17th Earl of Derby. B. 29 Jan. 1920; m. 5 Jan. 1965, Susan, only d. of Sir John Aubrey-Fletcher, Bart. (She died 1976). Educ. at Eton. Capt. Grenadier Guards. Heir Presumptive to the Earldom of Derby. Parliamentary Private Secretary to Rt. Hon. J.P.L. Thomas, First Lord of Admiralty, 1951-55. A Conservative. Elected for the North Fylde division of Lancashire in Feb. 1950 and sat until he retired in 1966. Joint Treasurer of Conservative Party 1962-66. Member of Gaming Board 1968-77.* [1966]

STEEL, Rt. Hon. David Martin Scott. House of Commons, London. Cherry Dene, Ettrick Bridge, Selkirkshire. S. of Very Rev. Dr. David Steel, Moderator of General Assembly of the Church of Scotland 1974-75. B. 31 Mar. 1938; m. 26 Oct. 1962, Judith, d. of W.D. MacGregor, Esq., C.B.E., of Dunblane, Perthshire, (2 s. 1 d.). Educ. at Prince of Wales School, Nairobi, George Watson's Coll., and Edinburgh University (M.A. 1960, LL.B. 1962). A Broadcaster and Journalist. President Edinburgh University Liberal Club 1960; President Edinburgh University Students' Representatives Council 1961. Assistant Secretary Scottish Liberal Party 1962-64. B.B.C. Television Interviewer in Scotland 1964-65. Sponsor of the Abortion Act 1967. Past President of the Anti-Apartheid Movement in Great Britain. Chairman Scottish Advisory Council of Shelter 1968-72. Liberal Chief Whip 1970-75. Member of British Council of Churches 1971-75. Liberal spokesman on Foreign Affairs 1975-76. Elected Leader of the Liberal Party in July 1976. PC. Jan. 1977. Author of *No Entry, The Background and Implications of the Commonwealth Immigrants Act 1968*. A Liberal. Unsuccessfully contested Roxburgh, Selkirk and Peebles at the general election in Oct. 1964. Elected for Roxburgh, Selkirk and Peebles at a by-election in Mar. 1965.* [1979]

STEELE, Thomas. Windyridge, Woodpark, Lesmahagow, Lanarkshire. S. of James Steele, Esq., of Coalburn, Lanarkshire. B. 15 Nov. 1905; m. 10 June 1939, Helen, d. of James Thomson, Esq., of Lochmaben. Educ. at Bellfield Public School. A Railway Station Master. Parliamentary Secretary Ministry of National Insurance Oct. 1946-Feb. 1950. An Opposition spokesman on Pensions and National Insurance to 1957 and on the Admiralty 1957-60. A Labour Member. Sat for Lanark from 1945 to Feb. 1950. Unsuccessfully contested Lanark in Feb. 1950. Elected for Dunbartonshire W. in Apr. 1950 and sat until he retired in 1970. Member of General Medical Council 1965-75. Chairman of Select Committee on Scottish Affairs 1969-70. Died 28 May 1979. [1970]

STEEN, Anthony David. 15 Sutherland Street, London. 15 Ullet Road, Liverpool. S. of Stephen Steen, Esq. B. 22 July 1939; m. 1966, Carolyn, d. of Colin Padfield, Esq., (1 s. 1 d.). Educ. at Westminster School and University Coll., London. Called to the bar 1962. A Barrister, Gray's Inn. A Youth Leader. Founder Task Force (Young helping the old) with Government grant 1964, first Director 1964-68. As Community and Social Worker intiated Young Volunteer Force Foundation, neo Government Community Development/Education Foundation, first Director 1968-74. Lecturer Ghana High Commission. Council of Legal Education. Ministry of Defence Court Martials Defence Counsel. Advisor to Federal and Provincial Canadian Governments on unemployment and youth problems. Board of Community Transport. Member of Council of V.S.O. Vice-Chairman of Task Force. A Conservative. Elected for the Wavertree division of Liverpool in Feb. 1974.* [1979]

STEPHEN, Campbell. 45 Brougham Street, Greenock. S. of Alexander Stephen, Esq. B. 29 Mar. 1884; m. 1945, Dorothy (MP. for Normich 1923-24), d. of Alderman George Jewson. Educ. at Townhead Elementary School, Glasgow University, Glasgow U.F. Theological Coll., and the Royal Technical Coll., M.A., B.Sc., B.D. Minister of the United Free Church at Ardrossan 1911-

351

18. Barrister-at-Law. An Independent Labour Party Member. Unsuccessfully contested Ayr Burghs in 1918. Unsuccessfully contested the Merthyr division of Merthyr Tydfil in June 1934. Member for the Camlachie division of Glasgow from Nov. 1922-Oct. 1931, when he was defeated and from 1935 until his death on 25 Oct. 1947. Resigned from the Independent Labour Party in July 1947. Joined the P.L.P. on 21 Oct. 1947. Member of governing body of British Film Institute Sept.-Oct. 1947. Died 25 Oct. 1947. [1947]

STEVENS, Geoffrey Paul. Hunter's Croft, Grayswood, Haslemere, Surrey. Royal Thames Yacht, United, and Cecil. S. of Alfred Stevens, Esq., of Hampstead. B. 1902; m. 1928, Evelyn Mitchell, d. of D.W. Marwick, Esq. Educ. at Westminster School. A Chartered Accountant. Served with R.A.F. 1939-45, retiring with rank of Wing-Commander. A Conservative. Unsuccessfully contested the Park division of Sheffield in 1945. Elected for the Langstone division of Portsmouth in Feb. 1950 and sat until he retired in 1964. Partner in Pannell Fitzpatrick and Company, Chartered Accountants, 1930-70.* [1964]

STEWARD, Harold Macdonald. House of Commons, London. S. of John Steward, Esq. B. 1904; m. 1941, Joyce Mary, d. of Thomas Nevison, Esq. Educ. at Rainhill, and Municipal Technical Coll., St. Helens. Radar Industrial Research during Second World War; member of Inter-Services Mission to ex-enemy countries; member of Liverpool City Council 1953-74, Alderman from 1961, Leader of the Council 1967-74 J.P. for Lancashire. A Consulting Engineer. A Conservative. Unsuccessfully contested the Edge Hill division of Liverpool in 1951. Elected for Stockport S. in Feb. 1955 and sat until 1964, when he was defeated. Chairman of Merseyside Passenger Transport Authority 1969-74. Knighted 1972. Died 3 Mar. 1977. [1964]

STEWARD, Sir William Arthur. 56 Curzon Street, London. Clandon Regis, West Clandon, Surrey. Carlton. S. of W.A. Steward, Esq., of Norwich. B. 20 Apr. 1901; m. 1939. Educ. at Norwich Model School, and Privately. Restaurateur and Farmer. Served

with R.A.F. 1938-45; Senior Catering Officer Air Ministry 1943-45, retired with Rank of Squadron-Leader. Member of London County Council Apr. 1949-1952; Freeman and Liveryman City of London; Chairman House of Commons Kitchen Committee from Nov. 1951 to Sept. 1959. Chairman of the Council of London Conservative Union from Apr. 1953 to 1955. Knight Bach. 1955. A Conservative. Unsuccessfully contested Southwark Central in 1945. Elected for Woolwich W. in Feb. 1950 and sat until he retired in 1959. Director of food manufacturing companies.* [1959]

STEWART, (Bernard Harold) Ian (Halley). House of Commons, London. S. of Professor Harold Stewart, C.B.E., M.D., D.L., K.St.J., F.R.S.E.B. 10 Aug. 1935; m. 8 Oct. 1966, Deborah Charlotte, d. of Hon. William Buchan, (1 s. 2d.). Educ. at Haileybury, and Jesus Coll., Cambridge. Served in R.N.V.R. 1954-56, R.D. (Lieut. Commander R.N.R.). Joined Brown, Shipley and Company Limited 1960, Director 1971. Parliamentary Private Secretary to Rt. Hon. Sir Geoffrey Howe, Chancellor of Exchequer from 1979. Fellow of Royal Numismatic Society, Society of Antiquaries and Society of Antiquaries (Scotland). Author of *The Scottish Coinage* 1955, revised 1966. Litt.D., Cambridge, 1978. A Conservative. Unsuccessfully contested Hammersmith N. in 1970. Sat for Hitchin from Feb. 1974.* [1979]

STEWART, Rt. Hon. Donald James. House of Commons, London. S. of Neil Stewart, Esq. B. 17 Oct. 1920; m. 1955, Christina Macaulay. Educ. at Nicolson Institute, Stornoway. Three terms as Provost of Stornoway; Honorary Sheriff Substitute. Leader of Scottish National Party in House of Commons. PC. 1977. A Scottish National Member. Elected for the Western Isles in June 1970.* [1979]

STEWART, James Henderson. See HENDERSON-STEWART, Sir James Henderson, Bart.

STEWART, Rt. Hon. (Robert) Michael Maitland, C.H. 11 Felden Street, London. Reform. S. of Robert Stewart, Esq. B. 6 Nov.

1906; m. 1941, Mary Elizabeth, J.P., created Baroness Stewart of Alvechurch 1974, d. of Herbert Birkinshaw, Esq. Educ. at Christ's Hospital, and St. John's Coll., Oxford, President of Oxford Union. A Teacher and Lecturer for the Workers Educational Association. Served in the Army Educational Corps. A Lord Commissioner of the Treasury Aug. 1945. Comptroller of H.M. Household Apr. 1946; Vice-Chamberlain Dec. 1946. Parliamentary Under-Secretary of State and Financial Secretary to the War Office Oct. 1947-May 1951. Parliamentary Secretary Ministry of Supply May-Oct. 1951. Opposition spokesman on War to 1956, on Education 1955-59 and on Housing 1959-64. Member of Parliamentary Committee of P.L.P. 1960-64. Secretary of State for Education and Science Oct. 1964-Jan. 1965. Secretary of State for Foreign Affairs Jan. 1965-Aug. 1966. Secretary of State for Economic Affairs Aug. 1966-Aug. 1967. First Secretary of State Aug. 1966-Mar. 1968. Secretary of State for Foreign Affairs Mar.-Oct. 1968. Secretary of State for Foreign and Commonwealth Affairs Oct. 1968-June 1970. Voted in favour of entry to E.E.C. on 28 Oct. 1971. Chairman of Select Committee on Parliamentary Commissioner for Administration 1970-74. Member of European Parliament and Leader of Labour Group July 1975-Nov. 1976. Honorary Fellow of St. John's Coll., Oxford, LL.D. (Hon. Causa) University of Leeds. D.Sc. (Hon. Causa) University of Benin. PC. 1964. Companion of Honour 1969. Created Baron Stewart of Fulham (Life Peerage) 1979. Freeman of the London borough of Hammersmith. President Economics Association 1971-73. Published *The British Approach to Politics and Modern Forms of Government.* A Labour Member. Unsuccessfully contested Lewisham W. in 1931 and 1935. Sat for Fulham E. from July 1945 to May 1955, for Fulham from May 1955 to Feb. 1974 and for the Fulham division of Hammersmith from Feb. 1974 to May 1979, when he retired.* [1979]

STEWART-SMITH, (Dudley) Geoffrey. Church House, Petersham, Surrey. Hayes Farm, Ticknall, Derby. S. of Dudley Cautley Steward-Smith, Esq. B. 28 Dec. 1933; m. 29 Sept. 1956, Kay Mary, d. of T.

Stewart-Johnstone, Esq. Educ. at Winchester and R.M.A. Sandhurst. Regular Officer The Black Watch 1952-60; Journalist *Financial Times*; Editor *East West Digest*; Director Foreign Affairs Publishing Company. Author of *The Defeat of Communism*, and *No Vision Here*. A Conservative. Elected for the Belper division of Derbyshire in June 1970 and sat until Feb. 1974, when he was defeated. Director of Foreign Affairs Research Institute from 1976.* [1974]

STODART, Rt. Hon. James Anthony. Lorimers, North Berwick. Caledonian. S. of Col. Thomas Stodart, C.I.E. B. 6 June 1916; m. 1940, Hazel Jean, eld. d. of Ronald James Usher, Esq. Educ. at Wellington. A Farmer from 1934. Executive Committee East Lothian N.F.U. 1948-51. Honorary President Edinburgh University Agricultural Society 1952. Joint Parliamentary Under-Secretary of State for Scotland Aug. 1963-Oct. 1964. Opposition spokesman on Scotland and Agriculture 1965-70. Parliamentary Secretary Ministry of Agriculture, Fisheries and Food June 1970-Apr. 1972. Minister of State, Ministry of Agriculture, Fisheries and Food Apr. 1972-Mar. 1974. A Conservative. Unsuccessfully contested Berwick and East Lothian in 1950 as a Liberal. Unsuccessfully contested Midlothian and Peebles in 1951 and Midlothian in 1955 as a Conservative. Elected for Edinburgh W. in 1959 and sat until he retired in Sept. 1974. PC. 1974. Chairman of Agricultural Credit Corporation Limited from 1975.*

[1974 2nd ed.]

STODDART, David Leonard. 'Sintra', 37a Bath Road, Reading. S. of Arthur L. Stoddart, Esq., Coal Miner. B. 4 May 1926; m. 24 June 1961, Jennifer, d. of L. Percival-Alwyn, Esq., (2 s.), (1 d. by previous marriage). Educ. at St. Clement Danes, and Henley Grammar Schools. A Power Station Clerical Worker 1951-70. Member of Reading County Borough Council 1954-72. Leader of the Labour Group on Council 1962-70. Served at various times as Chairman of Housing, Transport and Finance Committees. Member of various Boards including Thames Valley Board and Police Authority and the Court and Council of Reading

University. Member House of Commons Select Committee on Nationalised Industries. Parliamentary Private Secretary to Reg. Freeson, Minister for Housing and Construction 1974-75. Assistant Government Whip from Jan. 1975-Apr. 1976. Lord Commissioner of the Treasury Apr. 1976-Nov. 1977. A Labour Member. Unsuccessfully contested Newbury in 1959 and 1964 and Swindon in Oct. 1969. Elected for Swindon in June 1970.*   [1979]

STODDART-SCOTT, Sir Malcolm, O.B.E., T.D., D.L., M.D. Creskeld Hall, Arthington, Nr. Leeds. S. of John Stoddart-Scott, Esq. B. 23 Sept. 1901; m. May 1940, Elsie Mary, d. of B. Parkinson, Esq. J.P. Educ. at Elmfield Coll., York, Ashville Coll., Harrogate, and University of Leeds, M.B., Ch. B., M.D. Served in R.A.M.C. 1939-45. A.D.M.S. 48th Division 1942-45. T.D. 1943. O.B.E. 1945. Chairman British Group Inter-Parliamentary Union 1951-57; Chairman Yorkshire Provincial Area Conservative Association from 1957-65. Knighted 1957. Chairman Parliamentary Medical Committee 1955-64; past Secretary and Chairman of Conservative Health and Social Insurance Committee. Chairman Government Charterhouse Rheumatism Clinic. Chairman H.S.F. President Chippendale Society. Member of House of Laity of Church Assembly. Vice-Chairman Yorkshire Empire Cancer Campaign. Chairman Yorkshire Branch Heart Foundation. Dept.-Lieut. for the W. Riding of Yorkshire. A Conservative. Sat for the Pudsey and Otley division of the W. Riding of Yorkshire from July 1945 to Feb. 1950 and for the Ripon division of the W. Riding of Yorkshire from Feb. 1950 until his death on 15 June 1973.   [1973]

STOKES, John Heydon Romaine. House of Commons, London, Carlton. S. of Victor Romaine Stokes, Esq. B. 23 July 1917; m. 23 Dec. 1939, Barbara, youngest d. of R.E. Yorke, Esq. Educ. at Temple Grove, Hailey-bury Coll., and the Queen's Coll., Oxford. A Schoolmaster 1938-39. Served in the Infantry, Staff and Diplomatic Service 1939-46, wounded 1943. Maj. I.C.I. Limited, Personnel Officer 1946-51; British Celanese Limited and Courtaulds Limited, Personnel Manager

1951-59; Partner in Clive and Stokes, Personnel Consultants 1959. Member Parliamentary Delegation to Luxembourg 1972 and Belgium 1973. Chairman Gen. Purposes Committee, Primrose League. Vice-Chairman Royal Society of St. George. A Conservative. Unsuccessfully contested Gloucester in 1964 and Hitchin in 1966. Sat for Oldbury and Halesowen from 1970 to Feb. 1974. Elected for Halesowen and Stourbridge in Feb. 1974.*   [1979]

STOKES, Rt. Hon. Richard Rapier, M.C. 29 Palace Street, London. White's, and Garrick. S. of Philip Folliot Stokes, Esq., Barrister-at-Law. B. 27 Jan. 1897. Educ. at Downside Abbey, Royal Military Academy, Woolwich, and Trinity Coll., Cambridge. Served in France 1916-18; Maj. 1917. Had M.C. and Bar, French Croix de Guerre with Citation, and Order of the Nile. Reappointed Chairman and Managing Director of Ransomes and Rapier Limited, and Managing Director of Cochran and Company (Annan) Limited Nov. 1951. Minister of Works Feb. 1950-Apr. 1951. Lord Privy Seal, also Minister of Materials July-Oct. 1951. Member of P.L.P. Parliamentary Committee 1951-52 and 1955-56. Opposition spokesman on Defence 1955-56. PC. 1950. A Labour Member. Unsuccessfully contested Glasgow Central in 1935. Elected for Ipswich in Feb. 1938 and sat until his death on 3 Aug. 1957. Died 3 Aug. 1957.   [1957]

STONEHOUSE, Rt. Hon. John Thomson S. of W.M. Stonehouse, and Alderman Mrs. R.M. Stonehouse, of Southampton. B. 28 July 1925; m. 1948, Barbara, d. of Robert Smith, Esq., of London (divorced 1978). Educ. at Elementary School, Taunton's School, Southampton, and London School of Economics University of London, B.Sc. (Economics) Hons. Served 1944-47 with R.A.F. as pilot and education officer. Author of book *Prohibited Immigrant*, published by The Bodley Head Limited in Mar. 1960. Member of Islington Borough Council 1956-59. Director of London Co-operative Society 1956-62; President 1962-64. Delegate, Council of Europe and Western European Union Assemblies 1962-64. Parliamentary Secretary Ministry of Aviation Oct. 1964-Apr. 1966. Parliamentary Under-Secretary of State for the Colonies Apr. 1966-Jan. 1967. Minister of Aviation Jan.-Feb. 1967. Minister of State, Ministry of Technology from Feb. 1967 to June 1968. Postmaster-Gen. June 1968-Oct. 1969. Minister of Posts and Telecommunications Oct. 1969-June 1970. PC. 1968. A Labour and Co-operative Member. Unsuccessfully contested Twickenham in 1950 and Burton in 1951 as a Labour candidate. Sat for Wednesbury from Feb. 1957 to Feb. 1974. Elected for Walsall N. in Feb. 1974 and Sat until he resigned on 27 Aug. 1976. Reported missing in Miami on 21 Nov. 1974, re-appeared in Australia in Dec. 1974, resigned from the Labour Party and joined the English National Party in Apr. 1976, convicted on 18 charges of fraud, conspiracy and theft on 6 Aug. 1976, resigned from the Privy Council on 17 Aug. and from the House on 27 Aug. 1976. Sentenced to 7 years' imprisonment on 6 Aug. 1976 but released on 14 Aug. 1979. Granted citizenship of Bangladesh 1972.*   [1976]

STONES, William. House of Commons, London. S. of Thomas Stones, Esq. B. 1904; m. 1926, d. of Edward Armstrong, Esq. Educ. at Elementary School, and National Council of Labour Colls. Member of National Union of Mineworkers; a Mines Inspector. A Labour Member. Secretary of Stanley Labour Party 1940-55. Elected for the Consett division of Durham in 1955 and sat until he retired in 1966. President of District Nursing Association. Died 2 July 1969.
[1966]

STOREY, Sir Samuel, Bart. 12 Cowley Street, London. Settrington House, Malton, Yorkshire. Carlton. S. of Frederick George Storey, Esq., J.P. B. 18 Jan. 1896; m. 25 July 1929, Elisabeth, d. of Brigadier-Gen. W.J. Woodcock, D.S.O. (she died 1951). Educ. at Haileybury Coll., and Trinity Coll., Cambridge. Barrister-at-Law, Inner Temple, 1919. Member of Sunderland Borough Council 1927-30. Chairman of Press Association 1938 and of Reuters 1941. Parliamentary Private Secretary to Miss F. Horsbrugh, Parliamentary Secretary Ministry of Health Nov. 1939-42. Chairman of Conservative Social Services Committee 1942-45.

Chairman of Standing Committees and temporary Chairman of Committees of whole House 1957-64. Dept. Chairman Ways and Means from Nov. 1964 to Oct. 1965. Created Bart. 1960. Chairman Portsmouth and Sunderland Newspapers Limited, and of Envoy Journals Limited. President The Newspaper Society 1933-34. Member E. Riding County Council 1946-64. Dept. Speaker and Chairman of Ways and Means from Oct. 1965 to Mar. 1966. A Conservative. Sat for Sunderland from Oct. 1931 to July 1945, when he was defeated. Elected for Stretford in Feb. 1950 and sat until 1966, when he was defeated. Created Baron Buckton (Life Peerage) 1966. Died 17 Jan. 1978.   [1966]

STOTT, Roger. 10 Firs Park Crescent, Aspull, Wigan. S. of Richard Stott, Esq. B. 7 Aug. 1943; m. 7 June 1969, Irene, d. of Joseph Mills, Esq., (2 s.). Educ. at Rochdale Technical Coll. and Ruskin Coll., Oxford. Served in the Merchant Navy 1959-64. A G.P.O. Telephone Engineer 1964-73. Member P.O.E.U. Former member of Rochdale Council. Chairman Housing Committee 1970-73. Parliamentary Private Secretary to Rt. Hon. Eric Varley, Secretary of State for Energy 1974-75 and Secretary of State for Industry 1975-76. Parliamentary Private Secretary to Prime Minister Rt. Hon. James Callaghan, Oct. 1976-May 1979. Parliamentary Private Secretary to Rt. Hon. James Callaghan, Leader of Opposition from 1979. C.B.E. 1979. A Labour Member. Unsuccessfully contested the Cheadle division of Cheshire in 1970. Elected for the Westhoughton division of Lancashire in May 1973.*
[1979]

STRACHEY, Rt. Hon. Evelyn John St. Loe. The Old Rectory, Abridge, Essex. S. of John St. Loe Strachey. B. 21 Oct. 1901; m. 1st, 1924, Esther, d. of Patrick Murphy, Esq. (marriage dissolved on her petition 1933); 2ndly, 1933, Celia, d. of Rev. H. Simpson. Educ. at Eton and Magdalen Coll., Oxford. Served with the R.A.F. 1941-45. An Author. Parliamentary Under-Secretary of State for Air August 1945-May 1946. Minister of Food May 1946-Feb. 1950; PC. 1946. Secretary of State for War Feb. 1950-Oct.

1951. Opposition spokesman on War until 1960, on Aviation 1960-61, and on Colonial and Commonwealth Affairs 1961-63. A Labour Member. Unsuccessfully contested the Aston division of Birmingham as a Labour candidate in 1924 and as an Independent in 1931. Sat for the Aston division from 1929-31, and for Dundee from July 1945 to Feb. 1950. Elected for W. Dundee in Feb. 1950 and sat until his death on 15 July 1963. Resigned the Labour Whip in Feb. 1931 and joined Sir Oswald Mosley's New Party. Left the New Party in June 1931 and sat as an Independent. Rejoined the Labour Party and was adopted for Dundee in 1943. Member of Council of Institute for Strategic Studies. Heir-presumptive to Baronetcy of Strachey. Died 15 July 1963. [1963]

STRADLING THOMAS, John. See THOMAS, John Stradling.

STRANG, Gavin Steel. 80 Argyle Crescent, Edinburgh. S. of James S. Strang, Esq., Tenant Farmer. B. 10 July 1943; m. Aug. 1973 Bettina, Educ. at Edinburgh University, B.Sc. (Hons.), Churchill Coll., Cambridge Dip. Agri. Sci., and Edinburgh University, Ph.D. Scientist and Agricultural Research Council 1968-70. Parliamentary Secretary to Ministry of Agriculture Oct. 1974-May 1979. Member of Tayside Economic Planning Consultative Group 1966-68. Parliamentary Under-Secretary for Energy Mar.-Oct. 1974. An Opposition spokesman on Trade and Industry Dec. 1973-Mar. 1974 and on Agriculture from 1979. A Labour Member. Sat for Edinburgh E. from June 1970* [1979]

STARAUSS, Rt. Hon. George Russell. 1 Palace Green, London. Naylands, Slaugham, Sussex. S. of Arthur Strauss, Esq., MP. B. 18 July 1901; m. Patricia, d. of F. O'Flynn, Esq. Educ. at Rugby. Member London County Council 1925-31 and 32-46. Chairman of Highways Committee and Vice-Chairman of Finance Committee 1934-37; Chairman of Supplies Committee 1937-39; member of London and Home Counties Traffic Advisory Committee 1936-39. Expelled from Labour Party in Mar. 1939 as a Supporter of a Popular Front but re-admit-

ted in Feb. 1940. Parliamentary Private Secretary to the Rt. Hon. Herbert Morrison when Minister of Transport 1929-31, to the Rt. Hon. Sir Stafford Cripps, Lord Privy Seal Feb.-Nov. 1942, and when Minister of Aircraft Production Nov. 1942-May 1945. Parliamentary Secretary Ministry of War Transport Aug. 1945 and Ministry of Transport 1946-Oct. 1947. Minister of Supply Oct. 1947-Oct. 1951. Opposition spokesman on Transport to 1959 and 1960-64 and on Aviation 1959-60. Voted in favour of entry to E.E.C. on 28 Oct. 1971. PC. 1947. Father of the House 1974-79. Created Baron Strauss (Life Peerage) 1979. A Labour Member. Unsuccessfully contested Lambeth N. in 1924. Sat for Lambeth N. from 1929-31 when he was defeated and from Oct. 1934-50. Elected for the Vauxhall division of Lambeth in Feb. 1950 and sat until he retired in 1979.* [1979]

STRAUSS, Henry George, Q.C. 25 Cheyne Walk, London. Carlton, Beefsteak, and Pratt's. S. of A.H. Strauss, Esq. B. 24 June 1892; m. 1927, Anne, d. of J. Bowyer Nichols, Esq., of Lawford Hall, Manningtree. Educ. at Rugby, and Christ Church, Oxford, M.A., 1st Class Classical Hon. Mods., 1st Class Lit. Hum. Barrister-at-Law, Inner Temple, 1919. K.C. 1946. Member of Executive Committee National Trust. Parliamentary Private Secretary to Sir D. Somervell, Attorney-Gen. Mar. 1936. Joint Parliamentary Secretary Ministry of Works and Planning Mar. 1942-Feb. 1943. Parliamentary Secretary Ministry of Town and Country Planning Feb. 1943-Mar. 1945, when he resigned. Parliamentary Secretary Board of Trade Nov. 1951-Apr. 1955. A Conservative. Sat for Norwich from Nov. 1935-July 1945, when he was defeated, and for the Combined English Universities from Mar. 1946 to Feb. 1950. Elected for S. Norwich in Feb. 1950 and sat until Apr. 1955, when he was created Baron Conesford. Hon. Fellow of Royal Institute of British Architects 1965. Died 28 Aug. 1974. [1954]

STROSS, Sir Barnett. 11a Thorney Court, London. S. of Samuel Stross, Esq. B. 25 Dec. 1899; m. 1st. 1922, Olive Marion Reade (she died 1960); 2ndly, 1962, Gwendolen Ella Chesters. Educ. at Leeds Grammar School and University. Honorary Medical Adviser to National Society of Pottery Workers and North Staffordshire Miners' Federation. Alderman Stoke-on-Trent until 1952. Commissioner of The White Lion of Czechoslovakia. Parliamentary Secretary Ministry of Health Oct. 1964-Feb. 1965. Honorary Degree D.Sc. University of Keele 1965. A Labour Member. Sat for the Hanley division of Stoke-on-Trent from July 1945 to Feb. 1950. Elected for the Central division of Stoke-on-Trent in Feb. 1950 and sat until he retired in 1966. Member of Historic Buildings Council. Knighted 1964. Died 13 May 1967.   [1966]

STUART, Rt. Hon. James Gray, C.H., M.V.O., M.C. Harthill House, Redlynch, Salisbury. White's, and Turf. S. of 17th Earl of Moray. B. 9 Feb. 1897; m. 4 Aug. 1923, Lady Rachel Cavendish, d. of 9th Duke of Devonshire. Educ. at Eton. Capt. Royal Scots. Equerry to H.R.H. the Duke of York 1920-21; M.V.O. (4th class) 1921; a Lord Commissioner of the Treasury and Scottish Whip May 1935-Jan. 1941; Joint Parliamentary Secretary to the Treasury Jan. 1941-May 1945, Parliamentary Secretary to the Treasury May-July 1945, and Chief Conservative Whip 1941-48. Secretary of State for Scotland (Cabinet) Oct. 1951-Jan. 1957. PC. 1939. A Conservative. Elected for Moray and Nairn in Dec. 1923 and sat until he retired in 1959. Chairman of Unionist Party in Scotland 1950-62. C.H. 1957. Created Visct. Stuart of Findhorn 1959. Member of Royal Commission on Tribunals of Enquiry 1966-71. Dept.-Lieut. for Wiltshire. Author of memoirs, *Within the Fringe* (1967). Died 20 Feb. 1971.   [1959]

STUBBS, Albert Ernest. 5 Arbury Road, Cambridge. B. 1877. Former Machinist on Daily Paper. A Labour Party Organiser. Member of Cambridgeshire County Council in 1922 and 1931-62, Alderman 1942-62. Member of Cambridge City Council 1924-49. District Officer of Transport and General Workers Union 1929-44. A Labour Member. Unsuccessfully contested Cambridgeshire in 1918, 1922 and 1923 and the Melton division of Leicestershire in 1929, 1931 and 1935. Elected for Cambridgeshire in July 1945 and

sat until 1950, when he was defeated. President of Cambridge Trades Council and Labour Party. Died 4 Jan. 1962.   [1950]

STUDHOLME, Sir Henry Gray, Bart., C.V.O. 38 Knightsbridge Court, London. Wembury House, Plymouth. Carlton. S. of.William Paul Studholme, Esq., of Perridge House, Exeter. B. 13 June 1899; m. 10 Apr. 1929, Judith, d. of H.W. Whitbread, Esq., of Norton Bavant Manor, Wiltshire. Educ. at Eton, and Magdalen Coll., Oxford. Served with Scots Guards 1917-19; rejoined 1940; Staff Appointments 1941-44. Member of Paddington Borough Council 1935-44, of London County Council 1931-45. Parliamentary Private Secretary to Commander R.A. Brabner, Parliamentary Under-Secretary of State for Air Nov. 1944-Mar. 1945. Conservative Whip 1945-51; Vice-Chamberlain to H.M. Household Nov. 1951-April 1956. Joint Honorary Treasurer of Conservative Party Sept. 1956-62. C.V.O. 1953; created 1st Bart. 1956. A Conservative. Elected for the Tavistock division of Devonshire in Apr. 1942 and sat until he retired in 1966. Dept.-Lieut. for Devon 1969.*   [1966]

STUTTAFORD, Dr. (Irving) Thomas. Bramerton House, Bramerton, Norwich. Cavalry, Reform, St. Stephen's, and Norfolk (Norwich). S. of Dr. W.J.E. Stuttaford, M.C. B. 4 May 1931; m. 1 June 1957, Pamela, d. of Col. Richard Ropner. Educ. at Greshams, and Brasenose Coll., Oxford. 2nd Lieut. 10th Royal Hussars (P.W.O.) 1953-55; Jun. Hospital Appointments 1959-60; Gen. Practitioner 1960-70; member of Blofield and Flegg Rural District Council 1964-66 and of Norwich City Council 1969-71; Honorary member of British Cancer Council 1971. Member of the Management Committee Birth Control Campaign 1971; Secretary Conservative Health and Social Services Committee; member Council of Research Defence Society. A Conservative. Elected for Norwich S. in June 1970 and sat until Feb. 1974, when he was defeated. Unsuccessfully contested the Isle of Ely in Oct. 1974 and 1979.*   [1974]

SUMMERS, Sir (Gerard) Spencer. Thenford House, Nr. Banbury. Boodles'. S. of Frank Summers, Esq., of Froyle Place, Alton.

B. 27 Oct. 1902; m. 2 June 1930, Jean, adopted d. of John Pickering, Esq. Educ. at Wellington, and Trinity Coll., Cambridge. A Director of John Summers and Sons, iron and steel manufacturers. Director-Gen. of Regional Organisation, Ministry of Supply 1941-Mar. 1944. Secretary for Overseas Trade at end of Coalition and during Caretaker Government Mar.-July 1945. Knight Bach. 1956. A Conservative. Sat for Northampton from Dec. 1940 to July 1945, when he was defeated. Elected for the Aylesbury division of Buckinghamshire in Feb. 1950 and sat until he retired in 1970. Chairman of Outward Bound Trust 1947-75. President of British Direct Mail Advertising Association 1956-64. High Sheriff of Northamptonshire 1974. Vice-President of British Iron and Steel Federation. Died 19 Jan. 1976.   [1970]

SUMMERSKILL, Rt. Hon. Dr. Edith Clara, C.H. Pond House, Millfield Lane, Highgate, London. D. of Edith and William Summerskill. B. 19 Apr. 1901; m. Aug. 1925, Dr. E. Jeffrey Samuel. Educ. at King's Coll., and Charing Cross Hospital. A Physician from 1924. Member of Middlesex County Council 1934-41. Parliamentary Secretary Ministry of Food Aug. 1945-Feb. 1950; Minister of National Insurance Feb. 1950-Oct. 1951. Member of Parliamentary Committee of P.L.P. 1951-57 and 1958-59. Opposition spokesman on Health until 1961. PC. 1949. A Labour Member. Sat for Fulham W. from Apr. 1938 to May 1955. Elected for Warrington in May 1955 and sat until Jan. 1961, when she was created Baroness Summerskill (Life Peerage). Member of National Executive Committee of Labour Party 1944-58, Chairman 1954-55. C.H. 1966. Member of Political Honours Scrutiny Committee 1967-76. Died 4 Feb. 1980.   [1961]

SUMMERSKILL, Dr. The Hon. Shirley Catherine Wynne. House of Commons, London. D. of Dr. E. Jeffrey Samuel and Baroness Summerskill B. 9 Sept. 1931; m. 1957, John Ryman MP. for Blyth from 1974 (marriage dissolved in 1971). Educ. at St. Paul's Girls' School, Somerville Coll., Oxford, and St. Thomas's Hospital. Medical Practitioner. Joined the Labour Party in 1948. Member of Medical Practitioners'

Union. Ex-treasurer of the Oxford University Labour Club. Chairman of P.L.P. Health Group 1969. U.K. Delegate to U.N. Status of Women Commission 1968 and 1969. Delegate to Council of Europe and Western European Union 1968 and 1969. Opposition Health spokesman 1970-74. Under-Secretary of State at the Home Office Mar. 1974-May 1979. An Opposition spokesman on Home Affairs from 1979. A Labour Member. Unsuccessfully contested Blackpool N. at a by-election in 1962. Elected for Halifax in Oct. 1964.*   [1979]

SUMNER, (William) Donald Massey, O.B.E., Q.C. House of Commons, London. S. of Harold Sumner, Esq., of Standish Lancs. B. 1913. Educ. at Charterhouse, and Sidney Sussex Coll., Cambridge. Barrister-at-Law, Lincoln's Inn, 1937. Served with R.A. in Second World War, Lieut.-Col. and Assistant Adjutant-Gen. 21st Army Group. Member Orpington Urban District Council 1950-53. O.B.E. 1945, Order of the Crown of Belgium, Croix de Guerre and American Bronze Star. Parliamentary Private Secretary to Sir Jocelyn Simon, Solicitor-Gen. 1959-61. A Conservative. Elected for the Orpington division of Kent in Jan. 1955 and sat until Oct. 1961, when he was appointed a County Court Judge. Assistant Recorder of Plymouth 1954-61. Q.C. 1960. County Court Judge, later Circuit Judge, from 1961.*   [1962]

SUNDERLAND, John William. 29 Arthur Street, Great Harwood, Blackburn. B. about 1896; m. Hilda. Served in Army 1914-18. A Trade Union Secretary. Vice-Chairman of Weavers Amalgamation. Assistant Secretary of Todmorden Weavers Association 1925-29, Secretary from 1929. Member of Lancashire County Council 1934-45, Leader of Labour Group. A Congregationalist. A Labour Member. Elected for Preston July 1945 and sat until his death on 24 Nov. 1945. [1946]

SUTCLIFFE, Sir Harold. 3 Hare Court, Temple, London. Great Fosters, Egham, Surrey. May Royd, Hebden Bridge, Yorkshire. Carlton, and Bath. S. of William Henry Sutcliffe, Esq., Solicitor, of Hebden Bridge, Yorkshire. B. 11 Dec. 1897; m. 1st., 28 July 1926, Theodora, d. of Canon Cochrane, of

Yardley (whom he divorced in 1947); 2ndly, 1948, Eileen, d. of Lieut.-Col. J.T. Field. Educ. at Harrow, and Oriel Coll., Oxford. Barrister-at-Law, Inner Temple, 1925. Served in France 1917-18 with R.F.A. Parliamentary Private Secretary to Rt. Hon. William Mabane, Parliamentary Secretary Ministry of Home Security Dec. 1939-June 1942, and to Rt. Hon. Osbert Peake when Parliamentary Under-Secretary Home Office 1940-44, when Financial Secretary to the Treasury 1944-July 1945 and when Minister of National Insurance (later Pensions and National Insurance) from 1951 to 1955. Knighted 1953. A Conservative. Sat for the Royton division of Lancashire from 1931 to Feb. 1950. Elected for the Heywood and Royton division of Lancashire in Feb. 1950 and sat until he retired in 1955. Died 20 Jan. 1958. [1954]

SUTCLIFFE, John Harold Vick. Chapelgarth, Great Broughton, Middlesbrough. Teesside. St. Stephen's. S. of Sir Harold Sutcliffe, MP. B. 30 Apr. 1931; m. 25 July 1959, Cecilia Mary, eld. d. of Ralph Meredyth Turton, Esq. Educ. at Winchester Coll., and New Coll., Oxford. 2nd Lieut. R.A. 1950-51. Called to the bar, Inner Temple, 1956; practised on Midland Circuit to 1960; Company Director, Chairman North Riding and Teesside Association of Youth Clubs. A Conservative. Unsuccessfully contested Oldham W. in 1959, Chorley, Lancashire in 1964, and Middlesbrough W. in 1966. Elected for Middlesbrough W. in June 1970 and sat until Feb. 1974. Unsuccessfully contested the Thornaby division of Teesside in Oct. 1974. Voted against entry to E.E.C. on 28 Oct. 1971.* [1974]

SWAIN, Thomas Henry. House of Commons, London. S. of Thomas Henry Swain, Esq. of Burton-on-Trent. B. 1911; m. 1st., 1931, Ruth Wootton (she died 1969); 2ndly, 25 Oct. 1969, Rosemarie Fischer. Educ. at Broadway School, Burton-on-Trent. Member of Staveley Urban District Council 1944-56, of Derbyshire County Council 1946-49. Vice-President Derbyshire area executive of the National Union of Mineworkers and a Branch Secretary. A Labour Member. Elected for Derbyshire N.E. in 1959 and sat until

he was killed in a road accident on 2 Mar. 1979. [1979]

SWINGLER, Rt. Hon. Stephen Thomas. 6 Belsize Park Gardens, London. S. of Rev. H. Swingler. B. 2 Mar. 1915; m. 16 May 1936, Anne, d. of John Matthews, Esq., of Mitcham. Educ. at Stowe School, and New Coll., Oxford. Lecturer in Adult Education 1936-44. An Author. Served with Royal Armoured Corps 1941-45 as Capt. Royal Tank Regiment. Parliamentary Secretary to the Ministry of Transport Oct. 1964-Aug. 1967. Minister of State for Transport Aug. 1967-Nov. 1968. Minister of State for Health and Social Security Nov. 1968-Feb. 1969. PC. 1969. A Labour Member. Sat for the Stafford division from 1945-50, when he unsuccessfully contested Stafford and Stone. Elected for Newcastle-under-Lyme in 1951 and sat until his death on 19 Feb. 1969. [1968]

SYLVESTER, George Oscar. 70 Firville Street, Normanton, Yorkshire. S. of Osgood Sylvester, Esq., of Normanton. B. 1898; m. 1922, Mildred, d. of Frederick Arnold, Esq. Educ. at Normanton Council School. Member of Normanton Urban District Council 1927-47, and of W. Riding of Yorkshire County Council 1945-47. Branch Official Sharlston Branch N.U.M. 1925-47. A Labour Member. Sat for Normanton from Feb. 1947 to Feb. 1950. Elected for Pontefract in Feb. 1950 and sat until his death on 26 Oct. 1961. Member of Imperial War Graves Commission 1951-61. Died 26 Oct. 1961. [1961]

SYMONDS, Arthur Leslie, M.B.E. 66 St. Barnabas Road, Cambridge. S. of John Symonds, Esq., of Cambridge. B. 2 Oct. 1910; m. 3 Apr. 1946, Barbara Mary, d. of A.P. Draycon, Esq., of Ramsgate. Educ. at Perse School, and Jesus Coll., Cambridge. A Secondary School Master 1939-40. Served with H.M. Forces 1940-45. A Labour Member. Elected for Cambridge in July 1945 and sat until 1950, when he was defeated. Unsuccessfully contested Cambridge in 1951 and 1955. M.B.E. (Military) 1945; O.B.E. (Civil) 1959. Member of Cambridge City Council 1950-60, Alderman 1958-60. J.P. for Cambridge 1957. Died 25 Feb. 1960. [1950]

SYMONDS, Joseph Bede, O.B.E. House of Commons, London. B. 1900; m. 1921. Educ. at Bede's Higher School, Jarrow. A Roman Catholic. Mayor of Jarrow 1945-46; a Freeman of the Borough of Jarrow 1953. Member of Durham County Council 1946-60. Chairman of National Housing and Town Planning Council for four years, Executive Member for twenty-five years. O.B.E. 1957. A Labour Member. Elected for the Whitehaven division of Cumberland at a by-election in June 1959 and sat until he retired in 1970.* [1970]

TALBOT, John Ellis. Villa Sabina, Great Witley, Worcester. S. of Maj. E.W. Talbot, T.D., Solicitor. B. 24 Apr. 1906; m. 14 Aug. 1930, Sabina Emily Wood, second d. of Joseph Perrins, Esq. Educ. at Stubbington House, Fareham and Rossall. A Solicitor. Joint Manager Kidderminster Permanent Benefit Building Society 1938-61. Director and Chairman Kidderminster Equitable Building Society 1961. Master, Worshipful Company of Gardeners (London) 1962. Mayor of Kidderminster 1947-49, Councillor 1936, Alderman 1952-63. War Service 1941-45, Capt. R.A.O.C. Member of Worcestershire County Council 1952-55. Chairman Gardeners Royal Benevolent Society 1964. A Conservative. Elected for Brierley Hill in 1959 and sat until his death on 9 Jan. 1967. [1966 2nd ed.]

TAPSELL, Peter Hannay Bailey. Roughton Hall, Nr. Woodhall Spa, Lincolnshire. Albany, Carlton, and Hurlingham. S. of Eustace Tapsell, Esq. B. 1 Feb. 1930; m. 1st., 1963, Hon. Cecilia Hawke, d. of 9th Baron Hawke (marriage dissolved in 1971), (1s.); 2ndly, 1974, Mlle. Gabrielle, d. of Jean Mahieu. Educ. at Tonbridge School, and Merton Coll., Oxford. Commissioned, The Royal Sussex Regiment 1948-50. Conservative Research Department 1954-57. Personal Assistant to Sir Anthony Eden during 1955 general election campaign. Member London Stock Exchange 1976. Conservative Jun. Front Bench spokesman on Foreign and Commonwealth Affairs 1976-77. Jun. Conservative spokesman on Treasury and Economic Affairs Nov. 1977-Oct. 1978. A Conservative. Unsuccessfully contested Wednes-

bury in Feb. 1957. Sat for Nottingham W. from 1959-64, when he was defeated. Elected for the Horncastle division of Lincolnshire in Mar. 1966.* [1979]

TAVERNE, Dick, Q.C. Cambridge Street, London. S. of Dr. N.J.M. Taverne, Geologist. B. 18 Oct. 1928; m. 6 Aug. 1955, Janice, d. of Dr. and Mrs. R.S.F. Hennessey, (2 d.). Educ. at Charterhouse, and Balliol Coll., Oxford, First class honours, Greats 1951. Called to the bar, Middle Temple, Feb. 1954. Appointed Queens Counsel 1965. Parliamentary Private Secretary to Rt. Hon. Denis Healey, Minister of Defence, 1964-66. Parliamentary Under-Secretary of State Home Office Apr. 1966-Apr. 1968. Minister of State Treasury Apr. 1968-Oct. 1969. Financial Secretary Treasury Oct. 1969-June 1970. Voted in favour of entry to E.E.C. on 28 Oct. 1971. A Democratic Labour Member. Unsuccessfully contested Wandsworth, Putney as a Labour Candidate in 1959. Labour Member for Lincoln from Mar. 1962 to Oct. 1972, when he resigned. Elected as a Democratic Labour Member for Lincoln in Mar. 1973, defeating the official Labour candidate, re-elected in Feb. 1974 and sat until Oct. 1974, when he was defeated. Director of Institute for Fiscal Studies from 1970.* [1974 2nd ed.]

TAYLOR, Sir Charles Stuart, T.D., D.L. 4 Reeves House, Reeves Mews, London. 11 Fulbourne House, 56 Blackwater Road, Eastbourne, Sussex. Royal Thames Yacht. S. of Alfred George Taylor, Esq. B. 10 Apr. 1910; m. May 1936, Constance, d. of F.E. Shotter, Esq. Educ. at Epsom Coll., and Trinity Coll., Cambridge, M.A. President of Grosvenor House (Park Lane) Limited. Previously Chairman Grosvenor House and a Director of Unigate Limited and Cow and Gate Limited. Capt. R.A. (T.A.) Aug. 1939. T. Maj. 1940. Staff Coll. 6th War Course 1941 graduated *s.c.* Honorary Col. Dept.-Lieut. of Sussex 1948. Knight Bach. 1954. Honorary Freeman County Borough of Eastbourne 1971. S.B. St. J., P.S.L.J. (DATO) Brunei. A Conservative. Elected for the Eastbourne division of East Sussex in Mar. 1935 and sat until he retired in Feb. 1974 after his local association had declined to re-adopt him as their candidate. President

of Residential Hotels Association until 1948. Chairman of Onyx County Estates Limited.*
[1974]

TAYLOR, Edward Macmillan. 77 Newlands Road, Glasgow. S. of Edward Taylor, Esq. B. 18 Apr. 1937; m. 12 Dec. 1970, Miss Sheila Duncan, (2 s.). Educ. at The High School of Glasgow, and Glasgow University, M.A. (Hons). Commercial Editorial Staff of the *Glasgow Herald* Oct. 1958-Apr. 1959. Industrial Relations Officer with the Clyde Shipbuilders' Association Apr. 1959-Oct. 1964. Member of Glasgow Town Council representing Cathcart Ward Jan. 1960. Former Vice-Chairman of the Conservative Parliamentary Transport Committee and Secretary of the Conservative Parliamentary Shipbuilding Committee. Under-Secretary of State for Scotland June 1970-July 1971 when he resigned and Jan.-Mar. 1974. Voted against entry to E.E.C. on 28 Oct. 1971. An Opposition spokesman on Scottish Affairs 1974-76, on Trade Nov.-Dec. 1976 and on Scottish Affairs Dec. 1976-May 1979. Member of Shadow Cabinet Nov. 1976-May 1979. A Conservative. Unsuccessfully contested Springburn division of Glasgow 1959. Elected for the Cathcart division of Glasgow in Oct. 1964 and sat until 1979, when he was defeated. Elected for Southend E. at a by-election in Mar. 1980.* [1979]

TAYLOR, Edwin. 602 Tonge Moor Road, Bolton. Constitutional. S. of Lawrence Taylor, Esq. B. 13 Feb. 1905; m. 1933, Sarah Elizabeth, d. of William Rostron, Esq. Educ. at St. John's, Wingates, and Bolton Technical Coll. Served Bolton Town Council for Tonge Ward 1940-45 and 1947-73. Elected Alderman 1955; J.P. 1952; Mayor of Bolton 1959-60; Dept. Mayor 1960-61. Founder, Chairman and Past President of Bolton and District Master Bakers' Association. A Conservative. Elected for Bolton E. at a by-election in Nov. 1960 and sat until 1964, when he was defeated. Unsuccessfully contested Bolton E. in 1966. A Master Baker. Member of Greater Manchester County Council 1973. Died 25 Sept. 1973. [1964]

TAYLOR, Vice-Admiral Ernest Augustus, C.M.G., C.V.O. 1a Holland

Park, London. United Service, R.Y.S., and R.A.C. S. of Lieut.-Col. F.H. Taylor, R.A., of Rolvenden, Kent. B. 17 Apr. 1876; m. 1st., 18 June 1898, Rose, d. of Louis Alexander Campbell, Esq. (she died 1956); 2ndly, 1957, Hilda, widow of Maj. Horace Gough Turner. Educ. at Stubbington School, and in H.M.S. *Britannia.* C.V.O. 1919; C.M.G. 1920. Retired from Royal Navy 1924, rejoined 1940-46. Member London County Council for Finsbury 1925-28. A Conservative. Unsuccessfully contested E. Woolwich in Dec. 1923 and Finsbury in Oct. 1924. Elected for Paddington S. in Oct. 1930 as an Empire Crusader, with the support of the United Empire Party, defeating the official Conservative candidate. Accepted the Conservative Whip in Sept. 1931 and sat until he retired in 1950. Knighted 1952. Died 11 Mar. 1971. [1950]

TAYLOR, Frank Henry. 2a Barrie House, Lancaster Gate, London. Tinker Taylor, Sennen Cove, Cornwall. R.A.C., City Livery, British Sportsman's, and Constitutional. S. of G.H. Taylor, Esq., of Cambridgeshire. B. 10 Oct. 1907; m. 1st, 1936, Margaret Dora Mackay (she died 1944), (1 d.); 2ndly, 1948, Mabel Hills (she died 1974), (2 s.); 3rdly, 1978, Glenys Mary Edwards, M.B.E., of Bethesda. Educ. at Rutlish School, Merton, Surrey. F.C.I.S. 1929; F.C.A. 1930. Principal of two firms of Chartered Accountants: Frank H. Taylor and Company, City of London and W.T. Flower and Company, Wimbledon. Financial Director, Ministry of Food 1942-45. Lieut.-Col. Home Guard 1943. Freeman of the City of London. Gov. of Rutlish School 1946. A Conservative. Unsuccessfully contested Newcastle-under-Lyme in 1955 and Chorley in 1959. Elected for the Moss Side division of Manchester in Nov. 1961 and sat until Feb. 1974, when he was defeated.*
[1974]

TAYLOR, Harry Bernard, C.B.E. 47 Shakespeare Avenue, Mansfield Woodhouse, Nottinghamshire. S. of Henry Taylor, Esq., of Mansfield Woodhouse. B. 18 Sept. 1895; m. 26 Mar. 1921, Clara, d. of John Ashley, Esq. Educ. at Council Schools. A Coal Miner. Parliamentary Private Secretary to Ben Smith, Parliamentary Secretary to Ministry of Aircraft Production 1942, and to Rt. Hon. James Griffiths, Minister of National Insurance 1945-50; Parliamentary Secretary to Ministry of National Insurance Mar. 1950-Oct. 1951. A Labour Member. Elected for the Mansfield division of Nottinghamshire in Apr. 1941 and sat until he retired in 1966. C.B.E. Jan. 1966. Created Baron Taylor of Mansfield (Life Peerage) 1966. Author of *Uphill all the way.** [1966]

TAYLOR, John, J.P. 68 Ellingham Road, Hemel Hempstead, Hertfordshire. S. of John Taylor, Esq., Grocer and Lecturer, of Edinburgh. B. 22 July 1902; m. 30 Aug. 1930, Olive, youngest d. of Councillor J.K. Fox, of Lincoln, at one time Mayor of that city. Educ. at Sciennes School, Edinburgh. Docker, Journalist and Organiser. Member of Reading County Borough Council 1932-35. J.P. for Glasgow; Scottish Secretary of the Labour Party 1939-50. Opposition Whip 1953-59, Dept. Chief Whip 1959-61. A Labour Member. Elected for West Lothian in Oct. 1951 and sat until his death on 1 Mar. 1962. Member of National Union of Labour Organisers and Election Agents and of National Union of General and Municipal Workers. Died 1 Mar. 1962. [1962]

TAYLOR, Robert George. Hinterland House, Effingham Common, Surrey. Junior Carlton. East India Sports, and Public Schools. S. of Frederick Taylor, Esq. B. 7 Dec. 1932; m. 1964, Rosemary Ann, d. of Arthur Box, Esq., (1 s. 1 d.). Educ. at Cranleigh. Director G. and S. Allgood Limited; Chairman South African subsidiary G. and S. Allgood (Pty.) Limited. Former Director Syncronol Industries Limited. Chairman Council of the Building Materials Export Group. Voted against entry to E.E.C. on 28 Oct. 1971. Member of Select Committee on Public Accounts 1975. A Conservative. Unsuccessfully contested N. Battersea in 1959 and 1964. Elected for Croydon N.W. in June 1970.* [1979]

TAYLOR, Rt. Hon. Robert John, C.B.E. Crow Ash, Blyth, Northumberland. B. 1881. A Checkweighman. J.P. for Northumberland. Member of Blyth Council 1935-38 and Northumberland City Council. Chairman of

Morpeth division of Labour Party. English Whip 1939. A Lord Commissioner of the Treasury Aug. 1945-Oct. 1951 and Dept. Chief Whip from 1946-1951. PC. 1951. A Labour Member. Elected for the Morpeth division of Northumberland in 1935 and sat until his death on 19 July 1954. C.B.E. 1949. [1954]

TAYLOR, Stephen James Lake. Governor's House, Holloway Prison, London. S. of John Reginald Taylor, Esq. B. 30 Dec. 1910; m. 3 Oct. 1939, May Charity (M.B., B.S., Gov. of Holloway Prison 1945-59), d. of W.G. Clifford, Esq. Educ. at Stowe, and St. Thomas's Hospital, M.D., B.S., B.Sc., M.R.C.P. Late Grocers' Research Scholar, Medical Unit, St. Thomas's Hospital; Sen. Resident Medical Officer Royal Free Hospital; Assistant M.O. Maudsley Hospital; Assistant Editor *Lancet*; Surgeon Commander (Neuro-Psychiatric Specialist) R.N.V.R. Member N.W. Metropolitan Regional Hospital Board; Gov. of University Coll. Hospital; Vice-Chairman British Film Institute; Director of Home Intelligence and Social Survey, Ministry of Information 1941-45; Medical Correspondent *Daily Herald*; Parliamentary Private Secretary to the Rt. Hon. Herbert Morrison, Lord President of the Council Oct. 1947-Feb. 1950. A Labour Member. Elected for the Barnet division of Hertfordshire in July 1945 and sat until 1950, when he was defeated. Member of Harlow New Town Development Corporation 1950-64 and 1966-67. Consultant in Occupational Health, Richard Costain Limited, 1951-64 and 1966-67. Medical Director, Harlow Industrial Health Service 1955-64 and 1965-67. Created Baron Taylor (Life Peerage) 1958. F.R.C.P. 1960. Under-Secretary of State for Commonwealth Relations Oct. 1964-Oct. 1965. Vice-Chancellor, Memorial University of Newfoundland 1967-73, Visiting Professor of Medicine from 1973. Author of works on environmental health.* [1950]

TAYLOR, Sir William Johnson, Bart., C.B.E., D.L., J.P. Flat 19b, 36 Buckingham Gate, London. Bentwood, Cawthorne, Barnsley. Carlton, Royal Aero, and Royal Air Force. S. of Frank Taylor, Esq., of Wombwell, Yorkshire. B. 23 Oct. 1902; m.

Mary, d. of Thomas B. Hall, Esq., of Barnsley. Educ. at Archbishop Holgate's Grammar School, Barnsley, and University of Sheffield. Building and Civil Engineering Contractor and Director of Engineering Companies. Member of Lloyds. Member of Barnsley Borough Council 1933-45; J.P. and Dept.-Lieut. for the W. Riding and City of York. A Founder and Honorary Air Commodore of the Air Training Corps. Raised and Commanded First Cadet Battalion, The York and Lancaster Regiment 1943-45. O.B.E. 1943; C.B.E. 1951. Past Chairman Yorkshire Prov. Area Conservative and Unionist Association. Chairman mid-Yorkshire Conservative and National Liberal Federation. Parliamentary Secretary Ministry of Supply Jan. 1957-Oct. 1959; Parliamentary Under-Secretary of State for Air Oct. 1959-July 1962. Bart. 1963. A Conservative and National Liberal Member. Unsuccessfully contested Bradford E. in 1945. Elected for Bradford N. in Feb. 1950 and sat until 1964, when he was defeated. Chairman of Sheffield Diocesan Board of Finance. High Sheriff of Hallamshire 1968-69. Died 26 July 1972.   [1964]

TAYLOR, Winifred Ann. House of Commons, London. D. of John Walker, Esq. B. 2 July 1947; m. David Taylor, Esq. Educ. at Bolton School, and Bradford and Sheffield Universities. Part-time Tutor with Open University. Member of Holmfirth Urban District Council 1972-74. Parliamentary Private Secretary to Rt. Hon. F.W. Mulley, Secretary of State, Education and Science 1975-76. Secretary of State for Defence 1976-77. Assistant Government Whip Jan. 1977-May 1979. An Opposition spokesman on Education from 1979. A Labour Member. Unsuccessfully contested Bolton W. in Feb. 1974. Sat for Bolton W. from Oct. 1974.*   [1979]

TEBBIT, Norman Beresford. House of Commons, London. S. of Leonard Albert Tebbit, Esq. B. 29 Mar. 1931; m. 29 Sept. 1956, Margaret Elizabeth, d. of S. Daines, Esq., (2 s. 1 d.). Educ. at Edmonton County Grammar School. A Journalist 1947-49; R.A.F. Pilot Commissioned 1949-51; R.Aux.A.F. 604 Squadron 1952-55; Publicist and Publisher 1951-53; Airline Pilot 1953-70; Various Y.C. local and area offices

1946-55. Various offices Hemel Hempstead Conservative Association 1960-67. Former Officer B.A.L.P.A. Chairman Conservative Aviation Committee. Former Secretary New Towns Members of Parliament Group. Former Vice-Chairman and Secretary Conservative Housing Committee. Former Secretary Conservative Industry Committee. Parliamentary Private Secretary to Robin Chichester-Clark Minister of State, Department of Employment 1972-73. Under-Secretary of State for Trade from May 1979. Assistant Director of Information, National Federation Building Trades Employers. Member Select Committee on Science and Technology. A Conservative. Prospective Parliamentary candidate for S.W. Islington 1967-69. Sat for the Epping division of Essex from 1970 to Feb. 1974. Elected for the Chingford division of Waltham Forest in Feb. 1974.*   [1979]

TEELING, Sir Luke William Burke. 88 St. James Street, London. Carlton, St. James', Kildare Street, Dublin, and Press. S. of Luke Alexander Teeling, Esq., J.P., Accountant-Gen. Supreme Court, Dublin, of Ower House, Co. Galway. B. 5 Feb. 1903; m. 21 Jan. 1942, Mary Julia, d. of Charles O'Conor, Esq. (she died 22 June 1953). Educ. at Oratory School, and Magdalen Coll., Oxford, M.A. 1958. A Roman Catholic. Chairman of Catholic Emigration Society of Great Britain and Northern Ireland 1929-31. An Author and Traveller. Served in R.A.F. 1940-45. Chairman Parliamentary Channel Tunnel Committee; founder Chairman of Regency Society. Chairman Conservative Middle East and Mediterranean Sub-Committee. Kt. of Malta. Knighted 1962. A Conservative. Unsuccessfully contested the Silvertown division of West Ham in 1929. Sat for Brighton from Feb. 1944 to Feb. 1950 and for the Pavilion division of Brighton from Feb. 1950 until he resigned in Feb. 1969. Died 26 Oct. 1975.   [1968]

TEEVAN, Thomas Leslie. House of Commons, London. S. of R. Teevan, Esq., of Limavady. B. July 1927. Educ. at Limavady Academy and Queen's University, Belfast. An Ulster Unionist Member. Elected for W. Belfast 29 Nov. 1950 and sat until Oct. 1951, when he was defeated. Lecturer in Law, Queen's University, Belfast. Barrister-at-Law, Northern Ireland, 1952. Chairman of Limavady Urban District Council. Died 11 Oct. 1954. [1951]

TEMPLE, John Meredith, J.P. Picton Gorse, Nr. Chester. 126 Whitehall Court, London. Carlton, Racquet (Liverpool), City, and Grosvenor (Chester). S. of Tom Temple, Esq., of Heswall. B. 1910; m. 1942, Nancy Violet, d. of Brigadier-Gen. Robert William Hare, C.M.G., D.S.O., D.L., Cobh, Eire and Norwich, (1 s. 1 d.). Educ. at Charterhouse, and Clare Coll., Cambridge. Served in war 1939-45 (despatches); Aide-de-Camp to Gov. of South Australia 1941. President of National Council of Salmon Netsmen of England and Wales; Chester Conservative Club; Joint-President United Nations Association, Chester Branch. Vice-President Association of Municipal Corporations, Rural District Councils' Association, Association of River Authorities, Army Benevolent Fund, Chester Branch. Vice-Chairman British Group Inter-Parliamentary Union, Vice-President the Salmon and Trout Association; member of the Council of the Royal Agricultural Society of England; Chairman of Anglo-Colombian Society, the Anglo-Columbian Parliamentary Group; Vice-Chairman of the Conservative Finance Committee 1966-68; Secretary of Anglo-Peruvian Parliamentary Group, Chairman All-Party British Latin-American Parliamentary Group; and Chairman Conservative Party Latin American Group; member of the N.W. Regional Board of the Abbey National Building Society. A Conservative. Elected for the City of Chester division of Cheshire in Nov. 1956 and sat until he retired in Feb. 1974. J.P. for Cheshire 1949, Dept.-Lieut. 1975.* [1974]

TEMPLE-MORRIS, Peter. 7 Redington Road, London. Huntington Court, Huntington, Herefordshire. Carlton. S. of His Hon. Sir Owen Temple-Morris, Q.C. B. 12 Feb. 1938; m. 25 July 1964, Taheré, d. of His Excellency Senator Khozeime Alam, (2s. 2d.). Educ. at Malvern, and St. Catharine's Coll., Cambridge, M.A. (Cantab.). A Barrister, Inner Temple 1962. Chairman Cambridge University Conservative Association.

Member Cambridge Afro-Asian Expedition 1961. Member Iran Society Council. Member Royal Institute of International Affairs (special interest Middle East and South Africa). Chairman Bow Group Standing Committee on Home Affairs 1975. Secretary Conservative Parliamentary Transport Committee 1976. Secretary Anglo-Iranian Parliamentary Group and Treasurer Anglo-Lebanese Parliamentary Group. Member Executive British Branch of Inter-Parliamentary Union and Delegate on their fact finding mission on Namibia 1977. Secretary Conservative Parliamentary Legal Committee 1977. Parliamentary Private Secretary to Rt. Hon. Norman Fowler, Minister of Transport, from 1979. A Conservative. Unsuccessfully contested Newport in 1964 and 1966, and the Norwood division of Lambeth in 1970. Elected for Leominster in Feb. 1974.* [1979]

THATCHER, Rt. Hon. Margaret Hilda. House of Commons, London. D. of Alfred Roberts, Esq. B. 13 Oct. 1925; m. Dec. 1951, Denis Thatcher, (1 s. 1 d. twins). Educ. at Kesteven and Grantham High School, and Somerville Coll., Oxford, M.A., B.Sc. Research chemist 1947-51. Called to the bar, Lincoln's Inn, 1954. Parliamentary Secretary Minister of Pensions and National Insurance 1961-64. Front Bench spokesman for the Opposition on Pensions and National Insurance Oct. 1964-Oct. 1965; Opposition Front Bench spokesman on Housing and Land Oct. 1965-Apr. 1966, and for the Treasury Apr. 1966-Oct. 1967. Chief Opposition Front Bench spokesman on Power and a member of the Shadow Cabinet Oct. 1967-Nov. 1968. Shadow Minister of Transport Nov. 1968-Oct. 1969. Shadow Minister of Education Oct. 1969-June 1970. Secretary of State for Education and Science June 1970-Mar. 1974. PC. 1970. Shadow Secretary of State for the Environment Mar.-Oct. 1974. Opposition Treasury spokesman Oct. 1974-Feb. 1975. Elected Leader of the Conservative and Unionist Party and Leader of the Opposition Feb. 1975. Prime Minister from May 1979. A Conservative. Unsuccessfully contested Dartford in 1950 and 1951 under her maiden name of Roberts. Sat for Finchley from 1959 to Feb. 1974 and for the Finchley division of Barnet from Feb. 1974.* [1979]

THOMAS, Dafydd Elis. House of Commons, London. B. 18 Oct. 1946; m. 1970, Elen M. Williams, (1 s.). Educ. at University Coll. of N. Wales. A Tutor in Welsh Studies, Coleg Harlech 1970. A Lecturer, Department of English, University Coll. of N. Wales 1974. A Plaid Cymru Member. Unsuccessfully contested the Conway division of Caernarvonshire in 1970. Elected for Merioneth in Feb. 1974.*
[1979]

THOMAS, David Emlyn. 65 Broniestyn, Aberdare, Glamorgan. B. 16 Sept. 1892; m. Bessie Thomas (she died 1953). Educ. at Elementary Schools. Member of Executive of S. Wales Mineworkers Union. Miners' agent for Merthyr and Aberdare 1936-46. A Congregationalist deacon. A Labour Member. Sat for the Aberdare division of Merthyr Tydfil from Dec. 1946 to Feb. 1950 and for Aberdare from Feb. 1950 until his death on 20 June 1954.
[1954]

THOMAS, Iorwerth Rhys. 39 Tallis Street, Cwmpark, Glamorgan. S. of David William Thomas, Esq., of Cwmpark. B. 22 Jan. 1895; m. 22 Oct. 1920, Mary, d. of D.J. Davies, Esq. Educ. at Elementary School. A Colliery Checkweighman. Member of Rhondda Urban District Council from 1928. Member of S. Wales Electricity Board from 1947 to 1949. A Labour Member. Elected for Rhondda W. in Feb. 1950 and sat until his death on 3 Dec. 1966.
[1966 2nd ed.]

THOMAS, Ivor. 12 Edwardes Square, London. Athenaeum. S. of Alfred Ernest Thomas, Esq., of Cwmbran, Newport, Monmouth. Assumed the surname Bulmer-Thomas in lieu of Thomas 1952. B. 30 Nov. 1905; m. 1st, 5 Apr. 1932, Dilys, d. of Dr. W. Llewelyn Jones of Merthyr Tydfil (she died 16 Aug. 1938); 2ndly, 26 Dec. 1940, Margaret Joan, d. of E.F. Bulmer, Esq., of Adam's Hill, Hereford. Educ. at West Monmouth School, Pontypool, St. John's Coll., Oxford (Scholar), and Magdalen Coll., Oxford (Senior Demy). A Journalist and Author. Joined the Editorial Staff of *The Times* 1930. Chief Leader Writer to *The News Chronicle* 1937-39. Served with the Royal Fusiliers 1939-40, and with the Royal Norfolk Regiment 1940-42 and 1945. Parliamentary Secretary Ministry of Civil Aviation Aug. 1945-Oct. 1946. Parliamentary Under-Secretary of State for the Colonies Oct. 1946-Oct. 1947. Unsuccessfully contested the Spen Valley division of the W. Riding of Yorkshire as a Labour candidate in 1935. Sat for the Keighley division of the W. Riding of Yorkshire from Feb. 1942 to Feb. 1950. Resigned from the Labour Party in Oct. 1948 and joined the Conservative Party in Jan. 1949. Unsuccessfully contested Newport, Monmouthshire, as a Conservative in 1950. Acting Dept. Editor of *The Daily Telegraph* 1953-54. Member of Church Assembly 1950-70, of General Synod of Church of England from 1970. Chairman of Redundant Churches Fund 1969-76. Vice-President of Church Union. Fellow of Society of Antiquaries. Chairman of Ancient Monuments Society.*
[1950]

THOMAS, Ivor Owen. 26 Sumburgh Road, London. S. of Benjamin L. Thomas, Esq., of Briton Ferry. B. 1898; m. 1929, Beatrice, d. of William Davis, Esq. Educ. at Vernon Place School, Briton Ferry, and London Labour Coll. A Trades Union Official. Employed at Gwalia Tinplate Works, Briton Ferry, 1912-19, on Great Western Railway 1919-23, and at Head Office of National Union of Railwaymen 1925-45 and 1955-58. Member of Battersea Borough Council 1929-45. A Labour Member. Elected for The Wrekin division of Shropshire in July 1945 and sat until 1955, when he was defeated. On the staff of British Railways at Waterloo 1960-64 and of Westminster City Council Land Use Survey 1965-66.*
[1954]

THOMAS, Rt. Hon. James Purdon Lewes. Admiralty House, Whitehall, London. White's. S. of J. Lewes Thomas, Esq., J.P., of Caeglas, Llandilo, Carmarthenshire. B. 13 Oct. 1903. Unmarried. Educ. at Rugby, and Oriel Coll., Oxford. Member of Secretariat of Rt. Hon. Stanley Baldwin Nov. 1929; Assistant Private Secretary Sept. 1931; Parliamentary Private Secretary to Rt. Hon. J.H. Thomas, Secretary of State for Dominions Feb. 1932-Nov. 1935, and when Secretary of State for the Colonies Nov. 1935-May 1936, and to Rt. Hon. Anthony Eden, Secretary of State for Foreign Affairs Apr. 1937-Feb. 1938, and when Secretary of State for Dominions Sept. 1939-May 1940; Assistant Whip May 1940. A Lord Commissioner of the Treasury June 1940-Sept. 1943; Financial Secretary to the Admiralty Sept. 1943-July 1945. 1st Lord of the Admiralty Nov. 1951-Sept. 1956. PC. 1951. Vice-Chairman of the Conservative and Unionist Party Aug. 1945-Oct. 1951. A Gov. of Rugby School, Chairman of Governors 1958-60. A Conservative. Unsuccessfully contested the Llanelly division of Carmarthenshire in 1929. Elected for the Hereford division of Herefordshire in 1931 and sat until Jan. 1956, when he was created Visct. Cilcennin. Lord Lieut. of Herefordshire 1957-60. K. St. J. 1958. Died 13 July 1960. [1955]

THOMAS, Jeffrey, Q.C. 3 Temple Gardens, Temple, London. 60 Lamont Road, London. Reform. S. of John J. Thomas, Esq., Headmaster. B. 12 Nov. 1933; m. Apr. 1960, Margaret Jenkins, B.Sc. Educ. at Abertillery Grammar School, King's Coll., London, and Gray's Inn. President University of London Union 1955-56. A Barrister, called by Gray's Inn 1957. Q.C. 1974. Dept. Assistant Director Army Legal Services 1961. Recorder of Crown Court from 1975. Chairman British Caribbean Association. Member Council of Justice. Member E.C. Inter-Parliamentary Union. Parliamentary Private Secretary to John Morris, Q.C., Secretary of State for Wales 1977-79. An Opposition spokesman on Legal Affairs from 1979. A Labour Member. Unsuccessfully contested Barry in 1966. Elected for the Abertillery division of Monmouthshire in June 1970.* [1979]

THOMAS, John Richard. 128 Piccadilly, London. S. of Richard Thomas, Esq., of Wrexham. B. 8 Mar. 1897; m. 1920, Emma, d. of G.R. Coulthard, Esq. Served with Gloucestershire Regiment 1914-18 and with R.A.F. 1924-28. Partner of Coulthard, Thomas and Company, Chartered Accountants. A Labour Member. Elected for the Dover division of Kent in July 1945 and sat until he retired in 1950. Died 4 July 1968. [1950]

THOMAS, John Stradling. House of Commons, London. S. of Thomas Roger Thomas, Esq. B. 10 June 1925; m. 1957 Freda Rhys Evans, (1 s. 2 d.). Educ. at Rugby, and London University. Member Carmarthen Borough Council 1961-64. Member N.F.U. Council 1963-70. Member of Select Committee on Civil List 1970-71. Assistant Government Whip Nov. 1971-Oct. 1973. Lord Commissioner of Treasury Oct. 1973-Mar. 1974. Opposition Whip 1974-79. Treasurer of Royal Household and Government Dept. Chief Whip from May 1979. A Conservative. Unsuccessfully contested Aberavon in 1964, and Cardiganshire in 1966. Elected for Monmouth in 1970.* [1979]

THOMAS, Sir Leslie Montagu, M.B.E., T.D. House of Commons, London. Carlton. S. of Rt. Hon. J.H. Thomas, MP. B. 24 Apr. 1906; m. 5 Sept. 1929, Ursula, d. of H. Owen, Esq. Educ. at Elementary and Private Schools, and Dulwich Coll. Served 1939-45 in N. Africa and Italian Campaigns; Maj. R.A. Member of London Stock Exchange since 1931; member of Caterham Urban District Council and Chairman of Finance Committee 1931-35; of Whitstable Urban District Council 1950-52. M.B.E. 1945. Knight Bach. Jan. 1963. Parliamentary Private Secretary to Rt. Hon. Charles Hill, Chancellor of Duchy of Lancaster and Minister of Housing and Local Government 1961-62. A Conservative. Unsuccessfully contested the Leek division of Staffordshire as a National Labour candidate in 1935. Elected for the Canterbury division of Kent in Feb. 1953 and sat until he retired in 1966. Died 27 Nov. 1971. [1966]

THOMAS, Michael Stuart. House of Commons, London. Walker Social, Newcastle-upon-Tyne. S. of Arthur Edward Thomas, Esq. B. 24 May 1944. Educ. at Kings School, Macclesfield, and Liverpool University. President Liverpool University. Guild of Undergraduates 1965-66. Head Co-operative Party Research Department 1966-68. Sen. Research Officer, Political and Economic Planning 1968-73. Director Volunteer Centre 1973-74. Former member N.U.S. Executive. Member U.S.D.A.W. Parliamentary Private Secretary to Rt. Hon. Roy Hattersley, MP. from 1975 to 1976. Member Select Committee on Nationalised Industries. Founder of Parliament's weekly journal *The House Magazine*. A Labour and Co-operative Member. Unsuccessfully contested E. Hertfordshire in 1970. Elected for Newcastle-upon-Tyne E. in Oct. 1974.* [1979]

THOMAS, Rt. Hon. Peter John Mitchell, Q.C. 145 Kennington Road, London. Carlton. S. of David Thomas, Esq., Solicitor. B. 31 July 1920; m. 20 Dec. 1947, Frances Elizabeth Tessa, d. of Basil Dean, Esq., C.B.E. Educ. at Epworth Coll., Rhyl, and Jesus Coll., Oxford, M.A. A Theatrical Producer. Barrister-at-Law, Middle Temple 1947. Q.C. 1965. Master of the Bench 1971. War Service in R.A.F. Parliamentary Private Secretary to Sir Harry Hylton-Foster, Solicitor-Gen. 1954-59; Parliamentary Secretary to Ministry of Labour 1959-61; Parliamentary Under-Secretary of State, Foreign Office 1961-63; Minister of State for Foreign Affairs 1963-64. An Opposition spokesman on Legal Affairs 1965-66 and on Wales 1974-75. Dept. Chairman Cheshire Quarter Sessions 1966-70; Denbighshire Quarter Sessions 1968-70. Secretary of State for Wales and member of the Cabinet June 1970-Mar. 1974. Chairman Conservative Party July 1970-Apr. 1972. President National Union of Conservative and Unionist Associations 1974-76. Member of Shadow Cabinet 1974-75. A Recorder of the Crown Court from 1974. PC. 1964. A Conservative. Sat for Conway from 1951-66 when he was defeated. Sat for Hendon S. from 1970 to Feb. 1974 and for the Hendon S. division of Barnet from Feb. 1974.* [1979]

THOMAS, Ronald Richard. House of Commons, London. B. Mar. 1929. Educ. at Ruskin Coll., and Balliol, Oxford. A University Lecturer. Member of Bristol City Council 1972-75. A Labour Member. Unsuccessfully contested Bristol N.W. in Feb. 1974. Elected for Bristol N.W. in Oct. 1974 and sat until 1979, when he was defeated.* [1979]

THOMAS, Rt. Hon. Thomas George. Speaker's House, House of Commons, London. S. of Zachariah Thomas, Esq. B. 29 Jan. 1909. Unmarried. Educ. at Tonypandy Secondary School, and University Coll., Southampton. A Schoolmaster from 1931. Member of the Executive of National Union of Teachers 1940-45. Chairman Welsh P.L.P. 1950-51. Parliamentary Private Secretary to Lord Ogmore, Minister of Civil Aviation July-Nov. 1951. Member of Chairman's Panel, House of Commons 1951-64. President National Brotherhood Movement 1955. Chairman Welsh Parliamentary Party 1958-59. Vice-President of the Methodist Conference 1960-61. Parliamentary Under-Secretary of State, Home Office Oct. 1964-Apr. 1966. Minister of State, Welsh Office Apr. 1966-Jan. 1967. Minister of State, Commonwealth Office Jan. 1967-Apr. 1968. Secretary of State for Wales Apr. 1968-June 1970. Opposition spokesman on Wales 1970-74. PC. 1968. Freeman of Borough of Rhondda 1970. Elected Fellow University Coll. of Cardiff 1973. Dept. Speaker and Chairman of Ways and Means 1974-76. Freeman of the City of Cardiff Mar. 1975. Honorary Life member N.U.T. Apr. 1976, Honorary LL.D. Asbury University, U.S.A. June 1976, Honorary LL.D. University of Southampton July 1977, Honorary LL.D. University of Wales July 1977, Honorary LL.D. University of Birmingham 1978. Elected Speaker of the House of Commons from Feb. 1976. A Labour Member. Sat for Central Cardiff from July 1945 to Feb. 1950. Elected for the W. division of Cardiff in Feb. 1950.* [1979]

THOMPSON, Dr. Alan Eric. House of Commons, London. S. of Eric Joseph Thompson, Esq. B. 16 Sept. 1924; m. 1960 Mary Heather Long. Educ. at University of Edinburgh, M.A., Ph.D. Served in Army 1943-47. A Labour Member. Candidate for Galloway in 1950 and 1951. Elected for Dunfermline Burghs in 1959 and sat until he retired in 1964. Lecturer in Economics, University of Edinburgh 1953-59 and 1964-71. Parliamentary Adviser to Scottish Television 1966-76. Visiting Professor, Stanford University Graduate Business School 1966 and 1968. Member of Public Schools Commission Scottish Committee 1969-70. Chairman of Advisory Board on Economics Education 1970-76. Professor of the Economics of Government, Heriot-Watt University from 1972. Chairman of Northern Offshore Maritime Resources Study from 1974. Member of Royal Fine Art Commission for Scotland from 1975. Scottish Governor of B.B.C. from 1976.*

[1964]

THOMPSON, George Henry. House of Commons, London. B. 1928. Educ. at Dalry School, Kirkcudbright Academy, and Edinburgh University. A former S.N.P. Assistant National Secretary. A Teacher of Modern Languages. A Scottish National Party Member. Unsuccessfully contested Galloway in Feb. 1974. Elected for Galloway in Oct. 1974 and sat until 1979, when he was defeated.*

[1979]

THOMPSON, Sir Kenneth Pugh, Bart. House of Commons, London. S. of Ernest S. Thompson, Esq. B. 24 Dec. 1909; m. 1936, Nanne Broome, of Walton, (1 s. 1 d.). Educ. at Arnot Street School, and Bootle Grammar School. Served as Regional Officer with Ministry of Information during Second World War. Formerly member of Executive Committee National Union of Conservative and Unionist Associations, Council of Liverpool University, Lancashire and Merseyside Development Association, and Liverpool City Council 1938-58, Watch and Parks and Gardens Committees. Vice-President Liverpool Y.C.'s.; formerly Vice-President Association of Municipal Corporations. National Union of Manufacturers; Honorary President Liverpool Association of Chairframe Manufacturers; Secretary 1922 Committee 1951-58. Parliamentary Delegate to Brazil 1954 and to Liberia and Gambia in 1963. Assistant Postmaster-Gen. Jan. 1957-Oct. 1959. Parliamentary Secretary Ministry of Education Oct. 1959-July 1962. In Jan. 1963 was created a Bart. with the territorial designation of Walton-on-the-Hill in the City of Liverpool. A Conservative. Elected for the Walton division of Liverpool in 1950 and sat until 1964, when he was defeated. Unsuccessfully contested the Walton division of Liverpool in 1966. Member of Merseyside County Council from 1973, Chairman and Leader of the Council from 1977. Dept. Chairman of Merseyside Docklands Urban Development Corporation from 1980.*

[1964]

THOMPSON, Sir Richard Hilton Marler, Bart. Rhodes House, Sellindge, Kent. Carlton. S. of Richard Thompson, Esq., East India Merchant. B. 5 Oct. 1912; m. 9 Aug. 1939, Anne Christabel, d. of Philip de Vere Annesley, B.A. Educ. at Malvern Coll. Served in R.N. 1940-46; retired with rank of Lieut.-Commander. R.N.V.R. (despatches). Assistant Government Whip 1952; Lord Commissioner of the Treasury July 1954-Apr. 1956; Vice-Chamberlain H.M. Household Apr. 1956-Sept. 1957; Parliamentary Secretary Ministry of Health Sept. 1957-Oct. 1959; Under-Secretary of State, C.R.O. Oct. 1959-Oct. 1960; Parliamentary Secretary Ministry of Works Oct. 1960-July 1962; member Public Accounts Committee 1973; a Trustee of the British Museum; Chairman British Museum Society; Chairman Capital and Counties Property Company Limited 1971-77. A Conservative. Sat for Croydon W. from 1950-55 and Croydon S. from 1955-66, when he was defeated. Re-elected for Croydon S. in June 1970 and sat until he retired in Feb. 1974. Created Bart. 1963. President of British Property Federation 1976-77.*

[1974]

THOMSON, Rt. Hon. George Morgan. 7 Carver Road, London. S. of James Thomson, Esq., of Dundee. B. 16 Jan. 1921; m. 23 Dec. 1948, Grace, d. of Cunningham Jenkins, Esq., of Glasgow. Educ. at Grove Academy, Broughty Ferry. Served in R.A.F. 1940-45. A Journalist and former Editor of *Forward*. Joint Chairman Council for Education in the Commonwealth 1959-64. Minister of State, Foreign Office from Oct. 1964 to Apr. 1966 and Jan.-Aug. 1967. Chancellor of the Duchy of Lancaster Apr. 1966-Jan. 1967. PC. 1966. Secretary of State for Commonwealth Affairs Aug. 1967-Oct. 1968. Minister without Portfolio Oct. 1968-Oct. 1969. Chancellor of the Duchy of Lancaster Oct. 1969-June 1970. Shadow Defence Minister 1970-72. Chairman Labour Committee for Europe 1972. Chairman David Davies Institute of International Affairs 1971. Opposition spokesman on Colonies 1959-64 and on Defence 1970-72. A Labour Member. Voted in favour of entry to E.E.C. on 28 Oct. 1971. Unsuccessfully contested the Hillhead division of Glasgow in 1950. Elected for Dundee E. in July 1952 and sat until he resigned in Oct. 1972 on appointment as E.E.C. Commissioner-designate. Member of Commission of European Communities Jan. 1973-Jan. 1977. Member of Parliamentary Committee of P.L.P. from July 1970 to Apr. 1972, when he resigned. Chairman of Labour Committee for Europe 1972-73. Created Baron Thomson of Monifieth (Life Peerage) 1977. Chairman of Advertising Standards Authority 1977-80. Chairman of European Movement in Britain from 1977. First Crown Estate Commissioner 1977-80. Chancellor of Heriot-Watt University from 1977. Dept. Chairman and Chairman-designate of Independent Broadcasting Authority from 1980.* [1973]

THOMSON, Rt. Hon. George Reid, K.C. 44 Northumberland Street, Edinburgh. S. of the Rev. W.R. Thomson. B. 1893; m. 1925, Grace, d. of the Rev. D. Georgeson. Educ. at South African Coll., Capetown, and at Corpus Christi Coll., Oxford (Honorary Fellow). Capt. A. and S. Highlanders 1914-18. Called to the Scottish bar 1922. K.C. 1936. Advocate Depute 1940-45. PC. 1945. Lord Advocate for Scotland Aug. 1945-Oct. 1947. A Labour Member. Elected for Edinburgh E. in Oct. 1945 and sat until Oct. 1947, when he was appointed Lord Justice Clerk. Lord Justice Clerk, with the judicial title of Lord Thomson, 1947-62, Honorary LL.D. Edinburgh University 1957. Died in Gibraltar 15 Apr. 1962. [1947]

THOMSON, Sir (James) Douglas Wishart, Bart. 8 Egerton Place, London. S. of Sir Frederick Thomson, Bart., Conservative MP. for S. Aberdeen 1918-35. B. 30 Oct. 1905; m. 26 Sept. 1935, Bettina, d. of Lieut.-Commander David W.S. Douglas, R.N. Educ. at Eton, and at University Coll., Oxford. Succeeded as Bart. 1935. Parliamentary Private Secretary to William Mabane when Assistant Postmaster-Gen. June-Oct. 1939, to Rt. Hon. Sir John Gilmour, Oct. 1939, to Rt. Hon. R.S. Hudson Apr. 1940, and to Rt. Hon. Ronald Cross May 1940-May 1941, successively Ministers of Shipping, and to Col. The Rt. Hon. J.J. Llewellin, Joint Parliamentary Secretary Ministry of War Transport May 1941-Feb. 1942. A Conservative. Elected for S. Aber-

deen in May 1935 and sat until he resigned in Nov. 1946. Managing Director of William Thomson and Company, Shipowners. Chairman of Ben Line Steamers Limited 1964-70. Died 3 Jan. 1972. [1946]

THORNE, Stanley George. 17a Chislehurst Avenue, Liverpool. S. of Frederick George Thorne, Esq. B. 22 July 1918; m. 24 Oct. 1952, Catherine Mary Rand, (2 s. 3 d.). Educ. at Ruskin Coll., Oxford, and University of Liverpool, B.A. Hons., Oxford University Diploma in Social Studies. Former Coal Miner, Railwayman, and Lecturer. Member of Liverpool City Council 1963-66 and 1971-74. A Labour Member. Unsuccessfully contested the Wavertree division of Liverpool in 1964. Elected for Preston S. in Feb. 1974.* [1979]

THORNEYCROFT, Rt. Hon. George Edward Peter, C.H. House of Commons, London. Army & Navy. S. of Maj. Mervyn Thorneycroft, D.S.O. B. 26 July 1909; m. 1st, 3 May 1938, Sheila, d. of E.W. Page, Esq., of Wergs Road, Tettenhall, Wolverhampton (marriage dissolved 1949); 2ndly, 2 Apr. 1949, Carla Roberti, d. of Count Malagola Cappi of Ravenna. Educ. at Eton, and Royal Military Academy, Woolwich. Late Royal Artillery. Barrister-at-Law, Inner Temple, 1934; Parliamentary Secretary Ministry of War Transport May-July 1945. President of the Board of Trade (Cabinet) Nov. 1951-Jan. 1957; Chancellor of the Exchequer Jan. 1957-Jan. 1958, when he resigned; Minister of Aviation July 1960-July 1962. Minister of Defence July 1962-Apr. 1964. Secretary of State for Defence Apr.-Oct. 1964. Opposition spokesman on Defence 1964-65 and on Home Affairs 1965-66. Member of Shadow Cabinet 1964-66. PC. 1951. A Conservative. Sat for the Stafford division from June 1938 to July 1945, when he was defeated. Elected for the Monmouth division of Monmouthshire in Oct. 1945 and sat until 1966, when he was defeated. Created Baron Thorneycroft (Life Peerage) 1967. Chairman of Simplification of International Trade Procedures 1968-75. Chairman of British Overseas Trade Board 1972-75. Chairman of Conservative Party from 1975. Chairman of Pye of Cambridge Limited, Pirelli Limited and Trust Houses Forte Limited. C.H. 1980.* [1966]

THORNEYCROFT, Harry. 140 Droylsden Road, Newton Heath, Manchester. B. 21 Feb. 1892; m. 1924, Lily, d. of Edward Ford, Esq. (she died 1950). Educ. at Elementary School. Served overseas 1914-19. Member of Manchester City Council 1923, Alderman 1939. Parliamentary Private Secretary to the Rt. Hon. Lord Pethick-Lawrence, Secretary of State for India and Burma 1945-47, and to the Rt. Hon. Arthur Henderson, Secretary of State for Air 1947-51. A Labour Member. Unsuccessfully contested the Blackpool division in 1935. Elected for the Clayton division of Manchester in Oct. 1942 and sat until he retired in 1955. President of National Federation of Hairdressers. Died 7 Mar. 1956.   [1954]

THORNTON, Ernest, M.B.E. 6 Lyndhurst Avenue, Castleton, Rochdale, Lancashire. S. of Charles Thornton, Esq., of Burnley. B. 1905; m. 1930, Evelyn, d. of F. Ingham, Esq. Educ. at Walverden Council School, Nelson. Gen. Secretary United Textile Factory Workers' Association 1943-53. Member of Lord President's Advisory Council for Scientific and Industrial Research 1943-48, Member of Council of British Cotton Industry Research Association 1948-53. M.B.E. 1951. President Amalgamated Weavers' Association 1960-64. J.P. for Rochdale 1944; Mayor of Rochdale 1942-43. Parliamentary Secretary Ministry of Labour Oct. 1964-Apr. 1966. A Labour Member. Elected for the Farnworth division of Lancashire in Oct. 1952 and sat until he retired in 1970. Member of National Executive Committee of Labour Party 1962-63, Dept.-Lieut. for Lancashire, later for Greater Manchester, from 1970.*   [1970]

THORNTON-KEMSLEY, Sir Colin Norman, O.B.E., T.D. 80 Cheyne Court, Chelsea, London. Thornton Castle, Laurencekirk, Kincardineshire. Carlton, and Scottish Conservative. S. of Norman Kemsley, Esq., of Woodford Green, Essex. B. 2 Sept. 1903; m. 7 June 1930, Alice Helen, only child of William Thornton, Esq., of Thornton, assuming by Deed Poll the additional surname of Thornton on his marriage. Educ. at Chigwell School, and Wadham Coll., Oxford, M.A. Partner in Kemsleys Chartered Surveyors. F.R.I.C.S. Director John Lewis Properties

Roy King Properties and Thornton Farms Limited. Rejoined R.A. from T.A.R.O. Sept. 1939; Staff Coll. 1943; held many Staff appointments 1939-45; Area Commander with rank of Col. 1945. O.B.E. 1946. T.D. 1950. Knighted 1958. A Liberal Unionist Member. Sat for Kincardine and Western division of Kincardine and Aberdeenshire from Mar. 1939 to Feb. 1950. Elected for the N. Angus and Mearns division of Angus and Kincardine in Feb. 1950 and sat until he retired in 1964. Vice-President of Town and Country Planning Association. Chairman of National Liberal Parliamentary Party 1961-64. Died 17 July 1977.   [1964]

THORP, Brigadier Robert Allen Fenwick, O.B.E. Lincoln House, Basil Street, London. Cavalry. S. of Thomas Thorp, Esq. B. 1900; m. 1939, Sybil, d. of Francis Hall, Esq., of Melton Mowbray. Educ. at Charterhouse. Served with Skinners Horse 1919-21, with 1st Life Guards 1921-30, Northumberland Hussars 1929-34; p.s.c. 1937; Senior Officer School Sheerness 1938; War Office 1939, in France 1939-40, Palestine and Abyssinia 1941, E. Africa 1942; commanded Bde. 1943-45. O.B.E. 1941. Retired with rank of Brigadier 1945. Conservative Whip 1947-48. A Conservative. Elected for the Berwick-on-Tweed division of Northumberland in July 1945 and sat until he retired in 1951. Died 5 May 1966.   [1951]

THORPE, Rt. Hon. John Jeremy. Higher Chuggaton, Cobbaton Umberleigh, North Devon. National Liberal. S. of J.H. Thorpe, Esq., K.C., O.B.E., J.P., MP. B. 29 Apr. 1929; m. 1st, 31 May 1968, Caroline Allpass (she died 1970), (1 s.); 2ndly, 14 Mar. 1973, Marion Countess of Harewood, d. of Erwin Stein, Esq. Educ. at Eton, in America, and Trinity, Oxford. President of the Oxford Union. A Barrister-at-Law, Inner Temple 1954. Honorary Treasurer of Liberal Party 1965-67. Elected Leader of the Liberal Party Jan. 1967, resigned May 1976. PC. 1967. Liberal spokesman on Foreign Affairs 1976-78. A Liberal. Unsuccessfully contested N. Devon in 1955. Elected for N. Devon in 1959 and sat until 1979, when he was defeated. Honorary Fellow of Trinity Coll., Oxford 1972. Chairman of United Nations Association from 1976. Accused in Aug. 1978 of conspiracy to murder Norman Scott and of unlawfully inciting David Holmes to murder Norman Scott and committed for trial on 13 Dec. 1978. The trial was postponed until after the General Election and opened on 8 May 1979. Acquitted on both charges on 22 June 1979.* [1979]

THURTLE, Ernest. 2 Paper Buildings, Temple, London. S. of Philip Thurtle and Emma Robinson, of Norfolk. B. 11 Nov. 1884; m. 13 Aug. 1912, Dorothy, d. of George Lansbury, Esq., MP. for Bow and Bromley. Served in France etc. 1914-48. Parliamentary Private Secretary to F.O. Roberts, Minister of Pensions Jan.-Oct. 1924, and to the Rt. Hon. G. Lansbury when First Commissioner of Works June 1929; a Lord Commissioner of the Treasury Oct. 1930-Aug. 1931; Parliamentary Secretary Ministry of Information July 1941-May 1945. A Labour Member. Unsuccessfully contested S.W. Bethnal Green in 1918 and Shoreditch in 1922. Sat for Shoreditch from 1923-31, when he was defeated, and 1935-50. Opposition Whip Aug.-Oct. 1931. Elected for Shoreditch and Finsbury in Feb. 1950 and sat until his death on 22 Aug. 1954. [1954]

TIERNEY, Sydney. House of Commons, London. S. of James Tierney, Esq. of Goldthorpe. B. Sept. 1923; m. 1956 Audrey. Educ. at Plater Coll., Oxford. J.P. for Leicester. Parliamentary Private Secretary to Edward Bishop, Minister of State for Agriculture, Fisheries and Food Mar. 1976. President Union of Shop and Distributive and Allied Workers Apr. 1977 to 1979. Member of National Executive Committee of Labour Party from 1978. A Roman Catholic. A Labour Member. Sat for the Yardley division of Birmingham from Feb. 1974 until 1979 when he was defeated.* [1979]

TIFFANY, Stanley. 6 North Street, Peterborough. S. of Albert Tiffany, Esq., of Rothwell. B. 1908; m. 1st, 1935, Alice, d. of Guy Howells, Esq., of Farnley; 2ndly, 1967, Audrey, d. of Harry Taylor, Esq. Educ. at Leeds Boys' Modern School. An Electrical Engineer. Director of Peterborough and District Co-operative Society. A Labour Member. Elected for the Peterborough division of Northamptonshire in July 1945 and sat until 1950, when he was defeated. Member of Wakefield Borough Council 1952-67. C.B.E. 1967. Hotel Proprietor in Bridlington. Died 19 Mar. 1971. [1950]

TILEY, Arthur. House of Commons, London. S. of Aykroyd Tiley, Esq., of Bradford. B. 1910; m. 1936, Mary, d. of Craven Tankard, Esq. Educ. at Grange High School, Bradford. Treasurer Bradford Y.W.C.A. 1934-50; Senior Company Officer in National Fire Service during Second World War. An Insurance Broker and Marine Underwriter. A Conservative and National Liberal Member. Unsuccessfully contested Bradford Central in 1951. Elected for Bradford W. in 1955 and sat until 1966, when he was defeated. Member of Council, Churchill Memorial Trust 1965-76. J.P. for Bradford 1967. C.B.E. 1972. Chairman of Clarkson, Tiley and Hargreaves Limited, Northern Capital Limited and Bradford and Northern Housing Association Limited.* [1966]

TILLEY, John Vincent. House of Commons, London. B. June 1941; m. Tracey (1 d.). Educ. at Bemrose Grammar School and Trinity Hall, Cambridge. Formerly Industrial Correspondent of *The Scotsman.* Joined the Labour Party in 1967. Member N.U.J. and T.G.W.U. Elected to Wandsworth Borough Council 1971 and 1974. A Labour Member. Unsuccessfully contested Kensington in Feb. and Oct. 1974 general elections. Elected for the Central division of Lambeth in Apr. 1978.* [1979]

TILNEY, Sir John Dudley Robert Tarleton, T.D., J.P. 3 Victoria Square, London. 25 Fulwood Park, Liverpool. Carlton, Jesters, Royal Tennis Court, Liverpool Cricket, Royal Liverpool Golf, and Liverpool Racquet. S. of Col. R.H. Tilney, D.S.O. B. 19 Dec. 1907; m. 3 June 1954, Guinevere, d. of Sir Alfred Hamilton Grant, Bart., K.C.S.I., K.C.I.E. Educ. at Eton, and Magdalen Coll., Oxford. Member of the Liverpool Stock Exchange 1932 (later United Stock Exchange). Served overseas 1939-45, commanded 359 Med. Regiment R.A., T.A.; Honorary Col. 470 (3 W. Lancs.) L.A.A.

Regiment (R.A.)., T.A. 1957-61. J.P. for Liverpool 1946. Parliamentary Private Secretary to Rt. Hon. A.H. Head, Secretary of State for War 1951-55. Chairman British Group Inter-Parliamentary Union 1959-62. Parliamentary Private Secretary to Rt. Hon. A.E. Marples, Postmaster-Gen. 1957-59 and Minister of Transport 1959-62. Parliamentary Under-Secretary of State for Commonwealth Relations July 1962-Oct. 1964. Treasurer of U.K. Branch of the Commonwealth Parliamentary Association 1968-70. Chairman Winston Churchill Memorial Statue Appeal. Knight Bach. 1973. A Conservative. Elected for the Wavertree division of Liverpool in Feb. 1950 and sat until he retired in Feb. 1974. Member of Executive Committee of Conservative Political Centre from 1972.* [1974]

TIMMONS, John. House of Commons, London. B. 14 May 1890; m. Emily Connelly (she died 1958). Educ. at Elementary School and Coatbridge Technical Coll. Served in Royal Navy 1939-45. A Miner. Member of Lanark County Council 1938-45. A Labour Member. Elected for the Bothwell division of Lanarkshire in July 1945 and sat until he retired in Sept. 1964. Died 21 Nov. 1964. [1964]

TINN, James. 1 Norfolk Road, Moorside, Consett, Co. Durham. S. of James Tinn, Esq. B. 23 Aug. 1922. Educ. at Elementary School, Ruskin Coll., Oxford, Diploma in Politics, Science and Economics, and Jesus Coll., Oxford, B.A., P.P.E. A School Teacher, formerly Coke Oven Worker. Joined the Labour Party in 1950. Joined the N.U. Blastfurnacemen 1948, (Lodge Secretary). Member of the Fabian Society from 1955, N.U.T. from 1958, and Consett Co-operative Society from 1950. Parliamentary Private Secretary to Rt. Hon. Arthur Bottomley, Secretary of State, Commonwealth Relations 1965-66 and Minister of Overseas Development 1966-67. Chairman of Trade Union Group of Labour MPs. 1969-71. Assistant Government Whip June 1976-May 1979. Opposition Whip from May 1979. A Labour Member. Sat for Cleveland from 1964 to Feb. 1974. Elected for the Redcar division of Teesside in Feb. 1974.* [1979]

TITTERINGTON, Meredith Farrar. 38 Homestead, Menston-in-Wharfedale, Yorkshire. S. of George Titterington, Esq. B. 1886; m. 1913, Phyllis, d. of Thomas Midgley, Esq. Educ. at Bradford School and Technical Coll., Ruskin Coll., and Labour Coll., Oxford. Apprenticeship in Wool, Textile Dyeing and Finishing Industry. Acting Secretary of National Association of Unions in Textile Trade 1919; President 1930-36. Member of Bradford City Council 1919-45; Lord Mayor 1939-40; J.P. for Bradford. Chairman of Ministry of Information Committee and of Civil Defence Emergency Committee; member of Board of Trade Advisory Council 1930-33. A Labour Member. Elected for Bradford S. in 1945 and sat until his death on 28 Oct. 1949. [1949]

TOLLEY, Louis Byron. 25 Larches Road, Kidderminster. S. of Joseph Tolley, Esq., of Kidderminster. B. 1889; m. 1912, Beatrice, d. of John Gower, Esq. Member of Kidderminster Borough Council 1919-46 and 1951-59, Mayor 1942-43, 1943-44 and 1956-57. A Labour Member. Unsuccessfully contested the Kidderminster division of Worcestershire in 1923. Elected for the Kidderminster division of Worcestershire in July 1945 and sat until 1950, when he was defeated. Died 30 Apr. 1959. [1950]

TOMLINSON, Rt. Hon. George. 87 Park Mansions, Knightsbridge, London. S. of John Wesley Tomlinson, Esq., of Rishton. B. 21 Mar. 1890; m. 4 Sept. 1914, Ethel, d. of Humphrey Pursell, Esq., of Rishton. Educ. at Rishton Elementary School. Member of Lancashire County Council 1931-45. A Trade Union Secretary; Joint Parliamentary Secretary Ministry of Labour Feb. 1941-May 1945; Minister of Works Aug. 1945-Feb. 1947. Minister of Education with a Seat in the Cabinet Feb. 1947-Oct. 1951. PC. 1945. A Labour Member. Elected for the Farnworth division of Lancashire in Jan. 1938 and sat until his death on 22 Sept. 1952. A Methodist Lay Preacher. A Weaver for 25 years. J.P. for Lancashire. Died 22 Sept. 1952. [1952]

TOMLINSON, John Edward. House of Commons, London. S. of Frederick Edwin

Tomlinson, retired Headteacher. B. 1 Aug. 1939; m. 17 Aug. 1963, Marianne Sommar of Stockholm, (3 s.). Educ. at Westminster City School, Co-operative Coll., and Brunel University. Secretary Sheffield Co-operative Party 1963-68. Head of Research Department A.U.E.W. 1968-70. Lecturer in Industrial Relations 1970-74. Parliamentary Private Secretary to Rt. Hon. H. Wilson when Prime Minister 1975-76. Parliamentary Under-Secretary of State for Foreign and Commonwealth Affairs Apr. 1976-May 1979. Also Parliamentary Secretary Ministry of Overseas Development Feb. 1977-May 1979. A Labour Member. Unsuccessfully contested Bridlington in 1966 and Walthamstow E. in 1970. Elected for Meriden in Feb. 1974 and sat until 1979, when he was defeated.*

[1979]

TOMNEY, Frank. 446 Uxbridge Road, London. S. of Arthur Tomney, Esq., Textile Engineer. B. 1908; m. 12 Sept. 1936, Gladys, d. of Andrew Isham, Esq. A Marketing Analyst and Industrial Consultant. Official General and Municipal Workers Union 1940-50. Member Watford Town Council 1946-50 and Hertfordshire County Council 1949-58. Delegate Council of Europe 1960-64 and 1973. Delegate Western European Union 1960-64 and 1973. Voted in favour of entry to E.E.C. on 28 Oct. 1971. Member of European Parliament Nov. 1976-Mar. 1977. Member of European Movement. A Labour Member. Elected for Hammersmith N. in Feb. 1950 and sat until he retired in 1979.*

[1979]

TOPE, Graham Norman. House of Commons, London. S. of Leslie Tope, Esq. B. 30 Nov. 1943; m. 22 July 1972, Margaret, d. of Frank East, Esq. Educ. at Whitgift School, South Croydon. Chairman Sutton and Cheam Young Liberals 1967-69. Unsuccessfully contested Greater London Council elections in Sutton in 1970. Chairman South East England Young Liberals 1970-71. Vice-Chairman National League of Young Liberals 1971-73. A Liberal. Elected for Sutton and Cheam in Dec. 1972 and sat until Feb. 1974, when he unsuccessfully contested the Sutton and Cheam division of Sutton. Unsuccessfully con-

tested the same constituency in Oct. 1974. Councillor and Leader of Liberal group, London Borough of Sutton from 1974. Dept. General Secretary, Camden Council of Social Service from 1975. Joint author of *Liberals and the Community.** [1974]

TORNEY, Thomas William. House of Commons, London. B. July 1915; m. 1940. Member General Management Committee, Derby Labour Party and member and past Chairman North Midland Regional Joint Apprenticeship Council for catering industry. J.P. for Derbyshire. Labour Party Agent, Wembley N. 1945 and Derbyshire W. 1964. Derby and District Area Organizer, U.S.D.A.W. 1946-70. Member Parliamentary Select Committee Race Relations. Chairman Parliamentary Labour Party Agriculture Fish and Food Group. A Labour Member. Sat for Bradford S. from June 1970.* [1979]

TOUCHE, Rt. Hon. Sir Gordon Cosmo, Bart. 2 Anstie Grange, Holmwood, Surrey. Carlton, and R.A.C. S. of Sir George Touche, Bart. B. 8 July 1895; m. 7 Apr. 1926, Ruby, d. of Sir Duncan Macpherson, C.I.E. Educ. at Marlborough, and University Coll., Oxford, M.A. Served in Gallipoli, Palestine and Egypt 1915-18. Barrister-at-Law, Inner Temple, 1923. Knighted 1952. PC. 1959. Dept. Chairman of Ways and Means 1956-59. Chairman of Ways and Means Oct. 1959 to Jan. 1962. Created Bart. 1962. A Conservative. Unsuccessfully contested Ashton-under-Lyne in Oct. 1928 and N. Islington in 1929. Sat for the Reigate division of Surrey from 1931 to Feb. 1950. Elected for the Dorking division of Surrey in Feb. 1950 and sat until he retired in 1964. Died 19 May 1972. [1964]

TOWNSEND, Cyril David. House of Commons, London. S. of Lieut.-Col. C.M. Townsend. B. 21 Dec. 1937; m. 31 July 1976, Anita S.W. Walshe, d. of Lieut.-Col. F.G.W. Walshe, M.C., and Mrs. Walshe. Educ. at Bradfield Coll., and Royal Military Academy, Sandhurst. Commissioned The Durham Light Infantry, served in Berlin, U.K., Cyprus and Borneo. Adjutant 1966-68. Aide-de-Camp to H.E. The Gov. and C. in C.

Hong Kong, Sir David Trench, G.C.M.G., M.C., 1964-66. Personal Assistant to the Rt. Hon. Edward Heath, M.B.E., MP. 1968-70. Conservative Research Department 1970-74. Parliamentary Private Secretary to Rt. Hon. R.E. Prentice, Minister for Social Security, May-Dec. 1979. Member Council St. Christopher's Fellowship. Joint Secretary of the Conservative Greater London members. Member of Select Committee on Violence in the Family. Committee member of 'Friends of Cyprus'. Member Executive Committee S.E. London Industrial Consultative Group. Vice-President Greater London Young Conservatives. Chairman Bow Group Standing Committee on Foreign Affairs. A Conservative. Sat for the Bexleyheath division of Bexley from Feb. 1974.* [1979]

TRAFFORD, Dr. (Joseph) Anthony Porteous. 14B The Upper Drive, Hove, Sussex. S. of Dr. Harold Trafford. B. 20 July 1932; m. 1960, Helen, d. of Ralph Chalk, Esq. Educ. at St. Edmunds, Hindhead, Charterhouse, and Guy's Hospital Medical School, Lincoln's Inn. Graduated M.B., B.S. 1957; various medical appointments 1957-65; Consultant Physician, Brighton and Lewes Group from 1965. A Conservative. Elected for The Wrekin division of Shropshire in June 1970 and sat until Feb. 1974, when he was defeated.* [1974]

TREW, Peter John Edward, M.I.C.E. House of Commons, London. Naval and Military. S. of Antony Trew, Esq., D.S.C., Author. B. 30 Apr. 1932; m. 1955, Angela, d. of Kenneth Rush, Esq., C.B.E. Educ. at Diocesan Coll., Rondebosch, Cape. Royal Navy 1950-54; Chartered Institute of Secretaries Sir Ernest Clarke Prize 1955; Director of Rush and Tompkins Limited 1968, Rush and Tompkins Group Limited 1973; Joint Secretary Conservative Parliamentary Finance Committee 1972; member Select Committee Tax Credits 1972-73. A Conservative. Unsuccessfully contested Dartford in 1966. Elected for the Dartford division of Kent in June 1970 and sat until Feb. 1974, when he was defeated. Member of Council of C.B.I. from 1975.* [1974]

TROTTER, Neville Guthrie. Granville House, Granville Road, Newcastle-on-Tyne. Carlton, and R.A.F. S. of Capt. Alexander Trotter. B. 27 Jan. 1932. Educ. at Shrewsbury and King's Coll., Durham University, B.Com. A Chartered Accountant. Formerly Partner Thornton Baker and Company now Consultant. Member Newcastle City Council 1962-74, Alderman 1970. Member Northern Economic Planning Council 1968-74. J.P. for Newcastle-on-Tyne 1973. Member of Tyne and Wear County Council 1973-74. Member Civil Aviation Authority Airline Users' Committee. Member of Council Royal United Services Institute. Vice-Chairman Conservative Parliamentary Shipping and Shipbuilding Committee. Secretary Aviation Committee. Member Industry Sub-Committee of House of Commons Expenditure Committee. A Conservative. Unsuccessfully contested the Consett division of County Durham in 1970. Sat for Tynemouth from Feb. 1974.* [1979]

TUCK, Raphael Herman. 10 King's Bench Walk, Temple, London. S. of David Lionel Tuck, Esq. B. 5 Apr. 1910; m. 1959, Monica J. Ley Greaves. Educ. at St. Pauls School, London University, (L.S.E.), B.Sc. (Econ.). Trinity Hall, Cambridge, M.A., and Harvard University, LL.M. A Barrister-at-Law, Gray's Inn, 1951. Became a member of the London School of Economics Labour Party in 1936. On return from America rejoined the Labour Party in 1954. Member of the Society of Labour Lawyers from 1954. Member of 'Justice', Harvard Law Association of the U.K. Harvard Club of London. Vice-President Watford Society for Mentally Handicapped Children; Sea Lions Swimming Club for the Handicapped; National Association of Swimming Clubs for the Handicapped. Watford Operatic Society; Hertfordshire Association member Committee Patron Action for the Crippled Child Watford branch. Member of the Court, Reading University. Vice-President Watford Community Relations Council. Honorary member Hertfordshire Chamber of Commerce. Worked at the British Embassy, Washington 1940-41. A Lecturer and later Professor of Law, University of Saskatchewan, Canada 1941-45; Constitutional Adviser to the Premier of Manitoba, Canada 1943; Special Research Assistant, Ministry of Labour, Ottawa, Canada 1944; Professor of Political Science, McGill University, Montreal, Canada 1945-46. Professor of Political Science, Tulane University, New Orleans, U.S.A. 1947-49. Knighted June 1979. A Labour Member. Sat for Watford from Oct. 1964 until he retired in 1979.* [1979]

TUGENDHAT, Christopher Samuel. 1 Caroline Terrace, London. Carlton. S. of Dr. Georg Tugendhat. B. Feb. 1937; m. 1967, Julia Lissant Dobson, (2 s.). Educ. at Ampleforth Coll., Gonville and Caius Coll., Cambridge. President of the Union. *Financial Times* leader and feature writer 1960-70; Consultant, Wood Mackenzie 1968; Director Sunningdale Oils 1971-76; Director Phillips Petroleum International U.K. Limited 1972-76; Consultant 1976. Publications: *Oil, The Biggest Business* (1968), and *The Multinationals* (1971). Parliamentary Private Secretary to Rt. Hon. William Whitelaw, Secretary of State for Employment 1973-74. Opposition spokesman on Employment 1974-75 and on Foreign Affairs 1975-76. A Conservative. Sat for the Cities of London and Westminster from 1970 to Feb. 1974 and for the City of London and Westminster S. division of the Cities of London and Westminster from Feb. 1974 to Jan. 1977, when he was appointed a Member of the Commission of the European Communities. Member of the Commission of the European Communities, with responsibility for the Budget and Financial Control, Financial Institutions, Personnel and Administration from 1977.* [1977]

TURNER, Colin William Carstairs, D.F.C. 55 Rowantree Road, Enfield. Institute of Directors, Devonshire, R.A.F. Reserves. S. of Colin C.W. Turner, Esq. B. 4 Jan. 1922; m. 7 May 1949, Evelyn Mary, d. of Claude H. Buckard, Esq., of Ealing. Educ. at Highgate School. Served with R.A.F. 1940-45, Flying Officer, D.F.C. 1944. Enfield Young Conservatives 1945-53. National Executive National Union of Conservative Party 1946-53, 1968-73 and 1976-78. Chairman Enfield E. Conservative Association 1954-59. Dept. Chairman Enfield Borough Conserv-

ative Association 1954-59. Enfield Borough Council 1956-58. A Conservative. Unsuccessfully contested Enfield E. in 1950 and 1951. Elected for Woolwich W. in 1959 and sat until 1964, when he was defeated. Managing Director of Colin Turner and W. Ager Group of Companies. President of Overseas Press and Media Association 1965-67. Editor of *Overseas Media Guide* 1968-74. Chairman of Commonwealth Press Union P.R. Committee 1970-78. Chairman of Conservative Commonwealth and Overseas Council 1976-78.* [1964]

TURNER, Henry Frederic Lawrence. 165 High Holborn, London. Carlton. S. of G.F. Turner, Esq., M.B.E., Architect. B. 30 Dec. 1908; m. 8 Feb. 1938, Tessa, d. of C.R. Hartley, Esq., (1 s. 1 d.), (divorced 1966). Educ. at Radley, University of Reading and Exeter Coll., Oxford. Served in Royal Artillery 1939-45, imprisoned by the Japanese. Director of five companies. A Conservative. Unsuccessfully contested N. Paddington in Nov. 1946 and Feb. 1950. Elected for Oxford in Nov. 1950 and sat until he retired in 1959. Conservative Whip withdrawn May 1957-July 1958. Information Officer, Central Office of Information 1961-64. Died 17 Dec. 1977. [1959]

TURNER-SAMUELS, Moss, Q.C. 48 Pont Street, London. Abbot's Rill, Upton St. Leonards, Gloucestershire. B. 19 Oct. 1888; m. 1917, Gladys Deborah Belcher. Educ. at Newcastle-upon-Tyne Grammar School. Served with R.A.S.C. 1914-18. Solicitor 1914-21; Barrister-at-Law, Middle Temple 1922; K.C. 1946; member of Newcastle City Council 1921; High Sheriff of Gloucester 1945-46; Recorder of Halifax 1948-57; a Legal, Industrial and Political Writer. A Labour Member. Sat for the Barnard Castle division of Durham from 1923-24 when he was defeated. Unsuccessfully contested Leeds Central in 1931 and Gloucester in 1935. Elected for Gloucester in July 1945 and sat until his death on 6 June 1957. [1957]

TURTON, Rt. Hon. Sir Robert Hugh ('Robin'), K.B.E., M.C. 15 Greycoat Gardens, London. Upsall Castle, Thirsk, Yorkshire. S. of Maj. R.B. Turton. B. 8 Aug. 1903; m. 31 Mar. 1928, Ruby Christian, d. of R.T.

Scott, Esq. Educ. at Eton, and Balliol Coll., Oxford. J.P. for Yorkshire N. Riding. Barrister-at-Law, Inner Temple, Apr. 1926. J.P. for N. Riding of Yorkshire 1936. Served overseas 1940-43. M.C. 1942. Parliamentary Secretary Ministry of National Insurance Nov. 1951-Sept. 1953. Joint Parliamentary Secretary Ministry of Pensions and National Insurance Sept. 1953-Oct. 1954. Parliamentary Under-Secretary Foreign Affairs Oct. 1954-Dec. 1955. Minister of Health Dec. 1955-Jan. 1957. PC. 1955. Dept.-Lieut. for the N. Riding of Yorkshire 1962. Chairman Commonwealth Industries Association from 1963 to 1974. K.B.E. 1971; Chairman Select Committee on Procedure House of Commons 1970-74. Voted against entry to E.E.C. on 28 Oct. 1971. A Conservative. Elected for the Thirsk and Malton division of the N. Riding of Yorkshire in May 1929 and sat until he retired in Feb. 1974. Father of House of Commons Jan. 1965-Feb. 1974. Created Baron Tranmire (Life Peerage) 1974.*

[1974]

TWEEDSMUIR, Priscilla Jean Fortescue, The Lady. 40 Tufton Court, Westminster, London. Potterton House, Balmedie, Aberdeenshire. D. of Brigadier Alan Fortescue Thomson, D.S.O., of Craighall, Kennethmont, Aberdeenshire. B. 25 Jan. 1915; m. 1st, 14 May 1934, Sir Arthur Lindsay Grant of Monymusk, 11th Bart., of Cullen, who was killed in action in 1944, (2 d.); 2ndly, 27 July 1948, 2nd Baron Tweedsmuir, (1 d.). Member Council Royal Institute of International Affairs 1957-60. Delegate Council of Europe 1950-52; Chairman Scottish Advisory Panel British Council 1950-62; U.K. Delegate United Nations General Assembly 1960-61. Member of Committee of U.N. Commissioner for Refugees and Chairman 1961-62. Honorary Col. 316 (Scottish Command) Battalion W.R.A.C./T.A. 1958-61. Under-Secretary of State for Scotland Dec. 1962-Oct. 1964. Opposition spokesman on Foreign Affairs 1965-66. A Conservative. Unsuccessfully contested Aberdeen N. in 1945. Elected for Aberdeen S. in Nov. 1946 and sat until 1966, when she was defeated. Created Baroness Tweedsmuir of Belhevie (Life Peerage) 1970. Minister of State, Scottish Office June 1970-Apr. 1972. Minister of

State, Foreign and Commonwealth Office Apr. 1972-Mar. 1974. PC. 1974. Principal Dept. Chairman of Committee and Chairman of European Communities Committee, House of Lords 1974-77. Died 11 Mar. 1978.

[1966]

TYLER, Paul Archer. Viverdon, St. Mellion, Saltash, Cornwall. 29 Cleaver Square, London. S. of Oliver Walter Tyler, Esq. B. 29 Oct. 1941; m. 27 June 1970, Nicky, d. of Michael Ingram, Esq. Educ. at Sherborne School, Dorset, and Exeter Coll., Oxford. President Oxford University Liberal Club 1962. Councillor Devon County Council 1964-70. Member Devon and Cornwall Police Authority 1966-70. Administrative Staff, R.I.B.A. 1966-72, Director of Public Affairs 1972-73, Parliamentary Adviser 1974. Liberal spokesman on Housing and Transport 1974. A Liberal. Unsuccessfully contested Totnes in 1966 and Bodmin in 1970. Elected for Bodmin in Feb. 1974 and sat until Oct. 1974, when he was defeated. Unsuccessfully contested Bodmin in 1979. Chairman of Council for the Protection of Rural England Working Party on the Future of the Village 1974-78. Executive Director of *Cornwall Courier*.*

[1974 2nd ed.]

UNGOED-THOMAS, Sir (Arwyn) Lynn, Q.C. 4 King's Bench Walk, Temple, London. S. of the Rev. Evan Ungoed-Thomas, of Carmarthen. B. 29 June 1904; m. 19 Apr. 1933, Dorothy Travers, d. of Jasper Travers Wolfe, Esq., of Co. Cork. Educ. at Haileybury, and Magdalen Coll., Oxford, (Demy). Barrister-at-Law, Inner Temple, 1929, Chancery Bar; member Bar Council 1946; K.C. 1947; Master of the Bench of Lincoln's Inn 1951, Treasurer 1968. Chairman Chancery Bar Association 1957. Member of British Delegation to first Council of Europe 1949. Member of Leasehold Reform Committee and signed minority report in favour of leasehold enfranchisement; member of Court Martial Committee, Chairman Mr. Justice Pilcher. Solicitor-Gen. Apr.-Oct. 1951. Maj. R.A., served 1939-45. A Labour Member. Sat for Llandaff and Barry from July 1945 to Feb. 1950. Unsuccessfully contested Carmarthen in Feb. 1950. Elected for the N.E. division of Leicester in Sept. 1950 and sat until he was appointed a High Court Judge in Apr. 1962. Knighted 1951. Judge of the Chancery Division 1962-72. Died 4 Dec. 1972. [1962]

URWIN, Rt. Hon. Thomas William. 28 Stanhope Close, Houghton-le-Spring, Co. Durham. S. of Willie Urwin, Esq. of Hetton-le-Hole, Miner. B. 9 June 1912; m. 1934, Edith, d. of J. Scott, Esq., Miner. Educ. at Elementary School. A Trade Union Organiser. Joined the Labour Party in 1940 and Amalgamated Union of Building Trade Workers in 1928. Chairman of Houghton Urban District Council 1954-55, Councillor 1949-65; Chairman Housing and Planning Committee 1950-65; Leader of Labour Group. Minister of State Department of Economic Affairs Apr. 1968-Oct. 1969. Minister of State, Local Government and Regional Planning Oct. 1969-June 1970. Chairman Parliamentary Trade Union Group Mar. 1974. Leader of the British Parliamentary Delegation to the Council of Europe and Western European Union Apr. 1976. Chairman of Council of Europe Socialist Group May 1976. PC. 1979. A Labour Member. Sat for the Houghton-le-Spring division of Durham from Oct. 1964.* [1979]

USBORNE, Henry Charles. Totterdown, Aldington, Evesham, Worcestershire. S. of Charles Frederick Usborne, Esq. B. 16 Jan. 1909; m. 1936, Pamela, d. of H.D. Watson, Esq. Educ. at Bradfield, and Corpus Christi Coll., Cambridge. Managing Director of Nu-Way Heating Plants Limited. A Labour Member. Sat for the Acocks Green division of Birmingham from July 1945 to Feb. 1950. Elected for the Yardley division of Birmingham in Feb. 1950 and sat until 1959, when he was defeated. J.P. for Worcestershire 1964-79. Chairman of U.A. Engineering Limited, Sheffield.* [1959]

VAN STRAUBENZEE, William Radcliffe, M.B.E. 199 Westminster Bridge Road, London. 30 Rose Street, Wokingham, Berkshire. Carlton. S. of Brigadier A.B. van Straubenzee, D.S.O., M.C., and Mrs. A.B. van Straubenzee, of Richmond, Surrey. B. 1924. Unmarried. Educ. at Westminster. Served R.A. 1942-47. Maj., D.A.A. and

Q.M.G. Member Executive Committee of National Association of Conservative and Unionist Associations 1949-59. Member Conservative Overseas Bureau 1950-67. Admitted a Solicitor 1952. Chairman Young Conservative National Advisory Committee 1951-53. Honorary Secretary United and Cecil Club 1953-59 and Chairman 1964-68. Member of Richmond, Surrey Borough Council 1955-58. Parliamentary Private Secretary to Sir David Eccles, Minister of Education 1960-62. Past Chairman of Govs. Archbishop Tenison's Grammar School, Kennington. Former Chairman Westminster House Boys' Club, Camberwell. Honorary Secretary Federation of Conservative Students 1965-71. Member of the House of Laity of the Church Assembly for the Diocese of Oxford 1965-70 and of Gen. Synod from 1975. A Church Commissioner from 1968. An Opposition spokesman on Education and Science 1969-70 and Mar.-June 1974 and on Defence June-Oct. 1974. Member Court of Reading University. Honorary Vice-President National Union of Students. Joint Under-Secretary of State for Education and Science June 1970-Nov. 1972. Minister of State, Northern Ireland Office Nov. 1972-Mar. 1974. Member of Shadow Cabinet Mar.-June 1974. Chairman Select Committee on Assistance to Private Members 1975. Chairman National Council for Drama Training 1976. Chairman of Dioceses Commission from 1978. Second Church Estates Commissioner from 1979. M.B.E. (Civil) 1954. A Conservative. Unsuccessfully contested the Clapham division of Wandsworth in 1955. Elected for Wokingham, Berkshire in 1959.* [1979]

VANE, William Morgan Fletcher, T.D. 31 Marsham Court, London. Hutton in the Forest, Penrith, Cumberland. Junior Carlton, and Travellers'. S. of Col. Hon. William Lyonel Vane. B. 12 Apr. 1909; m. 28 July 1949, Mary, d. of Sir Richard Proby, Bart., of Elton Hall, Peterborough, (2 s.). Educ. at Charterhouse, and Trinity Coll., Cambridge, M.A. 1934. Assumed the surname of Fletcher-Vane in lieu of Vane 1931. Dept.-Lieut. for Westmorland 1946, for Cumbria 1974. A Landowner, Chartered Surveyor and Land Agent. Lieut.-Col. Durham Light Infantry (T.A.) 1943. Served overseas 1940-44 (despatches). Member Historic Buildings Council for England 1954-58. Parliamentary Private Secretary to Sir Thomas Dugdale, Minister of Agriculture 1951-54, to Rt. Hon. R.H. Turton, Under-Secretary Foreign Affairs 1954-55 and Minister of Health 1955-56; Joint Parliamentary Secretary to Ministry of Pensions and National Insurance Apr. 1958-Oct. 1960. Joint Parliamentary Secretary Ministry of Agriculture Oct. 1960-July 1962. A Conservative. Elected for Westmorland in July 1945 and sat until June 1964, when he was created Baron Inglewood. Chairman of Anglo-German Association from 1973.* [1964]

VARLEY, Rt. Hon. Eric Graham. House of Commons, London. S. of Frank Varley, Esq. B. 11 Aug. 1932; m. 1955, Marjorie, d. of Alfred Turner, Esq. Educ. at Secondary School, and Chesterfield Technical Coll. Three-year course Sheffield University Extra Mural Department (economics, industrial relations and political theory), Ruskin Coll., Oxford. A Craftsman, mining industry. Joined the Labour Party in 1955. Member of Derbyshire Area Executive Committee of N.U.M. 1956-64. Member of the National Union of Mineworkers. Assistant Government Whip July 1967-Nov. 1968. Parliamentary Private Secretary to Rt. Hon. Harold Wilson, Prime Minister Nov. 1968-Oct. 1969. Minister of State, Ministry of Technology Oct. 1969-June 1970. An Opposition spokesman on Industry and Power 1970-74 and on Employment from 1979. Chairman of Trade Union Group of Labour MPs. 1971-74. Secretary of State for Energy Mar. 1974-June 1975. Secretary of State for Industry from June 1975 to May 1979. Member of Parliamentary Committee of P.L.P. from 1979. PC. 1974. A Labour Member. Sat for Chesterfield from Oct. 1964.* [1979]

VAUGHAN, Gerard Folliott. House of Commons, London. S. of Leonard Vaughan, Esq., D.S.O., D.F.C. B. June 1923; m. 1955, Joyce Thurle. Educ. at London University, and Guy's Hospital Medical School. An Alderman London County Council 1955-61; Councillor for Streatham 1961-1964; Coun-

cillor for Lambeth 1967-70. Alderman Greater London Council 1970-72. Member of S.E. Economic Planning Council 1968-71. Fellow of the Royal Coll. of Physicians; Consultant Guy's Hospital. Parliamentary Private Secretary to William Whitelaw, Secretary of State for Northern Ireland 1974. Opposition Whip 1974-75. Opposition spokesman on Health 1975-79. Minister of State (Minister for Health) Department of Health and Social Security from May 1979. A Conservative. Unsuccessfully contested Poplar in 1955. Sat for Reading from 1970 to Feb. 1974. Elected for Reading S. in Feb. 1974.* [1979]

VAUGHAN-MORGAN, Rt. Hon. Sir John Kenyon, Bart. 36 Eaton Square, London. Ashcraft Lodge, Outwood, Redhill, Surrey. Brooks's, Carlton, and Hurlingham. S. of Sir Kenyon Vaughan-Morgan, O.B.E., MP. B. 2 Feb. 1905; m. 13 Mar. 1940, Emily, d. of W. Redmond Cross, Esq., of New York City, New York, U.S.A. Educ. at Eton, and Christ Church, Oxford. Lieut-Col. Welsh Guards, served overseas 1940-45 (despatches). G.S.O.1. Staff 21st Army Group. Member of Chelsea Borough Council 1928-31, of London County Council 1946-52. Director Morgan Crucible Company Limited. Parliamentary Secretary Ministry of Health Jan.-Sept. 1957; Minister of State Board of Trade Sept. 1957-Oct. 1959. Chairman Board of Governors Westminster Hospital 1963-74. A Conservative. Elected for the Reigate division of Surrey in Feb. 1950 and sat until he retired in 1970. Created Bart. 1960. PC. 1961. Created Baron Reigate (Life Peerage) 1970.* [1970]

VERNON, Maj. Wilfrid Foulston. 64 Kings Hall Road, Beckenham, Kent. Wyngarth, East Compton, Bristol. S. of George Thomas Vernon, Esq. B. 1882; m. 1st, 1907, Josephine, d. of Joseph Jervis, Esq., of Stafford (she died 1917); 2ndly, 1918, Laura Gladys, d. of Dr. H. Meade of Bradford (she died 1972). Educ. at Stationers' Company's School, and City and Guilds Technical Coll. An Electrical and Aeronautical Engineer. Lecturer on Technical and Social Subjects. Served with R.N.V.R., R.N.A.S. and R.A.F. 1914-18. Technical

Officer Air Ministry 1925-37; Instructor No. 1 Home Guard School 1940-42. A Labour Member. Elected for the Dulwich division of Camberwell in July 1945 and sat until 1951, when he was defeated. Unsuccessfully contested the Camberwell division of Dulwich in 1955. Member of London County Council 1952-55 and Camberwell Borough Council 1953-56. Died 1 Dec. 1975.　　　　[1951]

VIANT, Samuel Philip, C.B.E. 94 Doyle Gardens, Willesden, London. S. of Daniel W. Viant, Esq. B. at Plymouth 1882; m. 1911, Emily, d. of John Harvey, Esq. (she died 1956). Educ. at Devonport Higher Grade School and Ruskin Coll., Oxford. Foreman Carpenter and Joiner. Member of the London Labour Party Executive 1915-18; member of Willesden District Council; J.P. for Middlesex from 1928; Assistant Postmaster-Gen. June 1929-Aug. 1931; member of Select Committee on Parliamentary Procedure 1945-46 and on Members' Fund 1946, Chairman from 1946. C.B.E. 1948. Member of Select Committee on Members' Salaries and Expenses 1953-54, and of Committee of Privileges 1953-54 and 1954-55. A Labour Member. Unsuccessfully contested Willesden W. in 1918 and 1922. Sat for Willesden W. from Dec. 1923-Oct. 1931, when he was defeated, and from 1935 until he retired in 1959. Vice-Chairman of National Conciliation Board for Building Industry. Mayor of Willesden 1960-61. Died 19 May 1964.　　　　[1959]

VICKERS, Dame Joan Hilda, D.B.E. 6 Albemarle Villas, Devonport. D. of Horace Cecil Vickers, Esq. B. 1907. Educ. at St. Monica's Coll., Burgh Heath, and in Paris. Member London County Council 1937-46; served with B.R.C.S. in S.E. Asia; M.B.E. 1946; Netherlands Red Cross Distinguished Service Cross. Served in Colonial Service in Malaya 1946-50. A Conservative. Unsuccessfully contested S. Poplar in 1945. Elected for the Devonport division of Plymouth in 1955 and sat until Feb. 1974, when she was defeated. D.B.E. 1964. Delegate to Council of Europe and W.E.U. 1967-74. Unsuccessfully contested the Devonport division of Plymouth in Oct. 1974. Created Baroness Vickers (Life Peerage) 1974. Chairman of Anglo-Indonesian Society.*　　　[1974]

VIGGERS, Peter John. House of Commons, London. S. of John Sidney Viggers, Esq. B. 13 Mar. 1938; m. 7 Dec. 1968, Jennifer Mary, d. of Dr. R.B. McMillan. Educ. at Portsmouth Grammar School, and Trinity Hall, Cambridge, M.A. Hons (Cantab.). National Service R.A.F. 1956-58. Articled to Solicitor in Gosport, qualified 1967. Parliamentary Private Secretary to Sir Michael Havers, Attorney-General and to Sir Ian Percival, Solicitor-General from 1979. Director Energy, Finance and General Trust Limited, Premier Consolidated Oilfields Limited and the Sangers Group Limited. Underwriting member of Lloyds. Member of Bow Group. Territorial Army Officer for 5 years. A Conservative. Sat for Gosport from Feb. 1974.*　　　[1979]

VOSPER, Rt. Hon. Dennis Forwood, T.D. Henblas, Llanasa, Holywell, Flintshire. 68 Marsham Court, London. S. of Gerald Linn Vosper, of Heswall, Cheshire. B. 2 Jan. 1916; m. 1st, 26 July 1940, Margaret, d. of Sidney Ashford, Esq. (divorced 1966); 2ndly, 1966, Helen Norah, d. of Sir Crosland Graham. Educ. at Marlborough Coll., and Pembroke Coll., Cambridge, B.A. A Ship's Provision and Export Merchant. Served with T.A. Cheshire Regiment 1939-45, retired as Maj. T.D. 1950. Conservative agent for Knutsford 1946-50. Honorary Secretary Anglo-Turkish Society 1953. Member of Parliamentary Delegation to Israel Apr. 1951. Conservative Whip 1950. Government Whip and a Lord Commissioner of the Treasury Nov. 1951-Oct. 1954. Member of Parliamentary Delegation to Turkey June 1953; Leader Parliamentary Delegation W. Indies Apr. 1958. Parliamentary Secretary Ministry of Education Oct. 1954-Jan. 1957. Minister of Health Jan. 1957, resigned owing to illness Sept. 1957. PC. 1957. Joint Under-Secretary of State, Home Office Oct. 1959-Oct. 1960. Member of Albemarle Committee 1959. Minister of State, Home Office Oct. 1960-June 1961. Secretary for Technical Co-operation June 1961, resigned May 1963. A Conservative. Elected for the Runcorn division of Cheshire in Feb. 1950 and sat until Mar. 1964, when he was created Baron Runcorn (Life Peerage). Chairman of National Assistance Board 1964-66, of

Supplementary Benefits Commission 1966-68. Died 20 Jan. 1968. [1964]

WADDINGTON, David Charles, Q.C.
Flat 125, 4 Whitehall Court, London. Whins House, Sabden, Nr. Blackburn, Lancashire. S. of Charles Waddington, Esq., J.P., of The Old Vicarage, Read, Near Burnley, Lancashire. B. 2 Aug. 1929; m. 1958, Gillian, d. of Alan Green, Esq., MP., of Sabden, Blackburn. Educ. at Sedbergh, and Hertford Coll., Oxford. A Barrister, Gray's Inn, 1951. Served with Royal Lancers 1951-53, 2nd Lieut. Q.C. 1971. Parliamentary Private Secretary to Sir Peter Rawlinson, Attorney General 1970-74. A Conservative. Unsuccessfully contested Farnworth in 1955, Nelson and Colne in 1964 and Heywood and Royton in 1966. Elected for Nelson and Colne in June 1968 and sat until Oct. 1974, when he was defeated. Elected for Clitheroe at a by-election in Mar. 1979. A Company Director. A Recorder of the Crown Court from 1972. Lord Commissioner of the Treasury from May 1979.* [1974 2nd ed.]

WADE, Donald William. White Lodge, Ashleigh Road, Leeds. National Liberal. S. of William Mercer Wade, Esq., of Ilkley, Yorkshire. B. 16 June 1904; m. 18 June 1932, Ellenora, d. of F.H. Bentham, Esq. Educ. at Mill Hill School, and Trinity Hall, Cambridge. Partner in Leeds firm of Solicitors. Liberal Whip 1956-62. Dept. Leader 1962-64. A Liberal. Elected for Huddersfield W. in Feb. 1950 and sat until 1964, when he was defeated. Created Baron Wade (Life Peerage) 1964. Dept. Liberal Whip in the House of Lords 1965-67. President of Liberal Party 1967-68. Dept.-Lieut for W. Riding of Yorkshire 1967, for N. Yorkshire 1974.* [1964]

WADSWORTH, George. Foxholes Manor, E. Riding, Yorkshire. S. of Arnold Holroyd Wadsworth, Esq. B. 10 Dec. 1902; m. 24 July 1930, Guinivere, d. of Leonard Shepherd, Esq., of Halifax. Educ. at Heath Grammar School, Halifax, and Willaston Coll., Nantwich. Director of G. Wadsworth and Son Limited, and of Wadsworth, White Lead Company Limited, Halifax, and of Yorkshire Equipment Company Limited, Bridlington. Member of Public Accounts Committee

1945-47; with Parliamentary Mission to Hungary 1946. Member of Halifax Town Council 1938-49. A Liberal. Elected for the Buckrose division of the E. Riding of Yorkshire in July 1945 and sat until 1950, when he unsuccessfully contested the Bridlington division of the E. Riding of Yorkshire. Unsuccessfully contested the Hillsborough division of Sheffield in 1951 as a National Liberal and Conservative Candidate.* [1950]

WAINWRIGHT, Edwin. House of Commons, London. S. of John Wainwright, Esq. B. 1908; m. 1938, Dorothy Metcalfe. Educ. at Darfield County School, and Wombwell and Barnsley Technical Coll. Darfield Main Branch, N.U.M. Committee 5 years, Delegate 9 years, and Secretary 11 years. Member of Wombwell Urban District Council for 20 years 1939-59. Secretary/Agent Dearne Valley C.L.P. from 1950-59. Member of National Executive Committee of N.U.M. 1952-59. Secretary P.L.P.'s Trade Union Group 1966. Secretary Yorkshire Group of Labour Members of Parliament from 1966. Chairman Sub-Committee B, Select Committee on Nationalised Industries. B.E.M. 1957. A Labour Member. Sat for the Dearne Valley division of the W. Riding of Yorkshire from 1959.* [1979]

WAINWRIGHT, Richard Scurrah. The Heath, Adel, Leeds. Reform, and National Liberal. S. of Henry S. Wainwright, Esq., Chartered Accountant. B. 11 Apr. 1918; m. 3 Jan. 1948, Joyce Mary, d. of Arthur Hollis, Esq., (1 s. 2 d.). Educ. at Shrewsbury School, and Clare Coll., Cambridge. Served with Friends Ambulance Unit, N.W. Europe 1939-46. A Chartered Accountant. Formerly partner in Peat, Marwick, Mitchell and Company. Leeds Hospital Management Committee 1948-58. Honorary Director Rowntree Social Service Trust. Gov. of Ashville Coll. 1959-73. Vice-President Liberal Party 1959-66. Liberal Party, Economic Affairs spokesman 1966-70. Chairman Liberal Party 1971-72. Liberal spokesman on Trade and Industry 1974-79, on Prices and Consumer Protection 1974-76 and on Economic Affairs from 1979. A Methodist local preacher. A Liberal. Unsuccessfully contested Pudsey in 1950 and 1955 and the Colne

Valley division of the W. Riding of Yorkshire in 1959, Mar. 1963 and 1964. Sat for the Colne Valley division of the W. Riding of Yorkshire from Mar. 1966 to June 1970, when he was defeated, and again from Feb. 1974.*   [1979]

WAKEFIELD, Edward Birkbeck, C.I.E. Breadsall Lodge, Breadsall, Derby. Bath. S. of Roger William Wakefield, Esq., J.P., of Kendal. B. 24 July 1903; m. 7 Dec. 1929, Lalage, d. of Sir John Perronet Thompson, K.C.S.I., K.C.I.E. Educ. at Haileybury, and Trinity Coll., Cambridge. Joined I.C.S. 1927; Chief Minister Kalat State 1933-36, Nabha State 1939-41, Rewa State 1943-45. C.I.E. 1945. Joint Secretary Political Department Government of India 1946-47. Bronze Medal of Royal Humane Society 1936. Assistant Conservative Whip 1954; a Lord Commissioner of the Treasury Jan. 1956-Oct. 1958, Comptroller of the Household Oct. 1958-Jan 1959, Vice-Chamberlain Jan. 1959-June 1960. Treasurer June 1960-Mar. 1962. A Conservative. Elected for W. Derbyshire in Feb. 1950 and sat until Mar. 1962, when he was appointed Commissioner for Malta. Created Bart. 1962. Commissioner for Malta 1962-64. High Commissioner 1964-65. Died 14 Jan. 1969.   [1962]

WAKEFIELD, Flight-Lieut. Sir William Wavell. 32 Upper Brook Street, London. The Old House, Kendal, Westmorland. Carlton, and International Sportsmen's. S. of Roger William Wakefield, Esq., M.B., of Kendal. B. 10 Mar. 1898; m. 19 Nov. 1919, Rowena Doris, d. of the late Llewellyn Lewis, Esq., M.D., O.B.E. Educ. at Sedbergh School, and Pembroke Coll., Cambridge, M.A. Served with R.N.A.S. and R.A.F. 1917-23 and 1939-40. Director of Limited Companies; Parliamentary Private Secretary to the Marq. of Hartington, Parliamentary Under-Secretary Dominions Mar. 1936-May 1938, to the Rt. Hon. R.S. Hudson, Secretary of Overseas Trade Department Jan. 1939-Apr. 1940, to Capt. The Rt. Hon. H.H. Balfour, M.C., when Parliamentary Under-Secretary of State for Air Apr. 1940-Jan. 1942; Director of Air Training Corps Air Ministry Jan. 1942-44. Vice-President and member of Executive Council National Union of Manufacturers, of Executive Committee of National Playing Fields Association and of National Council of Y.M.C.A.; member of Council of Royal National Mission to Deep Sea Fishermen; President Industrial Transport Association and of Electric Vehicles Association. Member of Parliamentary Mission to East African Colonies and South Africa 1944. Member Council of Royal Albert Hall. Knight Bach. 1944. A Conservative. Unsuccessfully contested Swindon in Oct. 1934. Sat for the Swindon division from 1935-45 and for St. Marylebone division from 1945 until Nov. 1963, when he was created Baron Wakefield of Kendal. President of Metropolitan Association of Building Societies 1967-78. President of Rugby Football Union, sometime Captain of England.*   [1963]

WAKEHAM, John. House of Commons, London. St. Stephen's. S. of Maj. Walter John Wakeham. B. 22 June 1932; m. 9 Sept. 1965, Anne Roberta, d. of H.E. Bailey, Esq., (2 s.). Educ. at Charterhouse. A Chartered Accountant. J.P. for Inner London 1972. Assistant Government Whip from May 1979. A Conservative. Unsuccessfully contested Coventry E. in 1966 and Putney in 1970. Elected for Maldon in Feb. 1974.*   [1979]

WALDEN, (Alastair) Brian. House of Commons, London. S. of W.F. Walden, Esq. B. 8 July 1932; m. 1st 1957, Sybil Frances Brackstone (divorced 1968); 2ndly, 1969, Jane, d. of Sir Patrick McKenon (divorced 1975); 3rdly, 1975, Hazel, d. of William Downes, (3 s. by former marriages). Educ. at All Saints' Elementary School, West Bromwich Grammar School, Queen's Coll., and Nuffield Coll., Oxford. University Lecturer. Joined the Labour Party in 1951. Member of National Union of General and Municipal Workers, Association of University Teachers' and Staff Tutors' Association. Parliamentary Private Secretary to Rt. Hon. John Diamond, Chief Secretary to the Treasury 1964-Dec. 1966 (resigned). Appointed member of the Committee to examine operation of Section 2 of the Official Secrets Act 1971. Front Bench Opposition spokesman on Defence 1970-71; Treasury 1971-73. A Labour Member. Unsuccessfully contested Oswestry at a by-election in Nov. 1961. Sat for the All Saints division of Birmingham from Oct. 1964 to Feb. 1974. Elected for the Ladywood division of Birmingham in Feb. 1974 and sat until he resigned in June 1977. Member of General Advisory Committee of Independent Television Authority to 1967. Presenter of 'Weekend World' for London Weekend Television from 1977.* [1977]

WALDER, (Alan) David, E.R.D. The White House, Grimsargh, Nr. Preston, Lancashire. 45 Courtenay Street, London. Cavalry, and Guards. S. of James Walder, Esq. B. 13 Nov. 1928; m. 28 July 1956, Elspeth Margaret, d. of the Rt. Hon. Lord Milligan, (1 s. 3 d.). Educ. at Latymer School, and Christ Church, Oxford. A Barrister-at-Law, Inner Temple 1956. Maj. Queen's Royal Irish Hussars. Published *Bags of Swank, The Short List, The House Party, The Fair Ladies of Salamanca, The Chanak Affair, The Short, Victorious War*, and *Nelson*. Parliamentary Private Secretary to Under-Secretary of State for Scotland 1962-64, to Rt. Hon. Michael Noble, Minister for Trade 1970-72. U.K. Delegate to Council of Europe Assembly and Western European Union 1972-73. Assistant Government Whip Oct. 1973-Mar. 1974. Member of Executive of National Book League 1976-78. Member of the Executive of the 1922 Committee. Vice-Chairman Conservative Defence Committee. E.R.D. 1965. A Conservative. Unsuccessfully contested S.W. Leicester in 1959. Sat for High Peak from Mar. 1961 to Mar. 1966 when he was defeated. Elected for Clitheroe in 1970 and sat until his death on 26 Oct. 1978. [1978]

WALKDEN, Evelyn. Valdemosa, 9 All Saints Road, Sutton, Surrey. S. of Edmund Walkden, Esq., of Ashton-in-Makerfield, Lancashire. B. Oct. 1893; m. 1915, Margaret, d. of P. Croston, Esq. (she died 1968). Educ. at Public Elementary School. A Co-operative Employee 1906-28; Trade Union Officer 1928-41; Organiser of the National Union of Distributive and Allied Workers. Served with Lancashire Hussars and York and Lancaster Regiment 1914-19. Parliamentary Private Secretary to Sir William Jowitt, Minister of National Insurance Mar.-May 1945 and to the Rt. Hon. Sir Ben Smith,

Minister of Food Aug. 1945-May 1946. Member of Sutton and Cheam Borough Council. An Independent Member. Unsuccessfully contested Rossendale in 1935. Elected for the Doncaster division of Yorkshire in Feb. 1941 as a Labour Member and sat until he retired in 1950. Resigned the Labour Whip in Nov. 1947 and sat as an Independent, after being found guilty of a breach of privilege by the Committee of Privileges and being reprimanded by the speaker for 'corruptly accepting payment for information obtained from fellow members under the obligation of secrecy'. Died 12 Sept. 1970. [1950]

WALKER, George Henry. Exbury, 50 Oxenholm Road, Kendal, Westmorland. B. 1874; m. 1897. Educ. at Kendal School. A Linotype Operator; executive member of Typographical Association. A Methodist Local Preacher and Temperance Worker. A Labour Member. Unsuccessfully contested Blackburn in 1935. Elected for Rossendale in July 1945 and sat until he retired in 1950. J.P. for Westmorland. Member of Westmorland County Council 1937-49. Died 24 Jan. 1954. [1950]

WALKER, Rt. Hon. Harold. House of Commons, London. S. of Harold Walker, Esq. B. 12 July 1927; m. 1956, Barbara, d. of Cecil Hague, Esq., (1 d.). Educ. at Manchester Coll. of Technology. N.C.L.C. A Toolmaker. Industrial Administrator. Political and T.U. Lecturer/Tutor. Chairman of stewards and convenor A.E.U. Assistant Government Whip Apr. 1967-Apr. 1968. Parliamentary Under-Secretary of State at Department of Employment and Productivity Apr. 1968-June 1970. Front Bench Opposition spokesman on Employment 1970-74. Parliamentary Under-Secretary of State for Employment Mar. 1974-Apr. 1976. Minister of State, Employment Apr. 1976-May 1979. An Opposition spokesman on Employment from 1979. PC. 1979. A Labour Member. Sat for Doncaster from Oct. 1964.* [1979]

WALKER, Rt. Hon. Peter Edward. House of Commons, London. S. of Sydney Walker, Esq. B. 25 Mar. 1932; m. 22 Feb.

1969, Tessa, d. of Mr. and Mrs. G.I. Pout, of Sunbury-on-Thames, (3 s. 1 d.). Educ. at Latymer School. National Chairman of Young Conservatives 1958-60. Member of National Executive of Conservative Party until 1962. Parliamentary Private Secretary to Mr. Selwyn Lloyd, Leader of House of Commons 1963-64. Dept. Chairman of Slater Walker Securities Limited 1964-70. Appointed Conservative Front Bench spokesman on Financial Affairs Feb. 1965. Opposition spokesman for Transport Apr. 1966-Nov. 1968. Member of Shadow Cabinet 1966-70 and 1974-75. Opposition spokesman for Housing and Land Nov. 1968-Oct. 1969. Opposition spokesman for Housing and Local Government, Transport and Land Oct. 1969-June 1970. Minister of Housing and Local Government June 1970-Oct. 1970. Secretary of State for the Environment Oct. 1970-Nov. 1972. Secretary of State for Trade and Industry Nov. 1972-Mar. 1974. Opposition spokesman for Trade and Industry Mar.-June 1974. Opposition spokesman for Defence June 1974-Feb. 1975. Minister of Agriculture, Fisheries and Food from May 1979. M.B.E. 1960. PC. 1970. A Conservative. Unsuccessfully contested Dartford in 1955 and 1959. Sat for Worcester from Mar. 1961.* [1979]

WALKER, Terence William. House of Commons, London. S. of William Edwin and Lillian Grace Walker. B. 26 Oct. 1935; m. 17 Jan. 1959, Priscilla Dart, (2 s. 1 d.). Educ. at Grammar School, Bristol. An Accountant with Courage (Western) Limited, 1951-74. Second Church Estates Commissioner Nov. 1974-May 1979. Parliamentary Private Secretary to Rt. Hon. John Smith, Secretary of State for Trade 1978-79. A Labour Member. Sat for Kingswood from Feb. 1974 until 1979, when he was defeated.* [1979]

WALKER-SMITH, Rt. Hon. Sir Derek Colclough, Bart., Q.C. 25 Cavendish Close, London. 2 Paper Buildings, Temple, London. Carlton. S. of Sir Jonah Walker-Smith, MP. for Barrow-in-Furness 1931-45. B. 1910; m. 1938, Dorothy, d. of L. Etherton, Esq., of Rowlands Castle. Educ. at Rossall, and Christ Church, Oxford. A Barrister-at-Law, Middle Temple 1934; Q.C. 1955. Bencher of Middle Temple 1963. Associate of Royal Institution of Chartered Surveyors. Chairman Conservative and Unionist Members' '1922' Committee 1951-55, and of Conservative National Advisory Committee on Local Government 1954-55. Parliamentary Secretary Board of Trade Oct. 1955-Nov. 1956; Economic Secretary to the Treasury Nov. 1956-Jan. 1957; Minister of State, Board of Trade Jan.-Sept. 1957; Minister of Health Sept. 1957-July 1960. PC. 1957. Created Bart. 1960. Chairman of Society of Conservative Lawyers 1969-75. Voted against entry to E.E.C. on 28 Oct. 1971. Member of European Parliament 1973-79. Chairman of National House Building Council 1973-78. A Conservative. Sat for the Hertford division of Hertfordshire from July 1945 to May 1955 and for Hertfordshire E. from May 1955.* [1979]

WALL, Patrick Henry Bligh, M.C., V.R.D. 8 Westminster Gardens, Marsham Street, London. Brantinghamthorpe, Brough, East Yorkshire. Institute of Directors, and Royal Yacht Squadron. S. of Henry Benedict Wall, Esq., M.C. B. 1916; m. 1953, Sheila Elizabeth, d. of James Putnam, Esq., of Broadstone, Dorset. Educ. at Downside. Served with Royal Marines 1935-50; Commanded 47 Cdo. R.M.F.V.R. 1951-56. M.C. 1945; V.R.D. 1957. Member Westminster City Council 1953-63; Chairman Mediterranean Group of Conservative Commonwealth and Overseas Council 1959-67; Chairman Joint Africa Board 1965-75; Chairman Southern Africa Sub-Committee of Conservatives Foreign Affairs Committee 1970; Chairman Africa Centre 1961-65. Vice-Chairman Conservatives Defence Committee 1965. Vice-President Urban District Councils Association. Vice-Chairman Conservatives Commonwealth Affairs Committee 1960-68; Vice-Chairman Conservative Overseas Bureau 1963-72; Chairman Conservative Fisheries Sub-Committee 1970. President Yorkshire Young Conservatives 1956-61. Parliamentary Private Secretary to Rt. Hon. Derick Heathcoat-Amory, Minister of Agriculture, Fisheries and Food 1955-58 and Chancellor of the Exchequer 1958-59. British Representative,

17th General Assembly, U.N. 1962. Chairman Military Committee North Atlantic Assembly. Chairman Conservative/Christian Democrat Group North Atlantic Assembly. Treasurer British Group Inter-Parliamentary Union. Awarded Legion of Merit, U.S.A. A Roman Catholic. A Conservative. Unsuccessfully contested the Cleveland division of Yorkshire in 1951 and 1952. Sat for the Haltemprice division of Kingston-upon-Hull from Feb. 1954 to May 1955 and for the Haltemprice division of the E. Riding of Yorkshire from May 1955.*   [1979]

WALLACE, George Douglas. 44 Shuttle Close, Sidcup, Kent. S. of George Wallace, Esq., of Cheltenham. B. 18 Apr. 1906; m. 28 Mar. 1932, Vera, d. of W.J. Randall, Esq., of Guildford, Surrey, (1 s. 1 d.). Educ. at Cheltenham Central School. Served with R.A.F. Fighter Command, Sergeant. Office Manager. Joined Labour Party in 1935. Member of Chislehurst and Sidcup Urban District Council 1937-46. Member of the Transport and General Workers' Union from 1939 (previously member of the National Union of Clerks). On Parliamentary Panel of the Transport and General Workers' Union. Assistant Government Whip 1947-50. Member Commonwealth Parliamentary Association, Delegate to Inter-Parliamentary Union Conference, Stockholm 1949. Member of Kent County Council 1952-57. Member Speaker's Conference on Electoral Law. Parliamentary Private Secretary to Rt. Hon. H.W. Bowden, Lord President of the Council Nov. 1964-66. Delegate to Inter-Parliamentary Union Conference, Delhi 1969. Delegate to Commonwealth Parliamentary Association Conference Ottawa 1966. Parliamentary Private Secretary to Rt. Hon. H.W. Bowden, Secretary of State Commonwealth Affairs 1966-67. Parliamentary Private Secretary to Niall MacDermot, Minister of State Housing and Local Government 1967-68. Commissioner Commonwealth War Graves Commission from 1970. Member Mr. Speaker's Chairmen's Panel 1970-74. A Labour Member. Sat for Chislehurst from 1945-50, when he was defeated. Unsuccessfully contested Chislehurst in 1951 and 1955, and Norwich S. in 1959 general elections. Elected for Norwich N. in Oct. 1964

and sat until he retired in Feb. 1974. Created Baron Wallace of Coslany (Life Peerage) 1974. Vice-Chairman of Greenwich and Bexley Area Health Authority 1974-77. Delegate to Council of Europe and W.E.U. from 1975. Lord in Waiting and Government Whip in House of Lords from Feb. 1977 to May 1979. Opposition Whip from 1979.*   [1974]

WALLACE, Harry Wright, C.B.E. 31 Uffingham Road, West Norwood, London. S. of Henry Wallace, Esq., of Manchester. B. 11 Sept. 1885; m. 7 Aug. 1924, Margaret, d. of E.W. Gardiner, Esq., (1 s.). Educ. at Elementary School. Assistant Secretary Post Office Workers' Union until 1945. Alderman Lambeth Borough Council from 1937. Mayor, Lambeth Borough Council 1952-53. C.B.E. 1950. A Labour Member. Unsuccessfully contested Bury in 1918, 1922, 1923 and 1924. Sat for Walthamstow E. from 1929-31, when he was defeated, and from 1945 to 1955, when he was defeated. Unsuccessfully contested Walthamstow E. in 1935. Opposition Whip 1952-55. Died 30 Apr. 1973.   [1954]

WALTERS, Dennis Murray, M.B.E. 63 Warwick Square, London. Orchardleigh, Corton, Warminster, Wiltshire. Boodle's. S. of Douglas Walters, Esq. B. Nov. 1928; m. 1st, 1955 Vanora, d. of Sir Archibald McIndoe (marriage dissolved in 1969), (1 s. 1 d.). 2ndly, 15 May 1970, Mrs. Celia Kennedy, youngest d. of Rt. Hon. Lord Duncan-Sandys, PC., C.H., and Mrs. Diana Churchill. Educ. at Downside School, and St. Catherine's Coll., Cambridge University, B.A. (Hons.). Interned in Italy during the war; served for eleven months with the Italian Resistance Movement after the Armistice of 1943. Director of Investment companies and a Travel Agency. Formerly Personal Assistant to Visct. Hailsham (now Lord Hailsham) throughout his Chairmanship of the Conservative Party. Chairman Asthma Research Council. Vice-Chairman Council for the Advancement of Arab-British Understanding 1967-70; Chairman from 1970. Secretary Conservative Parliamentary Foreign Affairs Committee 1965-71. Vice-Chairman Conservative Party Foreign Affairs Committee 1974. Joint Chairman Euro-Arab Parliamentary Association 1978.

M.B.E. 1960. A Roman Catholic. A Conservative. Unsuccessfully contested Blyth in the general election of 1959 and the by-election of Nov. 1960. Elected for the Westbury division of Wiltshire in Oct. 1964.* [1979]

WARBEY, William Noble. Overlands, 1 The Ridgeway, Mill Hill, London. S. of Charles Noble Warbey, Esq., Stationer, of Hackney. B. 16 Aug. 1903; m. 22 Aug. 1931, Audrey Grace, d. of Harry Wicks, Esq. Educ. at Grocers' Company's School, King's Coll., London and London School of Economics. A School Teacher and Lecturer 1926-40. Chief English Press Officer to Norwegian Government in London 1941-45. Editor of Educational Journal *Look and Listen* 1952-55. A Labour Member. Prospective candidate for Wimbledon 1942-44. Sat for the Luton division of Bedfordshire from 1945-50. Unsuccessfully contested the Luton division of Bedfordshire in 1950 and 1951. Sat for the Broxtowe division of Nottinghamshire from Sept. 1953 to May 1955 and for the Ashfield division of Nottinghamshire from May 1955 until he retired in 1966. Executive Director of Organisation for World Political and Social Studies from 1965. Secretary of World Studies Trust from 1966. Chairman of Rossetti House Group from 1968. Biographer of Ho Chi Minh and author of books on Vietnam and Norway. Died 6 May 1980.[1966]

WARD, Christopher John Ferguson. 2 Pinkneys Road, Maidenhead, Berkshire. S. of Harry L.F. Ward, Maj. B. 26 Dec. 1942; m. Elizabeth Cunniff. Educ. at Magdalen Coll. School, Oxford. Solicitor 1965. Standing Conference on London and S.E. Regional Planning 1966. A Conservative. Elected for Swindon in Oct. 1969 and sat until June 1970, when he was defeated. Unsuccessfully contested Eton and Slough in 1979. Member of Berkshire County Council 1965-70 and from 1974, Dept. Leader of Council from 1976.* [1970]

WARD, Rt. Hon. George Reginald. 13 Lowndes Close, London. Carlton, and White's. S. of 2nd Earl of Dudley. B. 20 Nov. 1907; m. 1st, 1940, Anne Capel (divorced 1951); 2ndly, 1962, Hon. Mrs. Barbara Astor, former wife of Hon. Michael Astor, MP. Educ. at Eton, and Christ Church, Oxford. Joined Auxiliary Air Force 1929, Royal Air Force 1932-37 and 1939-45. Parliamentary Under-Secretary of State, Air Ministry Feb. 1952-Dec. 1955; Parliamentary and Financial Secretary to the Admiralty Dec. 1955-Jan. 1957; Secretary of State for Air Jan. 1957-Oct. 1960. PC. 1957. A Conservative. Elected for Worcester in July 1945 and sat until Oct. 1960, when he was created Visct. Ward of Witley.* [1960]

WARD, Dame Irene Mary Bewick, C.H., J.P. 4 Roseworth Terrace, Gosforth, Newcastle-upon-Tyne. D. of A.J. Bewick Ward, Esq. B. 1895. Educ. at Newcastle Church High School. J.P. for Newcastle-upon-Tyne 1949. C.B.E. 1929; D.B.E. 1955; C.H. 1973. Honorary Fellow of Lucy Cavendish Coll., Cambridge; Honorary Fellow of Royal Society of Arts. A Conservative. Unsuccessfully contested Morpeth in 1924 and 1929. Member for Wallsend Oct. 1931-July 1945, when she was defeated. Elected for Tynemouth in Feb. 1950 and sat until she retired in Feb. 1974. Created Baroness Ward of North Tyneside (Life Peerage) 1974. Died 26 April 1980. [1974]

WARD, Michael John. House of Commons, London. S. of Stanley William Ward, Esq., of Romford, Local Government Officer and Musician. B. 7 Apr. 1931; m. 1953, Lilian, d. of Mr. and Mrs. Frederick Lomas, of Romford, (2 d.). Educ. at Mawney Road Junior and Royal Liberty Schools, Romford, Bungay Grammar School and University of Manchester. Education Officer, R.A.F. 1953-57. Registrar, Chartered Institute of Secretaries 1958-60. Member of Romford Borough Council and London Borough of Havering 1958-78, Alderman 1971, Leader of Council 1971-74. Local Government Officer to the Labour Party 1961-65 and Press Officer Inner London Education Authority 1970-74 and from 1979. Member of Essex River Authority 1964-71. President London Government Public Relations Association 1977. Parliamentary Private Secretary to Rt. Hon. R.E. Prentice, Secretary of State for Education and Science 1975, Minister of Overseas Development 1975-76 and to Frank Judd, Minister of State F.C.O. 1977. Chairman British-Malawi Group 1977. A Labour Member. Unsuccessfully contested Peterborough in 1966, 1970 and Feb. 1974. Elected for Peterborough in Oct. 1974 and sat until 1979, when he was defeated.* [1979]

WARREN, Kenneth Robin. Woodfield House, Goudhurst, Kent. S. of Edward C. Warren, Esq., Lecturer. B. 15 Aug. 1926; m. 16 June 1962, Elizabeth Anne, M.A. (Cantab.), d. of Russell Chamberlain, Esq., of Northamptonshire. Educ. at Midsomer Norton, Aldenham, and London University, C. Eng., F.R.Ae.S., F.C.I.T. Served Apprenticeship, De Havilland Aircraft 1947-51; Research Engineer, B.O.A.C. 1951-57; Smiths Industries 1957-60; Elliott Automation 1960-69; Director of Warren Woodfield Associates Limited, Ventek Limited, and Parsons, Tozer and Newton Limited. Chairman Conservative Parliamentary Aviation Committee 1974-76. Chairman Parliamentary Committee on 'Offshore Technology' 1974-75. Sen. Chairman Western European Union Science, Technology and Aerospace Committee 1977. Parliamentary Private Secretary to Sir Keith Joseph, Secretary of State for Industry from 1979. A Conservative. Unsuccessfully contested St. Pancras N. in 1964. Sat for Hastings from June 1970.* [1979]

WATERHOUSE, Capt. Rt. Hon. Charles, M.C., D.L. Middleton Hall, Bakewell. Carlton, and Turf. S. of Thomas Crompton Waterhouse, Esq., of Lomberdale Hall, Bakewell. B. 1893; m. 1917, Beryl Chrystol, d. of Thomas Ford, Esq., of Sydney, N.S.W. (she died 1970). Educ. at Cheltenham, and Trinity Hall, Cambridge, M.A. Served in France 1914-18 with 1st Life Guards. Dept.-Lieut. and J.P. for Derbyshire. Parliamentary Private Secretary to Sir Philip Cunliffe Lister, President of Board of Trade 1928-29 and to Sir Henry Betterton, Minister of Labour Nov. 1931-July 1934; Assistant Whip Dec. 1935-May 1937; a Junior Lord of the Treasury May-Oct. 1937; Comptroller of H.M. Household Oct. 1937-Apr. 1939, Treasurer Apr.-Oct. 1939; Assistant Postmaster-Gen. Oct. 1939-Feb. 1941; Parliamentary Secretary Board of Trade Feb. 1941-July 1945. PC. 1944. A Conservative. Unsuccessfully contes-

ted N.E. Derbyshire in 1922 and 1923. Sat for S. Leicester from Oct. 1924 to July 1945, when he was defeated. Elected for S.E. Leicester in Feb. 1950 and sat until he resigned in Oct. 1957. Chairman of Public Accounts Committee 1950-51 and Estimates Committee 1953-57. Chairman of Tanganyika Concessions 1957-66. Leader of 'Suez Group' of Conservative MPs. Died 2 Mar. 1975. [1957]

WATKINS, David John. 1 Carisbrooke House, Courtlands, Sheen Road, Richmond, Surrey. S. of Thomas Watkins, Esq., Merchant Seaman. B. 27 Aug. 1925. Unmarried. Educ. at Grammar Schools, and Bristol Technical Coll. Member Bristol City Council 1954-57. Co-opted member Bristol Education Committee 1958-66. Governor-Manager various schools 1954-67. Member of the Labour Party from 1950. Member Amalgamated Union of Engineering Workers from 1942. Sponsored Candidate. Secretary A.E.U.W. Parliamentary Group June 1968-77. Introduced and piloted Employers' Liability (Compulsory Insurance) Act 1969 and Industrial Common Ownership Act 1976 as Private Members' Bills. Introduced Drained Weight Bill 1973. Founder member Labour Middle East Council, Treasurer until 1974, Chairman 1974. Author of *Labour and Palestine*, and *Industrial Common Ownership*. Member of Chairmen's Panel 1978. A Labour Member. Unsuccessfully contested Bristol N.W. in the 1964 general election. Elected for the Consett division of Durham in Mar. 1966.* [1979]

WATKINS, Tudor Elwyn. Bronafon, Penyfan Road, Brecon. S. of H. Watkins, Esq., of Abercrave. B. 9 May 1903; m. 13 Apr. 1936, Bronwen, d. of T. Stather, Esq. Educ. at Elementary Schools, and Coleg Harlech, North Wales. A Miner 1916-24. Gen. Secretary of Breconshire Association of Approved Societies 1937-48. Alderman, Breconshire County Council 1940-74. Chairman Specialist Committee on Agriculture 1966-68. A Labour Member. Political Agent for Brecon and Radnor 1928-33. Elected for Brecon and Radnor in July 1945 and sat until he retired in 1970. Parliamentary Private Secretary to Rt. Hon. James Griffiths, Secretary of State for Wales 1964-66 and to Rt. Hon. Cledwyn Hughes, Secretary of State for Wales 1966-67. Created Baron Watkins (Life Peerage) 1972. Chairman of Powys County Council 1974-77. Lieut. of Powys from 1975. Chairman of Brecon Beacons National Park Committee.*   [1970]

WATKINSON, Rt. Hon. Harold Arthur, C.H. House of Commons, London. Carlton, R.N.V.R., and Itchenor Sailing. S. of Arthur Watkinson, Esq., of Walton-on-Thames. B. 25 Jan. 1910; m. Nov. 1939, Vera, d. of John Langmead, Esq. Educ. at Queen's Coll., Taunton, and King's Coll., London. An Engineer and Company Director. Lieut.-Commander (G) R.N.V.R. 1939-45; Managing Director of Schweppes Group of companies from 1963 to 1968; Director Consolidated Trust Limited and The Plessey Company Limited. Chairman National Advisory Company on the Employment of Older Men and Women 1952-55; Gov. Welbeck Coll.; member of Council, British Institute of Management and of Regular Forces Employment Association. Parliamentary Private Secretary to Rt. Hon. J.S. Maclay, Minister of Transport 1951-52; Parliamentary Secretary to Ministry of Labour and National Service May 1952-Dec. 1955; Minister of Transport and Civil Aviation Dec. 1955-Oct. 1959; Minister of Defence Oct. 1959-July 1962; Cabinet Minister 1957-62. PC. 1955; C.H. 1962. A Conservative. Elected for the Woking division of Surrey in Feb. 1950 and sat until June 1964, when he was created Visct. Watkinson. Member of British National Export Council 1964-70. Chairman of Committee for Exports to United States 1964-67. Chairman of Cadbury Schweppes Limited 1969-74. Director of British Insulated Callender's Cables 1968-77. Chairman of British Institute of Management 1968-70, Vice-President 1970-73, President 1973-78. President of Grocers Institute 1970-71, of Institute of Grocery Distribution 1972-73. President of C.B.I. 1976-77. Director of Midland Bank.*   [1964]

WATKINSON, John Taylor. 10 Vernon Close, Leamington Spa, Warwickshire. S. of William Forshaw Watkinson, Esq. B. 25 Jan. 1941; m. 29 Aug. 1969, Jane Elizabeth Miller. Educ. at Bristol Grammar School, and Worcester Coll., Oxford. A Schoolmaster 1964-71. A Barrister, Middle Temple 1972. Parliamentary Private Secretary to A.W. Lyon, Minister of State, Home Office 1975-76. Member and Rapporteur, Council of Europe and W.E.U. 1976-79. Chairman Warwick and Leamington C.L.P. A Labour Member. Unsuccessfully contested Warwick and Leamington at the general election of 1970. Elected for Gloucestershire W. in Oct. 1974 and sat until 1979, when he was defeated.*   [1979]

WATSON, William McLean. 136 Halbeath Road, Dunfermline, Fife. S. of James and Catherine Watson of Cowdenbeath. B. 27 Oct. 1874 at Donibristle, Fife; m. 1908, Elizabeth Westwood. Educ. at Donibristle School, and Ruskin Coll., Oxford. A Miner until 1908; Miners' Political Organiser until 1922. Member of Fifeshire War Pensions Committee. Member of Fife County Council 1912-30. A Labour Member. Unsuccessfully contested Dunfermline Burghs in 1918. Sat for Dunfermline Burghs from Nov. 1922-Oct. 1931, when he was defeated, and from 1935 until he retired in 1950. Died 25 Apr. 1962.   [1950]

WATT, Hamish. House of Commons, London. S. of William Watt, Esq. B. 27 Dec. 1925; m. 1948, Mary Helen Grant. Educ. at Keith Grammar School and St. Andrew's University. Scottish National Party Whip 1976-78. Director of Aberdeen Milk Board from 1962. A Scottish National Member. Unsuccessfully contested Caithness and Sutherland as a Conservative in 1966. Unsuccessfully contested Banffshire in 1970. Elected for Banffshire in Feb. 1974 and sat until 1979, when he was defeated.*   [1979]

WATTS, James, T.D. 20 Chester Street, London. White's, Pratt's, and R.A.C. S. of James Watts, Esq., of Abney Hall, Cheadle, Cheshire. B. 1903. Educ. at Shrewsbury, and New Coll., Oxford. Served with Cheshire Regiment in France, Middle East and India 1939-45, Maj. T.D. 1945. Member of Manchester City Council 1933-39. A Conservative. Honorary Treasurer Manchester City Conservative Association 1933-51, Chairman

1951-53. Unsuccessfully contested the Gorton division of Manchester in 1950. Elected for the Moss Side division of Manchester in 1959 and sat until his death on 7 July 1961.

[1961]

WEATHERILL, Rt. Hon. (Bruce) Bernard. 98 Lupus Street, London. S. of Bernard Weatherill, Esq. B. 1920; m. 1949, Lyn, d. of H.T. Eatwell, Esq., (2 s. 1 d.). Educ. at Malvern Coll. At the outbreak of war enlisted with the Oxfordshire and Buckinghamshire Light Infantry and was commissioned in 1940 in the 4/7 Royal Dragoon Guards. Transferred to the 19th King George V's Own Lancers (Indian Army) 1941-45. Served in Burma and N.W. Europe. Joined his family business of Bernard Weatherill Limited, Tailors, of Dover Street, London 1939. Served five year apprenticeship, Managing Director from 1958. Honorary Treasurer of the Tailors' Benevolent Institute 1945-60. Formerly first Chairman of the Guildford Young Conservatives Divisional Committee. Chairman Guildford Division 1959-63. Vice-Chairman S.E. Area Council 1962-64. Appointed Opposition Whip Jan. 1967-June 1970. Lord Commissioner of H.M. Treasury June 1970-Nov. 1971. Vice-Chamberlain of the Royal Household Nov. 1971-Apr. 1972. Comptroller of the Royal Household Apr. 1972-Dec. 1973. Treasurer of the Household and Dept. Chief Whip Dec. 1973-Mar. 1974. Opposition Dept. Chief Whip 1974-79. Dept. Speaker and Chairman of Ways and Means from 1979. PC. 1980. A Conservative. Sat for Croydon N.E. from Oct. 1964.*

[1979]

WEBB, Rt. Hon. Maurice. Willow Cottage, Pinner Hill, Middlesex. Savage, and Press. S. of George Webb, Esq., of Lancaster. B. 26 Sept. 1904; m. 23 Sept. 1931, Mabel, d. of Edgar Hughes, Esq., of Lancaster. Educ. at Christ Church School, Lancaster. A Political Journalist and Broadcast Commentator; on Staff of *Daily Herald* 1935-44, *Sunday Express* 1944-45. Labour Party agent in Skipton 1925-29; Propaganda Officer at Labour Party Headquarters 1929-36. Chairman of P.L.P 1946-50. Minister of Food Feb. 1950-Oct. 1951. PC. 1950. A Labour Member. Elected for Bradford Central in July 1945 and

sat until 1955, when he unsuccessfully contested Bradford N. Methodist Local Preacher. Died 10 June 1956. [1954]

WEBBE, Sir (William) Harold, C.B.E., D.L. Ash Pollard, Merstham, Surrey. Athenaeum, Carlton, and Constitutional. S. of John Henry Webbe, Esq., of Birmingham. B. 30 Sept. 1885; m. 9 Nov. 1910, Constance Laura, d. of Walter Andrew Harrison, Esq., of Birmingham (she died 1956). Educ. at King Edward's School, and Queens' Coll., Cambridge, 1st Class Maths. Tripos. H.M. Inspector of Schools 1910-14; served in Ministry of Munitions 1916-20; a Director of Companies. C.B.E. 1920. Member London County Council 1925-49, Alderman 1934-45. Leader of M.R. Party 1934-45. Knight Bach. 1937. Dept.-Lieut. for Co. London. A Conservative. Sat for the Abbey division of Westminster from May 1939 to Feb. 1950. Elected for the Cities of London and Westminster in Feb. 1950 and sat until he retired in 1959. Died 22 Apr. 1965. [1959]

WEBSTER, David William Ernest. Auldcroft, Wedmore, Somerset. Carlton, and United University. S. of David W. Webster, Esq. B. 20 Oct. 1923; m. 26 July 1947, Irene I.S. Beasey. Educ. at Fettes Coll., and Downing Coll., Cambridge, M.A. Flight-Lieut. and Pilot with R.A.F. 1942-47 in India, Pakistan, Canada and U.S.A.; Parachute Jumping Instructor. Joined Stockbroking Firm 1956. Parliamentary Private Secretary to Joint Parliamentary Secretaries Ministry of Pensions and National Insurance 1958-60. Member Select Committee of Estimates 1958-62. Vice-Chairman 1962-63. Joint Secretary Conservative Parliamentary Transport Committee 1961-62. Chairman 1963-64. Vice-Chairman 1964-65. Delegate to Council of Europe, Strasbourg and Western European Union. Vice-Chairman Economic Committee 1965-66 (Council of Europe). Introduced Merchant Shipping Act 1964 for the Safety of Life at Sea. Member Speaker's Conference on Electoral Reform 1965-66; Opposition spokesman on Transport 1965. A Conservative. Unsuccessfully contested Bristol N.E. in 1955. Elected for the Weston-super-Mare division of Somerset in June 1958 and sat until his death on 7 Jan. 1969. [1968]

WEDGWOOD BENN, Rt. Hon. Anthony Neil. See Benn, Rt. Hon. Anthony Neil Wedgwood.

WEETCH, Kenneth Thomas. House of Commons, London. S. of Kenneth George Weetch, Esq. B. Sept. 1933; m. 1961, Audrey Wilson. Educ. at Newbridge Grammar School, and London School of Economics. A College Lecturer. Served with Army in Hong Kong 1955-57. Head of History Department, Hockerill Coll. of Educ. 1964-74. Parliamentary Private Secretary to Rt. Hon. William Rodgers, Secretary of State for Transport 1976-78. A Labour Member. Unsuccessfully contested Ipswich in Feb. 1974 and Saffron Walden in 1970. Elected for Ipswich in Oct. 1974.* [1979]

WEITZMAN, David, Q.C. Devereux Chamber, Devereux Court, Temple, London. S. of Percy Weitzman, Esq. B. 18 June 1898; m. 1st, 1925, Fanny (she died 1950); 2ndly, 1955, Mrs. Lena Dundon (she died 1969), 3rdly, 1972, Mrs. Vivienne Hammond. Educ. at Hutchesons School, Glasgow, and at Manchester Central School, and University, B.A. (Hons.). A Barrister-at-Law, Gray's Inn 1922. K.C. 1951. Served in the Manchester Regiment 1916. A Labour Member. Unsuccessfully contested Stoke Newington in 1935. Sat for Stoke Newington from July 1945-Feb. 1950. Sat for Stoke Newington and Hackney N. from Feb. 1950 to Feb. 1974 and for the N. and Stoke Newington division of Hackney from Feb. 1974 until he retired in 1979.* [1979]

WELLBELOVED, (Alfred) James. House of Commons, London. S. of Wilfred Henry Wellbeloved, Esq. B. 29 July 1926; m. 1948, Mavis Beryl, d. of Edgar Ratcliff, Esq., of Bexleyheath, Kent. Educ. at South East Technical Coll. A Volunteer Boy Seaman 1942-46. Commerical Representative and Publisher. Ex-Leader of Council, London borough of Bexley. Parliamentary Private Secretary to Rt. Hon. Gerald Reynolds, Minister for Defence Administration 1967-69 and to Rt. Hon. Michael Stewart, Foreign and Commonwealth Secretary 1969-70. Opposition Whip 1972-73. Under-Secretary of State for Defence for R.A.F. Apr. 1976-May 1979. A Labour Member. Sat for Erith and Crayford from Nov. 1965 to Feb. 1974 and for the Erith and Crayford division of Bexley from Feb. 1974.* [1979]

WELLS, John Julius. Mere House, Mereworth, Maidstone. S. of A.R.K. Wells, Esq. B. 30 Mar. 1925; m. 31 July 1948, Lucinda, d. of Francis Meath-Baker, Esq. Educ. at Eton, and Corpus Christi Coll., Oxford. Joined R.N.V.R. as Ordinary Seaman 1942; Commissioned 1943. Served in H.M. Submarines until 1946. Leamington Spa Borough Councillor 1953-55. Chairman Conservative Party Horticulture Committee 1965-71; Vice-Chairman Conservative Party Agriculture Committee 1970-71. Chairman of Parliamentary Waterways Group from 1974. Member Chairman's Panel from 1974. Master of the Fruiterers' Company 1977. Knight Commander of Order of Civil Merit (Spain) 1972. A Conservative. Unsuccessfully contested Smethwick in 1955. Elected for Maidstone in 1959.* [1979]

WELLS, Percy Lawrence. 4 Park Avenue, Sittingbourne, Kent. S. of William Alfred Wells, Esq. B. 8 June 1891; m. 26 Dec. 1919, Florence, d. of E.J. Fisher, Esq. Educ. at Church of England School, Stone. A Trade Union Official from 1920. J.P. for Kent; member of Central Agricultural Wages Board; Parliamentary Private Secretary to Rt. Hon. Ernest Bevin, Secretary of State for Foreign Affairs 1945-51 and Lord Privy Seal 1951. A Labour Member. Elected for the Faversham division of Kent in July 1945 and sat until his death on 3 Apr. 1964. [1964]

WELLS, William Thomas, Q.C. 3 Middle Temple Lane, Temple, London. Mymms Hall, Potters Bar, Hertfordshire. S. of William Collins Wells, Esq. B. 10 Aug. 1908; m. 1936, Angela, d. of Robert Noble, Esq. Educ. at Lancing, and Balliol Coll., Oxford. Barrister-at-Law, Middle Temple, 1932. Q.C. 1955, Bencher 1963. Served in the Army, mainly on General Staff, War Office 1940-45, with the rank of Maj. Member of Chairman's Panel 1948-50; Lord Chancellor's Committee on Practice and Procedure of Supreme Court 1947-53; Magistrates Courts Rules Committee from 1954 and of Inter-Departmental Committee on Homosexual Offences and Prostitution 1954-57. Dept. Chairman Hertfordshire Quarter Sessions 1961-71. Recorder King's Lynn 1965-71. A Recorder of the Crown Court from 1972. Voted in favour of entry to E.E.C. on 28 Oct. 1971. A Labour Member. Sat for Walsall from July 1945 to May 1955 and for Walsall N. from May 1955 until he retired in Feb. 1974. Q.C., Hong Kong, 1968. A Chairman of Industrial Tribunals from 1976.* [1974]

WELLWOOD, Capt. William, M.C. House of Commons, London. B. 1893. Served with Royal Marines 1914-18, M.C. and bar. An Ulster Unionist Member. Elected for Londonderry in May 1951 and sat until he retired in 1955. Died 28 June 1971. [1954]

WELSH, Andrew. House of Commons, London. Olympia Buildings, Arbroath, Angus. S. of William Welsh, Esq. B. Apr. 1944; m. 1971, Sheena Margaret Cannon. Educ. at Glasgow University. A Teacher. Stirling District Councillor. S.N.P. Parliamentary spokesman on Housing 1974-78, and on Small Businesses and Self-Employed Affairs 1975. S.N.P. Parliamentary Party Chief Whip 1978-79. S.N.P. Parliamentary spokesman on Agriculture 1977. A Scottish National Party Member. Unsuccessfully contested Dunbartonshire Central in Feb. 1974. Elected for South Angus in Oct. 1974 and sat until 1979, when he was defeated.* [1979]

WEST, Daniel Granville. Brynderwen, Abersychan, Pontypool. S. of John West, Esq., of Newbridge, Monmouthshire. B. 17 Mar. 1904; m. 12 Jan. 1937, Vera, d. of G. Hopkins, Esq., of Pontypool. Admitted a Solicitor 1929. Member of Abercarn Urban District Council 1934-38, and of Monmouthshire County Council 1938-47. Served in R.A.F.V.R. 1940-45. Parliamentary Private Secretary to Rt. Hon. J. Chuter Ede, Home Secretary, 1950-51. A Labour Member. Elected for the Pontypool division of Monmouthshire in July 1946 and sat until July 1958, when he was created Baron Granville-West (Life Peerage). Senior Partner, D. Granville West, Chivers and Morgan, Solicitors.* [1958]

WEST, Rt. Hon. Henry William. Rossahilly House, Enniskillen, Co. Fermanagh. S. of W.H. West, Esq. B. 1917; m. 1956, Maureen Elizabeth Hall. Educ. at Portora Royal School. A Farmer. Member of British Wool Marketing Board 1950-58. President of Ulster Farmers Union 1955-56. High Sheriff of Co. Fermanagh 1954. Member of Northern Ireland Parliament for Enniskillen 1954-72. PC. (Northern Ireland) 1960. Parliamentary Secretary to Northern Ireland Ministry of Agriculture 1958-60, Minister of Agriculture 1960-67 and 1971-72. Member of Northern Ireland Assembly for Fermanagh and S. Tyrone 1973-75, and of Constitutional Convention 1975-76. A United Ulster Unionist Coalition Member. Elected for Fermanagh and S. Tyrone in Feb. 1974 and sat until Oct. 1974, when he was defeated. Leader of U.U.U.C. Group 1974. Leader of Official Unionist Party Jan. 1974-July 1979. Unsuccessfully contested the Northern Ireland Constituency in the European Parliament election 1979.* [1974 2nd ed.]

WESTWOOD, Rt. Hon. Joseph. 50 Viewforth Street, Kirkcaldy. S. of Solomon Westwood, Esq., of Wollescote, Worcs. B. 1884; m. 1906, Frances, d. of James Scarlett, Esq. Educ. at Buckhaven Higher Grade School. A Draper's Apprentice, Messenger Boy and Miner. Industrial Organiser for Fife Miners 1916-18; Political Organiser for Scottish Miners 1918-29. Active member of Salvation Army. Member of Kirkcaldy Town Council and Education Committee; Parliamentary Private Secretary to Rt. Hon. William Adamson when Secretary of State for Scotland June 1929. Parliamentary Under-Secretary of State for Scotland Mar.-Aug. 1931. Dept. Commissioner for Civil Defence 1939. Parliamentary Under-Secretary of State for Scotland May 1940-May 1945; Secretary of State for Scotland July 1945-Oct. 1947. PC. 1943. J.P., F.E.I.S. A Labour Member. Sat for Peebles and Southern division of Peebles and Midlothian from Nov. 1922-Oct. 1931, when he was defeated. Unsuccessfully contested E. Fife in Feb. 1933. Sat for Stirling and Falkirk from 1935 until he was killed in a car accident on 17 July 1948. [1948]

WHEATLEY, Rt. Hon. John Thomas, Q.C. 15 Drummond Place, Edinburgh. S. of Patrick Wheatley, Esq., of Shettleston, Glasgow. B. 17 Jan. 1908; m. 5 Aug. 1935, Agnes, d. of Samuel Nichol, Esq. Educ. at St. Aloysius Coll., Glasgow, Mount St. Mary's Coll., Sheffield, and University of Glasgow, M.A. 1928, LL.B. 1930. Called to the Scottish Bar 1932, Advocate Depute 1945-47. Served with R.A. and with J.A.G. Branch 1939-45. Solicitor-Gen. for Scotland Mar.-Oct. 1947; Lord Advocate Oct. 1947-Oct. 1951. A Labour Member. Unsuccessfully contested Bute and N. Ayrshire in 1945 and the Bridgeton division of Glasgow in Aug. 1946 (when he was defeated by the I.L.P. candidate). Elected for Edinburgh E. in Nov. 1947 and sat until Jan. 1954, when he was appointed a Judge of the Court of Session, with the judicial title of Lord Wheatley. Judge of Court of Session from 1954, Lord Justice Clerk from 1972. Chairman of Scottish Nurses' Salaries Committee 1945-47, of Milk Enquiry in Scotland 1946-47. Chairman of Committee on Teaching Profession in Scotland 1961-63. Member of Royal Commission on Penal Reform 1946-66 and Royal Commission on Local Government in Scotland 1966-69. K.C. 1947. PC. 1947. Created Baron Wheatley (Life Peerage) 1970.* [1954]

WHEATLEY, Lieut.-Col. Mervyn James, C.B.E. Sandecotes Lodge, Parkstone, Dorset. Junior United Service, and St. Stephen's. S. of Lieut.-Col. F.G. Wheatley, V.D., T.D., of Poole. B. 24 Apr. 1880; m. 1st, 1909, Mary, d. of Arthur Cox, Esq., of Windholm, Parkstone (she died 1952); 2ndly, 1952, Mrs. Eileen Shelley. Educ. at Sutton Valence School. Commissioned Dorset Regiment 1900, retired 1918. Served in South African War 1900-02, and 1914-18 in Egyptian Army and Sudan Defence Force 1907-28, Private Secretary to Sirdar Egyptian Army and Gov.-Gen. of Sudan 1916-21; Gov. and O.C. Bahr-el-Ghazal Province; Battalion Commander Dorset Home Guard 1940-45; Lieut.-Col. 1941; Army Welfare Officer 1939-45; Chairman of E. Dorset Conservative Association 1938-45 and of Wessex Area Unionist and Conservative Association 1944-46. Cloth-worker and Freeman of London; Freeman of Poole; Alderman Dorset County Council and Poole Borough Council; J.P. and Dept.-Lieut. for Dorset; Mayor of Poole 1936. O.B.E. 1918; C.B.E. 1928; K.B.E. 1952. Commander of Order of the Nile, of Nahda and Officer of Osmanieh. Conservative Whip Nov. 1948-Oct. 1951. A Conservative. Sat for E. Dorset from July 1945 to Feb. 1950 and for Poole from Feb. 1950 until he retired in 1951. Died 26 Oct. 1974. [1951]

WHEELDON, William Edwin. House of Commons, London. S. of W.W. Wheeldon, Esq., of Crewe. B. 20 Feb. 1898; m. 1922, Annie, d. of Robert Davies, Esq., of Crewe. Educ. at Elementary School. Served with R.F.C. and R.A.F. 1914-18. Member of Birmingham City Council 1927-53, Alderman 1945-53, Chairman of Finance Committee 1946-49 and 1952-53. Secretary of Birmingham and District Co-operative Party 1935-60. Member of National Committee of Co-operative Party. A Labour and Co-operative Member. Elected for the Small Heath division of Birmingham in Nov. 1952 and sat until his death on 7 Oct. 1960. [1960]

WHITAKER, Benjamin Charles George. 13 Elsworthy Road, London. S. of Maj.-Gen. Sir John Whitaker, Bart. B. 15 Sept. 1934; m. 1964, Janet Alison Stewart, (1 s. 1 d.). Educ. at Eton, and New Coll., Oxford, B.A. A Barrister, Inner Temple, 1959, Writer and Journalist. Author of *The Police* (1964), *Crime and Society* (1967), *Parks for People* (1971), *The Foundations* (1974), *Police in Society* (1979), Editor of *A Radical Future* (1967), *Participation and Poverty* (1968), *The Fourth World* (1972) and *Sources for Contemporary Issues* (Series 1973-75). Parliamentary Private Secretary to Rt. Hon. Anthony Greenwood, MP. from 1966 to Mar. 1967. Parliamentary Secretary Ministry of Overseas Development Oct. 1969-June 1970. A Labour Member. Elected for Hampstead in Mar. 1966 and sat until 1970, when he was defeated. Vice-Chairman of Danilo Dolci Trust 1960-69. Lecturer in Law, London University 1963-64. Director of Minority Rights Group from 1971. Member of Goodman Committee on Charity Law Reform 1974-76. Chairman of U.N. Working Group on Slavery from 1976. Member of U.K. National Commission for UNESCO from 1978.* [1970]

WHITE, Charles Frederick. Tansley House, Tansley, Matlock. S. of Charles Frederick White, Esq., MP., of Bonsall, Matlock. B. 23 Jan. 1891; m. 10 Jan. 1915, Alice, d. of George Harrison Moore, Esq., of Matlock. Educ. at Elementary School, and Wirksworth Grammar School. Served with Sherwood Foresters 1914-17. A Lecturer and Organiser. Member of Derbyshire County Council from 1928 to 1931 and from 1936 to 1956, Alderman from 1937, Chairman 1946. Unsuccessfully contested the Hanley division of Stoke-on-Trent as a Liberal in 1929 and Derbyshire W. as a Labour candidate in June 1938. Elected for Derbyshire W. in Feb. 1944 as an Independent Labour Member and in July 1945 as a Labour Member. Sat until he retired in 1950. Labour Party Agent for Derbyshire W. 1929-30. Supporter of Sir Oswald Mosley's New Party in 1931. C.B.E. 1951. Chairman of Peak Park Planning Board 1951-56. Died 27 Nov. 1956. [1950]

WHITE, Eirene Lloyd. 36 Westminster Gardens, Marsham Street, London. D. of Dr. Thomas Jones, C.H. B. 1909; m. 1948, John Cameron White (he died 1968). Educ. at St. Paul's Girls' School, and Somerville Coll., Oxford. A Journalist from 1945, previously in Ministry of Labour. Member of National Executive Committee of Labour Party 1947-53, and from 1958 to 1972; Chairman Fabian Society 1959. Parliamentary Under-Secretary Colonial Office Oct. 1964-Apr. 1966. Minister of State for Foreign Affairs Apr. 1966-Jan. 1967. Minister of State for Wales Jan. 1967-June 1970. Chairman of the Labour Party 1968-69. A Labour Member. Unsuccessfully contested Flintshire in 1945. Elected for E. Flintshire in Feb. 1950 and sat until she retired in 1970. Member of Cinematograph Films Council 1946-64. President of Nursery Schools Association 1964-66. Created Baroness White (Life Peerage) 1970. Dept. Chairman of Metrication Board 1972-76. Chairman of International Committee of National Council of Social Service 1973-77. Member of Royal Commission on Environmental Pollution from 1974. Member of British Waterways Board from 1974. Chairman of Land Authority for Wales from 1975. Member of University Grants Committee from 1977. Governor of National Library of Wales. Chairman of Coleg Harlech. Chairman of Advisory Committee on Oil Pollution at Sea. Principal Dept. Chairman of Committees and Chairman of Select Committee on Europe, House of Lords from 1979.*
[1970]

WHITE, Frank Richard. House of Commons, London. S. of Arthur Leslie White, Esq., Royal Engineers. B. Nov. 1939; m. 27 Jan. 1967, Eileen, d. of Frank Crook, Esq., (2 s. 1 d.). Educ. at Bolton Technical Coll. An Industrial Relations Adviser. Member Bolton Council from 1963 to 1974. Elected to Greater Manchester County Council 1973-75. Parliamentary Private Secretary to Gregor Mackenzie, Minister of State for Industry 1975-76. Assistant Government Whip Apr. 1976-Oct. 1978. A Labour Member. Unsuccessfully contested Bury and Radcliffe in Feb. 1974. Elected for Bury and Radcliffe in Oct. 1974.*
[1979]

WHITE, Henry. Elmfields, Creswell, Worksop, Nottinghamshire. S. of William White, Esq., of Church Gresley. B. 5 Aug. 1890; m. 19 July 1912, d. of Frederick Cook, Esq. Educ. at Gresley Church of England School. A Coal Miner. Trades Union Secretary; Vice-President of Derbyshire Miners 1938-42; member of Wages Board, Dispute Board and Arbitration Board. A Labour Member. Elected for N.E. Derbyshire in Mar. 1942 and sat until he retired in 1959. Labour Agent for N.E. Derbyshire. Member of Derbyshire County Council 1933-45, Alderman 1945-49, and of Clowne Rural District Council to 1946. Died 4 Feb. 1964. [1959]

WHITE, James. House of Commons, London. S. of James White, Esq. of Glasgow. B. Apr. 1922; m. 1948, Mary E. Dempsey. Educ. at Knightswood Senior Secondary School, Glasgow. Member of the Labour Party for 20 years, Trade Union service for 34 years. Served in Army 1939-45. A Company Director. A Labour Member. Elected for the Pollok division of Glasgow in June 1970.* [1979]

WHITE, Lieut.-Col. John Baker. 24 Buckingham Palace Mansions, London. The Old Farm House, Street End, Nr. Canterbury, Kent. S. of John Wilfred Baker White,

Esq. B. 12 Aug. 1902; m. 21 Oct. 1925, Sybil, d. of E. Graham, Esq. Educ. at Stubbington House, Fareham, and Malvern Coll. Director of Economic League Central Council 1926-45, Publicity Adviser 1945-76. Served with Rifle Brigade, War Office, Political Intelligence Department Foreign Office and Political Warfare Executive Middle East with Military Rank of Lieut.-Col.; T.D. 1950. A Conservative. Elected for the Canterbury division of Kent in July 1945 and sat until he resigned in Jan. 1953. J.P. for Kent 1953. Author of *Dover-Nürnberg Return*, *The Soviet Spy System*, *The Big Lie*, *Pattern for Conquest*, *Sabotage is Suspected*, *True Blue*, an autobiography and other works.* [1953]

WHITE, Roger Lowrey, J.P. Sole Street House, Cobham-by-Gravesend, Kent. Carlton. S. of George F. White, Esq. B. 1 June 1928; m. 27 Jan. 1962, Angela, d. of Henry W. Orman, Esq. Educ. at St. Joseph's Coll., Beulah Hill. A Company Director. Founder member Conservative Commonwealth Council; admitted a Freeman of the City of London; J.P. for the Inner London Area 1965; National Vice-Chairman Young Conservatives 1958-59; member of Council London Borough of Bromley 1964-68. A Conservative. Unsuccessfully contested Stoke Newington and Hackney N. in 1959 and 1964 and the Gravesend division of Kent in 1966. Elected for the Gravesend division of Kent in June 1970 and sat until Feb. 1974, when he was defeated. Member of Asthma Research Council, Managing Director of Research Information Services (Westminster) Limited.* [1974]

WHITE, Sir (Rudolph) Dymoke, Bart. Southleigh Park, Havant, Hampshire. Salle Park, Norfolk. Cavalry, and Oxford & Cambridge. S. of Sir Woolmer White, 1st Bart. B. 11 June 1888; m. 26 June 1912, Isabelle, d. of James MacGowan, Esq. Educ. at Cheltenham, and Trinity Coll., Cambridge, M.A. Succeeded as Bart. 1931. High Sheriff for Co. Southampton 1935; Dept.-Lieut., J.P. and C.A. for Hampshire. Late Hampshire Carabiniers. Served in France 1916-19. A Conservative. Elected for the Fareham division of Hampshire in Oct. 1939 and sat until he retired in 1950. President of Royal Counties

Agricultural Society, Royal Norfolk Agricultural Association and British Horse Society. President of Coaching Club. Died 25 May 1968. [1950]

WHITEHEAD, Phillip. Mill House, Rowsley, Matlock, Derbyshire. S. of Harold Whitehead, Esq. B. 30 May 1937; m. 1967, Christine Usborne, (2 s. 1 d.). Educ. at Lady Manners Grammar School, Bakewell, and Exeter Coll., Oxford. Voted in favour of entry to E.E.C. on 28 Oct. 1971. Member of Annan Committee on Future of Broadcasting 1974-77. A Television Producer and Writer. Member P.L.P. Liaison Committee 1975. Vice-Chairman Fabian Society 1977-78, Chairman 1978-79. A Labour Member. Unsuccessfully contested W. Derbyshire in 1966. Elected for N. Derby in June 1970.* [1979]

WHITELAW, Rt. Hon. William Stephen Ian, C.H., M.C., D.L. Ennim, Penrith, Cumberland. Carlton. S. of William Alexander Whitelaw, Esq. B. 28 June 1918; m. 6 Feb. 1943, Cecilia, youngest d. of Maj. Mark Sport. Educ. at Winchester, and Trinity Coll., Cambridge. Regular Officer, Scots Guards 1939-47, Maj. 1942, Despatches, served in Germany and Palestine, resigned Commission in 1947. A Dept.-Lieut. for Dunbartonshire 1952-66 and for Cumberland 1967. British Walker Cup Golf Selector 1953. A Farmer. Parliamentary Private Secretary to Rt. Hon. Peter Thorneycroft, President of Board of Trade 1956-57 and Chancellor of Exchequer 1957-58. Assistant Government Whip 1959-61. Lord Commissioner of the Treasury Mar. 1961-July 1962. Parliamentary Secretary to the Ministry of Labour July 1962-Oct. 1964. Opposition Chief Whip 1964-70. PC. 1967. C.H. 1974. Capt. Royal and Ancient Golf Club St. Andrews 1969-70. Visiting Fellow of Nuffield Coll, Oxford from 1970. Lord President of the Council and Leader of the House of Commons June 1970-Mar. 1972; Secretary of State for Northern Ireland Mar. 1972-Dec. 1973, for Employment Dec. 1973-Mar. 1974. Member of Shadow Cabinet 1974-79. Opposition spokesman on Employment Mar.-June 1974, on Devolution Oct. 1974-Nov. 1976. Chairman Conservative Party June 1974-Feb. 1975. Dept. Leader of the Conservative Party from 1975. Opposition spokesman for Home Affairs Jan. 1976-May 1979. Home Secretary from May 1979. A Conservative. Unsuccessfully contested E. Dunbartonshire in 1950 and 1951. Sat for the Penrith and Border division of Cumberland from 1955.* [1979]

WHITELEY, Rt. Hon. William, C.H. Long Garth, White Smocks, Durham. S. of Samuel and Ellen Whiteley. B. 3 Oct. 1881; m. 5 Oct. 1901, Elizabeth Swordy, d. of James Jackson, Esq. Educ. at Brandon Colliery School, Co. Durham. A Methodist. A Miners' Agent from 1912. Member of Durham County Insurance Company and Education Committee. President of Durham Aged Mine Workers Homes Association and of Durham Miners Approved Society. Labour Whip 1927. A Lord Commissioner of the Treasury June 1929-Aug. 1931. Comptroller of the Royal Household May 1940-Mar. 1942. Joint Parliamentary Secretary to the Treasury and Chief Labour Whip Mar. 1942-May 1945; Chief Government Whip and Parliamentary Secretary to the Treasury Aug. 1945-Oct. 1951. Chief Whip of Labour Party 1942-55. Opposition Chief Whip May-July 1945 and Oct. 1951-June 1955. PC. 1943. A Labour Member. Unsuccessfully contested the Blaydon division of Durham in 1918. Sat for the Blaydon division of Durham from Nov. 1922 to Oct. 1931, when he was defeated. Re-elected in 1935 and sat until his death on 3 Nov. 1955. C.H. 1948. Dept.-Lieut. for Co. Durham. Died 3 Nov. 1955.
[1955]

WHITLOCK, William Charles. 51 Stoughton Road, Leicester. S. of George Whitlock, Esq., and Sarah Whitlock. B. 20 June 1918; m. 1943, Jessie Hilda, d. of George Victor Reardon, Esq., (5 s.). Educ. at Itchen Grammar School, and Southampton University. Former Area Organiser of the Union of Shop, Distributive and Allied Workers. War Service in the Army from 1939-46. President of the N.E. Leicester Constituency Labour Party 1955-56 and 1958-59. President of the Leicester and District Trades Council 1955-56. President of Leicester City Labour Party 1956-57, and Vice-President 1959-60. President East Midlands Regional Council of

Labour Party 1962-63. Appointed Opposition Whip Nov. 1962. Vice-Chamberlain of H.M. Household Oct. 1964-Mar. 1966. Lord Commissioner of the Treasury from Mar. 1966 to July 1966. Comptroller, H.M. Household from July 1966 to Mar. 1967. Dept. Chief Whip and Lord Commissioner of the Treasury Mar. 1967-July 1967. Parliamentary Under-Secretary of State for Commonwealth Affairs July 1967-Oct. 1968. Parliamentary Under-Secretary of State for Foreign and Commonwealth Affairs Oct. 1968-Oct. 1969. A Labour Member. Sat for Nottingham N. from 1959.* [1979]

WHITNEY, Raymond William, O.B.E. Dial House, Sunninghill, Berkshire. R.A.C. S. of George William Whitney, Esq., Hotel Keeper. B. 28 Nov. 1930; m. 31 Mar. 1956, Sheila Margot Beswick, d. of Walter Henry Prince, Esq., of Doncaster, (2 s.). Educ. at Wellingborough School, Royal Military Academy, Sandhurst, and London and Hong Kong Universities. Commissioned Northamptonshire Regiment 1951, service in Italy, Germany and Korea. Seconded Australian Government 1960-63. Diplomatic Service in Peking and Argentina 1964-72. Dept. High Commissioner Bangladesh 1973-76. Head of Information Research Department, Overseas Information Department, Foreign and Commonwealth Office 1977-78. Parliamentary Private Secretary to Nigel Lawson, Financial Secretary to Treasury and Peter Rees, Minister of State at Treasury from 1979. O.B.E. 1968. A Conservative. Elected for the Wycombe division of Buckinghamshire in Apr. 1978.* [1979]

WHITTAKER, John Edmondson. 121 Rosehill Road, Burnley, Lancashire. S. of James Whittaker, Esq., of Burnley. B. 1897; m. 1921, Alice, d. of Frank Marshall, Esq. Educ. at Burnley Municipal Coll., Sarisbury Court C. of E. Teachers Training Coll., Hampshire. Headmaster of Rosegrove County Modern School, Burnley to 1945. Served overseas 1915-19. A Labour Member. Elected for the Heywood and Radcliffe division of Lancashire in July 1945 and sat until he committed suicide on 9 Dec. 1945.
[1946]

WIGG, Rt. Hon. George Edward Cecil. 26A Warwick Square, London. 117 Newcastle Street, Trent Vale, Stoke-on-Trent. S. of Edward William Wigg, Esq. B. 28 Nov. 1900; m. 1930, Florence, d. of William Veal, Esq. Educ. at Queen Mary's Grammar School, Basingstoke. Parliamentary Private Secretary to the Rt. Hon. E. Shinwell, MP, Minister of Fuel and Power 1945-47, when Secretary of State for War 1947-50, and when Minister of Defence 1950-51. Served Regular Army 1919-37; rejoined 1940-46. Member of the Racecourse Betting Control Board 1958-61. Appointed by the Home Secretary to the Horserace Totalisator Board 1961-64. Paymaster Gen. Oct. 1964-Nov. 1967. PC. 1964. A Labour Member. Elected for Dudley in July 1945 and sat until Nov. 1967, when he was created Baron Wigg (Life Peerage) and appointed Chairman of Horserace Betting Levy Board. Opposition Whip 1951-52. Chairman of Horserace Betting Levy Board 1967-72. President of Betting Office Licensees' Association from 1973.* [1967]

WIGGIN, Alfred William (Jerry), T.D. The Court, Axbridge, Somerset. House of Commons, London. Beefsteak. S. of Col. Sir William Wiggin, K.C.B., D.S.O., T.D., D.L., J.P. B. 24 Feb. 1937; m. 1964, Rosemary Janet, d. of David Orr, Esq., of Wormley, Surrey, (2 s. 1 d.). Educ. at Eton, and Trinity Coll., Cambridge. 2nd Lieut. Queens Own Warwickshire and Worcestershire Yeomanry (T.A.) 1959, Maj. 1967. Maj. Royal Yeomanry 1975-78. Parliamentary Private Secretary to Lord Balniel, Minister of State for Defence 1970-72. Parliamentary Private Secretary to Ian Gilmour, Minister of State for Defence Procurement 1971-72. Parliamentary Private Secretary to Lord Balniel, Minister of State Foreign and Commonwealth Office 1972-74. Promoted Hallmarking Act 1973. Joint Secretary Conservative Defence Committee 1974-75. Vice-Chairman Agricultural Committee 1974. Rapporteur Economic Committee North Atlantic Assembly 1976. Chairman West Country Members 1978. Parliamentary Secretary to Minister of Agriculture from May 1979. T.D. 1970. A Conservative. Unsuccessfully contested Montgomeryshire in the general elections of 1964 and 1966. Elec-

ted for the Weston-super-Mare division of Somerset at a by-election in Mar. 1969.* [1979]

WIGLEY, Dafydd Wynne. Hen Efail, Bontnewydd, Caernarfon. S. of Elfyn Edward Wigley, Esq., B.A., F.S.A.A., F.I.M.T.A. B. 1 Apr. 1943; m. 26 Aug. 1967, Elinor, d. of Emrys Bennett Owen, Esq., (3 s. 1 d.). Educ. at Caernarvon Grammar School, Rydal School, Colwyn Bay, and Manchester University, B.Sc. 1964. Finance Staff, Ford Motor Company 1964-67. Chief Cost Accountant and Financial Planning Manager, Mars Limited 1967-71. Financial Controller, Hoover Limited, Merthyr Tydfil Plant 1971-74. Member Merthyr Tydfil County Borough Council 1972-74. Co-Author of *An Economic Plan for Wales* 1970. A Plaid Cymru Member. Unsuccessfully contested Merioneth in 1970. Elected for Caernarvon in Feb. 1974.* [1979]

WILCOCK, Group Capt. Clifford Arthur Bowman, O.B.E., A.F.C. 78 Buckingham Gate, London. B. 28 Apr. 1898. Educ. at St. Dunstan's Coll. and Edinburgh University. Served in Army, R.F.C. and R.A.F. 1914-18, A.F.C. Retired from R.A.F. as Group Captain 1938; in Air Ministry 1939-45. O.B.E. 1944. Chairman of Committee on Licensing, Recruitment and Training of Personnel for Civil Aviation; member of Lloyds; Director of Aviation Companies; a Freeman of the City of London; Gov. of Westminster Hospital; F.R.Ae.S. A Labour Member. Sat for Derby from July 1945 to Feb. 1950. Elected for N. Derby in Feb. 1950 and sat until his death on 14 Jan. 1962. [1962]

WILKES, Maj. Lyall. 37 The Drive, Gosforth, Northumberland. S. of George Wilkes, Esq., of Gosforth. B. 19 May 1914; m. 1946, Margaret, d. of Frederick Tait, Esq., of Gateshead. Educ. at Newcastle Grammar School, and Balliol Coll., Oxford, M.A. Barrister-at-Law, Middle Temple, 1947; practised on the N.E. Circuit. Chairman Oxford University Labour Club 1937; Secretary Oxford Union Society 1937. Joined Middlesex Regiment 1940; served overseas and with Special Mission to Greece; Maj. 1945 (despatches). A Labour Member. Elected for the Central division of Newcastle-on-Tyne in July 1945 and sat until he retired in 1951. Assistant Recorder of Sheffield and Newcastle-on-Tyne 1960-62. Dept. Chairman of Co. Durham Quarter Sessions 1961-64. County Court Judge, later Circuit Judge, from 1964.* [1951]

WILKINS, William Albert, C.B.E. 37 King Street, Two Mile Hill, Kingswood, Bristol. S. of W.A. Wilkins, Esq. B. 17 Jan. 1899; m. 1923, Violet, d. of Edward Reed, Esq. Educ. at Whitehall Elementary School, Bristol. Past President of Bristol Branch of Typographical Association. Assistant Whip Oct. 1947-Oct. 1959. Lord Commissioner of the Treasury Jan. 1950-Oct. 1951. Member of Bristol City Council 1936-46. A Labour Member. Elected for Bristol S. in July 1945 and sat until he retired in 1970. C.B.E. 1965.* [1970]

WILKINSON, Rt. Hon. Ellen Cicely. 14 Belgrave Square, London. Twixtlands Penn, Buckinghamshire. National Trades Union. D. of Richard and Ellen Wilkinson. B. 8 Oct. 1891. Educ. at Stretford Road Secondary School, and at University of Manchester. Organiser for National Union of Women's Suffrage Societies 1913-14. National Organiser of National Union of Distributive and Allied Workers from 1915; member of Manchester City Council 1923-26. Parliamentary Private Secretary to Susan Lawrence when Parliamentary Secretary to Ministry of Health June 1929-Aug. 1931; Parliamentary Secretary Ministry of Pensions May-Oct. 1940; Joint Parliamentary Secretary Ministry of Home Security Oct. 1940-May 1945; Minister of Education with a seat in the Cabinet July 1945-Feb. 1947. Member of National Executive Committee of Labour Party 1927-29 and1937-47, Chairman 1944-45. Chairman of the Labour Party 1944. PC. 1945. A Labour Member. Unsuccessfully contested Ashton-under-Lyne 1923. Member for Middlesbrough East division from Oct. 1924 to Oct. 1931, when she was defeated, and for the Jarrow division of Durham from 1935 until her death on 6 Feb. 1947. [1947]

WILKINSON, John Arbuthnot Ducane. House of Commons, London. R.A.F., United Service, and Royal Aero. S. of Denys Wilkinson, Esq., Schoolmaster. B. 23 Sept. 1940; m. 1969, Paula, d. of Joseph Adey, Esq., of Co. Durham. Educ. at Eton, R.A.F. Coll., Cranwell, and Churchill Coll., Cambridge. Commissioned into R.A.F. from Cranwell 1961; Flying Instructor No. 8 F.T.S. 1962; M.A. Hons. History Tripos Cambridge 1965; Flying Instructor R.A.F. Coll., Cranwell 1966-67; Head of University Department Conservative Central Office 1967-68; Aviation Specialist Conservative Research Department 1969; Sen. Administration Officer (Anglo/French Jaguar Project) Preston Division B.A.C. 1969-70; Secretary of Conservative Defence Committee and Secretary Conservative Aviation Committee from 1972. A Conservative. Elected for Bradford W. in June 1970 and sat until Feb. 1974, when he was defeated. Unsuccessfully contested Bradford W. in Oct. 1974. Elected for the Ruislip-Northwood division of Hillingdon in May 1979. Tutor, Open University 1970-71. Chief Flying Instructor, Skywork Limited, 1974-75. General Manager, General Aviation Division, Brooklands Aviation Limited 1975-76. Personal Assistant to Chairman of B.A.C. 1976-77. Senior Sales Executive, Eagle Aircraft Services Limited 1977-78. Sales Manager, Klingair Limited, 1978-79.* [1974]

WILLEY, Rt. Hon. Frederick Thomas. 11 North Square, London. S. of F. Willey, Esq., F.R.I.B.A. B. 1910; m. 1939, Eleanor, d. of W.H. Snowdon, Esq., (2 s. 1 d.). Educ. at Johnston School, and St. John's Coll., Cambridge, Foundation Scholar McMahon Studentship, Harmsworth Studentship, and Blackstone Prizeman. A Barrister-at-Law, Middle Temple 1936. Served in the London Fire Brigade. Parliamentary Private Secretary to the Rt. Hon. J. Chuter Ede, Home Secretary 1946-50. Formerly Director North Eastern Trading Estates Limited. Chairman of Select Committee on Estimates and member of Select Committees on Statutory Instruments and Public Accounts Mar.-Apr. 1950. Parliamentary Secretary to Ministry of Food Apr. 1950-Oct. 1951. Opposition spokesman on Agriculture and Food to 1960 and on

Education 1960-64. Member of Parliamentary Committee of P.L.P. 1956-64. Minister of Land and Natural Resources Oct. 1964-Feb. 1967. Minister of State, Ministry of Housing and Local Government Feb.-Aug. 1967. Chairman Select Committee on Education and Science 1968-70. Chairman Select Committees on Members Interests, Race Relations and Immigration, Abortion (Amendments) Bill and Selection and member of Select Committee on Privileges. Chairman Parliamentary and Scientific Committee. Voted in favour of entry to E.E.C. on 28 Oct. 1971. Vice-Chairman P.L.P. 1975-79. Chairman of P.L.P. from 1979. PC. 1964. A Labour Member. Sat for Sunderland from July 1945-Feb. 1950. Elected for N. Sunderland in Feb. 1950.* [1979]

WILLEY, Octavius George, C.B.E. 13 St. John's Grove, Upper Holloway, London. S. of Octavius Willey, Esq. B. 12 Jan. 1886; m. 1916, Fannie, d. of Lincoln Grunwell, Esq., of Bramley, Leeds. Educ. at London Board Schools and Fircroft Coll., Birmingham. A Lecturer in Economics and History and Political Organiser. Outside Meetings Officer for Ministry of Information 1940-41. Dept. Regional Commissioner Civil Defence N.E. Region 1941-45. A Labour Member. Unsuccessfully contested the Skipton division of the W. Riding of Yorkshire in 1923 and 1924 and W. Birmingham in 1929, 1931 and 1935. Elected for the Cleveland division of the N. Riding of Yorkshire in July 1945 and sat until his death on 12 July 1952. C.B.E. 1951. Died 12 July 1952. [1952]

WILLIAMS, Rt. Hon. Alan John. 96 Plunch Lane, Swansea. S. of Emlyn Williams, Esq., Coal Miner. B. 14 Oct. 1930; m. June 1967, Patricia Rees, (2 s. 1 d.). Educ. at Cardiff High School, in London, B.Sc. (Econ.), and University Coll., Oxford, B.A. Lecturer in Economics at the Welsh Coll. of Advanced Technology. Joined the Labour Party in 1950. Member of the Association of Teachers at Technical Institutes, affiliated to the N.U.T. from 1958. Member of the Fabian Society and the Co-operative Party. Visited Russia as a member of National Union of Students Delegation in 1954. Council of Europe and Western European Union 1966-67. Member Public Accounts Committee 1966-67. Chairman Welsh Parliamentary Labour Group 1966-67. Parliamentary Private Secretary to Rt. Hon. Edward Short, Postmaster Gen. July 1966-Aug. 1967. Parliamentary Under-Secretary of State, Department of Economic Affairs Aug. 1967-Oct. 1969. Joint Parliamentary Secretary Ministry of Technology Oct. 1969-June 1970. Opposition spokesman on Higher Education 1970-72, on Industry 1972-73, on Consumer Affairs 1973-Feb. 1974. Chairman All-Party Back Bench Committee on Minerals 1972. Minister of State, Prices and Consumer Protection Mar. 1974-Apr. 1976; Minister of State, Industry Apr. 1976-May. 1979. An Opposition spokesman on Welsh Affairs from 1979. PC. Jan. 1977. A Labour Member. Unsuccessfully contested Poole in 1959. Sat for Swansea W. from Oct. 1964.* [1979]

WILLIAMS, Alan Lee, O.B.E. House of Commons, London. Reform, Travellers, and Royal United Service Institute. S. of Alfred Edward Williams, Esq., Tug-Master. B. 29 Nov. 1930. Educ. at Roan School, Greenwich, and Ruskin Coll., Oxford. National Youth Officer of the Labour Party 1956-62. Delegate to the United Nations 1969. Dept. Director European Movement 1970-72. Director British Atlantic Committee 1972-74. Head of United Nations Youth Department for four years; Chairman of British National Committee, World Assembly of Youth; Vice-President of Council of European Youth Committees. Freeman of Company of Watermen and Lightermen; Freeman of the City of London. Member of the U.K. Delegation to the Western European Union and the Council of Europe 1967-70. Parliamentary Private Secretary to Rt. Hon. Denis Healey, Secretary of State for Defence 1969-70 and to Rt. Hon. Roy Mason, Secretary of State for Defence 1975-76 and Secretary of State for Northern Ireland 1976-79. Member of the Foreign Office Advisory Committee on Disarmament and Arms Control 1975. Member of the Advisory Council of the European Discussion Centre, Wilton Park 1975. Gov. of the Royal Greenwich Hospital School 1976. European Co-Chairman of the Transatlantic Policy Panel on Standardisation, Georgetown University 1976. Chairman of Transport on Water Association; Chairman All-Party Parliamentary Waterways Group Oct. 1974. Chairman of P.L.P. Defence Committee 1976-79. Director General of English-Speaking Union from 1979. O.B.E. 1973. Author of works of reference on international affairs. Member of United Nations Parliamentary Group. A Labour Member. Unsuccessfully contested Epsom in 1964. Sat for Hornchurch from 1966 to 1970, when he was defeated, and for the Hornchurch division of Havering from Feb. 1974 to 1979, when he was again defeated.* [1979]

WILLIAMS, Albert Clifford, B.E.M. "Brodawel", Abertillery Road, Blaina, Monmouthshire. S. of Daniel Williams, Esq., a Miner. B. 28 June 1905; m. 24 June 1930, Beatrice Annie, d. of Charles Garbett, Esq. Educ. at Primary School, Blaina, Monmouthshire. Started work in the mines at fourteen, Trade Union Officer N.U.M. 1934-64; J.P. from 1952. Chairman of Usk River Board for ten years; member of Hospital boards for thirty years. Awarded the B.E.M. 1957. A Labour Member. Elected for the Abertillery division of Monmouth at a by-election in Apr. 1965 and sat until he retired in 1970. Member of Monmouthshire County Council, Alderman 1964-74. Member of Sports Council for Wales 1972-75. Member of Welsh National Water Development Authority.* [1970]

WILLIAMS, Sir Brandon Meredith Rhys, Bart. See RHYS-WILLIAMS, Sir Brandon Meredith, Bart.

WILLIAMS, Rt. Hon. Charles. Rozel, Torquay. Caerhays Castle, Gorran, St. Austell, Cornwall. Carlton, Marlborough, and Windham. S. of John Charles Williams, Esq., MP., of Caerhays Castle, Cornwall. B. 21 Apr. 1886; m. 1915, Mary Frances, d. of T.B. Bolitho, Esq., MP. Educ. at Eton, and Trinity Coll., Cambridge. Late Lieut.-Commander R.N.V.R., served at Antwerp and Gallipoli. Parliamentary Private Secretary to Sir Arthur Griffith-Boscawen, Minister of Agriculture 1921-22. Dept. Chairman of Ways and Means Mar. 1943-May 1945, and Chairman of Ways and Means and Dept. Speaker May-July 1945.

PC. 1952. A Conservative. Unsuccessfully contested as a Liberal Unionist the Northwich division of Cheshire in Jan. 1910 and the Truro division of Cornwall in Dec. 1910. Represented the Tavistock division of Devon from 1918-22, when he was defeated. Unsuccessfully contested Torquay in 1923. Elected for Torquay in Oct. 1924 and sat until his death on 28 Oct. 1955. [1955]

WILLIAMS, David James. Delfryn, Penscynor, Neath, Glamorgan. S. of Morgan Williams, Esq., a Miner. B. 3 Feb. 1897; m. 1939, Janet Scott, d. of James Alexander, Esq. Educ. at Elementary School, and Central Labour Coll., London. A Coal Miner and Checkweigher. Member of Executive Council South Wales Miners' Federation and of Pontardawe Rural District Council 1931-45. Member of Miners' Delegation to Russia. A Labour Member. Elected for the Neath division of Glamorganshire in May 1945 and sat until he retired in 1964. Died 12 Sept. 1972. [1964]

WILLIAMS, Rt. Hon. Edward John. Riversdale, Bridgend, Glamorgan. S. of Emmanuel Williams, Esq., of Victoria, Monmouthshire. B. 1 July 1890; m. 10 June 1916, Evelyn, d. of David James, Esq., of Pontypridd. Educ. at Victoria Voluntary School, Hopkinstown Elementary School, and at Labour Coll., London. Miners' Secretary 1909-12. Labour Coll. 1912-15, Provincial Lecturer 1916. Miner, Checkweigher 1917-18; Miners' Agent 1919-31. Parliamentary Private Secretary to Rt. Hon. George Hall, Financial Secretary to the Admiralty 1942-43, and when Parliamentary Under-Secretary of State for Foreign Affairs 1943-45. Minister of Information Aug. 1945-Feb. 1946. PC. 1945. A Labour Member. Sat for the Ogmore division of Glamorganshire from May 1931 until May 1946, when he resigned on appointment as High Commissioner in Australia. Member of Glamorgan County Council 1928-31. High Commissioner in Australia 1946-52. K.C.M.G. 1952. Member of National Industrial Disputes Tribunal 1953-59. Died 16 May 1963. [1946]

WILLIAMS, Gerald Wellington. 10 Artillery Mansions, Victoria Street, London.

Shernfold Park, Frant, Tunbridge Wells. Carlton, and Pratt's. S. of W.A. Williams, Esq., of Shernfold Park, Frant. B. 1903; m. 1930, Mary, d. of Capt. Josceline Heber Percy. Educ. at Eton, and Christ Church, Oxford. Dept.-Lieut. and J.P., of East Lymden, Ticehurst. Chairman of Rye Divisional Conservative Association 1938-45; member of Uckfield Rural District Council 1938. Served with R.N.V.R. 1939-45, Lieut.-Commander. A Conservative. Elected for the Tonbridge division of Kent in July 1945 and sat until he resigned in May 1956. J.P. for Tunbridge Wells, High Sheriff of Kent 1968-69.* [1956]

WILLIAMS, Sir Herbert Geraint, Bart. 80 Ashley Gardens, London. 145 Abbey House, Victoria Street, London. Constitutional, and 1900. S. of Thomas Williams, Esq., M.A., LL.D., Schoolmaster, of Hooton, Cheshire. B. 2 Dec. 1884; m. 29 Jan. 1916, Dorothy Frances, d. of Barton Jones, Esq. Educ. at Hooton Grammar School, and University of Liverpool, M.Eng., M.Sc. A.M.Inst.C.E. 1911. Secretary of Machine Tools Trade Association 1911-28. Served in Ministry of Munitions and with R.A.O.C. 1914-18. Director of Empire Industries Association 1926-28 and 1931-41. Late member of Wimbledon Borough Council; Alderman London County Council 1940-44; Honorary Secretary of Empire Economic Union; Lieut. R.A.O.C. Director of Companies. Parliamentary Secretary to Board of Trade Jan. 1928-June 1929. Chairman of Executive of London Area of Conservative Council 1939-48, and of Special Enquiries Sub-Committee of Select Committee on National Expenditure. Chairman of Annual Conservative Conference (Llandudno) 1948. Knight Bach. 1939. Bart. 1953. A Conservative. Unsuccessfully contested the Combined English Universities in 1918 and Oct. 1931, Wednesbury 1922 and 1923. Sat for Reading from Oct. 1924-June 1929, when he was defeated. Member for Croydon S. Feb. 1932-July 1945, when he was defeated. Elected for E. Croydon in Feb. 1950 and sat until his death on 25 July 1954. [1954]

WILLIAMS, John Lloyd. 99 Hill Street, Glasgow. S. of John Williams, Esq. B. 1895;

m. Marion Porter. Educ. at National School, Machynlleth, and Labour Coll., London. A Journalist. Member of Glasgow Corporation 1938-45; Magistrate Glasgow 1943-45. A Labour Member. Elected for the Kelvingrove division of Glasgow in July 1945 and sat until 1950, when he was defeated. Unsuccessfully contested the Kelvingrove division of Glasgow in 1951 and 1955.* [1950]

WILLIAMS, Rev. Llywelyn. Hafod-y-Cwm, Old Pant Road, Newbridge, Monmouthshire. S. of W. Williams, Esq., of Llanelly. B. 22 July 1911; m. 17 Aug. 1938, the Hon. Elsie, eld. d. of Rt. Hon. Lord Macdonald of Gwaenysgor. Educ. at Llanelly Grammar School, and Swansea University, B.A. Minister of Religion (Congregational) 1936-50, at Bethesda, Bangor 1936-42, at Tabernacle, Abertillery 1943-46 and at Welsh Tabernacle, King's Cross, London 1946-50. A Labour Member. Elected for the Abertillery division of Monmouthshire in Nov. 1950 and sat until his death on 4 Feb. 1965. [1965]

WILLIAMS, Paul Glyn. Little Brook House, Over Wallop, Nr. Stockbridge, Hampshire. S. of Sam O. Williams, Esq., of Alnmouth, Northumberland. B. 14 Nov. 1922; m. 1st, 6 Sept. 1947, Barbara, d. of Alan Hardy, Esq., of Alnwick, Northumberland (divorced 1964); 2ndly, 1964, Gillian Foote, d. of A.G. Howland Jackson, Esq. and Mrs. E.J. Foote. Educ. at Marlborough, and Trinity Hall, Cambridge. Travelled in Canada, U.S.A., South Africa, East Africa, Europe and Scandinavia. Director Hodgkinson Partners Limited, and Adams Powel Equipment Limited. A Conservative. Unsuccessfully contested Newcastle on Tyne E. in 1950 and Sunderland S. in 1951. Elected for Sunderland S. in May 1953; re-elected 1955 and 1959 and sat until 1964, when he was defeated. Conservative Whip withdrawn May 1957-July 1958. Chairman of Monday Club 1964-69. Fellow of the Institute of Directors. Chairman of Backer Electric Company Limited.* [1964]

WILLIAMS, Rolf Dudley. See DUDLEY-WILLIAMS, Sir Rolf, Bart.

WILLIAMS, Ronald Watkins. 5 Briton Close, Sanderstead, Surrey. S. of Thomas Jenkin Watkins and adopted s. of Isaac Williams. B. 18 July 1907; m. 19 July 1934, Olive May, d. of I.N. Bazzard, Esq. Educ. at Council School, Briton Ferry, Glamorgan. Admitted a Solicitor 1930; Solicitor to Durham Miners' Association 1936-45, and to National Union of Mineworkers 1945-48. Member of Commission of Enquiry into Nigerian Disorders 1949-50 and of Inter-Parliamentary Union Delegation Nice 1949, Stockholm 1949 and of Commonwealth Parliamentary Delegation Malaya 1950. Council of Europe, Strasbourg 1951. Admitted Northern Rhodesian bar 1953. Member of Parliamentary Delegation to Kenya 1954, and Commonwealth Parliamentary Delegation to Kenya 1956. A Labour Member. Elected for Wigan in Mar. 1948 and sat until his death on 14 Mar. 1958.   [1957]

WILLIAMS, Rt. Hon. Shirley Vivien Teresa Brittain. House of Commons, London. D. of Sir George Catlin and Vera Brittain, B. 1930; m. 1955, Professor Bernard Williams, s. of Owen Williams, Esq. (marriage dissolved in 1974), (1 d.). Educ. at Elementary School, Summit School, Minnesota, U.S.A., St. Paul's Girls' School, and Open Scholar, Somerville Coll., Oxford, M.A. U.S. State Department Scholarship to Columbia University, New York. Employed on the *Daily Mirror* from 1952-54, and *Financial Times* 1954-58. General Secretary Fabian Society 1960-64. Joined the Labour Party in 1946. Member Association of Prof. Executive Clerical and Computer Staffs Union. First woman Chairman Oxford University Labour Club. Parliamentary Private Secretary to Rt. Hon. Kenneth Robinson, Minister of Health 1964-66. Parliamentary Secretary to Ministry of Labour 1966-67. Minister of State, Education and Science 1967-69; Minister of State, Home Office Oct. 1969-June 1970. Member of the Shadow Cabinet, Parliamentary Committee of P.L.P. 1970-74. Shadow spokesman on Social Services 1970-71. Shadow Home Secretary 1971-73. Voted in favour of entry to E.E.C. on 28 Oct. 1971. Shadow spokesman on Prices and Consumer Affairs 1973-74. Secretary of State for Prices and Consumer Protec-

tion Mar. 1974-Sept. 1976. Paymaster-Gen. Apr. 1976-May 1979. Secretary of State for Education and Science Sept. 1976-May 1979. Member National Executive Committee of the Labour Party from 1970. Visiting Fellow Nuffield Coll., Honorary Doctor Edinburgh (CNAA); Honorary Doctor of Political Economy, University of Leuven 1976, Professorial Fellow of Policy Studies Institute from 1979. PC. 1974. A Labour Member. Unsuccessfully contested Harwich at a by-election in 1954 and in the general election of 1955. Unsuccessfully contested the Test division of Southampton in 1959. Sat for the Hitchin division of Hertfordshire from 1964-Feb. 1974. Elected for Hertford and Stevenage in 1974 and sat until 1979 when she was defeated.*   [1979]

WILLIAMS, Rt. Hon. Thomas. Cartref, Town Moor Avenue, Doncaster. S. of James Williams, Esq.; of Wath. B. 18 Mar. 1888; m. 1910, Elizabeth Ann, d. of Thomas Andrews, Esq. Educ. at Elementary School. A Miner, Checkweighman. Parliamentary Private Secretary to Noel Buxton, Minister of Agriculture Jan.-Oct. 1924, to Rt. Hon. Margaret Bondfield, Minister of Labour June 1929-Aug. 1931. Parliamentary Secretary Ministry of Agriculture and Fisheries May 1940-May 1945; Minister of Agriculture and Fisheries July 1945-Oct. 1951. Member of Executive Committee of P.L.P. 1931-40. Member of Shadow Cabinet 1931-40. Opposition spokesman on Agriculture until 1959. PC. 1941. A Labour Member. Elected for the Don Valley division of the W. Riding of Yorkshire in Nov. 1922 and sat until he retired in 1959. Created Baron Williams of Barnburgh (Life Peerage) 1961. Member of Political Honours Scrutiny Committee 1961-67. Member of Doncaster Board of Guardians and Bolton-on-Dearne Urban District Council. Died 29 Mar. 1967.   [1959]

WILLIAMS, (William) Donald. Sexton Barns, Cockshot Road, Malvern, Worcestershire. Kendall, Wadley and Company, Chartered Accountants, Lyttelton House, Malvern. S. of Sydney Williams, Esq. B. 17 Oct. 1919; m. 26 July 1945, Cecilia Mary, d. of Basil Hirons, Esq. Educ. at Royal Grammar School, Worcester. Joined Worcester Regiment 1939. Taken prisoner on active service June 1940, and escaped through Russia Jan.-Mar. 1945. Qualified as Chartered Accountant 1949. A Financial Consultant. Partner in Kendall, Wadley and Company from Apr. 1950 to 1977. A Conservative. Unsuccessfully contested Dudley in Mar. 1966. Elected for Dudley at a by-election in Mar. 1968 and sat until 1970, when he was defeated. Unsuccessfully contested Dudley East in 1979. Member of Hereford & Worcester County Council from 1973.*   [1970]

WILLIAMS, William Richard. 53 Woodbury Drive, Sutton, Surrey. S. of O.E. Williams, Esq., of Llanrug. B. 7 Mar. 1895; m. 1926, Lillian Vaughan, d. of John Williams, Esq., of Liverpool. Educ. at Elementary Schools. Served in Post Office 1912-40. Assistant Secretary Union of Post Office Workers 1940-52. Opposition spokesman on Post Office Affairs 1960-63. A Labour Member. Sat for Heston and Isleworth from 1945-50, when he was defeated, and for Droylsden from 1951 to May 1955. Elected for the Openshaw division of Manchester in May 1955 and sat until his death on 11 Sept. 1963. Died 11 Sept. 1963.   [1963]

WILLIAMS, Sir William Thomas, Q.C. House of Commons, London. S. of David John Williams, Esq., of Aberdare. B. 1915; m. 28 Feb. 1942, Gwyneth, d. of Rev. D.G. Harries. Educ. at Aberdare Grammar School, University of Wales, M.A., B.D., and at St. Catherine's Society, Oxford, M.A. A Barrister-at-Law, Lincoln's Inn, 1951. Bursar and Tutor of Manchester Coll., Oxford 1946-49. Baptist Minister 1941-46, Chaplain and Welfare Office R.A.F. Prisoners of War Camp 1944-46. Parliamentary Private Secretary to Rt. Hon. H.A. Marquand, Minister of Pensions 1950-51 and Minister of Health 1951. Parliamentary Private Secretary to Sir Elwyn Jones, Attorney General and Sir Dingle Foot, Solicitor General 1964-67. Appointed a Q.C. 1964. Member of Advisory Council on Public Records 1965-71. Member of S.E. Metropolitan Regional Hospital Board 1965-71. Recorder of Birkenhead 1969-72; Recorder Crown Court 1972. Bencher Lincoln's Inn 1972. Chairman of Inter-Parliamentary Union 1974-77. Member of

Advisory Council on Statute Law from 1974. President World Council, Inter-Parliamentary Union 1976. Chairman Select Committee on Parliamentary Procedure from 1976. Knight Bachelor 1976. A Labour and Co-operative Member. Sat for S. Hammersmith from Feb. 1949-May 1955, and Barons Court from 1955-59, when he was defeated. Elected for Warrington in Apr. 1961.*   [1979]

WILLIAMSON, Thomas. 5 Endsleigh Gardens, London. 26 Elmcroft Drive, Surbiton. S. of James Williamson, Esq. B. 2 Sept. 1897; m. 24 Feb. 1925, Hilda, d. of John Hartley, Esq. Educ. at St. Helens, and at Workers' Educational Association Liverpool University. National Industrial Officer of National Union of General and Municipal Workers 1938; member Liverpool City Council 1929-35; J.P.; member of National Executive Labour Party 1940-47. Gen. Secretary National Union of General and Municipal Workers 1946-61. A Labour Member. Elected for the Brigg division of Lincoln and Rutland in July 1945 and sat until he resigned in Mar. 1948. C.B.E. 1950; knighted 1956; created Baron Williamson (Life Peerage) 1962. Chairman of British Productivity Council 1953-54. Director of Daily Herald Limited 1953-62. Chairman of T.U.C. 1956-57. Hon. LL.D. Cambridge University, 1959. Member of Iron and Steel Board 1960-67. Member of Independent Television Authority 1961-64. Trustee of Thomson Foundation 1962-78. Director of Securicor Limited from 1964.*   [1948]

WILLINK, Rt. Hon. Henry Urmston, M.C., K.C. 102 Hamilton Terrace, London. United University. S. of William Edward Willink, Esq., F.R.I.B.A., of Liverpool. B. 7 Mar. 1894; m. 1st, 11 Dec. 1923, Cynthia Frances, d. of H. Morley Fletcher, Esq., M.D., F.R.C.P. (she died 1959); 2ndly, 1964, Mrs. Doris Preston. Educ. at Eton, and Trinity Coll., Cambridge. Served overseas 1915-19, M.C., Barrister-at-Law, Inner Temple, 1920, Bencher 1942. K.C. 1935; Special Commissioner for Rehousing for London Region Sept. 1940-Sept. 1943. Minister of Health Nov. 1943-July 1945. PC. 1943. Chancellor of the Diocese of Rochester 1942-

43. A National Conservative Member. Unsuccessfully contested Ipswich in Feb. 1938. Sat for N. Croydon from June 1940 until he resigned in Jan. 1948. High Bailiff of Westminster 1942-67. Fellow of Eton Coll. 1946-56. Chancellor of Dioceses of Norwich and St. Edmundsbury and Ipswich 1948-55. Master of Magdalene Coll., Cambridge 1948-66. Vice-Chancellor of Cambridge University 1953-55. Dean of Court of Arches and Vicar-Gen. of Province of Canterbury 1955-70. Created Bart. 1957. Chairman of Royal Commission on Betting 1949, Committee on Medical Manpower 1955, Committee on Minorities in Nigeria 1957, Royal Commission on the Police 1960. Died 1 Jan. 1973.

[1948]

WILLIS, Rt. Hon. Eustace George. 31 Great King Street, Edinburgh. S. of Walter Willis, Esq. B. 7 Mar. 1903; m. 2 Nov. 1929, Mary Swan Ramsay Nisbet. Educ. at City of Norwich Secondary School. Served in R.N. 1919-30 and in R.A. 1942-45. Bookseller and Lecturer for National Council of Labour Colleges 1932-64. Minister of State for Scotland Oct. 1964-Jan. 1967. PC. 1967. Chairman of Scottish Labour Party 1954-55, of Scottish P.L.P. 1961-63. Opposition spokesman on Admiralty Affairs 1961-64. A Labour Member. Sat for Edinburgh N. from 1945-50, when he was defeated. Unsuccessfully contested Edinburgh N. in 1951. Sat for Edinburgh E. from Apr. 1954 until he retired in 1970. General Commissioner, Board of Inland Revenue 1972-78. Member of Scottish Parole Board.*   [1970]

WILLOUGHBY DE ERESBY, Gilbert James Heathcote-Drummond-Willoughby, Lord. Swinstead Hall, Grantham. S. of Gilbert, 2nd Earl of Ancaster. B. 8 Dec. 1907; m. 27 July 1933, Hon. Phyllis Astor, d. of Waldorf, 2nd Visct. Astor (she died 1975). Educ. at Eton, and Magdalene Coll., Cambridge, B.A. Maj. 153rd (Leicestershire Yeomanry) Field Regiment R.A., T.A. Served overseas (despatches 1944). T.D. 1945. Dept.-Lieut., and J.P. for Lincolnshire, Lord-Lieut. 1950-75. A Conservative. Elected for the Rutland and Stamford division of Lincolnshire in Nov. 1933 and sat until he retired in 1950. Lord Great Chamberlain 1950-52.

Called up to the House of Lords as Lord Willoughby de Eresby in Jan. 1951 and succeeded to the Earldom of Ancaster in Sept. 1951. Member of Kesteven County Council 1950-74, Alderman 1954-74. National President of British Limbless Ex-servicemen's Association from 1956. K.C.V.O. 1971.*

[1950]

WILLS, Edith Agnes. 23 St. Mark's Crescent, Regents Park, London. 34 Rupert Street, Birmingham. D. of John Wood, Esq. B. 21 Nov. 1892; m. 1921, Frank Wills, Esq. Educ. at Aston, Birmingham. Member of Birmingham City Council from 1930. J.P. 1934. A Labour Member. Elected for the Duddeston division of Birmingham in July 1945 and sat until she retired in 1950. Director of Birmingham Co-operative Society from 1932. Member of Tomato and Cucumber Marketing Board. O.B.E. 1966. Died 7 Apr. 1970.   [1950]

WILLS, Sir Gerald, M.B.E. 42 Eaton Square, London. Milton House, East Knoyle, Salisbury, Wiltshire. Bucks., Carlton, and Pratts. Adopted S. of R.D. Wills, Esq. B. 3 Oct. 1905; m. 19 July 1927, Amy Mary Louise, d. of Ivo Peters, Esq., of Corston, Somerset. Educ. privately, and at Trinity Coll., Cambridge. Barrister-at-Law, Middle Temple, 1932; J.P. for Wiltshire. Member of Lloyd's. Served with R.A. (T.A.) and on Staff 1939-45. M.B.E. 1945. Assistant Government Whip 1952-54. Lord Commissioner of the Treasury Oct. 1954-Jan. 1957; Comptroller of H.M. Household Jan. 1957-Oct. 1958. Knight Bach. 1958. A Conservative. Unsuccessfully contested the Bridgwater division of Somerset in 1945. Elected for Bridgwater in Feb. 1950 and sat until his death on 31 Oct. 1969.

[1969]

WILMOT, Rt. Hon. John Charles. 14 Stanhope Gate, London. Reform. S. of Charles Wilmot, Esq. B. 2 Apr. 1895; m. 8 Aug. 1928, Elsa, d. of George Slate, Esq., of Hastings. Educ. at Elementary School and Chelsea Polytechnic. Served in R.N.A.S. 1914-18. Member of Institute of Bankers; Alderman London County Council 1937-45; Chairman of London Fire Brigade Committee 1939-42; member of Cohen Committee on Company Law Reform, of Select Committee on Rebuilding House of Commons, of Executive Committee of Commonwealth Parliamentary Association; Councillor of Royal Empire Society; Gov. of Old Vic and Sadler's Wells Theatres. Parliamentary Private Secretary to the Rt. Hon. Hugh Dalton, when Minister of Economic Warfare 1940-42 and when President of Board of Trade 1942-44; Joint Parliamentary Secretary Ministry of Supply Nov. 1944-May 1945; Minister of Supply Aug. 1945-Oct. 1947 and Minister of Aircraft Production Aug. 1945-Apr. 1946. PC. 1945. J.P. for London. A Labour Member. Unsuccessfully contested E. Lewisham in 1924, 1929 and 1931. Sat for E. Fulham from Oct. 1933 until he was defeated in 1935, for the Kennington division of Lambeth from May 1939 to July 1945, and for Deptford from July 1945 until Jan. 1950, when he was created Baron Wilmot of Selmeston. Member of National Executive Committee of Labour Party Jan.-May 1939 and 1940-41. Died 22 July 1964.

[1950]

WILSON, Alexander. House of Commons, London. S. of James Wilson, Esq. B. June 1917; m. 1941. Educ. at Forth Grammar School. A Miner. Member 3rd district Council, Lanarkshire for 11 years. A Labour Member. Unsuccessfully contested Hamilton in 1967. Elected for the Hamilton division of Lanarkshire on 18 June 1970 and sat until his death on 23 Mar. 1978.   [1978]

WILSON, Hugh Geoffrey Birch. 36 Cleaver Square, London. S. of F.J. Wilson, Esq., C.I.E., of Sidmouth. B. 11 June 1903; m. 27 June 1935, Daphne, d. of Gordon Astley Wake, Esq. Educ. at Clifton Coll., and Pembroke Coll., Cambridge, M.A. Admitted a Solicitor 1929; in Solicitors' Department G.W.R. for 19 years, and one year with British Railways, Western Region. A Partner in London firm; Associate of the Institute of Transport. A Conservative. Elected for the Truro division of Cornwall in Feb. 1950 and sat until he retired in 1970. Chairman of Conservative Transport Committee 1955-63. C.B.E. 1973. Died 11 Apr. 1975.

[1970]

WILSON, Rt. Hon. Sir James Harold, K.G., O.B.E., F.R.S. House of Commons, London. Athenaeum. S. of Herbert Wilson, Esq., Chemist, of Huddersfield. B. 11 Mar. 1916; m. 1 Jan. 1940, Gladys Mary, d. of Rev. D. Baldwin, of Duxford, (2 s.). Educ. at Milnsbridge Council School, Royds Hall and Wirral Grammar Schools, and Jesus Coll., Oxford. A Lecturer in Economics, New Coll., Oxford 1938; Fellow of University Coll. 1938-39 and 1944-45. Member of the War Cabinet Secretariat 1940-41. Director of Economics and Statistics Ministry of Fuel and Power 1941-44. Parliamentary Secretary Ministry of Works Aug. 1945-Mar. 1947; Secretary for Overseas Trade Mar.-Oct. 1947. President of Board of Trade with a Seat in the Cabinet Oct. 1947-Apr. 1951. Member of National Executive Committee of Labour Party 1952-76, Chairman 1961-62. Member of Parliamentary Committee of P.L.P. from Apr. 1954. Chairman Public Accounts Committee from 1959-63. Unsuccessful candidate for leadership of Labour Party 1960. Opposition spokesman on Trade and Treasury Affairs to 1961, on Foreign Affairs 1961-63. Elected Leader of the Labour Party in Feb. 1963. Leader of Opposition 1963-64 and 1970-74. Chairman of Committee to Review the Functioning of Financial Institutions from 1976. Freeman of the City of Sheffield 1966; Freeman of the Borough of Merthyr Tydfil 1969. Elder Brother of Trinity House 1968. President Royal Statistical Society 1972. Fellow of the Royal Society. Prime Minister and First Lord of the Treasury Oct. 1964-June 1970 and Mar. 1974-Apr. 1976. Honorary D.C.L. (Oxford) 1965. A Freeman of the Borough of Huddersfield 1968. Chancellor of Bradford University 1966. O.B.E. 1945. PC. 1947. K.G. 1976. A Labour Member. Sat for Ormskirk from July 1945 to Mar. 1950. Elected for the Huyton division of Lancashire in Feb. 1950.*   [1979]

WILSON, (Robert) Gordon. House of Commons, London. S. of R.G. Wilson, Esq. B. Apr. 1938; m. 1965, Edith M. Hassall. Educ. at Douglas High School, and Edinburgh University. Former Law Practice Partner. National Secretary of S.N.P. 1963-71, Executive Vice-Chairman 1972-73, Senior Vice-Chairman 1973-74. Dept. Leader of S.N.P. in

House of Commons 1974-77. Chairman of S.N.P. from 1979. A Scottish National Party Member. Unsuccessfully contested Dundee E. in 1973. Elected for Dundee E. in Feb. 1974.* [1979]

WILSON, William. Avonside House, Barford, Warwickshire. S. of Charles Wilson, Esq. B. 28 June 1913; m. 15 Oct. 1939, Bernice, d. of Thomas and Henrietta Morran. Educ. at Elementary Schools, Coventry Technical School, and Birmingham University. Served in Army 1941-46. A Solicitor. Life-long Member of the Co-operative movement. Lecturer for W.E.A. on legal subjects. Elected to Warwickshire County Council 1958-70 and leader of the Labour Group on that council, re-elected 1972. Dept.-Lieut. for Warwickshire from 1967. A Labour Member. Unsuccessfully contested Warwick and Leamington in 1951, 1955 and 1959 general elections and a by-election 1957. Sat for Coventry S. from 1964 to Feb. 1974. Elected for S.E. Coventry in Feb. 1974.* [1979]

WINGFIELD DIGBY, Kenelm Simon Digby. See Digby, Kenelm Simon Digby Wingfield.

WINNICK, David Julian. House of Commons, London. S. of E.G. Winnick, Esq. B. 26 June 1933; m. 23 Sept. 1968, Miss Bengisu Rona. Educ. at Secondary School, L.S.E., and self-educ. Served in Army 1951-53. Branch Secretary, Clerical and Administrative Workers Union 1956-62. Member Willesden Borough Council 1959-64; member Brent Borough Council 1964, resigned 1966. Advertisement Manager of *Tribune* 1963-66. A Labour Member. Unsuccessfully contested Harwich at the general election of 1964. Elected for Croydon S. in Mar. 1966 and sat until 1970, when he was defeated. Unsuccessfully contested Croydon Central in Oct. 1974 and Walsall N. in Nov. 1976. Elected for Walsall N. in May 1979.* [1970]

WINSTANLEY, Dr. Michael Platt. House of Commons, London. S. of Dr. Sydney A. Winstanley. B. Aug. 1918; m. 1st, 1945, Nancy Penney (divorced 1952); 2ndly, 1955, Joyce M. Woodhouse. Educ. at Manchester

Grammar School, and Manchester University. President Manchester University Union. Member of Liberal Party Council from 1961 and of Party committee. A Medical Practitioner. Member of B.B.C.'s General Advisory Council 1967-70. Radio and television broadcaster. Author of *Home Truths for Home Doctors* (1963), *The Anatomy of First Aid* (1966), *The British Ombudsman* (1970), *Tell Me Doctor* (1972) and *Know Your Rights* (1975). A Liberal. Unsuccessfully contested Stretford in 1964. Sat for Cheadle from Mar. 1966-70, when he was defeated. Elected for Hazel Grove in Feb. 1974 and sat until Oct. 1974, when he was defeated. Dept. Liberal Whip Mar.-Oct. 1974. Created Baron Winstanley (Life Peerage) 1975. Member of Post Office Board from 1978. Chairman of Countryside Commission from 1978. Member of Water Space Amenity Commission from 1980.* [1974 2nd ed.]

WINTERBOTTOM, Ian. Old House, Clapton, Kettering, Northamptonshire. S. of G.H. Winterbottom, Esq., of Horton House, Northamptonshire. B. 6 Apr. 1913; m. Irene Eva, d. of Dr. Walter Munk, of Haifa. Educ. at Charterhouse, and Clare Coll., Cambridge. Worked in Textile and Engineering Industry in Manchester, Derby and Germany. Capt. Royal Horse Guards, served overseas; N.W. European Campaign. Aide-de-Camp to Regional Commissioner for Hamburg and on his Personal Staff until 1949. Private Secretary to Lord Pakenham when Minister for Civil Aviation 1949-50; member of Commission of Management of Papworth Village Settlement, and of Overseas Migration Board. A Labour Member. Elected for Nottingham Central in Feb. 1950 and sat until 1955, when he was defeated. Unsuccessfully contested Nottingham Central in 1959. Created Baron Winterbottom (Life Peerage) 1965. Parliamentary Under-Secretary for Defence for the Navy Apr. 1966-Jan. 1967. Parliamentary Secretary to Ministry of Public Building and Works Jan. 1967-Nov. 1968. Parliamentary Under-Secretary for Defence for the R.A.F. Nov. 1968-June 1970. Lord in Waiting and Government Whip in the House of Lords from Oct. 1974 to May 1979. Chairman of Venesta International 1972-74.* [1954]

WINTERBOTTOM, Richard Emanuel.
House of Commons, London. S. of Peter
Winterbottom, Esq. B. 1899; m. 1925, Lilian
Sumner. Educ. at Elementary School in
Oldham. Served with Royal Navy 1914-18.
Area Organiser for Union of Shop, Distribu-
tive and Allied Workers 1935-44, National
Organiser 1944-50. Parliamentary Private
Secretary to Rt. Hon. Ness Edwards, Post-
master-Gen. 1950-51. A Labour Member.
Elected for the Brightside division of Sheffield
in Feb. 1950 and sat until his death on 9 Feb.
1968.   [1967]

**WINTERTON, Edward Turnour, Rt.
Hon. Earl.** 61 Eccleston Square, London.
Shillinglee Park, Chiddingfold. Carlton,
Turf, and Beefsteak. S. of 5th Earl Winterton
and Lady Georgiana Hamilton, d. of 1st
Duke of Abercorn. B. 4 Apr. 1883; m. 28 Feb.
1924, Hon. Cecilia Monica Wilson, d. of
Charles, 2nd Baron Nunburnholme. Educ. at
Eton, and New Coll., Oxford. Succeeded his
father as 6th Earl Winterton in the Peerage of
Ireland 1907. Served in Gallipoli and Pales-
tine 1915, with Sussex Yeomanry, and after-
wards with Imperial Camel Corps. T.D. Had
Orders of the Nile and El Nahda. Under-
Secretary of State for India Mar. 1922-Jan.
1924, and Nov. 1924-June 1929. Parliament-
ary Private Secretary to Rt. Hon. George
Pretyman when Financial Secretary to the
Admiralty 1903-05. Chancellor of Duchy of
Lancaster May 1937-Jan. 1939. Dept. to
Secretary of State for Air and Vice-President
of Air Council Mar.-May 1938. Member of
the Cabinet Mar. 1938-Jan. 1939; Assistant
to Home Secretary June 1938. Chairman of
Intergovernmental Committee 1938-45. Pay-
master-Gen. Jan.-Nov. 1939. Dept.-Lieut.
and J.P. for Sussex. PC. 1924. Member of
Sussex T.A. A Conservative. Member for
Horsham division Nov. 1904-Dec. 1918, for
Horsham and Worthing division Dec. 1918-
July 1945, and for Horsham division from
July 1945 until he retired in Oct. 1951. Father
of the House of Commons 1945-51. Styled
Visct. Turnour until he succeeded to the
Earldom in 1907. Created Baron Turnour in
the U.K. Peerage 1952. Author of *Pre-War,
Fifty Tumultuous* and *Orders of the Day*. Died 26
Aug. 1962.   [1951]

WINTERTON, Nicholas Raymond.
House of Commons, London. Lighthouse,
and Associate Member Eccentric. S. of Norman Harry Winterton, Esq. B. 31 Mar. 1938;
m. 1960, Jane Ann, d. of J.R. Hodgson, Esq.,
(2 s. 1 d.). Educ. at Bilton Grange Preparatory School, and Rugby School. Commissioned 14th/20th Kings Hussars 1957-59.
Sales Executive Trainee Shell-Mex B.P.
Limited 1959-60; Sales and General Manager Stevens and Hodgson 1960-71. Elected to
Warwickshire County Council Apr. 1967; re-
elected 1970, resigned Dec. 1972. Chairman
County Youth Service Sub-Committee 1969-
72. Dept. Chairman Education Committee
1970-72. Joint Secretary Conservative Parliamentary Agriculture Committee. Vice-
Chairman All-Party Parliamentary Textile
Group. Chairman British-Sri Lanka Parliamentary Group. Vice-Chairman Anglo-
Danish Parliamentary Group. Joint Secretary Conservative Parliamentary Education
Committee. A Conservative. Unsuccessfully
contested Newcastle-under-Lyme at a by-
election in Oct. 1969 and at the general
election of 1970. Elected for the Macclesfield
division of Cheshire in Sept. 1971.* [1979]

WISE, (Alfred) Roy. House of Commons,
London. S. of Alfred Gascoyne Wise, Puisne
Judge, of Hong Kong. B. 1901; m. 1942,
Cassandra Noel, only d. of Lieut.-Col. B.E.
Coke, O.B.E., R.E. (Retd.), (1 s.). Educ. at
Repton School, and Oriel Coll., Oxford.
Assistant District Commissioner in Kenya
1923-26. A Conservative. Unsuccessfully con-
tested Smethwick in 1929. Sat for Smethwick
from 1931-45. Unsuccessfully contested
Epping in 1945. Elected for the Rugby di-
vision of Warwickshire in 1959 and sat until
1966, when he was defeated. M.B.E. 1941,
T.D. 1943. Served with the Queen's Royal
Regiment (W. Surrey) and with British Intelligence Organisation in Germany. Member
of Westminster City Council 1956-59. Died
21 Aug. 1974.   [1966]

WISE, Audrey. House of Commons, Lon-
don. D. of George Brown, Esq. B. 1935; m.
John Wise, Esq. Educ. at Rutherford High
School. Author of *Women and the Struggle for
Workers' Control* and *Eyewitness in Revolutionary
Portugal*. A Labour Member. Elected for

405

Coventry S.W. in Feb. 1974 and sat until 1979, when she was defeated.*   [1979]

WISE, Maj. Frederick John. The Windmill, Heacham, Norfolk. S. of Edward Wise, Esq., of Bury St. Edmunds. B. 10 Apr. 1887; m. 25 Nov. 1911, Kate, d. of John Sturgeon, Esq. Educ. at King Edward's School, Bury St. Edmunds. Fellow of Royal Institute of Chartered Surveyors. Member of Council of Royal Veterinary Coll. Served with Suffolk Regiment R.F.C. and R.A.F. 1915-19, and as Lands Officer R.A.F. 1940-42. A Labour Member. Unsuccessfully contested the Harborough division of Leicestershire in 1929 and 1931, the Lowestoft division of E. Suffolk in 1935 and, as an Independent Labour Candidate, the King's Lynn division of Norfolk in Feb. 1943. Elected for the King's Lynn division of Norfolk in July 1945 and sat until 1951, when he was defeated. Created Baron Wise 1951. Mayor of King's Lynn 1953-54. Dept.-Lieut. for Norfolk. Died 20 Nov. 1968.   [1951]

WOLRIGE-GORDON, Patrick. Ythan Lodge, Newburgh, Aberdeenshire. S. of Capt. Robert Wolrige-Gordon, M.C., J.P. and grandson of Dame Flora Macleod of Macleod. B. 10 Aug. 1935; m. 1962, Anne, only d. of Peter D. Howard, Esq., and Mrs. Howard, of Brent Eleigh, Suffolk, (1 s. 1 d.). Educ. at Eton, and New Coll., Oxford. Parliamentary Private Secretary to Anthony Barber, Economic Secretary to Treasury 1960-62, Financial Secretary to Treasury 1962-63 and Minister of Health 1963-64. A Conservative. Elected for Aberdeenshire E. in Nov. 1958 and sat until Feb. 1974, when he was defeated.*   [1974]

WOOD, Rt. Hon. Richard Frederick. Flat Top House, Bishop Wilton, Yorkshire. 49 Cadogan Place, London. S. of 1st Earl of Halifax, K.G., O.M., G.C.S.I., G.C.I.E. B. 5 Oct. 1920; m. 15 Apr. 1947, Diane, d. of Col. E.O. Kellett, D.S.O., MP., and Hon. Mrs. William McGowan, (1 s. 1 d.). Educ. at Eton, and New Coll., Oxford. Lieut. 60th Rifles 1941-43 (wounded). Parliamentary Private Secretary to D. Heathcoat-Amory 1951-55. Joint Parliamentary Secretary to Ministry of Pensions and National Insurance 1955-58.

Parliamentary Secretary to Ministry of Labour 1958-59; Minister of Power 1959-63; Minister of Pensions and National Insurance Oct. 1963-Oct. 1964. Opposition spokesman on Health 1964-65, on Labour and Social Services 1965-66, on Commonwealth Affairs 1966-67 and on Foreign Affairs 1967-70. Minister for Overseas Development 1970-74. Member of Hansard Society on Electoral Reform 1975-76. Honorary Col. Queen's Royal Rifles 1962, and of 4th Battalion, Royal Green Jackets 1967. Honorary LL.D. Sheffield University 1962; Honorary LL.D. Leeds 1978. Dept.-Lieut. for the E. Riding of Yorkshire 1968. Director of Hargreaves Group of Companies. PC. 1959. Created Baron Holderness (Life Peerage) 1979. A Conservative. Elected for the Bridlington division of the E. Riding of Yorkshire in Feb. 1950 and sat until he retired in 1979.*   [1979]

WOODALL, Alec. House of Commons, London. S. of William Woodall, Esq. B. 20 Sept. 1918; m. 22 July 1950, Mary, d. of Arthur William Scott, Esq., (1 s. 1 d.). Educ. at Hemsworth South Moor Road Elementary School. A Colliery official. Parliamentary Private Secretary to Rt. Hon. Edmund Dell, Secretary of State for Trade 1976-78. A Labour Member. Sat for Hemsworth from Feb. 1974.*   [1979]

WOODBURN, Rt. Hon. Arthur, PC., D.Litt. 83 Orchard Road, Edinburgh. S. of Matthew Woodburn, Esq., of Edinburgh. B. 1890; m. 1919, Barbara Halliday. Educ. at Bruntisfield, Boroughmuir Public Schools, and Heriot Watt Coll., Edinburgh. A Foreign Correspondent. President of the National Council of Labour Colleges from 1937; Scottish Secretary of Labour Party 1932-40; Lecturer in Economics and Finance, Labour Colls. from 1919. Member of Select Committee on National Expenditure 1939; Chairman of Sub-Committee on Finance and Establishments 1941 and of Speaker's Conference on Electoral Reform 1944. Member of Select Committees on Disqualification of Clergy 1952-53, on Delegated Legislation 1953 and on House of Commons Procedure 1956-57 and 1966-70. Leader of British Inter-Parliamentary Union Delegation in 1951 to Bonn Parliament. Was first outsider asked to address the West German Bundestag; British Parliamentary Delegate to Uruguay 1957; First British Parliamentary Delegate to Spain 1960. Parliamentary Private Secretary to the Rt. Hon. Thomas Johnston, Secretary of State for Scotland Feb. 1941-May 1945. Parliamentary Secretary Ministry of Aircraft Production Aug. 1945-Apr. 1946 and Joint Parliamentary Secretary Ministry of Supply Apr. 1946-Oct. 1947. Secretary of State for Scotland with a seat in the Cabinet Oct. 1947-Feb. 1950. Opposition spokesman on Scotland until 1959. PC. 1947. Member Historical Buildings Council Scotland, and Scottish National Trust. Trustee Scottish National Library. A Labour Member. Unsuccessfully contested Edinburgh S. in 1929 and Leith in 1931. Sat for the Clackmannan and Eastern division of Stirlingshire and Clackmannan from Oct. 1939 until he retired in 1970. Died 1 June 1978. [1970]

WOODHOUSE, Hon. Christopher Montague, D.S.O., O.B.E., M.A. Bois Mill, Latimer, Buckinghamshire. St. Stephen's. S. of the 3rd Lord Terrington. B. 11 May 1917; m. 28 Aug. 1945, Lady Davina, d. of Earl of Lytton, and widow of the Earl of Erne. Educ. at Winchester, and New Coll., Oxford. Army service 1939-45; Commander of the Allied Military Mission to the Greek Resistance 1943-44. D.S.O. 1943, O.B.E. 1944. Secretary-Gen. of Allied Mission for Observing Greek Elections 1946. Foreign Office 1945-46 and 1950-55; Director-Gen. Royal Institute of International Affairs 1955-59; Parliamentary Secretary Ministry of Aviation Oct. 1961-July 1962; Joint Parliamentary Under-Secretary of State Home Office July 1962-Oct. 1964. A Conservative. Sat for Oxford from 1959-66, when he was defeated, and from June 1970 until Oct. 1974, when he was again defeated. Assistant Secretary of Nuffield Foundation 1948-50. Director of Education and Training, C.B.I. 1966-70. Visiting Fellow, Nuffield Coll., Oxford 1956; Visiting Professor, King's Coll., London 1978. President of Classical Association 1968. Author of books on Greece and international relations.* [1974 2nd ed.]

WOODNUTT, Harold Frederick Martin ('Mark'). Portland House, Bembridge, Isle of Wight. Constitutional, and Bembridge Sailing. S. of Harold Frederick Woodnutt, Esq. B. 23 Nov. 1918; m. 1 Dec. 1945, Gwynneth, d. of William B. Lovely, Esq. Educ. at Isleworth Grammar School. Served in the ranks of the Army July-Dec. 1939. Commissioned in R.A. Dec. 1939. Active Service Norway, Egypt and Crete. P.O.W. 1941-45. Mentioned in despatches. Isle of Wight County Council 1952-74. County Alderman 1957-74. Chairman Bembridge Lifeboat Committee. Chartered Secretary. Director Charles Churchill Limited; Bembridge Harbour Improvements Company Limited; Chairman Southern Construction (Holdings) Limited; All-Party Anglo-Czechoslovakia Group; All-Party Tourists and Resorts Group. Vice-Chairman All-Party Hover Group. A Conservative. Elected for the Isle of Wight in 1959 and sat until Feb. 1974, when he was defeated. Died 6 Nov. 1974. [1974]

WOODS, Rev. George Saville. Hopgrove, York. S. of Thomas Woods, Esq. B. 13 Sept. 1886; m. 1 Aug. 1914, Edith Alice Mote, L.L.A. Educ. at Birmingham, and Manchester Coll., Oxford. Director of Co-op. Press Limited; member of Central Board of Co-op. Union Limited. Unitarian Minister of Mary Street Chapel, Taunton 1914-21 and of St. Saviourgate Chapel, York from 1921. President of Yorkshire Unitarian Union 1932-34. Member of York City Council. A Labour Member. Unsuccessfully contested the Taunton division of Somerset in 1918 and 1924, the Barkston Ash division of the W. Riding of Yorkshire in 1929 and 1931, and the Rusholme division of Manchester in Nov. 1933. Sat for Finsbury from Nov. 1935-July 1945, for Mossley July 1945-Feb. 1950. Elected for Droylsden in Feb. 1950 and sat until his death on 9 July 1951. [1951]

WOOF, Robert Edward. House of Commons, London. B. 1911; m. Mary Bell (she died 1971). Educ. at Elementary School. A Miner. Member of Durham County Council 1947-56. A Labour Member. Sat for the Blaydon division of Durham from Feb. 1956 until he retired in 1979.* [1979]

WOOLLAM, John Victor. 25 Queenscourt Road, Liverpool. S. of Thomas Woollam, Esq., Boilermaker. B. 14 Aug. 1927; m. 1964, Rosamund Ela, d. of S.R.E. Snow, Esq. Educ. at Liverpool University, B.A. Econ. Barrister-at-Law, Inner Temple, 1952. Parliamentary Election Agent for the Kirkdale division of Liverpool in 1951. Parliamentary Private Secretary to Rt. Hon. John Hare, Minister of Labour 1960-62. A Conservative. Unsuccessfully contested the Scotland division of Liverpool in 1950. Elected for the W. Derby division of Liverpool in Nov. 1954 and sat until 1964, when he was defeated.*

[1964]

WORSLEY, Sir William Marcus John, Bart. 25 Flood Street, London. Wool Knoll, Hovingham, Yorkshire. Carlton. S. of Sir William Worsley, 4th Bart., of Hovingham Hall. B. 6 Apr. 1925; m. Dec. 1955, Hon. Bridget Assheton, d. of 1st Baron Clitheroe. Educ. at Eton, and New Coll., Oxford. Served with the Green Howards 1943-47. Programme Assistant, B.B.C. European Service 1950-53. J.P. 1957. Parliamentary Private Secretary to Rt. Hon. Enoch Powell, Minister of Health 1960-61, to Rt. Hon. William Deedes, Minister without Portfolio 1962-64, and to Rt. Hon. William Whitelaw, Lord President of the Council 1970-72. Second Church Estates Commissioner 1970-74. A Conservative. Unsuccessfully contested Keighley in 1955. Sat for Keighley from 1959-64, when he was defeated. Sat for Chelsea from Mar. 1966 to Feb. 1974 and for the Chelsea division of Kensington and Chelsea from Feb. 1974 until he retired in Sept. 1974. Succeeded as Bart. 1973. A Church Commissioner from 1976.*

[1974 2nd ed.]

WRIGGLESWORTH, Ian William. House of Commons, London. S. of Edward Wrigglesworth, Esq., Foreman Fitter. B. Dec. 1939; m. June 1967, Patricia, d. of Hugh Truscott, Esq., (3 s.). Educ. at Stockton Grammar School, Stockton-Billingham Technical Coll., and Coll. of St. Mark and St. John, Chelsea. Formerly Personal Assistant to Sir Ronald Gould, Gen. Secretary of N.U.T.; Research Officer of the Co-operative Party; Press and Public Affairs Manager of the National Giro. Parliamentary Private Secretary to Alex Lyon, Minister of State, Home Office 1974 and to the Rt. Hon. Roy Jenkins, MP., Home Secretary from Nov. 1974 to Sept. 1976. Opposition spokesman on the Civil Service from 1979. Chairman Labour Economic, Finance and Taxation Association. Vice-Chairman P.L.P. Economic Group. A Labour and Co-operative Member. Sat for Teesside, Thornaby from 1974.*

[1979]

WRIGHT, Esmond. 15 Beaumont Gate, Glasgow. Constitutional. S. of Esmond Wright, Esq., of Newcastle-on-Tyne. B. 5 Nov. 1915; m. 16 Nov. 1945, Olive Adamson. Educ. at Heaton Grammar School, Newcastle, and Universities of Durham and Virginia. Served in Army 1940-46, Lieut.-Col. Lecturer 1946-57 and Professor 1957-67, of Modern History, University of Glasgow. A Conservative. Elected for the Pollok division of Glasgow in Mar. 1967 and sat until 1970, when he was defeated. Chairman of British Association for American Studies 1965-68. Dept. Chairman of Border Television. Fellow of Royal Historical Society. Director of Institute of United States Studies and Professor of American History, London University from 1971.*

[1970]

WYATT, Woodrow Lyle. House of Commons, London. S. of Robert Harvey Lyle Wyatt, Esq. B. 4 July 1918; m. 1st, 1957, Lady Moorea Hastings, d. of 15th Earl of Huntingdon (divorced 1966); 2ndly, 7 Dec. 1966, Mrs. Veronica Banszky. Educ. at Eastbourne Coll., and Worcester Coll., Oxford. Served in Army 1939-45, Maj. A Journalist, Writer and Broadcaster. Parliamentary Under-Secretary of State and Financial Secretary War Office May-Oct. 1951. A Labour Member. Sat for the Aston division of Birmingham from 1945-55, when he unsuccessfully contested the Grantham division of Lincolnshire. Elected for the Bosworth division of Leicestershire in 1959 and sat until 1970, when he was defeated. Member of Council of Zoological Society of London 1968-71 and 1973-77. Chairman of Horserace Totalisator Board from 1976.*

[1970]

WYLIE, Rt. Hon. Norman Russell, V.R.D., Q.C. 30 Lauder Road, Edinburgh 9. Constitutional, New (Edinburgh), and Royal Highland Yacht. S. of William Galloway Wylie, Esq. B. 26 Oct. 1923; m. 20 July 1963, Gillian Mary, d. of Dr. R.E. Verney, of Edinburgh, (3 s.). Educ. at Paisley Grammar School, St. Edmund Hall, Oxford, and Universities of Glasgow and Edinburgh. Served in Fleet Air Arm 1942-46, later with R.N.R., Lieut.-Commander. V.R.D. 1961. Called to Scottish bar 1952. Appointed Jun. Counsel in Scotland to Air Ministry 1956 and Advocate-Depute 1959. Q.C. 1964. Solicitor-Gen. for Scotland from Apr.-Oct. 1964. PC. 1970. Lord Advocate from June 1970-Feb. 1974. A Conservative. Unsuccessfully contested W. Fife in 1955 and Edinburgh Central in 1959. Elected for the Pentlands division of Edinburgh in 1964 and sat until Feb. 1974, when he was appointed a Judge of the Court of Session. Judge of the Court of Session, with the judicial title of Lord Wylie, from 1974.*
[1974]

YATES, Victor Francis. 7 Umberslade Road, Selly Oak, Birmingham. S. of James Yates, Esq., of Birmingham. B. 19 Apr. 1900. Unmarried. Educ. at Stirchley Elementary School, part-time Course at University of Birmingham, and one year at Ruskin Coll., Oxford. Late member of National Executive of Clerical and Administrative Workers' Union. Served on Birmingham City Council 1927-30 and 1934-37. Gov. King Edward's School, Birmingham for 29 years. Member of Select Committee on Estimates for six years. Chairman of P.L.P.'s Home Affairs Group. Vice-Chairman of the Trade Union Group of the P.L.P. Chairman of Labour Peace Fellowship. A Labour Member. Elected for the Ladywood division of Birmingham in July 1945 and sat (Labour Whip withdrawn Nov. 1954-Apr. 1955) until his death on 19 Jan. 1969.
[1968]

YATES, William. House of Commons, London. S. of William Yates, Esq. B. 1921; m. 1st, 1946, Hon. Rosemary Elton, d. of 1st Baron Elton (divorced 1955); 2ndly, 1957, Camilla, d. of E.W.D. Tennant, Esq. Educ. at Uppingham, and Hertford Coll., Oxford. Served in the 8th Army with The Queen's Bays 1942; Capt. Shropshire Yeomanry, T.A. 1956. Legal Officer in Tripoli to report on State Lands 1950. Myron Taylor Lecturer in International Affairs, Cornell University, 1958 and 1966. A Conservative. Elected for The Wrekin division of Shropshire in 1955 and sat until 1966, when he was defeated. Withdrew as prospective candidate for The Wrekin in Aug. 1967 after disagreeing with the local Conservative Association over the Arab-Israeli War. Senior Partner, World Wide Industrial Consultants. Liberal Member of House of Representatives for Holt, Victoria in the Parliament of the Commonwealth of Australia from 1975.*
[1966]

YORK, Christopher. Long Marston Manor, York. S. of Col. Edward York, of Hutton Hall, Long Marston, York, and Violet Helen, d. of Rt. Hon. Sir Frederick Milner, 7th Bart., G.C.V.O. B. 27 July 1909; m. 16 Oct. 1934, Pauline Rosemary, d. of Sir Lionel Fletcher, C.B.E. Educ. at Eton, and at Royal Military Coll., Sandhurst. A Land Agent; Maj. Royal Dragoons. A Conservative. Sat for the Ripon division from Feb. 1939 to Feb. 1950. Elected for the Harrogate division of the W. Riding of Yorkshire in Feb. 1950 and sat until he resigned in Feb. 1954. Dept.-Lieut. for W. Riding of Yorkshire, later for N. Yorkshire, from 1954. High Sheriff of Yorkshire 1966.*
[1954]

YOUNG, Sir Arthur Stewart Leslie, Bart. 1 The Grove, Highgate, London. Carlton, and R.Y.S. S. of D.H.L. Young, Esq., of Glasgow. B. 10 Oct. 1889; m. 21 Nov. 1913, Dorothy, d. of Sir W. Baldwin Spencer, K.C.M.G., Professor of Biology at University of Melbourne. Educ. at Glasgow Academy, Fettes Coll., and abroad. A Carpet Manufacturer. J.P. for Glasgow; Chairman of Jun. Imperial Union of Scottish Unionist Association 1925-28; Treasurer of Western Division Council of Scottish Unionist Association 1934; Commissioned 8th Scottish Rifles (T.) 1909, served overseas 1914-18, retired as Maj. 1919; Parliamentary Private Secretary to H.J. Scrymgeour-Wedderburn when Parliamentary Under-Secretary of State for Scotland Nov. 1936-Sept. 1939, to Rt. Hon. D. J. Colville, Secretary of State for Scotland Sept. 1939-May 1940, and to Rt. Hon. Ernest

Brown, Secretary of State for Scotland May 1940-Feb. 1941; Scottish Unionist Whip Feb. 1941. A Lord Commissioner of the Treasury Feb. 1942-July 1944; Vice-Chamberlain of H.M. Household July 1944-July 1945. Created Bart. 1945. Opposition Whip 1945-50. A Conservative. Sat for the Partick division of Glasgow from 1935-50, and for the Scotstoun division of Glasgow from Feb. 1950 until his death in France on 14 Aug. 1950.

[1950]

YOUNG, David Wright. House of Commons, London. B. Oct. 1930; m. Grace. Educ. at Greenock Academy, St. Paul's Coll., Cheltenham, and Glasgow University. Chairman of Coventry E. Constituency Labour Party 1964-68. Member of Nuneaton Borough Council 1973-76. Parliamentary Private Secretary to Mr. Mulley, Secretary of State for Defence Feb. 1977-May 1979. A Labour Member. Unsuccessfully contested Worcestershire S. in 1959, Banbury in 1966 and Bath in 1970. Elected for Bolton E. in Feb. 1974.*   [1979]

YOUNG, Sir George Samuel Knatchbull, Bart. House of Commons, London. S. of Sir George Young, Bart., C.M.G. B. 16 July 1941; m. 11 July 1964, Aurelia Nemon-Stuart. Educ. at Eton, and Christ Church, Oxford. Economist with National Economic Development Office 1966-67, Research Fellow, University of Surrey 1967-69. Councillor London Borough of Lambeth 1968-71. Economic Adviser, Post Office 1969-74. Greater London Council member for Ealing 1970-73. Opposition Whip 1976-79. Under-Secretary of State for Health and Social Security from May 1979. Author of *Tourism-Blessing or Blight.* Succeeded to Baronetcy 1960. A Conservative. Sat for the Acton division of Ealing from Feb. 1974.*   [1979]

YOUNG, Sir Robert, O.B.E. 213 Barry Road, Dulwich, London. B. at Glasgow 26 Jan. 1872; m. 1910, Bessie Laurina, d. of C.J. Choldcroft, Esq., of Oxford (she died 1950). Educ. at Monsbank School, and Ruskin Coll., Oxford. For fifteen years with Messrs. Dubs and Company, Locomotive Engineers, Glasgow. Member of Amalgamated Society of Engineers Trade Union Staff, Jan. 1906;

Assistant Secretary Jan. 1908; Gen. Secretary Oct. 1913-19. O.B.E. 1917. Independent Chairman Ophthalmic Benefit Approved Committee 1937-48. Chairman of National Temperance Federation from 1935. President of Workers' Temperance League from 1944. Lecturer for Ruskin Coll., Oxford to Trade Unions, Co-operative Societies, etc. 1904-05. Chairman of Committee of Ways and Means and Dept. Speaker Jan.-Oct. 1924 and June 1929-Oct. 1931; Temporary Chairman of Committees 1935-48. Knight Bach. 1931. Member of Select Committee on National Expenditure 1940-44. Chairman of Select Committee on House of Commons Procedure 1945-46. A Labour Member. Sat for the Newton division of Lancashire from Dec. 1918-Oct. 1931, when he was defeated, and from Nov. 1935 until he retired in 1950. Died 13 July 1957.   [1950]

YOUNGER, Rt. Hon. George Kenneth Hotson. Easter Leckie, Gargunnock, Stirlingshire. S. of 3rd Visct. Younger of Leckie. B. 22 Sept. 1931; m. 1954, Diana, d. of Capt. Tuck, D.S.O., R.N., (3 s. 1 d.). Educ. at Winchester, and New Coll., Oxford. Former Governor of the Royal Scottish Academy of Music. Heir to the Viscountcy. Served with Argyll and Sutherland Highlanders 1950-51 and in T.A. 1951-65, T.D. 1964. Director of George Younger and Son Limited 1958-68 and Tennant Caledonian Breweries Limited 1977-79. Scottish Conservative Whip 1965-67. Dept. Chairman of Conservative Party in Scotland from 1967-70. Dept.-Lieut. for Stirlingshire 1968. Parliamentary Under-Secretary of State for Development, Scottish Office June 1970-Jan. 1974. Minister of State for Defence Jan.-Mar. 1974. Opposition spokesman on Defence Mar. 1974-Jan. 1976 and on Scottish Affairs Nov. 1976-May 1979. Member of Shadow Cabinet Feb. 1975-Jan. 1976. Secretary of State for Scotland from May 1979. Member of Royal Company of Archers. PC. 1979. Chairman Conservative Party in Scotland June 1974. A Conservative. Unsuccessfully contested Lanarkshire N. in 1959. Prospective candidate for Kinross and W. Perthshire in 1963 but withdrew in favour of Sir Alec Douglas-Home, who became Prime Minister in Oct. and was elected for the constituency in Nov. 1963. Sat for the Ayr division of Ayrshire and Bute from Oct. 1964.* [1979]

YOUNGER, Rt. Hon. Kenneth Gilmour. 3 Clareville Grove, London. S. of 2nd Visct. Younger of Leckie. B. 15 Dec. 1908; m. 23 Aug. 1934, Elizabeth, d. of W.D. Stewart, Esq., of Achara, Duror, Argyll. Educ. at Winchester and New Coll., Oxford, B.A. Barrister-at-Law, Inner Temple, 1932. Served in Intelligence Corps 1940-45. Parliamentary Private Secretary to Philip Noel-Baker, Minister of State 1945-46 and Secretary of State for Air 1946-47. Chairman of U.N.R.R.A. Committee of Council for Europe June 1946. Under-Secretary of State for Home Affairs Oct. 1947-Feb. 1950. Minister of State for Foreign Affairs Feb. 1950-Oct. 1951. Opposition spokesman on Foreign Affairs until 1959, and Chief spokesman on Home Office Affairs 1955-57. Member of P.L.P. Parliamentary Committee 1955-57. Member of Supreme Court Committee on Practice and Procedure 1947. PC. 1951. A Labour Member. Elected for Grimsby in July 1945 and sat until he retired in 1959. Director of Royal Institute of International Affairs 1959-71. Chairman of Howard League for Penal Reform 1960-73. Chairman of Advisory Council on Penal System 1966. Chairman of Committee of Enquiry on Privacy 1970-72. K.B.E. 1972. Chairman of Data Protection Committee 1976. Died 19 May 1976. [1959]

ZILLIACUS, Konni. 75 Warrington Crescent, Maida Vale, London. S. of Konni Zilliacus, Esq., Author and Journalist. B. 13 Sept. 1894; m. 1st, 1918, Eugenia Nonicka; 2ndly, 1942, Janet Harris. Educ. at Lundsbergs Skola, Vaemland, Sweden, Bedales School, and Yale University, U.S.A. R.F.C. and Intelligence Officer, British Mission, Siberia, in First World War; member of Information Section, League of Nations Secretariat General 1919-39; in Ministry of Information in Second World War. A Writer, Lecturer and Broadcaster and has written sixteen books and numerous pamphlets and articles on international affairs. A Labour Member. Sat for Gateshead from 1945-50, when he unsuccessfully contested Gateshead E. as an Independent Labour candidate. Expelled from the Labour Party in May 1949, re-admitted in Feb. 1952. Member of Labour Independent Group 1949-50. Elected for the Gorton division of Manchester in 1955 and sat (Labour Whip withdrawn Mar. 1961-May 1963) until his death on 6 July 1967. [1967]

Index of Names

Index of Names

This index lists all Members of Parliament who sat in the House of Commons between 1945 and 1979. Cross references are given where necessary. All names appear in the same order as in the text.